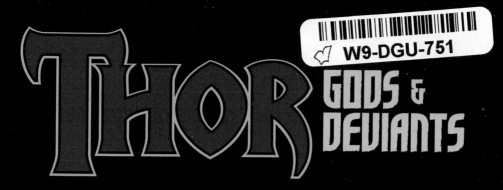

THOR GODS & DEVIANTS

Robert Rodi
WRITER

LOKI

Esad Ribić
ARTIST & COLORIST

VC's Cory Petit with Randy Gentile (#4)
LETTERERS

Esad Ribić
COVER ART

Special Thanks to Robert Glavak

THOR: FOR ASGARD

Simone Bianchi
PENCILER

Simone Bianchi with Andrea Silvestri (#3-6)
INKS & INKWASH

Simone Peruzzi
COLORIST

VC's Cory Petit
LETTERER

Simone Bianchi with Andrea Silvestri (#2-3) & Simone Peruzzi (#1-3)
COVER ART

ASTONISHING THOR

Mike Choi
ARTIST

Frank D'Armata
COLORIST

VC's Joe Caramagna
LETTERER

Esad Ribić (#1), Ed McGuinness & Laura Martin (#2-3), Mike Choi (#4-5)
COVER ART

THOR: THE DEVIANTS SAGA

Stephen Segovia
PENCILER

Jason Paz (#1-3) & Stephen Segovia (#4-5) with Jeff Huet (#3)
INKS & INKWASH

Andy Troy with John Rauch (#2) & Wil Quintana (#3 & #5)
COLORISTS

Jeff Eckleberry
LETTERER

Stephen Segovia
COVER ART

John Miesegaes, Cory Sedlmeier, Sebastian Girner, Charlie Beckerman & John Denning
ASSISTANT EDITORS

Axel Alonso & Ralph Macchio
EDITORS

COLLECTION EDITOR: MARK D. BEAZLEY
ASSISTANT EDITOR: CAITLIN O'CONNELL
ASSOCIATE MANAGING EDITOR: KATERI WOODY
ASSOCIATE MANAGER, DIGITAL ASSETS: JOE HOCHSTEIN
SENIOR EDITOR, SPECIAL PROJECTS: JENNIFER GRÜNWALD

VP PRODUCTION & SPECIAL PROJECTS: JEFF YOUNGQUIST
RESEARCH: DARON JENSEN
LAYOUT: JEPH YORK
BOOK DESIGNER: ADAM DEL RE
SVP PRINT, SALES & MARKETING: DAVID GABRIEL

EDITOR IN CHIEF: AXEL ALONSO
CHIEF CREATIVE OFFICER: JOE QUESADA
PRESIDENT: DAN BUCKLEY
EXECUTIVE PRODUCER: ALAN FINE

THOR CREATED BY STAN LEE, LARRY LIEBER & JACK KIRBY

THOR: GODS & DEVIANTS. Contains material originally published in magazine form as LOKI #1-4, THOR: FOR ASGARD #1-6, ASTONISHING THOR #1-5 and THOR: THE DEVIANTS SAGA #1-5. First printing 2017. ISBN# 978-1-302-90787-7. Published by MARVEL WORLDWIDE, INC., a subsidiary of MARVEL ENTERTAINMENT, LLC. OFFICE OF PUBLICATION: 135 West 50th Street, New York, NY 10020. Printed in the U.S.A. [illegible] Manufactured between 8/25/2017 and 9/26/2017 by LSC COMMUNICATIONS INC., KENDALLVILLE, IN, USA.

10 9 8 7 6 5 4 3 2 1

INTRODUCTION

Robert Rodi and I go back a long way to that ancient era when we were both what was referred to as "letterhacks," sending in a constant stream of comments to various Mighty Marvel letters pages, hoping to see them published. Rodi's missives were always so thought-provoking and smartly written. Eventually, he made the jump to professional comics scripter and produced all of the gems you'll be savoring in this superb volume.

It was then Editor Axel Alonso who first brought the redoubtable Mr. Rodi into the fold on *Loki*, the first entry collected here. This is a four-issue masterpiece brilliantly painted by Esad Ribić that centers on the source of so much agony in Asgard—Loki. In this tale of Asgard, the God of Evil actually has achieved his goal: the throne of the fabled realm itself! It is then that the epic's true nature unfolds as Loki is plagued by primal doubts because the Fates themselves have ruled against his ever retaining the title of liege. His destiny, as he learns, is ultimately to be defeated and disgraced by his hated adopted brother, the Mighty Thor. No matter what he does, he's locked in to that. Sophocles' *Oedipus* has nothing on this poor soul. Rodi gets right to the heart of what animates this relentless, fascinating figure and plays it out in an incredibly imaginative fashion brimming with mythic overtones.

My winged helmet is off to Editor Axel for placing Esad Ribić on this project, whose every illustration on *Loki* is suitable for framing. As you gaze at these incredibly powerful images, you almost believe that Ribić himself has journeyed to Asgard and committed what he saw to memory. The gods, goddesses, architectural structures and natural landscapes all bespeak an authenticity to be treasured. You simply fall into this wondrous world Ribić has painted and become part of it.

I recall someone asking me once who my favorite Marvel villain was and I quickly responded: Loki (although "villain" is too small a word to encompass the scope of his grand designs). What I love about him is that he is both majestic and petty. Remember, he is both God of Mischief and God of Evil. While his ultimate goal is to step outside of destiny's design, which is an awesome task, Loki still lets no slight inflicted upon him be forgiven. Frankly, he will mess with you and your loved ones if you look at him sideways, all the while contemplating matters of cosmic scope. That is the paradox that fuels Loki's inner fires, and Rodi and Ribić explore it here so effectively.

Flipping the coin, Rodi next tackled a story that examines the trials and travails of another Asgardian who gains the throne: the Mighty Thor, in *Thor: For Asgard*. And he does so

with equal zeal and talent. Here he teams with another artist who also must have taken the express bus to Asgard: Simone Bianchi. This epic is a counterpoint to *Loki* because here Rodi imagines an Asgard in which the God of Thunder assumes the lordship of the Realm Eternal and his hateful adopted brother is barely around. It's an understatement to say that in this story, uneasy hangs the head that wears the crown. Everything goes wrong both in the golden city and in the lands subjugated by the Asgardians. And no answer is forthcoming despite Thor's endless pondering of the problems, until...well, I won't give it away, but you'll be shocked. Suffice it to say that this rich character study in the qualities of leadership is no less compelling than the masterful *Loki*, allowing you to examine each god's respective approach to acquiring ultimate authority. Bianchi's art carries the tale forth with a scintillating artistic excellence that makes it seem as if you could reach out and touch the players. This is an unforgettable excursion into the domain of politics and power; food for thought on multiple levels. And you thought you were just reading a comic book collection.

Rodi and I both share a fascination with the Mighty Thor and his incredible Asgardian environs. So, it seemed inevitable that our paths would cross on a Thor project or two. Luckily, it did. In a limited series titled *Astonishing Thor*, Rodi and Mike Choi bring to life a titanic tale of cosmic meddling by a favorite of mine: the Stranger. No, I'm not referring to Albert Camus' existential anti-hero. I'm talking about Marvel's spacefaring scientist supreme, whose origins and ultimate motivations are shrouded in mystery. And, by the way, he is a being whose power is simply incalculable. He was the perfect motivating force for the story Rodi and I envisioned.

One of the more fascinating of the Lee/Kirby concepts introduced in that impossibly fertile period they had in *The Mighty Thor* back in the 1960s was Ego, the Living Planet. I loved the character, but something about the concept has always bugged me: The numerous origins attributed to Ego. I found none of them either compelling or even satisfactory. They didn't work for me, and I determined that should I ever edit or write a tale with this planetary powerhouse in it, I'd make sure he got a worthy origin. Apparently, Rodi felt the same. So, the two of us got together to craft what we hoped would be the definitive origin of this singular, sentient world. I was extremely happy with the result of our collaboration, especially as it put the Stranger at the very center of the action. For good measure, we tossed in ol' Taneleer Tivan, better known as the Collector, one of the Elders of the

Universe, to play an important role. This intermingling of cosmic concepts and characters was just what the doctor ordered for **Astonishing Thor**. And we had the perfect penciler to bring it all to vibrant, visual life: Mike Choi, whose amazing artistic acumen is evident on every page. His achievement is all the more stunning when you consider the logistical difficulty of juxtaposing an object as large as a planet with something as relatively miniscule as a human-sized figure within the same panel. In some magical way, Choi made it work spectacularly well. This became one of those blessed projects to which any editor would be proud to see his name attached. Rereading it now, there is nothing I would've changed or added. There are precious few endeavors an editor can say that about.

It was only a short time later that Rodi and I had the chance to work together again, this time with the highly talented then newcomer Stephen Segovia, who's since become a force to be reckoned with in this field. I've always been a huge fan of Jack Kirby's final creative masterwork for Marvel: **Eternals**. When they first appeared back in the mid-1970s, I hadn't yet begun my tenure at Marvel. I recall penning impassioned pleas (which were published) that the Eternals not be integrated into the mainstream Marvel Universe, rather they be allowed to blossom unimpeded by continuity restrictions in their own separate reality. Kirby's wonderful idea was that the Eternals and their subterranean-dwelling opposites, the Deviants, were the inspiration for the many myths and legends about gods and demons that arose in mankind's past. I thought that was brilliant. But it was a concept that was an odd fit with the existing Marvel cosmos, in which actual gods existed apart from the Eternals. So, making them part of the mainstream continuity could have watered down or outright contradicted the substructure of this fantastic idea. Needless to say, without re-litigating the whole affair, the Powers-That-Be (or were) disagreed with my objections, and Kirby's creations found a nice niche in mainstream Marvel, where they've resided ever since. In fact, I both edited and wrote a number of the stories where the Eternals ran smack up against the already existing mythological pantheons and we got some real fireworks.

That brings me to the final entry in this colorful collection: **Thor: The Deviants Saga**. My goal here was to ultimately bring back to Olympia all the wandering Eternals who had left their mountaintop city and make them one big happy family again. Much as I love those sky-dwelling deities, I am equally wowed by the Deviants. I wanted to alter their status quo, as well, while I had the chance. They are a fascinating race cursed with genetic instability, misshapen and misanthropic, through no fault of their own. I actually admire them because the Deviants, despite their genetic disadvantages, rose to conquer the Earth in ancient days, until they were cast down by their makers, the unfathomable Celestials. The Eternals are like the elite with every advantage nature could bestow on one. But the ever-ambitious Deviants have had to scrap and struggle for everything they have. Once they achieved actual mastery of the planet, it was all taken away from them by cosmic forces beyond their ken. Let's face it, there's a terrific metaphor in there somewhere, right?

Once again Rob Rodi and I were on the same page, and we were able to get inside Deviant society and expose its dark underbelly to the light of day. Their subsea home, Lemuria, is but a remnant of a once-great civilization, now crumbling and decayed. Its denizens are monstrous beings who still tragically dream of recapturing long-lost glory. So much story material to mine there. Of course, Rob made our blond-haired Thunder God a major player in the story, weaving him in perfectly with the Celestials' disparate offspring. It wasn't the first time they had encountered each other, but that's a tale for another tome. Newcomer Segovia gave us some startling interpretations of all the various players. I was amazed at the energy he put into every panel. This became another of those charmed series, and I'm sure my buddy Rodi feels the same.

Now, the time has come to cross the radiant Rainbow Bridge into a mythological realm of gods and Frost Giants and fire demons. It is a land seen in both your most aspirational dreams and dreaded nightmares. And the most deadly of all its denizens is the one who wears the jewel-encrusted crown of king. His name is Loki Laufeyson, and his unforgettable fable begins now. Pray Odin he does not look upon you with disfavor.

Enjoy

Ralph Macchio

Ralph Macchio

Ralph Macchio spent over 35 years at Marvel, starting as an assistant editor and later writing Avengers, Thor and many others. As editor, he oversaw books across the Marvel line, including shepherding the Ultimate line into existence, and editing all of Stephen King's Marvel adaptations.

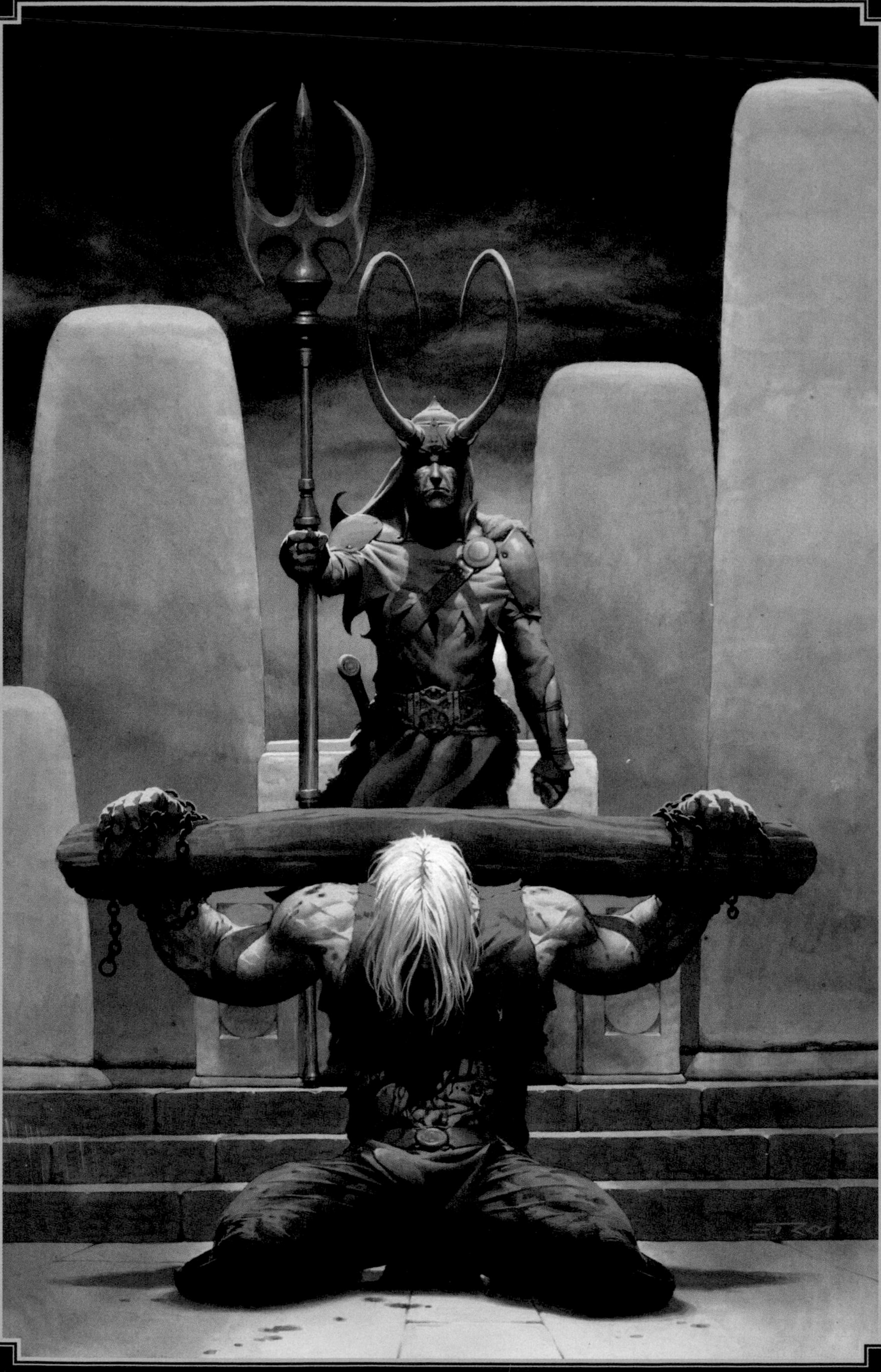

Loki 1

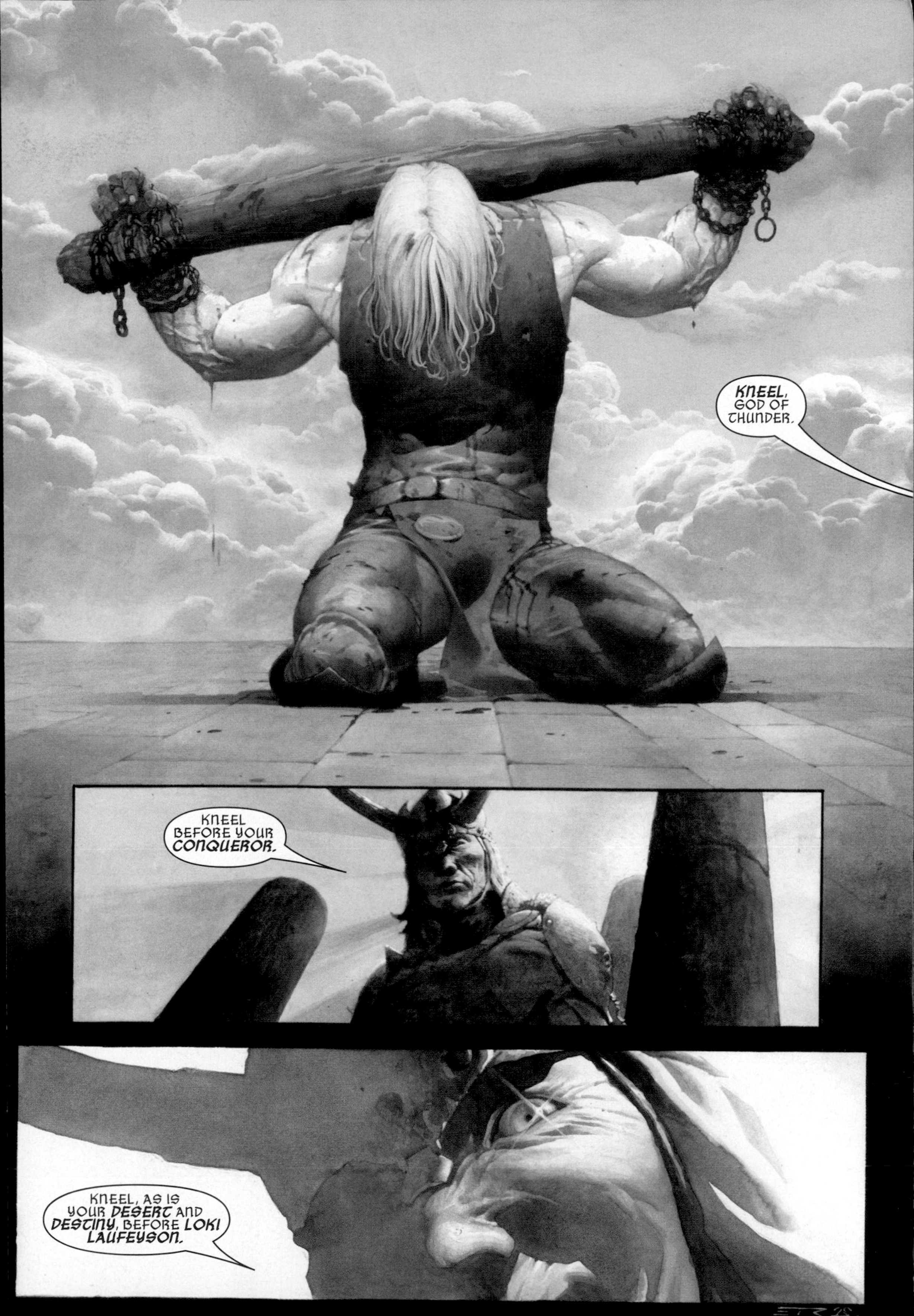
KNEEL, GOD OF THUNDER.
KNEEL BEFORE YOUR CONQUEROR.
KNEEL, AS IS YOUR DESERT AND DESTINY, BEFORE LOKI LAUFEYSON.

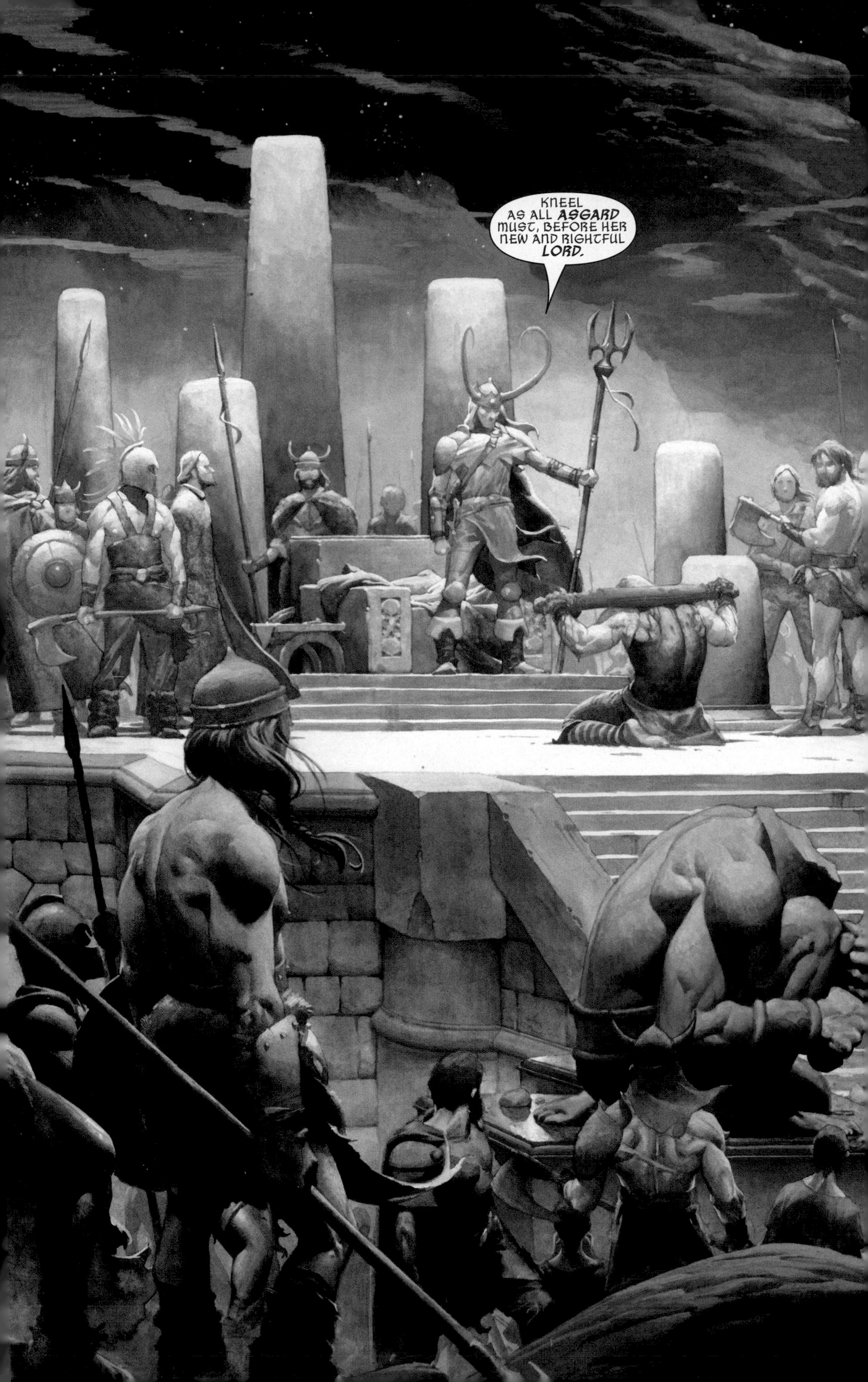

KNEEL AS ALL ASGARD MUST, BEFORE HER NEW AND RIGHTFUL LORD.

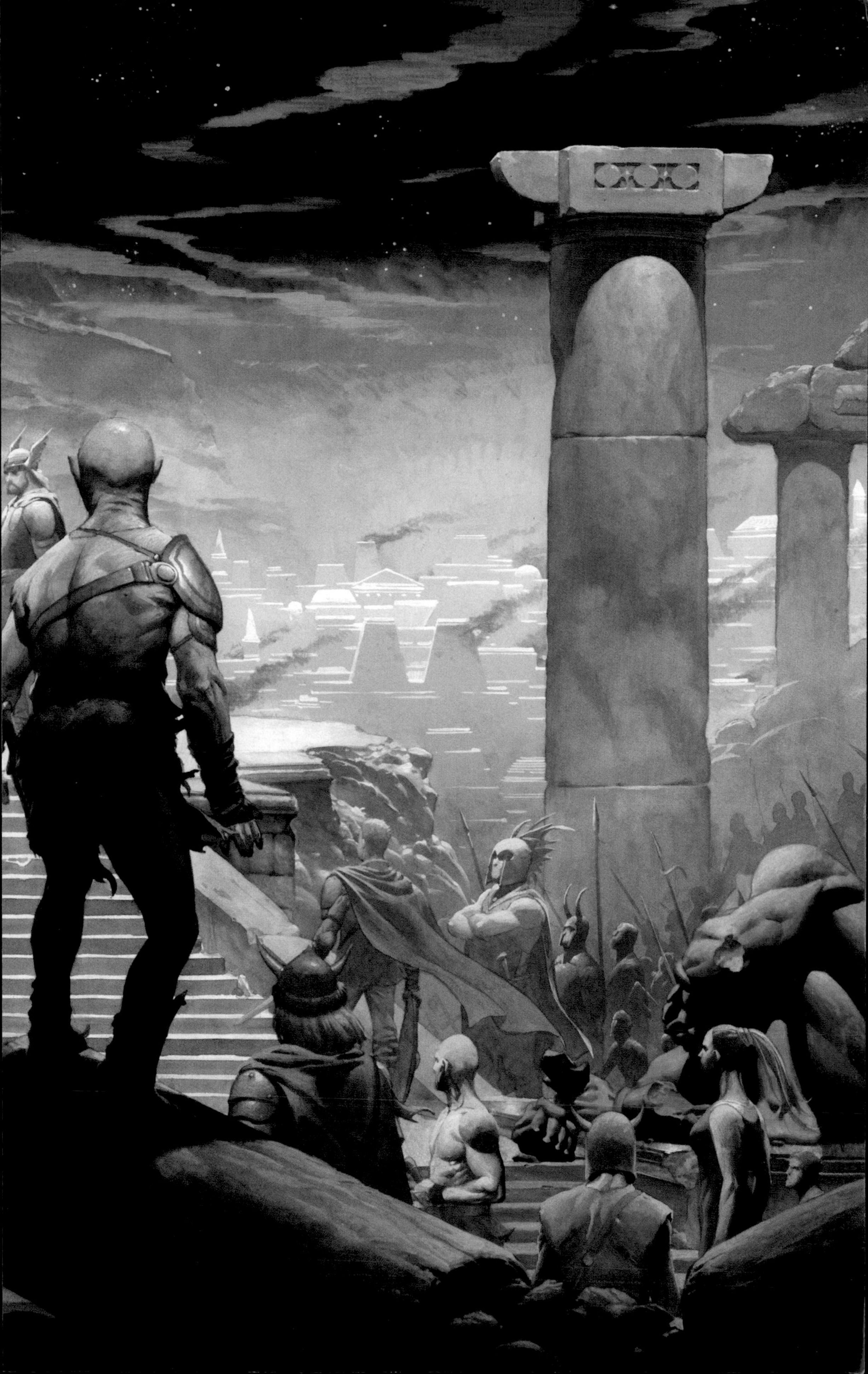

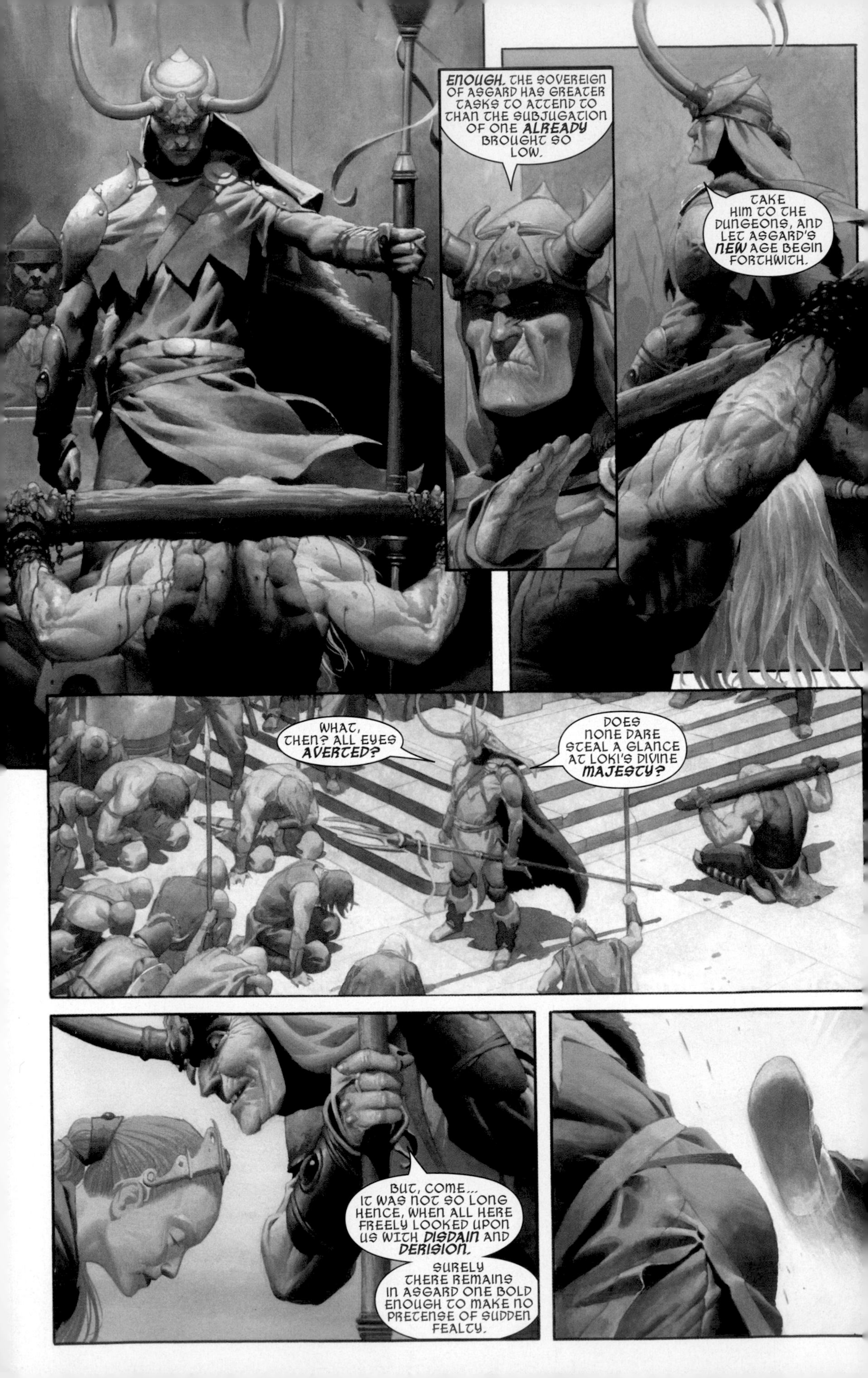
ENOUGH. THE SOVEREIGN OF ASGARD HAS GREATER TASKS TO ATTEND TO THAN THE SUBJUGATION OF ONE ALREADY BROUGHT SO LOW.
TAKE HIM TO THE DUNGEONS, AND LET ASGARD'S NEW AGE BEGIN FORTHWITH.
WHAT, THEN? ALL EYES AVERTED?
DOES NONE DARE STEAL A GLANCE AT LOKI'S DIVINE MAJESTY?
BUT, COME... IT WAS NOT SO LONG HENCE, WHEN ALL HERE FREELY LOOKED UPON US WITH DISDAIN AND DERISION.
SURELY THERE REMAINS IN ASGARD ONE BOLD ENOUGH TO MAKE NO PRETENSE OF SUDDEN FEALTY.

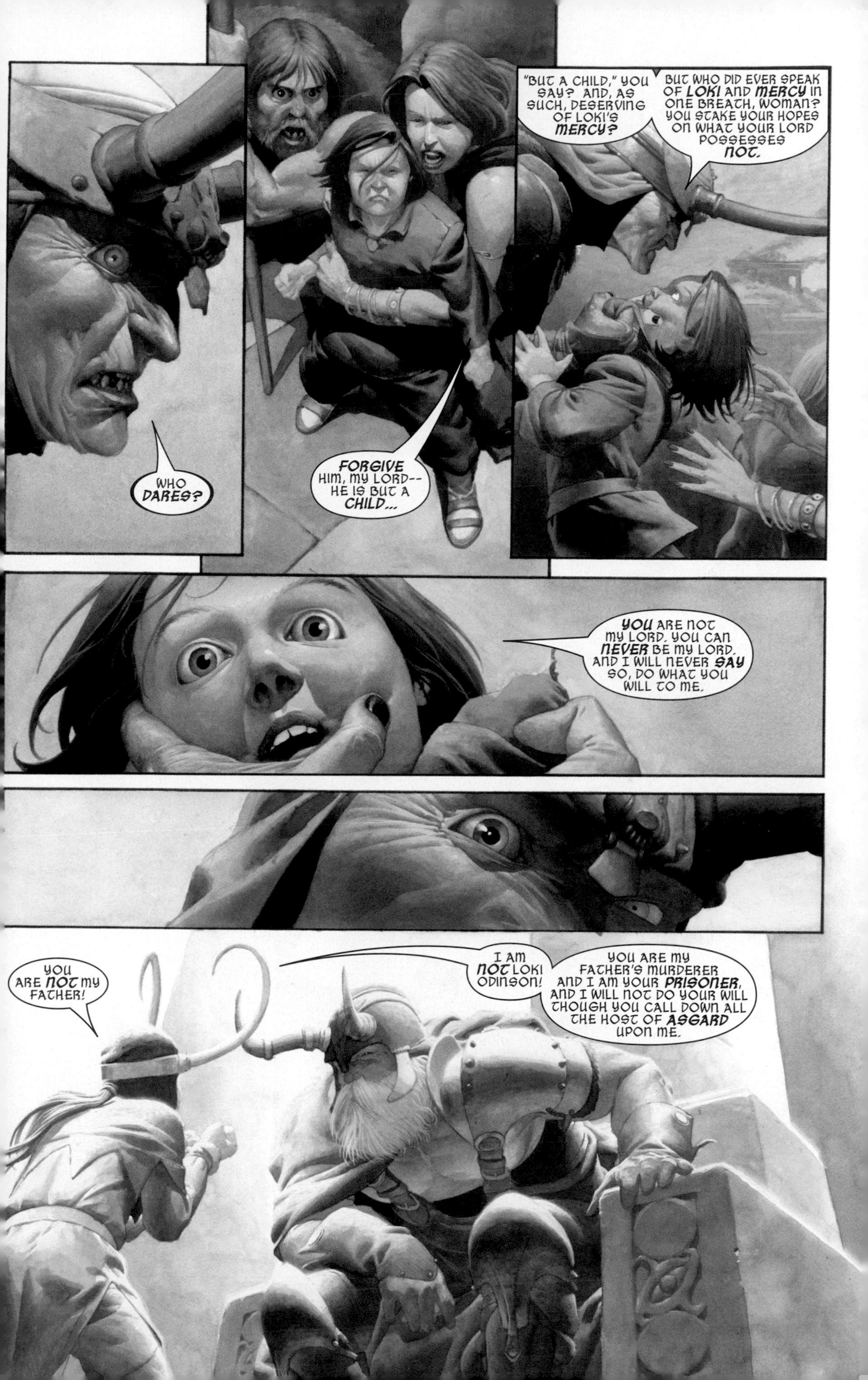
WHO DARES?
FORGIVE HIM, MY LORD-- HE IS BUT A CHILD...
"BUT A CHILD," YOU SAY? AND, AS SUCH, DESERVING OF LOKI'S MERCY?
BUT WHO DID EVER SPEAK OF LOKI AND MERCY IN ONE BREATH, WOMAN? YOU STAKE YOUR HOPES ON WHAT YOUR LORD POSSESSES NOT.
YOU ARE NOT MY LORD. YOU CAN NEVER BE MY LORD. AND I WILL NEVER SAY SO, DO WHAT YOU WILL TO ME.
YOU ARE NOT MY FATHER!
I AM NOT LOKI ODINSON!
YOU ARE MY FATHER'S MURDERER AND I AM YOUR PRISONER, AND I WILL NOT DO YOUR WILL THOUGH YOU CALL DOWN ALL THE HOST OF ASGARD UPON ME.

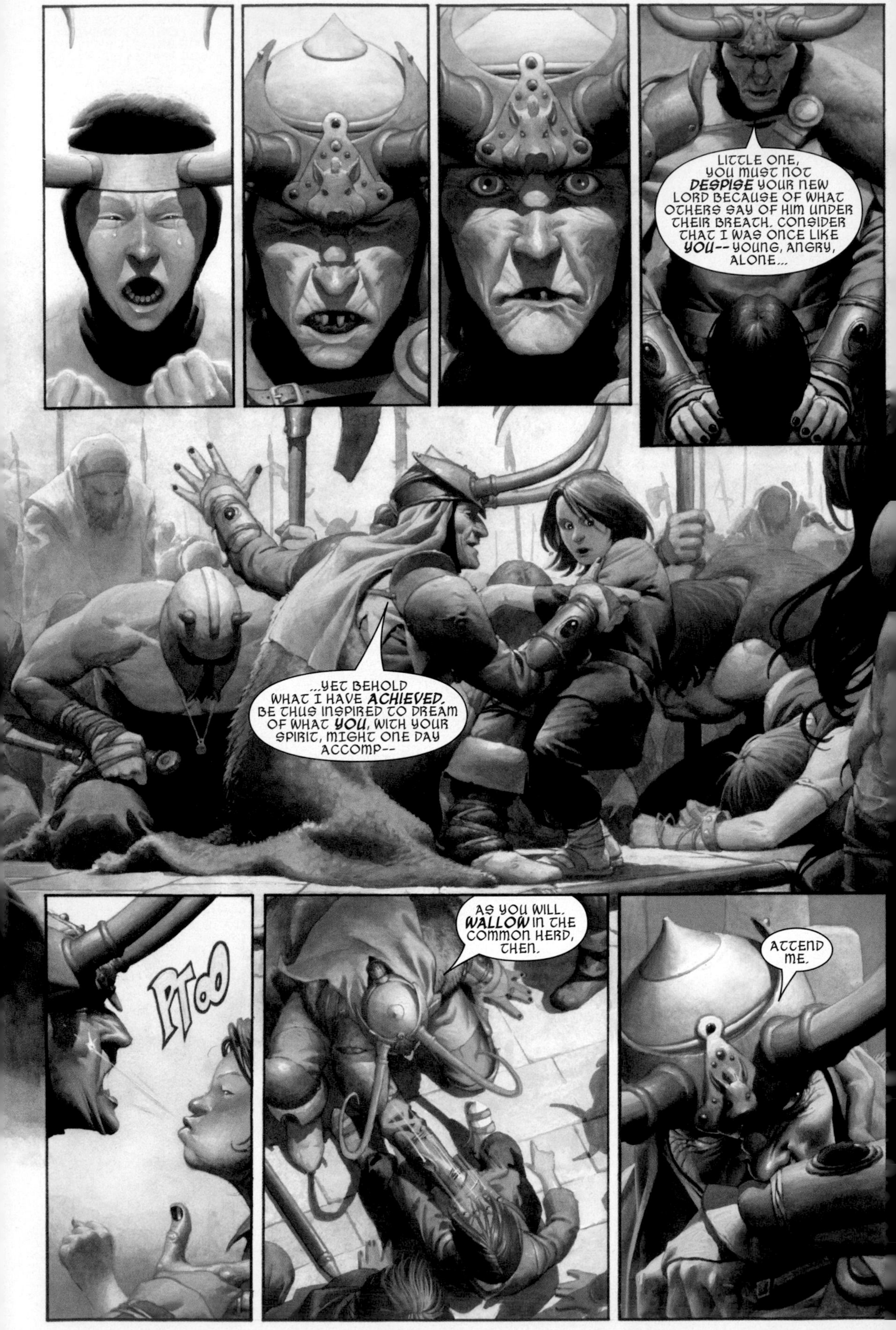
LITTLE ONE, YOU MUST NOT DESPISE YOUR NEW LORD BECAUSE OF WHAT OTHERS SAY OF HIM UNDER THEIR BREATH. CONSIDER THAT I WAS ONCE LIKE YOU-- YOUNG, ANGRY, ALONE...
...YET BEHOLD WHAT I HAVE ACHIEVED. BE THUS INSPIRED TO DREAM OF WHAT YOU, WITH YOUR SPIRIT, MIGHT ONE DAY ACCOMP--
PTOO
AS YOU WILL. WALLOW IN THE COMMON HERD, THEN.
ATTEND ME.

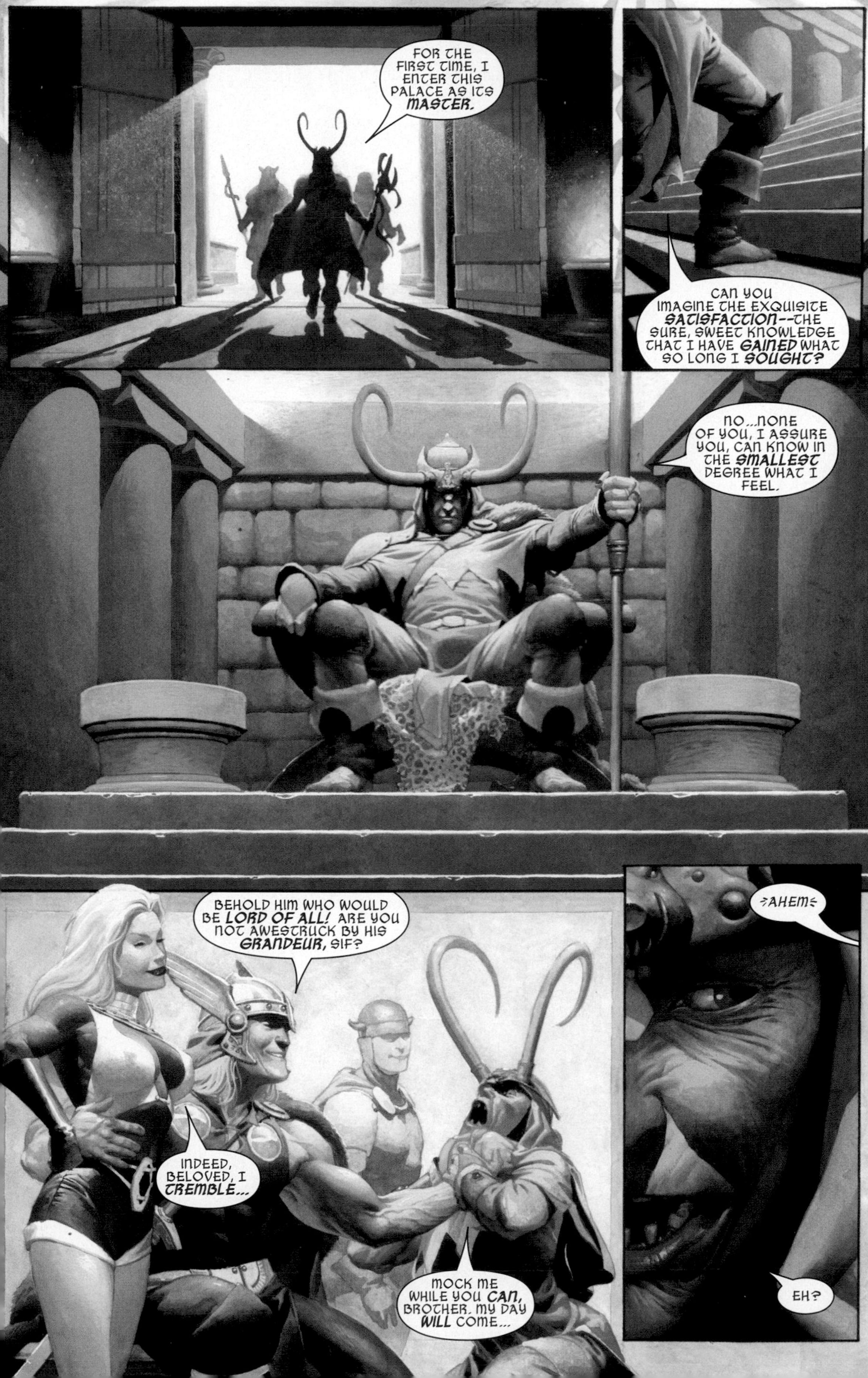

FOR THE FIRST TIME, I ENTER THIS PALACE AS ITS MASTER.
CAN YOU IMAGINE THE EXQUISITE SATISFACTION--THE SURE, SWEET KNOWLEDGE THAT I HAVE GAINED WHAT SO LONG I SOUGHT?
NO...NONE OF YOU, I ASSURE YOU, CAN KNOW IN THE SMALLEST DEGREE WHAT I FEEL.
BEHOLD HIM WHO WOULD BE LORD OF ALL! ARE YOU NOT AWESTRUCK BY HIS GRANDEUR, SIF?
INDEED, BELOVED, I TREMBLE...
MOCK ME WHILE YOU CAN, BROTHER. MY DAY WILL COME...
AHEM
EH?

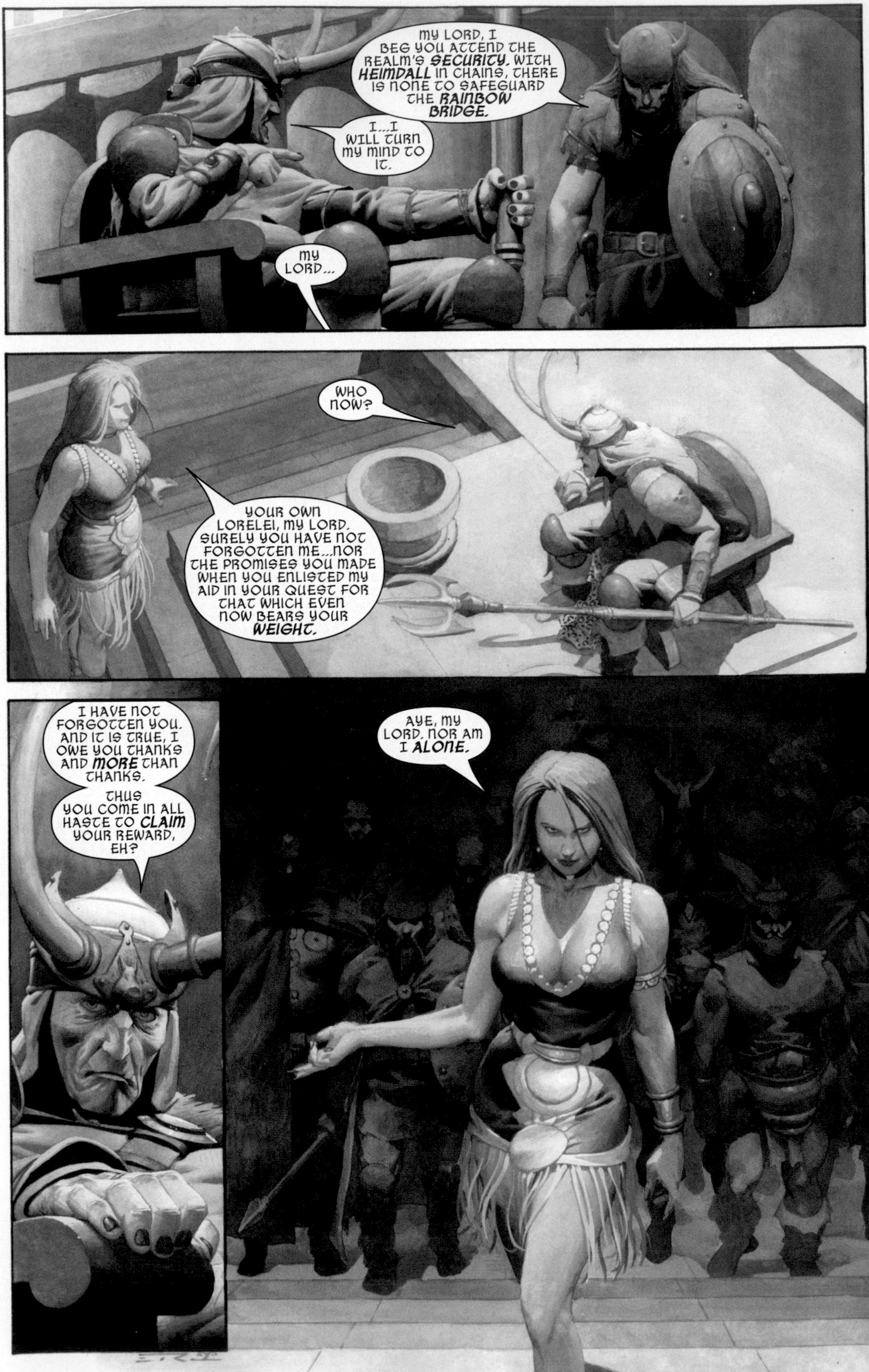
MY LORD, I BEG YOU ATTEND THE REALM'S SECURITY. WITH HEIMDALL IN CHAINS, THERE IS NONE TO SAFEGUARD THE RAINBOW BRIDGE.
I...I WILL TURN MY MIND TO IT.
MY LORD...
WHO NOW?
YOUR OWN LORELEI, MY LORD. SURELY YOU HAVE NOT FORGOTTEN ME...NOR THE PROMISES YOU MADE WHEN YOU ENLISTED MY AID IN YOUR QUEST FOR THAT WHICH EVEN NOW BEARS YOUR WEIGHT.
I HAVE NOT FORGOTTEN YOU. AND IT IS TRUE, I OWE YOU THANKS AND MORE THAN THANKS.
THUS YOU COME IN ALL HASTE TO CLAIM YOUR REWARD, EH?
AYE, MY LORD. NOR AM I ALONE.

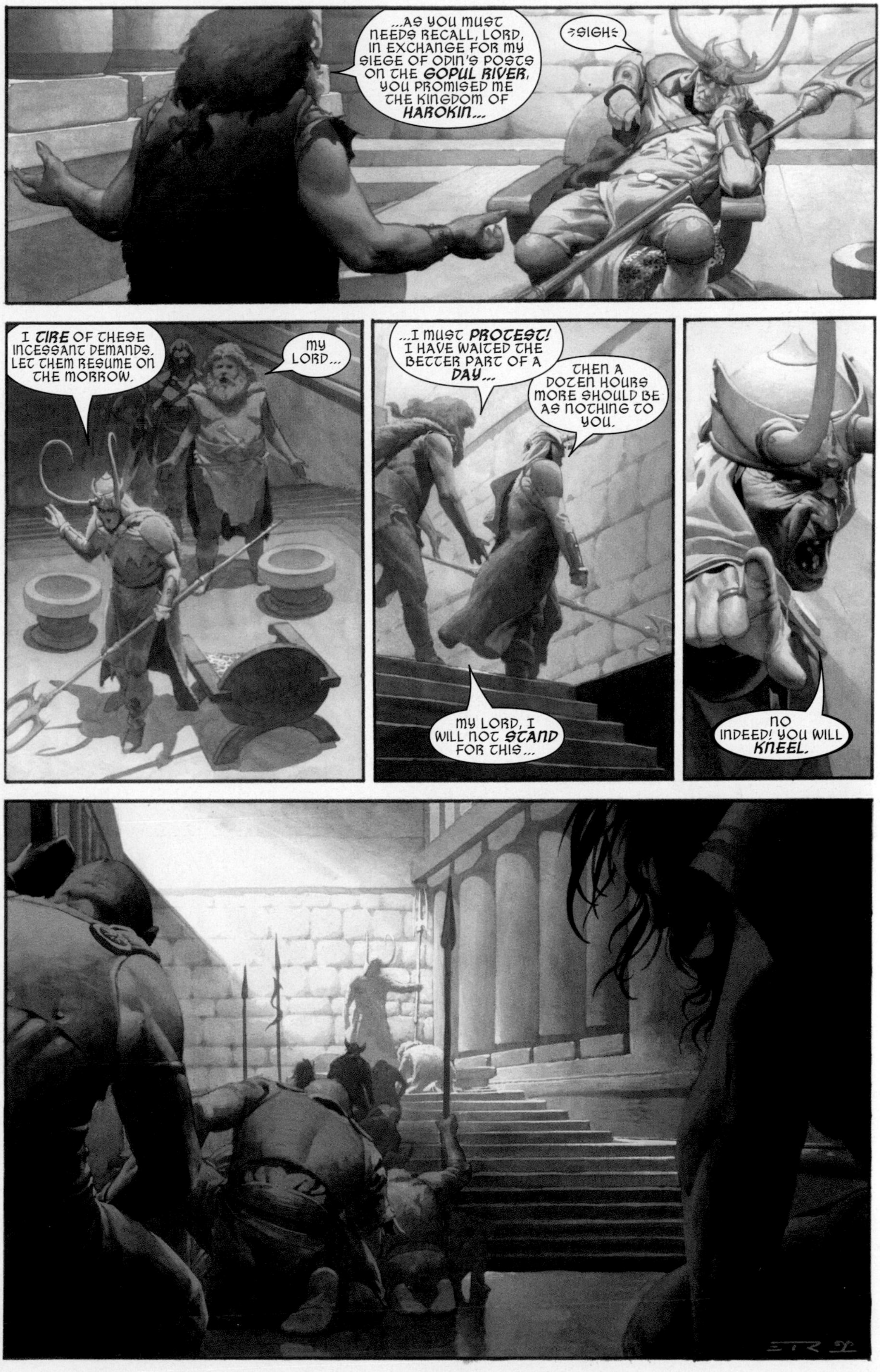
...AS YOU MUST NEEDS RECALL, LORD, IN EXCHANGE FOR MY SIEGE OF ODIN'S POSTS ON THE GOPUL RIVER, YOU PROMISED ME THE KINGDOM OF HAROKIN...
>SIGH<
I TIRE OF THESE INCESSANT DEMANDS. LET THEM RESUME ON THE MORROW.
MY LORD...
...I MUST PROTEST! I HAVE WAITED THE BETTER PART OF A DAY...
THEN A DOZEN HOURS MORE SHOULD BE AS NOTHING TO YOU.
MY LORD, I WILL NOT STAND FOR THIS...
NO INDEED! YOU WILL KNEEL.

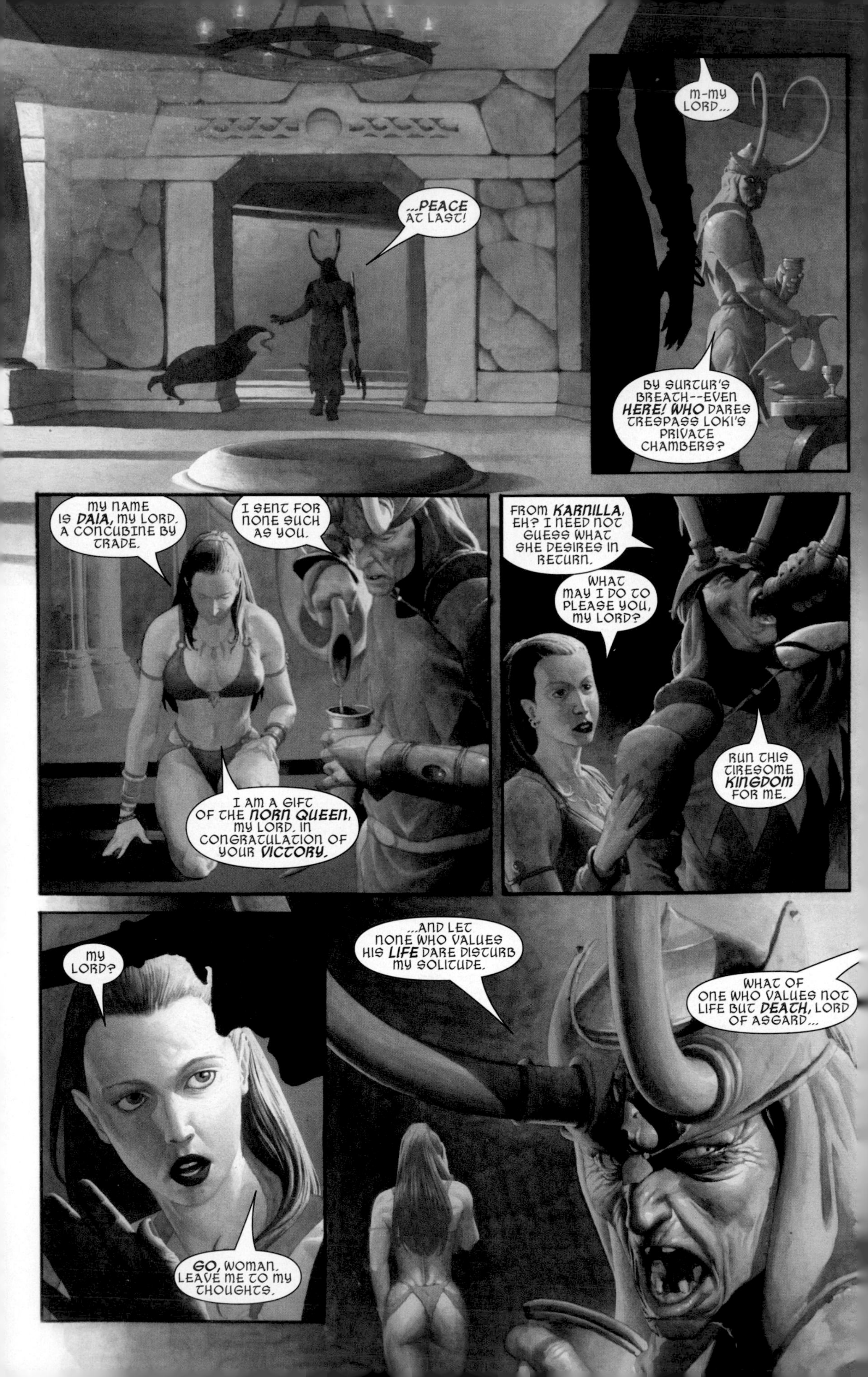
...PEACE AT LAST!
M-MY LORD...
BY SURTUR'S BREATH--EVEN HERE! WHO DARES TRESPASS LOKI'S PRIVATE CHAMBERS?
MY NAME IS DAIA, MY LORD. A CONCUBINE BY TRADE.
I SENT FOR NONE SUCH AS YOU.
I AM A GIFT OF THE NORN QUEEN, MY LORD. IN CONGRATULATION OF YOUR VICTORY.
FROM KARNILLA, EH? I NEED NOT GUESS WHAT SHE DESIRES IN RETURN.
WHAT MAY I DO TO PLEASE YOU, MY LORD?
RUN THIS TIRESOME KINGDOM FOR ME.
MY LORD?
GO, WOMAN. LEAVE ME TO MY THOUGHTS.
...AND LET NONE WHO VALUES HIS LIFE DARE DISTURB MY SOLITUDE.
WHAT OF ONE WHO VALUES NOT LIFE BUT DEATH, LORD OF ASGARD...

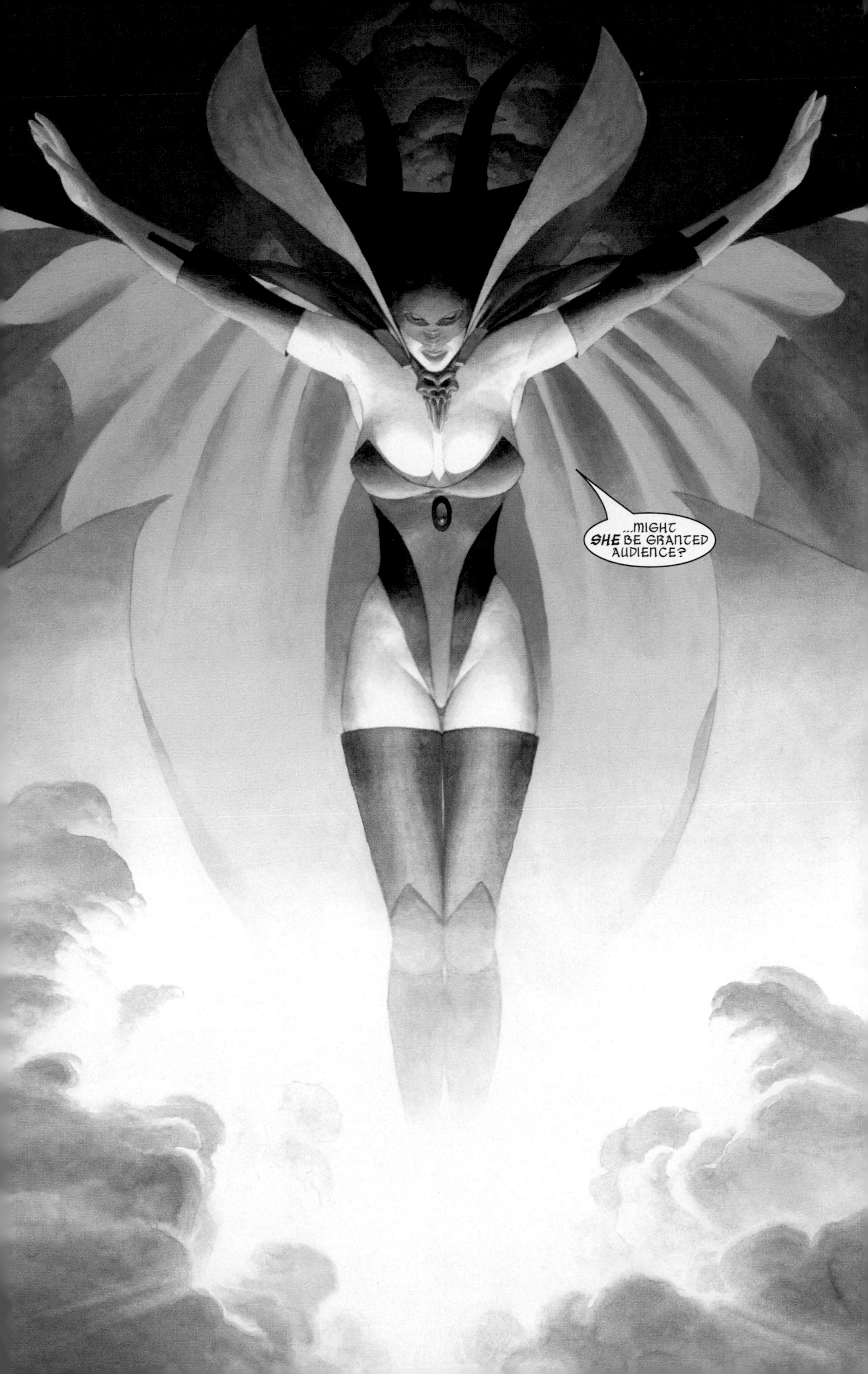
...MIGHT SHE BE GRANTED AUDIENCE?

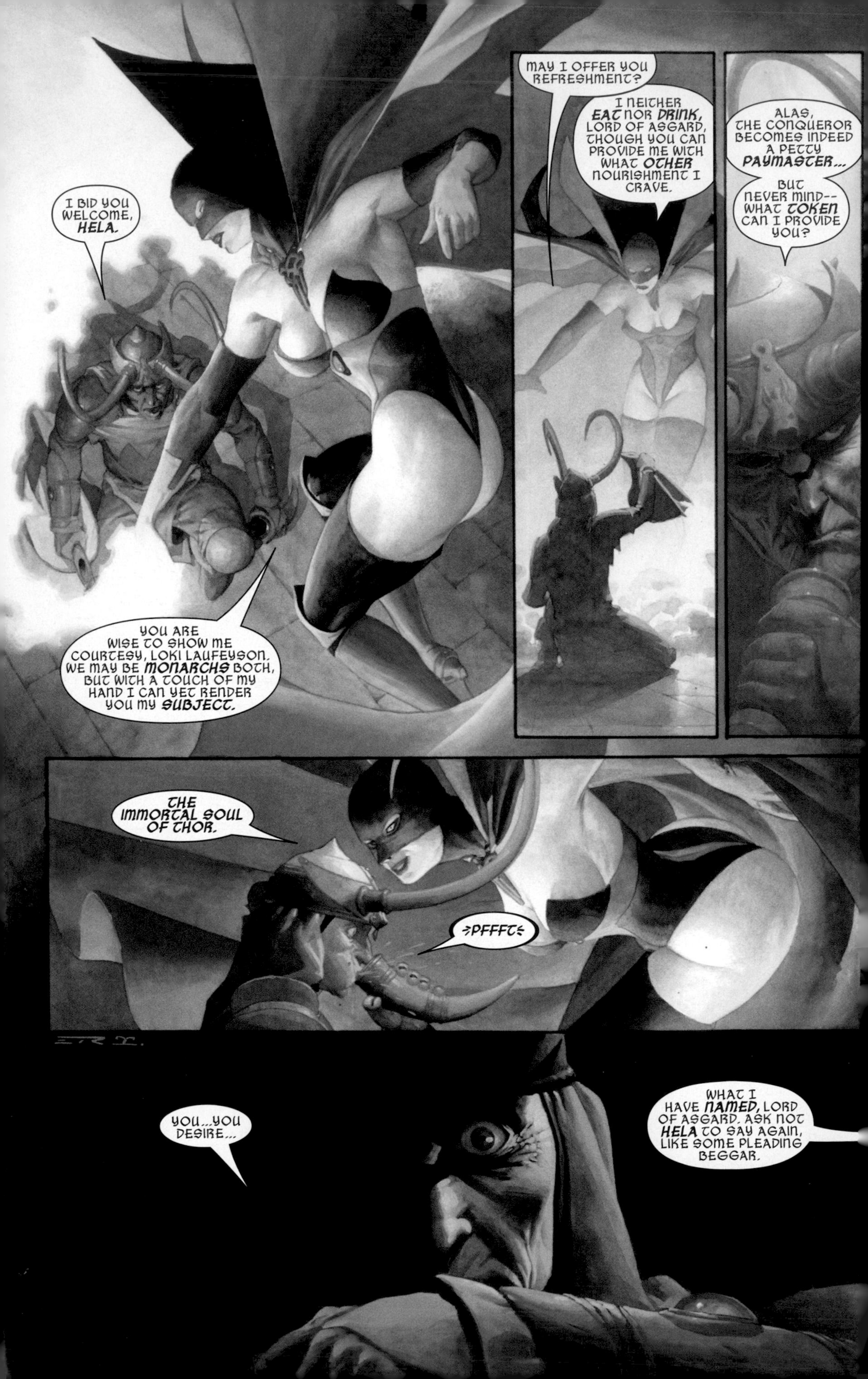
I BID YOU WELCOME, HELA.
YOU ARE WISE TO SHOW ME COURTESY, LOKI LAUFEYSON. WE MAY BE MONARCHS BOTH, BUT WITH A TOUCH OF MY HAND I CAN YET RENDER YOU MY SUBJECT.
MAY I OFFER YOU REFRESHMENT?
I NEITHER EAT NOR DRINK, LORD OF ASGARD, THOUGH YOU CAN PROVIDE ME WITH WHAT OTHER NOURISHMENT I CRAVE.
ALAS, THE CONQUEROR BECOMES INDEED A PETTY PAYMASTER...
BUT NEVER MIND-- WHAT TOKEN CAN I PROVIDE YOU?
THE IMMORTAL SOUL OF THOR.
PFFFT
YOU...YOU DESIRE...
WHAT I HAVE NAMED, LORD OF ASGARD. ASK NOT HELA TO SAY AGAIN, LIKE SOME PLEADING BEGGAR.

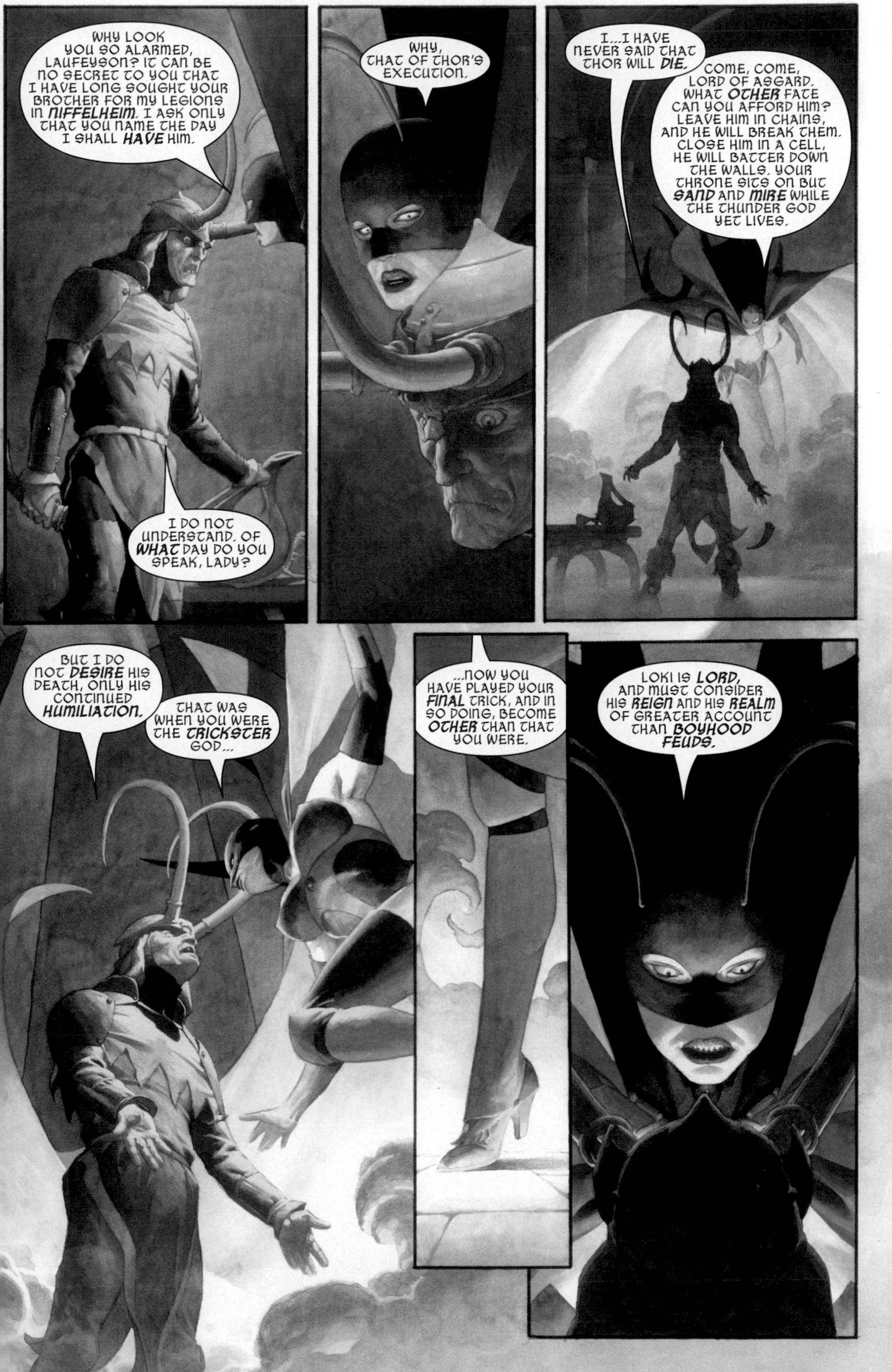
WHY LOOK YOU SO ALARMED, LAUFEYSON? IT CAN BE NO SECRET TO YOU THAT I HAVE LONG SOUGHT YOUR BROTHER FOR MY LEGIONS IN NIFFELHEIM. I ASK ONLY THAT YOU NAME THE DAY I SHALL HAVE HIM.
I DO NOT UNDERSTAND. OF WHAT DAY DO YOU SPEAK, LADY?
WHY, THAT OF THOR'S EXECUTION.
I...I HAVE NEVER SAID THAT THOR WILL DIE.
COME, COME, LORD OF ASGARD. WHAT OTHER FATE CAN YOU AFFORD HIM? LEAVE HIM IN CHAINS, AND HE WILL BREAK THEM. CLOSE HIM IN A CELL, HE WILL BATTER DOWN THE WALLS. YOUR THRONE SITS ON BUT SAND AND MIRE WHILE THE THUNDER GOD YET LIVES.
BUT I DO NOT DESIRE HIS DEATH, ONLY HIS CONTINUED HUMILIATION.
THAT WAS WHEN YOU WERE THE TRICKSTER GOD...
...NOW YOU HAVE PLAYED YOUR FINAL TRICK, AND IN SO DOING, BECOME OTHER THAN THAT YOU WERE.
LOKI IS LORD, AND MUST CONSIDER HIS REIGN AND HIS REALM OF GREATER ACCOUNT THAN BOYHOOD FEUDS.

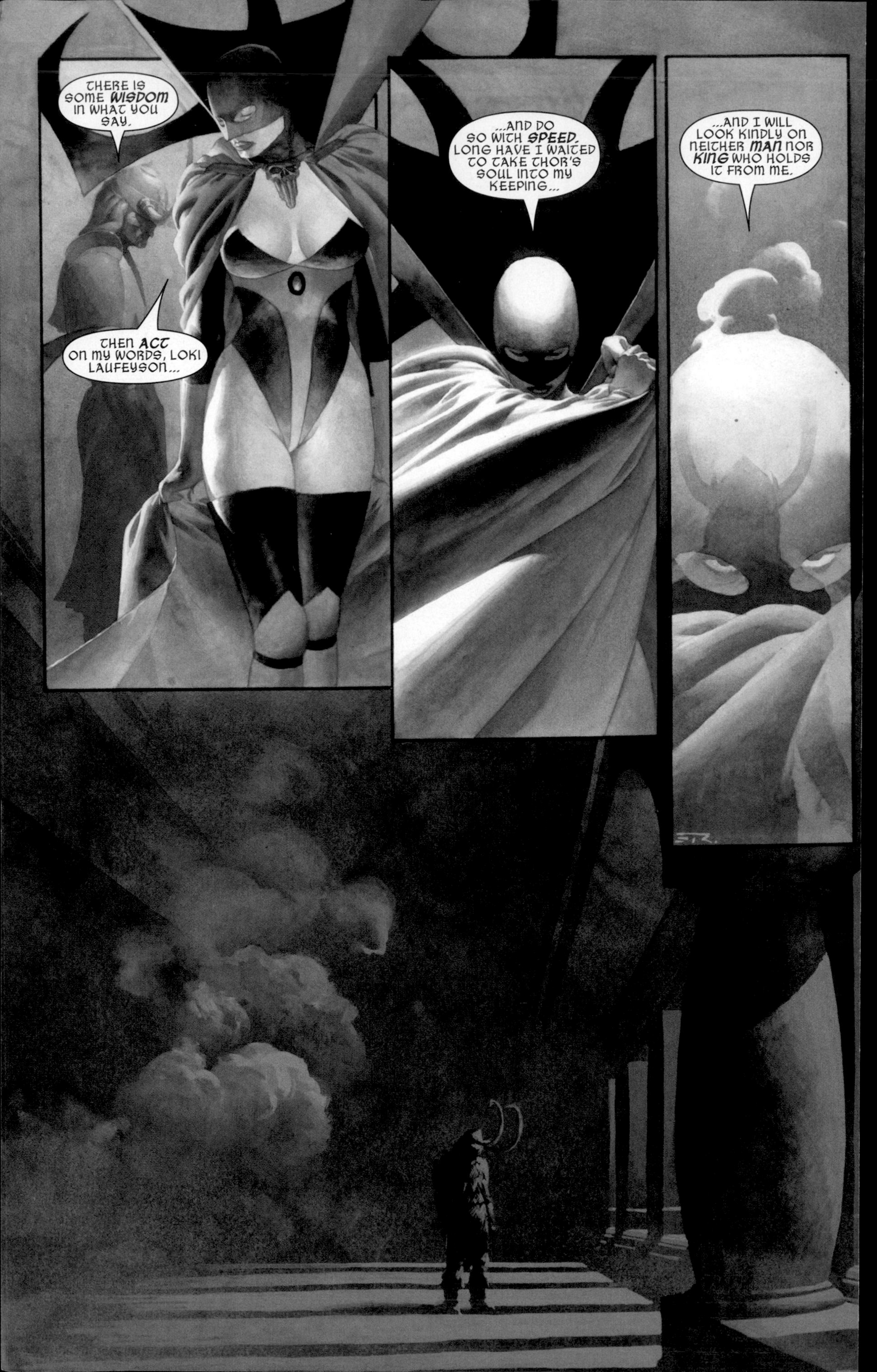
THERE IS SOME WISDOM IN WHAT YOU SAY.
THEN ACT ON MY WORDS, LOKI LAUFEYSON...
...AND DO SO WITH SPEED. LONG HAVE I WAITED TO TAKE THOR'S SOUL INTO MY KEEPING...
...AND I WILL LOOK KINDLY ON NEITHER MAN NOR KING WHO HOLDS IT FROM ME.

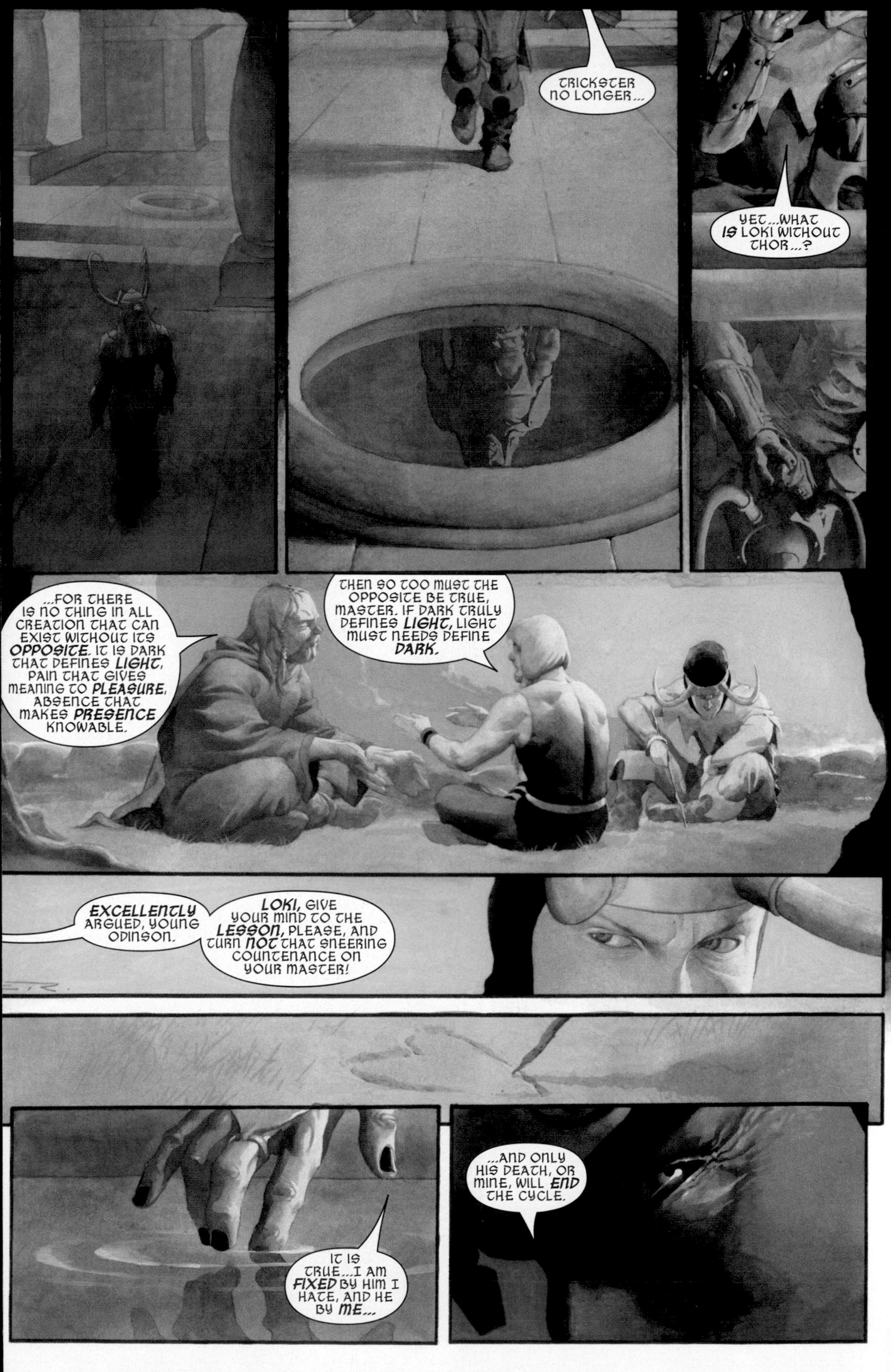
TRICKSTER NO LONGER...
YET...WHAT IS LOKI WITHOUT THOR...?
...FOR THERE IS NO THING IN ALL CREATION THAT CAN EXIST WITHOUT ITS OPPOSITE. IT IS DARK THAT DEFINES LIGHT, PAIN THAT GIVES MEANING TO PLEASURE, ABSENCE THAT MAKES PRESENCE KNOWABLE.
THEN SO TOO MUST THE OPPOSITE BE TRUE, MASTER. IF DARK TRULY DEFINES LIGHT, LIGHT MUST NEEDS DEFINE DARK.
EXCELLENTLY ARGUED, YOUNG ODINSON.
LOKI, GIVE YOUR MIND TO THE LESSON, PLEASE, AND TURN NOT THAT SNEERING COUNTENANCE ON YOUR MASTER!
IT IS TRUE...I AM FIXED BY HIM I HATE, AND HE BY ME...
...AND ONLY HIS DEATH, OR MINE, WILL END THE CYCLE.

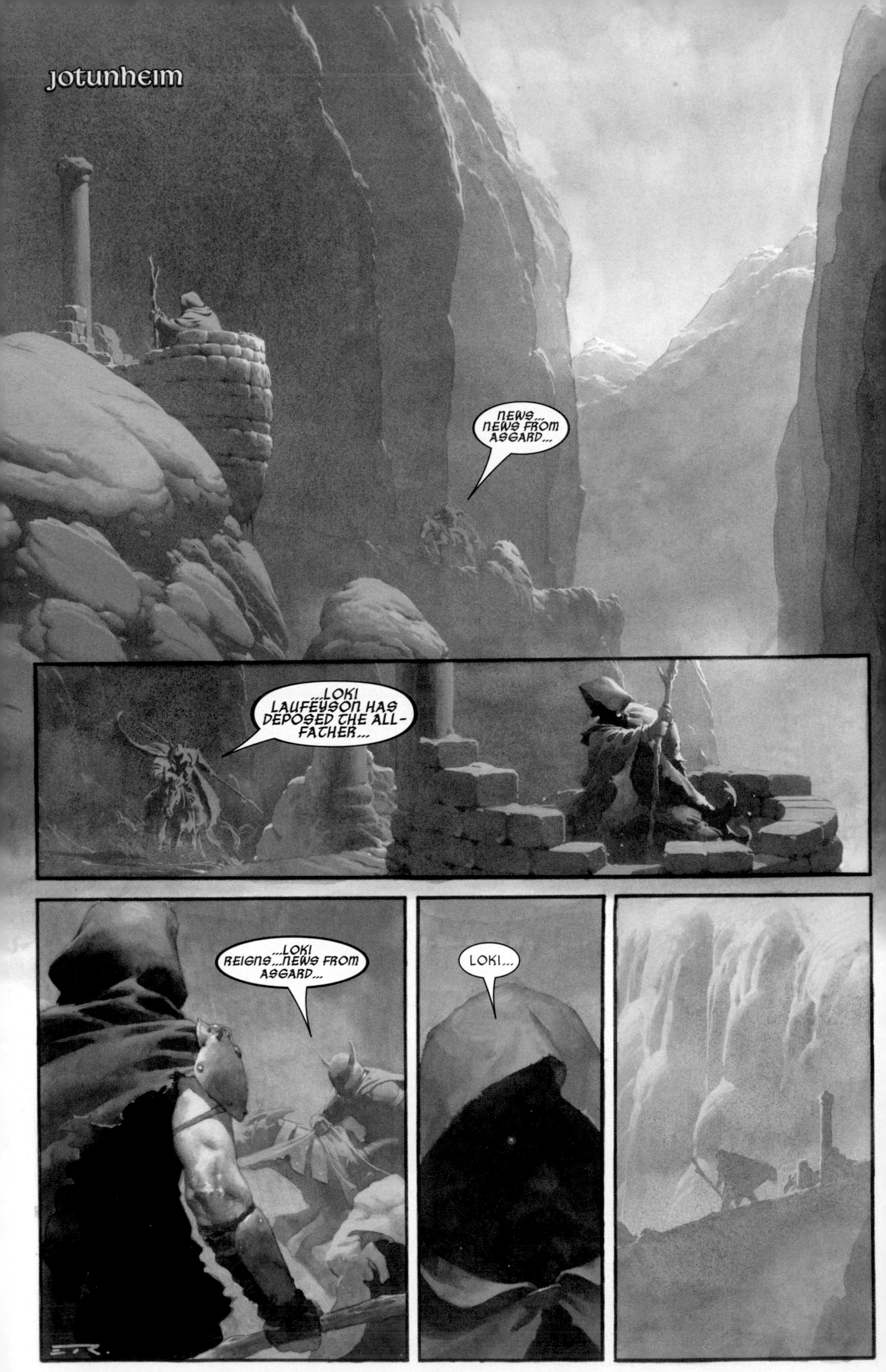
JOTUNHEIM
NEWS... NEWS FROM ASGARD...
...LOKI LAUFEYSON HAS DEPOSED THE ALL-FATHER...
...LOKI REIGNS...NEWS FROM ASGARD...
LOKI...

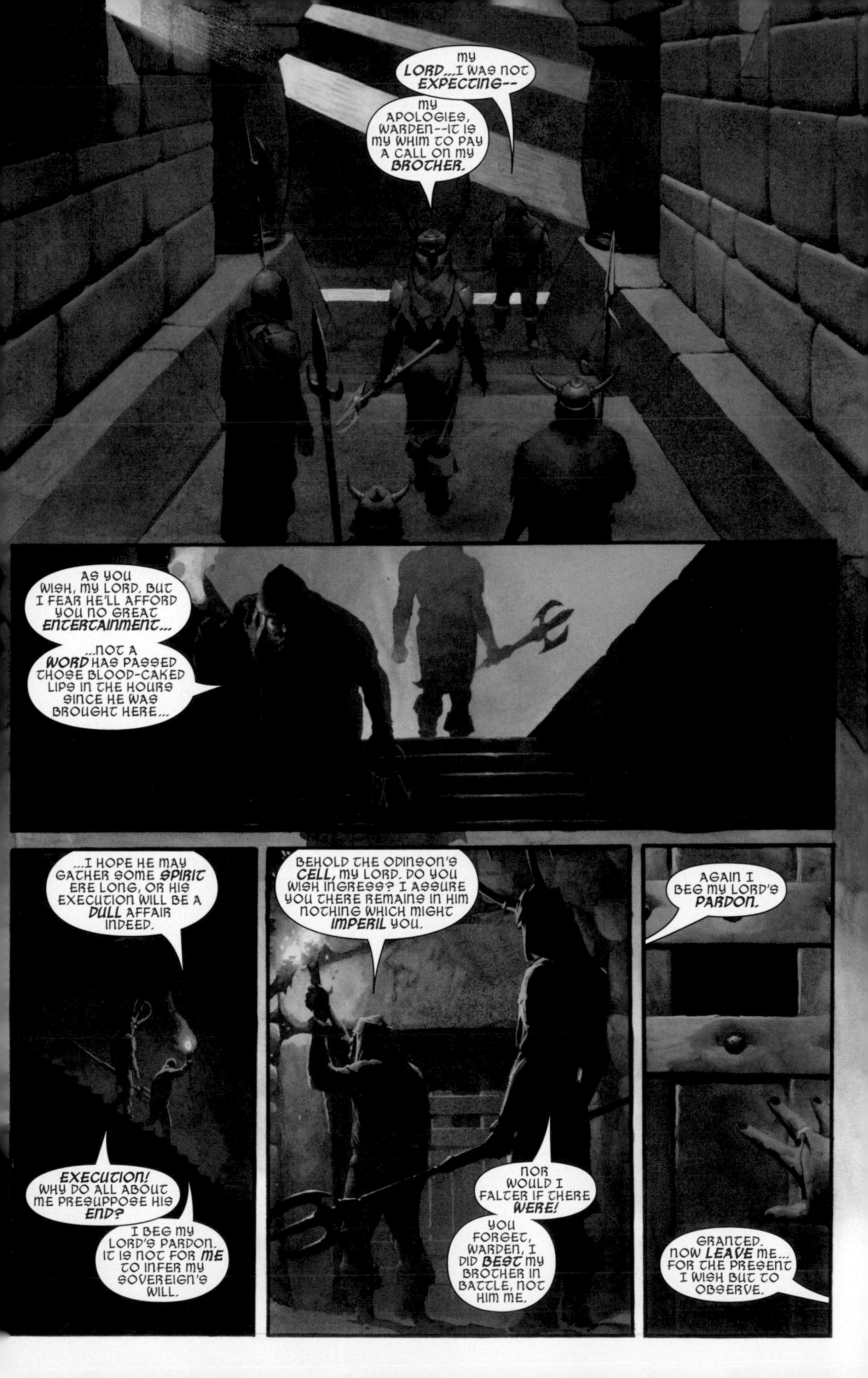
MY LORD...I WAS NOT EXPECTING--
MY APOLOGIES, WARDEN--IT IS MY WHIM TO PAY A CALL ON MY BROTHER.
AS YOU WISH, MY LORD. BUT I FEAR HE'LL AFFORD YOU NO GREAT ENTERTAINMENT...
...NOT A WORD HAS PASSED THOSE BLOOD-CAKED LIPS IN THE HOURS SINCE HE WAS BROUGHT HERE...
...I HOPE HE MAY GATHER SOME SPIRIT ERE LONG, OR HIS EXECUTION WILL BE A DULL AFFAIR INDEED.
EXECUTION! WHY DO ALL ABOUT ME PRESUPPOSE HIS END?
I BEG MY LORD'S PARDON. IT IS NOT FOR ME TO INFER MY SOVEREIGN'S WILL.
BEHOLD THE ODINSON'S CELL, MY LORD. DO YOU WISH INGRESS? I ASSURE YOU THERE REMAINS IN HIM NOTHING WHICH MIGHT IMPERIL YOU.
NOR WOULD I FALTER IF THERE WERE!
YOU FORGET, WARDEN, I DID BEST MY BROTHER IN BATTLE, NOT HIM ME.
AGAIN I BEG MY LORD'S PARDON.
GRANTED. NOW LEAVE ME... FOR THE PRESENT I WISH BUT TO OBSERVE.

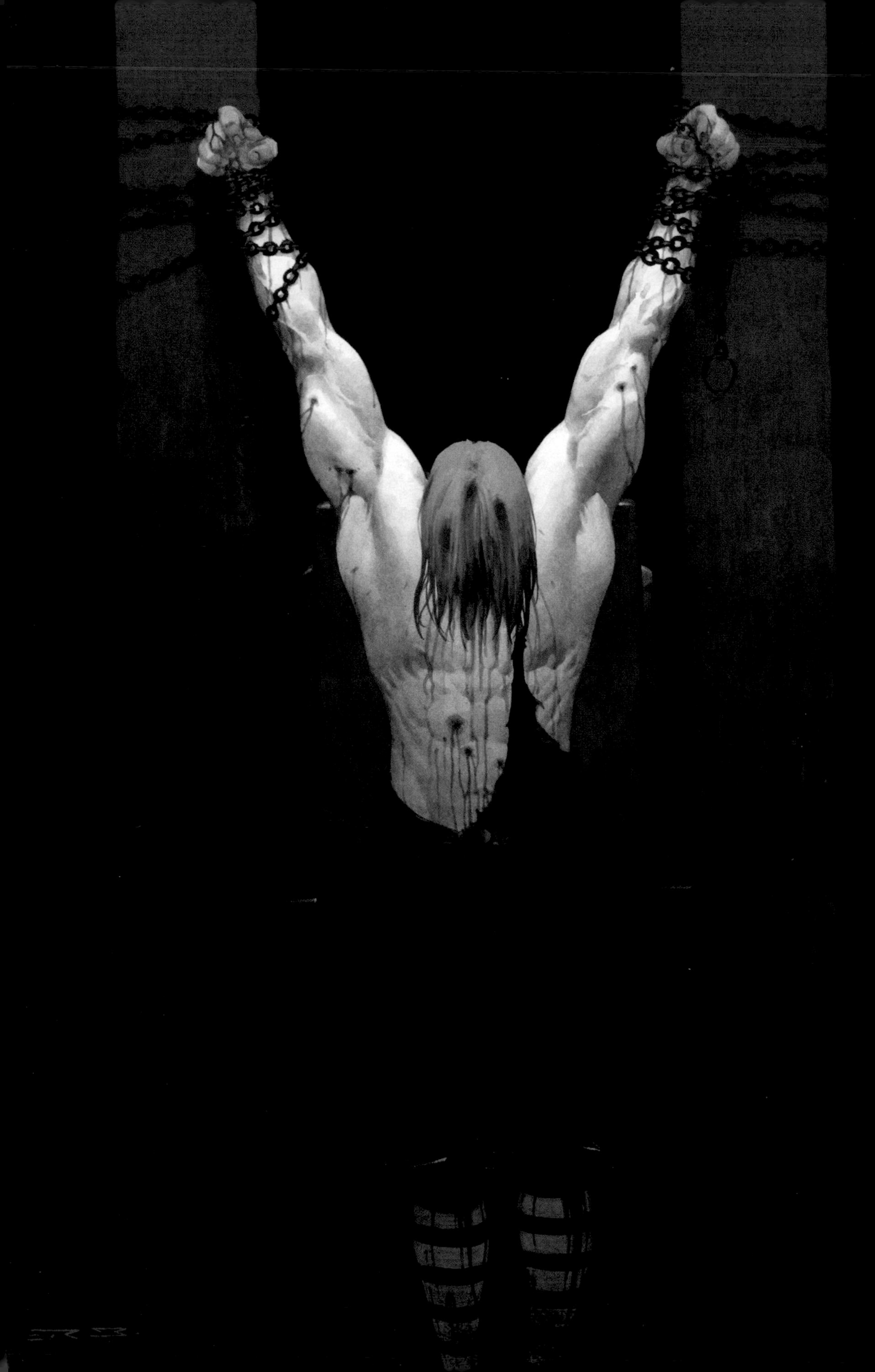

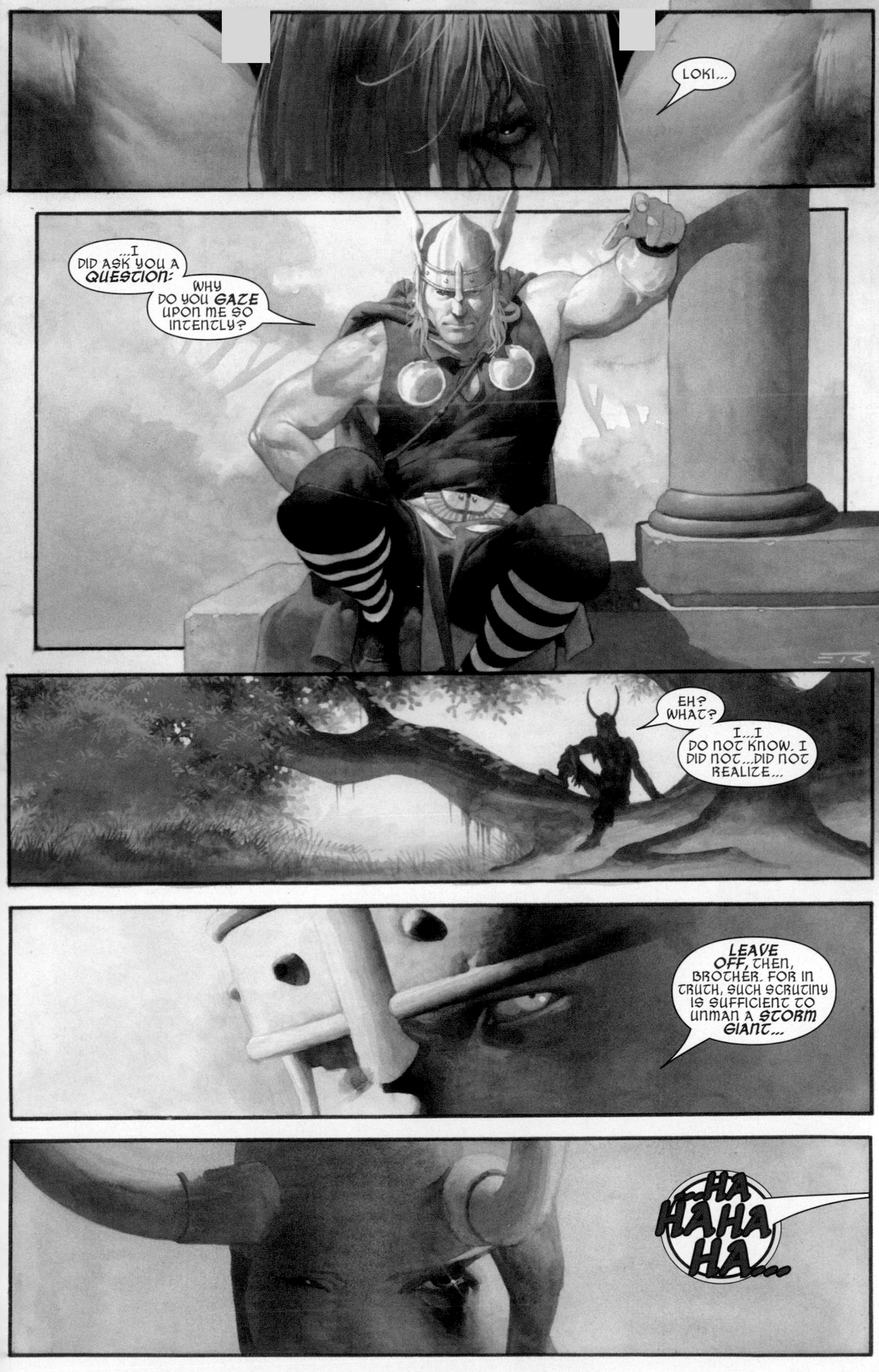
LOKI...
...I DID ASK YOU A QUESTION: WHY DO YOU GAZE UPON ME SO INTENTLY?
EH? WHAT?
I...I DO NOT KNOW. I DID NOT...DID NOT REALIZE...
LEAVE OFF, THEN, BROTHER. FOR IN TRUTH, SUCH SCRUTINY IS SUFFICIENT TO UNMAN A STORM GIANT...
HA HAHAHA HA...

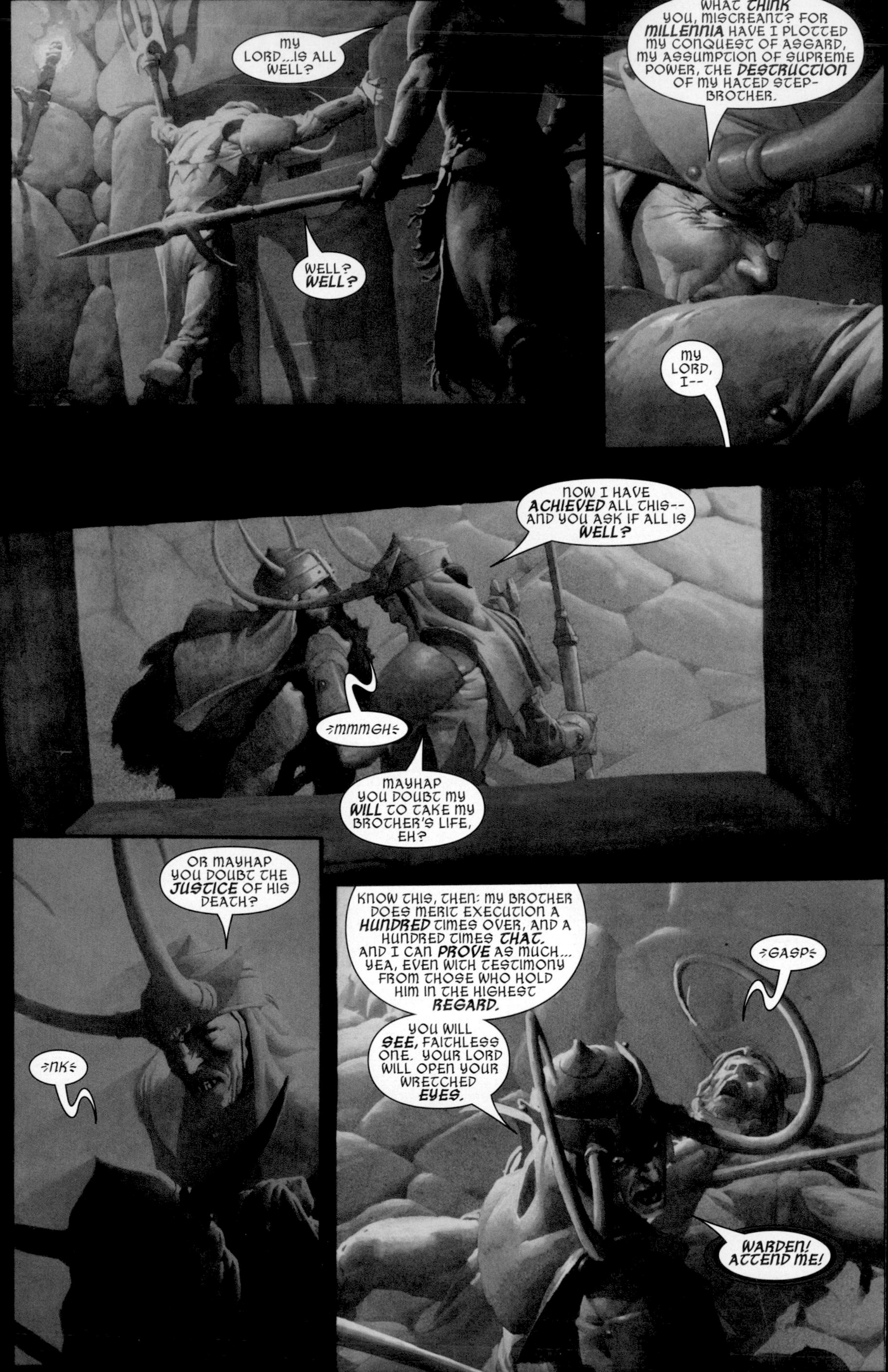
MY LORD...IS ALL WELL?
WELL? WELL?
WHAT THINK YOU, MISCREANT? FOR MILLENNIA HAVE I PLOTTED MY CONQUEST OF ASGARD, MY ASSUMPTION OF SUPREME POWER, THE DESTRUCTION OF MY HATED STEP-BROTHER.
MY LORD, I--
NOW I HAVE ACHIEVED ALL THIS-- AND YOU ASK IF ALL IS WELL?
MMMGH
MAYHAP YOU DOUBT MY WILL TO TAKE MY BROTHER'S LIFE, EH?
OR MAYHAP YOU DOUBT THE JUSTICE OF HIS DEATH?
NK
KNOW THIS, THEN: MY BROTHER DOES MERIT EXECUTION A HUNDRED TIMES OVER, AND A HUNDRED TIMES THAT. AND I CAN PROVE AS MUCH... YEA, EVEN WITH TESTIMONY FROM THOSE WHO HOLD HIM IN THE HIGHEST REGARD.
YOU WILL SEE, FAITHLESS ONE. YOUR LORD WILL OPEN YOUR WRETCHED EYES.
GASP
WARDEN! ATTEND ME!

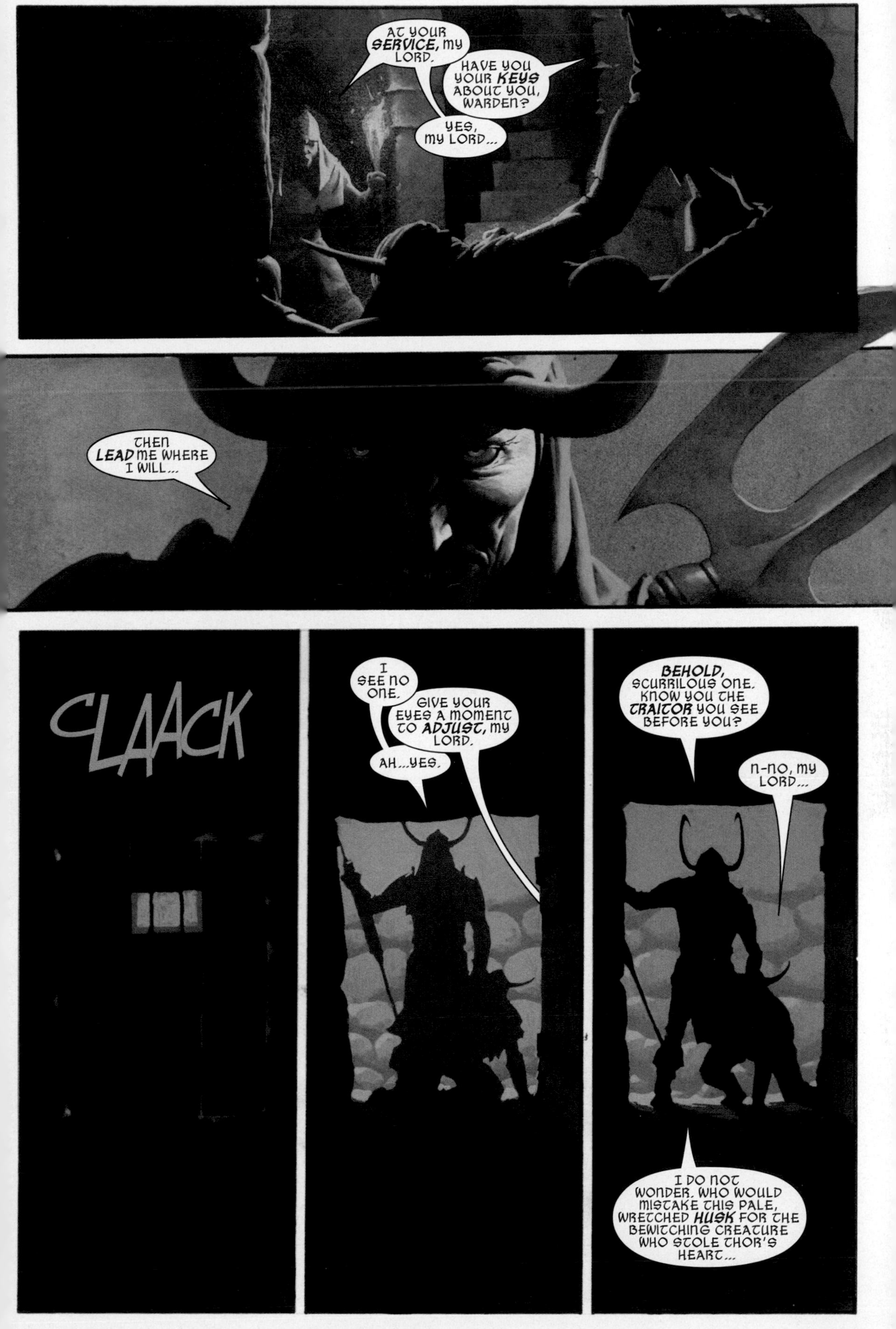

AT YOUR SERVICE, MY LORD.
HAVE YOU YOUR KEYS ABOUT YOU, WARDEN?
YES, MY LORD...
THEN LEAD ME WHERE I WILL...
CLAACK
I SEE NO ONE.
GIVE YOUR EYES A MOMENT TO ADJUST, MY LORD.
AH...YES.
BEHOLD, SCURRILOUS ONE. KNOW YOU THE TRAITOR YOU SEE BEFORE YOU?
N-NO, MY LORD...
I DO NOT WONDER. WHO WOULD MISTAKE THIS PALE, WRETCHED HUSK FOR THE BEWITCHING CREATURE WHO STOLE THOR'S HEART...

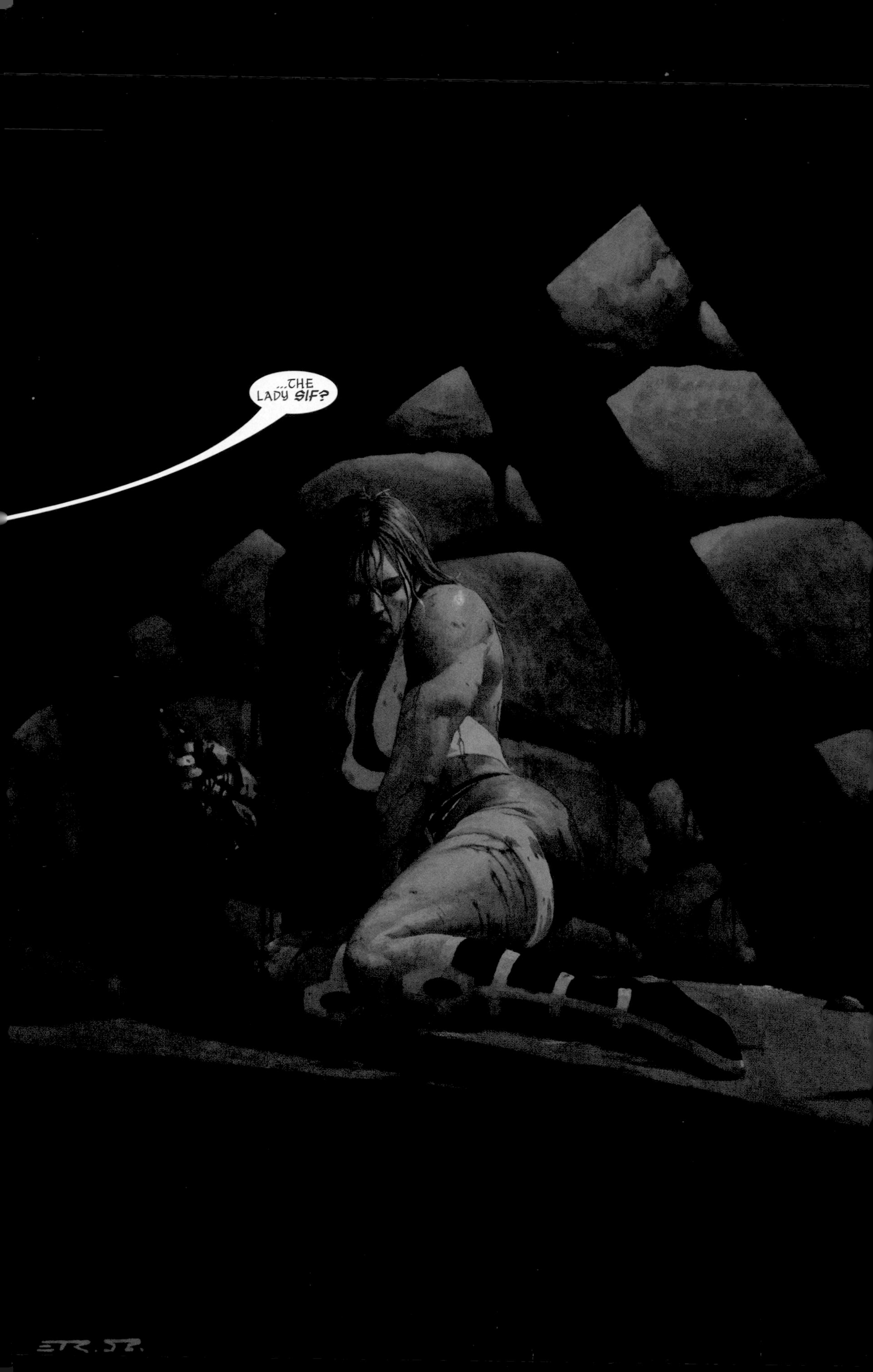
...THE LADY SIF?

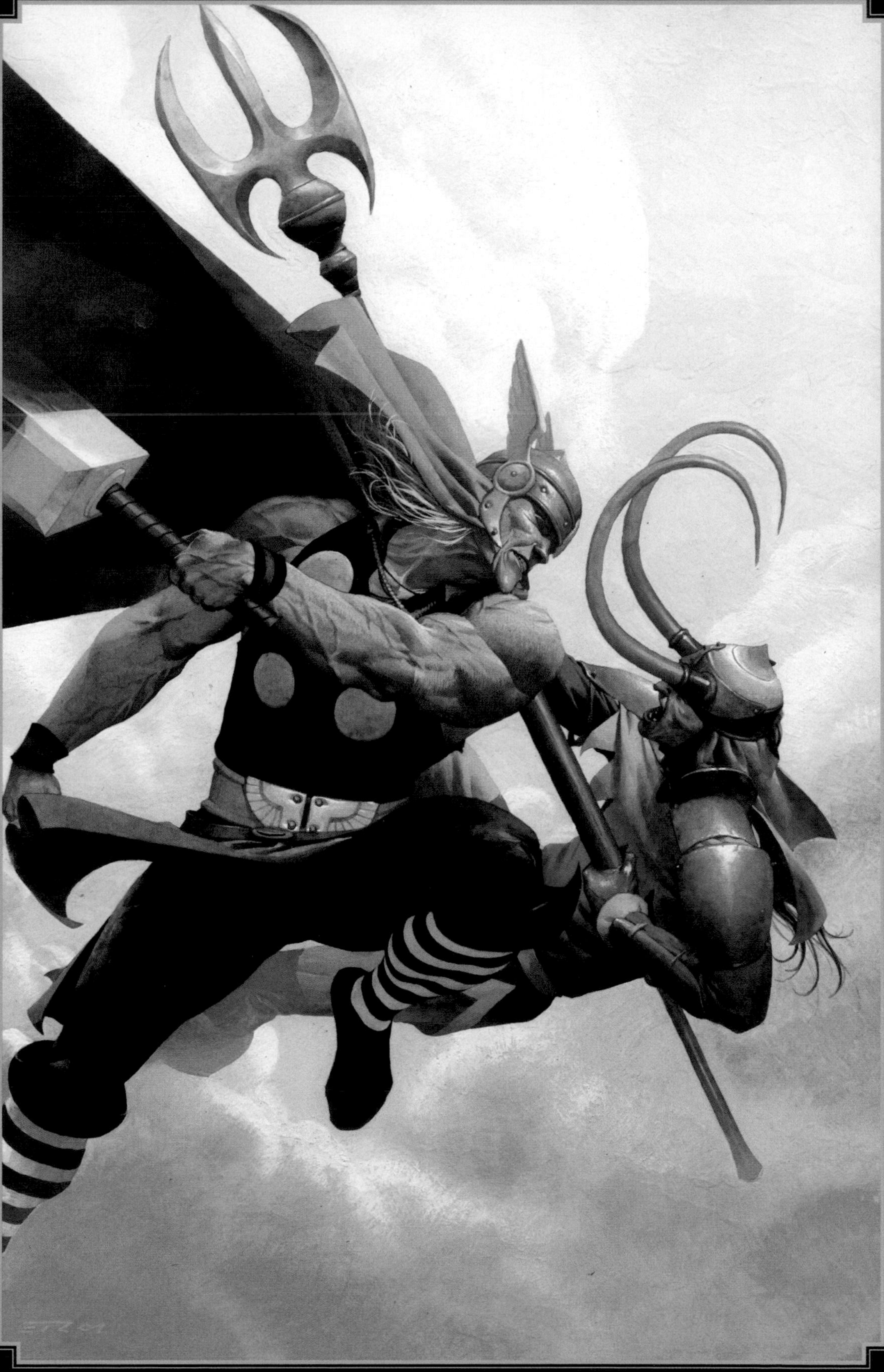

Loki 2

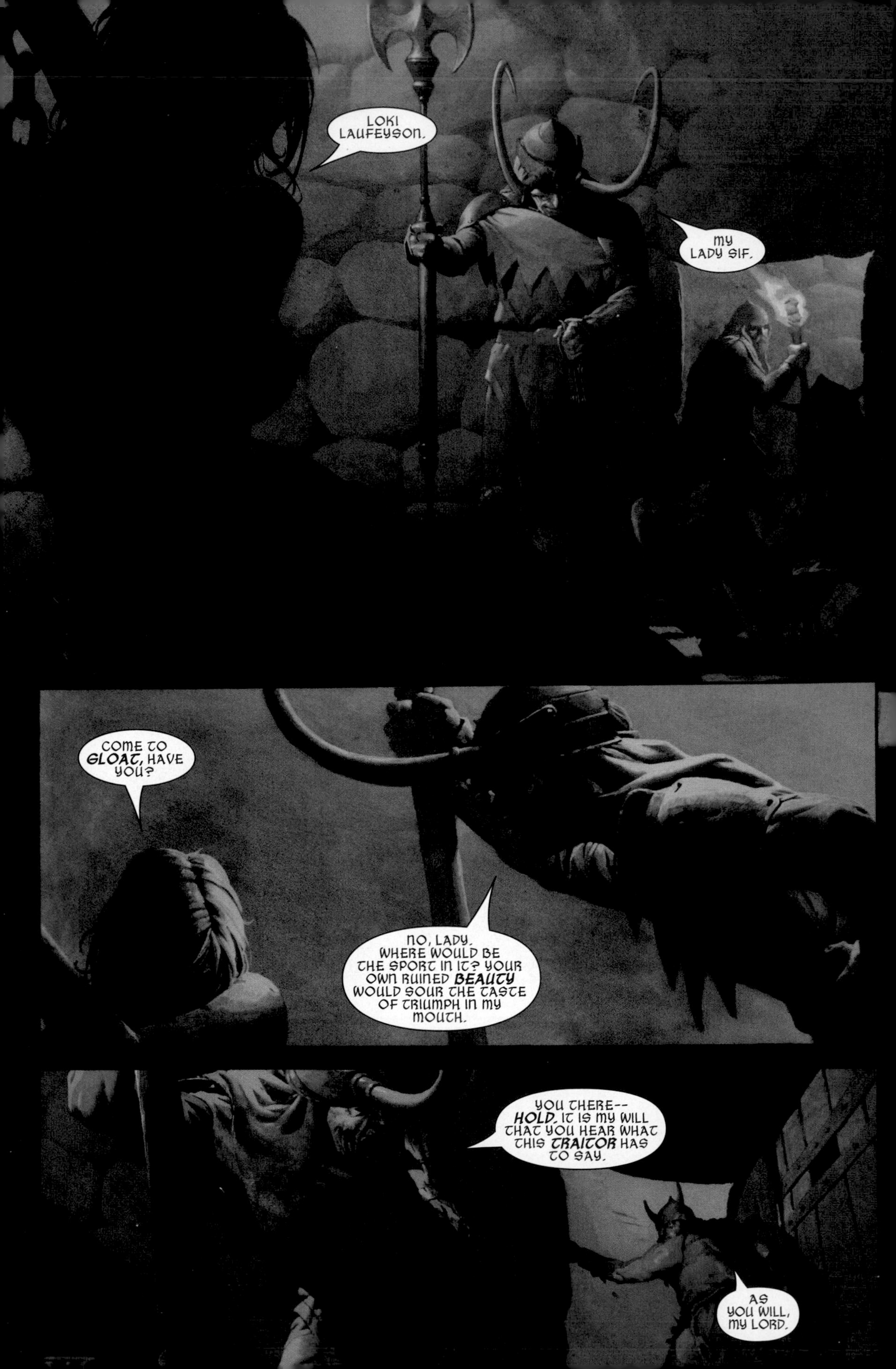
LOKI LAUFEYSON.
MY LADY SIF.
COME TO GLOAT, HAVE YOU?
NO, LADY. WHERE WOULD BE THE SPORT IN IT? YOUR OWN RUINED BEAUTY WOULD SOUR THE TASTE OF TRIUMPH IN MY MOUTH.
YOU THERE-- HOLD. IT IS MY WILL THAT YOU HEAR WHAT THIS TRAITOR HAS TO SAY.
AS YOU WILL, MY LORD.

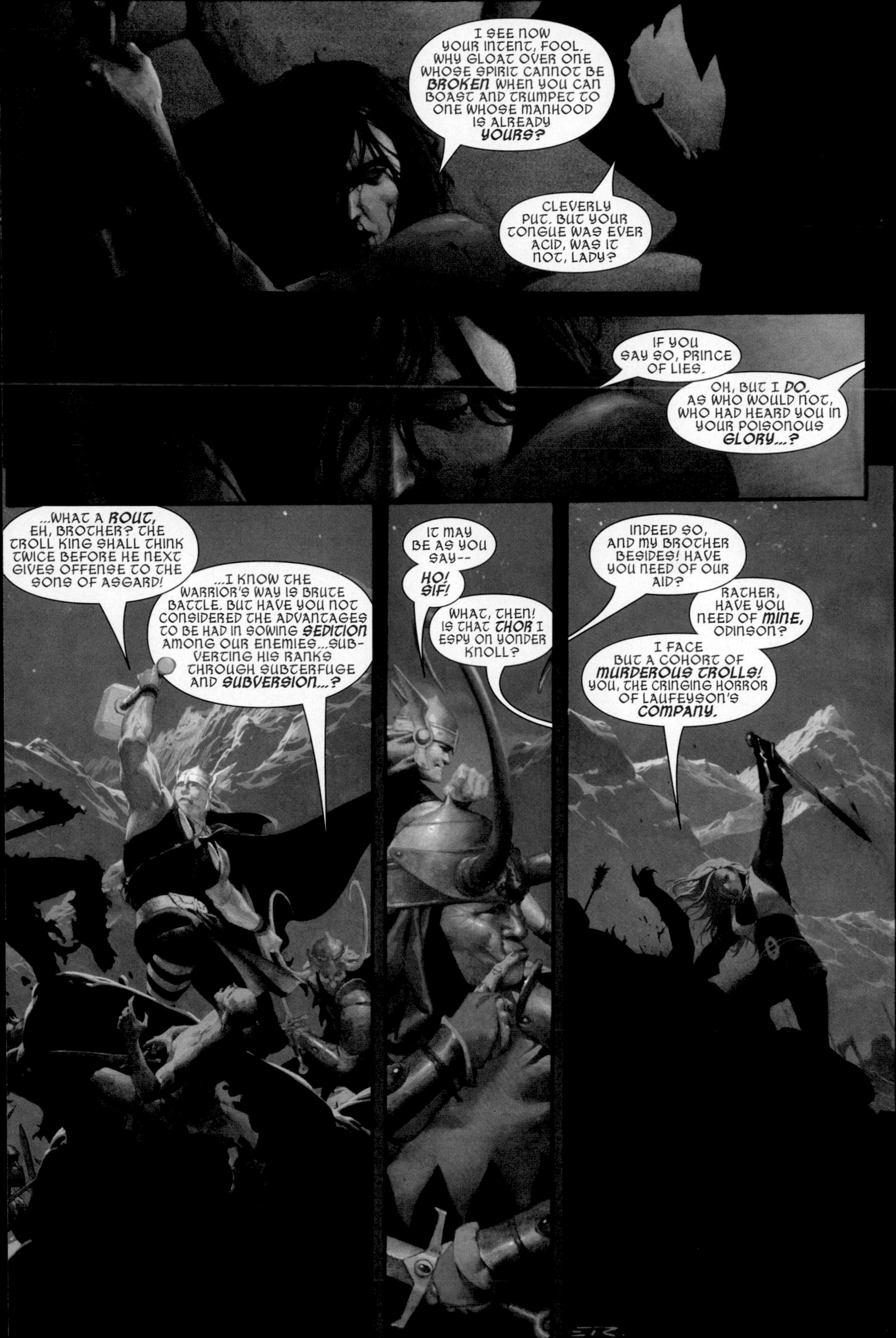
I SEE NOW YOUR INTENT, FOOL. WHY GLOAT OVER ONE WHOSE SPIRIT CANNOT BE BROKEN WHEN YOU CAN BOAST AND TRUMPET TO ONE WHOSE MANHOOD IS ALREADY YOURS?
CLEVERLY PUT. BUT YOUR TONGUE WAS EVER ACID, WAS IT NOT, LADY?
IF YOU SAY SO, PRINCE OF LIES.
OH, BUT I DO. AS WHO WOULD NOT, WHO HAD HEARD YOU IN YOUR POISONOUS GLORY...?
...WHAT A ROUT, EH, BROTHER? THE TROLL KING SHALL THINK TWICE BEFORE HE NEXT GIVES OFFENSE TO THE SONS OF ASGARD!
...I KNOW THE WARRIOR'S WAY IS BRUTE BATTLE. BUT HAVE YOU NOT CONSIDERED THE ADVANTAGES TO BE HAD IN SOWING SEDITION AMONG OUR ENEMIES...SUB-VERTING HIS RANKS THROUGH SUBTERFUGE AND SUBVERSION...?
IT MAY BE AS YOU SAY--
HO! SIF!
WHAT, THEN! IS THAT THOR I ESPY ON YONDER KNOLL?
INDEED SO, AND MY BROTHER BESIDES! HAVE YOU NEED OF OUR AID?
RATHER, HAVE YOU NEED OF MINE, ODINSON?
I FACE BUT A COHORT OF MURDEROUS TROLLS! YOU, THE CRINGING HORROR OF LAUFEYSON'S COMPANY.

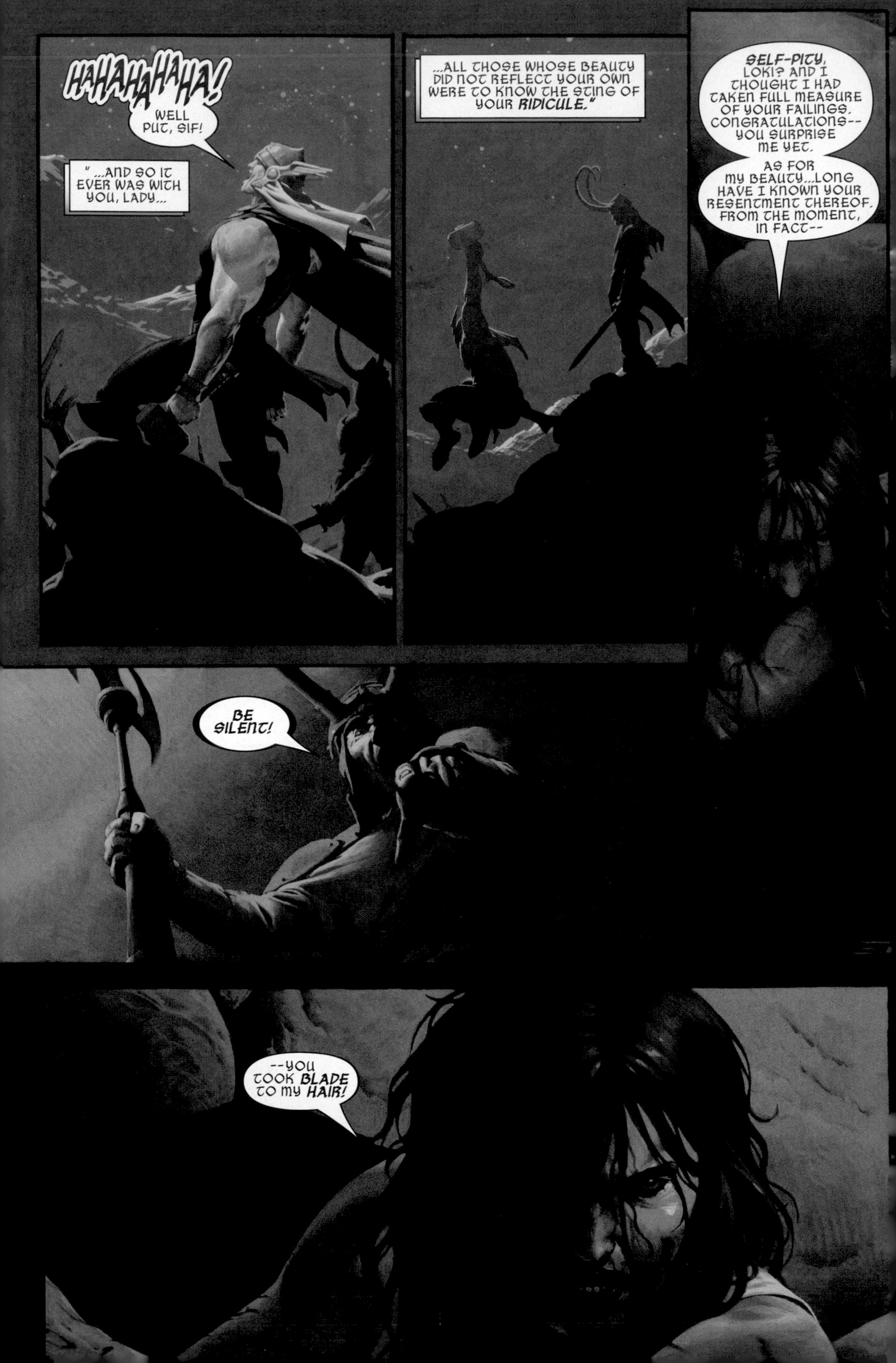
HAHAHAHAHAHA!
WELL PUT, SIF!
"...AND SO IT EVER WAS WITH YOU, LADY...
...ALL THOSE WHOSE BEAUTY DID NOT REFLECT YOUR OWN WERE TO KNOW THE STING OF YOUR RIDICULE."
SELF-PITY, LOKI? AND I THOUGHT I HAD TAKEN FULL MEASURE OF YOUR FAILINGS. CONGRATULATIONS--YOU SURPRISE ME YET.
AS FOR MY BEAUTY...LONG HAVE I KNOWN YOUR RESENTMENT THEREOF. FROM THE MOMENT, IN FACT--
BE SILENT!
--YOU TOOK BLADE TO MY HAIR!

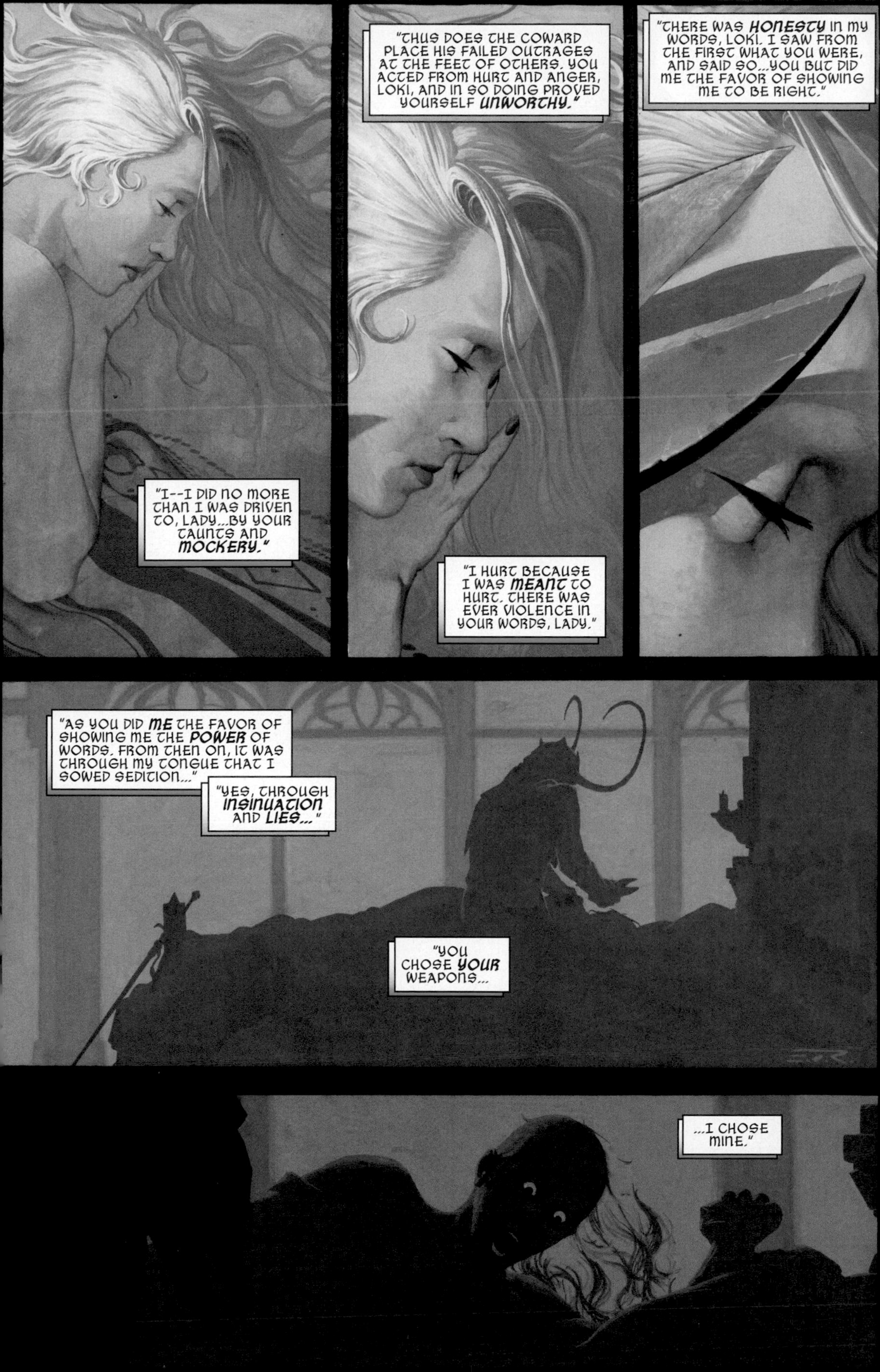
"I--I DID NO MORE THAN I WAS DRIVEN TO, LADY...BY YOUR TAUNTS AND MOCKERY."
"THUS DOES THE COWARD PLACE HIS FAILED OUTRAGES AT THE FEET OF OTHERS. YOU ACTED FROM HURT AND ANGER, LOKI, AND IN SO DOING PROVED YOURSELF UNWORTHY."
"I HURT BECAUSE I WAS MEANT TO HURT. THERE WAS EVER VIOLENCE IN YOUR WORDS, LADY."
"THERE WAS HONESTY IN MY WORDS, LOKI. I SAW FROM THE FIRST WHAT YOU WERE, AND SAID SO...YOU BUT DID ME THE FAVOR OF SHOWING ME TO BE RIGHT."
"AS YOU DID ME THE FAVOR OF SHOWING ME THE POWER OF WORDS. FROM THEN ON, IT WAS THROUGH MY TONGUE THAT I SOWED SEDITION..."
"YES, THROUGH INSINUATION AND LIES..."
"YOU CHOSE YOUR WEAPONS...
...I CHOSE MINE."

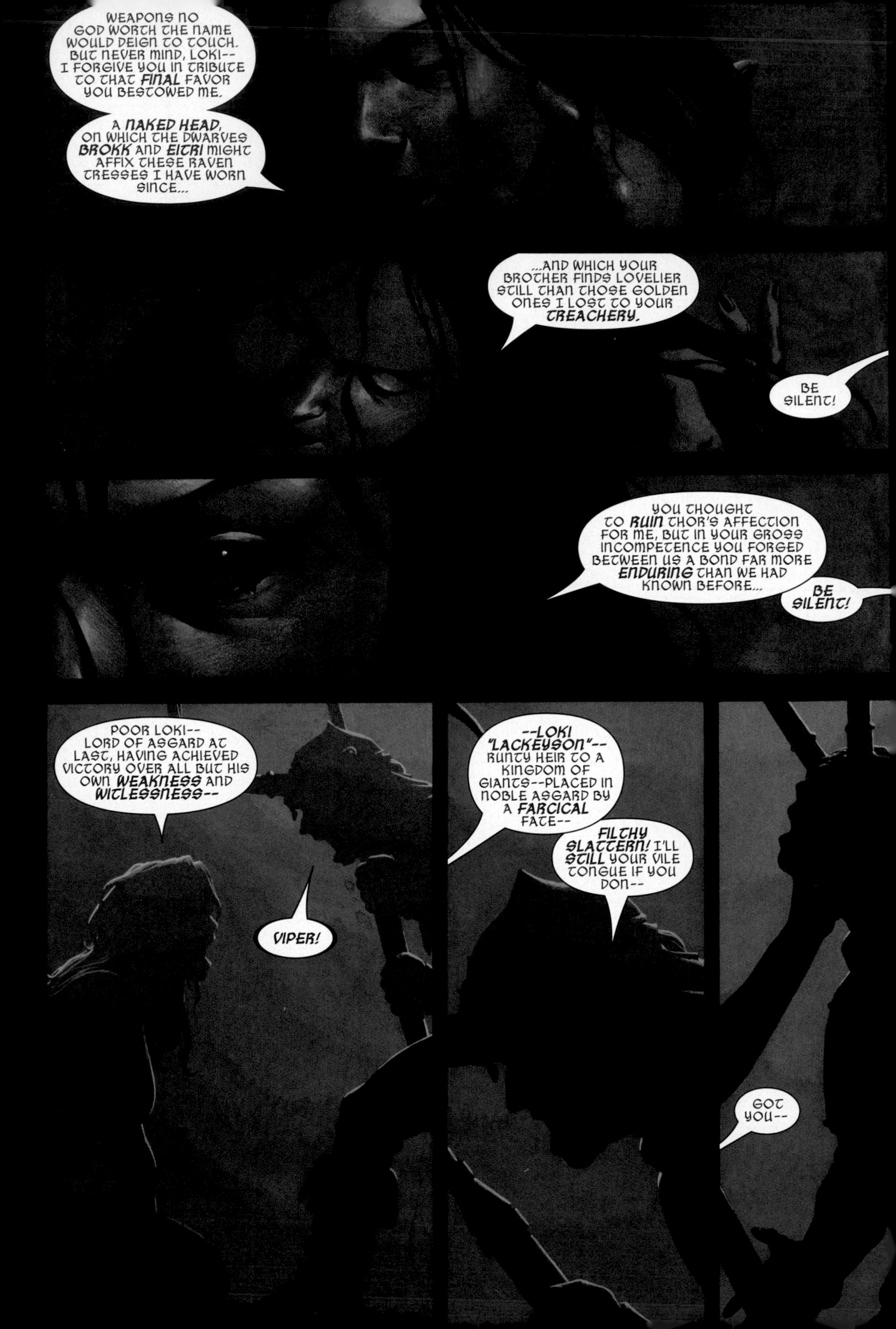
WEAPONS NO GOD WORTH THE NAME WOULD DEIGN TO TOUCH. BUT NEVER MIND, LOKI-- I FORGIVE YOU IN TRIBUTE TO THAT FINAL FAVOR YOU BESTOWED ME.
A NAKED HEAD, ON WHICH THE DWARVES BROKK AND EITRI MIGHT AFFIX THESE RAVEN TRESSES I HAVE WORN SINCE...
...AND WHICH YOUR BROTHER FINDS LOVELIER STILL THAN THOSE GOLDEN ONES I LOST TO YOUR TREACHERY.
BE SILENT!
YOU THOUGHT TO RUIN THOR'S AFFECTION FOR ME, BUT IN YOUR GROSS INCOMPETENCE YOU FORGED BETWEEN US A BOND FAR MORE ENDURING THAN WE HAD KNOWN BEFORE...
BE SILENT!
POOR LOKI-- LORD OF ASGARD AT LAST, HAVING ACHIEVED VICTORY OVER ALL BUT HIS OWN WEAKNESS AND WITLESSNESS--
VIPER!
--LOKI "LACKEYSON"-- RUNTY HEIR TO A KINGDOM OF GIANTS--PLACED IN NOBLE ASGARD BY A FARCICAL FATE--
FILTHY SLATTERN! I'LL STILL YOUR VILE TONGUE IF YOU DON--
GOT YOU--

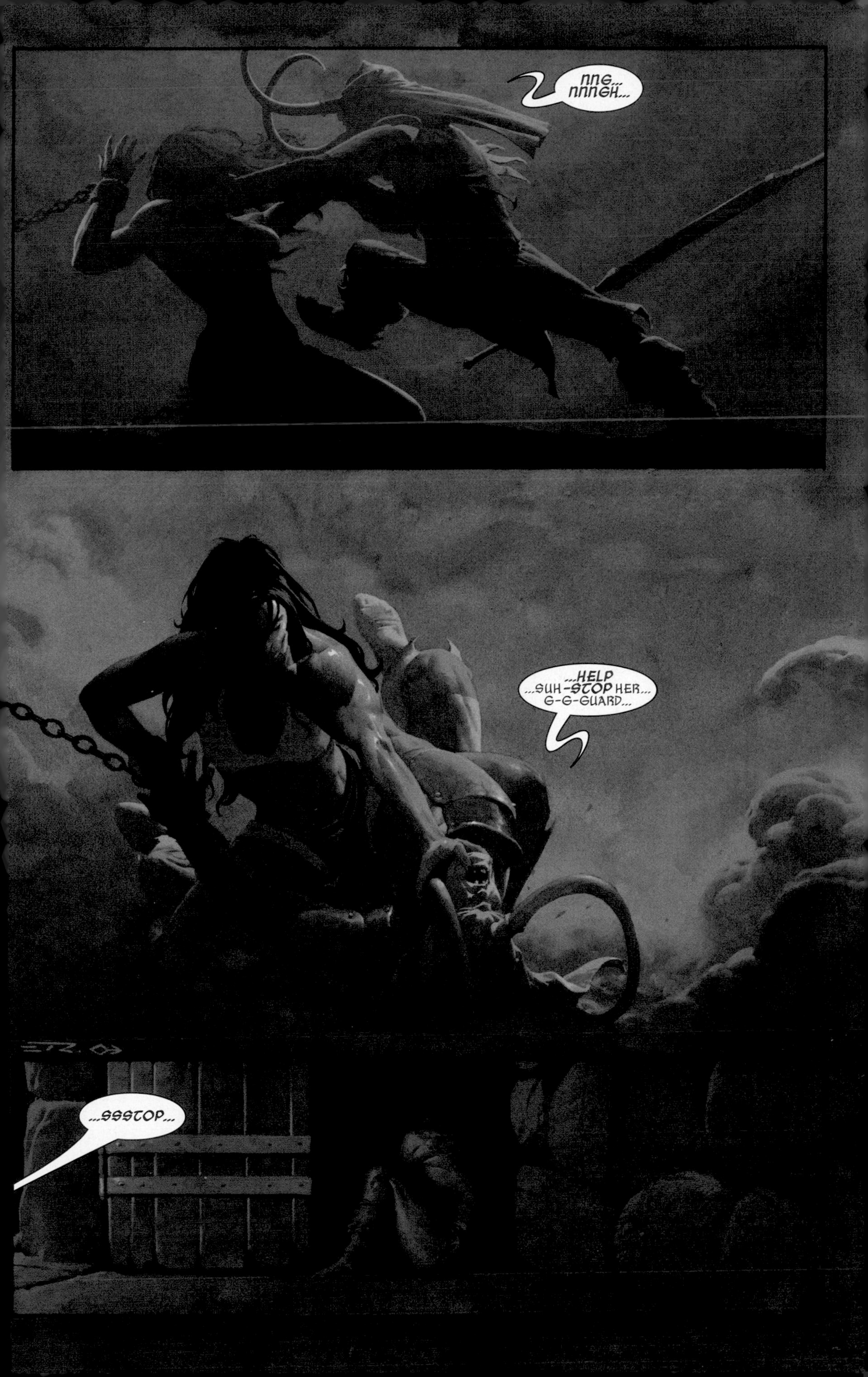
NNG... NNNGH...
...HELP ...SUH-STOP HER... G-G-GUARD...
...SSSTOP...

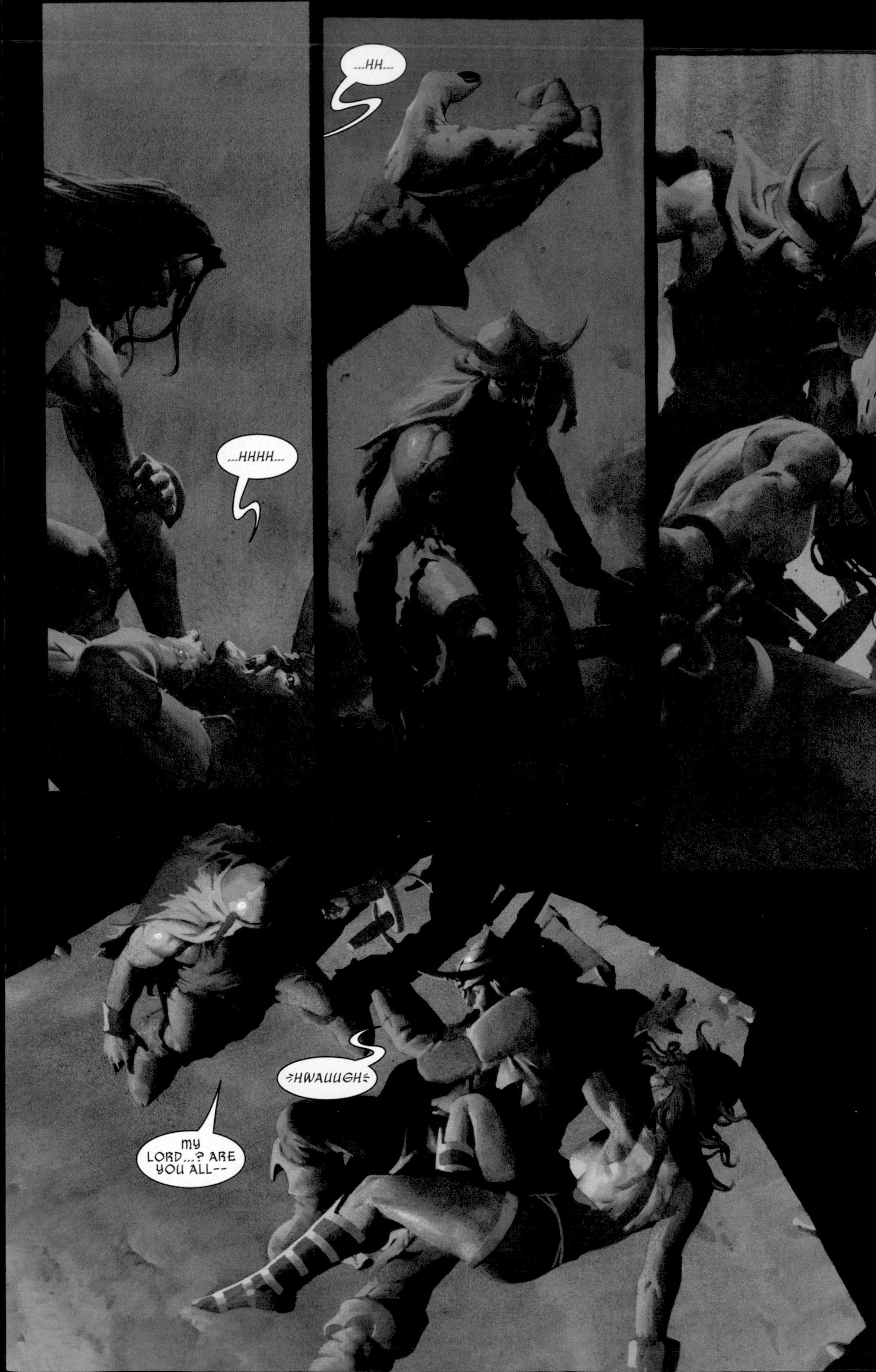
...HHHH...
...HH...
MY LORD...? ARE YOU ALL--
HWAUUGH

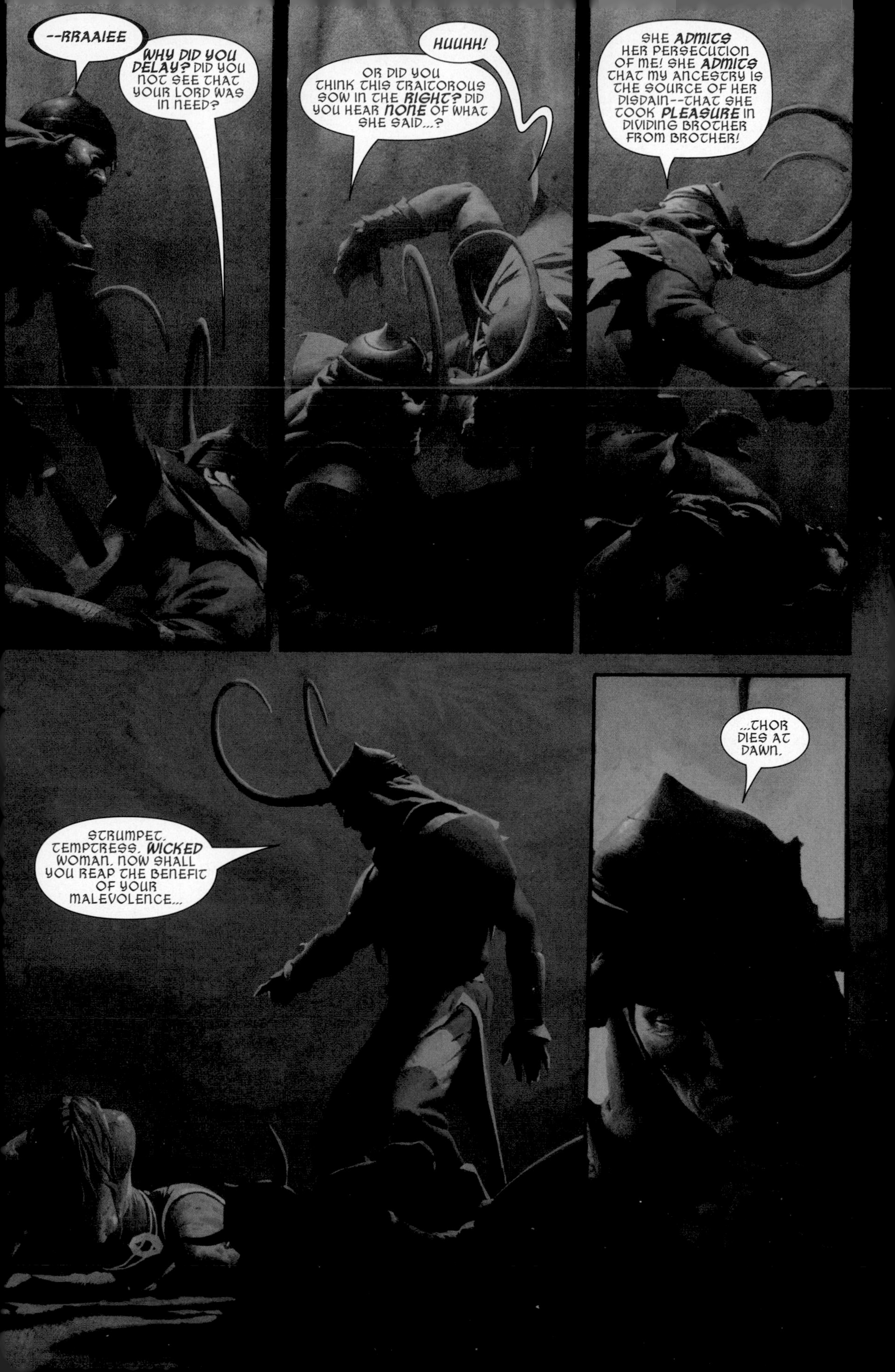
--BRAAIEE
WHY DID YOU DELAY? DID YOU NOT SEE THAT YOUR LORD WAS IN NEED?
HUUHH!
OR DID YOU THINK THIS TRAITOROUS SOW IN THE RIGHT? DID YOU HEAR NONE OF WHAT SHE SAID...?
SHE ADMITS HER PERSECUTION OF ME! SHE ADMITS THAT MY ANCESTRY IS THE SOURCE OF HER DISDAIN--THAT SHE TOOK PLEASURE IN DIVIDING BROTHER FROM BROTHER!
STRUMPET. TEMPTRESS. WICKED WOMAN. NOW SHALL YOU REAP THE BENEFIT OF YOUR MALEVOLENCE...
...THOR DIES AT DAWN.

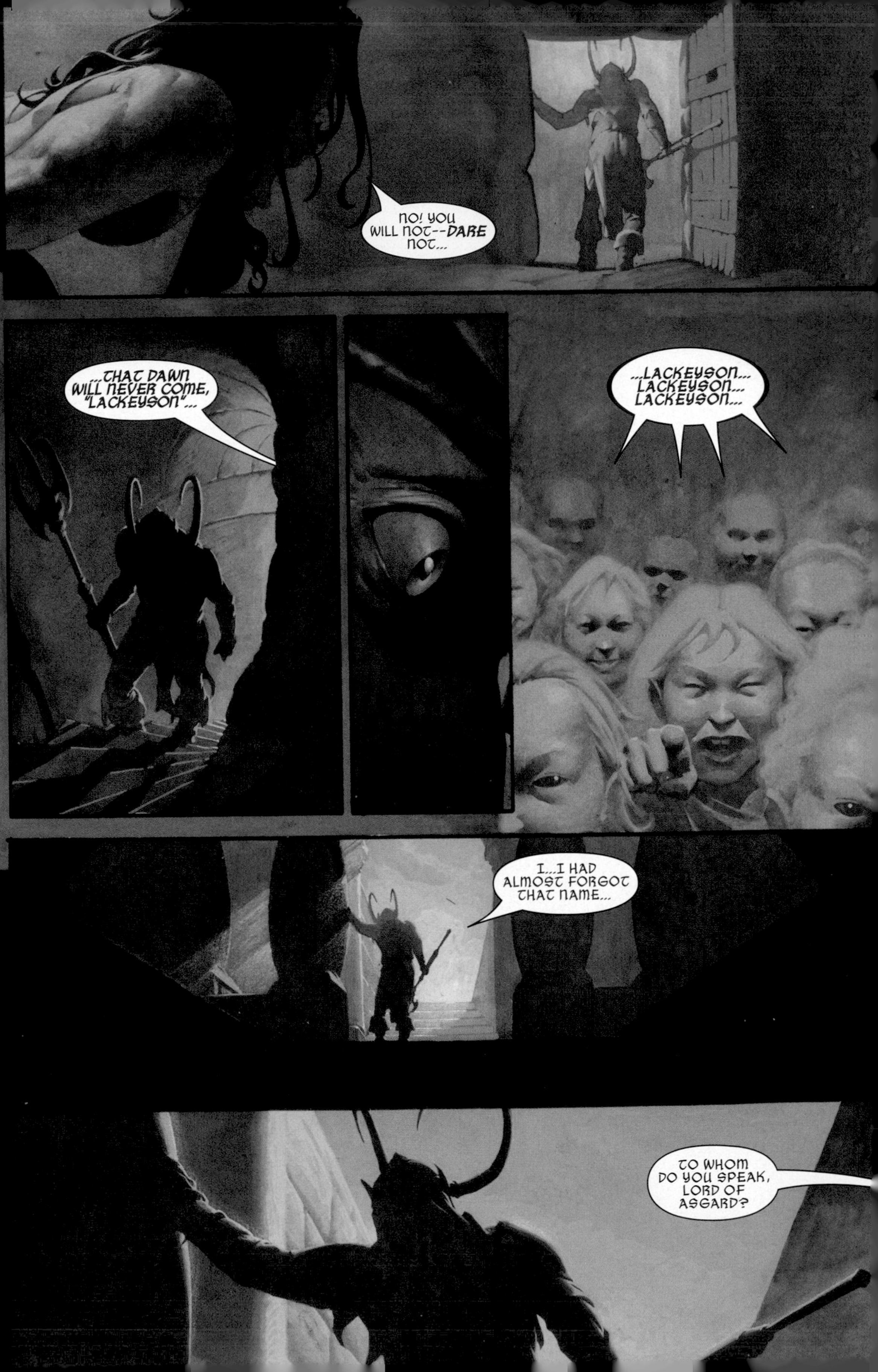
NO! YOU WILL NOT--DARE NOT...
...THAT DAWN WILL NEVER COME, "LACKEYSON"...
...LACKEYSON... LACKEYSON... LACKEYSON...
I...I HAD ALMOST FORGOT THAT NAME...
TO WHOM DO YOU SPEAK, LORD OF ASGARD?

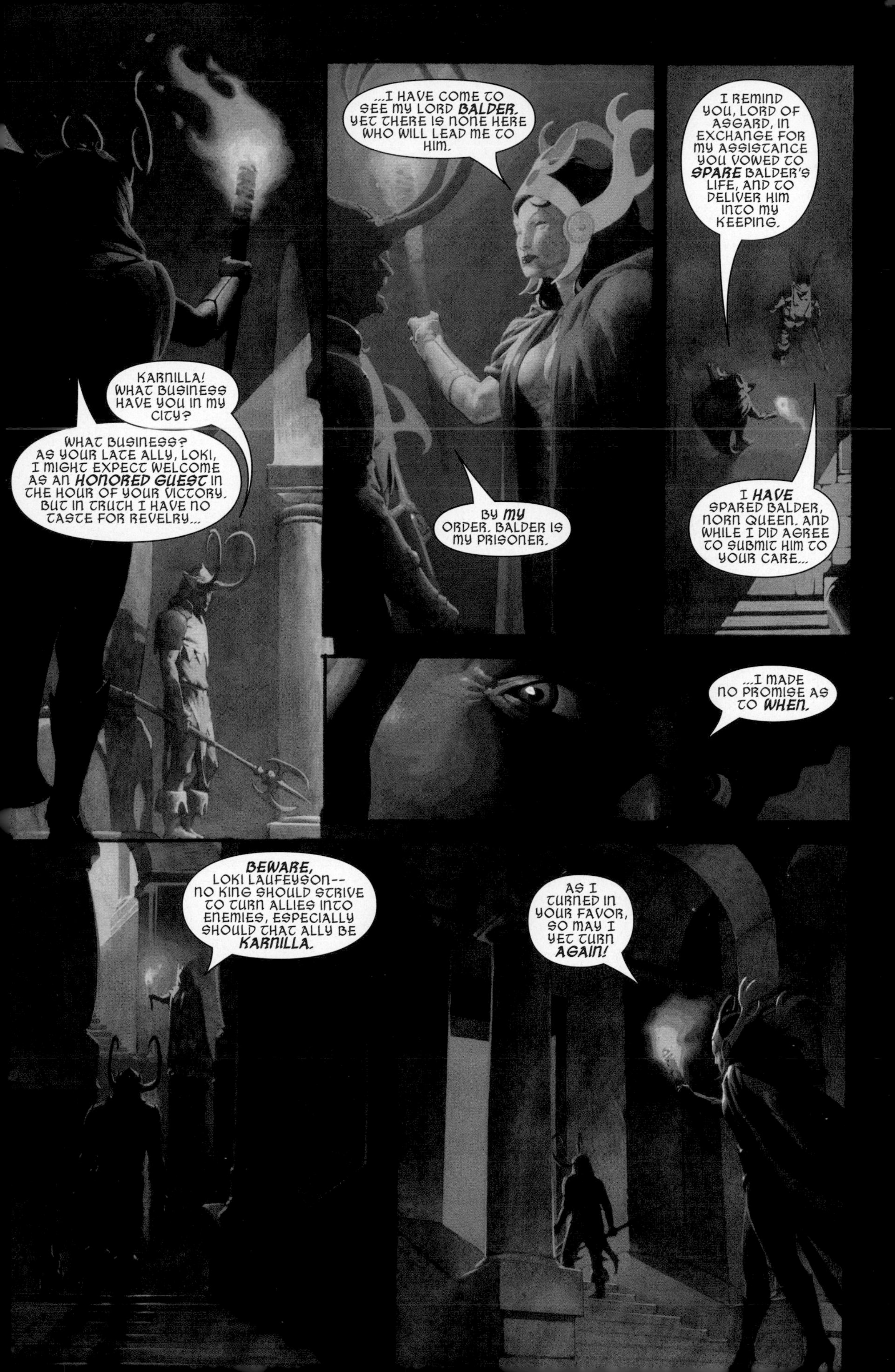
KARNILLA! WHAT BUSINESS HAVE YOU IN MY CITY?
WHAT BUSINESS? AS YOUR LATE ALLY, LOKI, I MIGHT EXPECT WELCOME AS AN HONORED GUEST IN THE HOUR OF YOUR VICTORY. BUT IN TRUTH I HAVE NO TASTE FOR REVELRY...
...I HAVE COME TO SEE MY LORD BALDER. YET THERE IS NONE HERE WHO WILL LEAD ME TO HIM.
BY MY ORDER. BALDER IS MY PRISONER.
I REMIND YOU, LORD OF ASGARD, IN EXCHANGE FOR MY ASSISTANCE YOU VOWED TO SPARE BALDER'S LIFE, AND TO DELIVER HIM INTO MY KEEPING.
I HAVE SPARED BALDER, NORN QUEEN. AND WHILE I DID AGREE TO SUBMIT HIM TO YOUR CARE...
...I MADE NO PROMISE AS TO WHEN.
BEWARE, LOKI LAUFEYSON-- NO KING SHOULD STRIVE TO TURN ALLIES INTO ENEMIES, ESPECIALLY SHOULD THAT ALLY BE KARNILLA.
AS I TURNED IN YOUR FAVOR, SO MAY I YET TURN AGAIN!

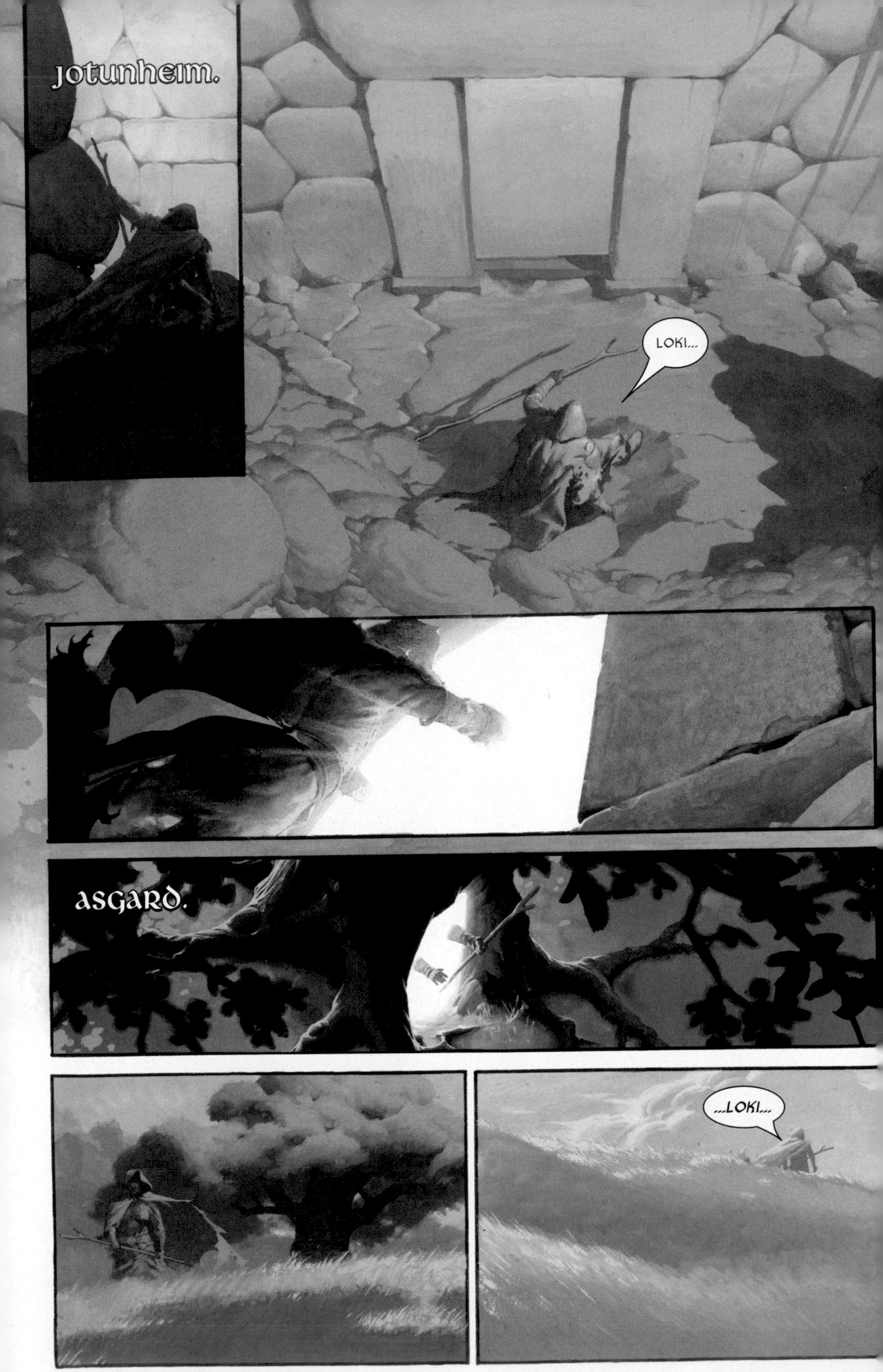
JOTUNHEIM.
LOKI...
ASGARD.
...LOKI...

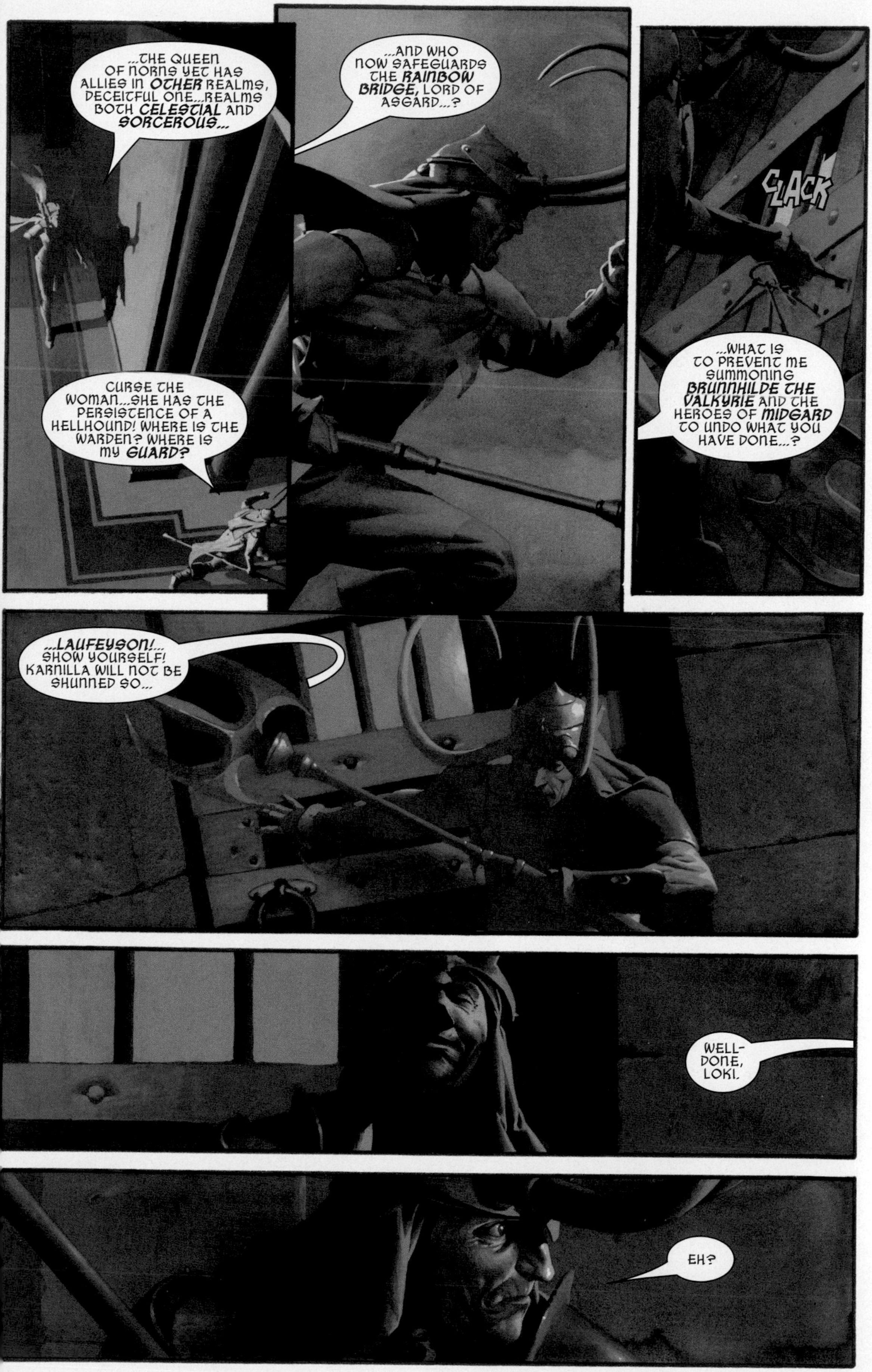
...THE QUEEN OF NORNS YET HAS ALLIES IN OTHER REALMS, DECEITFUL ONE...REALMS BOTH CELESTIAL AND SORCEROUS...
...AND WHO NOW SAFEGUARDS THE RAINBOW BRIDGE, LORD OF ASGARD...?
CURSE THE WOMAN...SHE HAS THE PERSISTENCE OF A HELLHOUND! WHERE IS THE WARDEN? WHERE IS MY GUARD?
CLACK
...WHAT IS TO PREVENT ME SUMMONING BRUNNHILDE THE VALKYRIE AND THE HEROES OF MIDGARD TO UNDO WHAT YOU HAVE DONE...?
...LAUFEYSON!... SHOW YOURSELF! KARNILLA WILL NOT BE SHUNNED SO...
WELL-DONE, LOKI.
EH?

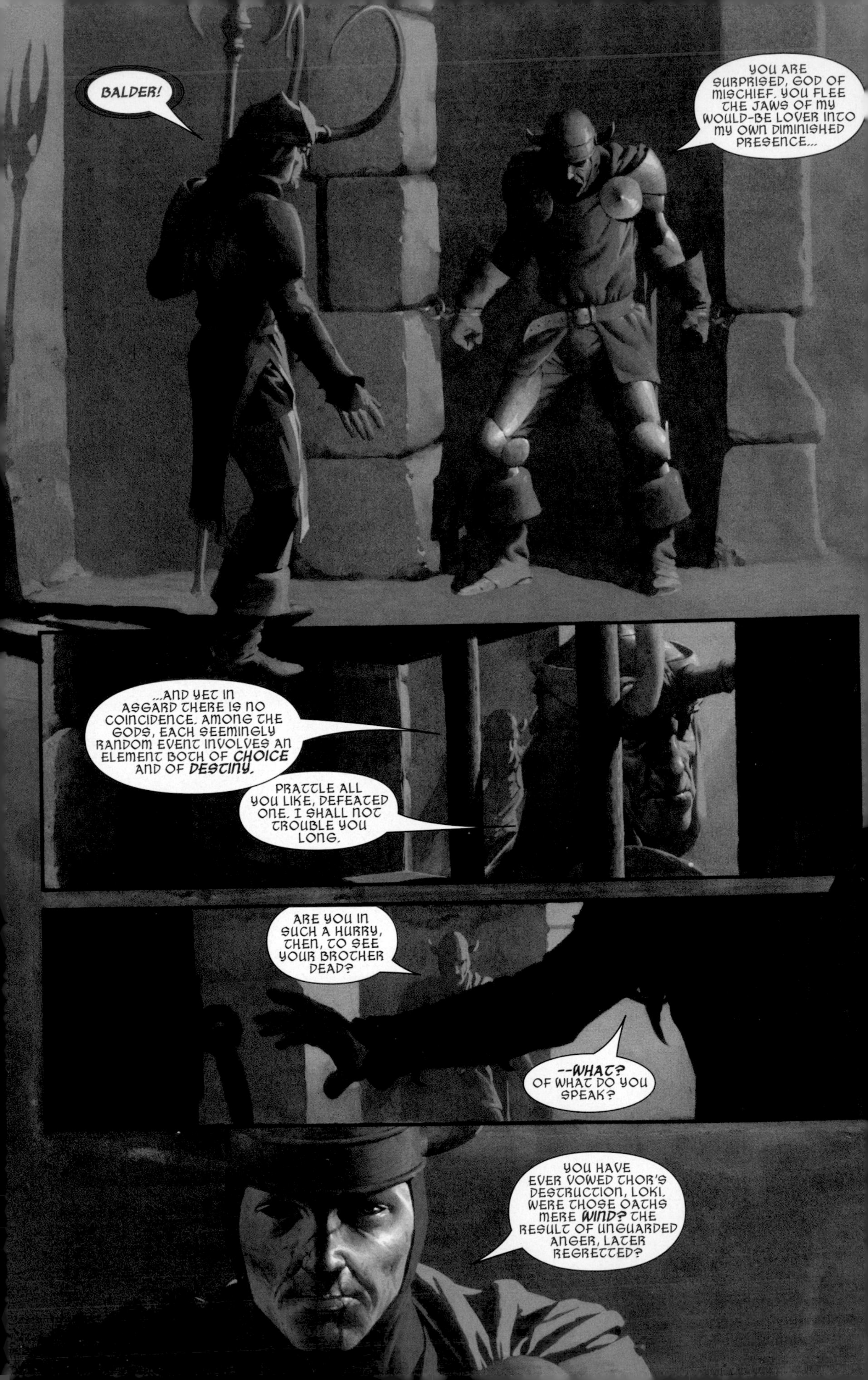
BALDER!
YOU ARE SURPRISED, GOD OF MISCHIEF. YOU FLEE THE JAWS OF MY WOULD-BE LOVER INTO MY OWN DIMINISHED PRESENCE...
...AND YET IN ASGARD THERE IS NO COINCIDENCE. AMONG THE GODS, EACH SEEMINGLY RANDOM EVENT INVOLVES AN ELEMENT BOTH OF CHOICE AND OF DESTINY.
PRATTLE ALL YOU LIKE, DEFEATED ONE. I SHALL NOT TROUBLE YOU LONG.
ARE YOU IN SUCH A HURRY, THEN, TO SEE YOUR BROTHER DEAD?
--WHAT? OF WHAT DO YOU SPEAK?
YOU HAVE EVER VOWED THOR'S DESTRUCTION, LOKI. WERE THOSE OATHS MERE WIND? THE RESULT OF UNGUARDED ANGER, LATER REGRETTED?

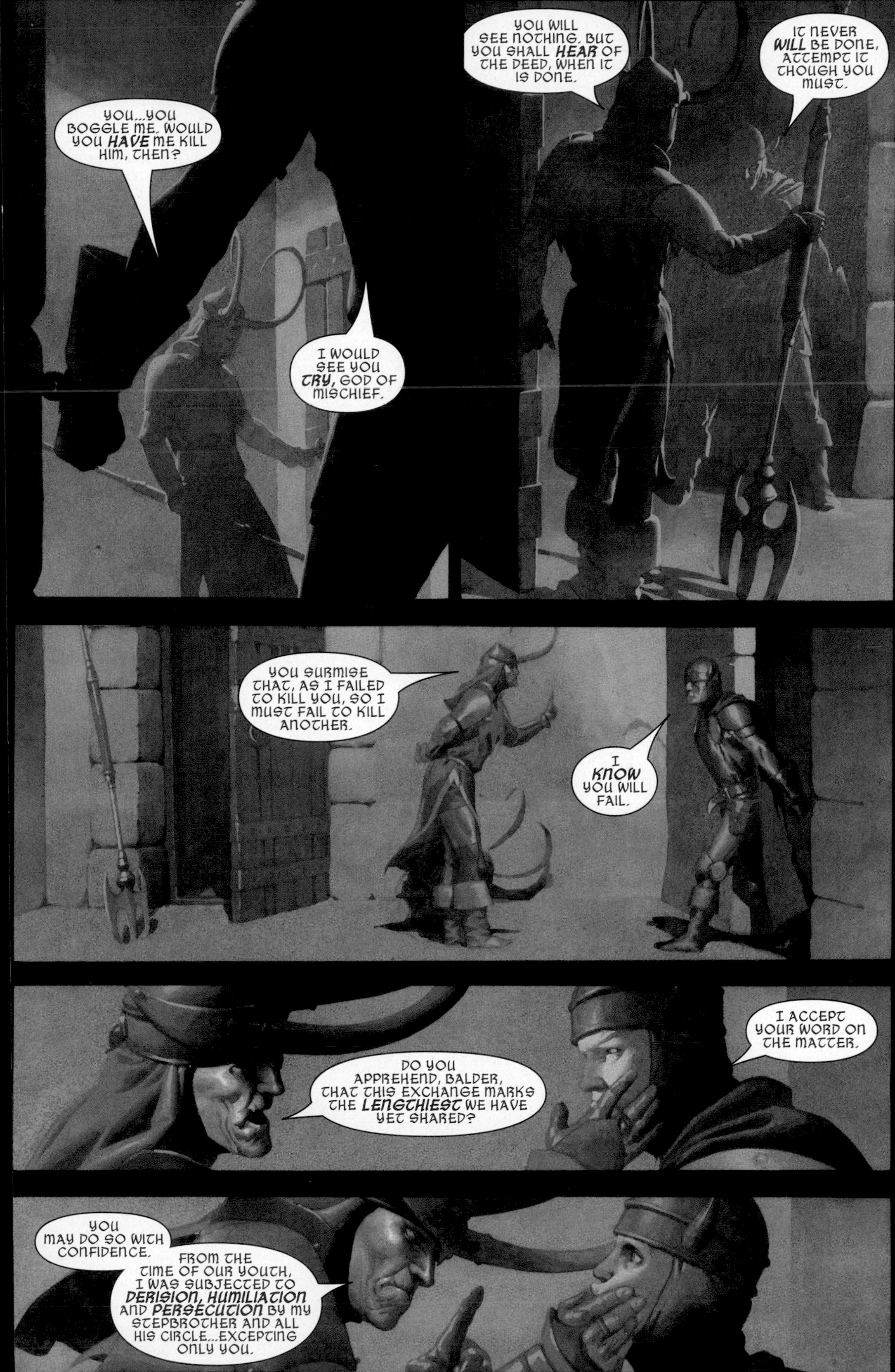
YOU...YOU BOGGLE ME. WOULD YOU HAVE ME KILL HIM, THEN?
I WOULD SEE YOU TRY, GOD OF MISCHIEF.
YOU WILL SEE NOTHING, BUT YOU SHALL HEAR OF THE DEED, WHEN IT IS DONE.
IT NEVER WILL BE DONE, ATTEMPT IT THOUGH YOU MUST.
YOU SURMISE THAT, AS I FAILED TO KILL YOU, SO I MUST FAIL TO KILL ANOTHER.
I KNOW YOU WILL FAIL.
DO YOU APPREHEND, BALDER, THAT THIS EXCHANGE MARKS THE LENGTHIEST WE HAVE YET SHARED?
I ACCEPT YOUR WORD ON THE MATTER.
YOU MAY DO SO WITH CONFIDENCE.
FROM THE TIME OF OUR YOUTH, I WAS SUBJECTED TO DERISION, HUMILIATION AND PERSECUTION BY MY STEPBROTHER AND ALL HIS CIRCLE...EXCEPTING ONLY YOU.

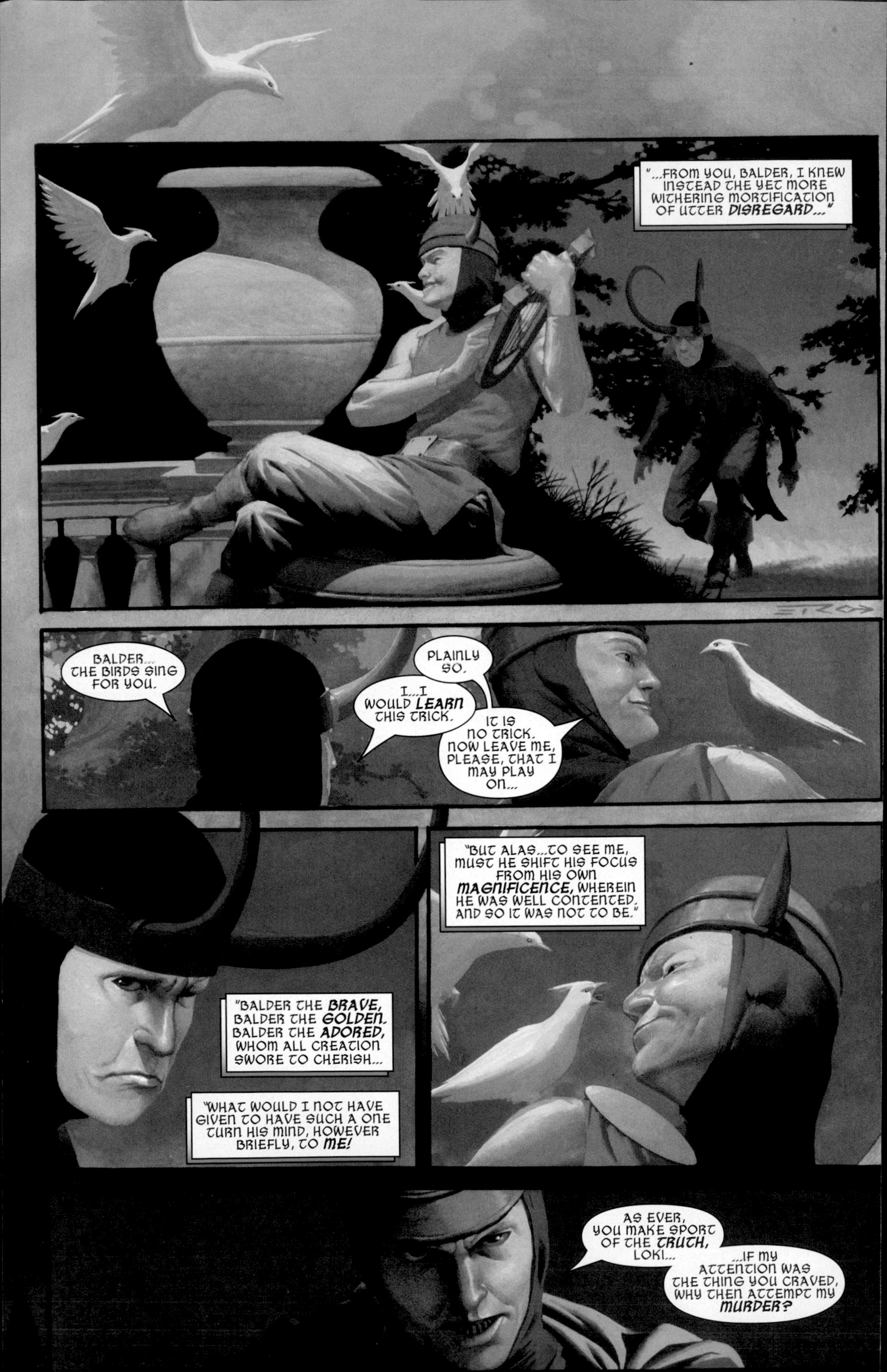
"...FROM YOU, BALDER, I KNEW INSTEAD THE YET MORE WITHERING MORTIFICATION OF UTTER DISREGARD..."
BALDER... THE BIRDS SING FOR YOU.
PLAINLY SO.
I...I WOULD LEARN THIS TRICK.
IT IS NO TRICK. NOW LEAVE ME, PLEASE, THAT I MAY PLAY ON...
"BUT ALAS...TO SEE ME, MUST HE SHIFT HIS FOCUS FROM HIS OWN MAGNIFICENCE, WHEREIN HE WAS WELL CONTENTED, AND SO IT WAS NOT TO BE."
"BALDER THE BRAVE, BALDER THE GOLDEN, BALDER THE ADORED, WHOM ALL CREATION SWORE TO CHERISH...
"WHAT WOULD I NOT HAVE GIVEN TO HAVE SUCH A ONE TURN HIS MIND, HOWEVER BRIEFLY, TO ME!
AS EVER, YOU MAKE SPORT OF THE TRUTH, LOKI...
...IF MY ATTENTION WAS THE THING YOU CRAVED, WHY THEN ATTEMPT MY MURDER?

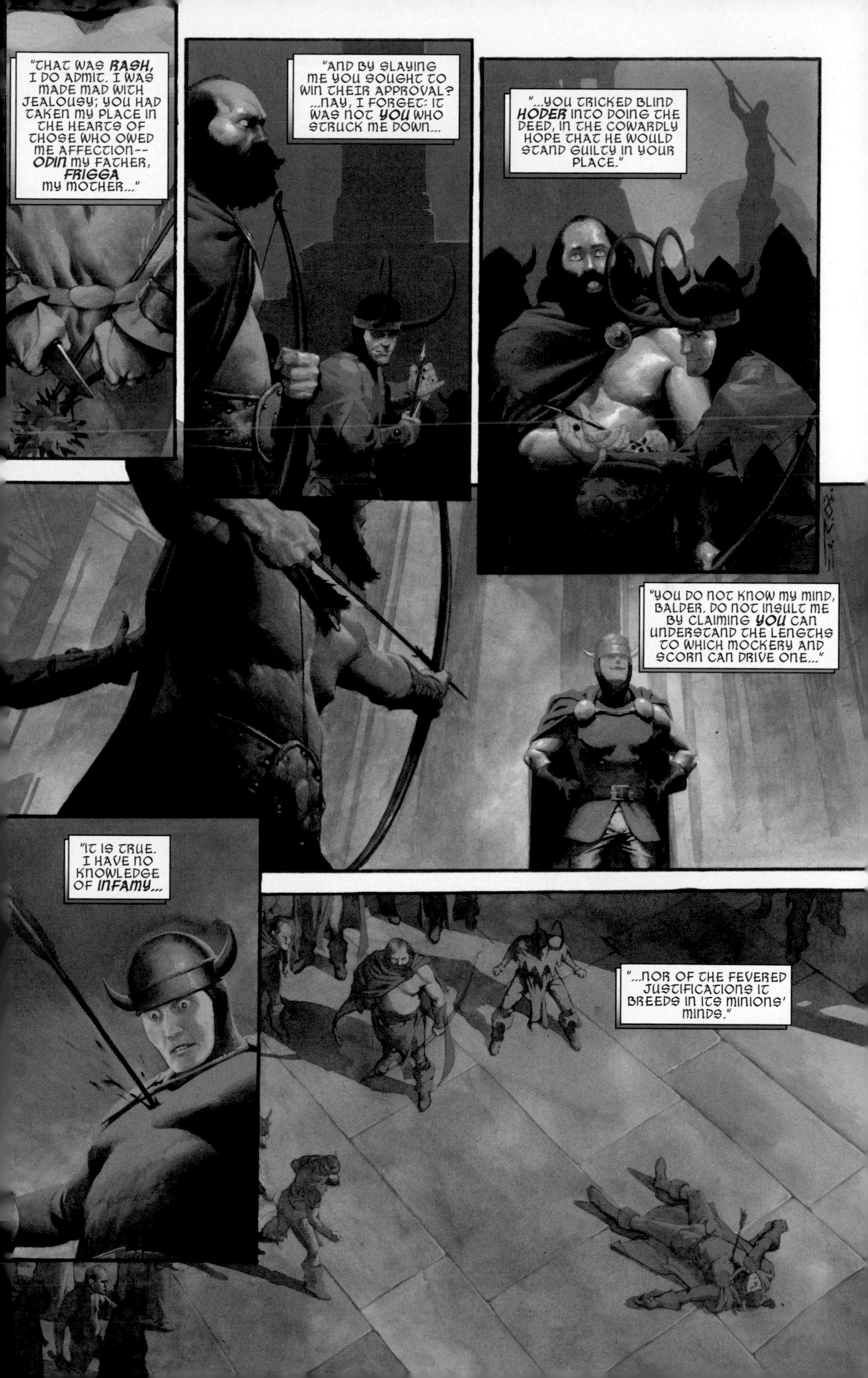
"THAT WAS RASH, I DO ADMIT. I WAS MADE MAD WITH JEALOUSY; YOU HAD TAKEN MY PLACE IN THE HEARTS OF THOSE WHO OWED ME AFFECTION-- ODIN MY FATHER, FRIGGA MY MOTHER..."
"AND BY SLAYING ME YOU SOUGHT TO WIN THEIR APPROVAL? ...NAY, I FORGET: IT WAS NOT YOU WHO STRUCK ME DOWN...
"...YOU TRICKED BLIND HODER INTO DOING THE DEED, IN THE COWARDLY HOPE THAT HE WOULD STAND GUILTY IN YOUR PLACE."
"YOU DO NOT KNOW MY MIND, BALDER. DO NOT INSULT ME BY CLAIMING YOU CAN UNDERSTAND THE LENGTHS TO WHICH MOCKERY AND SCORN CAN DRIVE ONE..."
"IT IS TRUE. I HAVE NO KNOWLEDGE OF INFAMY...
"...NOR OF THE FEVERED JUSTIFICATIONS IT BREEDS IN ITS MINIONS' MINDS."

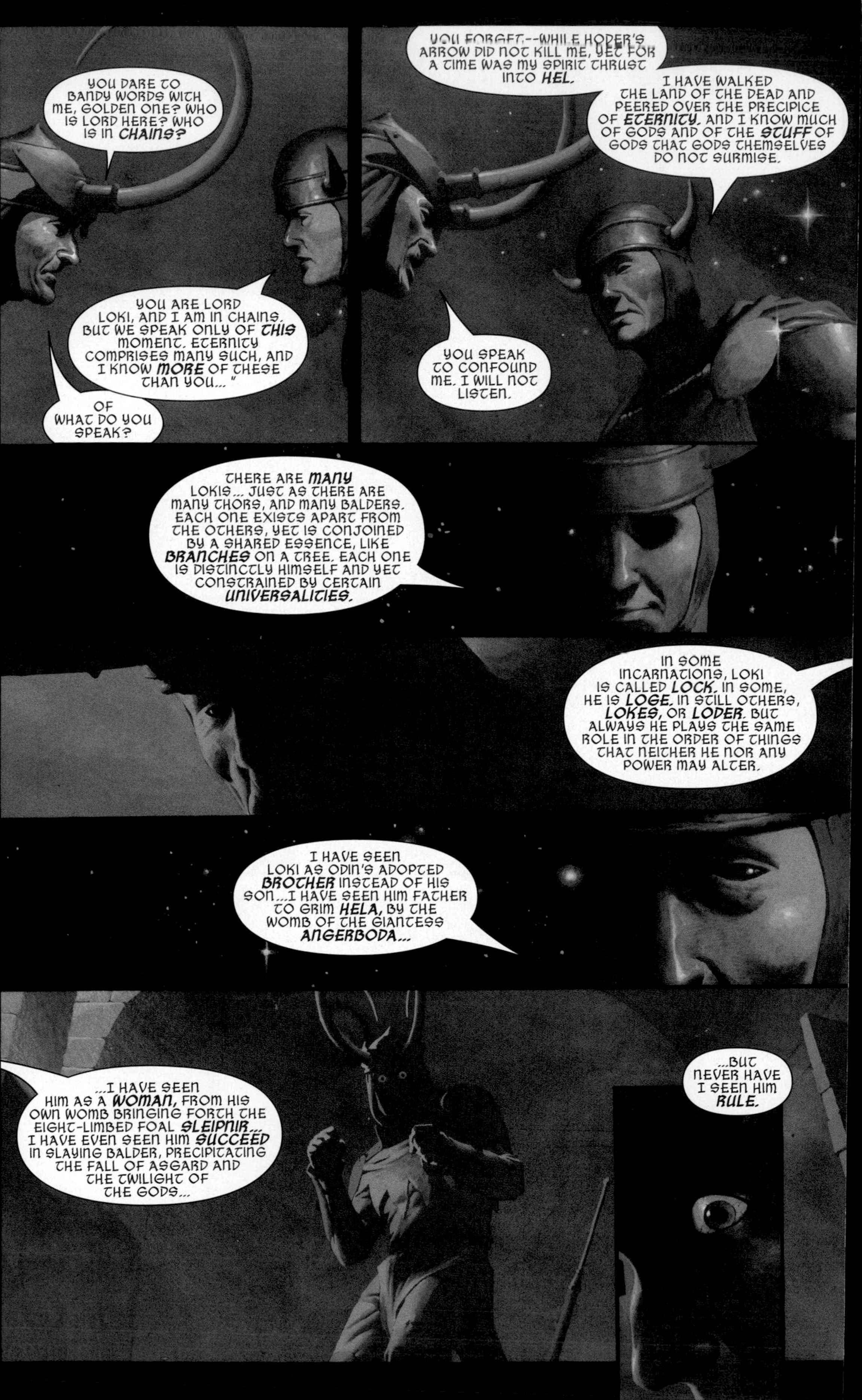
YOU DARE TO BANDY WORDS WITH ME, GOLDEN ONE? WHO IS LORD HERE? WHO IS IN CHAINS?
YOU ARE LORD LOKI, AND I AM IN CHAINS. BUT WE SPEAK ONLY OF THIS MOMENT. ETERNITY COMPRISES MANY SUCH, AND I KNOW MORE OF THESE THAN YOU... "
OF WHAT DO YOU SPEAK?
YOU FORGET,--WHILE HODER'S ARROW DID NOT KILL ME, YET FOR A TIME WAS MY SPIRIT THRUST INTO HEL.
I HAVE WALKED THE LAND OF THE DEAD AND PEERED OVER THE PRECIPICE OF ETERNITY, AND I KNOW MUCH OF GODS AND OF THE STUFF OF GODS THAT GODS THEMSELVES DO NOT SURMISE.
YOU SPEAK TO CONFOUND ME. I WILL NOT LISTEN.
THERE ARE MANY LOKIS... JUST AS THERE ARE MANY THORS, AND MANY BALDERS. EACH ONE EXISTS APART FROM THE OTHERS, YET IS CONJOINED BY A SHARED ESSENCE, LIKE BRANCHES ON A TREE. EACH ONE IS DISTINCTLY HIMSELF AND YET CONSTRAINED BY CERTAIN UNIVERSALITIES.
IN SOME INCARNATIONS, LOKI IS CALLED LOCK. IN SOME, HE IS LOGE. IN STILL OTHERS, LOKES, OR LODER. BUT ALWAYS HE PLAYS THE SAME ROLE IN THE ORDER OF THINGS THAT NEITHER HE NOR ANY POWER MAY ALTER.
I HAVE SEEN LOKI AS ODIN'S ADOPTED BROTHER INSTEAD OF HIS SON...I HAVE SEEN HIM FATHER TO GRIM HELA, BY THE WOMB OF THE GIANTESS ANGERBODA...
...I HAVE SEEN HIM AS A WOMAN, FROM HIS OWN WOMB BRINGING FORTH THE EIGHT-LIMBED FOAL SLEIPNIR... I HAVE EVEN SEEN HIM SUCCEED IN SLAYING BALDER, PRECIPITATING THE FALL OF ASGARD AND THE TWILIGHT OF THE GODS...
...BUT NEVER HAVE I SEEN HIM RULE.

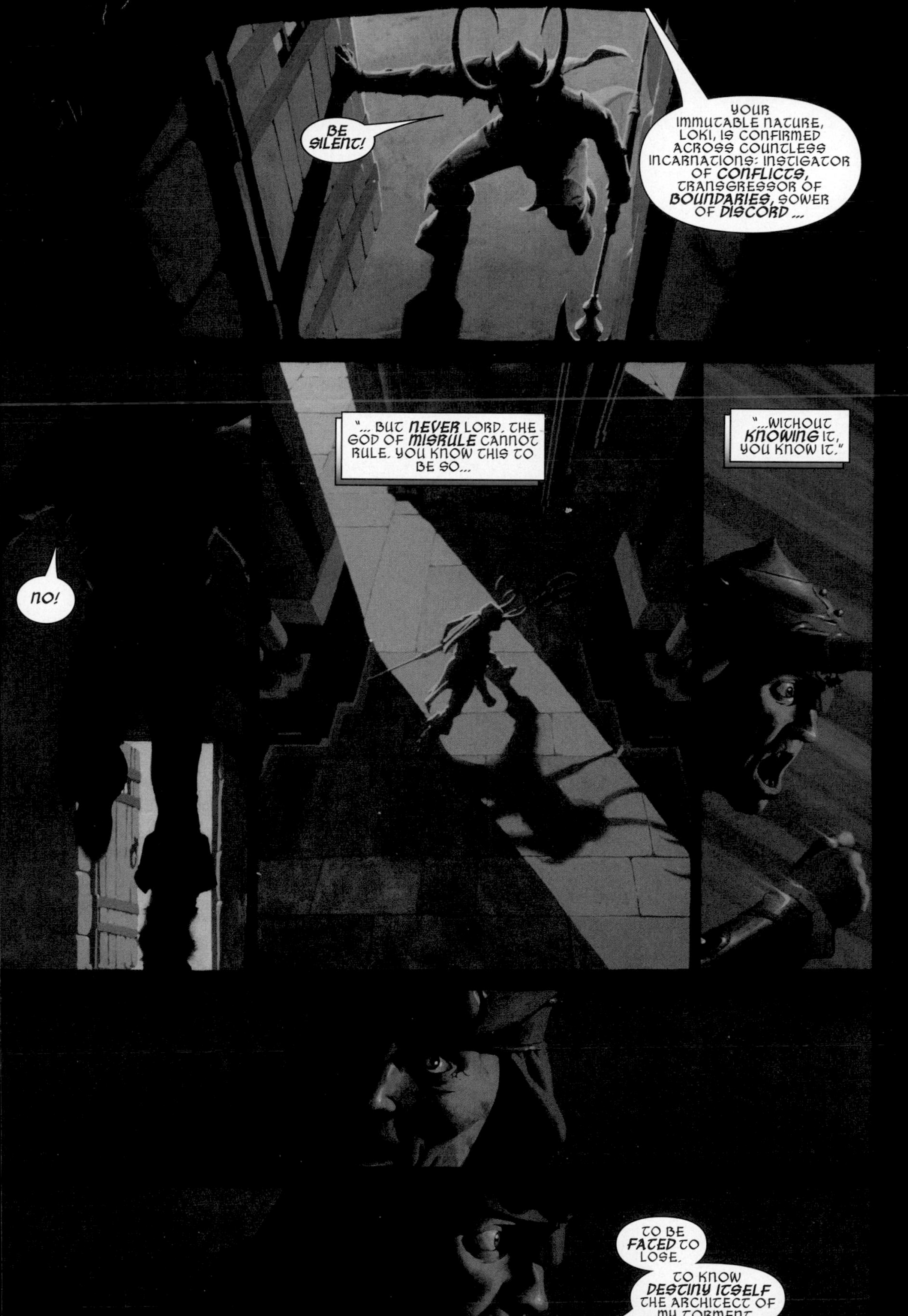
BE SILENT!
YOUR IMMUTABLE NATURE, LOKI, IS CONFIRMED ACROSS COUNTLESS INCARNATIONS: INSTIGATOR OF CONFLICTS, TRANSGRESSOR OF BOUNDARIES, SOWER OF DISCORD ...
"... BUT NEVER LORD. THE GOD OF MISRULE CANNOT RULE. YOU KNOW THIS TO BE SO...
"...WITHOUT KNOWING IT, YOU KNOW IT."
NO!
TO BE FATED TO LOSE.
TO KNOW DESTINY ITSELF THE ARCHITECT OF MY TORMENT.

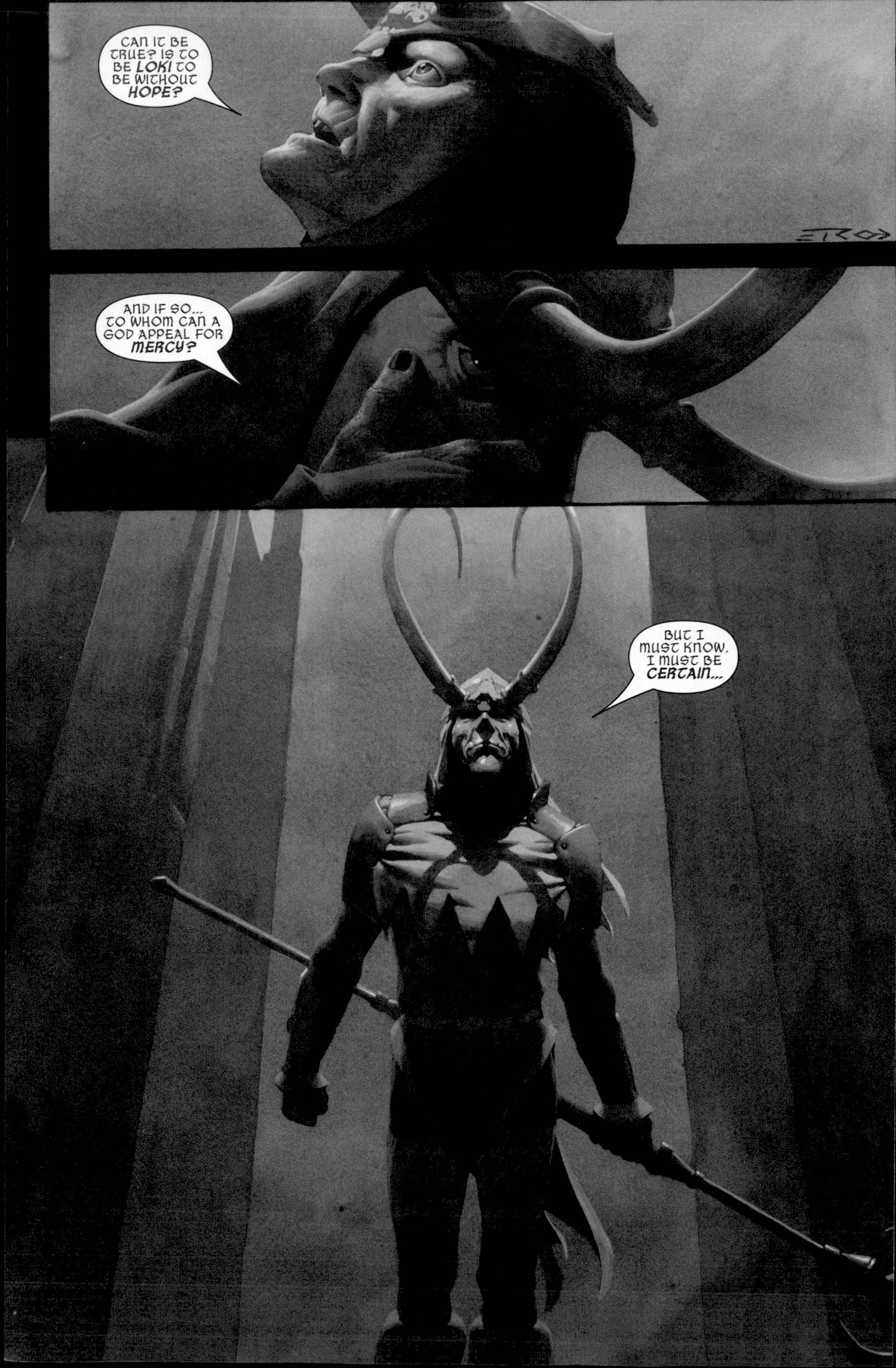
CAN IT BE TRUE? IS TO BE LOKI TO BE WITHOUT HOPE?
AND IF SO... TO WHOM CAN A GOD APPEAL FOR MERCY?
BUT I MUST KNOW. I MUST BE CERTAIN...

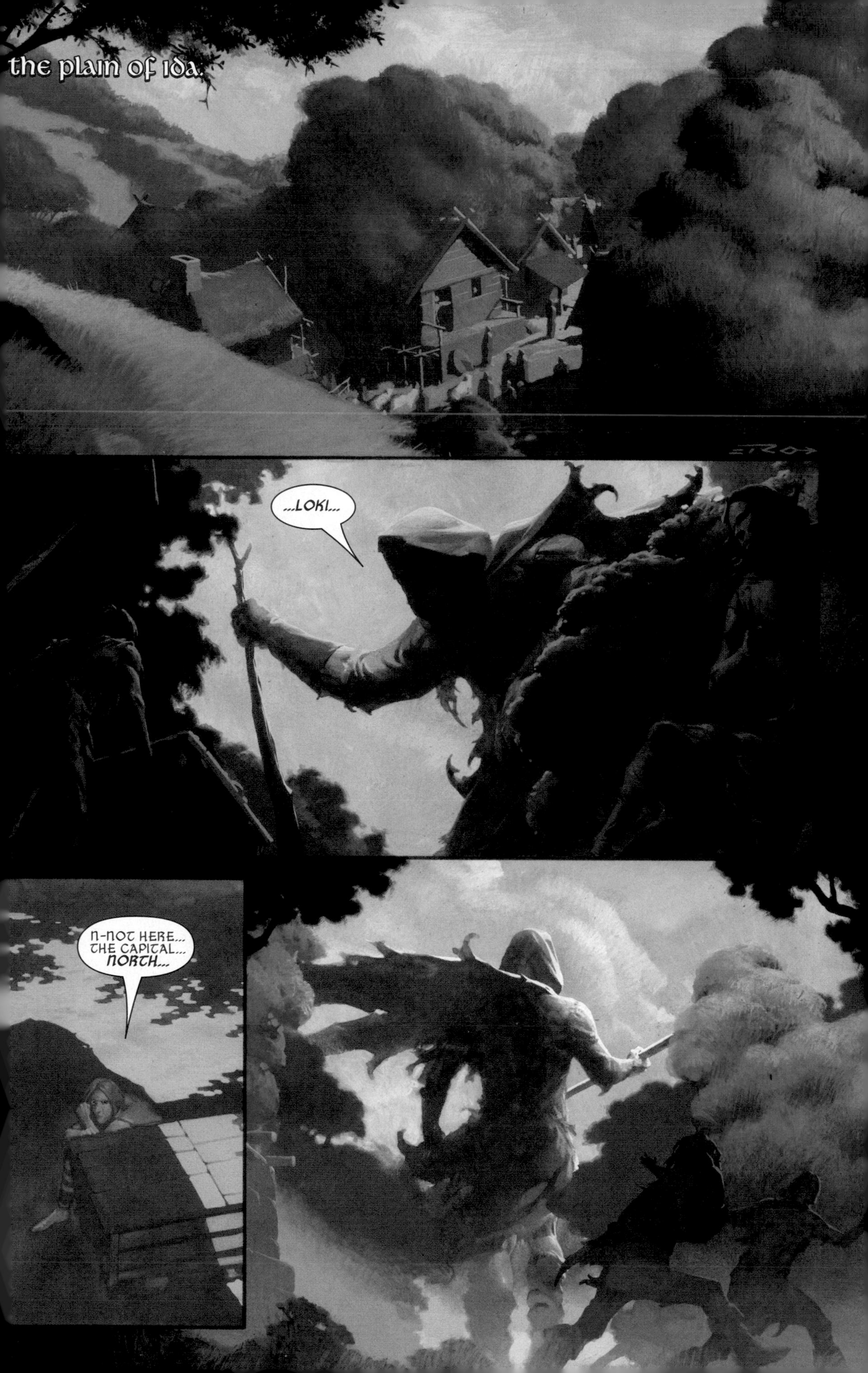
the plain of ida.
...LOKI...
N-NOT HERE... THE CAPITAL... NORTH...

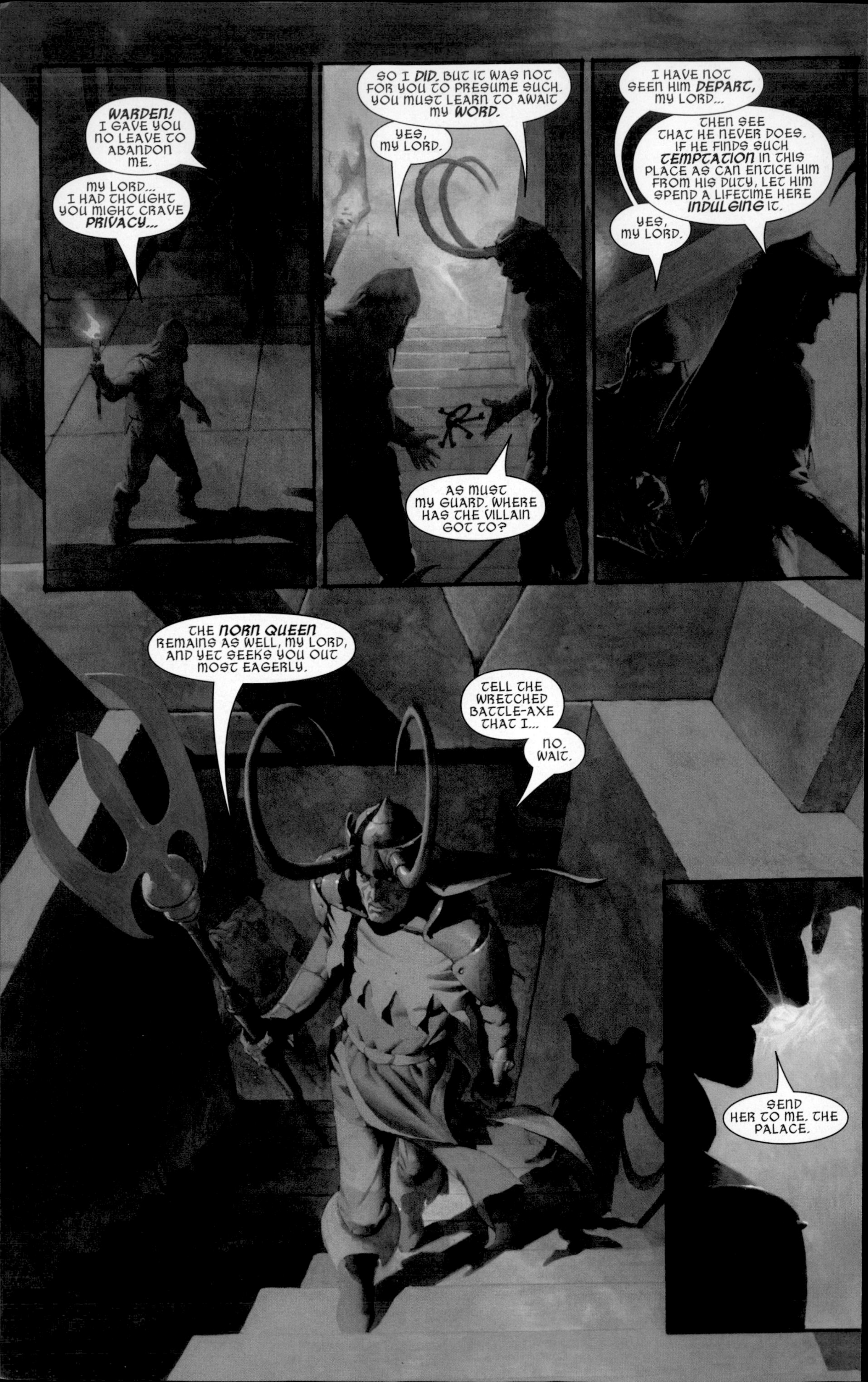
WARDEN! I GAVE YOU NO LEAVE TO ABANDON ME.
MY LORD... I HAD THOUGHT YOU MIGHT CRAVE PRIVACY...
SO I DID. BUT IT WAS NOT FOR YOU TO PRESUME SUCH. YOU MUST LEARN TO AWAIT MY WORD.
YES, MY LORD.
AS MUST MY GUARD. WHERE HAS THE VILLAIN GOT TO?
I HAVE NOT SEEN HIM DEPART, MY LORD...
THEN SEE THAT HE NEVER DOES. IF HE FINDS SUCH TEMPTATION IN THIS PLACE AS CAN ENTICE HIM FROM HIS DUTY, LET HIM SPEND A LIFETIME HERE INDULGING IT.
YES, MY LORD.
THE NORN QUEEN REMAINS AS WELL, MY LORD, AND YET SEEKS YOU OUT MOST EAGERLY.
TELL THE WRETCHED BATTLE-AXE THAT I...
NO. WAIT.
SEND HER TO ME. THE PALACE.

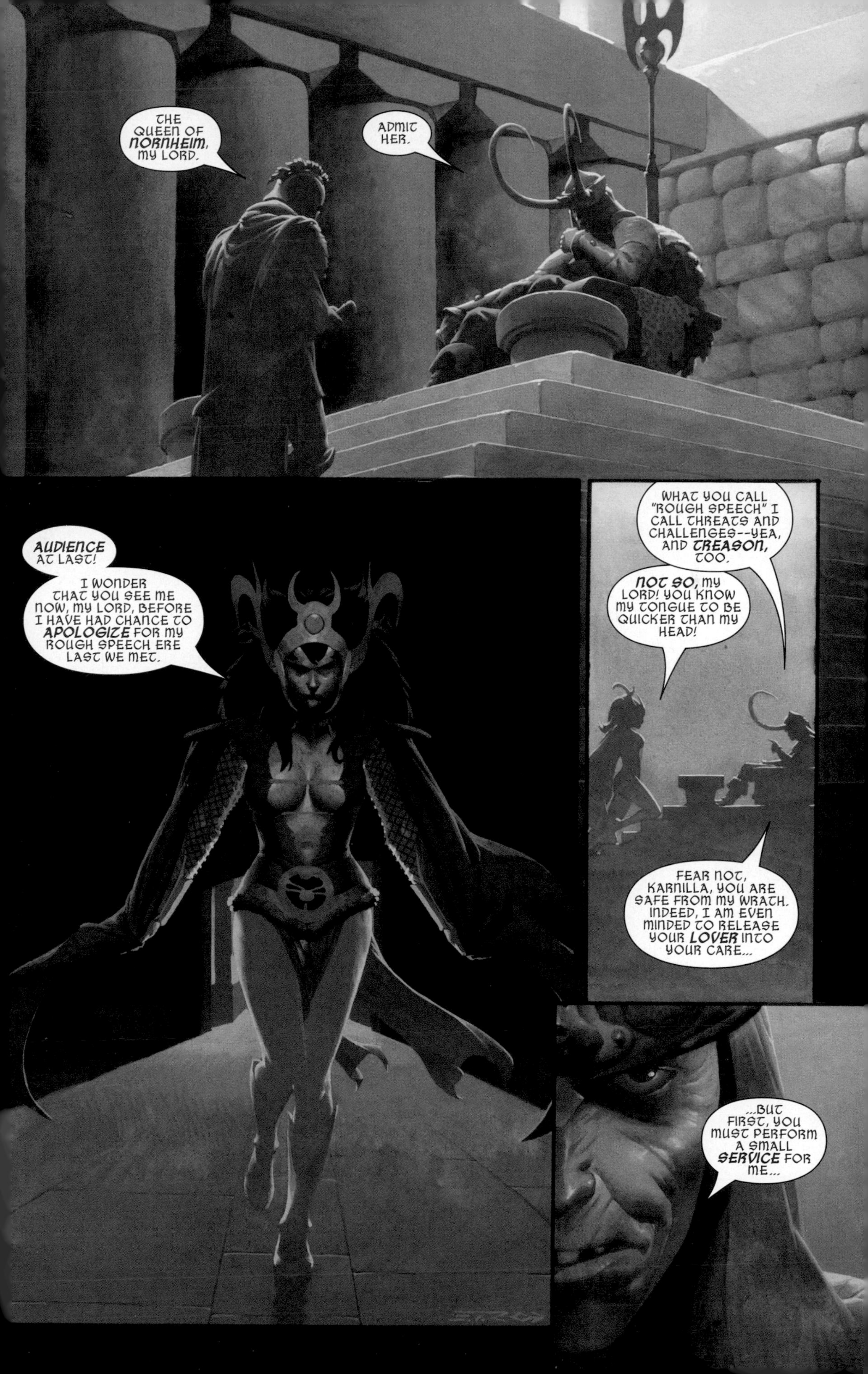
THE QUEEN OF NORNHEIM, MY LORD.
ADMIT HER.
AUDIENCE AT LAST!
I WONDER THAT YOU SEE ME NOW, MY LORD, BEFORE I HAVE HAD CHANCE TO APOLOGIZE FOR MY ROUGH SPEECH ERE LAST WE MET.
WHAT YOU CALL "ROUGH SPEECH" I CALL THREATS AND CHALLENGES--YEA, AND TREASON, TOO.
NOT SO, MY LORD! YOU KNOW MY TONGUE TO BE QUICKER THAN MY HEAD!
FEAR NOT, KARNILLA, YOU ARE SAFE FROM MY WRATH. INDEED, I AM EVEN MINDED TO RELEASE YOUR LOVER INTO YOUR CARE...
...BUT FIRST, YOU MUST PERFORM A SMALL SERVICE FOR ME...

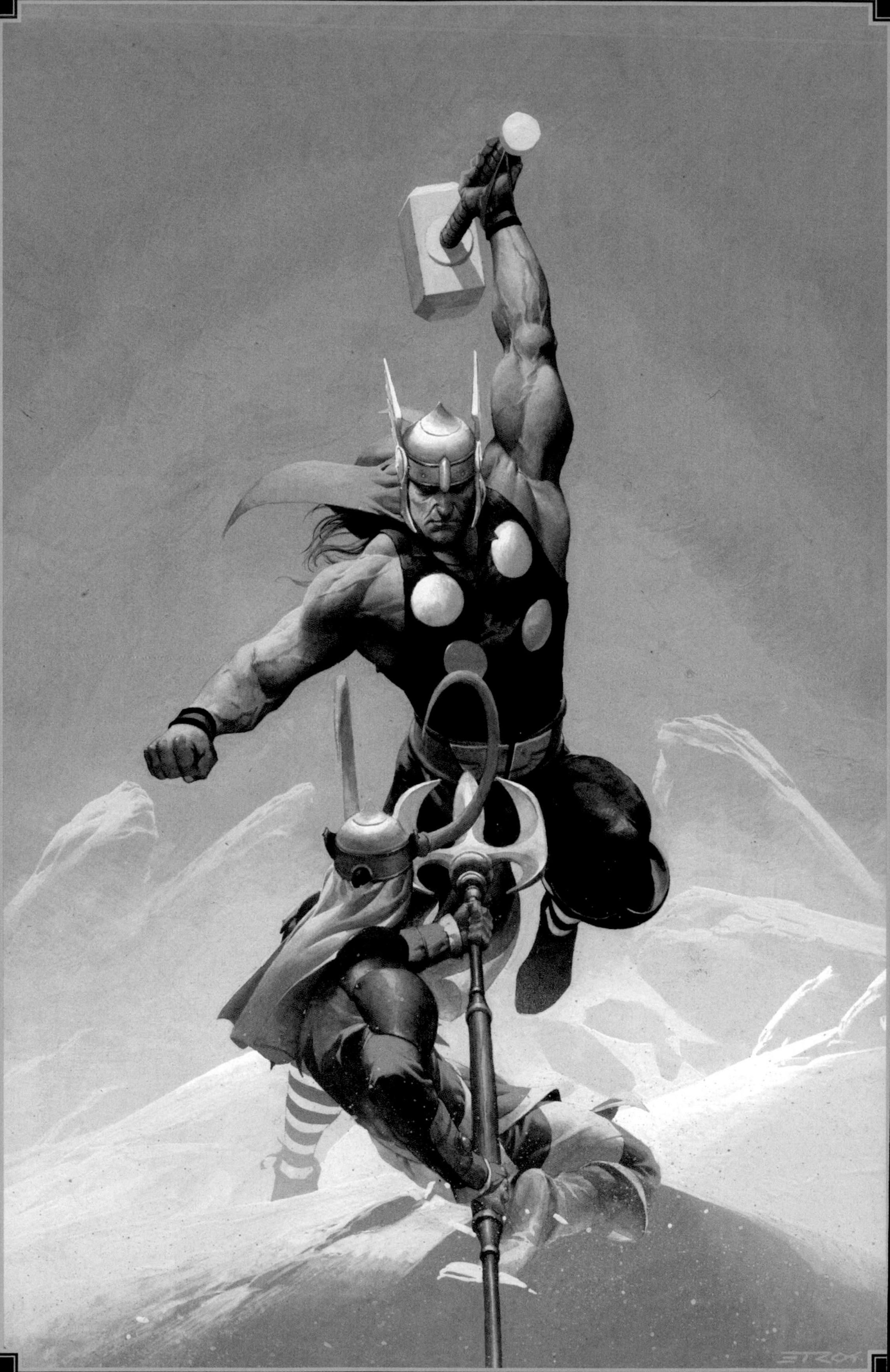
E TROY

Loki 3

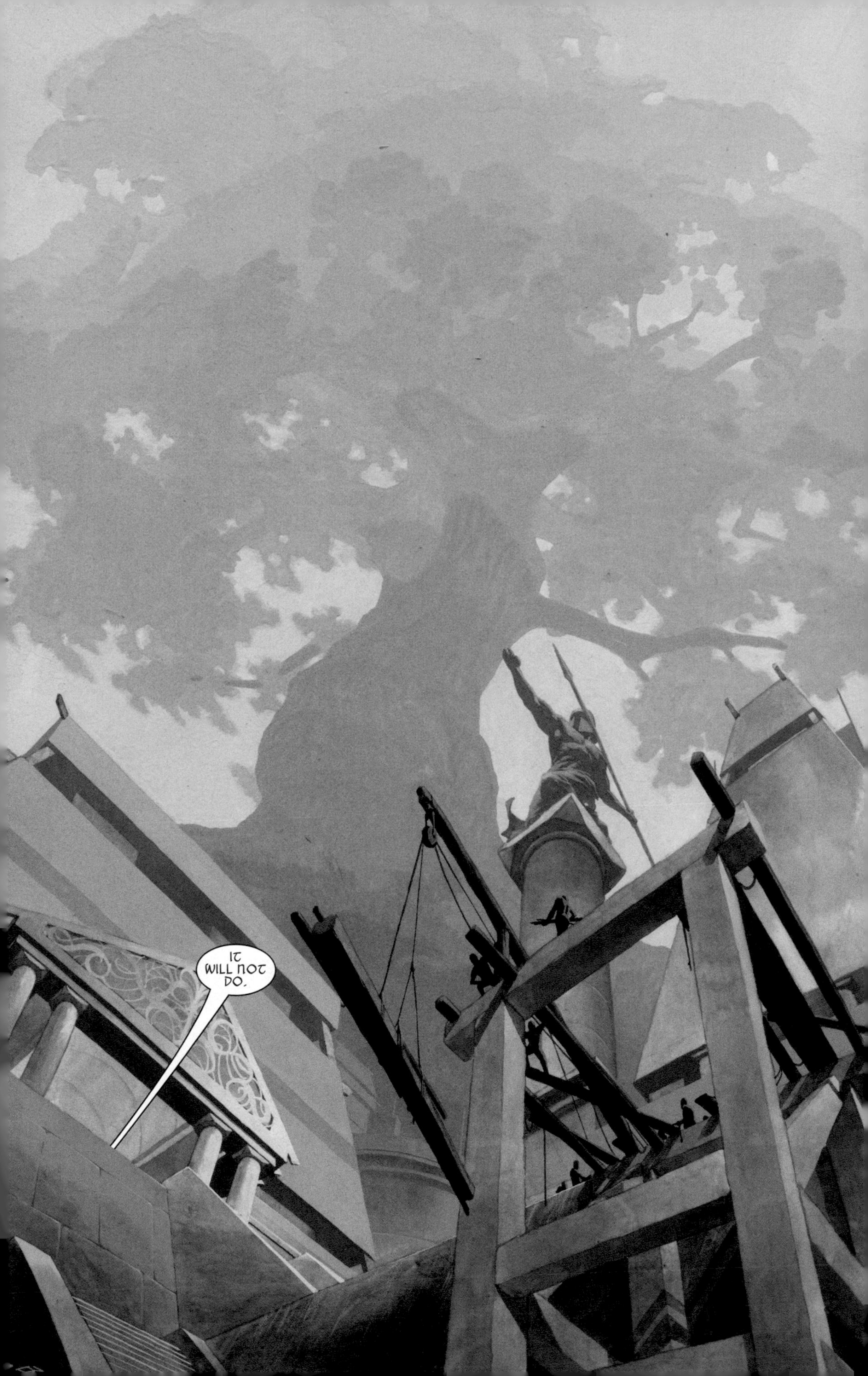
IT WILL NOT DO.

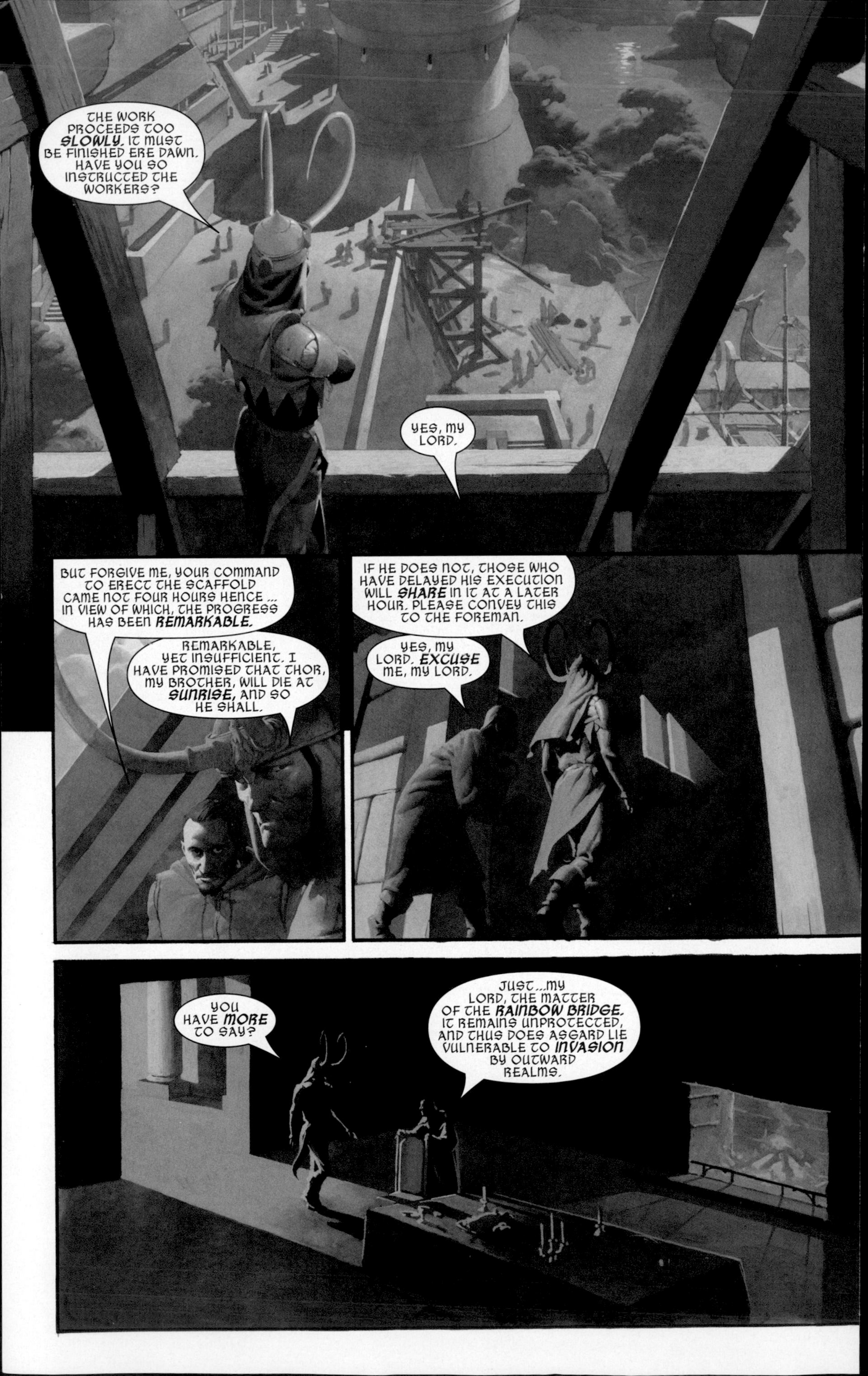
THE WORK PROCEEDS TOO SLOWLY. IT MUST BE FINISHED ERE DAWN. HAVE YOU SO INSTRUCTED THE WORKERS?
YES, MY LORD.
BUT FORGIVE ME, YOUR COMMAND TO ERECT THE SCAFFOLD CAME NOT FOUR HOURS HENCE ... IN VIEW OF WHICH, THE PROGRESS HAS BEEN REMARKABLE.
REMARKABLE, YET INSUFFICIENT. I HAVE PROMISED THAT THOR, MY BROTHER, WILL DIE AT SUNRISE, AND SO HE SHALL.
IF HE DOES NOT, THOSE WHO HAVE DELAYED HIS EXECUTION WILL SHARE IN IT AT A LATER HOUR. PLEASE CONVEY THIS TO THE FOREMAN.
YES, MY LORD. EXCUSE ME, MY LORD.
YOU HAVE MORE TO SAY?
JUST...MY LORD, THE MATTER OF THE RAINBOW BRIDGE. IT REMAINS UNPROTECTED, AND THUS DOES ASGARD LIE VULNERABLE TO INVASION BY OUTWARD REALMS.

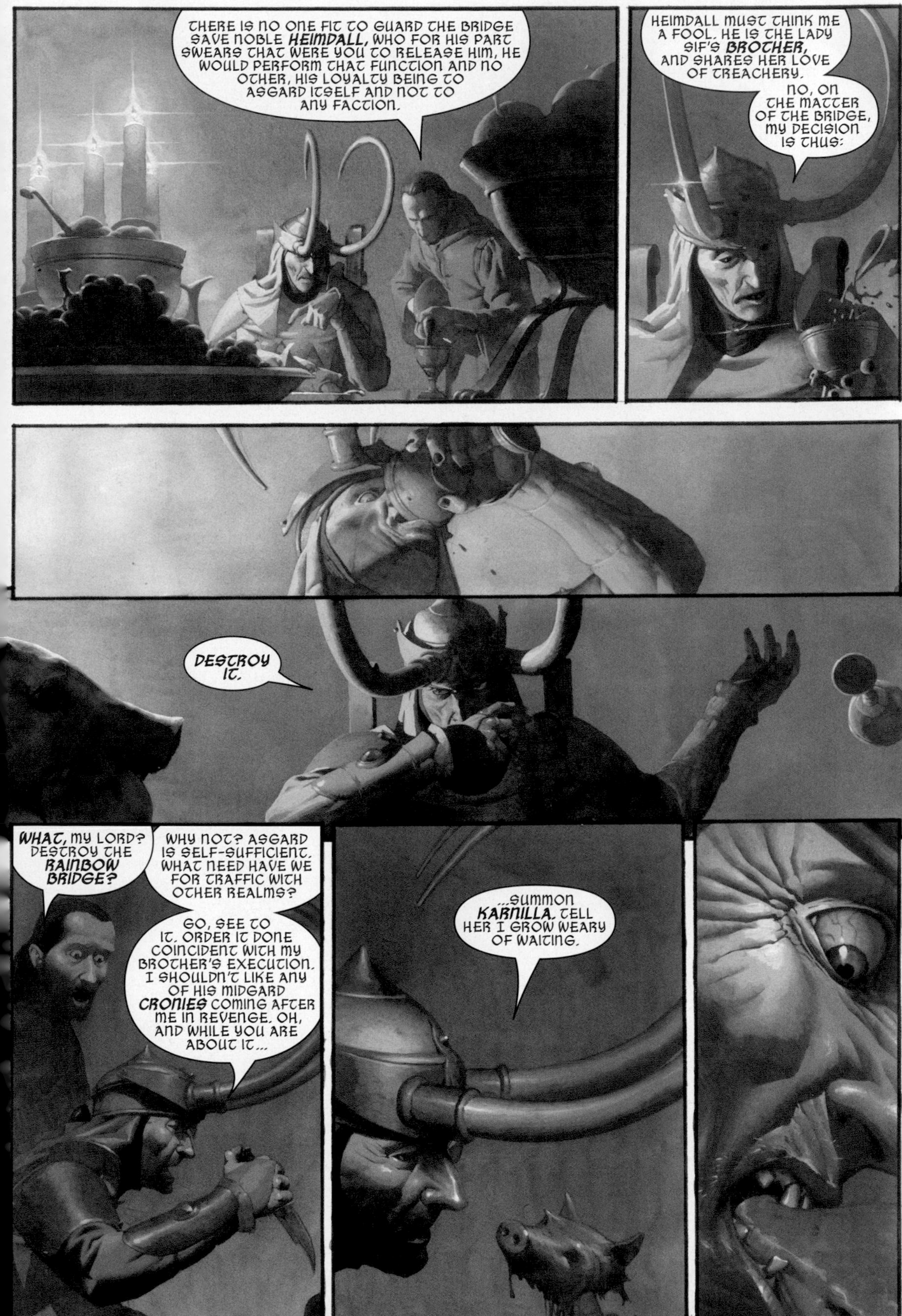
THERE IS NO ONE FIT TO GUARD THE BRIDGE SAVE NOBLE HEIMDALL, WHO FOR HIS PART SWEARS THAT WERE YOU TO RELEASE HIM, HE WOULD PERFORM THAT FUNCTION AND NO OTHER, HIS LOYALTY BEING TO ASGARD ITSELF AND NOT TO ANY FACTION.
HEIMDALL MUST THINK ME A FOOL. HE IS THE LADY SIF'S BROTHER, AND SHARES HER LOVE OF TREACHERY.
NO, ON THE MATTER OF THE BRIDGE, MY DECISION IS THUS:
DESTROY IT.
WHAT, MY LORD? DESTROY THE RAINBOW BRIDGE?
WHY NOT? ASGARD IS SELF-SUFFICIENT. WHAT NEED HAVE WE FOR TRAFFIC WITH OTHER REALMS?
GO, SEE TO IT. ORDER IT DONE COINCIDENT WITH MY BROTHER'S EXECUTION. I SHOULDN'T LIKE ANY OF HIS MIDGARD CRONIES COMING AFTER ME IN REVENGE. OH, AND WHILE YOU ARE ABOUT IT...
...SUMMON KARNILLA. TELL HER I GROW WEARY OF WAITING.

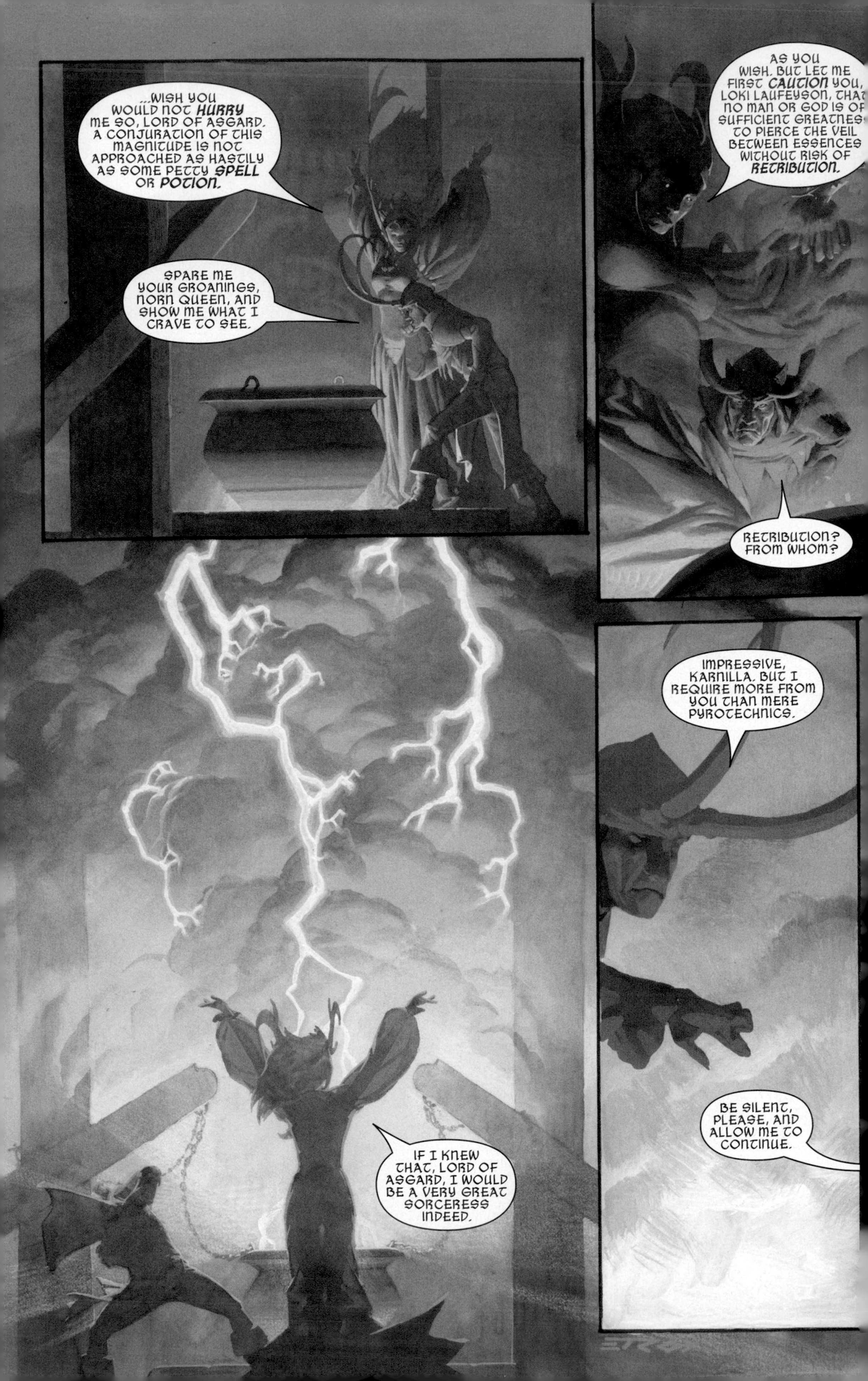
...WISH YOU WOULD NOT HURRY ME SO, LORD OF ASGARD. A CONJURATION OF THIS MAGNITUDE IS NOT APPROACHED AS HASTILY AS SOME PETTY SPELL OR POTION.
SPARE ME YOUR GROANINGS, NORN QUEEN, AND SHOW ME WHAT I CRAVE TO SEE.
AS YOU WISH. BUT LET ME FIRST CAUTION YOU, LOKI LAUFEYSON, THAT NO MAN OR GOD IS OF SUFFICIENT GREATNESS TO PIERCE THE VEIL BETWEEN ESSENCES WITHOUT RISK OF RETRIBUTION.
RETRIBUTION? FROM WHOM?
IF I KNEW THAT, LORD OF ASGARD, I WOULD BE A VERY GREAT SORCERESS INDEED.
IMPRESSIVE, KARNILLA. BUT I REQUIRE MORE FROM YOU THAN MERE PYROTECHNICS.
BE SILENT, PLEASE, AND ALLOW ME TO CONTINUE.

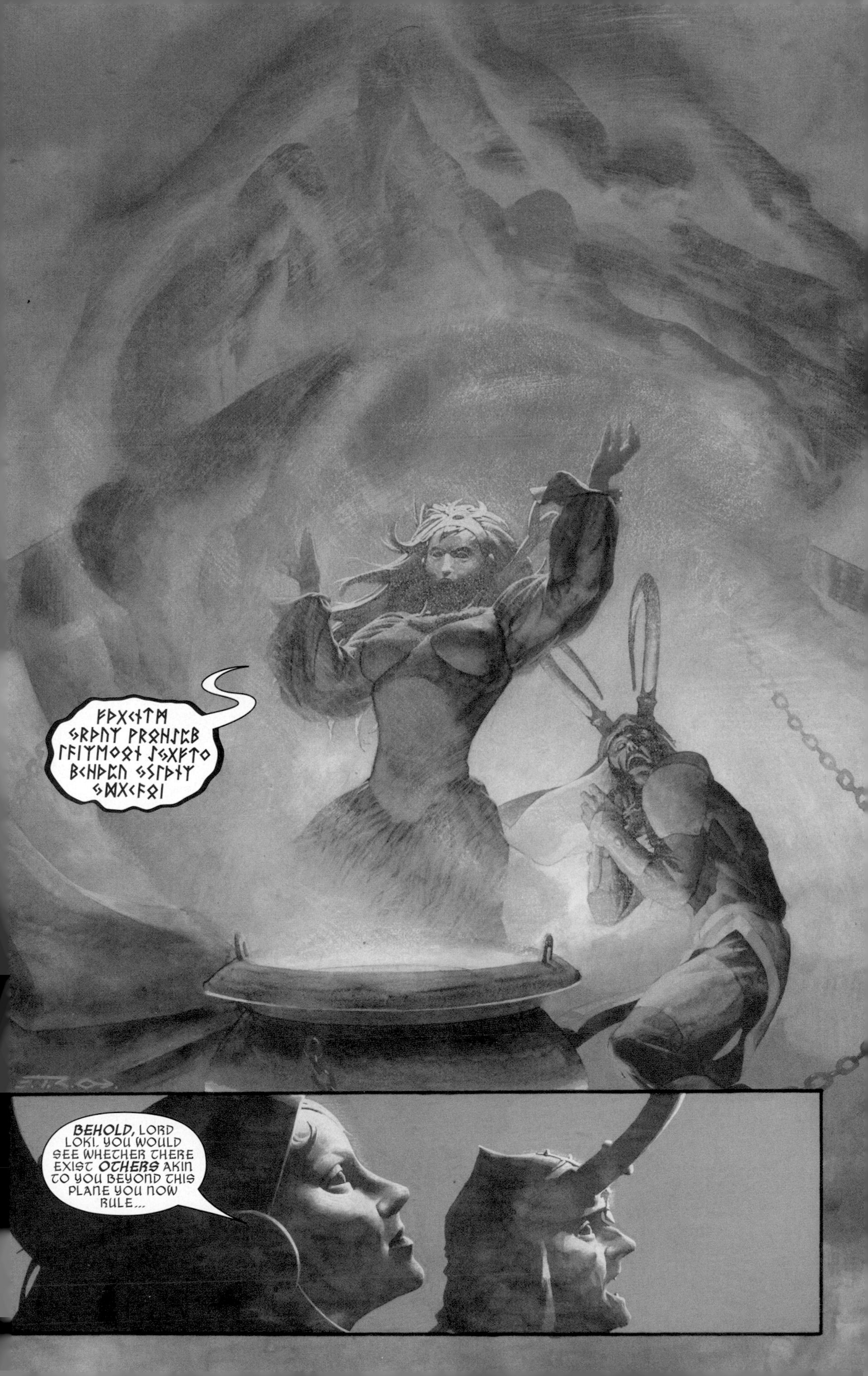
BEHOLD, LORD LOKI. YOU WOULD SEE WHETHER THERE EXIST **OTHERS** AKIN TO YOU BEYOND THIS PLANE YOU NOW RULE...

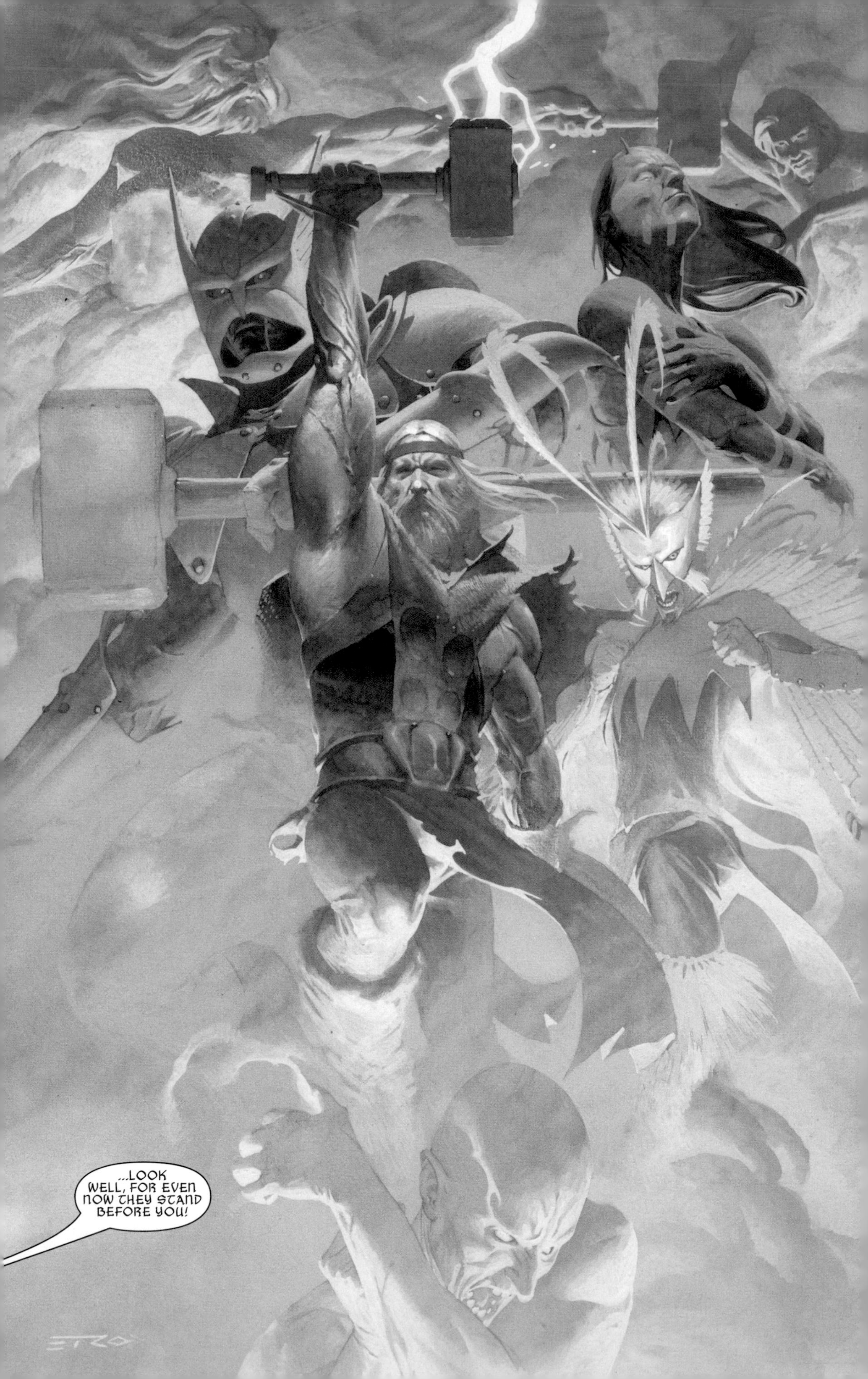
...LOOK WELL, FOR EVEN NOW THEY STAND BEFORE YOU!
ETRO

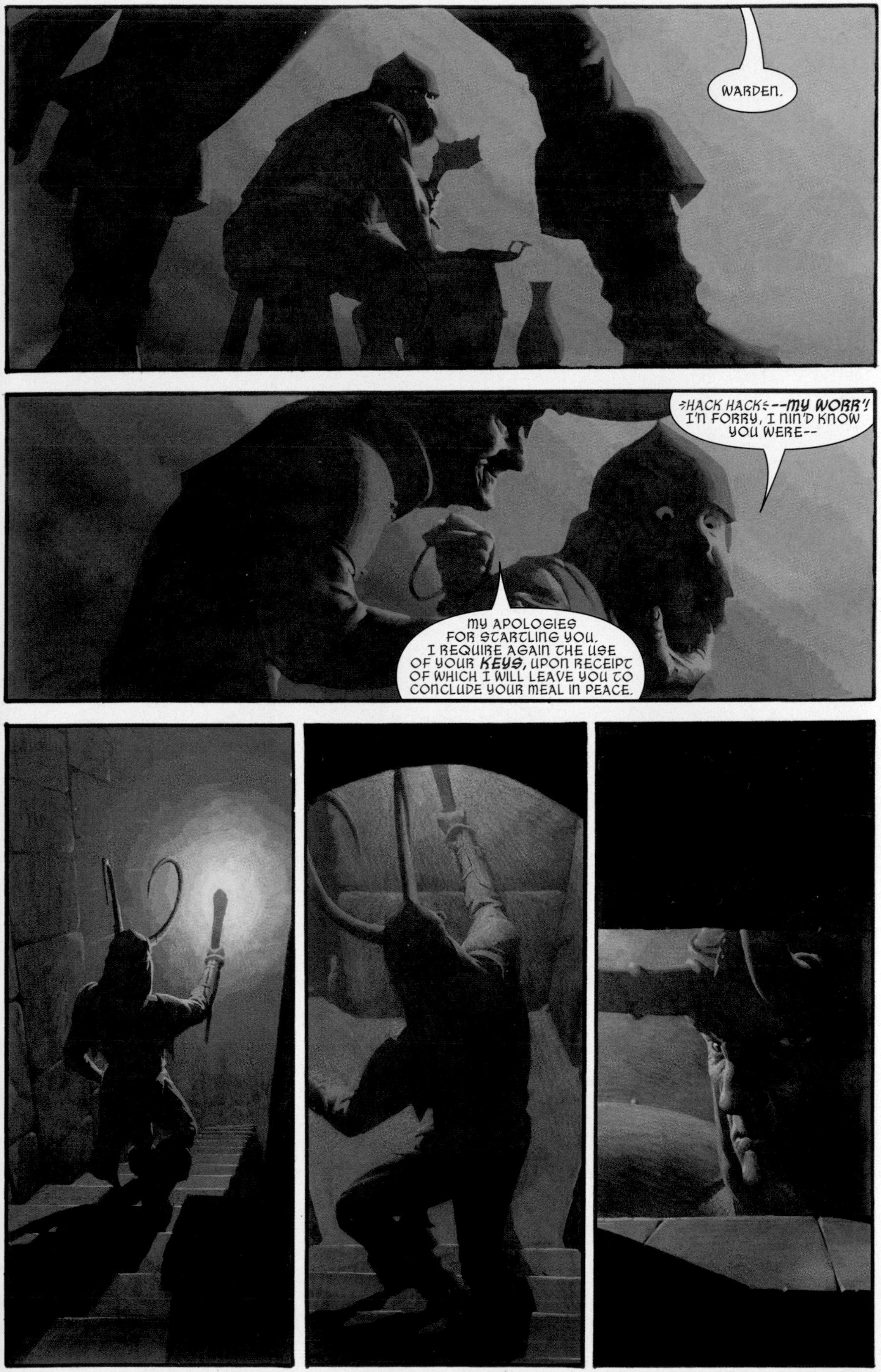
WARDEN.
>HACK HACK< --MY WORR'! I'N FORRY, I NIN'D KNOW YOU WERE--
MY APOLOGIES FOR STARTLING YOU. I REQUIRE AGAIN THE USE OF YOUR KEYS, UPON RECEIPT OF WHICH I WILL LEAVE YOU TO CONCLUDE YOUR MEAL IN PEACE.

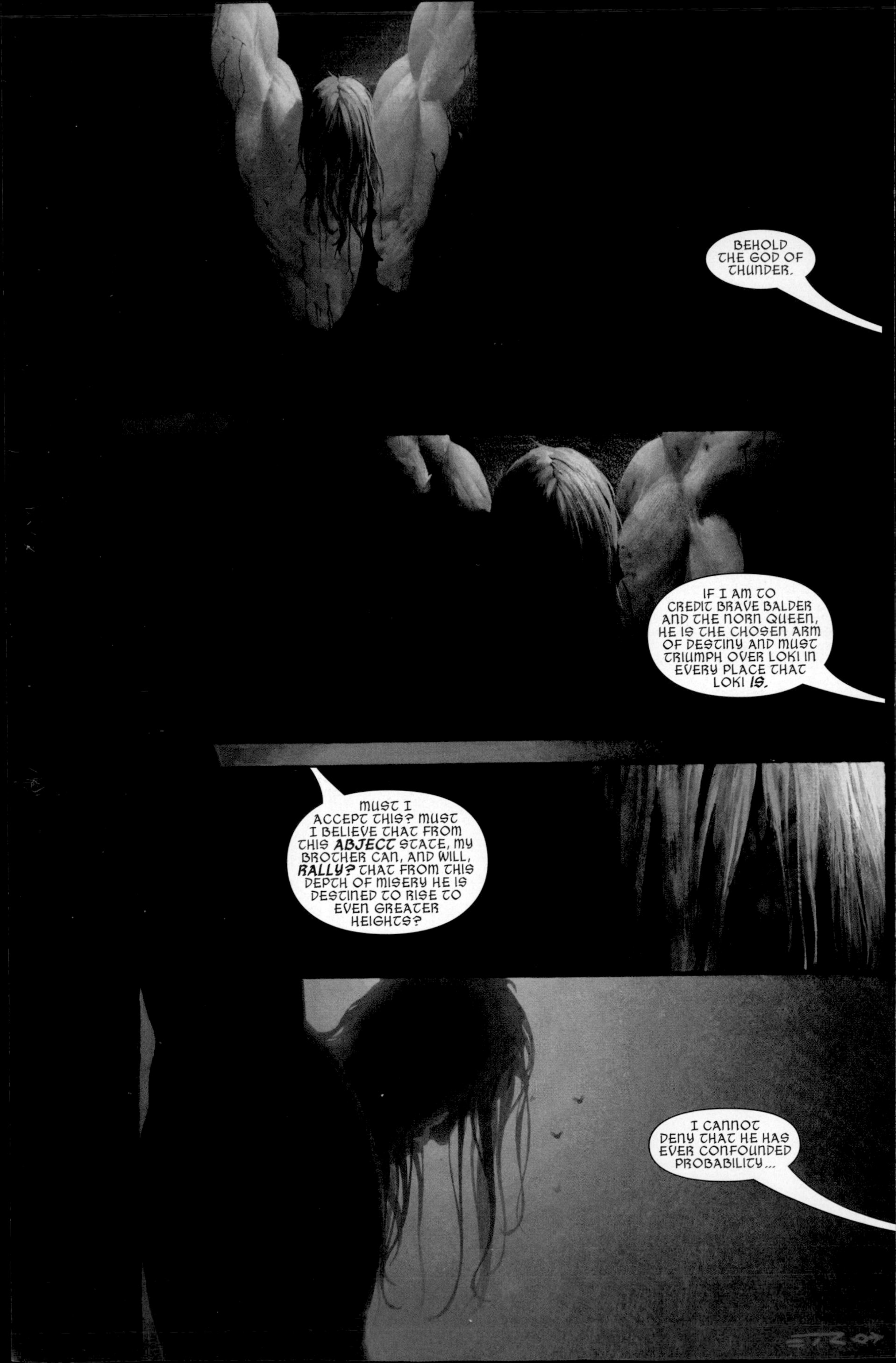
BEHOLD THE GOD OF THUNDER.
IF I AM TO CREDIT BRAVE BALDER AND THE NORN QUEEN, HE IS THE CHOSEN ARM OF DESTINY AND MUST TRIUMPH OVER LOKI IN EVERY PLACE THAT LOKI IS.
MUST I ACCEPT THIS? MUST I BELIEVE THAT FROM THIS ABJECT STATE, MY BROTHER CAN, AND WILL, RALLY? THAT FROM THIS DEPTH OF MISERY HE IS DESTINED TO RISE TO EVEN GREATER HEIGHTS?
I CANNOT DENY THAT HE HAS EVER CONFOUNDED PROBABILITY...

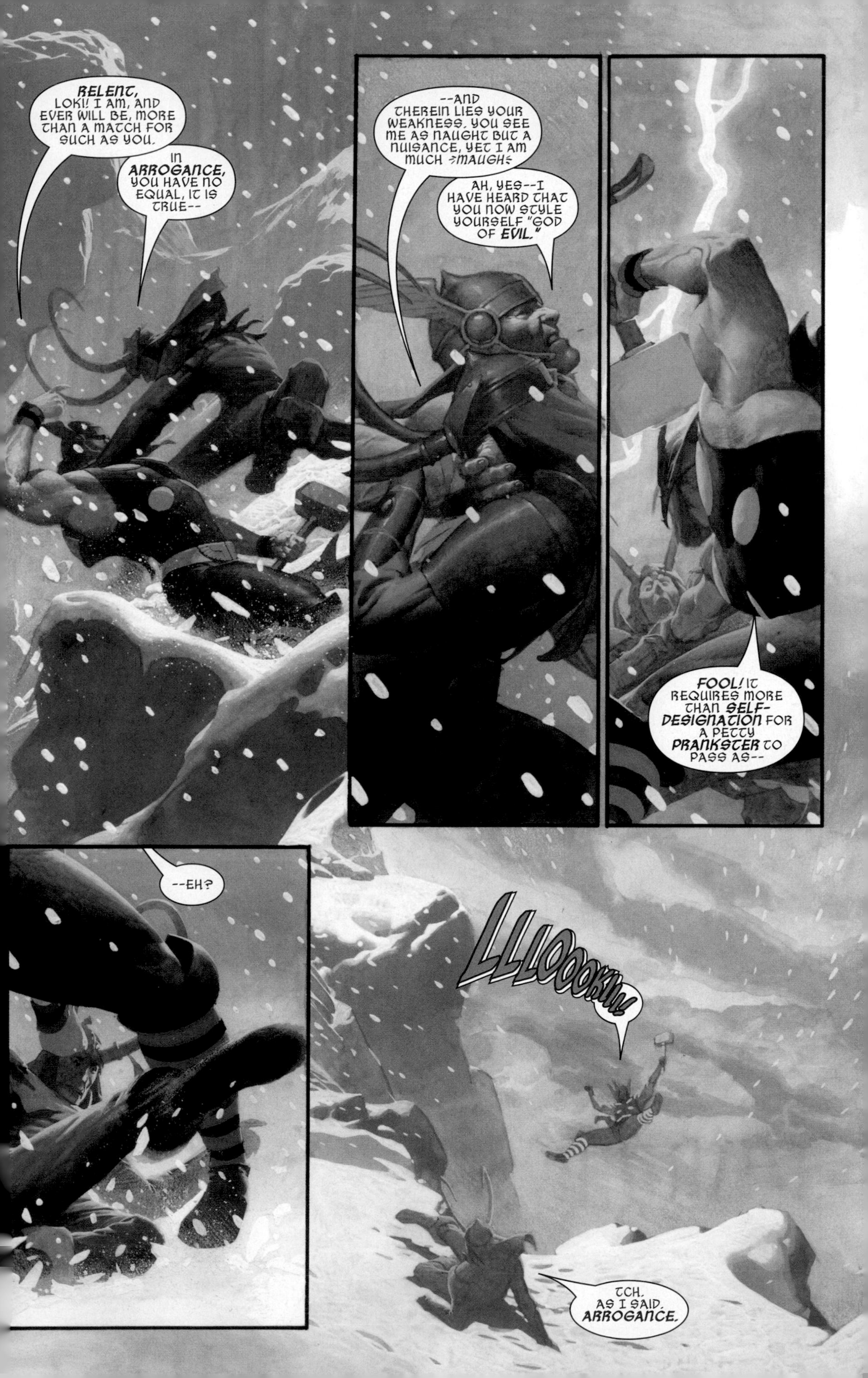

RELENT, LOKI! I AM, AND EVER WILL BE, MORE THAN A MATCH FOR SUCH AS YOU.
IN ARROGANCE, YOU HAVE NO EQUAL, IT IS TRUE--
--AND THEREIN LIES YOUR WEAKNESS. YOU SEE ME AS NAUGHT BUT A NUISANCE, YET I AM MUCH *MAUGH*
AH, YES--I HAVE HEARD THAT YOU NOW STYLE YOURSELF "GOD OF EVIL."
FOOL! IT REQUIRES MORE THAN SELF-DESIGNATION FOR A PETTY PRANKSTER TO PASS AS--
--EH?
LLLOOOKIII!
TCH. AS I SAID. ARROGANCE.

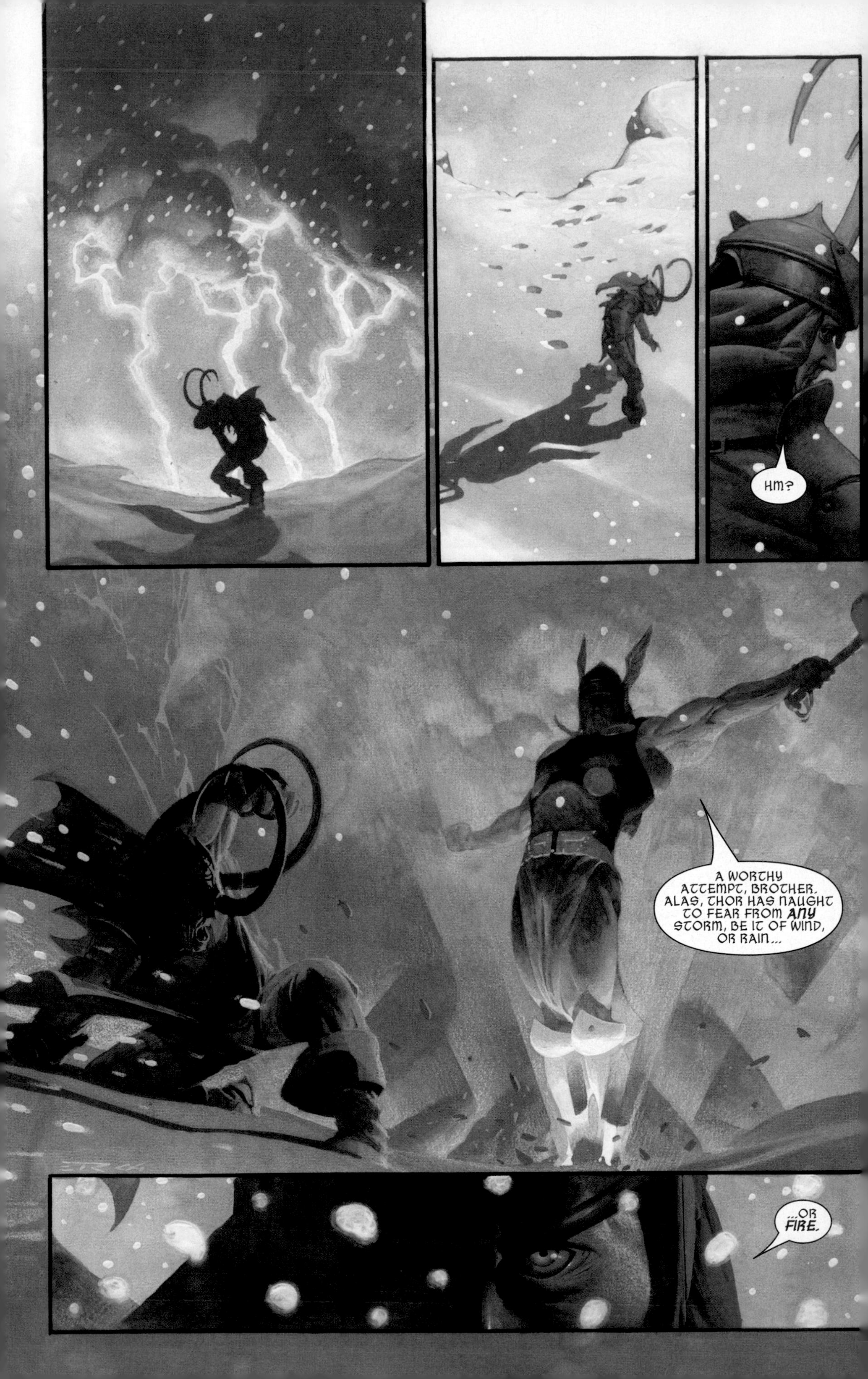
HM?
A WORTHY ATTEMPT, BROTHER. ALAS, THOR HAS NAUGHT TO FEAR FROM ANY STORM, BE IT OF WIND, OR RAIN...
...OR FIRE.

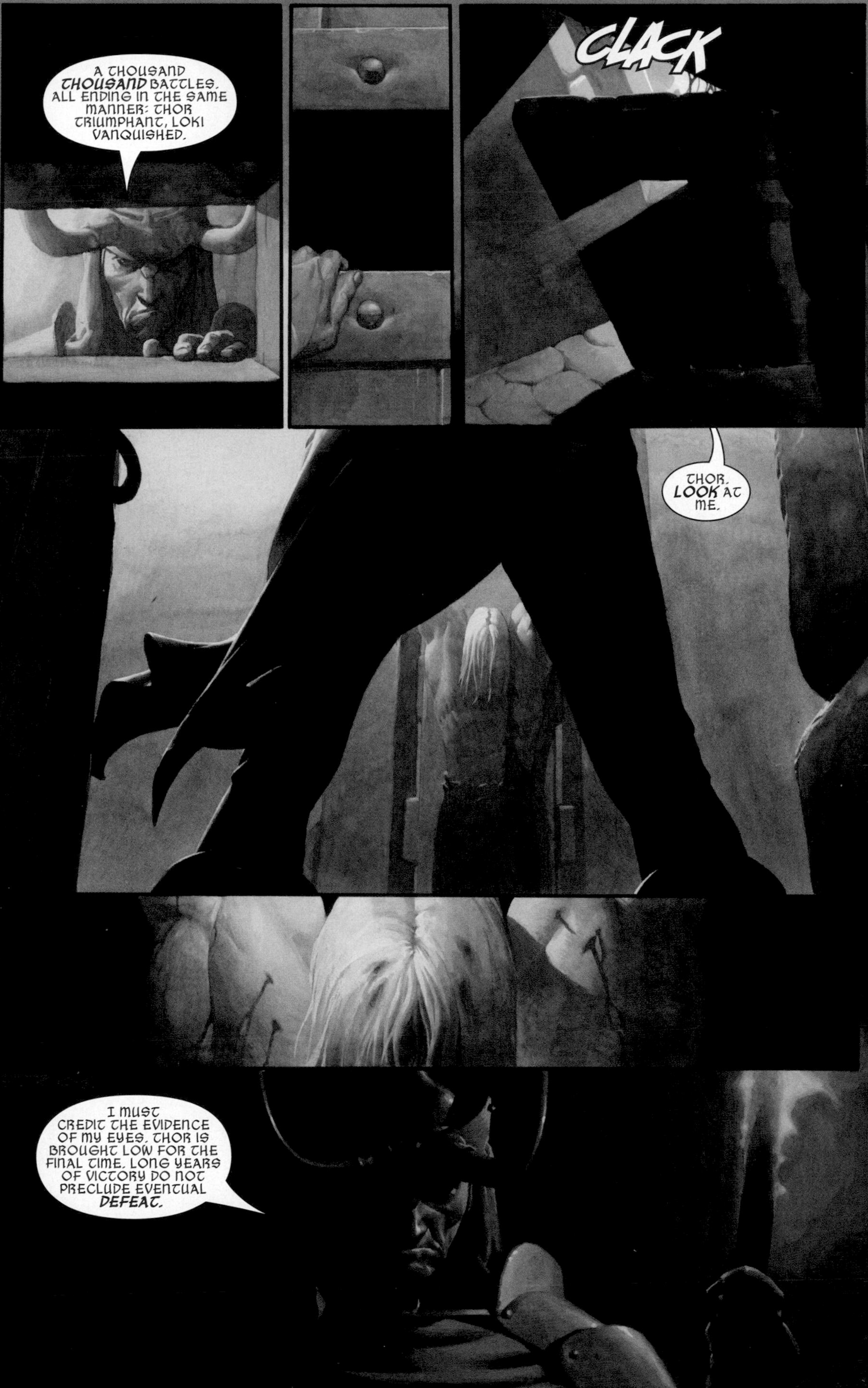
A THOUSAND THOUSAND BATTLES. ALL ENDING IN THE SAME MANNER: THOR TRIUMPHANT, LOKI VANQUISHED.
CLACK
THOR. LOOK AT ME.
I MUST CREDIT THE EVIDENCE OF MY EYES. THOR IS BROUGHT LOW FOR THE FINAL TIME. LONG YEARS OF VICTORY DO NOT PRECLUDE EVENTUAL DEFEAT.

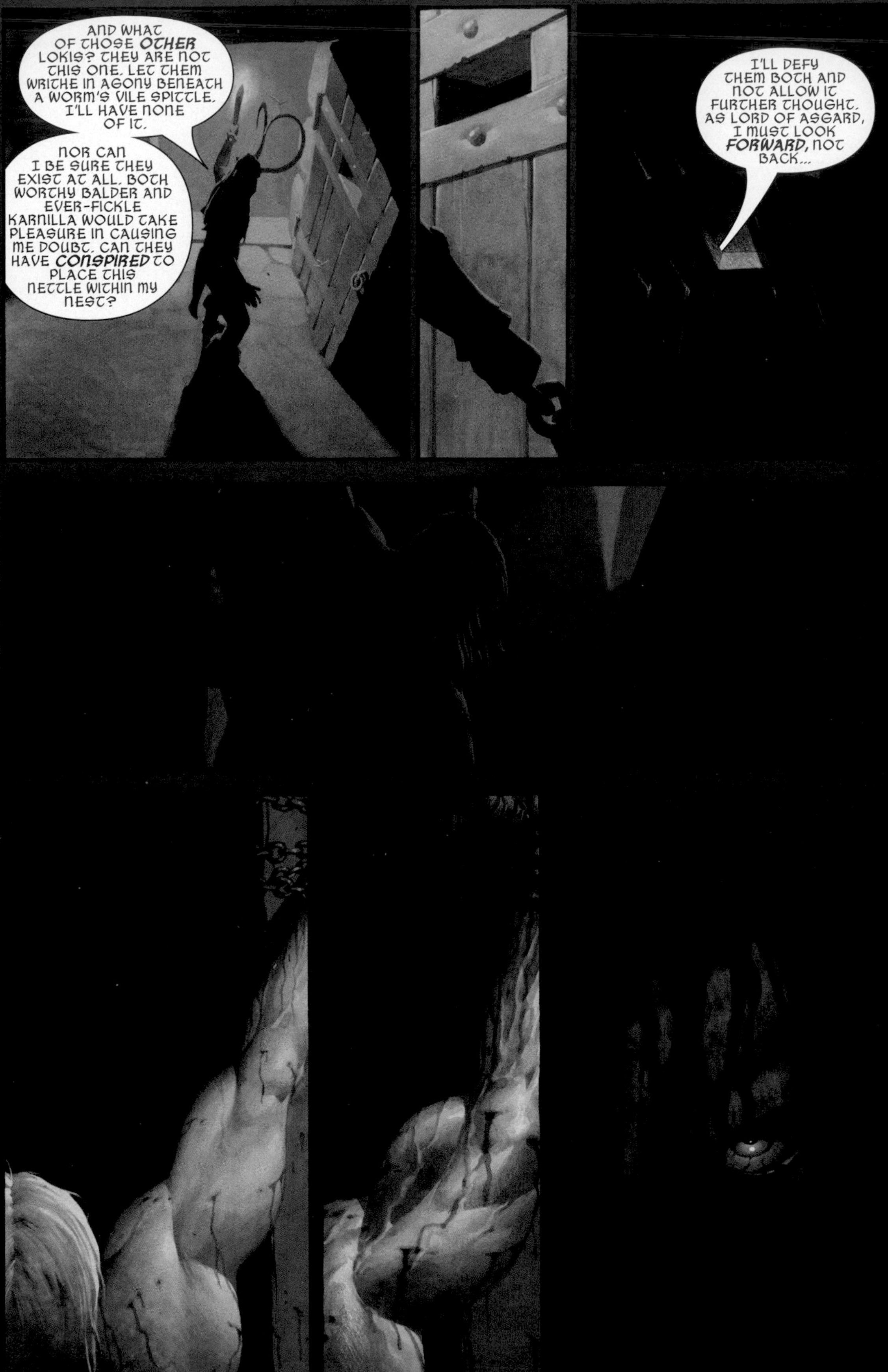
AND WHAT OF THOSE OTHER LOKIS? THEY ARE NOT THIS ONE. LET THEM WRITHE IN AGONY BENEATH A WORM'S VILE SPITTLE. I'LL HAVE NONE OF IT.
NOR CAN I BE SURE THEY EXIST AT ALL. BOTH WORTHY BALDER AND EVER-FICKLE KARNILLA WOULD TAKE PLEASURE IN CAUSING ME DOUBT. CAN THEY HAVE CONSPIRED TO PLACE THIS NETTLE WITHIN MY NEST?
I'LL DEFY THEM BOTH AND NOT ALLOW IT FURTHER THOUGHT. AS LORD OF ASGARD, I MUST LOOK FORWARD, NOT BACK...

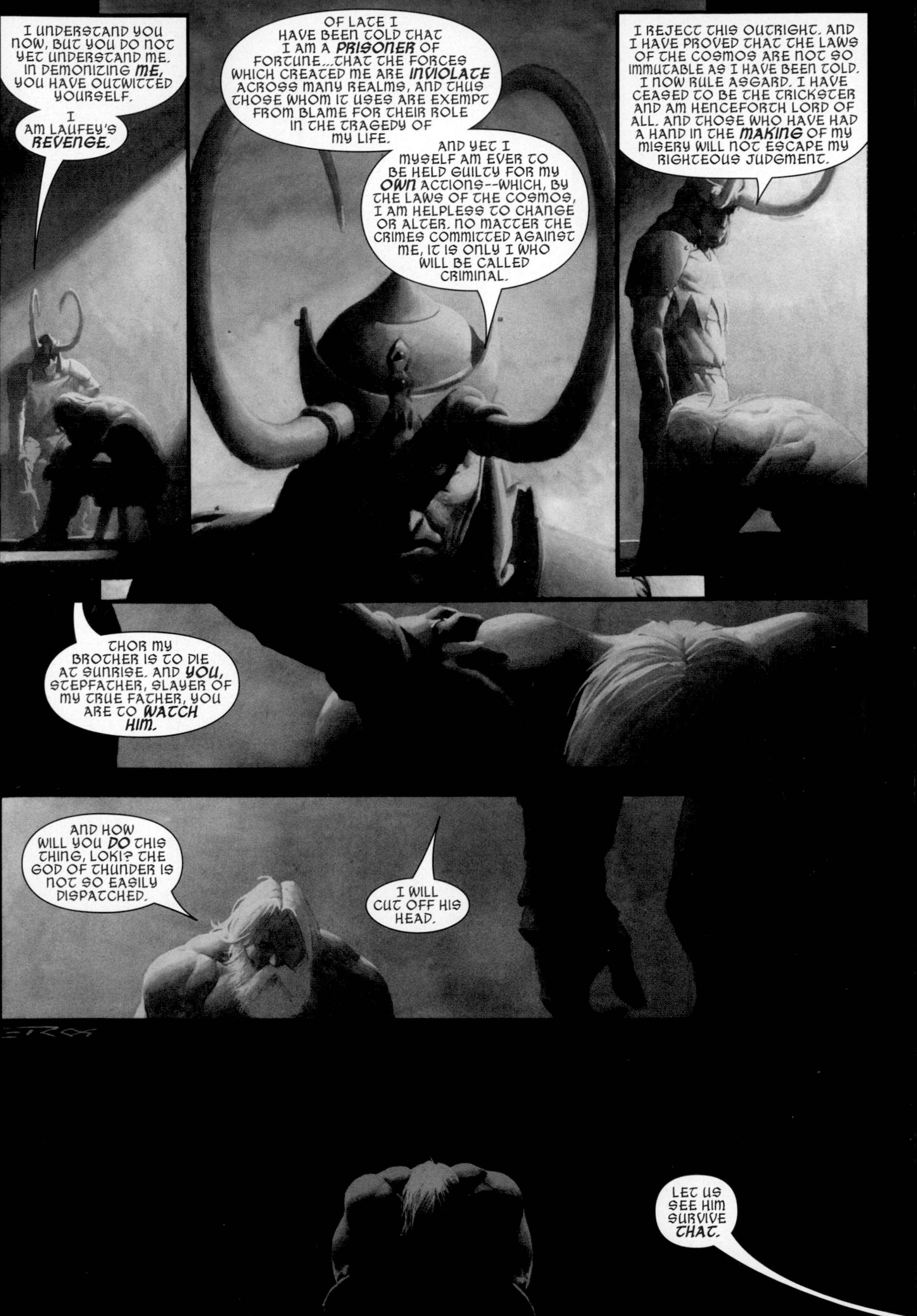
I UNDERSTAND YOU NOW, BUT YOU DO NOT YET UNDERSTAND ME. IN DEMONIZING ME, YOU HAVE OUTWITTED YOURSELF.
I AM LAUFEY'S REVENGE.
OF LATE I HAVE BEEN TOLD THAT I AM A PRISONER OF FORTUNE...THAT THE FORCES WHICH CREATED ME ARE INVIOLATE ACROSS MANY REALMS, AND THUS THOSE WHOM IT USES ARE EXEMPT FROM BLAME FOR THEIR ROLE IN THE TRAGEDY OF MY LIFE.
AND YET I MYSELF AM EVER TO BE HELD GUILTY FOR MY OWN ACTIONS--WHICH, BY THE LAWS OF THE COSMOS, I AM HELPLESS TO CHANGE OR ALTER. NO MATTER THE CRIMES COMMITTED AGAINST ME, IT IS ONLY I WHO WILL BE CALLED CRIMINAL.
I REJECT THIS OUTRIGHT. AND I HAVE PROVED THAT THE LAWS OF THE COSMOS ARE NOT SO IMMUTABLE AS I HAVE BEEN TOLD. I NOW RULE ASGARD. I HAVE CEASED TO BE THE TRICKSTER AND AM HENCEFORTH LORD OF ALL. AND THOSE WHO HAVE HAD A HAND IN THE MAKING OF MY MISERY WILL NOT ESCAPE MY RIGHTEOUS JUDGMENT.
THOR MY BROTHER IS TO DIE AT SUNRISE. AND YOU, STEPFATHER, SLAYER OF MY TRUE FATHER, YOU ARE TO WATCH HIM.
AND HOW WILL YOU DO THIS THING, LOKI? THE GOD OF THUNDER IS NOT SO EASILY DISPATCHED.
I WILL CUT OFF HIS HEAD.
LET US SEE HIM SURVIVE THAT.

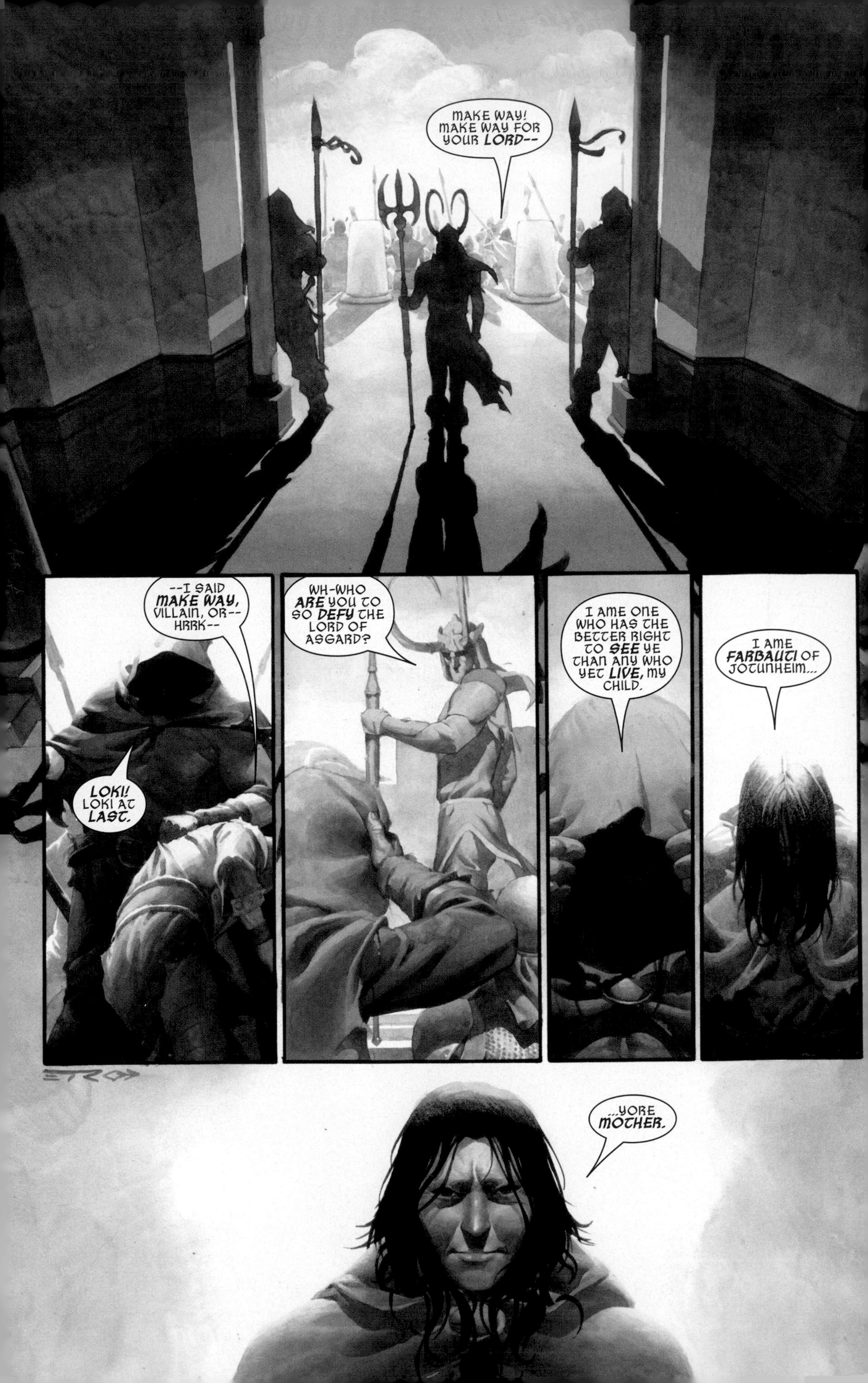
MAKE WAY! MAKE WAY FOR YOUR LORD--
--I SAID MAKE WAY, VILLAIN, OR-- HRRK--
LOKI! LOKI AT LAST.
WH-WHO ARE YOU TO SO DEFY THE LORD OF ASGARD?
I AME ONE WHO HAS THE BETTER RIGHT TO SEE YE THAN ANY WHO YET LIVE, MY CHILD.
I AME FARBAUTI OF JOTUNHEIM...
...YORE MOTHER.

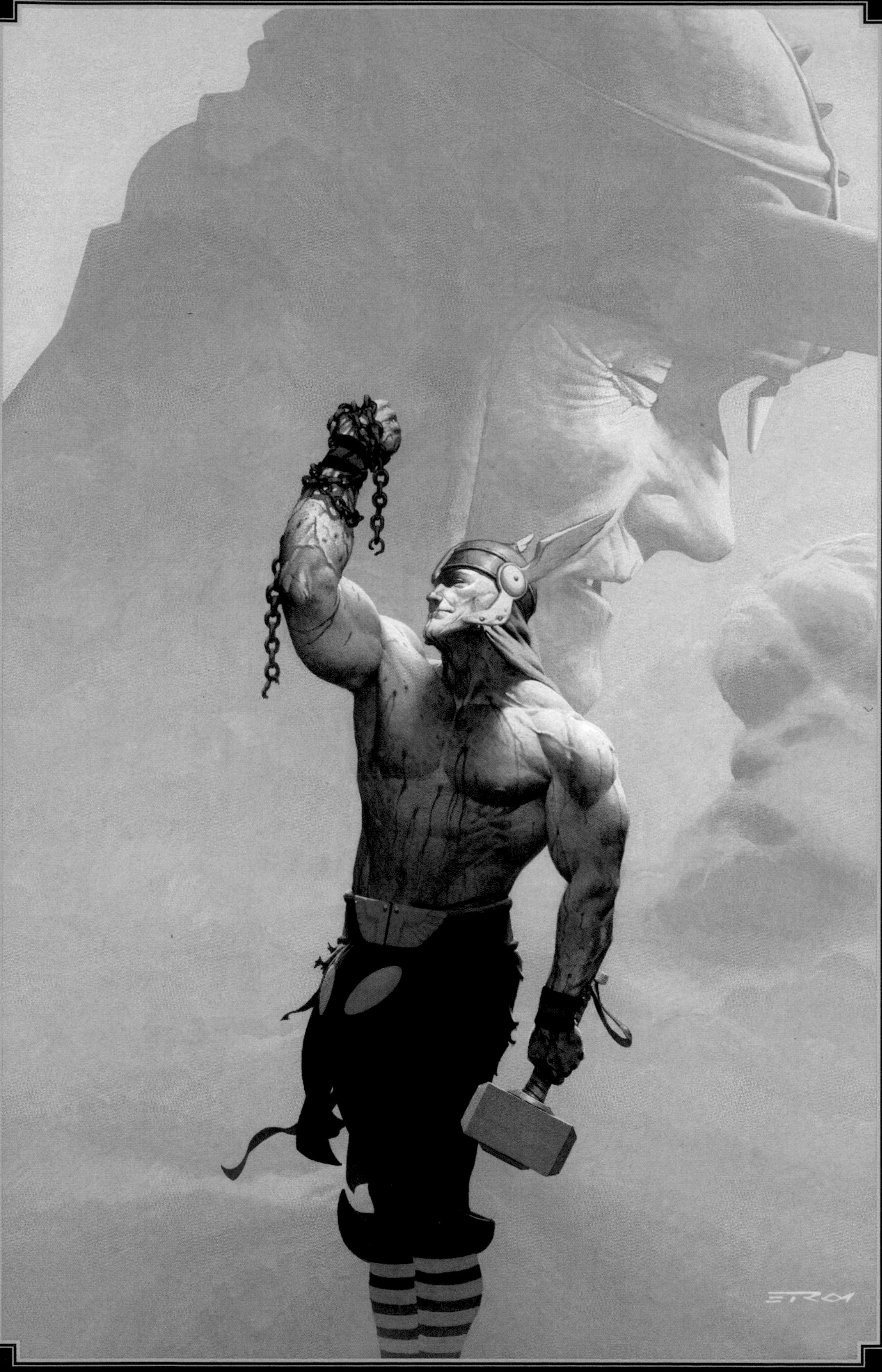
ETRO

Loki 4

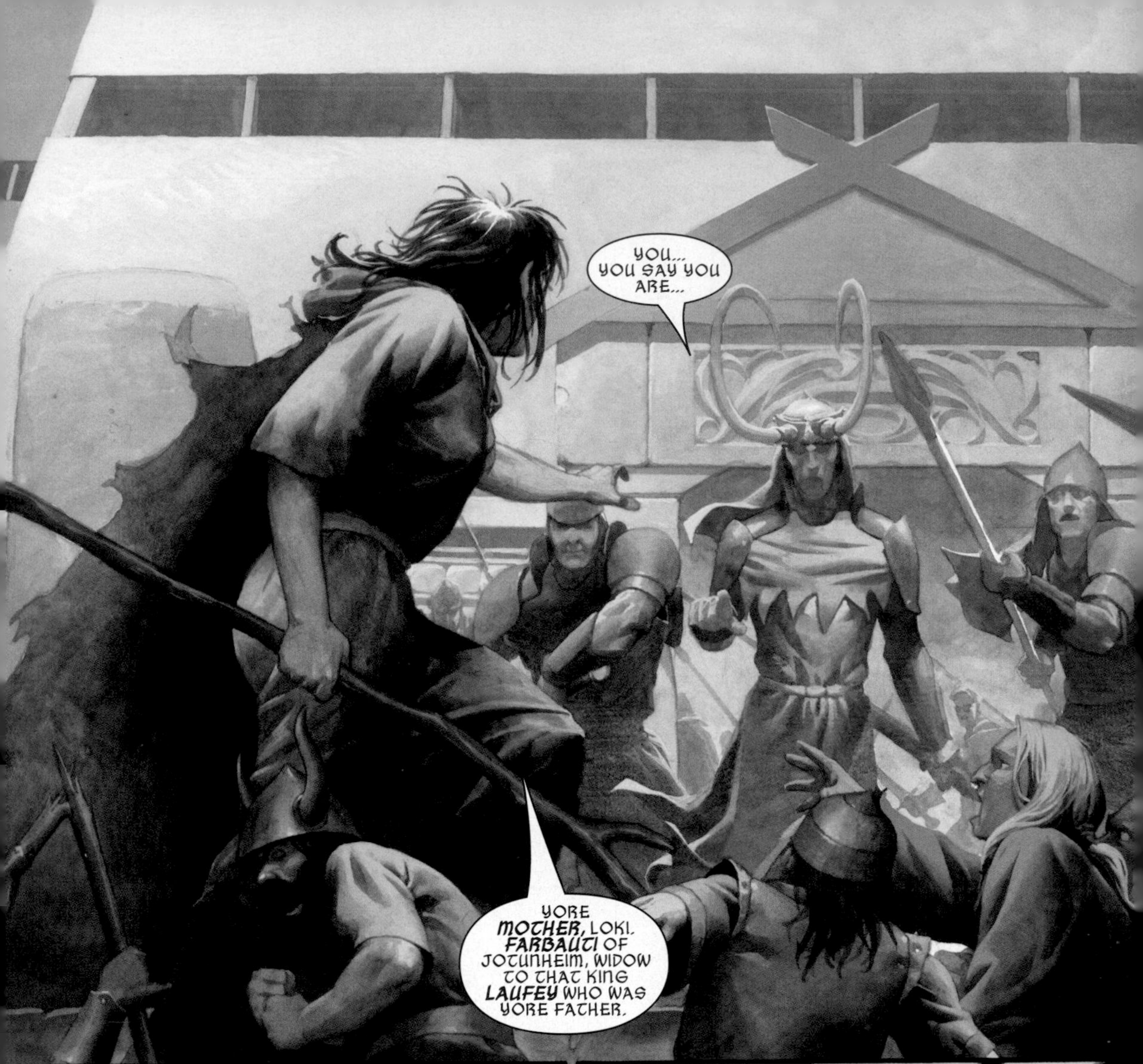
YOU...
YOU SAY YOU ARE...
YORE MOTHER, LOKI. FARBAUTI OF JOTUNHEIM, WIDOW TO THAT KING LAUFEY WHO WAS YORE FATHER.

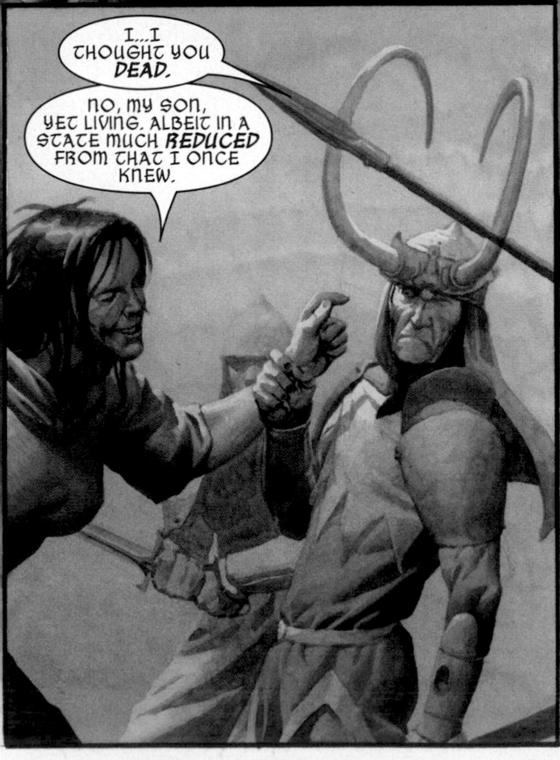
I...I THOUGHT YOU DEAD.
NO, MY SON, YET LIVING. ALBEIT IN A STATE MUCH REDUCED FROM THAT I ONCE KNEW.

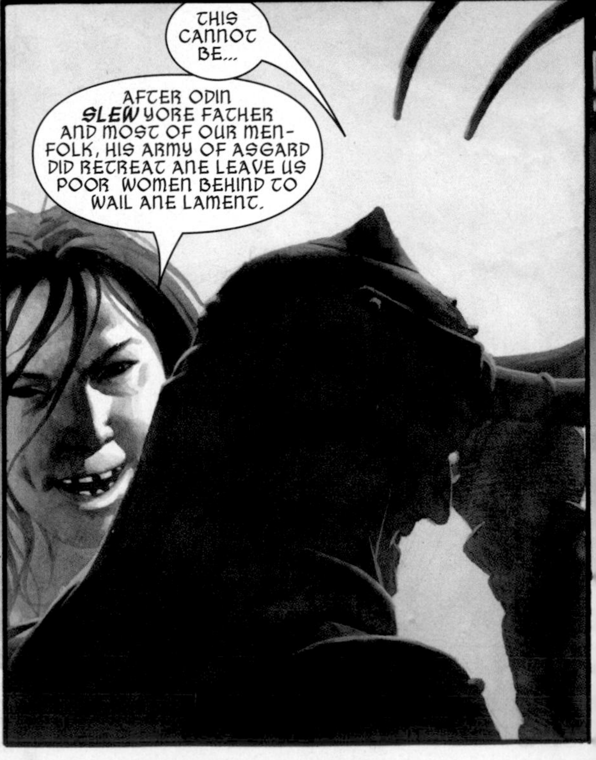
THIS CANNOT BE...
AFTER ODIN SLEW YORE FATHER AND MOST OF OUR MEN-FOLK, HIS ARMY OF ASGARD DID RETREAT ANE LEAVE US POOR WOMEN BEHIND TO WAIL ANE LAMENT.

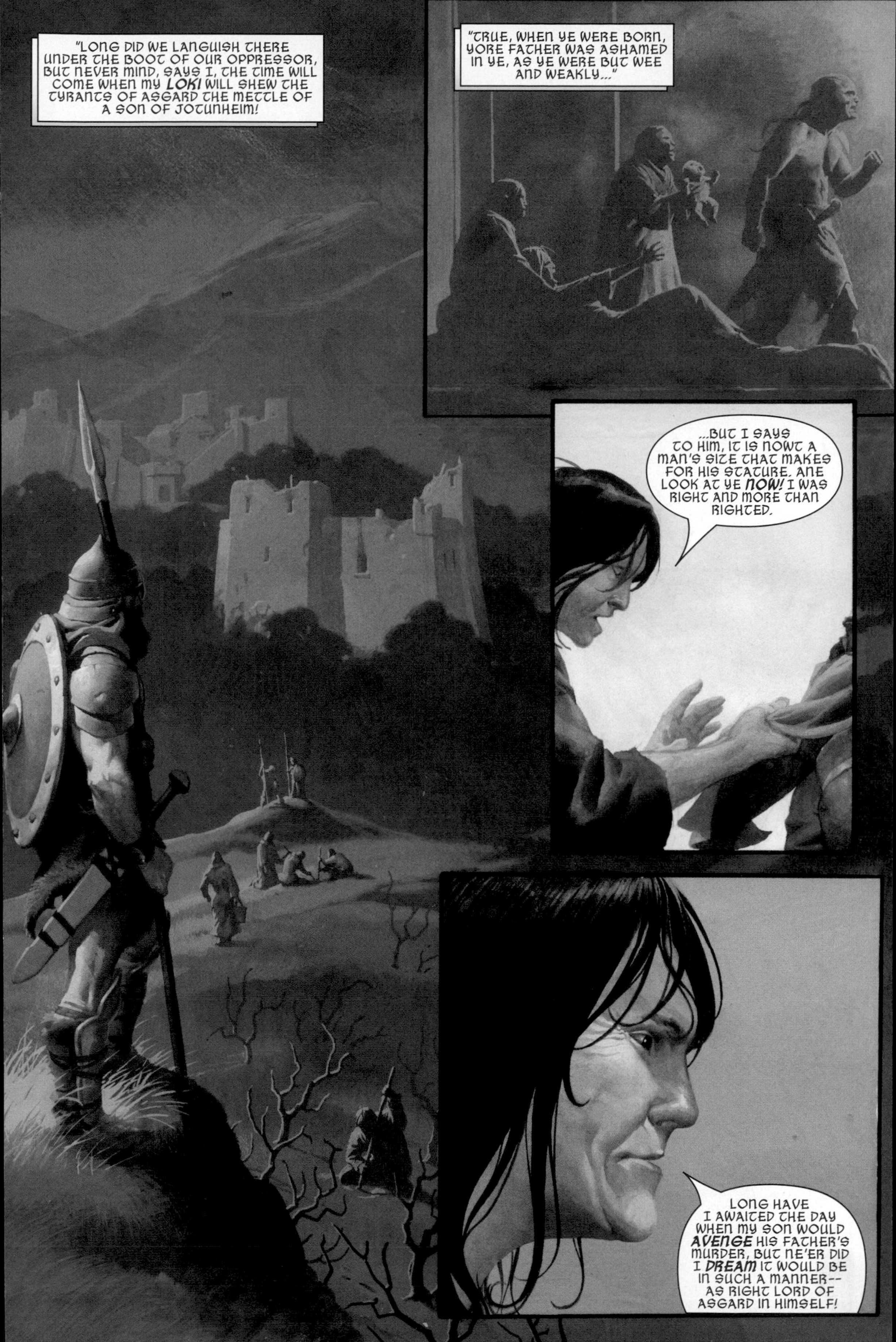
"LONG DID WE LANGUISH THERE UNDER THE BOOT OF OUR OPPRESSOR, BUT NEVER MIND, SAYS I, THE TIME WILL COME WHEN MY LOKI WILL SHEW THE TYRANTS OF ASGARD THE METTLE OF A SON OF JOTUNHEIM!
"TRUE, WHEN YE WERE BORN, YORE FATHER WAS ASHAMED IN YE, AS YE WERE BUT WEE AND WEAKLY..."
...BUT I SAYS TO HIM, IT IS NOWT A MAN'S SIZE THAT MAKES FOR HIS STATURE. ANE LOOK AT YE NOW! I WAS RIGHT AND MORE THAN RIGHTED.
LONG HAVE I AWAITED THE DAY WHEN MY SON WOULD AVENGE HIS FATHER'S MURDER, BUT NE'ER DID I DREAM IT WOULD BE IN SUCH A MANNER-- AS RIGHT LORD OF ASGARD IN HIMSELF!

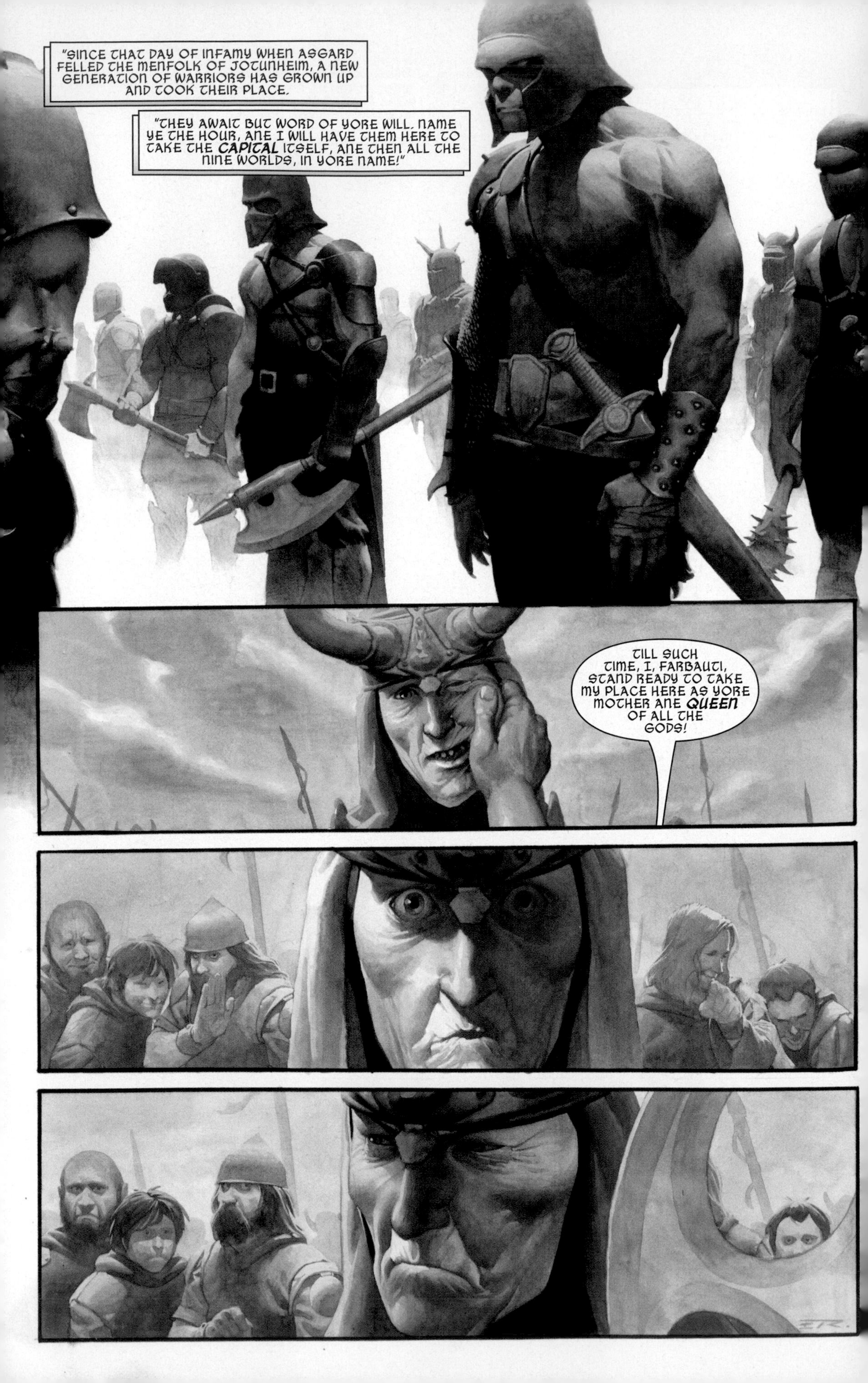
"SINCE THAT DAY OF INFAMY WHEN ASGARD FELLED THE MENFOLK OF JOTUNHEIM, A NEW GENERATION OF WARRIORS HAS GROWN UP AND TOOK THEIR PLACE.
"THEY AWAIT BUT WORD OF YORE WILL. NAME YE THE HOUR, ANE I WILL HAVE THEM HERE TO TAKE THE CAPITAL ITSELF, ANE THEN ALL THE NINE WORLDS, IN YORE NAME!"
TILL SUCH TIME, I, FARBAUTI, STAND READY TO TAKE MY PLACE HERE AS YORE MOTHER ANE QUEEN OF ALL THE GODS!

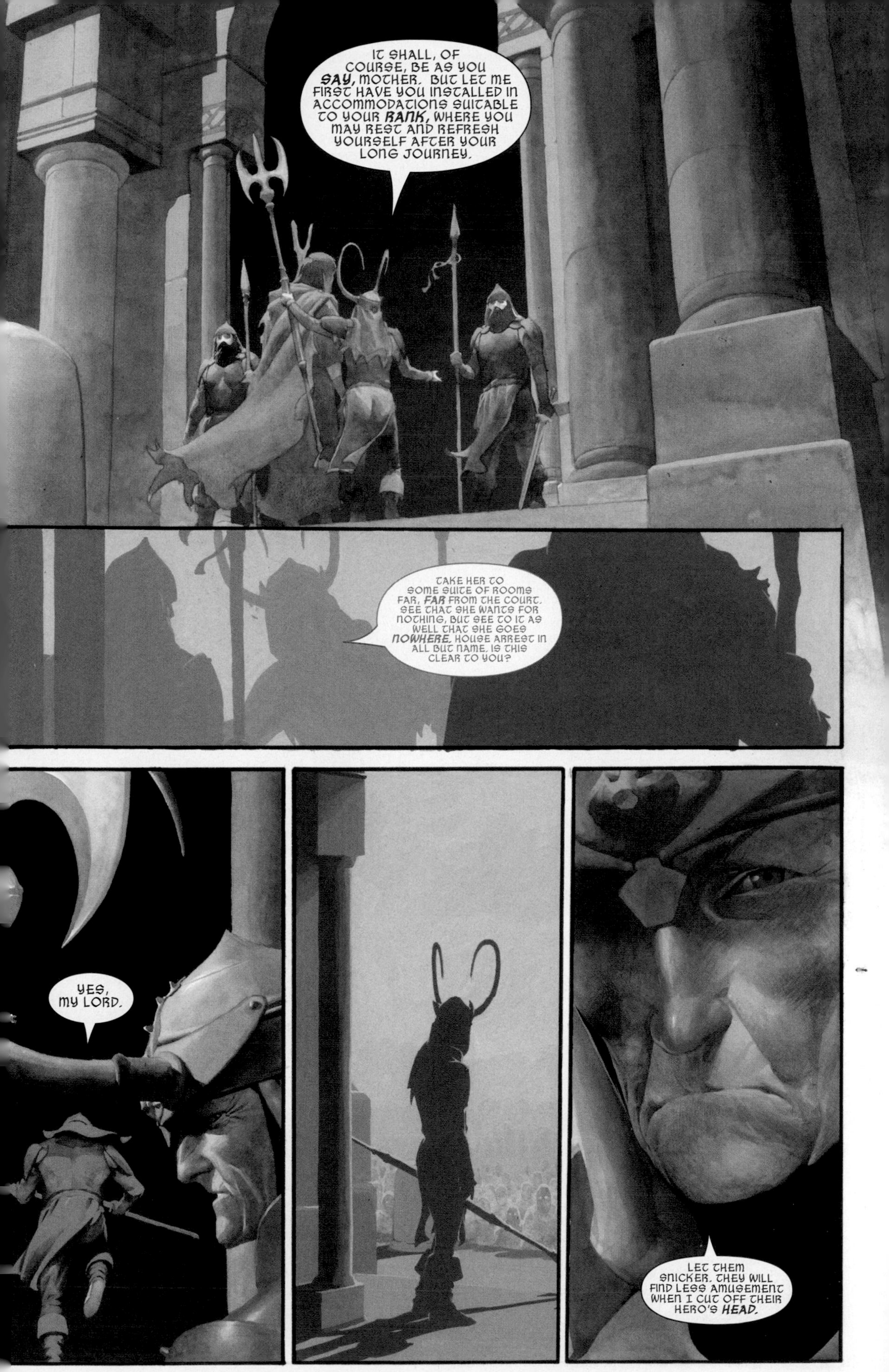
IT SHALL, OF COURSE, BE AS YOU SAY, MOTHER. BUT LET ME FIRST HAVE YOU INSTALLED IN ACCOMMODATIONS SUITABLE TO YOUR RANK, WHERE YOU MAY REST AND REFRESH YOURSELF AFTER YOUR LONG JOURNEY.
TAKE HER TO SOME SUITE OF ROOMS FAR, FAR FROM THE COURT. SEE THAT SHE WANTS FOR NOTHING, BUT SEE TO IT AS WELL THAT SHE GOES NOWHERE. HOUSE ARREST IN ALL BUT NAME. IS THIS CLEAR TO YOU?
YES, MY LORD.
LET THEM SNICKER. THEY WILL FIND LESS AMUSEMENT WHEN I CUT OFF THEIR HERO'S HEAD.

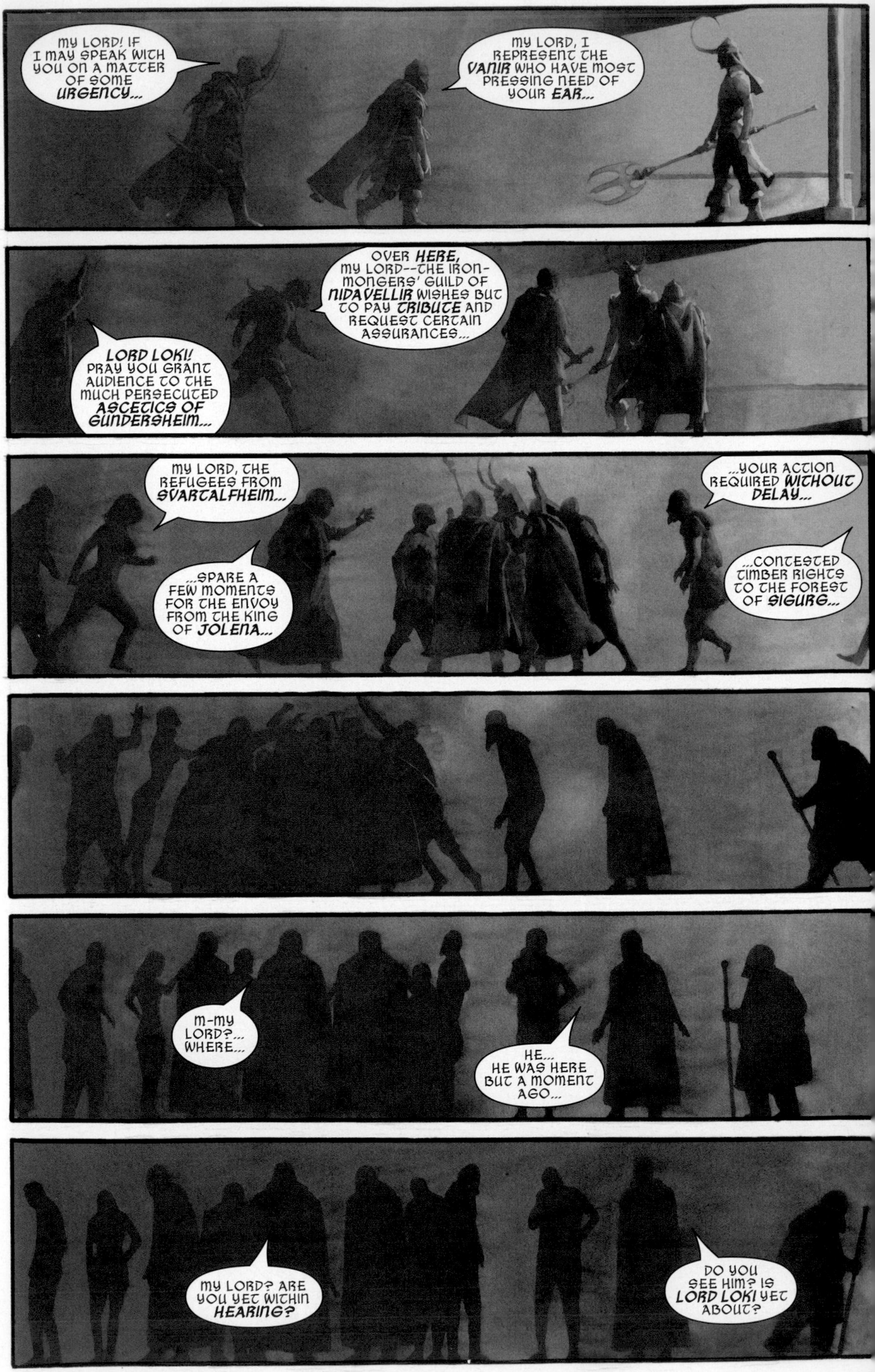

MY LORD! IF I MAY SPEAK WITH YOU ON A MATTER OF SOME URGENCY...
MY LORD, I REPRESENT THE VANIR WHO HAVE MOST PRESSING NEED OF YOUR EAR...
OVER HERE, MY LORD--THE IRON-MONGERS' GUILD OF NIDAVELLIR WISHES BUT TO PAY TRIBUTE AND REQUEST CERTAIN ASSURANCES...
LORD LOKI! PRAY YOU GRANT AUDIENCE TO THE MUCH PERSECUTED ASCETICS OF GUNDERSHEIM...
MY LORD, THE REFUGEES FROM SVARTALFHEIM...
...SPARE A FEW MOMENTS FOR THE ENVOY FROM THE KING OF JOLENA...
...YOUR ACTION REQUIRED WITHOUT DELAY...
...CONTESTED TIMBER RIGHTS TO THE FOREST OF SIGURG...
M-MY LORD?... WHERE...
HE... HE WAS HERE BUT A MOMENT AGO...
MY LORD? ARE YOU YET WITHIN HEARING?
DO YOU SEE HIM? IS LORD LOKI YET ABOUT?

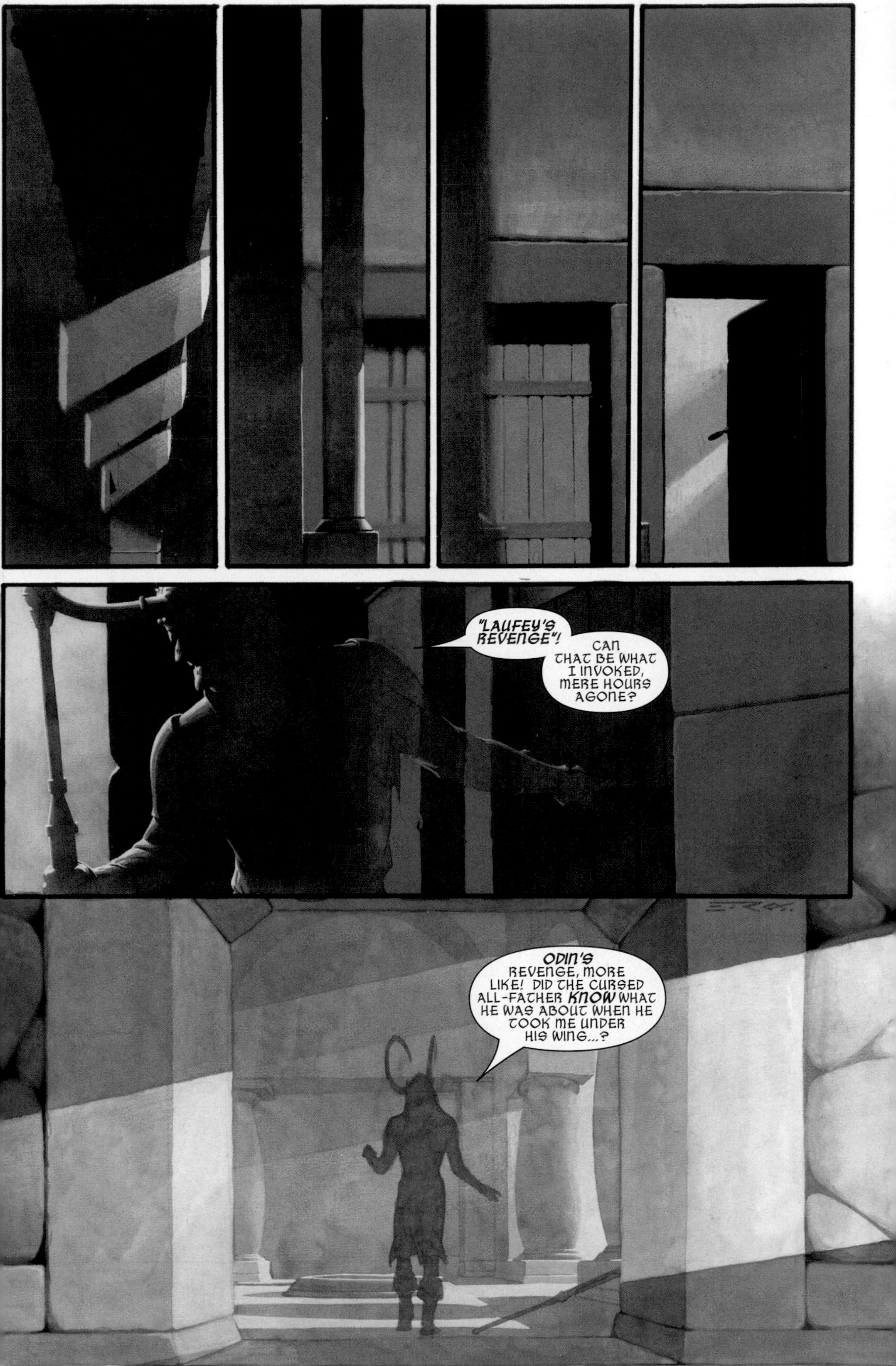
"LAUFEY'S REVENGE"!
CAN THAT BE WHAT I INVOKED, MERE HOURS AGONE?
ODIN'S REVENGE, MORE LIKE! DID THE CURSED ALL-FATHER KNOW WHAT HE WAS ABOUT WHEN HE TOOK ME UNDER HIS WING...?

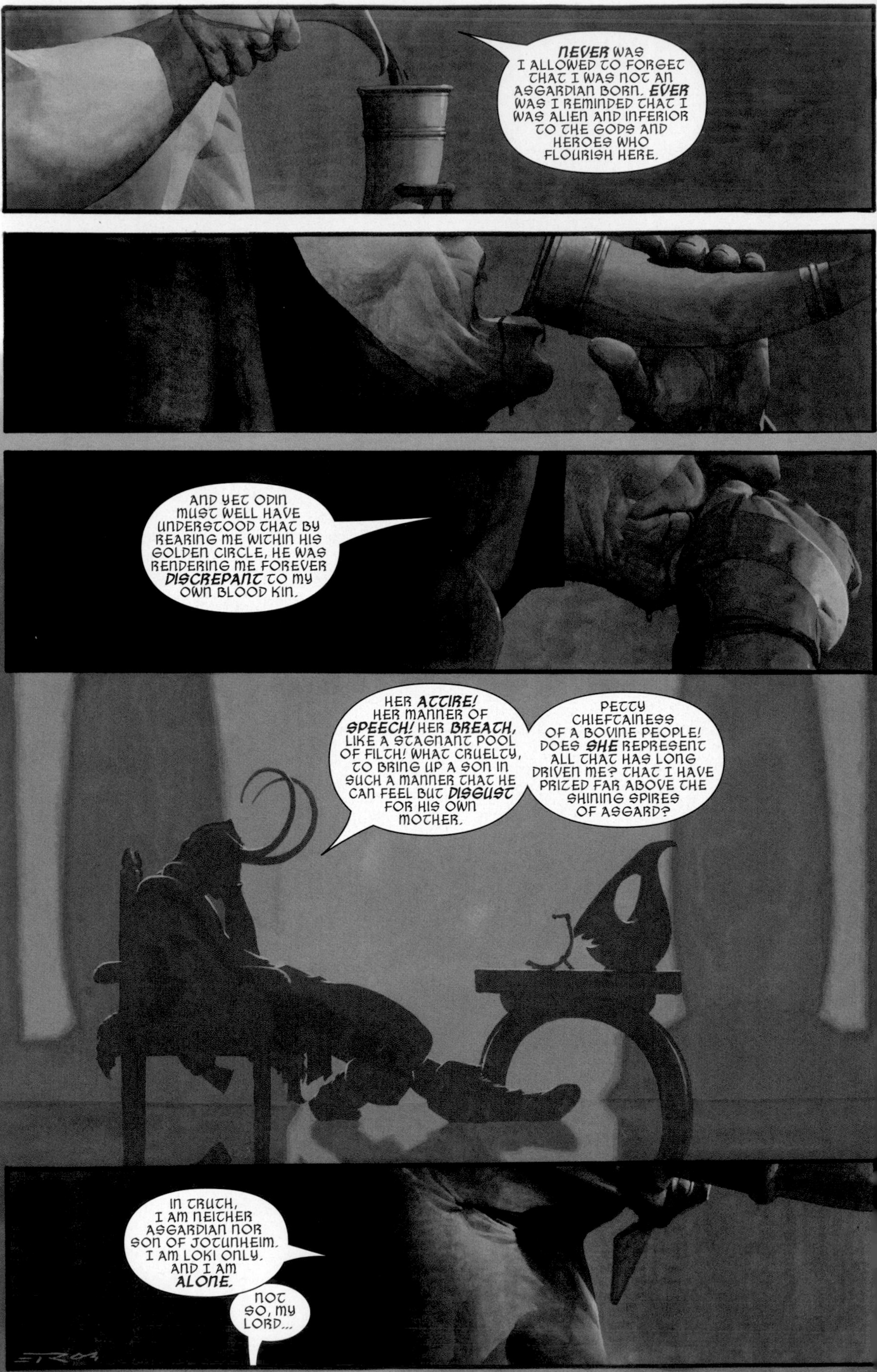
NEVER WAS I ALLOWED TO FORGET THAT I WAS NOT AN ASGARDIAN BORN. EVER WAS I REMINDED THAT I WAS ALIEN AND INFERIOR TO THE GODS AND HEROES WHO FLOURISH HERE.
AND YET ODIN MUST WELL HAVE UNDERSTOOD THAT BY REARING ME WITHIN HIS GOLDEN CIRCLE, HE WAS RENDERING ME FOREVER DISCREPANT TO MY OWN BLOOD KIN.
HER ATTIRE! HER MANNER OF SPEECH! HER BREATH, LIKE A STAGNANT POOL OF FILTH! WHAT CRUELTY, TO BRING UP A SON IN SUCH A MANNER THAT HE CAN FEEL BUT DISGUST FOR HIS OWN MOTHER.
PETTY CHIEFTAINESS OF A BOVINE PEOPLE! DOES SHE REPRESENT ALL THAT HAS LONG DRIVEN ME? THAT I HAVE PRIZED FAR ABOVE THE SHINING SPIRES OF ASGARD?
IN TRUTH, I AM NEITHER ASGARDIAN NOR SON OF JOTUNHEIM. I AM LOKI ONLY, AND I AM ALONE.
NOT SO, MY LORD...

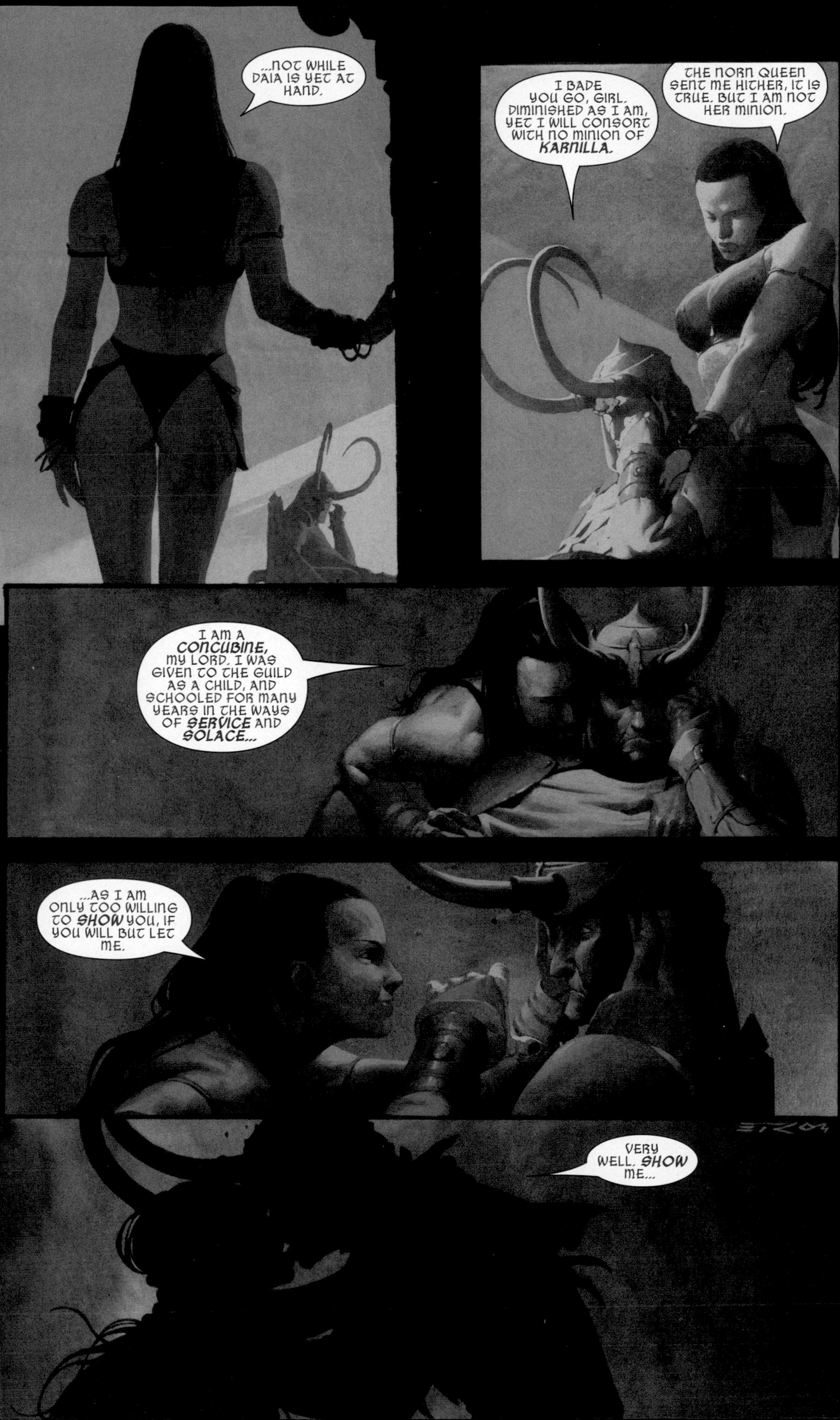

...NOT WHILE DAIA IS YET AT HAND.
I BADE YOU GO, GIRL. DIMINISHED AS I AM, YET I WILL CONSORT WITH NO MINION OF KARNILLA.
THE NORN QUEEN SENT ME HITHER, IT IS TRUE. BUT I AM NOT HER MINION.
I AM A CONCUBINE, MY LORD. I WAS GIVEN TO THE GUILD AS A CHILD, AND SCHOOLED FOR MANY YEARS IN THE WAYS OF SERVICE AND SOLACE...
...AS I AM ONLY TOO WILLING TO SHOW YOU, IF YOU WILL BUT LET ME.
VERY WELL. SHOW ME...

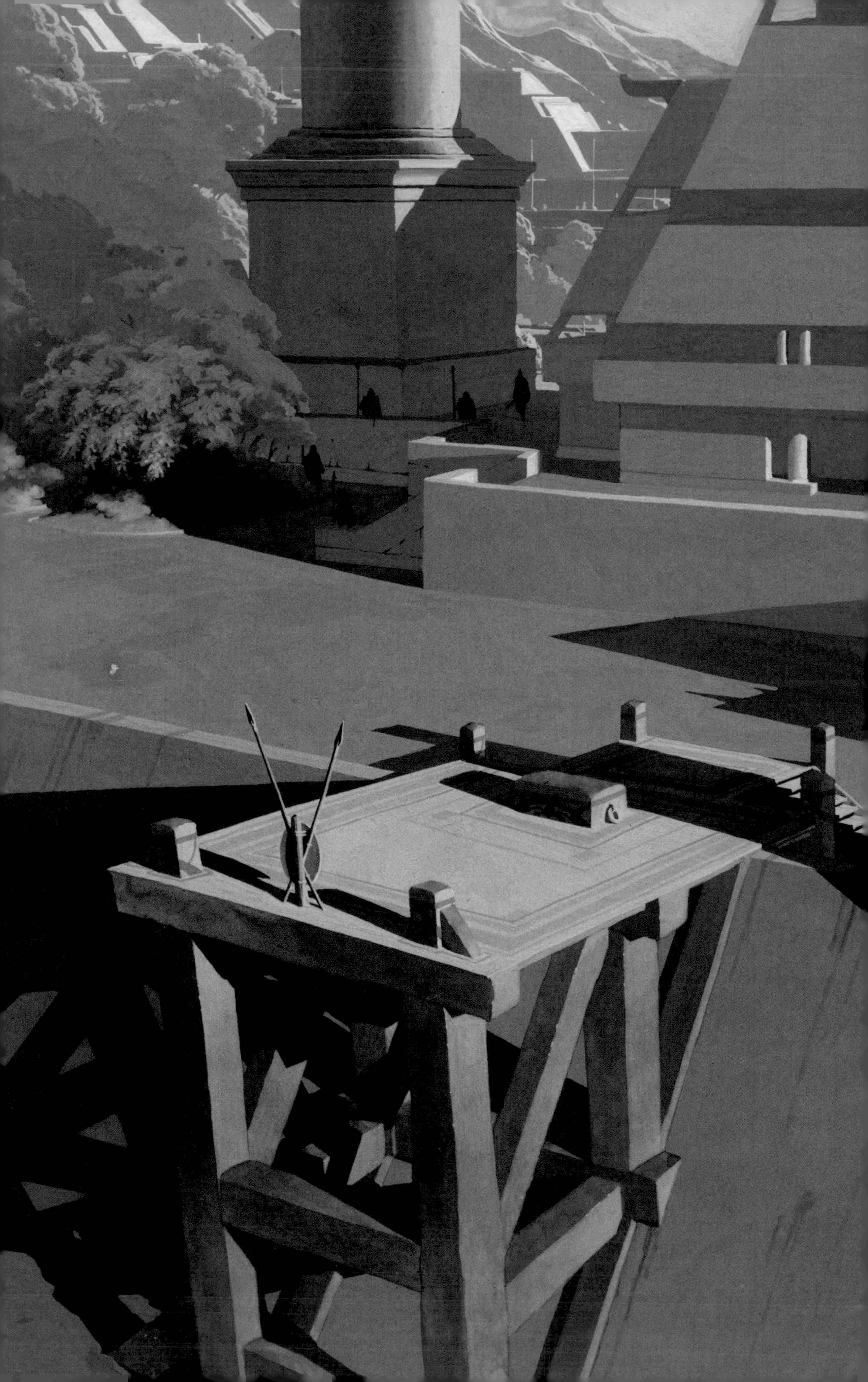

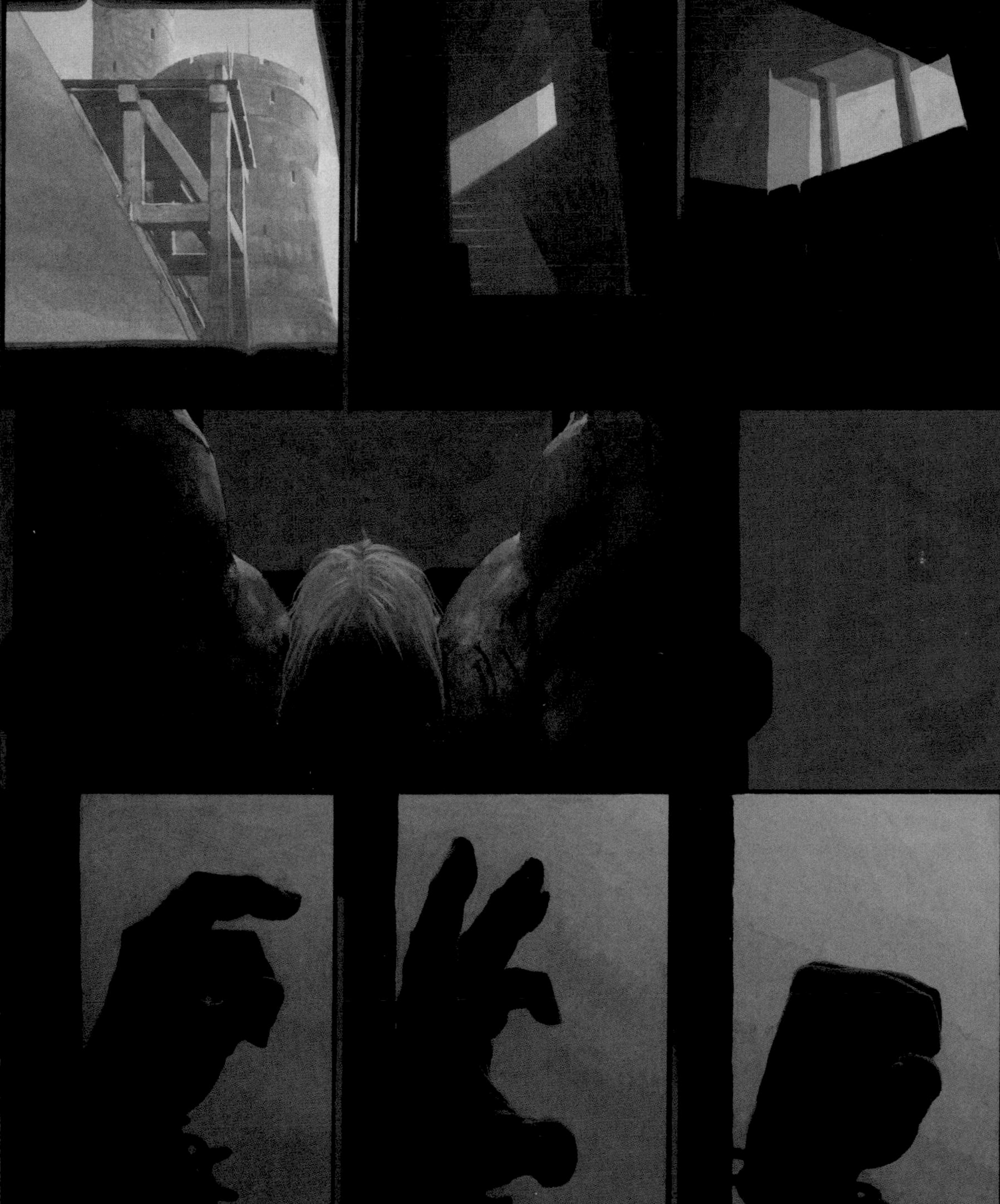

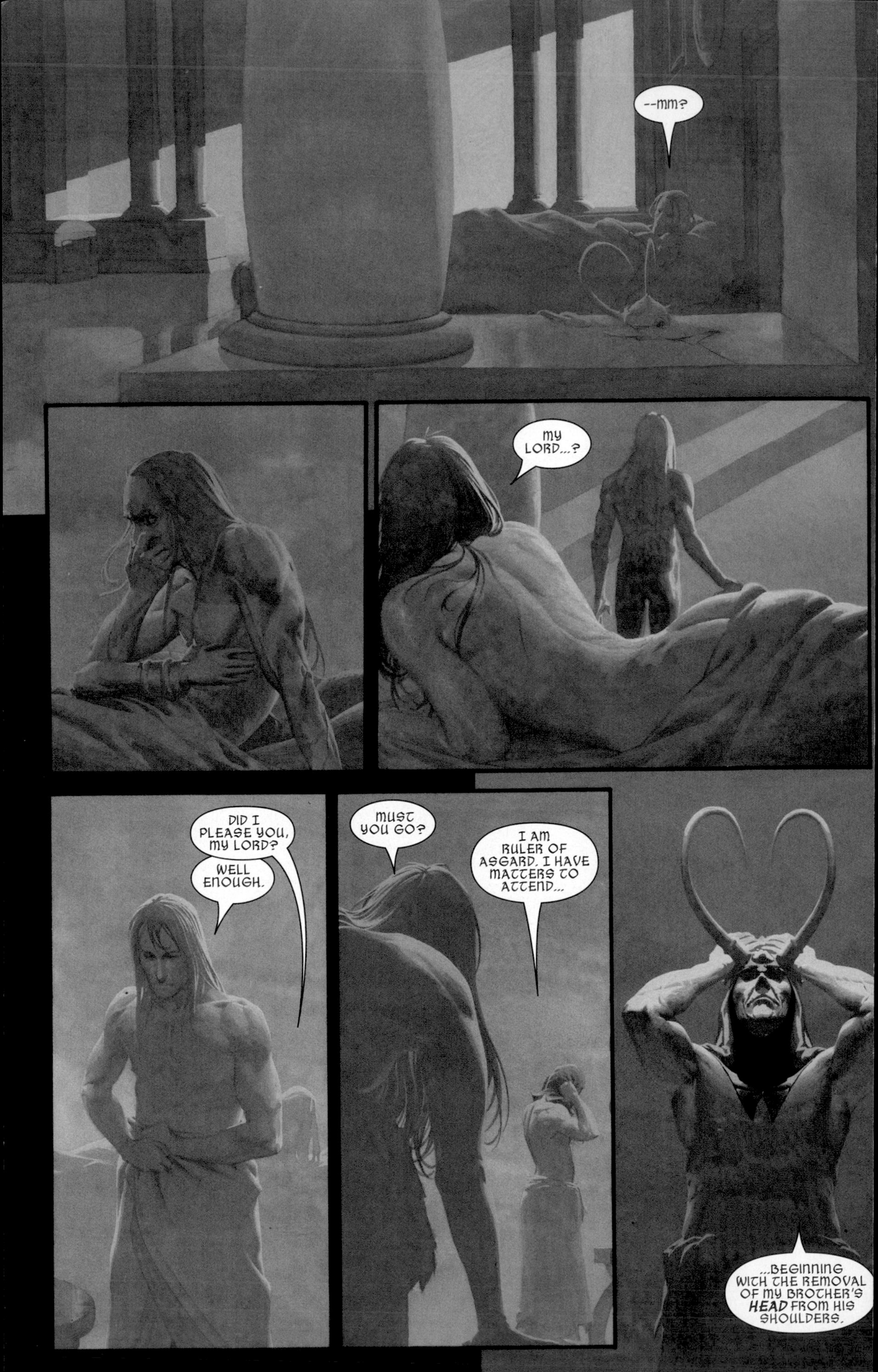
--mm?
MY LORD...?
DID I PLEASE YOU, MY LORD?
WELL ENOUGH.
MUST YOU GO?
I AM RULER OF ASGARD. I HAVE MATTERS TO ATTEND...
...BEGINNING WITH THE REMOVAL OF MY BROTHER'S **HEAD** FROM HIS SHOULDERS.

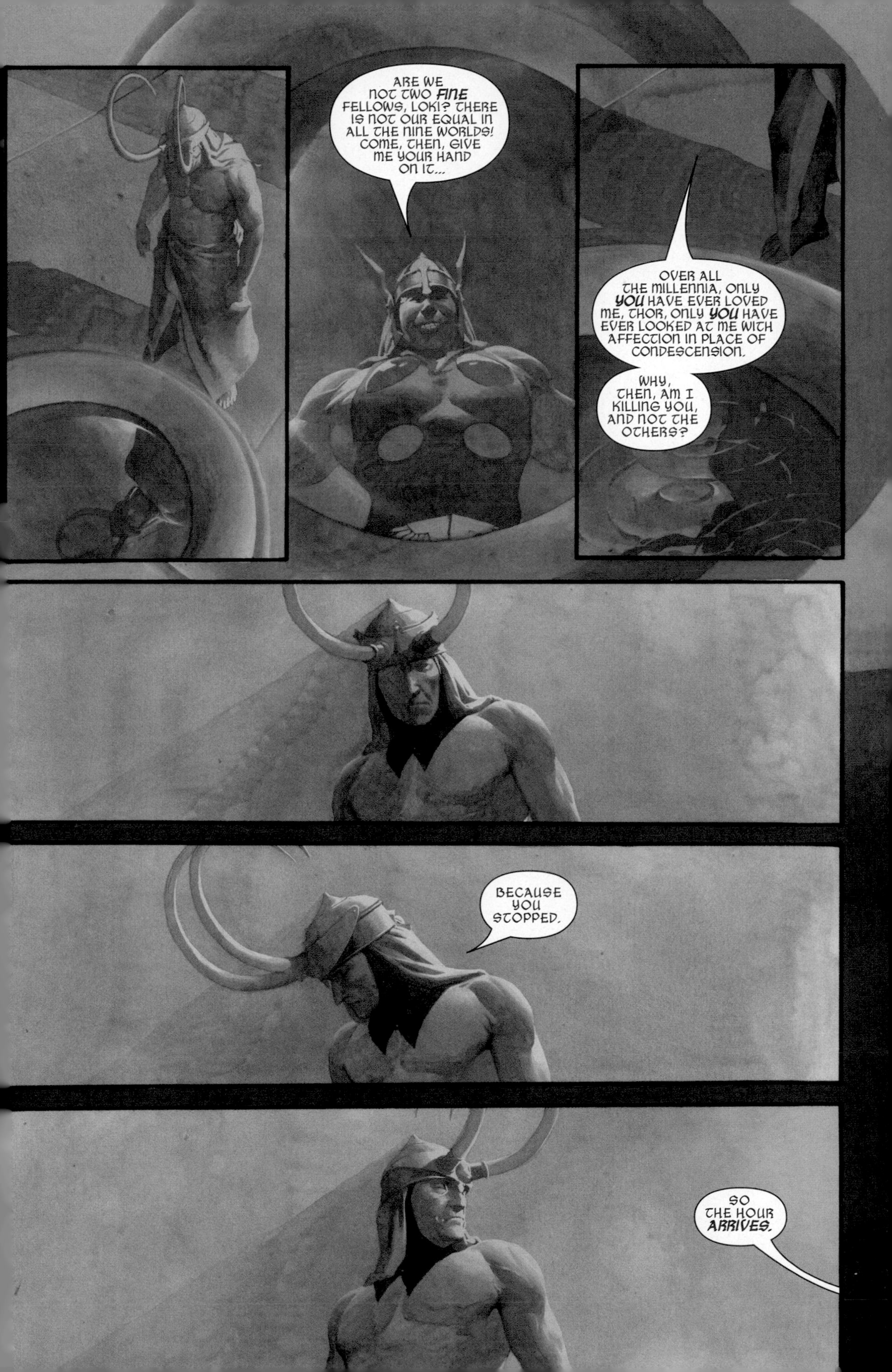
ARE WE NOT TWO FINE FELLOWS, LOKI? THERE IS NOT OUR EQUAL IN ALL THE NINE WORLDS! COME, THEN, GIVE ME YOUR HAND ON IT...
OVER ALL THE MILLENNIA, ONLY YOU HAVE EVER LOVED ME, THOR, ONLY YOU HAVE EVER LOOKED AT ME WITH AFFECTION IN PLACE OF CONDESCENSION.
WHY, THEN, AM I KILLING YOU, AND NOT THE OTHERS?
BECAUSE YOU STOPPED.
SO THE HOUR ARRIVES.

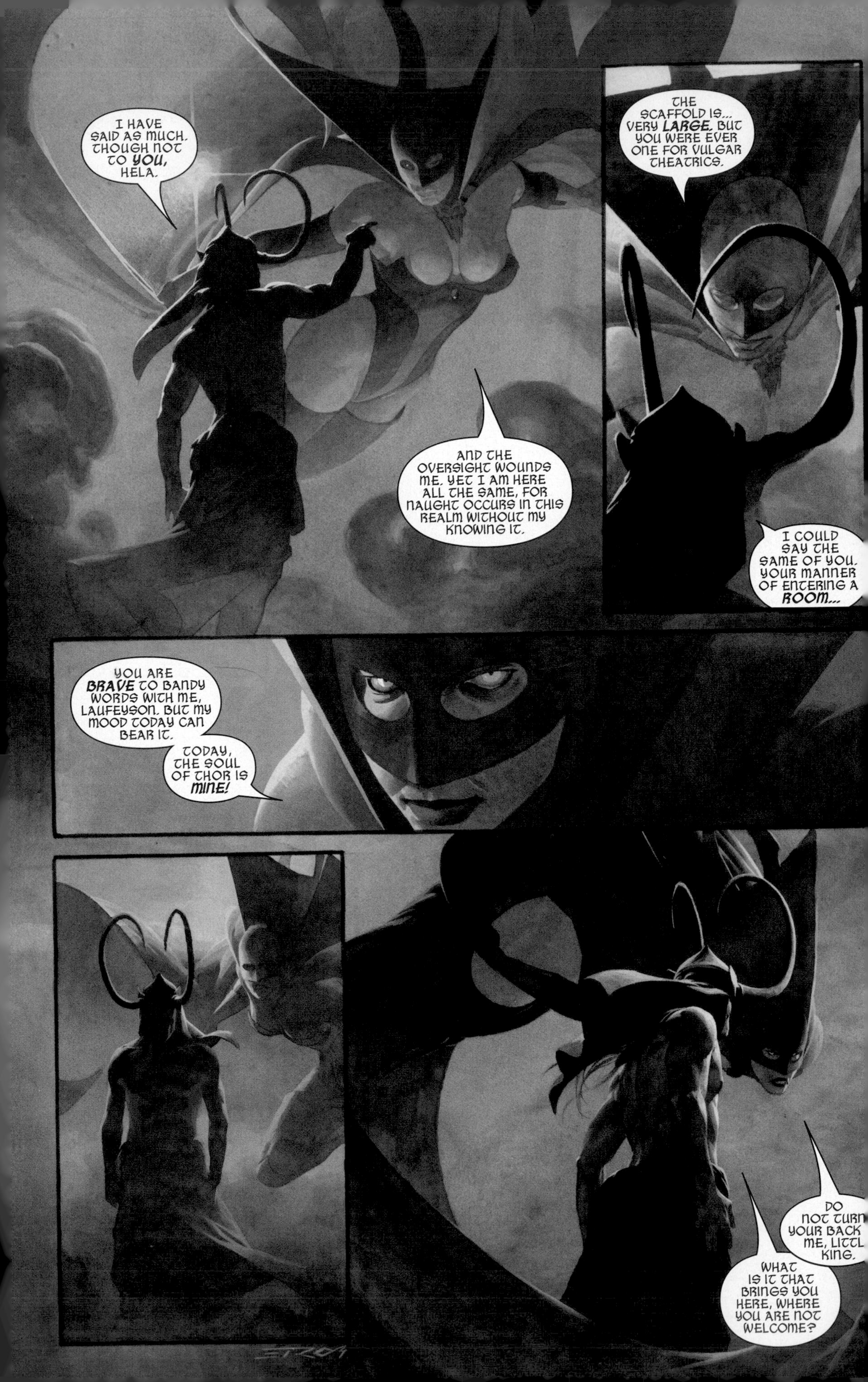

I HAVE SAID AS MUCH. THOUGH NOT TO YOU, HELA.
AND THE OVERSIGHT WOUNDS ME. YET I AM HERE ALL THE SAME, FOR NAUGHT OCCURS IN THIS REALM WITHOUT MY KNOWING IT.
THE SCAFFOLD IS... VERY LARGE. BUT YOU WERE EVER ONE FOR VULGAR THEATRICS.
I COULD SAY THE SAME OF YOU. YOUR MANNER OF ENTERING A ROOM...
YOU ARE BRAVE TO BANDY WORDS WITH ME, LAUFEYSON. BUT MY MOOD TODAY CAN BEAR IT.
TODAY, THE SOUL OF THOR IS MINE!
DO NOT TURN YOUR BACK ME, LITTL KING.
WHAT IS IT THAT BRINGS YOU HERE, WHERE YOU ARE NOT WELCOME?

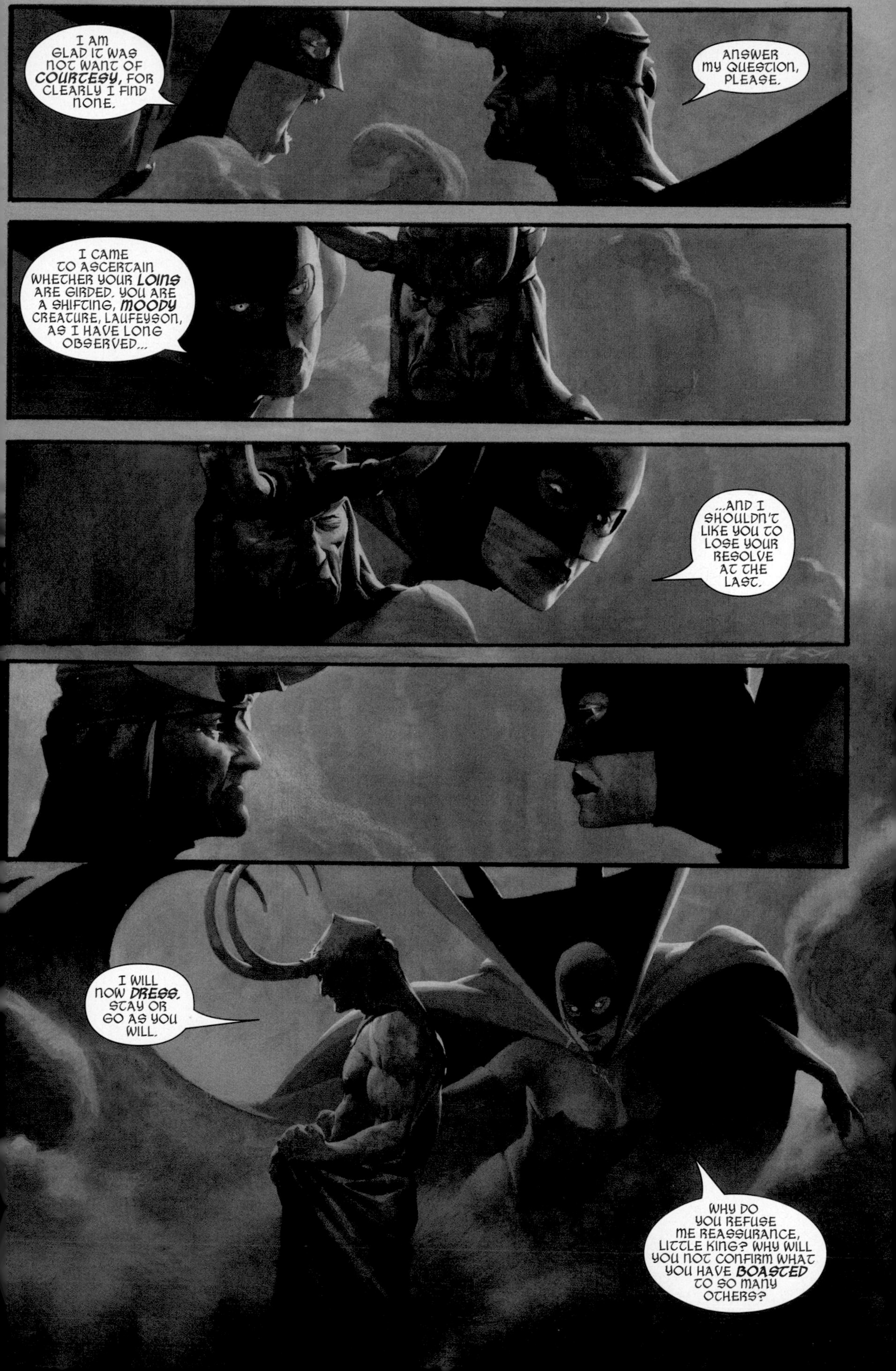
I AM GLAD IT WAS NOT WANT OF COURTESY, FOR CLEARLY I FIND NONE.
ANSWER MY QUESTION, PLEASE.
I CAME TO ASCERTAIN WHETHER YOUR LOINS ARE GIRDED. YOU ARE A SHIFTING, MOODY CREATURE, LAUFEYSON, AS I HAVE LONG OBSERVED...
...AND I SHOULDN'T LIKE YOU TO LOSE YOUR RESOLVE AT THE LAST.
I WILL NOW DRESS. STAY OR GO AS YOU WILL.
WHY DO YOU REFUSE ME REASSURANCE, LITTLE KING? WHY WILL YOU NOT CONFIRM WHAT YOU HAVE BOASTED TO SO MANY OTHERS?

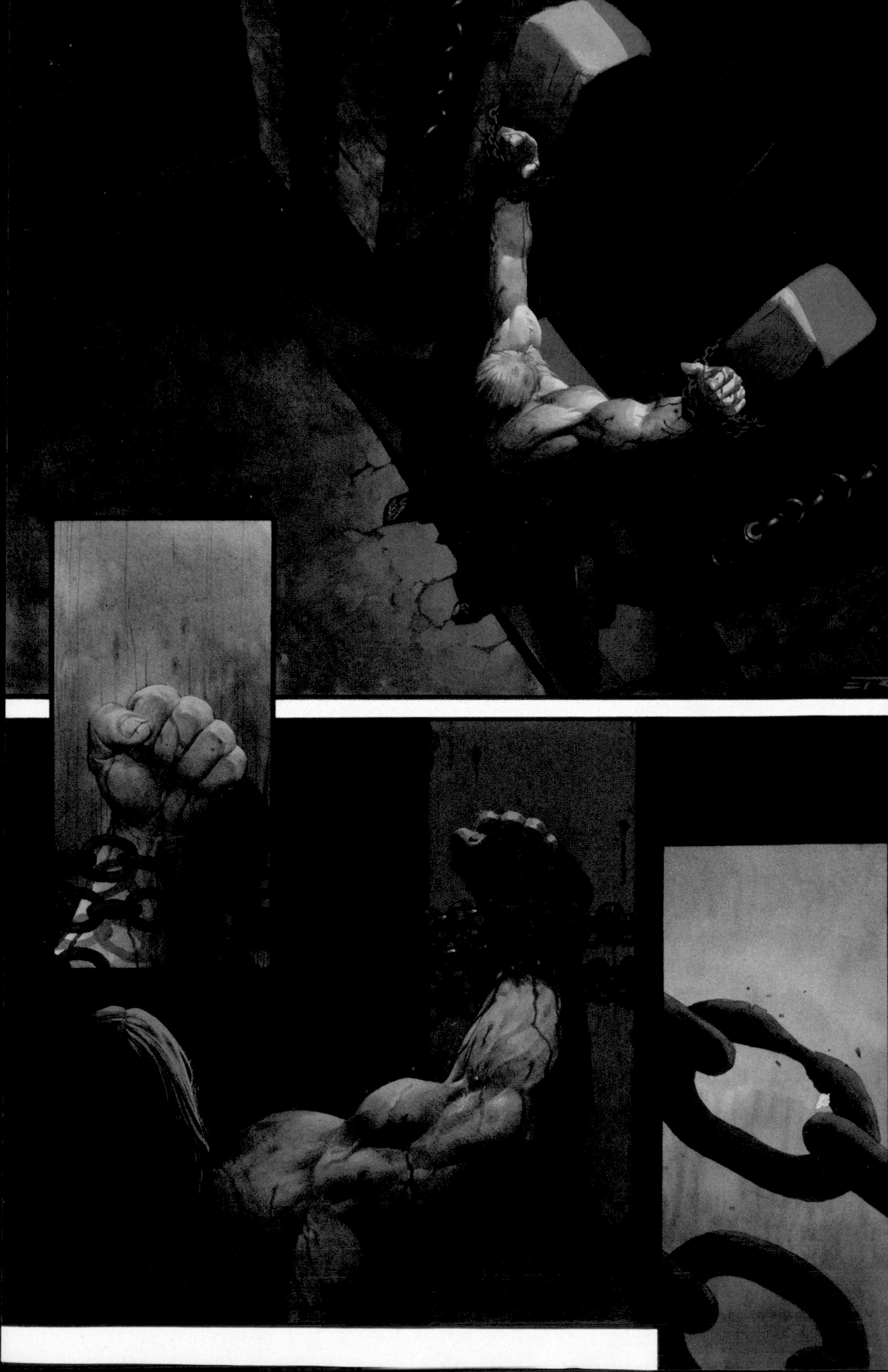

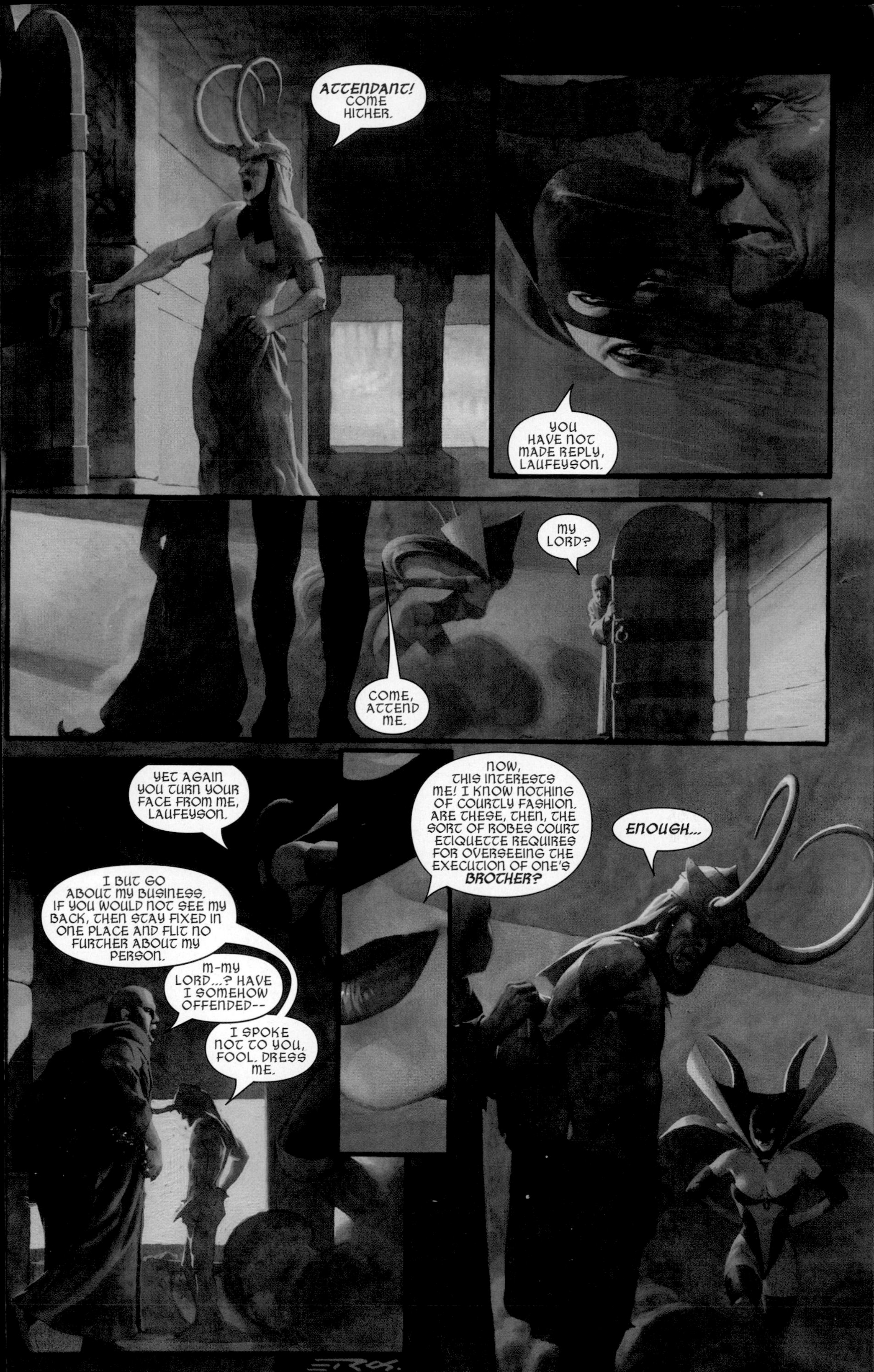
ATTENDANT! COME HITHER.
YOU HAVE NOT MADE REPLY, LAUFEYSON.
MY LORD?
COME, ATTEND ME.
YET AGAIN YOU TURN YOUR FACE FROM ME, LAUFEYSON.
I BUT GO ABOUT MY BUSINESS. IF YOU WOULD NOT SEE MY BACK, THEN STAY FIXED IN ONE PLACE AND FLIT NO FURTHER ABOUT MY PERSON.
M-MY LORD...? HAVE I SOMEHOW OFFENDED--
I SPOKE NOT TO YOU, FOOL. DRESS ME.
NOW, THIS INTERESTS ME! I KNOW NOTHING OF COURTLY FASHION. ARE THESE, THEN, THE SORT OF ROBES COURT ETIQUETTE REQUIRES FOR OVERSEEING THE EXECUTION OF ONE'S BROTHER?
ENOUGH...

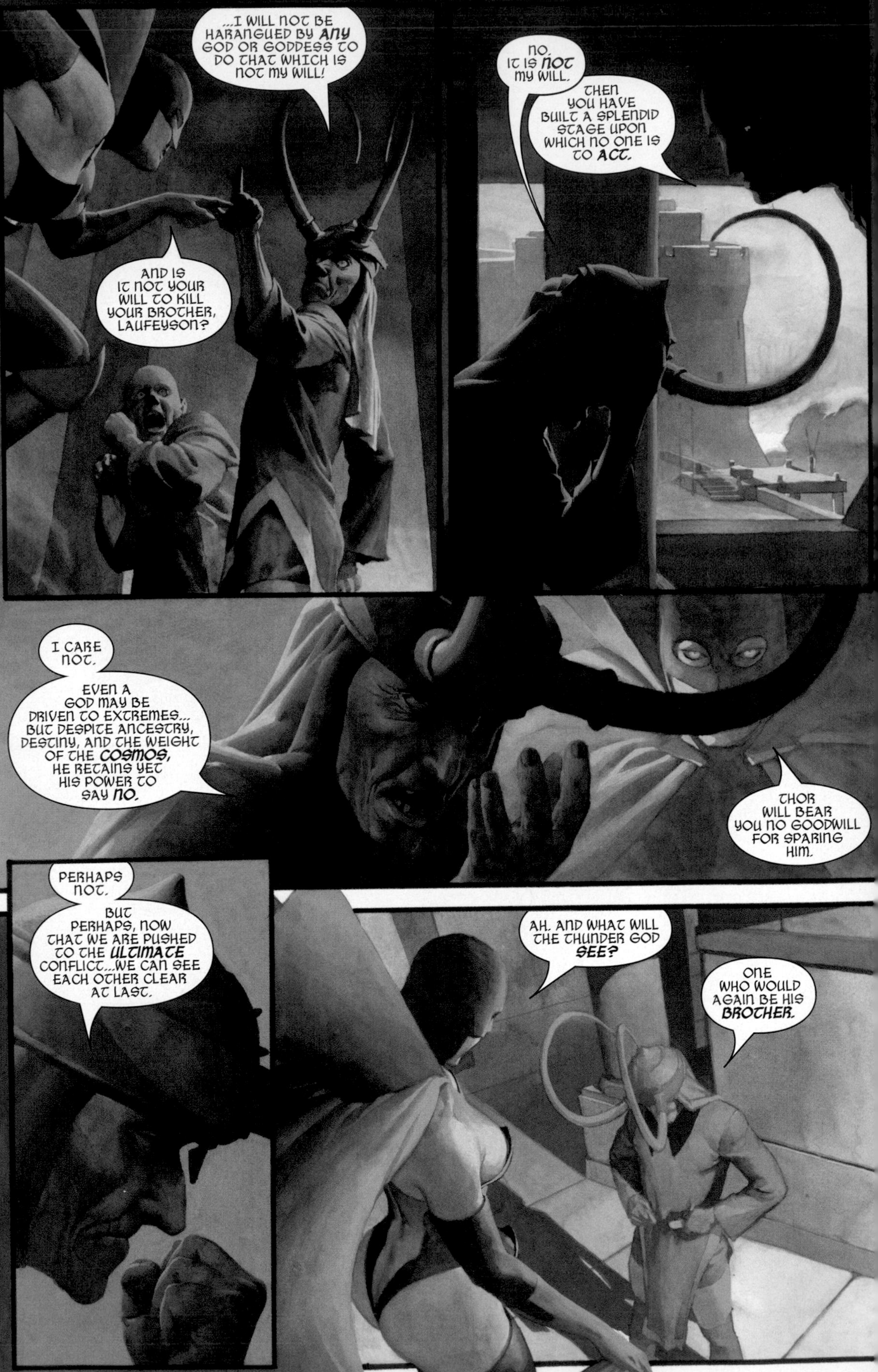
...I WILL NOT BE HARANGUED BY ANY GOD OR GODDESS TO DO THAT WHICH IS NOT MY WILL!
AND IS IT NOT YOUR WILL TO KILL YOUR BROTHER, LAUFEYSON?
NO. IT IS NOT MY WILL.
THEN YOU HAVE BUILT A SPLENDID STAGE UPON WHICH NO ONE IS TO ACT.
I CARE NOT.
EVEN A GOD MAY BE DRIVEN TO EXTREMES... BUT DESPITE ANCESTRY, DESTINY, AND THE WEIGHT OF THE COSMOS, HE RETAINS YET HIS POWER TO SAY NO.
THOR WILL BEAR YOU NO GOODWILL FOR SPARING HIM.
PERHAPS NOT.
BUT PERHAPS, NOW THAT WE ARE PUSHED TO THE ULTIMATE CONFLICT...WE CAN SEE EACH OTHER CLEAR AT LAST.
AH. AND WHAT WILL THE THUNDER GOD SEE?
ONE WHO WOULD AGAIN BE HIS BROTHER.

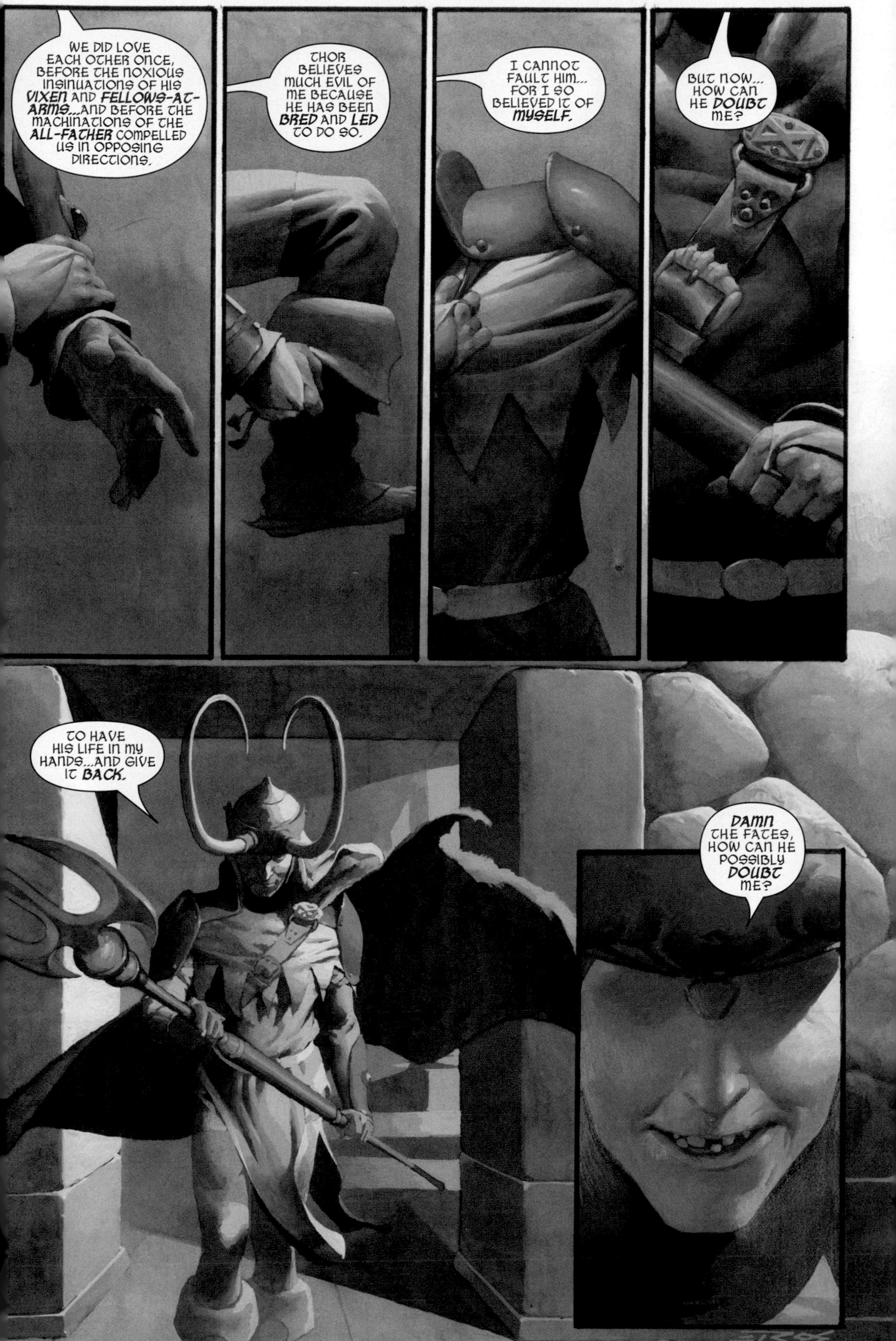
WE DID LOVE EACH OTHER ONCE, BEFORE THE NOXIOUS INSINUATIONS OF HIS VIXEN AND FELLOWS-AT-ARMS... AND BEFORE THE MACHINATIONS OF THE ALL-FATHER COMPELLED US IN OPPOSING DIRECTIONS.
THOR BELIEVES MUCH EVIL OF ME BECAUSE HE HAS BEEN BRED AND LED TO DO SO.
I CANNOT FAULT HIM... FOR I SO BELIEVED IT OF MYSELF.
BUT NOW... HOW CAN HE DOUBT ME?
TO HAVE HIS LIFE IN MY HANDS... AND GIVE IT BACK.
DAMN THE FATES, HOW CAN HE POSSIBLY DOUBT ME?

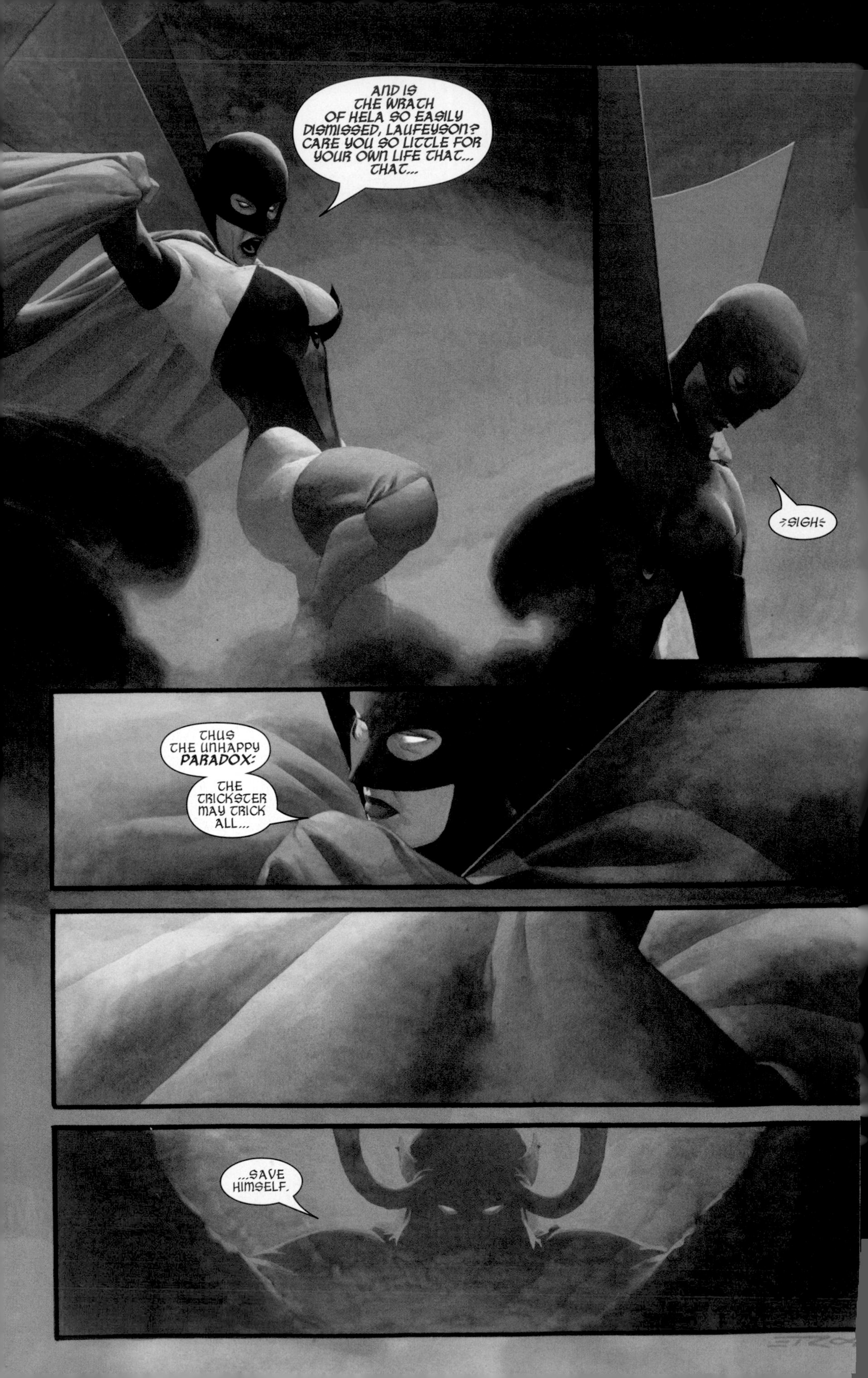
AND IS THE WRATH OF HELA SO EASILY DISMISSED, LAUFEYSON? CARE YOU SO LITTLE FOR YOUR OWN LIFE THAT... THAT...
SIGH
THUS THE UNHAPPY PARADOX:
THE TRICKSTER MAY TRICK ALL...
...SAVE HIMSELF.

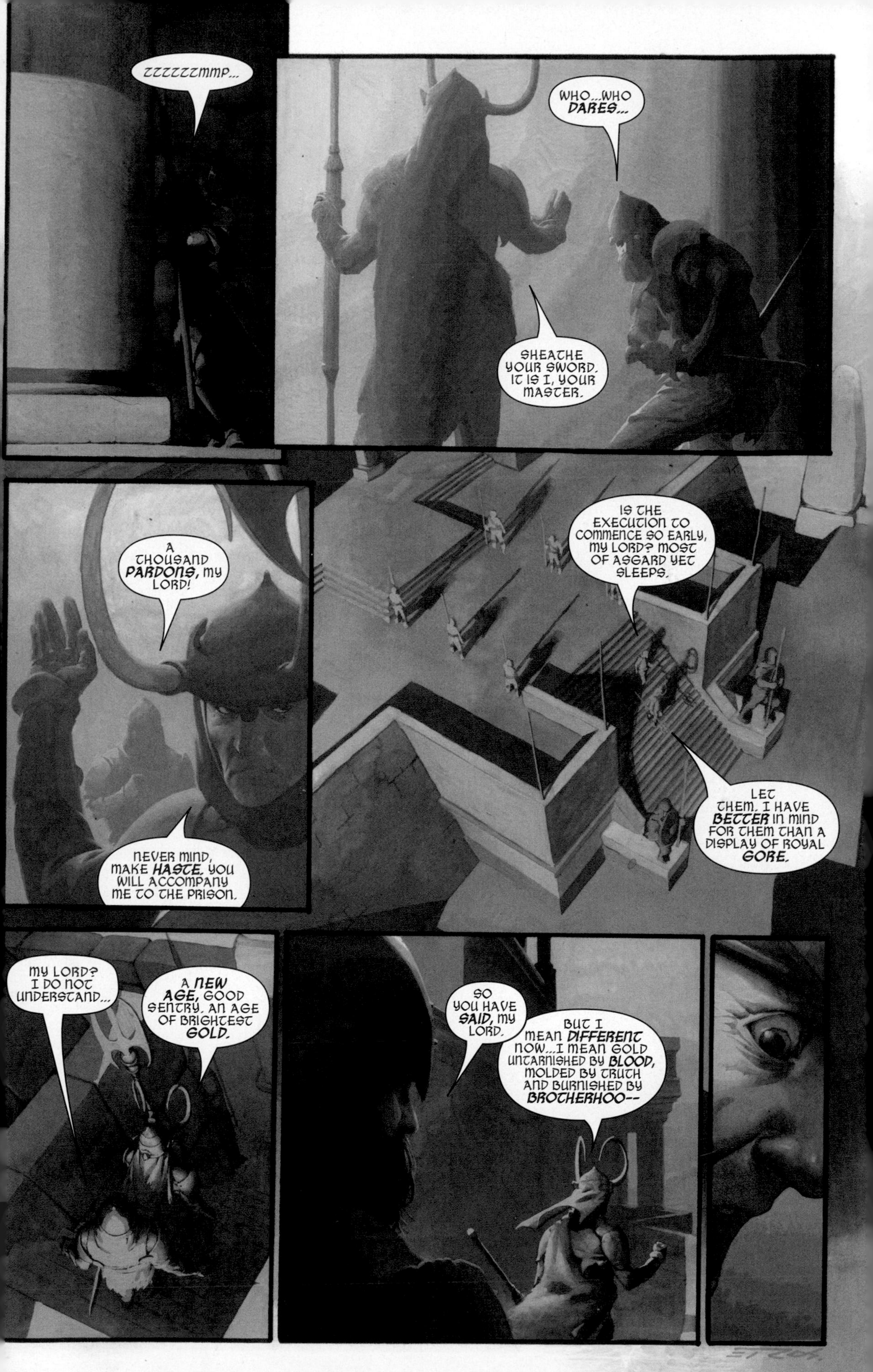
ZZZZZZMMP...
WHO...WHO DARES...
SHEATHE YOUR SWORD. IT IS I, YOUR MASTER.
A THOUSAND PARDONS, MY LORD!
NEVER MIND, MAKE HASTE. YOU WILL ACCOMPANY ME TO THE PRISON.
IS THE EXECUTION TO COMMENCE SO EARLY, MY LORD? MOST OF ASGARD YET SLEEPS.
LET THEM. I HAVE BETTER IN MIND FOR THEM THAN A DISPLAY OF ROYAL GORE.
MY LORD? I DO NOT UNDERSTAND...
A NEW AGE, GOOD SENTRY. AN AGE OF BRIGHTEST GOLD.
SO YOU HAVE SAID, MY LORD.
BUT I MEAN DIFFERENT NOW...I MEAN GOLD UNTARNISHED BY BLOOD, MOLDED BY TRUTH AND BURNISHED BY BROTHERHOO--

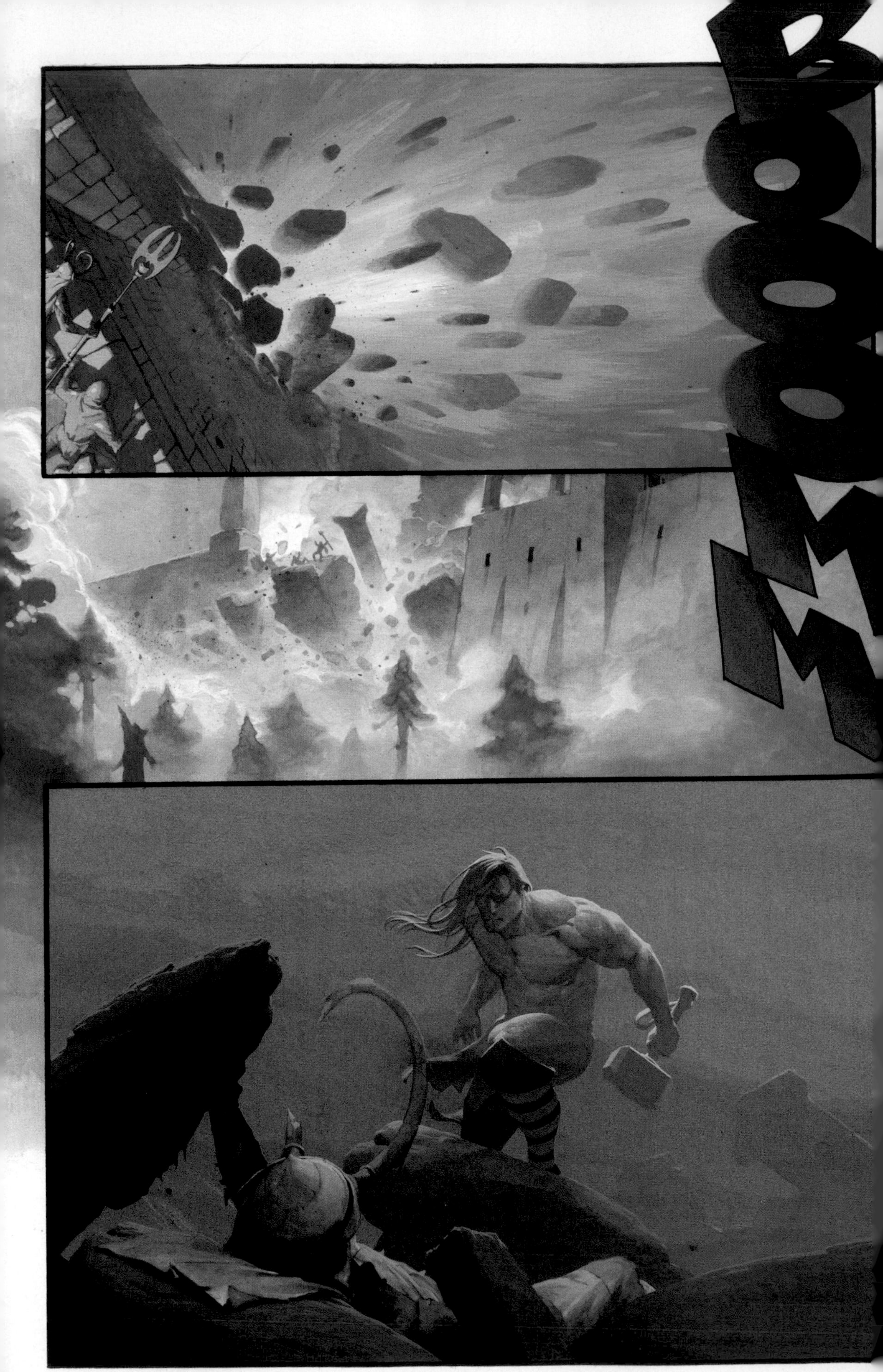
BOOOMM

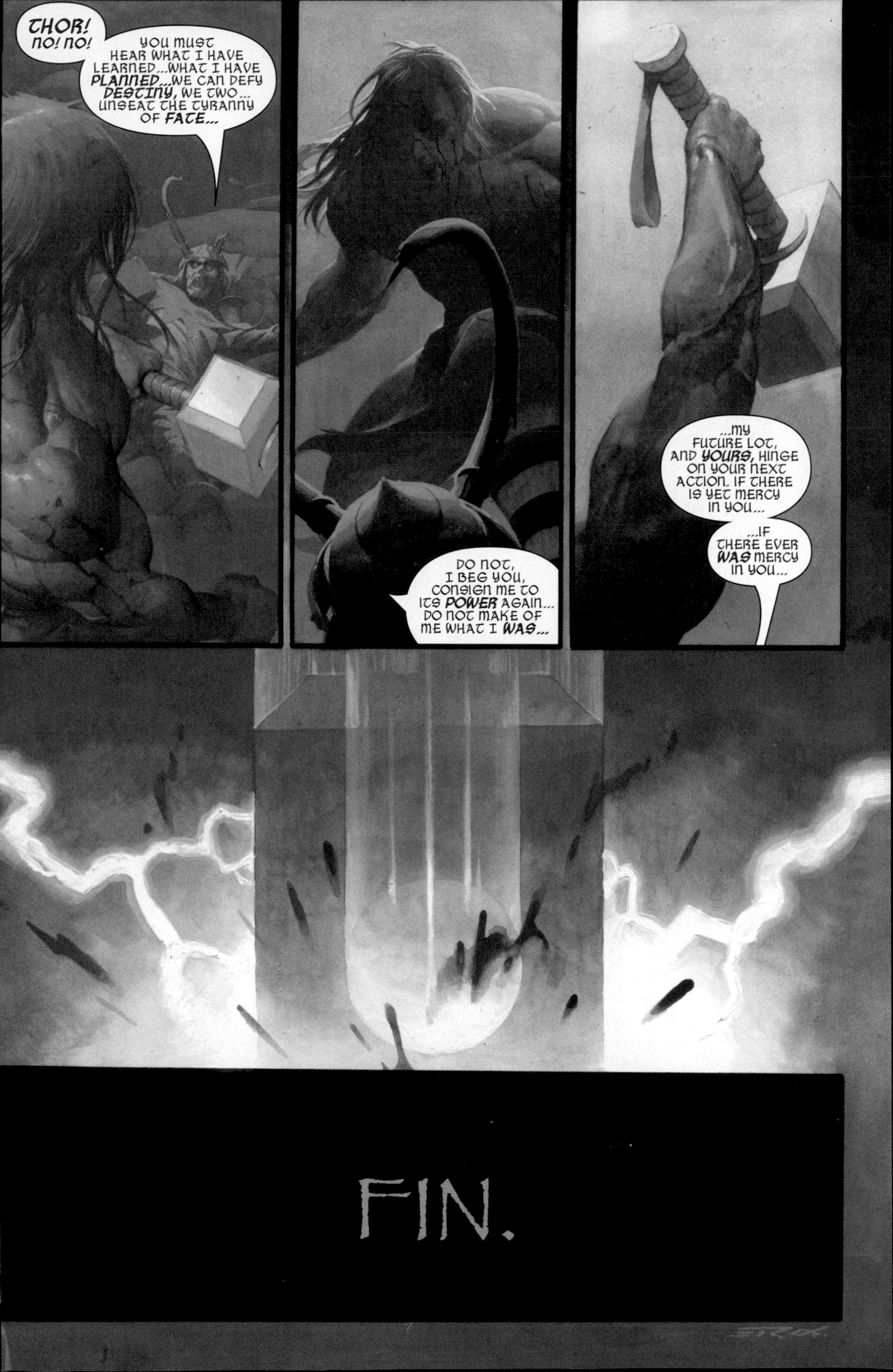
THOR! NO! NO!
YOU MUST HEAR WHAT I HAVE LEARNED...WHAT I HAVE PLANNED...WE CAN DEFY DESTINY, WE TWO... UNSEAT THE TYRANNY OF FATE...
DO NOT, I BEG YOU, CONSIGN ME TO ITS POWER AGAIN... DO NOT MAKE OF ME WHAT I WAS...
...MY FUTURE LOT, AND YOURS, HINGE ON YOUR NEXT ACTION. IF THERE IS YET MERCY IN YOU...
...IF THERE EVER WAS MERCY IN YOU...
FIN.

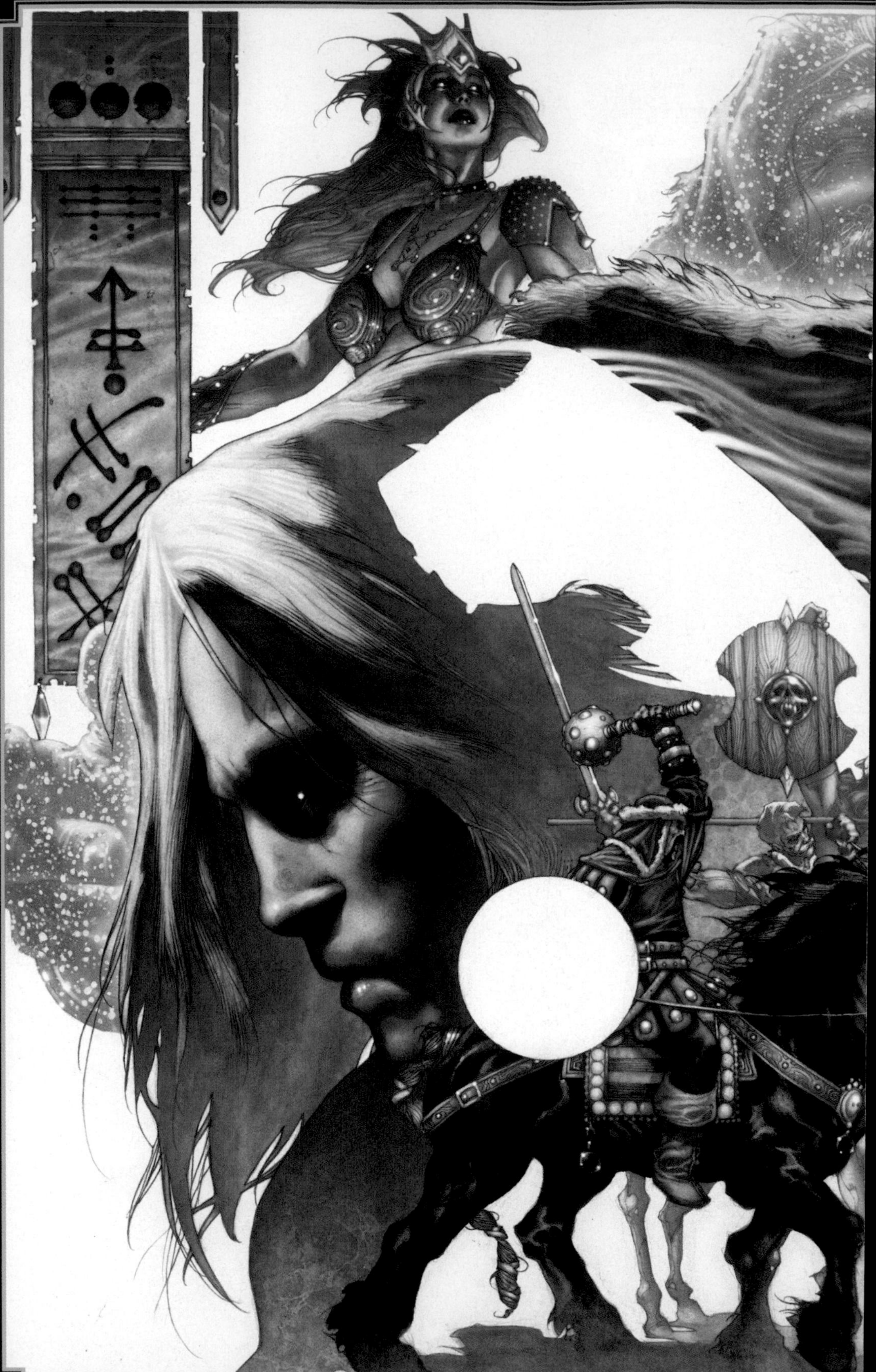

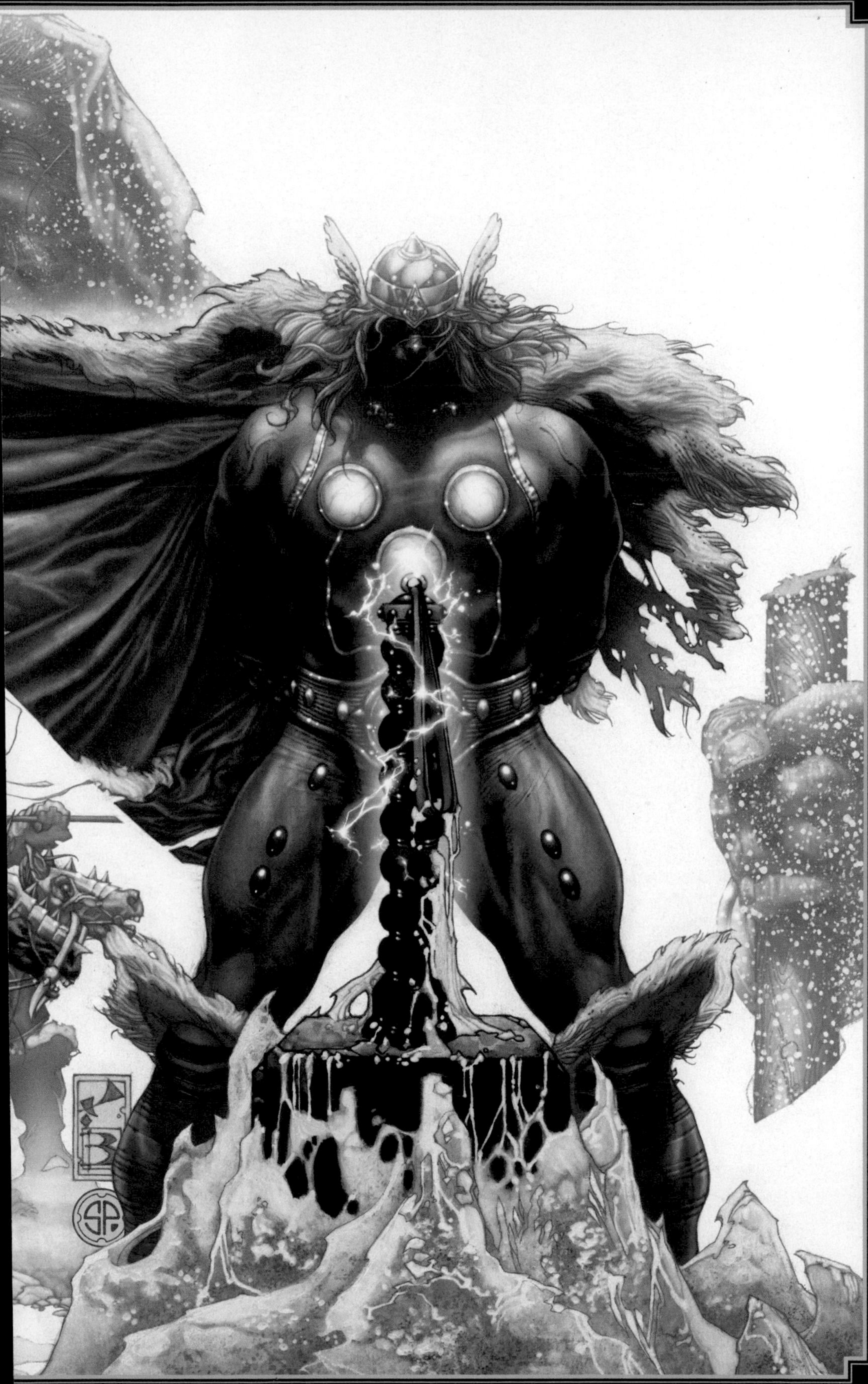

Thor: For Asgard 1

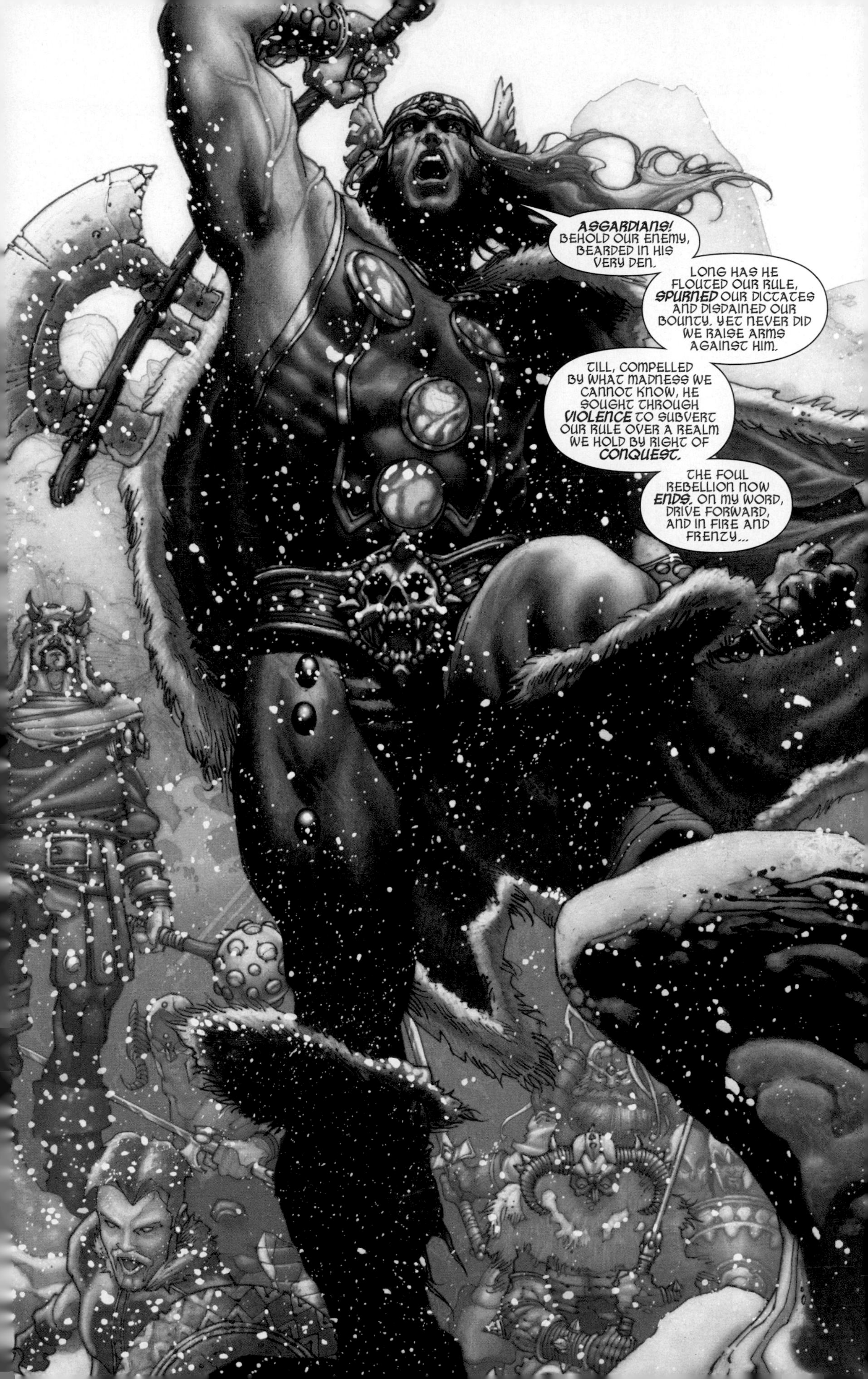
ASGARDIANS! BEHOLD OUR ENEMY, BEARDED IN HIS VERY DEN.
LONG HAS HE FLOUTED OUR RULE, SPURNED OUR DICTATES AND DISDAINED OUR BOUNTY. YET NEVER DID WE RAISE ARMS AGAINST HIM.
TILL, COMPELLED BY WHAT MADNESS WE CANNOT KNOW, HE SOUGHT THROUGH VIOLENCE TO SUBVERT OUR RULE OVER A REALM WE HOLD BY RIGHT OF CONQUEST.
THE FOUL REBELLION NOW ENDS. ON MY WORD, DRIVE FORWARD, AND IN FIRE AND FRENZY...

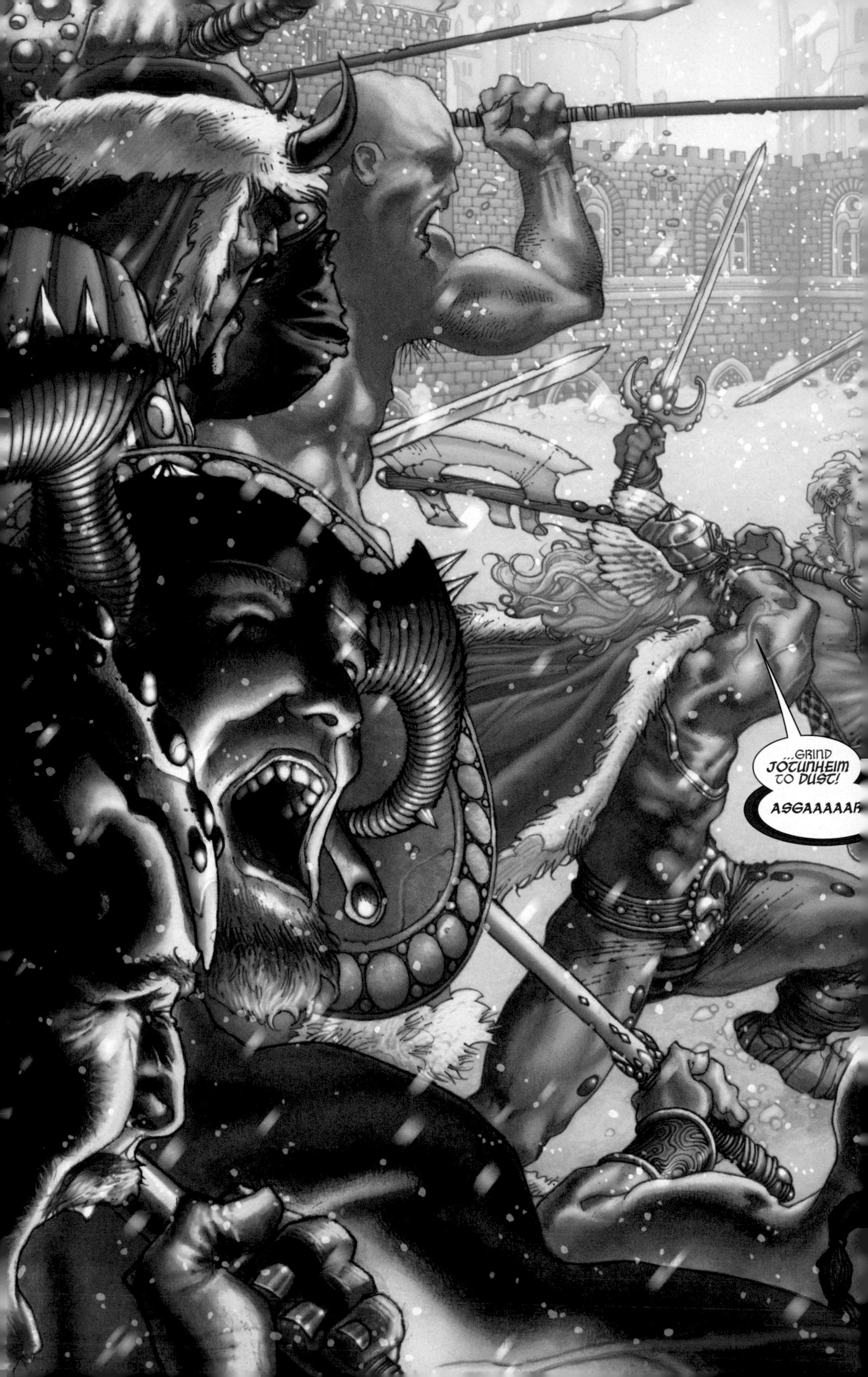
...GRIND JÖTUNHEIM TO DUST!
ASGAAAAAR

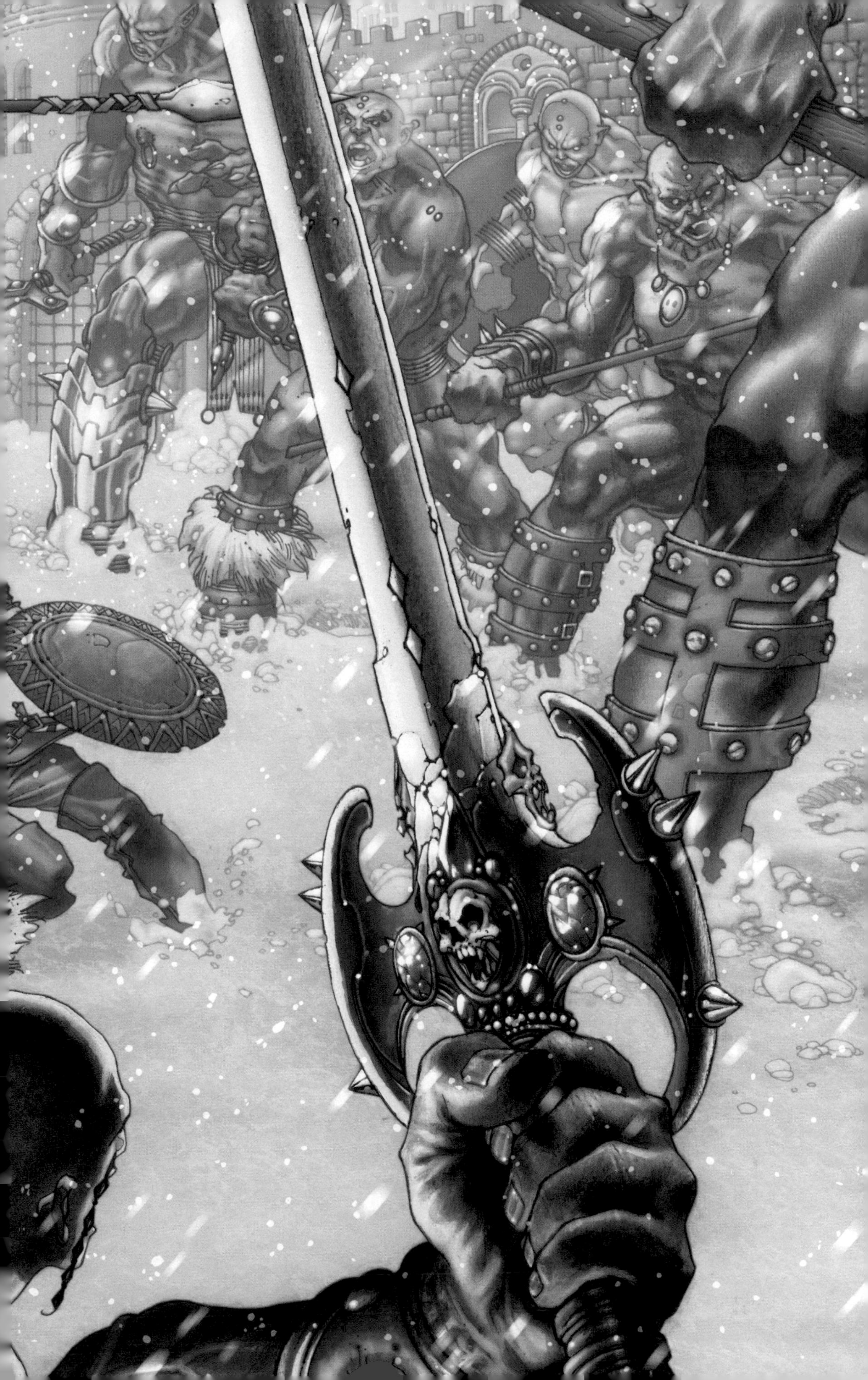

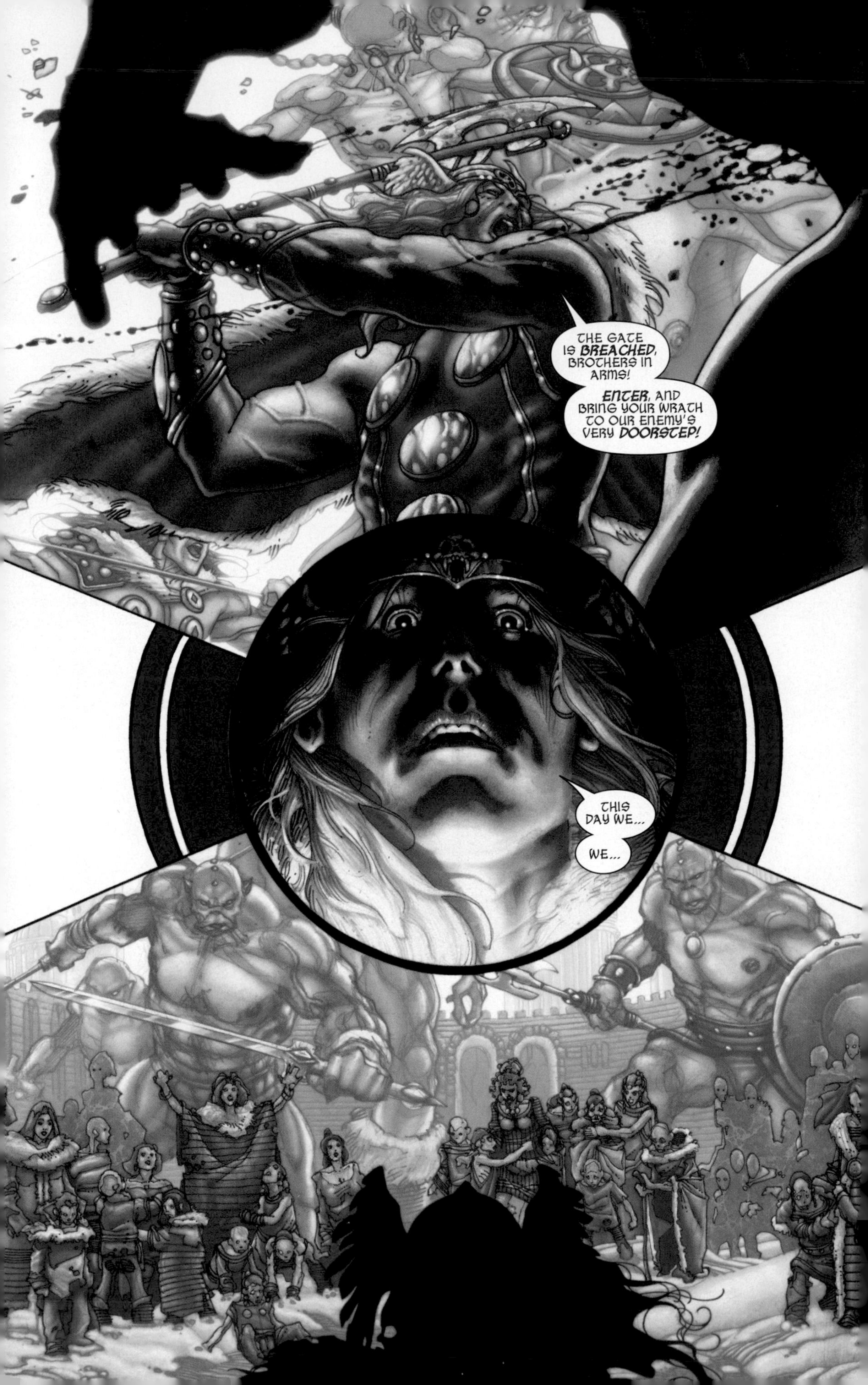
THE GATE IS BREACHED, BROTHERS IN ARMS!
ENTER, AND BRING YOUR WRATH TO OUR ENEMY'S VERY DOORSTEP!
THIS DAY WE...
WE...

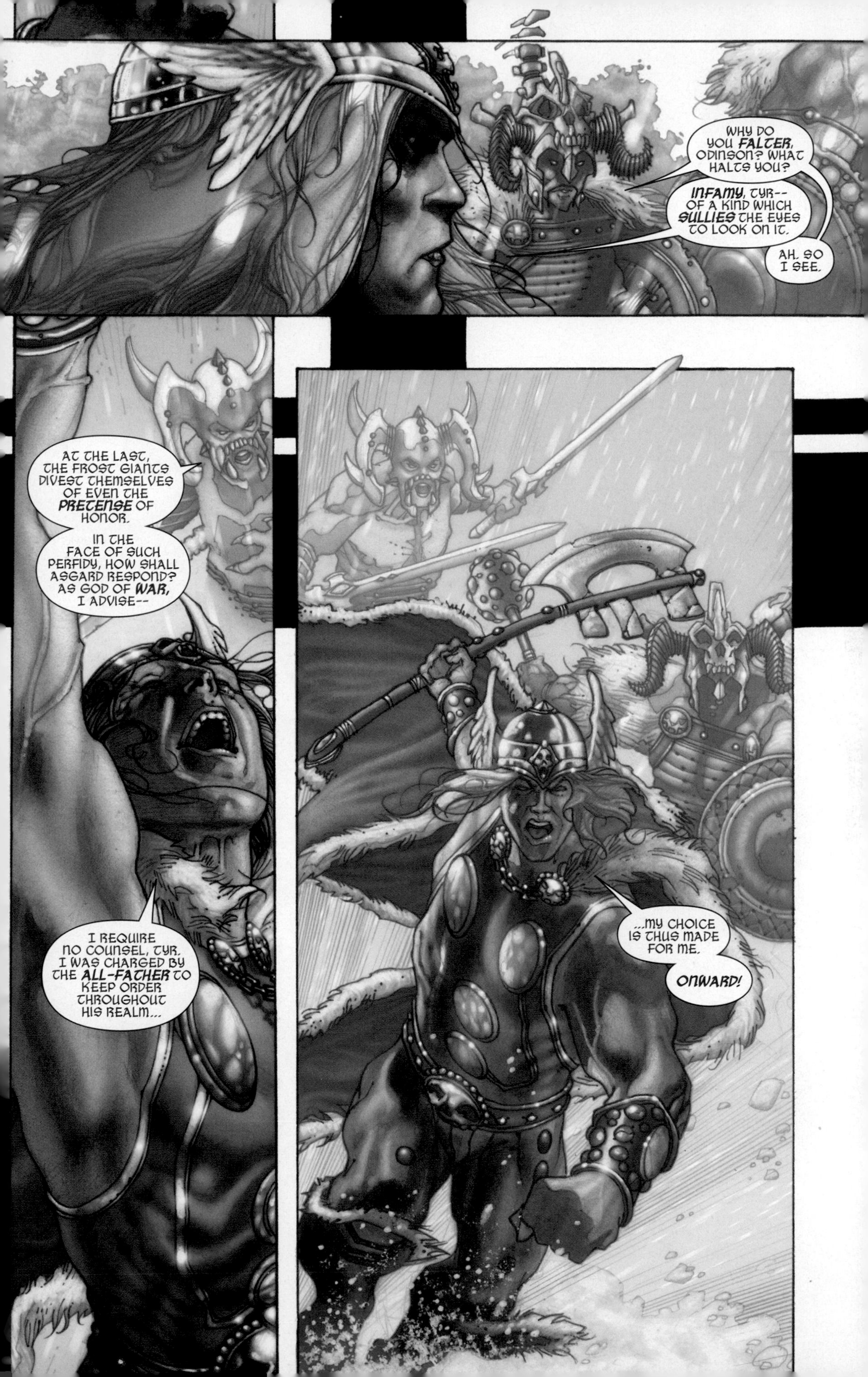
WHY DO YOU FALTER, ODINSON? WHAT HALTS YOU?
INFAMY, TYR-- OF A KIND WHICH SULLIES THE EYES TO LOOK ON IT.
AH. SO I SEE.
AT THE LAST, THE FROST GIANTS DIVEST THEMSELVES OF EVEN THE PRETENSE OF HONOR.
IN THE FACE OF SUCH PERFIDY, HOW SHALL ASGARD RESPOND? AS GOD OF WAR, I ADVISE--
I REQUIRE NO COUNSEL, TYR. I WAS CHARGED BY THE ALL-FATHER TO KEEP ORDER THROUGHOUT HIS REALM...
...MY CHOICE IS THUS MADE FOR ME.
ONWARD!

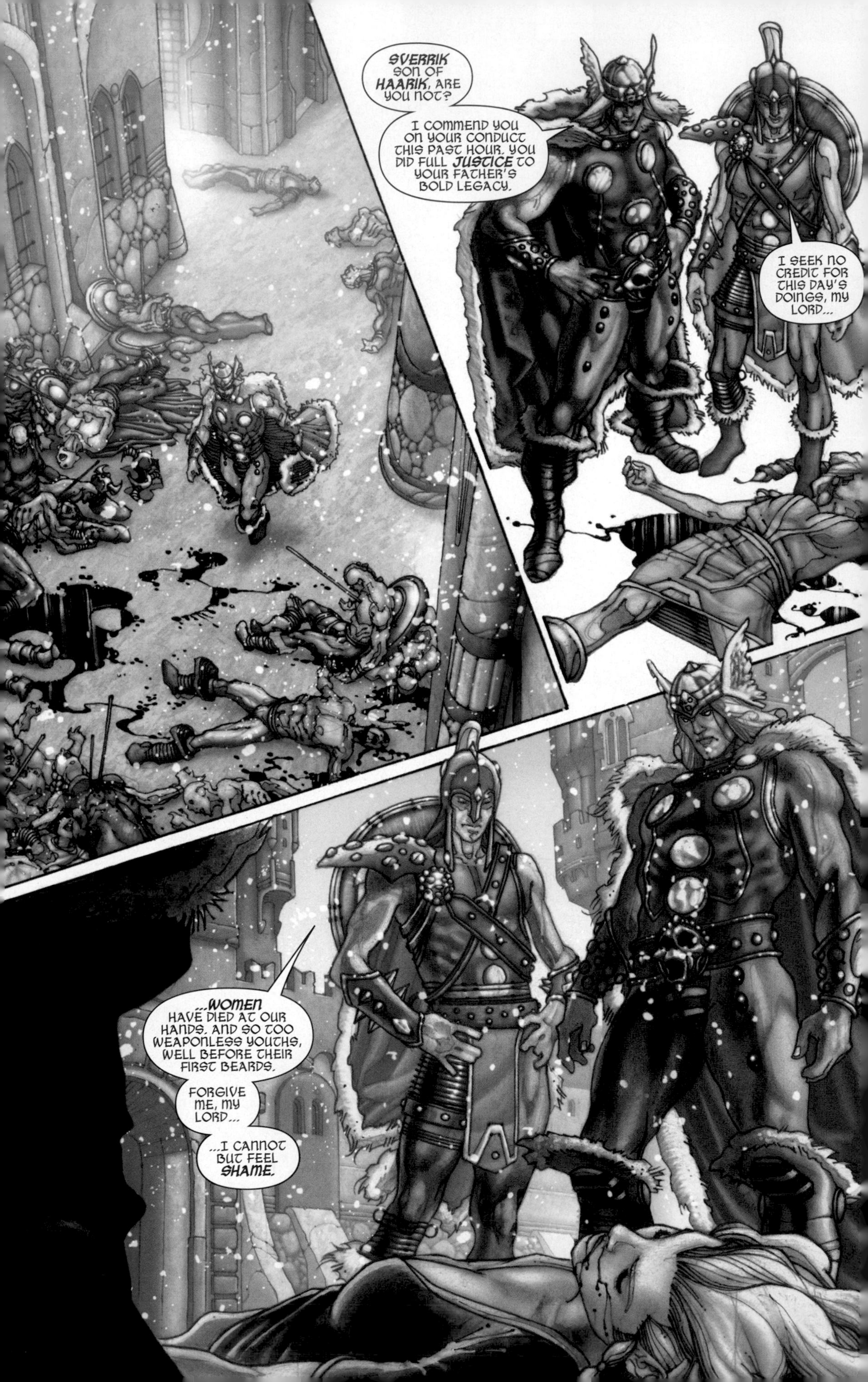
SVERRIK SON OF HAARIK, ARE YOU NOT?
I COMMEND YOU ON YOUR CONDUCT THIS PAST HOUR. YOU DID FULL JUSTICE TO YOUR FATHER'S BOLD LEGACY.
I SEEK NO CREDIT FOR THIS DAY'S DOINGS, MY LORD...
...WOMEN HAVE DIED AT OUR HANDS. AND SO TOO WEAPONLESS YOUTHS, WELL BEFORE THEIR FIRST BEARDS.
FORGIVE ME, MY LORD...
...I CANNOT BUT FEEL SHAME.

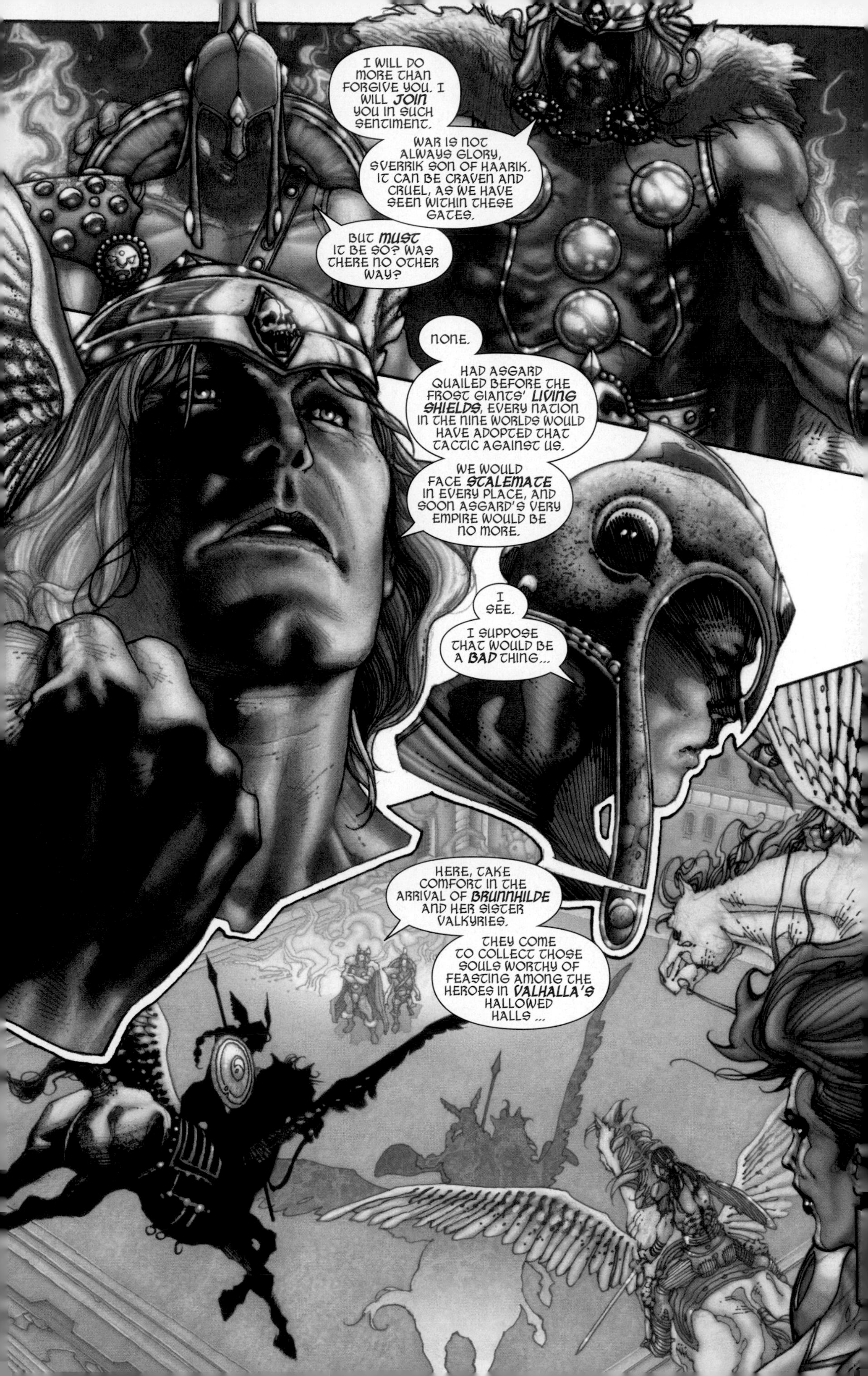
I WILL DO MORE THAN FORGIVE YOU. I WILL JOIN YOU IN SUCH SENTIMENT.
WAR IS NOT ALWAYS GLORY, SVERRIK SON OF HAARIK. IT CAN BE CRAVEN AND CRUEL, AS WE HAVE SEEN WITHIN THESE GATES.
BUT MUST IT BE SO? WAS THERE NO OTHER WAY?
NONE.
HAD ASGARD QUAILED BEFORE THE FROST GIANTS' LIVING SHIELDS, EVERY NATION IN THE NINE WORLDS WOULD HAVE ADOPTED THAT TACTIC AGAINST US.
WE WOULD FACE STALEMATE IN EVERY PLACE, AND SOON ASGARD'S VERY EMPIRE WOULD BE NO MORE.
I SEE.
I SUPPOSE THAT WOULD BE A BAD THING...
HERE, TAKE COMFORT IN THE ARRIVAL OF BRUNNHILDE AND HER SISTER VALKYRIES.
THEY COME TO COLLECT THOSE SOULS WORTHY OF FEASTING AMONG THE HEROES IN VALHALLA'S HALLOWED HALLS ...

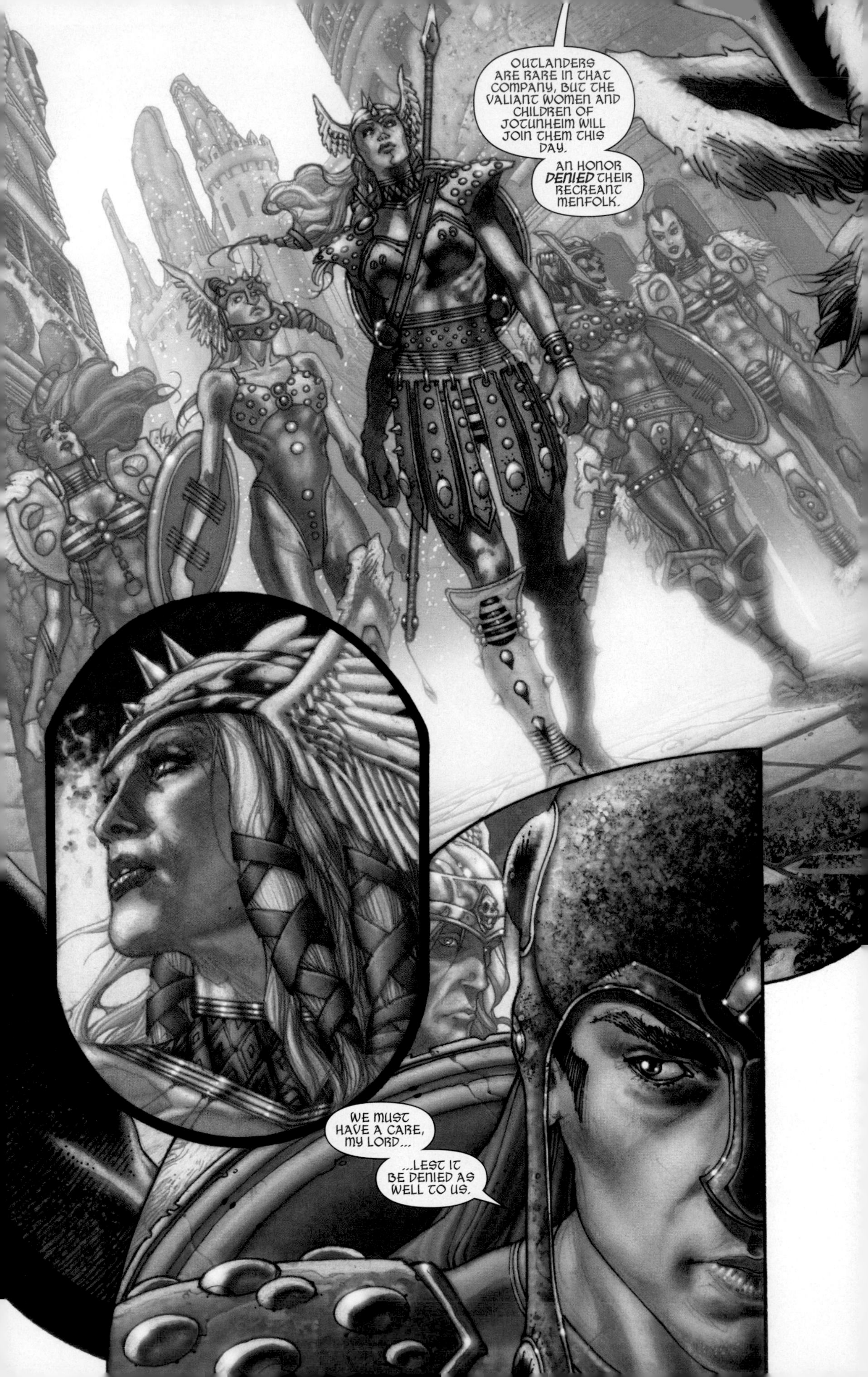
OUTLANDERS ARE RARE IN THAT COMPANY, BUT THE VALIANT WOMEN AND CHILDREN OF JOTUNHEIM WILL JOIN THEM THIS DAY.
AN HONOR DENIED THEIR RECREANT MENFOLK.
WE MUST HAVE A CARE, MY LORD...
...LEST IT BE DENIED AS WELL TO US.

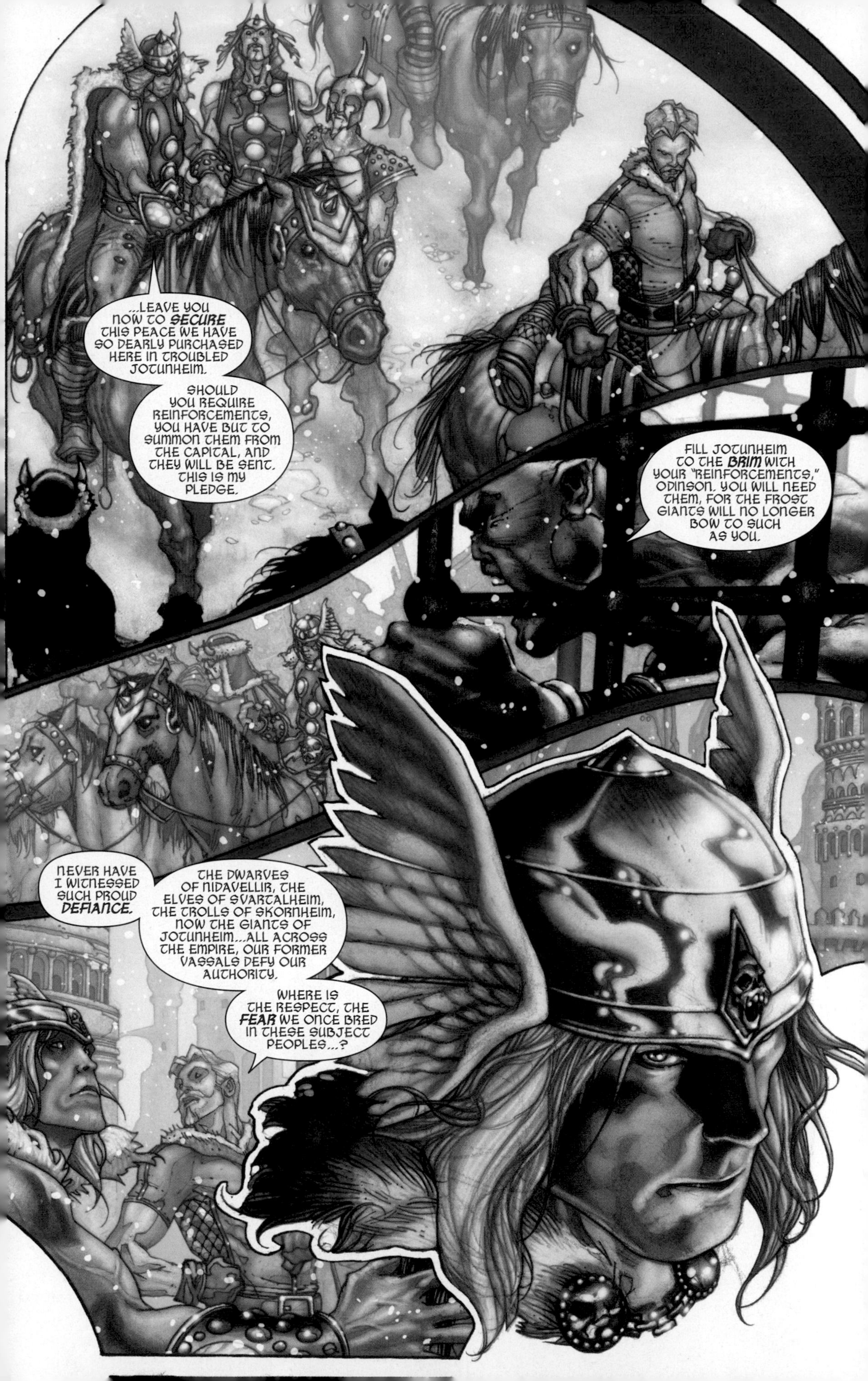
...LEAVE YOU NOW TO SECURE THIS PEACE WE HAVE SO DEARLY PURCHASED HERE IN TROUBLED JOTUNHEIM.
SHOULD YOU REQUIRE REINFORCEMENTS, YOU HAVE BUT TO SUMMON THEM FROM THE CAPITAL, AND THEY WILL BE SENT. THIS IS MY PLEDGE.
FILL JOTUNHEIM TO THE BRIM WITH YOUR "REINFORCEMENTS," ODINSON. YOU WILL NEED THEM, FOR THE FROST GIANTS WILL NO LONGER BOW TO SUCH AS YOU.
NEVER HAVE I WITNESSED SUCH PROUD DEFIANCE.
THE DWARVES OF NIDAVELLIR, THE ELVES OF SVARTALHEIM, THE TROLLS OF SKORNHEIM, NOW THE GIANTS OF JOTUNHEIM...ALL ACROSS THE EMPIRE, OUR FORMER VASSALS DEFY OUR AUTHORITY.
WHERE IS THE RESPECT, THE FEAR WE ONCE BRED IN THESE SUBJECT PEOPLES...?

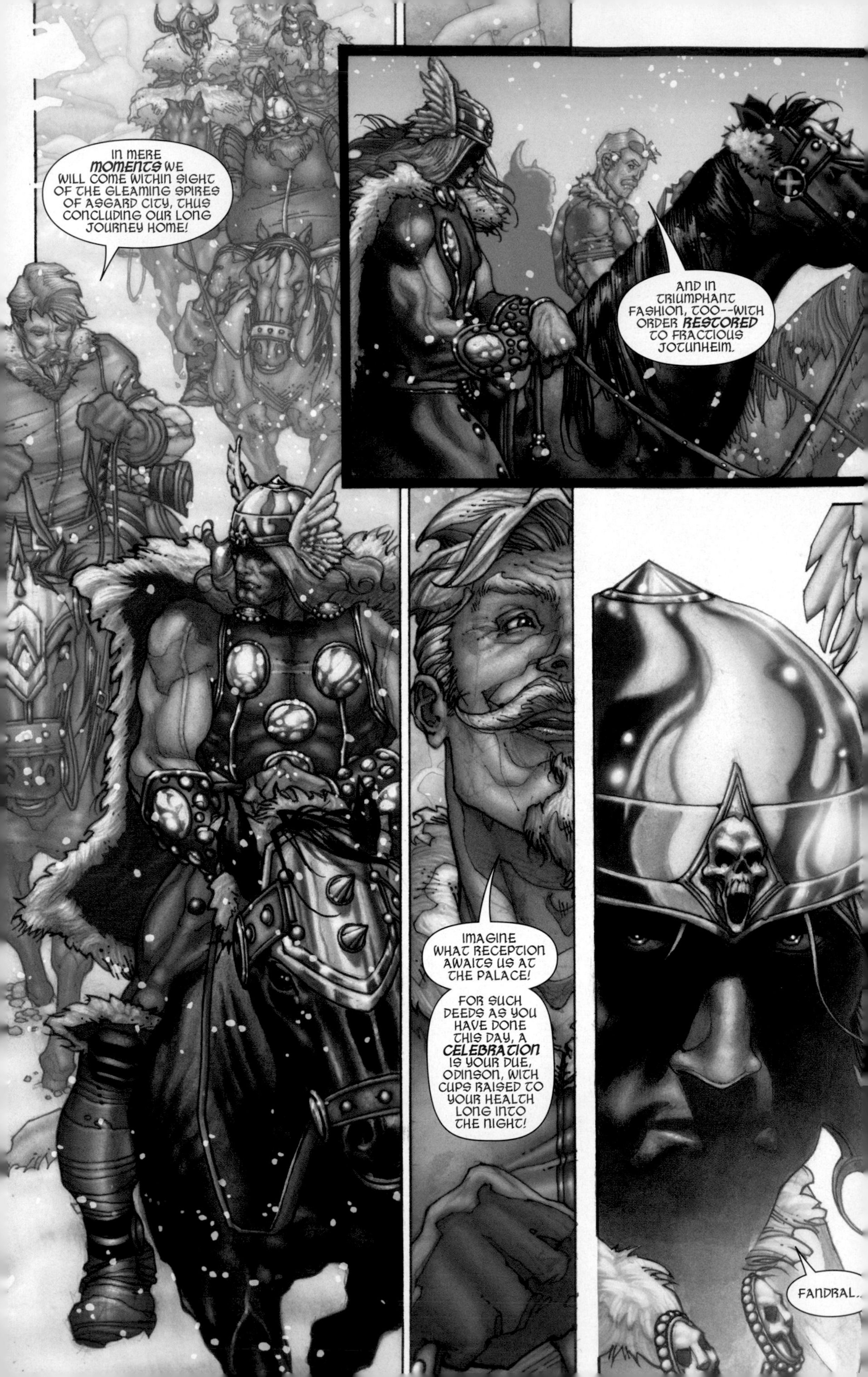
IN MERE MOMENTS WE WILL COME WITHIN SIGHT OF THE GLEAMING SPIRES OF ASGARD CITY, THUS CONCLUDING OUR LONG JOURNEY HOME!
AND IN TRIUMPHANT FASHION, TOO--WITH ORDER RESTORED TO FRACTIOUS JOTUNHEIM.
IMAGINE WHAT RECEPTION AWAITS US AT THE PALACE!
FOR SUCH DEEDS AS YOU HAVE DONE THIS DAY, A CELEBRATION IS YOUR DUE, ODINSON, WITH CUPS RAISED TO YOUR HEALTH LONG INTO THE NIGHT!
FANDRAL...

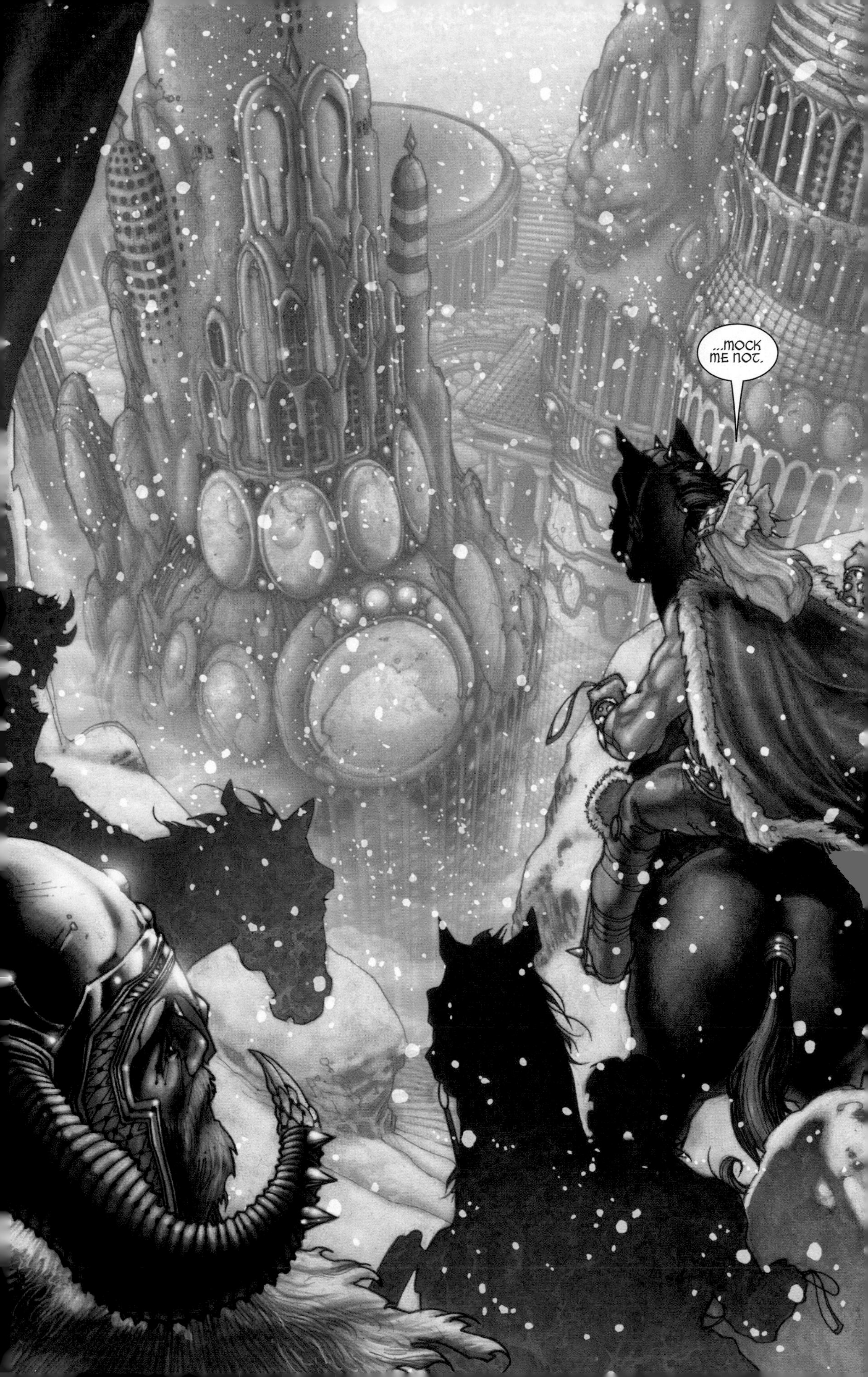
...MOCK ME NOT.

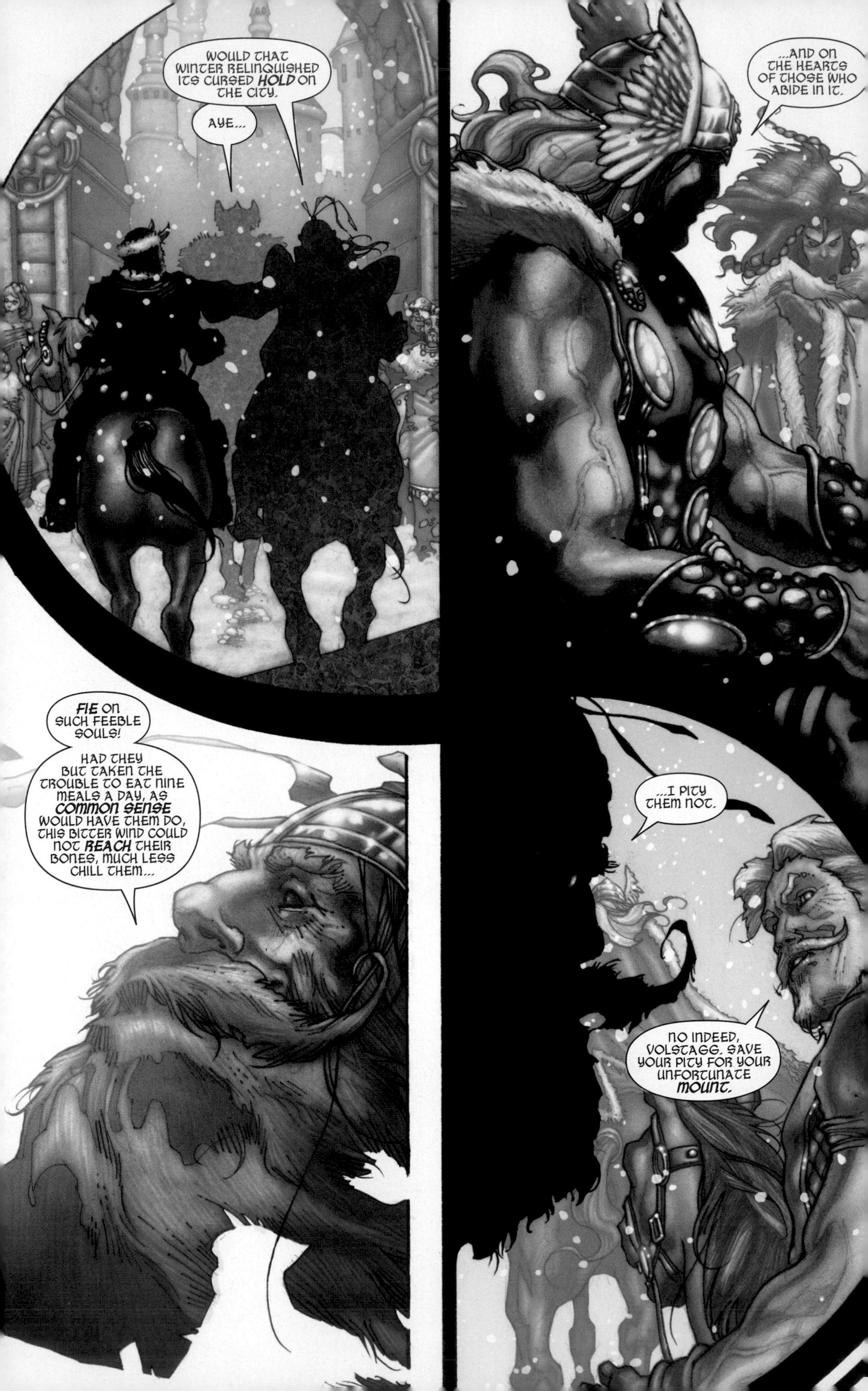
WOULD THAT WINTER RELINQUISHED ITS CURSED HOLD ON THE CITY.
AYE...
...AND ON THE HEARTS OF THOSE WHO ABIDE IN IT.
FIE ON SUCH FEEBLE SOULS!
HAD THEY BUT TAKEN THE TROUBLE TO EAT NINE MEALS A DAY, AS COMMON SENSE WOULD HAVE THEM DO, THIS BITTER WIND COULD NOT REACH THEIR BONES, MUCH LESS CHILL THEM...
...I PITY THEM NOT.
NO INDEED, VOLSTAGG. SAVE YOUR PITY FOR YOUR UNFORTUNATE MOUNT.

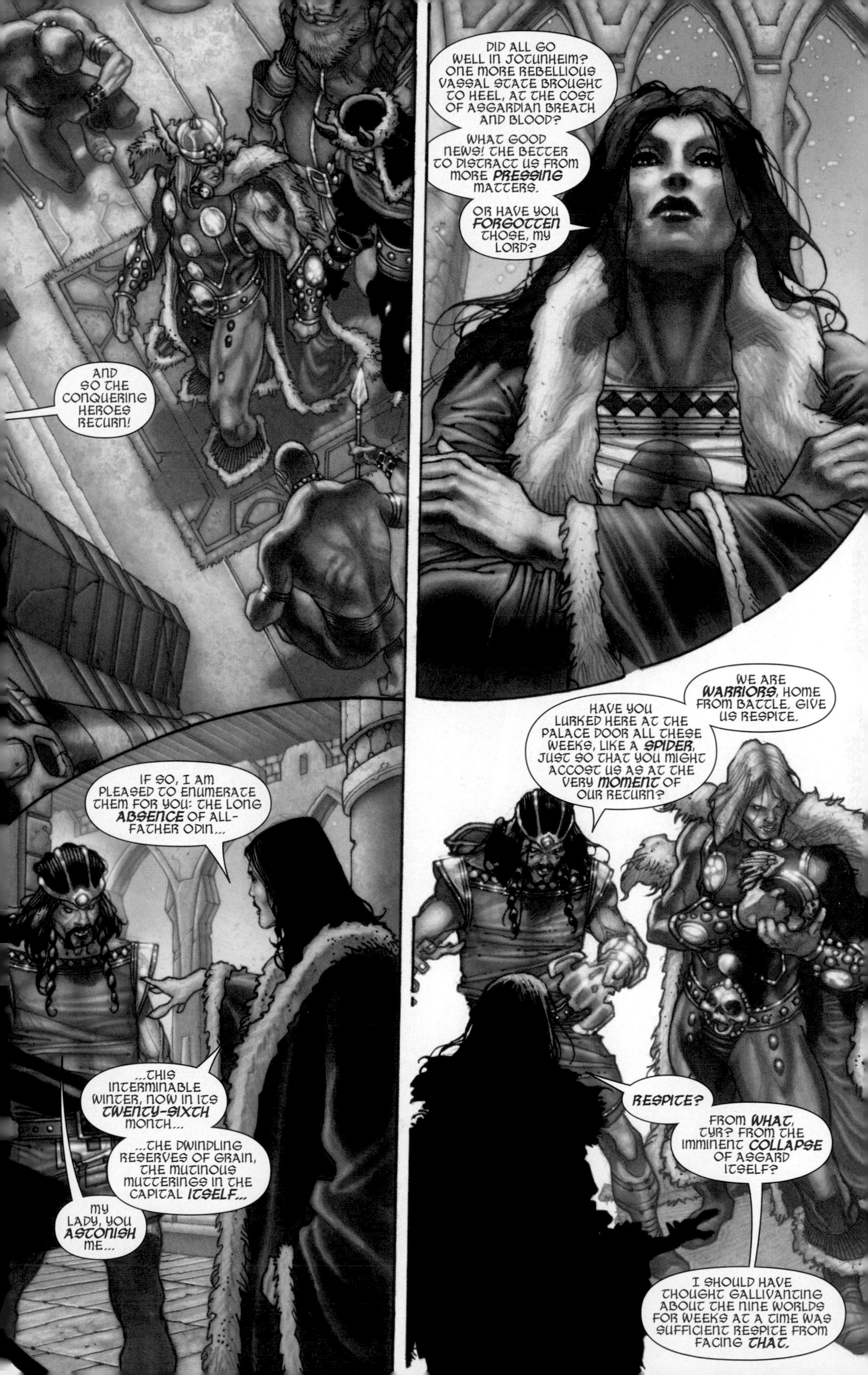
AND SO THE CONQUERING HEROES RETURN!
DID ALL GO WELL IN JOTUNHEIM? ONE MORE REBELLIOUS VASSAL STATE BROUGHT TO HEEL, AT THE COST OF ASGARDIAN BREATH AND BLOOD?
WHAT GOOD NEWS! THE BETTER TO DISTRACT US FROM MORE PRESSING MATTERS.
OR HAVE YOU FORGOTTEN THOSE, MY LORD?
IF SO, I AM PLEASED TO ENUMERATE THEM FOR YOU: THE LONG ABSENCE OF ALL-FATHER ODIN...
...THIS INTERMINABLE WINTER, NOW IN ITS TWENTY-SIXTH MONTH...
...THE DWINDLING RESERVES OF GRAIN, THE MUTINOUS MUTTERINGS IN THE CAPITAL ITSELF...
MY LADY, YOU ASTONISH ME...
HAVE YOU LURKED HERE AT THE PALACE DOOR ALL THESE WEEKS, LIKE A SPIDER, JUST SO THAT YOU MIGHT ACCOST US AS AT THE VERY MOMENT OF OUR RETURN?
WE ARE WARRIORS, HOME FROM BATTLE. GIVE US RESPITE.
RESPITE?
FROM WHAT, TYR? FROM THE IMMINENT COLLAPSE OF ASGARD ITSELF?
I SHOULD HAVE THOUGHT GALLIVANTING ABOUT THE NINE WORLDS FOR WEEKS AT A TIME WAS SUFFICIENT RESPITE FROM FACING THAT.

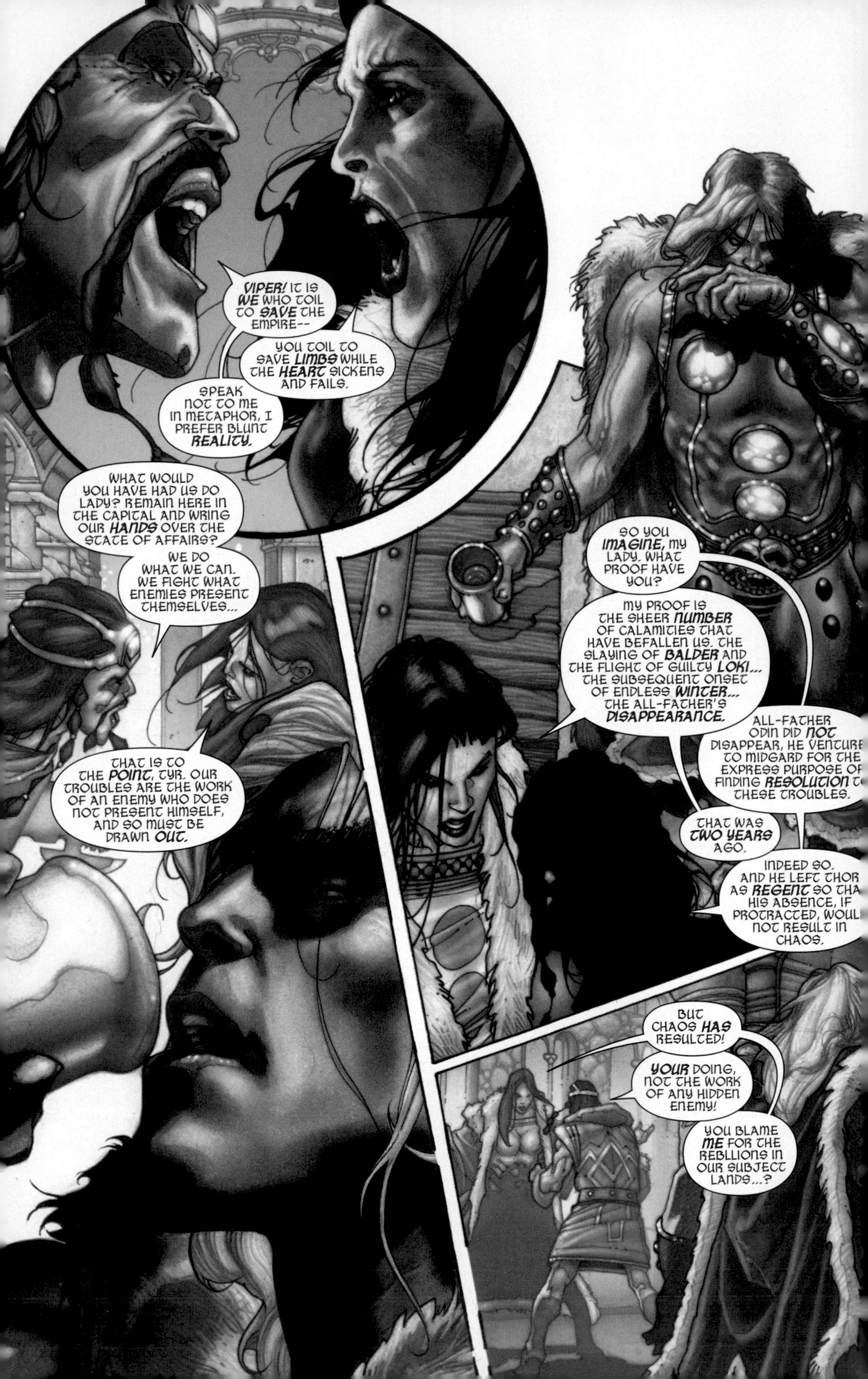
VIPER! IT IS WE WHO TOIL TO SAVE THE EMPIRE--
YOU TOIL TO SAVE LIMBS WHILE THE HEART SICKENS AND FAILS.
SPEAK NOT TO ME IN METAPHOR, I PREFER BLUNT REALITY.
WHAT WOULD YOU HAVE HAD US DO LADY? REMAIN HERE IN THE CAPITAL AND WRING OUR HANDS OVER THE STATE OF AFFAIRS?
WE DO WHAT WE CAN. WE FIGHT WHAT ENEMIES PRESENT THEMSELVES...
THAT IS TO THE POINT, TYR. OUR TROUBLES ARE THE WORK OF AN ENEMY WHO DOES NOT PRESENT HIMSELF, AND SO MUST BE DRAWN OUT.
SO YOU IMAGINE, MY LADY. WHAT PROOF HAVE YOU?
MY PROOF IS THE SHEER NUMBER OF CALAMITIES THAT HAVE BEFALLEN US. THE SLAYING OF BALDER AND THE FLIGHT OF GUILTY LOKI... THE SUBSEQUENT ONSET OF ENDLESS WINTER... THE ALL-FATHER'S DISAPPEARANCE.
ALL-FATHER ODIN DID NOT DISAPPEAR, HE VENTURE TO MIDGARD FOR THE EXPRESS PURPOSE OF FINDING RESOLUTION TO THESE TROUBLES.
THAT WAS TWO YEARS AGO.
INDEED SO. AND HE LEFT THOR AS REGENT SO THA HIS ABSENCE, IF PROTRACTED, WOUL NOT RESULT IN CHAOS.
BUT CHAOS HAS RESULTED!
YOUR DOING, NOT THE WORK OF ANY HIDDEN ENEMY!
YOU BLAME ME FOR THE REBLLIONS IN OUR SUBJECT LANDS...?

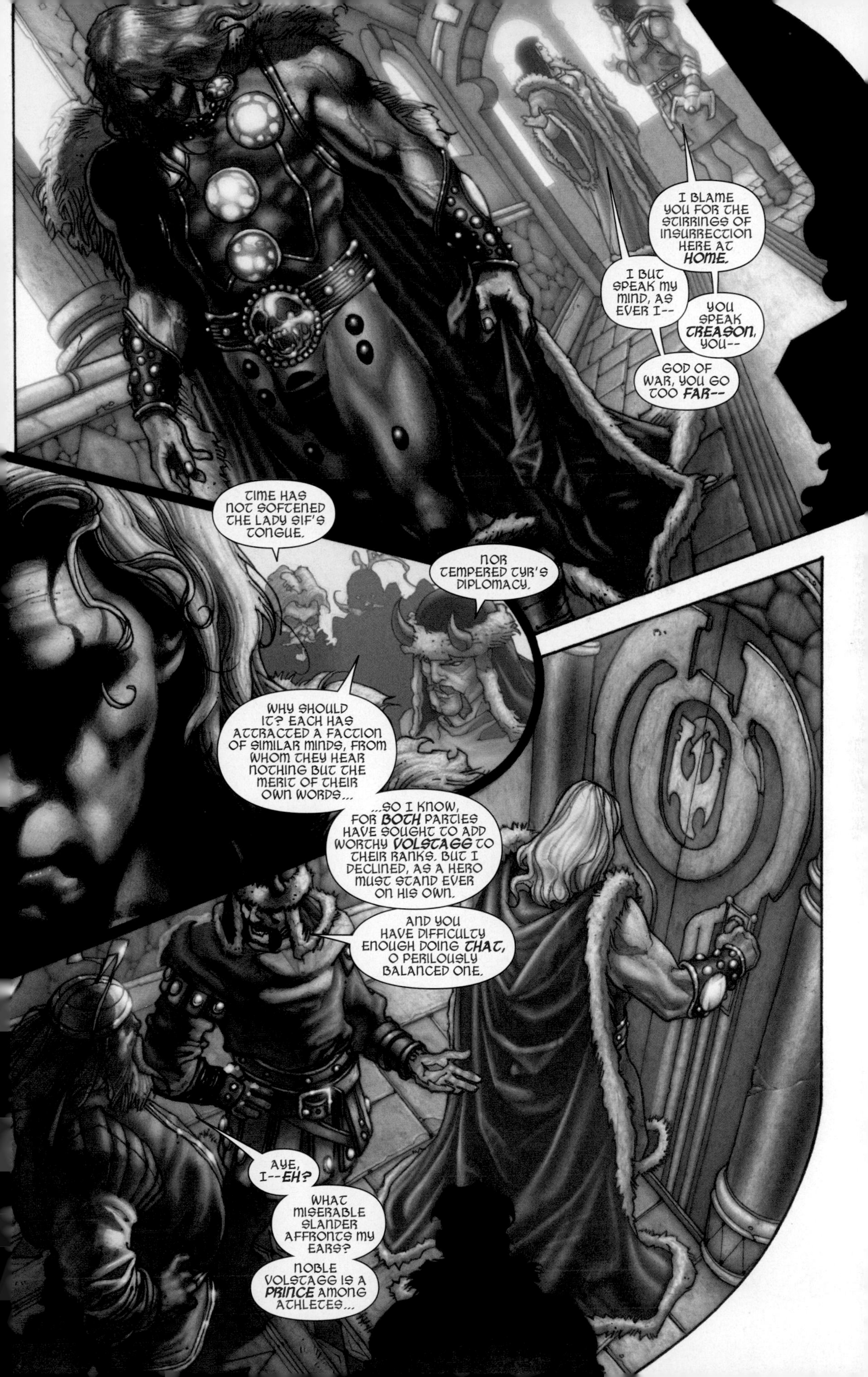
I BLAME YOU FOR THE STIRRINGS OF INSURRECTION HERE AT HOME.
I BUT SPEAK MY MIND, AS EVER I--
YOU SPEAK TREASON, YOU--
GOD OF WAR, YOU GO TOO FAR--
TIME HAS NOT SOFTENED THE LADY SIF'S TONGUE.
NOR TEMPERED TYR'S DIPLOMACY.
WHY SHOULD IT? EACH HAS ATTRACTED A FACTION OF SIMILAR MINDS, FROM WHOM THEY HEAR NOTHING BUT THE MERIT OF THEIR OWN WORDS...
...SO I KNOW, FOR BOTH PARTIES HAVE SOUGHT TO ADD WORTHY VOLSTAGG TO THEIR RANKS. BUT I DECLINED, AS A HERO MUST STAND EVER ON HIS OWN.
AND YOU HAVE DIFFICULTY ENOUGH DOING THAT, O PERILOUSLY BALANCED ONE.
AYE, I--EH?
WHAT MISERABLE SLANDER AFFRONTS MY EARS?
NOBLE VOLSTAGG IS A PRINCE AMONG ATHLETES...

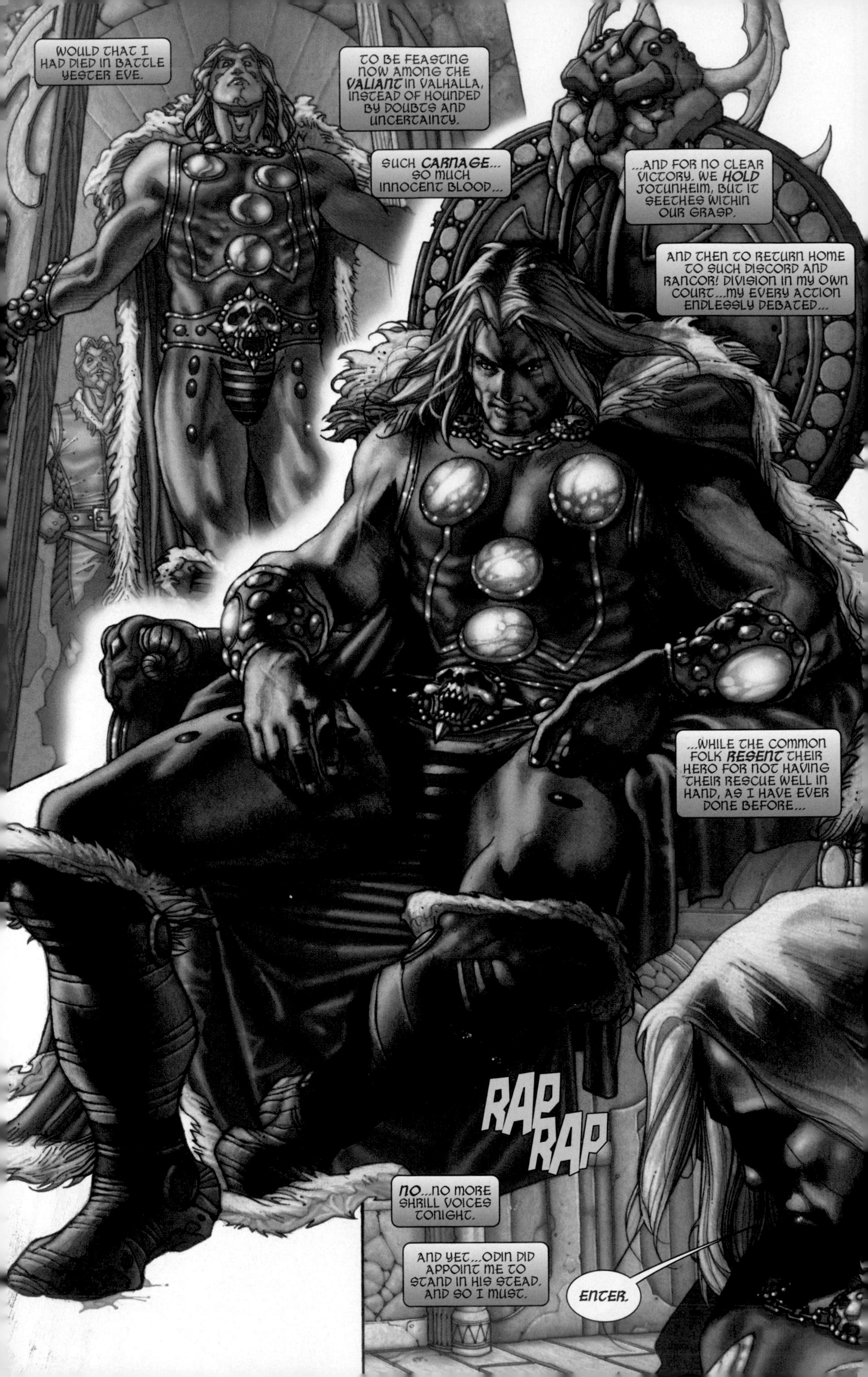
WOULD THAT I HAD DIED IN BATTLE YESTER EVE.
TO BE FEASTING NOW AMONG THE VALIANT IN VALHALLA, INSTEAD OF HOUNDED BY DOUBTS AND UNCERTAINTY.
SUCH CARNAGE... SO MUCH INNOCENT BLOOD...
...AND FOR NO CLEAR VICTORY. WE HOLD JOTUNHEIM, BUT IT SEETHES WITHIN OUR GRASP.
AND THEN TO RETURN HOME TO SUCH DISCORD AND RANCOR! DIVISION IN MY OWN COURT...MY EVERY ACTION ENDLESSLY DEBATED...
...WHILE THE COMMON FOLK RESENT THEIR HERO FOR NOT HAVING THEIR RESCUE WELL IN HAND, AS I HAVE EVER DONE BEFORE...
RAP RAP
NO...NO MORE SHRILL VOICES TONIGHT.
AND YET...ODIN DID APPOINT ME TO STAND IN HIS STEAD, AND SO I MUST.
ENTER.

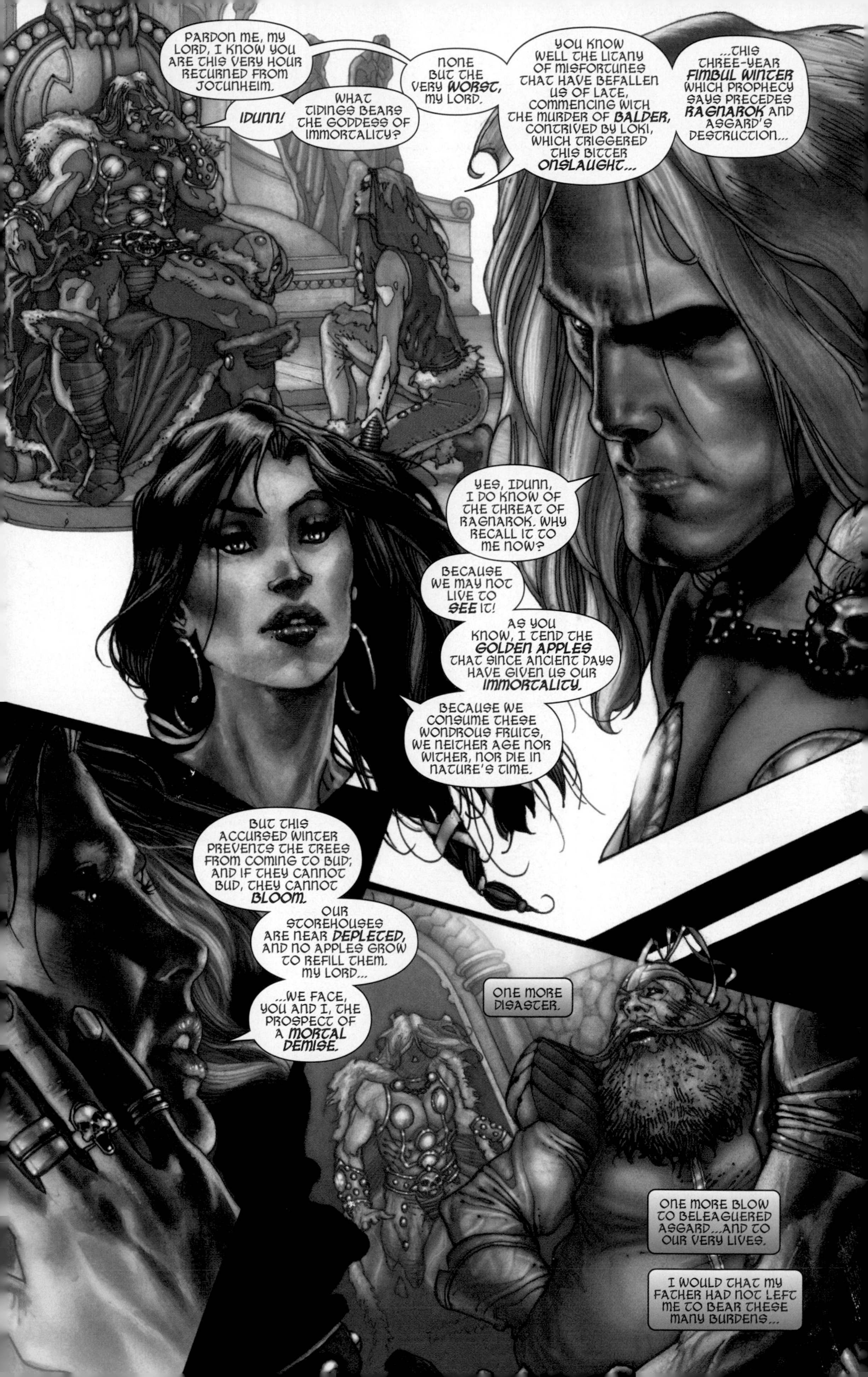

PARDON ME, MY LORD, I KNOW YOU ARE THIS VERY HOUR RETURNED FROM JOTUNHEIM.
IDUNN!
WHAT TIDINGS BEARS THE GODDESS OF IMMORTALITY?
NONE BUT THE VERY WORST, MY LORD.
YOU KNOW WELL THE LITANY OF MISFORTUNES THAT HAVE BEFALLEN US OF LATE, COMMENCING WITH THE MURDER OF BALDER, CONTRIVED BY LOKI, WHICH TRIGGERED THIS BITTER ONSLAUGHT...
...THIS THREE-YEAR FIMBUL WINTER WHICH PROPHECY SAYS PRECEDES RAGNAROK AND ASGARD'S DESTRUCTION...
YES, IDUNN, I DO KNOW OF THE THREAT OF RAGNAROK. WHY RECALL IT TO ME NOW?
BECAUSE WE MAY NOT LIVE TO SEE IT!
AS YOU KNOW, I TEND THE GOLDEN APPLES THAT SINCE ANCIENT DAYS HAVE GIVEN US OUR IMMORTALITY.
BECAUSE WE CONSUME THESE WONDROUS FRUITS, WE NEITHER AGE NOR WITHER, NOR DIE IN NATURE'S TIME.
BUT THIS ACCURSED WINTER PREVENTS THE TREES FROM COMING TO BUD; AND IF THEY CANNOT BUD, THEY CANNOT BLOOM.
OUR STOREHOUSES ARE NEAR DEPLETED, AND NO APPLES GROW TO REFILL THEM. MY LORD...
...WE FACE, YOU AND I, THE PROSPECT OF A MORTAL DEMISE.
ONE MORE DISASTER.
ONE MORE BLOW TO BELEAGUERED ASGARD...AND TO OUR VERY LIVES.
I WOULD THAT MY FATHER HAD NOT LEFT ME TO BEAR THESE MANY BURDENS...

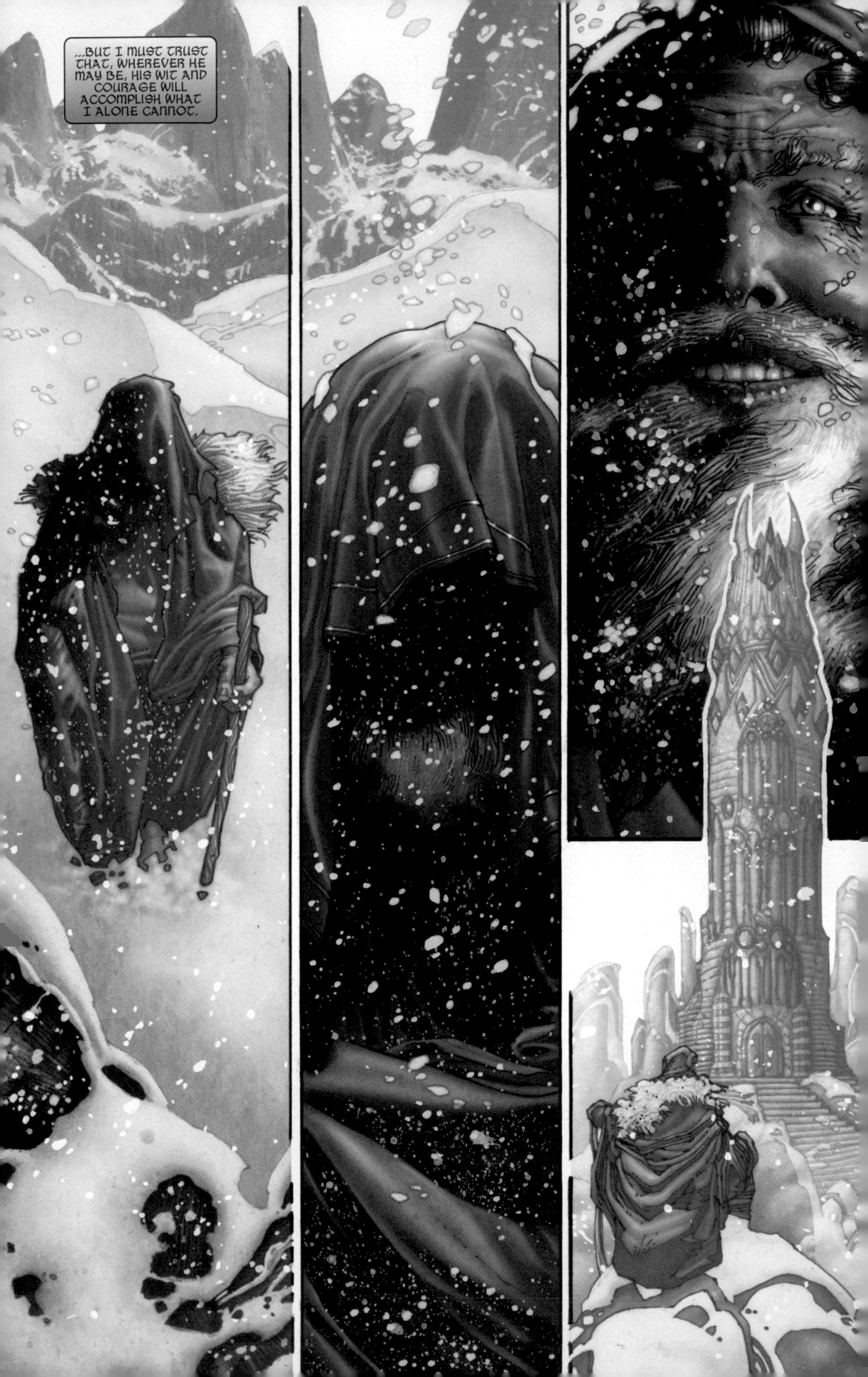
...BUT I MUST TRUST THAT, WHEREVER HE MAY BE, HIS WIT AND COURAGE WILL ACCOMPLISH WHAT I ALONE CANNOT.

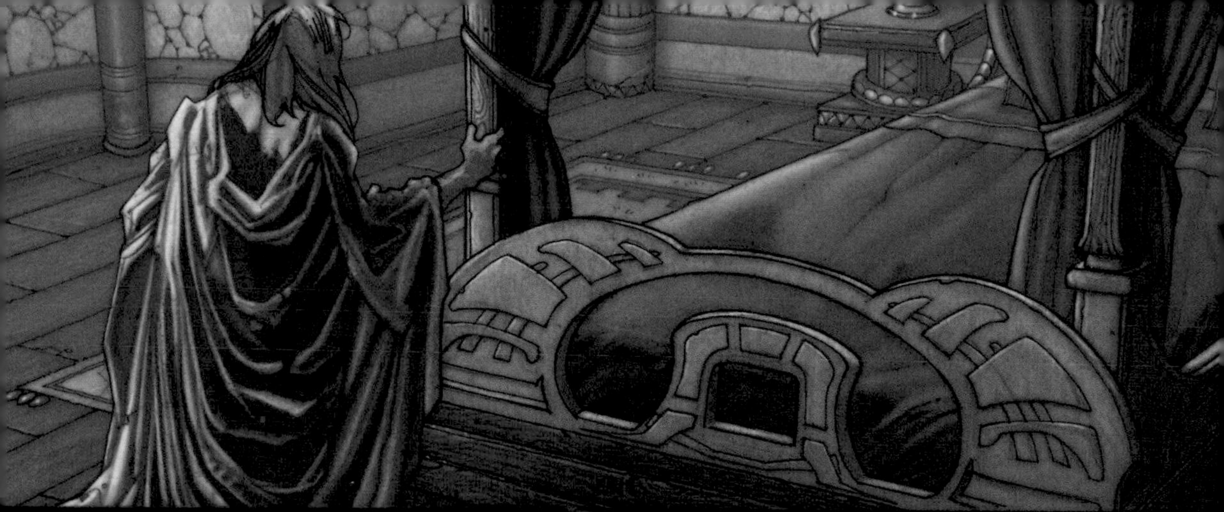

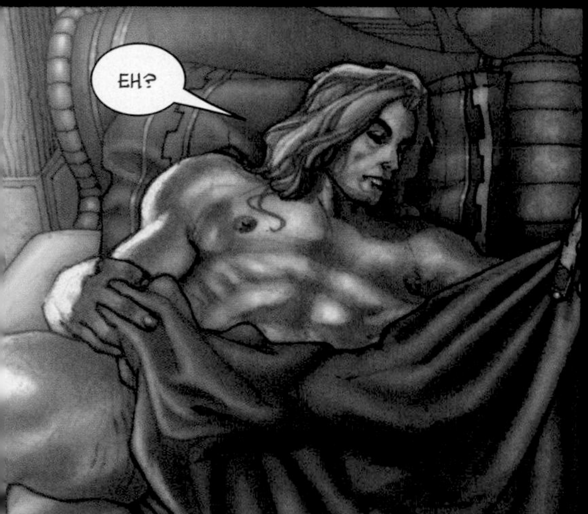
EH?

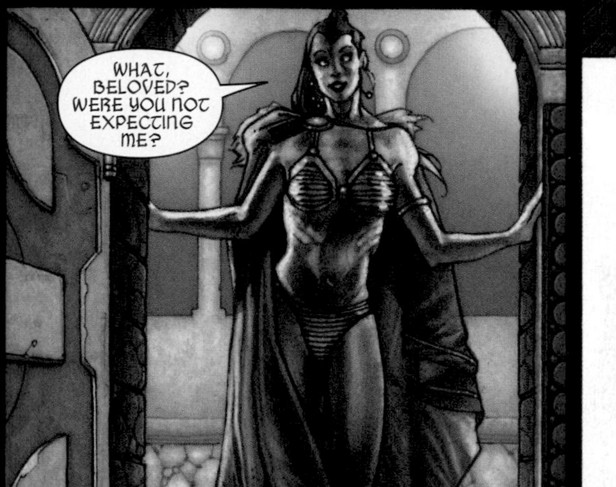
WHAT, BELOVED? WERE YOU NOT EXPECTING ME?

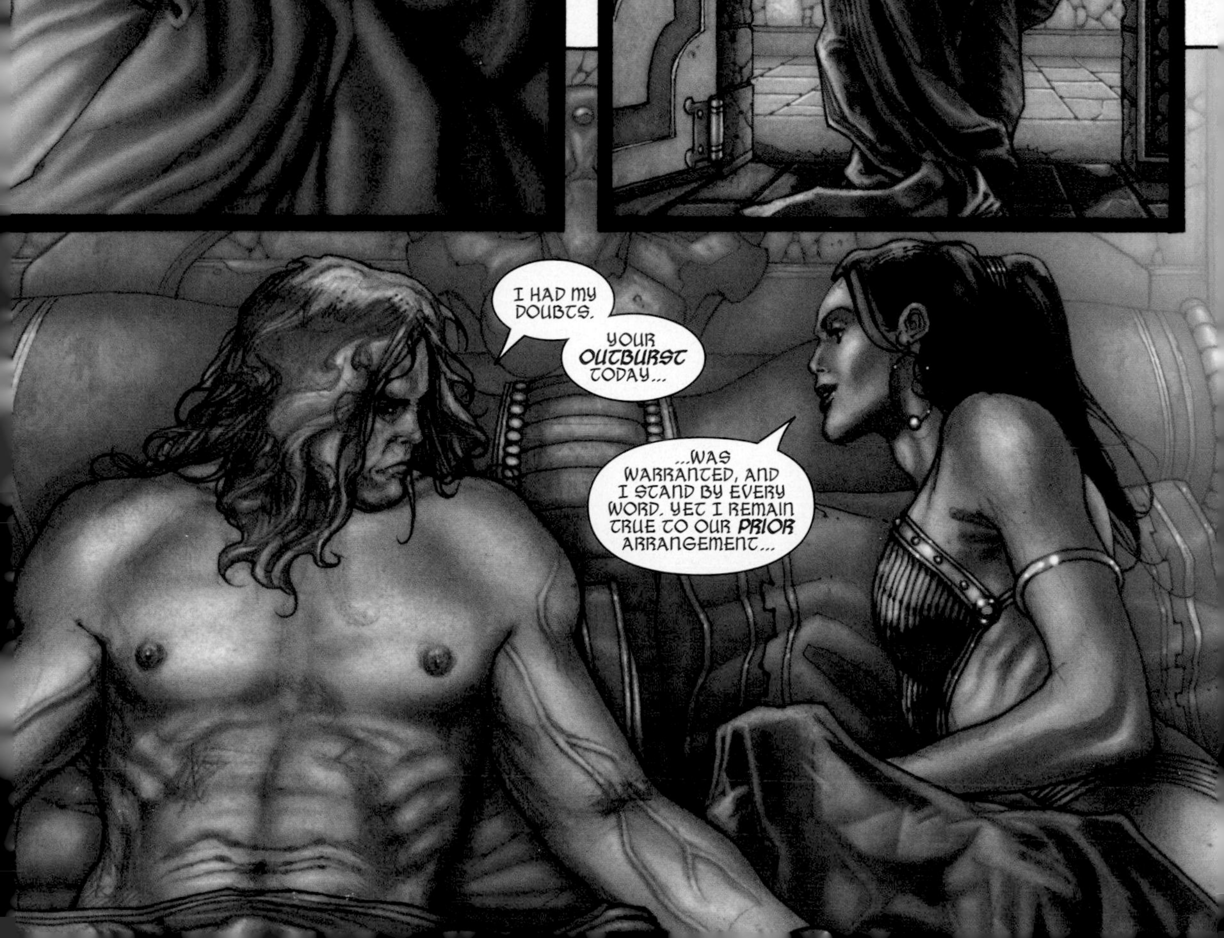
I HAD MY DOUBTS.
YOUR OUTBURST TODAY...
...WAS WARRANTED, AND I STAND BY EVERY WORD. YET I REMAIN TRUE TO OUR PRIOR ARRANGEMENT...

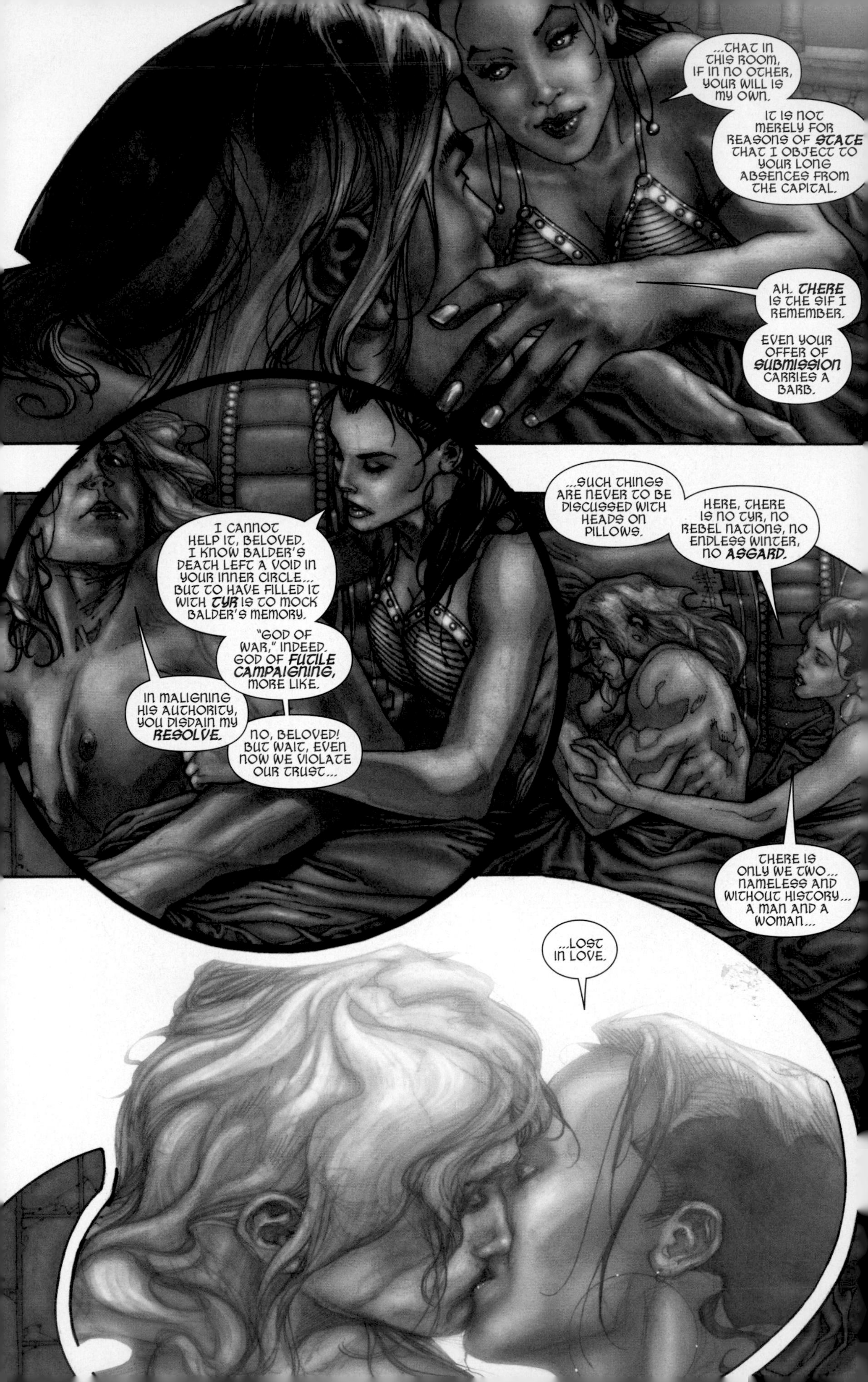
...THAT IN THIS ROOM, IF IN NO OTHER, YOUR WILL IS MY OWN.
IT IS NOT MERELY FOR REASONS OF STATE THAT I OBJECT TO YOUR LONG ABSENCES FROM THE CAPITAL.
AH. THERE IS THE SIF I REMEMBER.
EVEN YOUR OFFER OF SUBMISSION CARRIES A BARB.
I CANNOT HELP IT, BELOVED. I KNOW BALDER'S DEATH LEFT A VOID IN YOUR INNER CIRCLE... BUT TO HAVE FILLED IT WITH TYR IS TO MOCK BALDER'S MEMORY.
"GOD OF WAR," INDEED. GOD OF FUTILE CAMPAIGNING, MORE LIKE.
IN MALIGNING HIS AUTHORITY, YOU DISDAIN MY RESOLVE.
NO, BELOVED! BUT WAIT, EVEN NOW WE VIOLATE OUR TRUST...
...SUCH THINGS ARE NEVER TO BE DISCUSSED WITH HEADS ON PILLOWS.
HERE, THERE IS NO TYR, NO REBEL NATIONS, NO ENDLESS WINTER, NO ASGARD.
THERE IS ONLY WE TWO... NAMELESS AND WITHOUT HISTORY... A MAN AND A WOMAN...
...LOST IN LOVE.

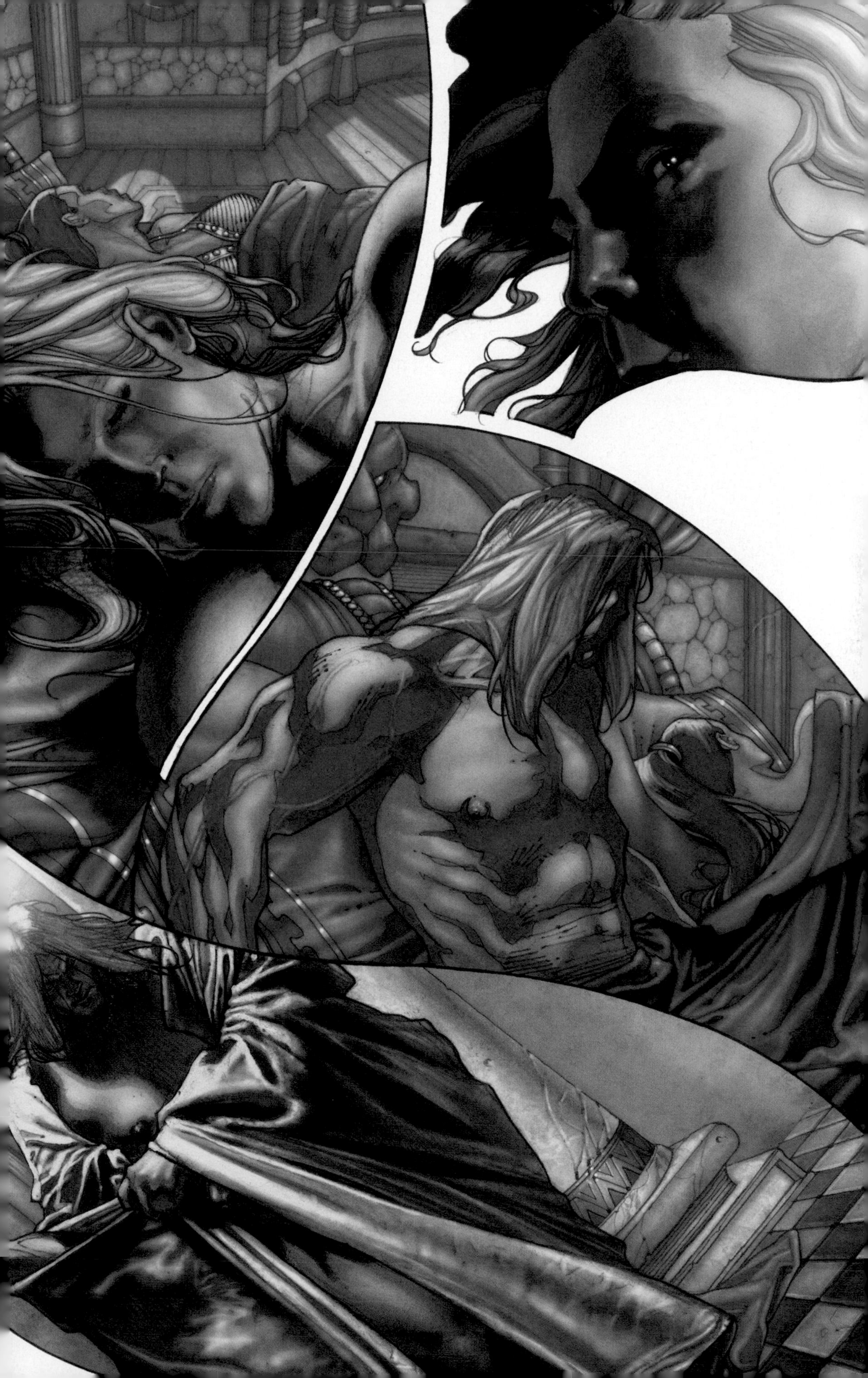

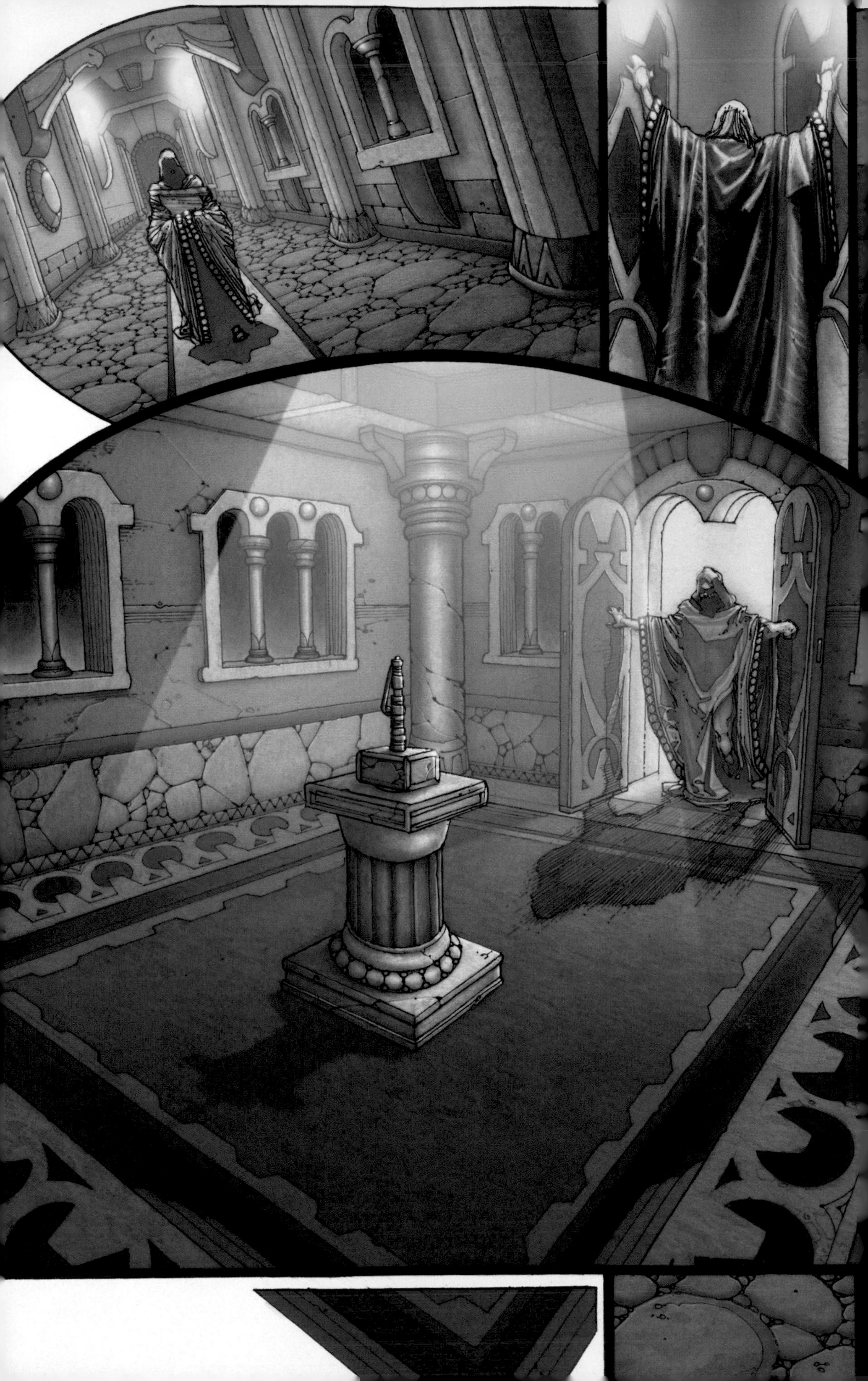

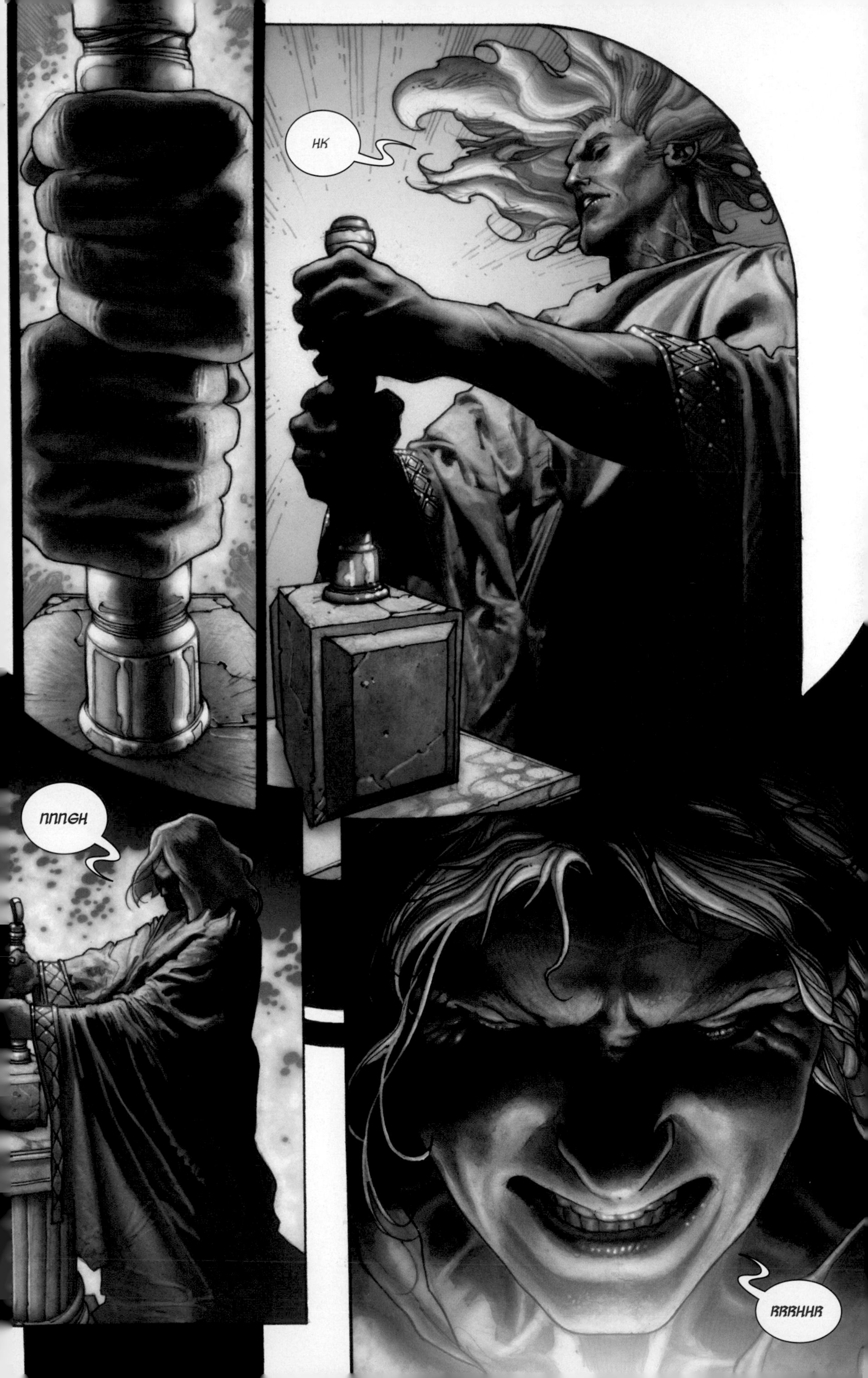
HK
NNNGH
RRRHHR

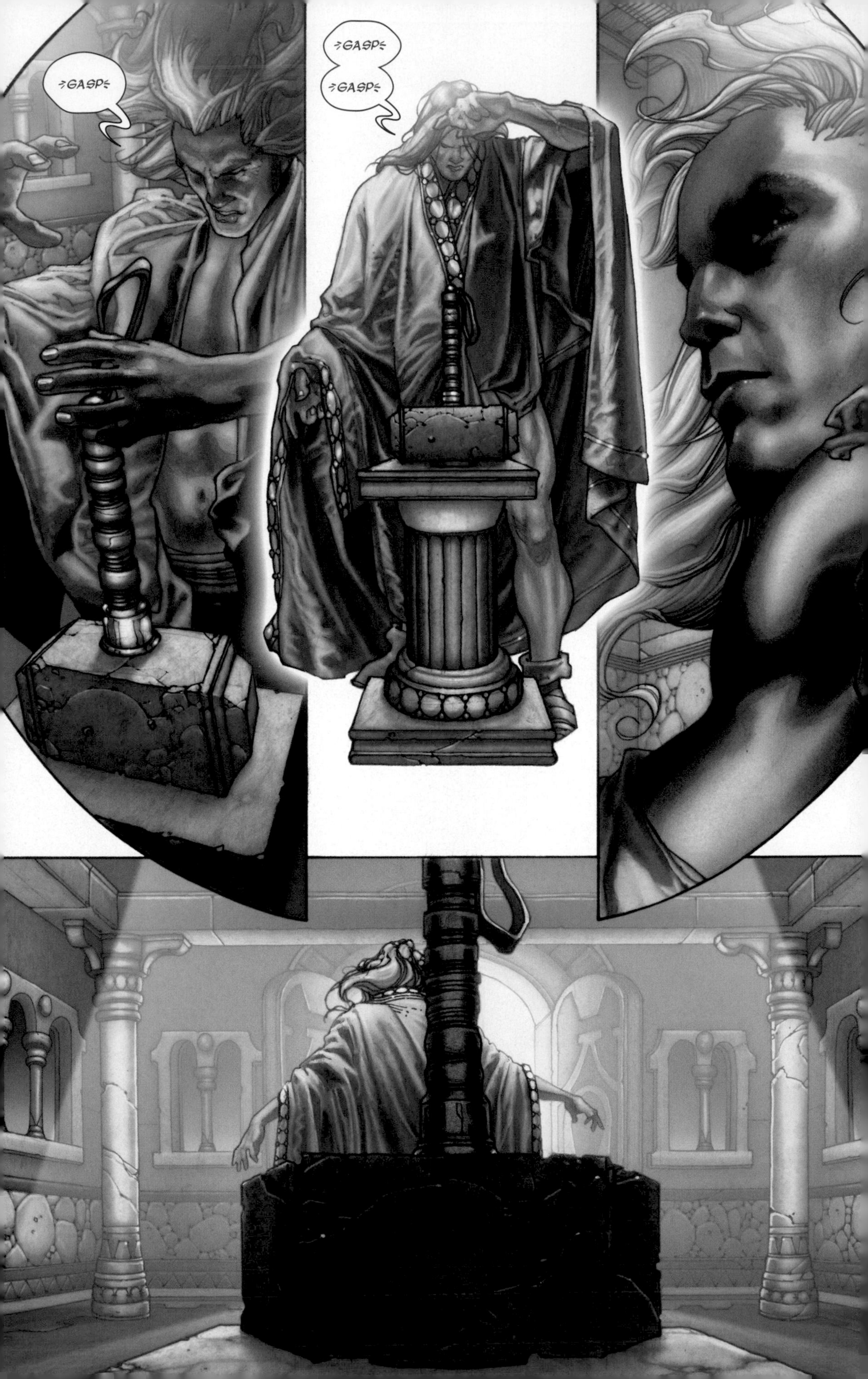
GASP
GASP
GASP

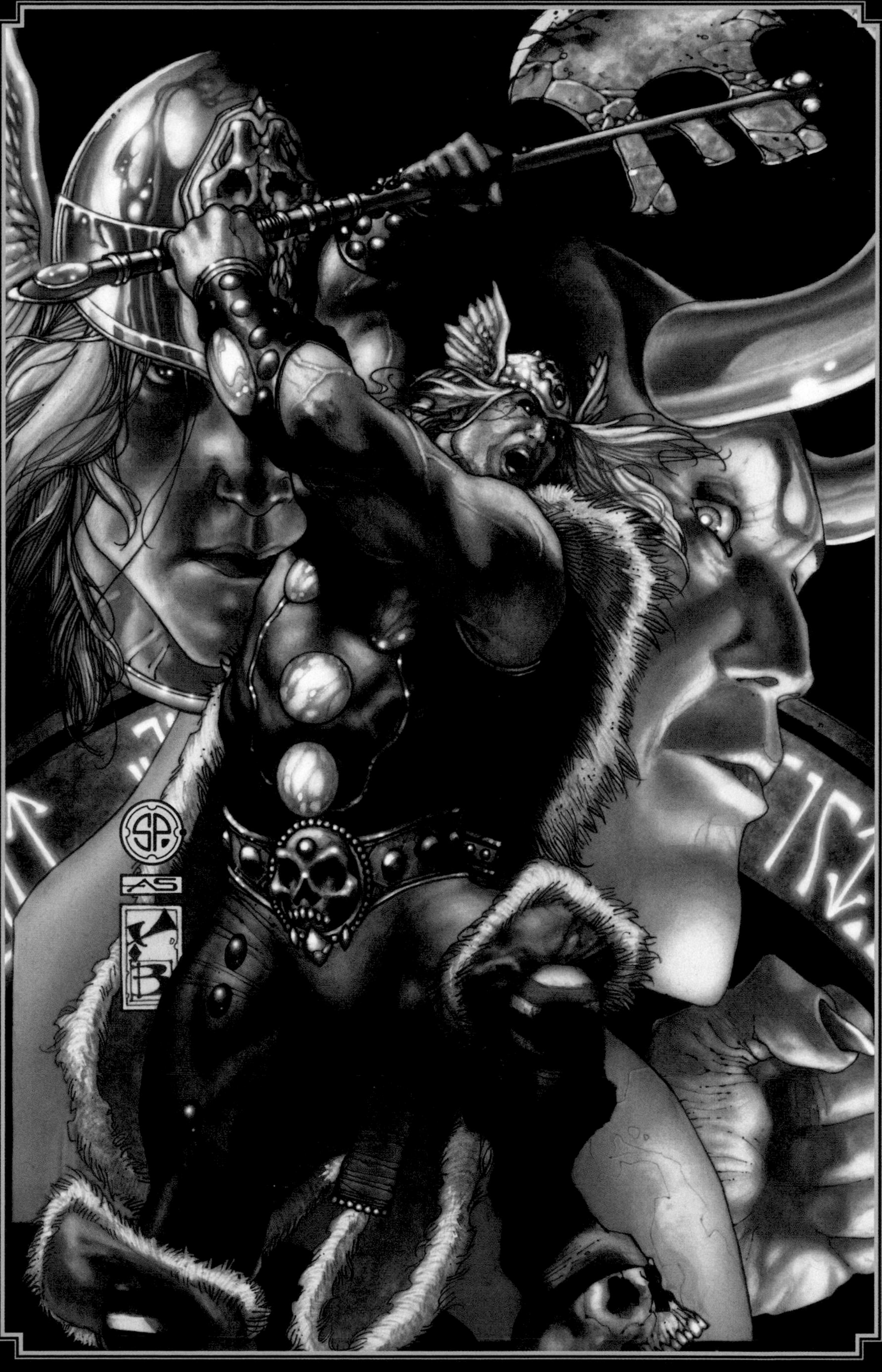

Thor: For Asgard 2

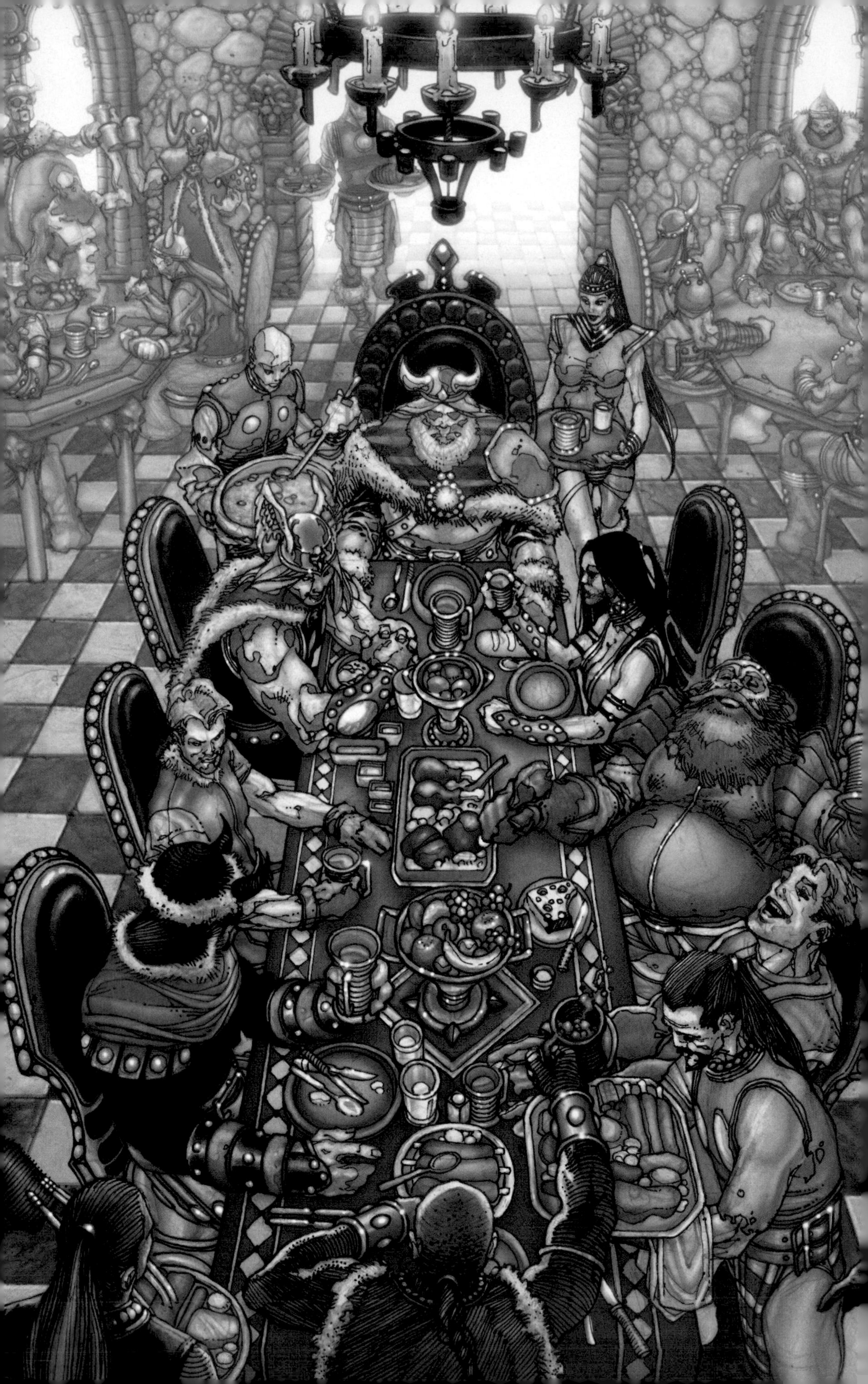

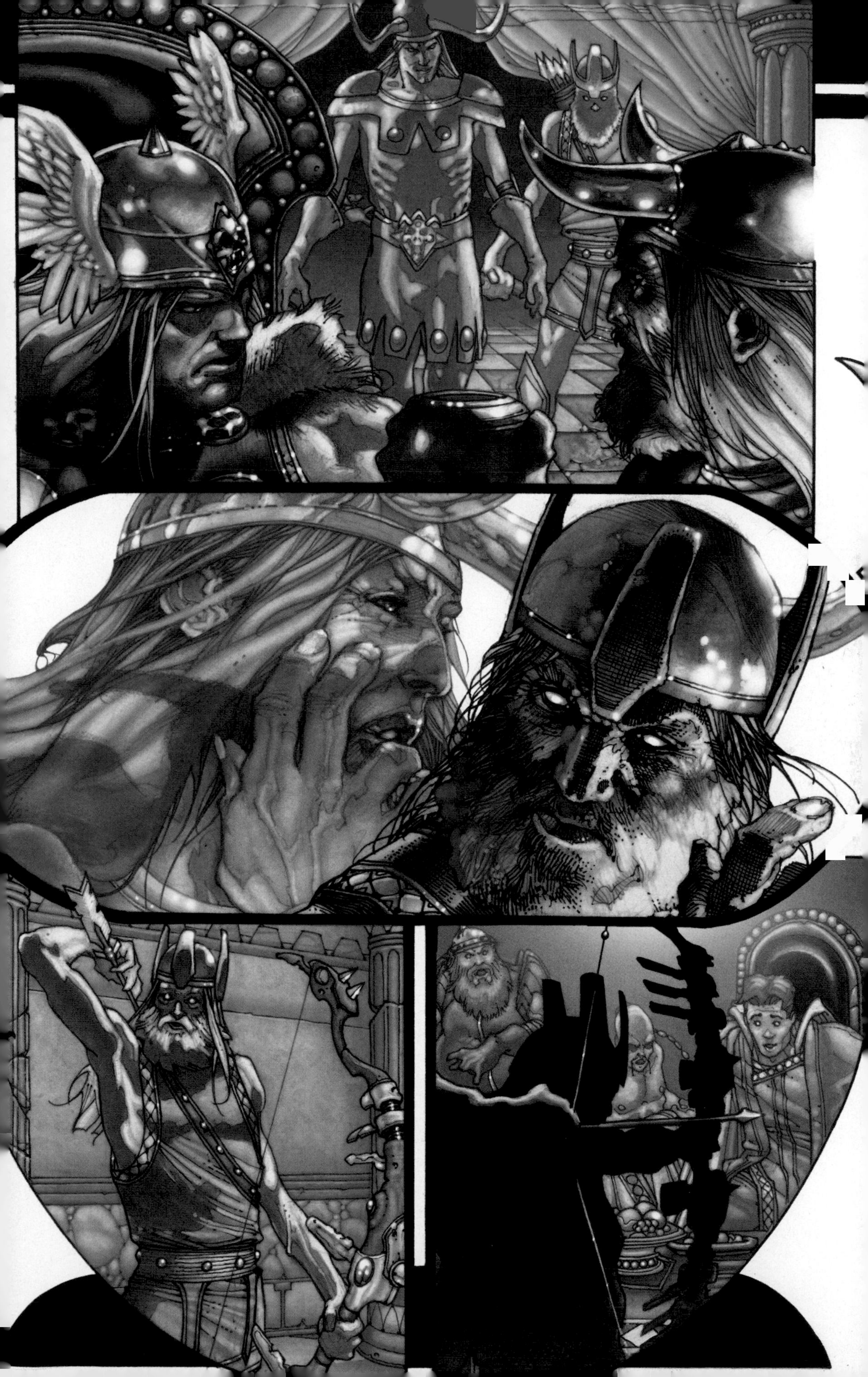

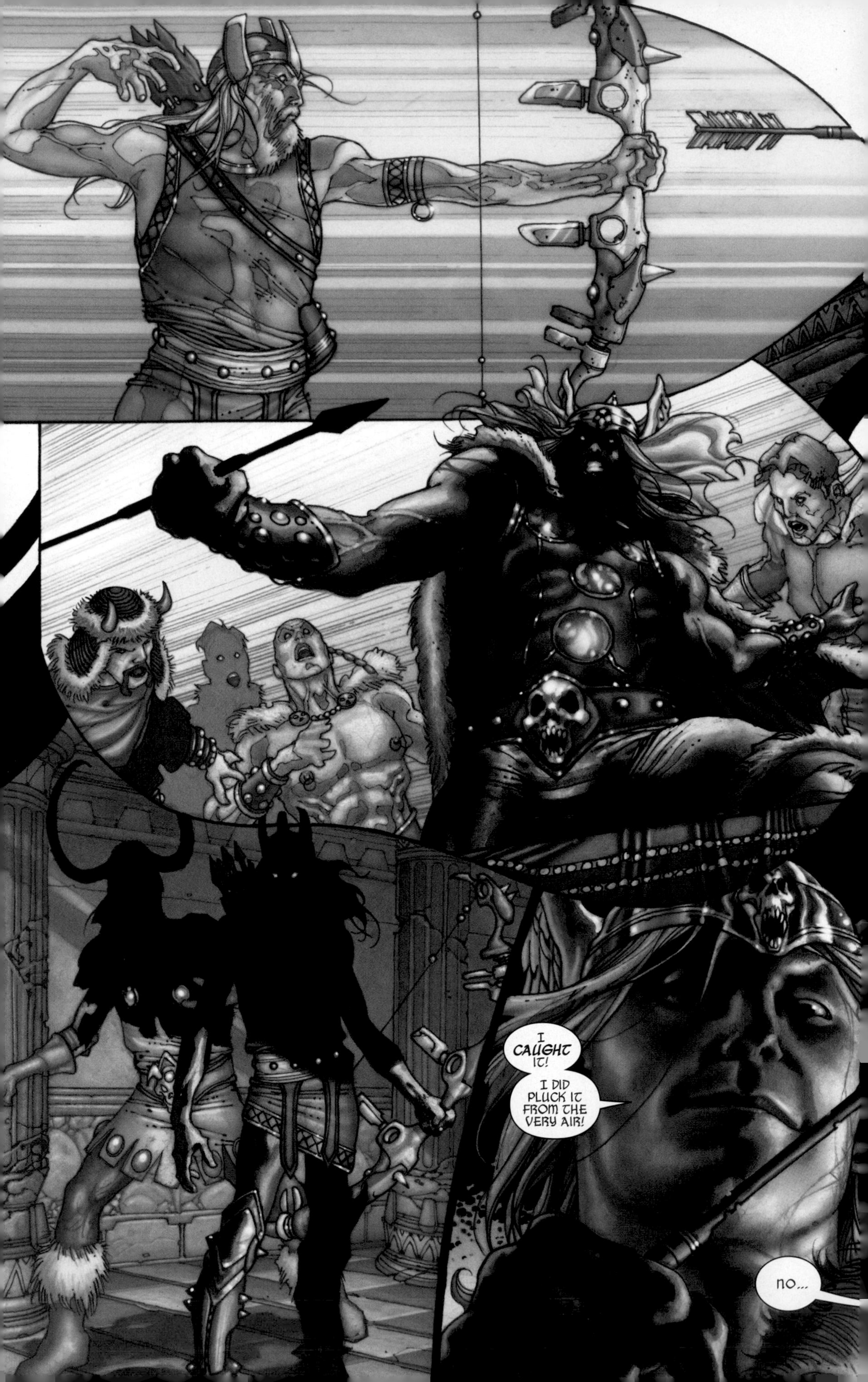
I CAUGHT IT!
I DID PLUCK IT FROM THE VERY AIR!
no...

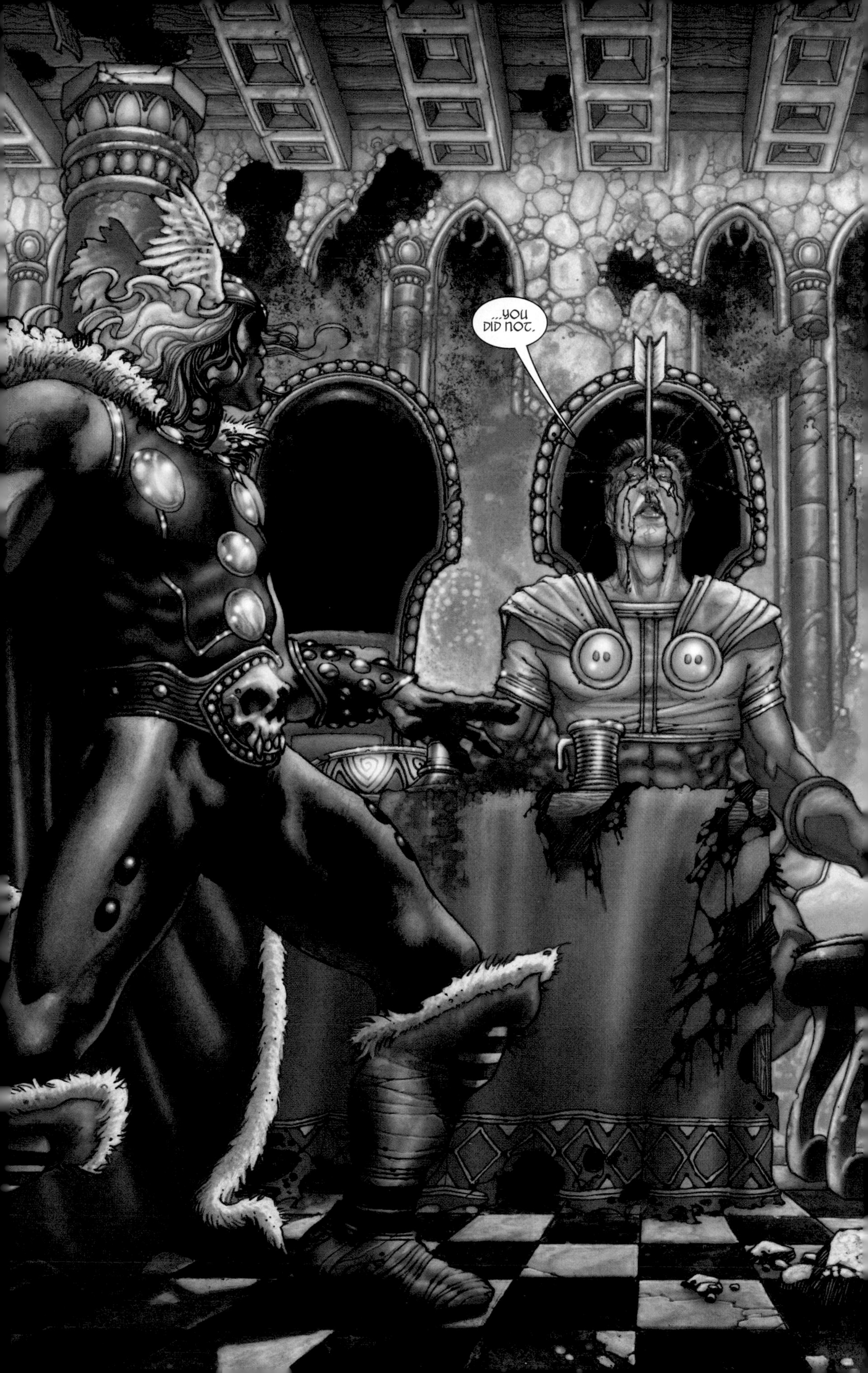
...YOU DID NOT.

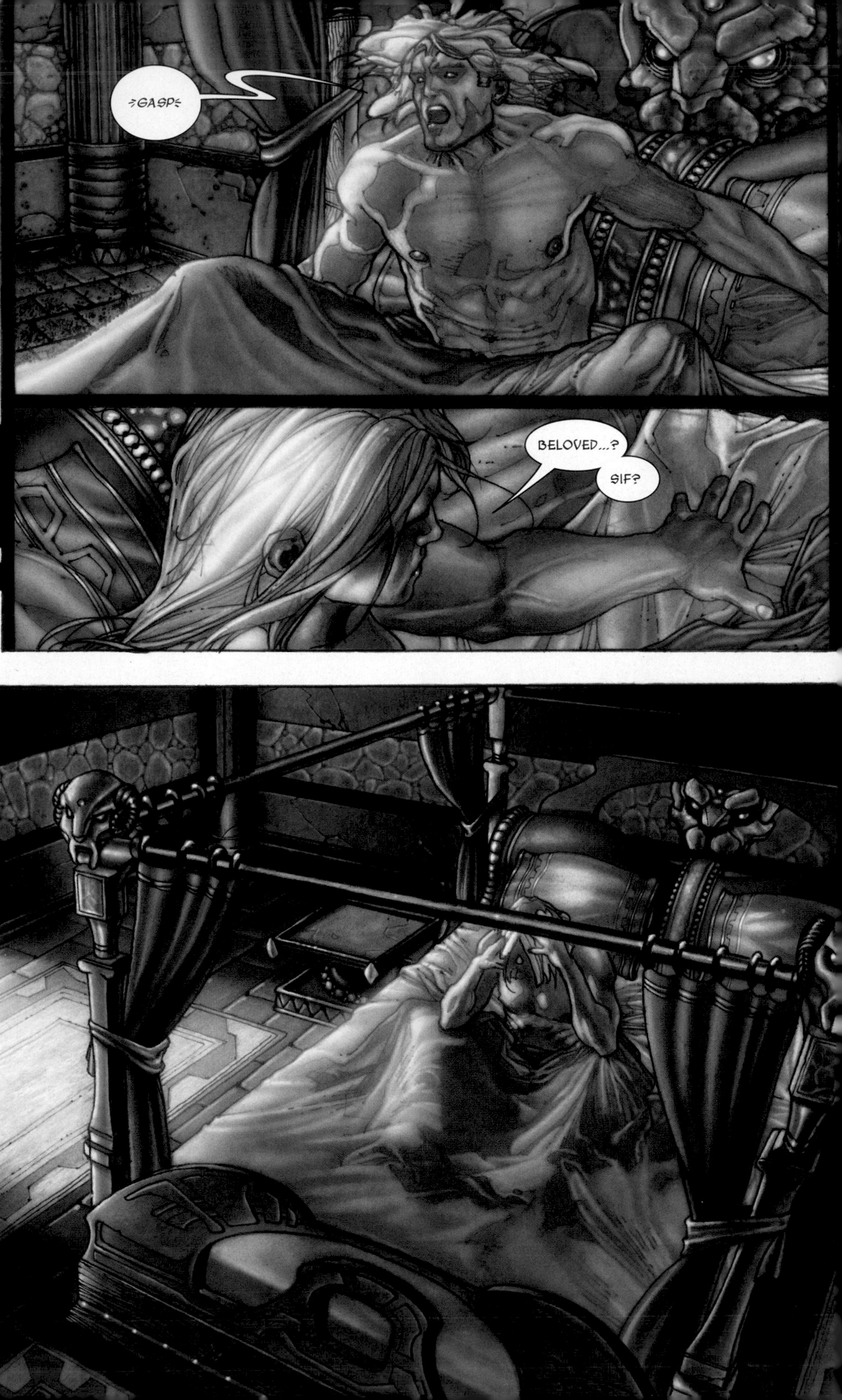

=GASP=
BELOVED...?
SIF?

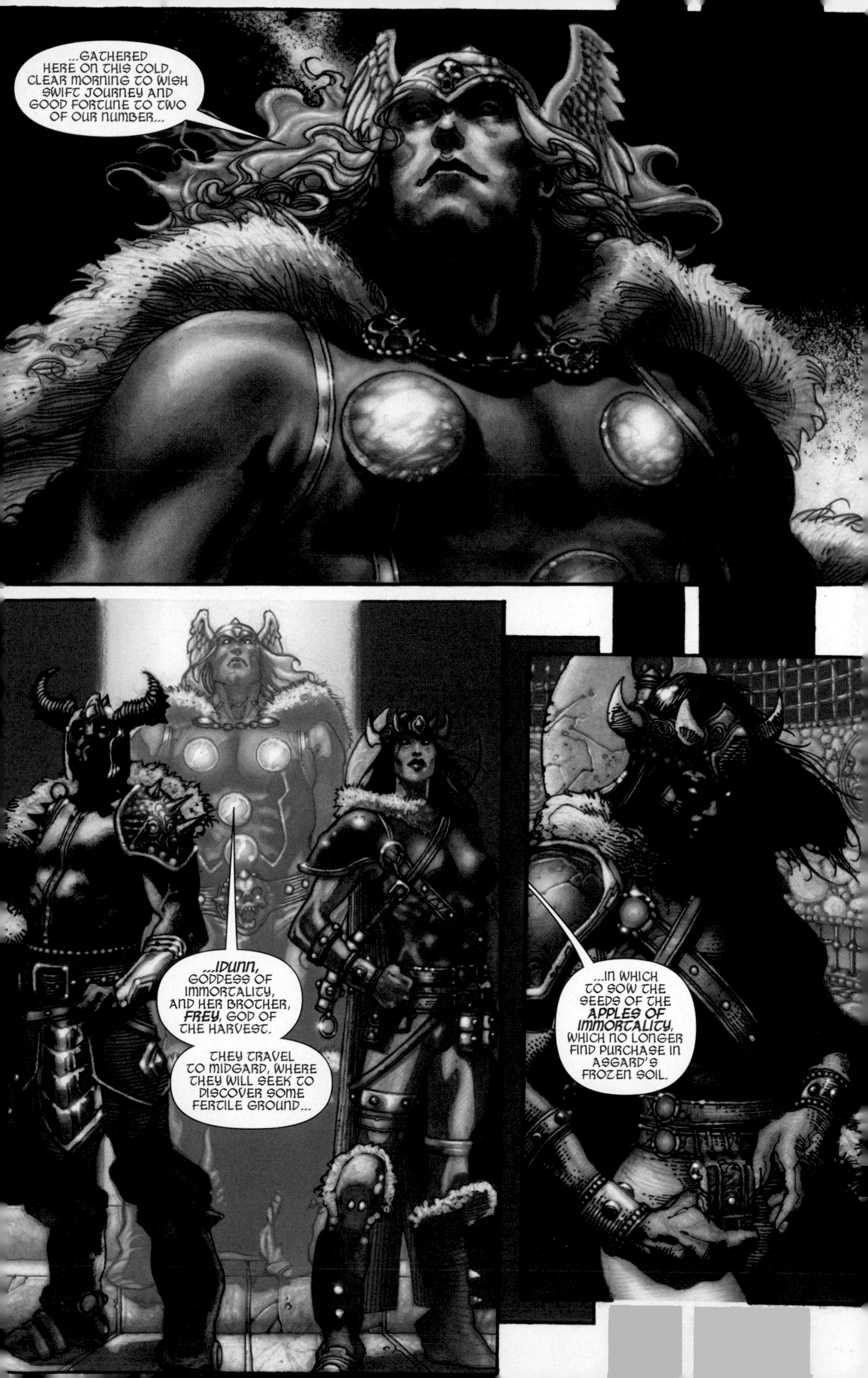
...GATHERED HERE ON THIS COLD, CLEAR MORNING TO WISH SWIFT JOURNEY AND GOOD FORTUNE TO TWO OF OUR NUMBER...
...IDUNN, GODDESS OF IMMORTALITY, AND HER BROTHER, FREY, GOD OF THE HARVEST.
THEY TRAVEL TO MIDGARD, WHERE THEY WILL SEEK TO DISCOVER SOME FERTILE GROUND...
...IN WHICH TO SOW THE SEEDS OF THE APPLES OF IMMORTALITY, WHICH NO LONGER FIND PURCHASE IN ASGARD'S FROZEN SOIL.

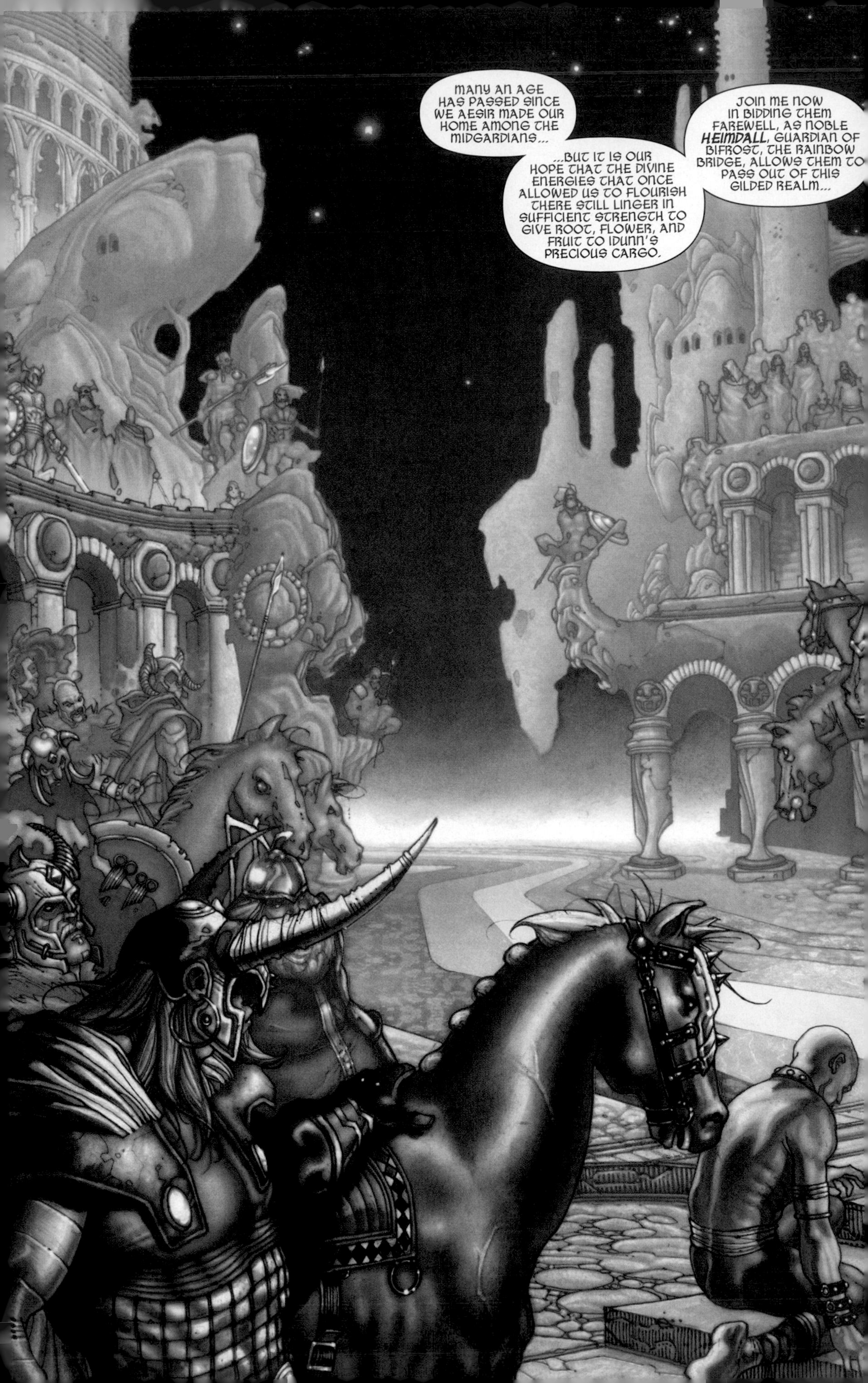
MANY AN AGE HAS PASSED SINCE WE AESIR MADE OUR HOME AMONG THE MIDGARDIANS...
...BUT IT IS OUR HOPE THAT THE DIVINE ENERGIES THAT ONCE ALLOWED US TO FLOURISH THERE STILL LINGER IN SUFFICIENT STRENGTH TO GIVE ROOT, FLOWER, AND FRUIT TO IDUNN'S PRECIOUS CARGO.
JOIN ME NOW IN BIDDING THEM FAREWELL, AS NOBLE HEIMDALL, GUARDIAN OF BIFROST, THE RAINBOW BRIDGE, ALLOWS THEM TO PASS OUT OF THIS GILDED REALM...

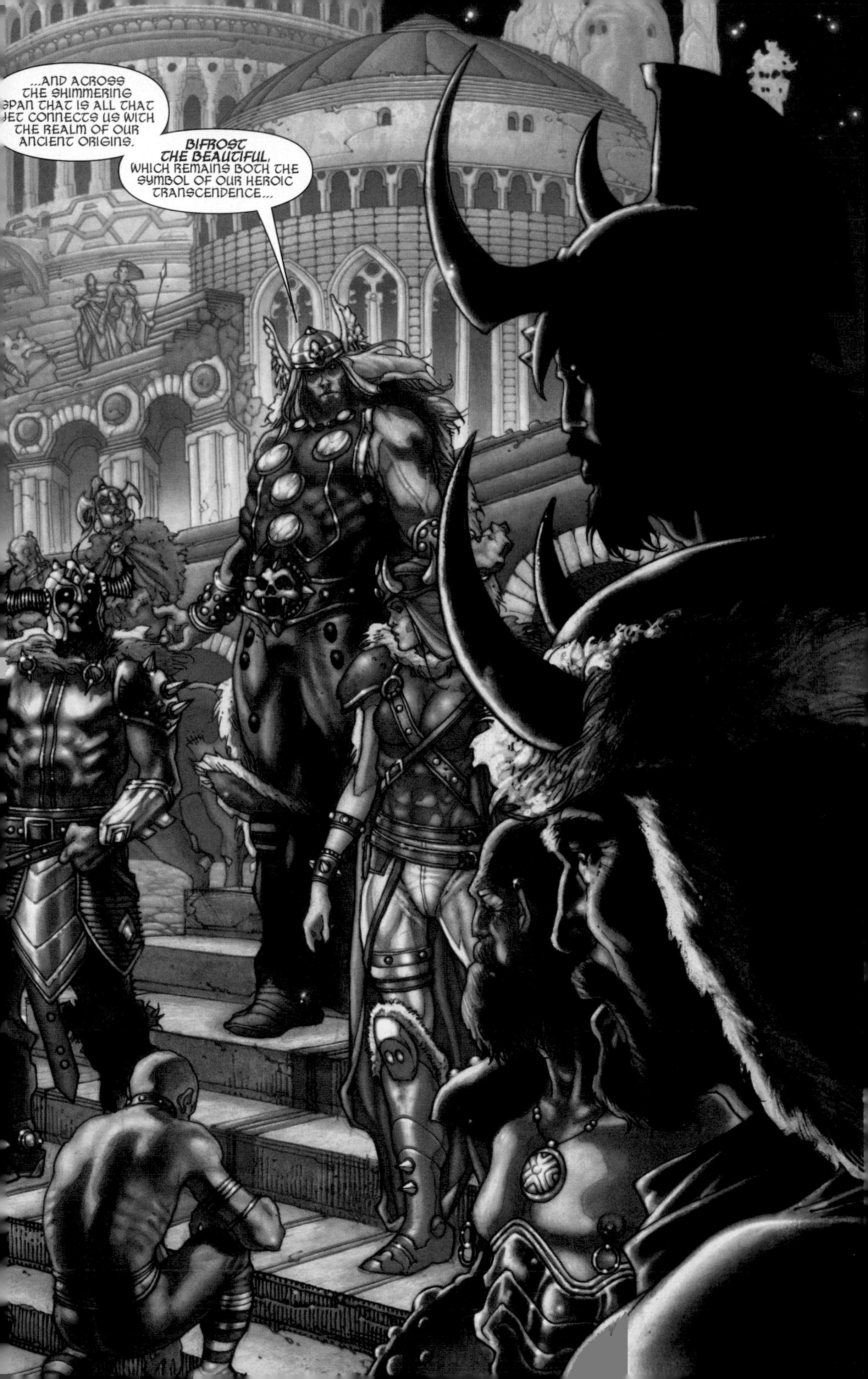
...AND ACROSS THE SHIMMERING SPAN THAT IS ALL THAT YET CONNECTS US WITH THE REALM OF OUR ANCIENT ORIGINS.
BIFROST THE BEAUTIFUL, WHICH REMAINS BOTH THE SYMBOL OF OUR HEROIC TRANSCENDENCE...

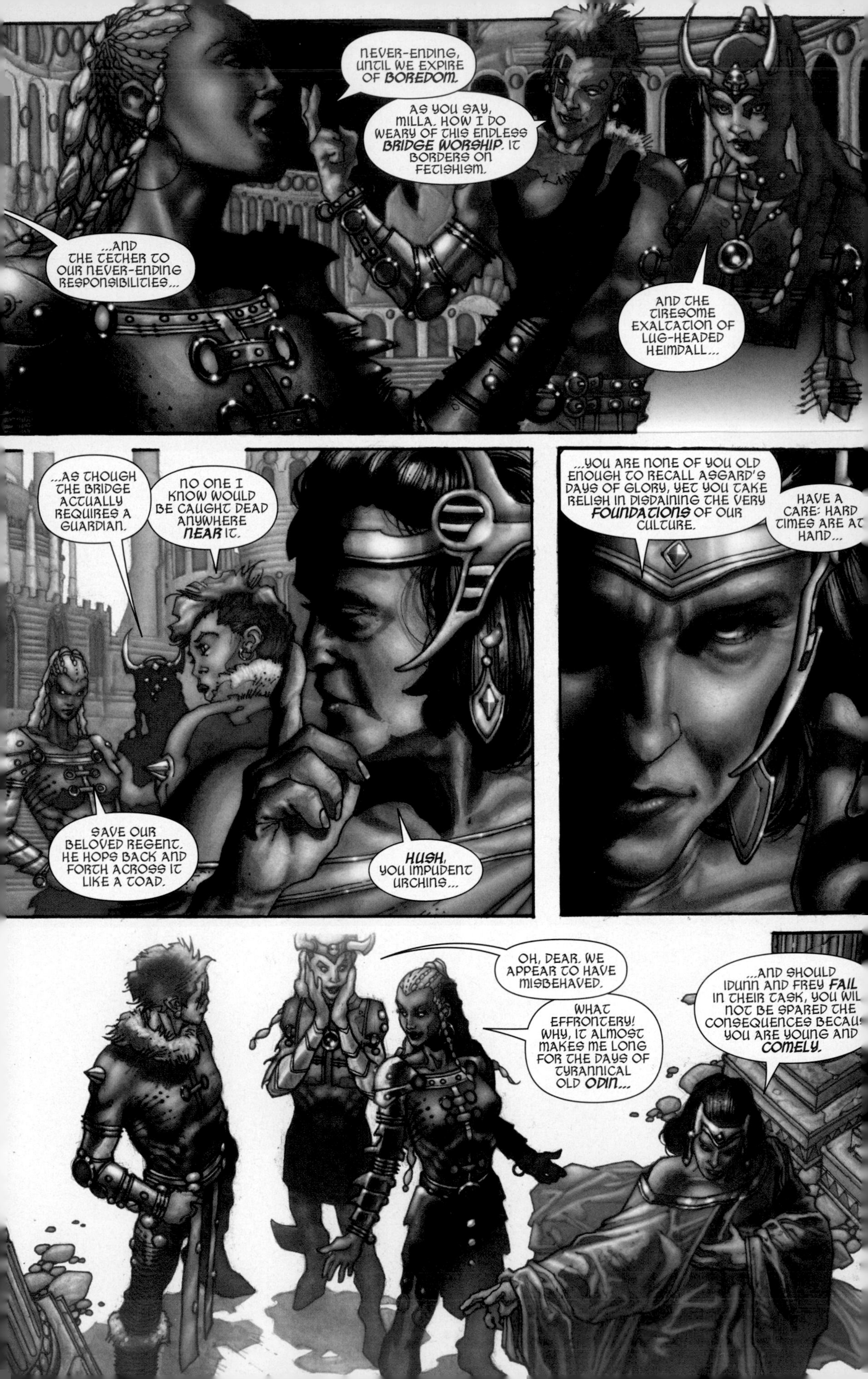

NEVER-ENDING, UNTIL WE EXPIRE OF BOREDOM.
AS YOU SAY, MILLA. HOW I DO WEARY OF THIS ENDLESS BRIDGE WORSHIP. IT BORDERS ON FETISHISM.
...AND THE TETHER TO OUR NEVER-ENDING RESPONSIBILITIES...
AND THE TIRESOME EXALTATION OF LUG-HEADED HEIMDALL...
...AS THOUGH THE BRIDGE ACTUALLY REQUIRES A GUARDIAN.
NO ONE I KNOW WOULD BE CAUGHT DEAD ANYWHERE NEAR IT.
SAVE OUR BELOVED REGENT. HE HOPS BACK AND FORTH ACROSS IT LIKE A TOAD.
HUSH, YOU IMPUDENT URCHINS...
...YOU ARE NONE OF YOU OLD ENOUGH TO RECALL ASGARD'S DAYS OF GLORY, YET YOU TAKE RELISH IN DISDAINING THE VERY FOUNDATIONS OF OUR CULTURE.
HAVE A CARE: HARD TIMES ARE AT HAND...
OH, DEAR. WE APPEAR TO HAVE MISBEHAVED.
WHAT EFFRONTERY! WHY, IT ALMOST MAKES ME LONG FOR THE DAYS OF TYRANNICAL OLD ODIN...
...AND SHOULD IDUNN AND FREY FAIL IN THEIR TASK, YOU WIL NOT BE SPARED THE CONSEQUENCES BECAU YOU ARE YOUNG AND COMELY.

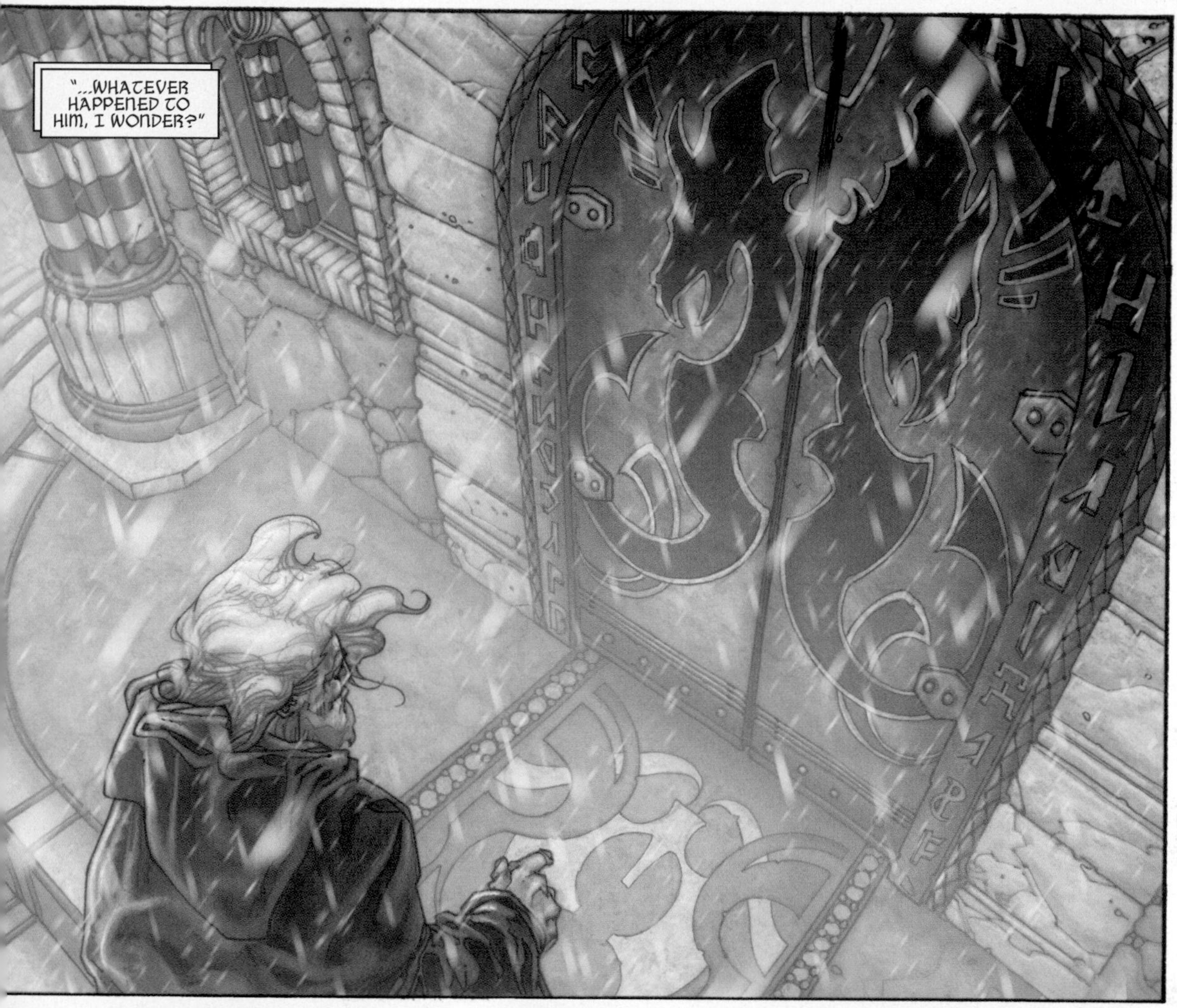
"...WHATEVER HAPPENED TO HIM, I WONDER?"

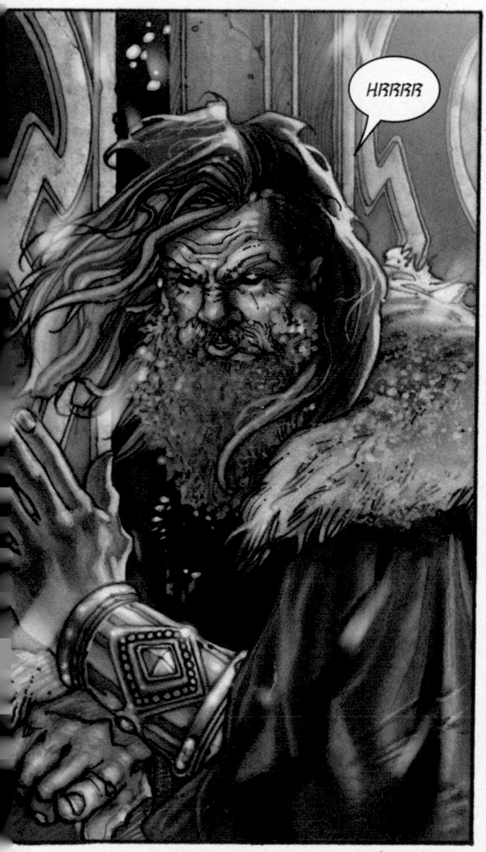
HRRRR

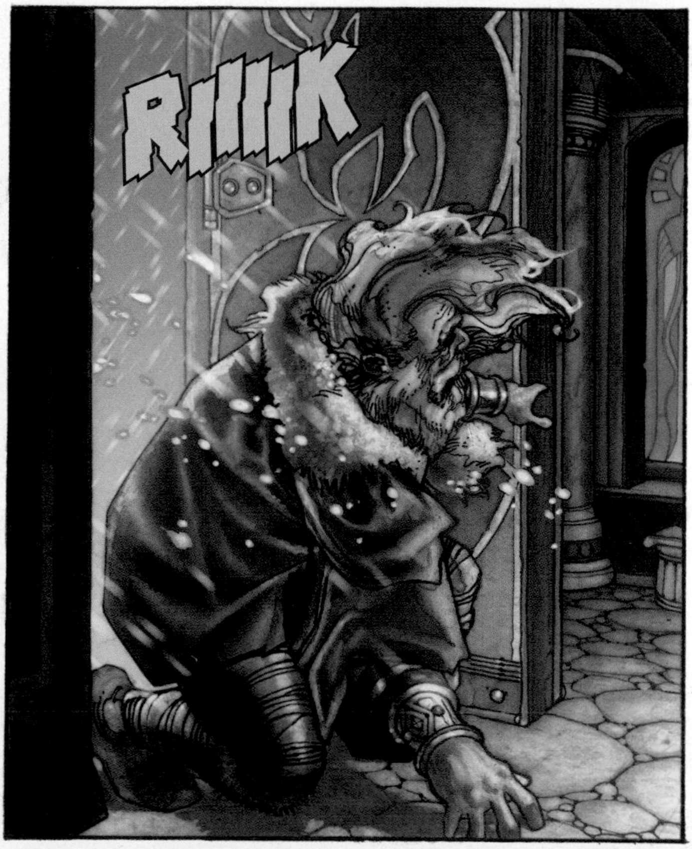
RIIIIK

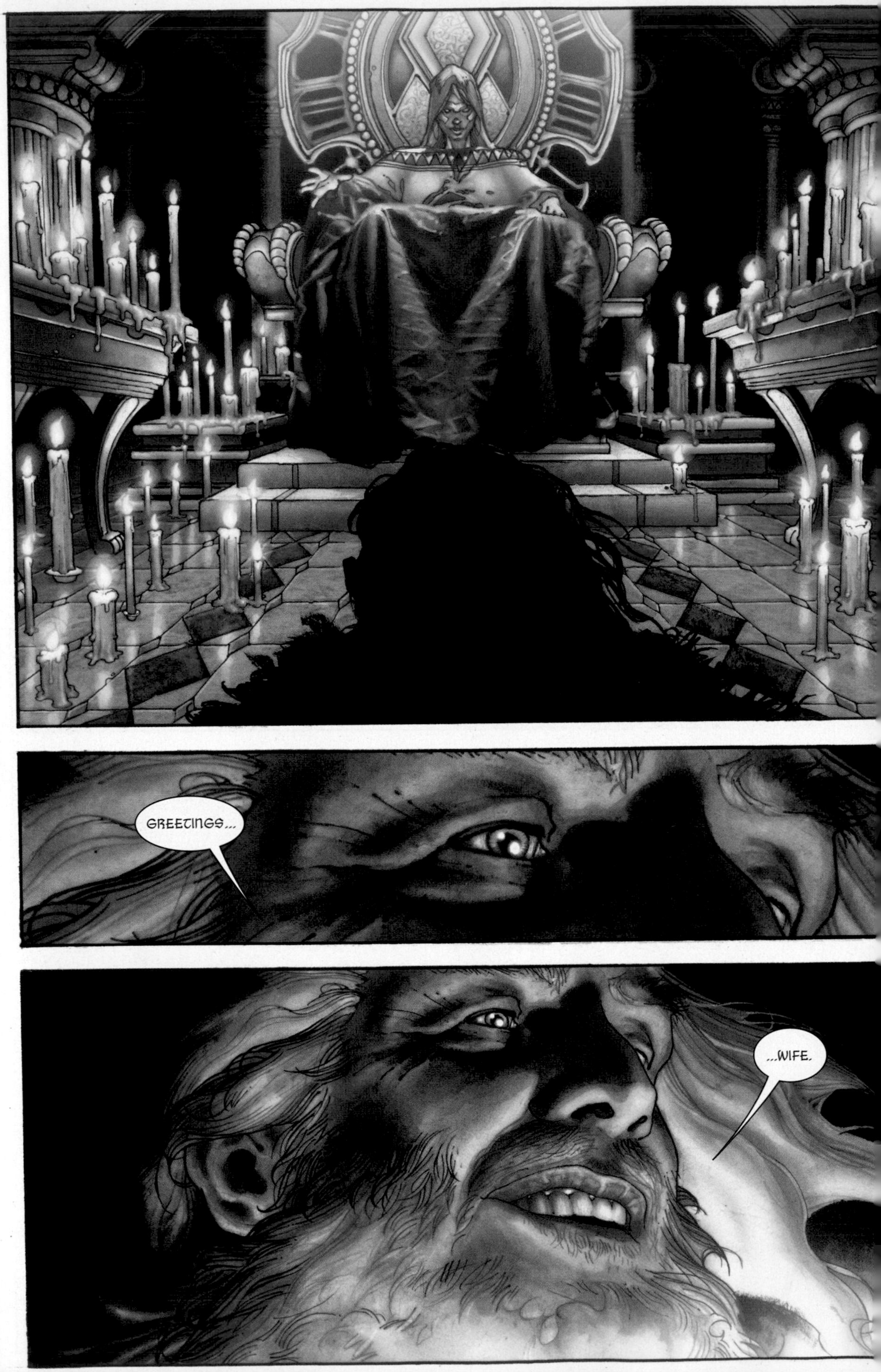
GREETINGS...
...WIFE.

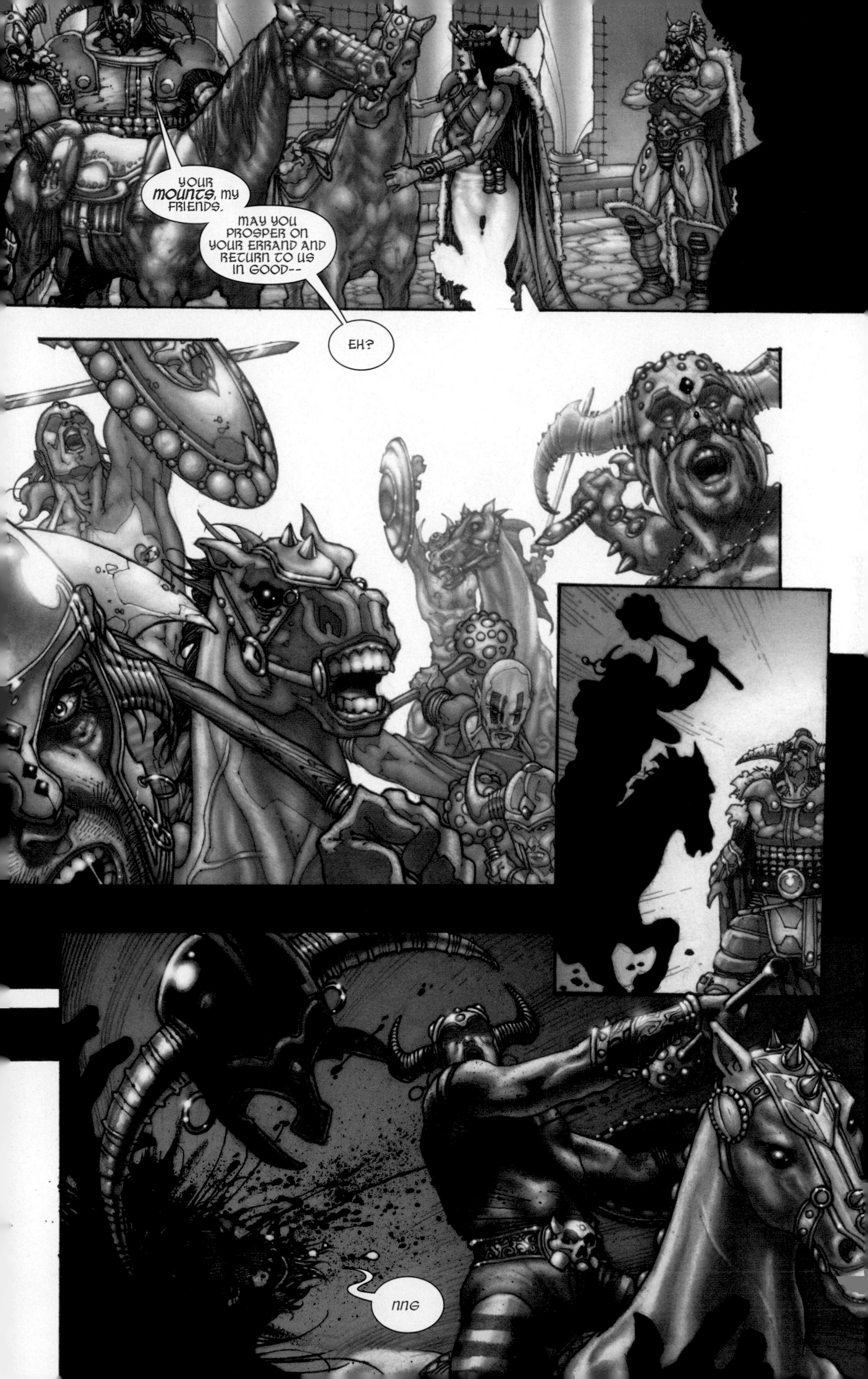
YOUR *MOUNTS*, MY FRIENDS.
MAY YOU PROSPER ON YOUR ERRAND AND RETURN TO US IN GOOD--
EH?
NNG

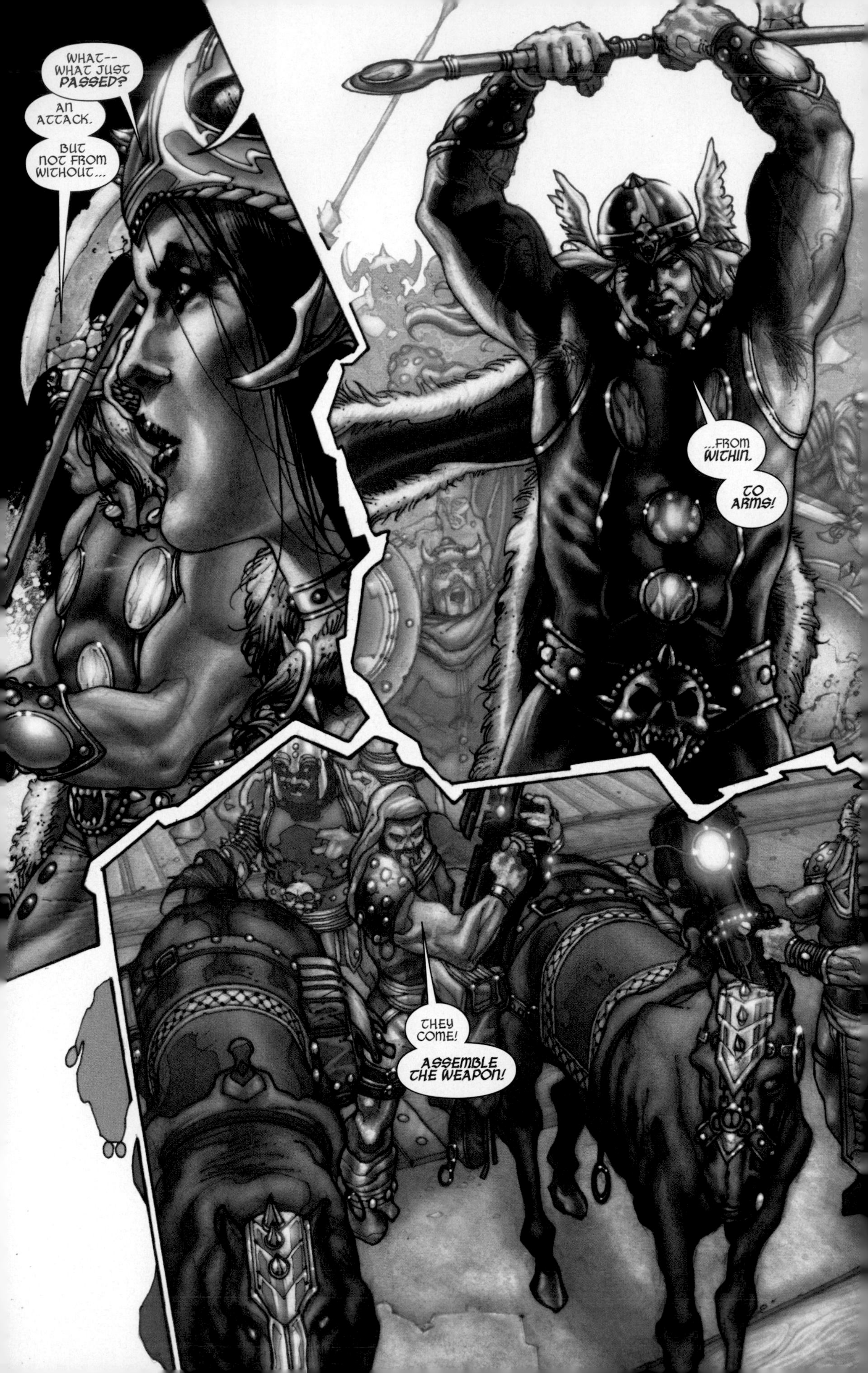
WHAT-- WHAT JUST PASSED?
AN ATTACK.
BUT NOT FROM WITHOUT...
...FROM WITHIN.
TO ARMS!
THEY COME!
ASSEMBLE THE WEAPON!

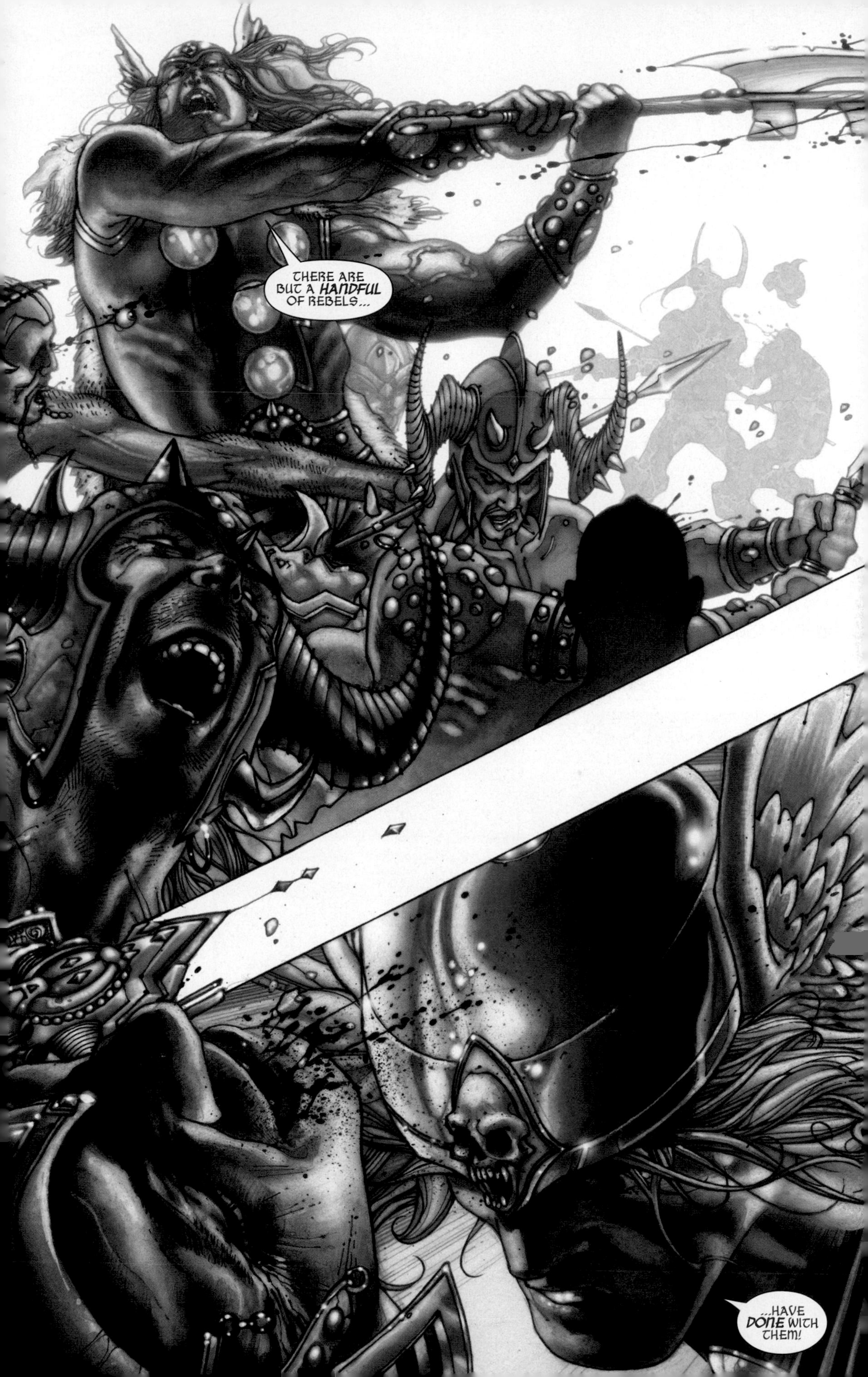
THERE ARE BUT A HANDFUL OF REBELS...
...HAVE DONE WITH THEM!

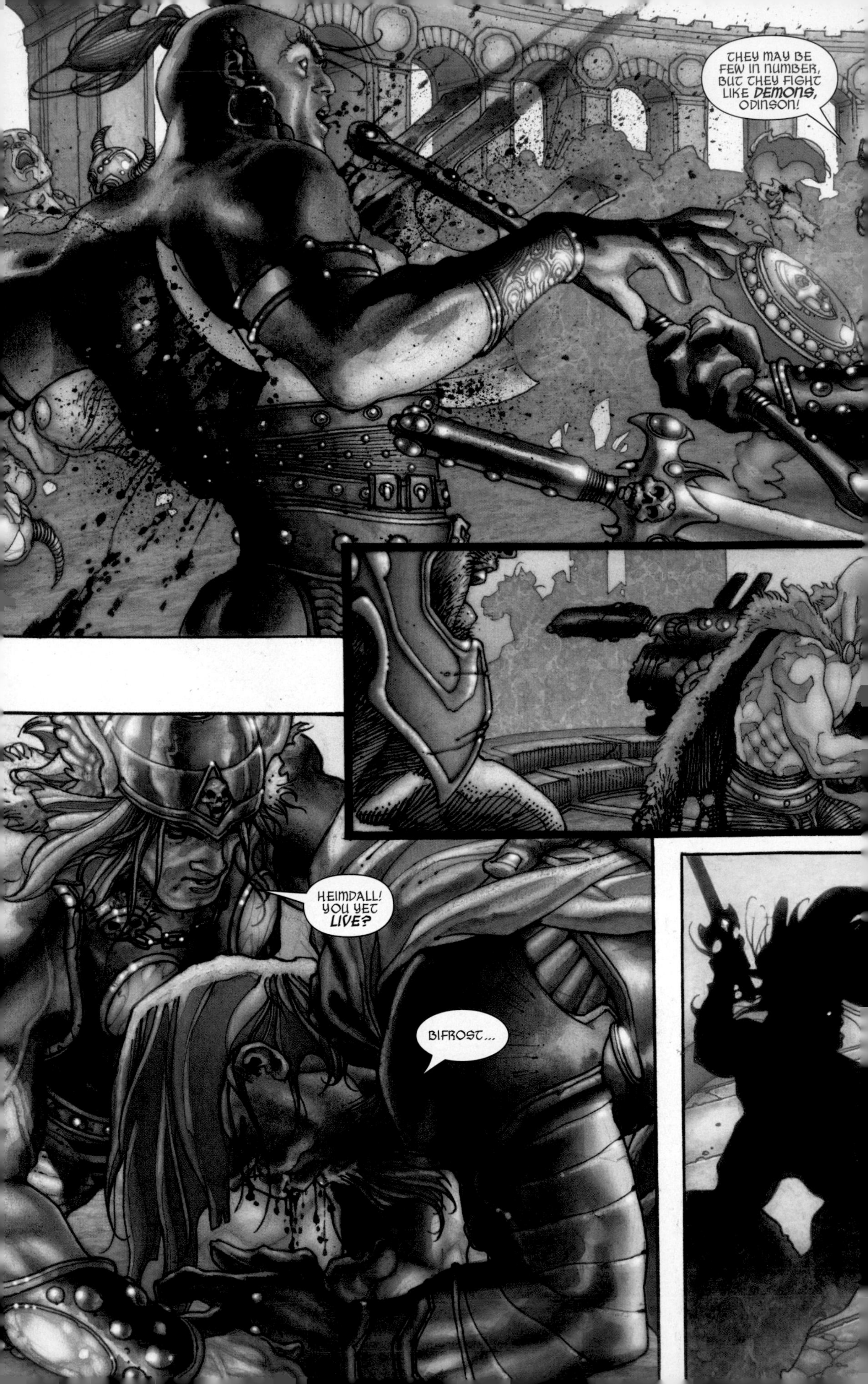
THEY MAY BE FEW IN NUMBER, BUT THEY FIGHT LIKE DEMONS, ODINSON!
HEIMDALL! YOU YET LIVE?
BIFROST...

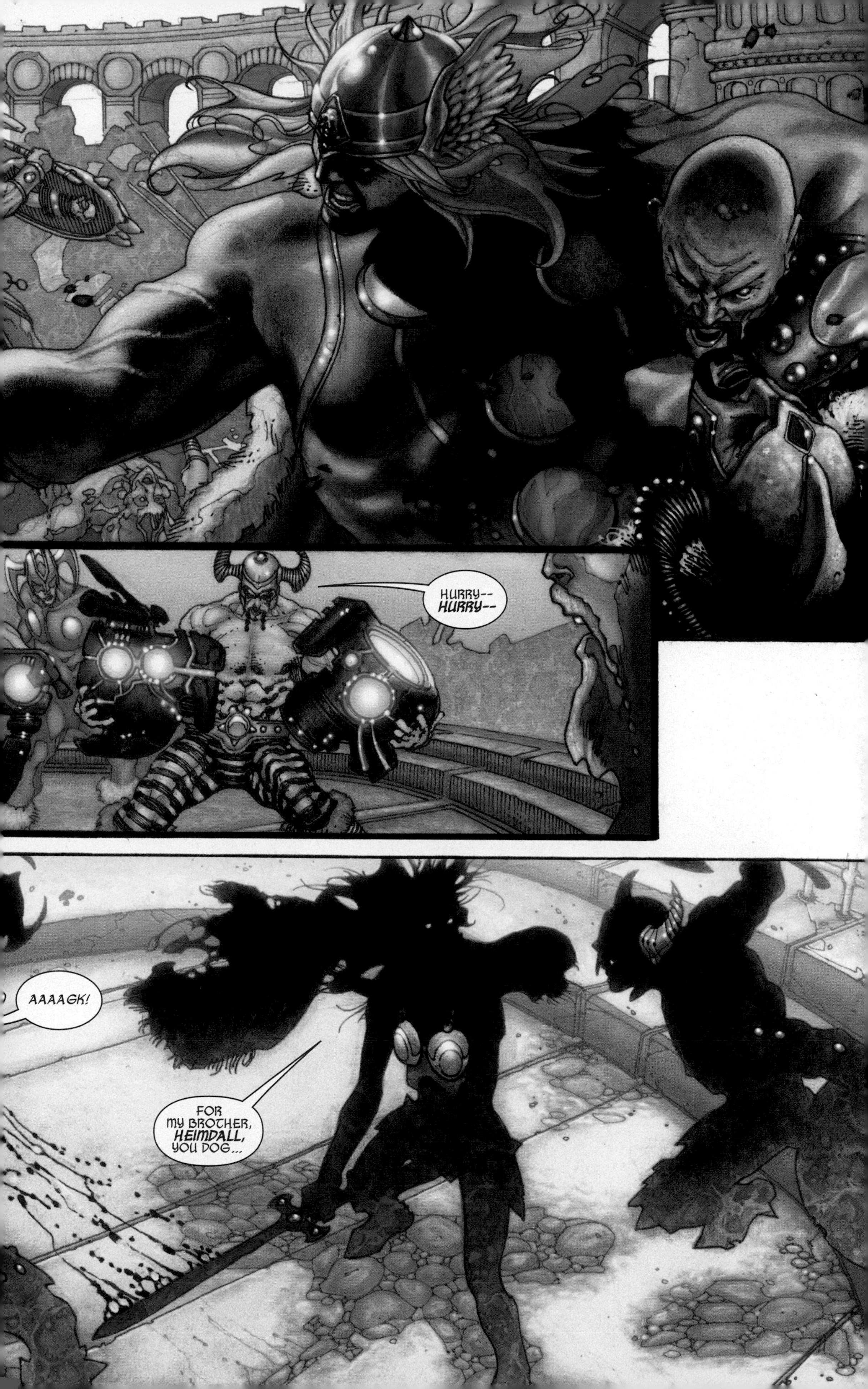
HURRY--
HURRY--
AAAAGK!
FOR MY BROTHER, HEIMDALL, YOU DOG...

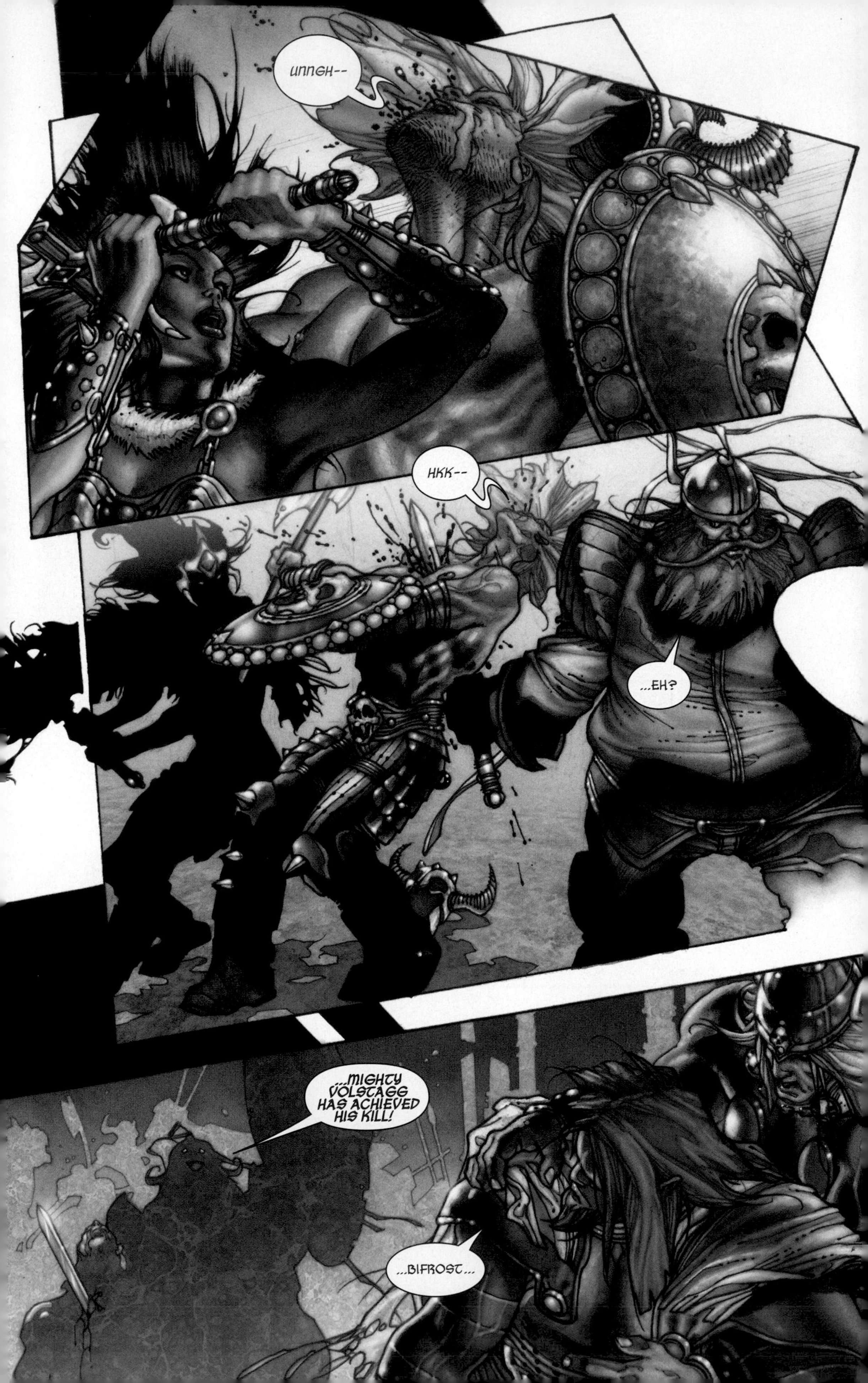
UNNGH--
HKK--
...EH?
...MIGHTY VOLSTAGG HAS ACHIEVED HIS KILL!
...BIFROST...

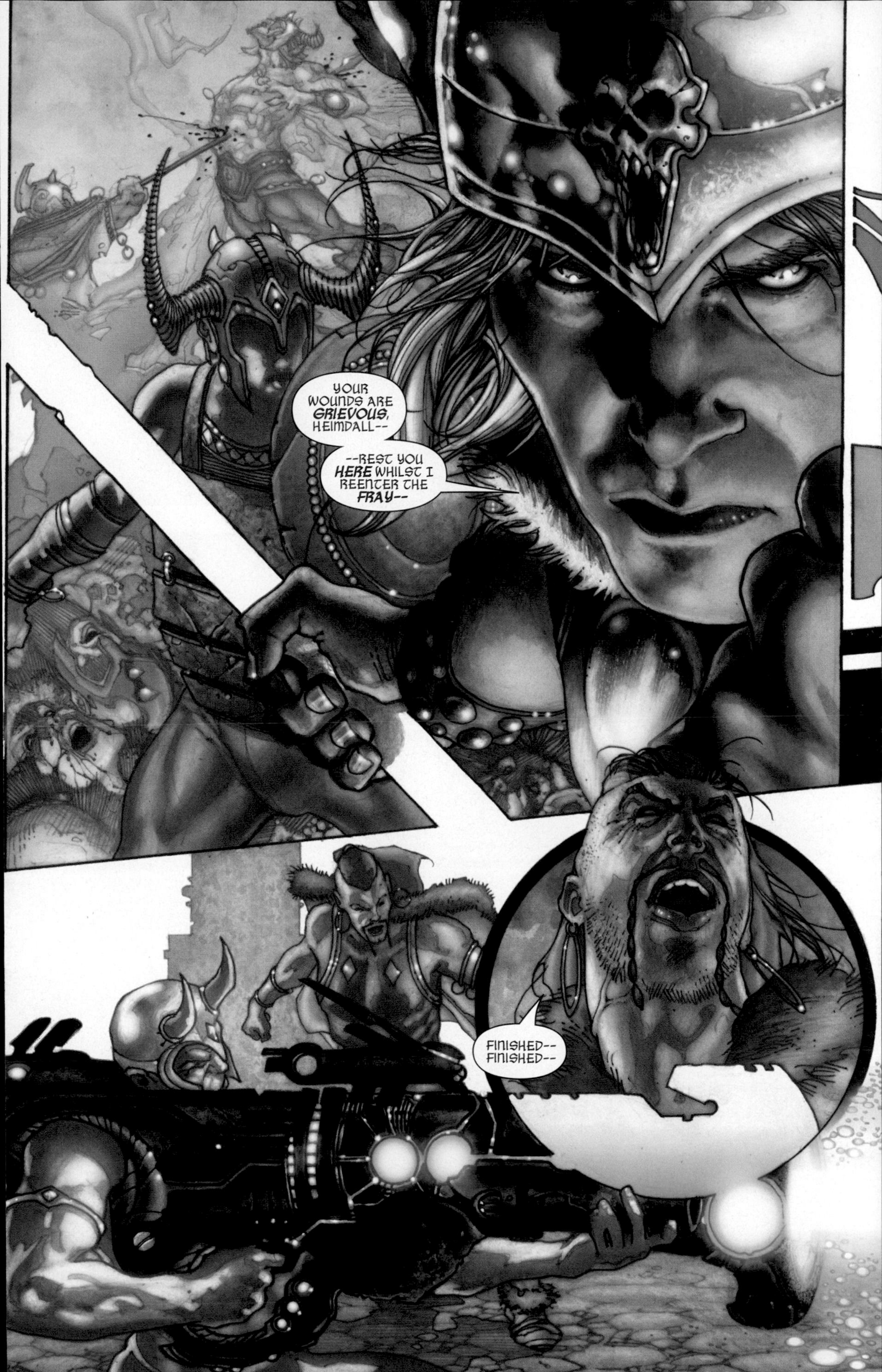
YOUR WOUNDS ARE GRIEVOUS, HEIMDALL--
--REST YOU HERE WHILST I REENTER THE FRAY--
FINISHED-- FINISHED--

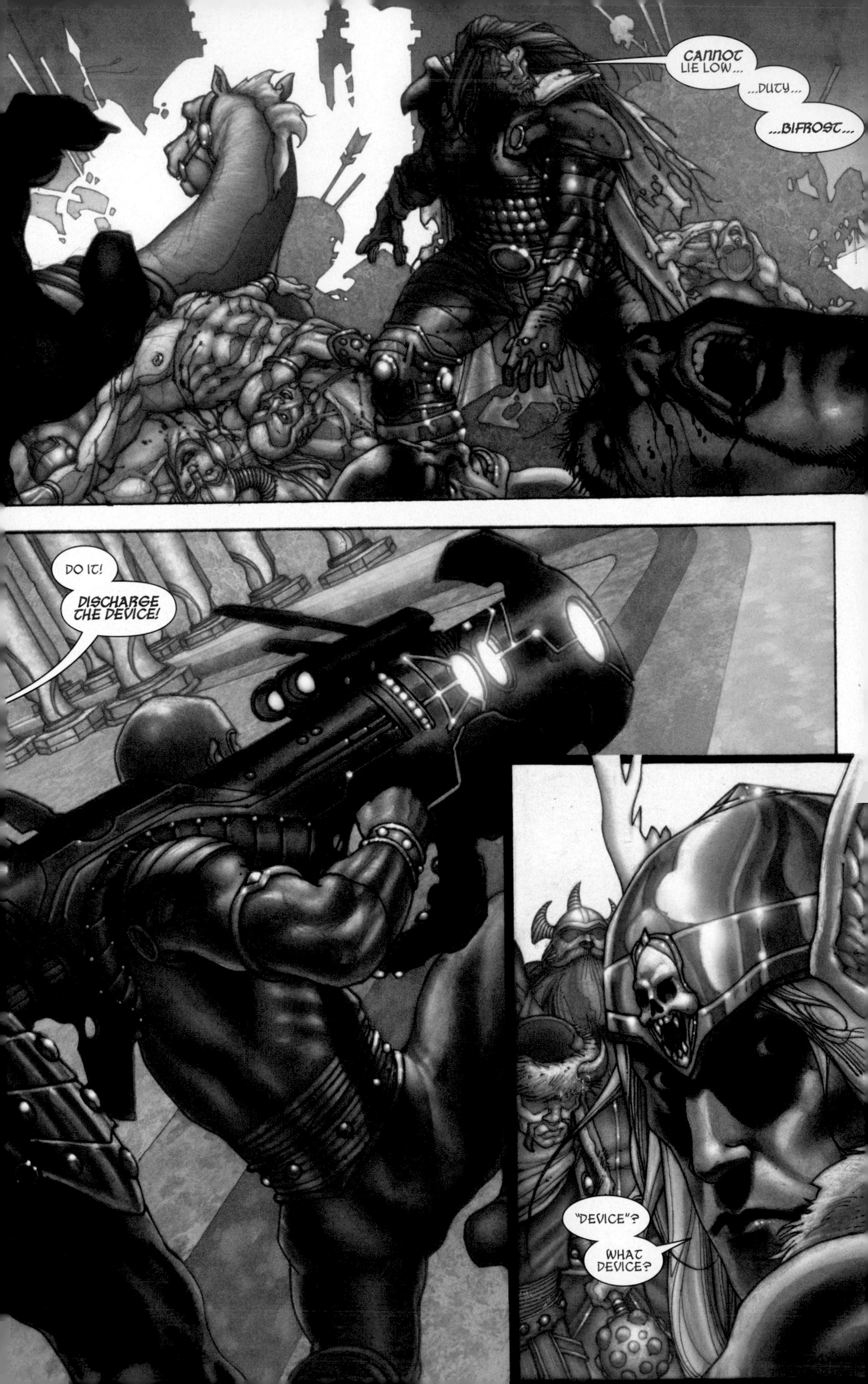
CANNOT LIE LOW...
...DUTY...
...BIFROST...
DO IT!
DISCHARGE THE DEVICE!
"DEVICE"?
WHAT DEVICE?

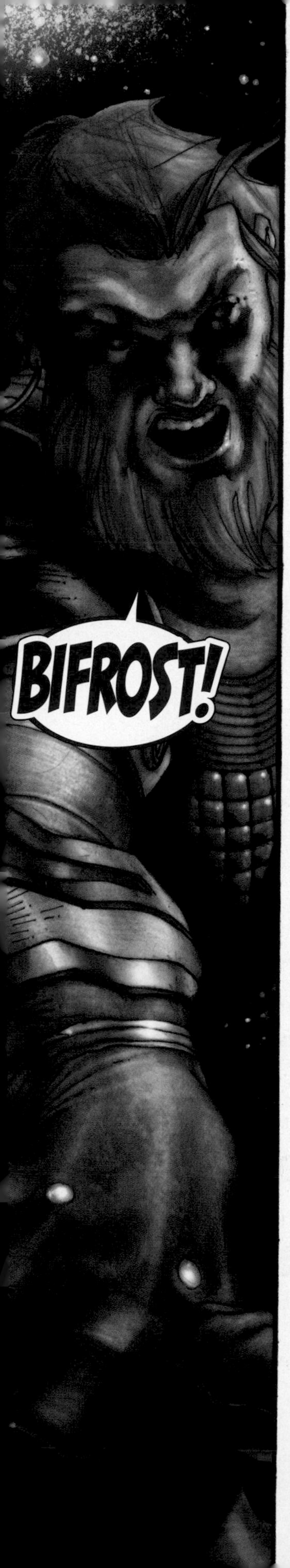
BIFROST!

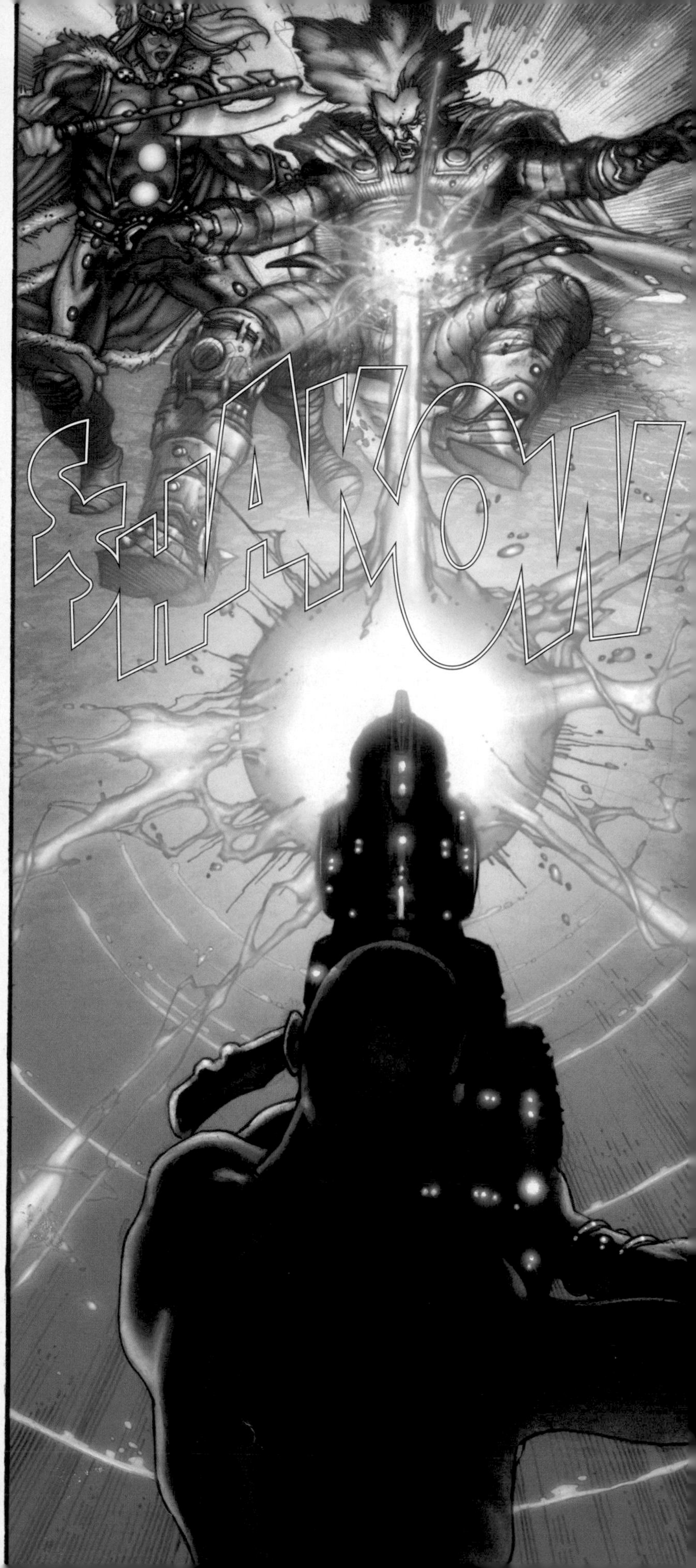
SHAKOW

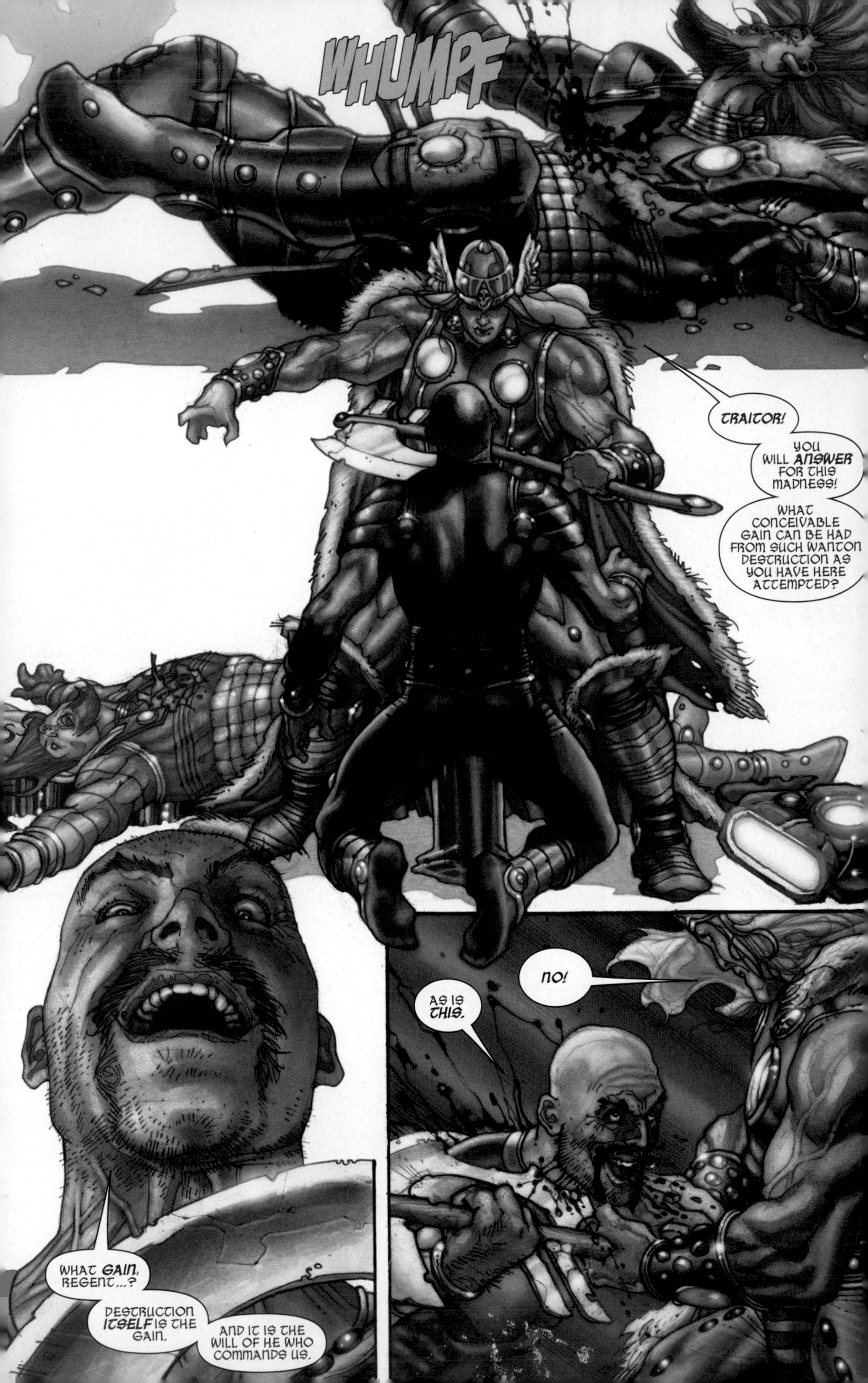
WHUMPF
TRAITOR!
YOU WILL ANSWER FOR THIS MADNESS!
WHAT CONCEIVABLE GAIN CAN BE HAD FROM SUCH WANTON DESTRUCTION AS YOU HAVE HERE ATTEMPTED?
WHAT GAIN, REGENT...?
DESTRUCTION ITSELF IS THE GAIN.
AND IT IS THE WILL OF HE WHO COMMANDS US.
NO!
AS IS THIS.

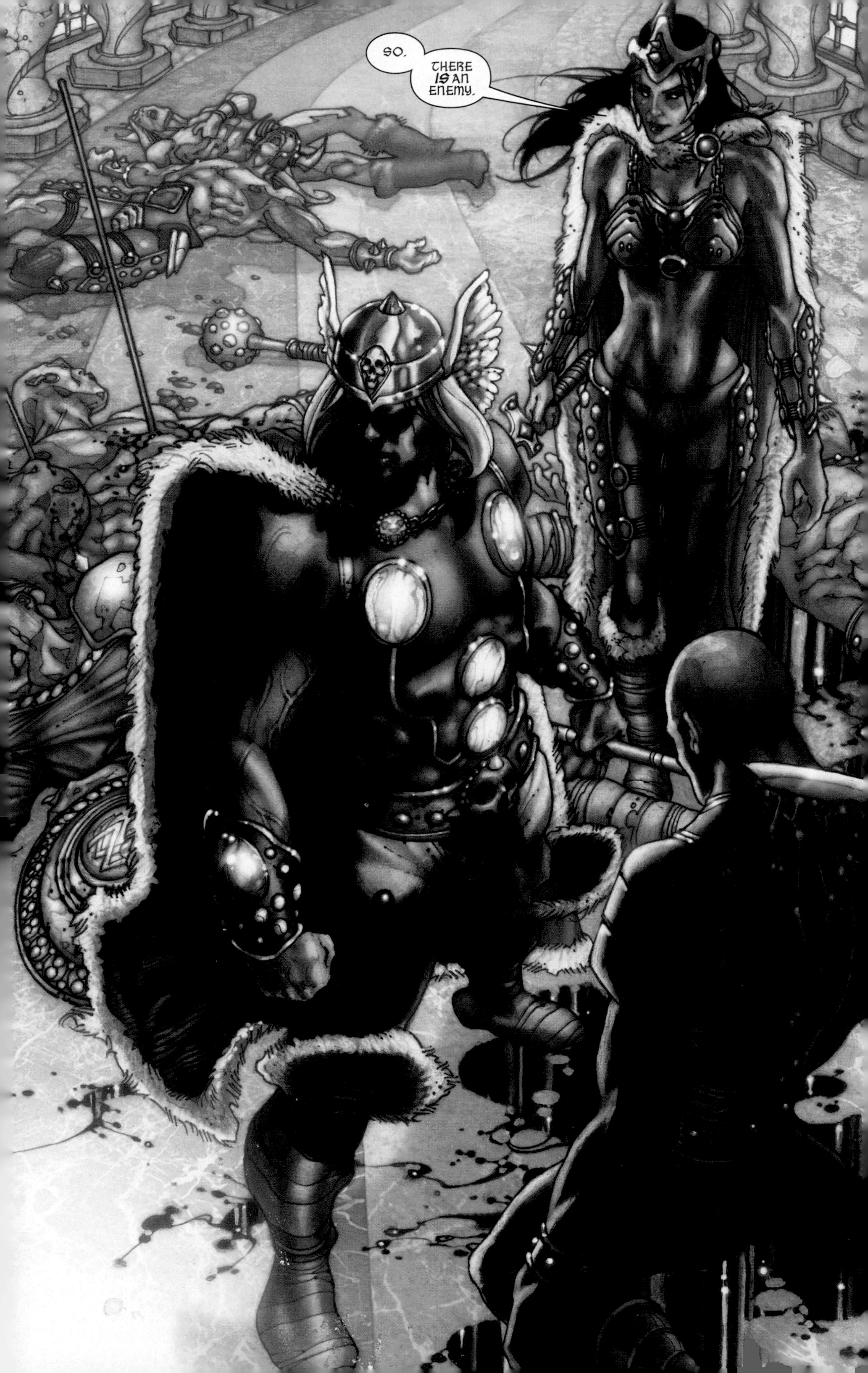
SO.
THERE IS AN ENEMY.

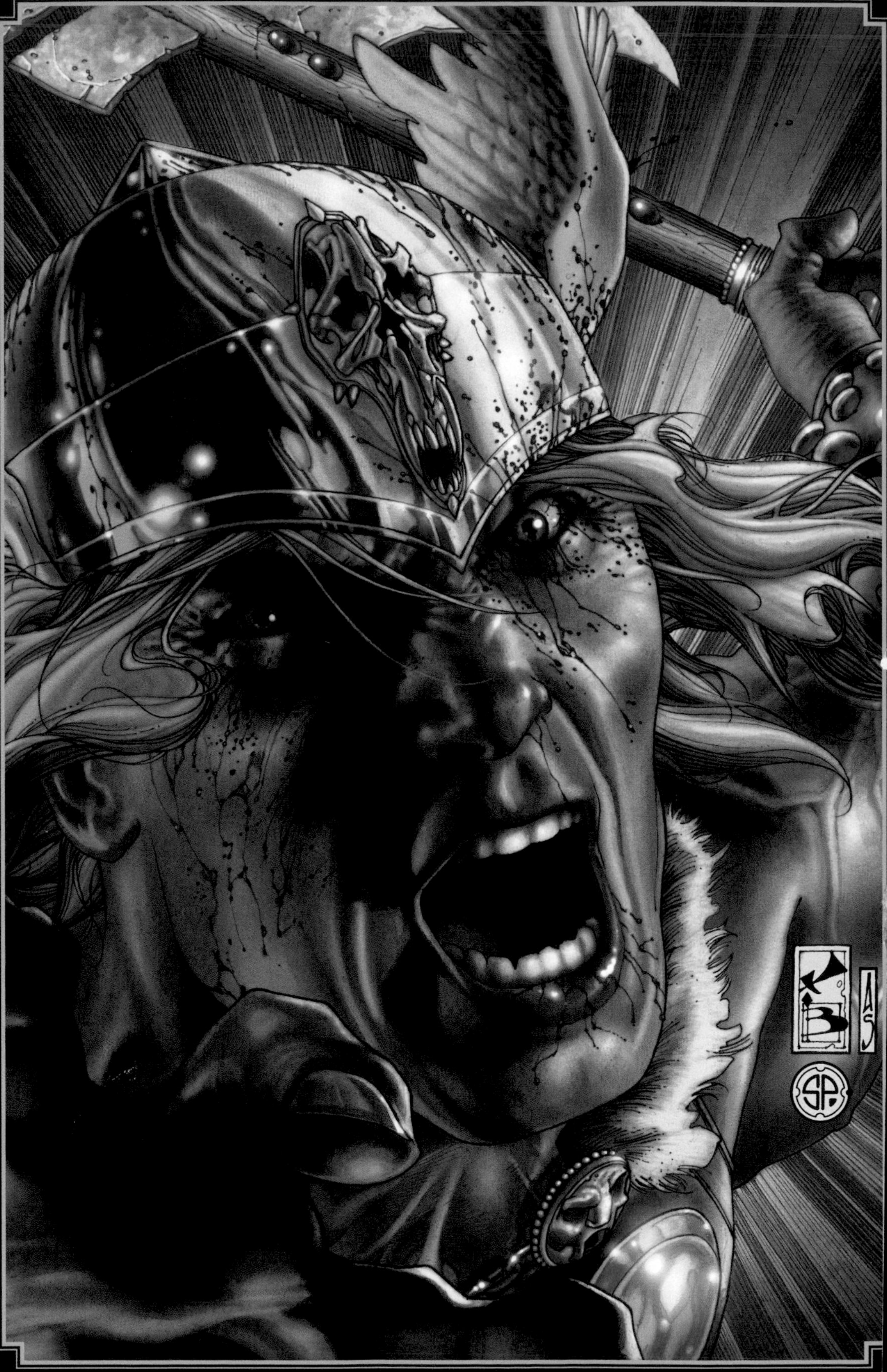

Thor: For Asgard 3

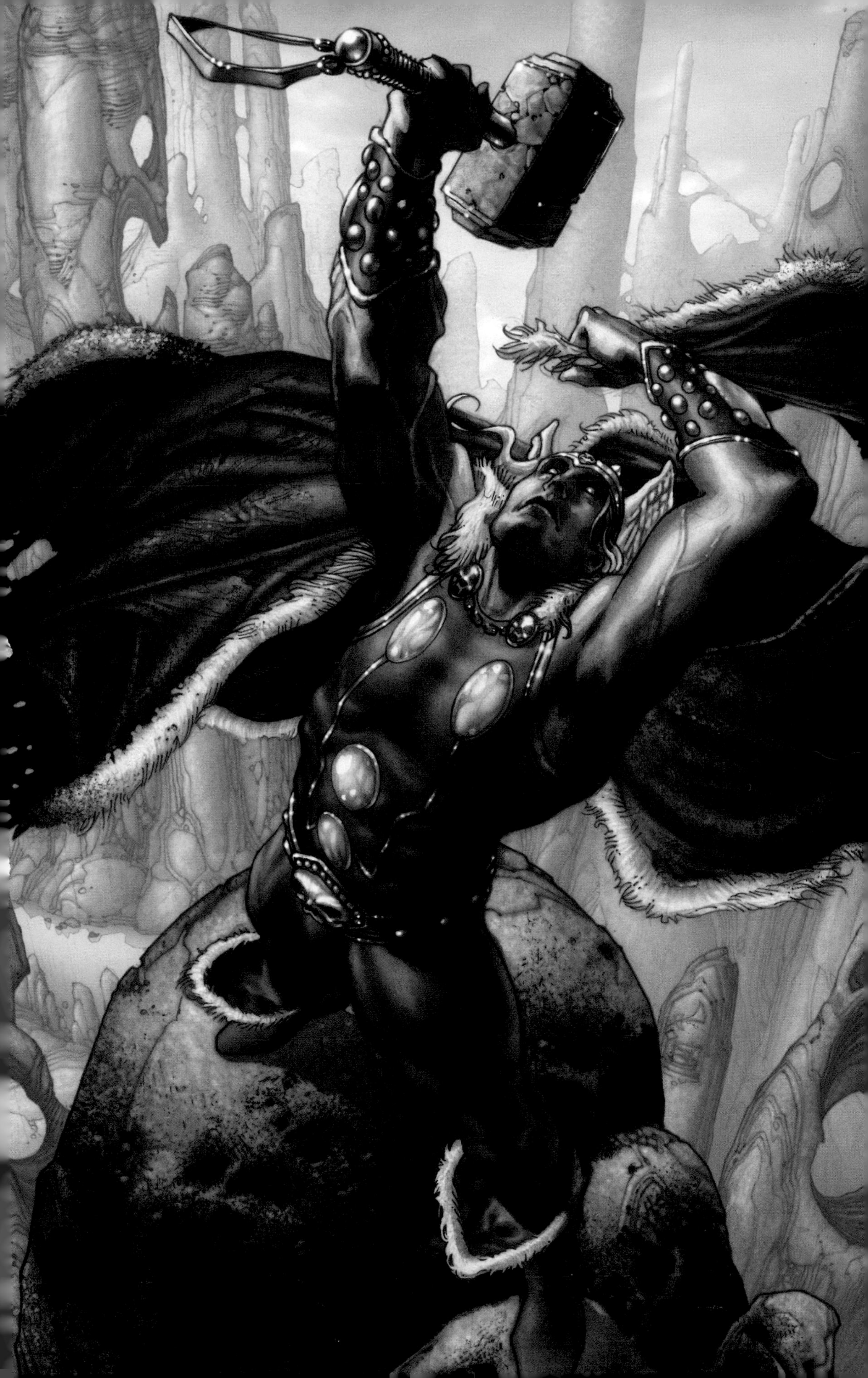

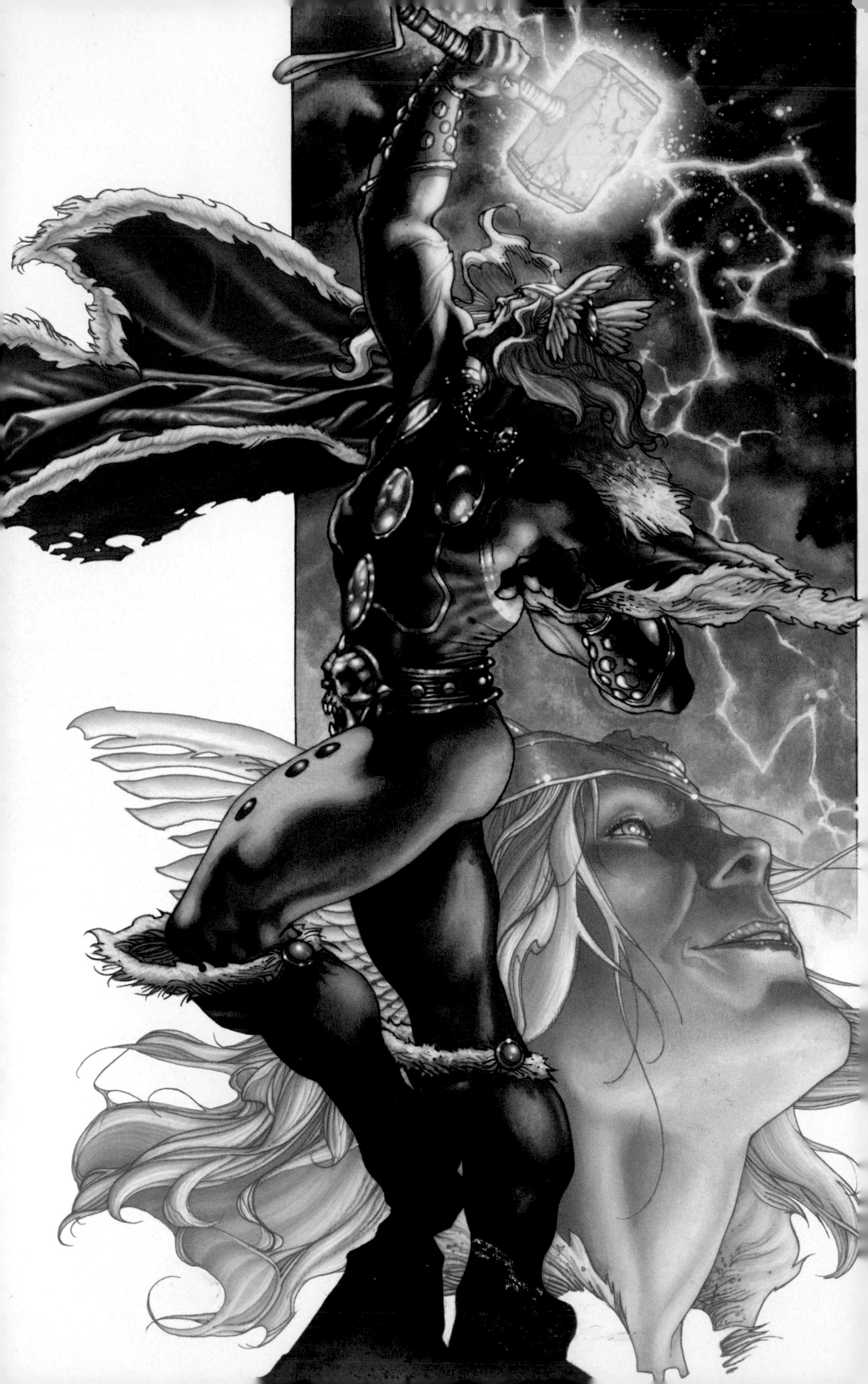

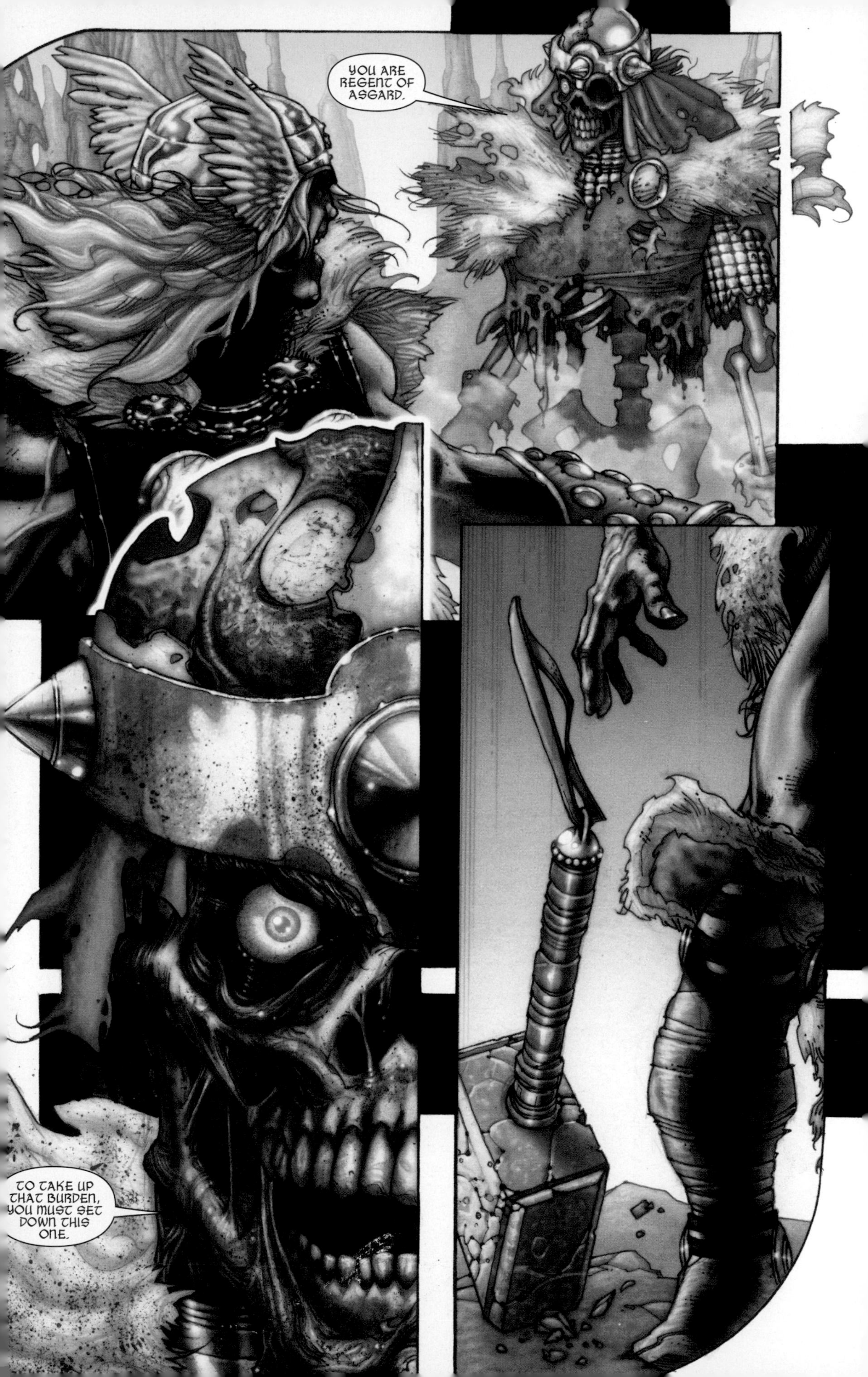
YOU ARE REGENT OF ASGARD.
TO TAKE UP THAT BURDEN, YOU MUST SET DOWN THIS ONE.

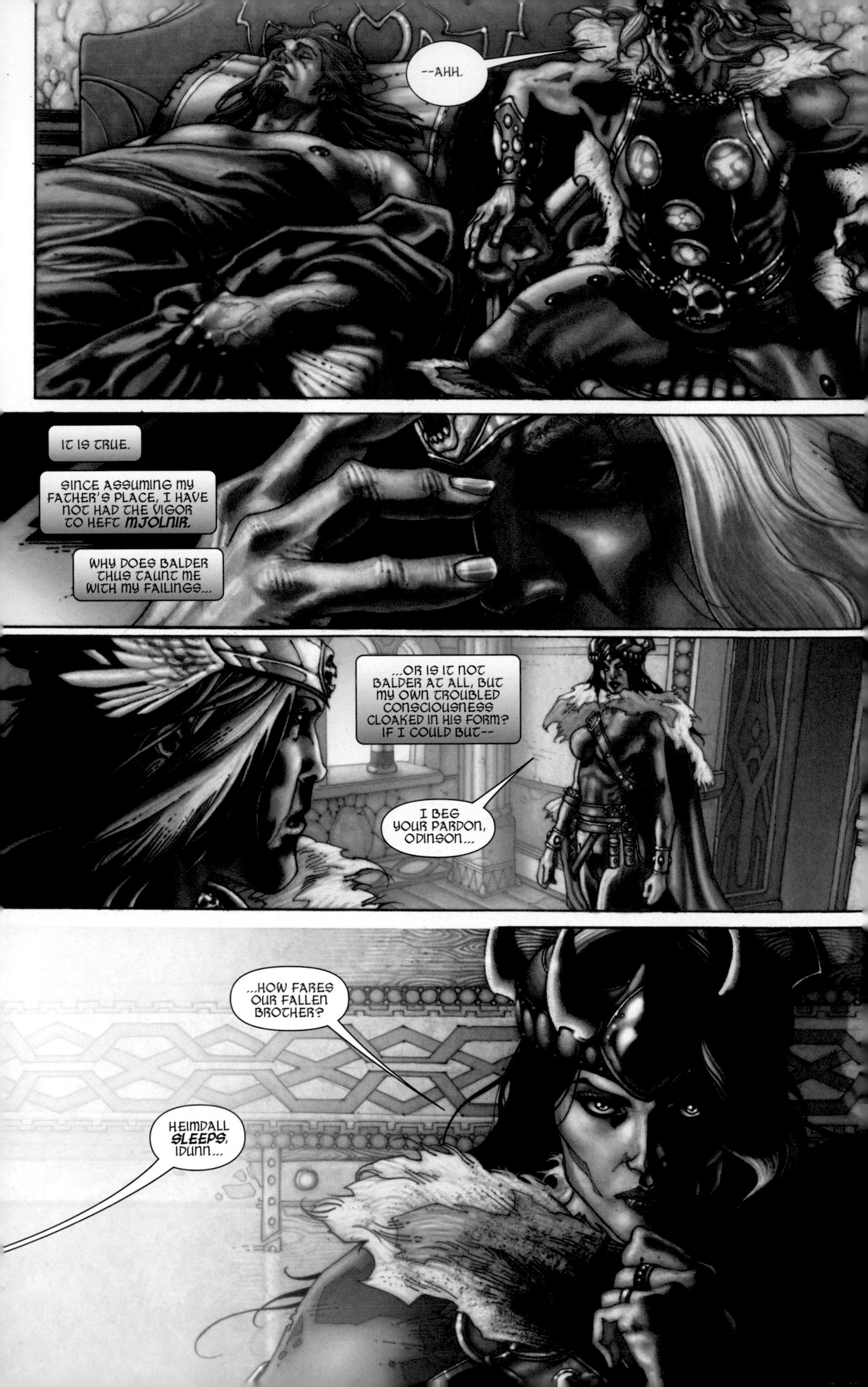
--AHH.
IT IS TRUE.
SINCE ASSUMING MY FATHER'S PLACE, I HAVE NOT HAD THE VIGOR TO HEFT MJOLNIR.
WHY DOES BALDER THUS TAUNT ME WITH MY FAILINGS...
...OR IS IT NOT BALDER AT ALL, BUT MY OWN TROUBLED CONSCIOUSNESS CLOAKED IN HIS FORM? IF I COULD BUT--
I BEG YOUR PARDON, ODINSON...
...HOW FARES OUR FALLEN BROTHER?
HEIMDALL SLEEPS, IDUNN...

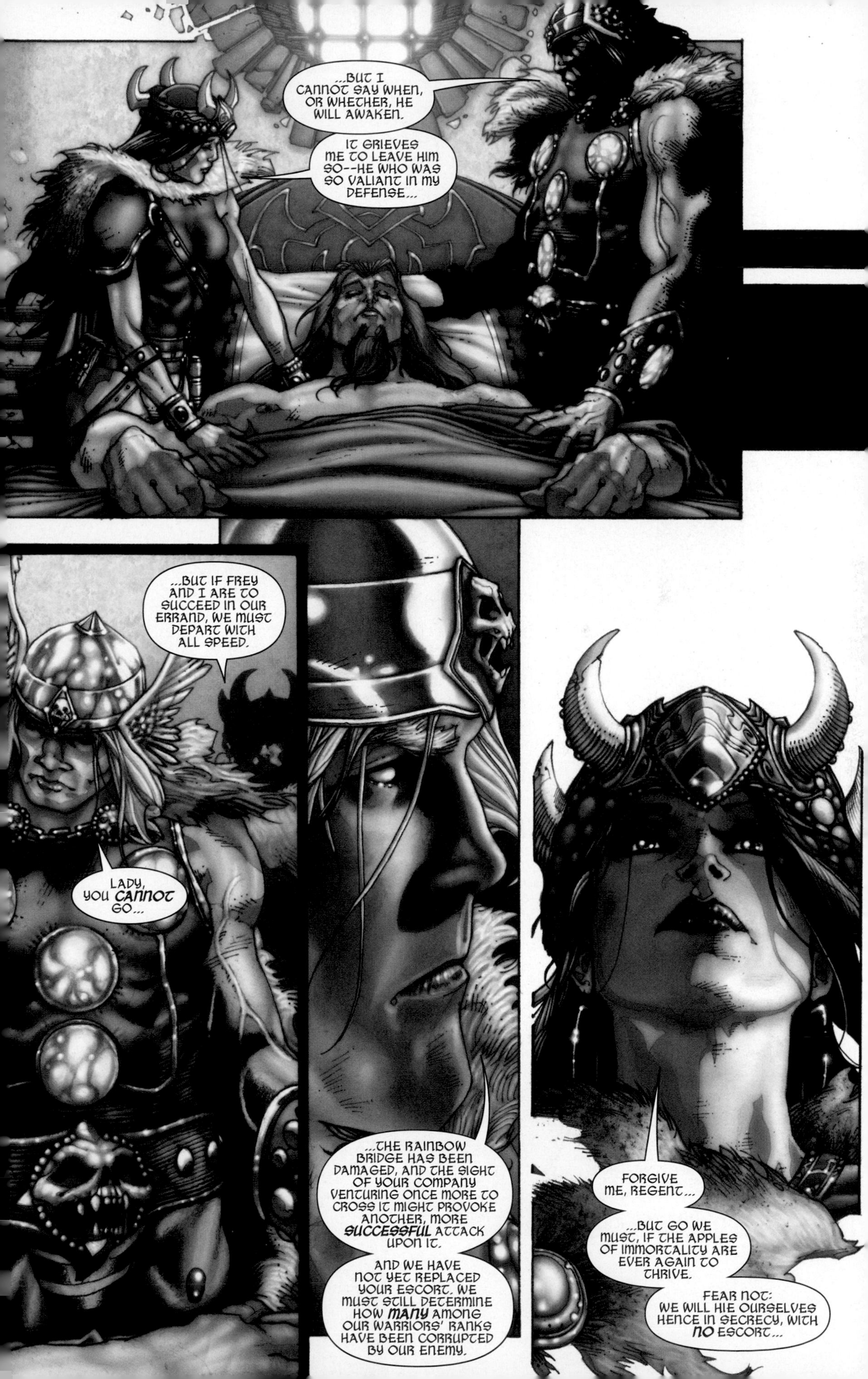
...BUT I CANNOT SAY WHEN, OR WHETHER, HE WILL AWAKEN.
IT GRIEVES ME TO LEAVE HIM SO--HE WHO WAS SO VALIANT IN MY DEFENSE...
...BUT IF FREY AND I ARE TO SUCCEED IN OUR ERRAND, WE MUST DEPART WITH ALL SPEED.
LADY, YOU CANNOT GO...
...THE RAINBOW BRIDGE HAS BEEN DAMAGED, AND THE SIGHT OF YOUR COMPANY VENTURING ONCE MORE TO CROSS IT MIGHT PROVOKE ANOTHER, MORE SUCCESSFUL ATTACK UPON IT.
AND WE HAVE NOT YET REPLACED YOUR ESCORT. WE MUST STILL DETERMINE HOW MANY AMONG OUR WARRIORS' RANKS HAVE BEEN CORRUPTED BY OUR ENEMY.
FORGIVE ME, REGENT...
...BUT GO WE MUST, IF THE APPLES OF IMMORTALITY ARE EVER AGAIN TO THRIVE.
FEAR NOT: WE WILL HIE OURSELVES HENCE IN SECRECY, WITH NO ESCORT...

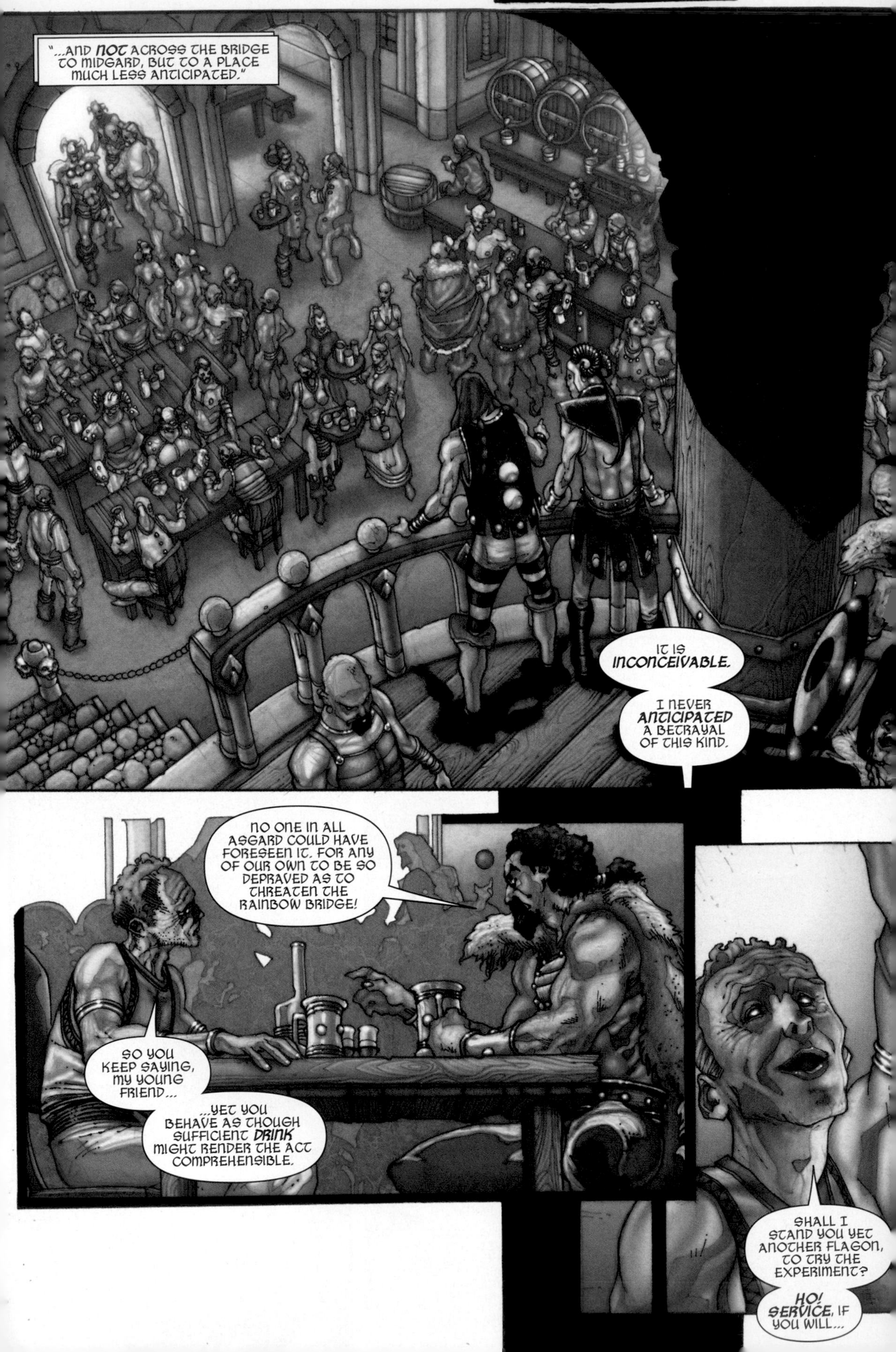
"...AND NOT ACROSS THE BRIDGE TO MIDGARD, BUT TO A PLACE MUCH LESS ANTICIPATED."
IT IS INCONCEIVABLE.
I NEVER ANTICIPATED A BETRAYAL OF THIS KIND.
NO ONE IN ALL ASGARD COULD HAVE FORESEEN IT. FOR ANY OF OUR OWN TO BE SO DEPRAVED AS TO THREATEN THE RAINBOW BRIDGE!
SO YOU KEEP SAYING, MY YOUNG FRIEND...
...YET YOU BEHAVE AS THOUGH SUFFICIENT DRINK MIGHT RENDER THE ACT COMPREHENSIBLE.
SHALL I STAND YOU YET ANOTHER FLAGON, TO TRY THE EXPERIMENT?
HO! SERVICE, IF YOU WILL...

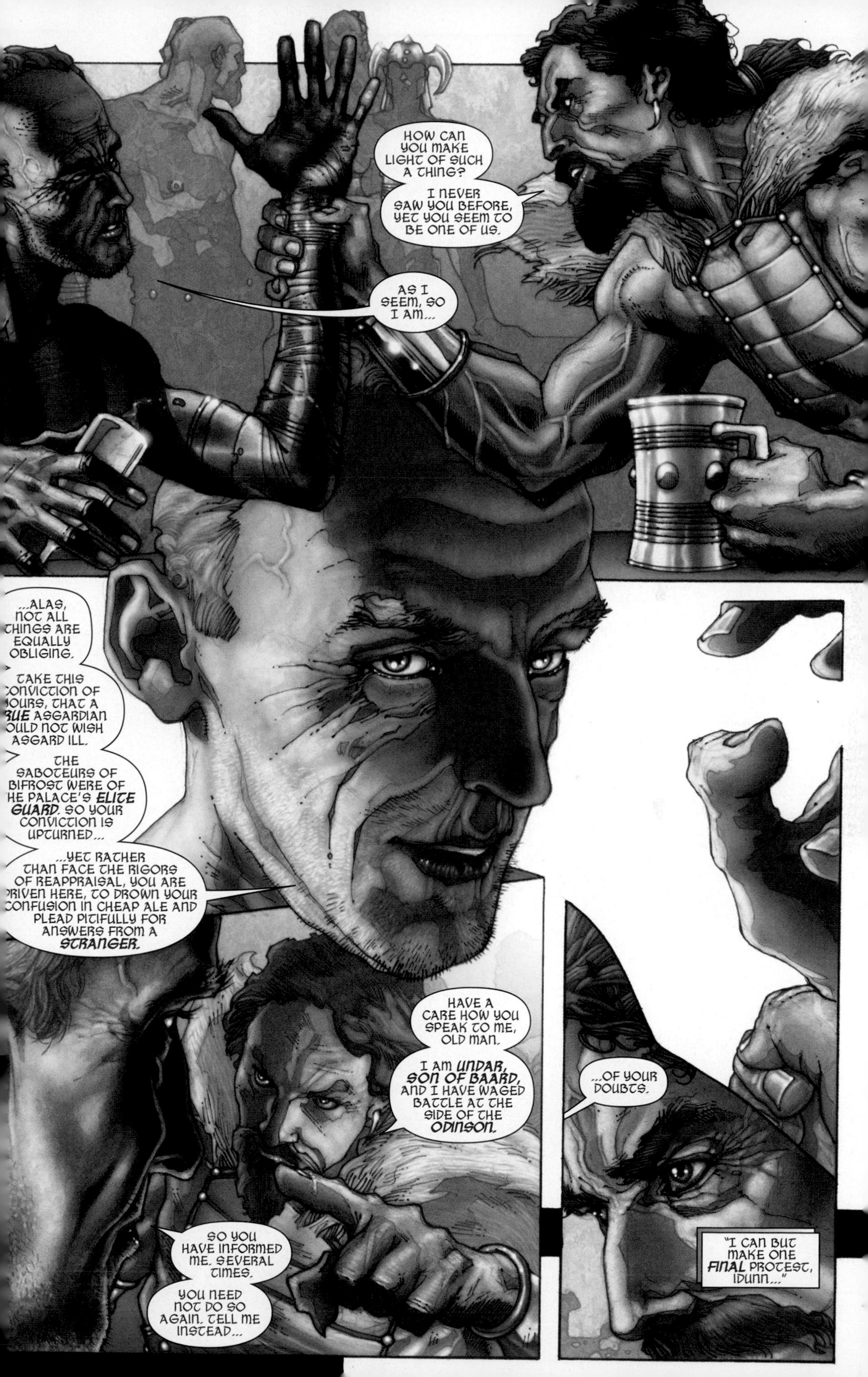
HOW CAN YOU MAKE LIGHT OF SUCH A THING?
I NEVER SAW YOU BEFORE, YET YOU SEEM TO BE ONE OF US.
AS I SEEM, SO I AM...
...ALAS, NOT ALL THINGS ARE EQUALLY OBLIGING.
TAKE THIS CONVICTION OF YOURS, THAT A TRUE ASGARDIAN COULD NOT WISH ASGARD ILL.
THE SABOTEURS OF BIFROST WERE OF THE PALACE'S ELITE GUARD. SO YOUR CONVICTION IS UPTURNED...
...YET RATHER THAN FACE THE RIGORS OF REAPPRAISAL, YOU ARE DRIVEN HERE, TO DROWN YOUR CONFUSION IN CHEAP ALE AND PLEAD PITIFULLY FOR ANSWERS FROM A STRANGER.
HAVE A CARE HOW YOU SPEAK TO ME, OLD MAN.
I AM UNDAR, SON OF BAARD, AND I HAVE WAGED BATTLE AT THE SIDE OF THE ODINSON.
SO YOU HAVE INFORMED ME. SEVERAL TIMES.
YOU NEED NOT DO SO AGAIN. TELL ME INSTEAD...
...OF YOUR DOUBTS.
"I CAN BUT MAKE ONE FINAL PROTEST, IDUNN..."

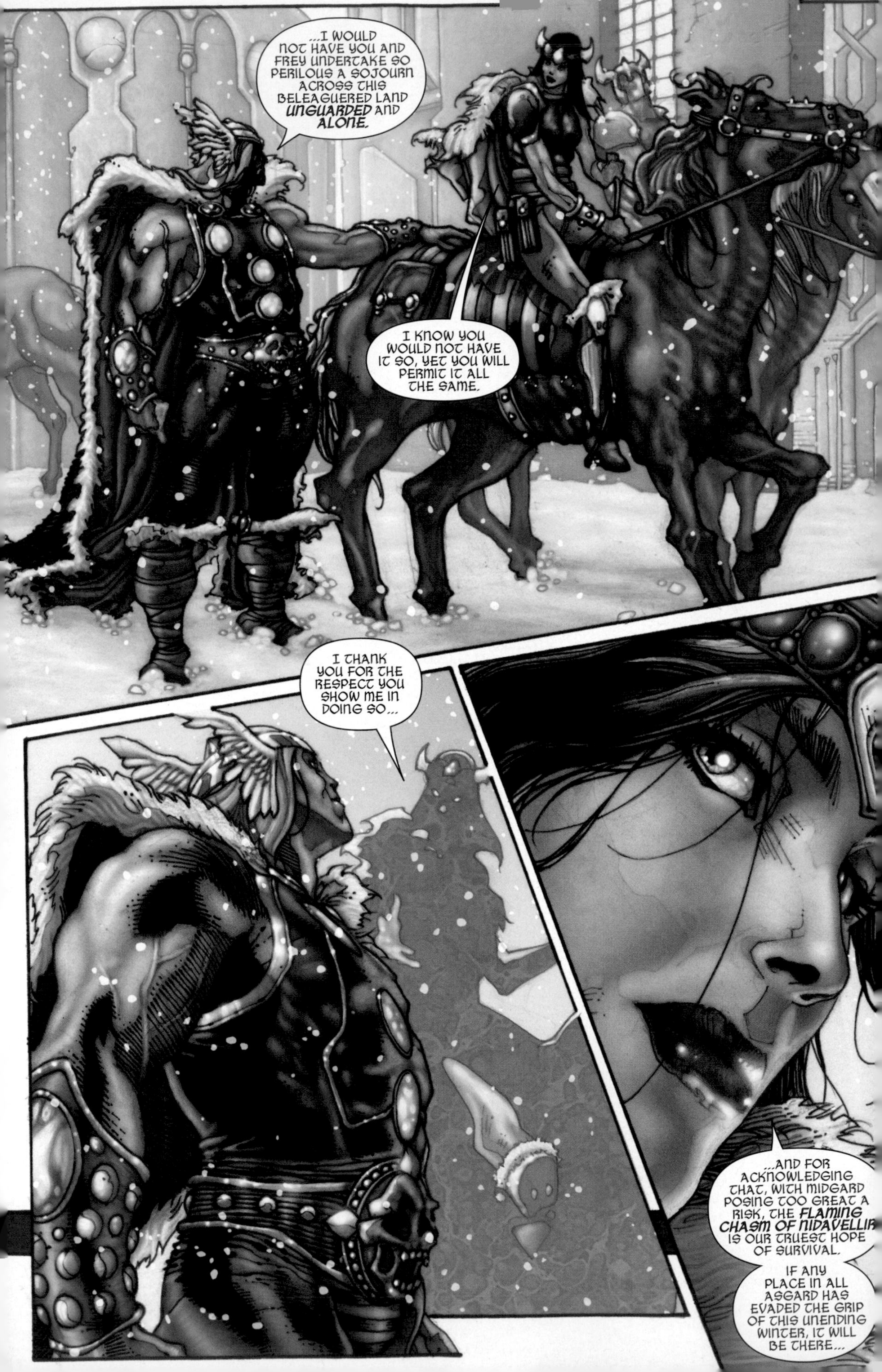
...I WOULD NOT HAVE YOU AND FREY UNDERTAKE SO PERILOUS A SOJOURN ACROSS THIS BELEAGUERED LAND UNGUARDED AND ALONE.
I KNOW YOU WOULD NOT HAVE IT SO, YET YOU WILL PERMIT IT ALL THE SAME.
I THANK YOU FOR THE RESPECT YOU SHOW ME IN DOING SO...
...AND FOR ACKNOWLEDGING THAT, WITH MIDGARD POSING TOO GREAT A RISK, THE FLAMING CHASM OF NIDAVELLIR IS OUR TRUEST HOPE OF SURVIVAL.
IF ANY PLACE IN ALL ASGARD HAS EVADED THE GRIP OF THIS UNENDING WINTER, IT WILL BE THERE...

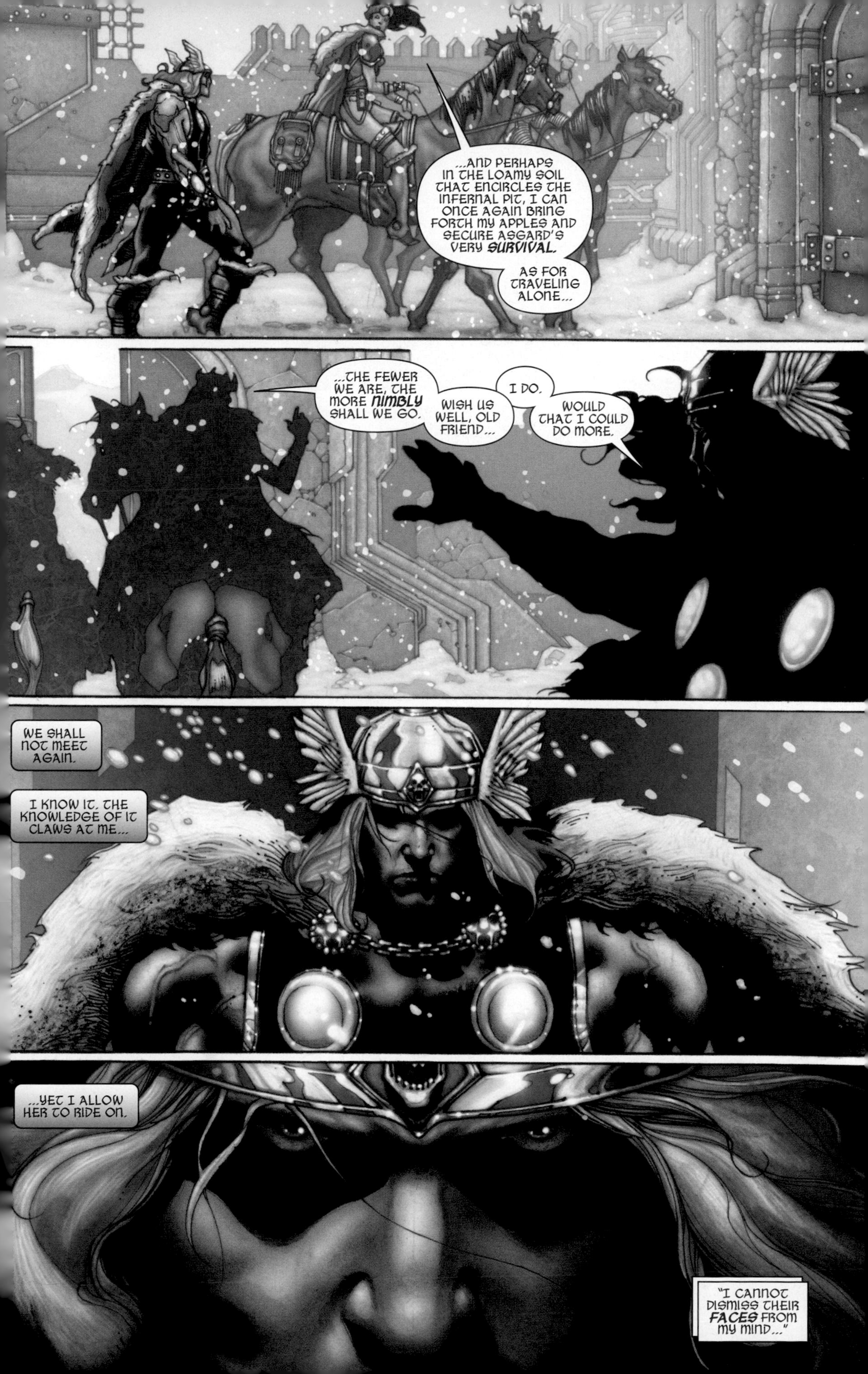
...AND PERHAPS IN THE LOAMY SOIL THAT ENCIRCLES THE INFERNAL PIT, I CAN ONCE AGAIN BRING FORTH MY APPLES AND SECURE ASGARD'S VERY SURVIVAL.
AS FOR TRAVELING ALONE...
...THE FEWER WE ARE, THE MORE NIMBLY SHALL WE GO.
WISH US WELL, OLD FRIEND...
I DO.
WOULD THAT I COULD DO MORE.
WE SHALL NOT MEET AGAIN.
I KNOW IT. THE KNOWLEDGE OF IT CLAWS AT ME...
...YET I ALLOW HER TO RIDE ON.
"I CANNOT DISMISS THEIR FACES FROM MY MIND..."

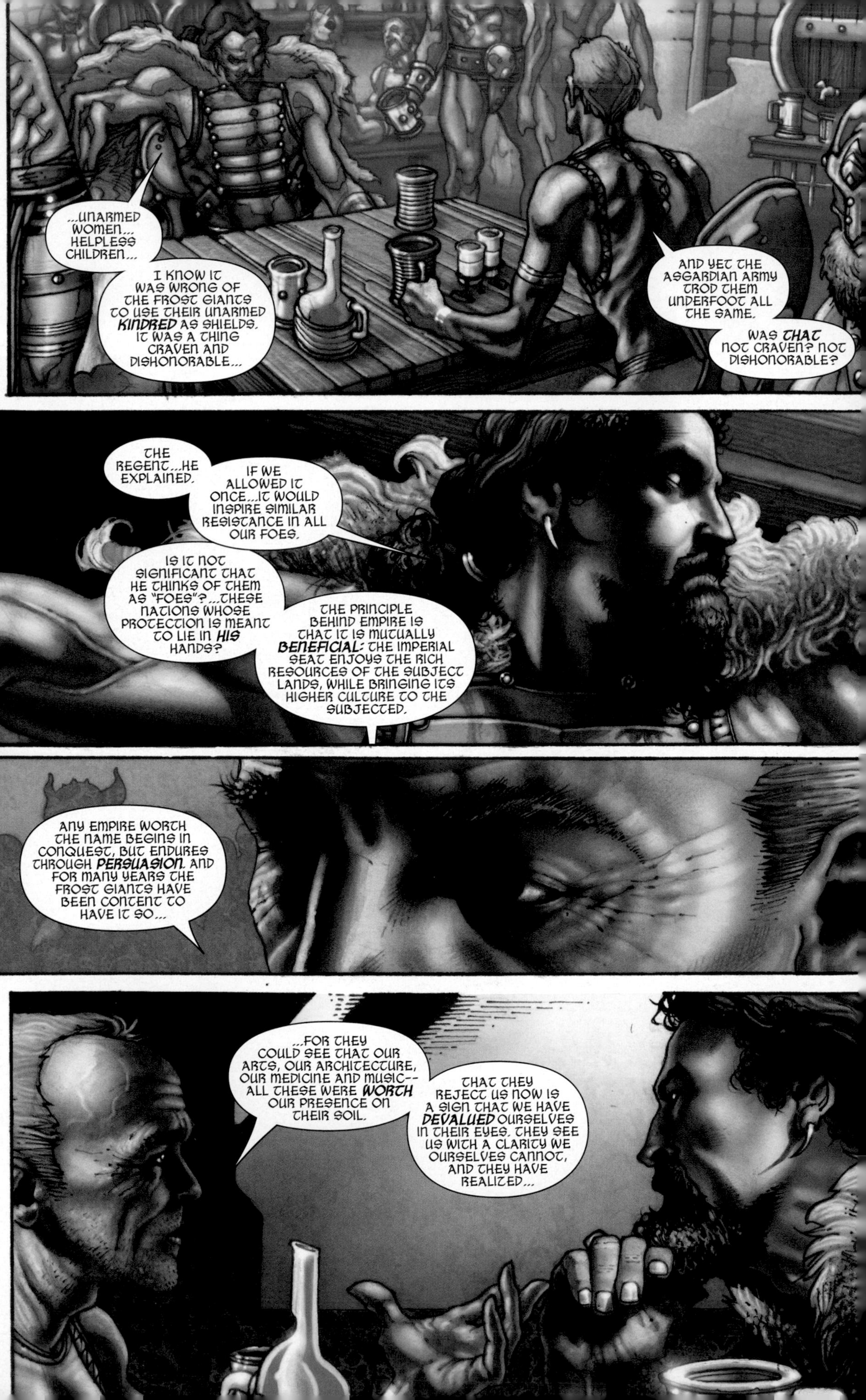
...UNARMED WOMEN... HELPLESS CHILDREN...
I KNOW IT WAS WRONG OF THE FROST GIANTS TO USE THEIR UNARMED KINDRED AS SHIELDS. IT WAS A THING CRAVEN AND DISHONORABLE...
AND YET THE ASGARDIAN ARMY TROD THEM UNDERFOOT ALL THE SAME.
WAS THAT NOT CRAVEN? NOT DISHONORABLE?
THE REGENT...HE EXPLAINED.
IF WE ALLOWED IT ONCE...IT WOULD INSPIRE SIMILAR RESISTANCE IN ALL OUR FOES.
IS IT NOT SIGNIFICANT THAT HE THINKS OF THEM AS "FOES"?...THESE NATIONS WHOSE PROTECTION IS MEANT TO LIE IN HIS HANDS?
THE PRINCIPLE BEHIND EMPIRE IS THAT IT IS MUTUALLY BENEFICIAL: THE IMPERIAL SEAT ENJOYS THE RICH RESOURCES OF THE SUBJECT LANDS, WHILE BRINGING ITS HIGHER CULTURE TO THE SUBJECTED.
ANY EMPIRE WORTH THE NAME BEGINS IN CONQUEST, BUT ENDURES THROUGH PERSUASION. AND FOR MANY YEARS THE FROST GIANTS HAVE BEEN CONTENT TO HAVE IT SO...
...FOR THEY COULD SEE THAT OUR ARTS, OUR ARCHITECTURE, OUR MEDICINE AND MUSIC--ALL THESE WERE WORTH OUR PRESENCE ON THEIR SOIL.
THAT THEY REJECT US NOW IS A SIGN THAT WE HAVE DEVALUED OURSELVES IN THEIR EYES. THEY SEE US WITH A CLARITY WE OURSELVES CANNOT, AND THEY HAVE REALIZED...

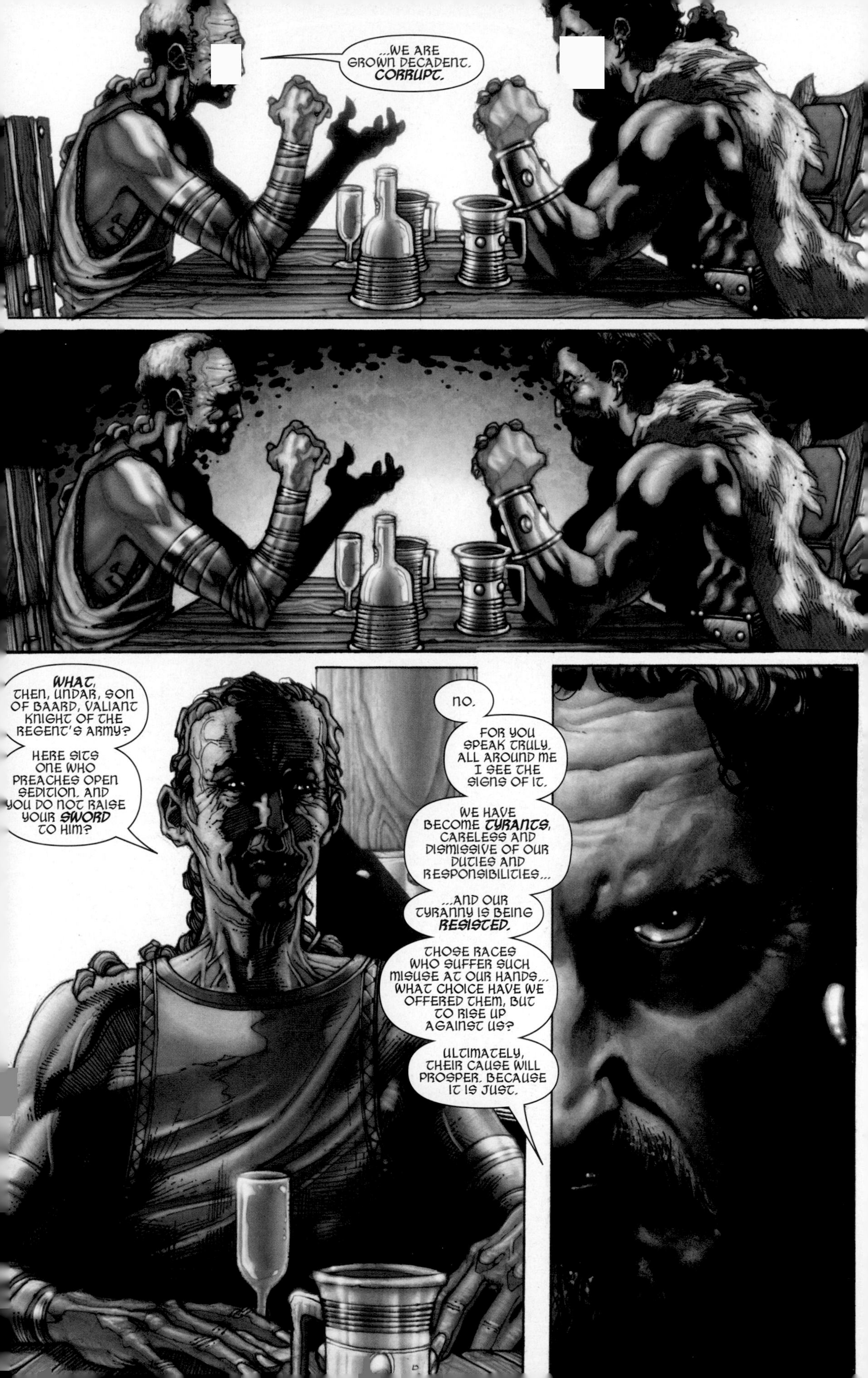
...WE ARE GROWN DECADENT. **CORRUPT.**
WHAT, THEN, UNDAR, SON OF BAARD, VALIANT KNIGHT OF THE REGENT'S ARMY?
HERE SITS ONE WHO PREACHES OPEN SEDITION. AND YOU DO NOT RAISE YOUR **SWORD** TO HIM?
NO.
FOR YOU SPEAK TRULY. ALL AROUND ME I SEE THE SIGNS OF IT.
WE HAVE BECOME **TYRANTS,** CARELESS AND DISMISSIVE OF OUR DUTIES AND RESPONSIBILITIES...
...AND OUR TYRANNY IS BEING **RESISTED.**
THOSE RACES WHO SUFFER SUCH MISUSE AT OUR HANDS... WHAT CHOICE HAVE WE OFFERED THEM, BUT TO RISE UP AGAINST US?
ULTIMATELY, THEIR CAUSE WILL PROSPER. BECAUSE IT IS JUST.

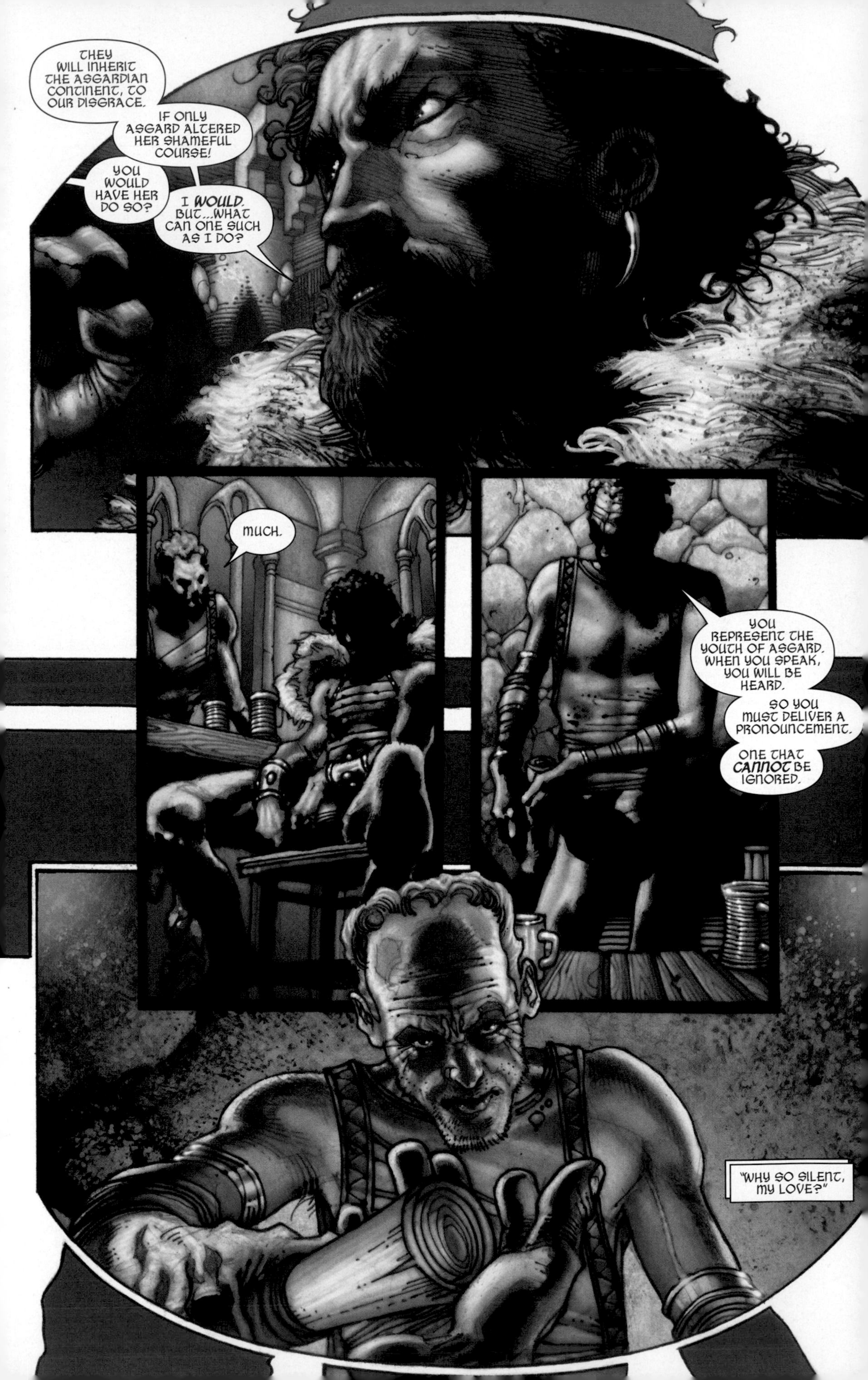
THEY WILL INHERIT THE ASGARDIAN CONTINENT, TO OUR DISGRACE.
IF ONLY ASGARD ALTERED HER SHAMEFUL COURSE!
YOU WOULD HAVE HER DO SO?
I WOULD. BUT...WHAT CAN ONE SUCH AS I DO?
MUCH.
YOU REPRESENT THE YOUTH OF ASGARD. WHEN YOU SPEAK, YOU WILL BE HEARD.
SO YOU MUST DELIVER A PRONOUNCEMENT.
ONE THAT CANNOT BE IGNORED.
"WHY SO SILENT, MY LOVE?"

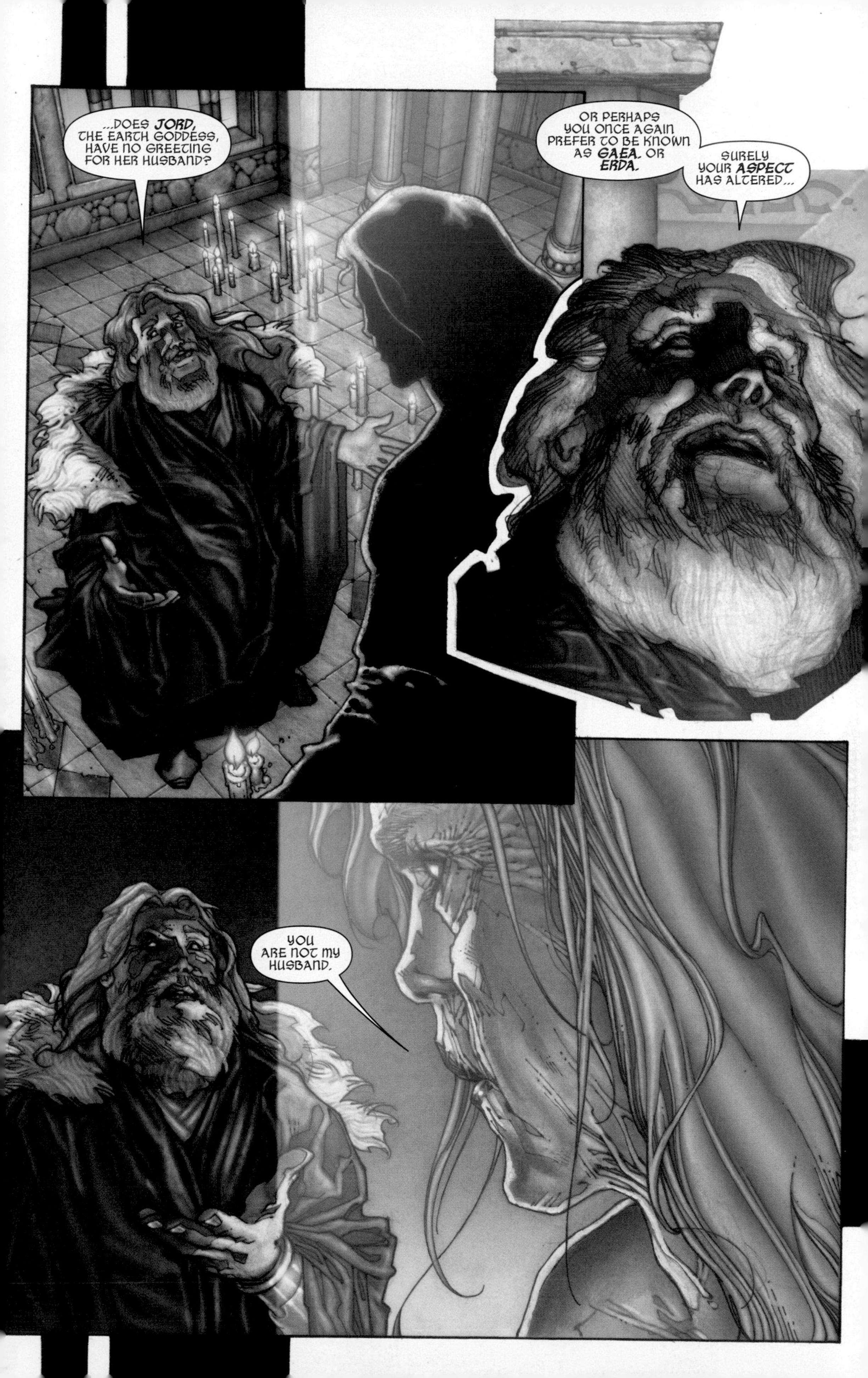
...DOES JORD, THE EARTH GODDESS, HAVE NO GREETING FOR HER HUSBAND?
OR PERHAPS YOU ONCE AGAIN PREFER TO BE KNOWN AS GAEA, OR ERDA.
SURELY YOUR ASPECT HAS ALTERED...
YOU ARE NOT MY HUSBAND.

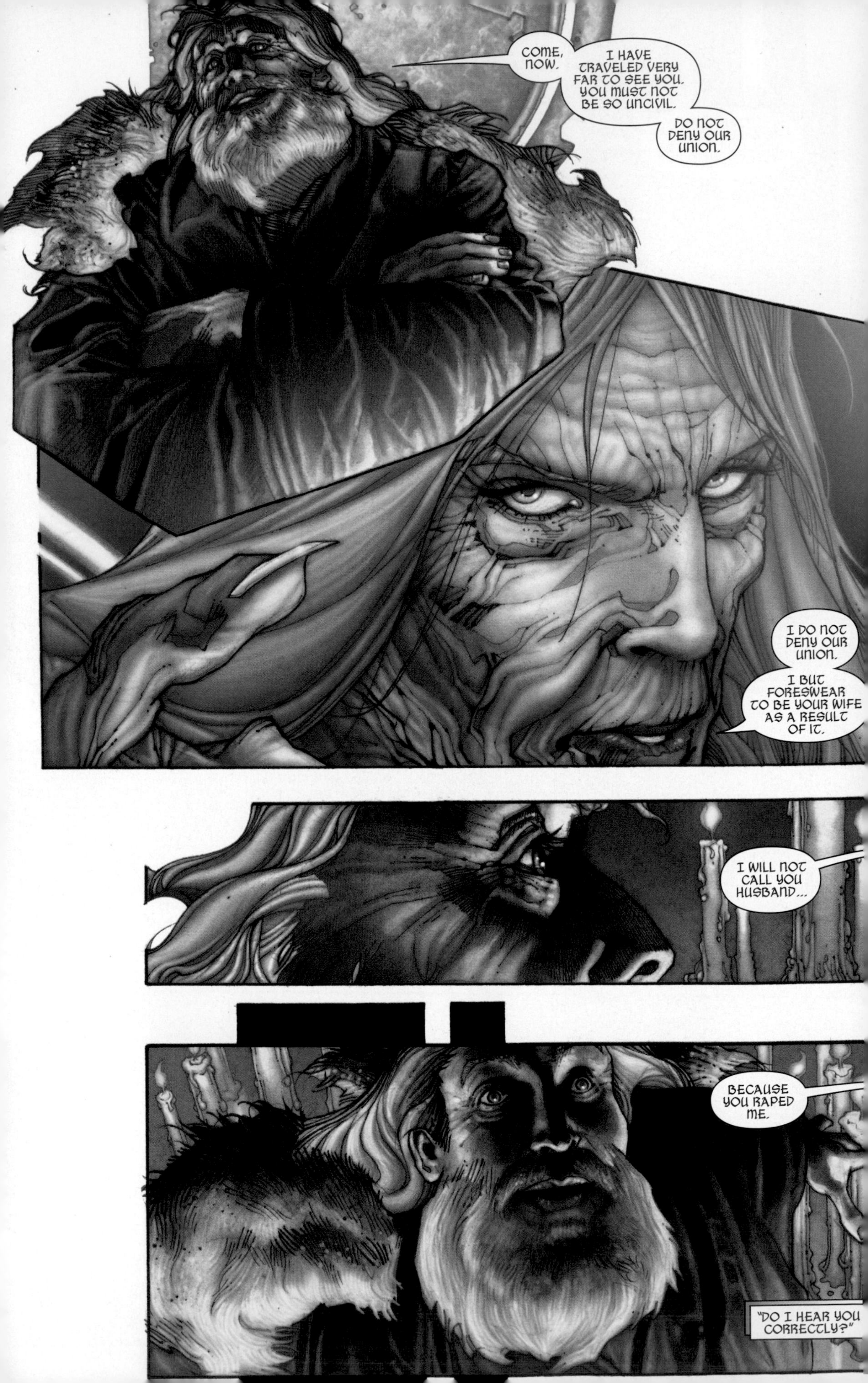

COME, NOW.
I HAVE TRAVELED VERY FAR TO SEE YOU. YOU MUST NOT BE SO UNCIVIL.
DO NOT DENY OUR UNION.
I DO NOT DENY OUR UNION.
I BUT FORESWEAR TO BE YOUR WIFE AS A RESULT OF IT.
I WILL NOT CALL YOU HUSBAND...
BECAUSE YOU RAPED ME.
"DO I HEAR YOU CORRECTLY?"

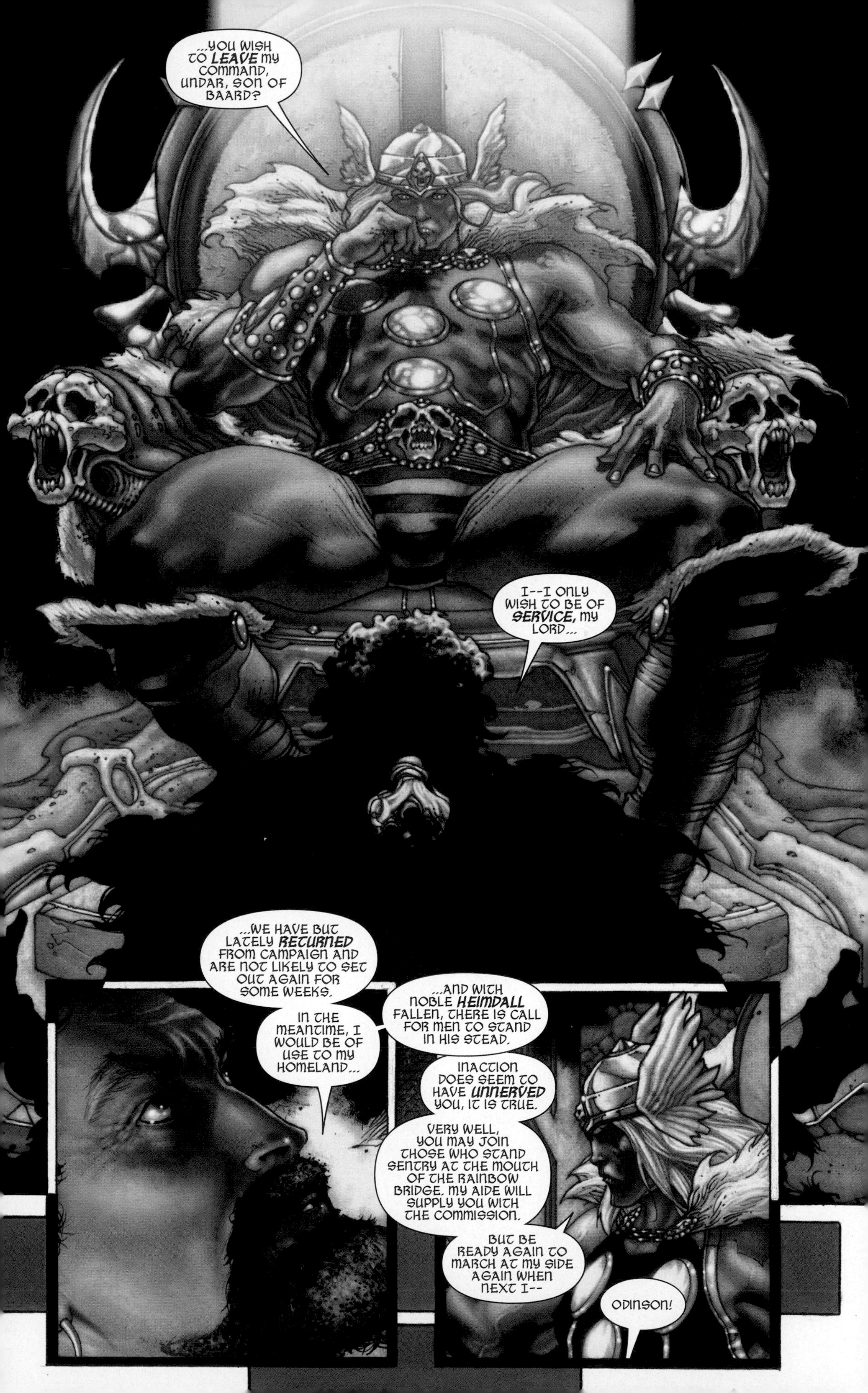
...YOU WISH TO LEAVE MY COMMAND, UNDAR, SON OF BAARD?
I--I ONLY WISH TO BE OF SERVICE, MY LORD...
...WE HAVE BUT LATELY RETURNED FROM CAMPAIGN AND ARE NOT LIKELY TO SET OUT AGAIN FOR SOME WEEKS.
IN THE MEANTIME, I WOULD BE OF USE TO MY HOMELAND...
...AND WITH NOBLE HEIMDALL FALLEN, THERE IS CALL FOR MEN TO STAND IN HIS STEAD.
INACTION DOES SEEM TO HAVE UNNERVED YOU, IT IS TRUE.
VERY WELL, YOU MAY JOIN THOSE WHO STAND SENTRY AT THE MOUTH OF THE RAINBOW BRIDGE. MY AIDE WILL SUPPLY YOU WITH THE COMMISSION.
BUT BE READY AGAIN TO MARCH AT MY SIDE AGAIN WHEN NEXT I--
ODINSON!

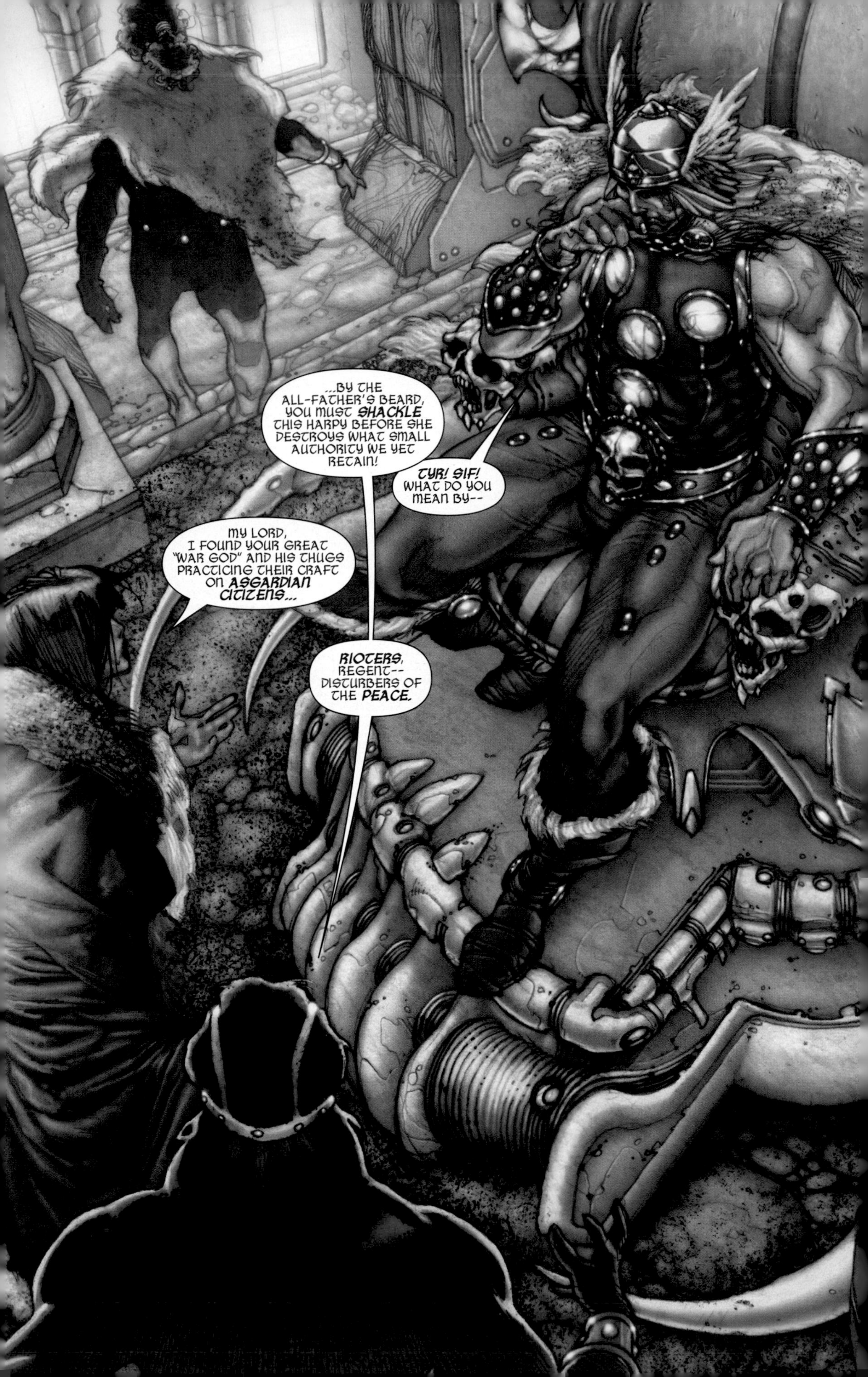

MY LORD, I FOUND YOUR GREAT "WAR GOD" AND HIS THUGS PRACTICING THEIR CRAFT ON ASGARDIAN CITIZENS...
...BY THE ALL-FATHER'S BEARD, YOU MUST SHACKLE THIS HARPY BEFORE SHE DESTROYS WHAT SMALL AUTHORITY WE YET RETAIN!
TYR! SIF! WHAT DO YOU MEAN BY--
RIOTERS, REGENT-- DISTURBERS OF THE PEACE.

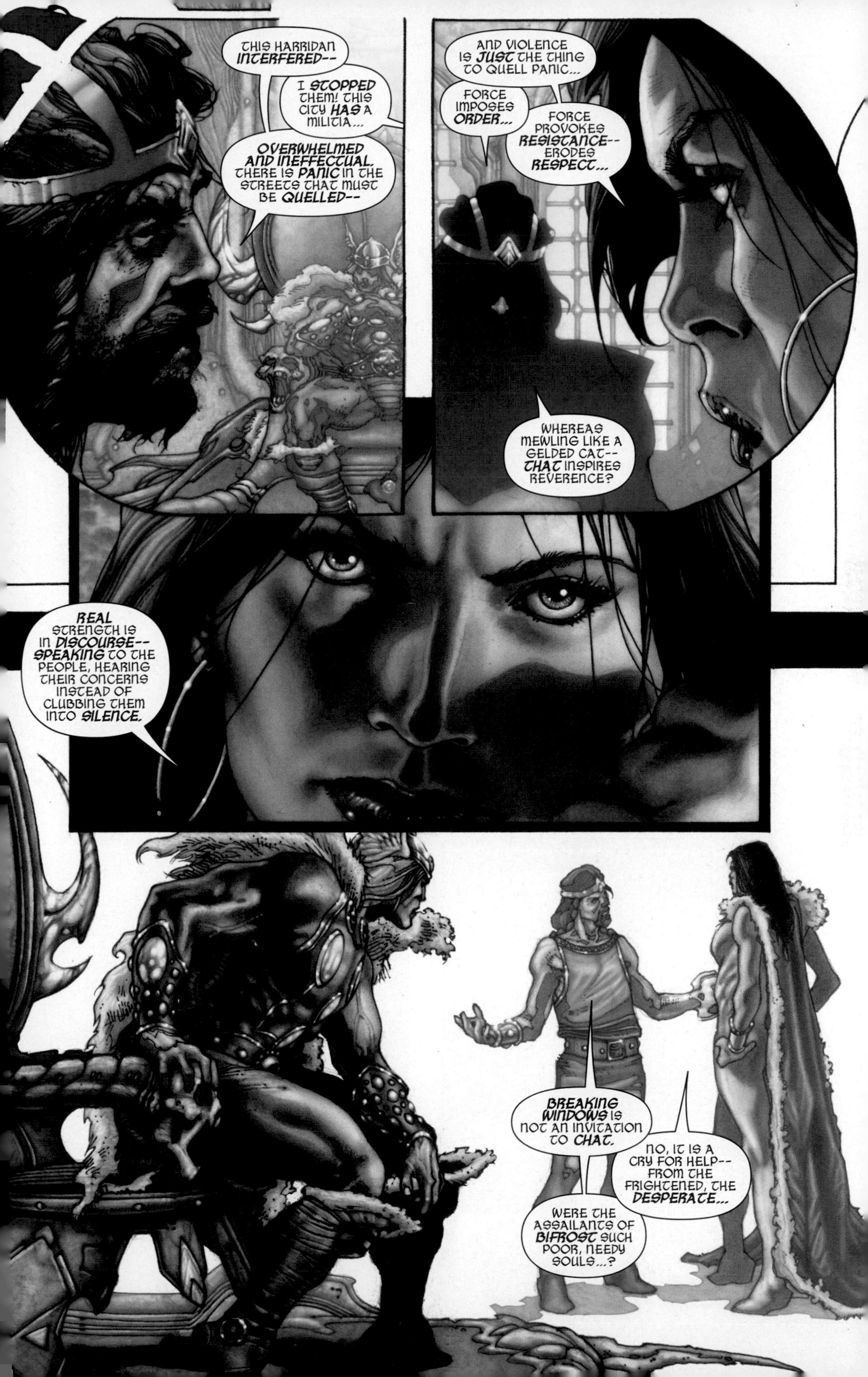
THIS HARRIDAN INTERFERED--
I STOPPED THEM! THIS CITY HAS A MILITIA...
OVERWHELMED AND INEFFECTUAL. THERE IS PANIC IN THE STREETS THAT MUST BE QUELLED--
AND VIOLENCE IS JUST THE THING TO QUELL PANIC...
FORCE IMPOSES ORDER...
FORCE PROVOKES RESISTANCE-- ERODES RESPECT...
WHEREAS MEWLING LIKE A GELDED CAT-- THAT INSPIRES REVERENCE?
REAL STRENGTH IS IN DISCOURSE-- SPEAKING TO THE PEOPLE, HEARING THEIR CONCERNS INSTEAD OF CLUBBING THEM INTO SILENCE.
BREAKING WINDOWS IS NOT AN INVITATION TO CHAT.
NO, IT IS A CRY FOR HELP-- FROM THE FRIGHTENED, THE DESPERATE...
WERE THE ASSAILANTS OF BIFROST SUCH POOR, NEEDY SOULS...?

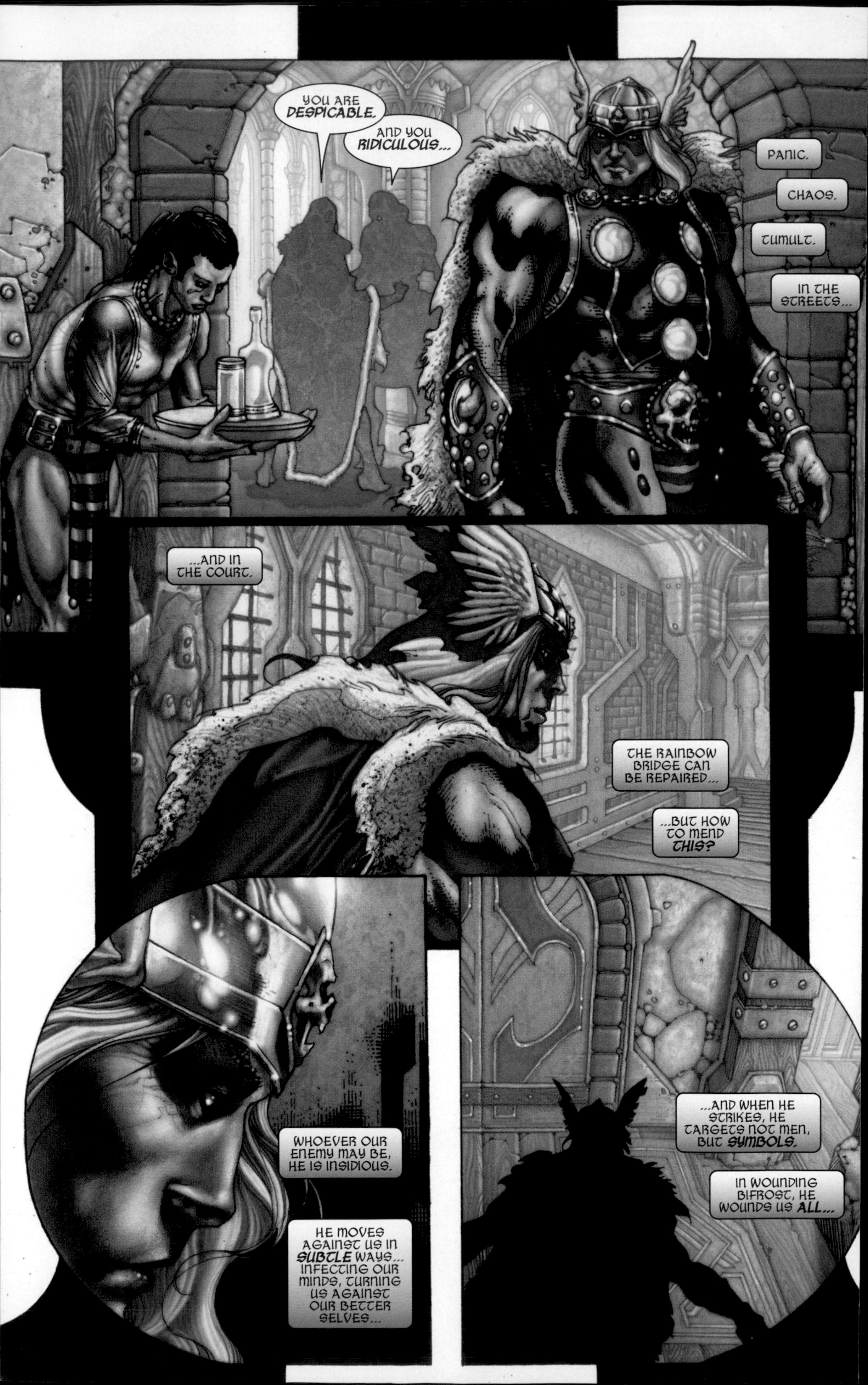
YOU ARE DESPICABLE.
AND YOU RIDICULOUS...
PANIC.
CHAOS.
TUMULT.
IN THE STREETS...
...AND IN THE COURT.
THE RAINBOW BRIDGE CAN BE REPAIRED...
...BUT HOW TO MEND THIS?
WHOEVER OUR ENEMY MAY BE, HE IS INSIDIOUS.
HE MOVES AGAINST US IN SUBTLE WAYS... INFECTING OUR MINDS, TURNING US AGAINST OUR BETTER SELVES...
...AND WHEN HE STRIKES, HE TARGETS NOT MEN, BUT SYMBOLS.
IN WOUNDING BIFROST, HE WOUNDS US ALL...

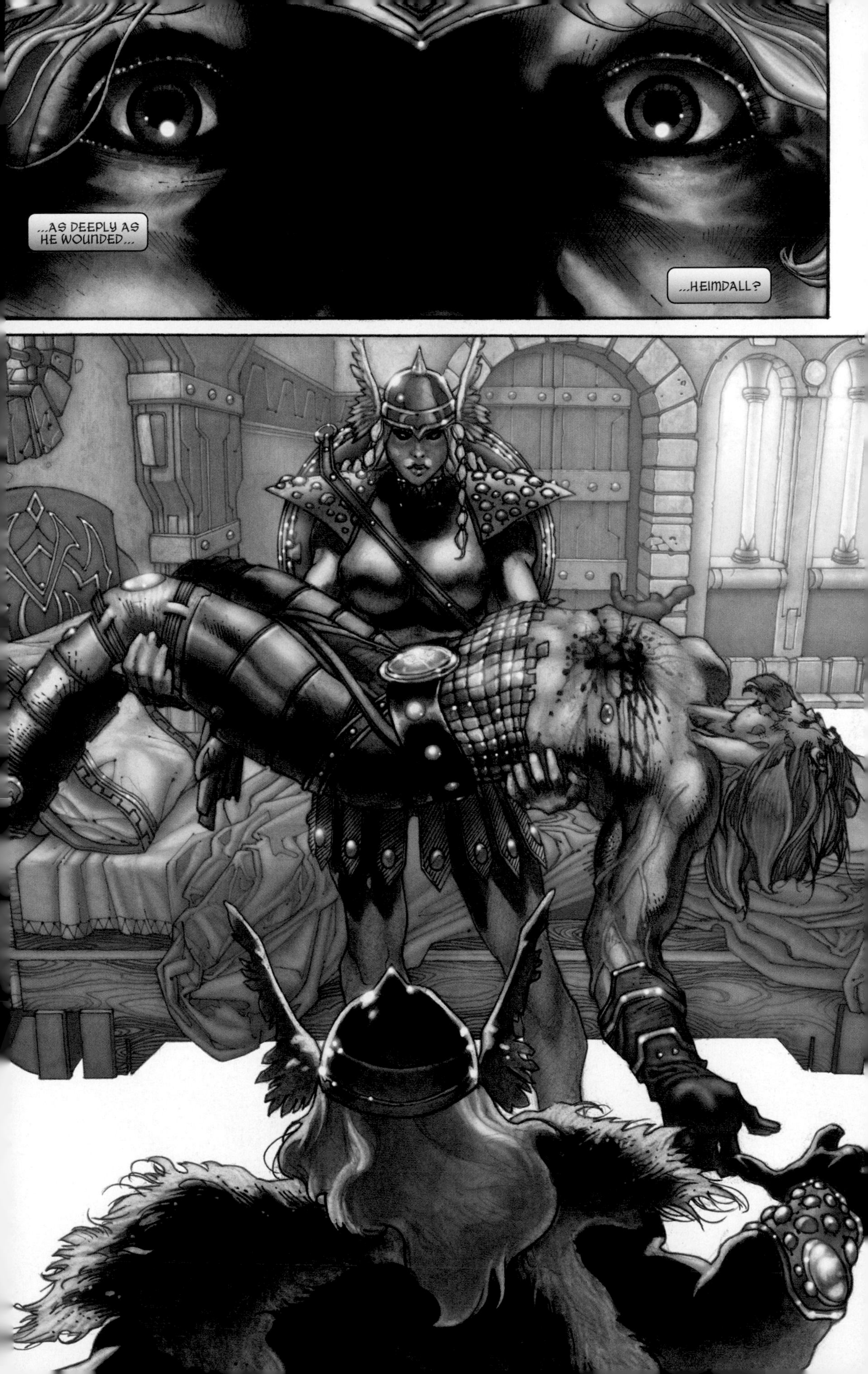
...AS DEEPLY AS HE WOUNDED...
...HEIMDALL?

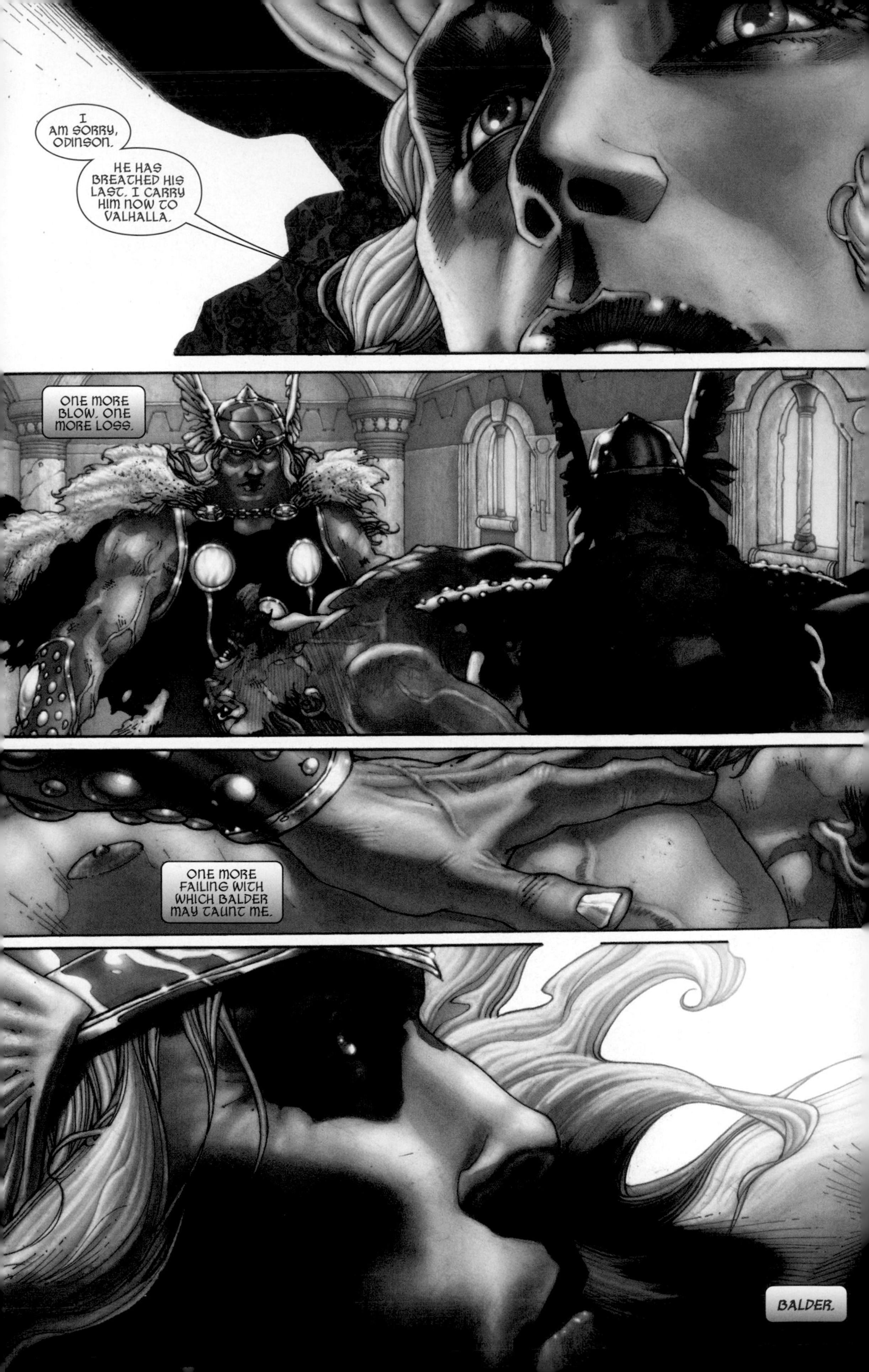
I AM SORRY, ODINSON.
HE HAS BREATHED HIS LAST. I CARRY HIM NOW TO VALHALLA.
ONE MORE BLOW. ONE MORE LOSS.
ONE MORE FAILING WITH WHICH BALDER MAY TAUNT ME.
BALDER.

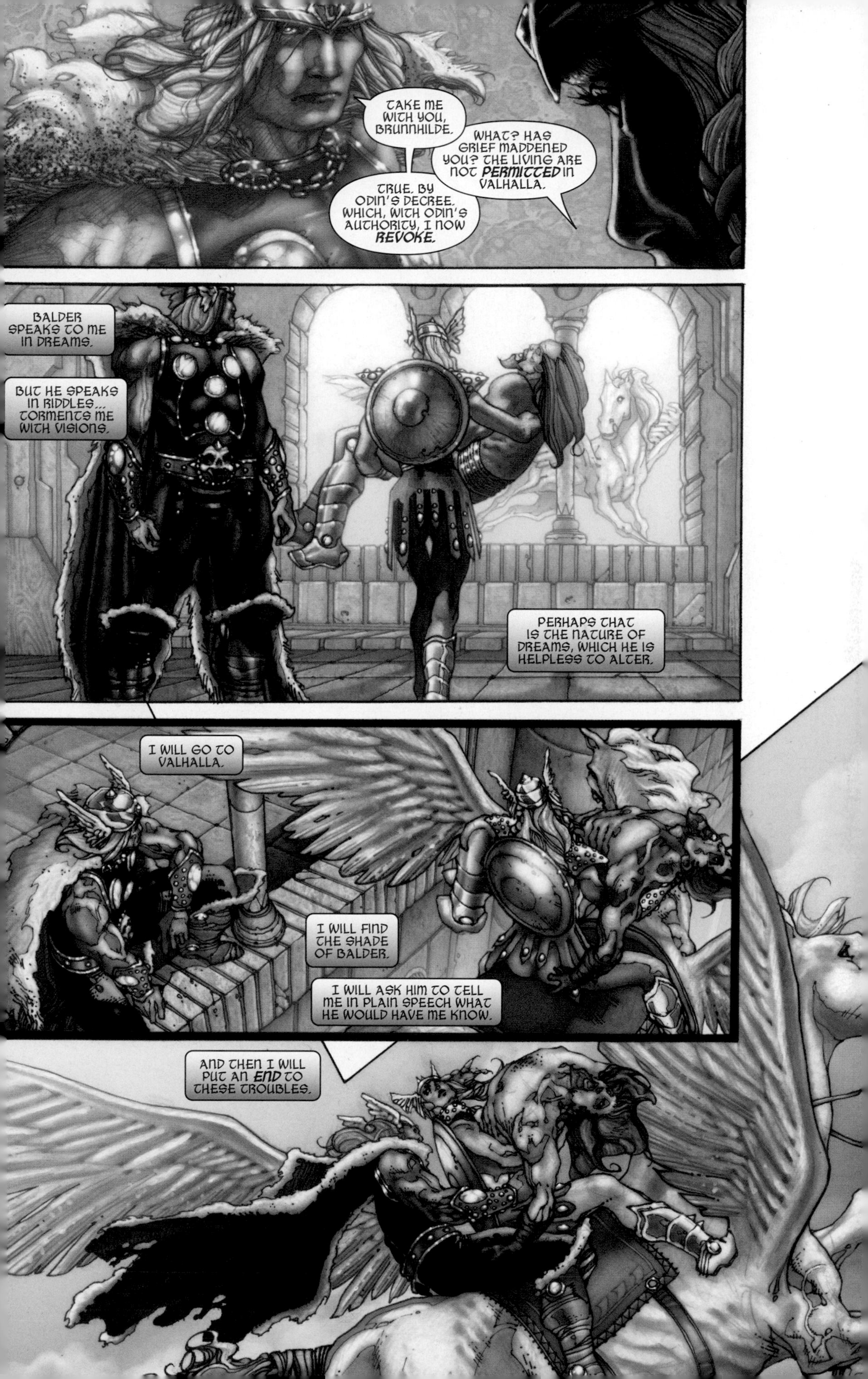

TAKE ME WITH YOU, BRUNNHILDE.
WHAT? HAS GRIEF MADDENED YOU? THE LIVING ARE NOT PERMITTED IN VALHALLA.
TRUE. BY ODIN'S DECREE. WHICH, WITH ODIN'S AUTHORITY, I NOW REVOKE.
BALDER SPEAKS TO ME IN DREAMS.
BUT HE SPEAKS IN RIDDLES... TORMENTS ME WITH VISIONS.
PERHAPS THAT IS THE NATURE OF DREAMS, WHICH HE IS HELPLESS TO ALTER.
I WILL GO TO VALHALLA.
I WILL FIND THE SHADE OF BALDER.
I WILL ASK HIM TO TELL ME IN PLAIN SPEECH WHAT HE WOULD HAVE ME KNOW.
AND THEN I WILL PUT AN END TO THESE TROUBLES.

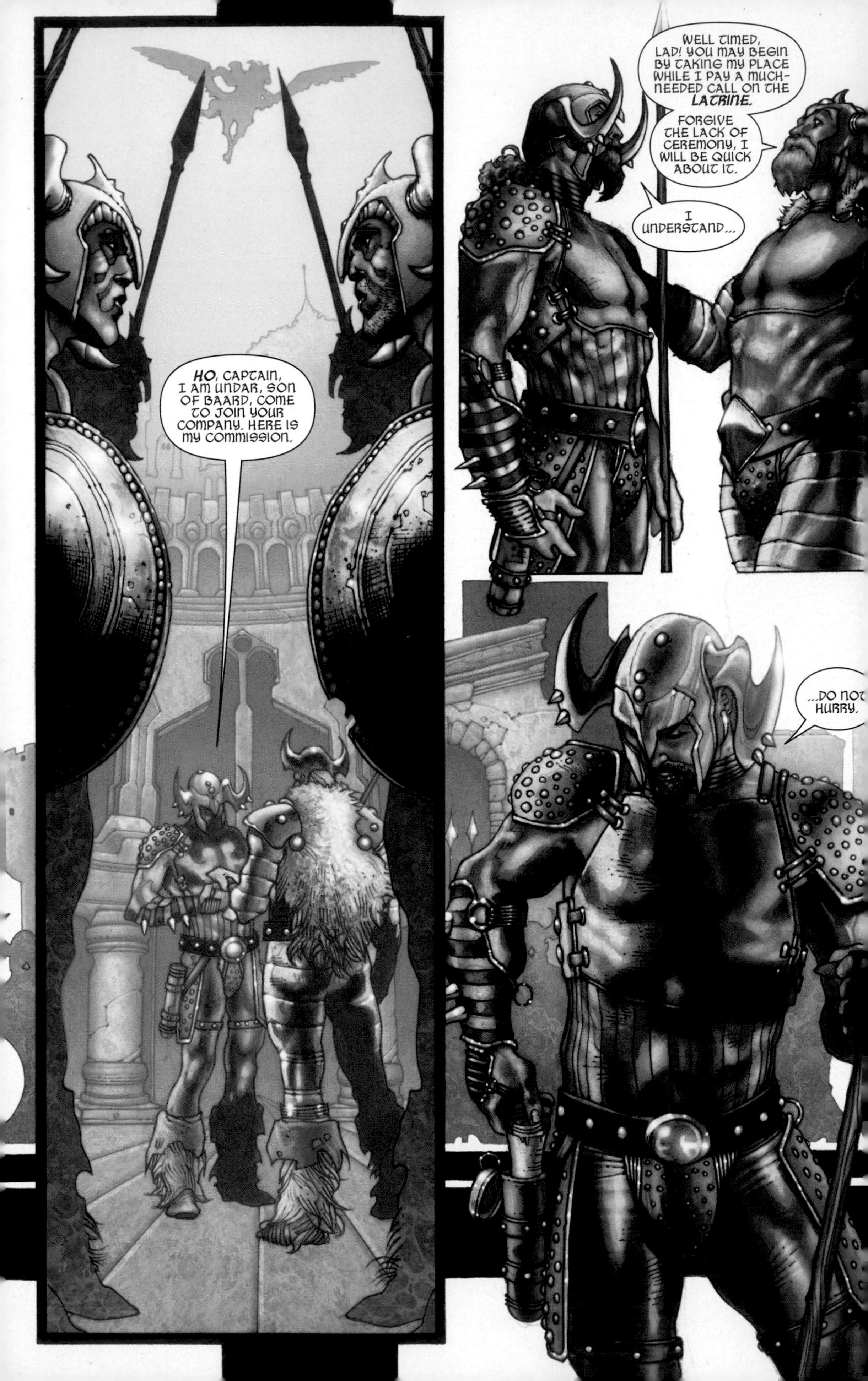

HO, CAPTAIN, I AM UNDAR, SON OF BAARD, COME TO JOIN YOUR COMPANY. HERE IS MY COMMISSION.
WELL TIMED, LAD! YOU MAY BEGIN BY TAKING MY PLACE WHILE I PAY A MUCH-NEEDED CALL ON THE LATRINE.
FORGIVE THE LACK OF CEREMONY, I WILL BE QUICK ABOUT IT.
I UNDERSTAND...
...DO NOT HURRY.

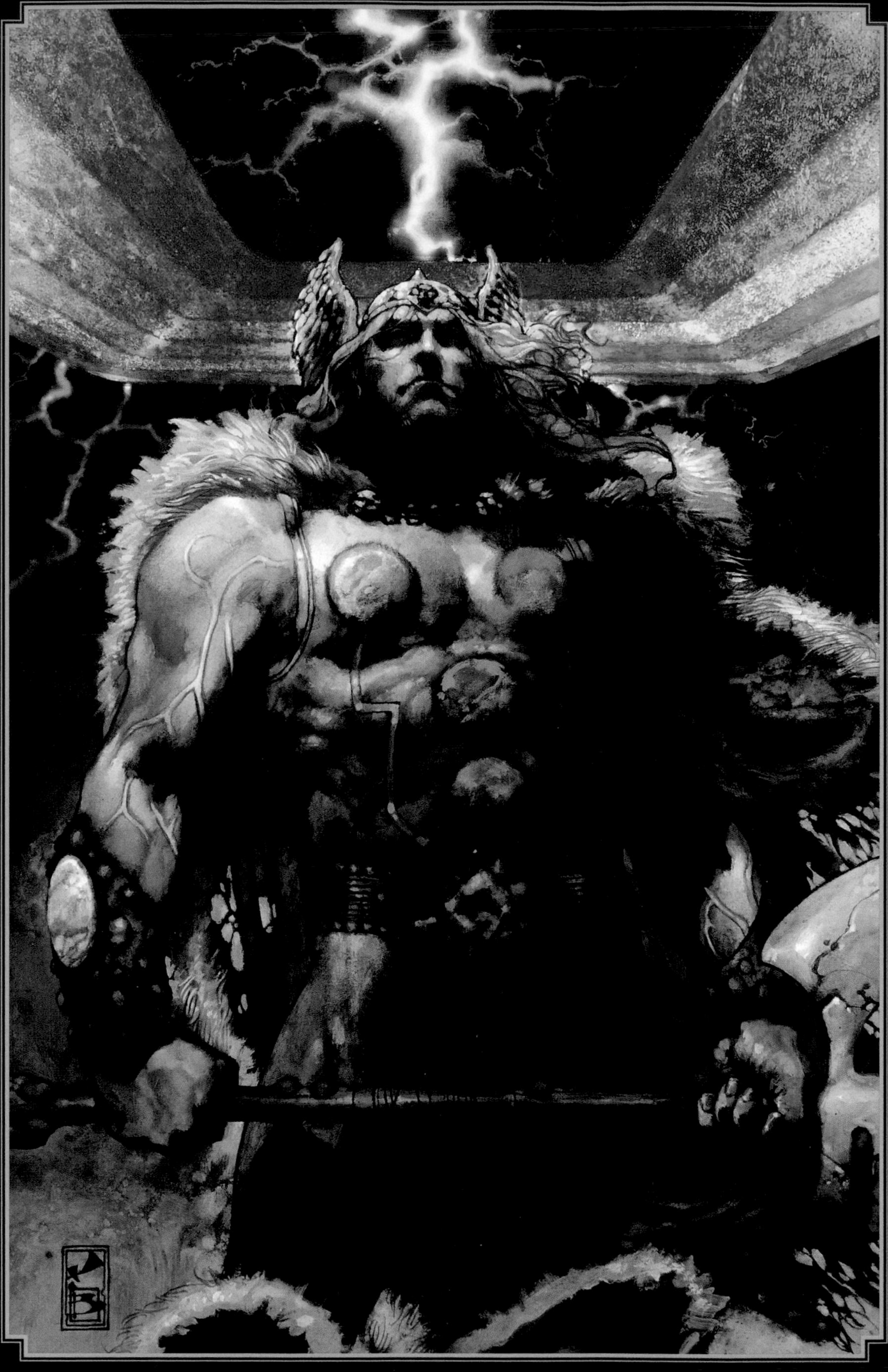

Thor: For Asgard 4

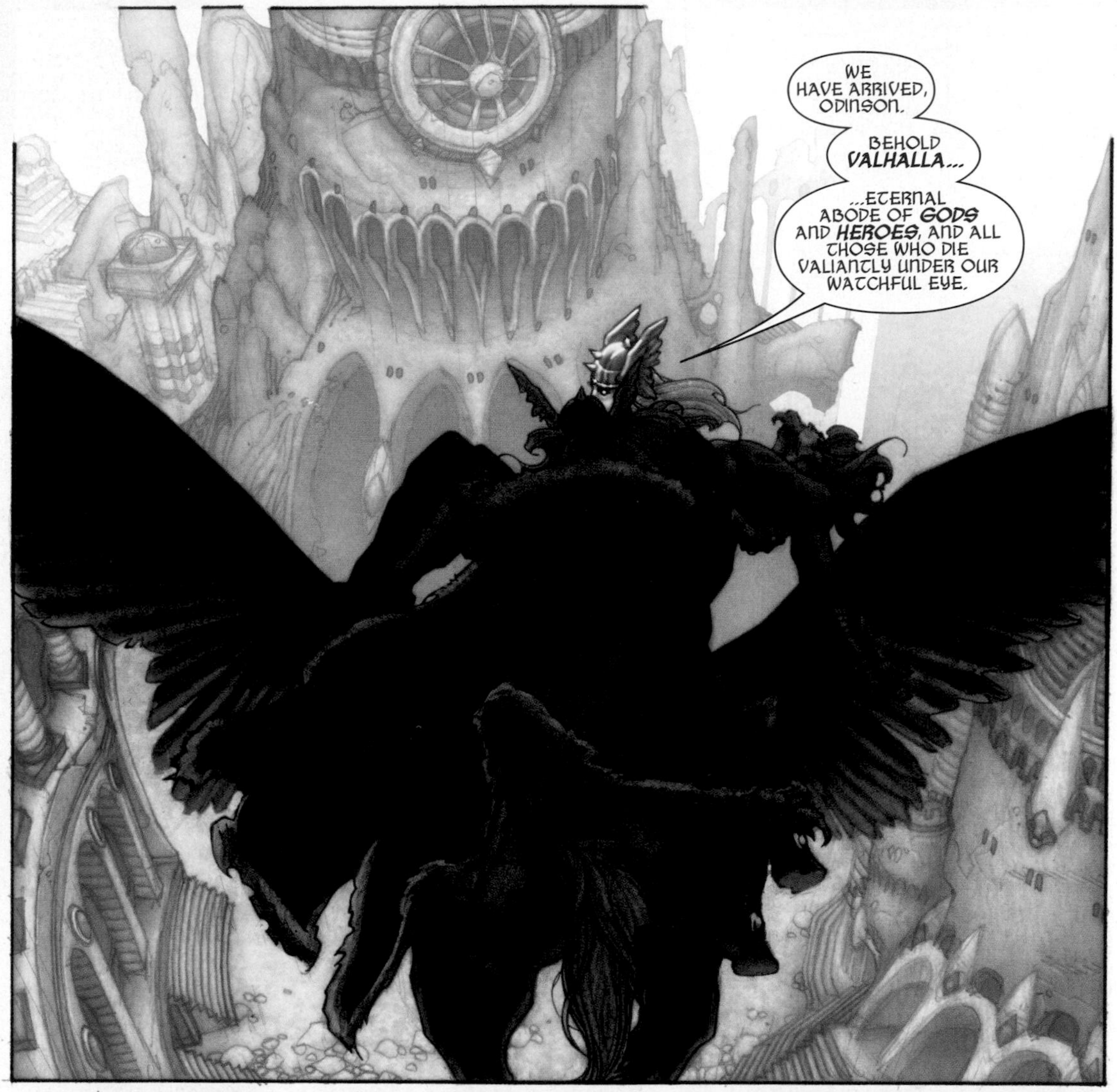
WE HAVE ARRIVED, ODINSON.
BEHOLD VALHALLA...
...ETERNAL ABODE OF GODS AND HEROES, AND ALL THOSE WHO DIE VALIANTLY UNDER OUR WATCHFUL EYE.

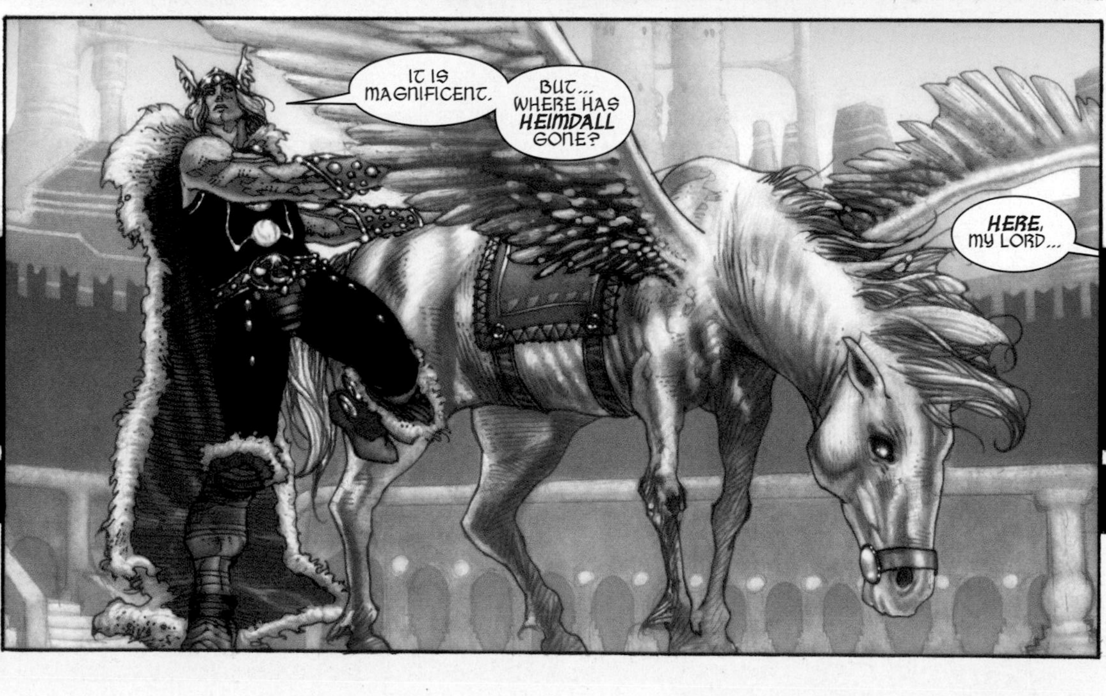
IT IS MAGNIFICENT.
BUT... WHERE HAS HEIMDALL GONE?
HERE, MY LORD...

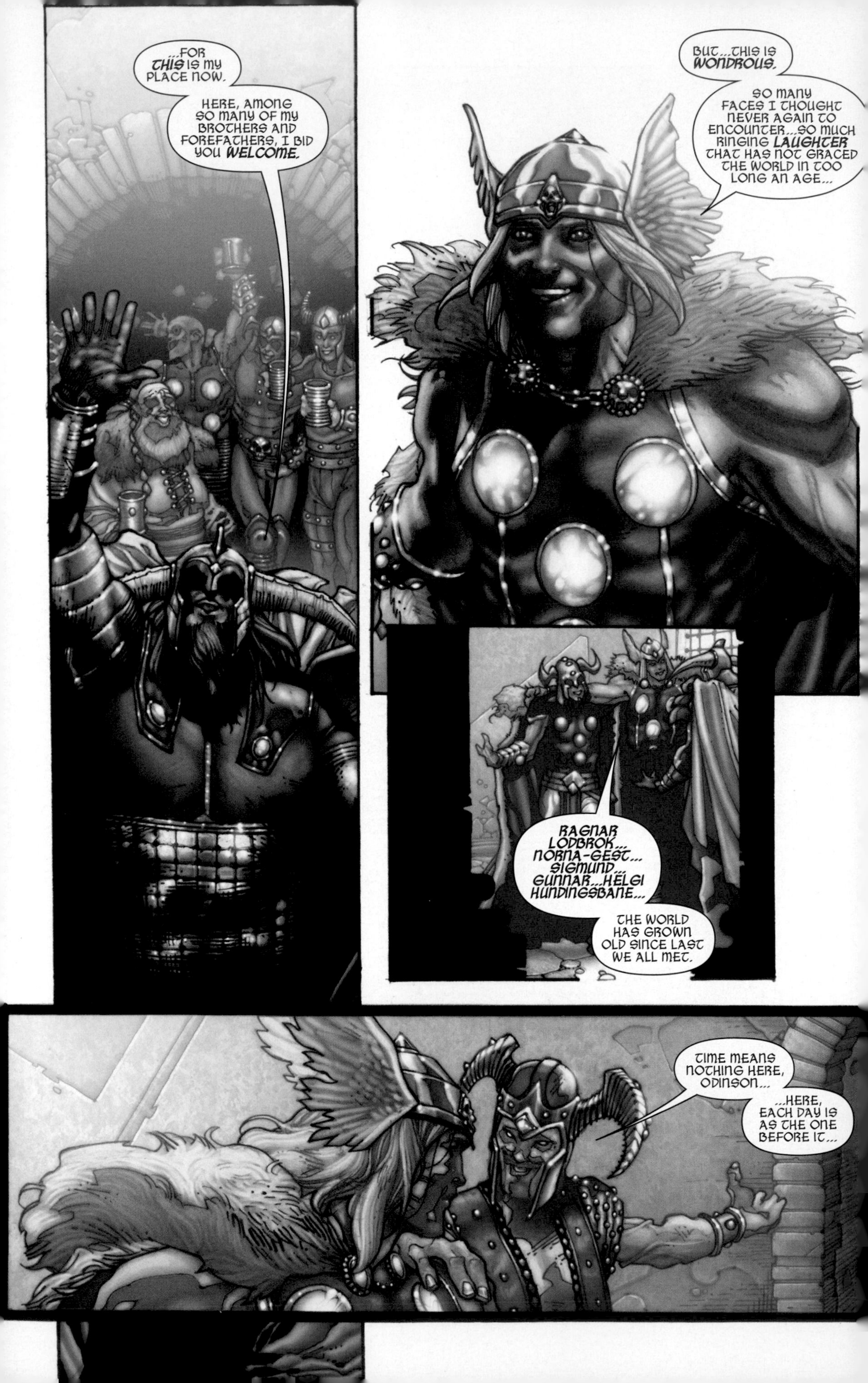

...FOR THIS IS MY PLACE NOW.
HERE, AMONG SO MANY OF MY BROTHERS AND FOREFATHERS, I BID YOU WELCOME.
BUT...THIS IS WONDROUS.
SO MANY FACES I THOUGHT NEVER AGAIN TO ENCOUNTER...SO MUCH RINGING LAUGHTER THAT HAS NOT GRACED THE WORLD IN TOO LONG AN AGE...
RAGNAR LODBROK... NORNA-GEST... SIGMUND... GUNNAR...HELGI HUNDINGSBANE...
THE WORLD HAS GROWN OLD SINCE LAST WE ALL MET.
TIME MEANS NOTHING HERE, ODINSON...
...HERE, EACH DAY IS AS THE ONE BEFORE IT...

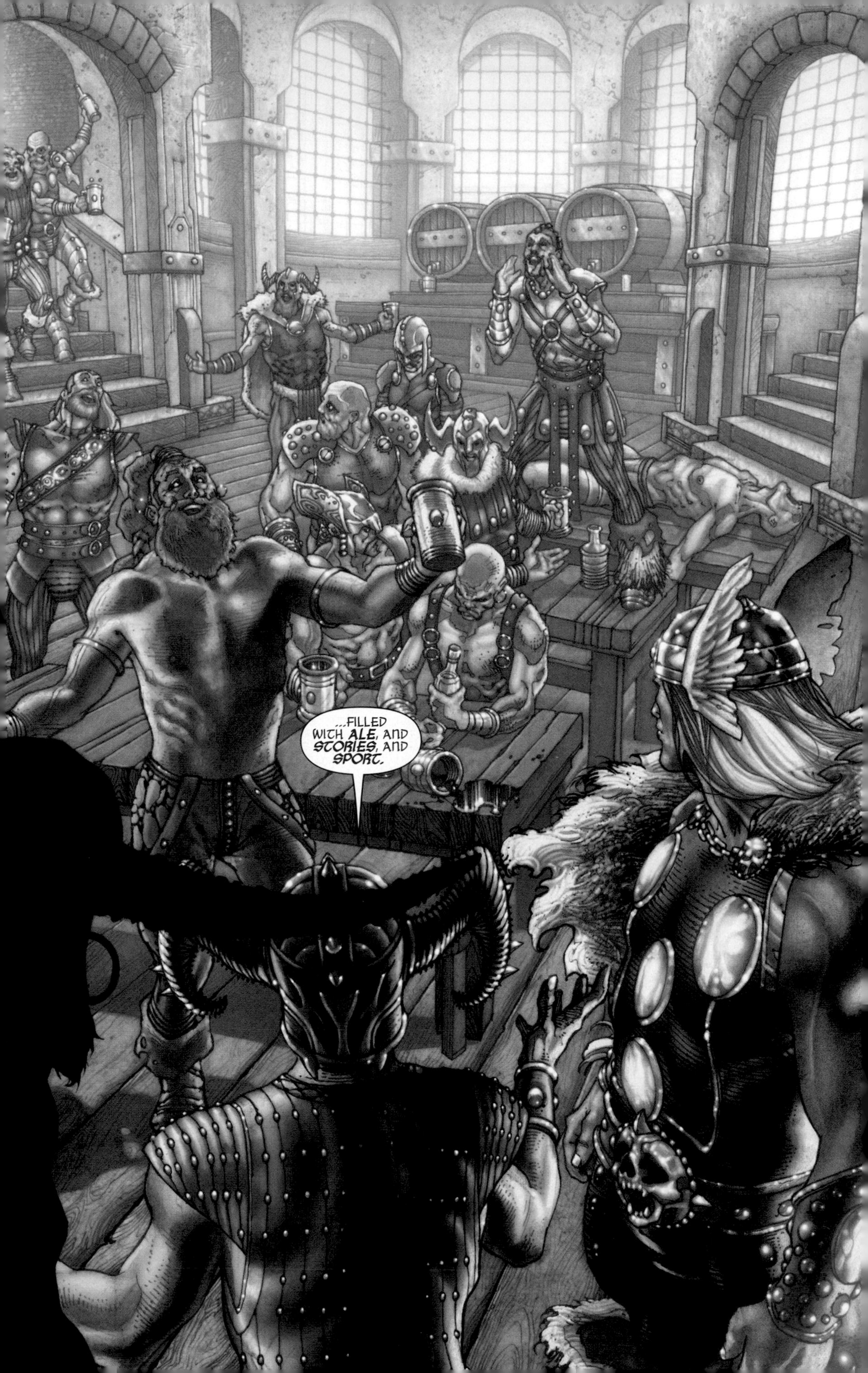
...FILLED WITH ALE, AND STORIES, AND SPORT.

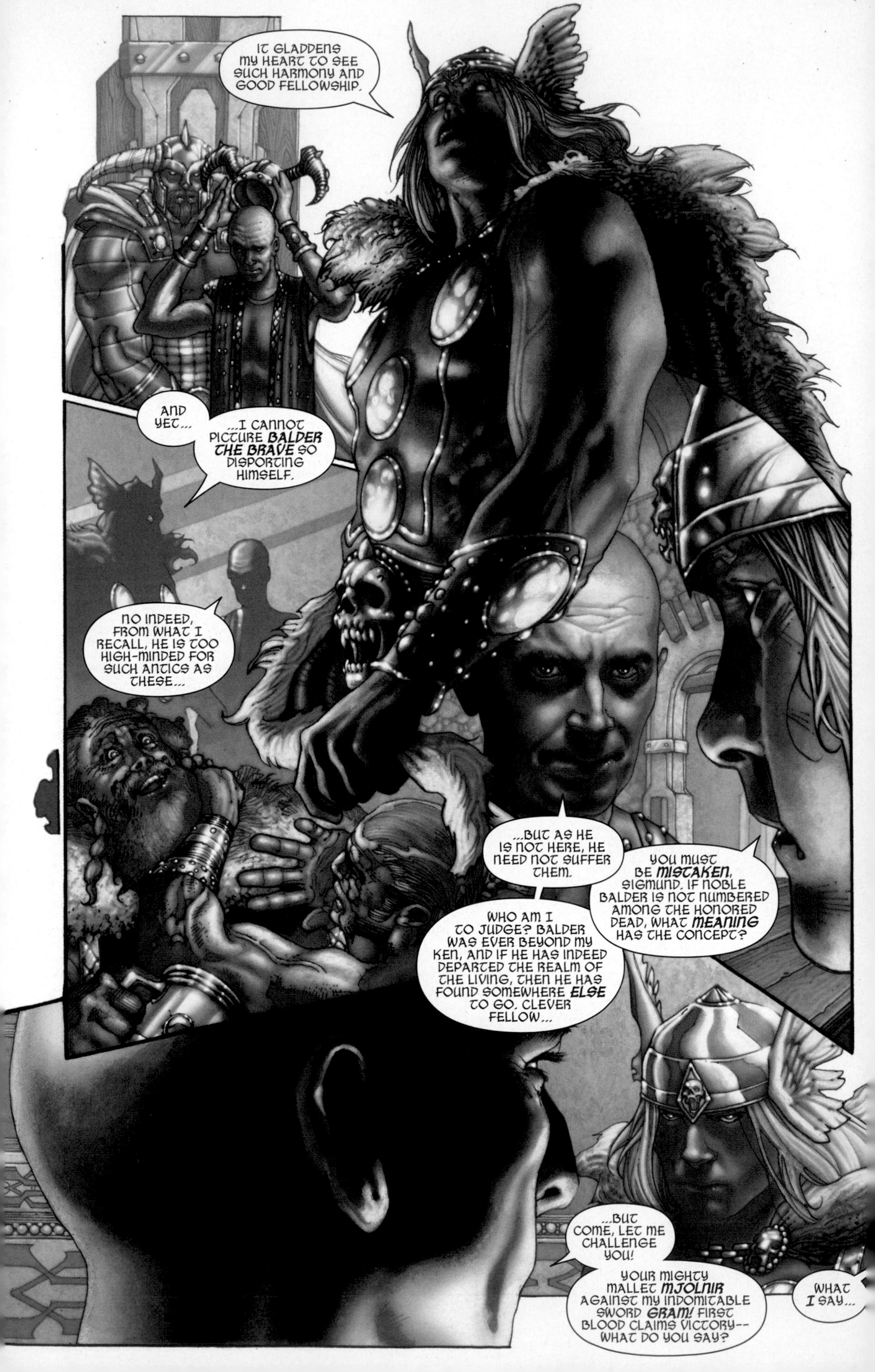
IT GLADDENS MY HEART TO SEE SUCH HARMONY AND GOOD FELLOWSHIP.
AND YET...
...I CANNOT PICTURE **BALDER THE BRAVE** SO DISPORTING HIMSELF.
NO INDEED, FROM WHAT I RECALL, HE IS TOO HIGH-MINDED FOR SUCH ANTICS AS THESE...
...BUT AS HE IS NOT HERE, HE NEED NOT SUFFER THEM.
YOU MUST BE **MISTAKEN**, SIGMUND. IF NOBLE BALDER IS NOT NUMBERED AMONG THE HONORED DEAD, WHAT **MEANING** HAS THE CONCEPT?
WHO AM I TO JUDGE? BALDER WAS EVER BEYOND MY KEN, AND IF HE HAS INDEED DEPARTED THE REALM OF THE LIVING, THEN HE HAS FOUND SOMEWHERE **ELSE** TO GO. CLEVER FELLOW...
...BUT COME, LET ME CHALLENGE YOU!
YOUR MIGHTY MALLET **MJOLNIR** AGAINST MY INDOMITABLE SWORD **GRAM!** FIRST BLOOD CLAIMS VICTORY-- WHAT DO YOU SAY?
WHAT **I** SAY...

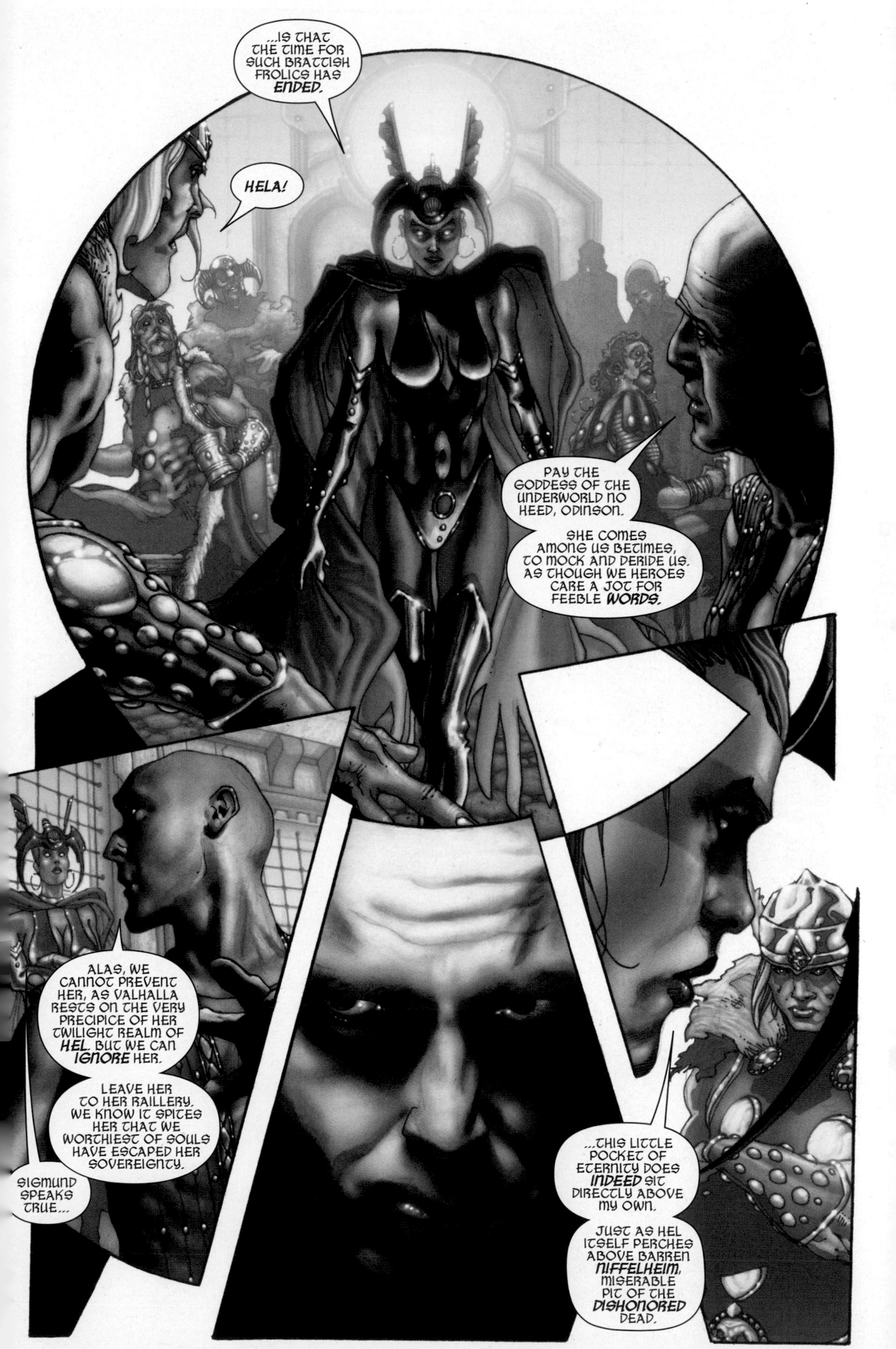
...IS THAT THE TIME FOR SUCH BRATTISH FROLICS HAS ENDED.
HELA!
PAY THE GODDESS OF THE UNDERWORLD NO HEED, ODINSON.
SHE COMES AMONG US BETIMES, TO MOCK AND DERIDE US. AS THOUGH WE HEROES CARE A JOT FOR FEEBLE WORDS.
ALAS, WE CANNOT PREVENT HER, AS VALHALLA RESTS ON THE VERY PRECIPICE OF HER TWILIGHT REALM OF HEL. BUT WE CAN IGNORE HER.
LEAVE HER TO HER RAILLERY. WE KNOW IT SPITES HER THAT WE WORTHIEST OF SOULS HAVE ESCAPED HER SOVEREIGNTY.
SIGMUND SPEAKS TRUE...
...THIS LITTLE POCKET OF ETERNITY DOES INDEED SIT DIRECTLY ABOVE MY OWN.
JUST AS HEL ITSELF PERCHES ABOVE BARREN NIFFELHEIM, MISERABLE PIT OF THE DISHONORED DEAD.

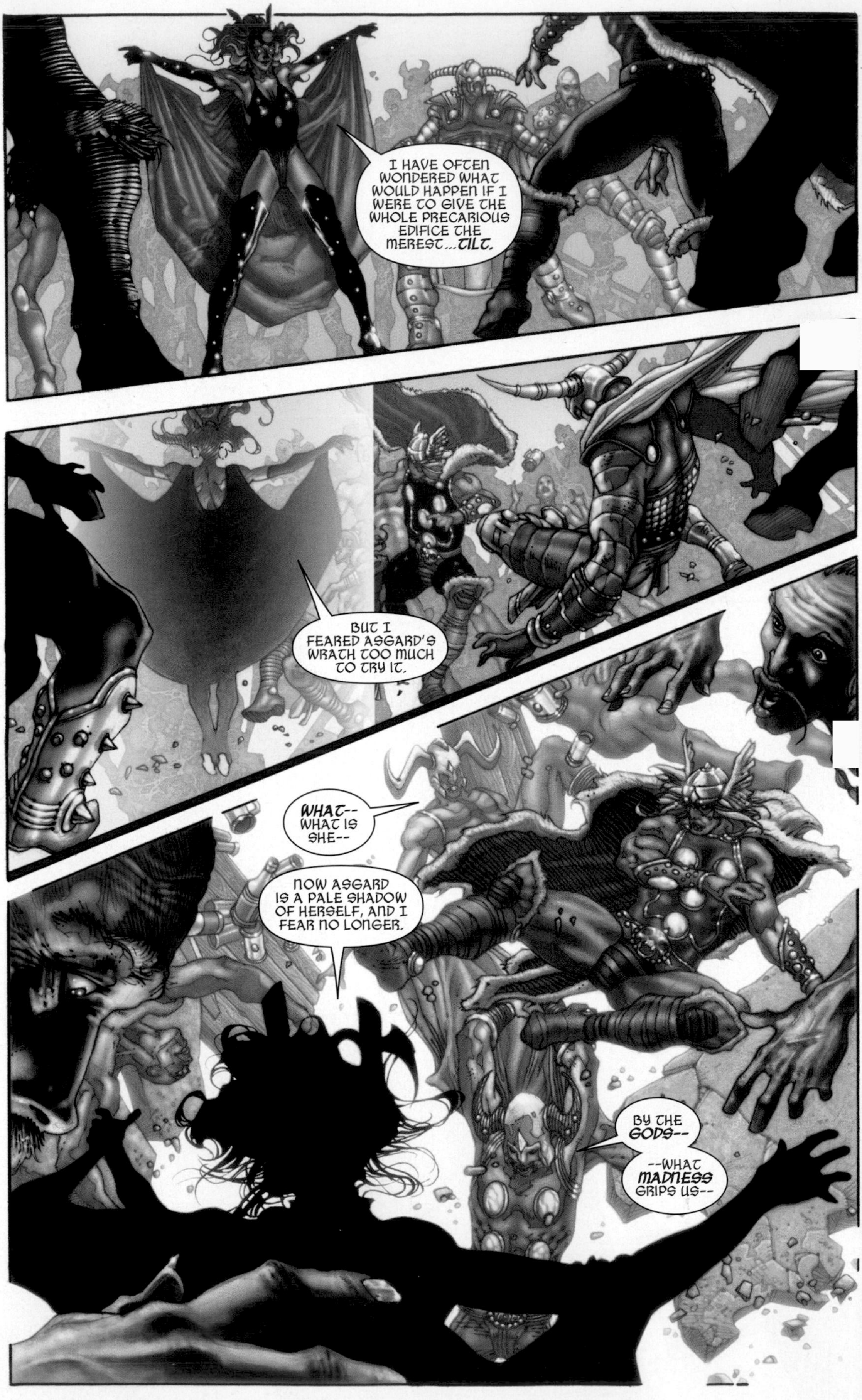
I HAVE OFTEN WONDERED WHAT WOULD HAPPEN IF I WERE TO GIVE THE WHOLE PRECARIOUS EDIFICE THE MEREST...TILT.
BUT I FEARED ASGARD'S WRATH TOO MUCH TO TRY IT.
WHAT-- WHAT IS SHE--
NOW ASGARD IS A PALE SHADOW OF HERSELF, AND I FEAR NO LONGER.
BY THE GODS--
--WHAT MADNESS GRIPS US--

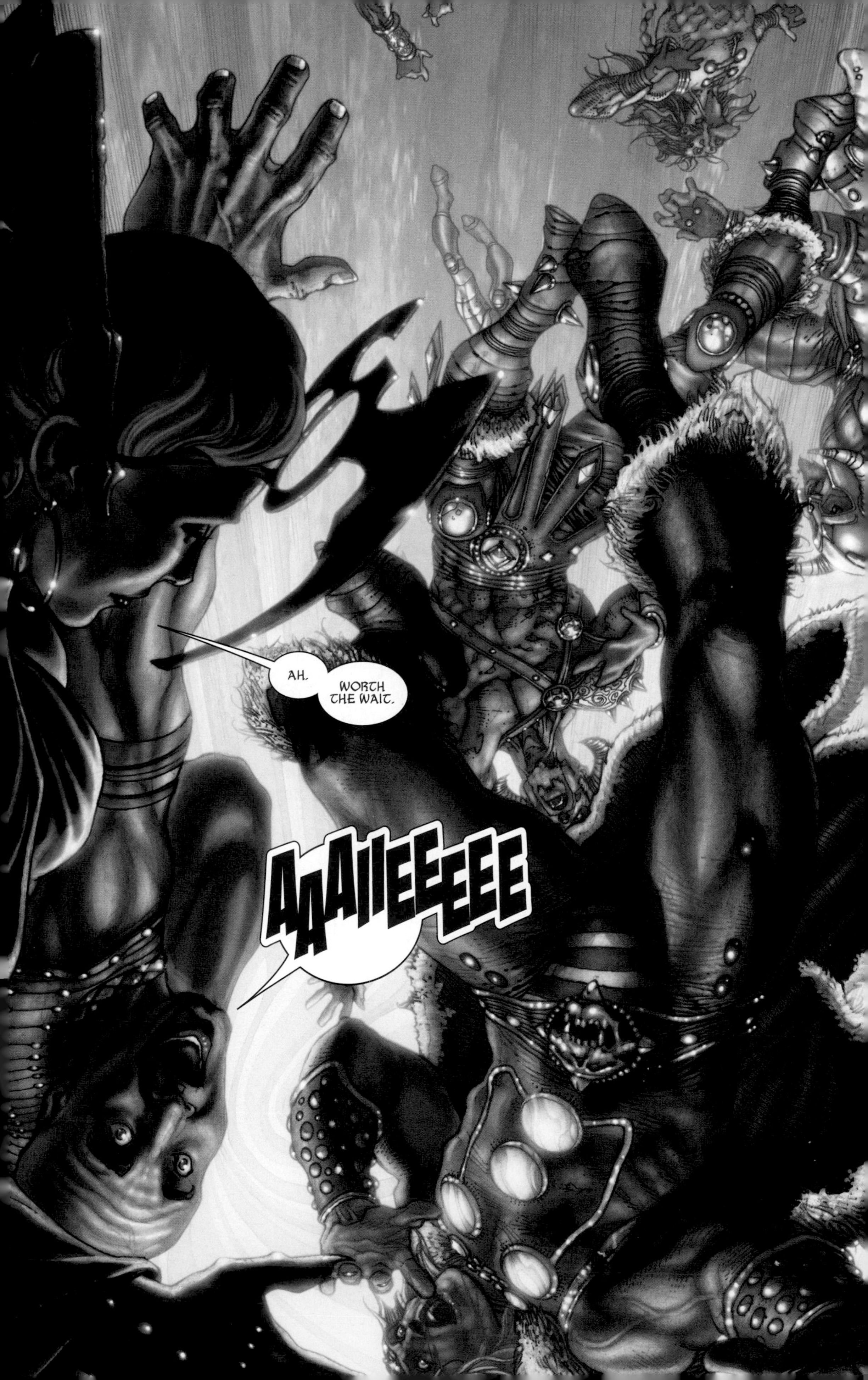
AH.
WORTH THE WAIT.
AAAIIEEEEE

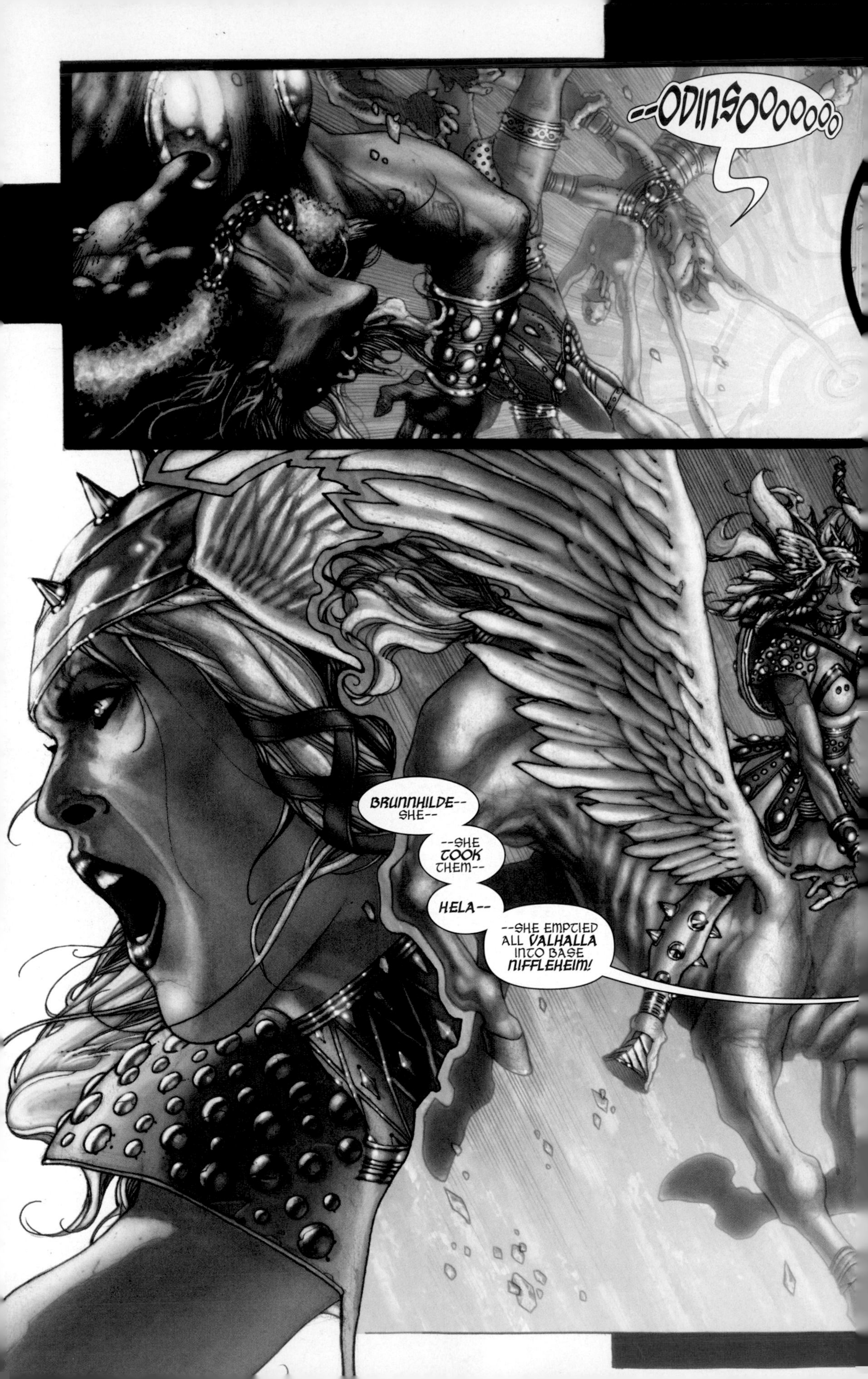
--ODINSOOOOOO
BRUNNHILDE-- SHE--
--SHE TOOK THEM--
HELA--
--SHE EMPTIED ALL VALHALLA INTO BASE NIFFLEHEIM!

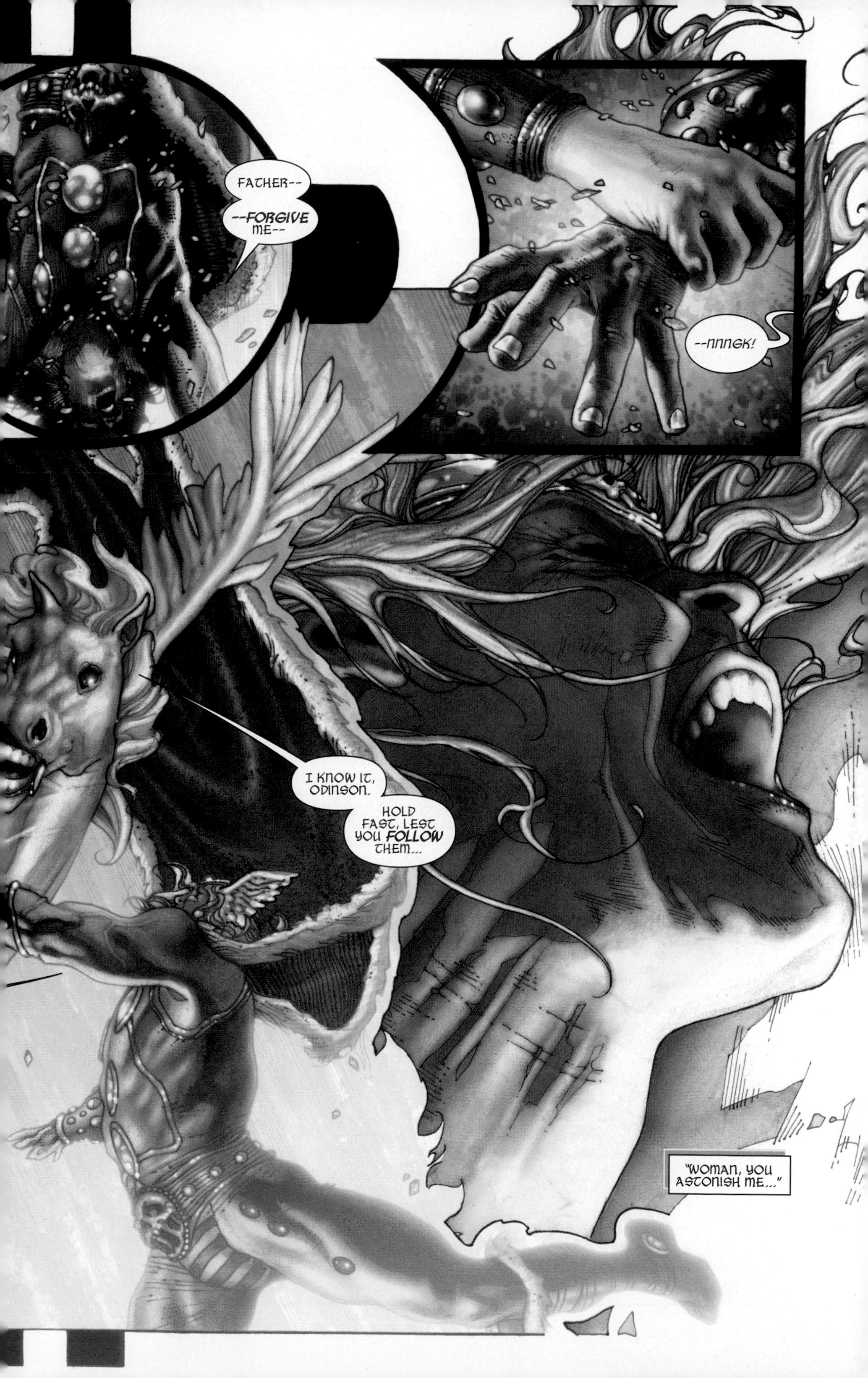
FATHER--
--FORGIVE ME--
--NNNGK!
I KNOW IT, ODINSON.
HOLD FAST, LEST YOU FOLLOW THEM...
"WOMAN, YOU ASTONISH ME..."

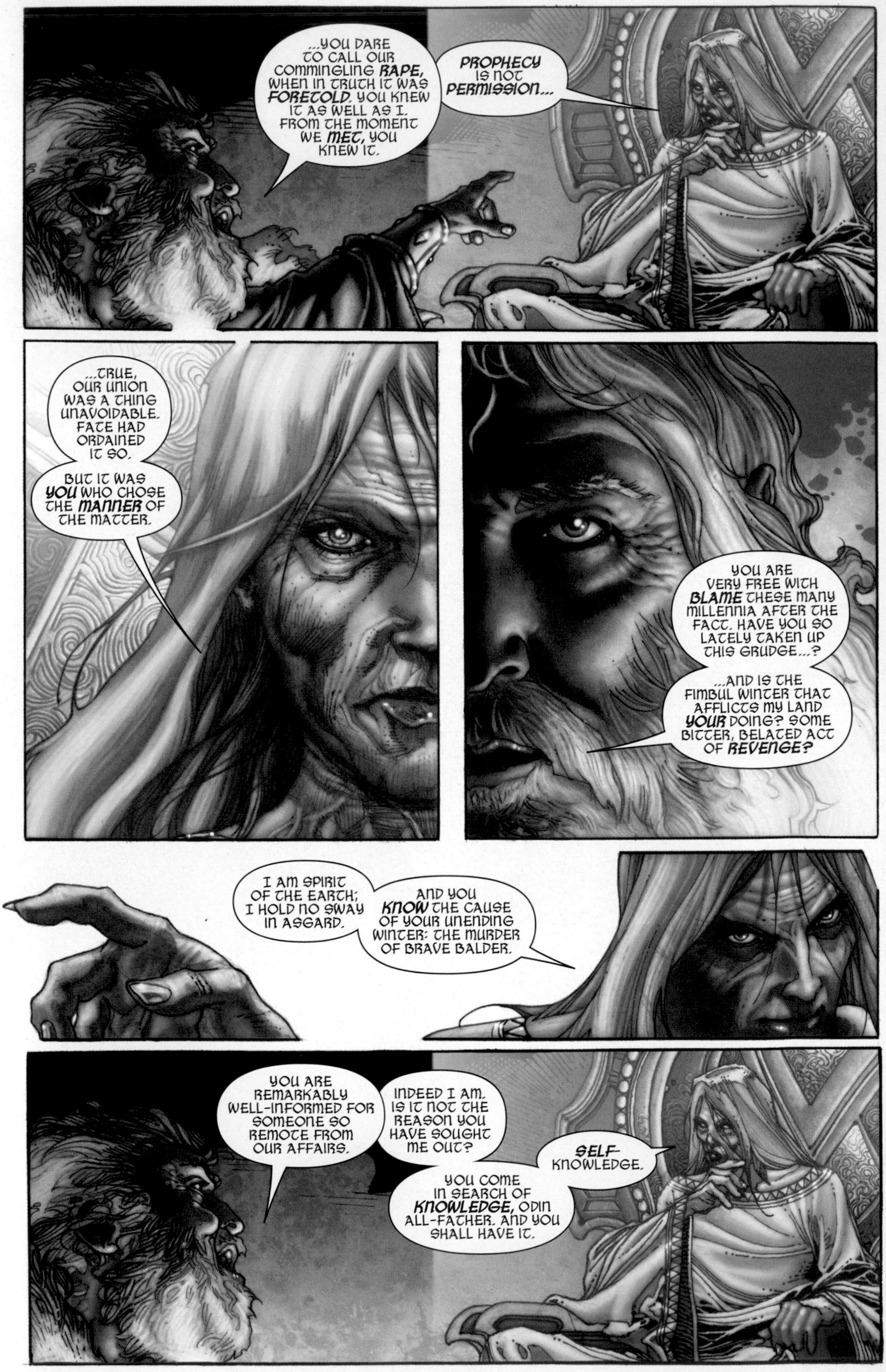
...YOU DARE TO CALL OUR COMMINGLING RAPE, WHEN IN TRUTH IT WAS FORETOLD. YOU KNEW IT AS WELL AS I. FROM THE MOMENT WE MET, YOU KNEW IT.
PROPHECY IS NOT PERMISSION...
...TRUE, OUR UNION WAS A THING UNAVOIDABLE. FATE HAD ORDAINED IT SO.
BUT IT WAS YOU WHO CHOSE THE MANNER OF THE MATTER.
YOU ARE VERY FREE WITH BLAME THESE MANY MILLENNIA AFTER THE FACT. HAVE YOU SO LATELY TAKEN UP THIS GRUDGE...?
...AND IS THE FIMBUL WINTER THAT AFFLICTS MY LAND YOUR DOING? SOME BITTER, BELATED ACT OF REVENGE?
I AM SPIRIT OF THE EARTH; I HOLD NO SWAY IN ASGARD.
AND YOU KNOW THE CAUSE OF YOUR UNENDING WINTER: THE MURDER OF BRAVE BALDER.
YOU ARE REMARKABLY WELL-INFORMED FOR SOMEONE SO REMOTE FROM OUR AFFAIRS.
INDEED I AM. IS IT NOT THE REASON YOU HAVE SOUGHT ME OUT?
SELF-KNOWLEDGE.
YOU COME IN SEARCH OF KNOWLEDGE, ODIN ALL-FATHER. AND YOU SHALL HAVE IT.

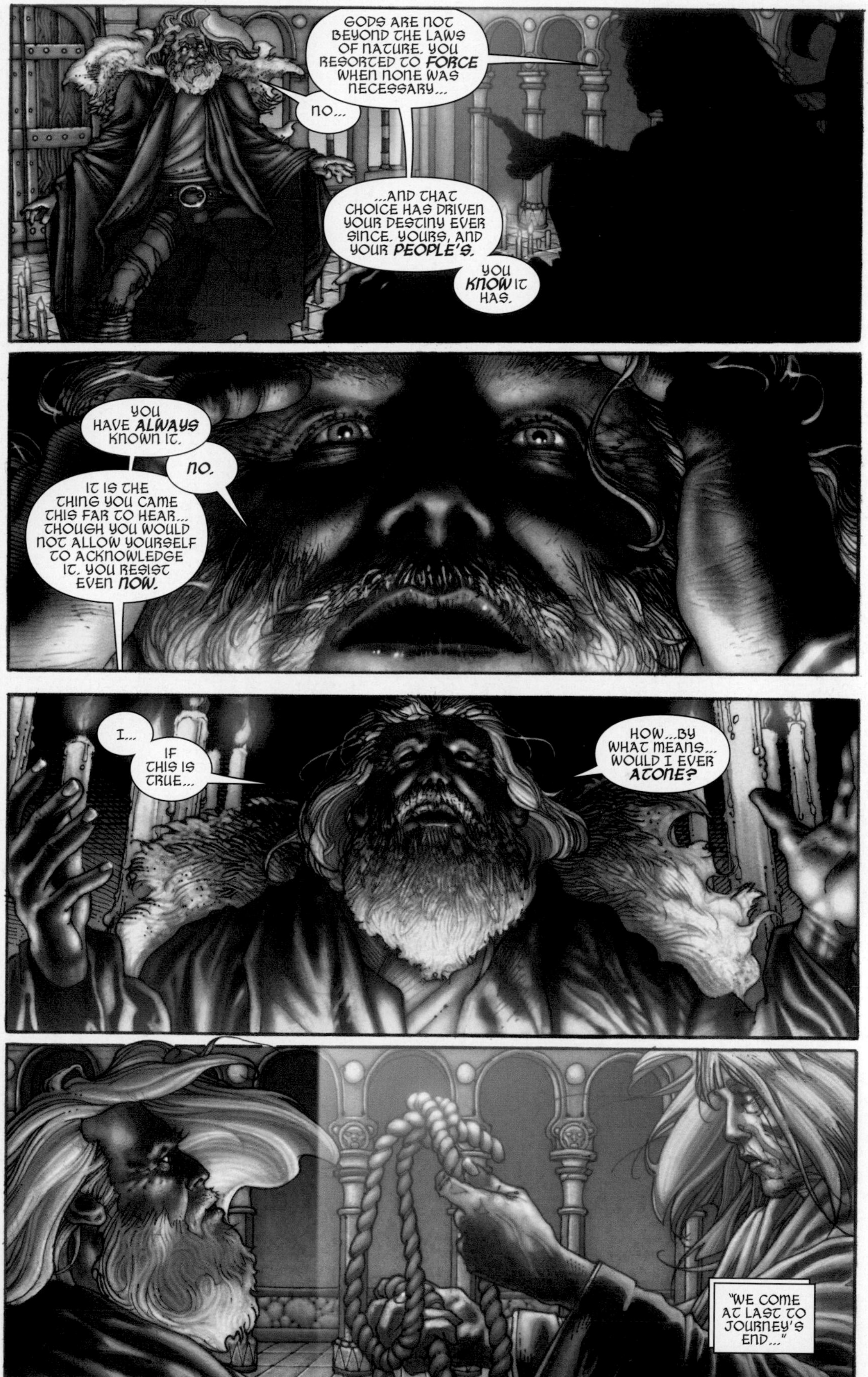
GODS ARE NOT BEYOND THE LAWS OF NATURE. YOU RESORTED TO FORCE WHEN NONE WAS NECESSARY...
NO...
...AND THAT CHOICE HAS DRIVEN YOUR DESTINY EVER SINCE. YOURS, AND YOUR PEOPLE'S.
YOU KNOW IT HAS.
YOU HAVE ALWAYS KNOWN IT.
NO.
IT IS THE THING YOU CAME THIS FAR TO HEAR... THOUGH YOU WOULD NOT ALLOW YOURSELF TO ACKNOWLEDGE IT. YOU RESIST EVEN NOW.
I...
IF THIS IS TRUE...
HOW...BY WHAT MEANS... WOULD I EVER ATONE?
"WE COME AT LAST TO JOURNEY'S END..."

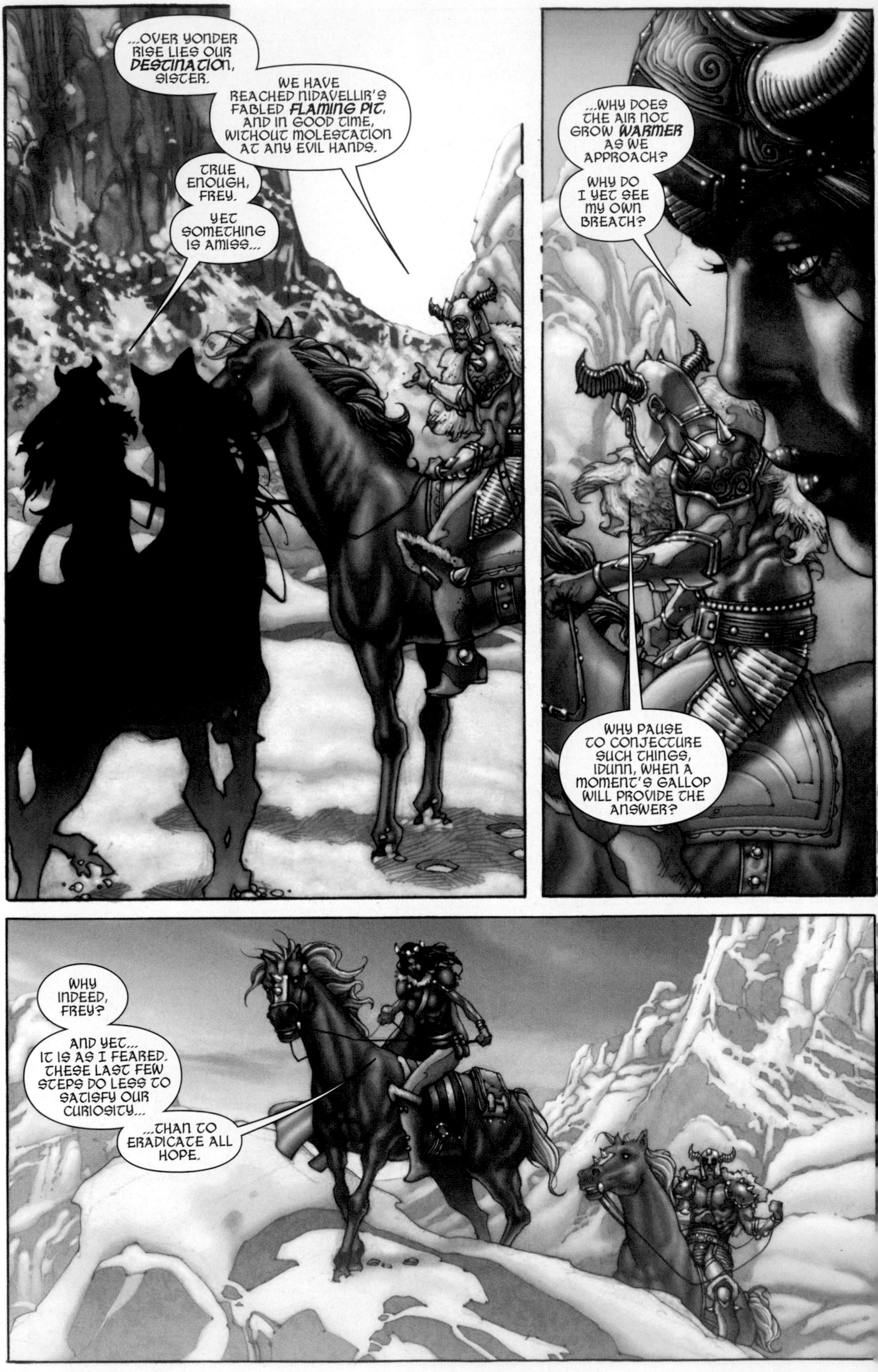
...OVER YONDER RISE LIES OUR DESTINATION, SISTER.
WE HAVE REACHED NIDAVELLIR'S FABLED FLAMING PIT, AND IN GOOD TIME, WITHOUT MOLESTATION AT ANY EVIL HANDS.
TRUE ENOUGH, FREY.
YET SOMETHING IS AMISS...
...WHY DOES THE AIR NOT GROW WARMER AS WE APPROACH?
WHY DO I YET SEE MY OWN BREATH?
WHY PAUSE TO CONJECTURE SUCH THINGS, IDUNN, WHEN A MOMENT'S GALLOP WILL PROVIDE THE ANSWER?
WHY INDEED, FREY?
AND YET... IT IS AS I FEARED. THESE LAST FEW STEPS DO LESS TO SATISFY OUR CURIOSITY...
...THAN TO ERADICATE ALL HOPE.

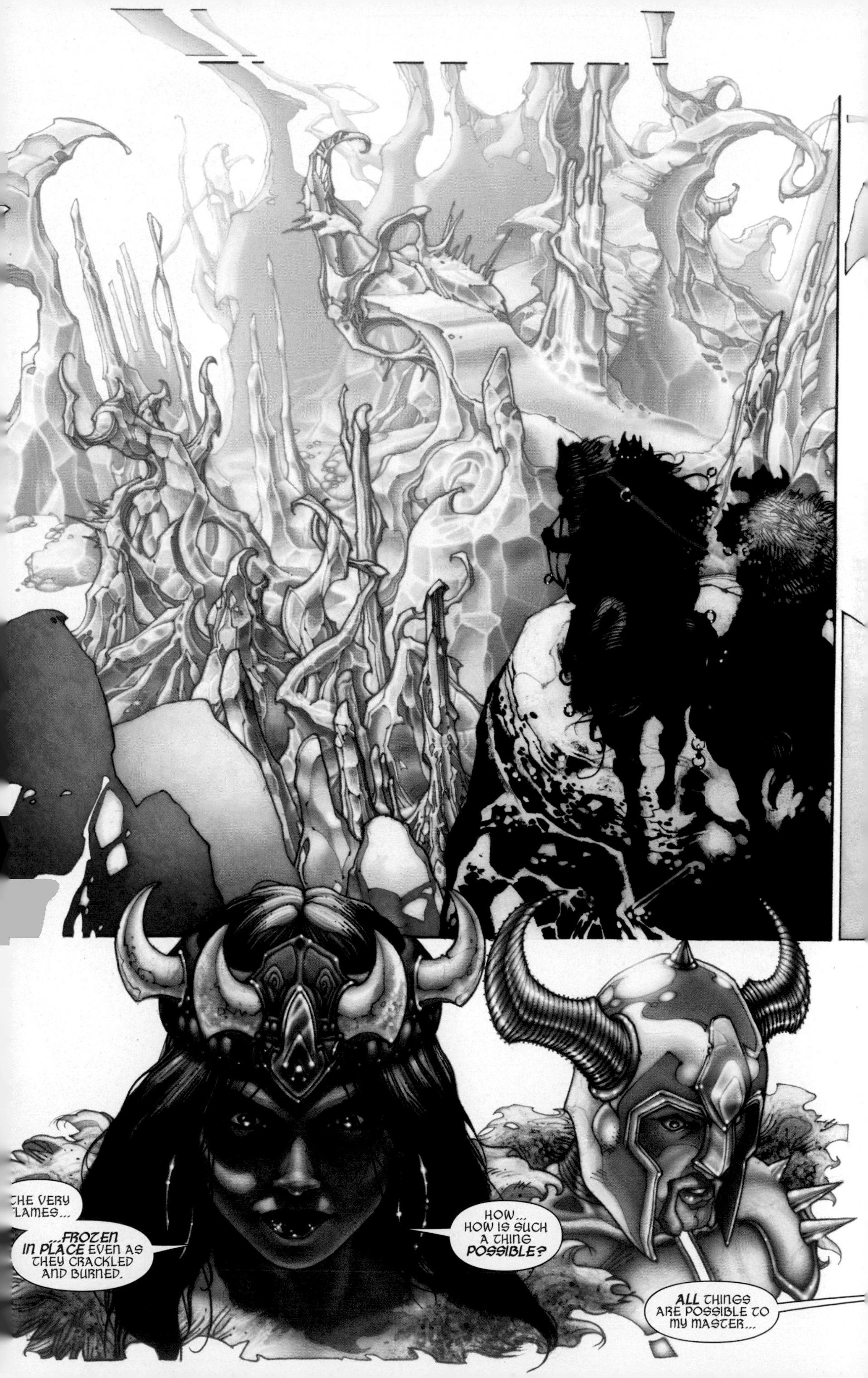

THE VERY FLAMES...
...FROZEN IN PLACE EVEN AS THEY CRACKLED AND BURNED.
HOW... HOW IS SUCH A THING POSSIBLE?
ALL THINGS ARE POSSIBLE TO MY MASTER...

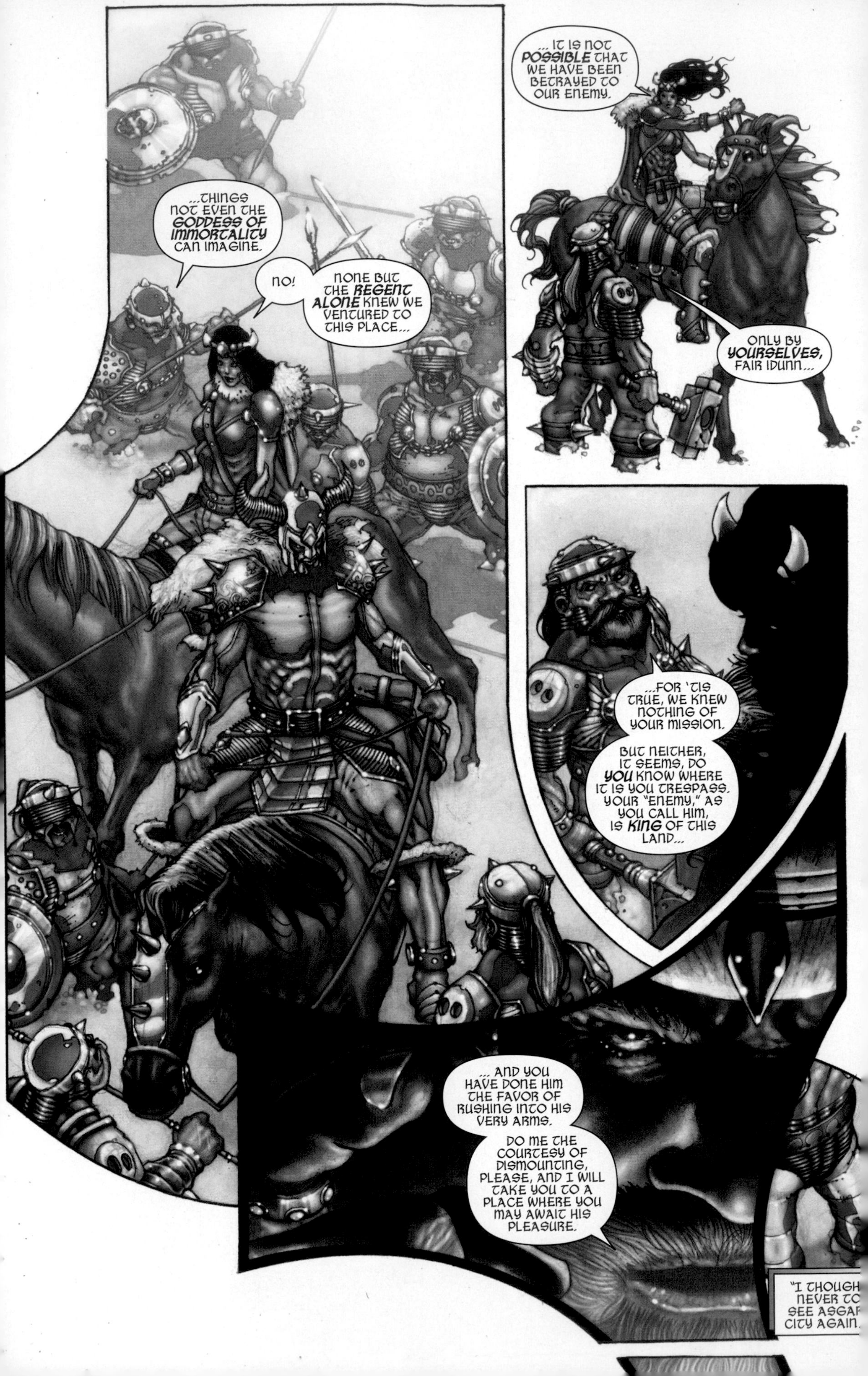

...THINGS NOT EVEN THE GODDESS OF IMMORTALITY CAN IMAGINE.
NO!
NONE BUT THE REGENT ALONE KNEW WE VENTURED TO THIS PLACE...
...IT IS NOT POSSIBLE THAT WE HAVE BEEN BETRAYED TO OUR ENEMY.
ONLY BY YOURSELVES, FAIR IDUNN...
...FOR 'TIS TRUE, WE KNEW NOTHING OF YOUR MISSION.
BUT NEITHER, IT SEEMS, DO YOU KNOW WHERE IT IS YOU TRESPASS. YOUR "ENEMY," AS YOU CALL HIM, IS KING OF THIS LAND...
...AND YOU HAVE DONE HIM THE FAVOR OF RUSHING INTO HIS VERY ARMS.
DO ME THE COURTESY OF DISMOUNTING, PLEASE, AND I WILL TAKE YOU TO A PLACE WHERE YOU MAY AWAIT HIS PLEASURE.

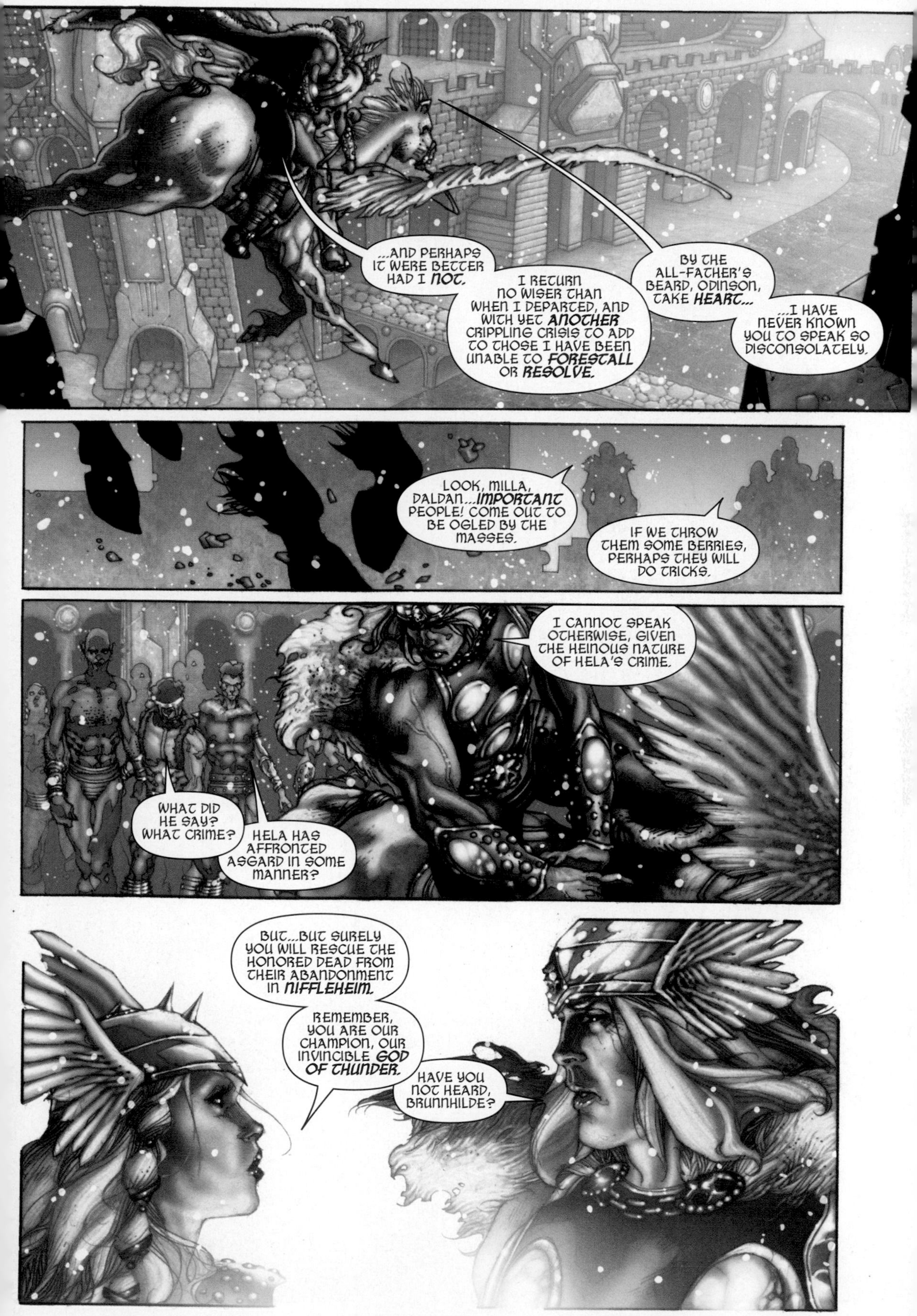
...AND PERHAPS IT WERE BETTER HAD I NOT.
I RETURN NO WISER THAN WHEN I DEPARTED, AND WITH YET ANOTHER CRIPPLING CRISIS TO ADD TO THOSE I HAVE BEEN UNABLE TO FORESTALL OR RESOLVE.
BY THE ALL-FATHER'S BEARD, ODINSON, TAKE HEART...
...I HAVE NEVER KNOWN YOU TO SPEAK SO DISCONSOLATELY.
LOOK, MILLA, DALDAN...IMPORTANT PEOPLE! COME OUT TO BE OGLED BY THE MASSES.
IF WE THROW THEM SOME BERRIES, PERHAPS THEY WILL DO TRICKS.
I CANNOT SPEAK OTHERWISE, GIVEN THE HEINOUS NATURE OF HELA'S CRIME.
WHAT DID HE SAY? WHAT CRIME?
HELA HAS AFFRONTED ASGARD IN SOME MANNER?
BUT...BUT SURELY YOU WILL RESCUE THE HONORED DEAD FROM THEIR ABANDONMENT IN NIFFLEHEIM.
REMEMBER, YOU ARE OUR CHAMPION, OUR INVINCIBLE GOD OF THUNDER.
HAVE YOU NOT HEARD, BRUNNHILDE?

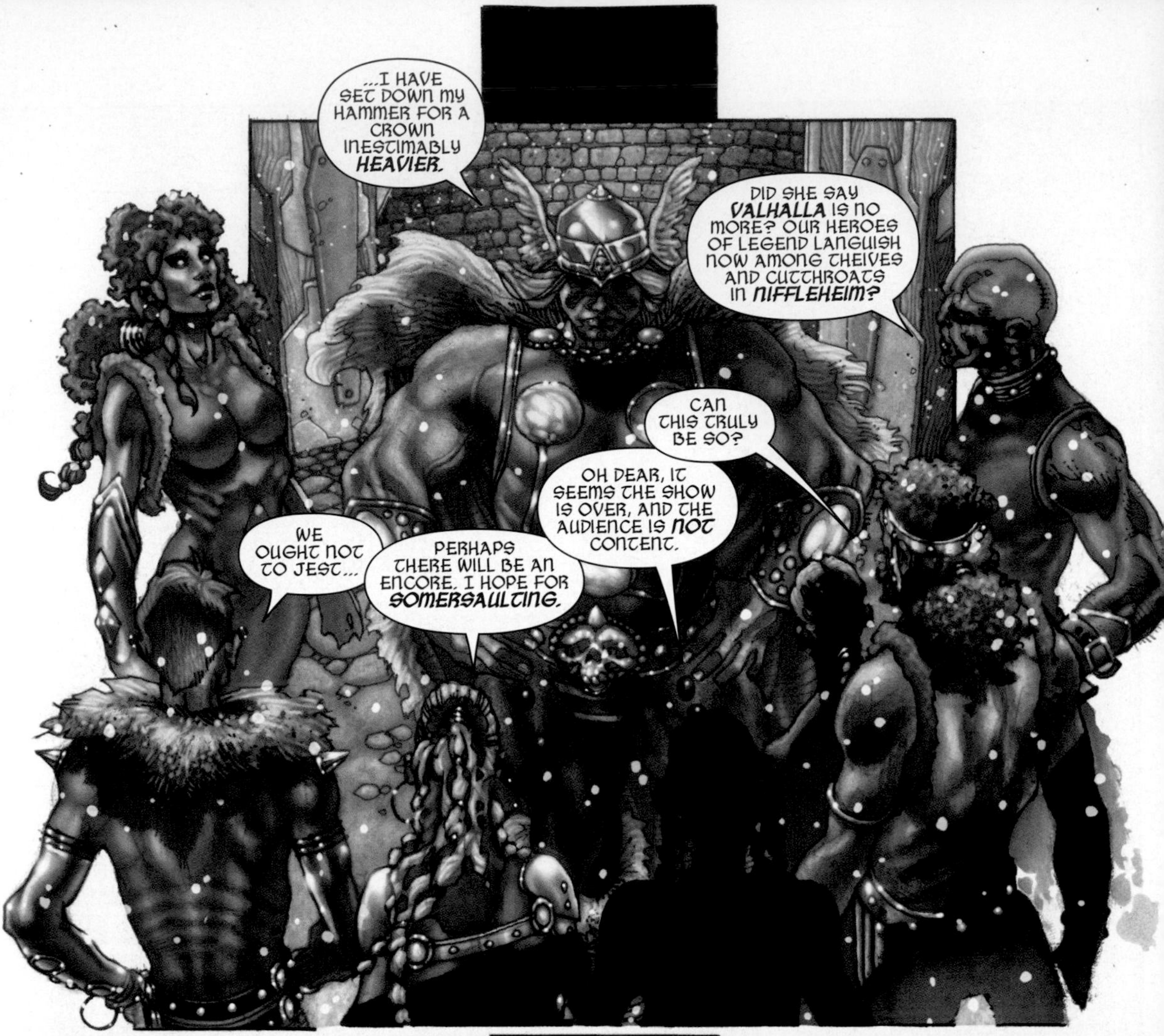
...I HAVE SET DOWN MY HAMMER FOR A CROWN INESTIMABLY HEAVIER.
DID SHE SAY VALHALLA IS NO MORE? OUR HEROES OF LEGEND LANGUISH NOW AMONG THEIVES AND CUTTHROATS IN NIFFLEHEIM?
CAN THIS TRULY BE SO?
OH DEAR, IT SEEMS THE SHOW IS OVER, AND THE AUDIENCE IS NOT CONTENT.
WE OUGHT NOT TO JEST...
PERHAPS THERE WILL BE AN ENCORE. I HOPE FOR SOMERSAULTING.

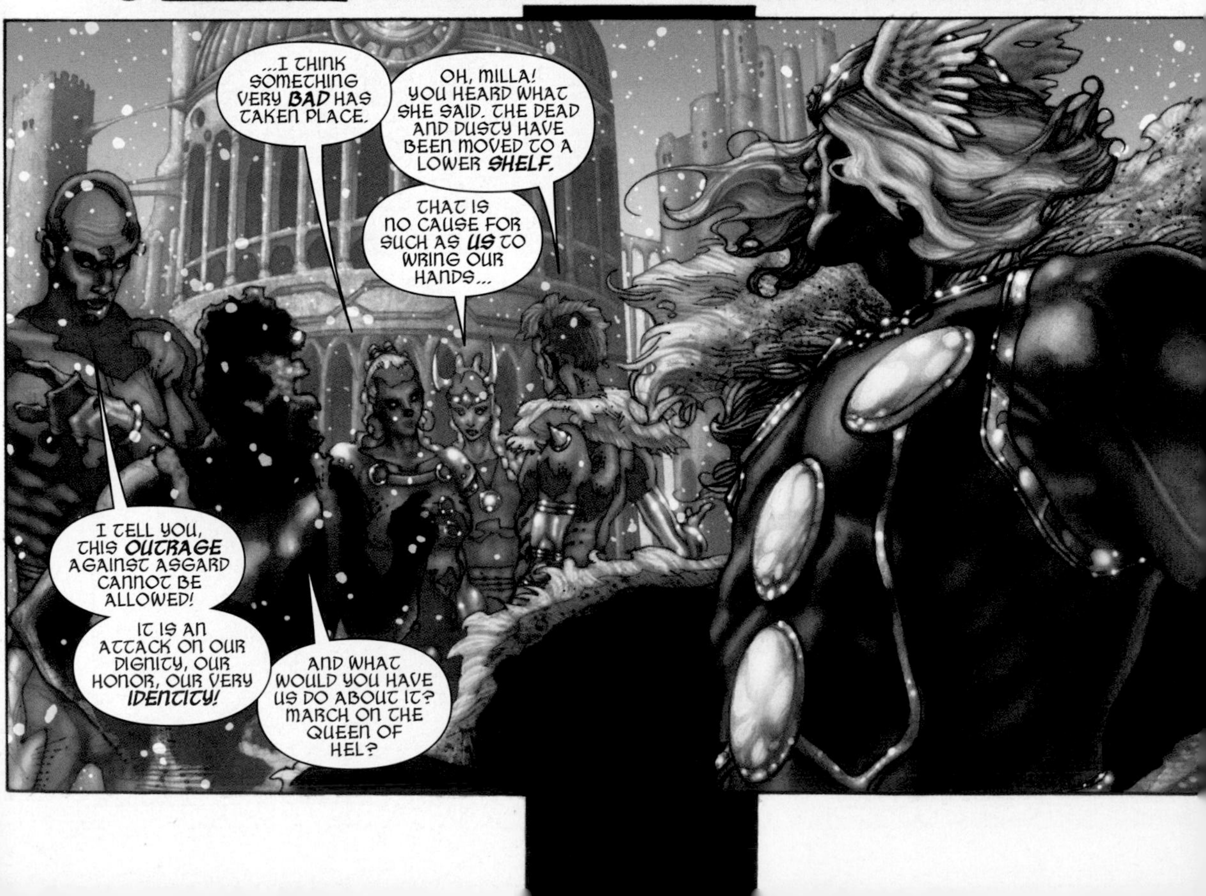
...I THINK SOMETHING VERY BAD HAS TAKEN PLACE.
OH, MILLA! YOU HEARD WHAT SHE SAID. THE DEAD AND DUSTY HAVE BEEN MOVED TO A LOWER SHELF.
THAT IS NO CAUSE FOR SUCH AS US TO WRING OUR HANDS...
I TELL YOU, THIS OUTRAGE AGAINST ASGARD CANNOT BE ALLOWED!
IT IS AN ATTACK ON OUR DIGNITY, OUR HONOR, OUR VERY IDENTITY!
AND WHAT WOULD YOU HAVE US DO ABOUT IT? MARCH ON THE QUEEN OF HEL?

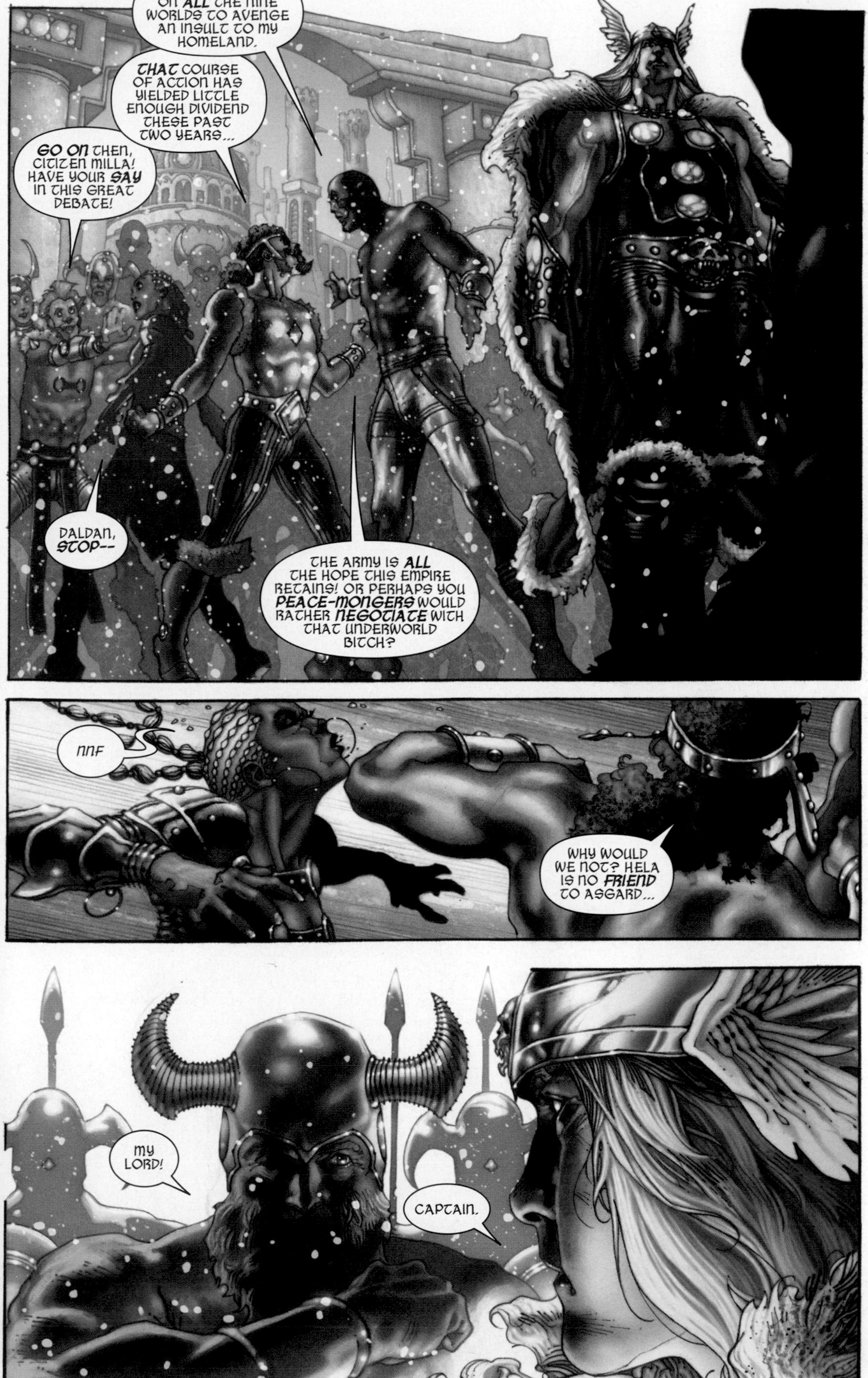
I WOULD MARCH ON ALL THE NINE WORLDS TO AVENGE AN INSULT TO MY HOMELAND.
THAT COURSE OF ACTION HAS YIELDED LITTLE ENOUGH DIVIDEND THESE PAST TWO YEARS...
GO ON THEN, CITIZEN MILLA! HAVE YOUR SAY IN THIS GREAT DEBATE!
DALDAN, STOP--
THE ARMY IS ALL THE HOPE THIS EMPIRE RETAINS! OR PERHAPS YOU PEACE-MONGERS WOULD RATHER NEGOTIATE WITH THAT UNDERWORLD BITCH?
NNF
WHY WOULD WE NOT? HELA IS NO FRIEND TO ASGARD...
MY LORD!
CAPTAIN.

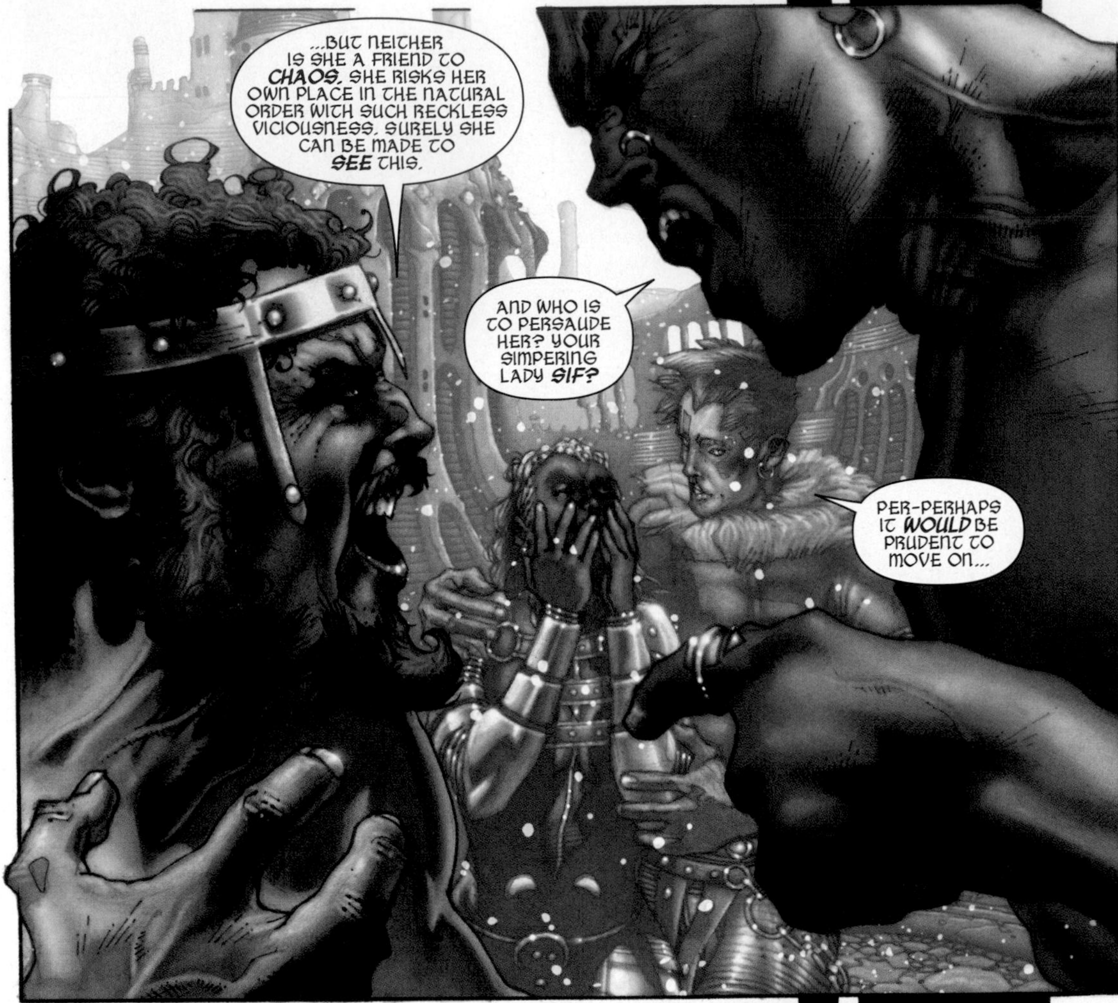
...BUT NEITHER IS SHE A FRIEND TO CHAOS. SHE RISKS HER OWN PLACE IN THE NATURAL ORDER WITH SUCH RECKLESS VICIOUSNESS. SURELY SHE CAN BE MADE TO SEE THIS.
AND WHO IS TO PERSAUDE HER? YOUR SIMPERING LADY SIF?
PER-PERHAPS IT WOULD BE PRUDENT TO MOVE ON...

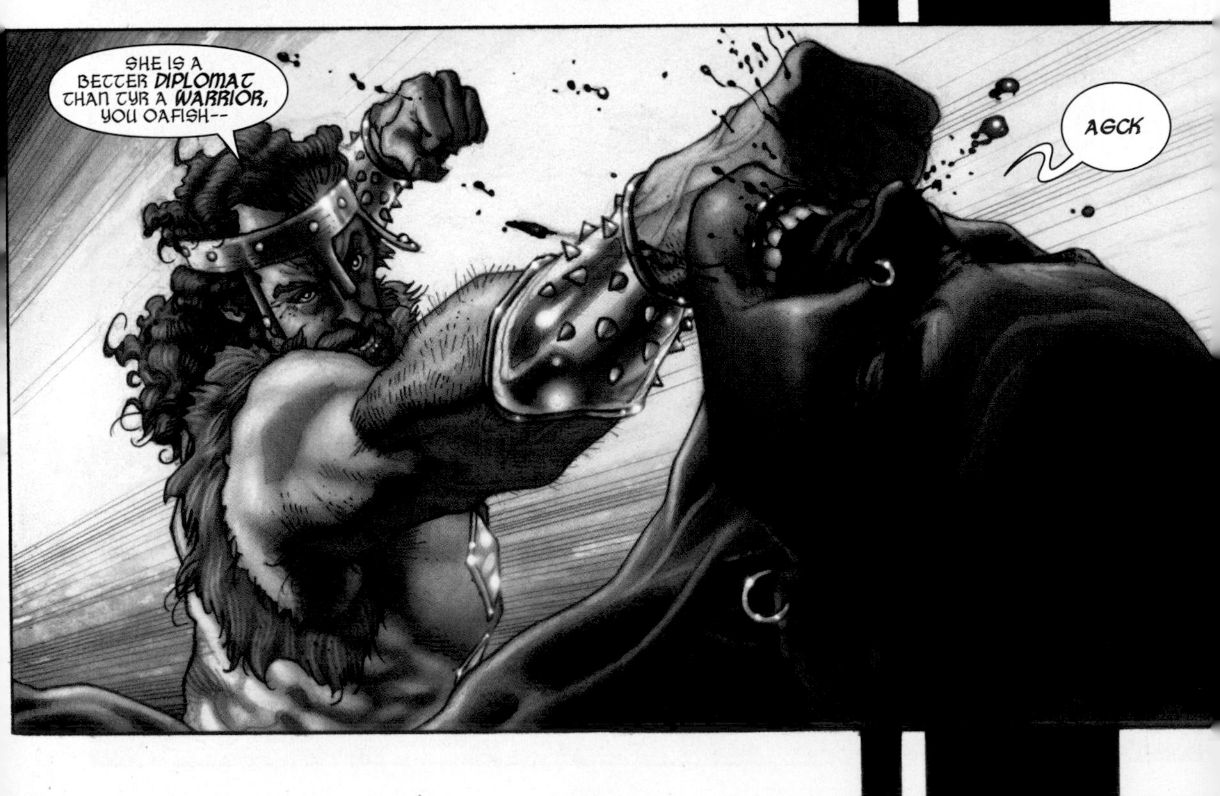
SHE IS A BETTER DIPLOMAT THAN TYR A WARRIOR, YOU OAFISH--
AGCK

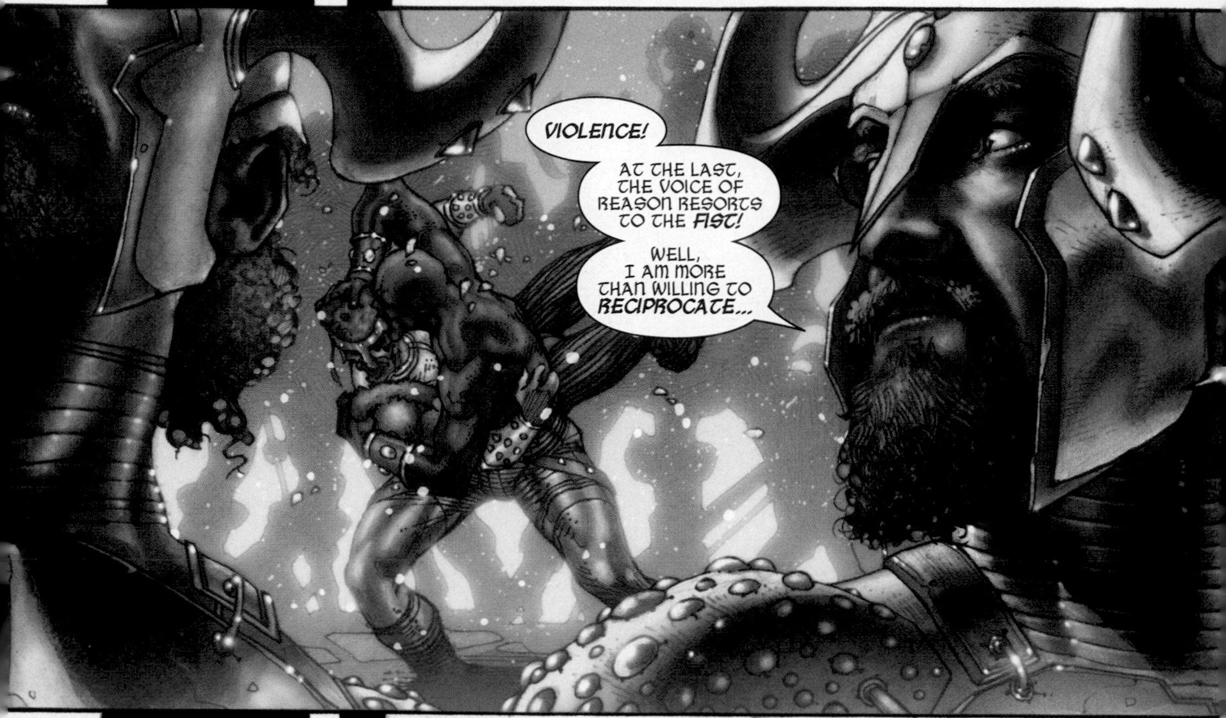
VIOLENCE!
AT THE LAST, THE VOICE OF REASON RESORTS TO THE FIST!
WELL, I AM MORE THAN WILLING TO RECIPROCATE...

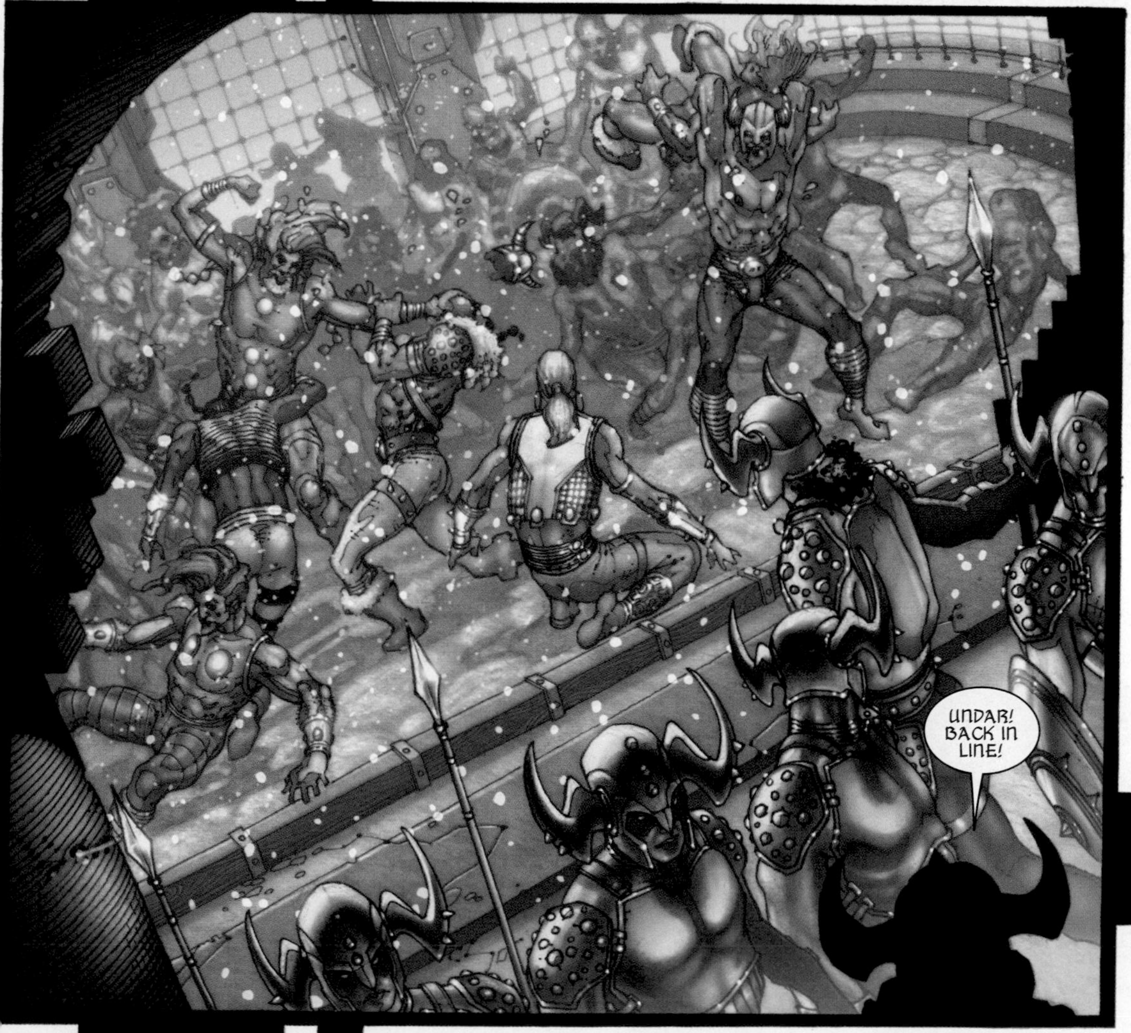
UNDAR! BACK IN LINE!

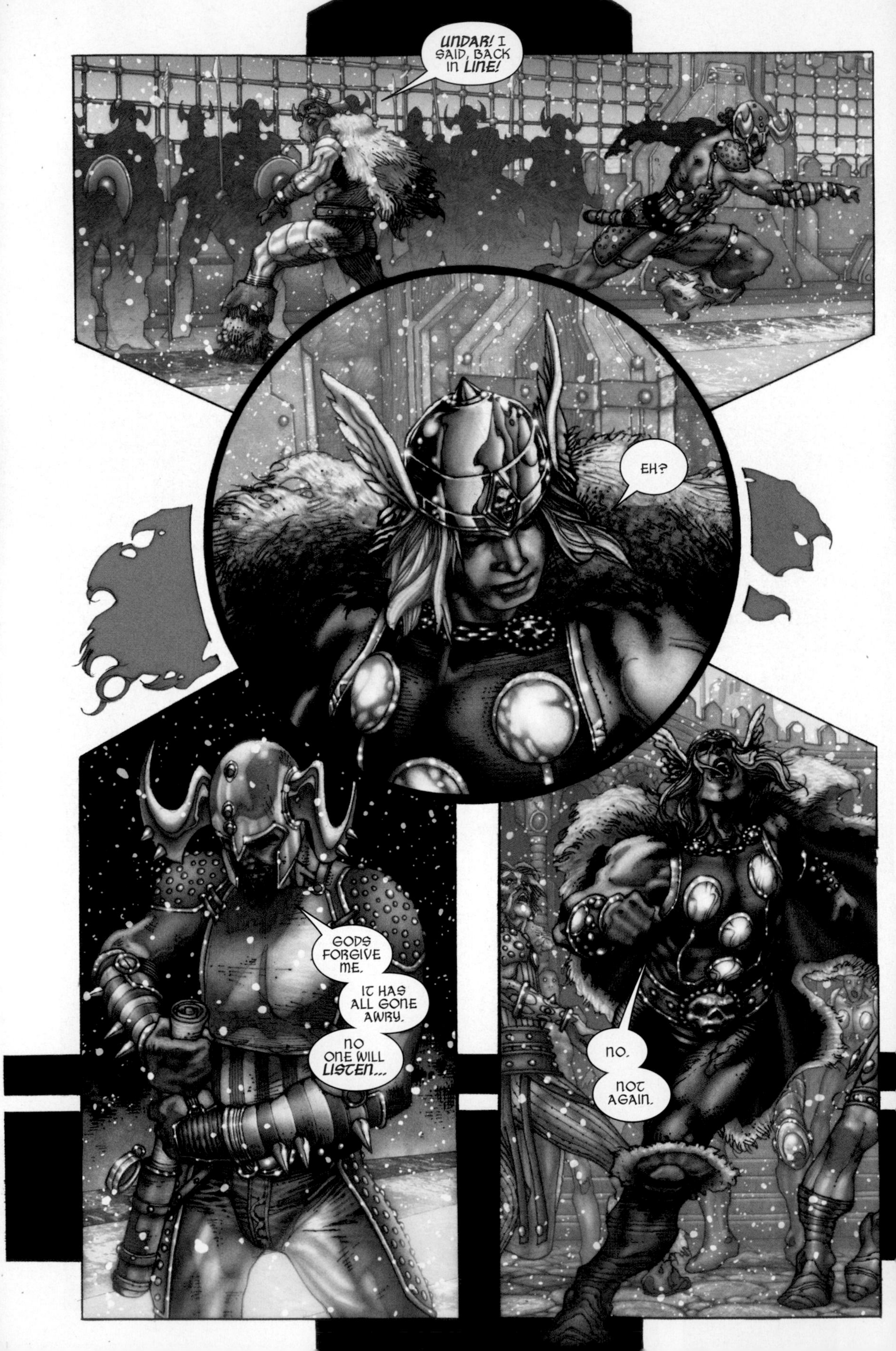
UNDAR! I SAID, BACK IN LINE!
EH?
GODS FORGIVE ME.
IT HAS ALL GONE AWRY.
NO ONE WILL LISTEN...
NO.
NOT AGAIN.

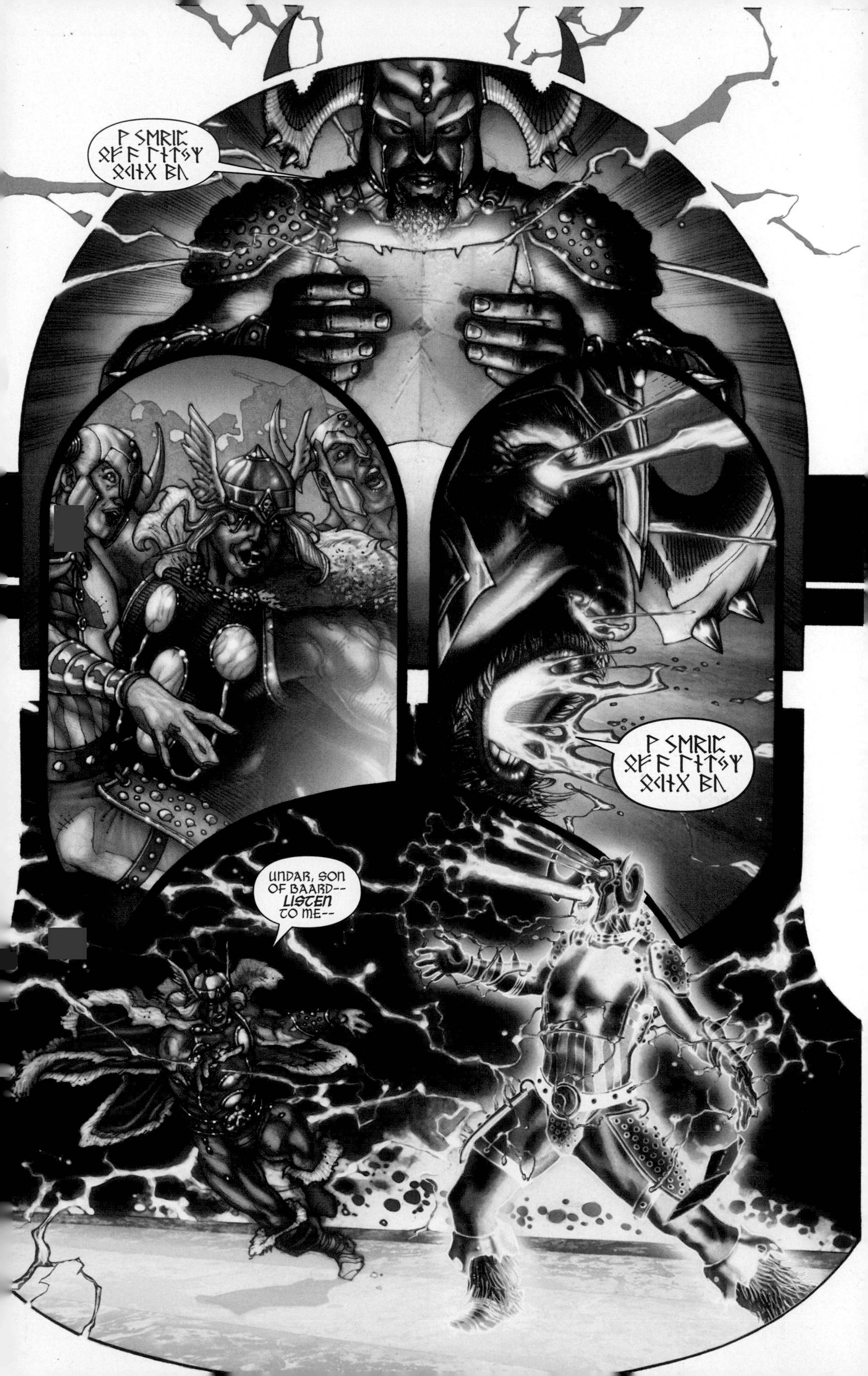
UNDAR, SON OF BAARD-- LISTEN TO ME--

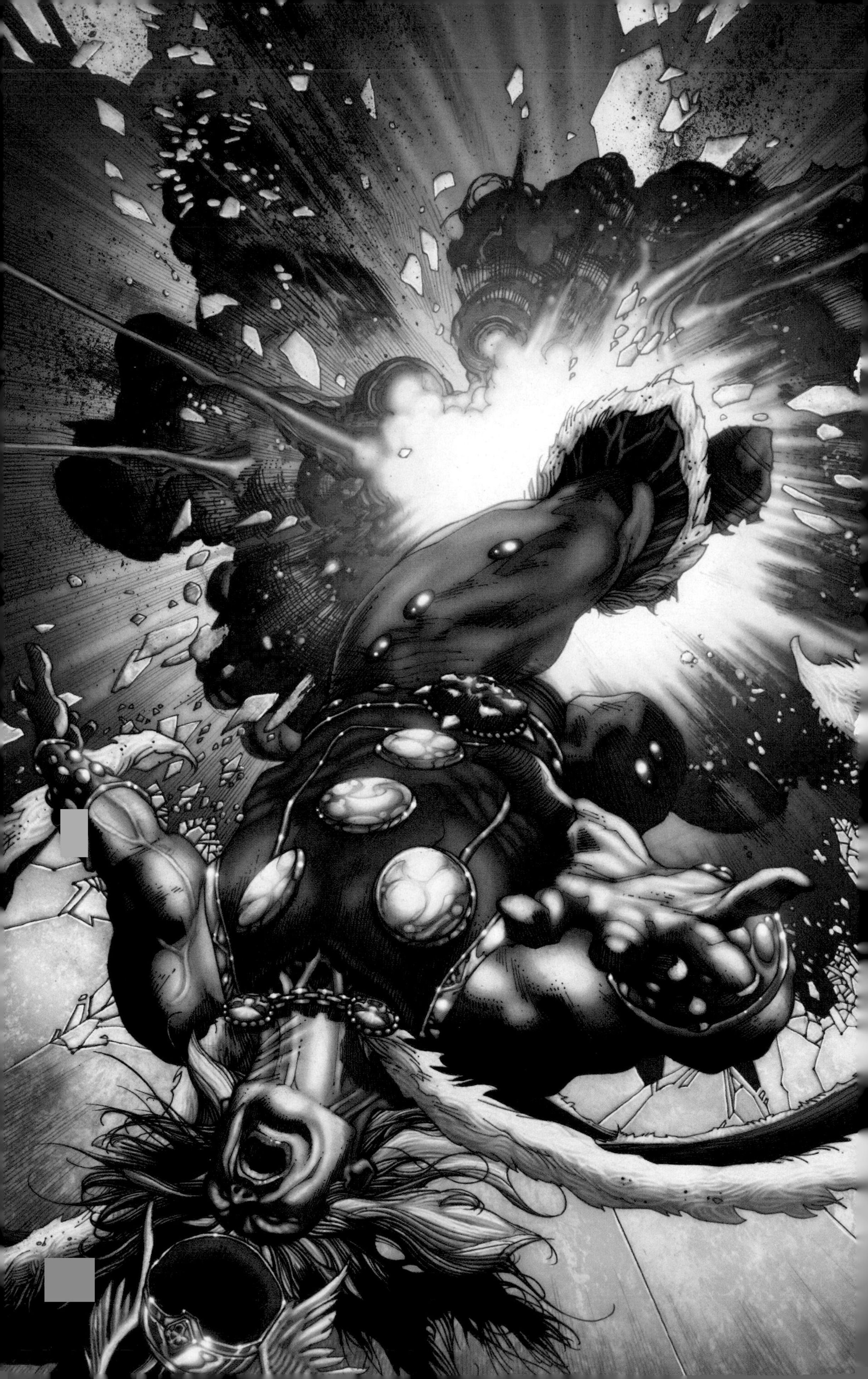

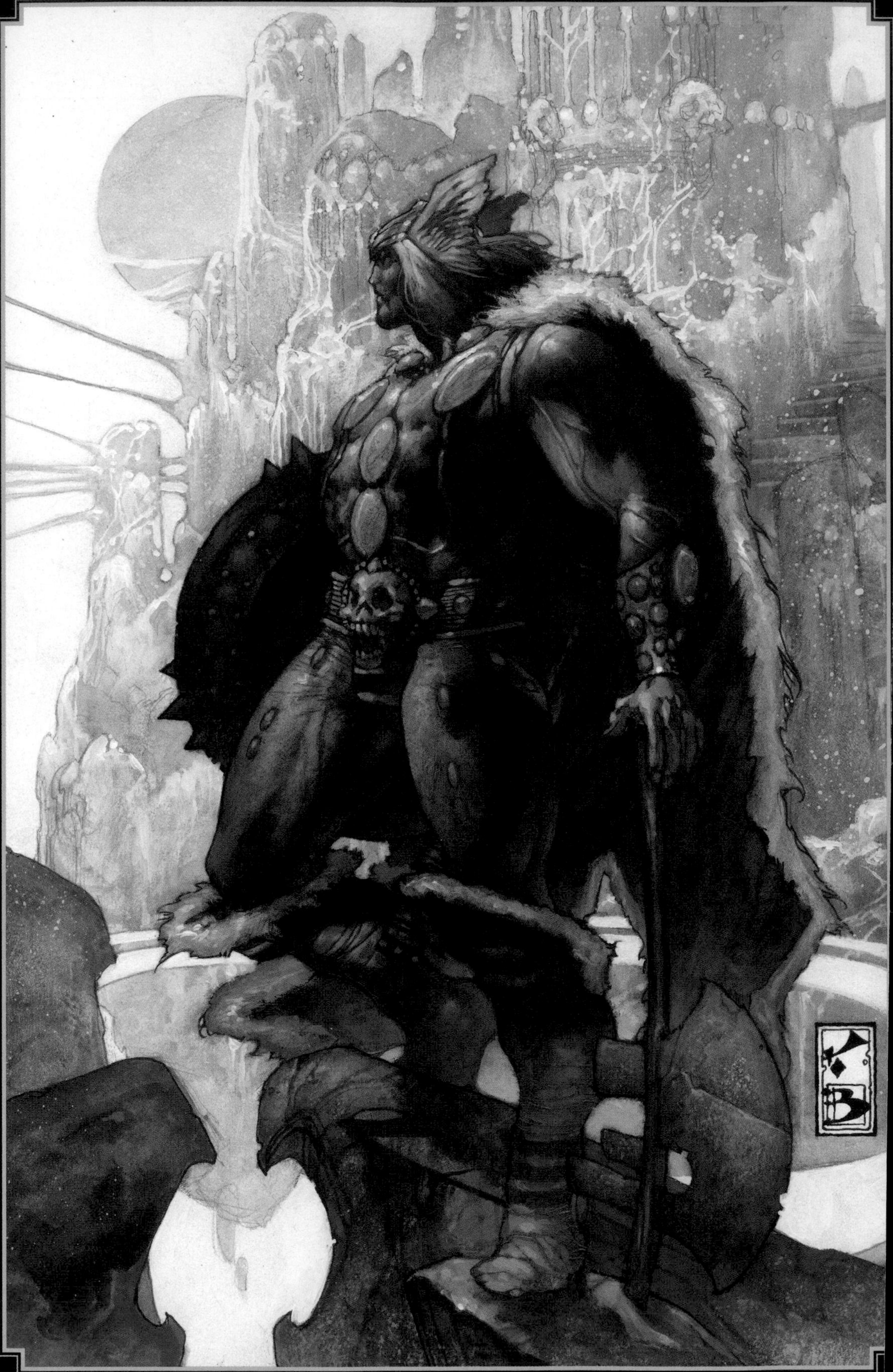

Thor: For Asgard 5

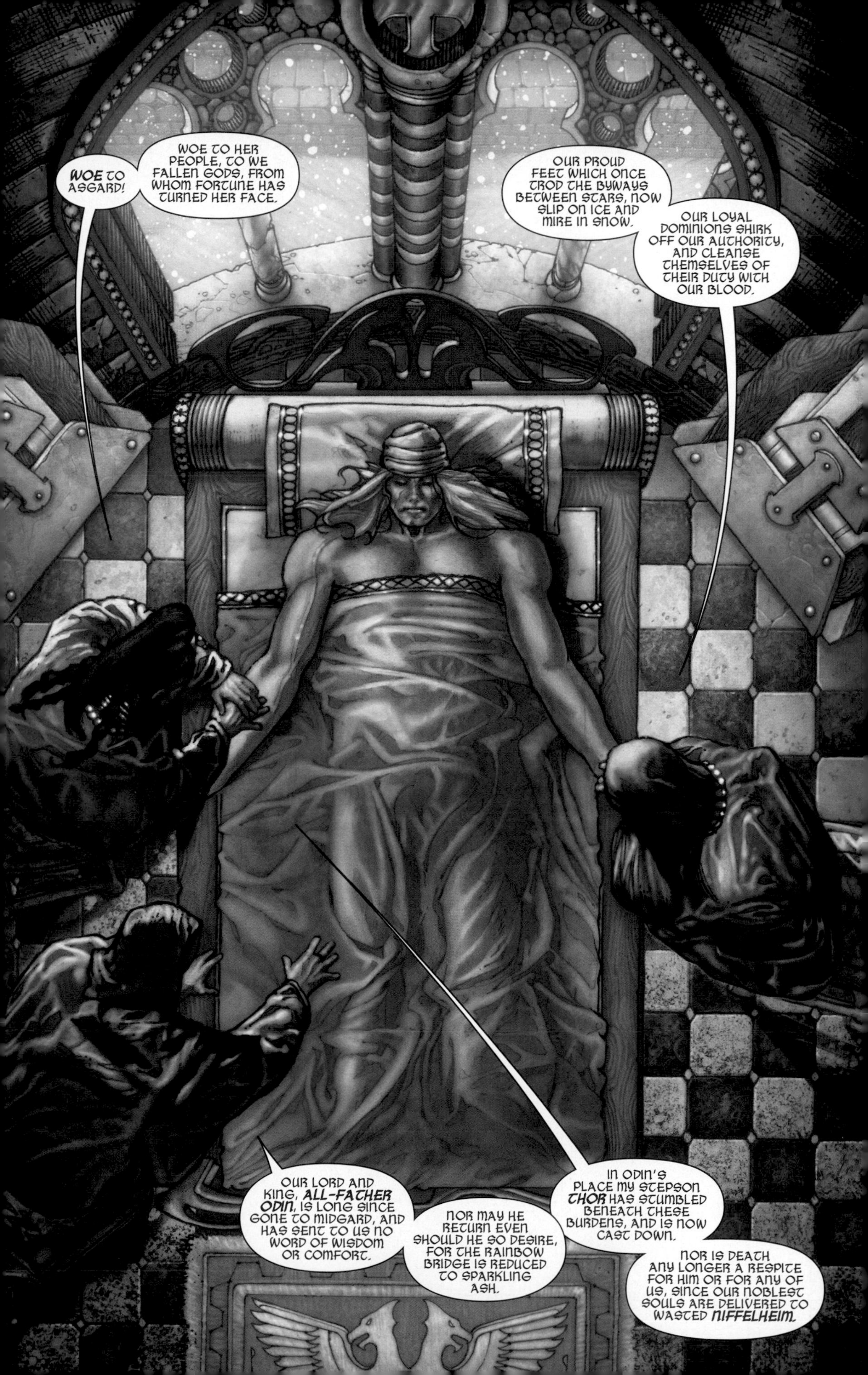

WOE TO ASGARD!
WOE TO HER PEOPLE, TO WE FALLEN GODS, FROM WHOM FORTUNE HAS TURNED HER FACE.
OUR PROUD FEET WHICH ONCE TROD THE BYWAYS BETWEEN STARS, NOW SLIP ON ICE AND MIRE IN SNOW.
OUR LOYAL DOMINIONS SHIRK OFF OUR AUTHORITY, AND CLEANSE THEMSELVES OF THEIR DUTY WITH OUR BLOOD.
OUR LORD AND KING, ALL-FATHER ODIN, IS LONG SINCE GONE TO MIDGARD, AND HAS SENT TO US NO WORD OF WISDOM OR COMFORT.
NOR MAY HE RETURN EVEN SHOULD HE SO DESIRE, FOR THE RAINBOW BRIDGE IS REDUCED TO SPARKLING ASH.
IN ODIN'S PLACE MY STEPSON THOR HAS STUMBLED BENEATH THESE BURDENS, AND IS NOW CAST DOWN.
NOR IS DEATH ANY LONGER A RESPITE FOR HIM OR FOR ANY OF US, SINCE OUR NOBLEST SOULS ARE DELIVERED TO WASTED NIFFELHEIM.

WOE TO ASGARD.
WOE TO THE SON OF ODIN.
WOE.
WOE.
HO, GOD OF THUNDER...

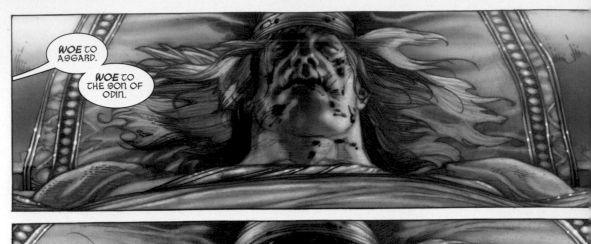

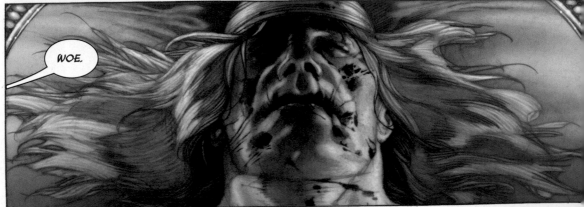

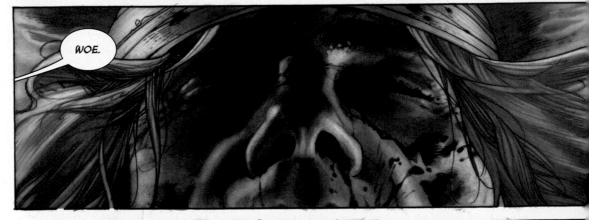

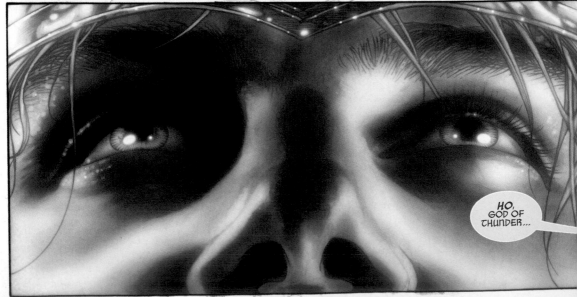

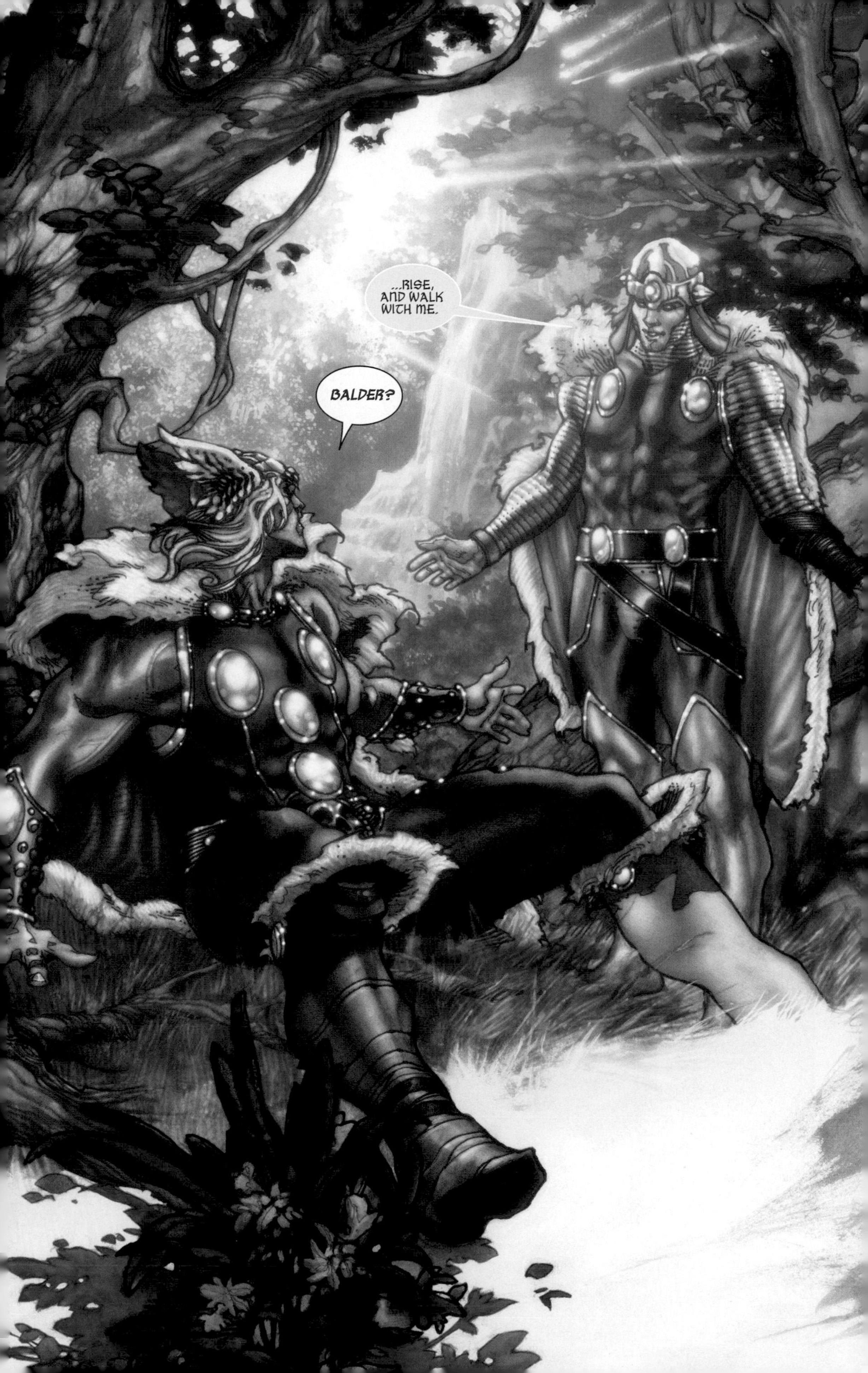
...RISE, AND WALK WITH ME.
BALDER?

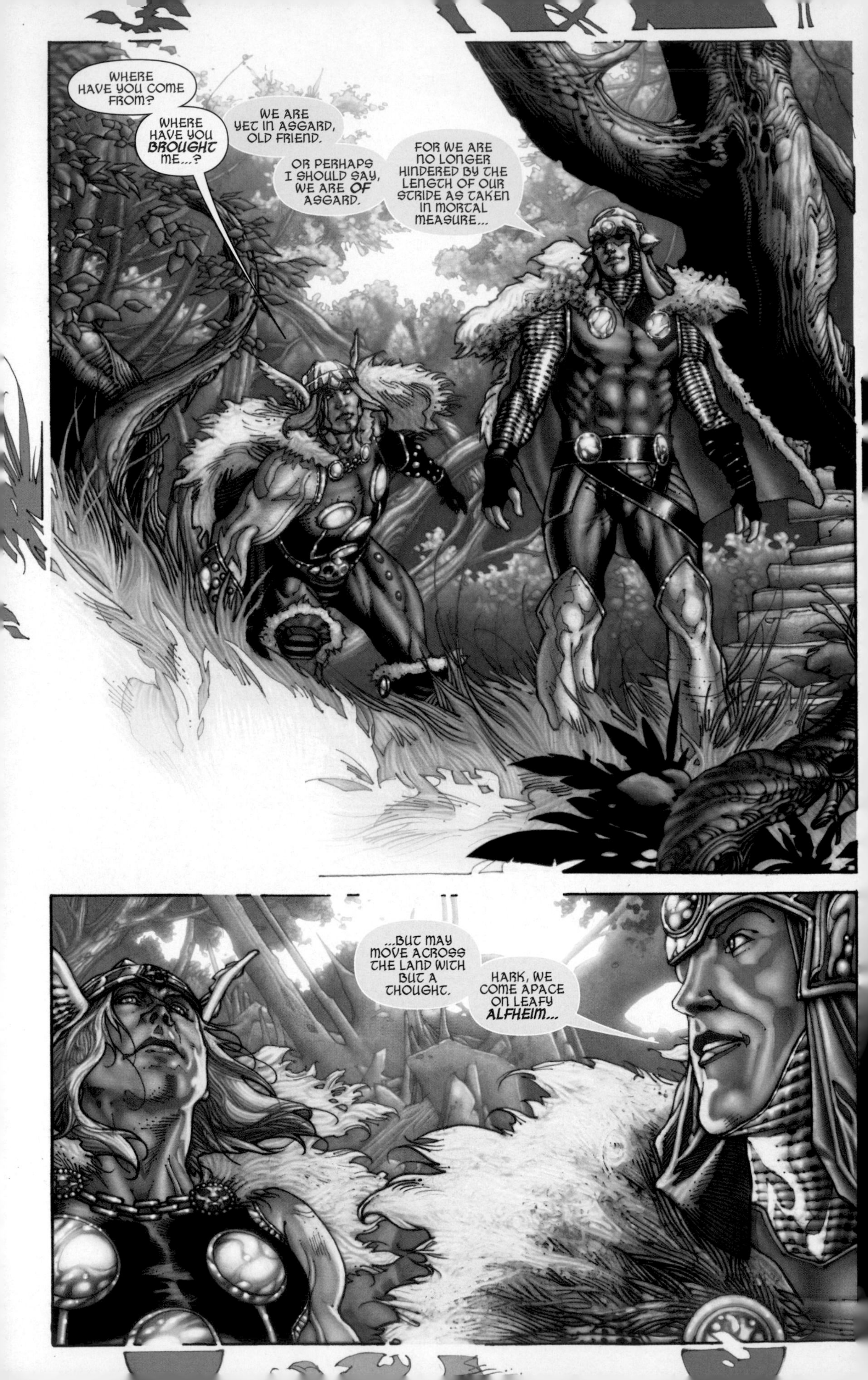
WHERE HAVE YOU COME FROM?
WHERE HAVE YOU BROUGHT ME...?
WE ARE YET IN ASGARD, OLD FRIEND.
OR PERHAPS I SHOULD SAY, WE ARE OF ASGARD.
FOR WE ARE NO LONGER HINDERED BY THE LENGTH OF OUR STRIDE AS TAKEN IN MORTAL MEASURE...
...BUT MAY MOVE ACROSS THE LAND WITH BUT A THOUGHT.
HARK, WE COME APACE ON LEAFY ALFHEIM...

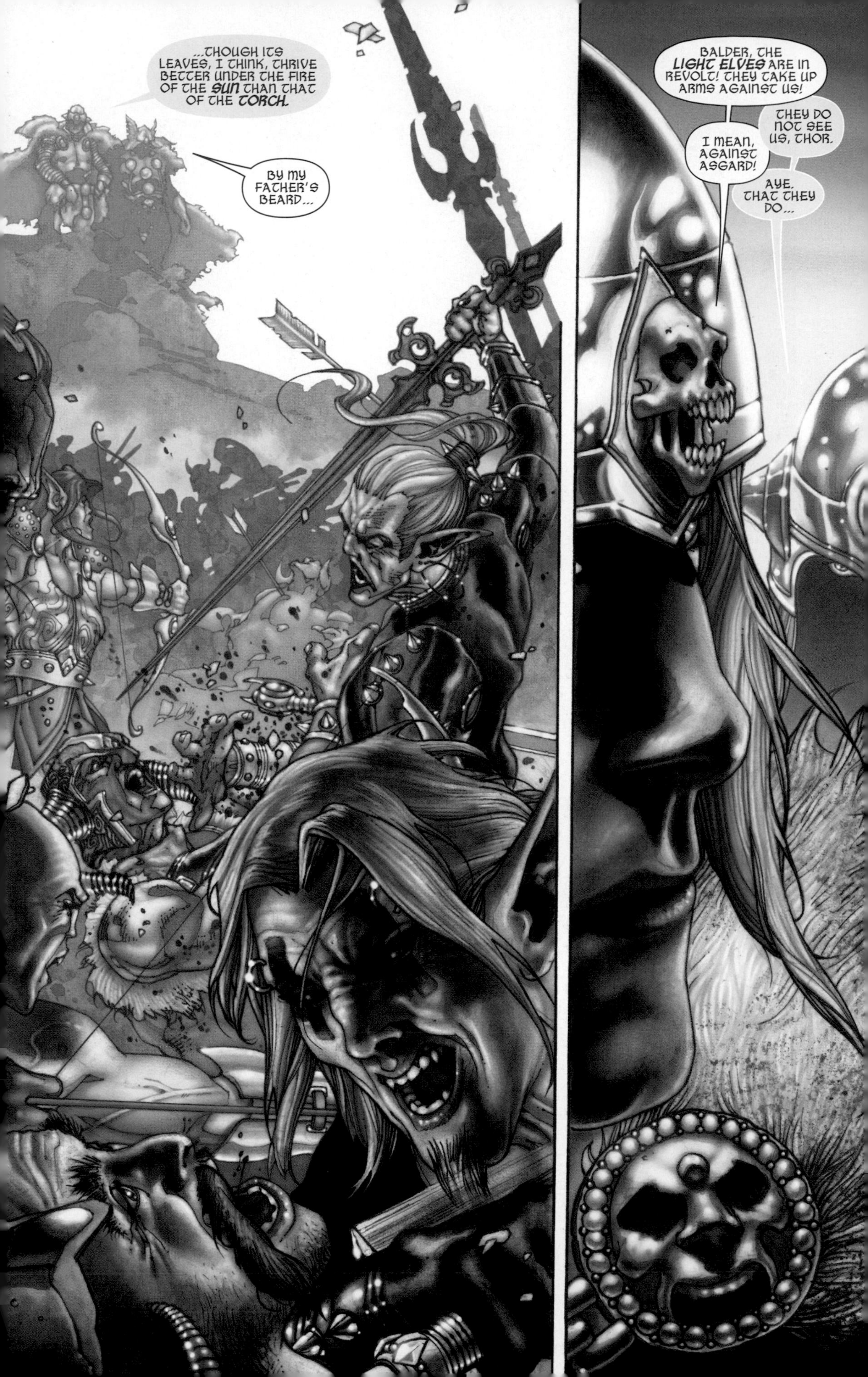
...THOUGH ITS LEAVES, I THINK, THRIVE BETTER UNDER THE FIRE OF THE SUN THAN THAT OF THE TORCH.
BY MY FATHER'S BEARD...
BALDER, THE LIGHT ELVES ARE IN REVOLT! THEY TAKE UP ARMS AGAINST US!
I MEAN, AGAINST ASGARD!
THEY DO NOT SEE US, THOR.
AYE. THAT THEY DO...

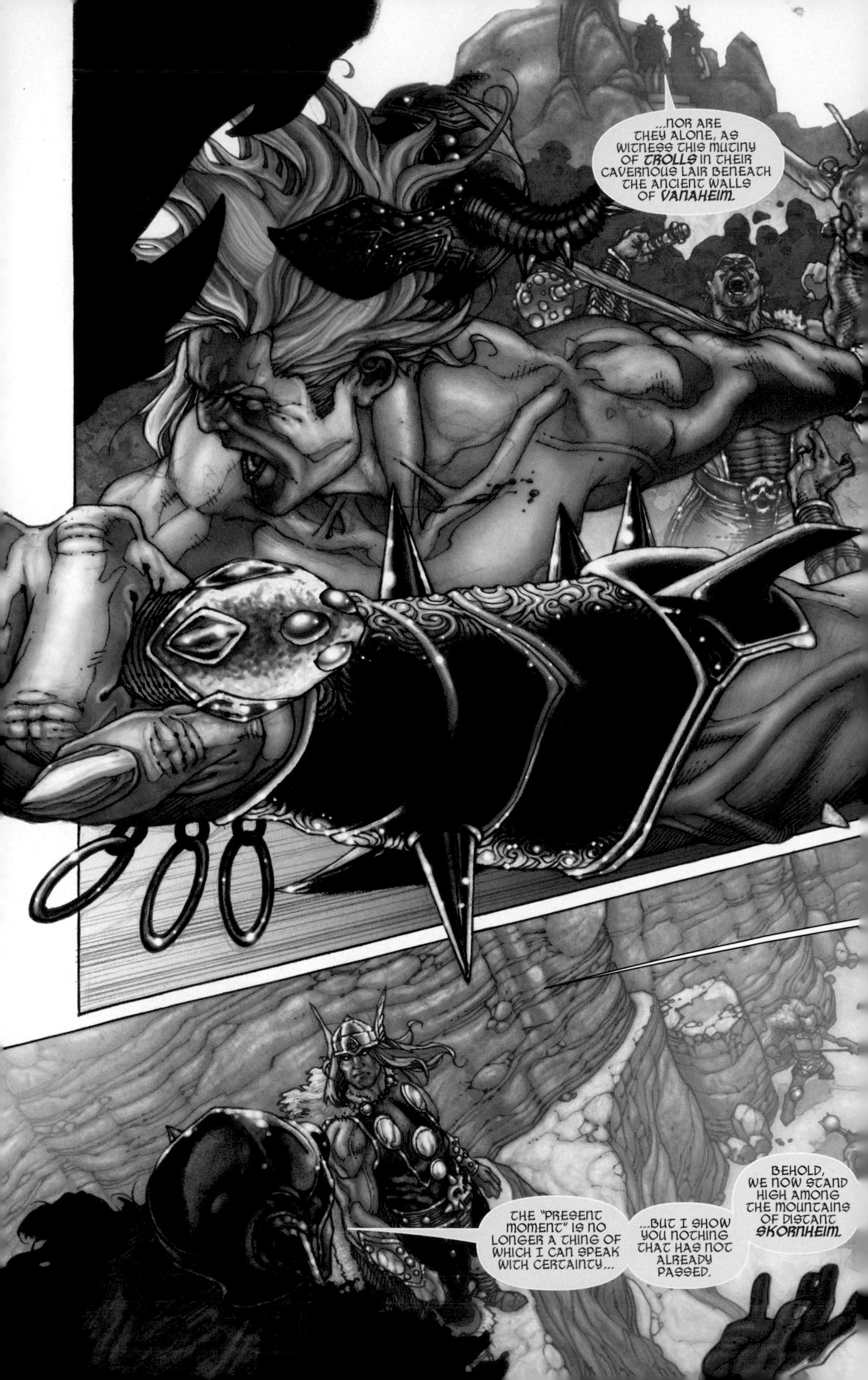
...NOR ARE THEY ALONE, AS WITNESS THIS MUTINY OF TROLLS IN THEIR CAVERNOUS LAIR BENEATH THE ANCIENT WALLS OF VANAHEIM.
BEHOLD, WE NOW STAND HIGH AMONG THE MOUNTAINS OF DISTANT SKORNHEIM.
...BUT I SHOW YOU NOTHING THAT HAS NOT ALREADY PASSED.
THE "PRESENT MOMENT" IS NO LONGER A THING OF WHICH I CAN SPEAK WITH CERTAINTY...

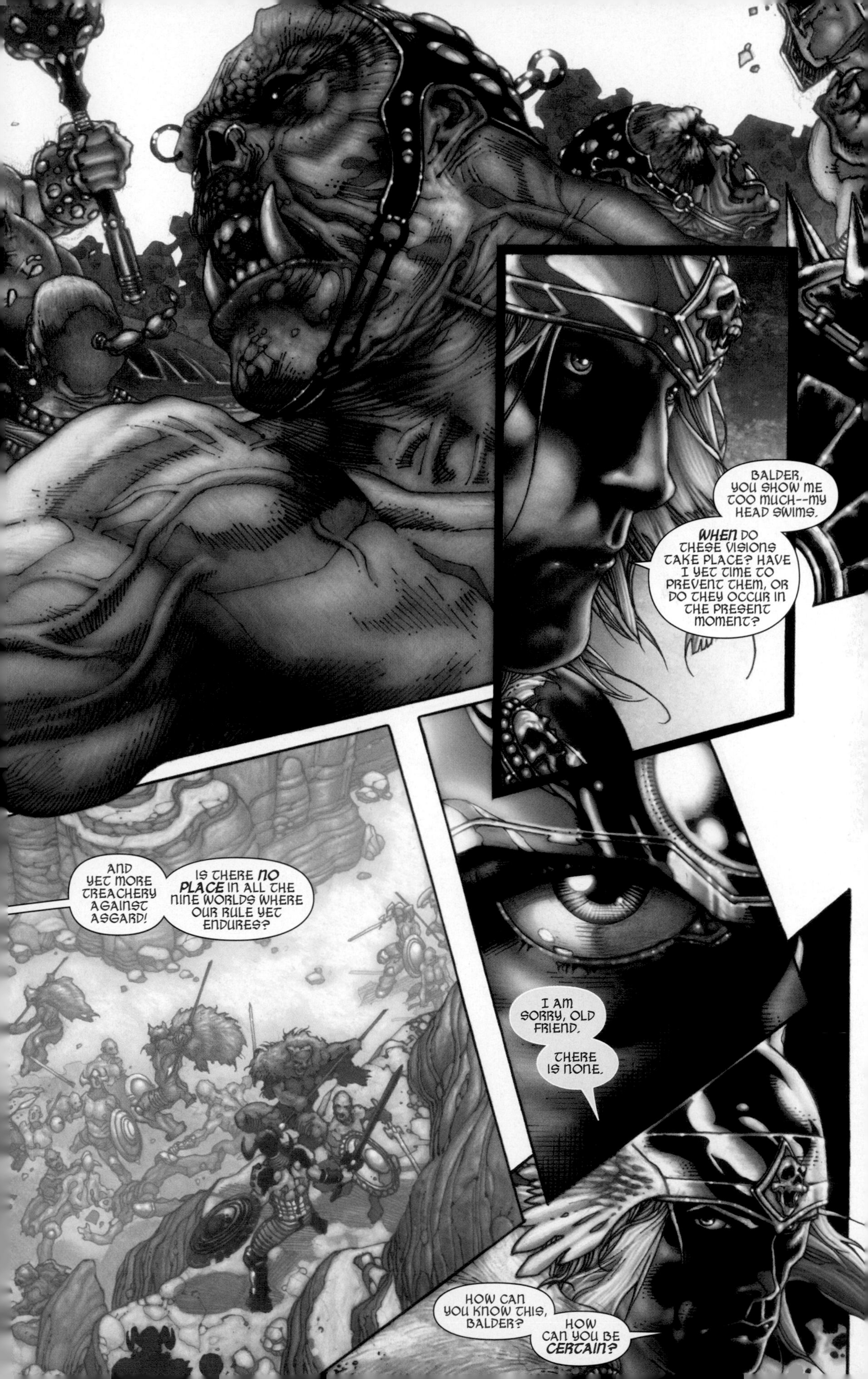
BALDER, YOU SHOW ME TOO MUCH--MY HEAD SWIMS.
WHEN DO THESE VISIONS TAKE PLACE? HAVE I YET TIME TO PREVENT THEM, OR DO THEY OCCUR IN THE PRESENT MOMENT?
AND YET MORE TREACHERY AGAINST ASGARD!
IS THERE NO PLACE IN ALL THE NINE WORLDS WHERE OUR RULE YET ENDURES?
I AM SORRY, OLD FRIEND.
THERE IS NONE.
HOW CAN YOU KNOW THIS, BALDER?
HOW CAN YOU BE CERTAIN?

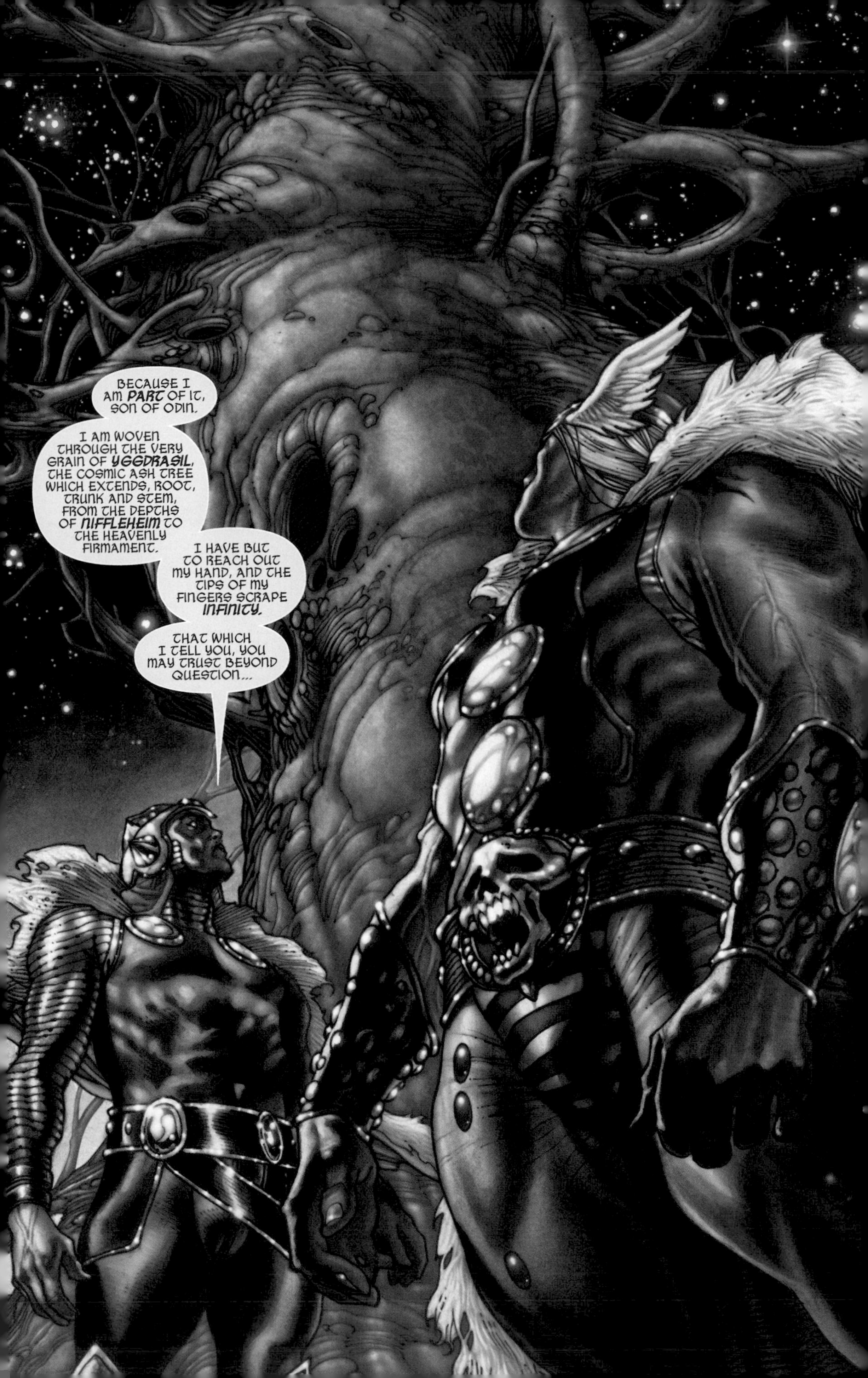
BECAUSE I AM PART OF IT, SON OF ODIN.
I AM WOVEN THROUGH THE VERY GRAIN OF YGGDRASIL, THE COSMIC ASH TREE WHICH EXTENDS, ROOT, TRUNK AND STEM, FROM THE DEPTHS OF NIFFLEHEIM TO THE HEAVENLY FIRMAMENT.
I HAVE BUT TO REACH OUT MY HAND, AND THE TIPS OF MY FINGERS SCRAPE INFINITY.
THAT WHICH I TELL YOU, YOU MAY TRUST BEYOND QUESTION...

...WERE OUR LONG FRIENDSHIP NOT SUFFICIENT GUARANTEE.

BALDER...

...WHAT ARE YOU?

I AM LIFE.

BUT... YOU DIED.

I AM DEATH AS WELL.

I AM THE CYCLE, THOR...

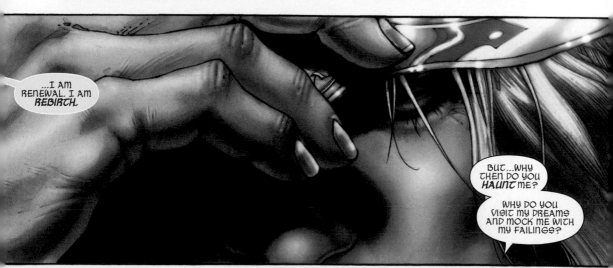

...I AM RENEWAL. I AM REBIRTH.

BUT...WHY THEN DO YOU HAUNT ME?

WHY DO YOU VISIT MY DREAMS AND MOCK ME WITH MY FAILINGS?

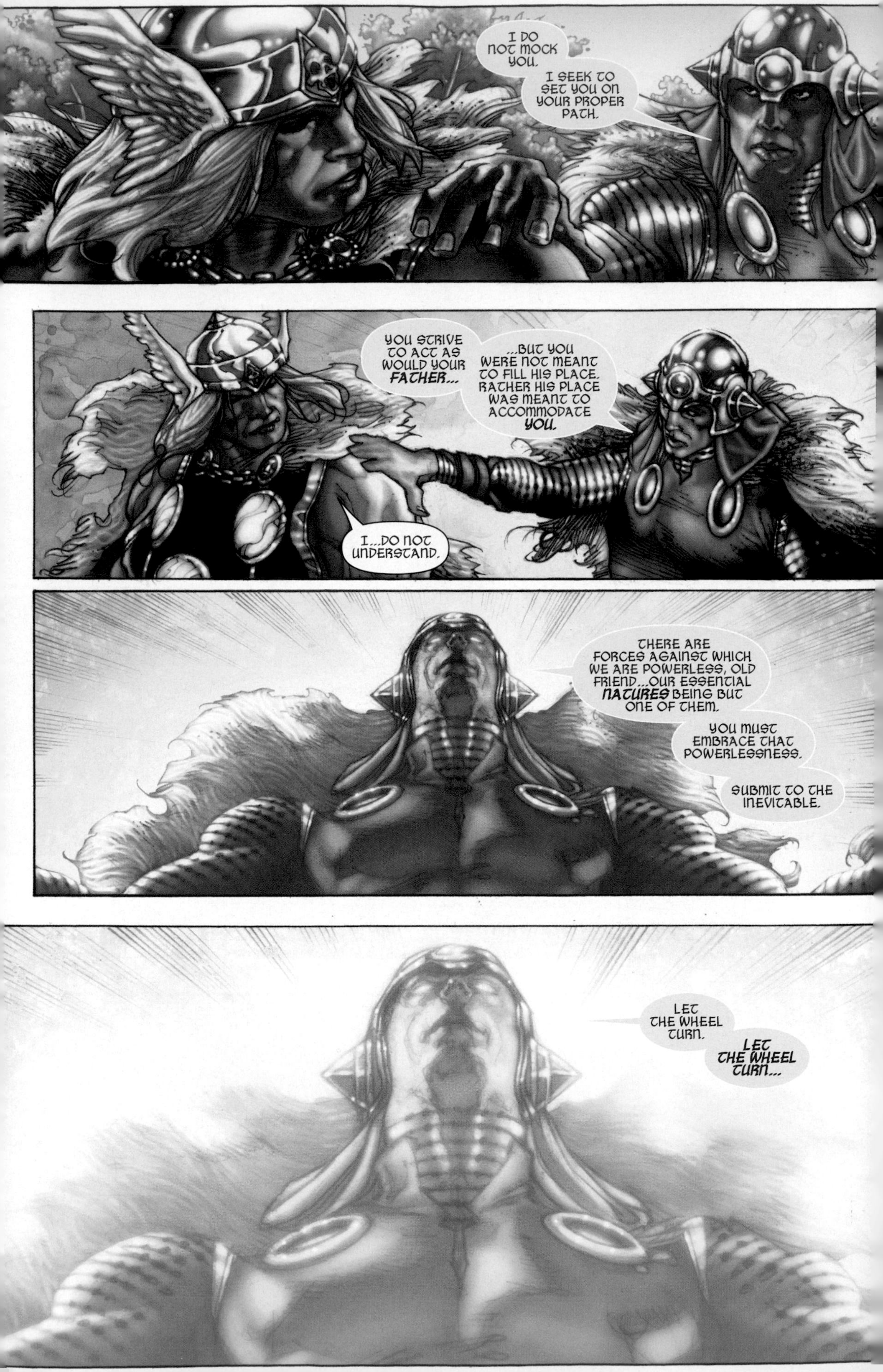
I DO NOT MOCK YOU.
I SEEK TO SET YOU ON YOUR PROPER PATH.
YOU STRIVE TO ACT AS WOULD YOUR FATHER...
...BUT YOU WERE NOT MEANT TO FILL HIS PLACE. RATHER HIS PLACE WAS MEANT TO ACCOMMODATE YOU.
I...DO NOT UNDERSTAND.
THERE ARE FORCES AGAINST WHICH WE ARE POWERLESS, OLD FRIEND...OUR ESSENTIAL NATURES BEING BUT ONE OF THEM.
YOU MUST EMBRACE THAT POWERLESSNESS.
SUBMIT TO THE INEVITABLE.
LET THE WHEEL TURN.
LET THE WHEEL TURN...

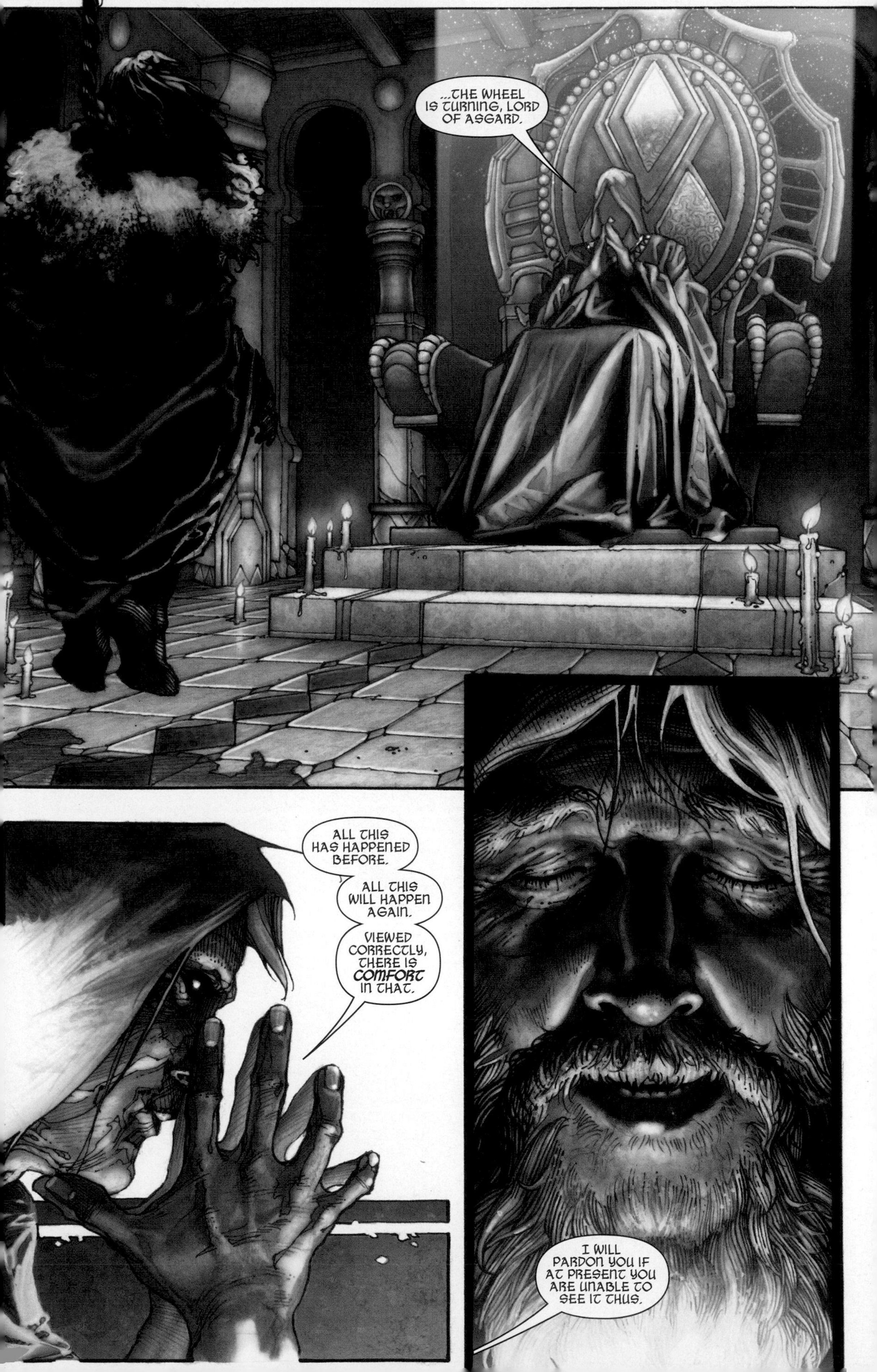
...THE WHEEL IS TURNING, LORD OF ASGARD.
ALL THIS HAS HAPPENED BEFORE.
ALL THIS WILL HAPPEN AGAIN.
VIEWED CORRECTLY, THERE IS COMFORT IN THAT.
I WILL PARDON YOU IF AT PRESENT YOU ARE UNABLE TO SEE IT THUS.

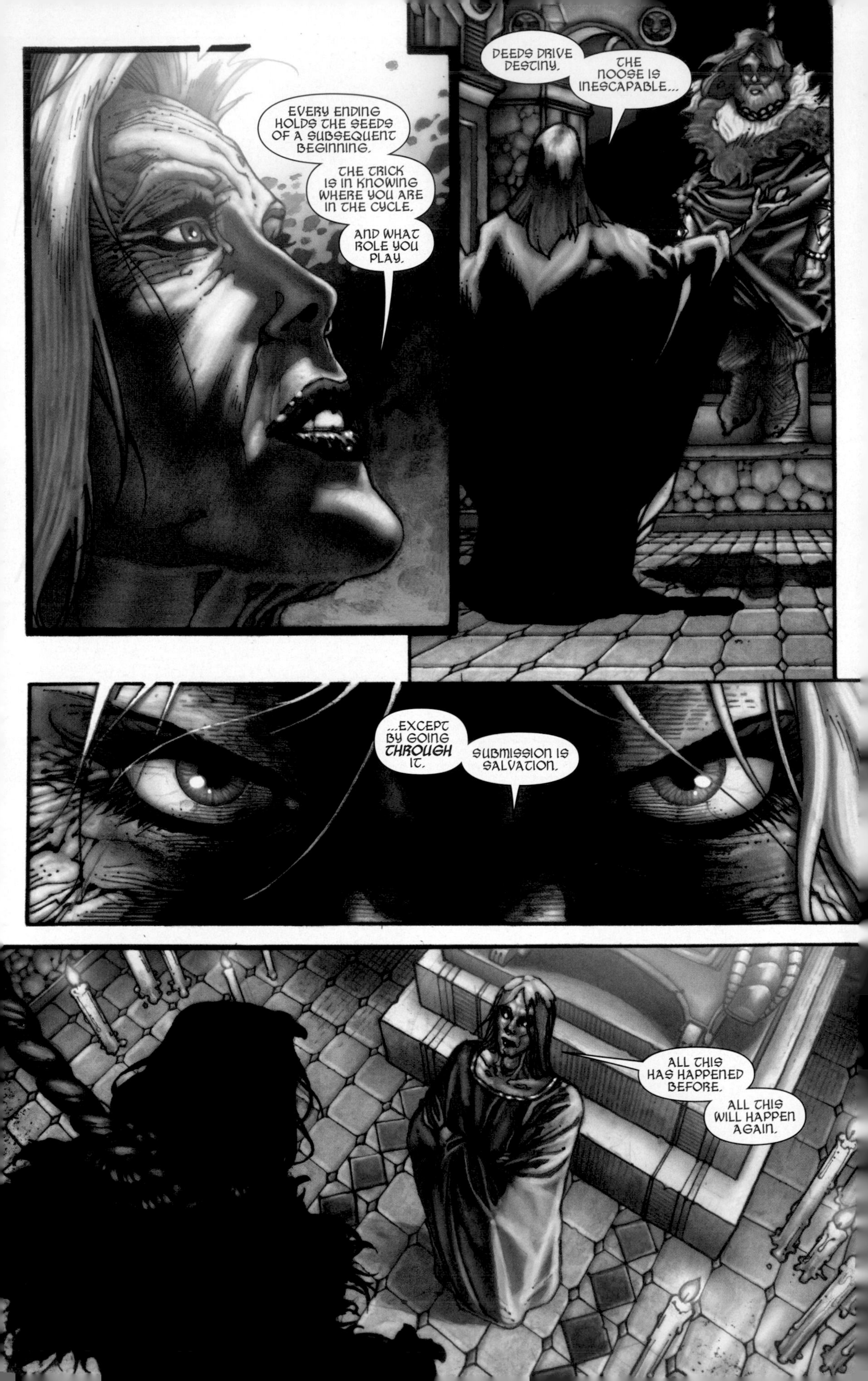
EVERY ENDING HOLDS THE SEEDS OF A SUBSEQUENT BEGINNING.
THE TRICK IS IN KNOWING WHERE YOU ARE IN THE CYCLE.
AND WHAT ROLE YOU PLAY.
DEEDS DRIVE DESTINY.
THE NOOSE IS INESCAPABLE...
...EXCEPT BY GOING **THROUGH** IT.
SUBMISSION IS SALVATION.
ALL THIS HAS HAPPENED BEFORE.
ALL THIS WILL HAPPEN AGAIN.

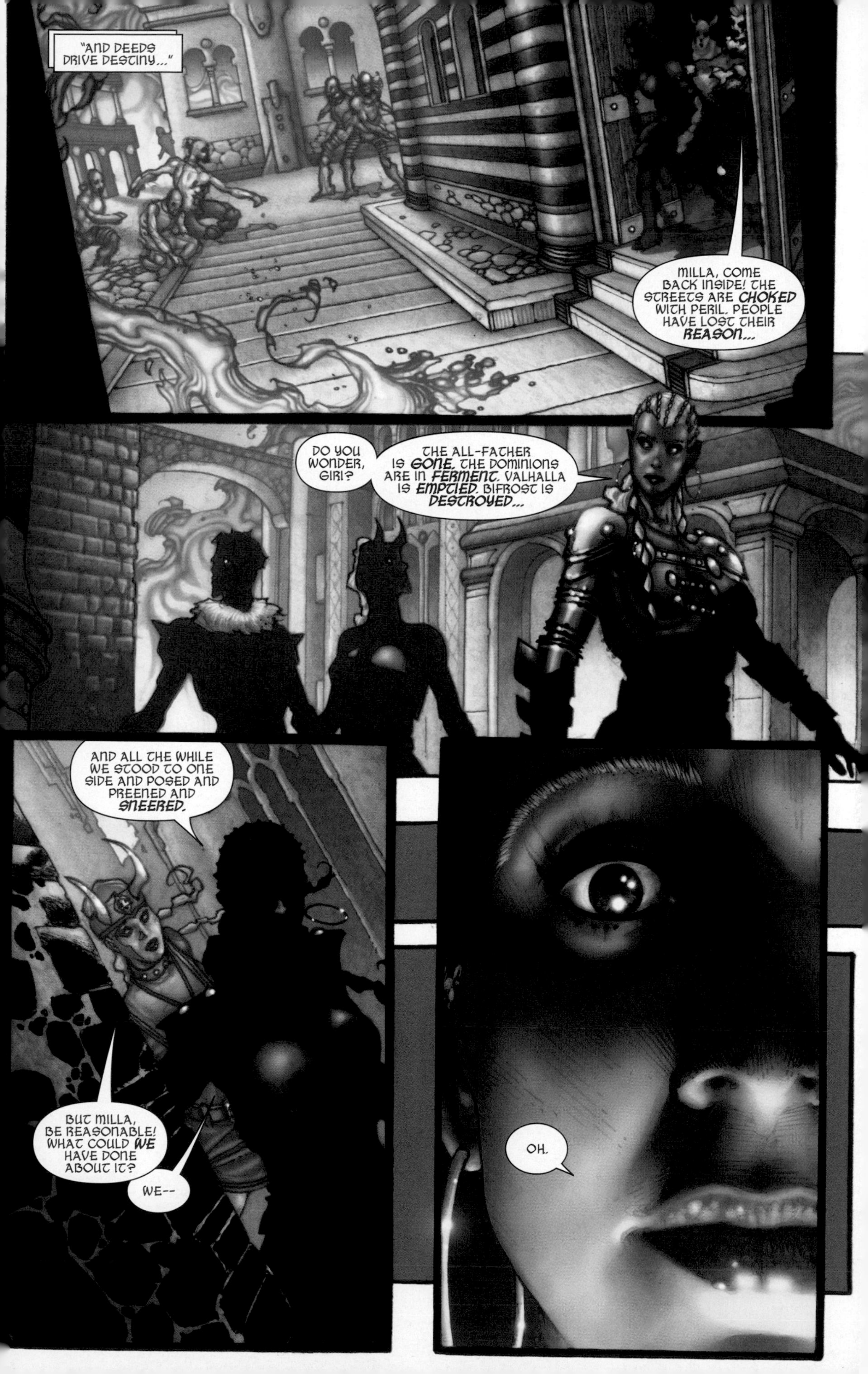
"AND DEEDS DRIVE DESTINY..."
MILLA, COME BACK INSIDE! THE STREETS ARE CHOKED WITH PERIL. PEOPLE HAVE LOST THEIR REASON...
DO YOU WONDER, GIRL?
THE ALL-FATHER IS GONE. THE DOMINIONS ARE IN FERMENT. VALHALLA IS EMPTIED. BIFROST IS DESTROYED...
AND ALL THE WHILE WE STOOD TO ONE SIDE AND POSED AND PREENED AND SNEERED.
BUT MILLA, BE REASONABLE! WHAT COULD WE HAVE DONE ABOUT IT?
WE--
OH.

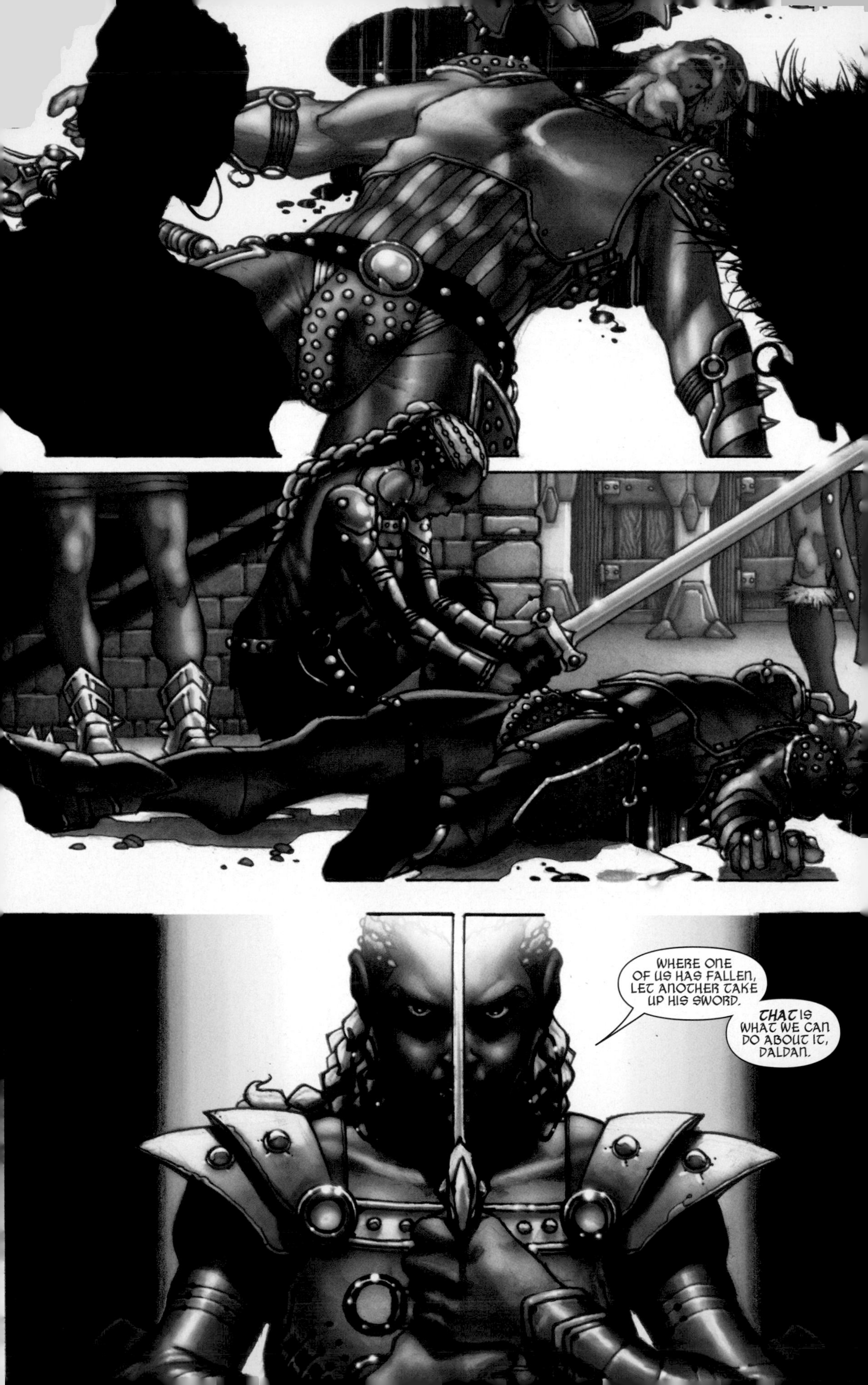
WHERE ONE OF US HAS FALLEN, LET ANOTHER TAKE UP HIS SWORD.
THAT IS WHAT WE CAN DO ABOUT IT, DALDAN.

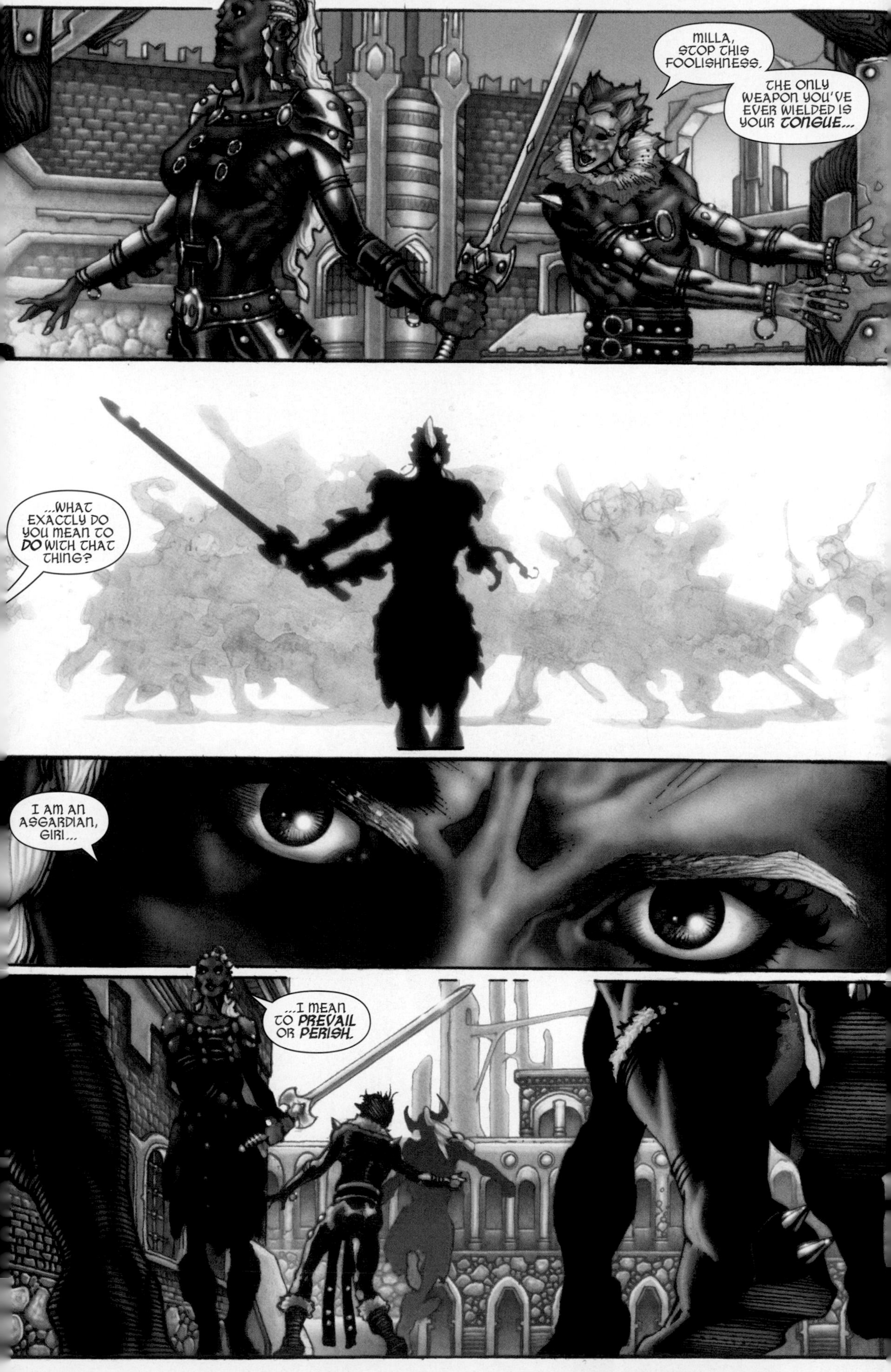
MILLA, STOP THIS FOOLISHNESS.
THE ONLY WEAPON YOU'VE EVER WIELDED IS YOUR TONGUE...
...WHAT EXACTLY DO YOU MEAN TO DO WITH THAT THING?
I AM AN ASGARDIAN, GIRL...
...I MEAN TO PREVAIL OR PERISH.

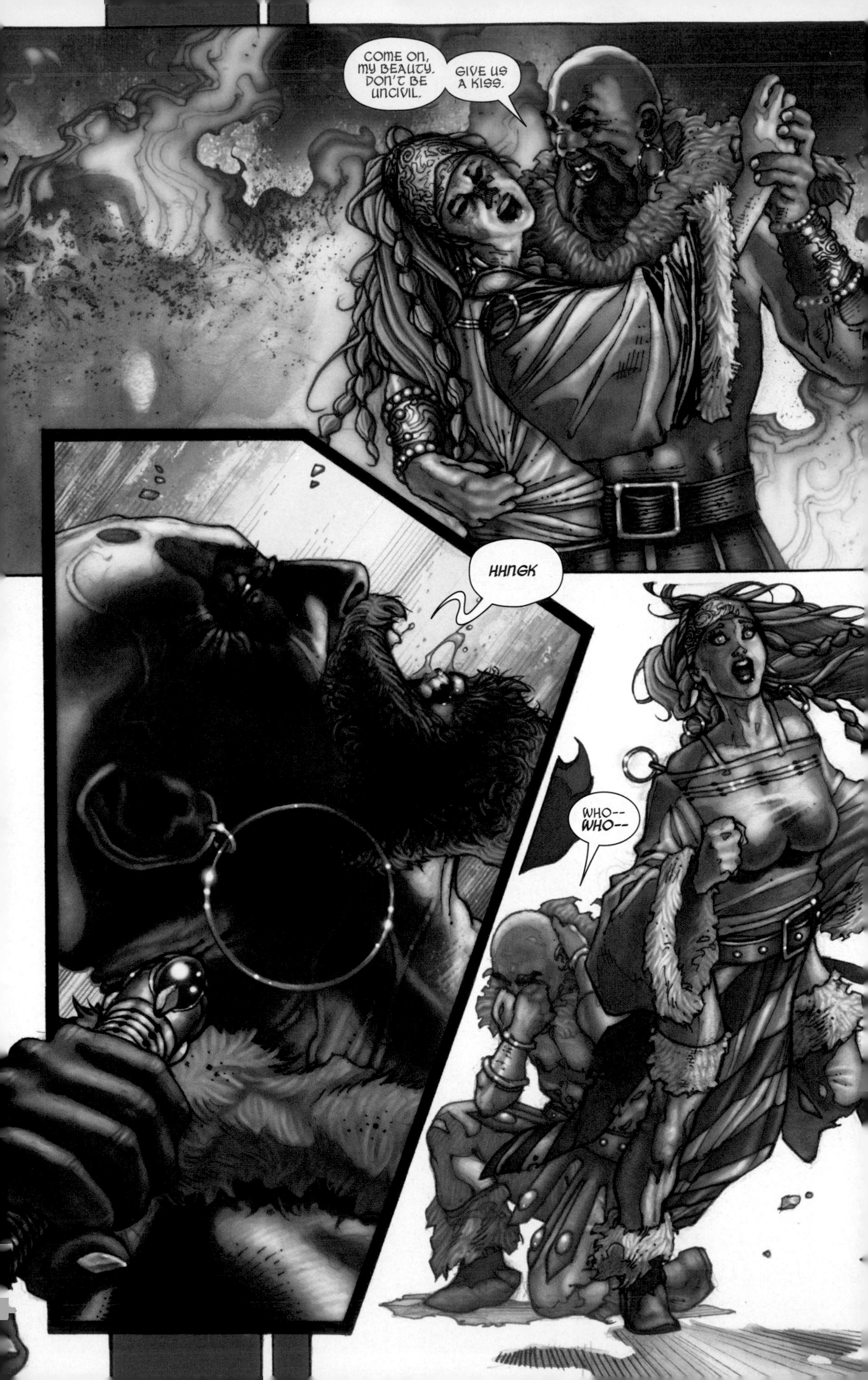
COME ON, MY BEAUTY. DON'T BE UNCIVIL.
GIVE US A KISS.
HHNGK
WHO-- WHO--

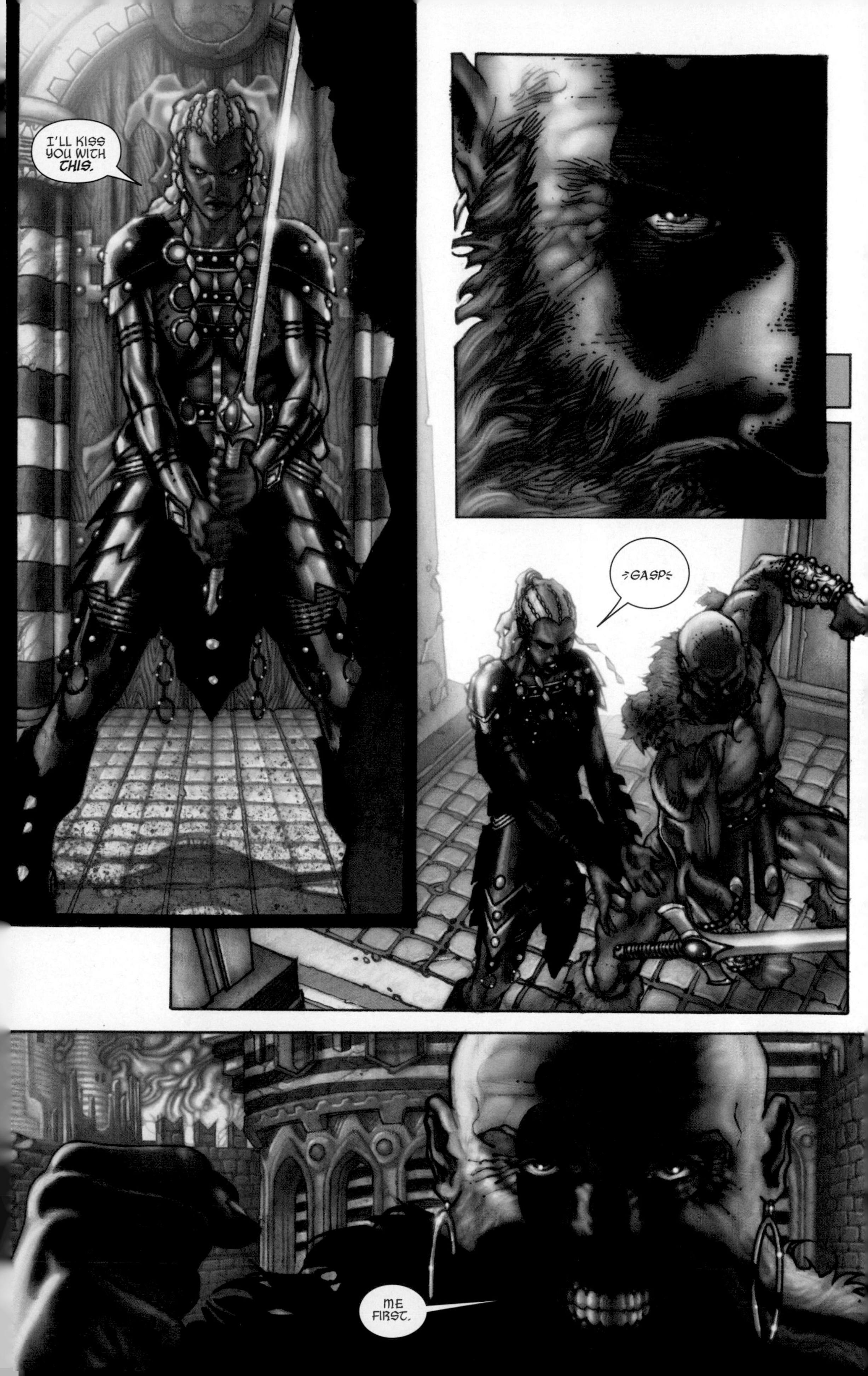
I'LL KISS YOU WITH THIS.
GASP
ME FIRST.

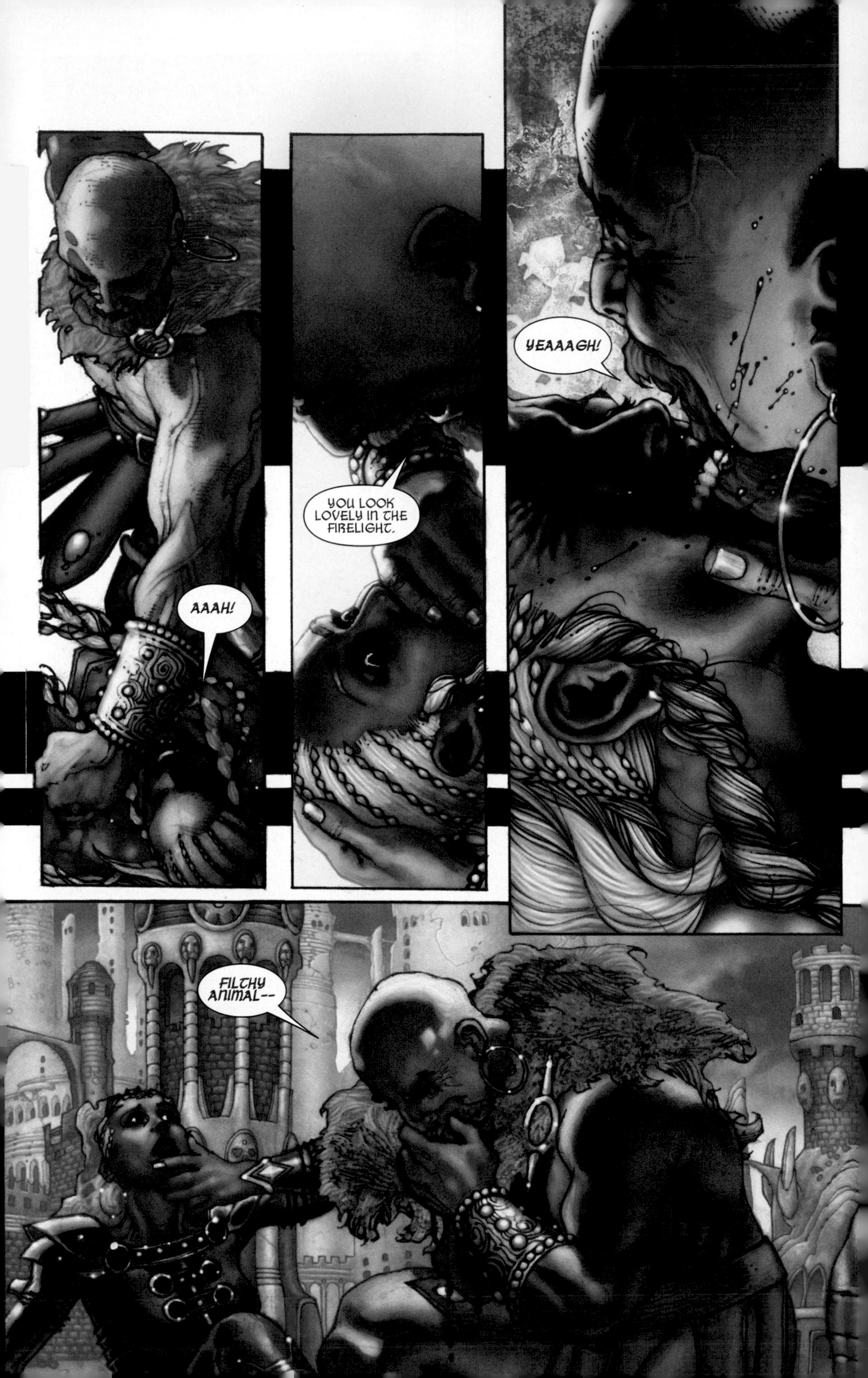

AAAH!
YOU LOOK LOVELY IN THE FIRELIGHT.
YEAAAGH!
FILTHY ANIMAL--

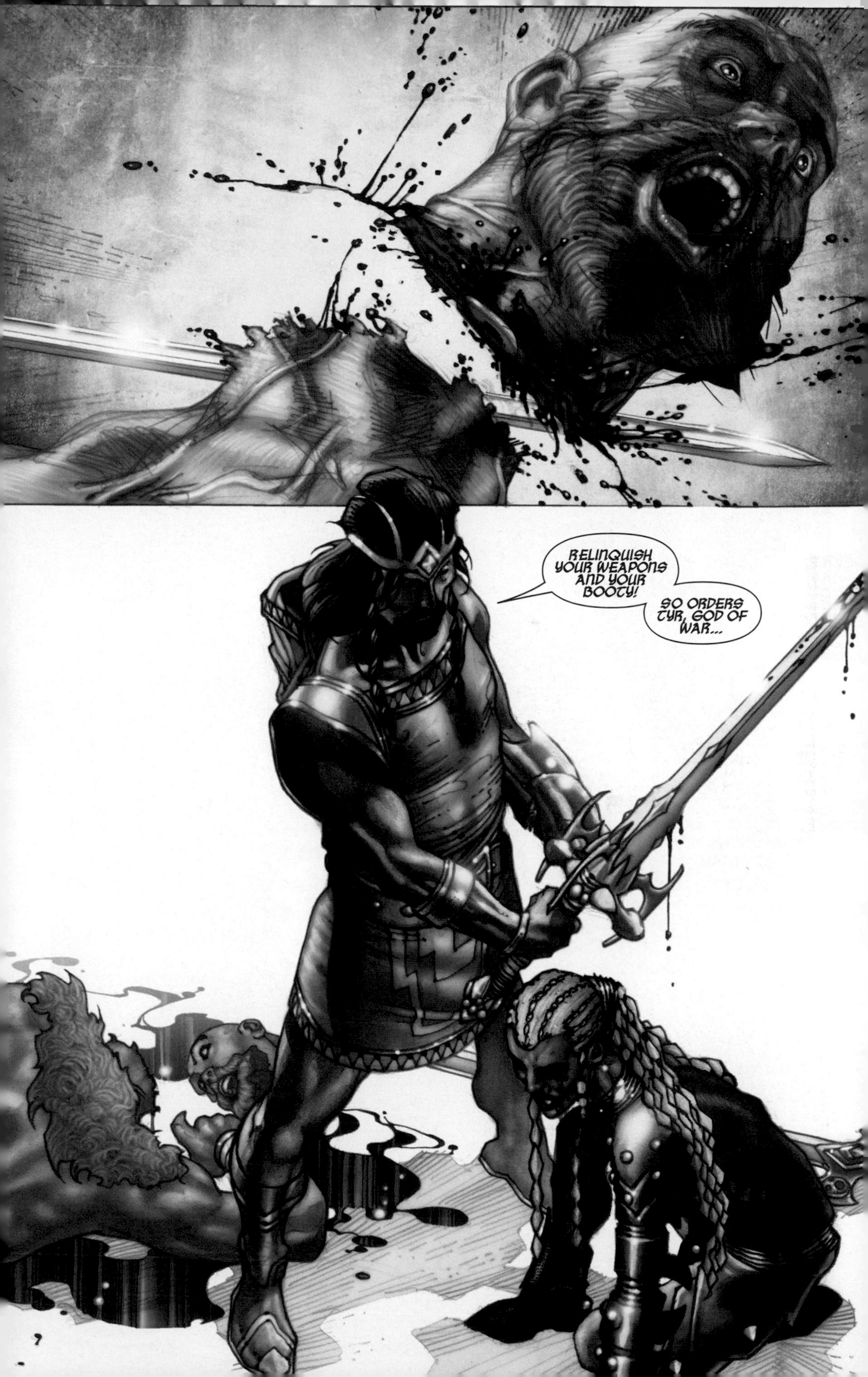
RELINQUISH YOUR WEAPONS AND YOUR BOOTY!
SO ORDERS TYR, GOD OF WAR...

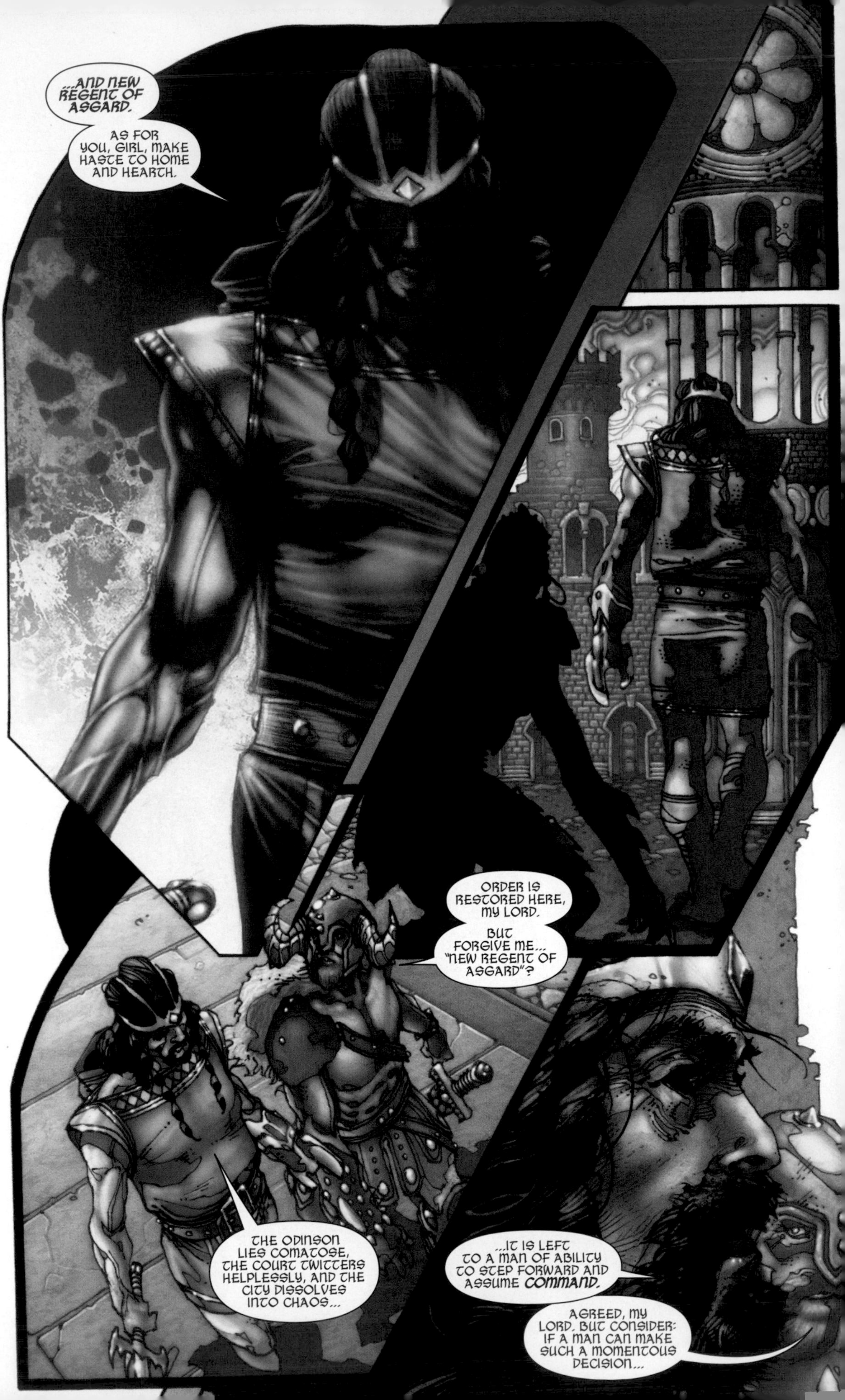
...AND NEW REGENT OF ASGARD.
AS FOR YOU, GIRL, MAKE HASTE TO HOME AND HEARTH.
ORDER IS RESTORED HERE, MY LORD.
BUT FORGIVE ME... "NEW REGENT OF ASGARD"?
THE ODINSON LIES COMATOSE, THE COURT TWITTERS HELPLESSLY, AND THE CITY DISSOLVES INTO CHAOS...
...IT IS LEFT TO A MAN OF ABILITY TO STEP FORWARD AND ASSUME COMMAND.
AGREED, MY LORD. BUT CONSIDER: IF A MAN CAN MAKE SUCH A MOMENTOUS DECISION...

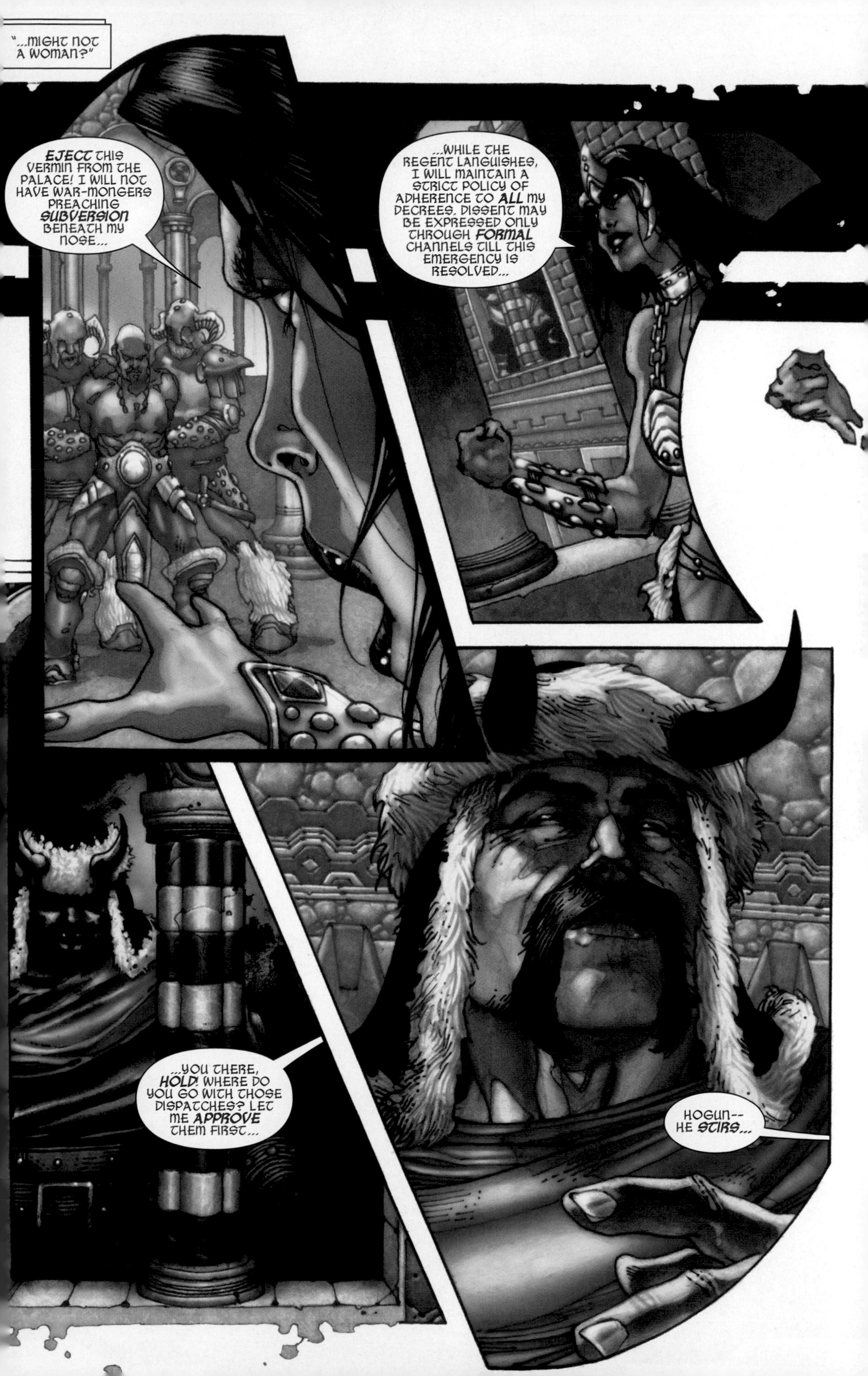
"...MIGHT NOT A WOMAN?"
EJECT THIS VERMIN FROM THE PALACE! I WILL NOT HAVE WAR-MONGERS PREACHING SUBVERSION BENEATH MY NOSE...
...WHILE THE REGENT LANGUISHES, I WILL MAINTAIN A STRICT POLICY OF ADHERENCE TO ALL MY DECREES. DISSENT MAY BE EXPRESSED ONLY THROUGH FORMAL CHANNELS TILL THIS EMERGENCY IS RESOLVED...
...YOU THERE, HOLD! WHERE DO YOU GO WITH THOSE DISPATCHES? LET ME APPROVE THEM FIRST...
HOGUN-- HE STIRS...

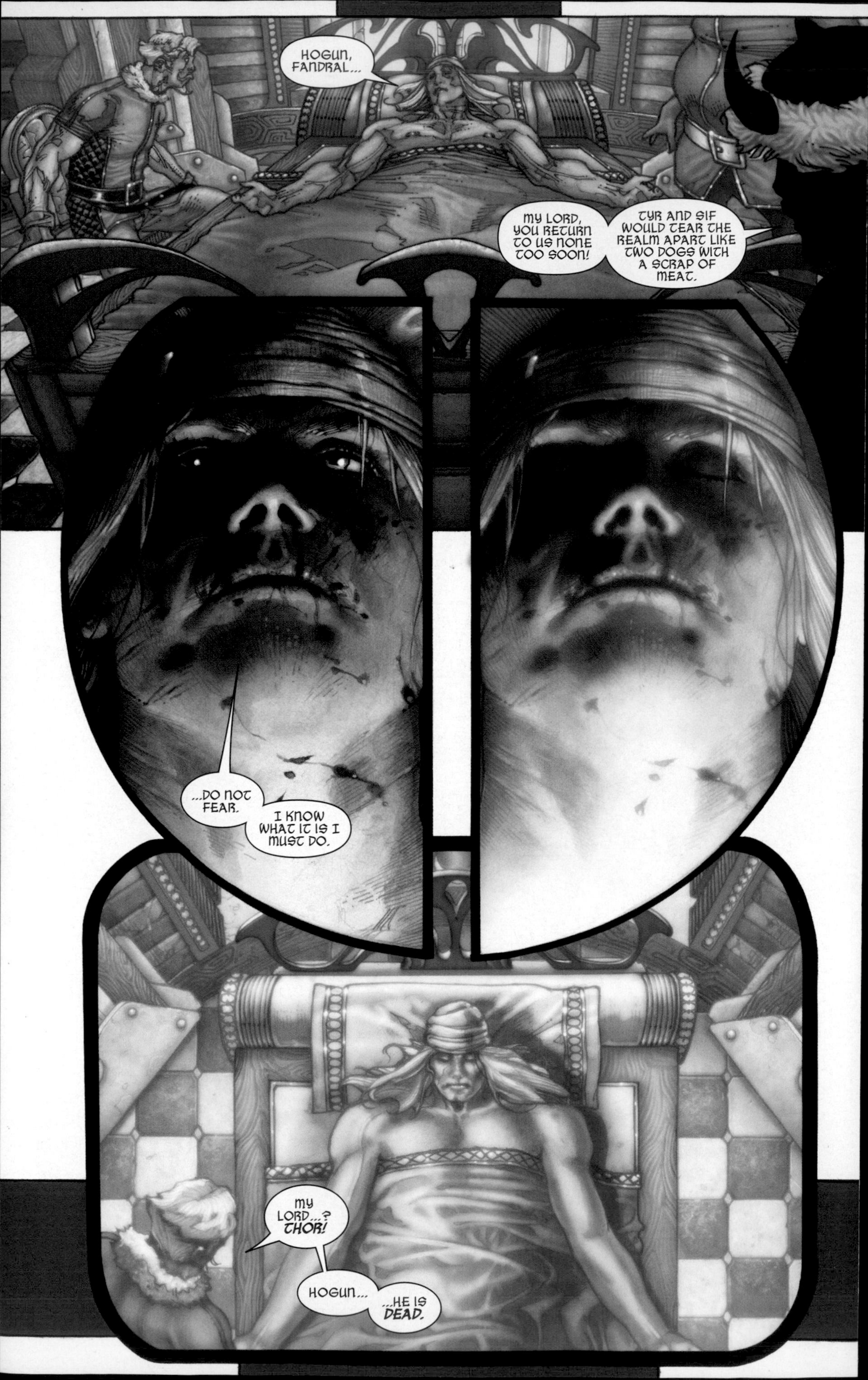
HOGUN, FANDRAL...
MY LORD, YOU RETURN TO US NONE TOO SOON!
TYR AND SIF WOULD TEAR THE REALM APART LIKE TWO DOGS WITH A SCRAP OF MEAT.
...DO NOT FEAR.
I KNOW WHAT IT IS I MUST DO.
MY LORD...? THOR!
HOGUN...
...HE IS DEAD.

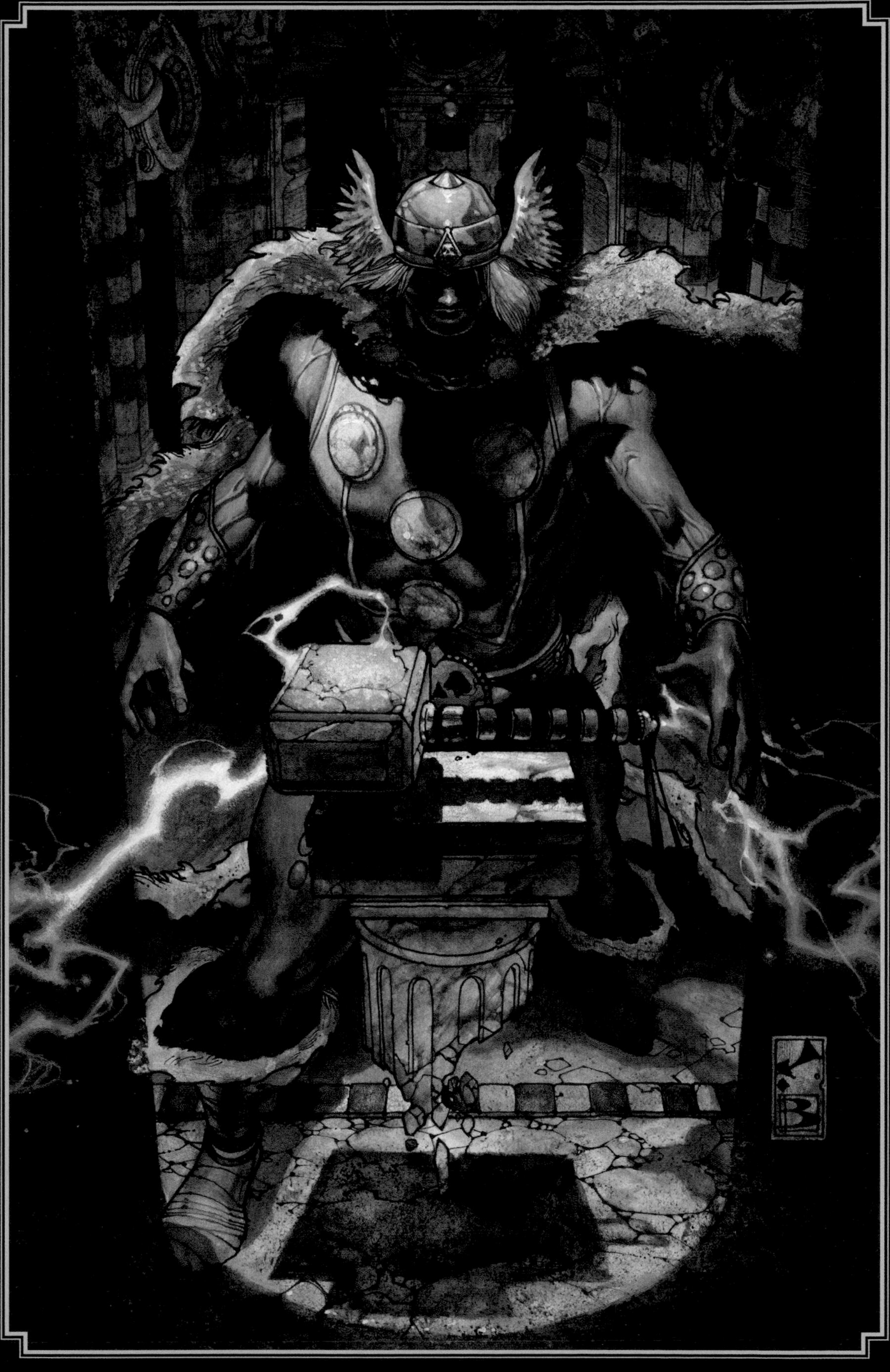

Thor: For Asgard 6

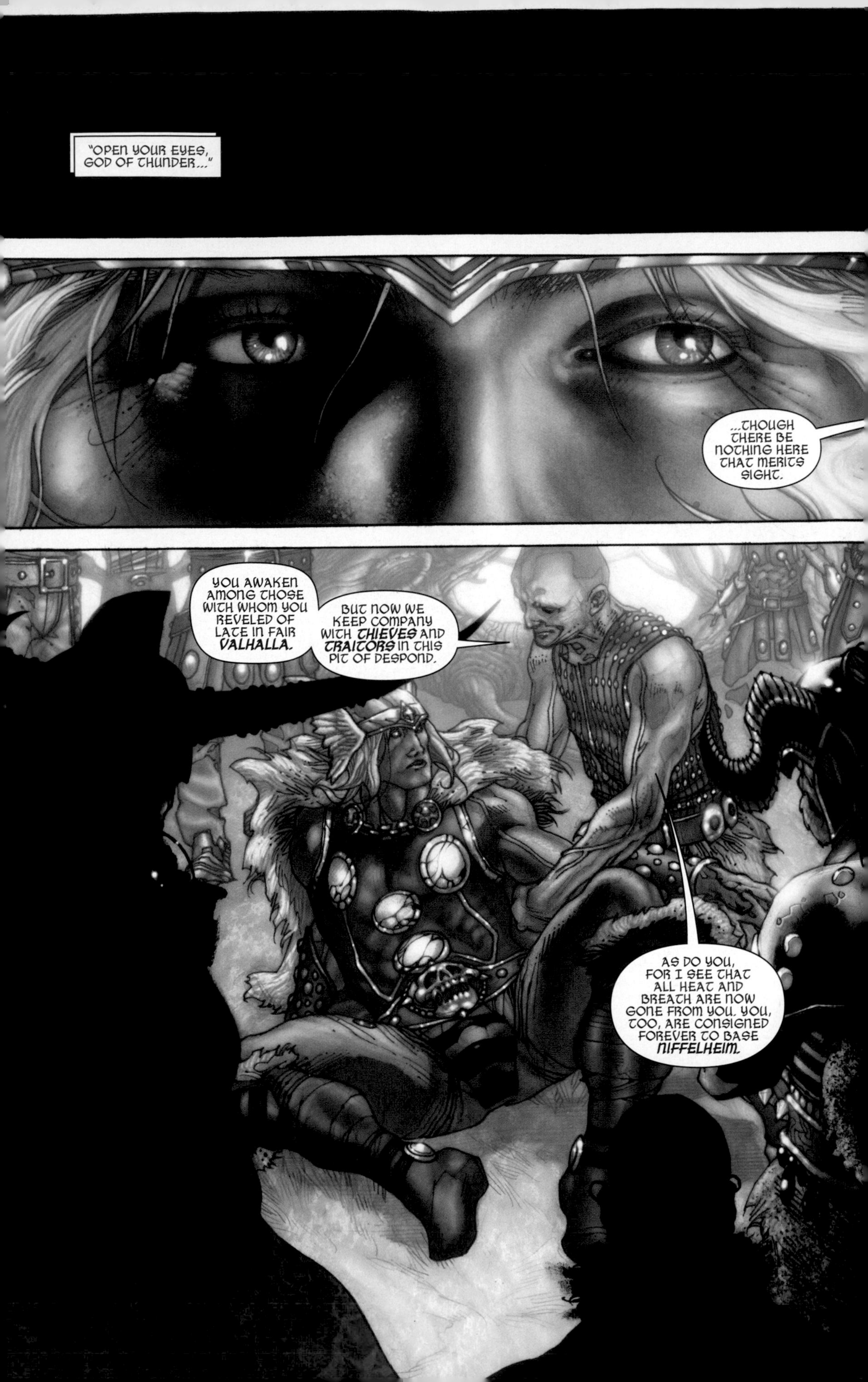
"OPEN YOUR EYES, GOD OF THUNDER..."
...THOUGH THERE BE NOTHING HERE THAT MERITS SIGHT.
YOU AWAKEN AMONG THOSE WITH WHOM YOU REVELED OF LATE IN FAIR VALHALLA.
BUT NOW WE KEEP COMPANY WITH THIEVES AND TRAITORS IN THIS PIT OF DESPOND.
AS DO YOU, FOR I SEE THAT ALL HEAT AND BREATH ARE NOW GONE FROM YOU. YOU, TOO, ARE CONSIGNED FOREVER TO BASE NIFFELHEIM.

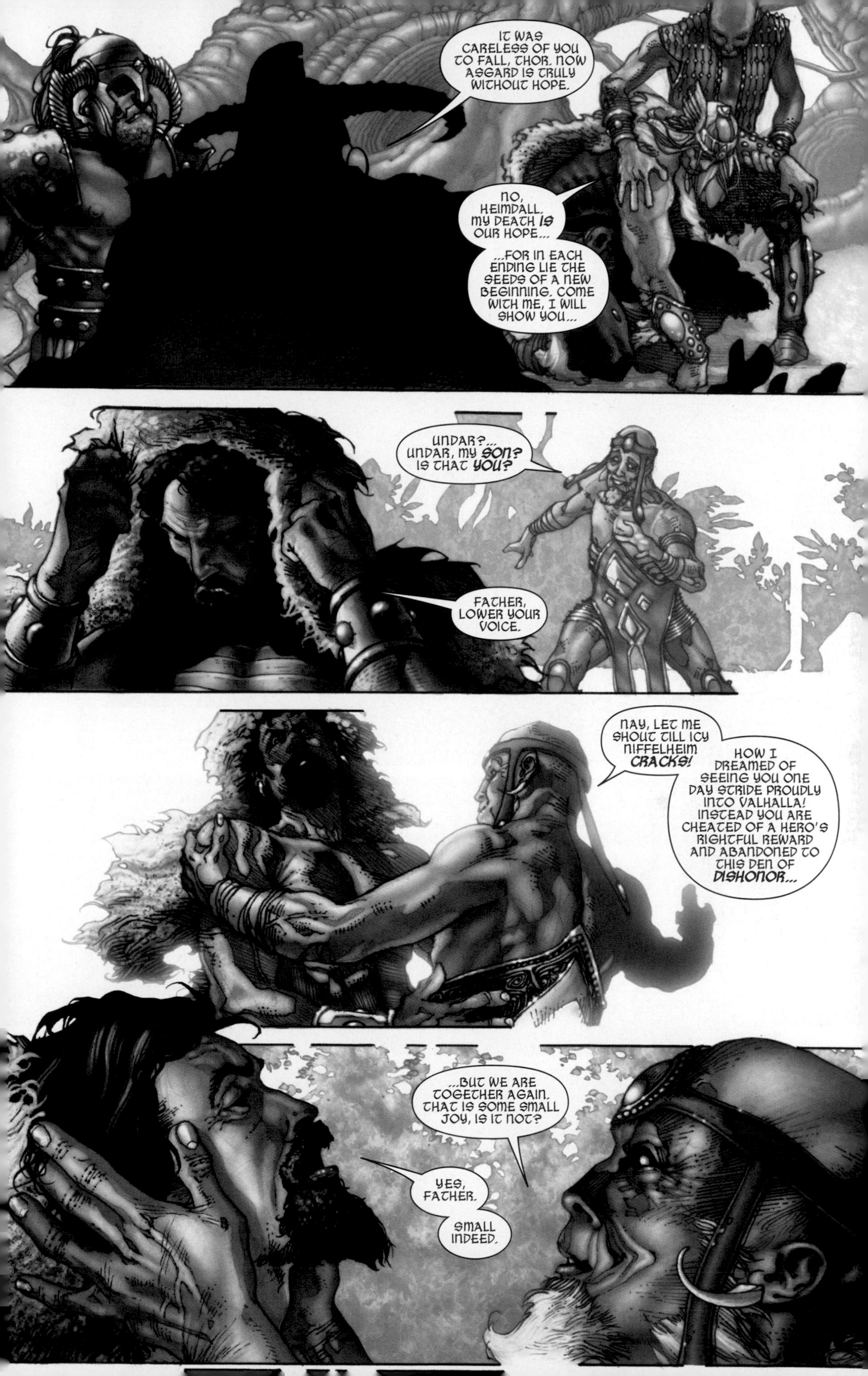
IT WAS CARELESS OF YOU TO FALL, THOR. NOW ASGARD IS TRULY WITHOUT HOPE.
NO, HEIMDALL. MY DEATH *IS* OUR HOPE...
...FOR IN EACH ENDING LIE THE SEEDS OF A NEW BEGINNING. COME WITH ME, I WILL SHOW YOU...
UNDAR?... UNDAR, MY *SON?* IS THAT *YOU?*
FATHER, LOWER YOUR VOICE.
NAY, LET ME SHOUT TILL ICY NIFFELHEIM *CRACKS!*
HOW I DREAMED OF SEEING YOU ONE DAY STRIDE PROUDLY INTO VALHALLA! INSTEAD YOU ARE CHEATED OF A HERO'S RIGHTFUL REWARD AND ABANDONED TO THIS DEN OF *DISHONOR...*
...BUT WE ARE TOGETHER AGAIN. THAT IS SOME SMALL JOY, IS IT NOT?
YES, FATHER.
SMALL INDEED.

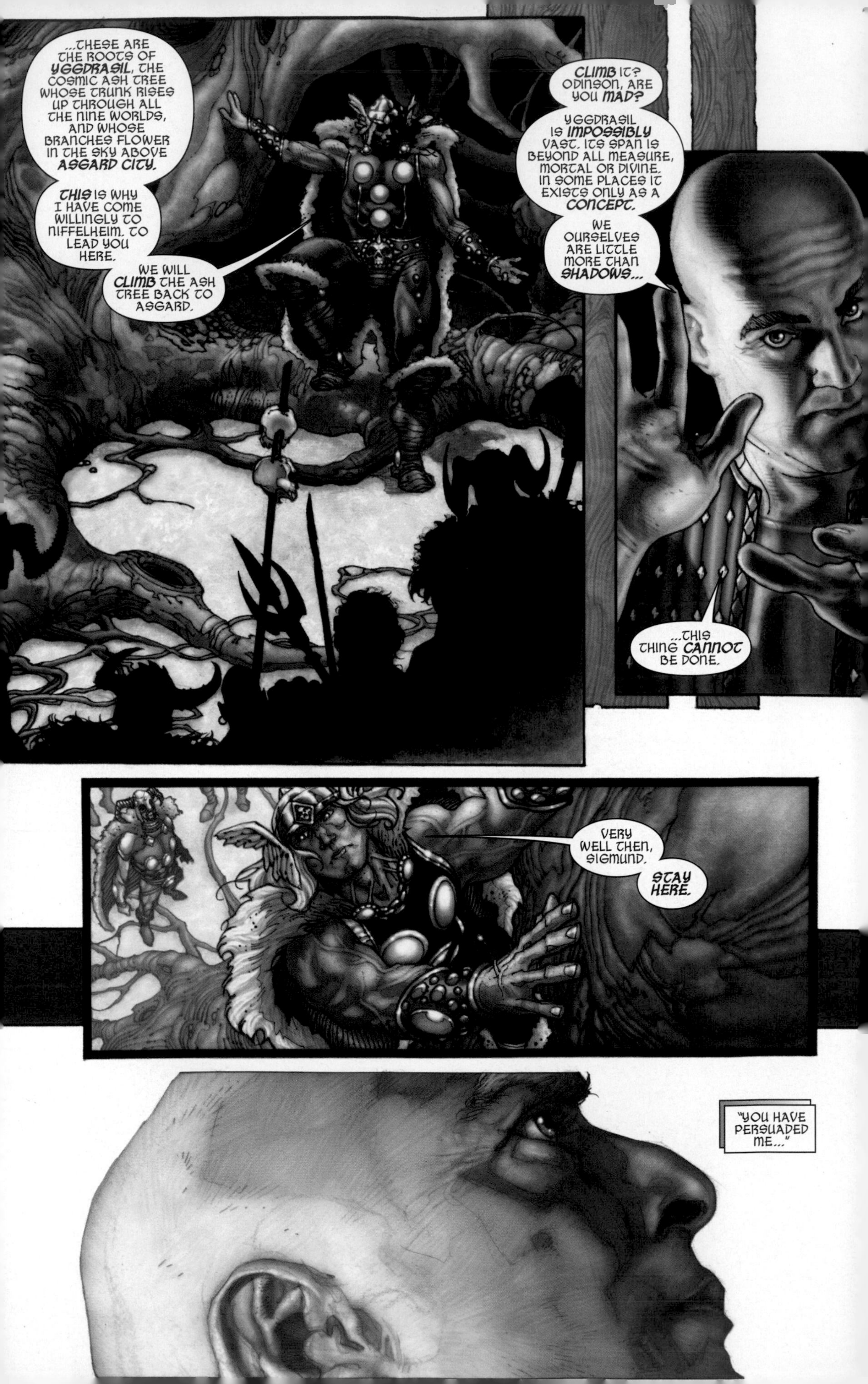

...THESE ARE THE ROOTS OF YGGDRASIL, THE COSMIC ASH TREE WHOSE TRUNK RISES UP THROUGH ALL THE NINE WORLDS, AND WHOSE BRANCHES FLOWER IN THE SKY ABOVE ASGARD CITY.
THIS IS WHY I HAVE COME WILLINGLY TO NIFFELHEIM. TO LEAD YOU HERE.
WE WILL CLIMB THE ASH TREE BACK TO ASGARD.
CLIMB IT? ODINSON, ARE YOU MAD?
YGGDRASIL IS IMPOSSIBLY VAST. ITS SPAN IS BEYOND ALL MEASURE, MORTAL OR DIVINE. IN SOME PLACES IT EXISTS ONLY AS A CONCEPT.
WE OURSELVES ARE LITTLE MORE THAN SHADOWS...
...THIS THING CANNOT BE DONE.
VERY WELL THEN, SIGMUND.
STAY HERE.
"YOU HAVE PERSUADED ME..."

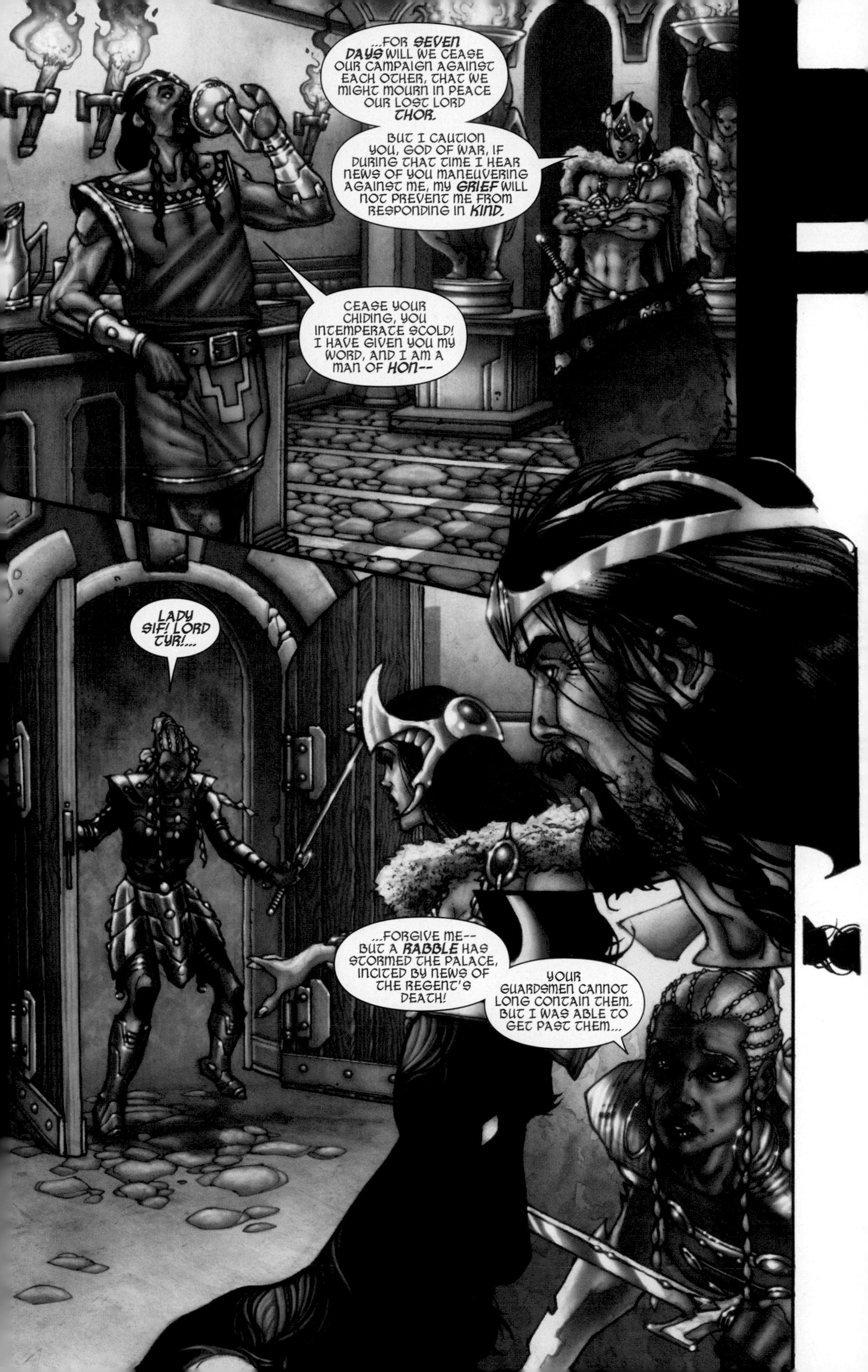
...FOR SEVEN DAYS WILL WE CEASE OUR CAMPAIGN AGAINST EACH OTHER, THAT WE MIGHT MOURN IN PEACE OUR LOST LORD THOR.
BUT I CAUTION YOU, GOD OF WAR, IF DURING THAT TIME I HEAR NEWS OF YOU MANEUVERING AGAINST ME, MY GRIEF WILL NOT PREVENT ME FROM RESPONDING IN KIND.
CEASE YOUR CHIDING, YOU INTEMPERATE SCOLD! I HAVE GIVEN YOU MY WORD, AND I AM A MAN OF HON--
LADY SIF! LORD TYR!...
...FORGIVE ME-- BUT A RABBLE HAS STORMED THE PALACE, INCITED BY NEWS OF THE REGENT'S DEATH!
YOUR GUARDSMEN CANNOT LONG CONTAIN THEM. BUT I WAS ABLE TO GET PAST THEM...

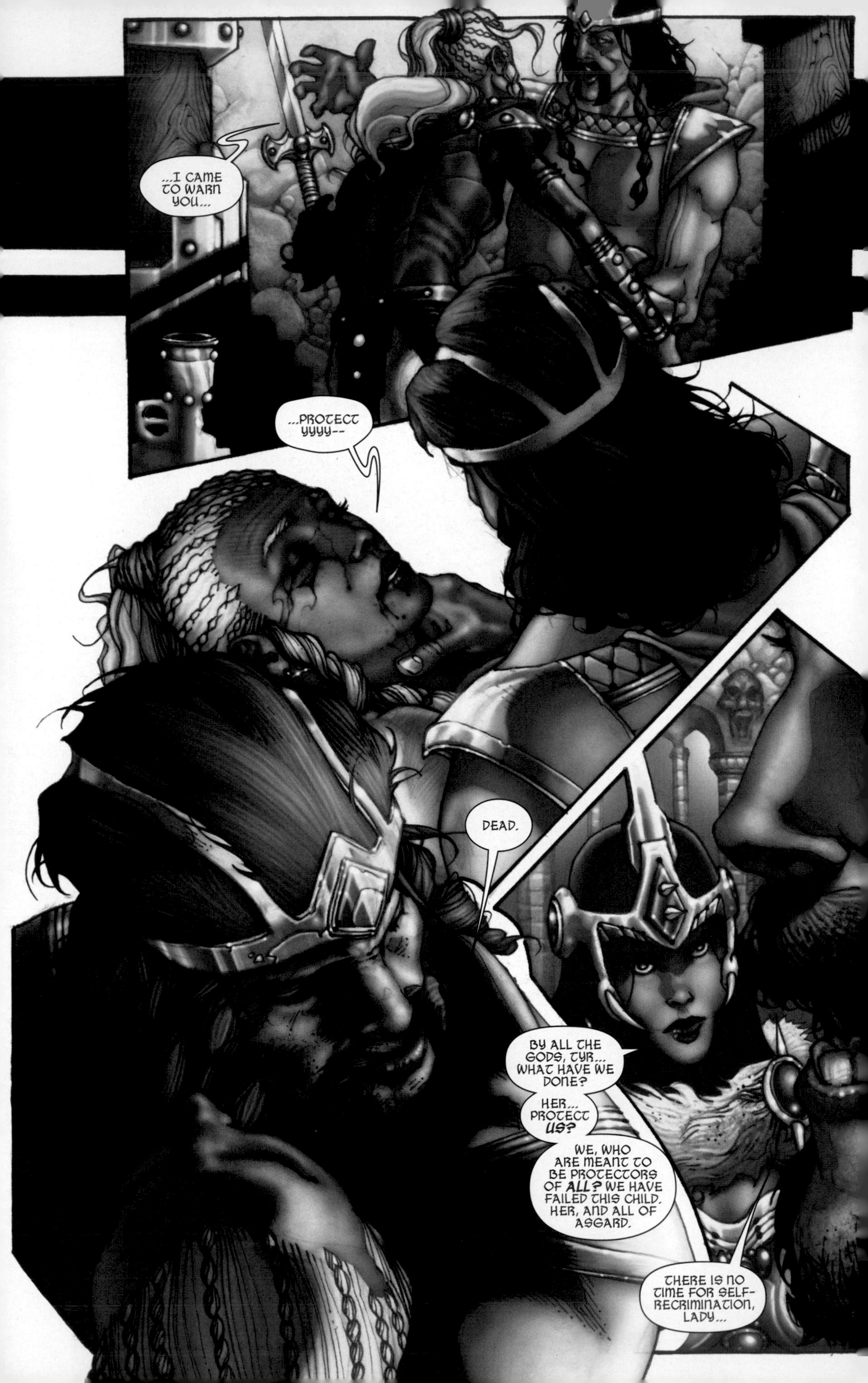
...I CAME TO WARN YOU...
...PROTECT YYYY--
DEAD.
BY ALL THE GODS, TYR... WHAT HAVE WE DONE?
HER... PROTECT US?
WE, WHO ARE MEANT TO BE PROTECTORS OF ALL? WE HAVE FAILED THIS CHILD. HER, AND ALL OF ASGARD.
THERE IS NO TIME FOR SELF-RECRIMINATION, LADY...

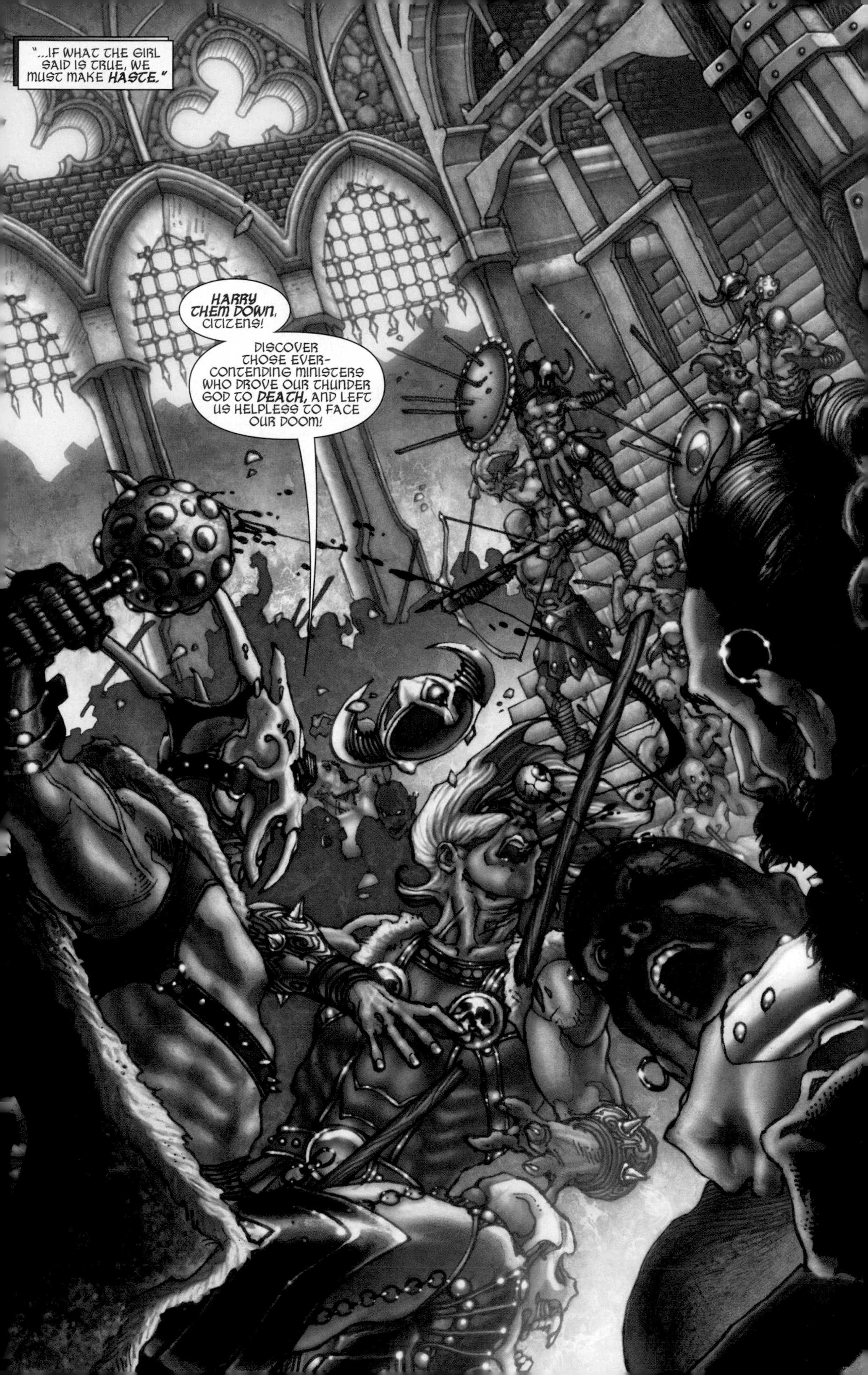
"...IF WHAT THE GIRL SAID IS TRUE, WE MUST MAKE HASTE."
HARRY THEM DOWN, CITIZENS!
DISCOVER THOSE EVER-CONTENDING MINISTERS WHO DROVE OUR THUNDER GOD TO DEATH, AND LEFT US HELPLESS TO FACE OUR DOOM!

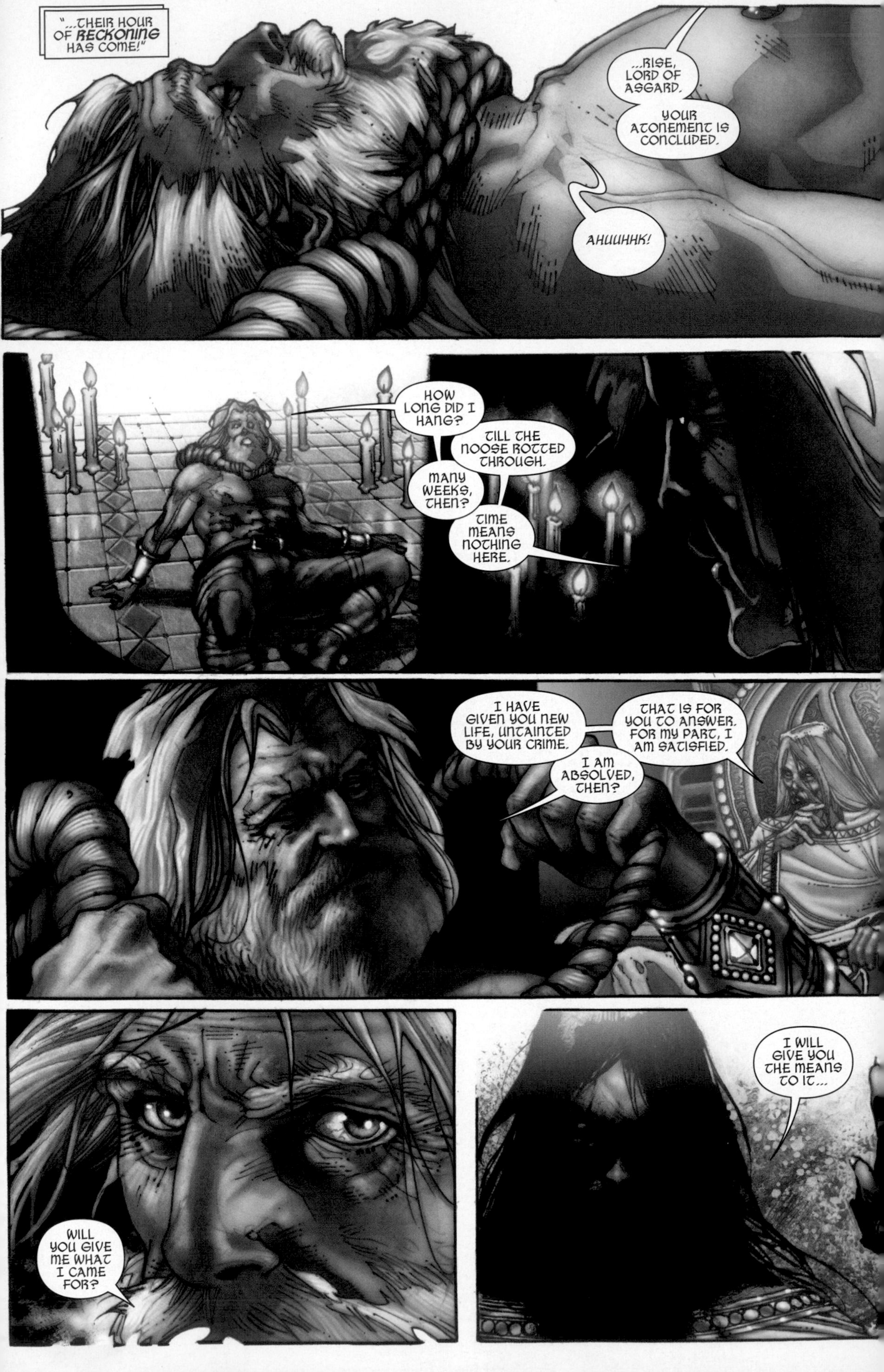
"...THEIR HOUR OF RECKONING HAS COME!"
...RISE, LORD OF ASGARD.
YOUR ATONEMENT IS CONCLUDED.
AHUUHHK!
HOW LONG DID I HANG?
TILL THE NOOSE ROTTED THROUGH.
MANY WEEKS, THEN?
TIME MEANS NOTHING HERE.
I HAVE GIVEN YOU NEW LIFE, UNTAINTED BY YOUR CRIME.
I AM ABSOLVED, THEN?
THAT IS FOR YOU TO ANSWER. FOR MY PART, I AM SATISFIED.
WILL YOU GIVE ME WHAT I CAME FOR?
I WILL GIVE YOU THE MEANS TO IT...

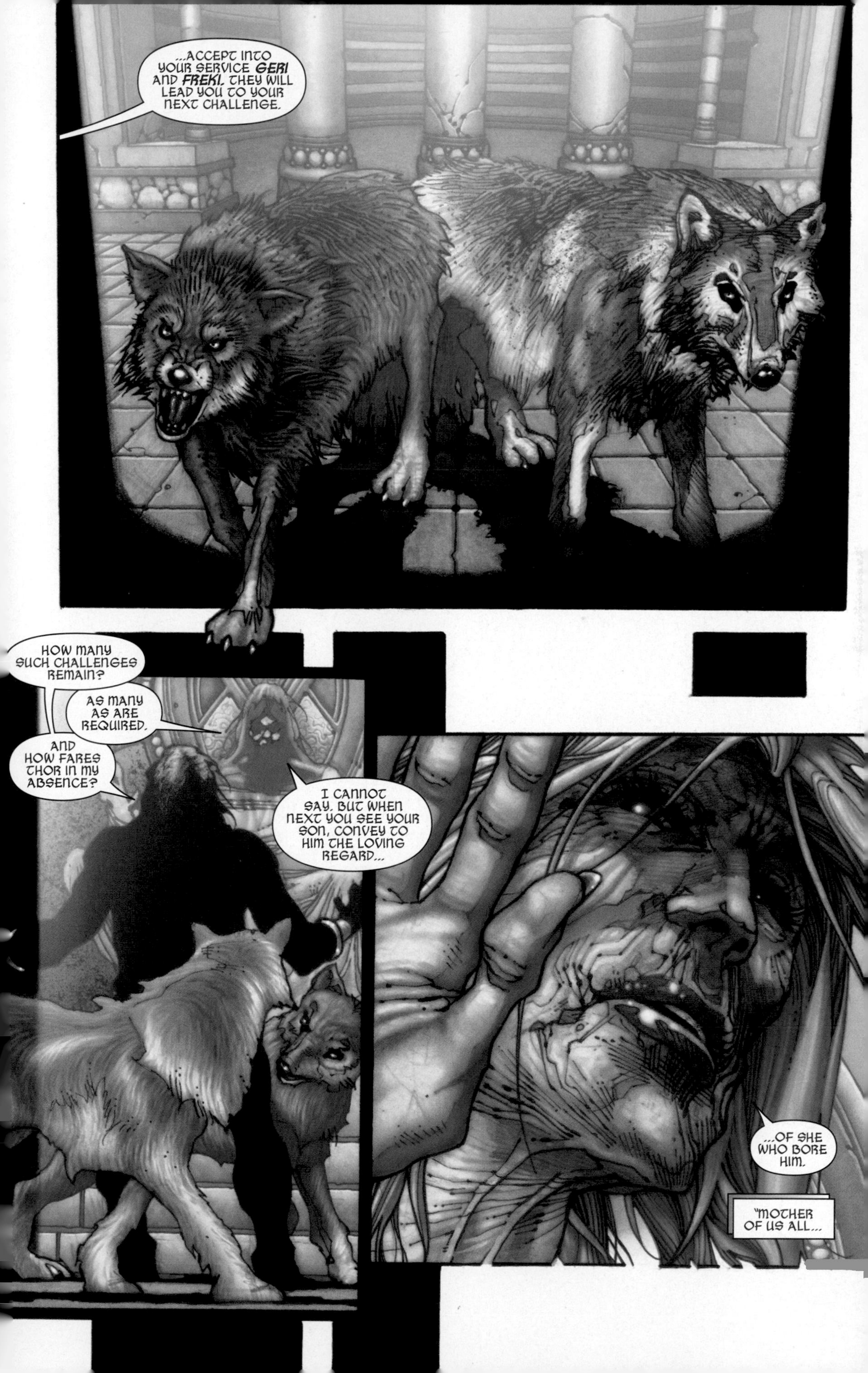
...ACCEPT INTO YOUR SERVICE GERI AND FREKI. THEY WILL LEAD YOU TO YOUR NEXT CHALLENGE.
HOW MANY SUCH CHALLENGES REMAIN?
AS MANY AS ARE REQUIRED.
AND HOW FARES THOR IN MY ABSENCE?
I CANNOT SAY. BUT WHEN NEXT YOU SEE YOUR SON, CONVEY TO HIM THE LOVING REGARD...
...OF SHE WHO BORE HIM.
"MOTHER OF US ALL...

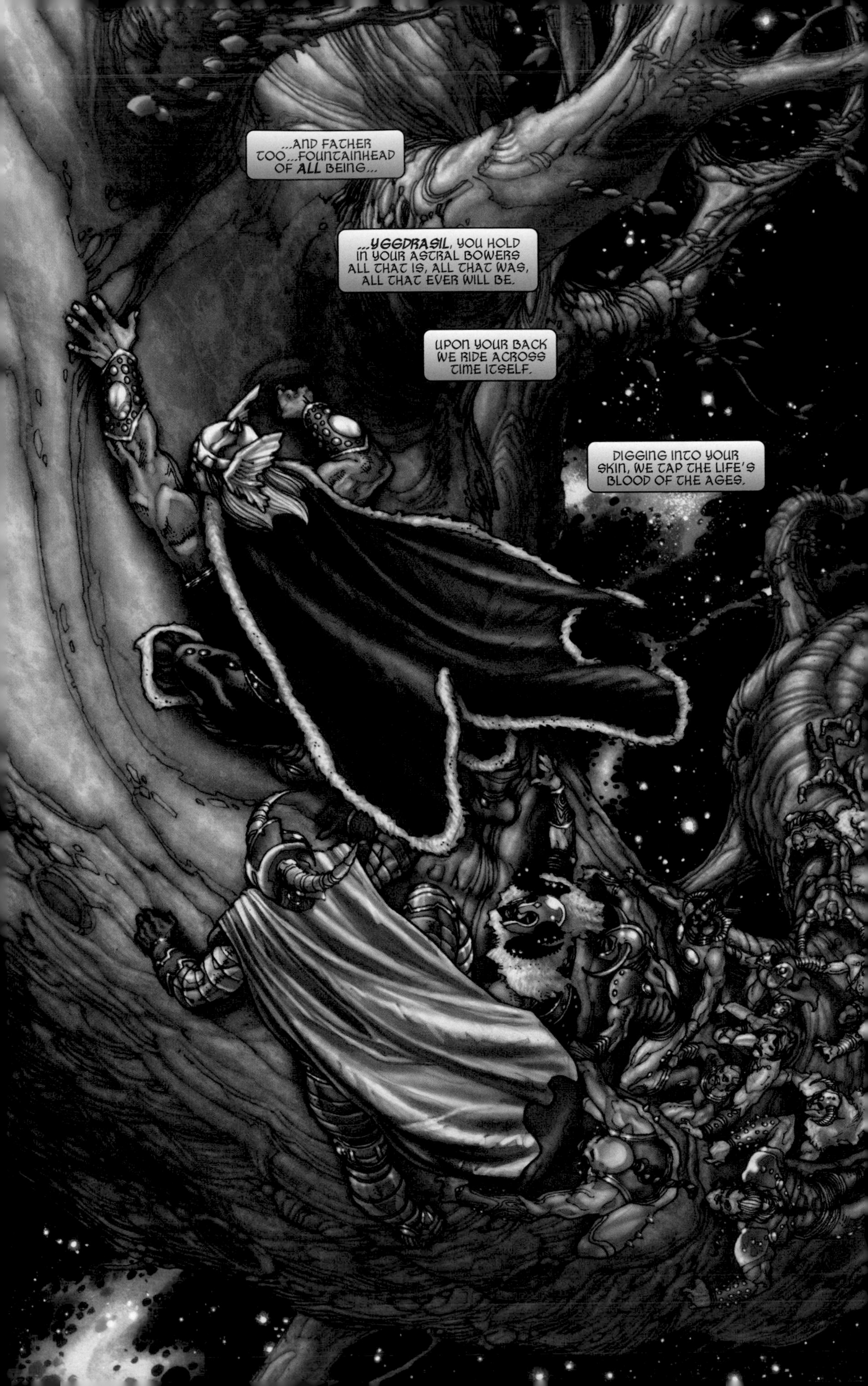
...AND FATHER TOO...FOUNTAINHEAD OF ALL BEING...
...YGGDRASIL, YOU HOLD IN YOUR ASTRAL BOWERS ALL THAT IS, ALL THAT WAS, ALL THAT EVER WILL BE.
UPON YOUR BACK WE RIDE ACROSS TIME ITSELF.
DIGGING INTO YOUR SKIN, WE TAP THE LIFE'S BLOOD OF THE AGES.

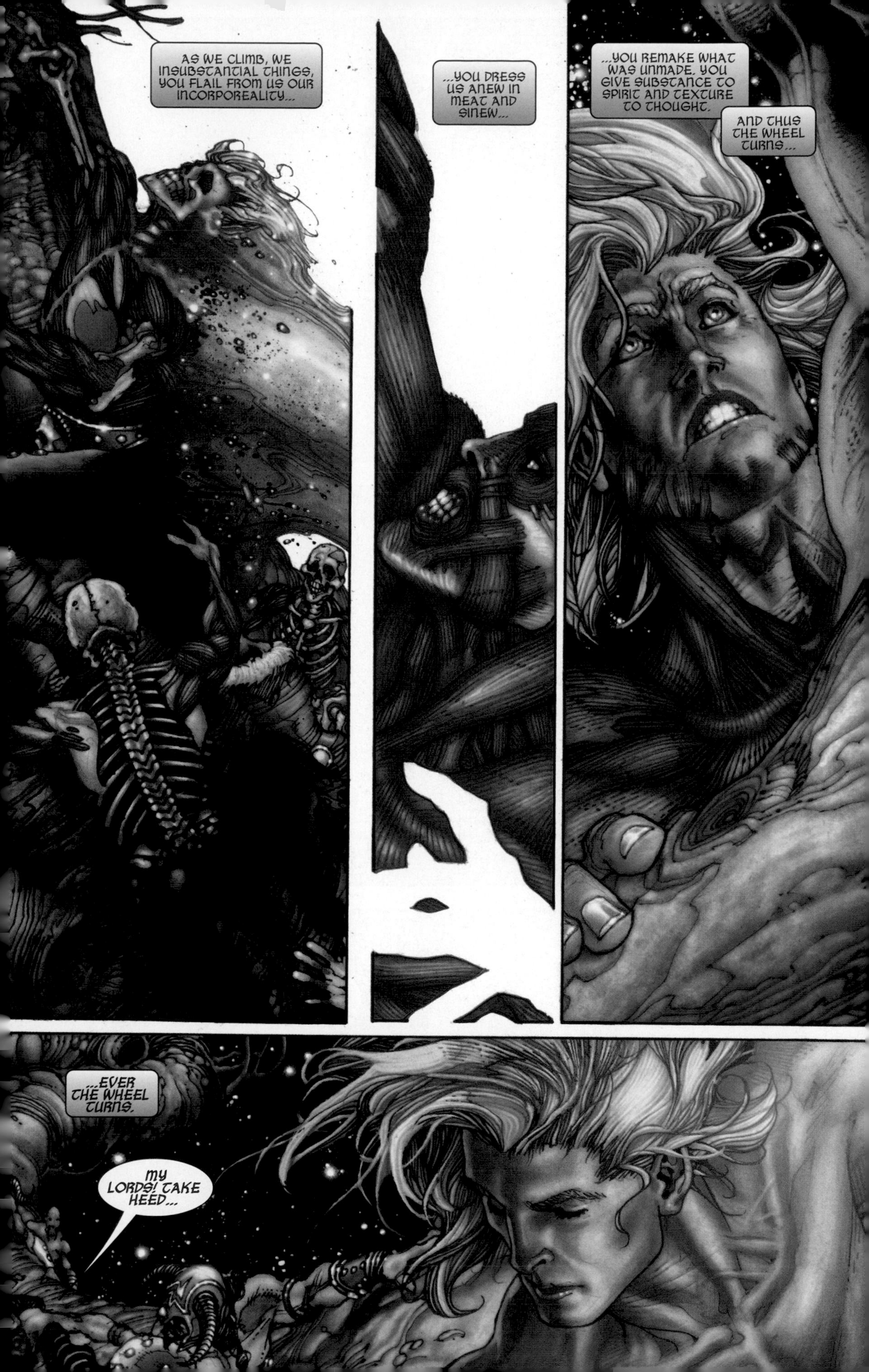
AS WE CLIMB, WE INSUBSTANTIAL THINGS, YOU FLAIL FROM US OUR INCORPOREALITY...
...YOU DRESS US ANEW IN MEAT AND SINEW...
...YOU REMAKE WHAT WAS UNMADE. YOU GIVE SUBSTANCE TO SPIRIT AND TEXTURE TO THOUGHT.
AND THUS THE WHEEL TURNS...
...EVER THE WHEEL TURNS.
MY LORDS! TAKE HEED...

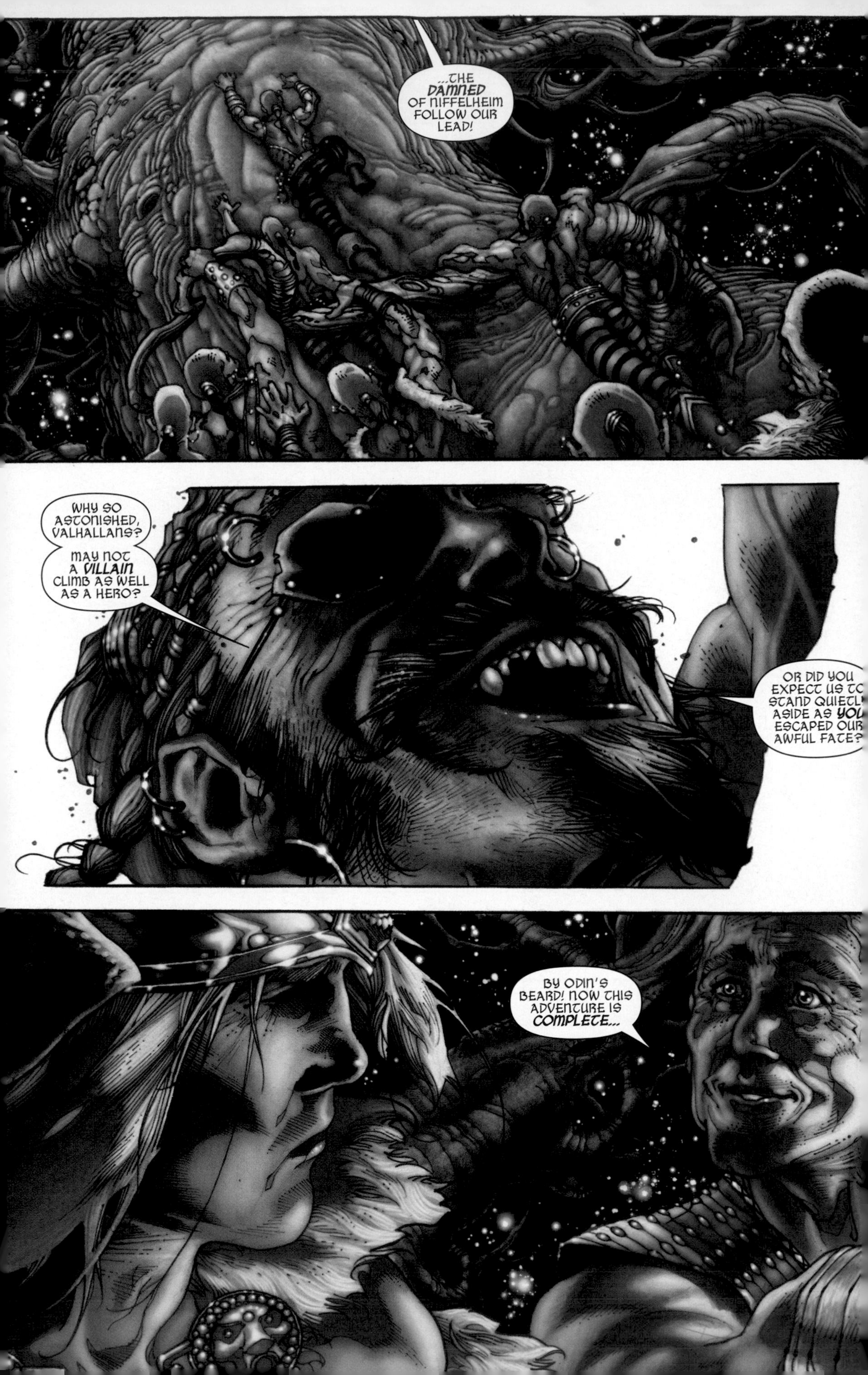
...THE DAMNED OF NIFFELHEIM FOLLOW OUR LEAD!
WHY SO ASTONISHED, VALHALLANS?
MAY NOT A VILLAIN CLIMB AS WELL AS A HERO?
OR DID YOU EXPECT US TO STAND QUIETLY ASIDE AS YOU ESCAPED OUR AWFUL FATE?
BY ODIN'S BEARD! NOW THIS ADVENTURE IS COMPLETE...

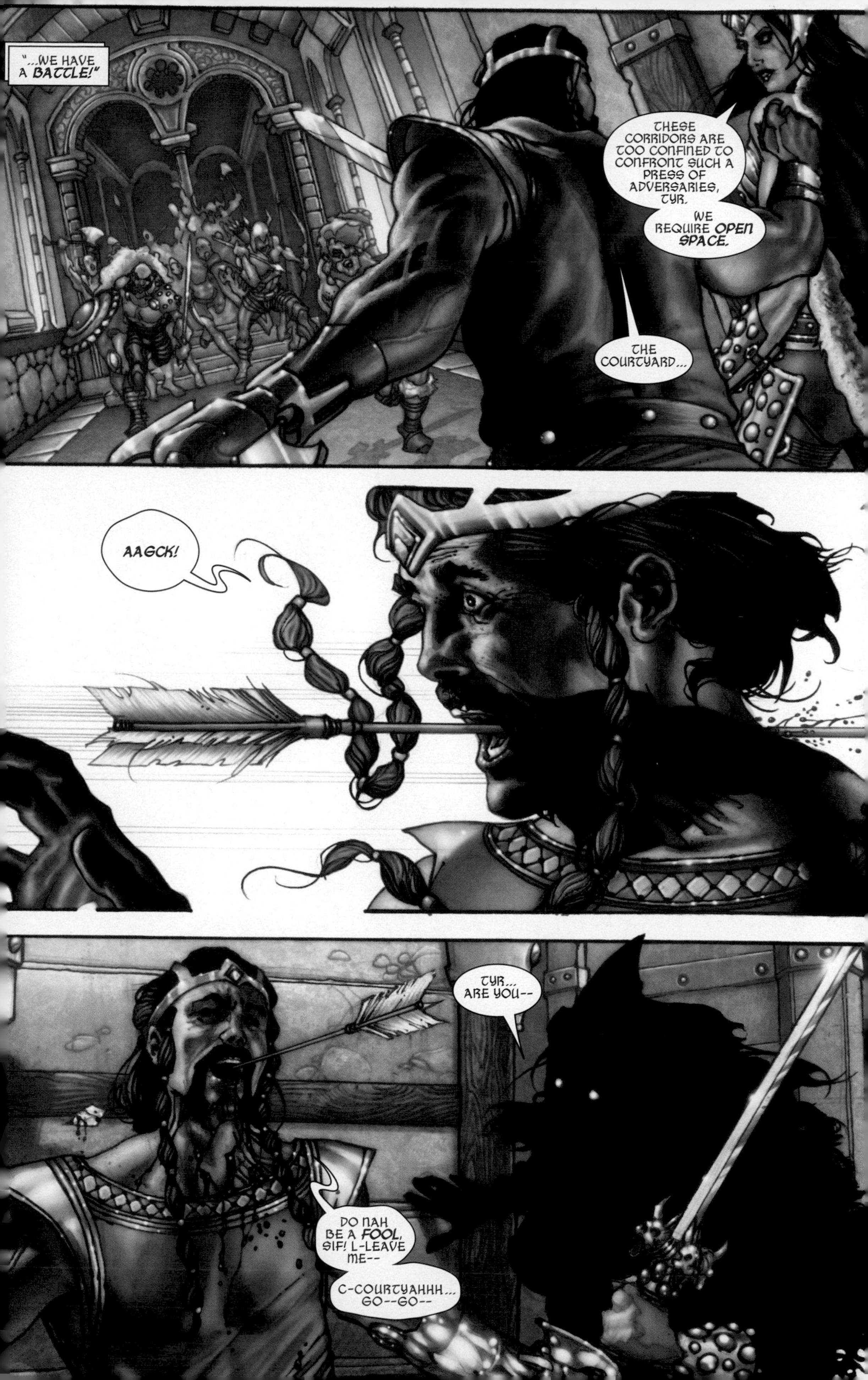
"...WE HAVE A BATTLE!"
THESE CORRIDORS ARE TOO CONFINED TO CONFRONT SUCH A PRESS OF ADVERSARIES, TYR.
WE REQUIRE OPEN SPACE.
THE COURTYARD...
AAGCK!
TYR... ARE YOU--
DO NAH BE A FOOL, SIF! L-LEAVE ME--
C-COURTYAHHH... GO--GO--

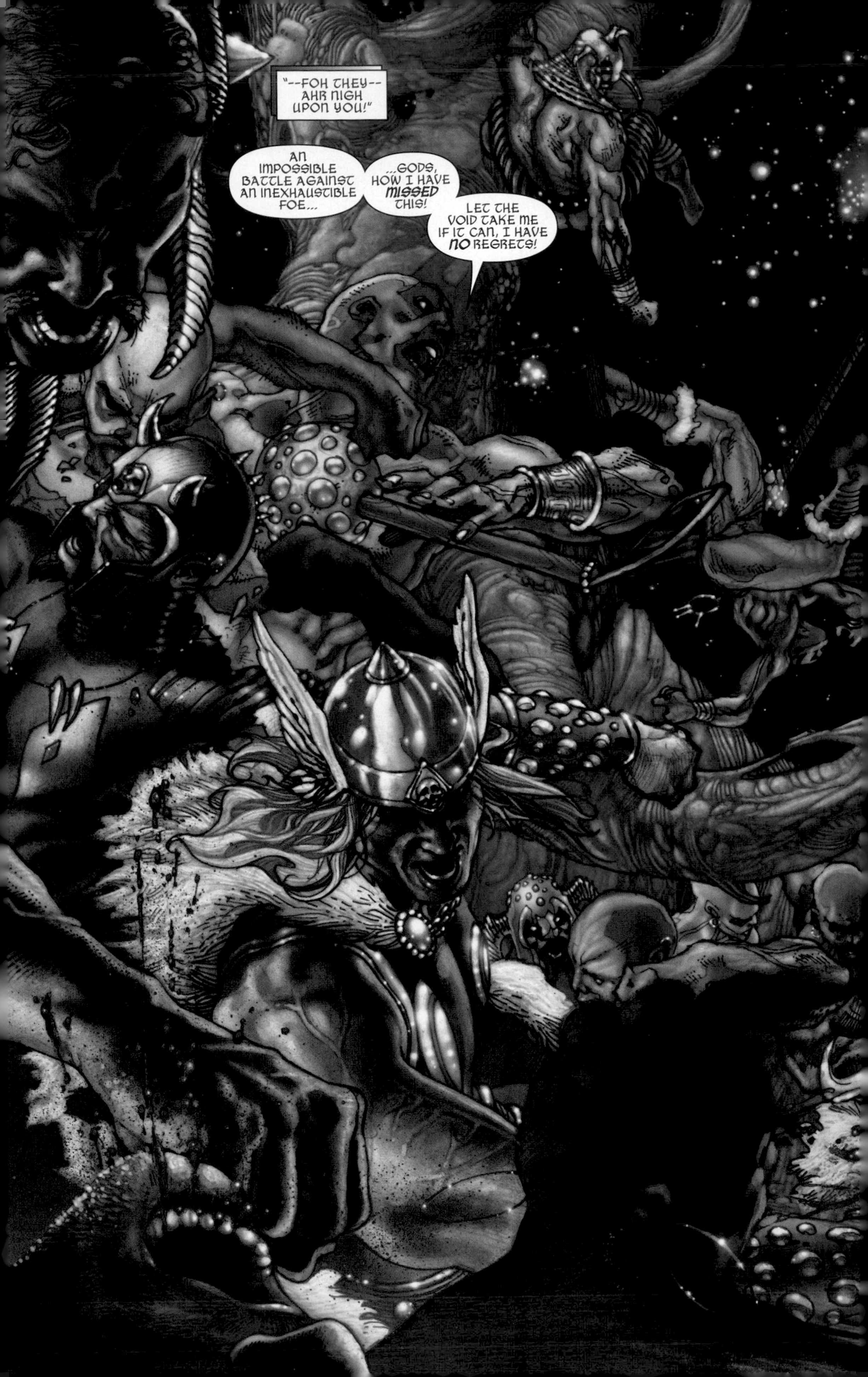
"--FOH THEY-- AHR NIGH UPON YOU!"
AN IMPOSSIBLE BATTLE AGAINST AN INEXHAUSTIBLE FOE...
...GODS, HOW I HAVE MISSED THIS!
LET THE VOID TAKE ME IF IT CAN, I HAVE NO REGRETS!

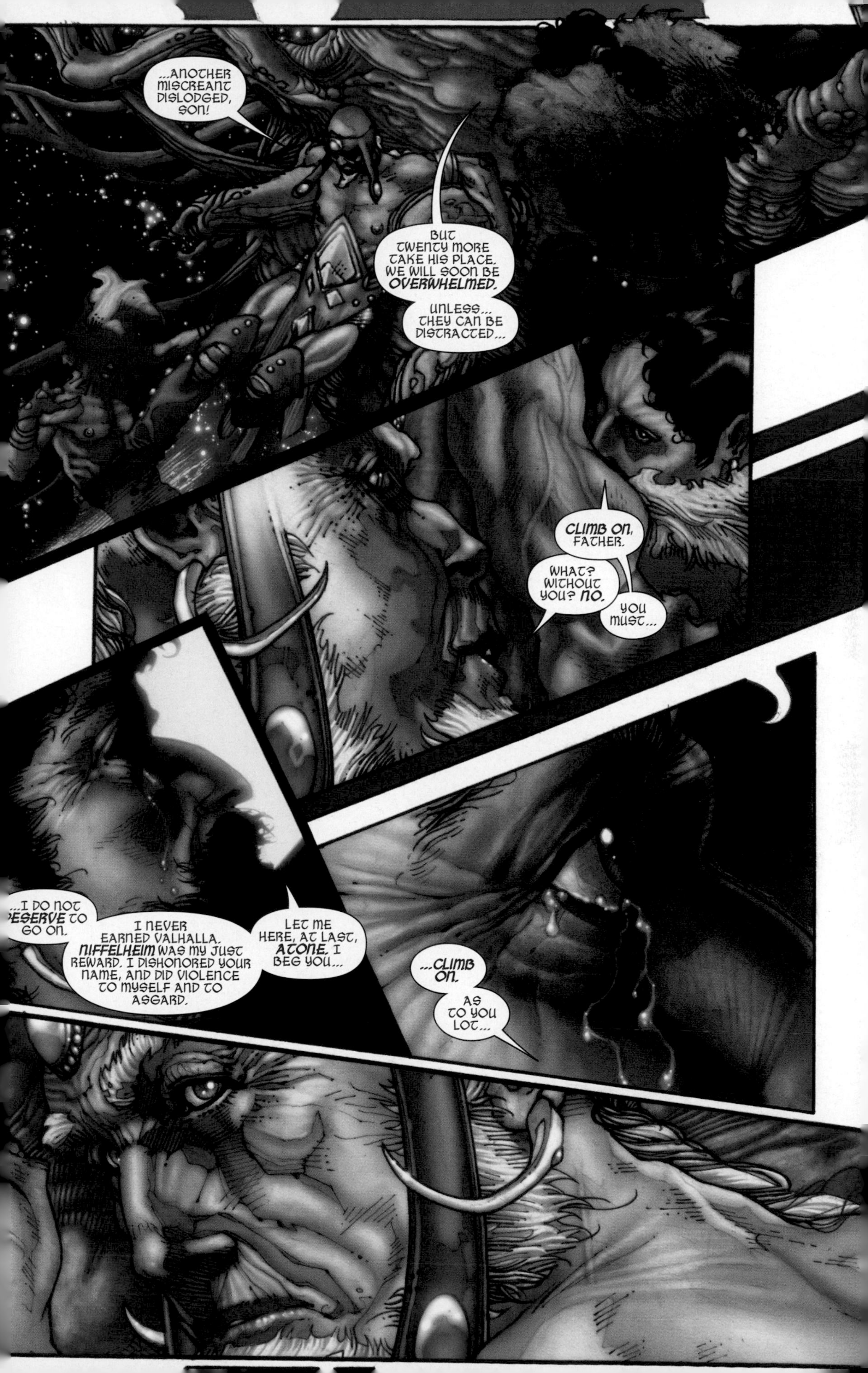
...ANOTHER MISCREANT DISLODGED, SON!
BUT TWENTY MORE TAKE HIS PLACE. WE WILL SOON BE **OVERWHELMED.**
UNLESS... THEY CAN BE DISTRACTED...
CLIMB ON, FATHER.
WHAT? WITHOUT YOU? **NO.**
YOU MUST...
...I DO NOT **DESERVE** TO GO ON.
I NEVER EARNED VALHALLA. **NIFFELHEIM** WAS MY JUST REWARD. I DISHONORED YOUR NAME, AND DID VIOLENCE TO MYSELF AND TO ASGARD.
LET ME HERE, AT LAST, **ATONE.** I BEG YOU...
...CLIMB ON.
AS TO YOU LOT...

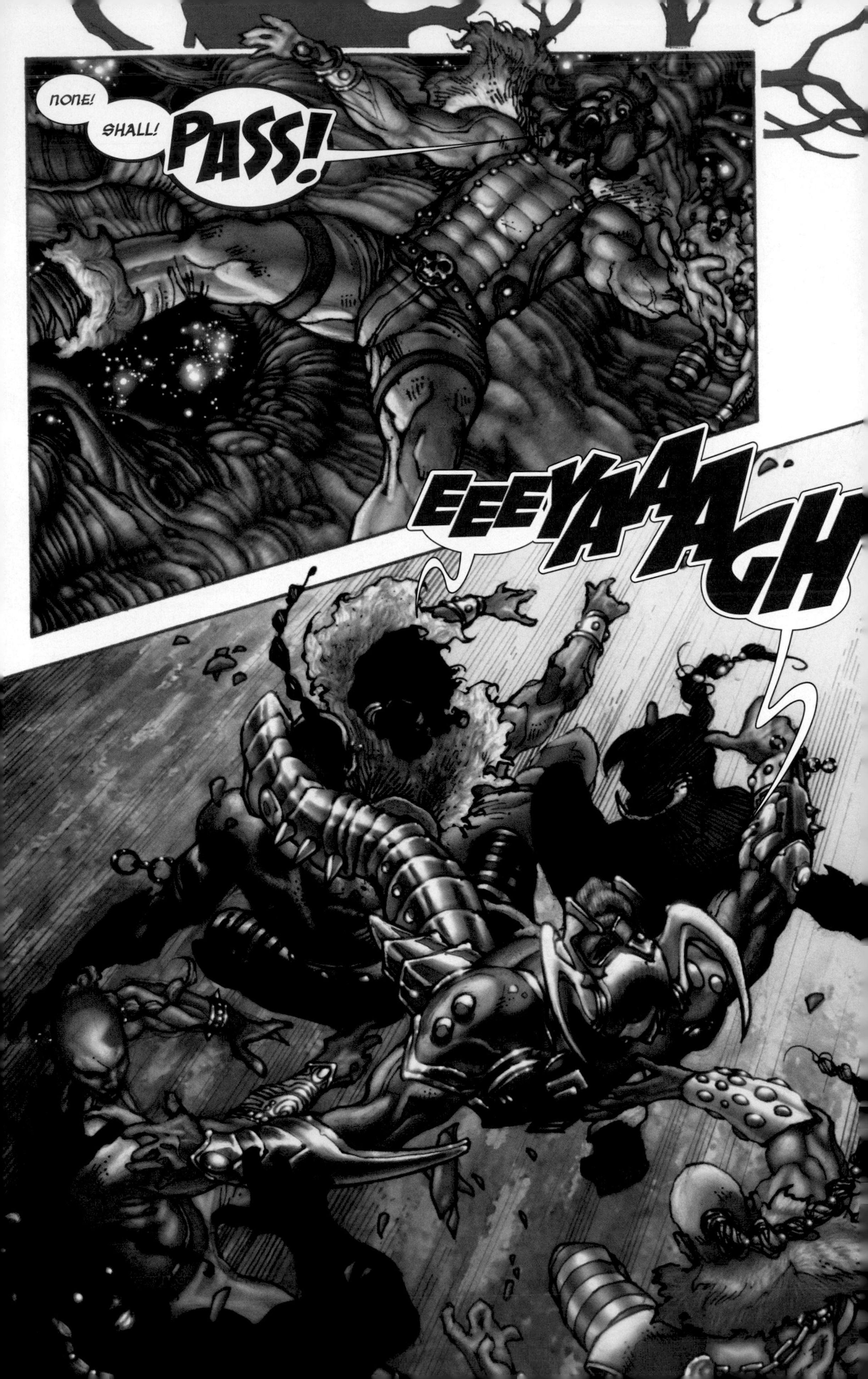
NONE!
SHALL!
PASS!
EEEYAAACH

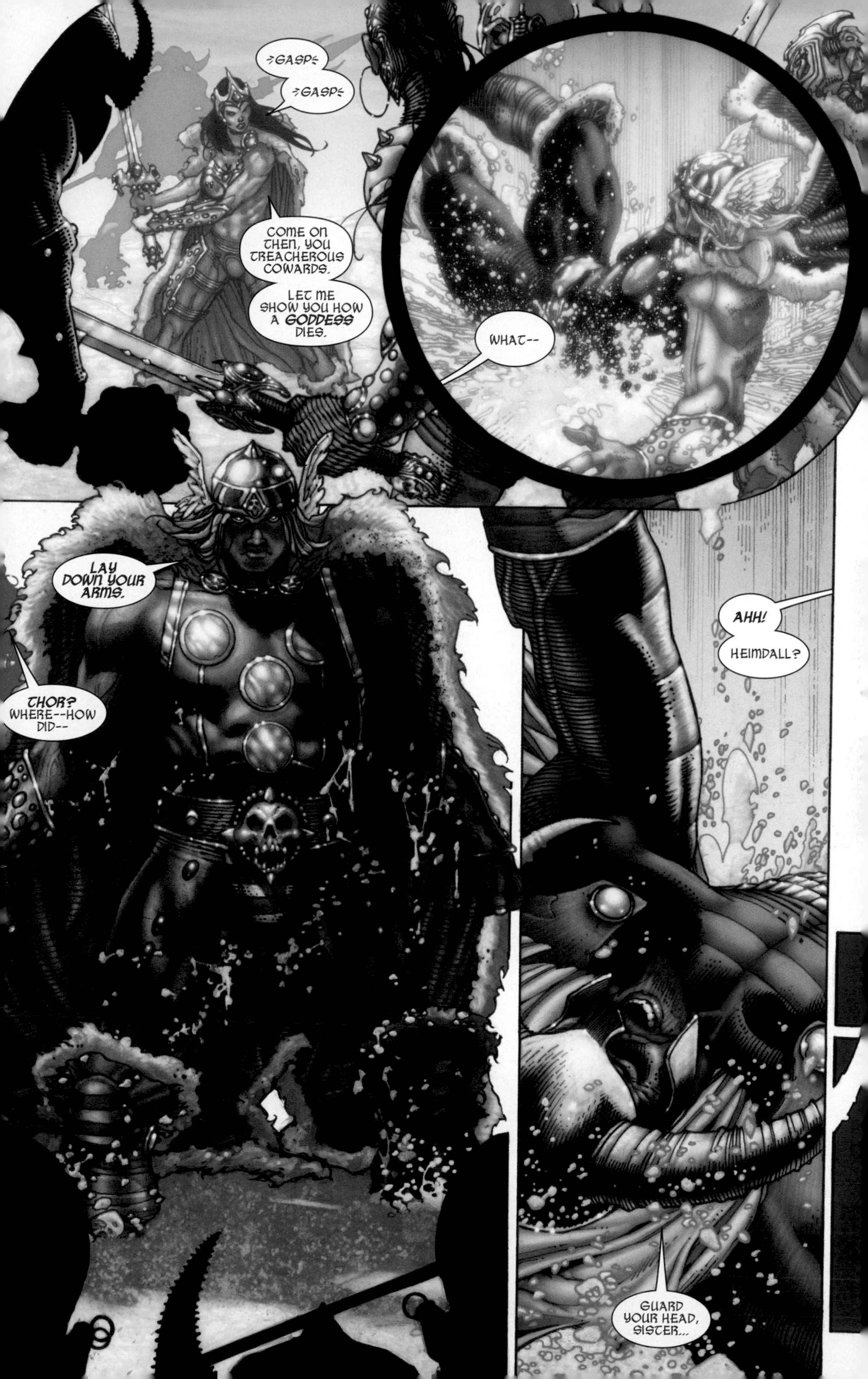

-GASP-
-GASP-
COME ON THEN, YOU TREACHEROUS COWARDS.
LET ME SHOW YOU HOW A GODDESS DIES.
WHAT--
LAY DOWN YOUR ARMS.
THOR? WHERE--HOW DID--
AHH!
HEIMDALL?
GUARD YOUR HEAD, SISTER...

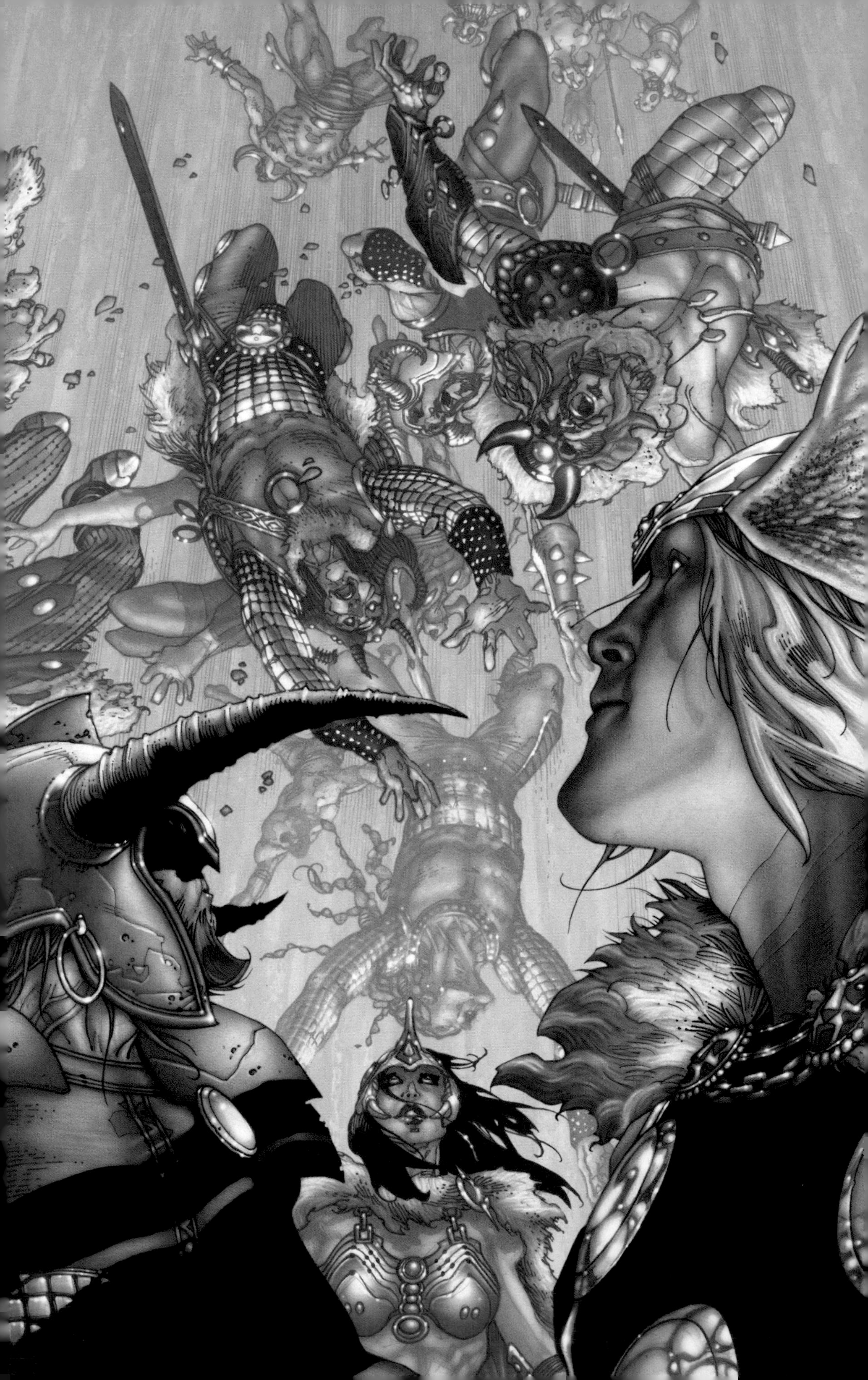

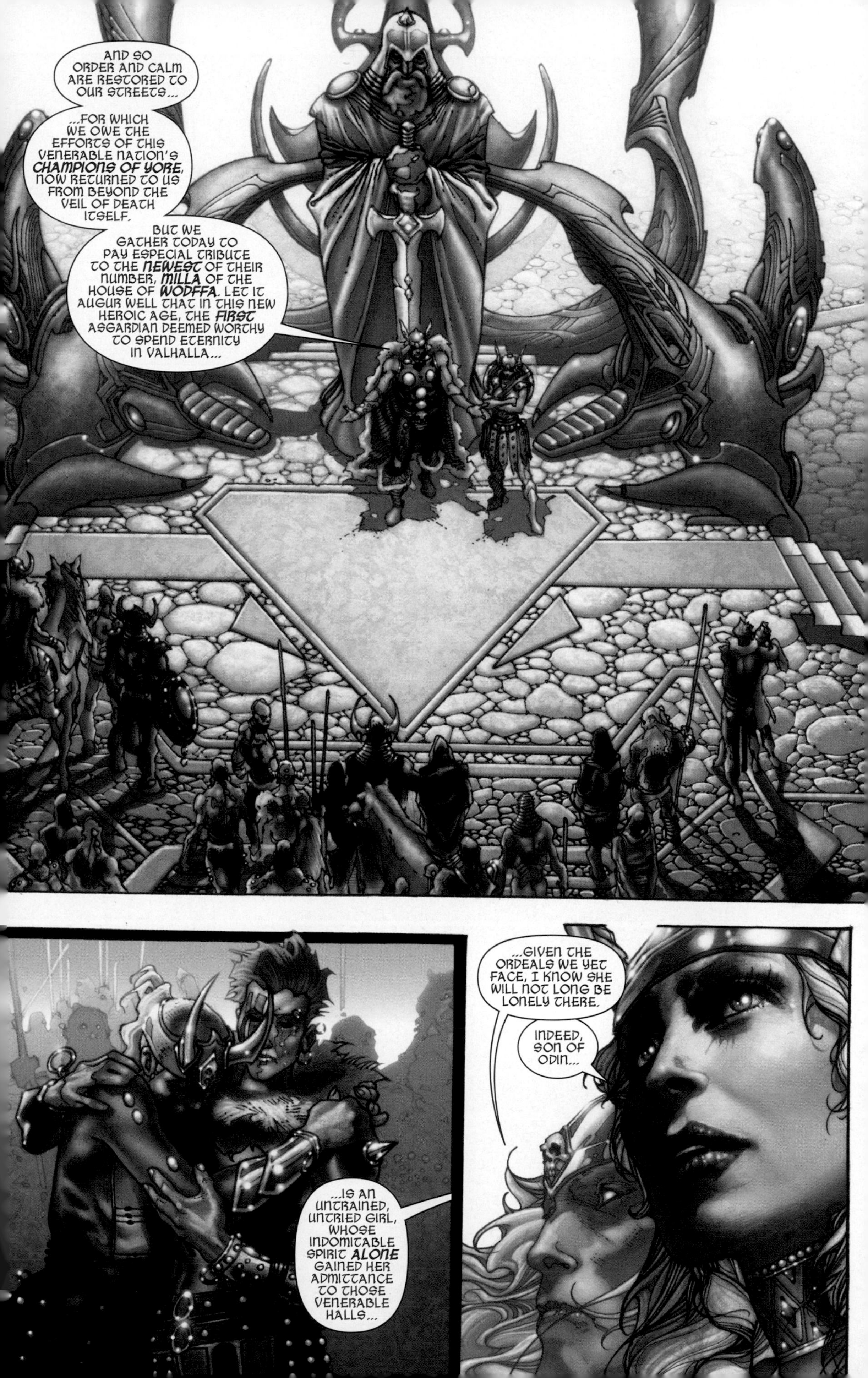
AND SO ORDER AND CALM ARE RESTORED TO OUR STREETS...
...FOR WHICH WE OWE THE EFFORTS OF THIS VENERABLE NATION'S **CHAMPIONS OF YORE**, NOW RETURNED TO US FROM BEYOND THE VEIL OF DEATH ITSELF.
BUT WE GATHER TODAY TO PAY ESPECIAL TRIBUTE TO THE **NEWEST** OF THEIR NUMBER, **MILLA** OF THE HOUSE OF **WODFFA**. LET IT AUGUR WELL THAT IN THIS NEW HEROIC AGE, THE **FIRST** ASGARDIAN DEEMED WORTHY TO SPEND ETERNITY IN VALHALLA...
...IS AN UNTRAINED, UNTRIED GIRL, WHOSE INDOMITABLE SPIRIT **ALONE** GAINED HER ADMITTANCE TO THOSE VENERABLE HALLS...
...GIVEN THE ORDEALS WE YET FACE, I KNOW SHE WILL NOT LONG BE LONELY THERE.
INDEED, SON OF ODIN...

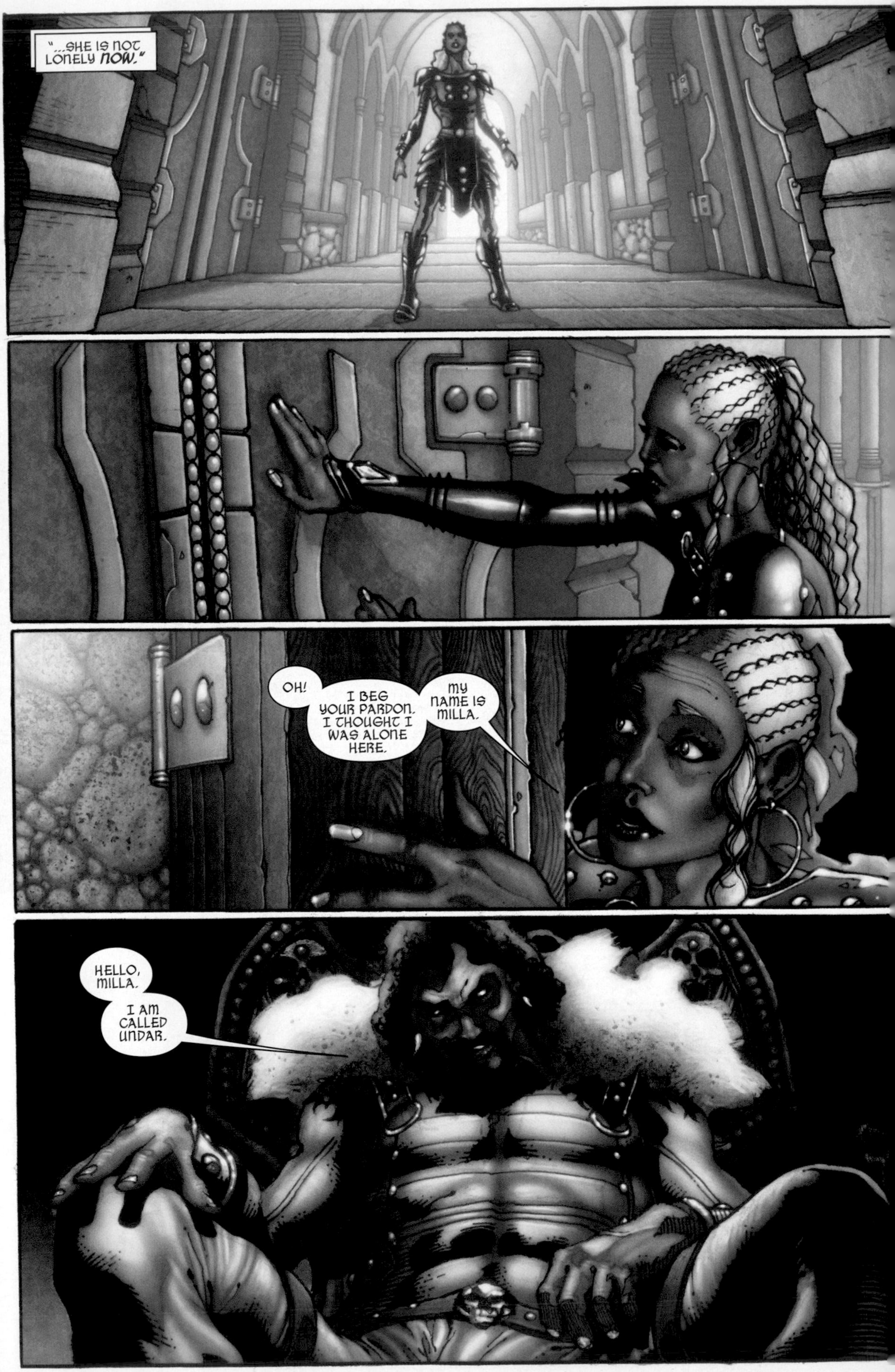
"...SHE IS NOT LONELY NOW."
OH!
I BEG YOUR PARDON. I THOUGHT I WAS ALONE HERE.
MY NAME IS MILLA.
HELLO, MILLA.
I AM CALLED UNDAR.

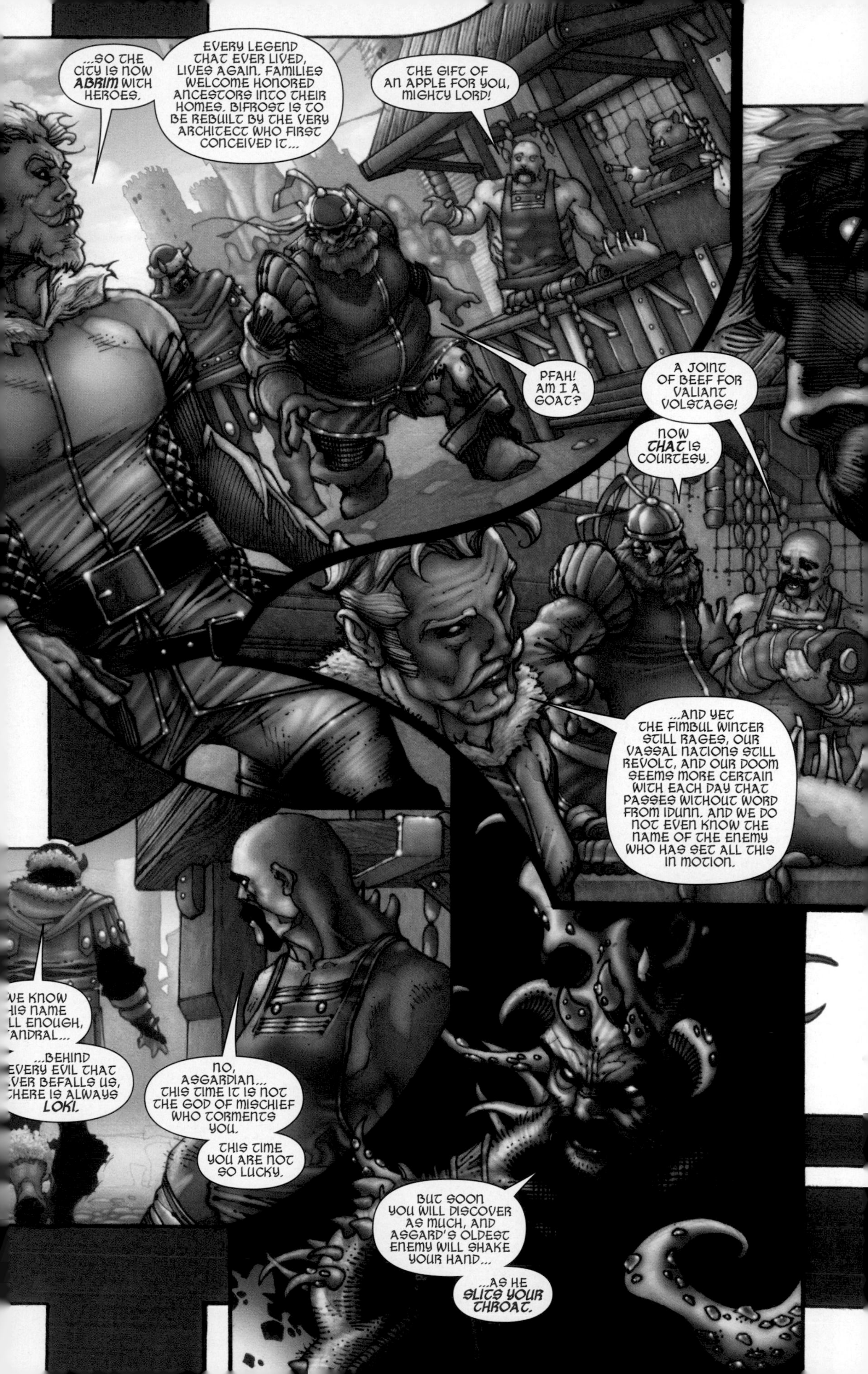
...SO THE CITY IS NOW ABRIM WITH HEROES.
EVERY LEGEND THAT EVER LIVED, LIVES AGAIN. FAMILIES WELCOME HONORED ANCESTORS INTO THEIR HOMES. BIFROST IS TO BE REBUILT BY THE VERY ARCHITECT WHO FIRST CONCEIVED IT...
THE GIFT OF AN APPLE FOR YOU, MIGHTY LORD!
PFAH! AM I A GOAT?
A JOINT OF BEEF FOR VALIANT VOLSTAGG!
NOW THAT IS COURTESY.
...AND YET THE FIMBUL WINTER STILL RAGES, OUR VASSAL NATIONS STILL REVOLT, AND OUR DOOM SEEMS MORE CERTAIN WITH EACH DAY THAT PASSES WITHOUT WORD FROM IDUNN. AND WE DO NOT EVEN KNOW THE NAME OF THE ENEMY WHO HAS SET ALL THIS IN MOTION.
...BEHIND EVERY EVIL THAT EVER BEFALLS US, THERE IS ALWAYS LOKI.
NO, ASGARDIAN... THIS TIME IT IS NOT THE GOD OF MISCHIEF WHO TORMENTS YOU.
THIS TIME YOU ARE NOT SO LUCKY.
BUT SOON YOU WILL DISCOVER AS MUCH, AND ASGARD'S OLDEST ENEMY WILL SHAKE YOUR HAND...
...AS HE SLITS YOUR THROAT.

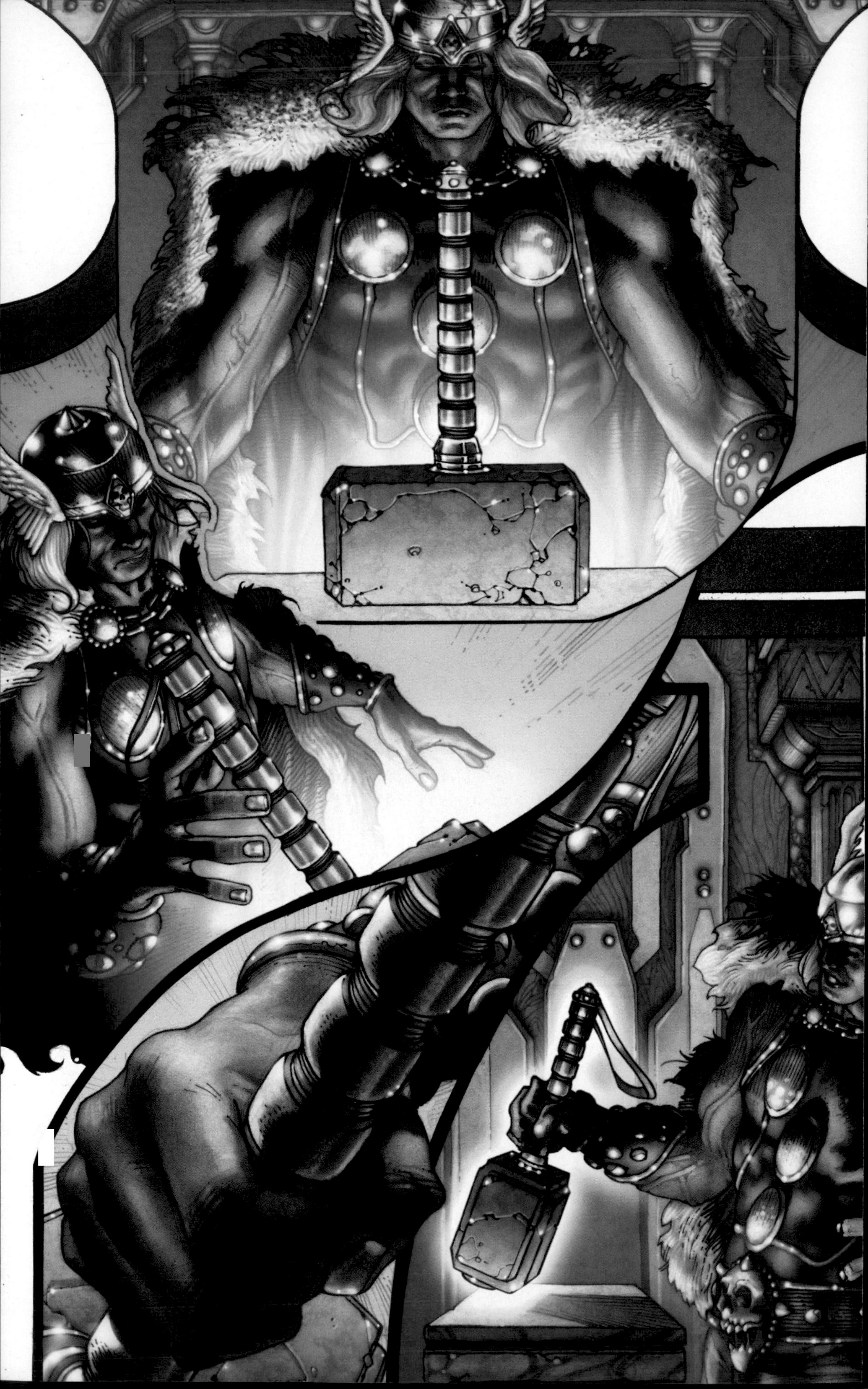

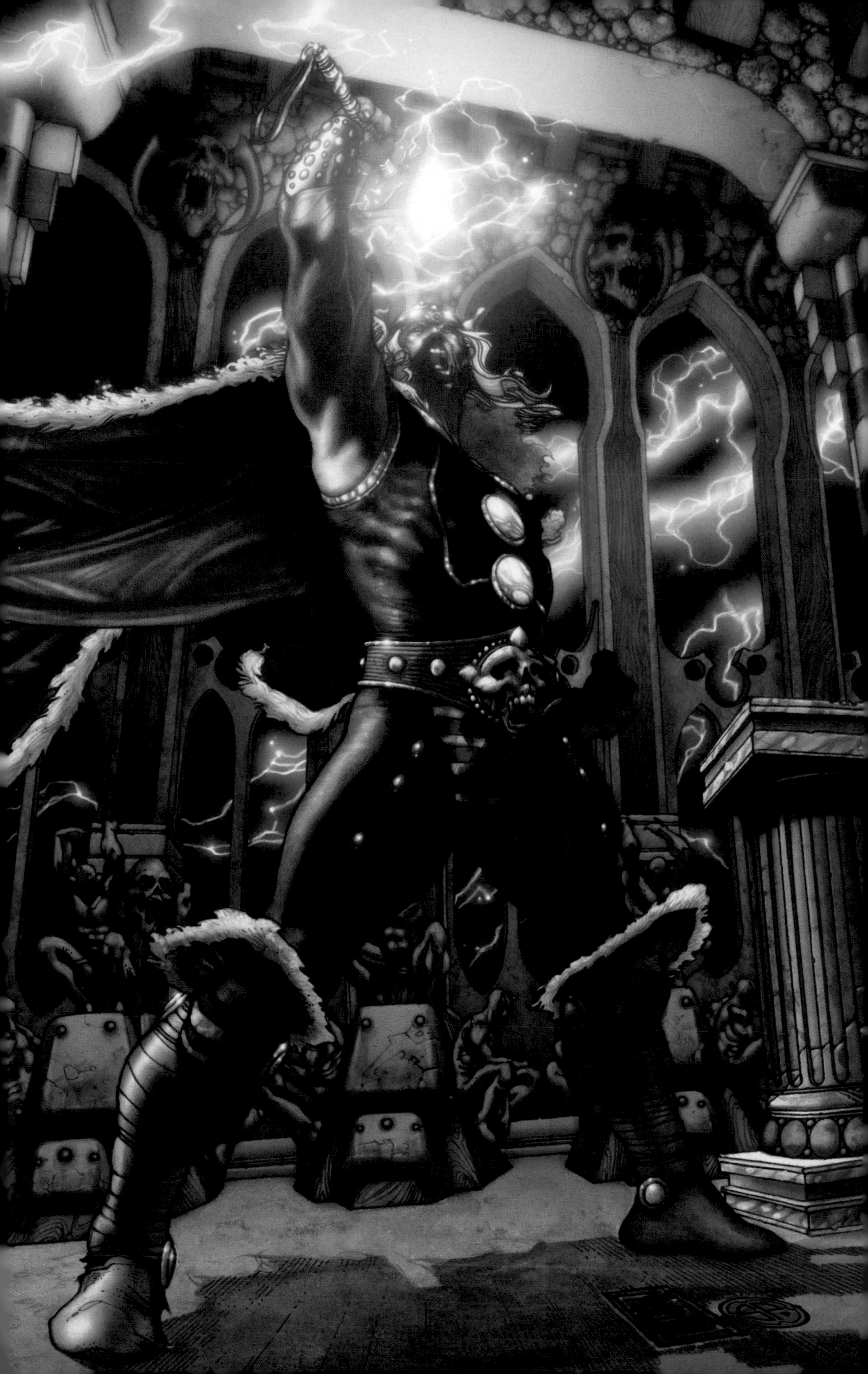

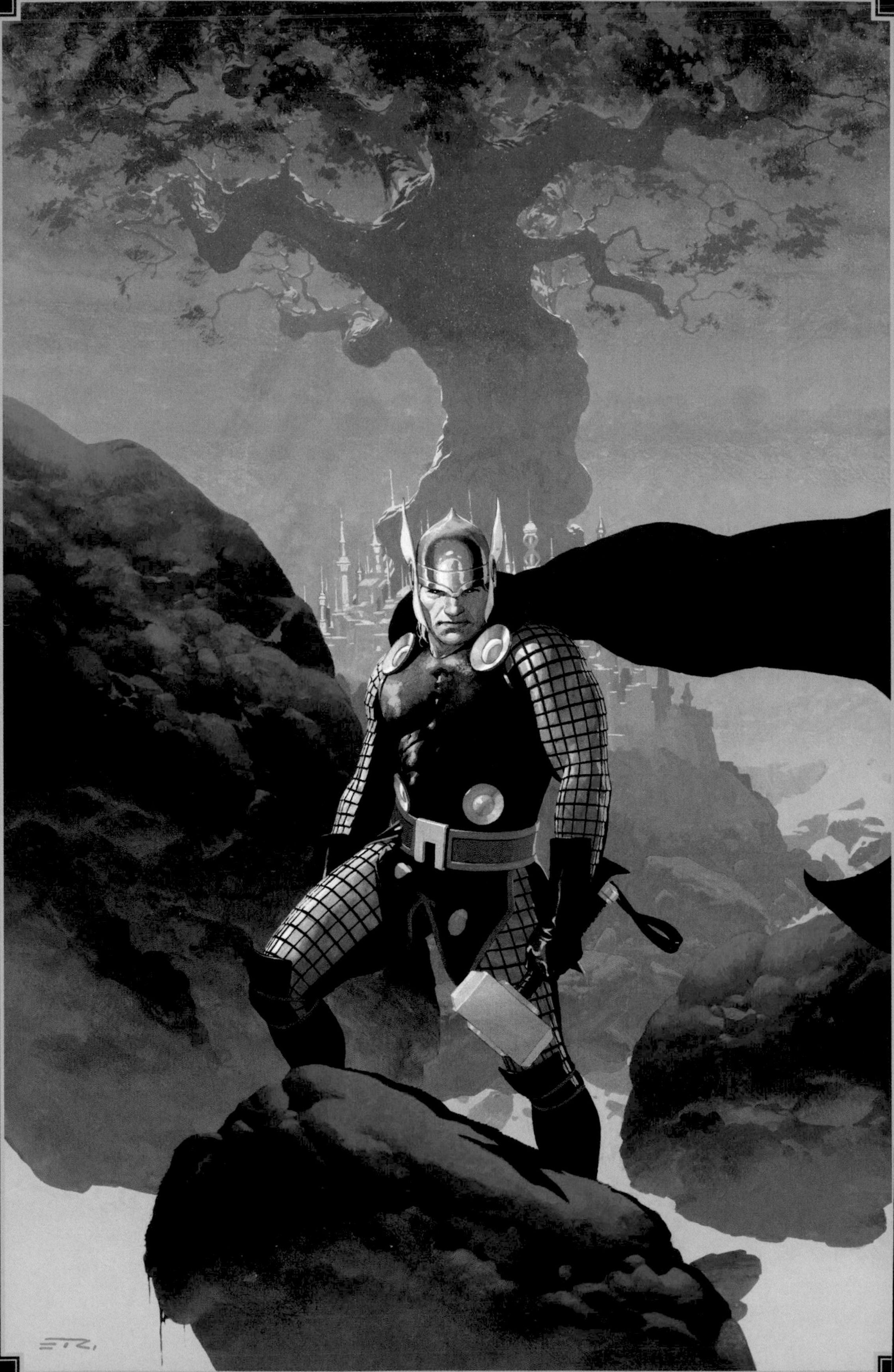
ETRI

Astonishing Thor 1

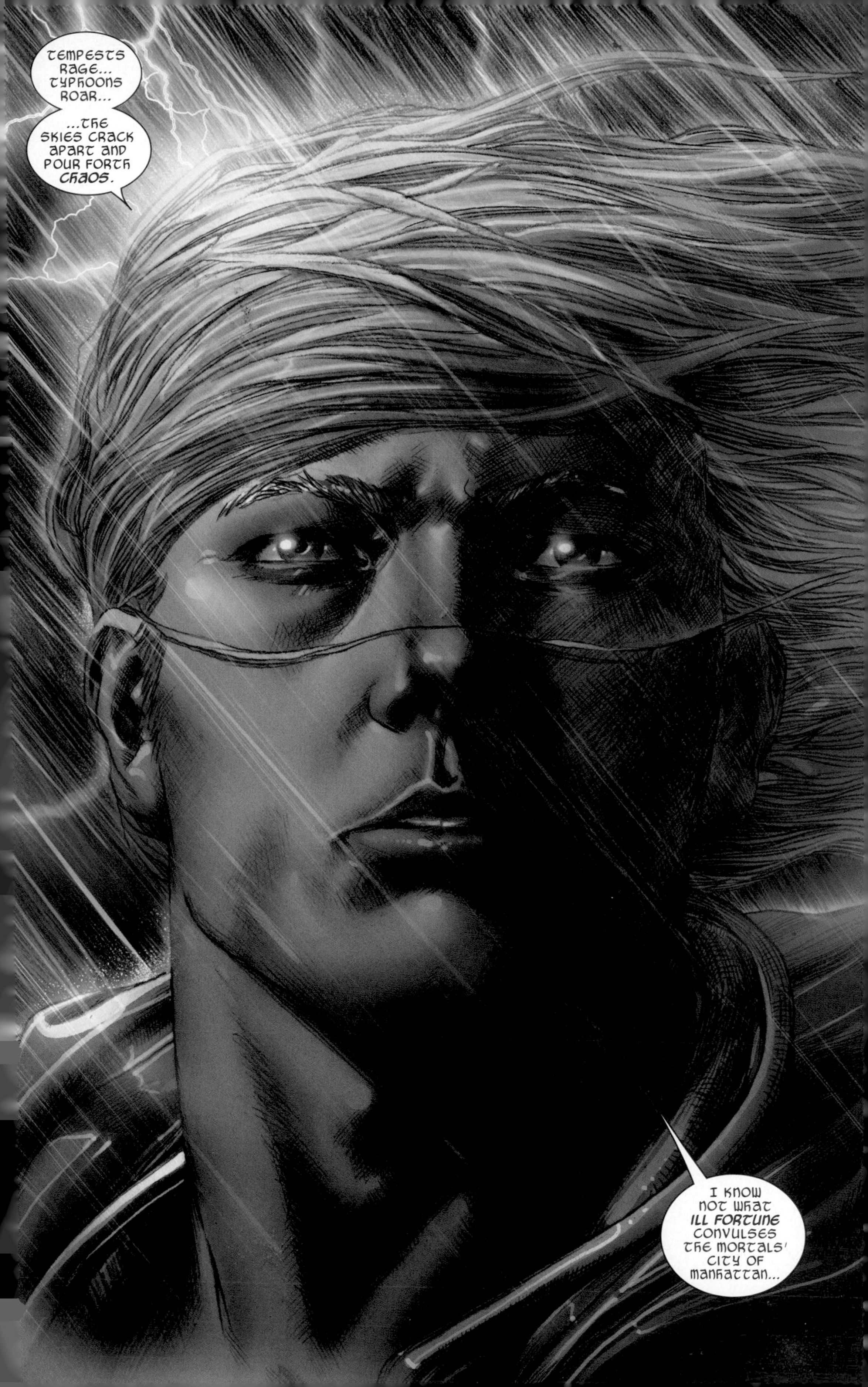
TEMPESTS RAGE... TYPHOONS ROAR...
...THE SKIES CRACK APART AND POUR FORTH *CHAOS*.
I KNOW NOT WHAT ***ILL FORTUNE*** CONVULSES THE MORTALS' CITY OF MANHATTAN...

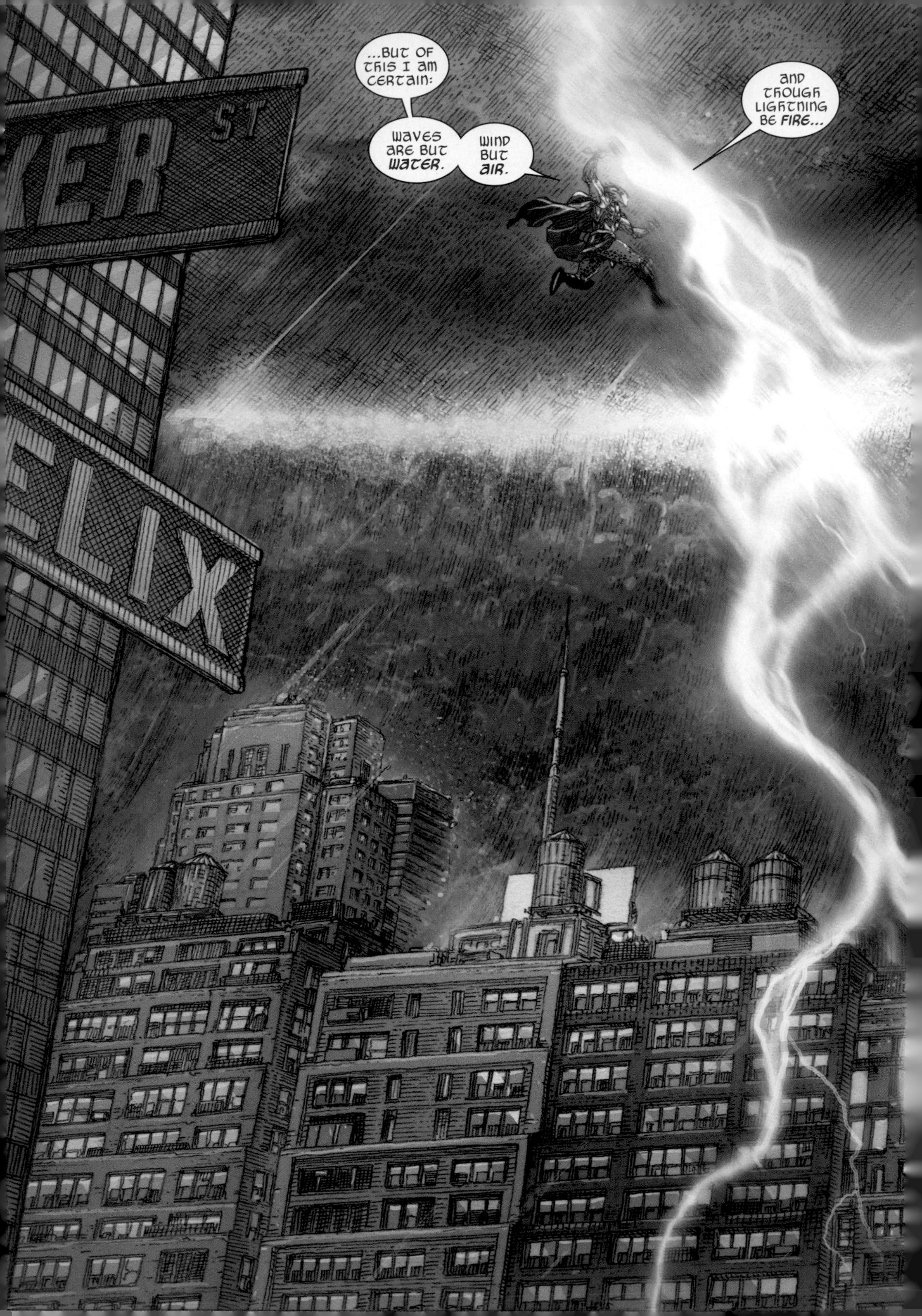

...BUT OF THIS I AM CERTAIN:
WAVES ARE BUT WATER.
WIND BUT AIR.
AND THOUGH LIGHTNING BE FIRE...

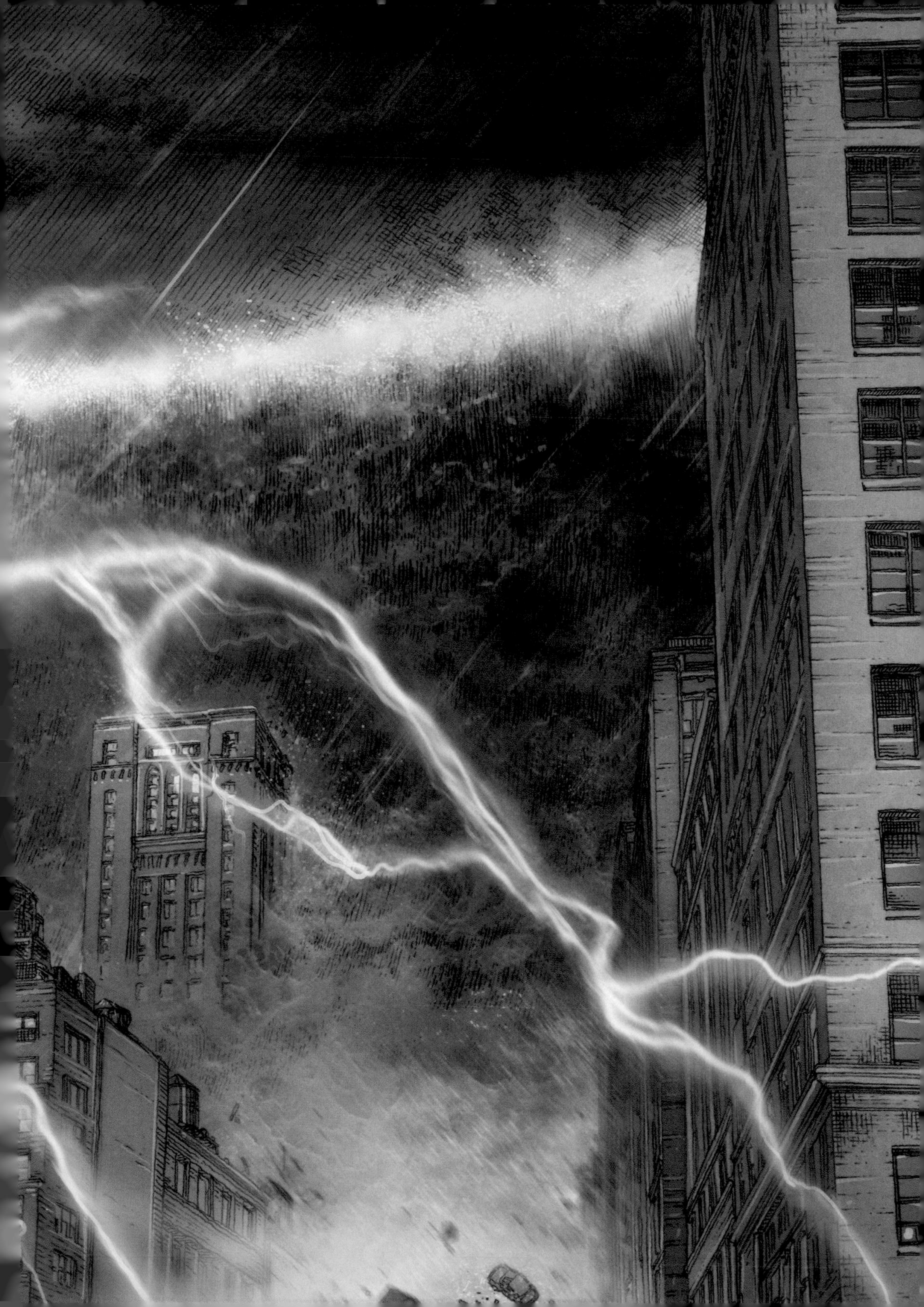

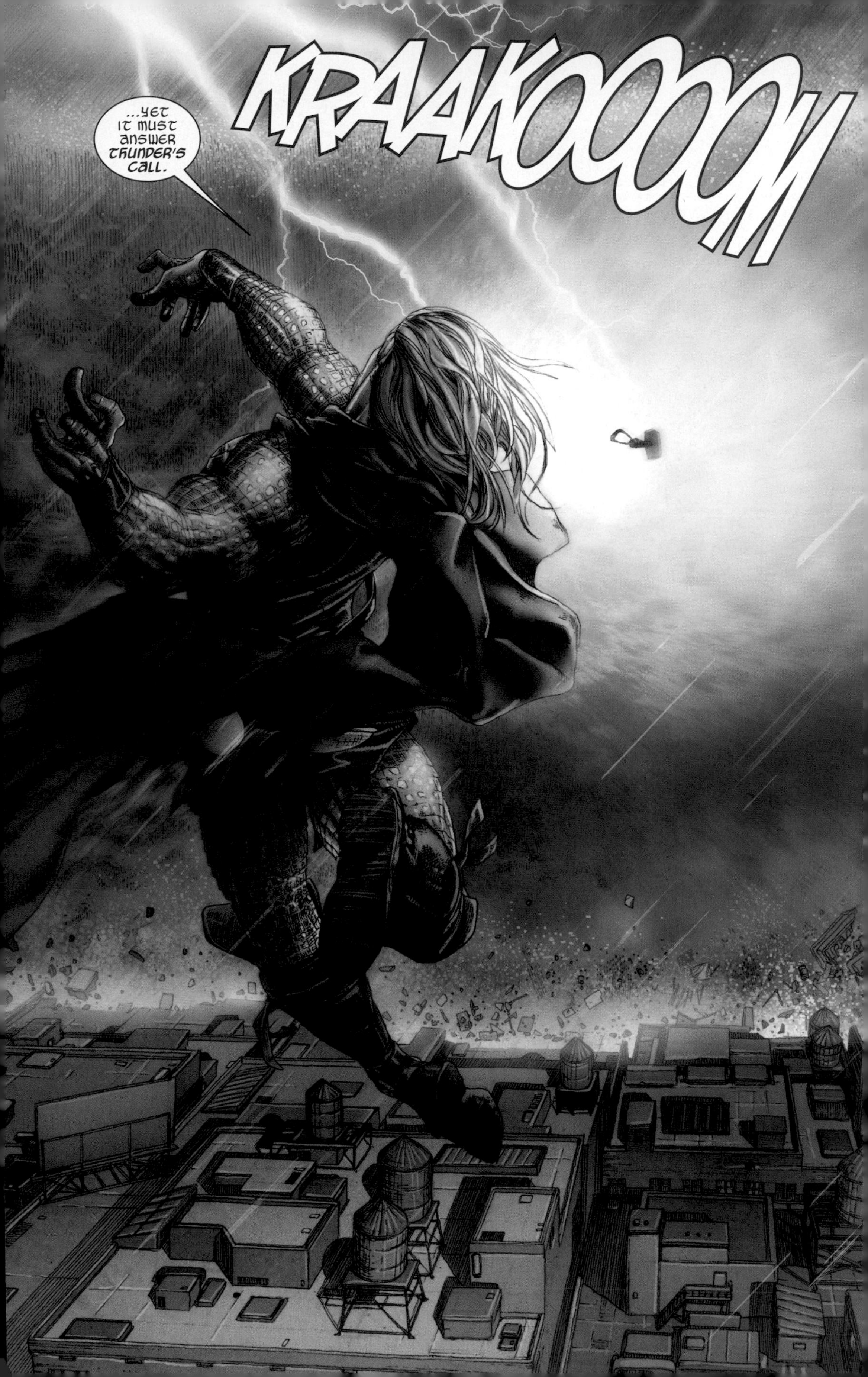
...YET IT MUST ANSWER THUNDER'S CALL.
KRAAKOOOOM

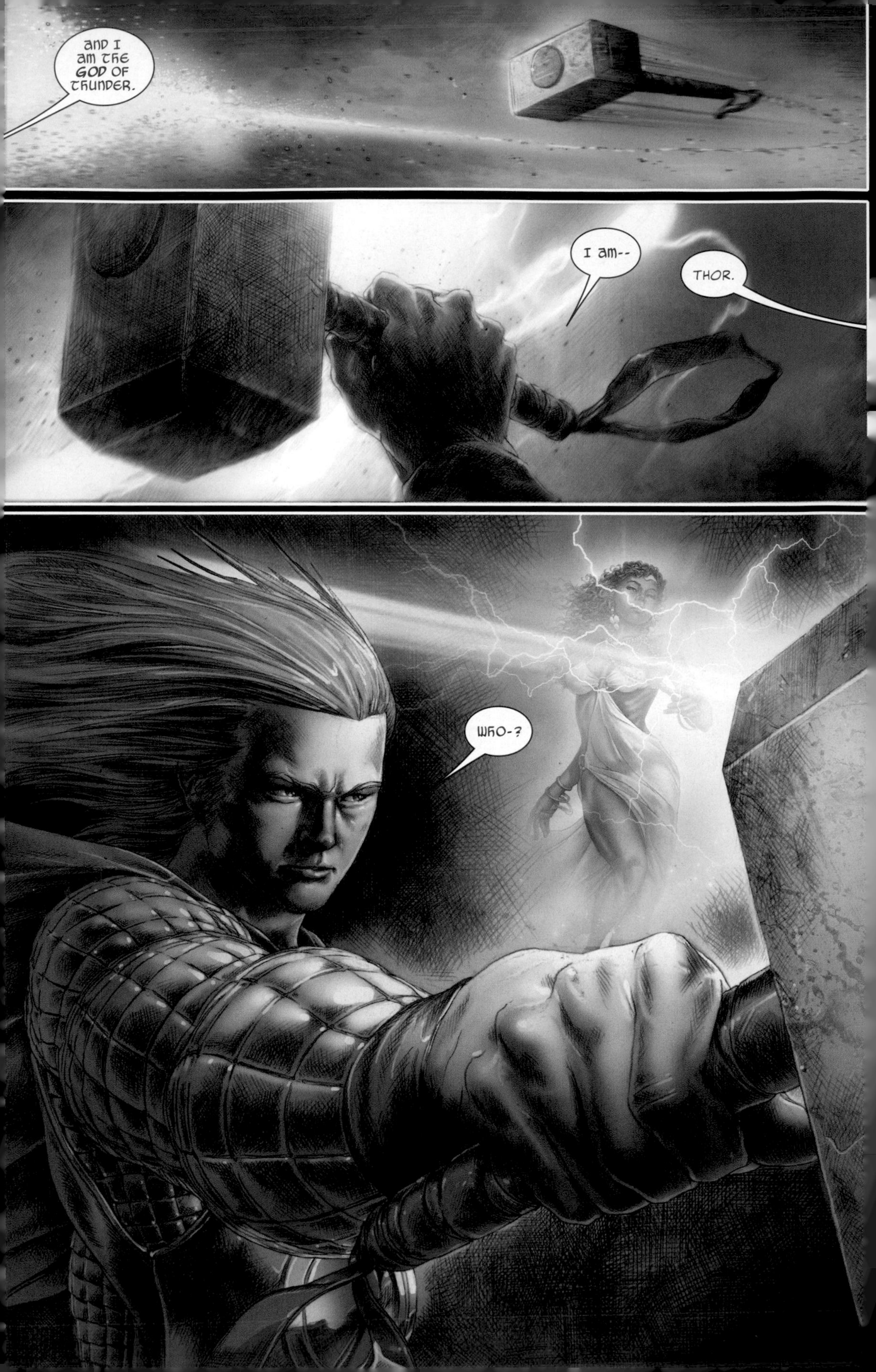

AND I AM THE GOD OF THUNDER.
I AM--
THOR.
WHO-?

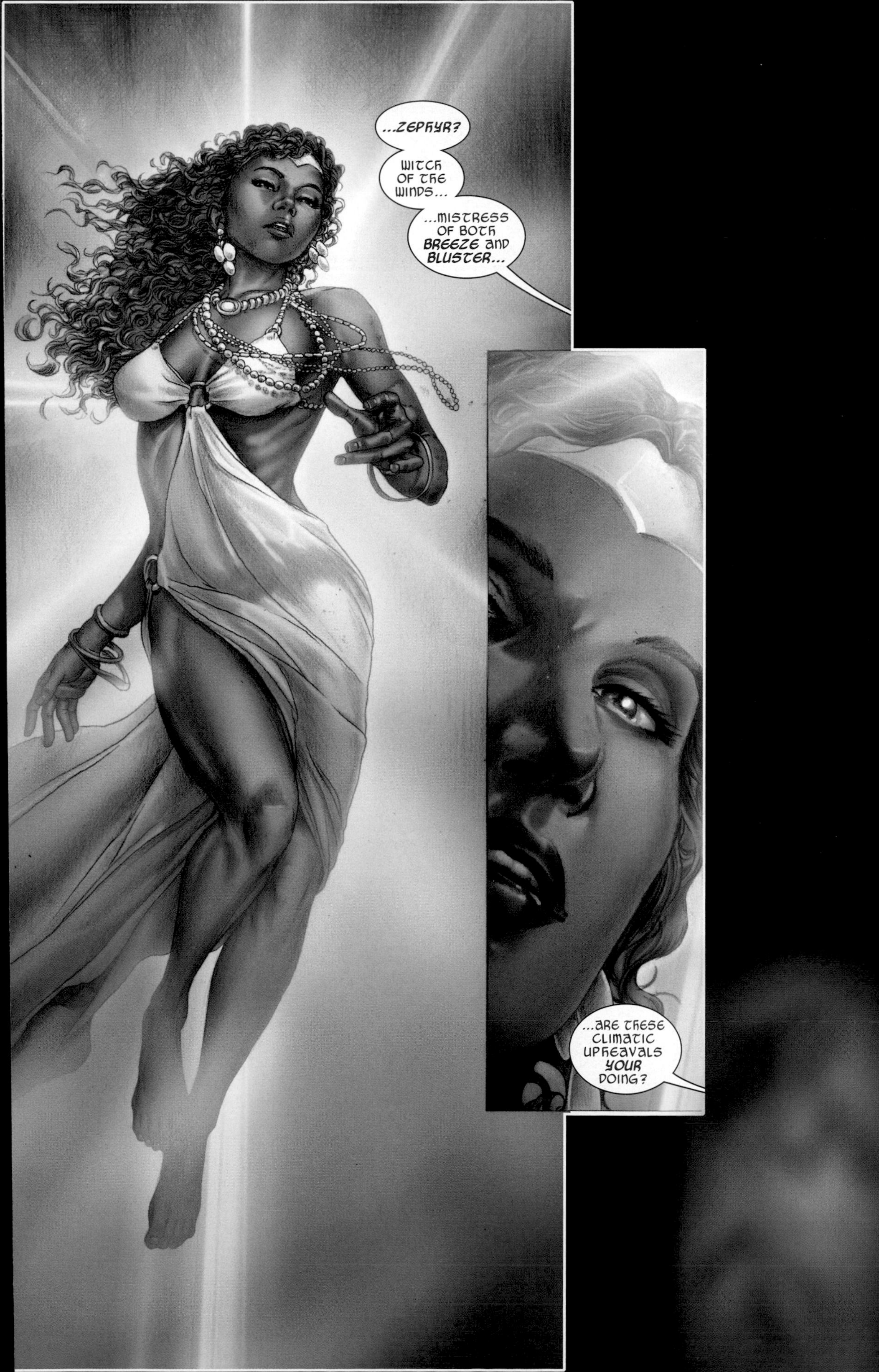
...ZEPHYR?
WITCH OF THE WINDS...
...MISTRESS OF BOTH BREEZE AND BLUSTER...
...ARE THESE CLIMATIC UPHEAVALS YOUR DOING?

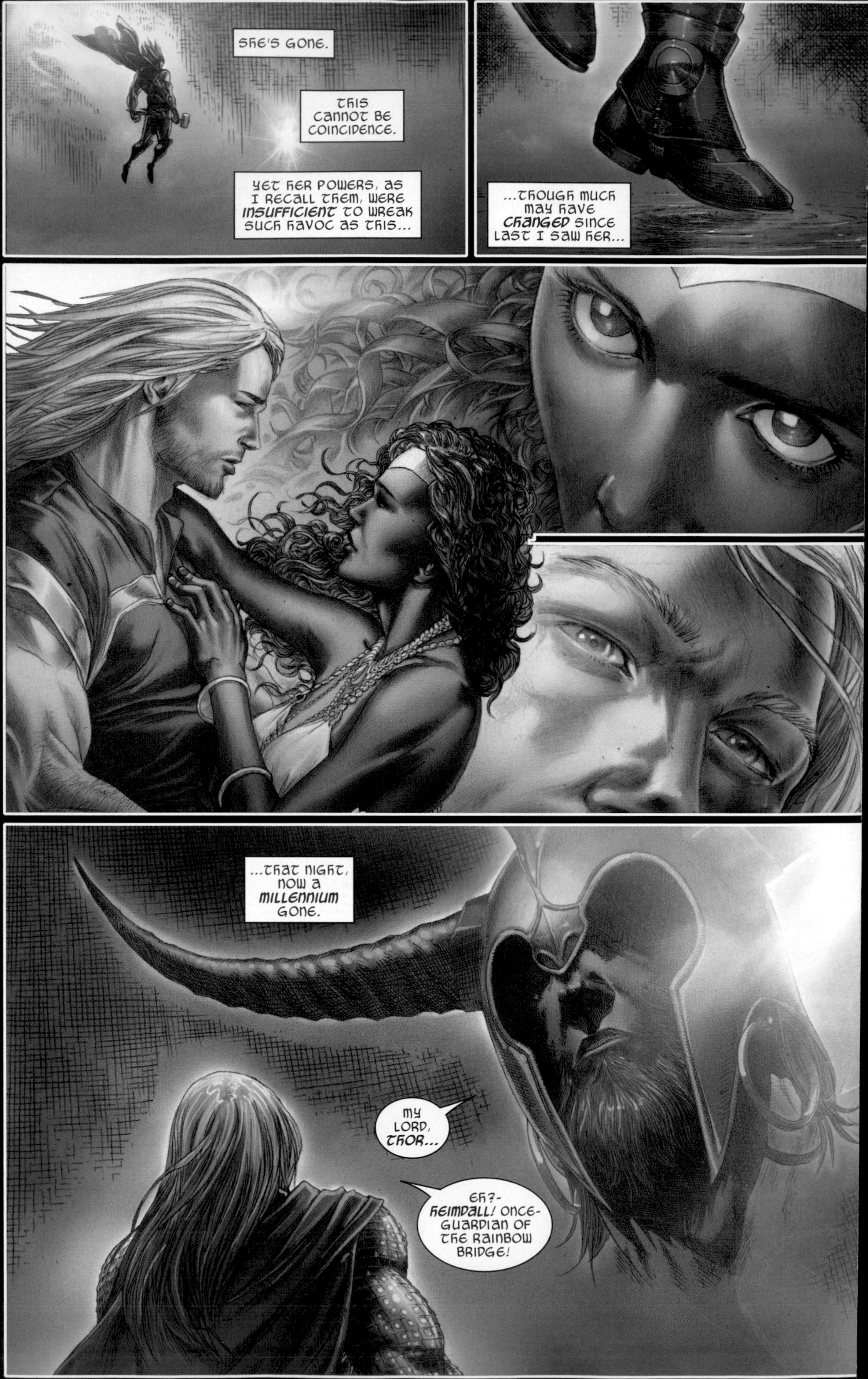
SHE'S GONE.
THIS CANNOT BE COINCIDENCE.
YET HER POWERS, AS I RECALL THEM, WERE INSUFFICIENT TO WREAK SUCH HAVOC AS THIS...
...THOUGH MUCH MAY HAVE CHANGED SINCE LAST I SAW HER...
...THAT NIGHT, NOW A MILLENNIUM GONE.
MY LORD, THOR...
EH?- HEIMDALL! ONCE-GUARDIAN OF THE RAINBOW BRIDGE!

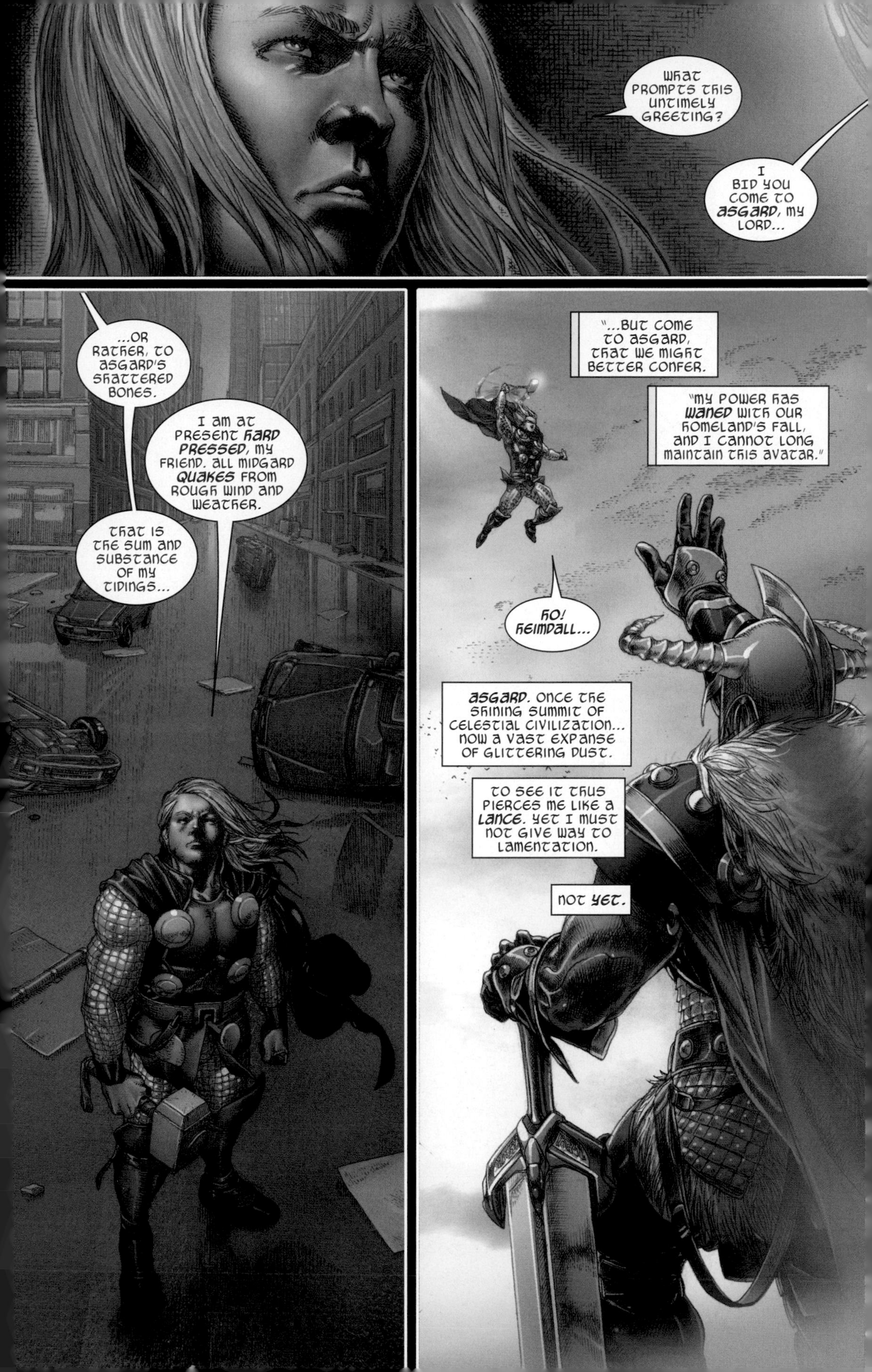
WHAT PROMPTS THIS UNTIMELY GREETING?
I BID YOU COME TO ASGARD, MY LORD...
...OR RATHER, TO ASGARD'S SHATTERED BONES.
THAT IS THE SUM AND SUBSTANCE OF MY TIDINGS...
I AM AT PRESENT HARD PRESSED, MY FRIEND. ALL MIDGARD QUAKES FROM ROUGH WIND AND WEATHER.
"...BUT COME TO ASGARD, THAT WE MIGHT BETTER CONFER.
"MY POWER HAS WANED WITH OUR HOMELAND'S FALL, AND I CANNOT LONG MAINTAIN THIS AVATAR."
HO! HEIMDALL...
ASGARD. ONCE THE SHINING SUMMIT OF CELESTIAL CIVILIZATION... NOW A VAST EXPANSE OF GLITTERING DUST.
TO SEE IT THUS PIERCES ME LIKE A LANCE. YET I MUST NOT GIVE WAY TO LAMENTATION.
NOT YET.

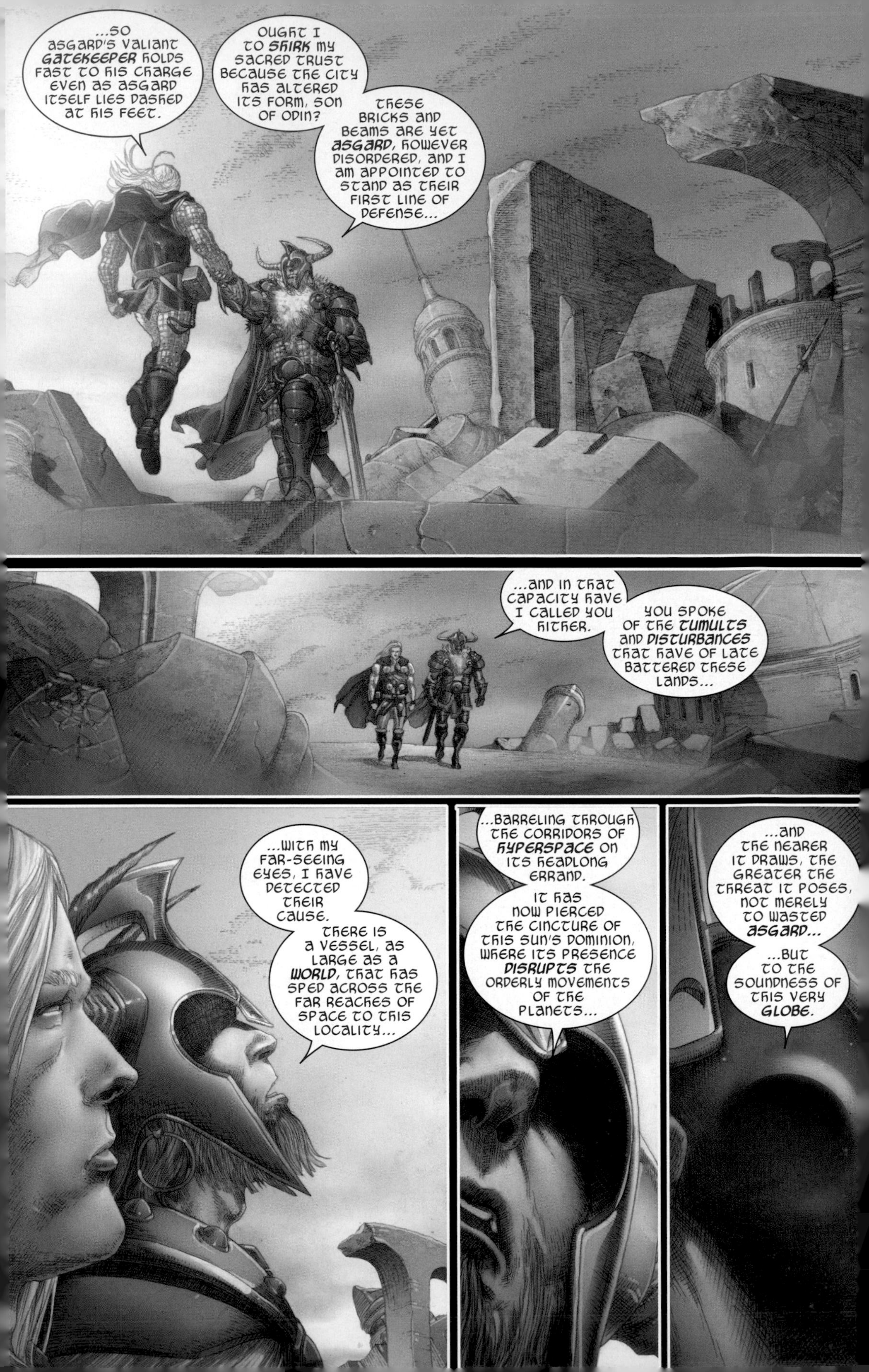
...SO ASGARD'S VALIANT GATEKEEPER HOLDS FAST TO HIS CHARGE EVEN AS ASGARD ITSELF LIES DASHED AT HIS FEET.
OUGHT I TO SHIRK MY SACRED TRUST BECAUSE THE CITY HAS ALTERED ITS FORM, SON OF ODIN?
THESE BRICKS AND BEAMS ARE YET ASGARD, HOWEVER DISORDERED, AND I AM APPOINTED TO STAND AS THEIR FIRST LINE OF DEFENSE...
...AND IN THAT CAPACITY HAVE I CALLED YOU HITHER.
YOU SPOKE OF THE TUMULTS AND DISTURBANCES THAT HAVE OF LATE BATTERED THESE LANDS...
...WITH MY FAR-SEEING EYES, I HAVE DETECTED THEIR CAUSE.
THERE IS A VESSEL, AS LARGE AS A WORLD, THAT HAS SPED ACROSS THE FAR REACHES OF SPACE TO THIS LOCALITY...
...BARRELING THROUGH THE CORRIDORS OF HYPERSPACE ON ITS HEADLONG ERRAND.
IT HAS NOW PIERCED THE CINCTURE OF THIS SUN'S DOMINION, WHERE ITS PRESENCE DISRUPTS THE ORDERLY MOVEMENTS OF THE PLANETS...
...AND THE NEARER IT DRAWS, THE GREATER THE THREAT IT POSES, NOT MERELY TO WASTED ASGARD...
...BUT TO THE SOUNDNESS OF THIS VERY GLOBE.

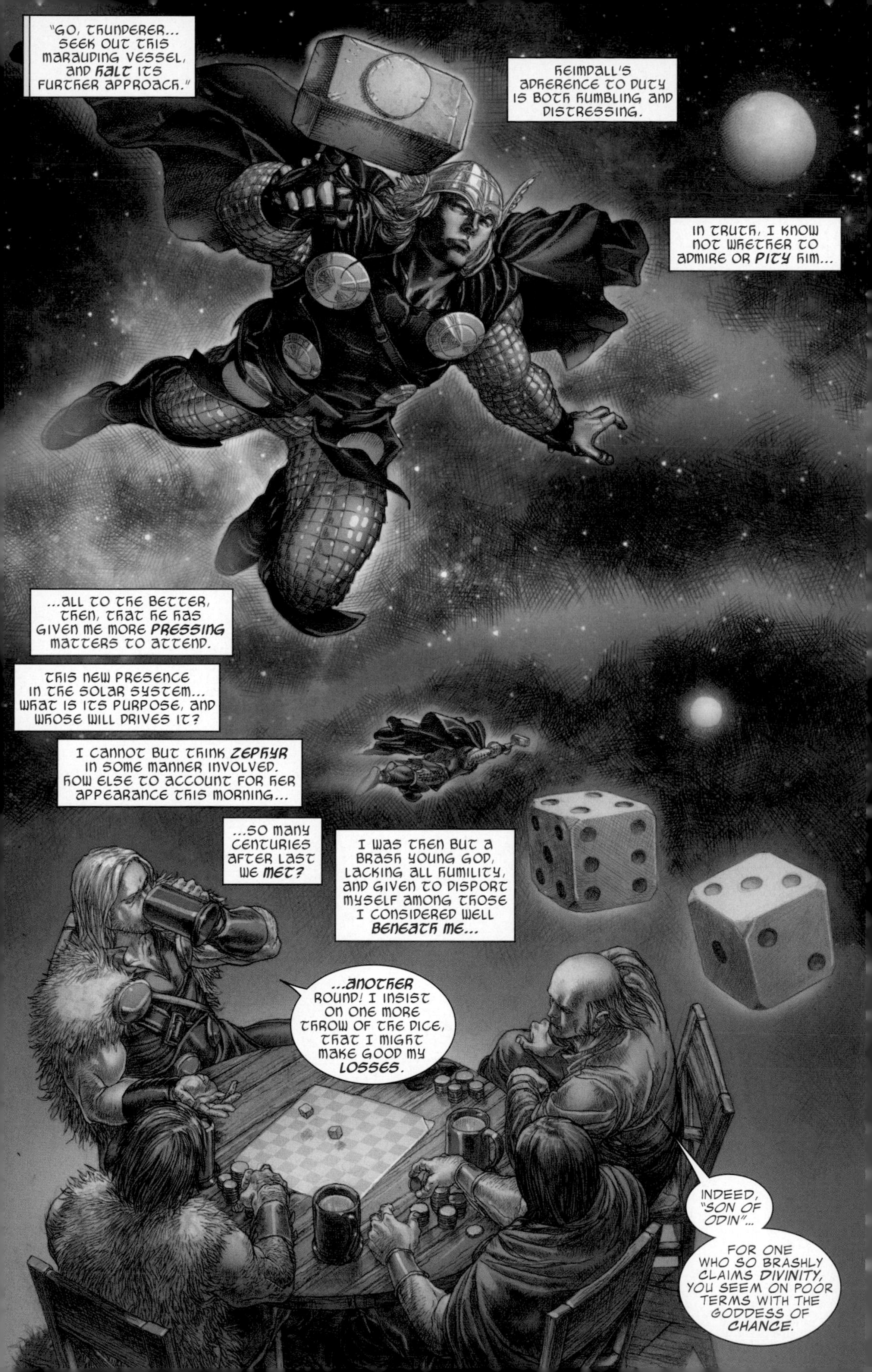
"GO, THUNDERER... SEEK OUT THIS MARAUDING VESSEL, AND HALT ITS FURTHER APPROACH."
HEIMDALL'S ADHERENCE TO DUTY IS BOTH HUMBLING AND DISTRESSING.
IN TRUTH, I KNOW NOT WHETHER TO ADMIRE OR PITY HIM...
...ALL TO THE BETTER, THEN, THAT HE HAS GIVEN ME MORE PRESSING MATTERS TO ATTEND.
THIS NEW PRESENCE IN THE SOLAR SYSTEM... WHAT IS ITS PURPOSE, AND WHOSE WILL DRIVES IT?
I CANNOT BUT THINK ZEPHYR IN SOME MANNER INVOLVED. HOW ELSE TO ACCOUNT FOR HER APPEARANCE THIS MORNING...
...SO MANY CENTURIES AFTER LAST WE MET?
I WAS THEN BUT A BRASH YOUNG GOD, LACKING ALL HUMILITY, AND GIVEN TO DISPORT MYSELF AMONG THOSE I CONSIDERED WELL BENEATH ME...
...ANOTHER ROUND! I INSIST ON ONE MORE THROW OF THE DICE, THAT I MIGHT MAKE GOOD MY LOSSES.
INDEED, "SON OF ODIN"...
FOR ONE WHO SO BRASHLY CLAIMS DIVINITY, YOU SEEM ON POOR TERMS WITH THE GODDESS OF CHANCE.

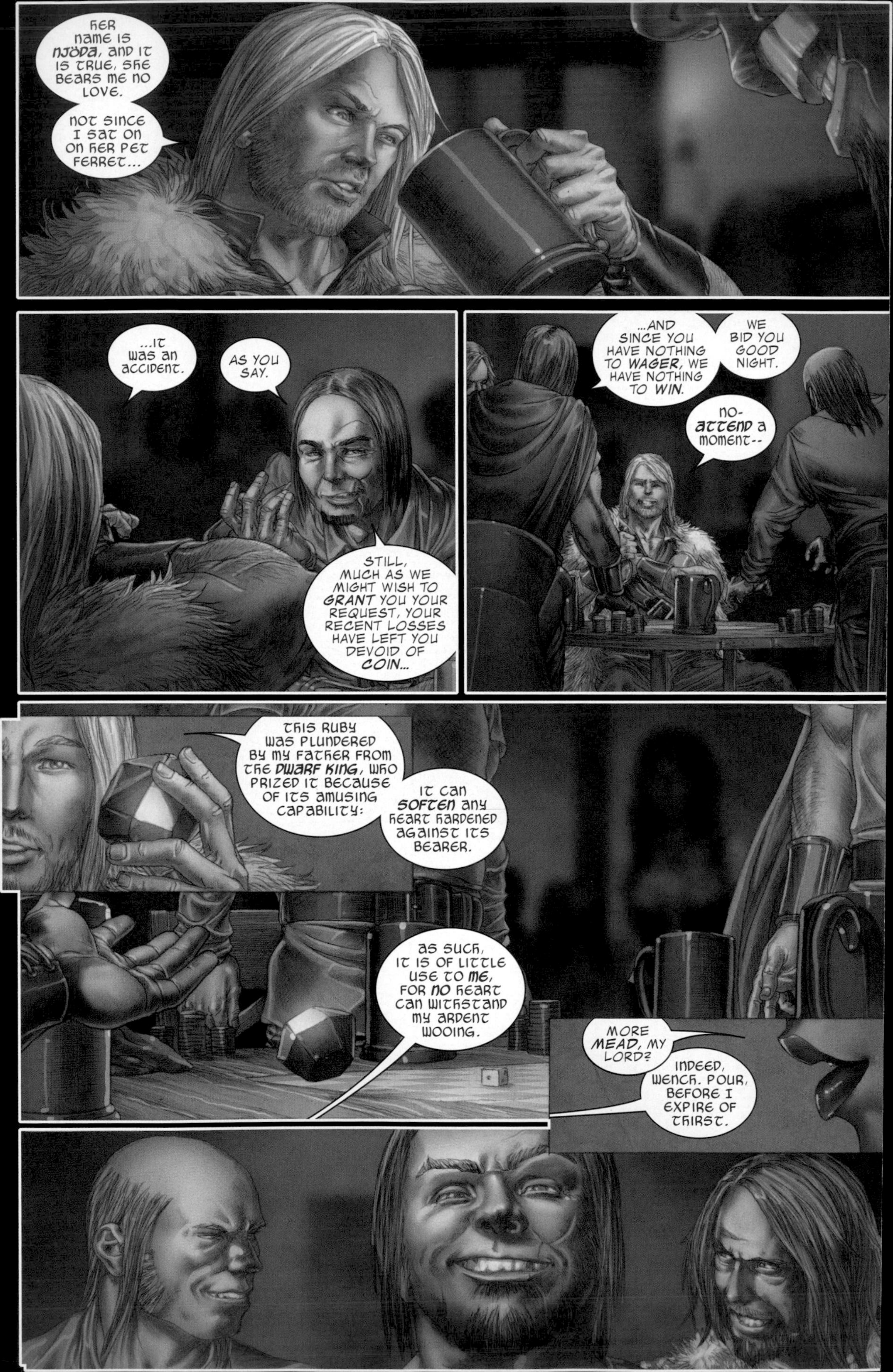
HER NAME IS NJÖDA, AND IT IS TRUE, SHE BEARS ME NO LOVE.
NOT SINCE I SAT ON ON HER PET FERRET...
...IT WAS AN ACCIDENT.
AS YOU SAY.
STILL, MUCH AS WE MIGHT WISH TO GRANT YOU YOUR REQUEST, YOUR RECENT LOSSES HAVE LEFT YOU DEVOID OF COIN...
...AND SINCE YOU HAVE NOTHING TO WAGER, WE HAVE NOTHING TO WIN.
WE BID YOU GOOD NIGHT.
NO- ATTEND A MOMENT--
THIS RUBY WAS PLUNDERED BY MY FATHER FROM THE DWARF KING, WHO PRIZED IT BECAUSE OF ITS AMUSING CAPABILITY:
IT CAN SOFTEN ANY HEART HARDENED AGAINST ITS BEARER.
AS SUCH, IT IS OF LITTLE USE TO ME, FOR NO HEART CAN WITHSTAND MY ARDENT WOOING.
MORE MEAD, MY LORD?
INDEED, WENCH. POUR, BEFORE I EXPIRE OF THIRST.

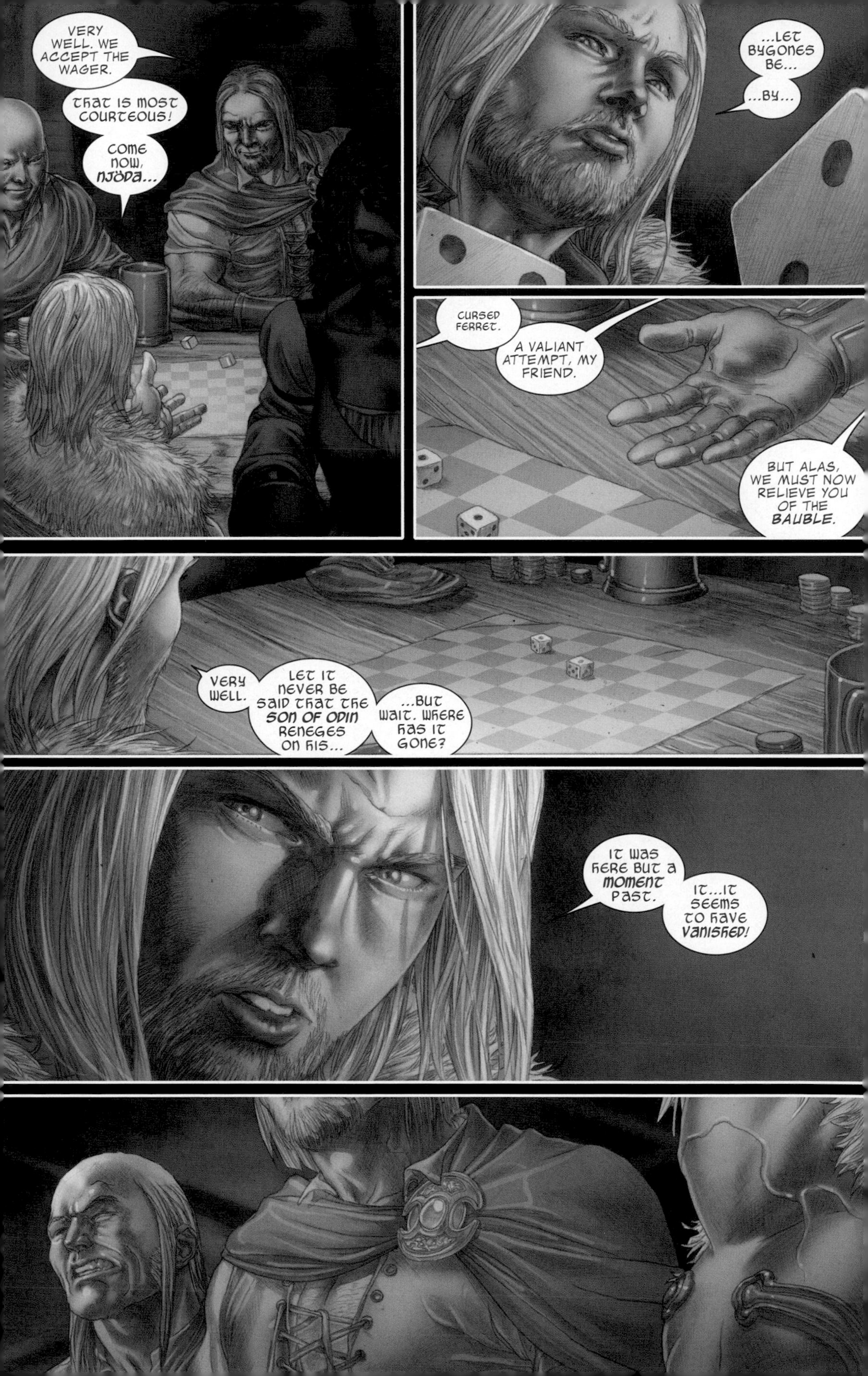
VERY WELL. WE ACCEPT THE WAGER.
THAT IS MOST COURTEOUS!
COME NOW, NJÖDA...
...LET BYGONES BE...
...BY...
CURSED FERRET.
A VALIANT ATTEMPT, MY FRIEND.
BUT ALAS, WE MUST NOW RELIEVE YOU OF THE BAUBLE.
VERY WELL.
LET IT NEVER BE SAID THAT THE SON OF ODIN RENEGES ON HIS...
...BUT WAIT. WHERE HAS IT GONE?
IT WAS HERE BUT A MOMENT PAST.
IT...IT SEEMS TO HAVE VANISHED!

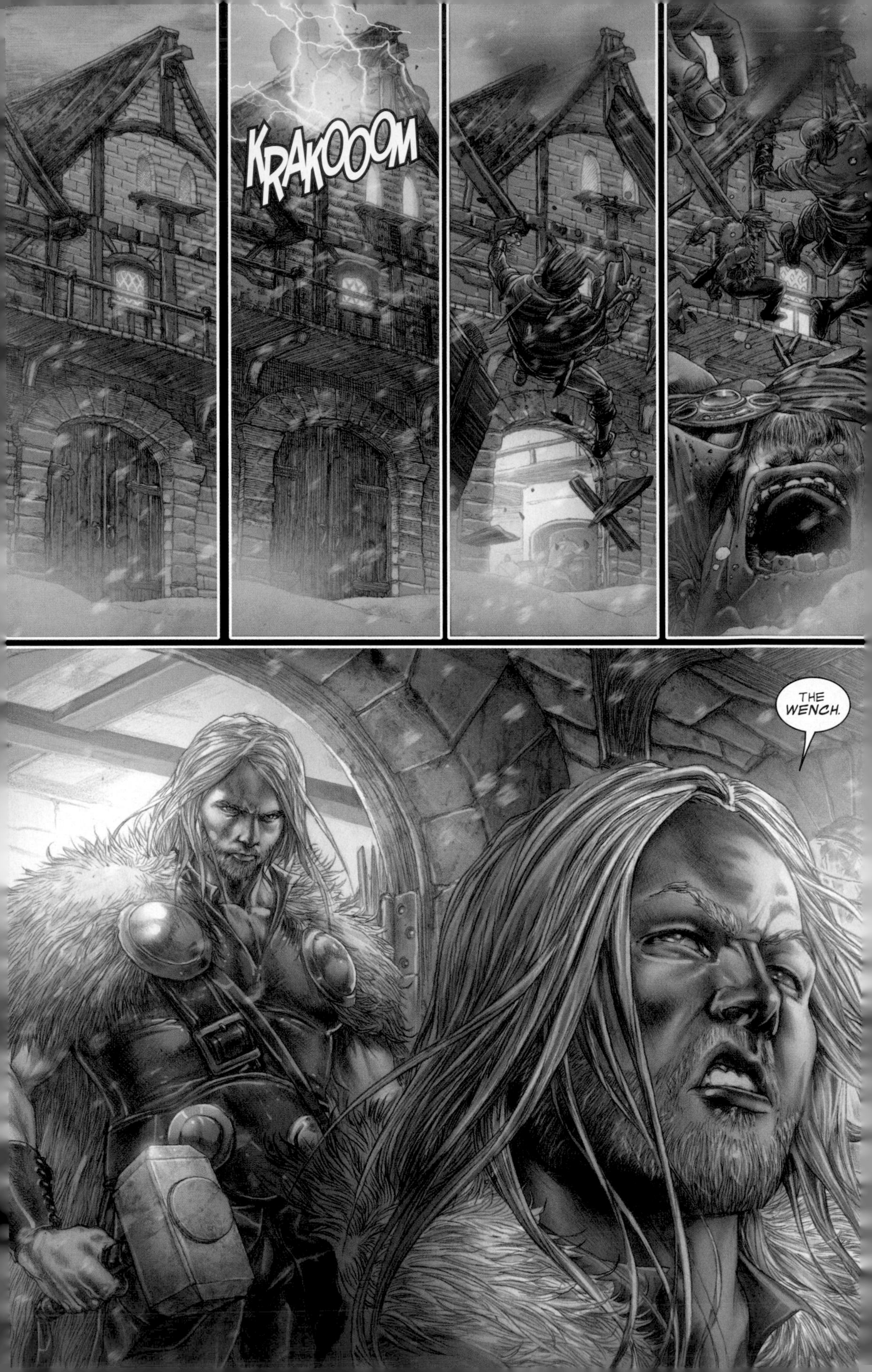
KRAKOOOM
THE WENCH.

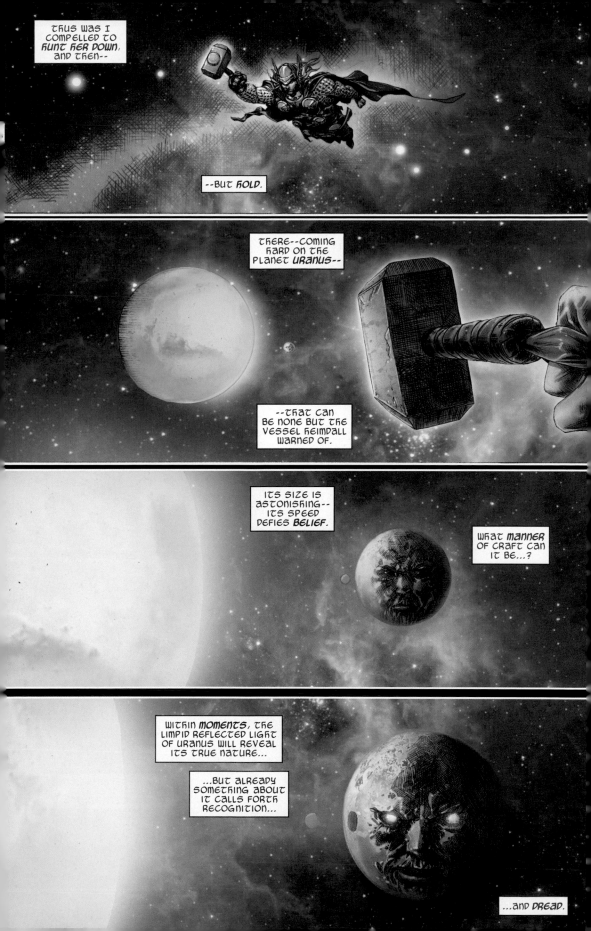

THUS WAS I COMPELLED TO *HUNT HER DOWN*, AND THEN--

--BUT *HOLD.*

THERE--COMING HARD ON THE PLANET *URANUS*--

--THAT CAN BE NONE BUT THE VESSEL HEIMDALL WARNED OF.

ITS SIZE IS ASTONISHING-- ITS SPEED DEFIES *BELIEF.*

WHAT *MANNER* OF CRAFT CAN IT BE...?

WITHIN *MOMENTS*, THE LIMPID REFLECTED LIGHT OF URANUS WILL REVEAL ITS TRUE NATURE...

...BUT ALREADY SOMETHING ABOUT IT CALLS FORTH RECOGNITION...

...AND *DREAD.*

AS WELL IT MIGHT...
...FOR THAT IS NO VESSEL.
THAT IS EGO, THE LIVING PLANET.
I HOPED NEVER AGAIN TO ENCOUNTER THIS COSMIC ABERRATION...

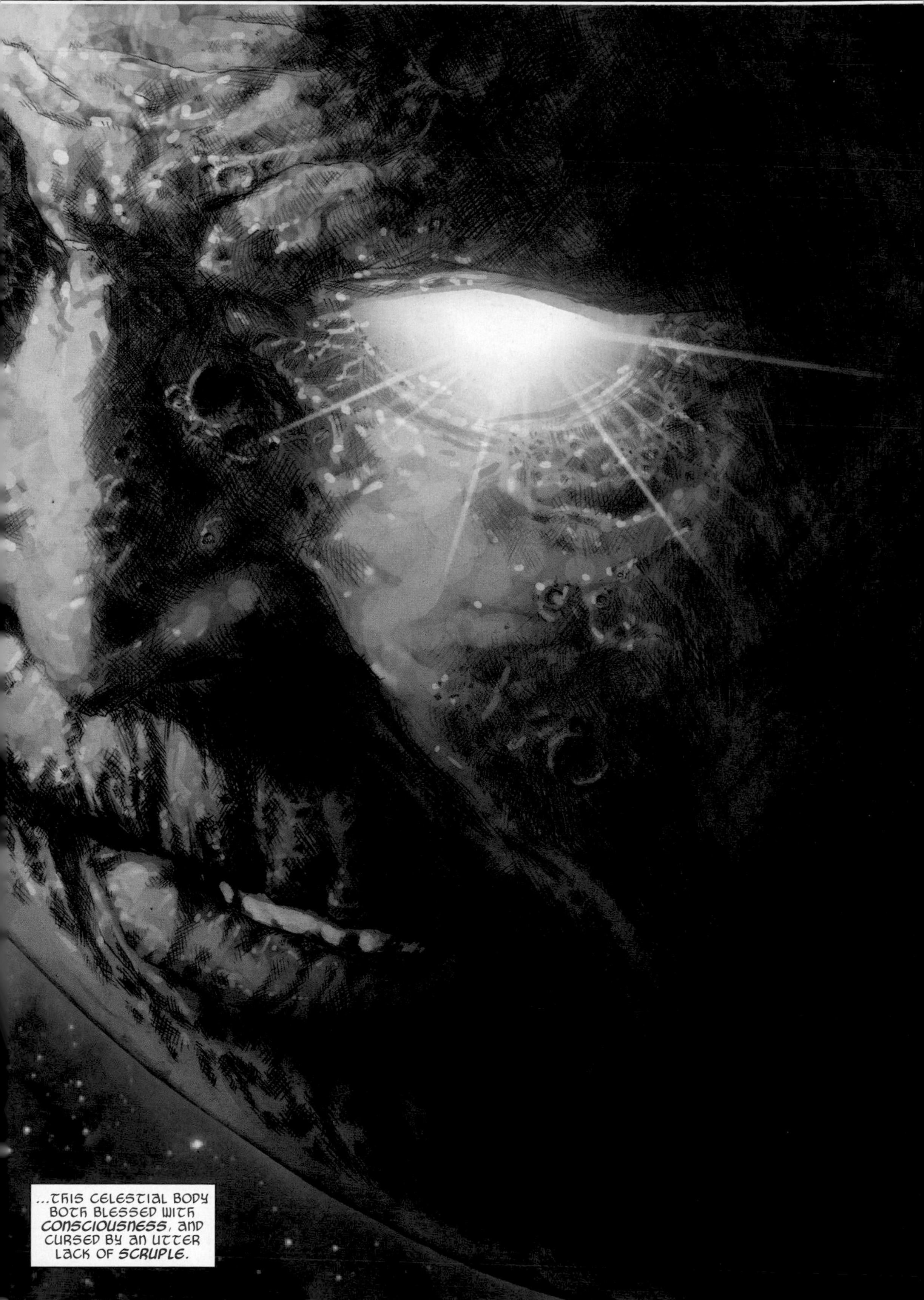
...THIS CELESTIAL BODY BOTH BLESSED WITH CONSCIOUSNESS, AND CURSED BY AN UTTER LACK OF SCRUPLE.

BUT...HOW IS IT
POSSIBLE THAT EGO
SHOULD BE HERE?

BY WHAT MEANS
DID HE BREAK FREE
OF HIS ORBIT IN THE
BLACK GALAXY?

HOW DOES HE TRAVEL
ACROSS THE VOID OF
SPACE, UNAIDED?

AND WHERE DID
HE ACQUIRE THE
MEANS TO ACCESS
HYPERSPACE?

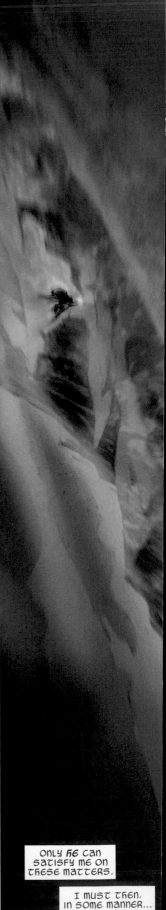

ONLY HE CAN
SATISFY ME ON
THESE MATTERS.

I MUST THEN,
IN SOME MANNER...

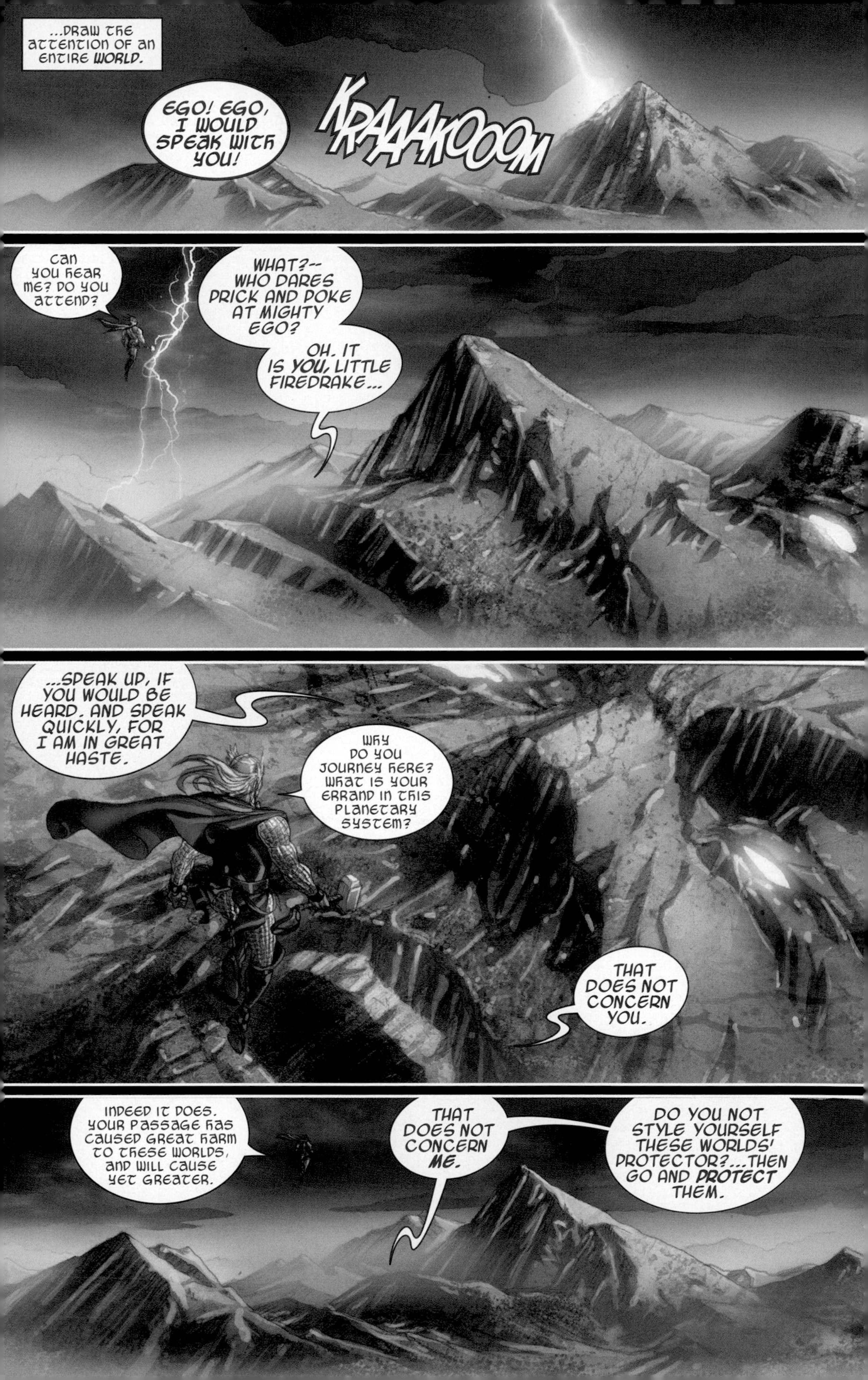
...DRAW THE ATTENTION OF AN ENTIRE WORLD.
EGO! EGO, I WOULD SPEAK WITH YOU!
KRAAAKOOOM
CAN YOU HEAR ME? DO YOU ATTEND?
WHAT?-- WHO DARES PRICK AND POKE AT MIGHTY EGO?
OH. IT IS YOU, LITTLE FIREDRAKE...
...SPEAK UP, IF YOU WOULD BE HEARD. AND SPEAK QUICKLY, FOR I AM IN GREAT HASTE.
WHY DO YOU JOURNEY HERE? WHAT IS YOUR ERRAND IN THIS PLANETARY SYSTEM?
THAT DOES NOT CONCERN YOU.
INDEED IT DOES. YOUR PASSAGE HAS CAUSED GREAT HARM TO THESE WORLDS, AND WILL CAUSE YET GREATER.
THAT DOES NOT CONCERN ME.
DO YOU NOT STYLE YOURSELF THESE WORLDS' PROTECTOR?...THEN GO AND PROTECT THEM.

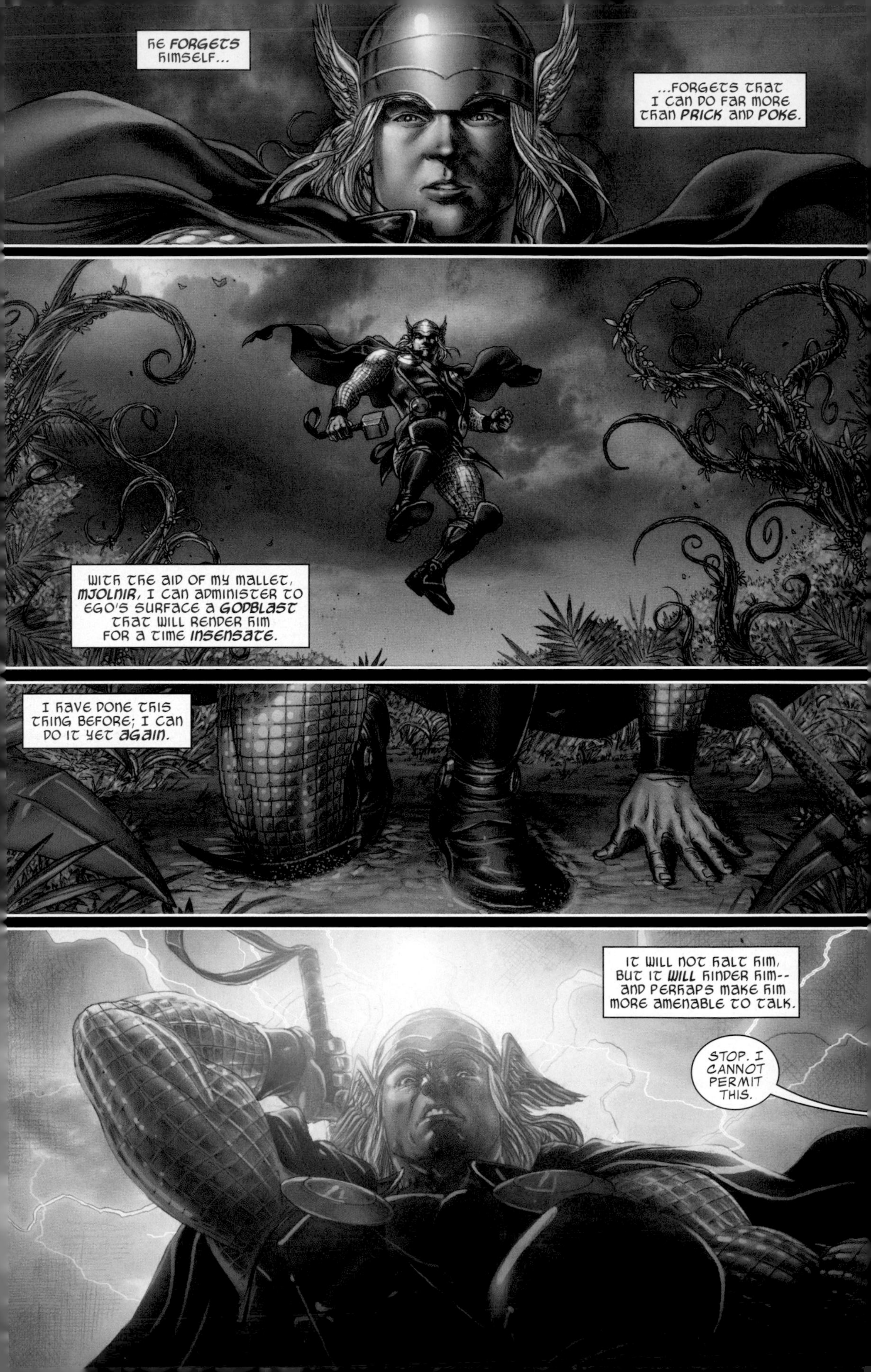
HE FORGETS HIMSELF...
...FORGETS THAT I CAN DO FAR MORE THAN PRICK AND POKE.
WITH THE AID OF MY MALLET, MJOLNIR, I CAN ADMINISTER TO EGO'S SURFACE A GODBLAST THAT WILL RENDER HIM FOR A TIME INSENSATE.
I HAVE DONE THIS THING BEFORE; I CAN DO IT YET AGAIN.
IT WILL NOT HALT HIM, BUT IT WILL HINDER HIM--AND PERHAPS MAKE HIM MORE AMENABLE TO TALK.
STOP. I CANNOT PERMIT THIS.

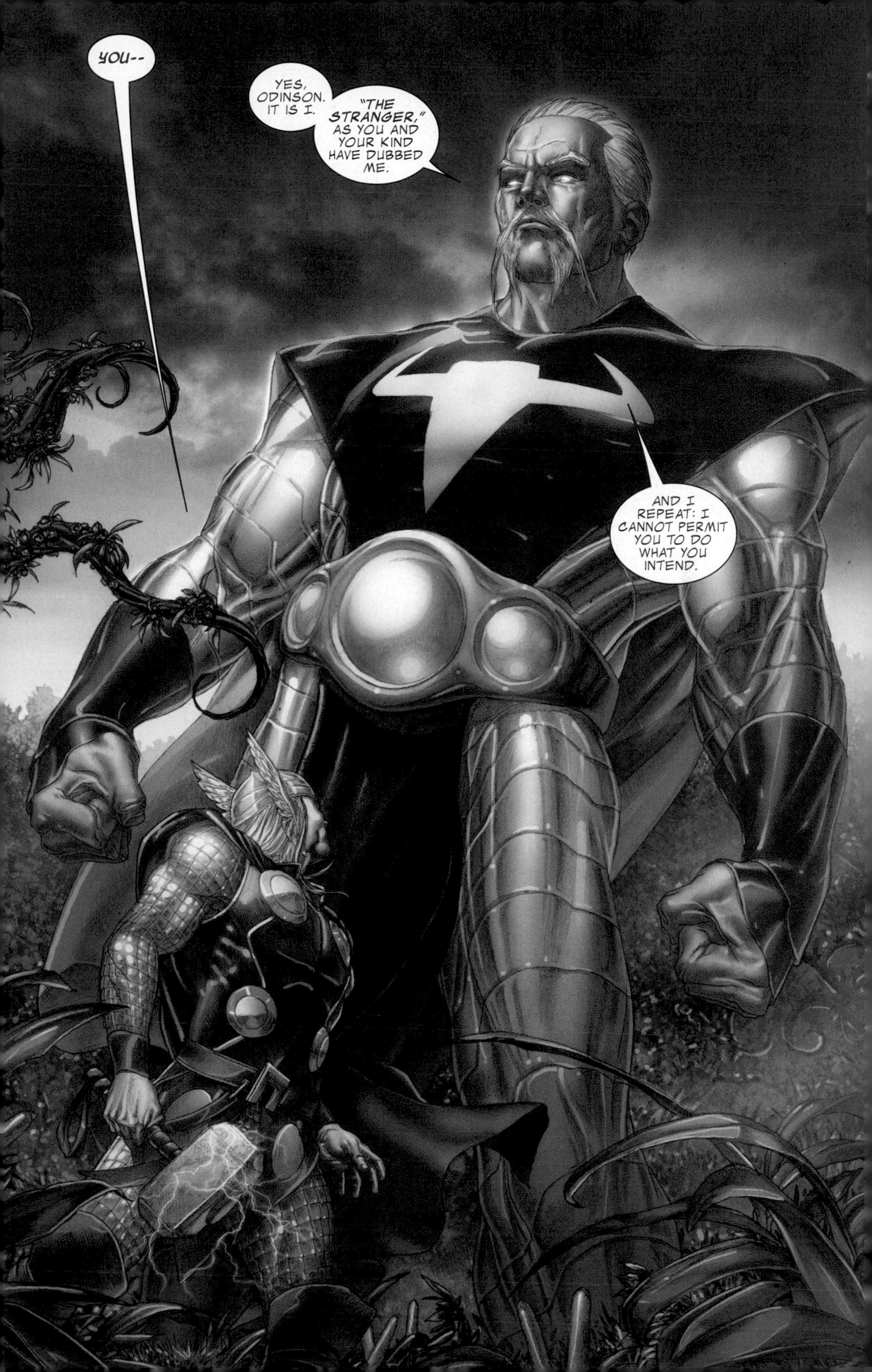
YOU--
YES, ODINSON. IT IS I.
"THE STRANGER," AS YOU AND YOUR KIND HAVE DUBBED ME.
AND I REPEAT: I CANNOT PERMIT YOU TO DO WHAT YOU INTEND.

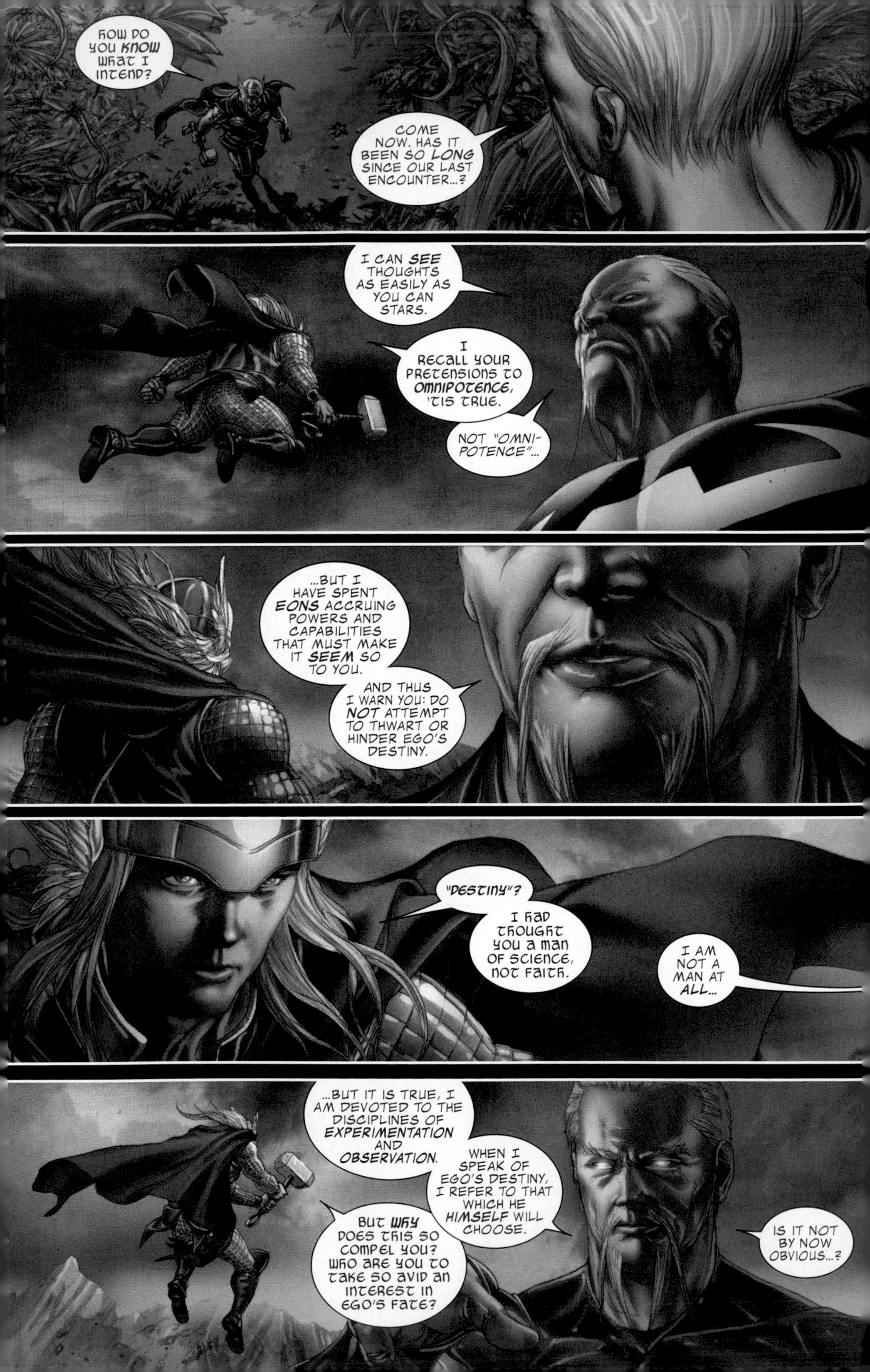
HOW DO YOU KNOW WHAT I INTEND?
COME NOW. HAS IT BEEN SO LONG SINCE OUR LAST ENCOUNTER...?
I CAN SEE THOUGHTS AS EASILY AS YOU CAN STARS.
I RECALL YOUR PRETENSIONS TO OMNIPOTENCE, 'TIS TRUE.
NOT "OMNI-POTENCE"...
...BUT I HAVE SPENT EONS ACCRUING POWERS AND CAPABILITIES THAT MUST MAKE IT SEEM SO TO YOU.
AND THUS I WARN YOU: DO NOT ATTEMPT TO THWART OR HINDER EGO'S DESTINY.
"DESTINY"?
I HAD THOUGHT YOU A MAN OF SCIENCE, NOT FAITH.
I AM NOT A MAN AT ALL...
...BUT IT IS TRUE, I AM DEVOTED TO THE DISCIPLINES OF EXPERIMENTATION AND OBSERVATION.
WHEN I SPEAK OF EGO'S DESTINY, I REFER TO THAT WHICH HE HIMSELF WILL CHOOSE.
BUT WHY DOES THIS SO COMPEL YOU? WHO ARE YOU TO TAKE SO AVID AN INTEREST IN EGO'S FATE?
IS IT NOT BY NOW OBVIOUS...?

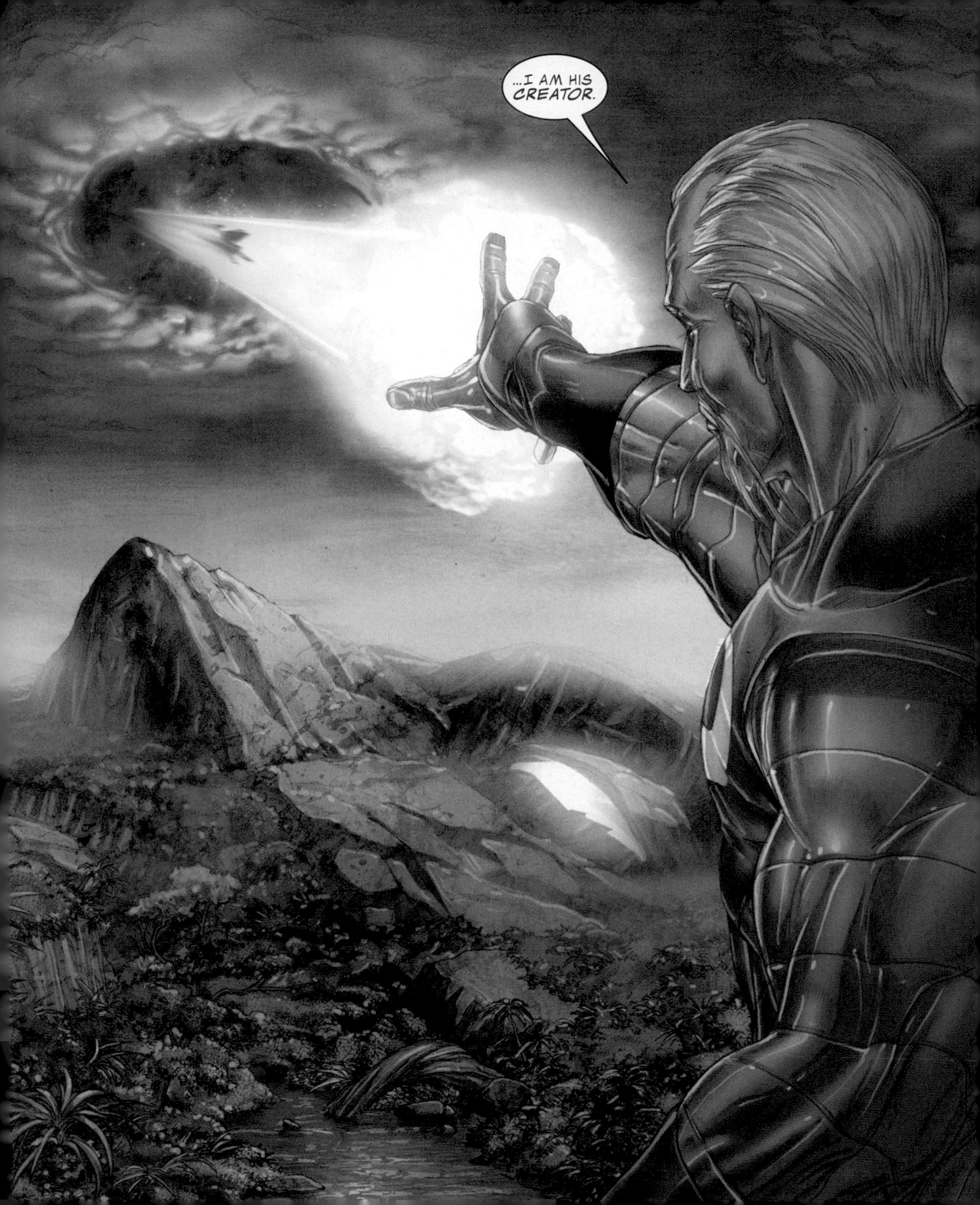
...I AM HIS CREATOR.

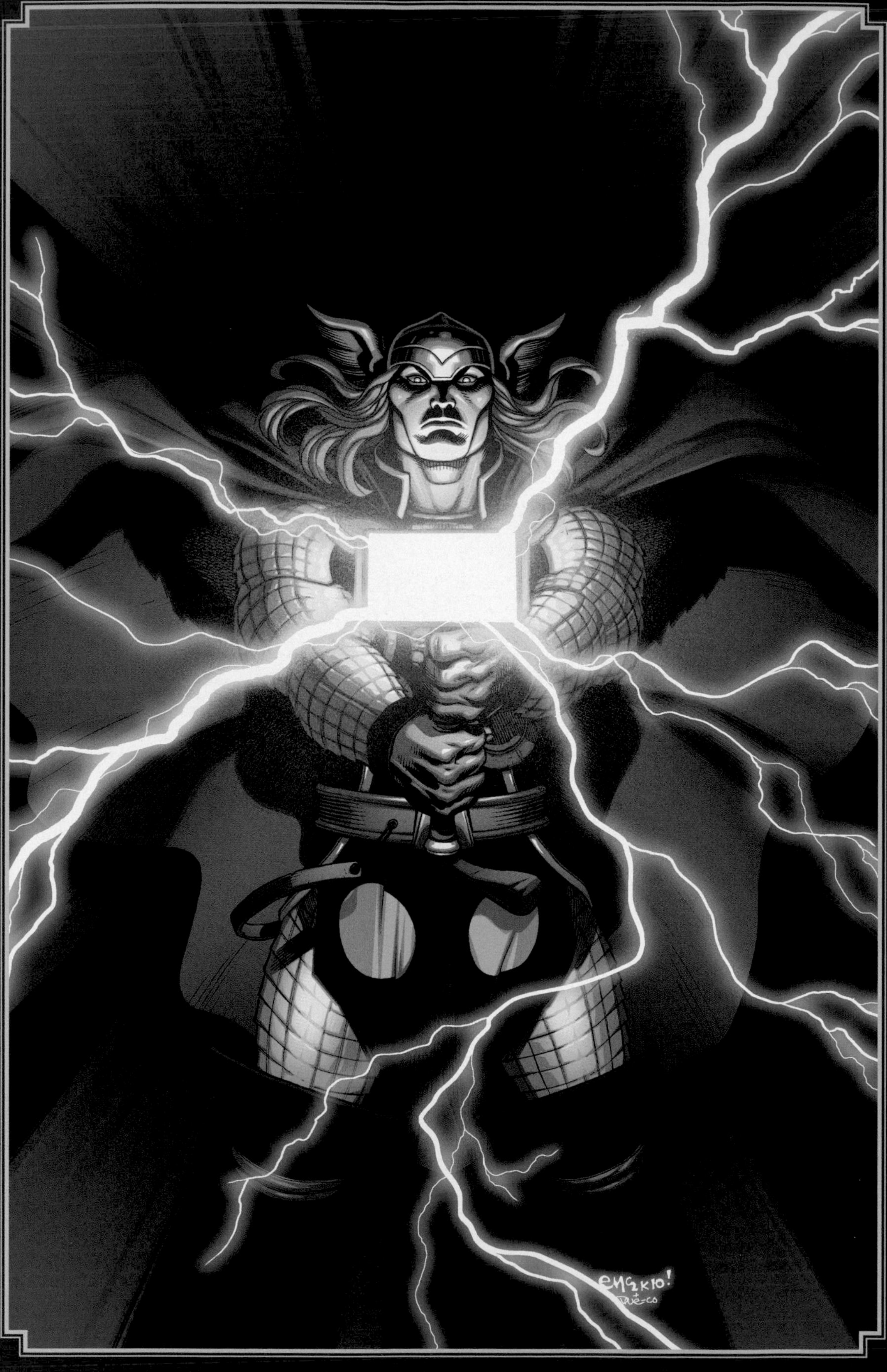

Astonishing Thor 2

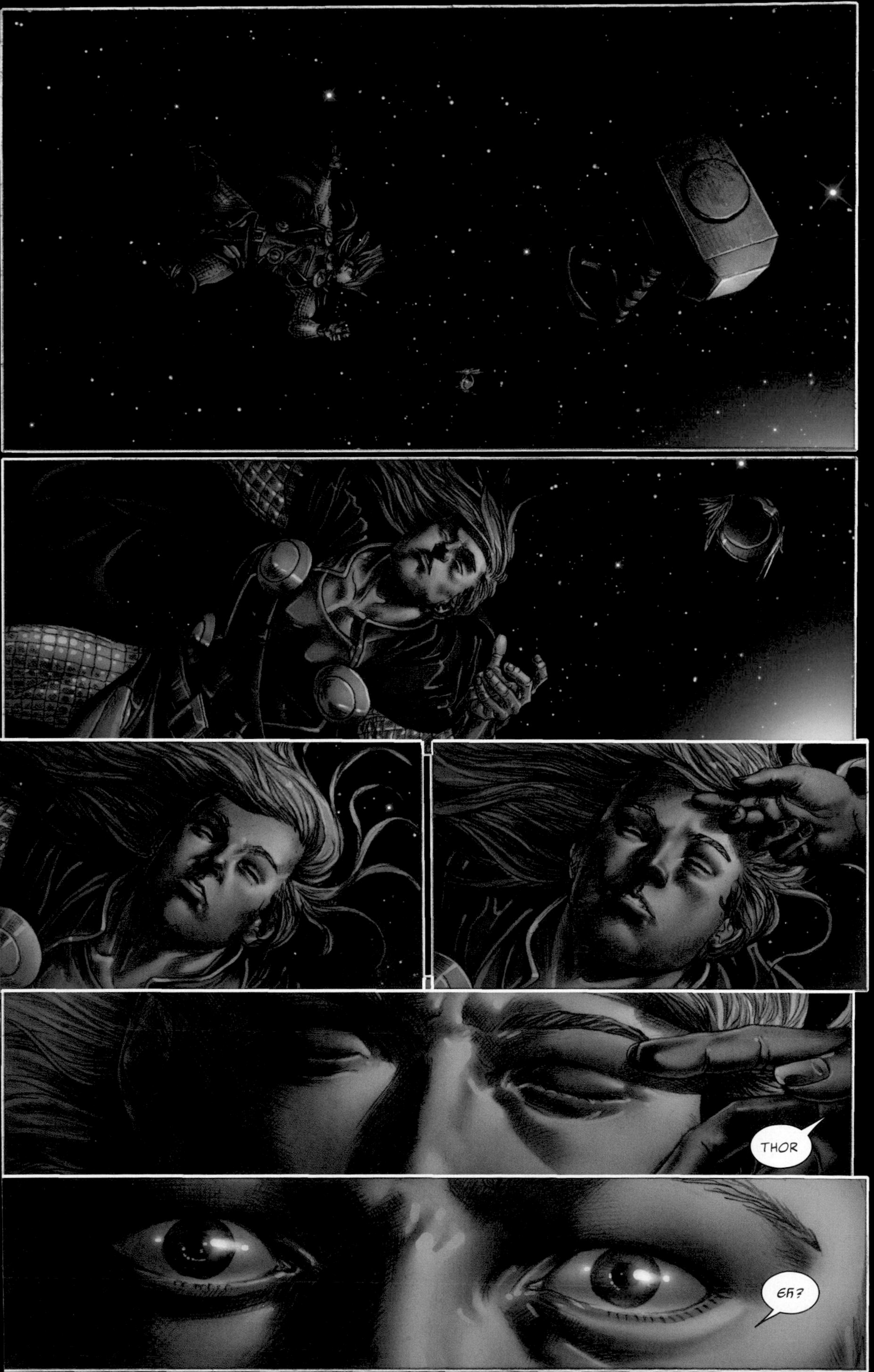
THOR
EH?

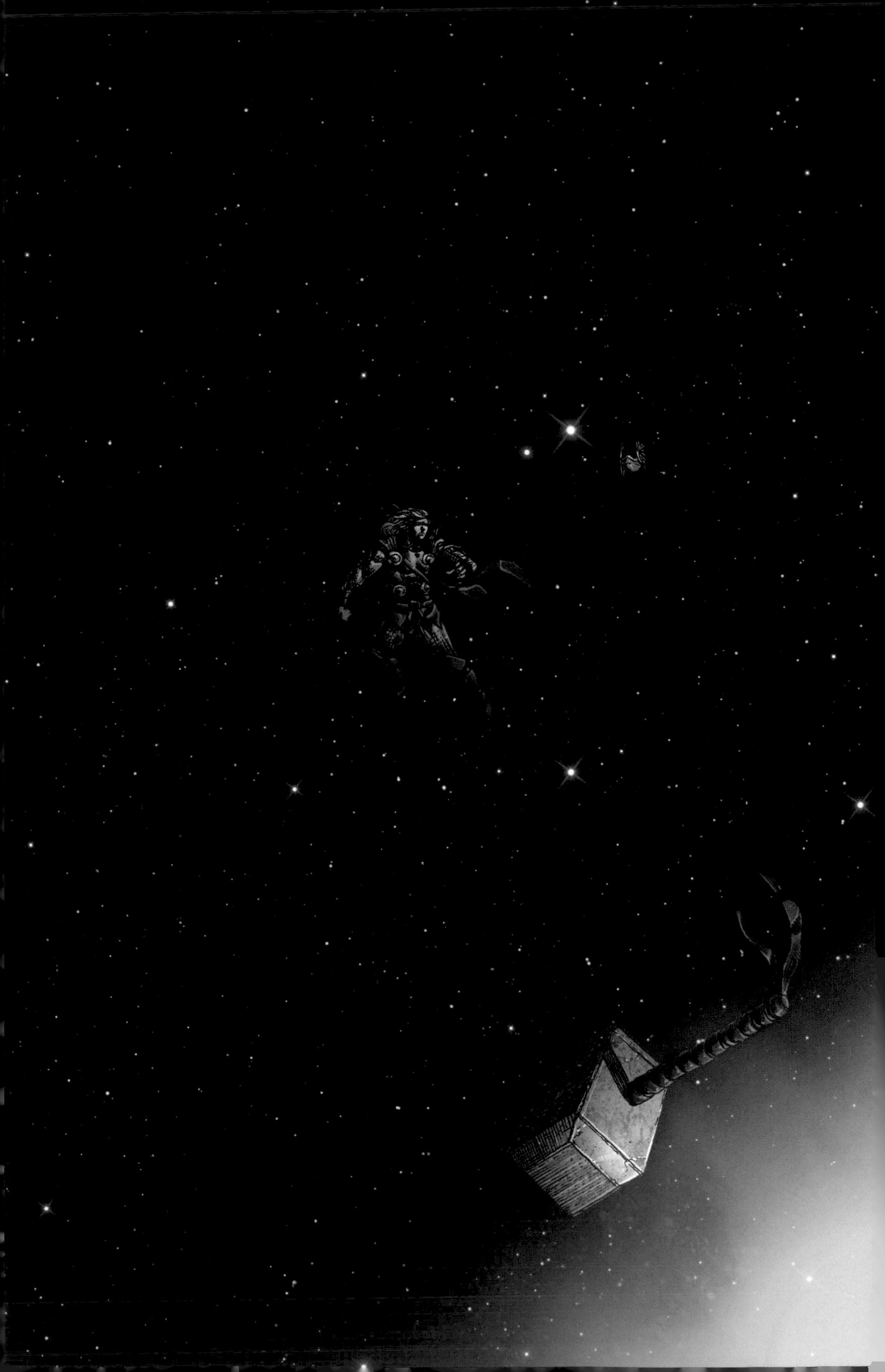

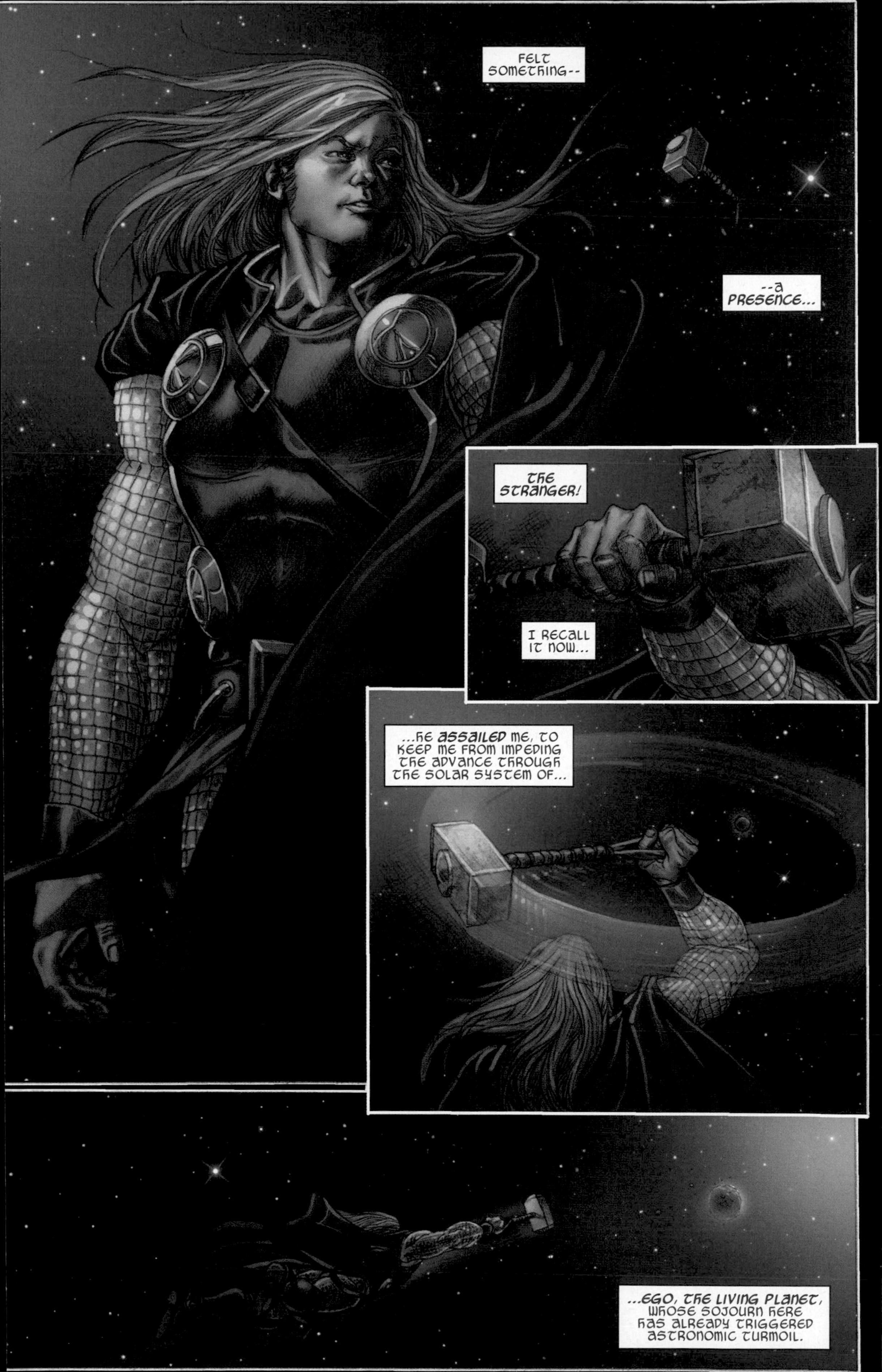
FELT SOMETHING--
--A PRESENCE...
THE STRANGER!
I RECALL IT NOW...
...HE ASSAILED ME, TO KEEP ME FROM IMPEDING THE ADVANCE THROUGH THE SOLAR SYSTEM OF...
...EGO, THE LIVING PLANET, WHOSE SOJOURN HERE HAS ALREADY TRIGGERED ASTRONOMIC TURMOIL.

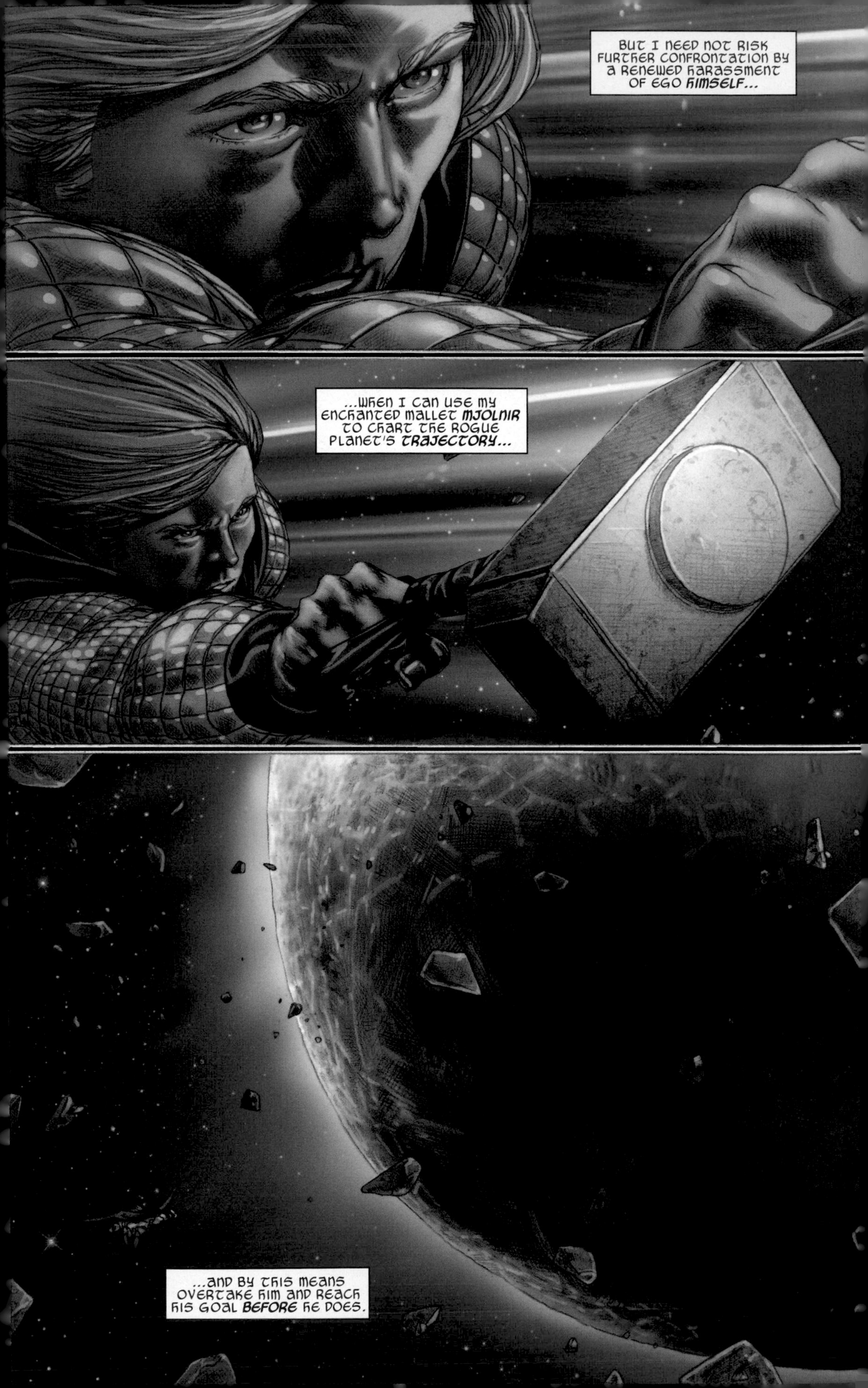
BUT I NEED NOT RISK FURTHER CONFRONTATION BY A RENEWED HARASSMENT OF EGO HIMSELF...
...WHEN I CAN USE MY ENCHANTED MALLET MJOLNIR TO CHART THE ROGUE PLANET'S TRAJECTORY...
...AND BY THIS MEANS OVERTAKE HIM AND REACH HIS GOAL BEFORE HE DOES.

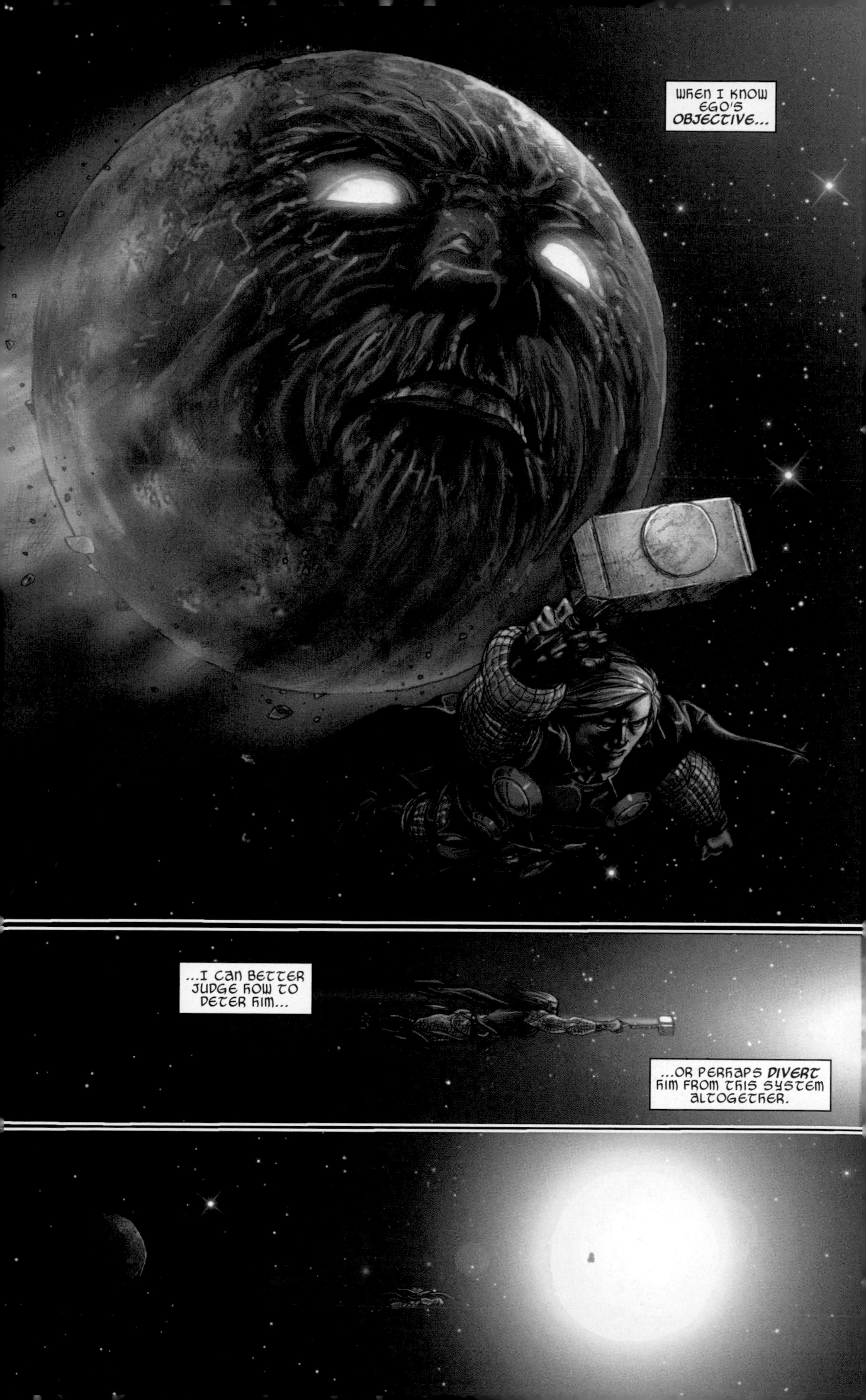
WHEN I KNOW EGO'S OBJECTIVE...
...I CAN BETTER JUDGE HOW TO DETER HIM...
...OR PERHAPS DIVERT HIM FROM THIS SYSTEM ALTOGETHER.

THUS DO I ARRIVE AT EGO'S DESTINATION, ON THE *OPPOSING* EDGE OF THE SOLAR SYSTEM...

...ONLY TO FIND THAT YET *ANOTHER* ANCIENT AND VASTLY POWERFUL ENTITY IS ENTWINED IN THIS BUSINESS.

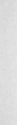

FOR THAT IS THE MUSEUM OF *TANELEER TIVAN*...

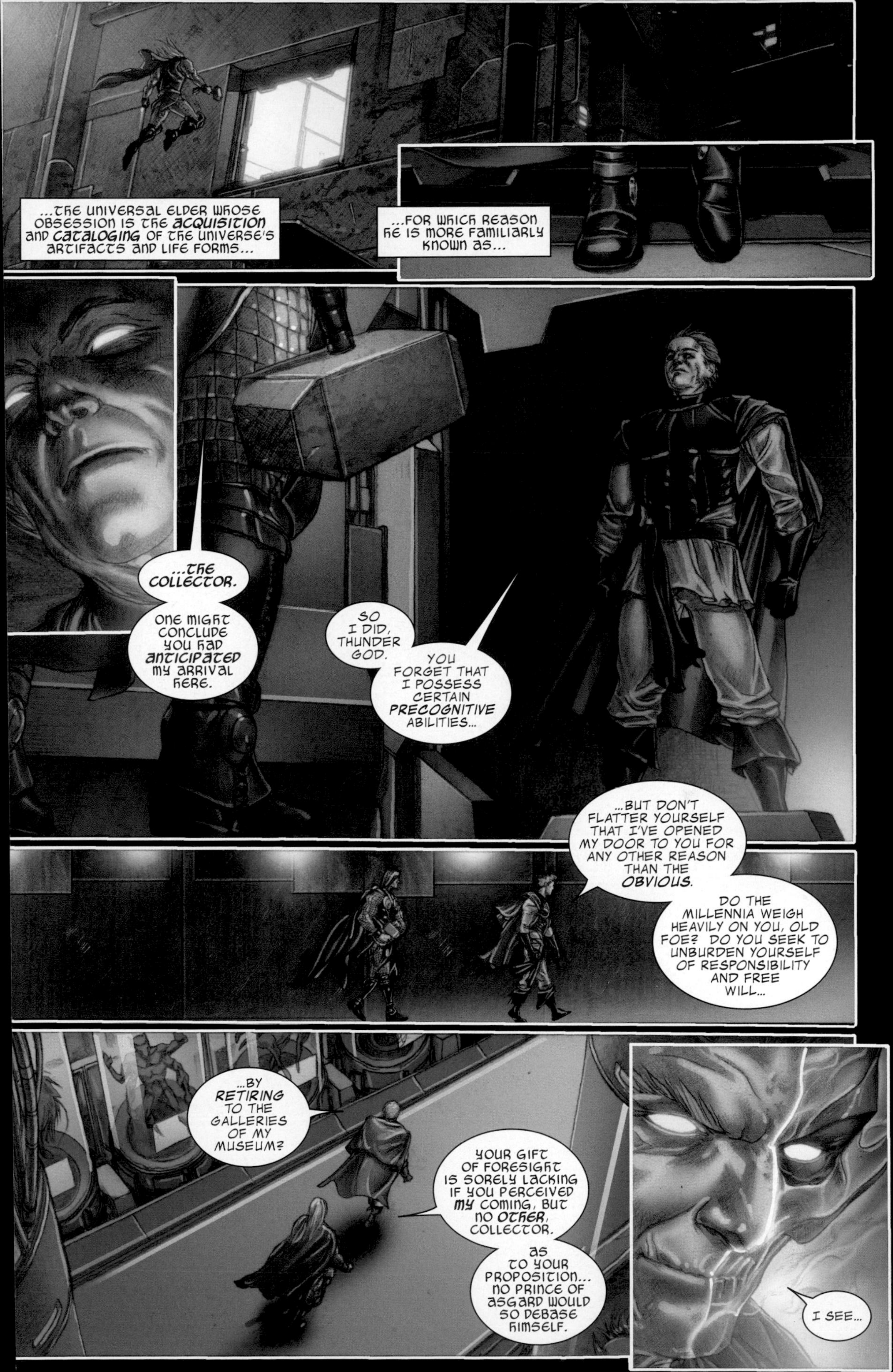
...THE UNIVERSAL ELDER WHOSE OBSESSION IS THE ACQUISITION AND CATALOGING OF THE UNIVERSE'S ARTIFACTS AND LIFE FORMS...
...FOR WHICH REASON HE IS MORE FAMILIARLY KNOWN AS...
...THE COLLECTOR.
ONE MIGHT CONCLUDE YOU HAD ANTICIPATED MY ARRIVAL HERE.
SO I DID, THUNDER GOD.
YOU FORGET THAT I POSSESS CERTAIN PRECOGNITIVE ABILITIES...
...BUT DON'T FLATTER YOURSELF THAT I'VE OPENED MY DOOR TO YOU FOR ANY OTHER REASON THAN THE OBVIOUS.
DO THE MILLENNIA WEIGH HEAVILY ON YOU, OLD FOE? DO YOU SEEK TO UNBURDEN YOURSELF OF RESPONSIBILITY AND FREE WILL...
...BY RETIRING TO THE GALLERIES OF MY MUSEUM?
YOUR GIFT OF FORESIGHT IS SORELY LACKING IF YOU PERCEIVED MY COMING, BUT NO OTHER, COLLECTOR.
AS TO YOUR PROPOSITION... NO PRINCE OF ASGARD WOULD SO DEBASE HIMSELF.
I SEE...

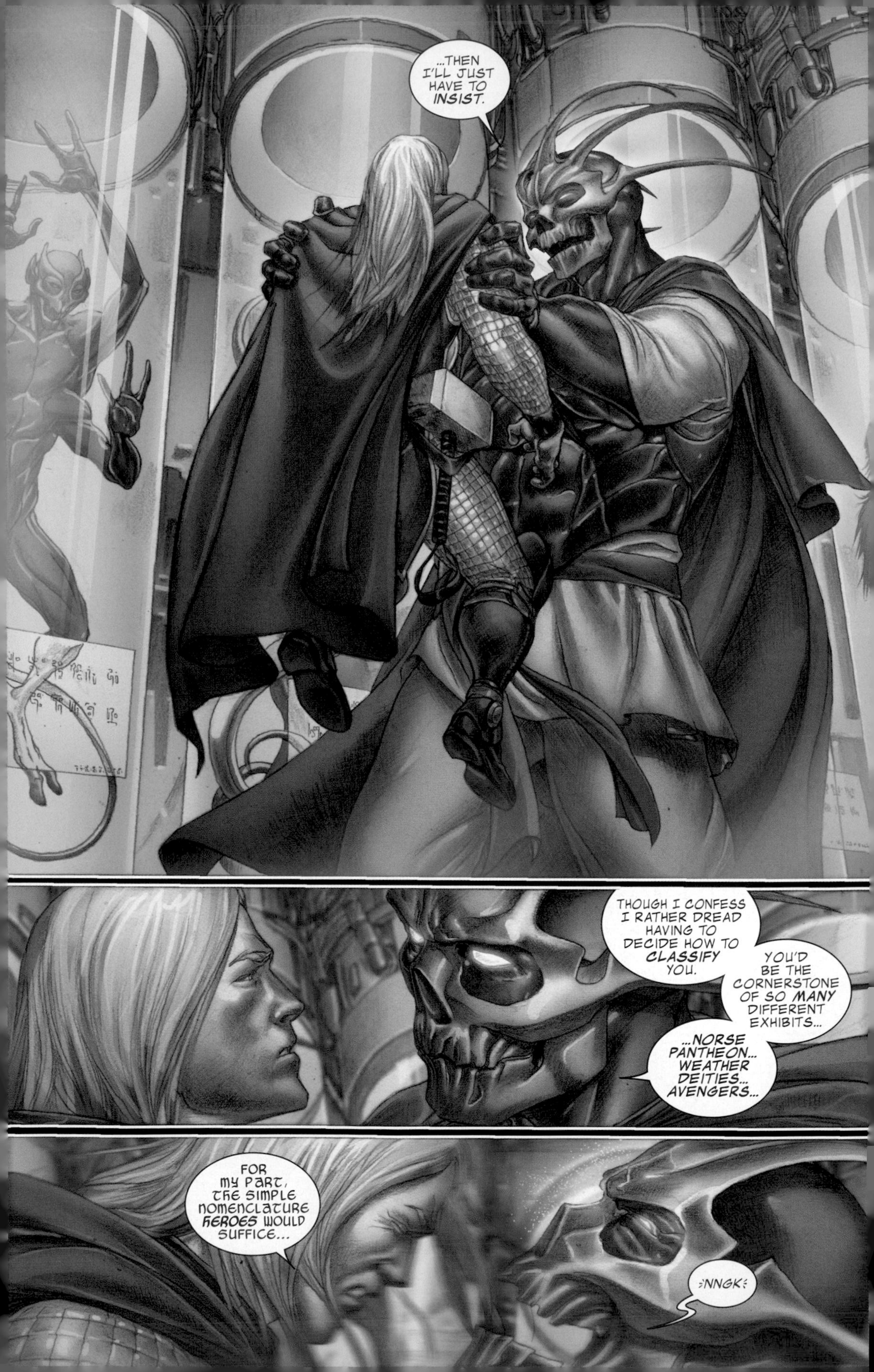
...THEN I'LL JUST HAVE TO INSIST.
THOUGH I CONFESS I RATHER DREAD HAVING TO DECIDE HOW TO CLASSIFY YOU.
YOU'D BE THE CORNERSTONE OF SO MANY DIFFERENT EXHIBITS...
...NORSE PANTHEON... WEATHER DEITIES... AVENGERS...
FOR MY PART, THE SIMPLE NOMENCLATURE HEROES WOULD SUFFICE...
NNGK

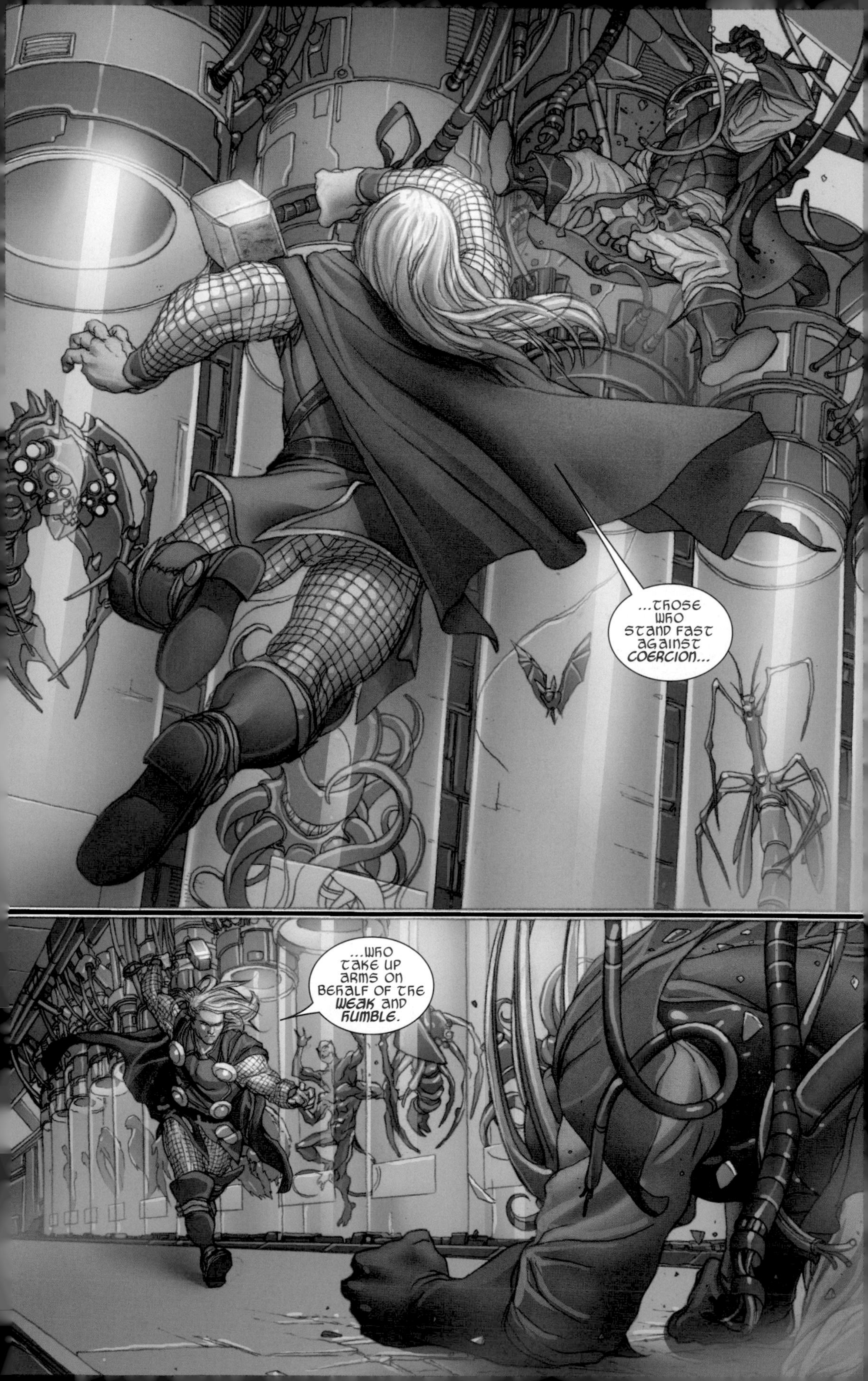
...THOSE WHO STAND FAST AGAINST COERCION...
...WHO TAKE UP ARMS ON BEHALF OF THE WEAK AND HUMBLE.

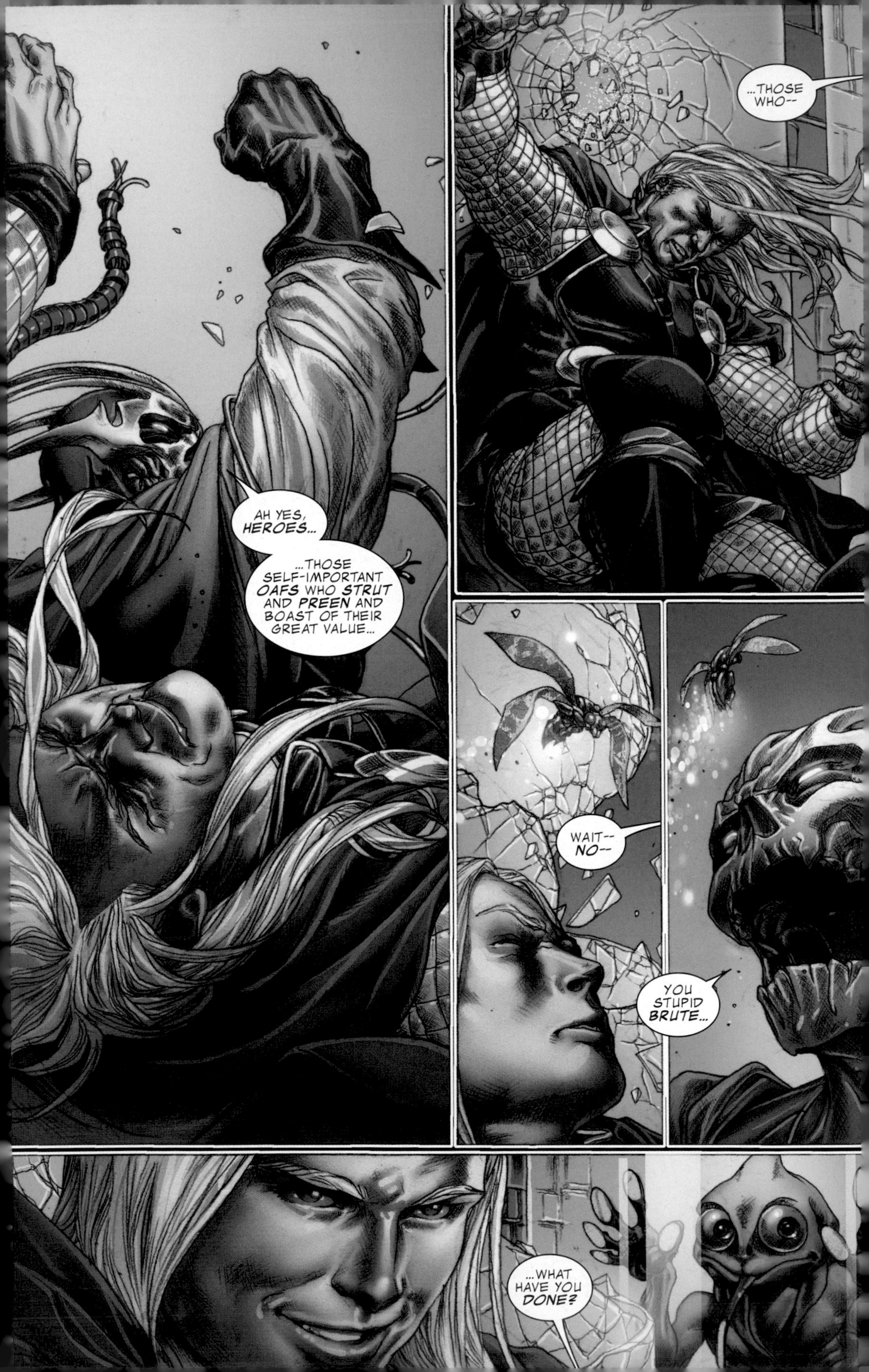
AH YES, HEROES...
...THOSE SELF-IMPORTANT OAFS WHO STRUT AND PREEN AND BOAST OF THEIR GREAT VALUE...
...THOSE WHO--
WAIT-- NO--
YOU STUPID BRUTE...
...WHAT HAVE YOU DONE?

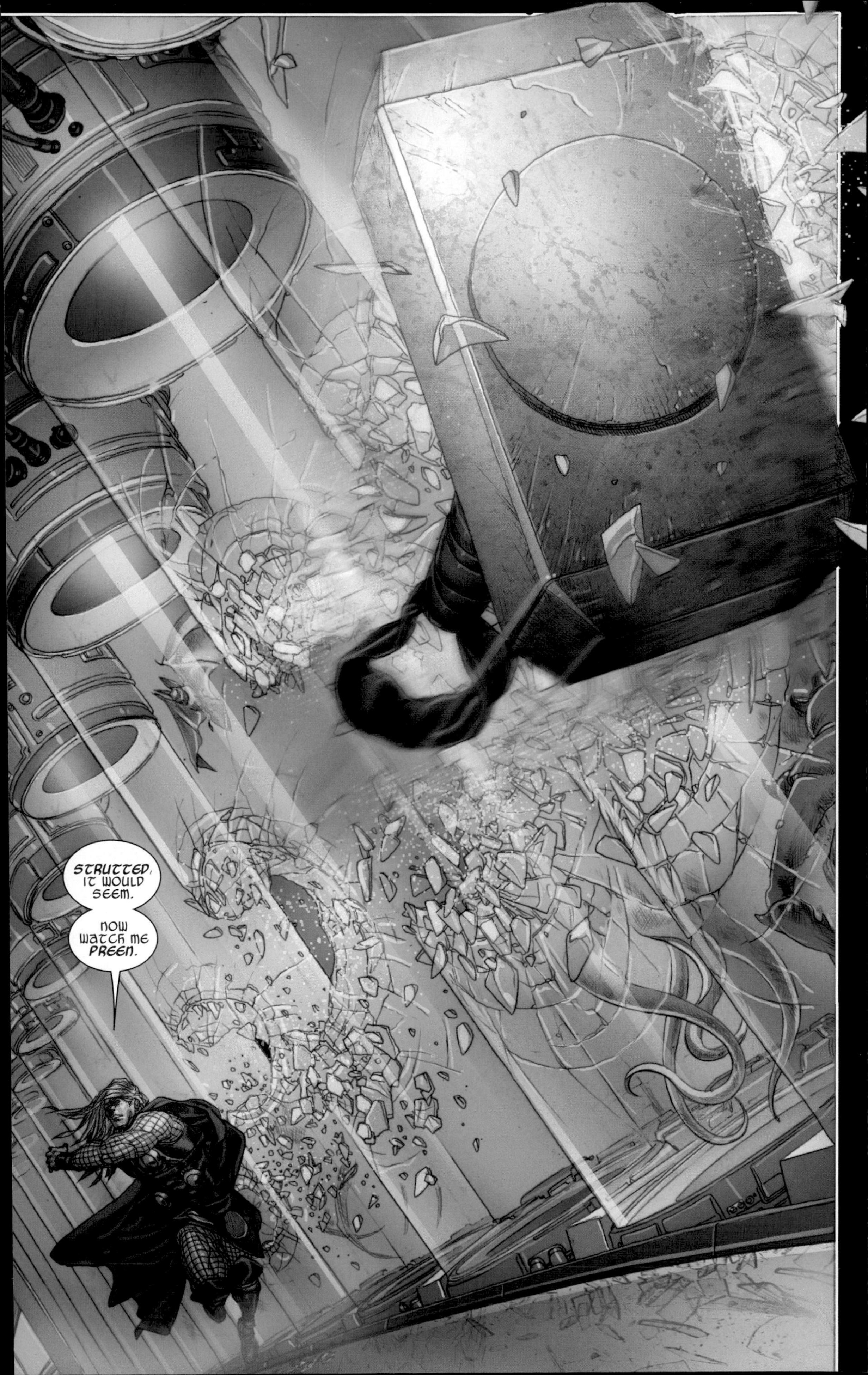
STRUTTED, IT WOULD SEEM.
NOW WATCH ME PREEN.

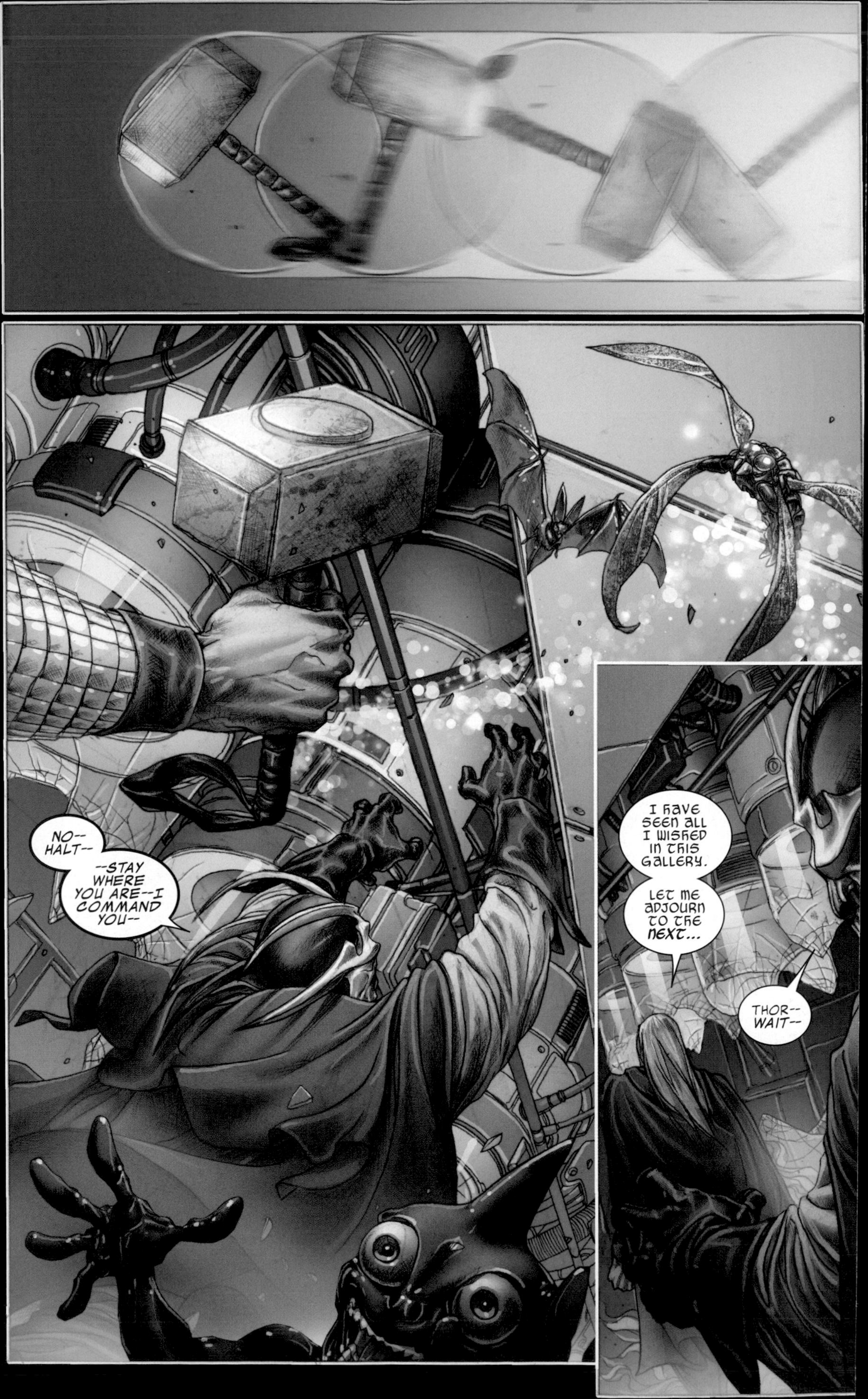
NO--
HALT--
--STAY WHERE YOU ARE--I COMMAND YOU--
I HAVE SEEN ALL I WISHED IN THIS GALLERY.
LET ME ADJOURN TO THE NEXT...
THOR--
WAIT--

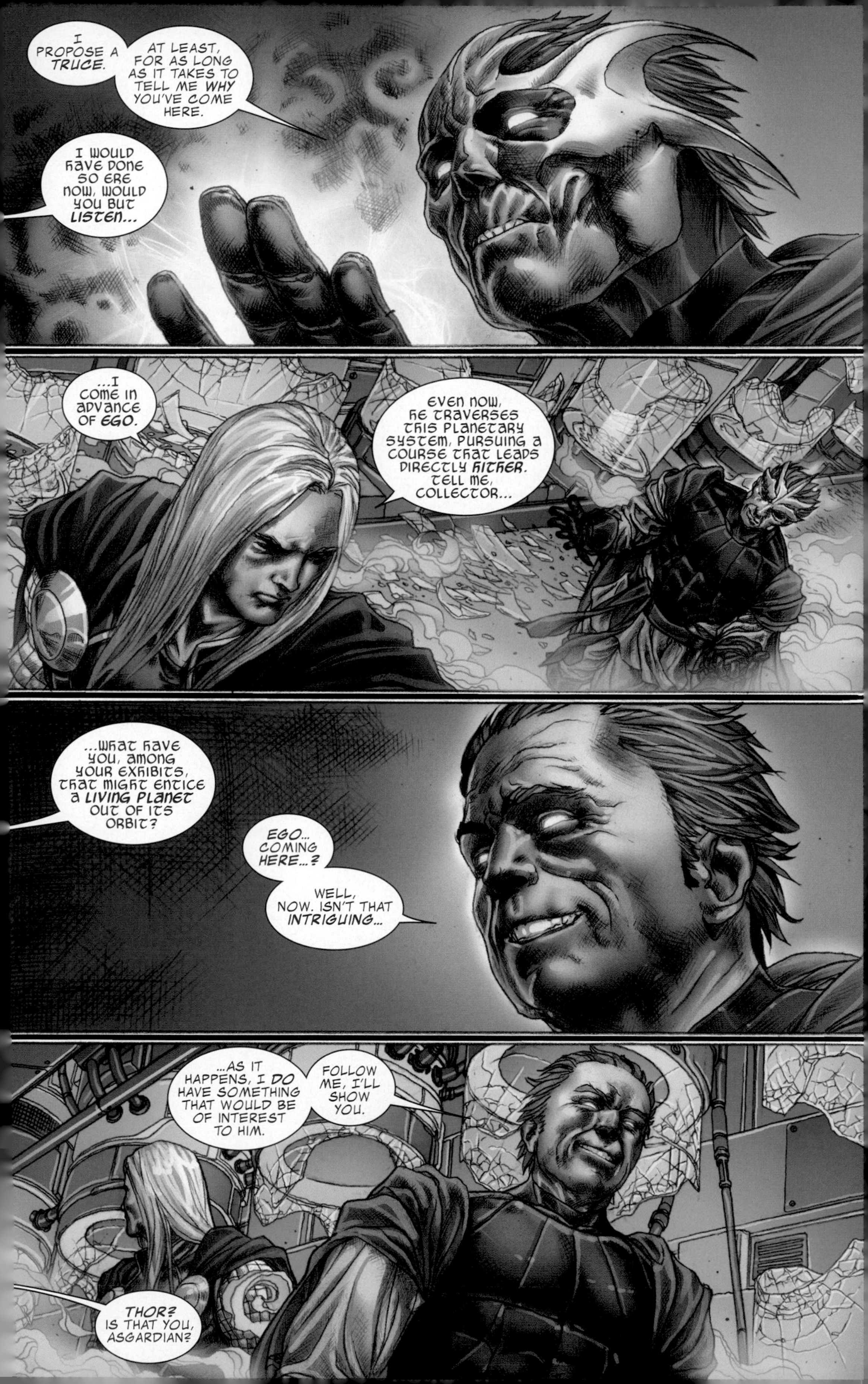
I PROPOSE A TRUCE.
AT LEAST, FOR AS LONG AS IT TAKES TO TELL ME WHY YOU'VE COME HERE.
I WOULD HAVE DONE SO ERE NOW, WOULD YOU BUT LISTEN...
...I COME IN ADVANCE OF EGO.
EVEN NOW, HE TRAVERSES THIS PLANETARY SYSTEM, PURSUING A COURSE THAT LEADS DIRECTLY HITHER. TELL ME, COLLECTOR...
...WHAT HAVE YOU, AMONG YOUR EXHIBITS, THAT MIGHT ENTICE A LIVING PLANET OUT OF ITS ORBIT?
EGO... COMING HERE...?
WELL, NOW. ISN'T THAT INTRIGUING...
...AS IT HAPPENS, I DO HAVE SOMETHING THAT WOULD BE OF INTEREST TO HIM.
FOLLOW ME, I'LL SHOW YOU.
THOR? IS THAT YOU, ASGARDIAN?

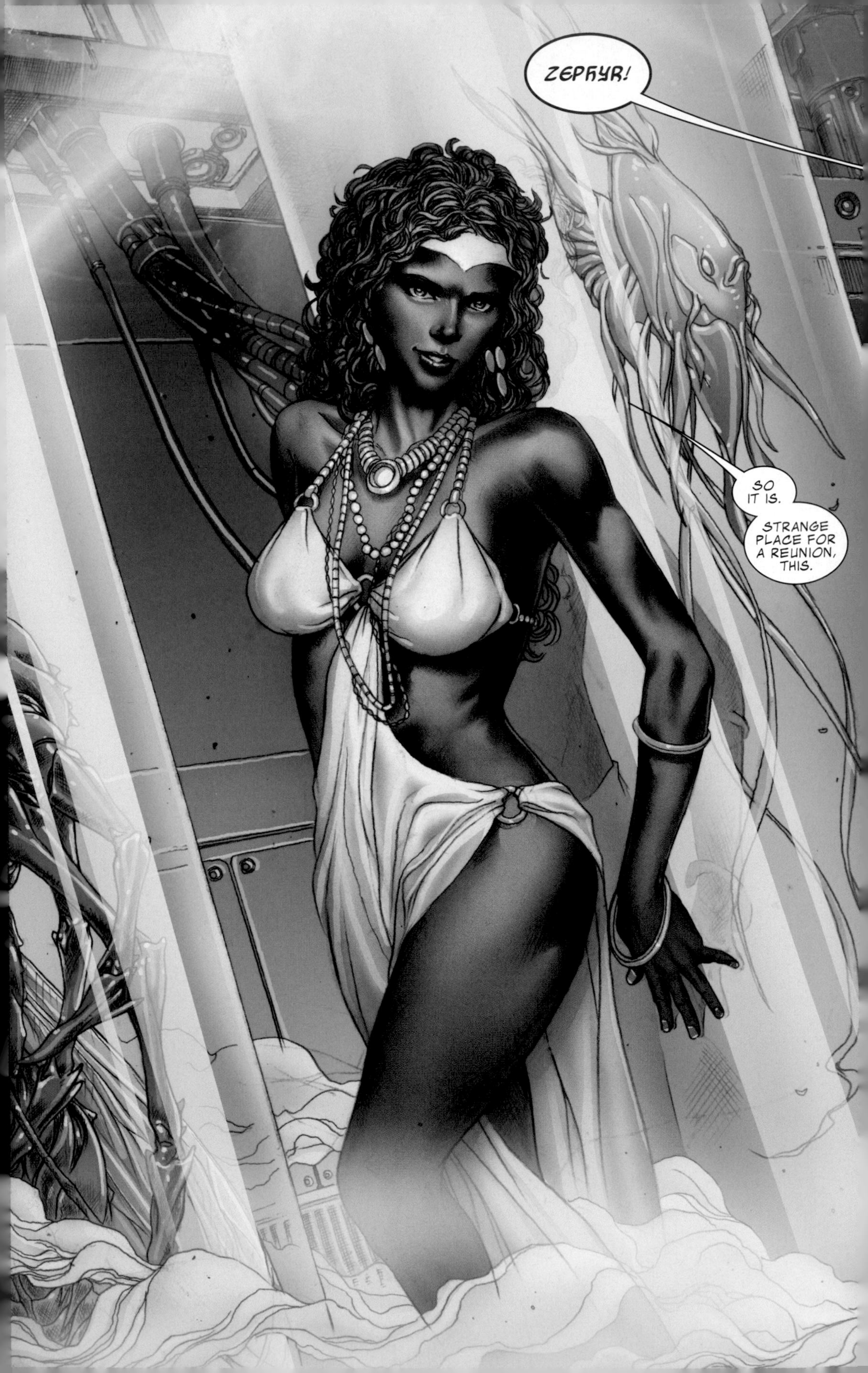
ZEPHYR!
SO IT IS.
STRANGE PLACE FOR A REUNION, THIS.

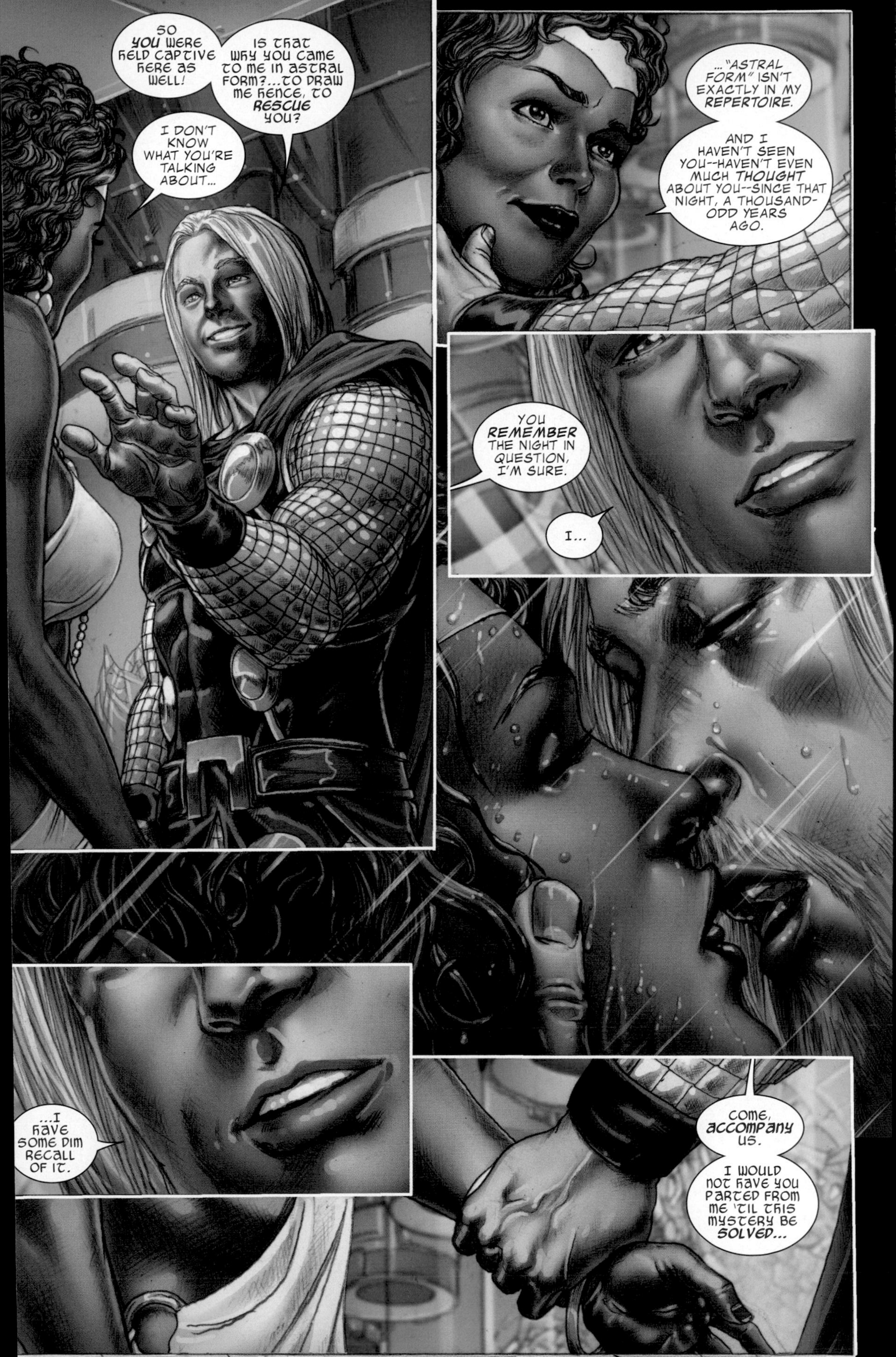
SO YOU WERE HELD CAPTIVE HERE AS WELL!
IS THAT WHY YOU CAME TO ME IN ASTRAL FORM?...TO DRAW ME HENCE, TO RESCUE YOU?
I DON'T KNOW WHAT YOU'RE TALKING ABOUT...
..."ASTRAL FORM" ISN'T EXACTLY IN MY REPERTOIRE.
AND I HAVEN'T SEEN YOU--HAVEN'T EVEN MUCH THOUGHT ABOUT YOU--SINCE THAT NIGHT, A THOUSAND-ODD YEARS AGO.
YOU REMEMBER THE NIGHT IN QUESTION, I'M SURE.
I...
...I HAVE SOME DIM RECALL OF IT.
COME, ACCOMPANY US.
I WOULD NOT HAVE YOU PARTED FROM ME 'TIL THIS MYSTERY BE SOLVED...

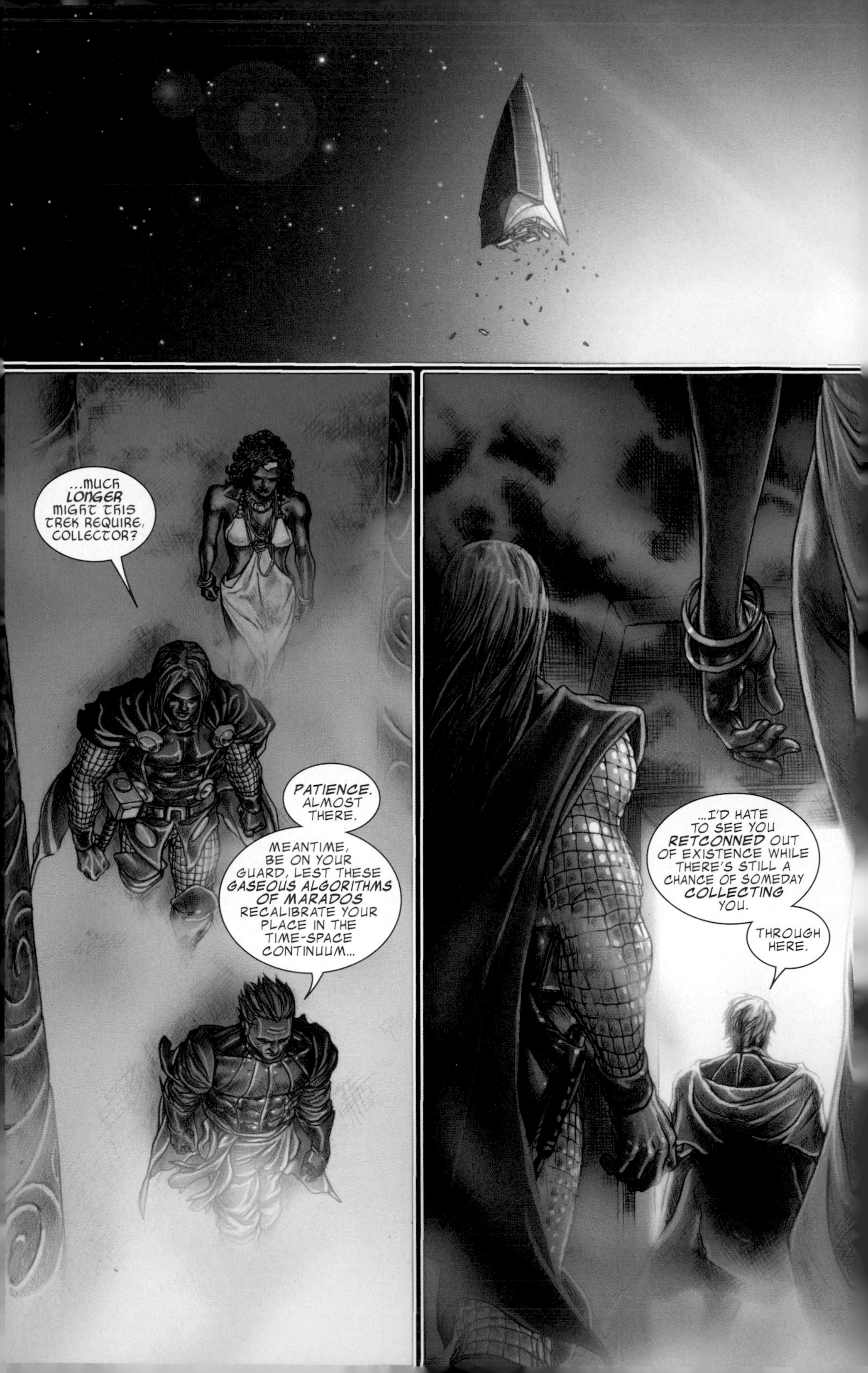

...MUCH LONGER MIGHT THIS TREK REQUIRE, COLLECTOR?
PATIENCE. ALMOST THERE.
MEANTIME, BE ON YOUR GUARD, LEST THESE GASEOUS ALGORITHMS OF MARADOS RECALIBRATE YOUR PLACE IN THE TIME-SPACE CONTINUUM...
...I'D HATE TO SEE YOU RETCONNED OUT OF EXISTENCE WHILE THERE'S STILL A CHANCE OF SOMEDAY COLLECTING YOU.
THROUGH HERE.

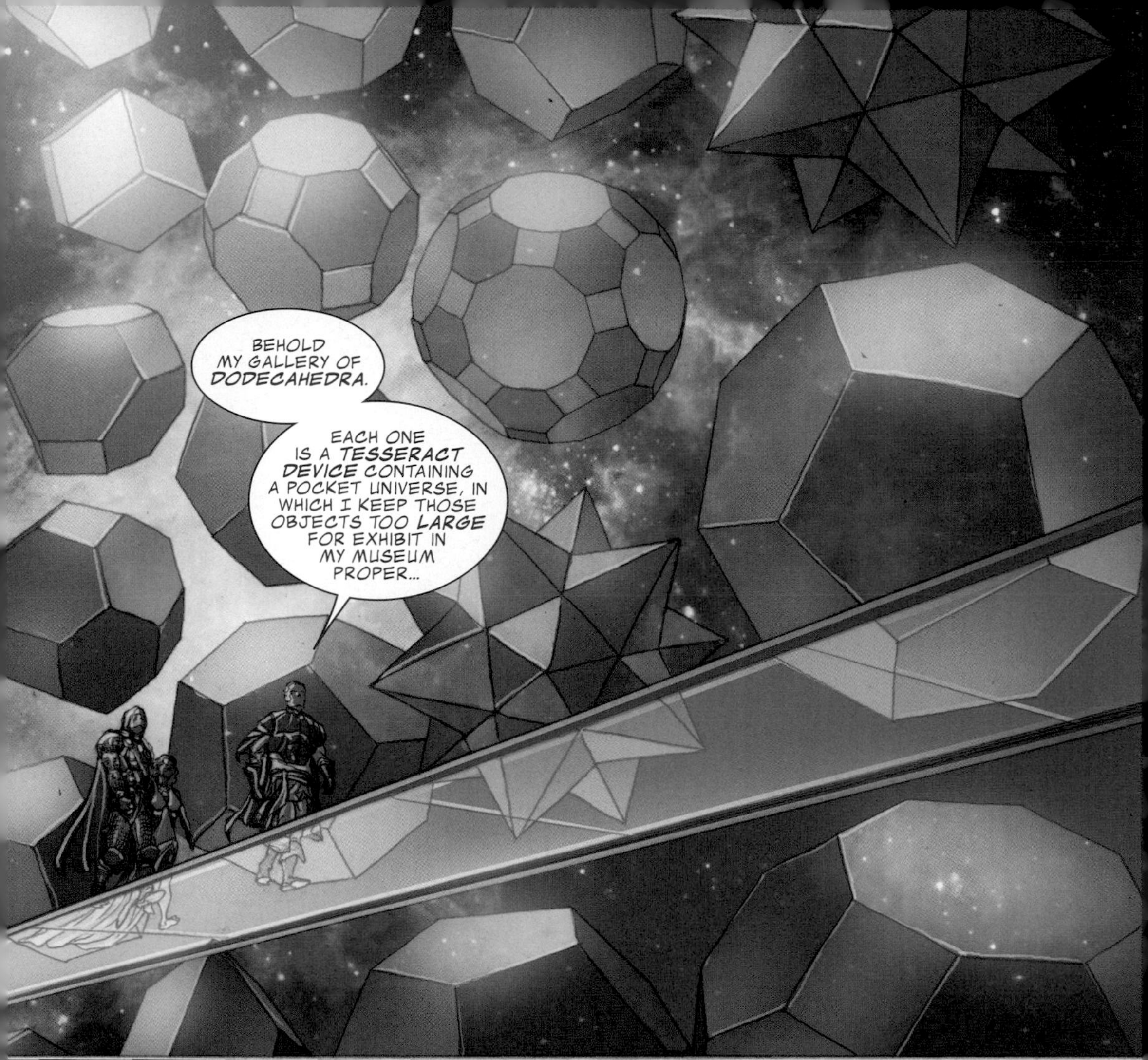
BEHOLD MY GALLERY OF DODECAHEDRA.
EACH ONE IS A TESSERACT DEVICE CONTAINING A POCKET UNIVERSE, IN WHICH I KEEP THOSE OBJECTS TOO LARGE FOR EXHIBIT IN MY MUSEUM PROPER...
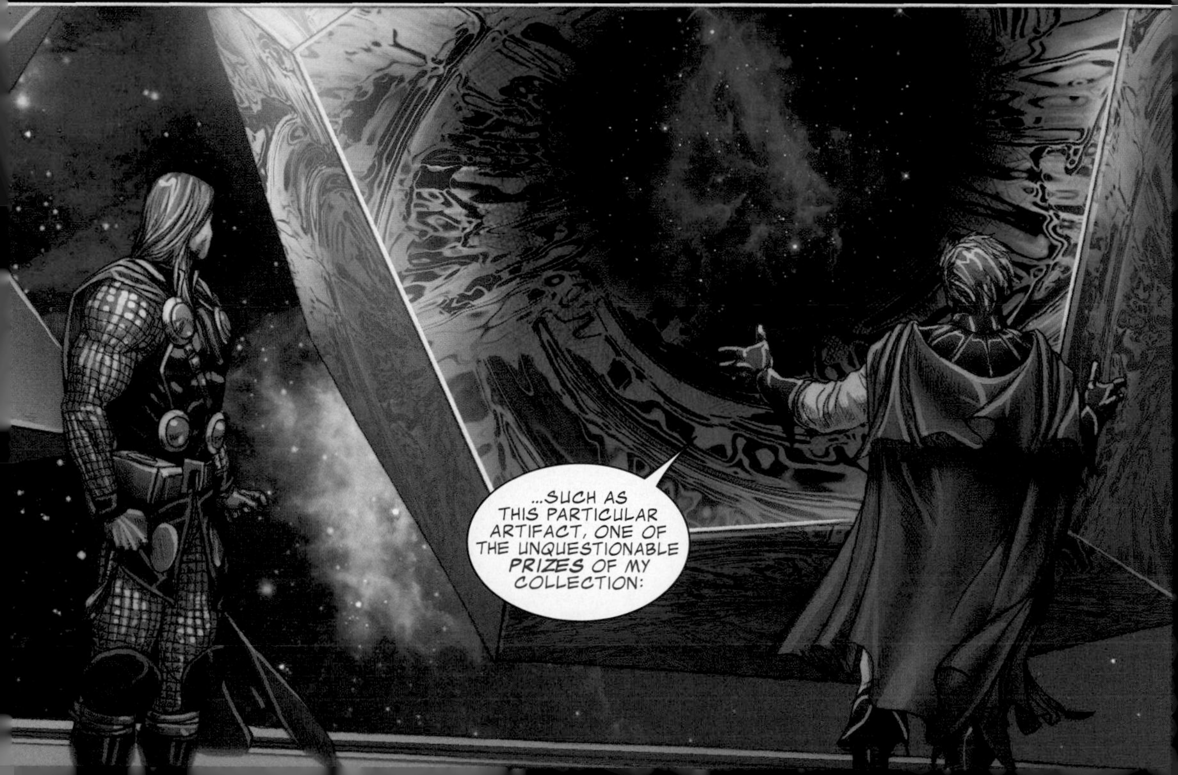
...SUCH AS THIS PARTICULAR ARTIFACT, ONE OF THE UNQUESTIONABLE PRIZES OF MY COLLECTION:

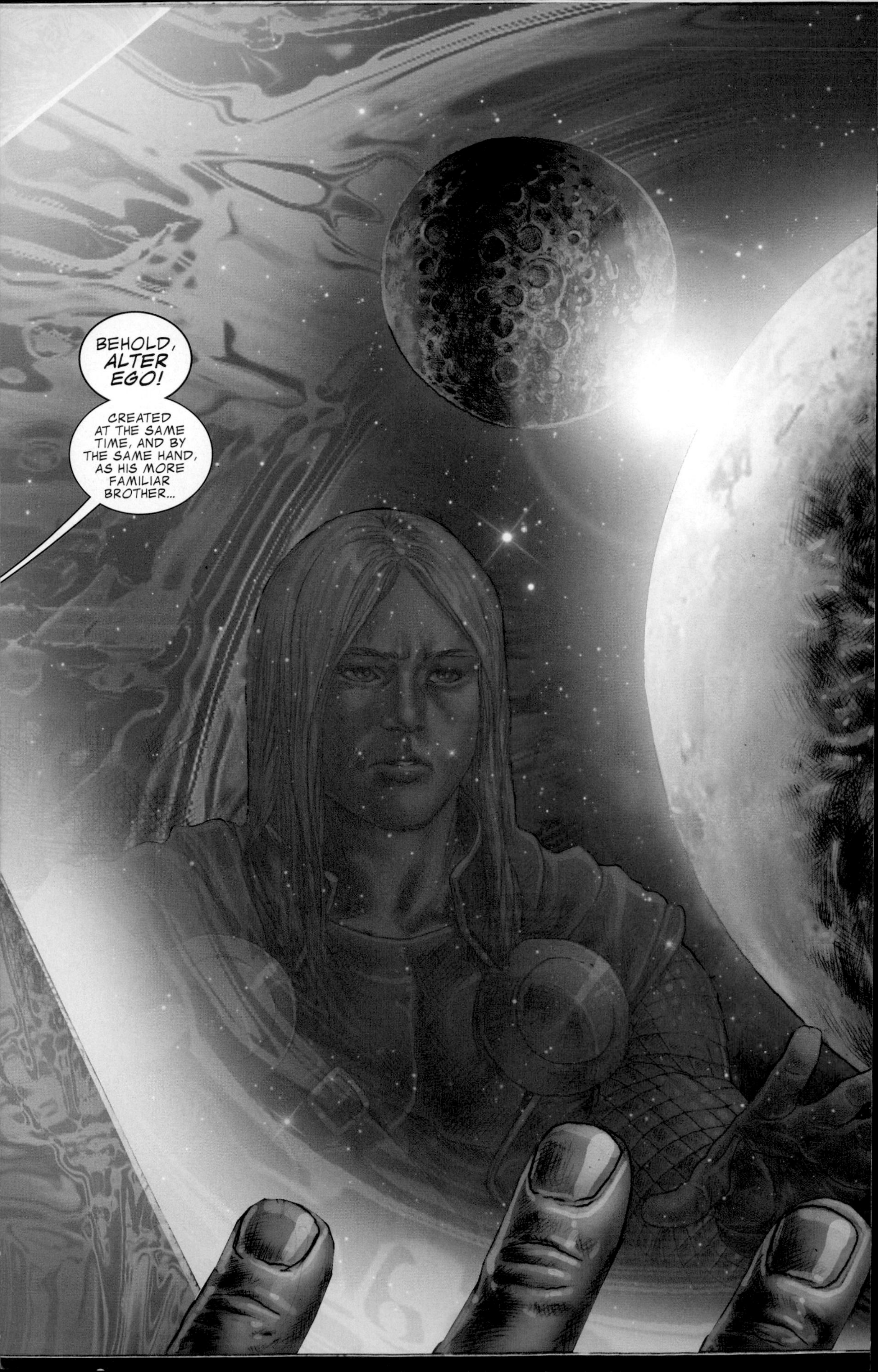
BEHOLD, ALTER EGO!
CREATED AT THE SAME TIME, AND BY THE SAME HAND, AS HIS MORE FAMILIAR BROTHER...

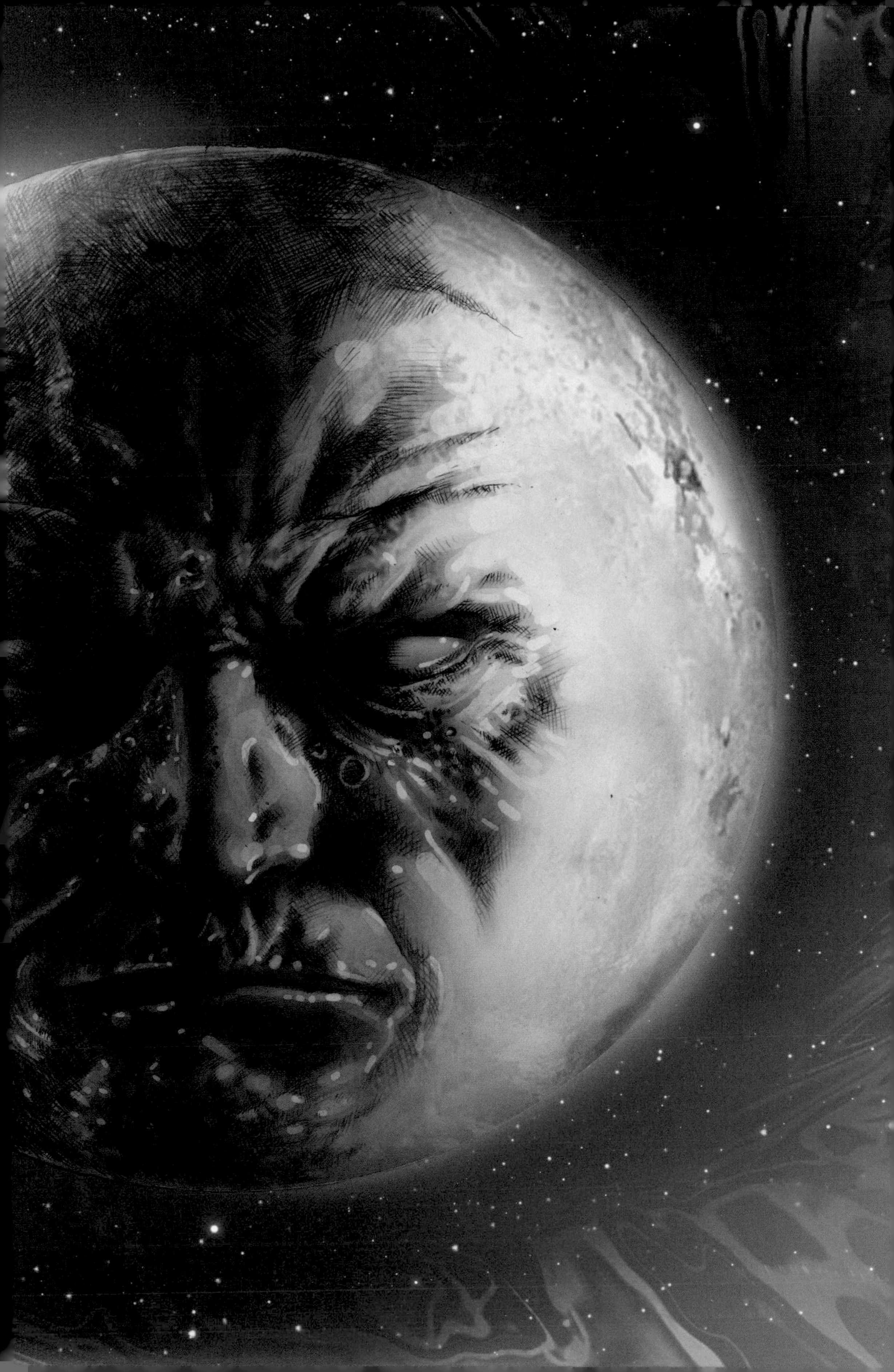

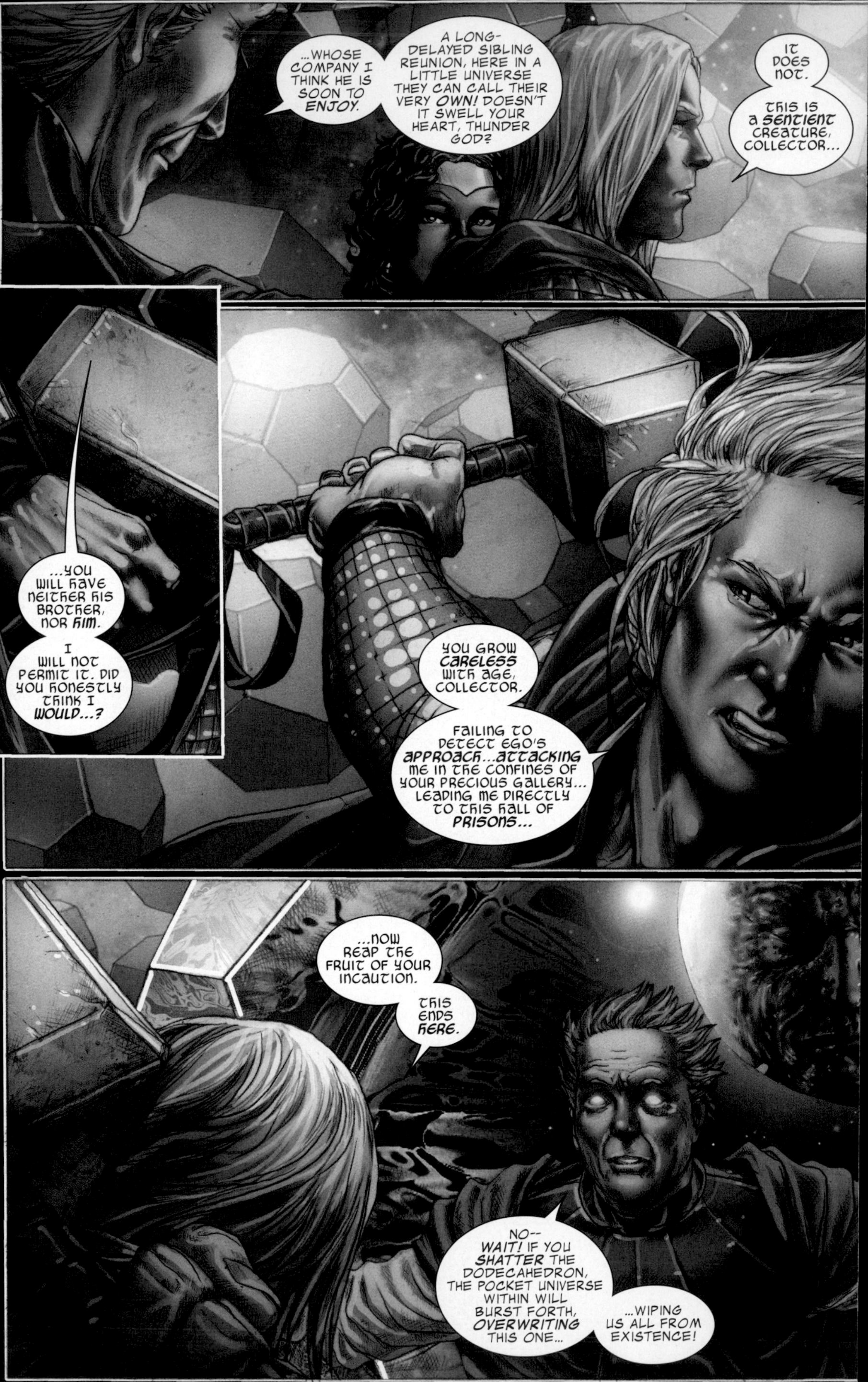
...WHOSE COMPANY I THINK HE IS SOON TO ENJOY.
A LONG-DELAYED SIBLING REUNION, HERE IN A LITTLE UNIVERSE THEY CAN CALL THEIR VERY OWN! DOESN'T IT SWELL YOUR HEART, THUNDER GOD?
IT DOES NOT.
THIS IS A SENTIENT CREATURE, COLLECTOR...
...YOU WILL HAVE NEITHER HIS BROTHER, NOR HIM.
I WILL NOT PERMIT IT. DID YOU HONESTLY THINK I WOULD...?
YOU GROW CARELESS WITH AGE, COLLECTOR.
FAILING TO DETECT EGO'S APPROACH...ATTACKING ME IN THE CONFINES OF YOUR PRECIOUS GALLERY... LEADING ME DIRECTLY TO THIS HALL OF PRISONS...
...NOW REAP THE FRUIT OF YOUR INCAUTION.
THIS ENDS HERE.
NO-- WAIT! IF YOU SHATTER THE DODECAHEDRON, THE POCKET UNIVERSE WITHIN WILL BURST FORTH, OVERWRITING THIS ONE...
...WIPING US ALL FROM EXISTENCE!

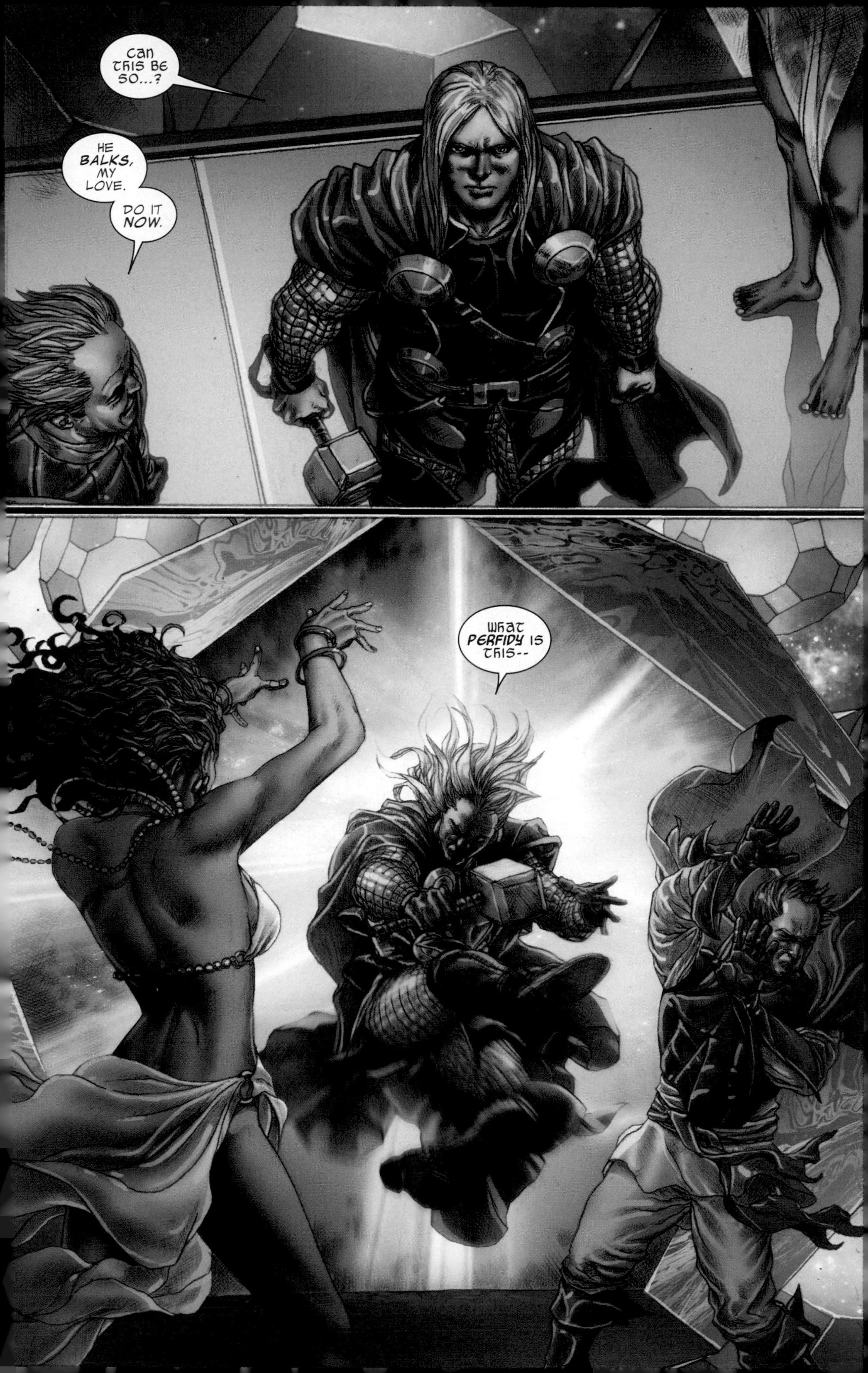
CAN THIS BE SO...?
HE BALKS, MY LOVE.
DO IT NOW.
WHAT PERFIDY IS THIS--

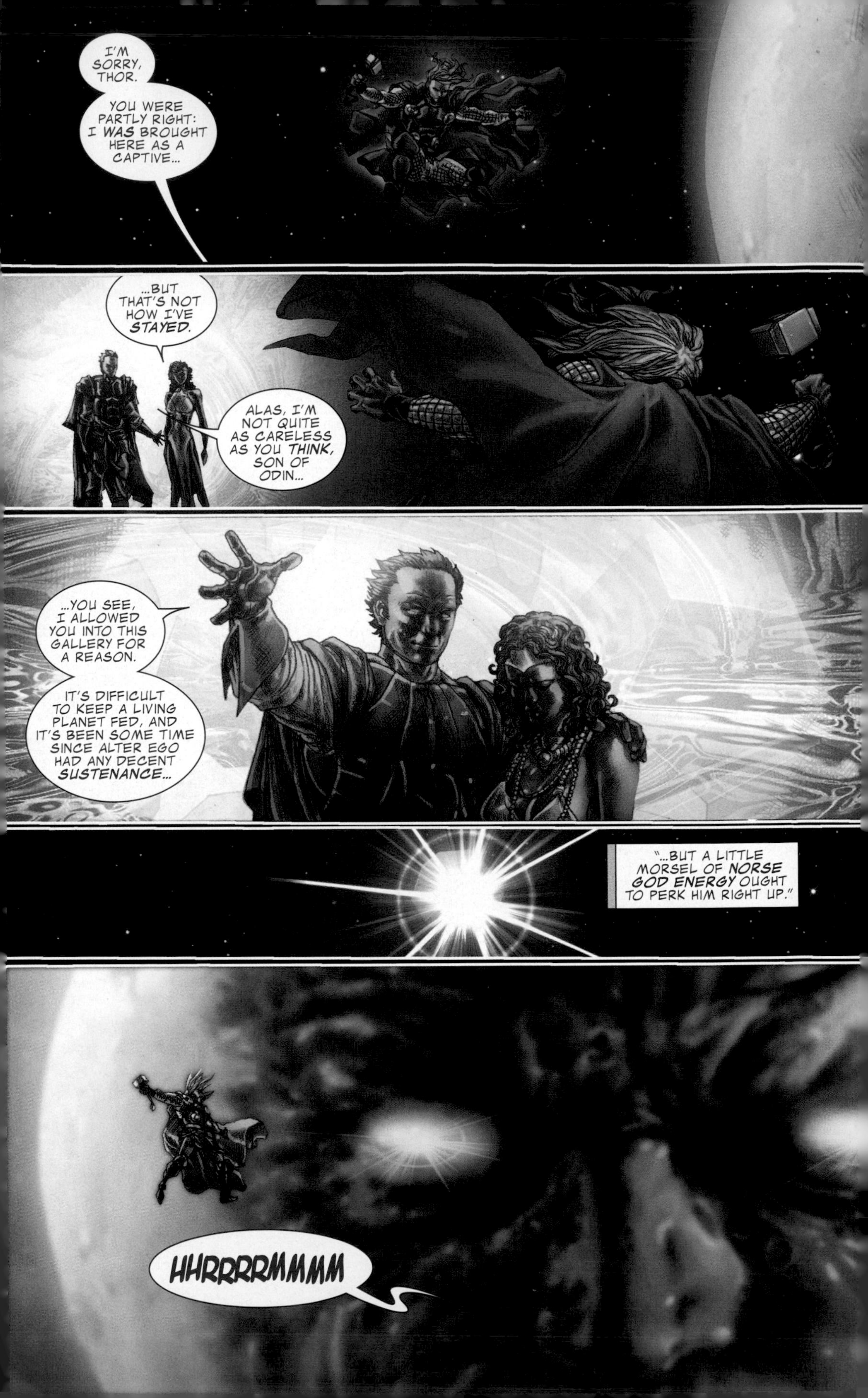
I'M SORRY, THOR.
YOU WERE PARTLY RIGHT: I WAS BROUGHT HERE AS A CAPTIVE...
...BUT THAT'S NOT HOW I'VE STAYED.
ALAS, I'M NOT QUITE AS CARELESS AS YOU THINK, SON OF ODIN...
...YOU SEE, I ALLOWED YOU INTO THIS GALLERY FOR A REASON.
IT'S DIFFICULT TO KEEP A LIVING PLANET FED, AND IT'S BEEN SOME TIME SINCE ALTER EGO HAD ANY DECENT SUSTENANCE...
"...BUT A LITTLE MORSEL OF NORSE GOD ENERGY OUGHT TO PERK HIM RIGHT UP."
HHRRRRMMMM

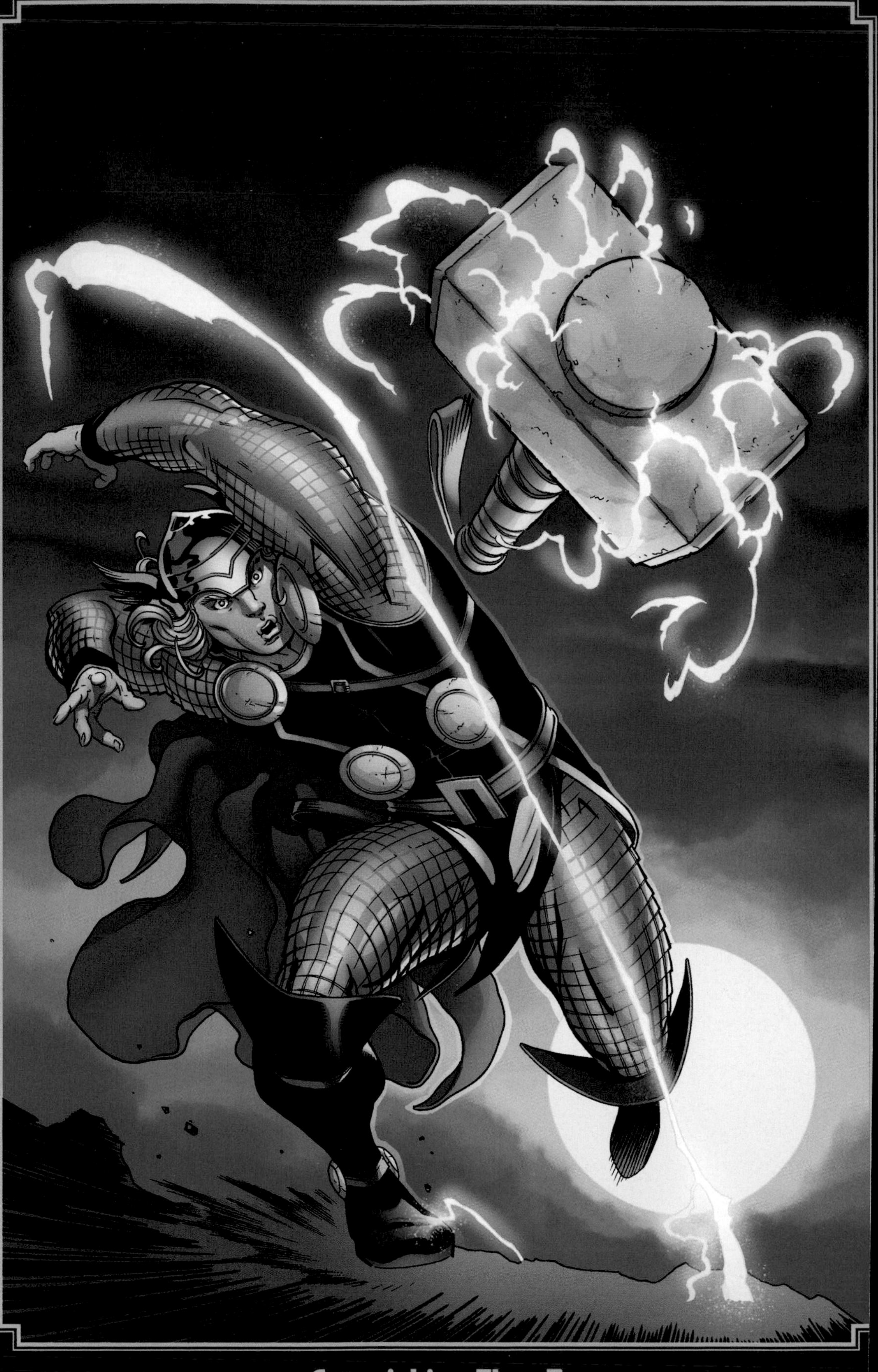

Astonishing Thor 3

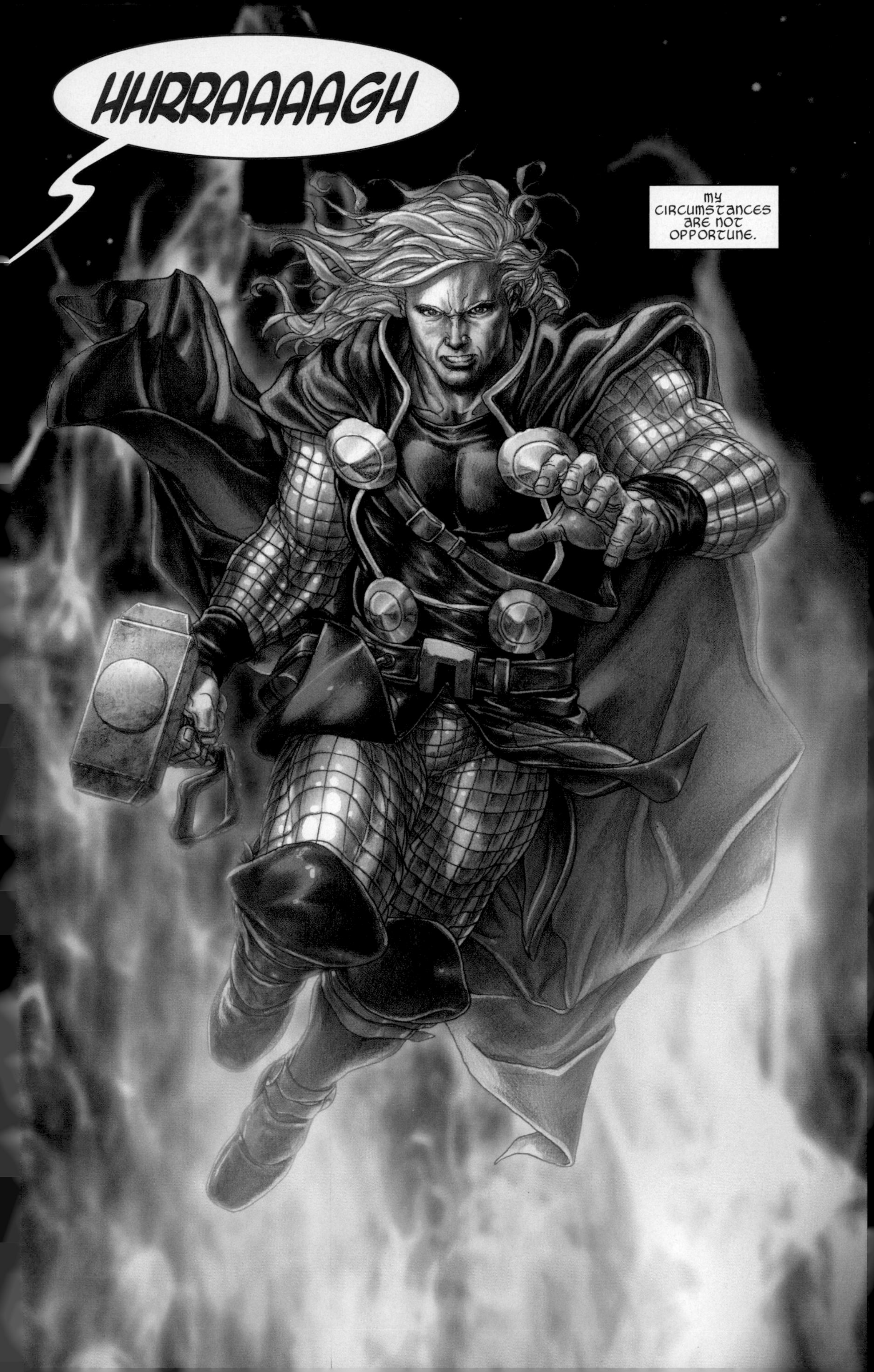
HHRRAAAAAGH
MY CIRCUMSTANCES ARE NOT OPPORTUNE.

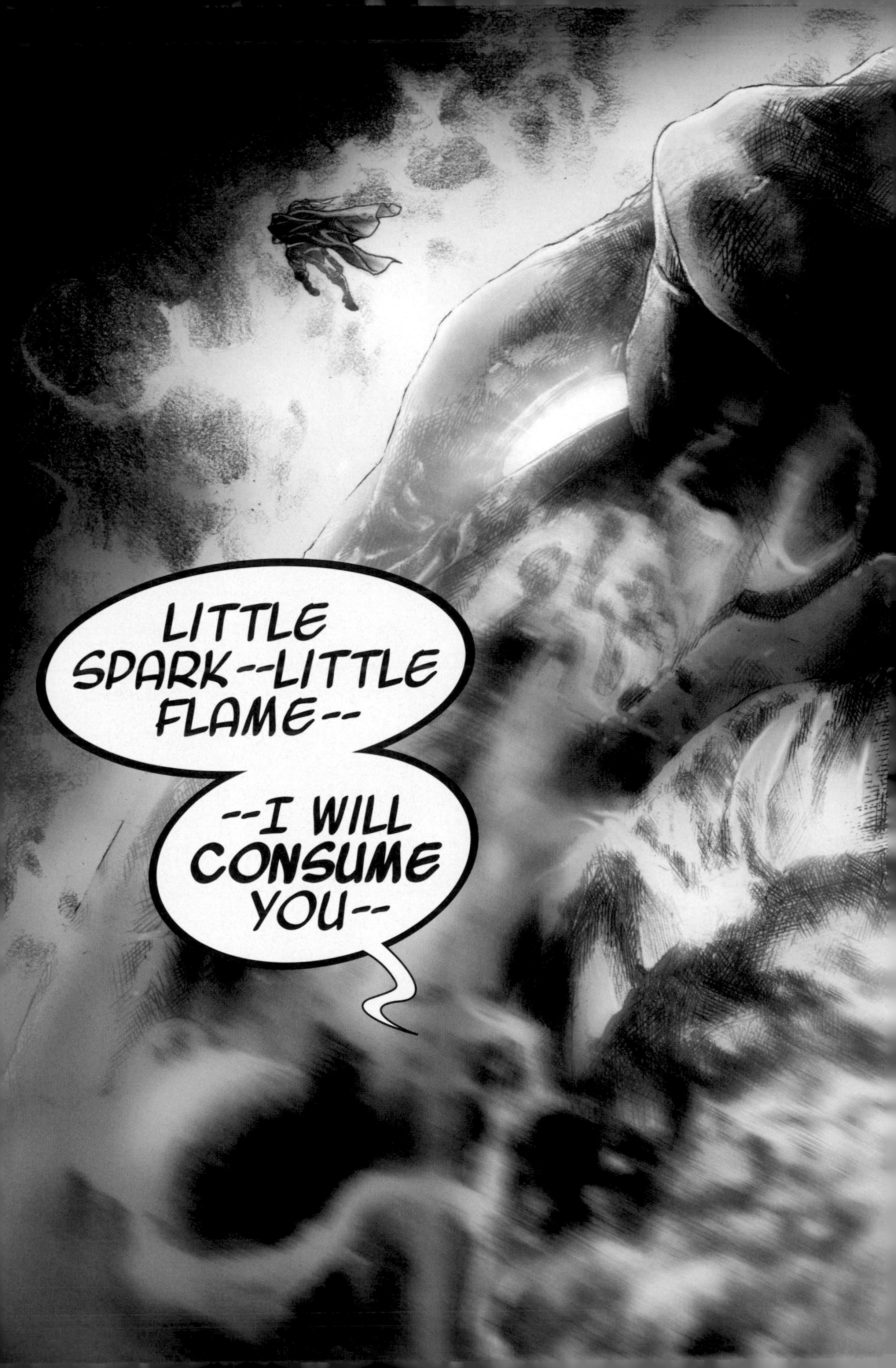
LITTLE SPARK--LITTLE FLAME--
--I WILL CONSUME YOU--

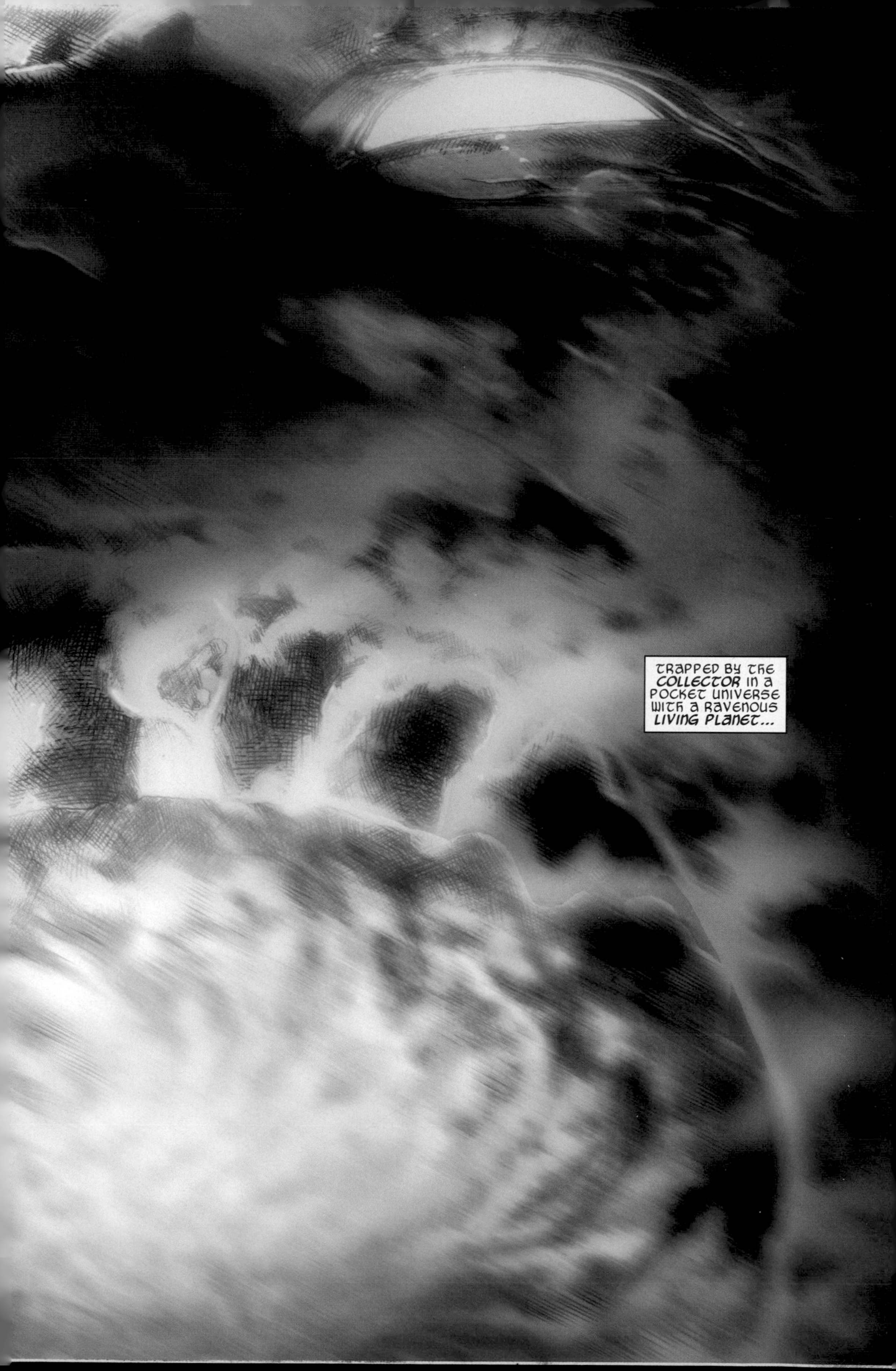
TRAPPED BY THE COLLECTOR IN A POCKET UNIVERSE WITH A RAVENOUS LIVING PLANET...

...AND THOUGH I AM THE LORD OF *STORM* AND *FURY*...

COME BACK LITTLE SPARK--

...THOSE ARE THE *LEAST* OF THE WEAPONS AT ALTER EGO'S DISPATCH.

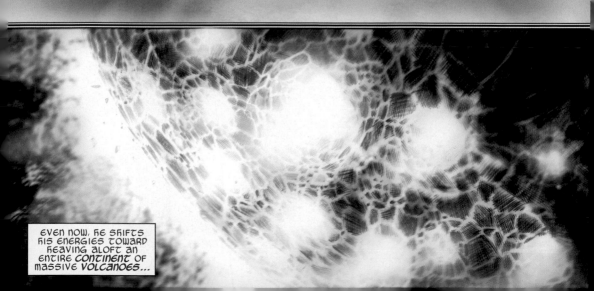

EVEN NOW, HE SHIFTS HIS ENERGIES TOWARD HEAVING ALOFT AN ENTIRE *CONTINENT* OF MASSIVE *VOLCANOES*...

...TO SERVE AS A GLOBAL-SCALE PROPULSION ENGINE.

I SAID COME BACK!

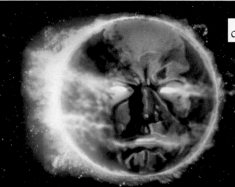

I CAN EASILY OUTDISTANCE HIM...

YOU CANNOT ESCAPE ME...

...BUT TO WHAT END? THIS UNIVERSE IS OTHERWISE EMPTY OF LIFE.

THERE IS NO SAFE HARBOR HERE.

NO HARBOR OF ANY KIND.

IN TIME, EVEN MY GODLY STAMINA WILL WANE...

...COME BACK...

...AND THE LIVING PLANET WILL BE UPON ME.

UNLESS...

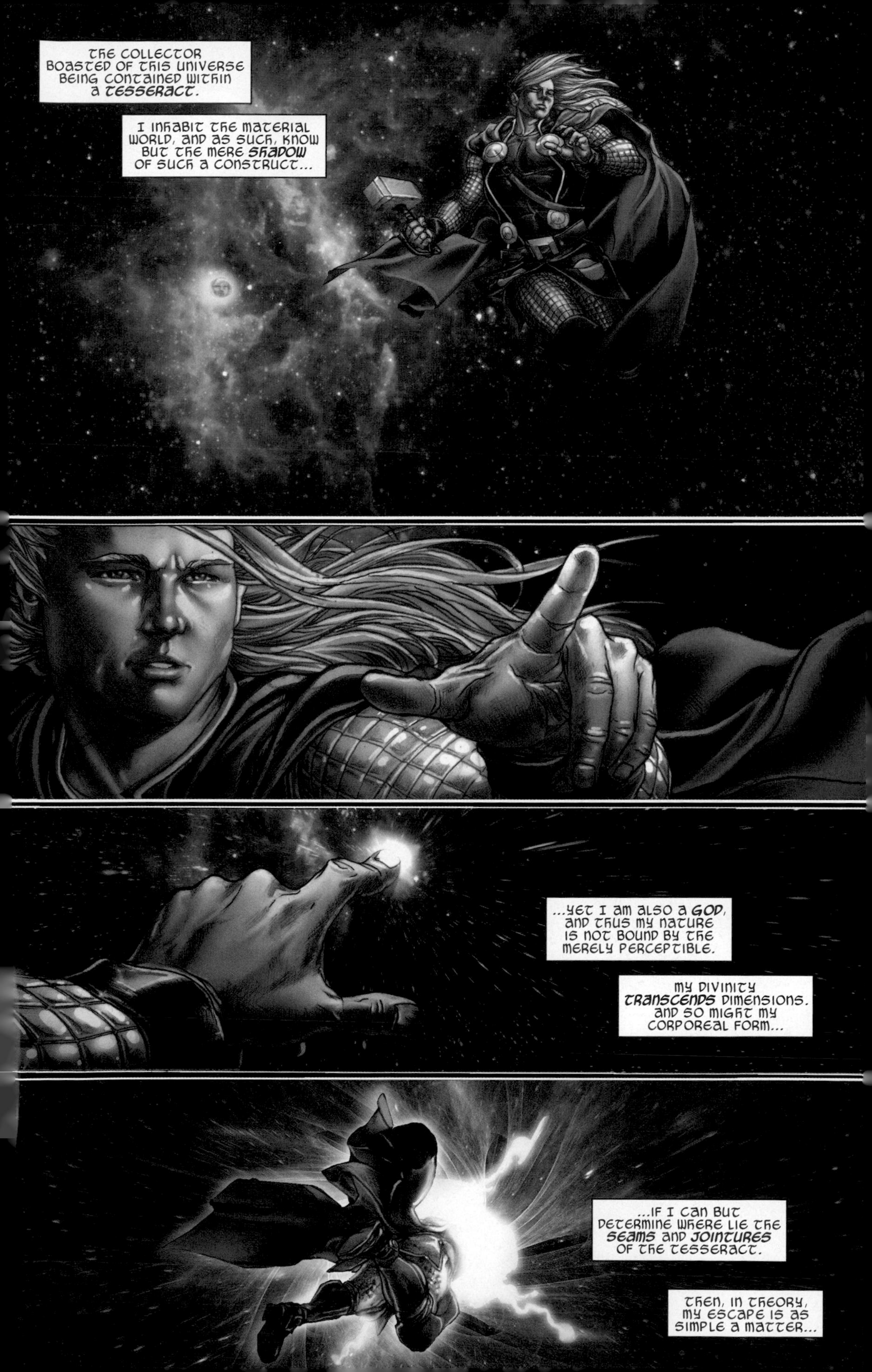
THE COLLECTOR BOASTED OF THIS UNIVERSE BEING CONTAINED WITHIN A TESSERACT.
I INHABIT THE MATERIAL WORLD, AND AS SUCH, KNOW BUT THE MERE SHADOW OF SUCH A CONSTRUCT...
...YET I AM ALSO A GOD, AND THUS MY NATURE IS NOT BOUND BY THE MERELY PERCEPTIBLE.
MY DIVINITY TRANSCENDS DIMENSIONS. AND SO MIGHT MY CORPOREAL FORM...
...IF I CAN BUT DETERMINE WHERE LIE THE SEAMS AND JOINTURES OF THE TESSERACT.
THEN, IN THEORY, MY ESCAPE IS AS SIMPLE A MATTER...

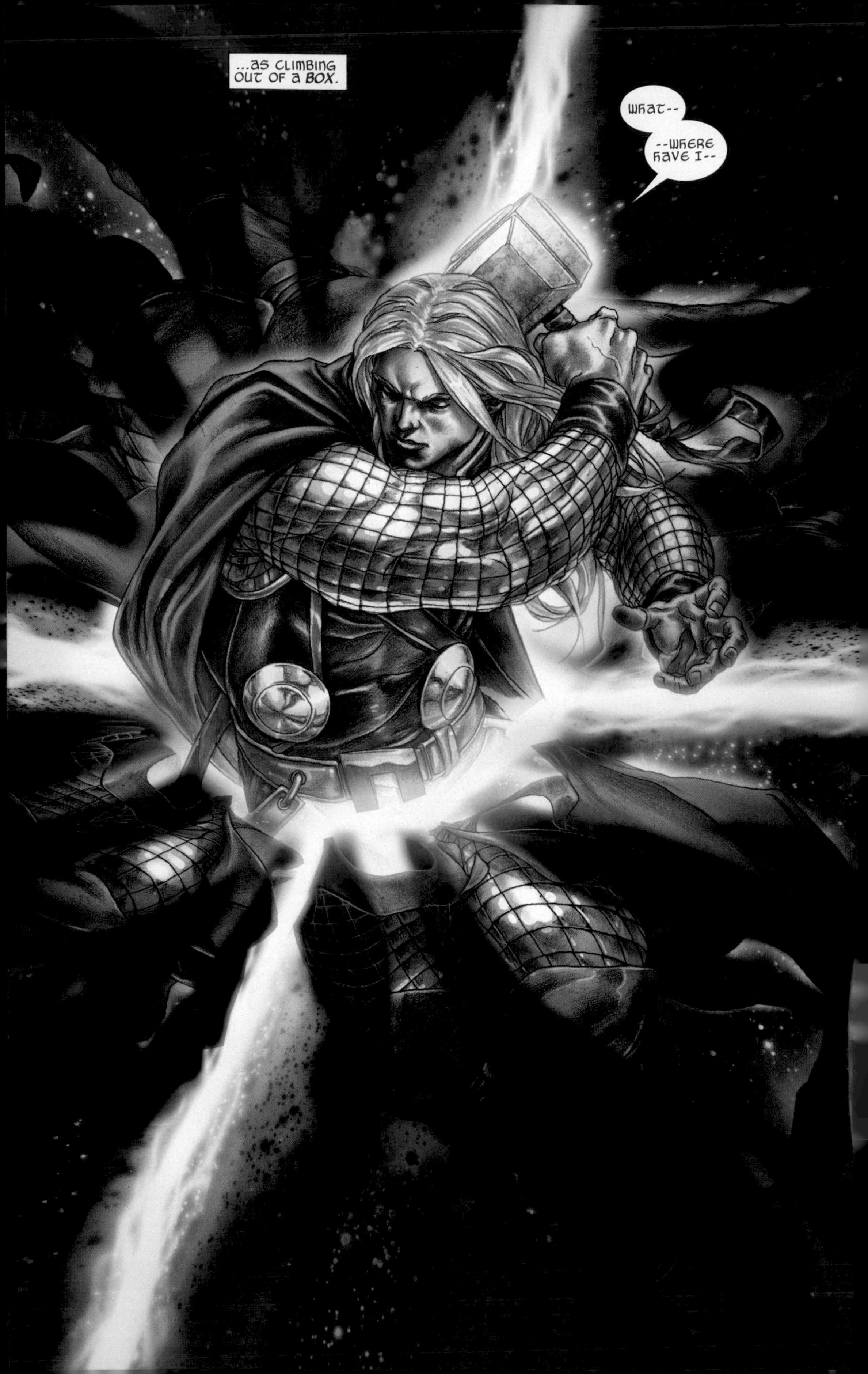
...AS CLIMBING OUT OF A BOX.
WHAT--
--WHERE HAVE I--

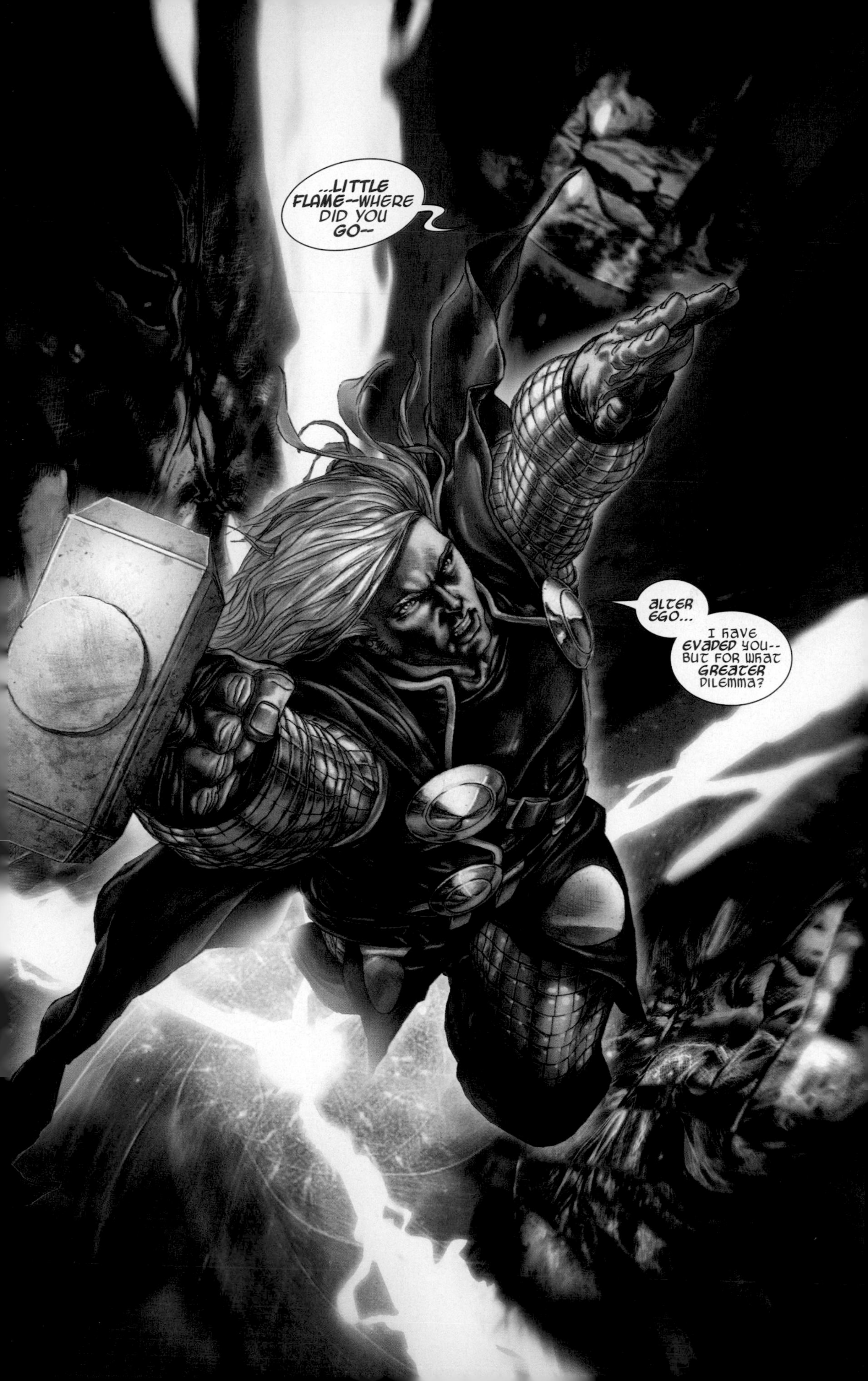
...LITTLE FLAME--WHERE DID YOU GO--
ALTER EGO...
I HAVE EVADED YOU-- BUT FOR WHAT GREATER DILEMMA?

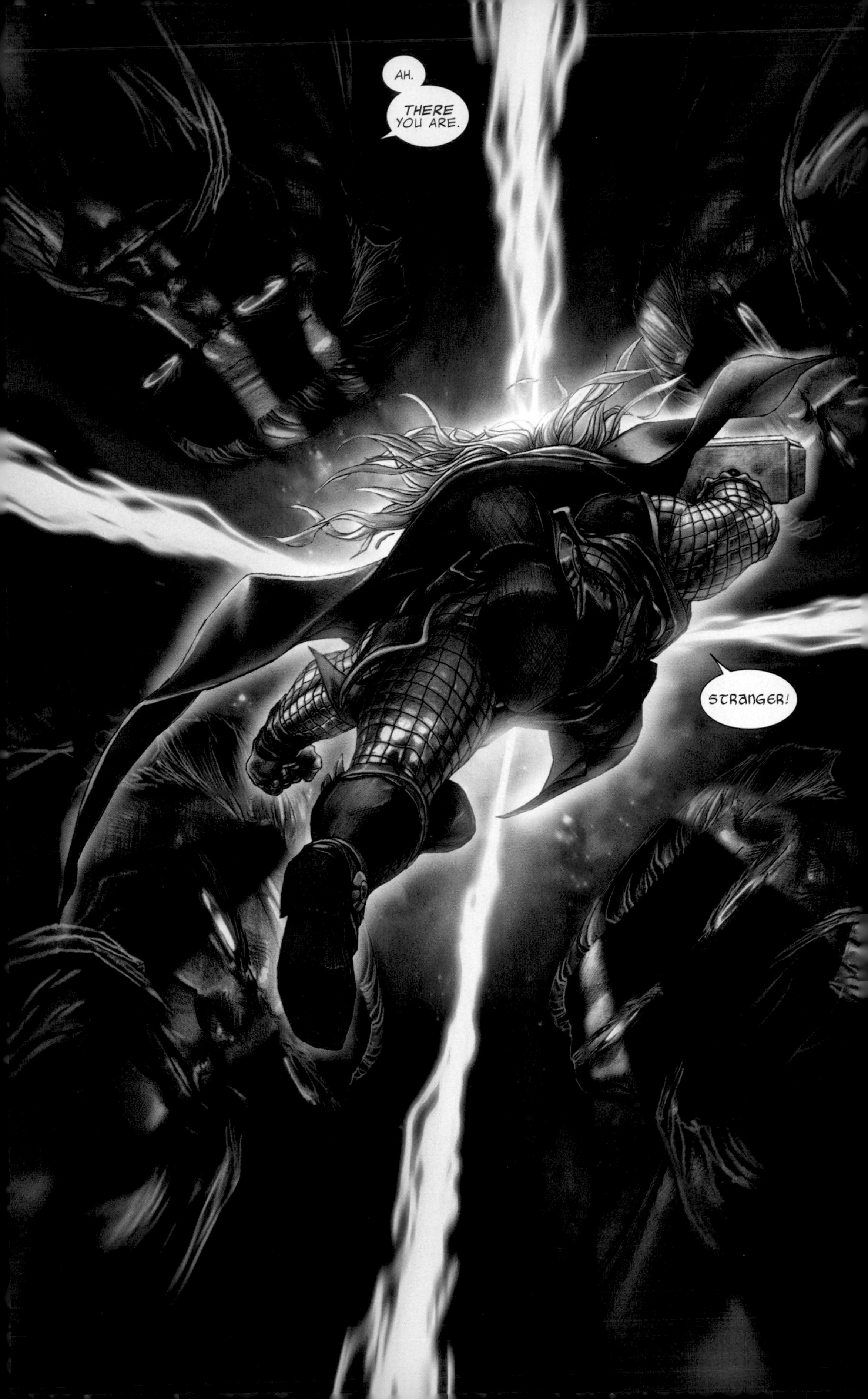
AH.
THERE YOU ARE.
STRANGER!

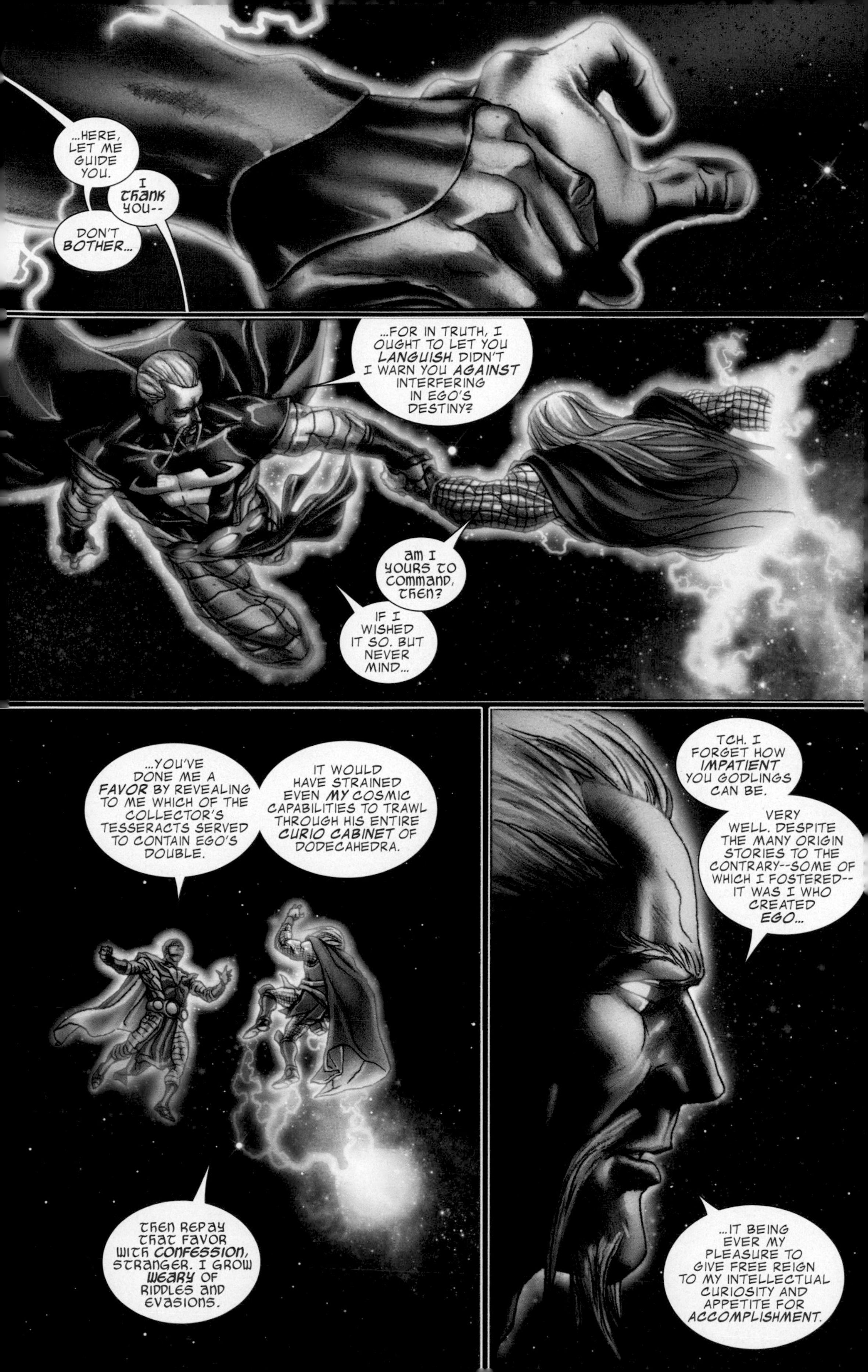
...HERE, LET ME GUIDE YOU.
I THANK YOU--
DON'T BOTHER...
...FOR IN TRUTH, I OUGHT TO LET YOU LANGUISH. DIDN'T I WARN YOU AGAINST INTERFERING IN EGO'S DESTINY?
AM I YOURS TO COMMAND, THEN?
IF I WISHED IT SO. BUT NEVER MIND...
...YOU'VE DONE ME A FAVOR BY REVEALING TO ME WHICH OF THE COLLECTOR'S TESSERACTS SERVED TO CONTAIN EGO'S DOUBLE.
IT WOULD HAVE STRAINED EVEN MY COSMIC CAPABILITIES TO TRAWL THROUGH HIS ENTIRE CURIO CABINET OF DODECAHEDRA.
THEN REPAY THAT FAVOR WITH CONFESSION, STRANGER. I GROW WEARY OF RIDDLES AND EVASIONS.
TCH. I FORGET HOW IMPATIENT YOU GODLINGS CAN BE.
VERY WELL. DESPITE THE MANY ORIGIN STORIES TO THE CONTRARY--SOME OF WHICH I FOSTERED--IT WAS I WHO CREATED EGO...
...IT BEING EVER MY PLEASURE TO GIVE FREE REIGN TO MY INTELLECTUAL CURIOSITY AND APPETITE FOR ACCOMPLISHMENT.

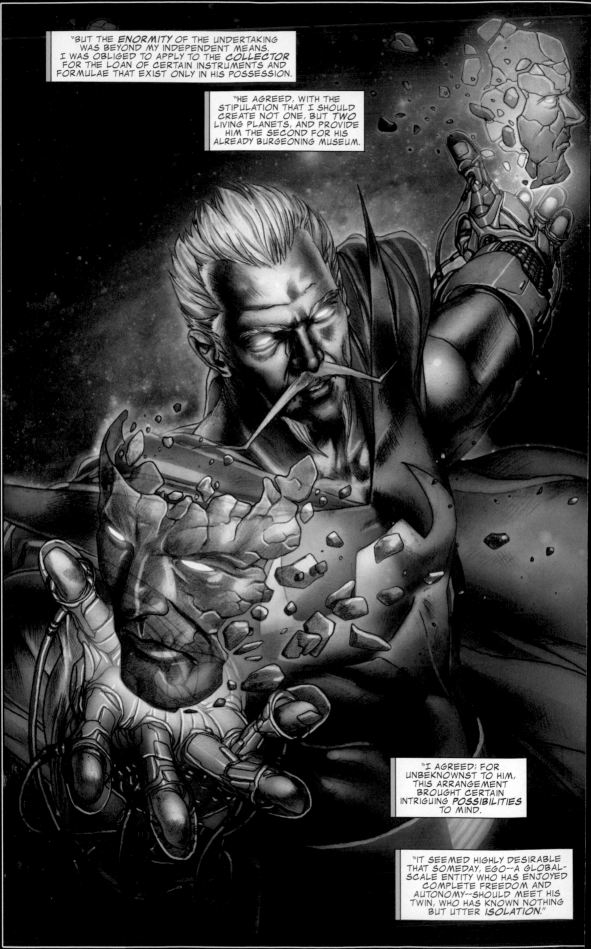

"BUT THE *ENORMITY* OF THE UNDERTAKING WAS BEYOND MY INDEPENDENT MEANS. I WAS OBLIGED TO APPLY TO THE *COLLECTOR* FOR THE LOAN OF CERTAIN INSTRUMENTS AND FORMULAE THAT EXIST ONLY IN HIS POSSESSION.

"HE AGREED, WITH THE STIPULATION THAT I SHOULD CREATE NOT ONE, BUT *TWO* LIVING PLANETS, AND PROVIDE HIM THE SECOND FOR HIS ALREADY BURGEONING MUSEUM.

"I AGREED; FOR UNBEKNOWNST TO HIM, THIS ARRANGEMENT BROUGHT CERTAIN INTRIGUING *POSSIBILITIES* TO MIND.

"IT SEEMED HIGHLY DESIRABLE THAT SOMEDAY, EGO--A GLOBAL-SCALE ENTITY WHO HAS ENJOYED COMPLETE FREEDOM AND AUTONOMY--SHOULD MEET HIS TWIN, WHO HAS KNOWN NOTHING BUT UTTER *ISOLATION*."

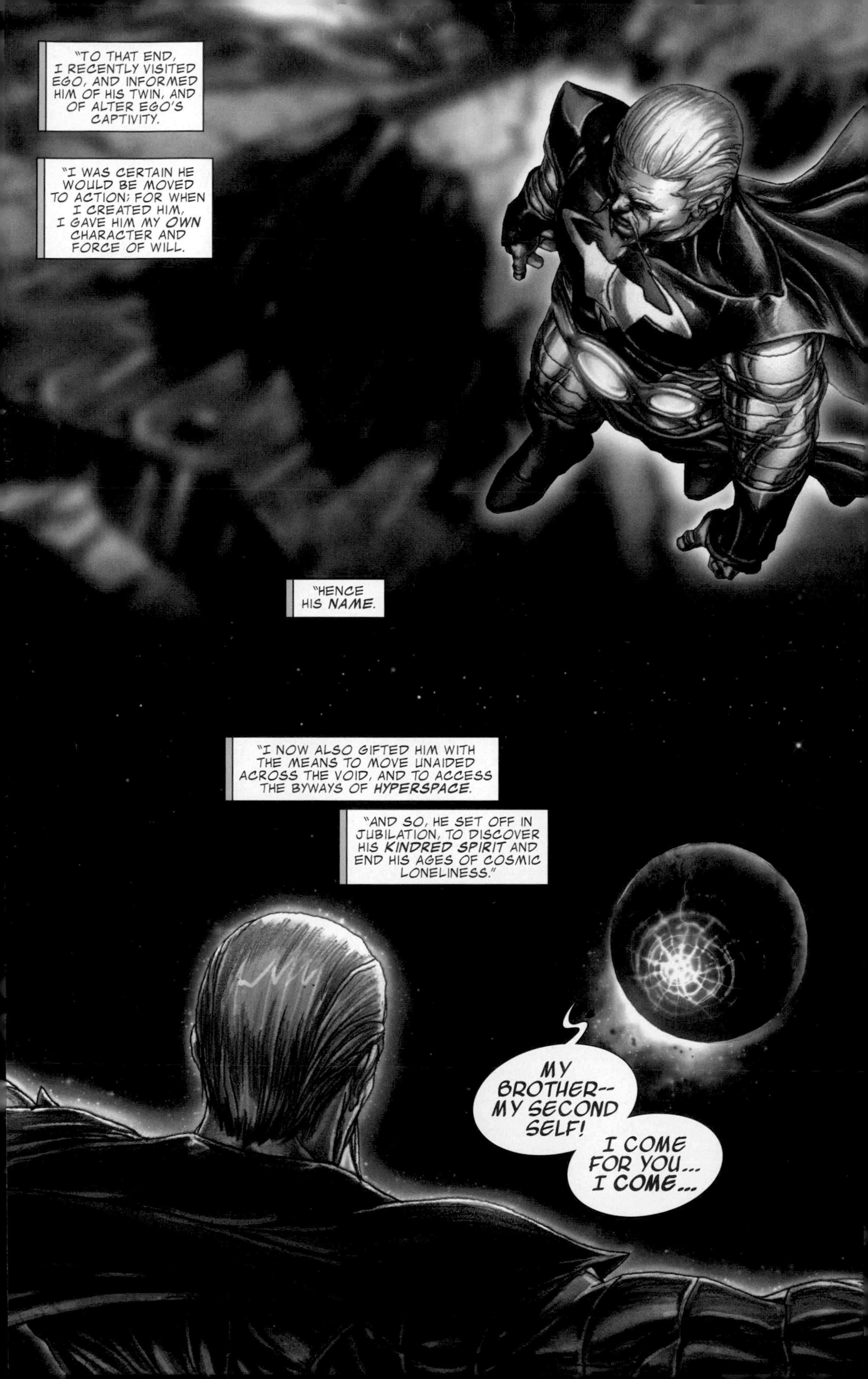
"TO THAT END, I RECENTLY VISITED EGO, AND INFORMED HIM OF HIS TWIN, AND OF ALTER EGO'S CAPTIVITY.
"I WAS CERTAIN HE WOULD BE MOVED TO ACTION; FOR WHEN I CREATED HIM, I GAVE HIM MY OWN CHARACTER AND FORCE OF WILL.
"HENCE HIS NAME.
"I NOW ALSO GIFTED HIM WITH THE MEANS TO MOVE UNAIDED ACROSS THE VOID, AND TO ACCESS THE BYWAYS OF HYPERSPACE.
"AND SO, HE SET OFF IN JUBILATION, TO DISCOVER HIS KINDRED SPIRIT AND END HIS AGES OF COSMIC LONELINESS."
MY BROTHER-- MY SECOND SELF!
I COME FOR YOU... I COME...

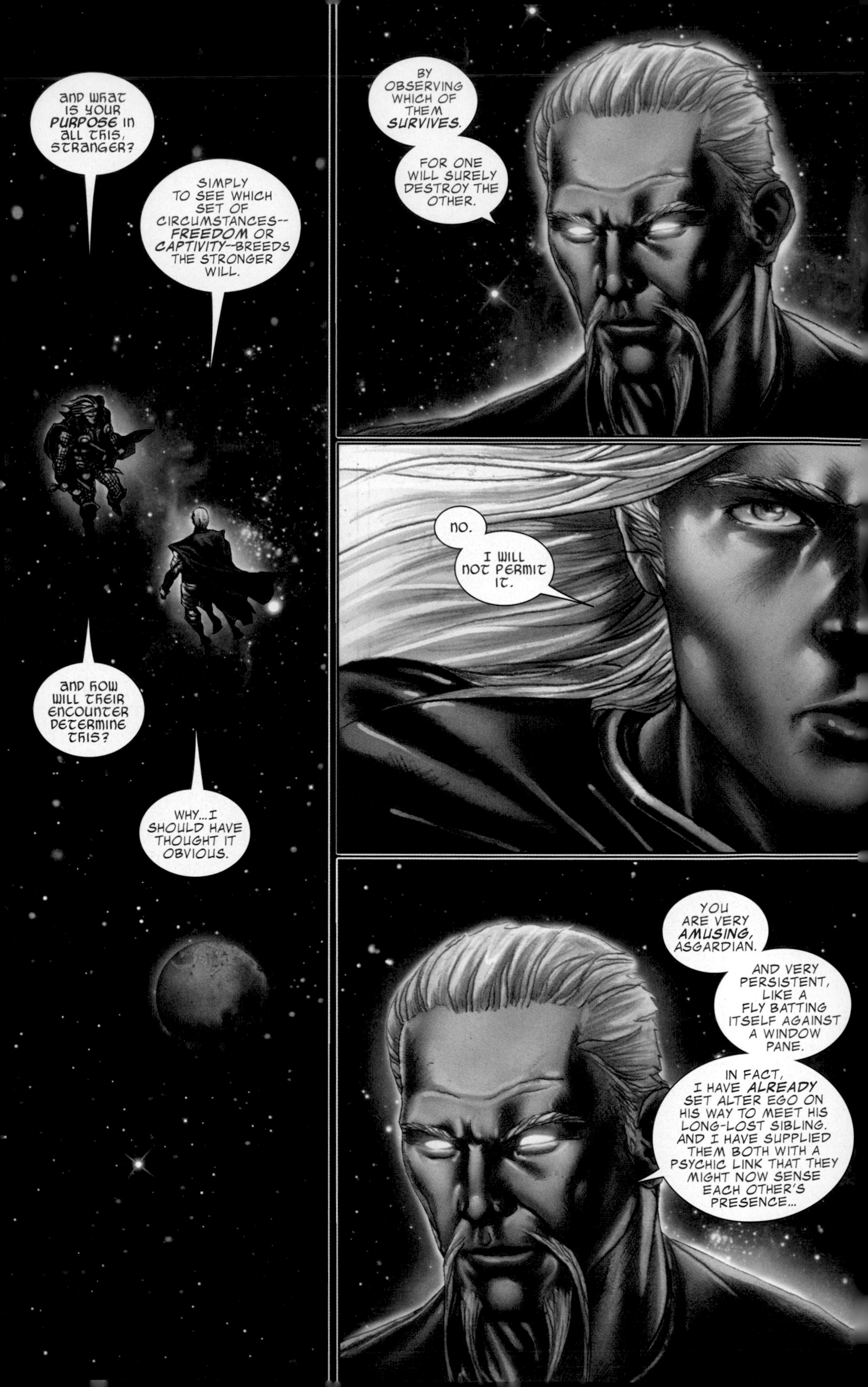
AND WHAT IS YOUR PURPOSE IN ALL THIS, STRANGER?
SIMPLY TO SEE WHICH SET OF CIRCUMSTANCES-- FREEDOM OR CAPTIVITY--BREEDS THE STRONGER WILL.
AND HOW WILL THEIR ENCOUNTER DETERMINE THIS?
WHY...I SHOULD HAVE THOUGHT IT OBVIOUS.
BY OBSERVING WHICH OF THEM SURVIVES.
FOR ONE WILL SURELY DESTROY THE OTHER.
NO.
I WILL NOT PERMIT IT.
YOU ARE VERY AMUSING, ASGARDIAN.
AND VERY PERSISTENT, LIKE A FLY BATTING ITSELF AGAINST A WINDOW PANE.
IN FACT, I HAVE ALREADY SET ALTER EGO ON HIS WAY TO MEET HIS LONG-LOST SIBLING. AND I HAVE SUPPLIED THEM BOTH WITH A PSYCHIC LINK THAT THEY MIGHT NOW SENSE EACH OTHER'S PRESENCE...

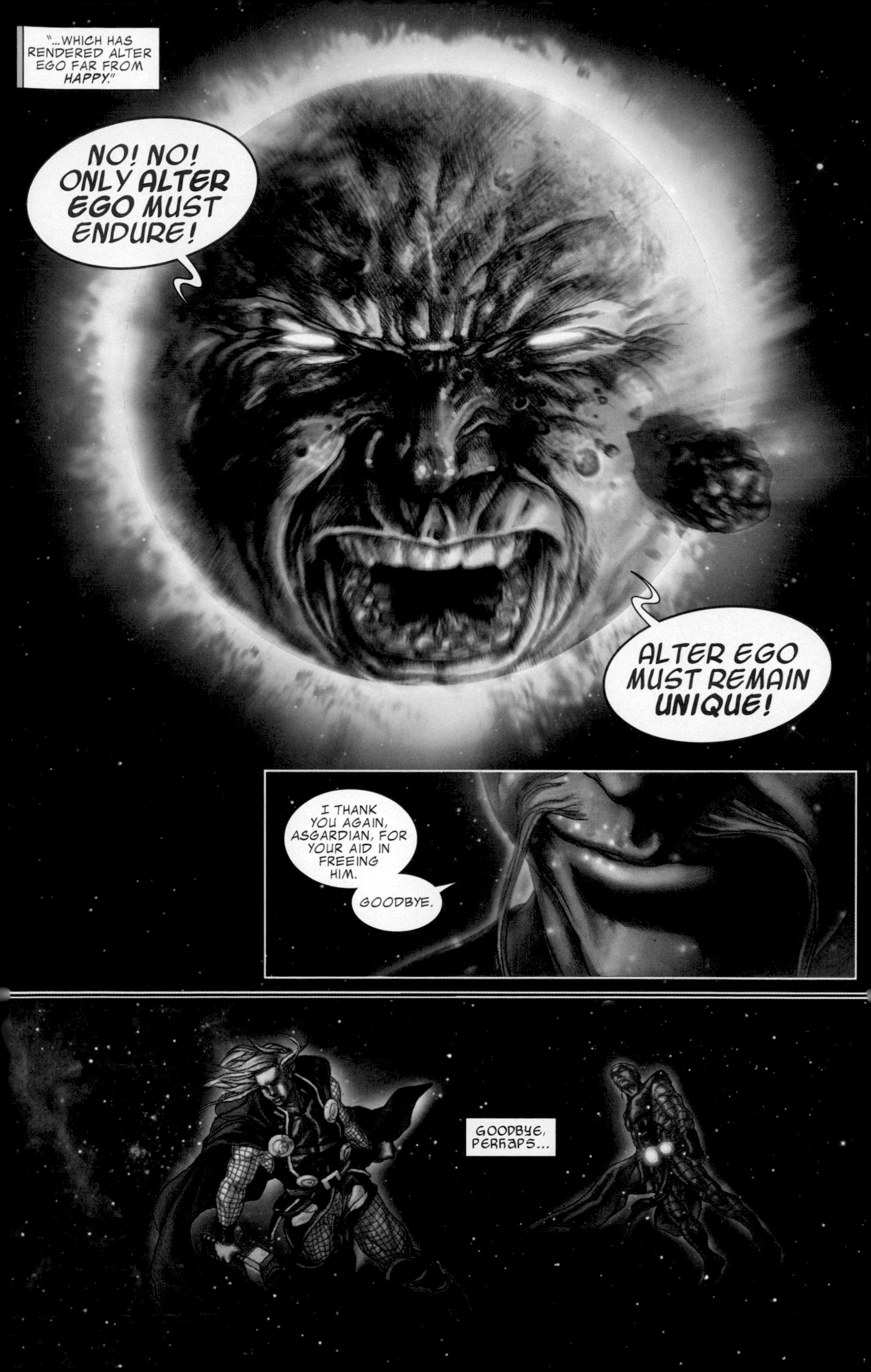
"...WHICH HAS RENDERED ALTER EGO FAR FROM HAPPY."
NO! NO! ONLY ALTER EGO MUST ENDURE!
ALTER EGO MUST REMAIN UNIQUE!
I THANK YOU AGAIN, ASGARDIAN, FOR YOUR AID IN FREEING HIM.
GOODBYE.
GOODBYE, PERHAPS...

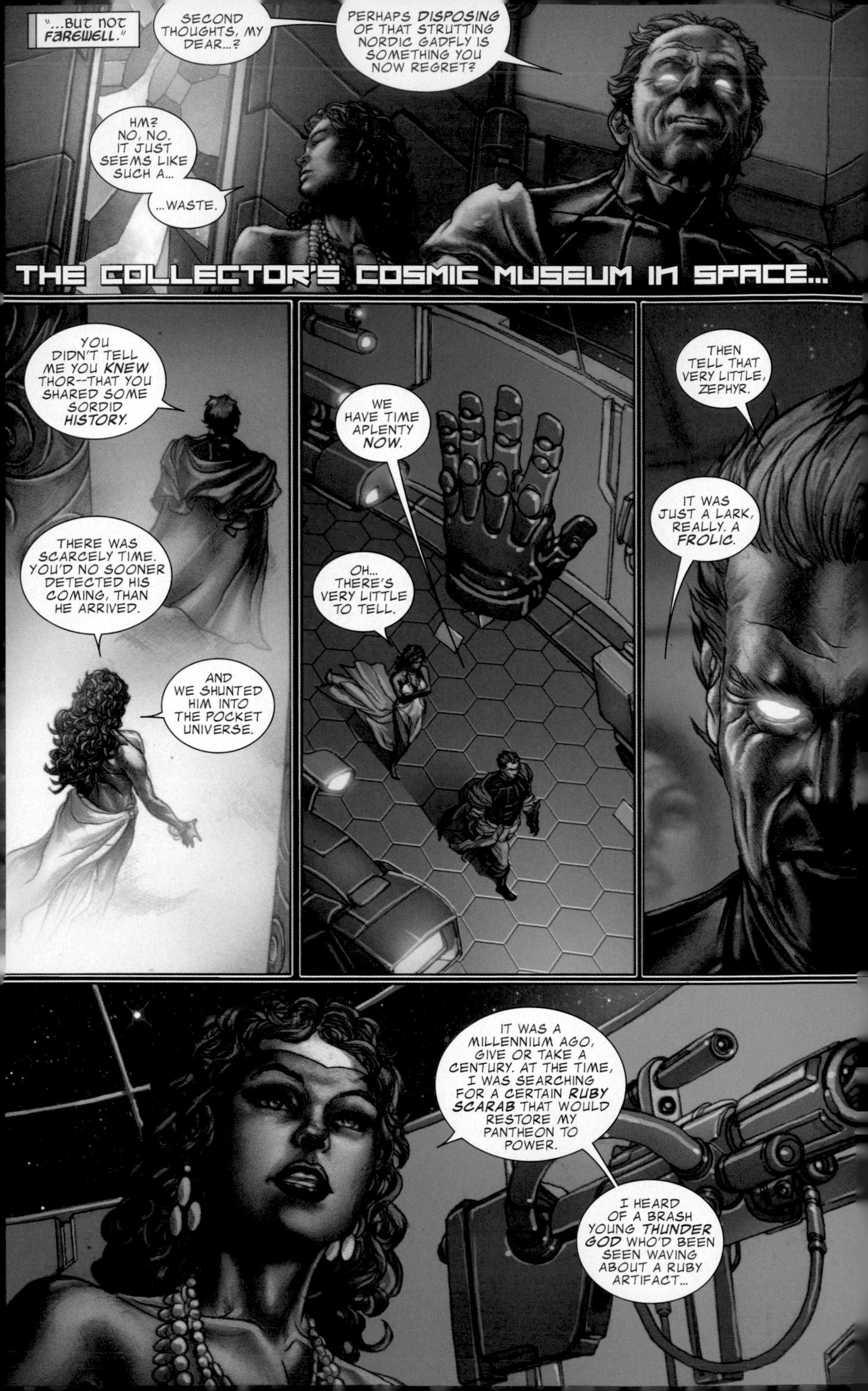
"...BUT NOT FAREWELL."
SECOND THOUGHTS, MY DEAR...?
PERHAPS DISPOSING OF THAT STRUTTING NORDIC GADFLY IS SOMETHING YOU NOW REGRET?
HM? NO, NO. IT JUST SEEMS LIKE SUCH A...
...WASTE.
THE COLLECTOR'S COSMIC MUSEUM IN SPACE...
YOU DIDN'T TELL ME YOU KNEW THOR--THAT YOU SHARED SOME SORDID HISTORY.
THERE WAS SCARCELY TIME. YOU'D NO SOONER DETECTED HIS COMING, THAN HE ARRIVED.
AND WE SHUNTED HIM INTO THE POCKET UNIVERSE.
WE HAVE TIME APLENTY NOW.
OH... THERE'S VERY LITTLE TO TELL.
THEN TELL THAT VERY LITTLE, ZEPHYR.
IT WAS JUST A LARK, REALLY. A FROLIC.
IT WAS A MILLENNIUM AGO, GIVE OR TAKE A CENTURY. AT THE TIME, I WAS SEARCHING FOR A CERTAIN RUBY SCARAB THAT WOULD RESTORE MY PANTHEON TO POWER.
I HEARD OF A BRASH YOUNG THUNDER GOD WHO'D BEEN SEEN WAVING ABOUT A RUBY ARTIFACT...

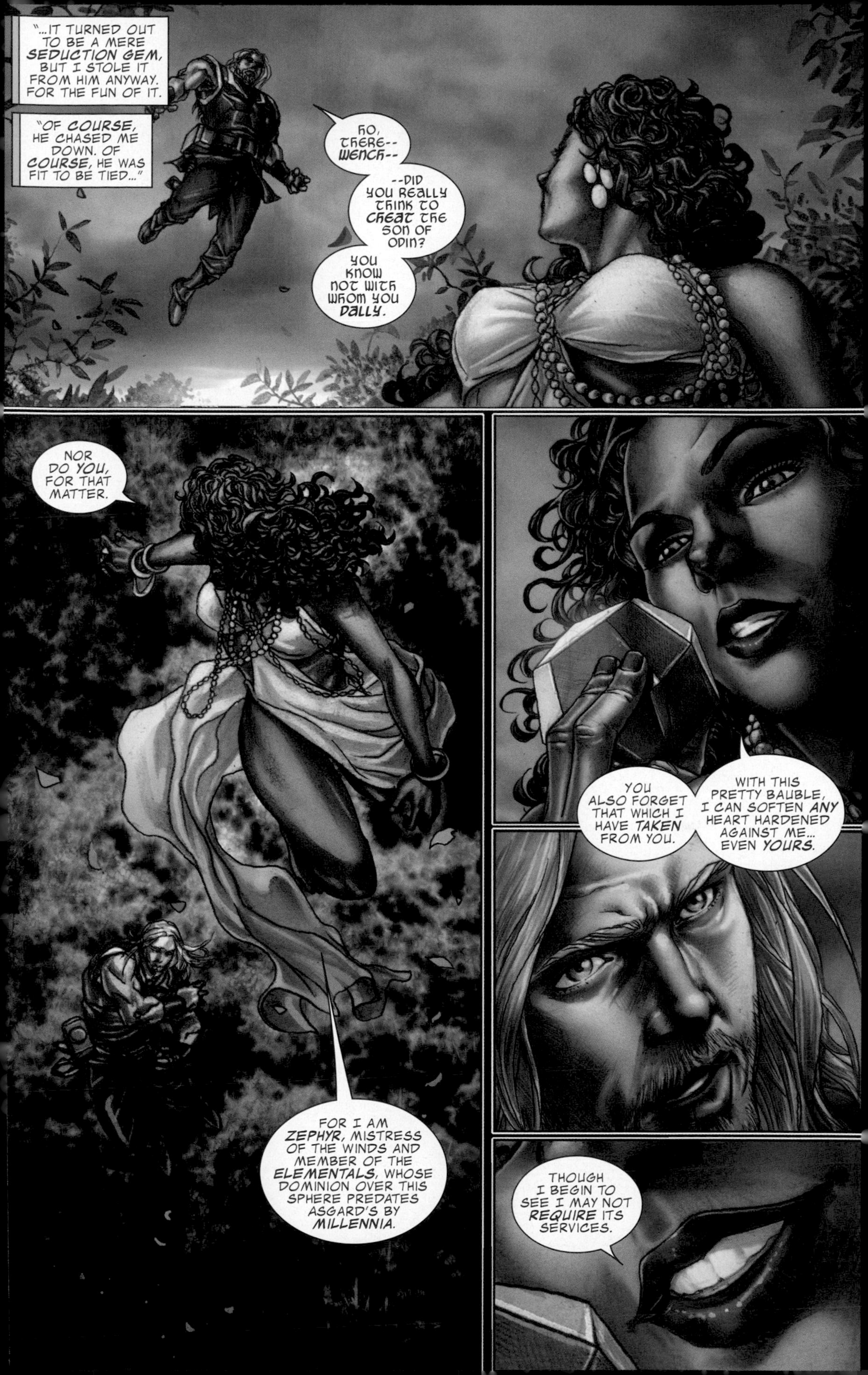
"...IT TURNED OUT TO BE A MERE SEDUCTION GEM, BUT I STOLE IT FROM HIM ANYWAY. FOR THE FUN OF IT.
"OF COURSE, HE CHASED ME DOWN. OF COURSE, HE WAS FIT TO BE TIED..."
HO, THERE--WENCH--
--DID YOU REALLY THINK TO CHEAT THE SON OF ODIN?
YOU KNOW NOT WITH WHOM YOU DALLY.
NOR DO YOU, FOR THAT MATTER.
FOR I AM ZEPHYR, MISTRESS OF THE WINDS AND MEMBER OF THE ELEMENTALS, WHOSE DOMINION OVER THIS SPHERE PREDATES ASGARD'S BY MILLENNIA.
YOU ALSO FORGET THAT WHICH I HAVE TAKEN FROM YOU.
WITH THIS PRETTY BAUBLE, I CAN SOFTEN ANY HEART HARDENED AGAINST ME... EVEN YOURS.
THOUGH I BEGIN TO SEE I MAY NOT REQUIRE ITS SERVICES.

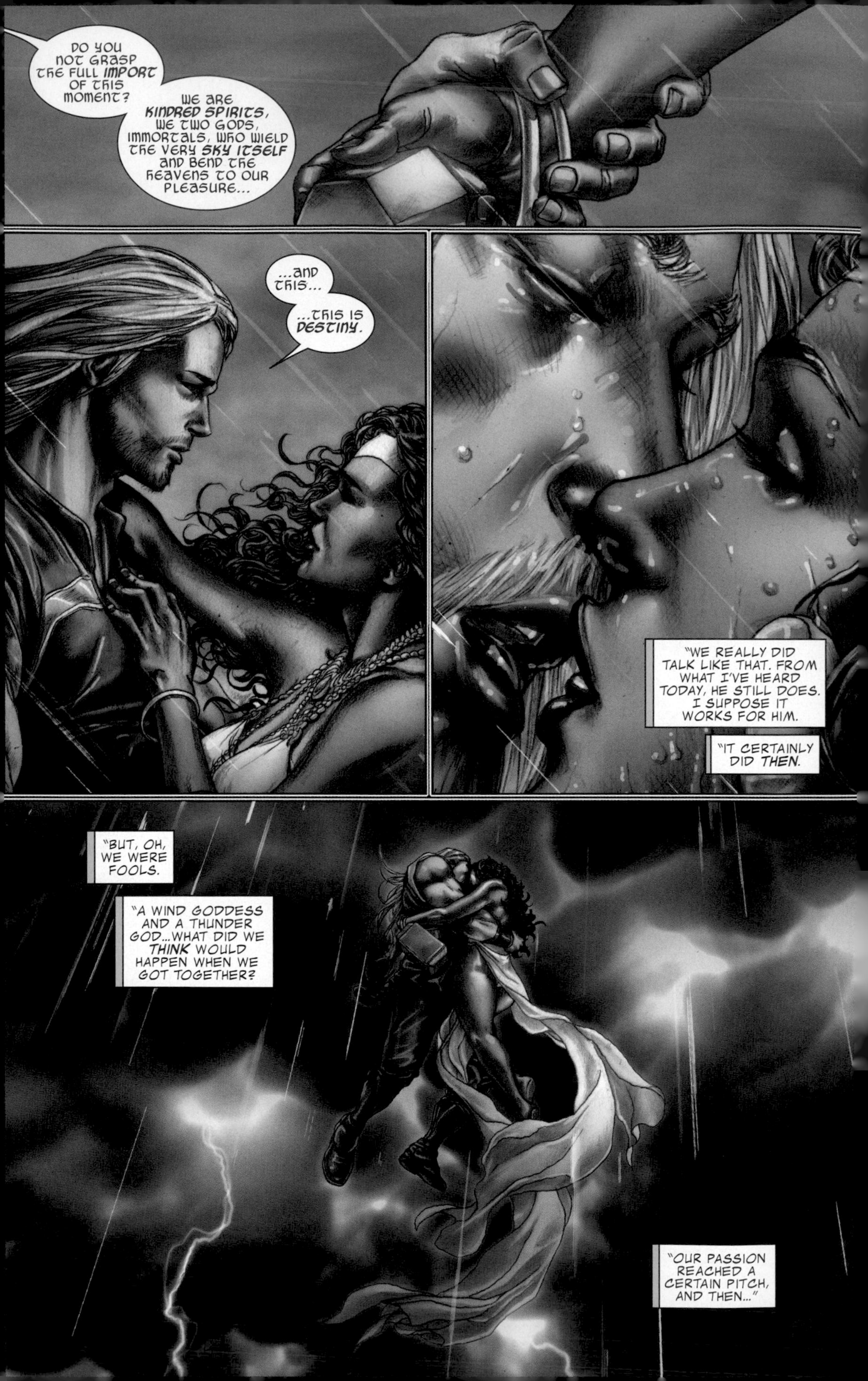
DO YOU NOT GRASP THE FULL IMPORT OF THIS MOMENT?
WE ARE KINDRED SPIRITS, WE TWO GODS, IMMORTALS, WHO WIELD THE VERY SKY ITSELF AND BEND THE HEAVENS TO OUR PLEASURE...
...AND THIS...
...THIS IS DESTINY.
"WE REALLY DID TALK LIKE THAT. FROM WHAT I'VE HEARD TODAY, HE STILL DOES. I SUPPOSE IT WORKS FOR HIM.
"IT CERTAINLY DID THEN.
"BUT, OH, WE WERE FOOLS.
"A WIND GODDESS AND A THUNDER GOD...WHAT DID WE THINK WOULD HAPPEN WHEN WE GOT TOGETHER?
"OUR PASSION REACHED A CERTAIN PITCH, AND THEN..."

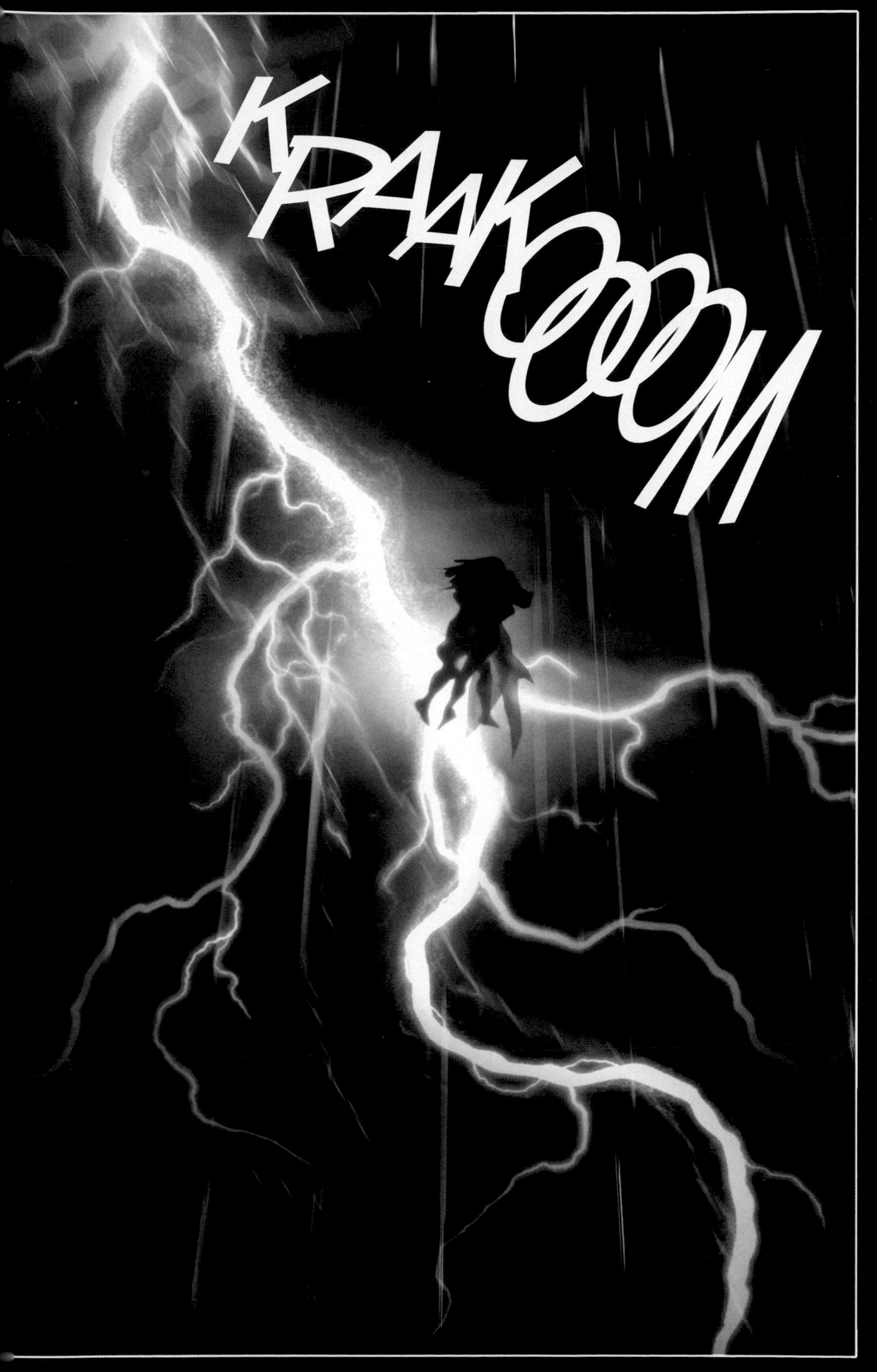
KRAAKOOOM

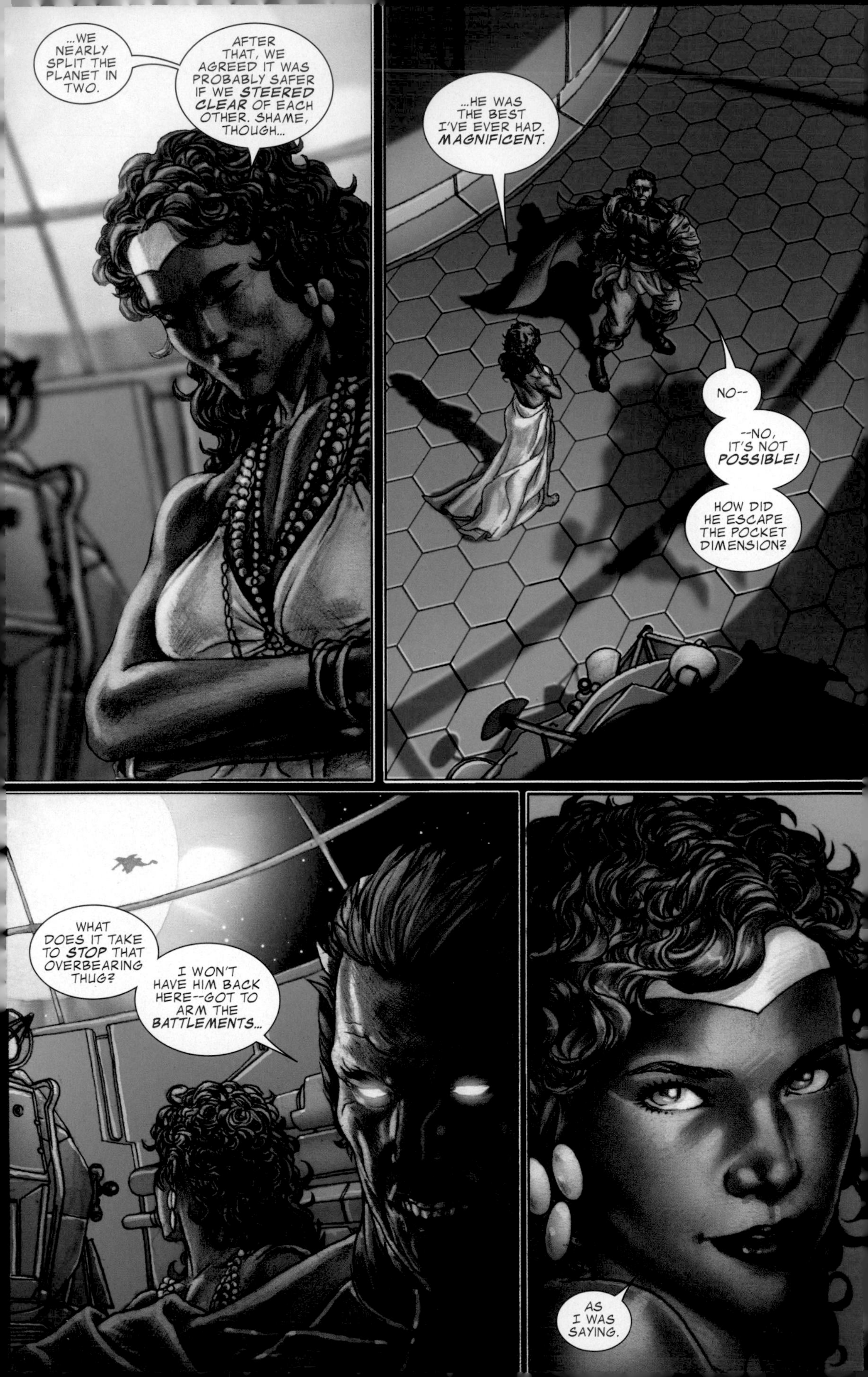
...WE NEARLY SPLIT THE PLANET IN TWO.
AFTER THAT, WE AGREED IT WAS PROBABLY SAFER IF WE STEERED CLEAR OF EACH OTHER. SHAME, THOUGH...
...HE WAS THE BEST I'VE EVER HAD. MAGNIFICENT.
NO--
--NO, IT'S NOT POSSIBLE!
HOW DID HE ESCAPE THE POCKET DIMENSION?
WHAT DOES IT TAKE TO STOP THAT OVERBEARING THUG?
I WON'T HAVE HIM BACK HERE--GOT TO ARM THE BATTLEMENTS...
AS I WAS SAYING.

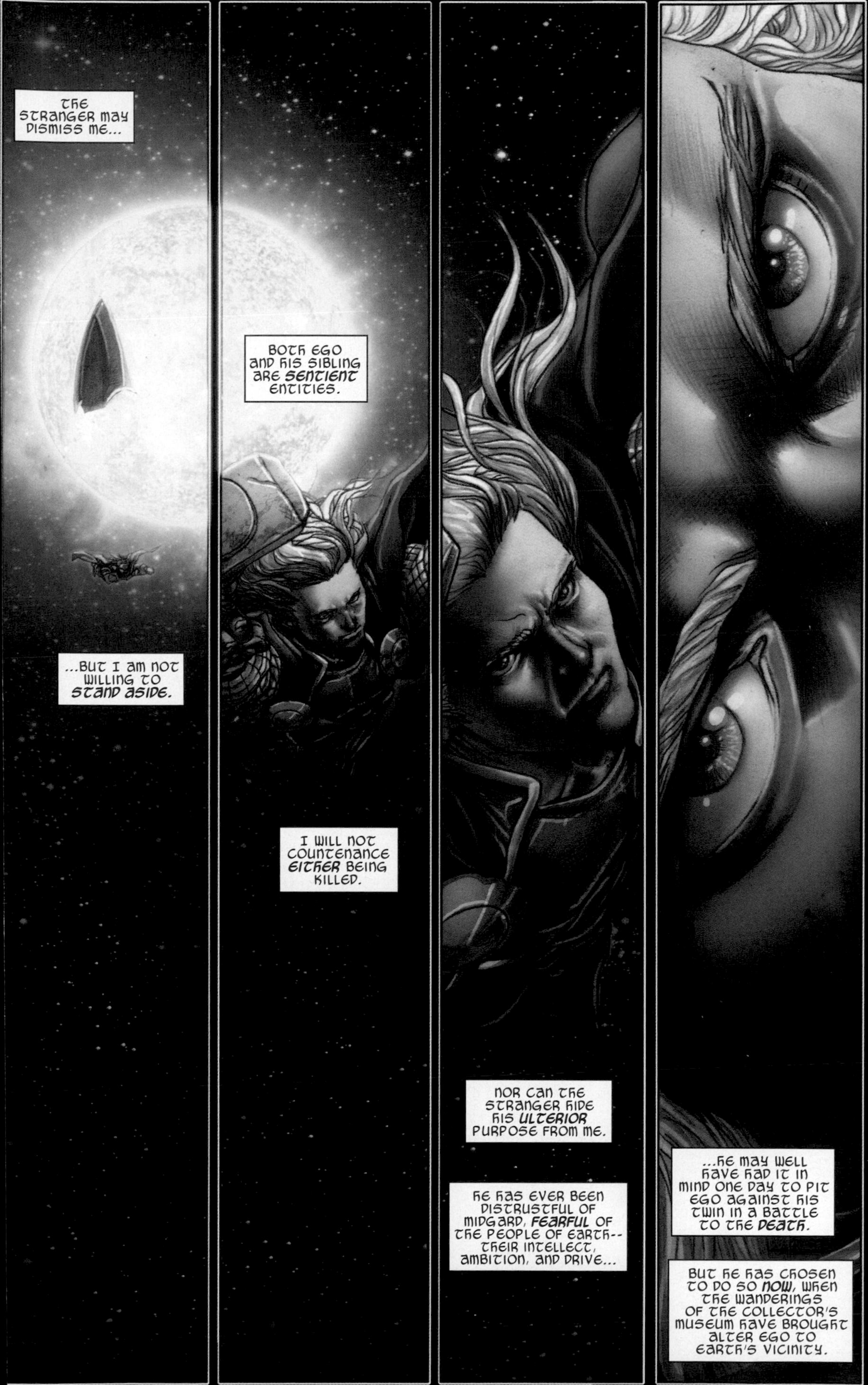
THE STRANGER MAY DISMISS ME...
...BUT I AM NOT WILLING TO STAND ASIDE.
BOTH EGO AND HIS SIBLING ARE SENTIENT ENTITIES.
I WILL NOT COUNTENANCE EITHER BEING KILLED.
NOR CAN THE STRANGER HIDE HIS ULTERIOR PURPOSE FROM ME.
HE HAS EVER BEEN DISTRUSTFUL OF MIDGARD, FEARFUL OF THE PEOPLE OF EARTH-- THEIR INTELLECT, AMBITION, AND DRIVE...
...HE MAY WELL HAVE HAD IT IN MIND ONE DAY TO PIT EGO AGAINST HIS TWIN IN A BATTLE TO THE DEATH.
BUT HE HAS CHOSEN TO DO SO NOW, WHEN THE WANDERINGS OF THE COLLECTOR'S MUSEUM HAVE BROUGHT ALTER EGO TO EARTH'S VICINITY.

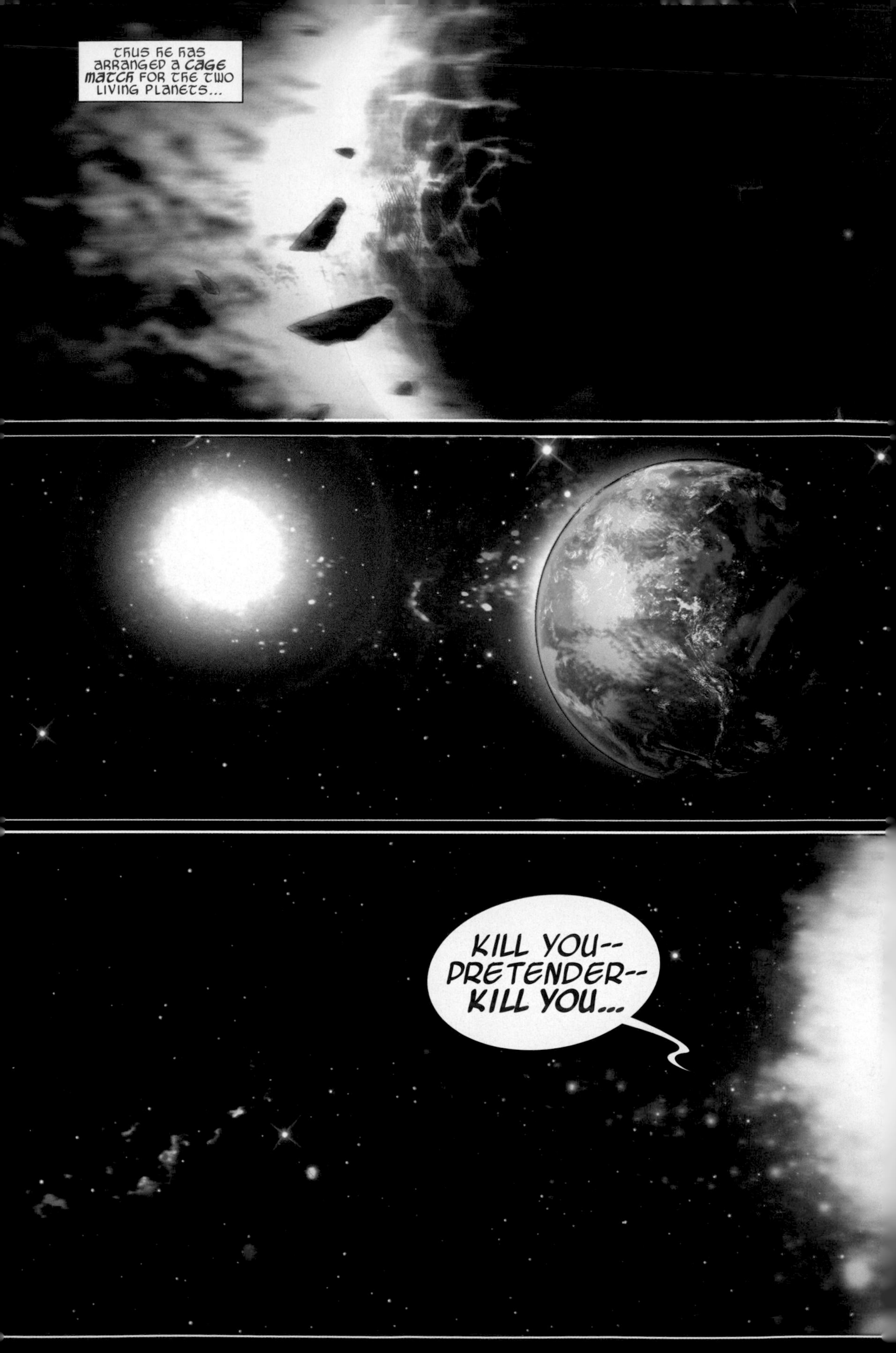
THUS HE HAS ARRANGED A *CAGE MATCH* FOR THE TWO LIVING PLANETS...
KILL YOU-- PRETENDER-- KILL YOU...

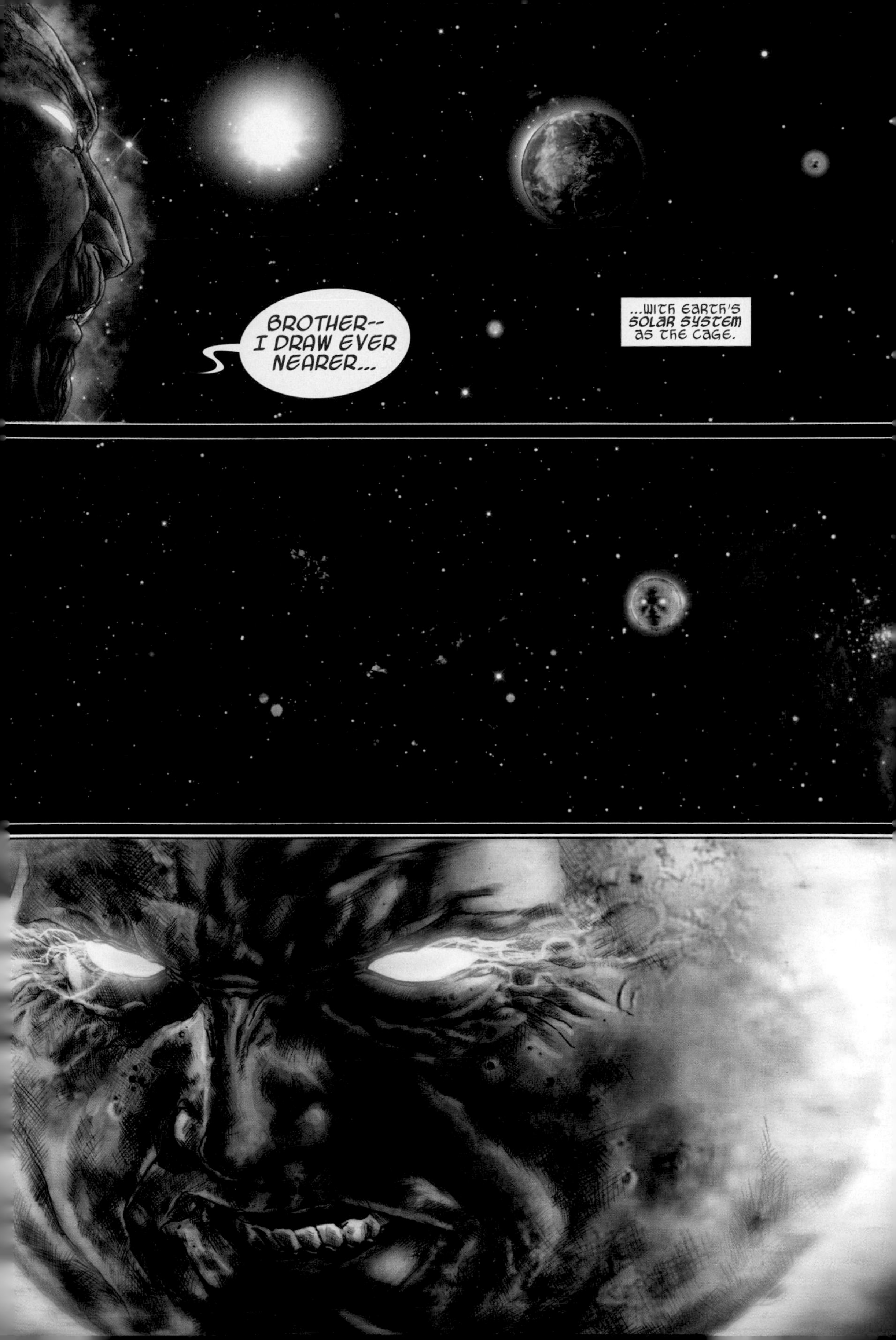

BROTHER-- I DRAW EVER NEARER...
...WITH EARTH'S SOLAR SYSTEM AS THE CAGE.

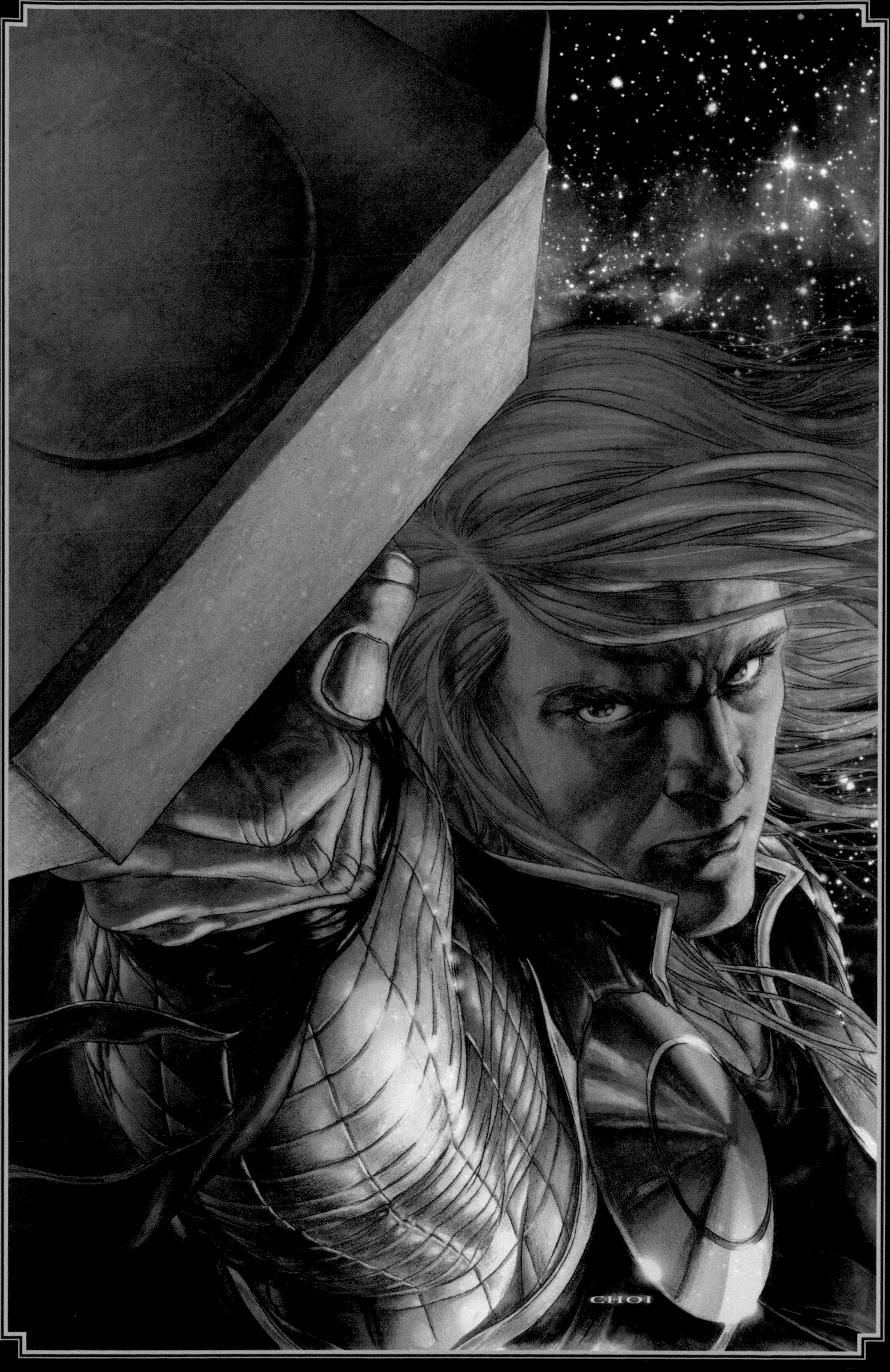
CHOI

Astonishing Thor 4

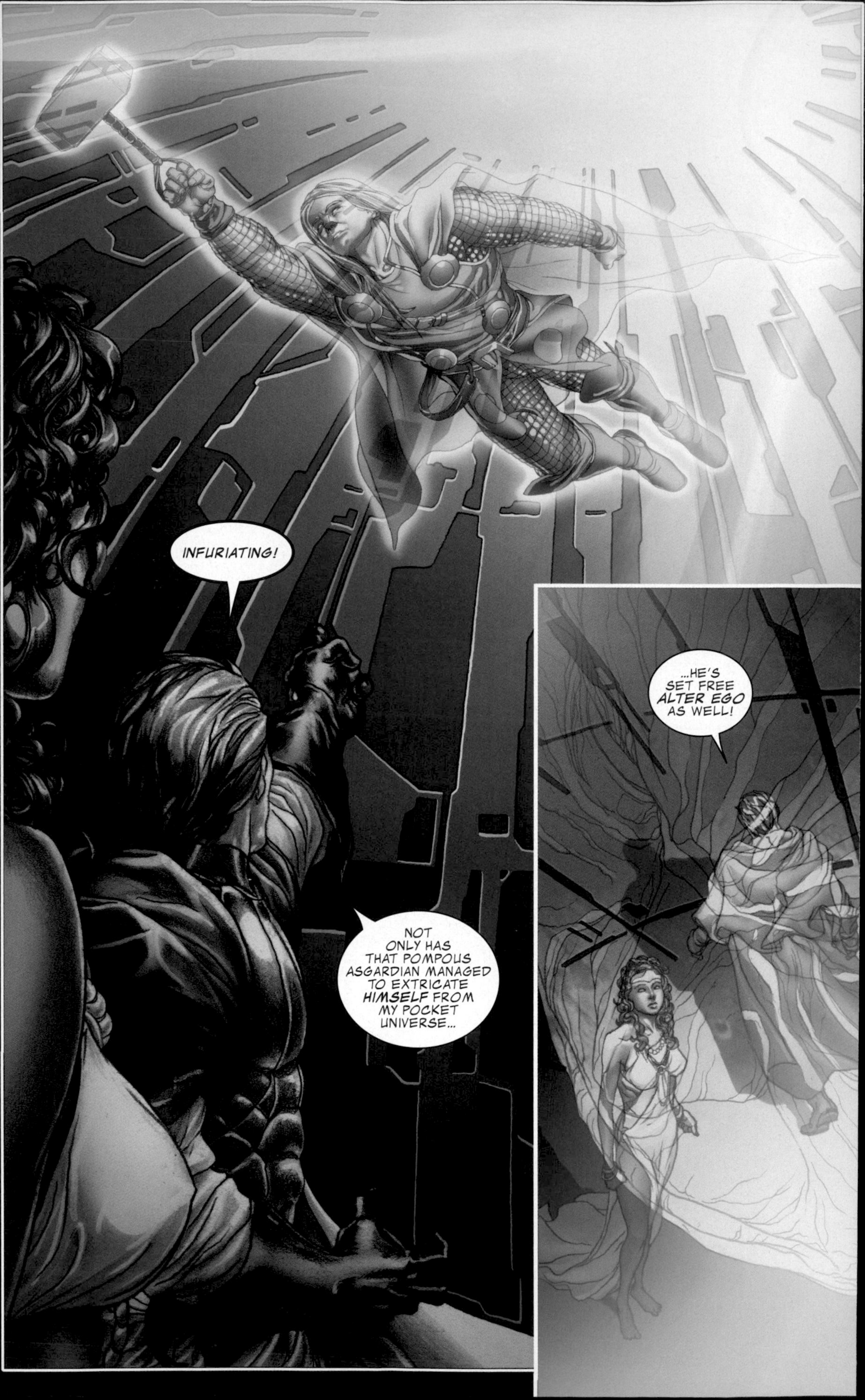
INFURIATING!
NOT ONLY HAS THAT POMPOUS ASGARDIAN MANAGED TO EXTRICATE HIMSELF FROM MY POCKET UNIVERSE...
...HE'S SET FREE ALTER EGO AS WELL!

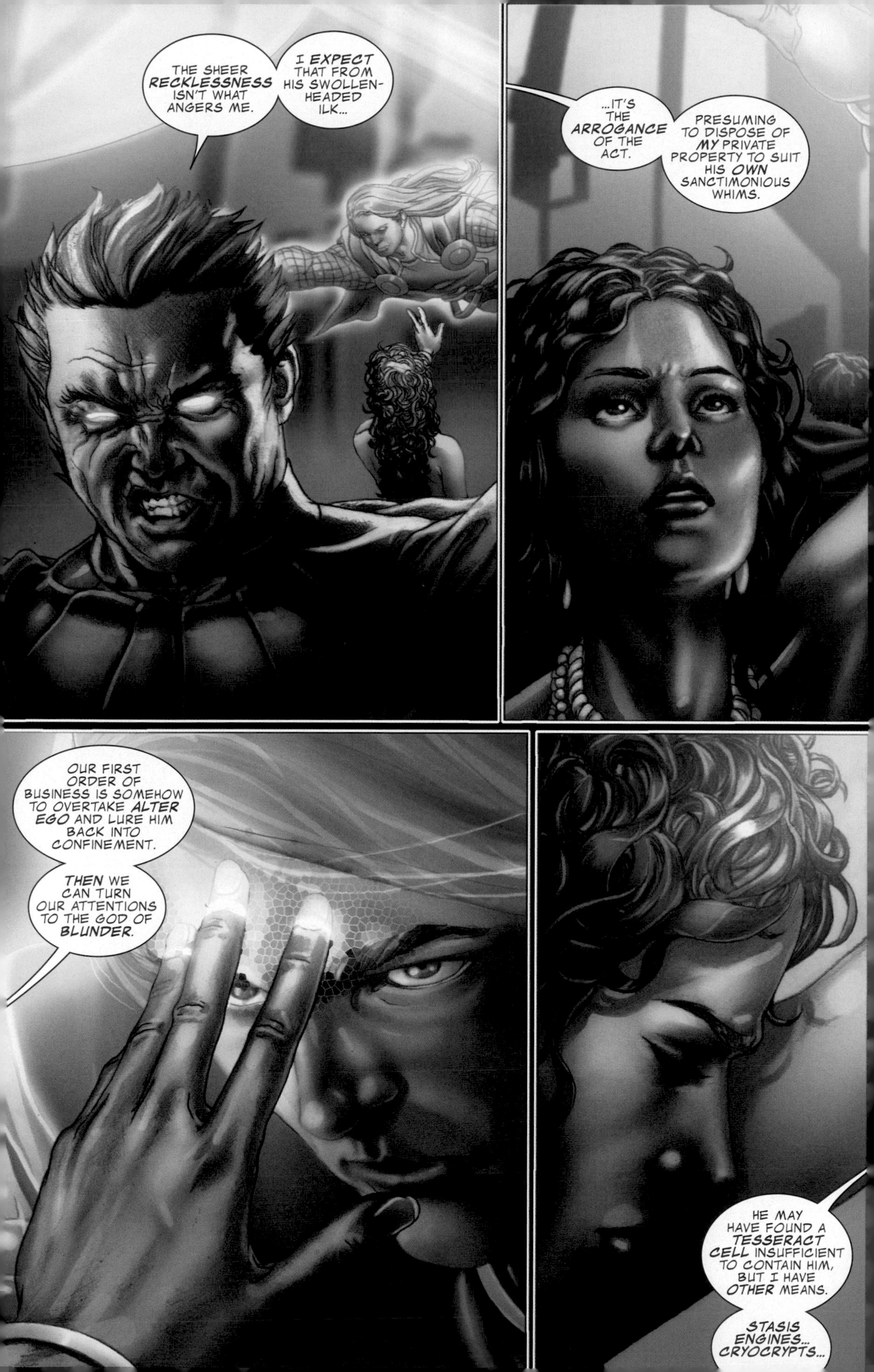
THE SHEER RECKLESSNESS ISN'T WHAT ANGERS ME.
I EXPECT THAT FROM HIS SWOLLEN-HEADED ILK...
...IT'S THE ARROGANCE OF THE ACT.
PRESUMING TO DISPOSE OF MY PRIVATE PROPERTY TO SUIT HIS OWN SANCTIMONIOUS WHIMS.
OUR FIRST ORDER OF BUSINESS IS SOMEHOW TO OVERTAKE ALTER EGO AND LURE HIM BACK INTO CONFINEMENT.
THEN WE CAN TURN OUR ATTENTIONS TO THE GOD OF BLUNDER.
HE MAY HAVE FOUND A TESSERACT CELL INSUFFICIENT TO CONTAIN HIM, BUT I HAVE OTHER MEANS.
STASIS ENGINES... CRYOCRYPTS...

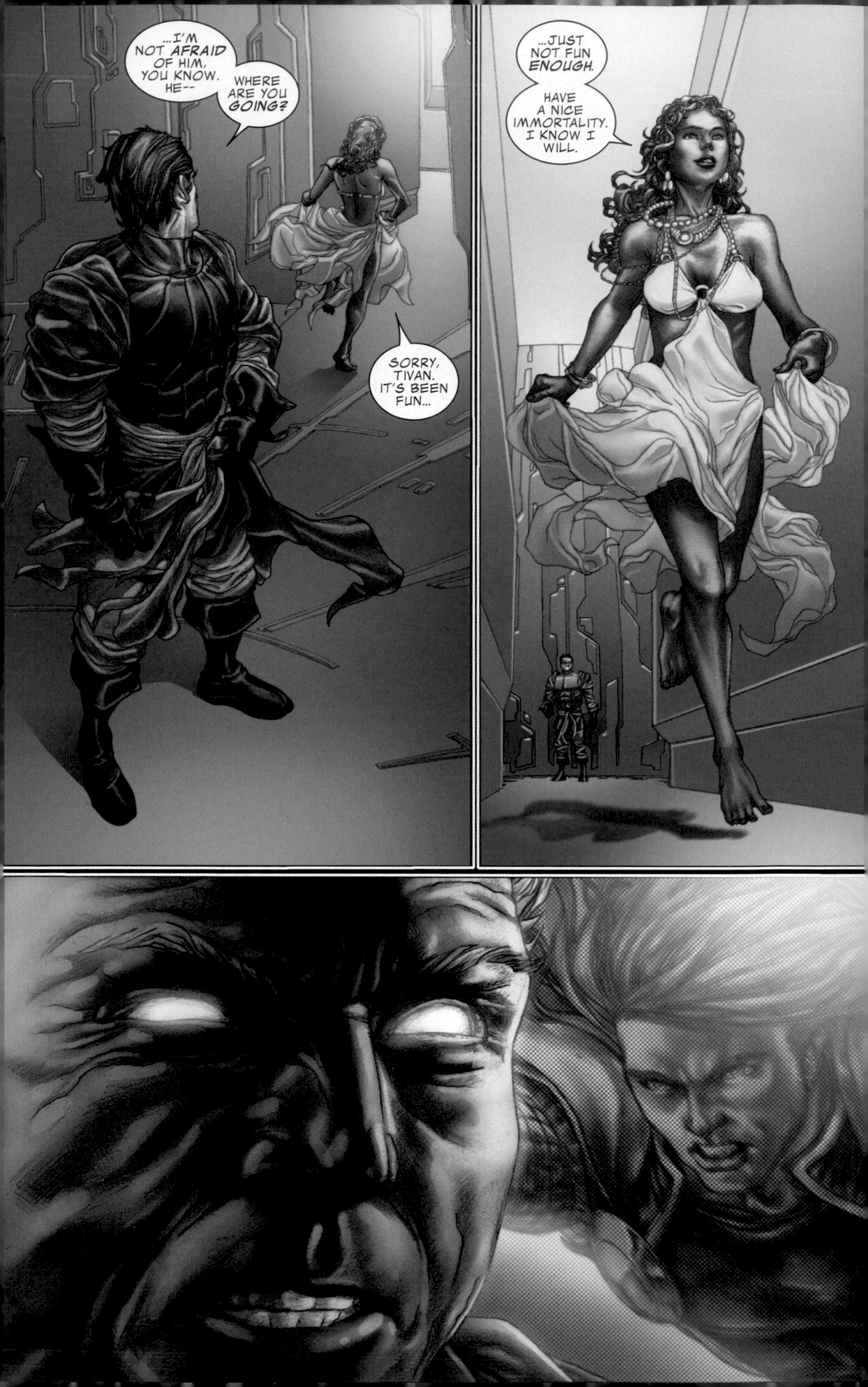
...I'M NOT AFRAID OF HIM, YOU KNOW. HE--
WHERE ARE YOU GOING?
SORRY, TIVAN. IT'S BEEN FUN...
...JUST NOT FUN ENOUGH.
HAVE A NICE IMMORTALITY. I KNOW I WILL.

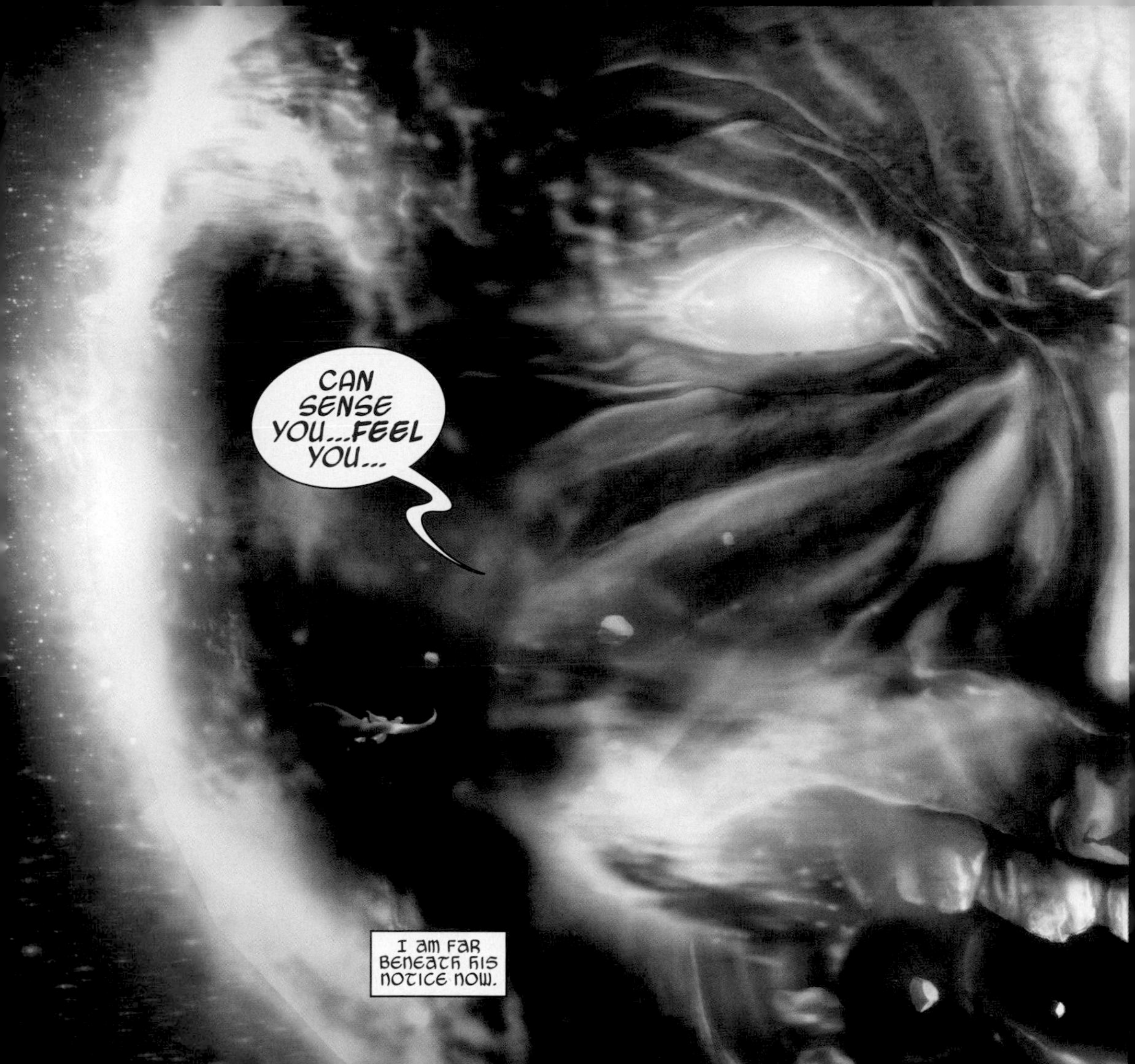
CAN SENSE YOU...FEEL YOU...
I AM FAR BENEATH HIS NOTICE NOW.

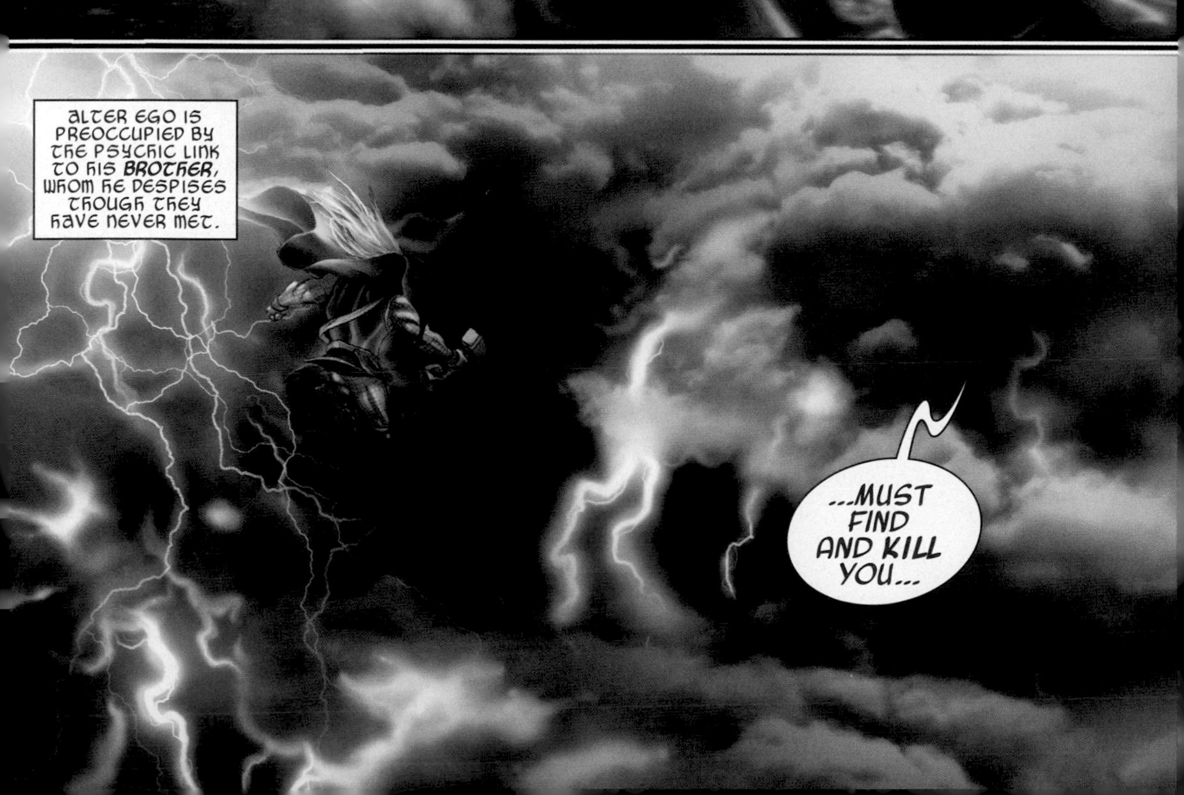
ALTER EGO IS PREOCCUPIED BY THE PSYCHIC LINK TO HIS BROTHER, WHOM HE DESPISES THOUGH THEY HAVE NEVER MET.
...MUST FIND AND KILL YOU...

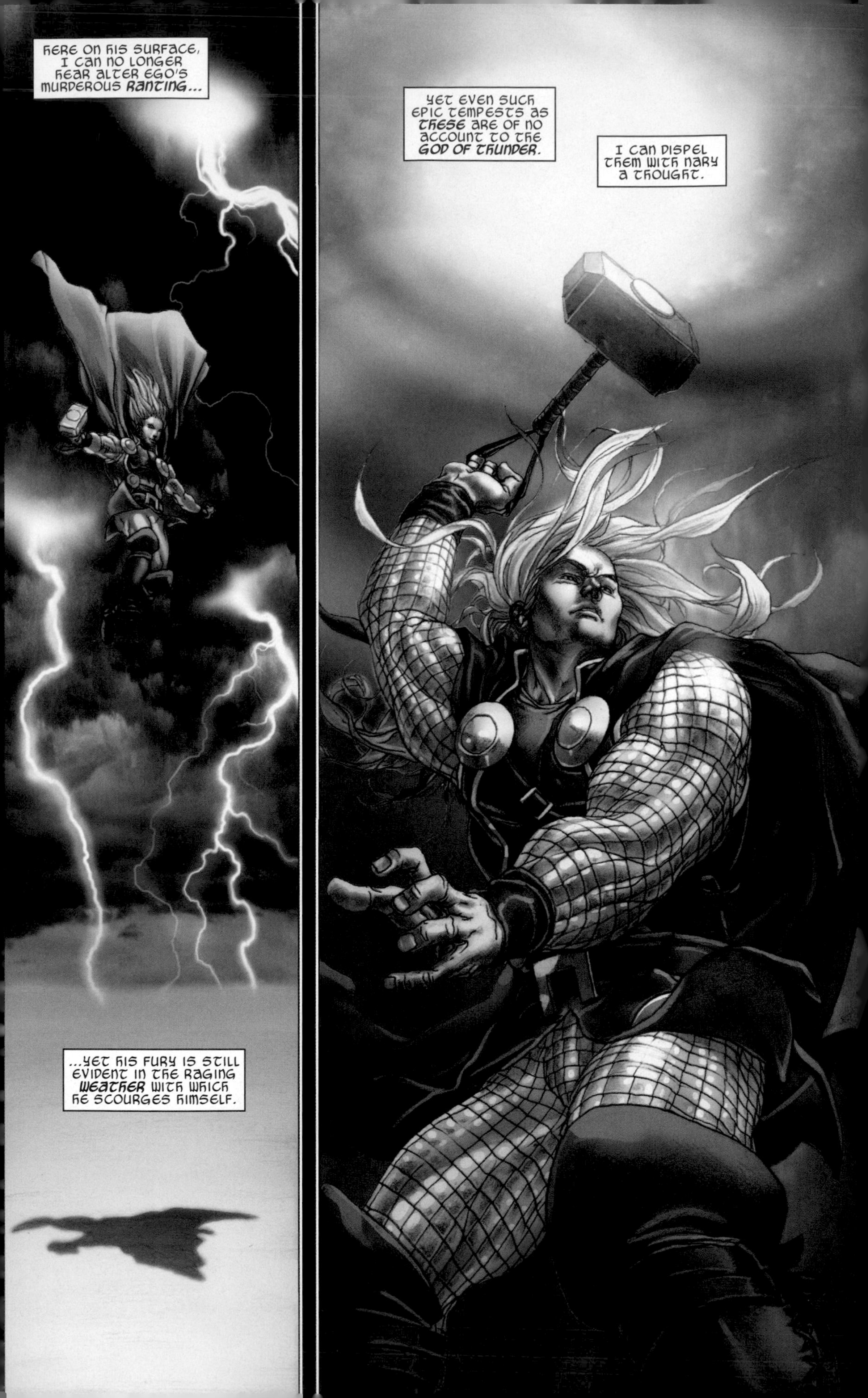
HERE ON HIS SURFACE, I CAN NO LONGER HEAR ALTER EGO'S MURDEROUS RANTING...
...YET HIS FURY IS STILL EVIDENT IN THE RAGING WEATHER WITH WHICH HE SCOURGES HIMSELF.
YET EVEN SUCH EPIC TEMPESTS AS THESE ARE OF NO ACCOUNT TO THE GOD OF THUNDER.
I CAN DISPEL THEM WITH NARY A THOUGHT.

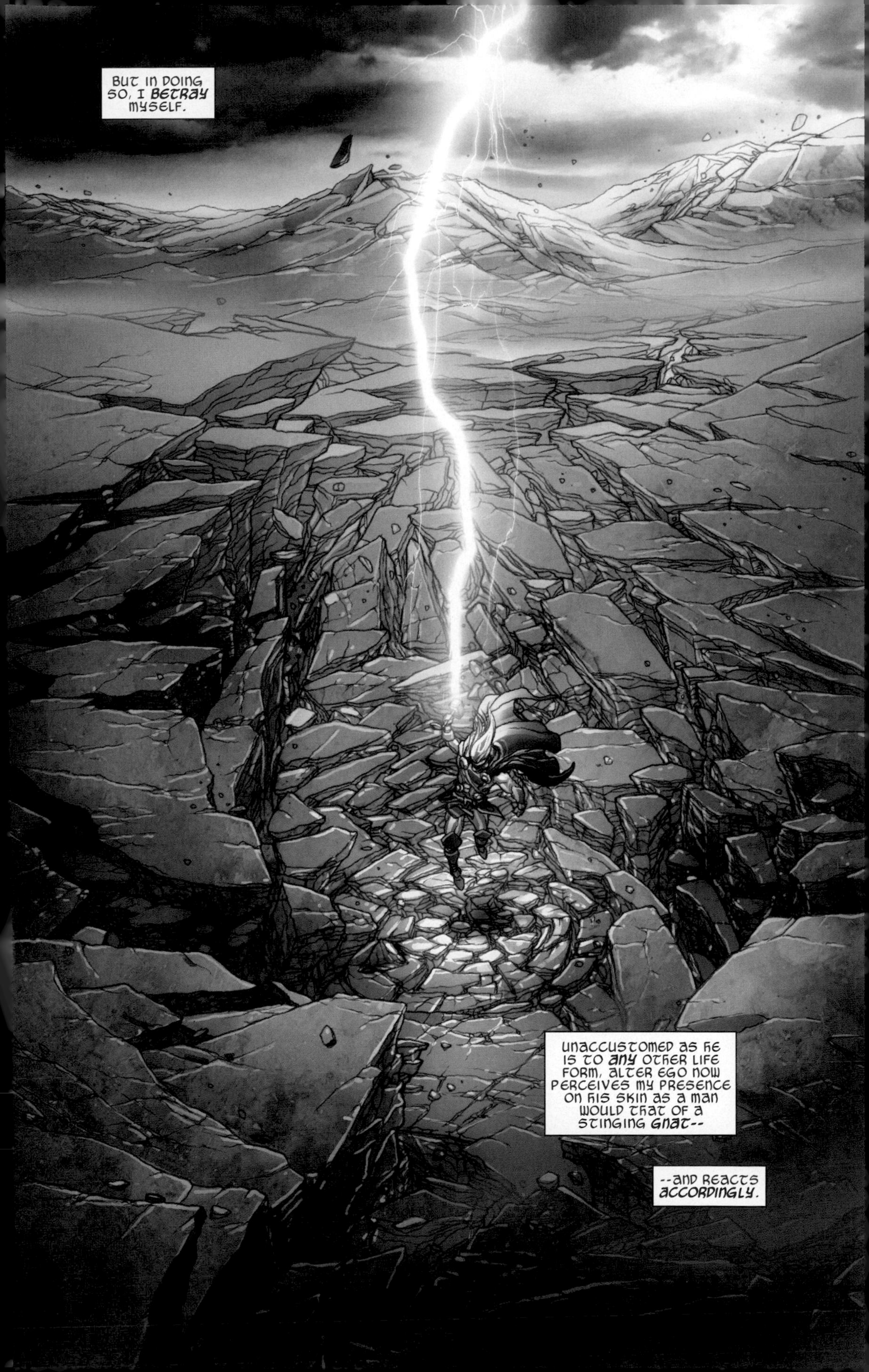
BUT IN DOING SO, I BETRAY MYSELF.
UNACCUSTOMED AS HE IS TO ANY OTHER LIFE FORM, ALTER EGO NOW PERCEIVES MY PRESENCE ON HIS SKIN AS A MAN WOULD THAT OF A STINGING GNAT--
--AND REACTS ACCORDINGLY.

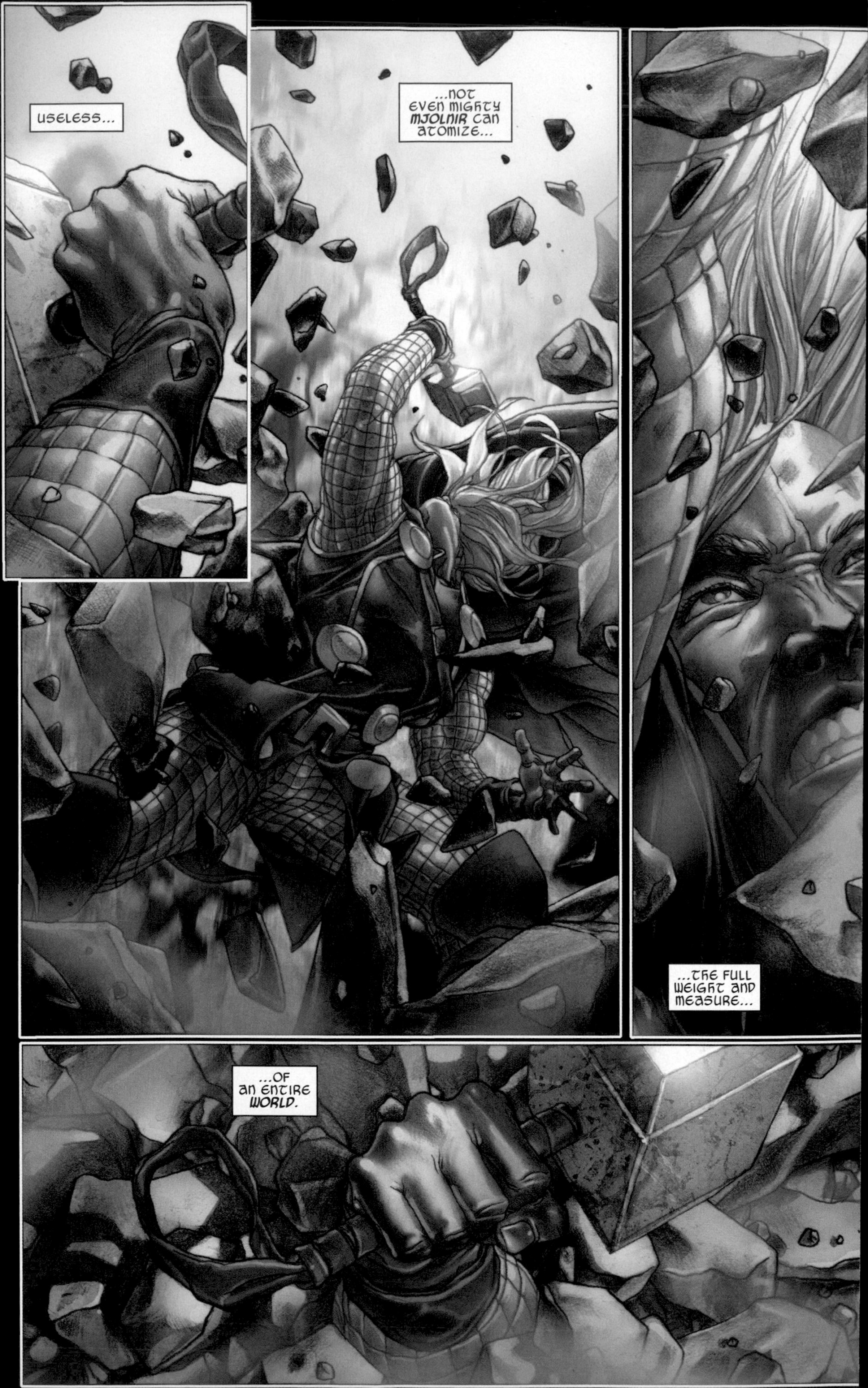
USELESS...
...NOT EVEN MIGHTY MJOLNIR CAN ATOMIZE...
...THE FULL WEIGHT AND MEASURE...
...OF AN ENTIRE WORLD.

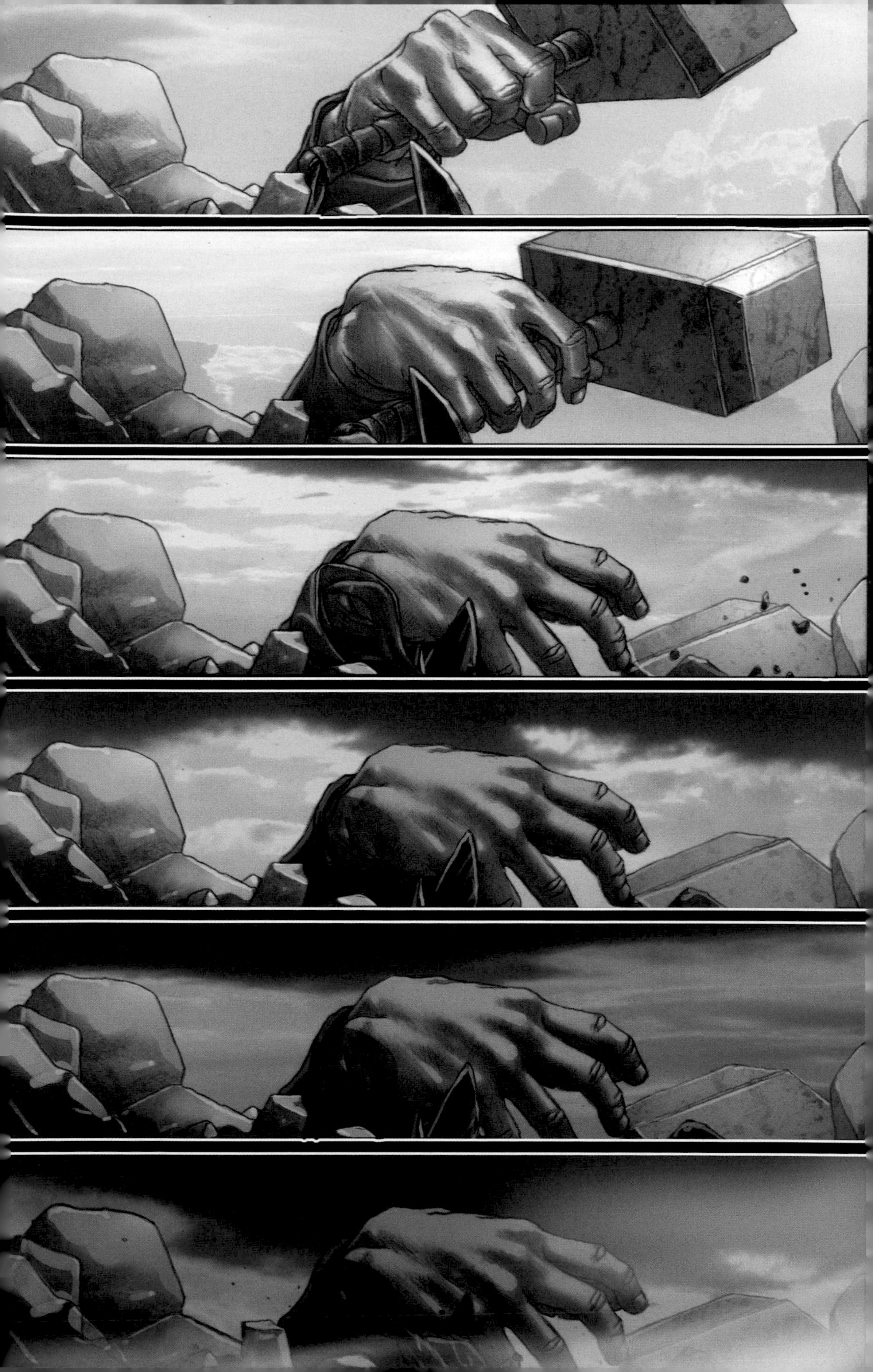

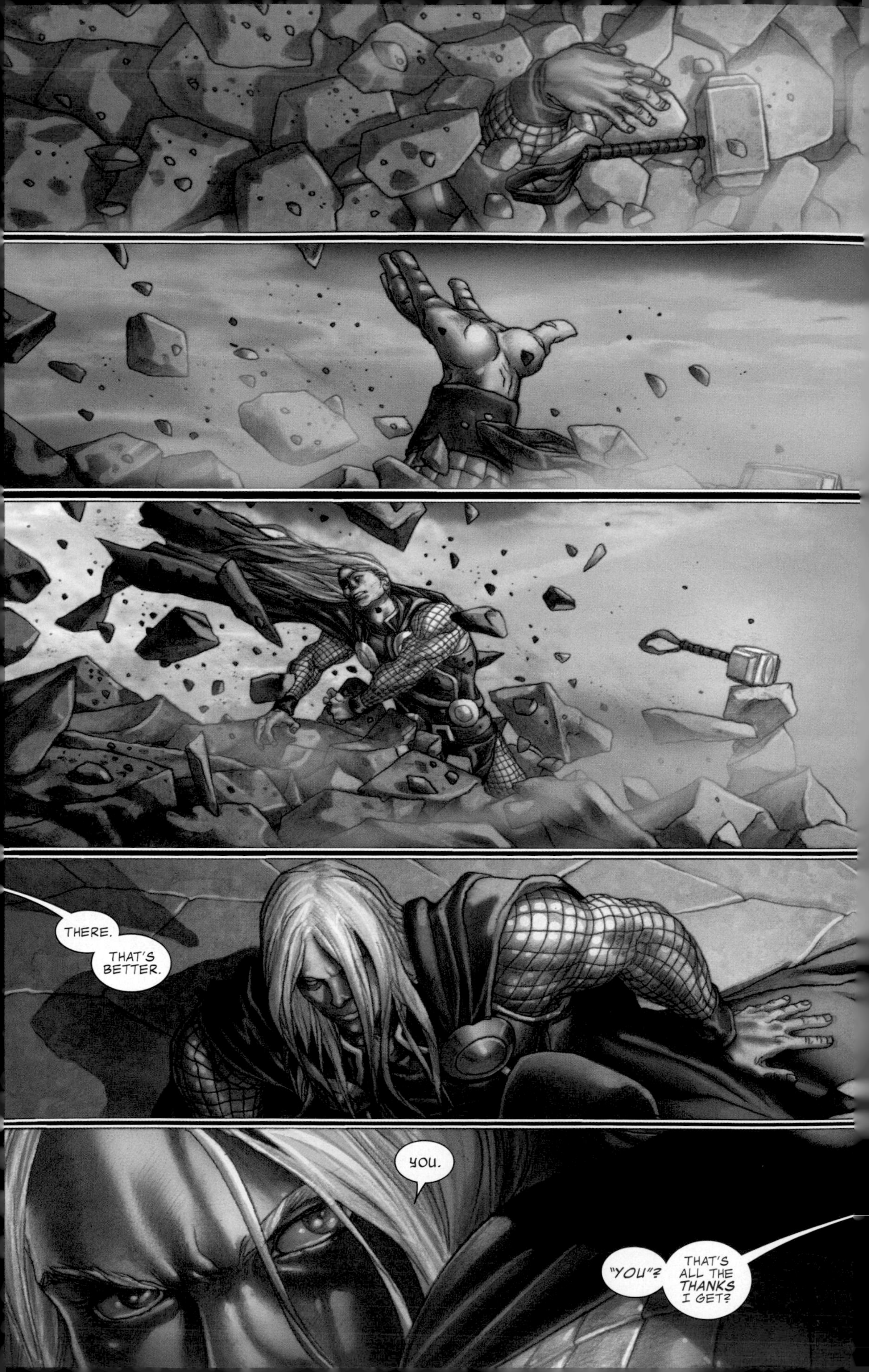
THERE.
THAT'S BETTER.
YOU.
"YOU"?
THAT'S ALL THE THANKS I GET?

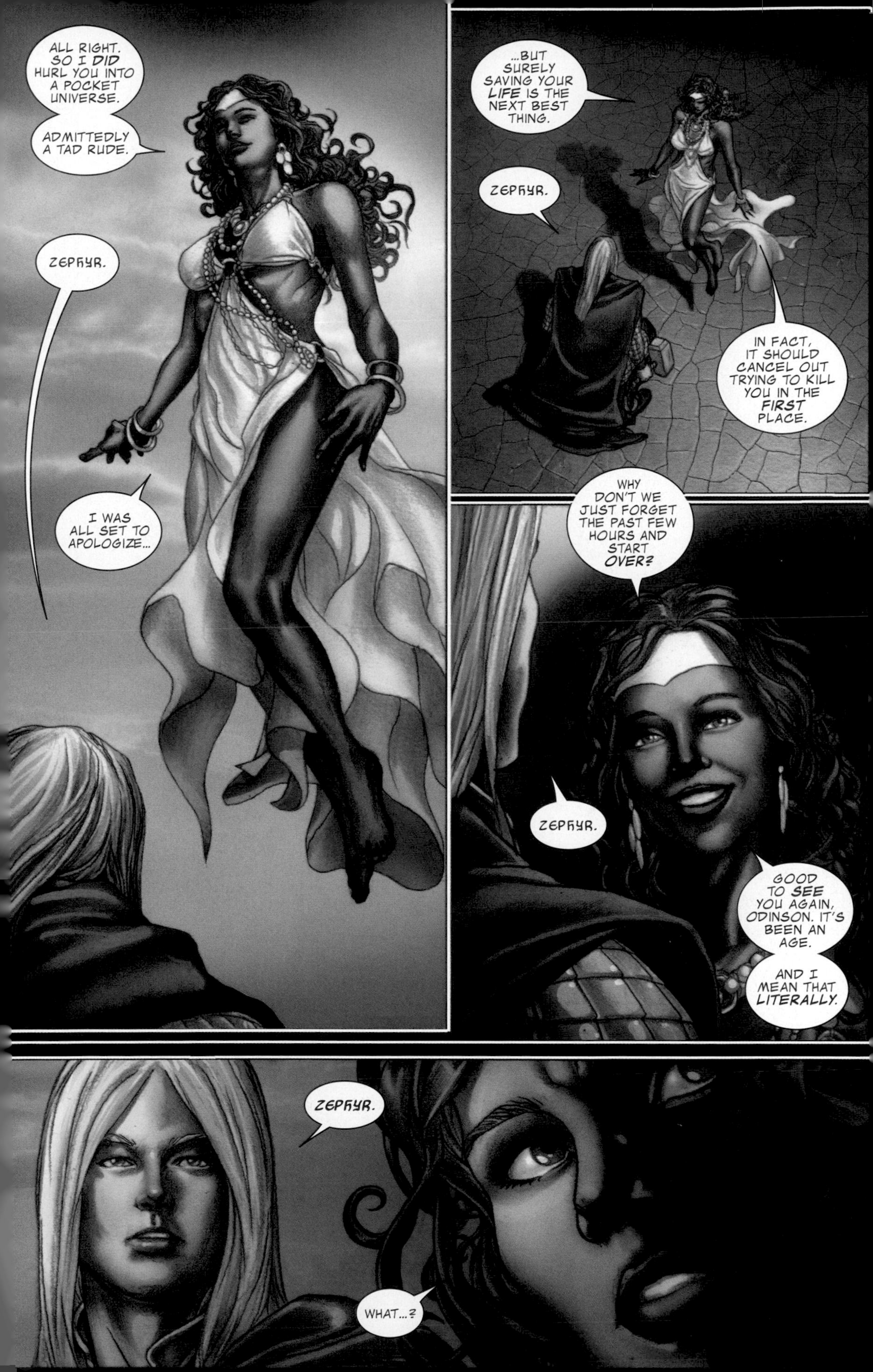
ALL RIGHT. SO I DID HURL YOU INTO A POCKET UNIVERSE.
ADMITTEDLY A TAD RUDE.
ZEPHYR.
I WAS ALL SET TO APOLOGIZE...
...BUT SURELY SAVING YOUR LIFE IS THE NEXT BEST THING.
ZEPHYR.
IN FACT, IT SHOULD CANCEL OUT TRYING TO KILL YOU IN THE FIRST PLACE.
WHY DON'T WE JUST FORGET THE PAST FEW HOURS AND START OVER?
ZEPHYR.
GOOD TO SEE YOU AGAIN, ODINSON. IT'S BEEN AN AGE.
AND I MEAN THAT LITERALLY.
ZEPHYR.
WHAT...?

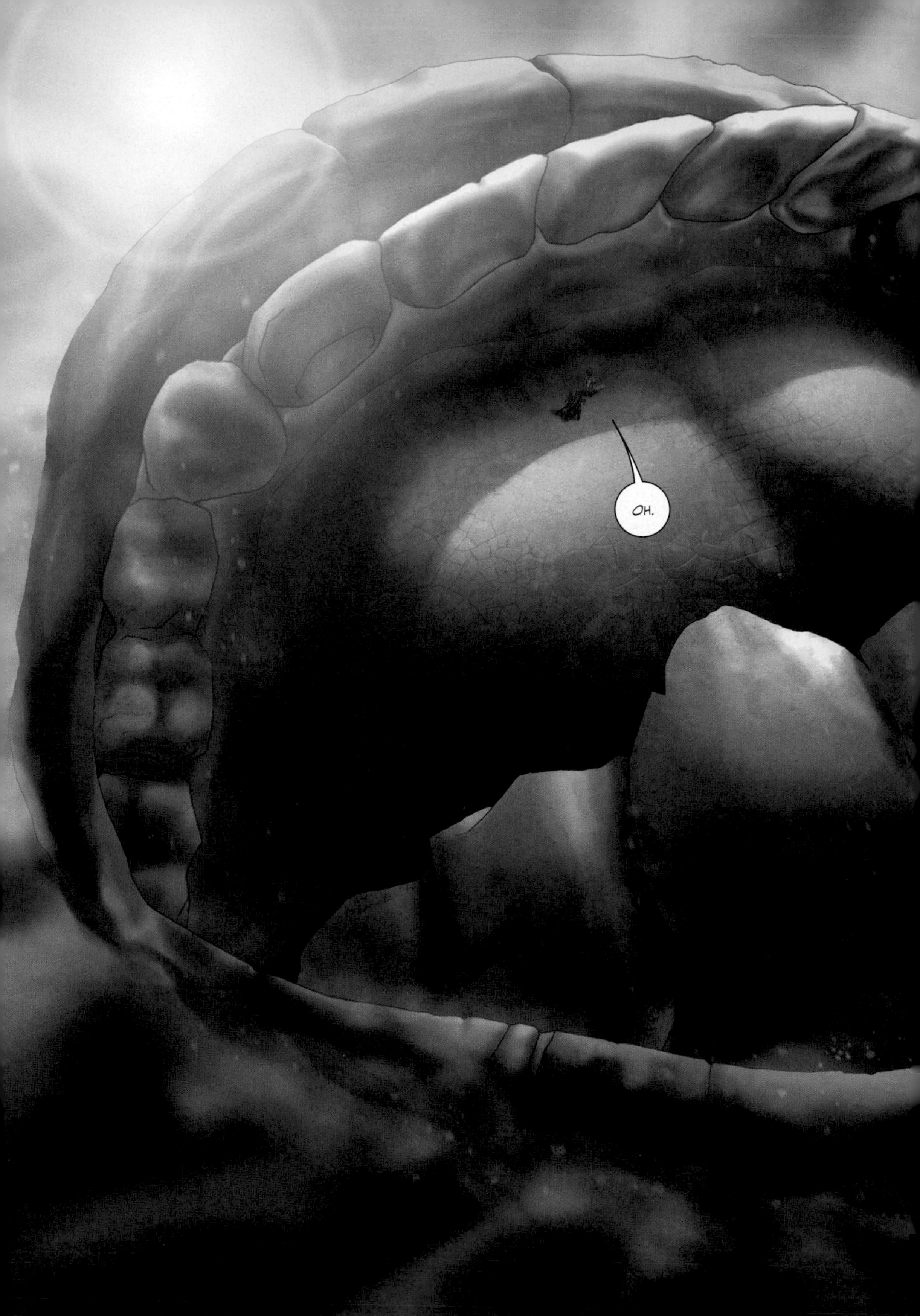
OH.

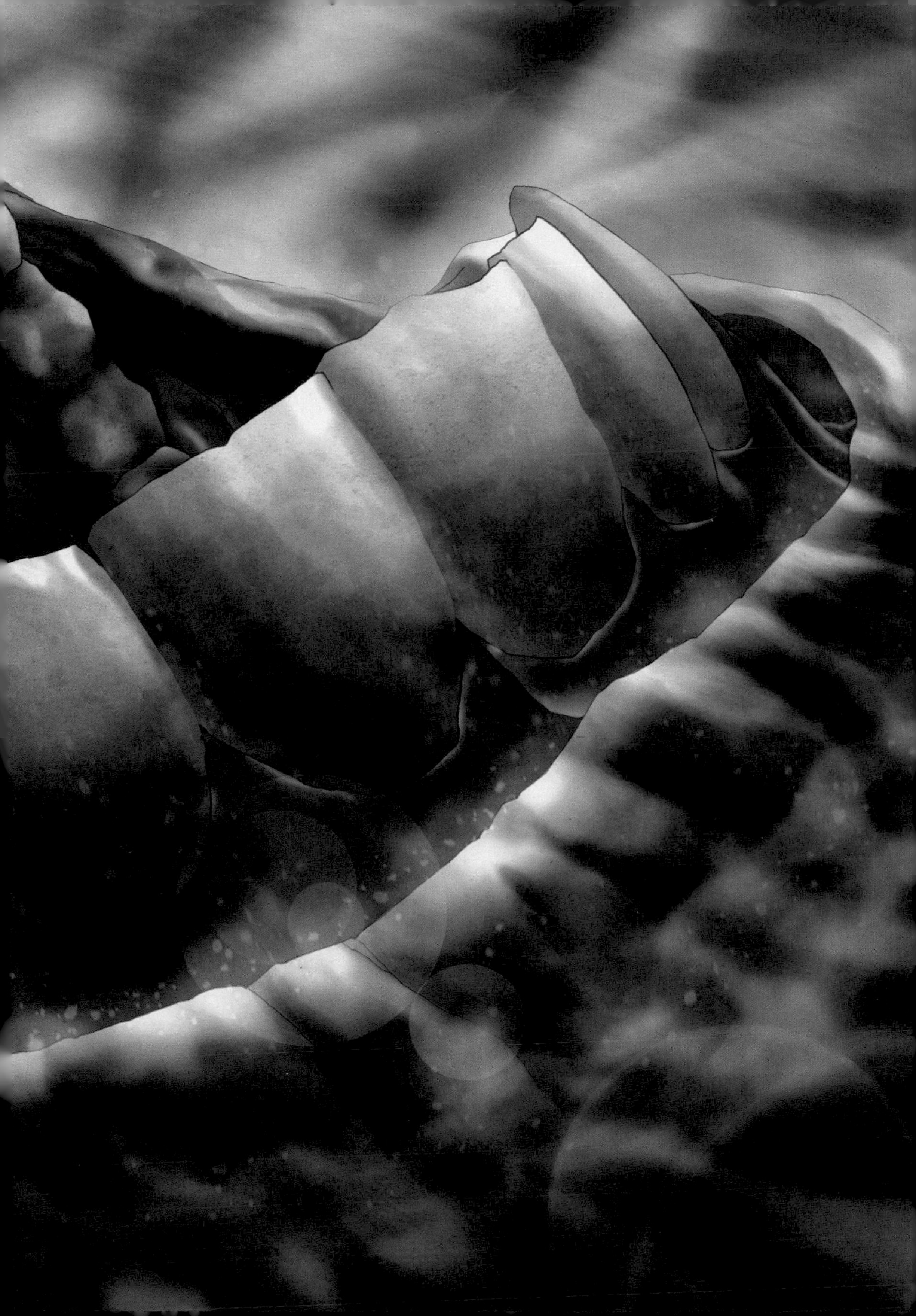

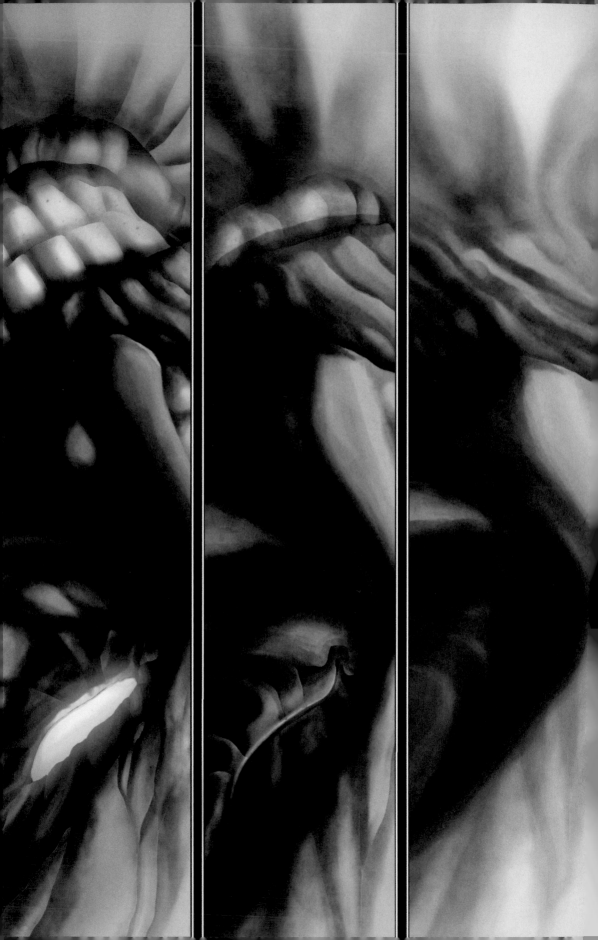

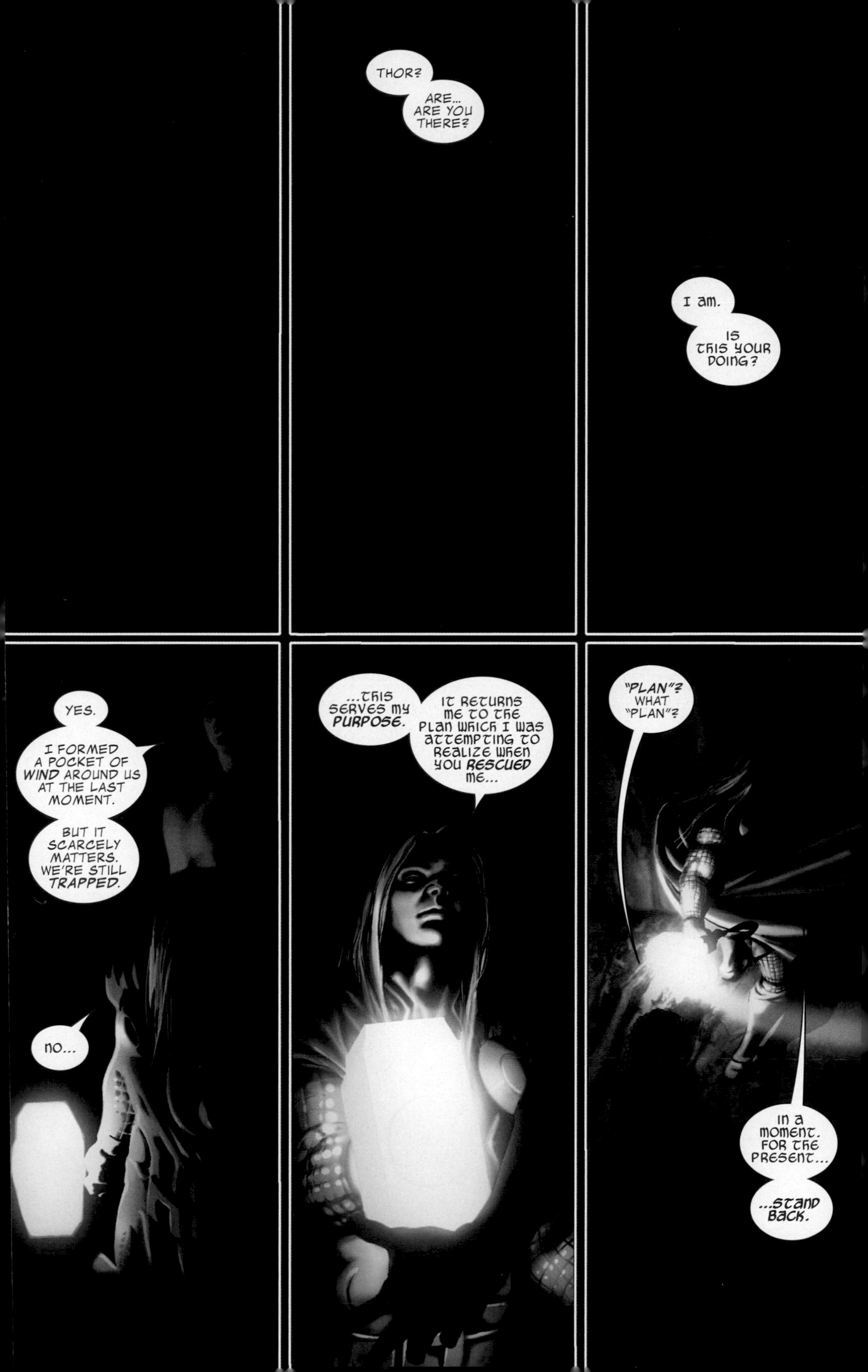
THOR?
ARE... ARE YOU THERE?
I AM.
IS THIS YOUR DOING?
YES.
I FORMED A POCKET OF WIND AROUND US AT THE LAST MOMENT.
BUT IT SCARCELY MATTERS. WE'RE STILL TRAPPED.
NO...
...THIS SERVES MY PURPOSE.
IT RETURNS ME TO THE PLAN WHICH I WAS ATTEMPTING TO REALIZE WHEN YOU RESCUED ME...
"PLAN"? WHAT "PLAN"?
IN A MOMENT. FOR THE PRESENT...
...STAND BACK.

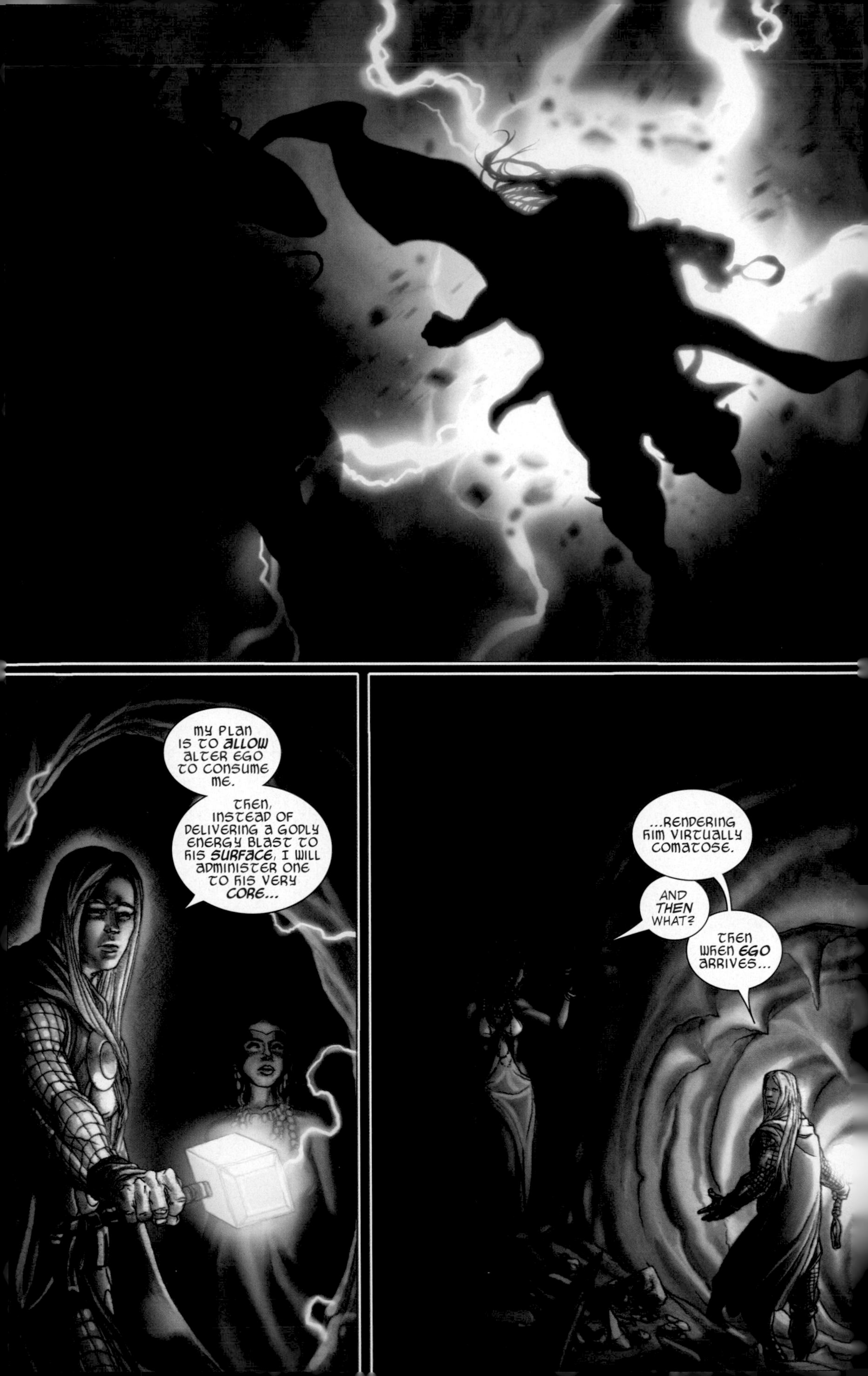
MY PLAN IS TO ALLOW ALTER EGO TO CONSUME ME.
THEN, INSTEAD OF DELIVERING A GODLY ENERGY BLAST TO HIS SURFACE, I WILL ADMINISTER ONE TO HIS VERY CORE...
...RENDERING HIM VIRTUALLY COMATOSE.
AND THEN WHAT?
THEN WHEN EGO ARRIVES...

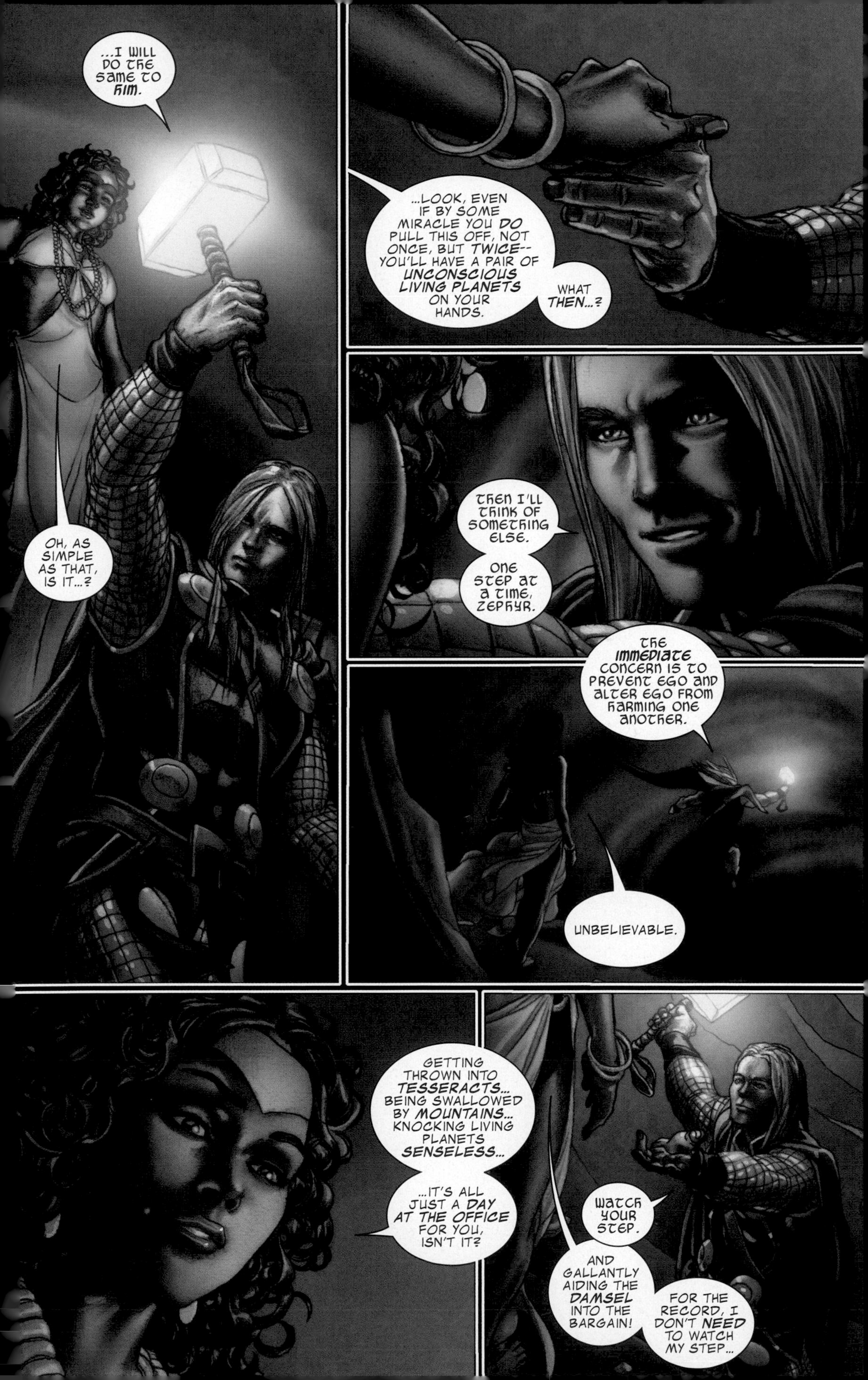

...I WILL DO THE SAME TO HIM.
OH, AS SIMPLE AS THAT, IS IT...?
...LOOK, EVEN IF BY SOME MIRACLE YOU DO PULL THIS OFF, NOT ONCE, BUT TWICE-- YOU'LL HAVE A PAIR OF UNCONSCIOUS LIVING PLANETS ON YOUR HANDS.
WHAT THEN...?
THEN I'LL THINK OF SOMETHING ELSE.
ONE STEP AT A TIME, ZEPHYR.
THE IMMEDIATE CONCERN IS TO PREVENT EGO AND ALTER EGO FROM HARMING ONE ANOTHER.
UNBELIEVABLE.
GETTING THROWN INTO TESSERACTS... BEING SWALLOWED BY MOUNTAINS... KNOCKING LIVING PLANETS SENSELESS...
...IT'S ALL JUST A DAY AT THE OFFICE FOR YOU, ISN'T IT?
WATCH YOUR STEP.
AND GALLANTLY AIDING THE DAMSEL INTO THE BARGAIN!
FOR THE RECORD, I DON'T NEED TO WATCH MY STEP...

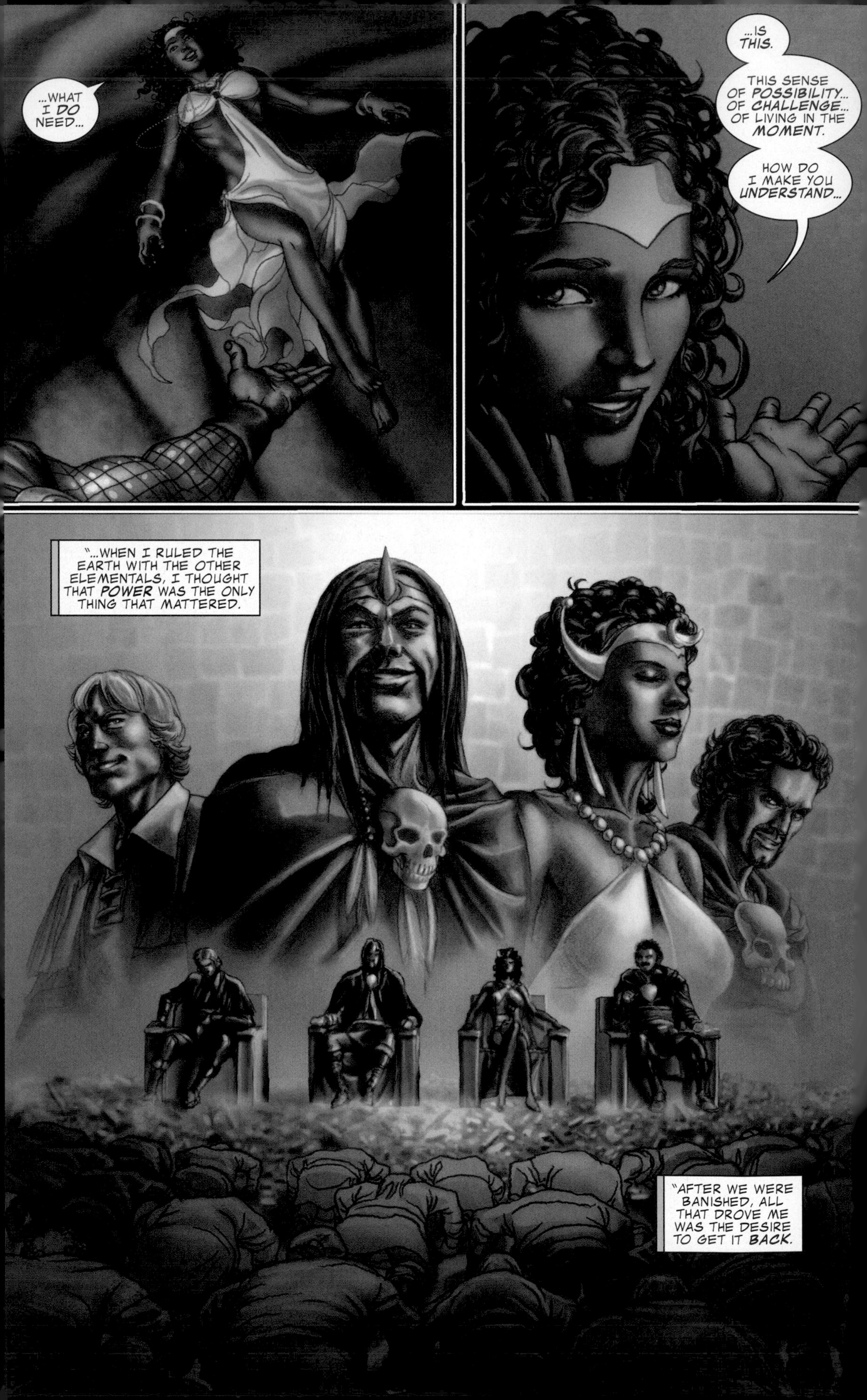
...WHAT I DO NEED...
...IS THIS.
THIS SENSE OF POSSIBILITY... OF CHALLENGE... OF LIVING IN THE MOMENT.
HOW DO I MAKE YOU UNDERSTAND...
"...WHEN I RULED THE EARTH WITH THE OTHER ELEMENTALS, I THOUGHT THAT POWER WAS THE ONLY THING THAT MATTERED.
"AFTER WE WERE BANISHED, ALL THAT DROVE ME WAS THE DESIRE TO GET IT BACK.

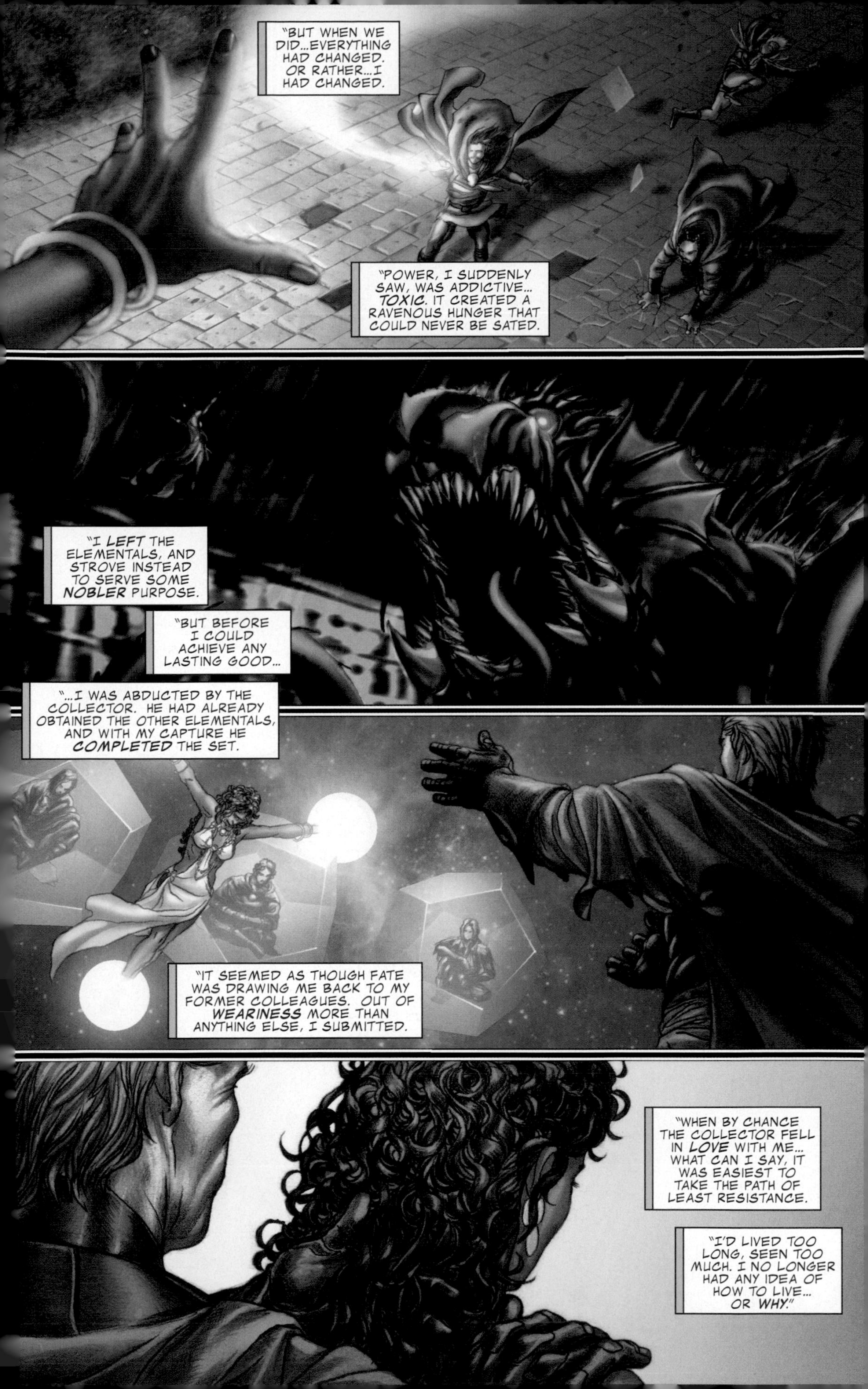
"BUT WHEN WE DID...EVERYTHING HAD CHANGED. OR RATHER...I HAD CHANGED.
"POWER, I SUDDENLY SAW, WAS ADDICTIVE... TOXIC. IT CREATED A RAVENOUS HUNGER THAT COULD NEVER BE SATED.
"I LEFT THE ELEMENTALS, AND STROVE INSTEAD TO SERVE SOME NOBLER PURPOSE.
"BUT BEFORE I COULD ACHIEVE ANY LASTING GOOD...
"...I WAS ABDUCTED BY THE COLLECTOR. HE HAD ALREADY OBTAINED THE OTHER ELEMENTALS, AND WITH MY CAPTURE HE COMPLETED THE SET.
"IT SEEMED AS THOUGH FATE WAS DRAWING ME BACK TO MY FORMER COLLEAGUES. OUT OF WEARINESS MORE THAN ANYTHING ELSE, I SUBMITTED.
"WHEN BY CHANCE THE COLLECTOR FELL IN LOVE WITH ME... WHAT CAN I SAY, IT WAS EASIEST TO TAKE THE PATH OF LEAST RESISTANCE.
"I'D LIVED TOO LONG, SEEN TOO MUCH. I NO LONGER HAD ANY IDEA OF HOW TO LIVE... OR WHY."

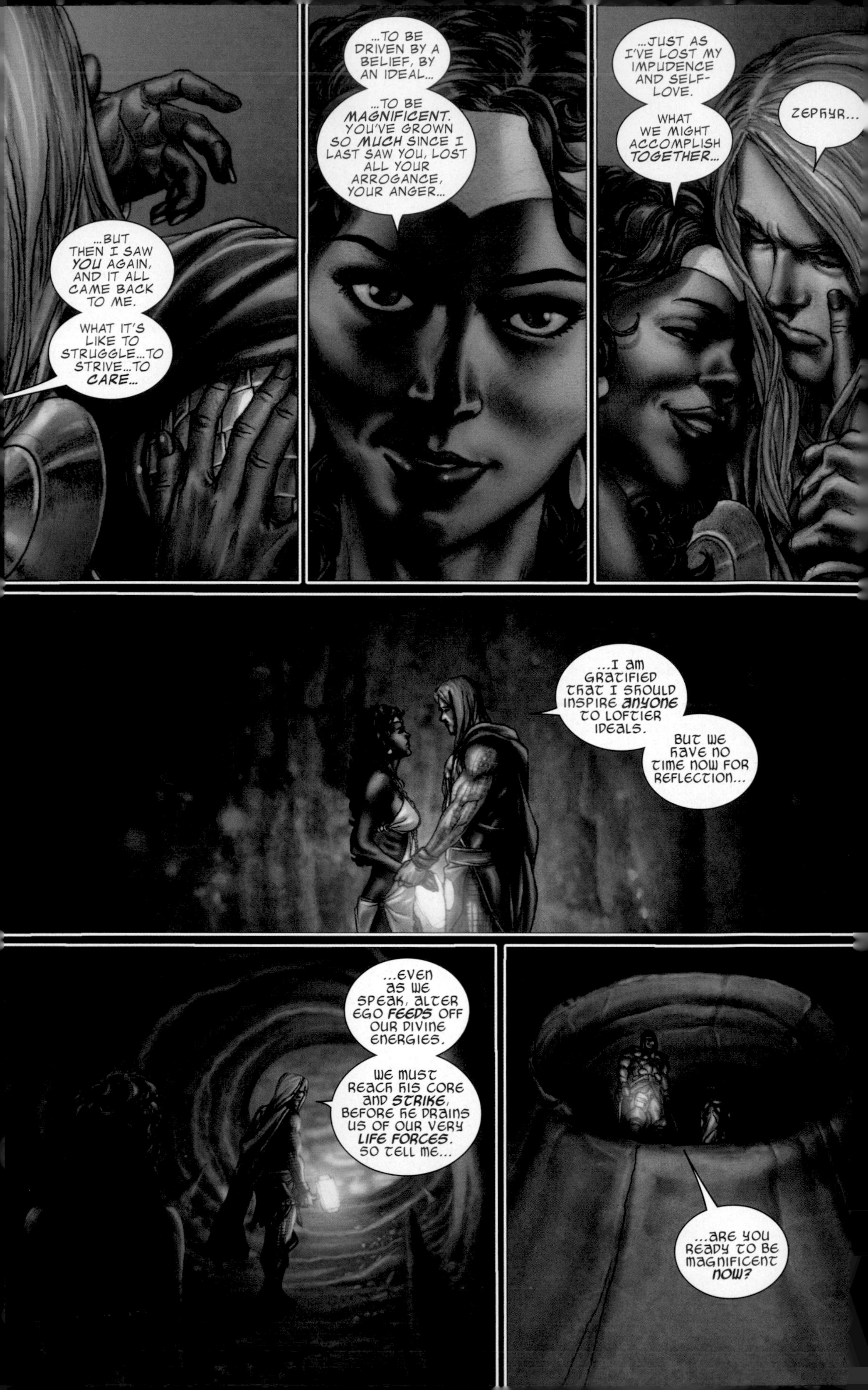
...BUT THEN I SAW YOU AGAIN, AND IT ALL CAME BACK TO ME.
WHAT IT'S LIKE TO STRUGGLE...TO STRIVE...TO CARE...
...TO BE DRIVEN BY A BELIEF, BY AN IDEAL...
...TO BE MAGNIFICENT. YOU'VE GROWN SO MUCH SINCE I LAST SAW YOU, LOST ALL YOUR ARROGANCE, YOUR ANGER...
...JUST AS I'VE LOST MY IMPUDENCE AND SELF-LOVE.
WHAT WE MIGHT ACCOMPLISH TOGETHER...
ZEPHYR...
...I AM GRATIFIED THAT I SHOULD INSPIRE ANYONE TO LOFTIER IDEALS.
BUT WE HAVE NO TIME NOW FOR REFLECTION...
...EVEN AS WE SPEAK, ALTER EGO FEEDS OFF OUR DIVINE ENERGIES.
WE MUST REACH HIS CORE AND STRIKE, BEFORE HE DRAINS US OF OUR VERY LIFE FORCES. SO TELL ME...
...ARE YOU READY TO BE MAGNIFICENT NOW?

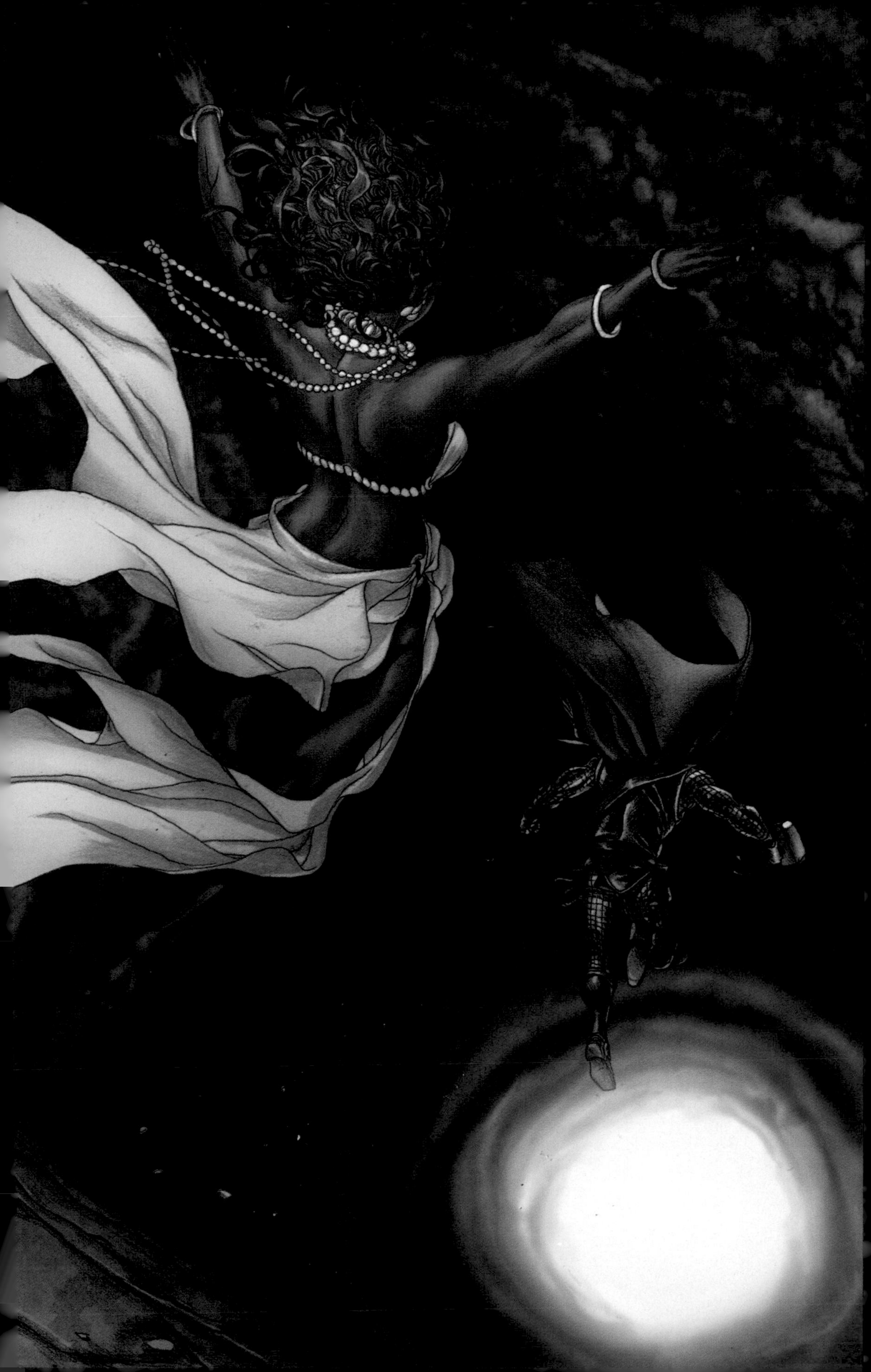

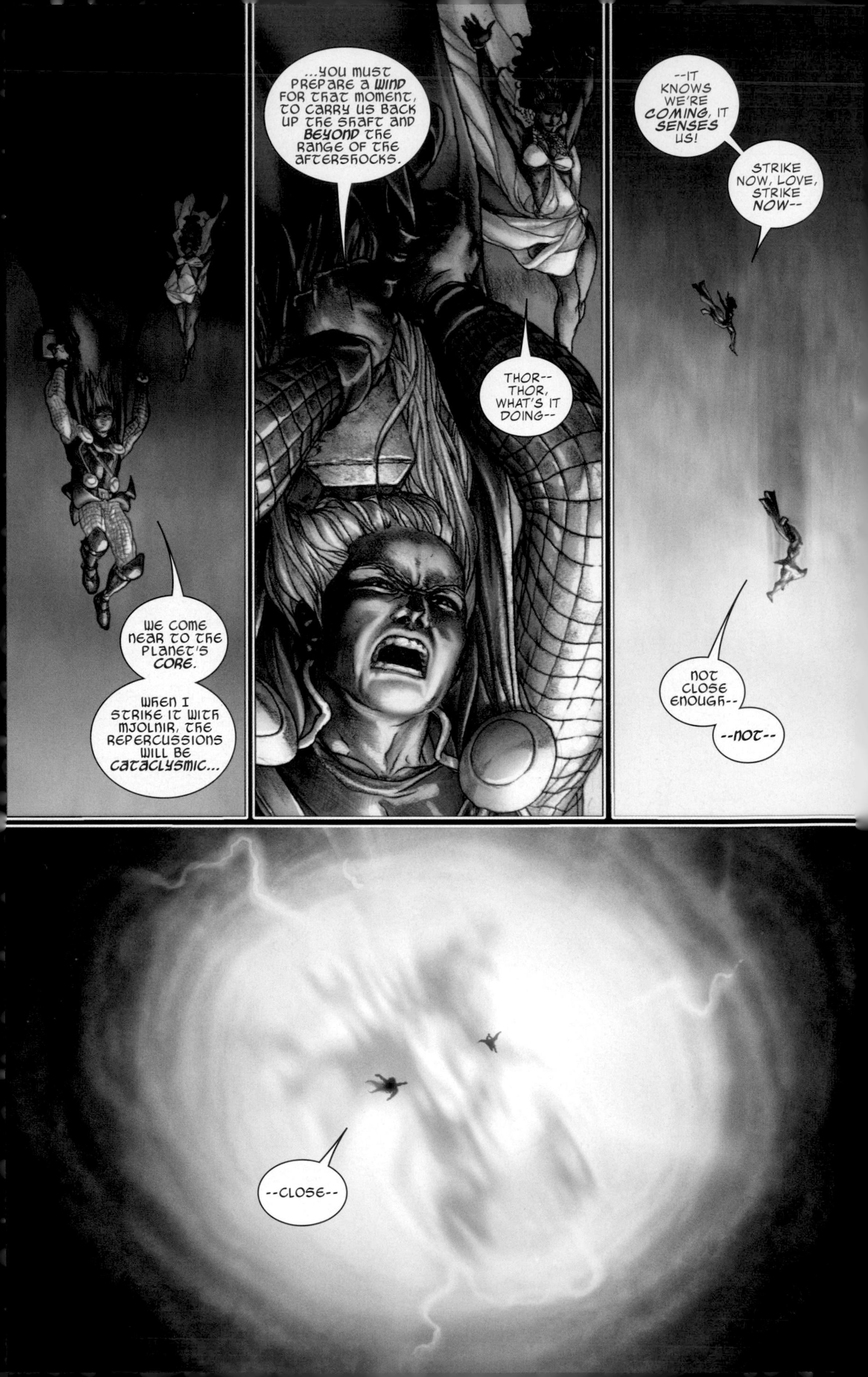
WE COME NEAR TO THE PLANET'S CORE.
WHEN I STRIKE IT WITH MJOLNIR, THE REPERCUSSIONS WILL BE CATACLYSMIC...
...YOU MUST PREPARE A WIND FOR THAT MOMENT, TO CARRY US BACK UP THE SHAFT AND BEYOND THE RANGE OF THE AFTERSHOCKS.
THOR-- THOR, WHAT'S IT DOING--
--IT KNOWS WE'RE COMING, IT SENSES US!
STRIKE NOW, LOVE, STRIKE NOW--
NOT CLOSE ENOUGH--
--NOT--
--CLOSE--

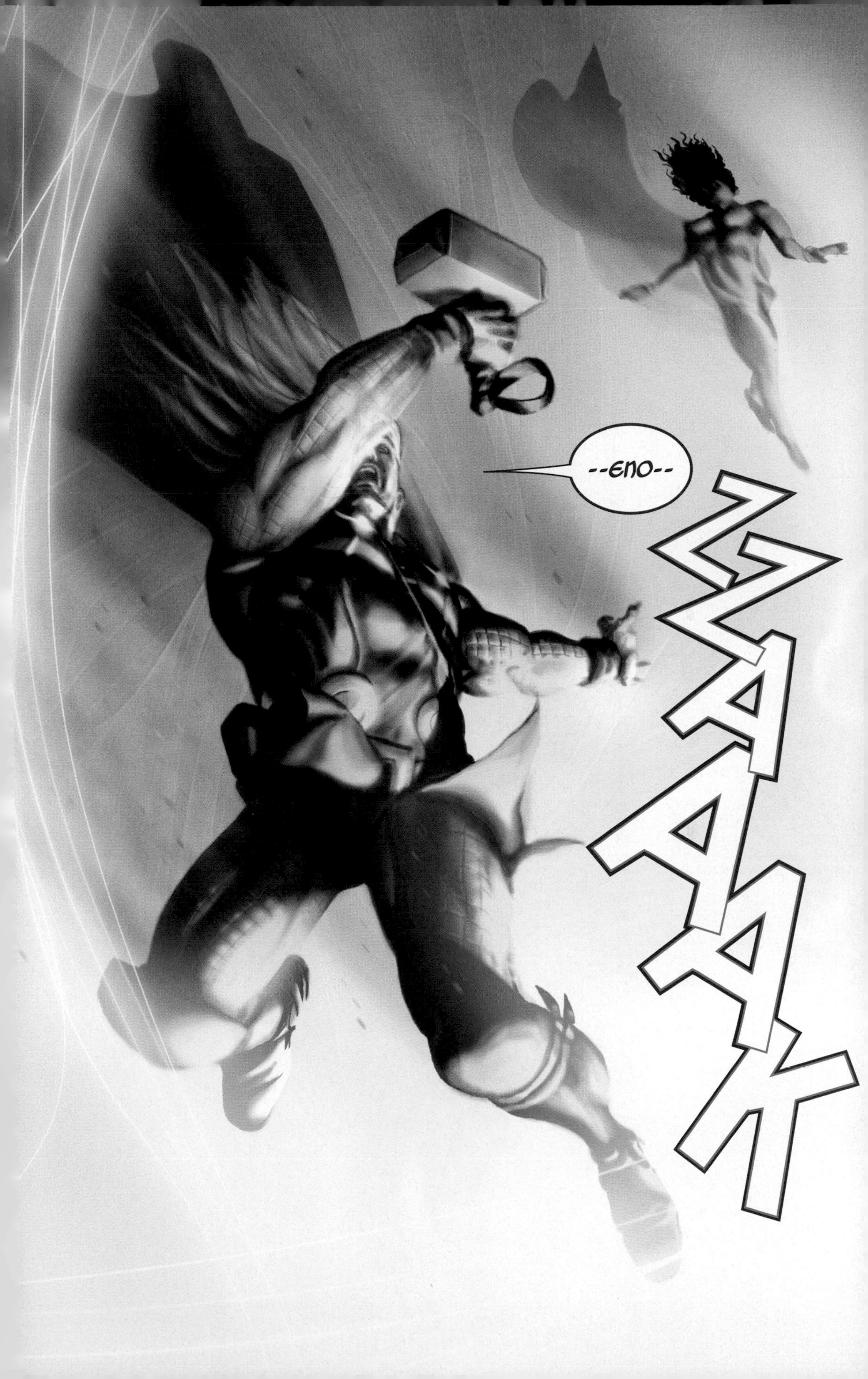
--END--
ZZAAAK

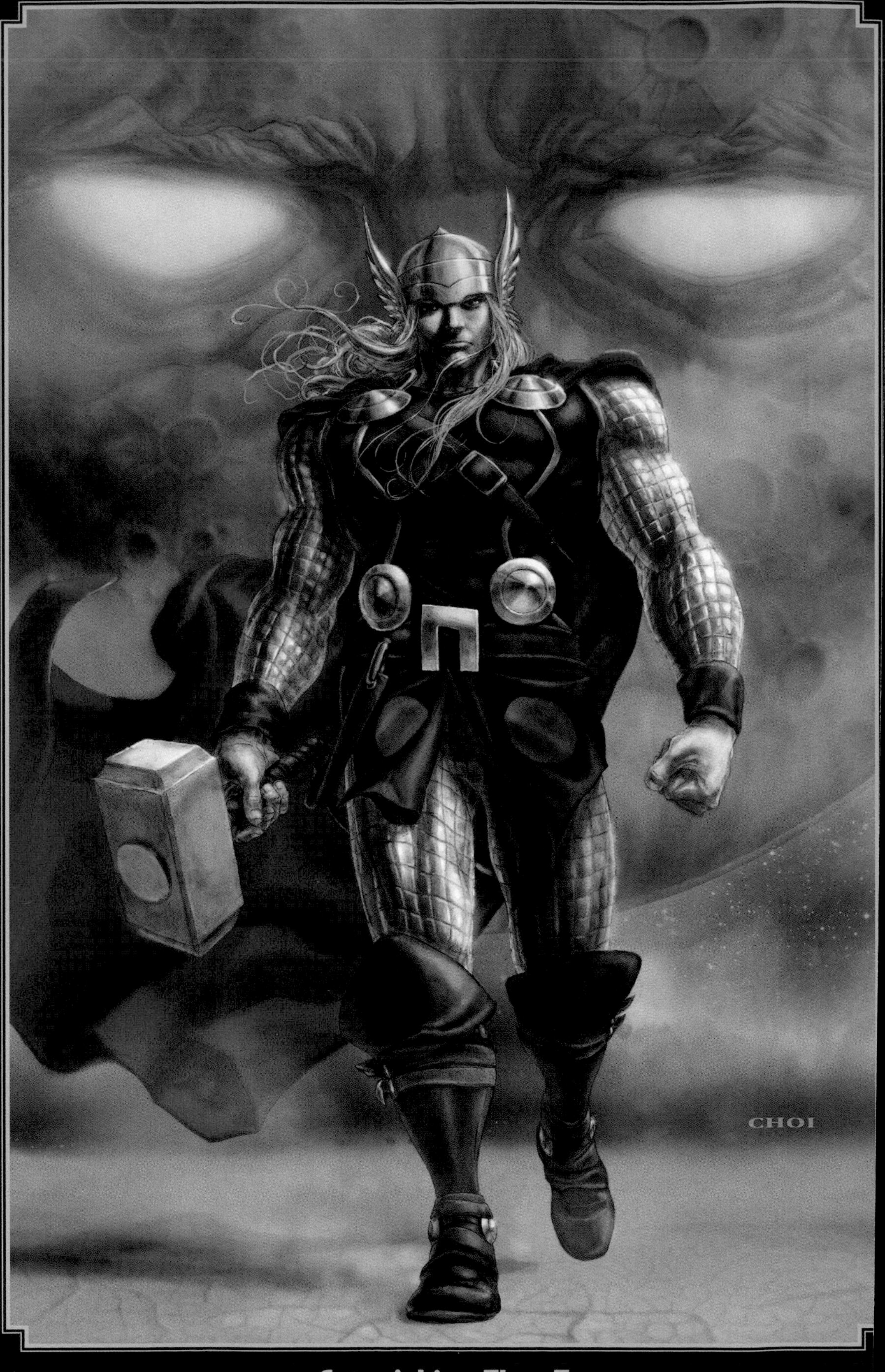
CHOI

Astonishing Thor 5

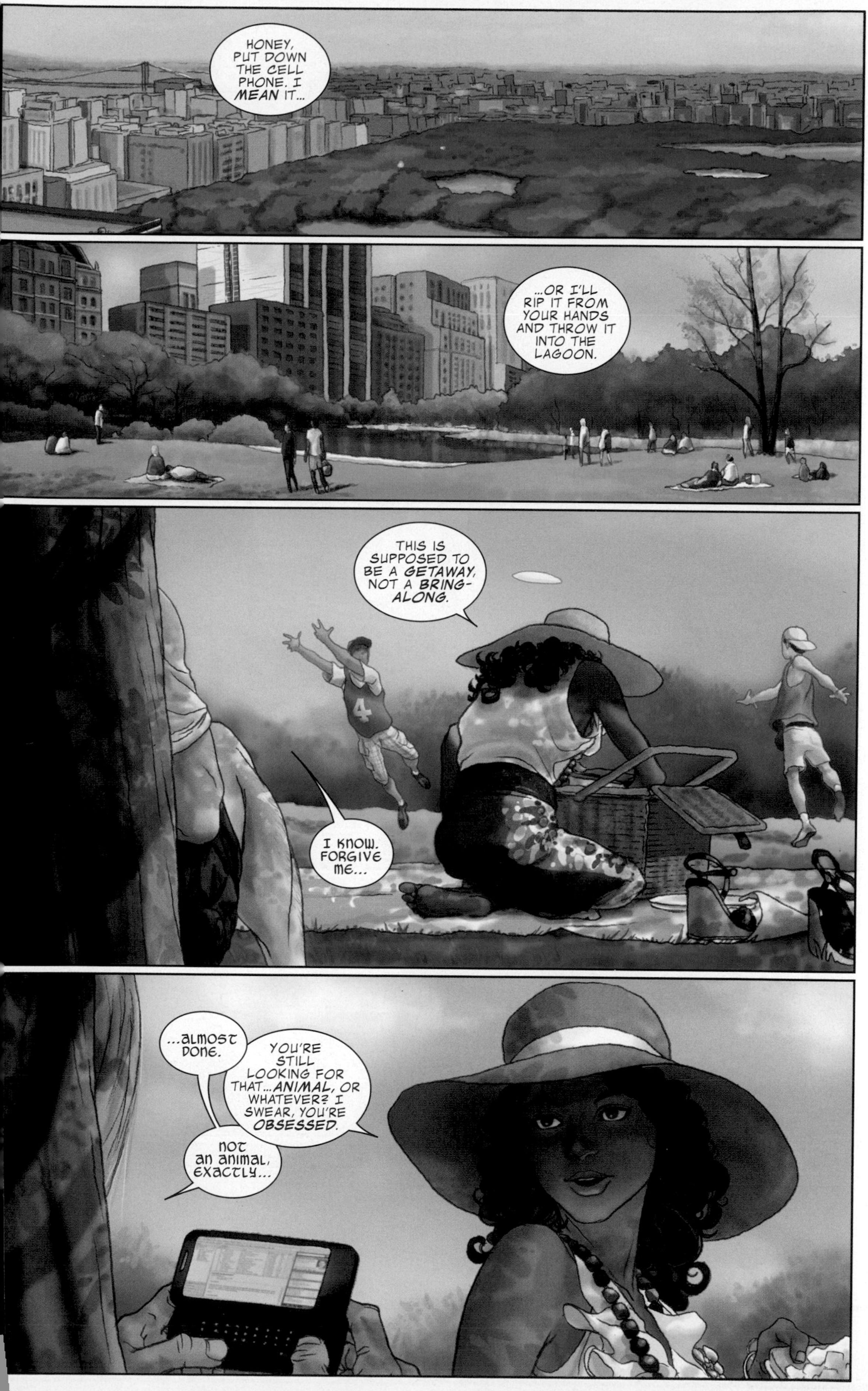
HONEY, PUT DOWN THE CELL PHONE. I MEAN IT...
...OR I'LL RIP IT FROM YOUR HANDS AND THROW IT INTO THE LAGOON.
THIS IS SUPPOSED TO BE A GETAWAY, NOT A BRING-ALONG.
I KNOW. FORGIVE ME...
...ALMOST DONE.
YOU'RE STILL LOOKING FOR THAT...ANIMAL, OR WHATEVER? I SWEAR, YOU'RE OBSESSED.
NOT AN ANIMAL, EXACTLY...

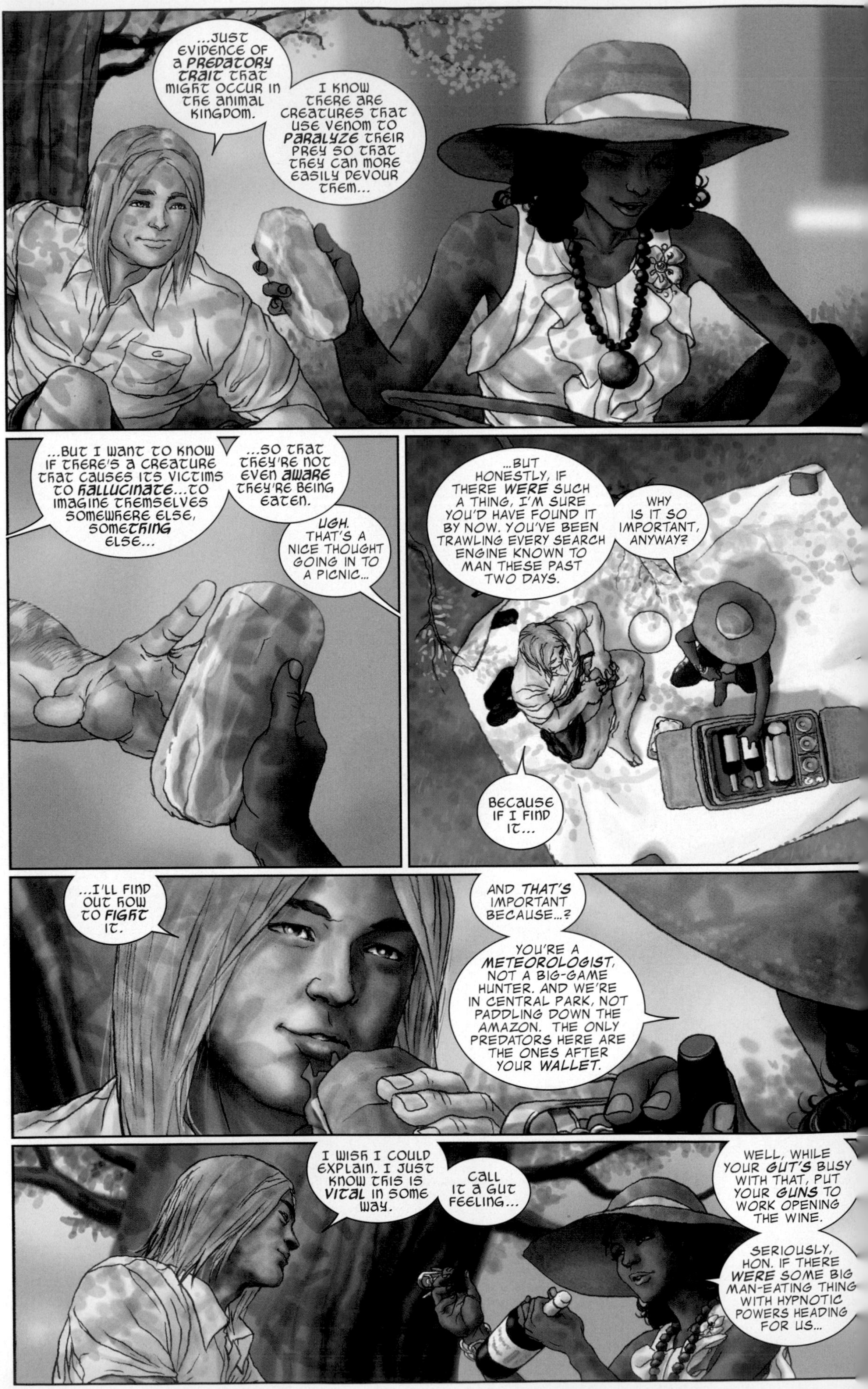
...JUST EVIDENCE OF A PREDATORY TRAIT THAT MIGHT OCCUR IN THE ANIMAL KINGDOM.
I KNOW THERE ARE CREATURES THAT USE VENOM TO PARALYZE THEIR PREY SO THAT THEY CAN MORE EASILY DEVOUR THEM...
...BUT I WANT TO KNOW IF THERE'S A CREATURE THAT CAUSES ITS VICTIMS TO HALLUCINATE...TO IMAGINE THEMSELVES SOMEWHERE ELSE, SOMETHING ELSE...
...SO THAT THEY'RE NOT EVEN AWARE THEY'RE BEING EATEN.
UGH. THAT'S A NICE THOUGHT GOING IN TO A PICNIC...
...BUT HONESTLY, IF THERE WERE SUCH A THING, I'M SURE YOU'D HAVE FOUND IT BY NOW. YOU'VE BEEN TRAWLING EVERY SEARCH ENGINE KNOWN TO MAN THESE PAST TWO DAYS.
WHY IS IT SO IMPORTANT, ANYWAY?
BECAUSE IF I FIND IT...
...I'LL FIND OUT HOW TO FIGHT IT.
AND THAT'S IMPORTANT BECAUSE...?
YOU'RE A METEOROLOGIST, NOT A BIG-GAME HUNTER. AND WE'RE IN CENTRAL PARK, NOT PADDLING DOWN THE AMAZON. THE ONLY PREDATORS HERE ARE THE ONES AFTER YOUR WALLET.
I WISH I COULD EXPLAIN. I JUST KNOW THIS IS VITAL IN SOME WAY.
CALL IT A GUT FEELING...
WELL, WHILE YOUR GUT'S BUSY WITH THAT, PUT YOUR GUNS TO WORK OPENING THE WINE.
SERIOUSLY, HON. IF THERE WERE SOME BIG MAN-EATING THING WITH HYPNOTIC POWERS HEADING FOR US...

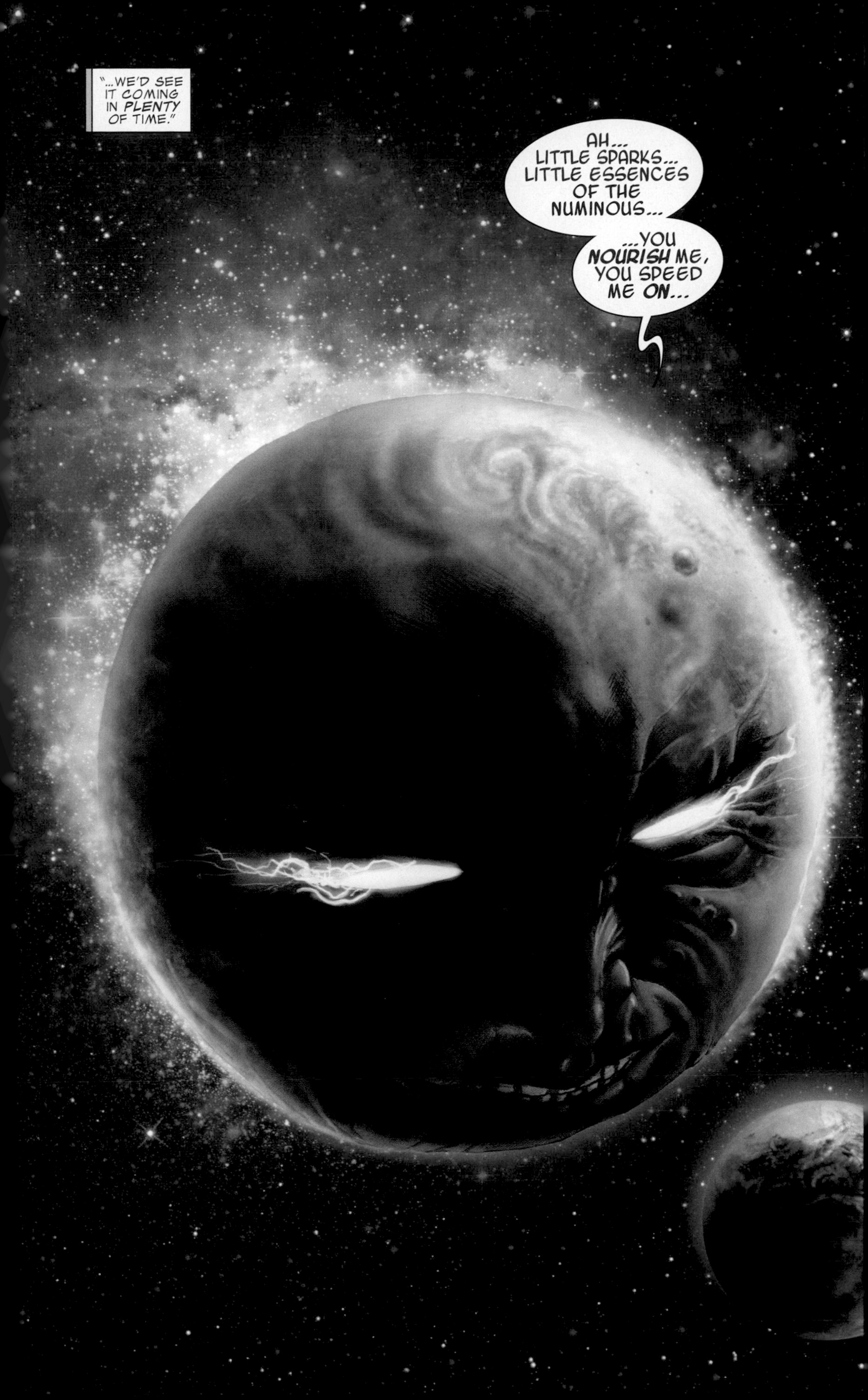
"...WE'D SEE IT COMING IN PLENTY OF TIME."
AH... LITTLE SPARKS... LITTLE ESSENCES OF THE NUMINOUS...
...YOU NOURISH ME, YOU SPEED ME ON...

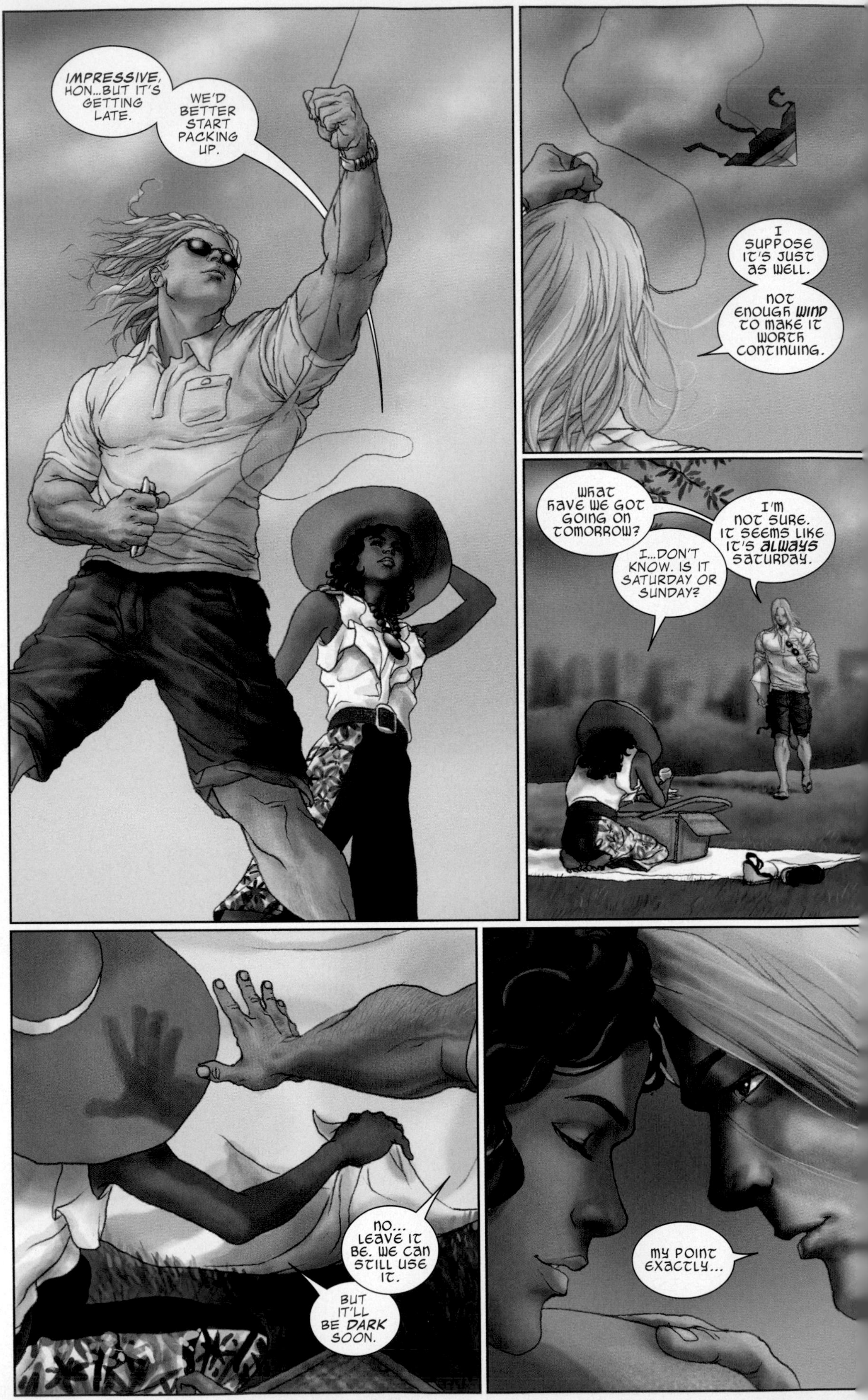
IMPRESSIVE, HON...BUT IT'S GETTING LATE.
WE'D BETTER START PACKING UP.
I SUPPOSE IT'S JUST AS WELL.
NOT ENOUGH WIND TO MAKE IT WORTH CONTINUING.
WHAT HAVE WE GOT GOING ON TOMORROW?
I...DON'T KNOW. IS IT SATURDAY OR SUNDAY?
I'M NOT SURE. IT SEEMS LIKE IT'S ALWAYS SATURDAY.
NO... LEAVE IT BE. WE CAN STILL USE IT.
BUT IT'LL BE DARK SOON.
MY POINT EXACTLY...

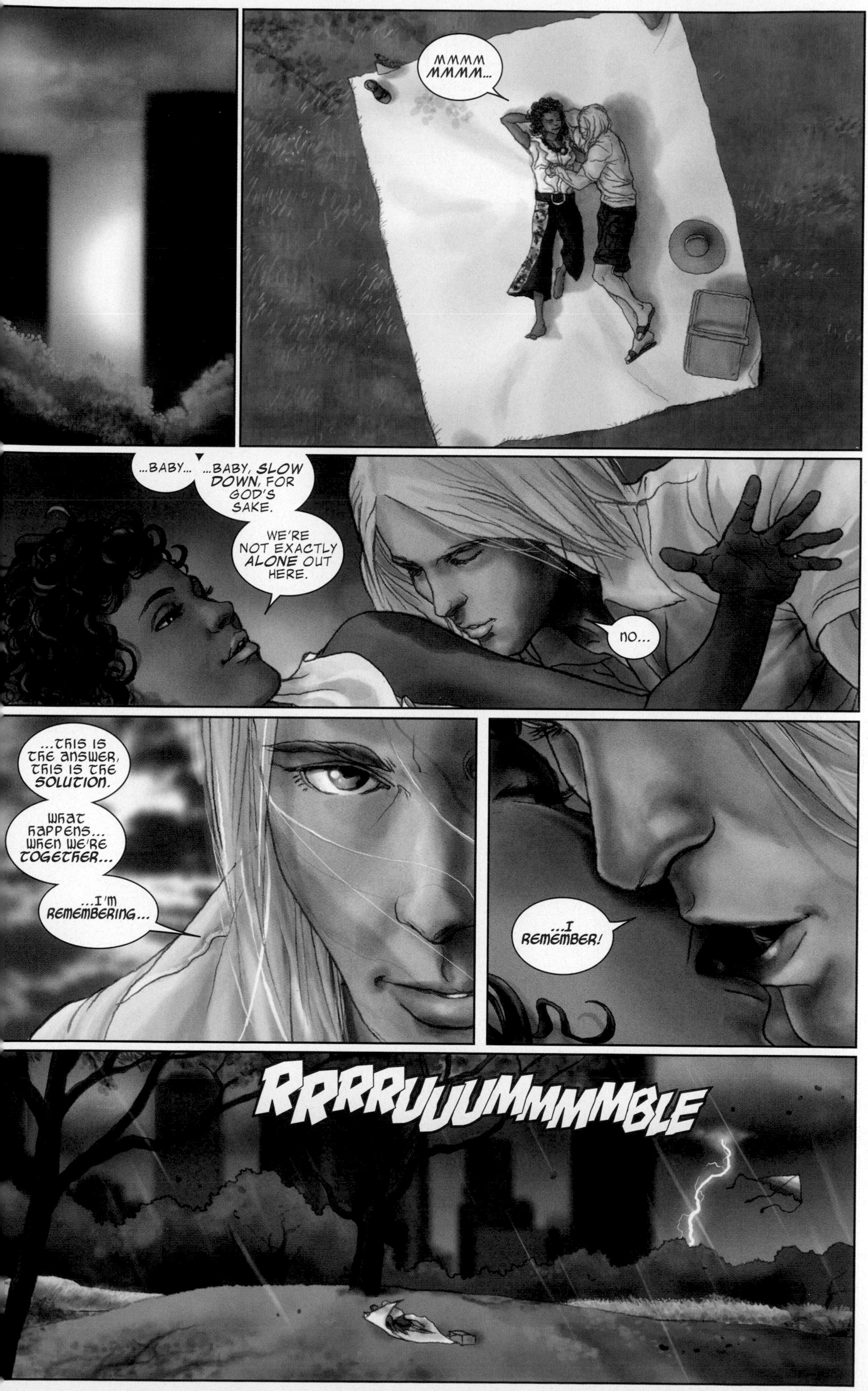
MMMM
MMMM...
...BABY...
...BABY, SLOW DOWN, FOR GOD'S SAKE.
WE'RE NOT EXACTLY ALONE OUT HERE.
NO...
...THIS IS THE ANSWER, THIS IS THE SOLUTION.
WHAT HAPPENS... WHEN WE'RE TOGETHER...
...I'M REMEMBERING...
...I REMEMBER!
RRRRUUUMMMMMBLE

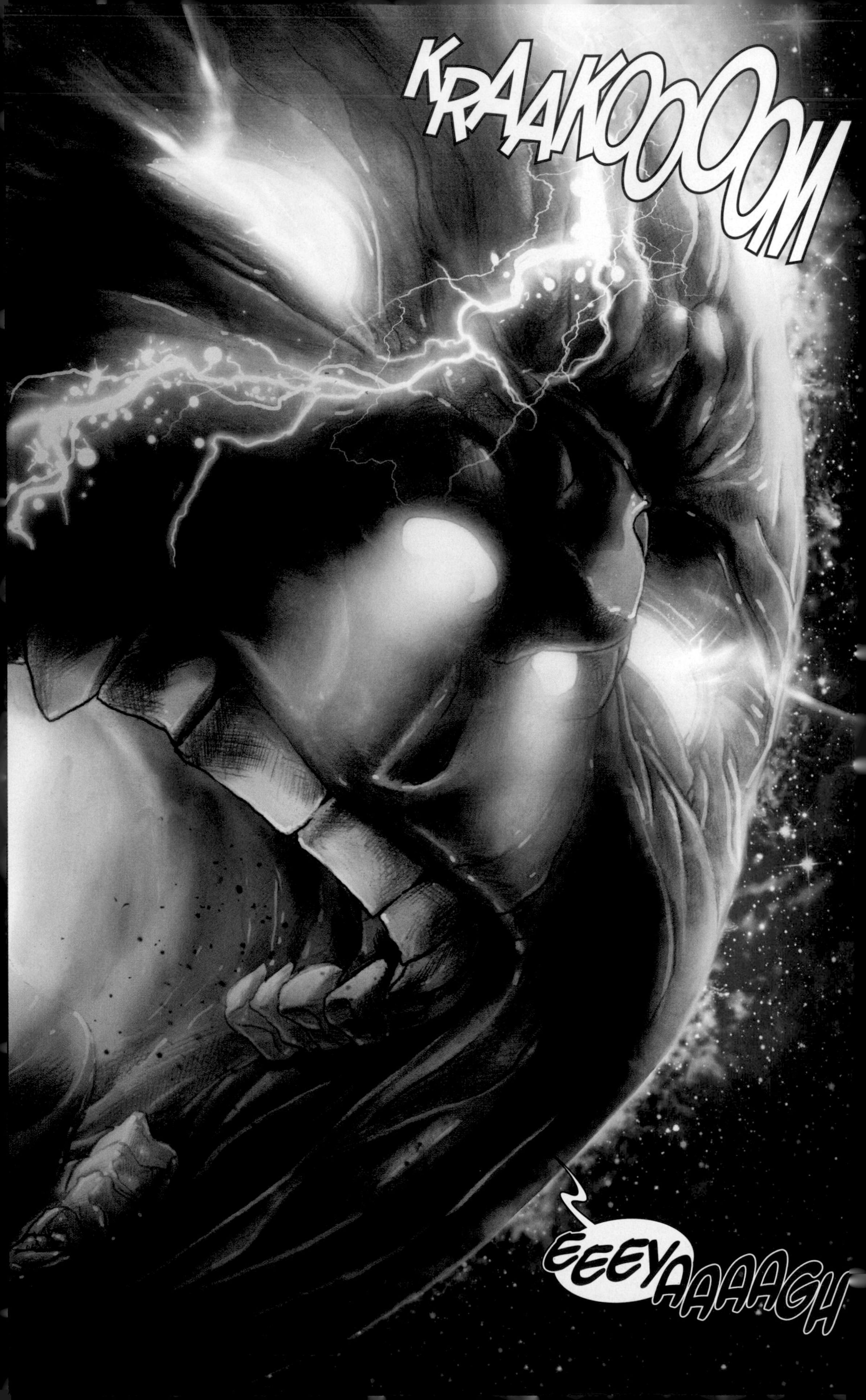
KRAAKOOOOOM
EEEYAAAAAGH

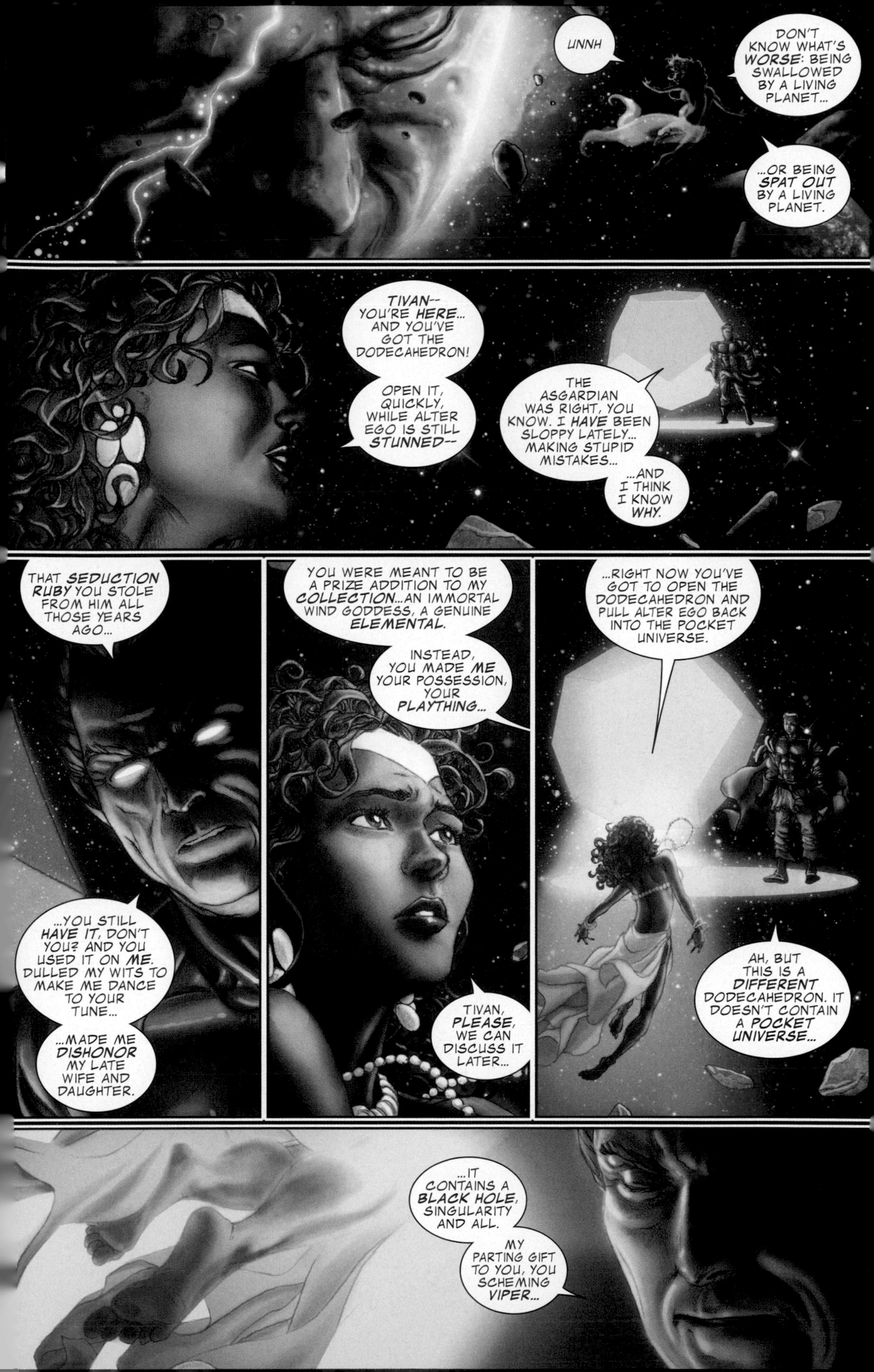

UNNH
DON'T KNOW WHAT'S WORSE: BEING SWALLOWED BY A LIVING PLANET...
...OR BEING SPAT OUT BY A LIVING PLANET.
TIVAN-- YOU'RE HERE... AND YOU'VE GOT THE DODECAHEDRON!
OPEN IT, QUICKLY, WHILE ALTER EGO IS STILL STUNNED--
THE ASGARDIAN WAS RIGHT, YOU KNOW. I HAVE BEEN SLOPPY LATELY... MAKING STUPID MISTAKES...
...AND I THINK I KNOW WHY.
THAT SEDUCTION RUBY YOU STOLE FROM HIM ALL THOSE YEARS AGO...
...YOU STILL HAVE IT, DON'T YOU? AND YOU USED IT ON ME. DULLED MY WITS TO MAKE ME DANCE TO YOUR TUNE...
...MADE ME DISHONOR MY LATE WIFE AND DAUGHTER.
YOU WERE MEANT TO BE A PRIZE ADDITION TO MY COLLECTION...AN IMMORTAL WIND GODDESS, A GENUINE ELEMENTAL.
INSTEAD, YOU MADE ME YOUR POSSESSION, YOUR PLAYTHING...
TIVAN, PLEASE, WE CAN DISCUSS IT LATER...
...RIGHT NOW YOU'VE GOT TO OPEN THE DODECAHEDRON AND PULL ALTER EGO BACK INTO THE POCKET UNIVERSE.
AH, BUT THIS IS A DIFFERENT DODECAHEDRON. IT DOESN'T CONTAIN A POCKET UNIVERSE...
...IT CONTAINS A BLACK HOLE, SINGULARITY AND ALL.
MY PARTING GIFT TO YOU, YOU SCHEMING VIPER...

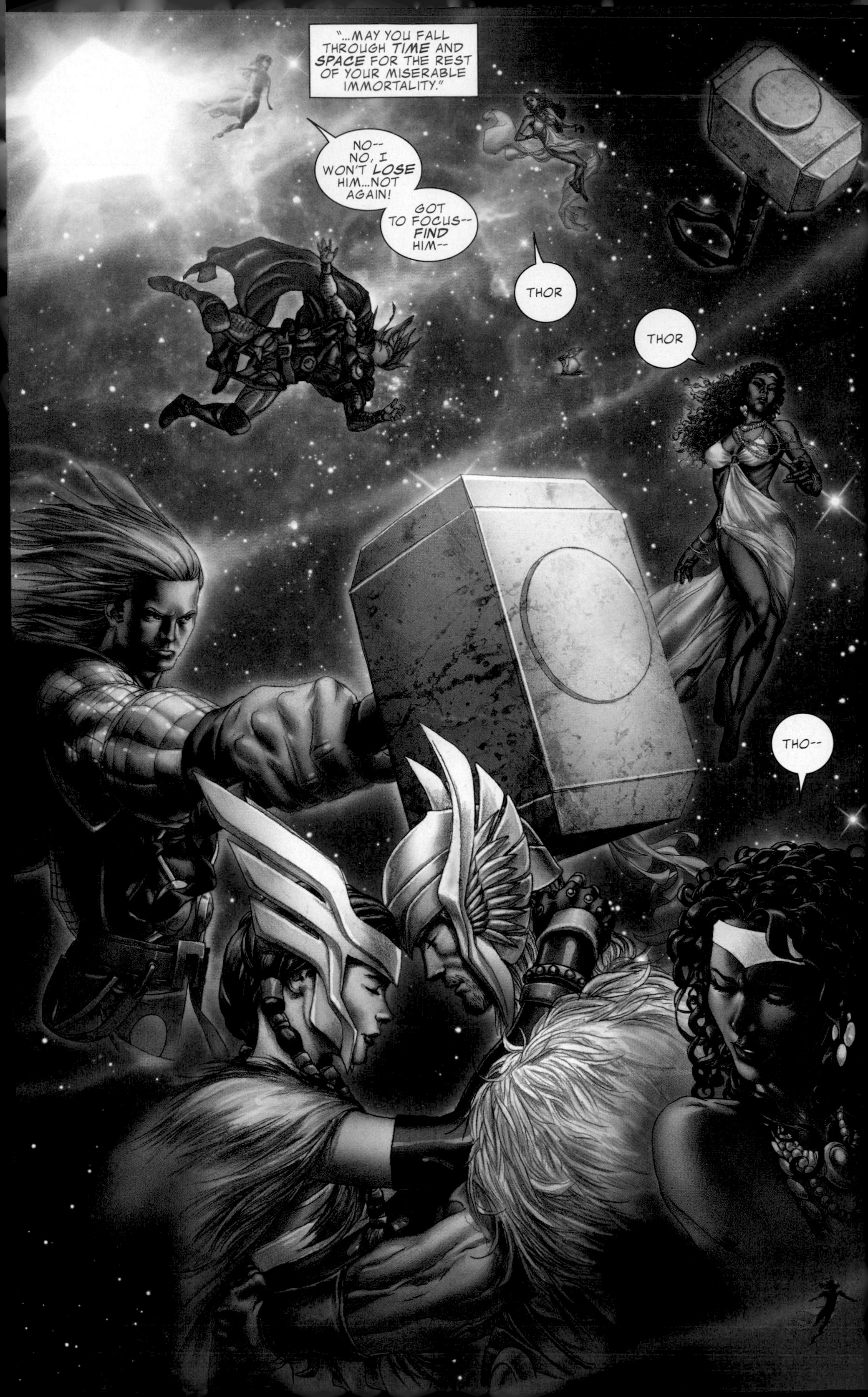
"...MAY YOU FALL THROUGH TIME AND SPACE FOR THE REST OF YOUR MISERABLE IMMORTALITY."
NO-- NO, I WON'T LOSE HIM...NOT AGAIN!
GOT TO FOCUS-- FIND HIM--
THOR
THOR
THO--

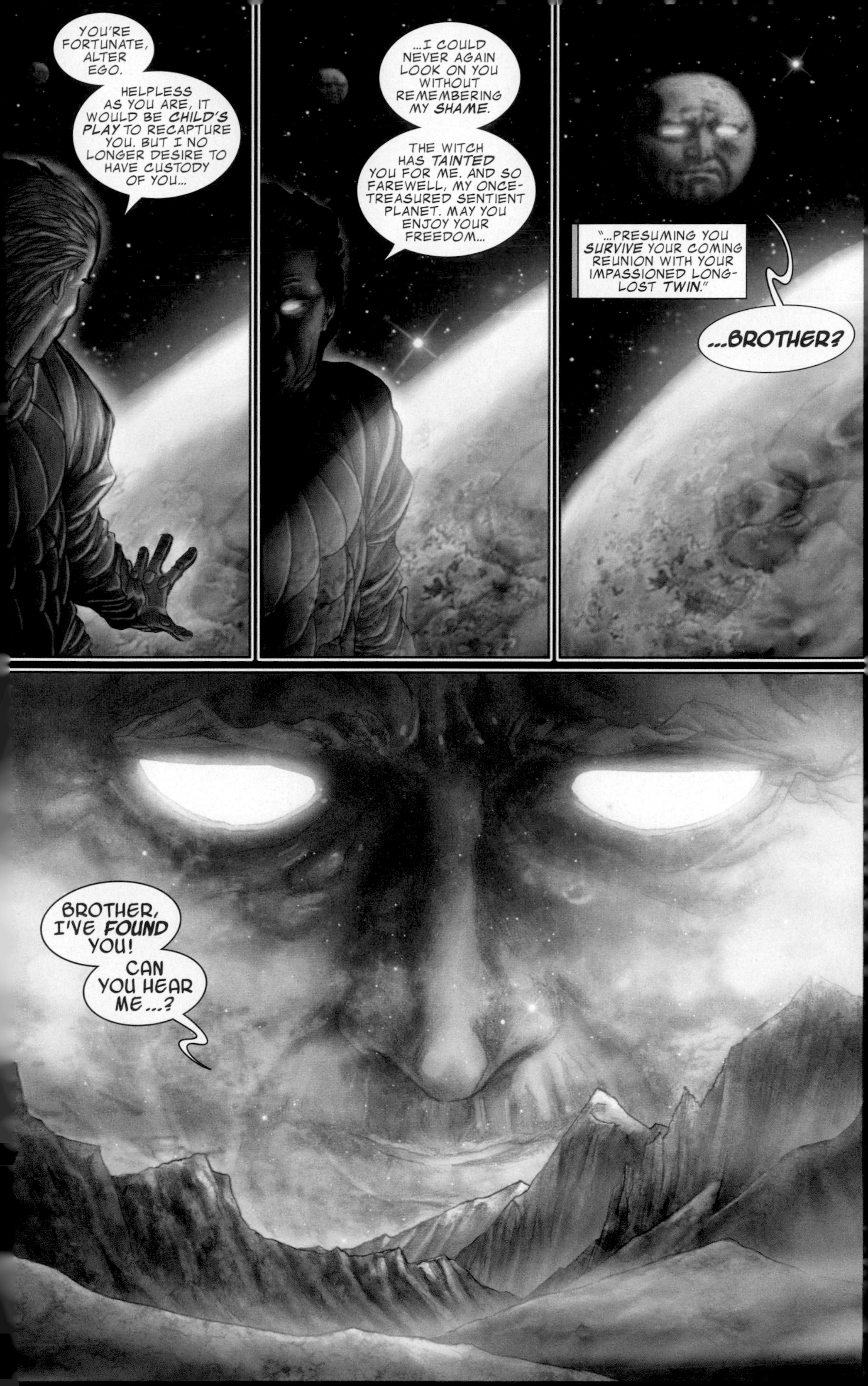
YOU'RE FORTUNATE, ALTER EGO.
HELPLESS AS YOU ARE, IT WOULD BE CHILD'S PLAY TO RECAPTURE YOU. BUT I NO LONGER DESIRE TO HAVE CUSTODY OF YOU...
...I COULD NEVER AGAIN LOOK ON YOU WITHOUT REMEMBERING MY SHAME.
THE WITCH HAS TAINTED YOU FOR ME. AND SO FAREWELL, MY ONCE-TREASURED SENTIENT PLANET. MAY YOU ENJOY YOUR FREEDOM...
"...PRESUMING YOU SURVIVE YOUR COMING REUNION WITH YOUR IMPASSIONED LONG-LOST TWIN."
...BROTHER?
BROTHER, I'VE FOUND YOU!
CAN YOU HEAR ME...?

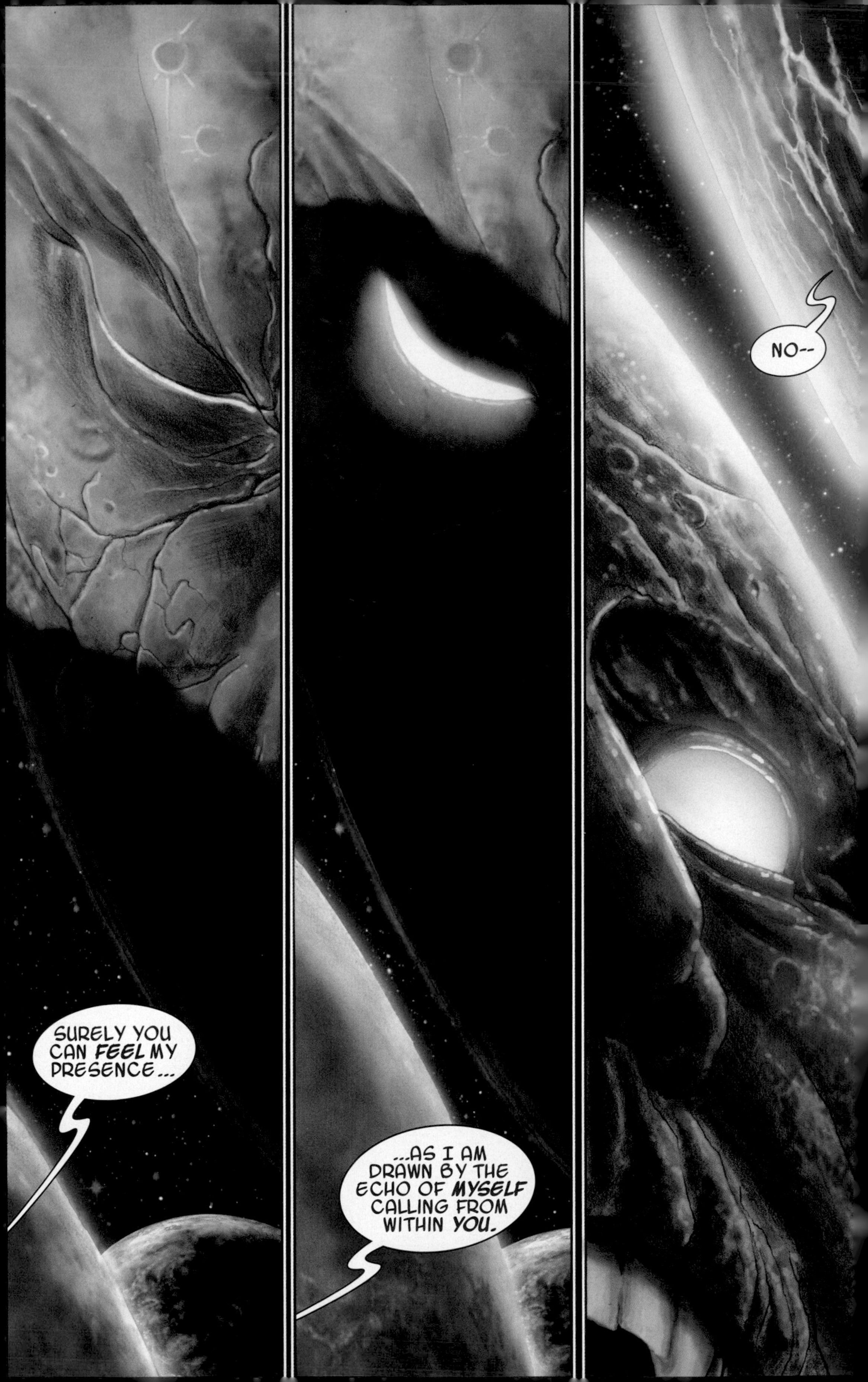
SURELY YOU CAN FEEL MY PRESENCE...
...AS I AM DRAWN BY THE ECHO OF MYSELF CALLING FROM WITHIN YOU.
NO--

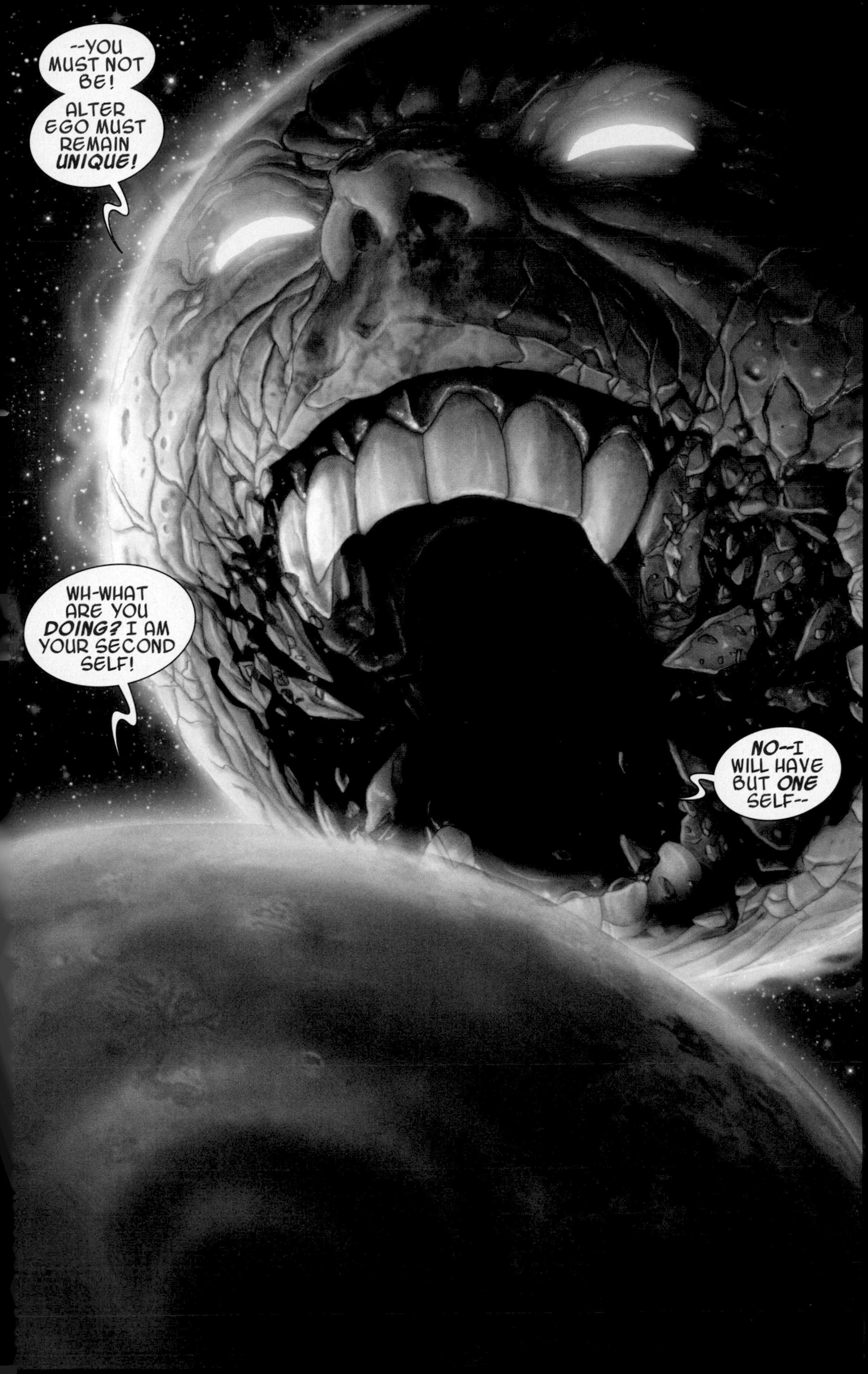
--YOU MUST NOT BE!
ALTER EGO MUST REMAIN *UNIQUE!*
WH-WHAT ARE YOU *DOING?* I AM YOUR SECOND SELF!
NO--I WILL HAVE BUT *ONE* SELF--

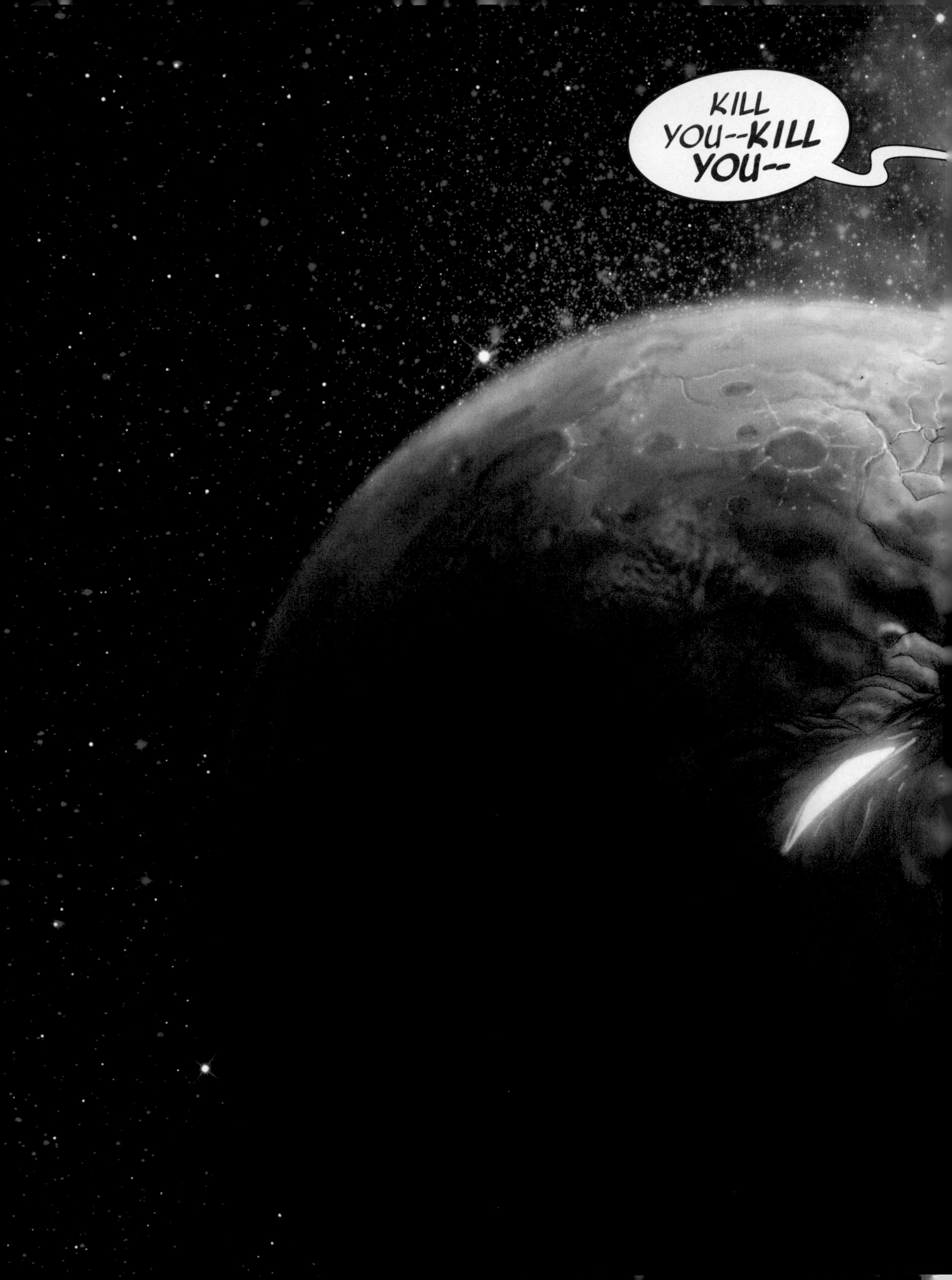
KILL YOU--KILL YOU--

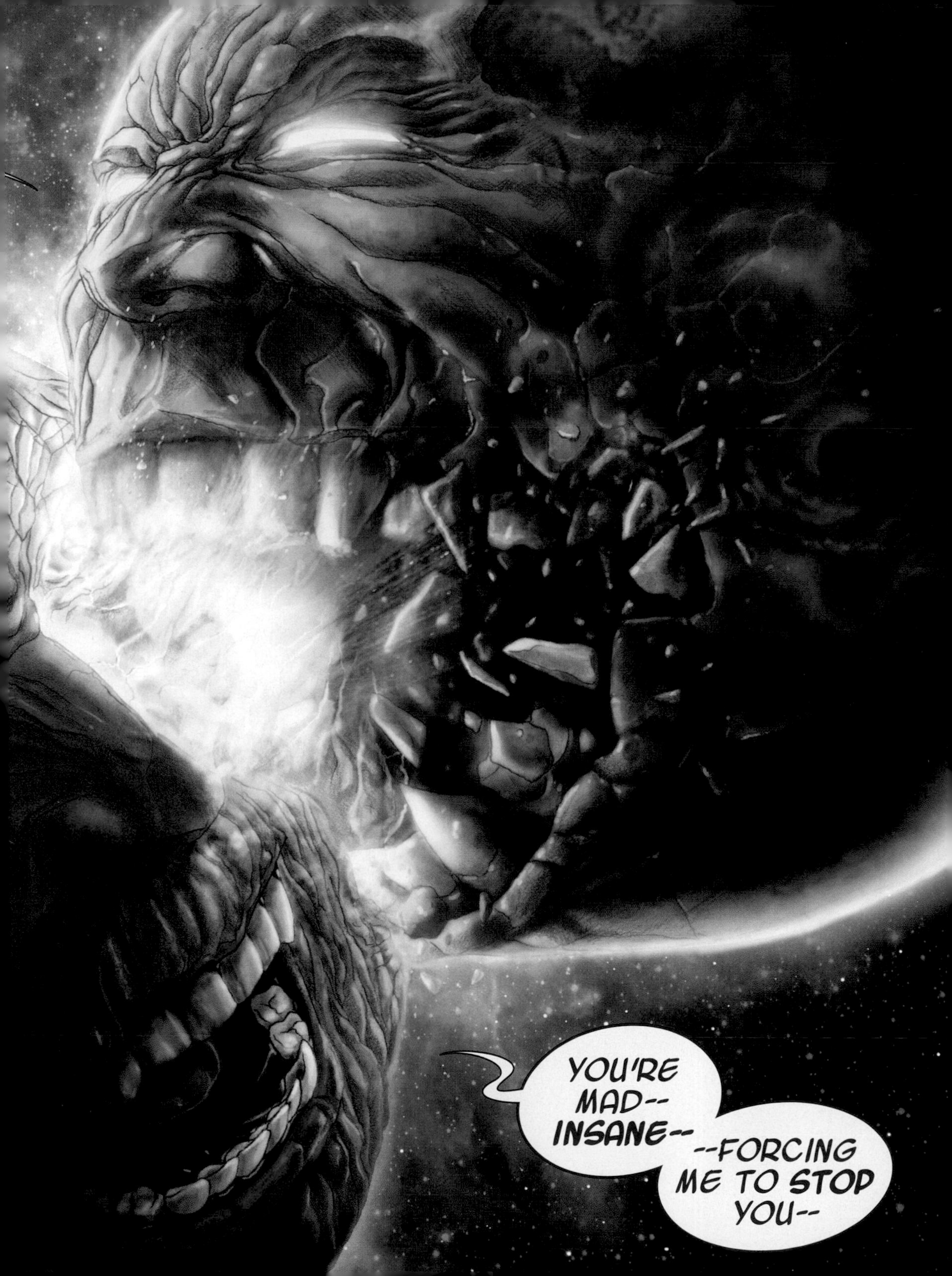
YOU'RE MAD-- INSANE--
--FORCING ME TO STOP YOU--

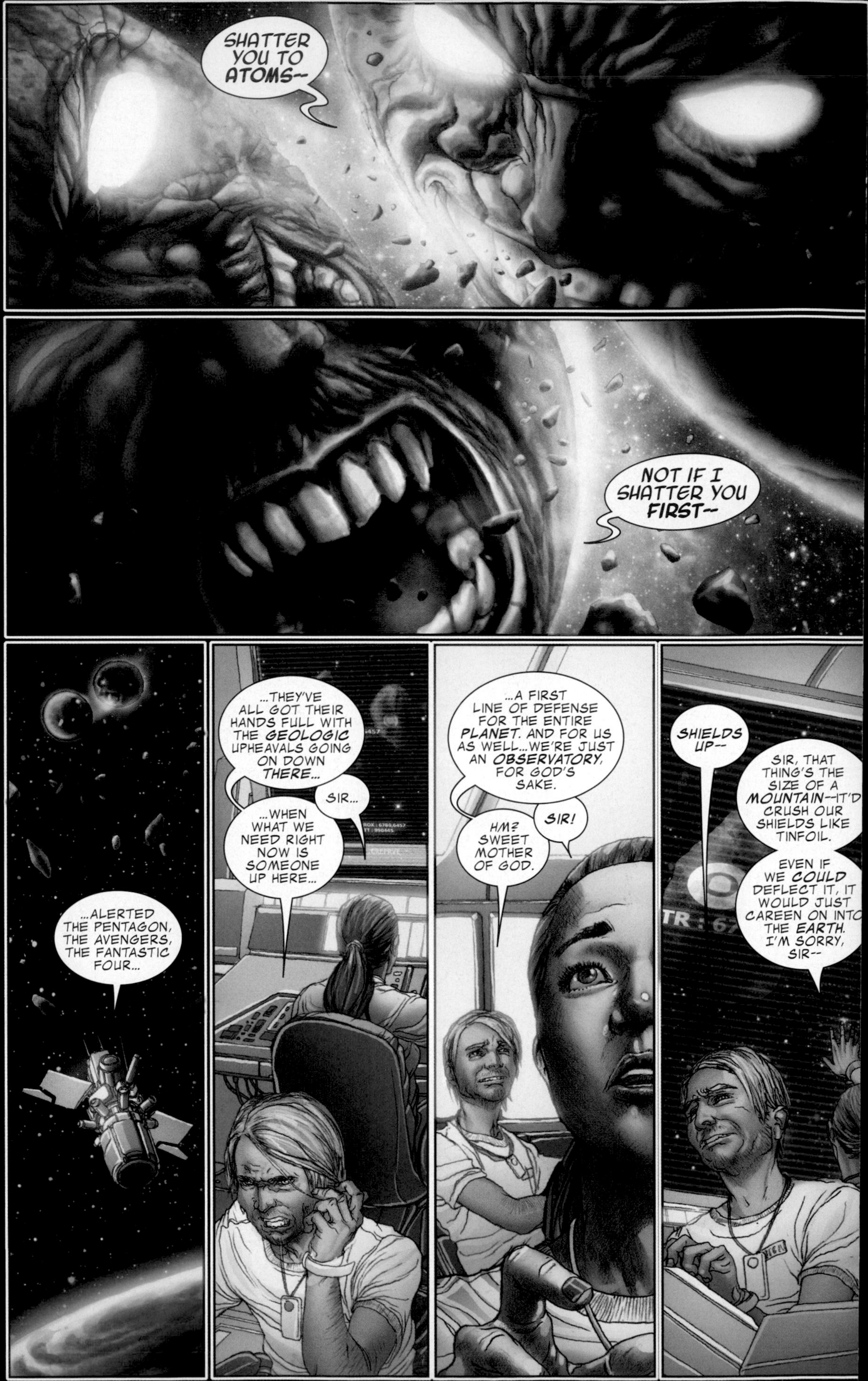

SHATTER YOU TO ATOMS--
NOT IF I SHATTER YOU FIRST--
...ALERTED THE PENTAGON, THE AVENGERS, THE FANTASTIC FOUR...
...THEY'VE ALL GOT THEIR HANDS FULL WITH THE GEOLOGIC UPHEAVALS GOING ON DOWN THERE...
SIR...
...WHEN WHAT WE NEED RIGHT NOW IS SOMEONE UP HERE...
...A FIRST LINE OF DEFENSE FOR THE ENTIRE PLANET. AND FOR US AS WELL...WE'RE JUST AN OBSERVATORY, FOR GOD'S SAKE.
SIR!
H/M? SWEET MOTHER OF GOD.
SHIELDS UP--
SIR, THAT THING'S THE SIZE OF A MOUNTAIN--IT'D CRUSH OUR SHIELDS LIKE TINFOIL.
EVEN IF WE COULD DEFLECT IT, IT WOULD JUST CAREEN ON INTO THE EARTH. I'M SORRY, SIR--

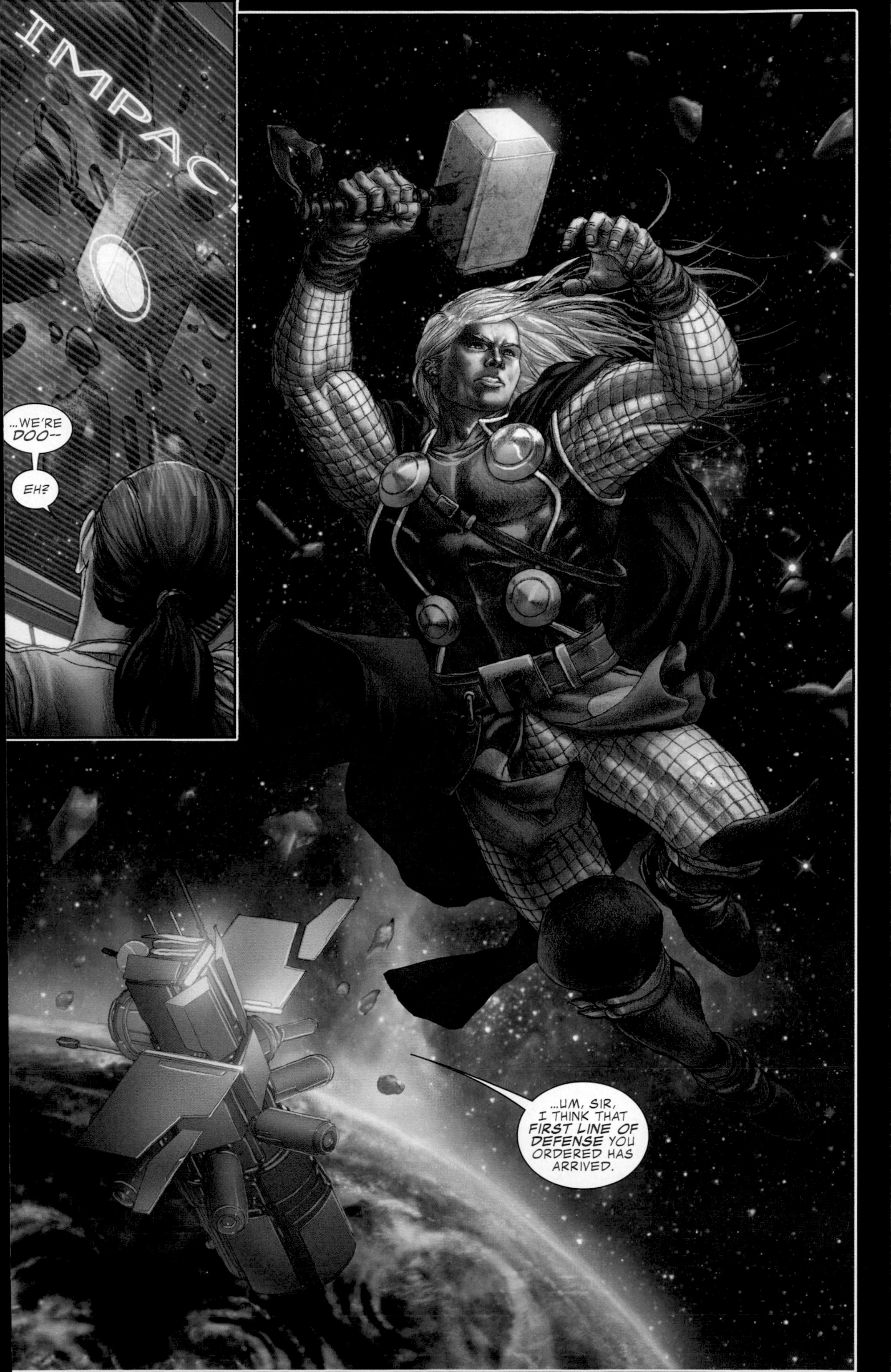
IMPACT
...WE'RE DOO--
EH?
...UM, SIR, I THINK THAT FIRST LINE OF DEFENSE YOU ORDERED HAS ARRIVED.

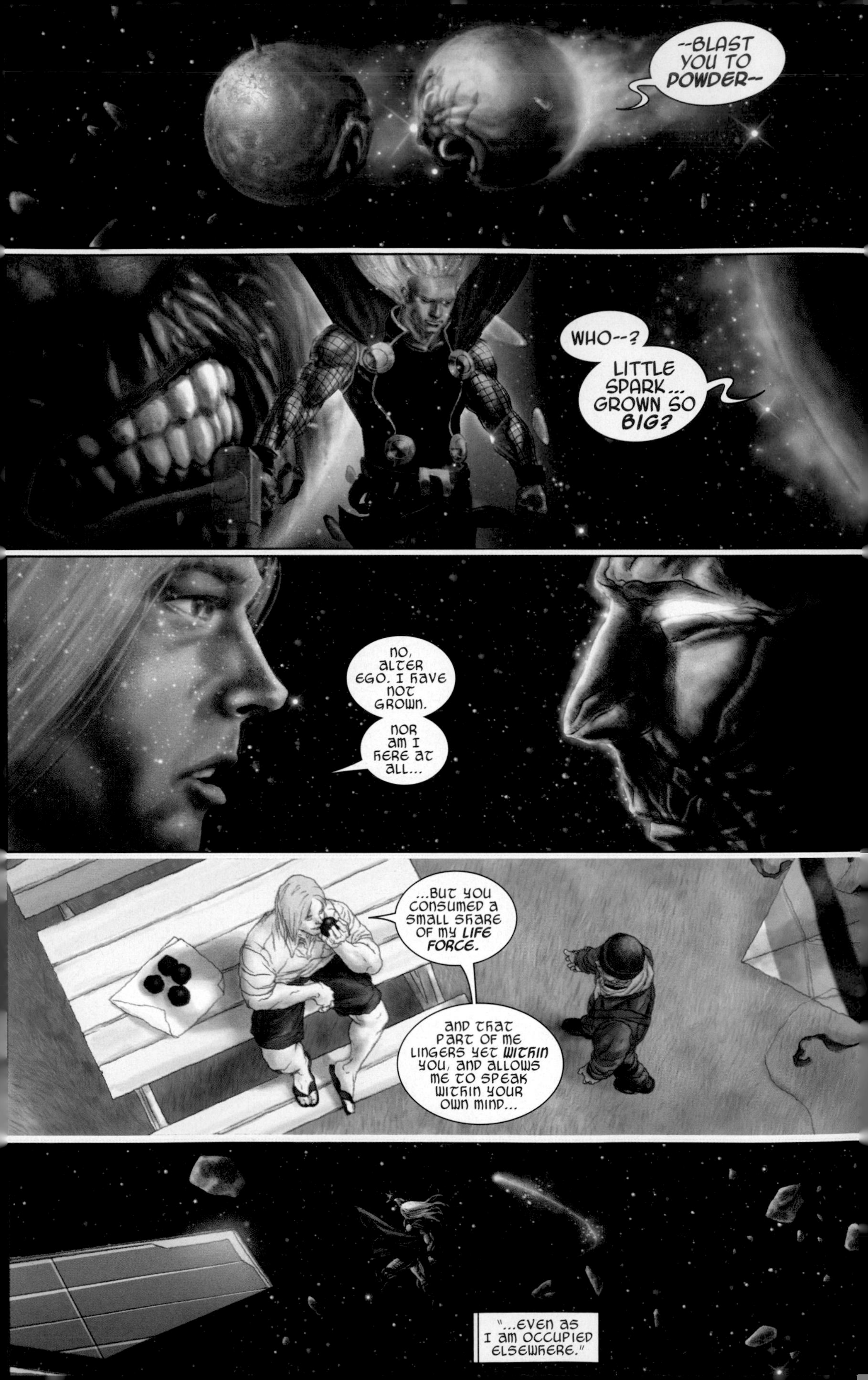
--BLAST YOU TO POWDER--
WHO--?
LITTLE SPARK... GROWN SO BIG?
NO, ALTER EGO. I HAVE NOT GROWN.
NOR AM I HERE AT ALL...
...BUT YOU CONSUMED A SMALL SHARE OF MY LIFE FORCE.
AND THAT PART OF ME LINGERS YET WITHIN YOU, AND ALLOWS ME TO SPEAK WITHIN YOUR OWN MIND...
"...EVEN AS I AM OCCUPIED ELSEWHERE."

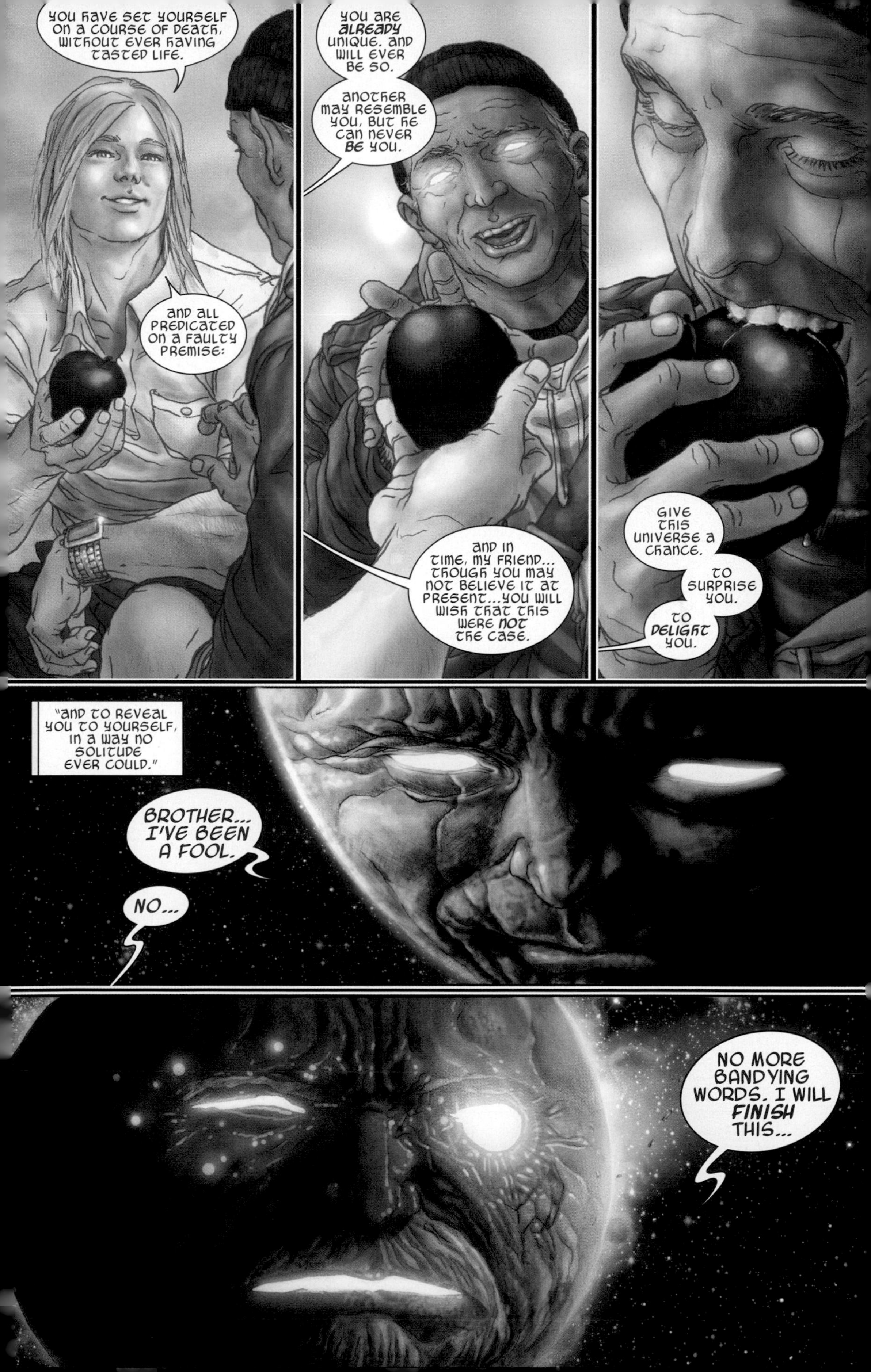
YOU HAVE SET YOURSELF ON A COURSE OF DEATH, WITHOUT EVER HAVING TASTED LIFE.
AND ALL PREDICATED ON A FAULTY PREMISE:
YOU ARE ALREADY UNIQUE. AND WILL EVER BE SO.
ANOTHER MAY RESEMBLE YOU, BUT HE CAN NEVER BE YOU.
AND IN TIME, MY FRIEND... THOUGH YOU MAY NOT BELIEVE IT AT PRESENT...YOU WILL WISH THAT THIS WERE NOT THE CASE.
GIVE THIS UNIVERSE A CHANCE.
TO SURPRISE YOU.
TO DELIGHT YOU.
"AND TO REVEAL YOU TO YOURSELF, IN A WAY NO SOLITUDE EVER COULD."
BROTHER... I'VE BEEN A FOOL.
NO...
NO MORE BANDYING WORDS. I WILL FINISH THIS...

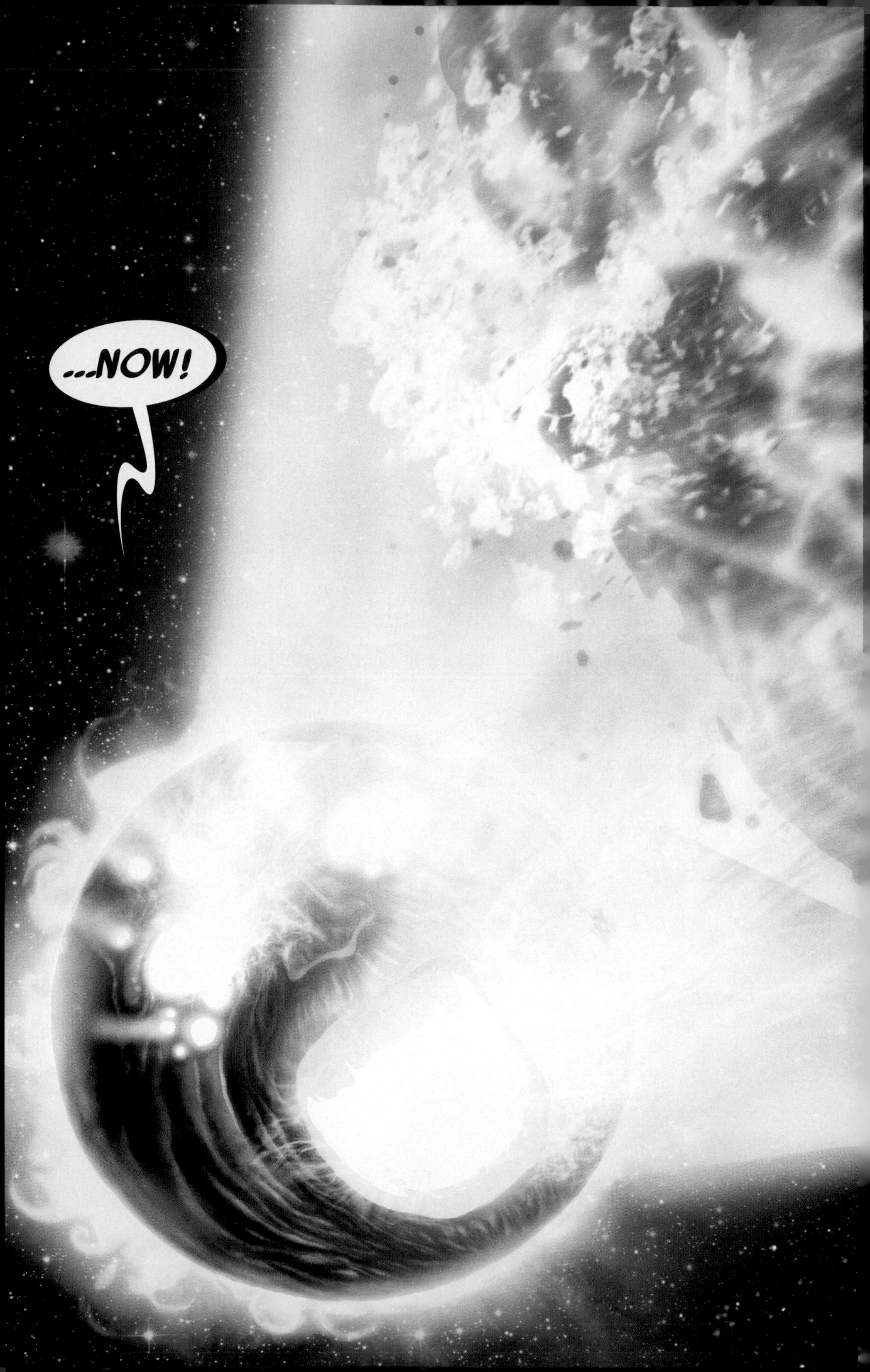
...NOW!

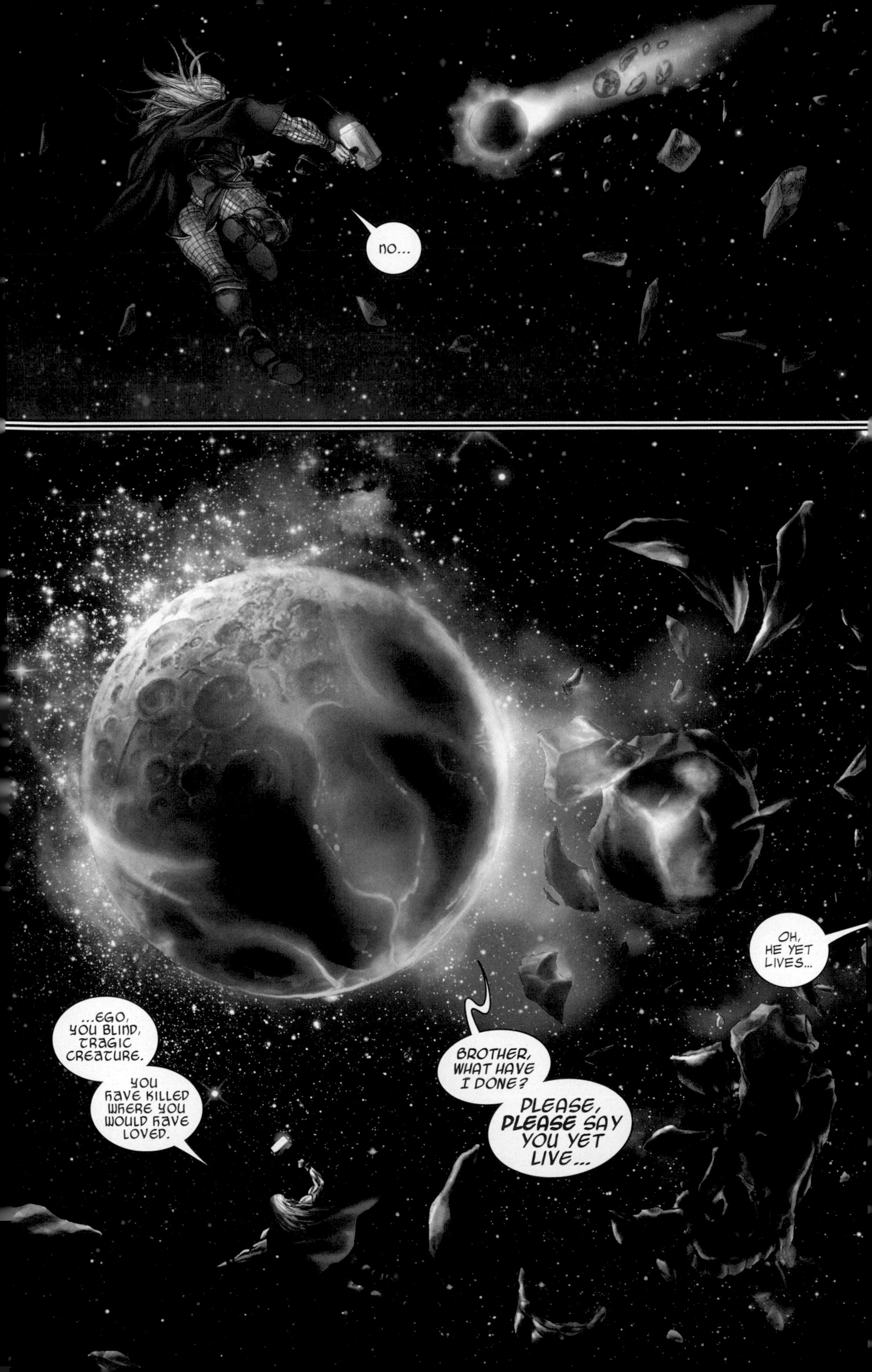
no...
OH, HE YET LIVES...
...EGO, YOU BLIND, TRAGIC CREATURE.
YOU HAVE KILLED WHERE YOU WOULD HAVE LOVED.
BROTHER, WHAT HAVE I DONE?
PLEASE, PLEASE SAY YOU YET LIVE...

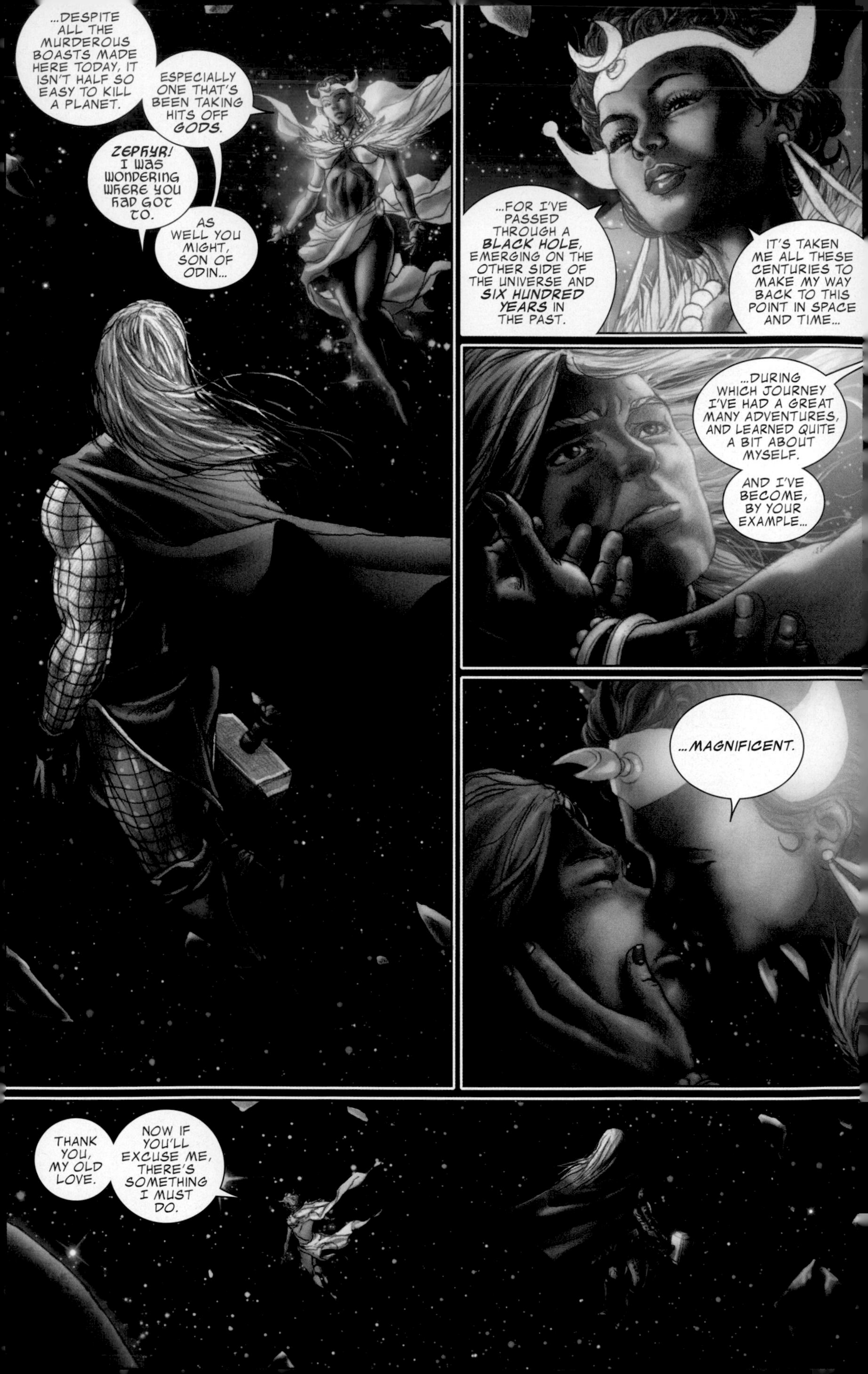
...DESPITE ALL THE MURDEROUS BOASTS MADE HERE TODAY, IT ISN'T HALF SO EASY TO KILL A PLANET.
ESPECIALLY ONE THAT'S BEEN TAKING HITS OFF GODS.
ZEPHYR! I WAS WONDERING WHERE YOU HAD GOT TO.
AS WELL YOU MIGHT, SON OF ODIN...
...FOR I'VE PASSED THROUGH A BLACK HOLE, EMERGING ON THE OTHER SIDE OF THE UNIVERSE AND SIX HUNDRED YEARS IN THE PAST.
IT'S TAKEN ME ALL THESE CENTURIES TO MAKE MY WAY BACK TO THIS POINT IN SPACE AND TIME...
...DURING WHICH JOURNEY I'VE HAD A GREAT MANY ADVENTURES, AND LEARNED QUITE A BIT ABOUT MYSELF.
AND I'VE BECOME, BY YOUR EXAMPLE...
...MAGNIFICENT.
THANK YOU, MY OLD LOVE.
NOW IF YOU'LL EXCUSE ME, THERE'S SOMETHING I MUST DO.

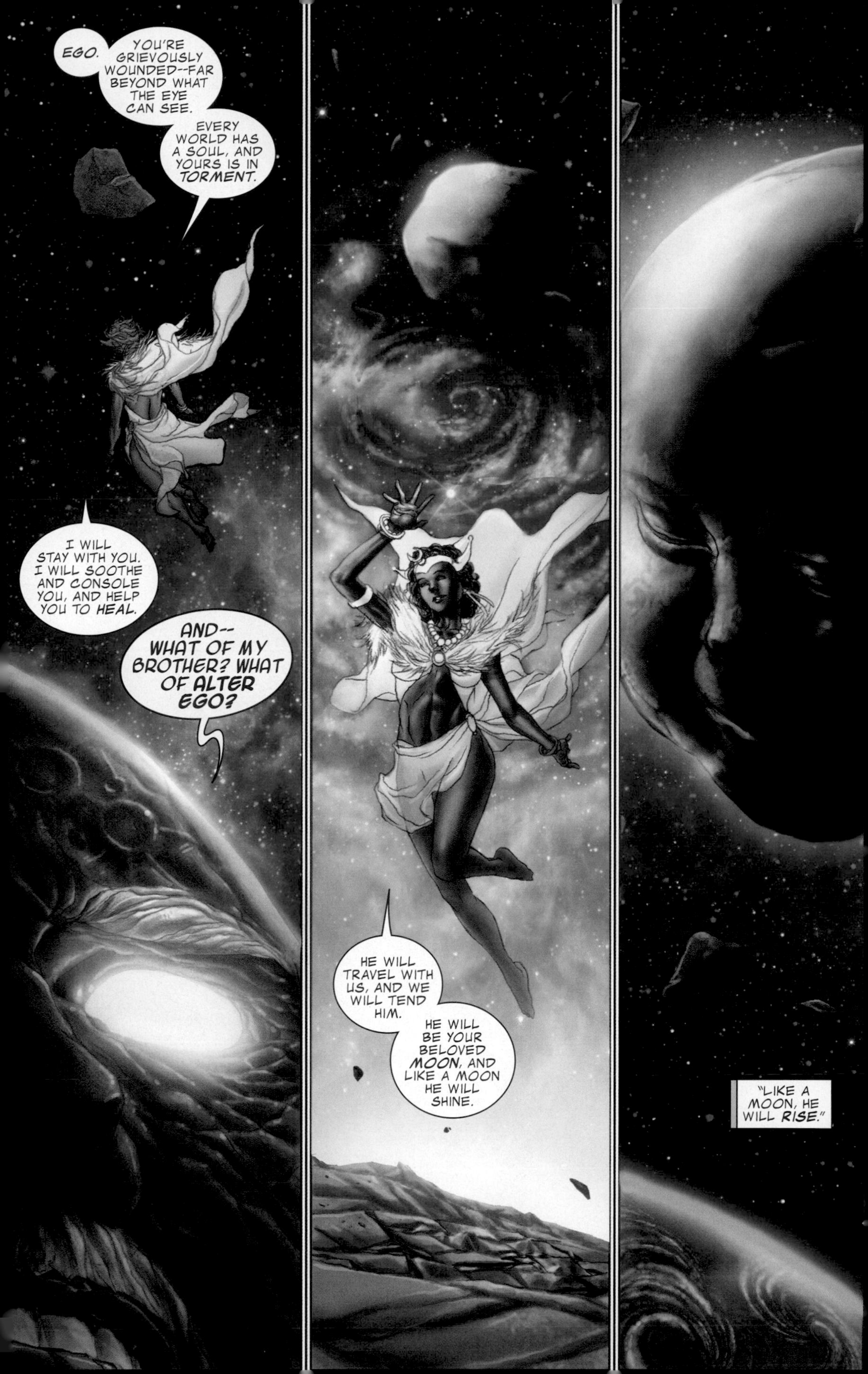

EGO.
YOU'RE GRIEVOUSLY WOUNDED--FAR BEYOND WHAT THE EYE CAN SEE.
EVERY WORLD HAS A SOUL, AND YOURS IS IN TORMENT.
I WILL STAY WITH YOU. I WILL SOOTHE AND CONSOLE YOU, AND HELP YOU TO HEAL.
AND-- WHAT OF MY BROTHER? WHAT OF ALTER EGO?
HE WILL TRAVEL WITH US, AND WE WILL TEND HIM.
HE WILL BE YOUR BELOVED MOON, AND LIKE A MOON HE WILL SHINE.
"LIKE A MOON, HE WILL RISE."

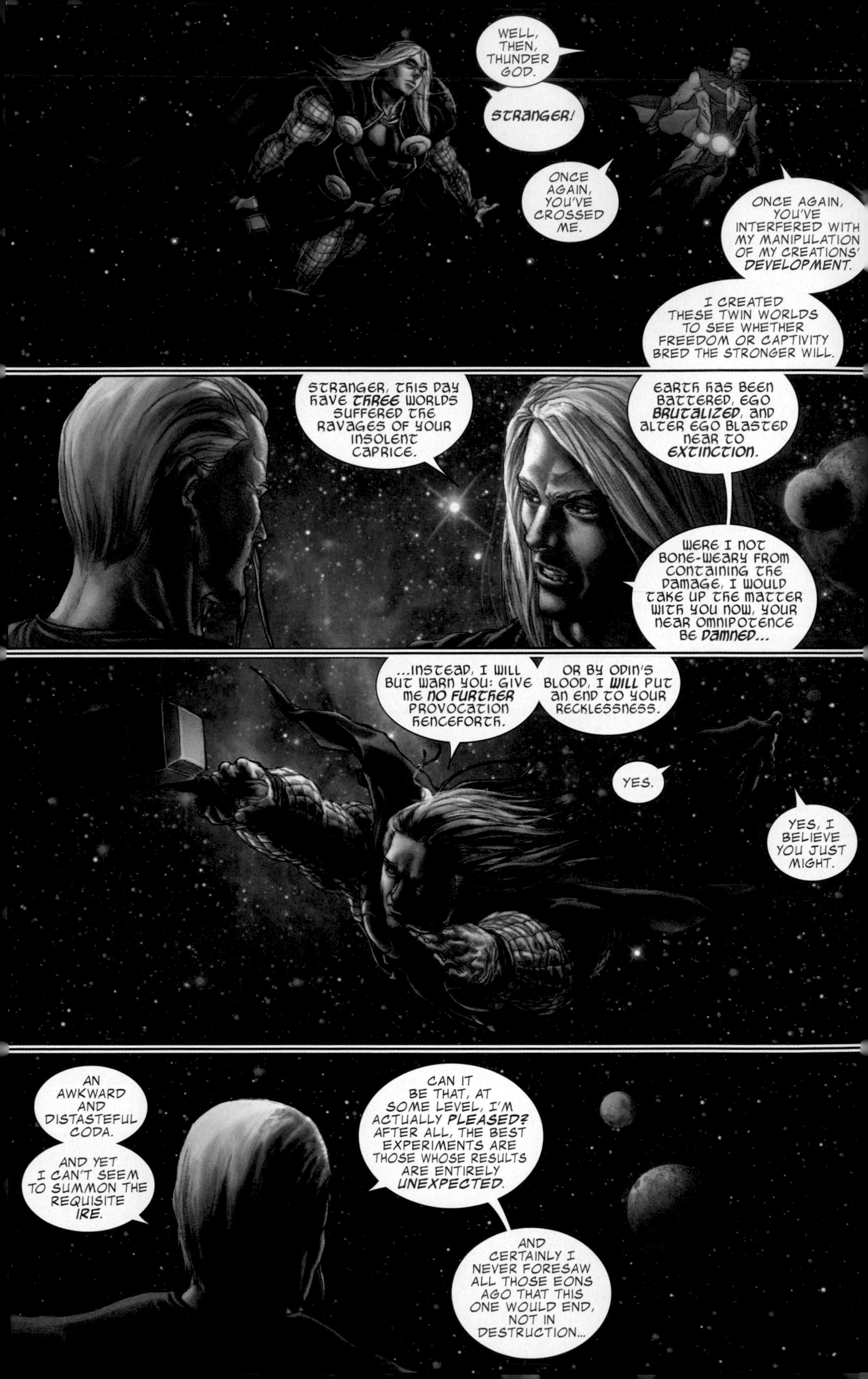
WELL, THEN, THUNDER GOD.
STRANGER!
ONCE AGAIN, YOU'VE CROSSED ME.
ONCE AGAIN, YOU'VE INTERFERED WITH MY MANIPULATION OF MY CREATIONS' DEVELOPMENT.
I CREATED THESE TWIN WORLDS TO SEE WHETHER FREEDOM OR CAPTIVITY BRED THE STRONGER WILL.
STRANGER, THIS DAY HAVE THREE WORLDS SUFFERED THE RAVAGES OF YOUR INSOLENT CAPRICE.
EARTH HAS BEEN BATTERED, EGO BRUTALIZED, AND ALTER EGO BLASTED NEAR TO EXTINCTION.
WERE I NOT BONE-WEARY FROM CONTAINING THE DAMAGE, I WOULD TAKE UP THE MATTER WITH YOU NOW, YOUR NEAR OMNIPOTENCE BE DAMNED...
...INSTEAD, I WILL BUT WARN YOU: GIVE ME NO FURTHER PROVOCATION HENCEFORTH.
OR BY ODIN'S BLOOD, I WILL PUT AN END TO YOUR RECKLESSNESS.
YES.
YES, I BELIEVE YOU JUST MIGHT.
AN AWKWARD AND DISTASTEFUL CODA.
AND YET I CAN'T SEEM TO SUMMON THE REQUISITE IRE.
CAN IT BE THAT, AT SOME LEVEL, I'M ACTUALLY PLEASED? AFTER ALL, THE BEST EXPERIMENTS ARE THOSE WHOSE RESULTS ARE ENTIRELY UNEXPECTED.
AND CERTAINLY I NEVER FORESAW ALL THOSE EONS AGO THAT THIS ONE WOULD END, NOT IN DESTRUCTION...

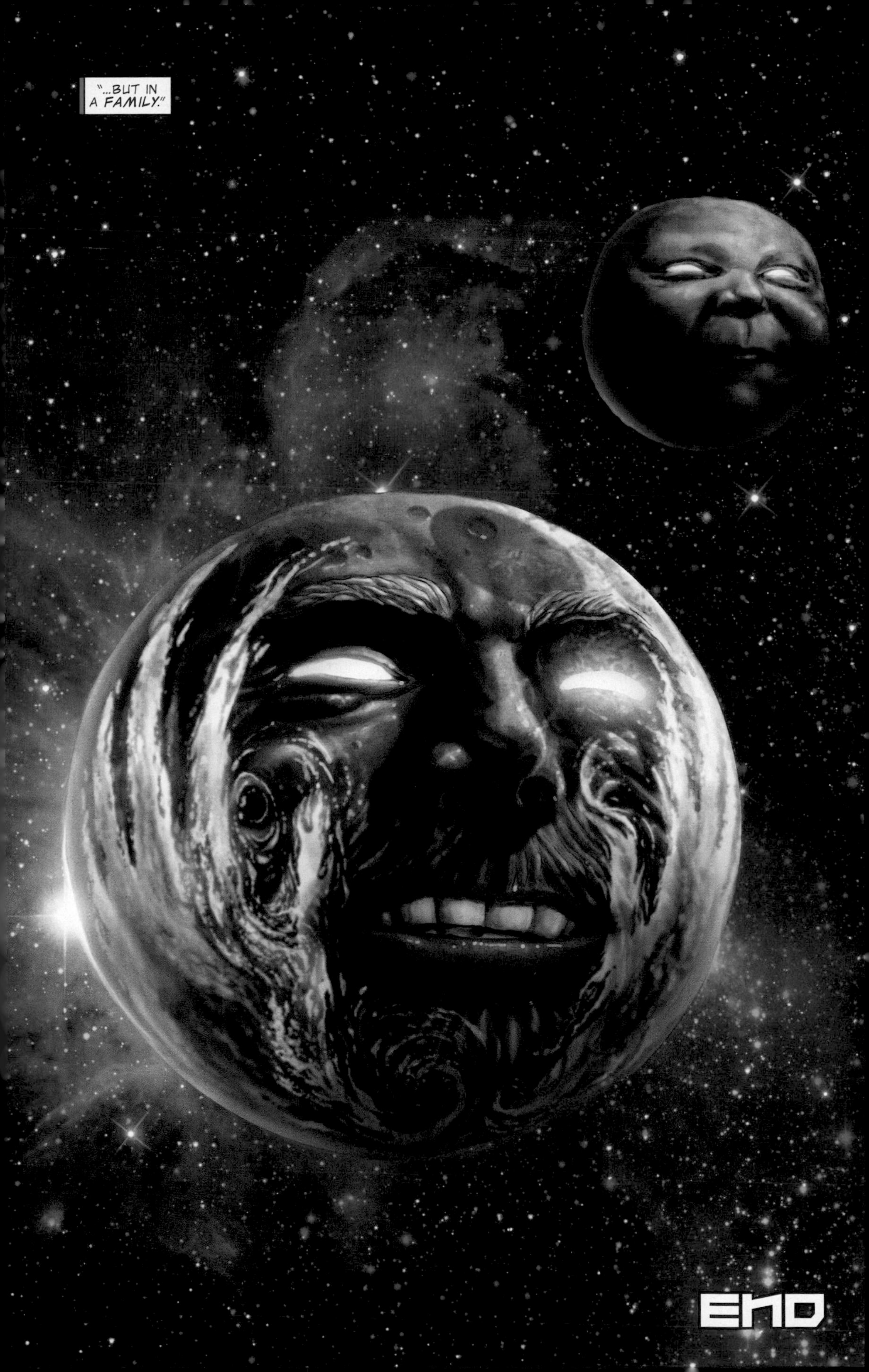
"...BUT IN A FAMILY."
END

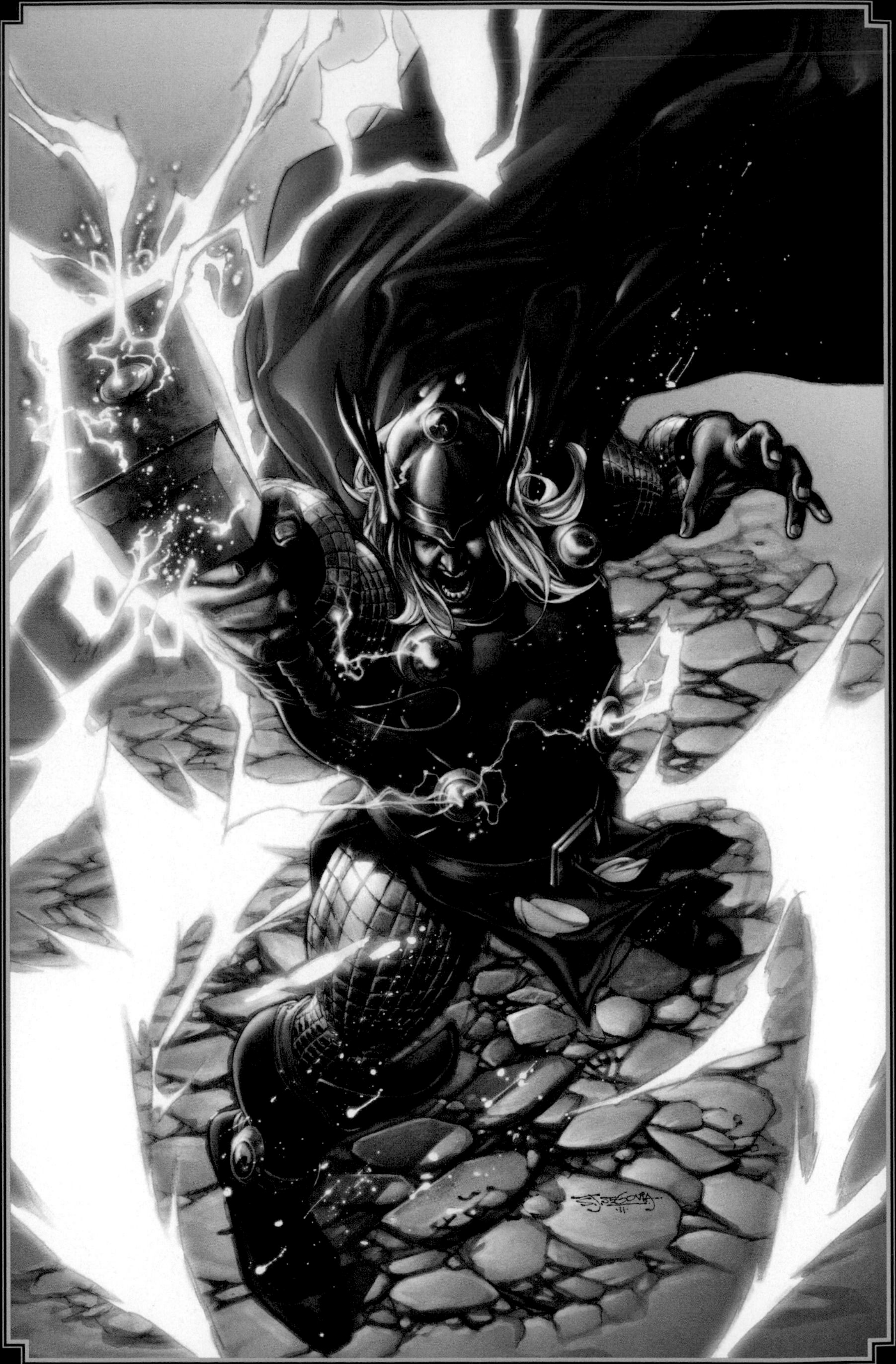

Thor: The Deviants Saga 1

I WAS BORN UNDER THE GROUND, IN A CITY OF GENETIC *DEVIANTS.*

THERE I SCROUNGED AND SCAVENGED FOR MY LIVELIHOOD.

BUT I WAS DRIVEN...I HAD *AMBITION.*

I STOLE THE NAME AND ASPECT OF A *GODDESS,* AND TOOK HER PLACE IN THE WORLD OF MEN.

AND SO I THRIVED.

YET AS TIME PASSED, I GREW BORED.

MY AMBITION DROVE ME FURTHER...*TOO* FAR.

I STOLE THE MEANS TO *INFINITE* POWER, AND ATTEMPTED TO RULE *ALL.*

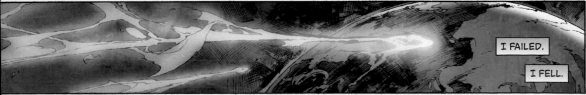

I FAILED.

I FELL.

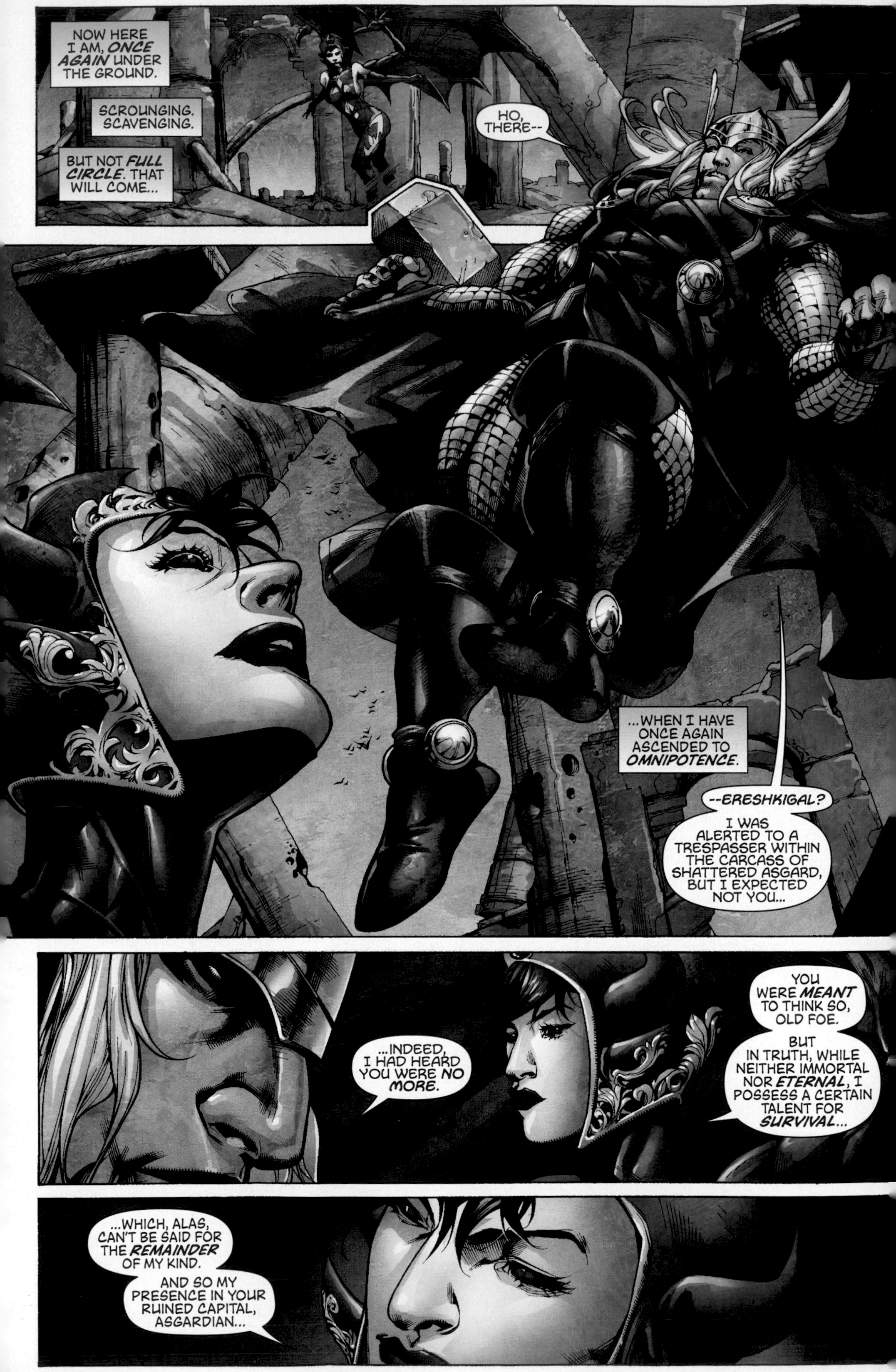
NOW HERE I AM, ONCE AGAIN UNDER THE GROUND.
SCROUNGING. SCAVENGING.
BUT NOT FULL CIRCLE. THAT WILL COME...
HO, THERE--
...WHEN I HAVE ONCE AGAIN ASCENDED TO OMNIPOTENCE.
--ERESHKIGAL?
I WAS ALERTED TO A TRESPASSER WITHIN THE CARCASS OF SHATTERED ASGARD, BUT I EXPECTED NOT YOU...
...INDEED, I HAD HEARD YOU WERE NO MORE.
YOU WERE MEANT TO THINK SO, OLD FOE.
BUT IN TRUTH, WHILE NEITHER IMMORTAL NOR ETERNAL, I POSSESS A CERTAIN TALENT FOR SURVIVAL...
...WHICH, ALAS, CAN'T BE SAID FOR THE REMAINDER OF MY KIND.
AND SO MY PRESENCE IN YOUR RUINED CAPITAL, ASGARDIAN...

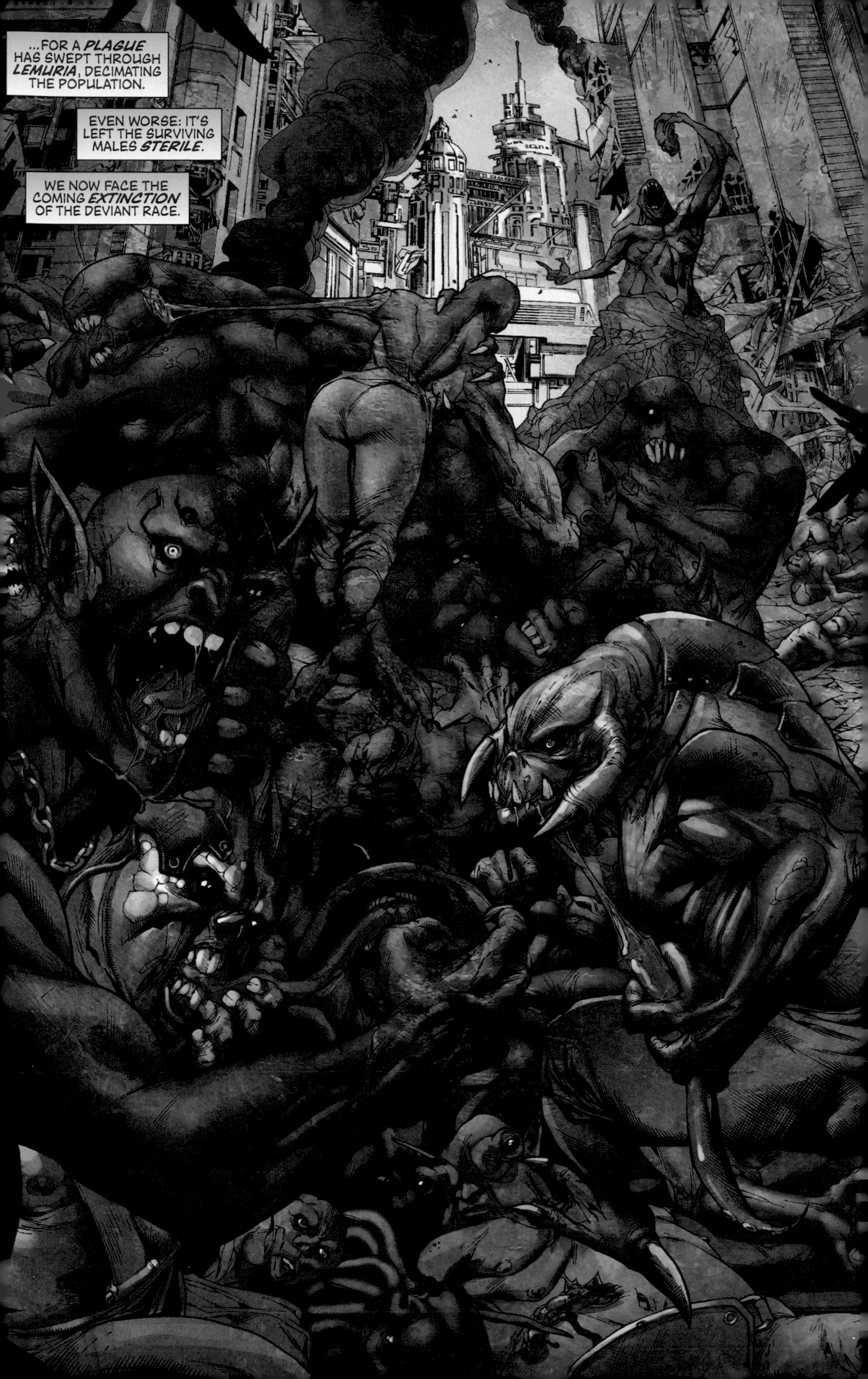
...FOR A PLAGUE HAS SWEPT THROUGH LEMURIA, DECIMATING THE POPULATION.
EVEN WORSE: IT'S LEFT THE SURVIVING MALES STERILE.
WE NOW FACE THE COMING EXTINCTION OF THE DEVIANT RACE.

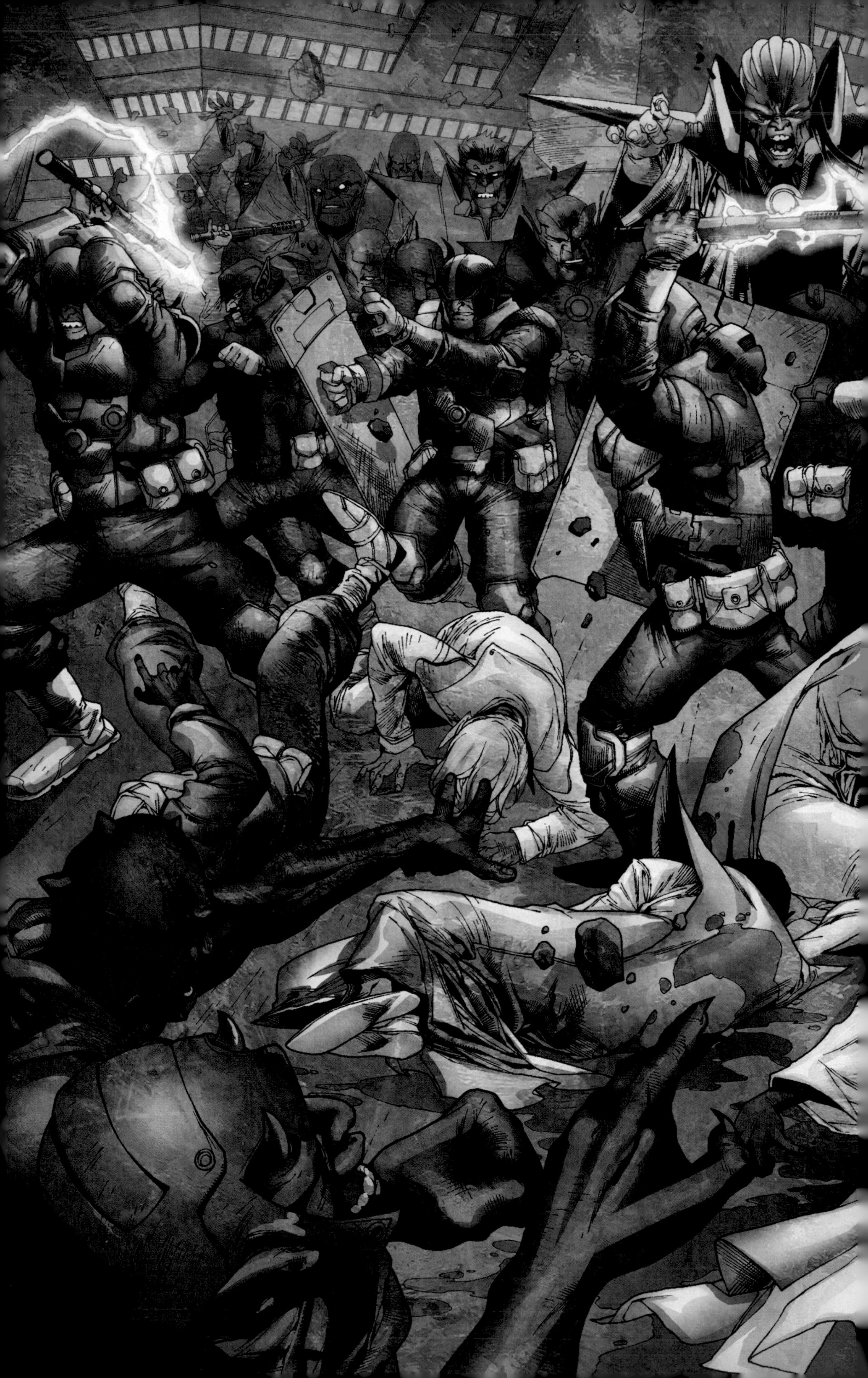

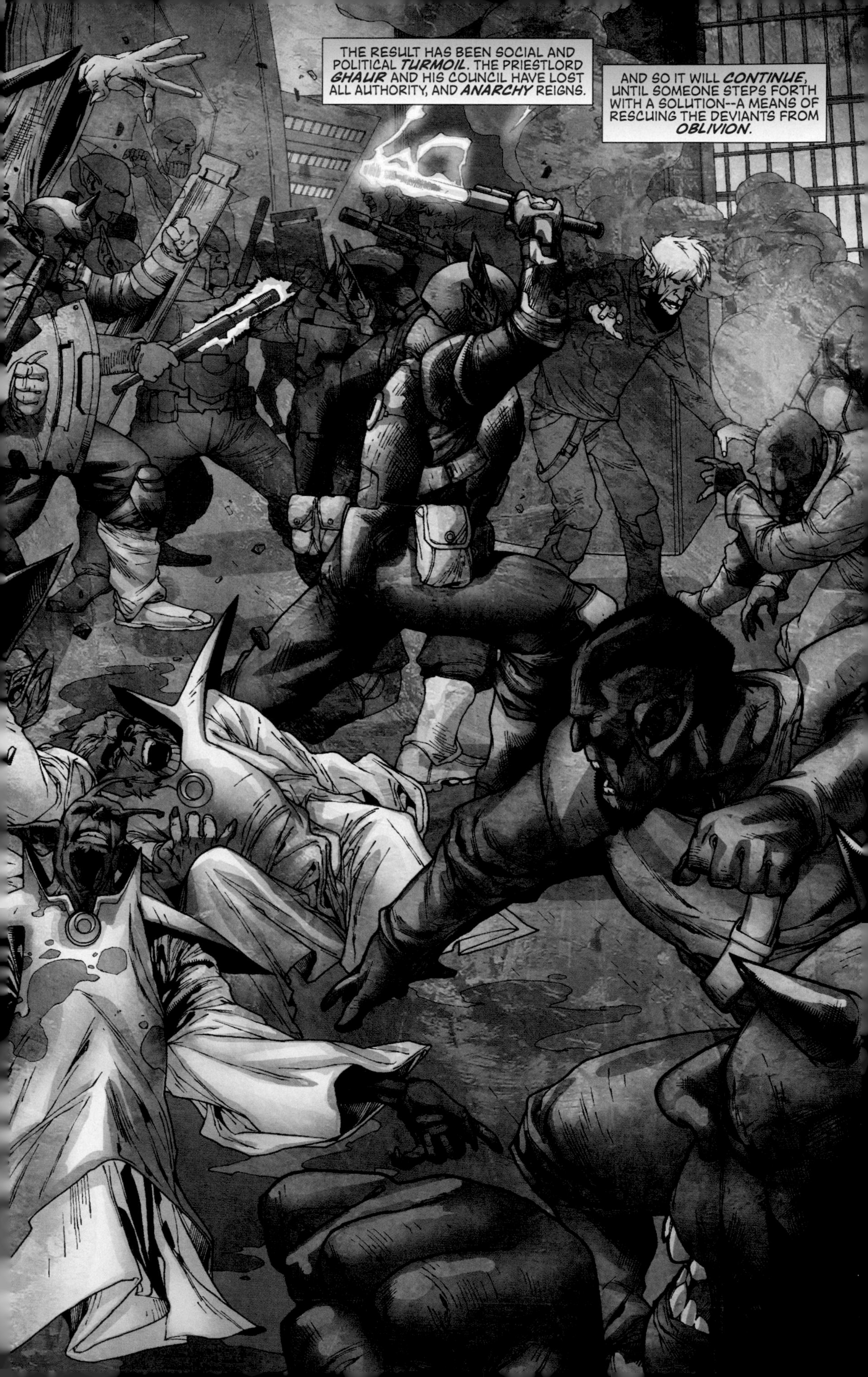
THE RESULT HAS BEEN SOCIAL AND POLITICAL TURMOIL. THE PRIESTLORD GHAUR AND HIS COUNCIL HAVE LOST ALL AUTHORITY, AND ANARCHY REIGNS.
AND SO IT WILL CONTINUE, UNTIL SOMEONE STEPS FORTH WITH A SOLUTION--A MEANS OF RESCUING THE DEVIANTS FROM OBLIVION.

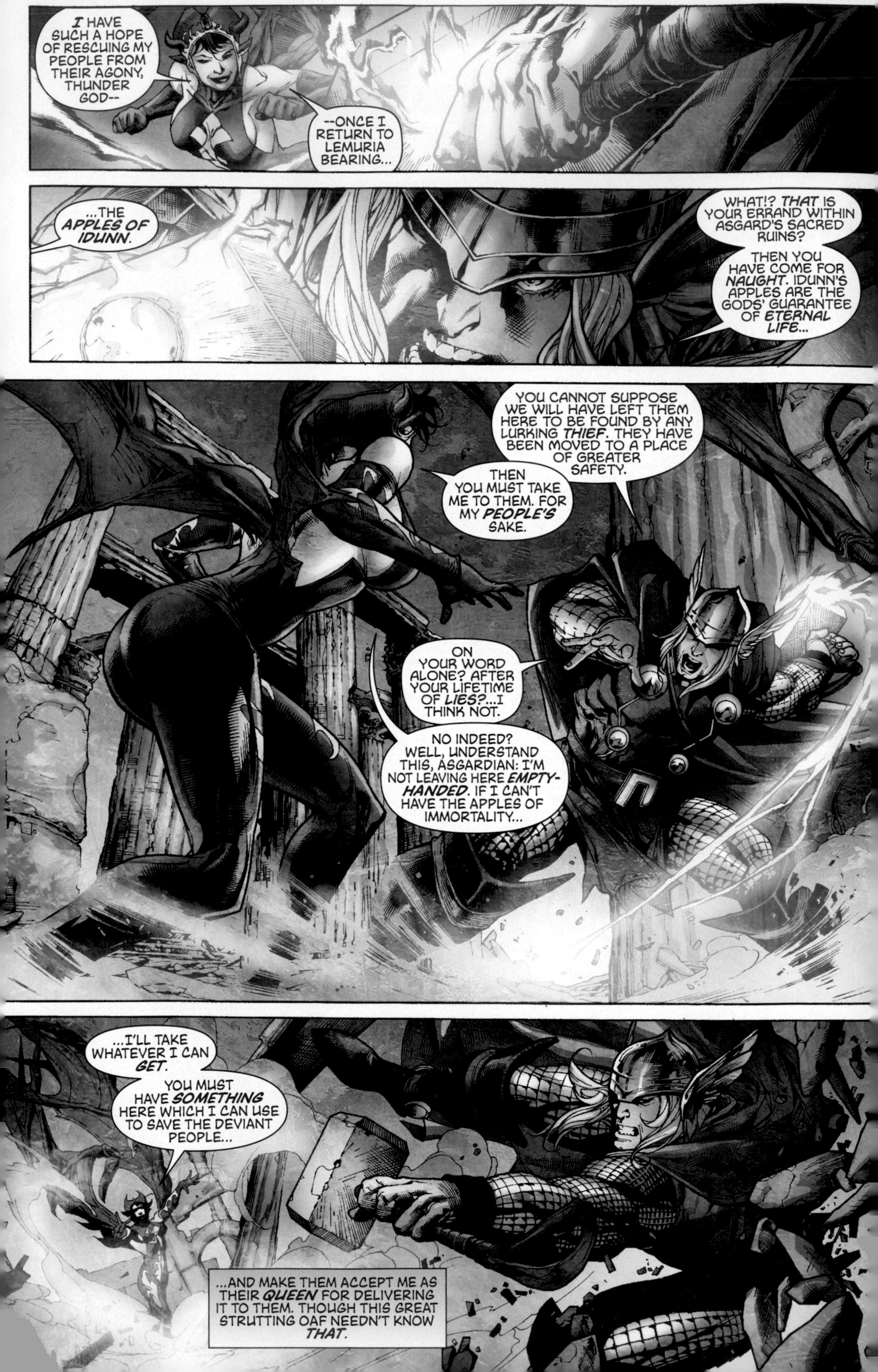
I HAVE SUCH A HOPE OF RESCUING MY PEOPLE FROM THEIR AGONY, THUNDER GOD--
--ONCE I RETURN TO LEMURIA BEARING...
...THE APPLES OF IDUNN.
WHAT!? THAT IS YOUR ERRAND WITHIN ASGARD'S SACRED RUINS?
THEN YOU HAVE COME FOR NAUGHT. IDUNN'S APPLES ARE THE GODS' GUARANTEE OF ETERNAL LIFE...
YOU CANNOT SUPPOSE WE WILL HAVE LEFT THEM HERE TO BE FOUND BY ANY LURKING THIEF. THEY HAVE BEEN MOVED TO A PLACE OF GREATER SAFETY.
THEN YOU MUST TAKE ME TO THEM. FOR MY PEOPLE'S SAKE.
ON YOUR WORD ALONE? AFTER YOUR LIFETIME OF LIES?...I THINK NOT.
NO INDEED? WELL, UNDERSTAND THIS, ASGARDIAN: I'M NOT LEAVING HERE EMPTY-HANDED. IF I CAN'T HAVE THE APPLES OF IMMORTALITY...
...I'LL TAKE WHATEVER I CAN GET.
YOU MUST HAVE SOMETHING HERE WHICH I CAN USE TO SAVE THE DEVIANT PEOPLE...
...AND MAKE THEM ACCEPT ME AS THEIR QUEEN FOR DELIVERING IT TO THEM. THOUGH THIS GREAT STRUTTING OAF NEEDN'T KNOW THAT.

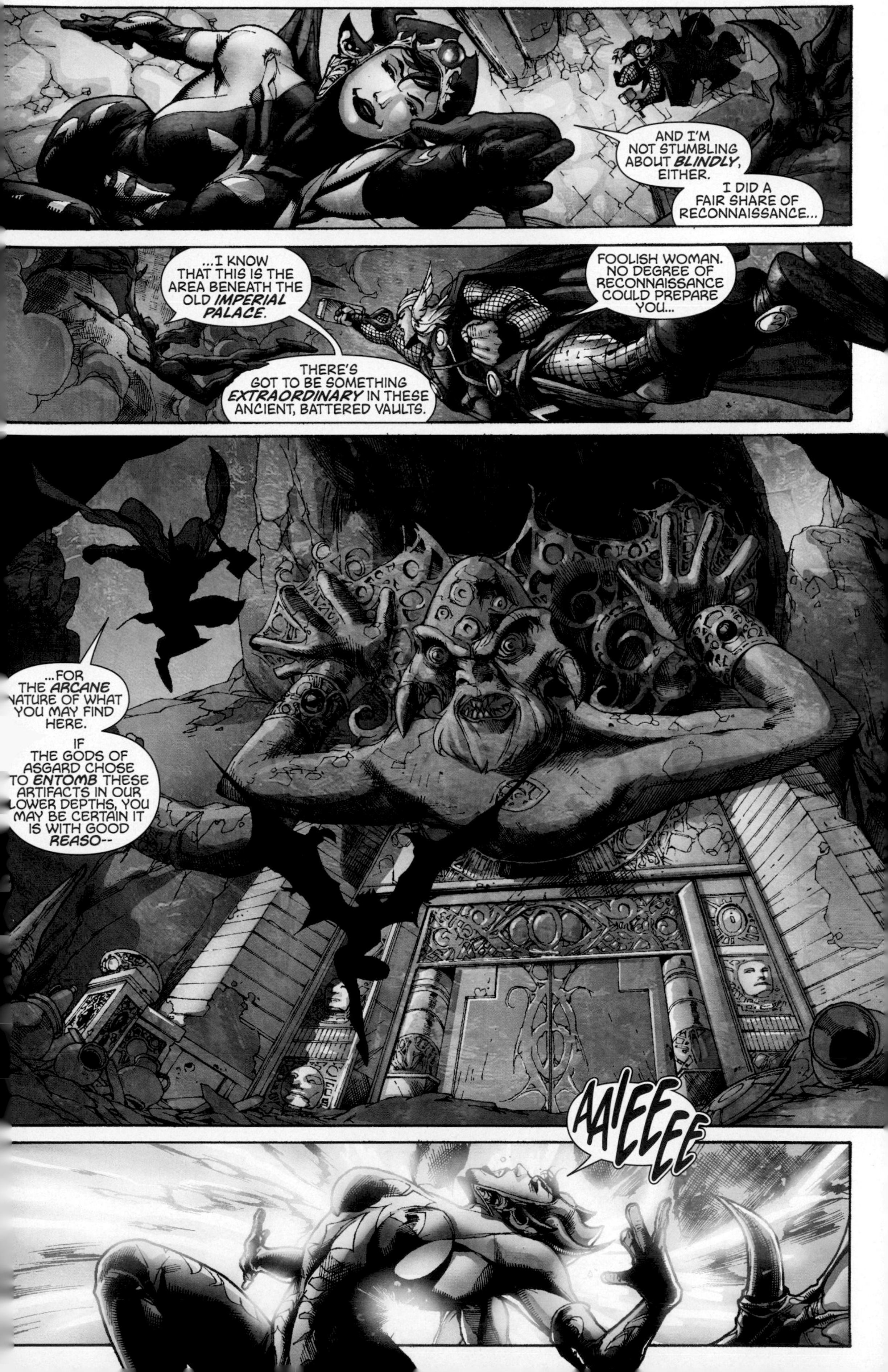

AND I'M NOT STUMBLING ABOUT BLINDLY, EITHER.
I DID A FAIR SHARE OF RECONNAISSANCE...
...I KNOW THAT THIS IS THE AREA BENEATH THE OLD IMPERIAL PALACE.
THERE'S GOT TO BE SOMETHING EXTRAORDINARY IN THESE ANCIENT, BATTERED VAULTS.
FOOLISH WOMAN. NO DEGREE OF RECONNAISSANCE COULD PREPARE YOU...
...FOR THE ARCANE NATURE OF WHAT YOU MAY FIND HERE.
IF THE GODS OF ASGARD CHOSE TO ENTOMB THESE ARTIFACTS IN OUR LOWER DEPTHS, YOU MAY BE CERTAIN IT IS WITH GOOD REASO--
AAIEEEE

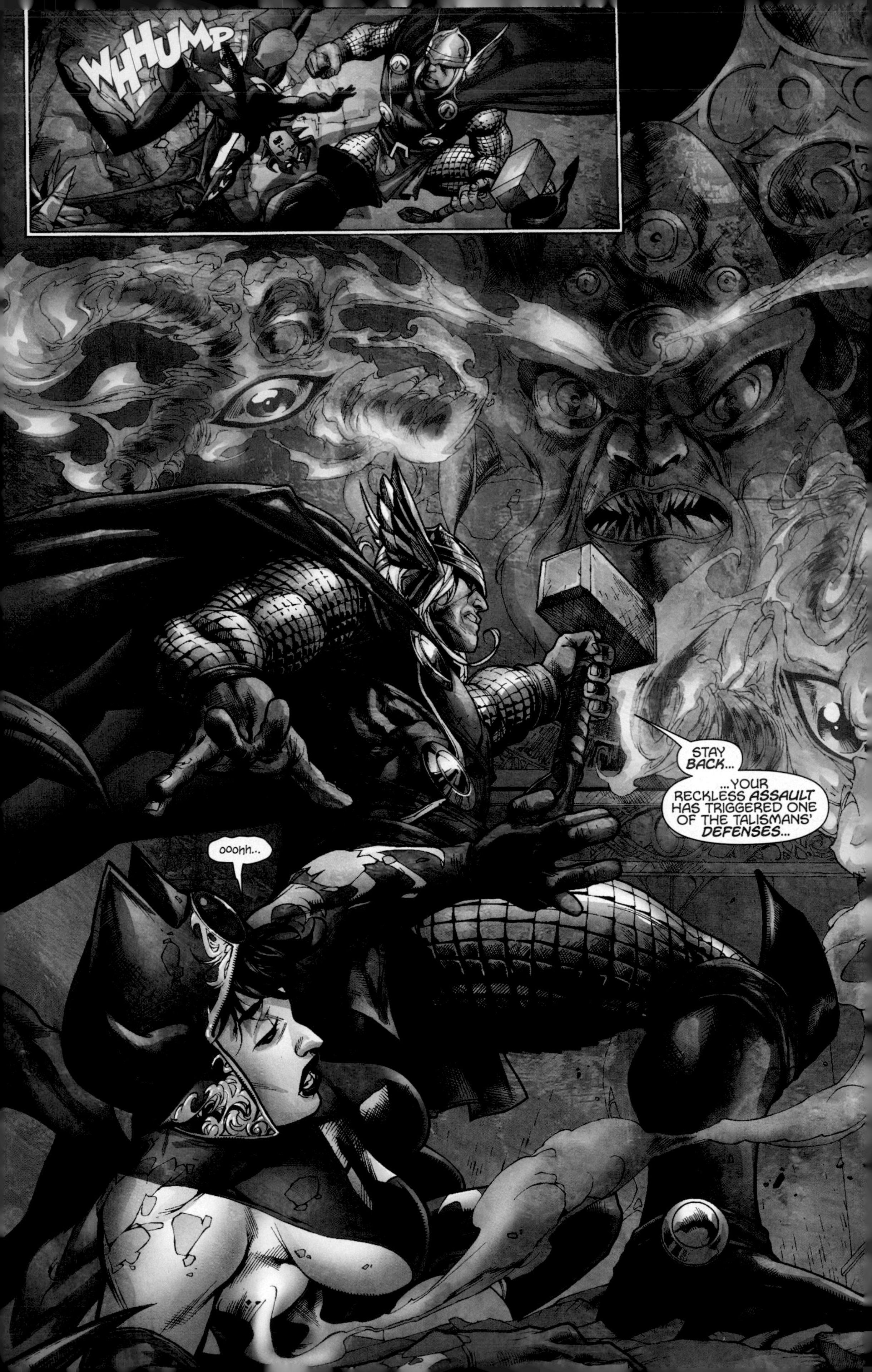
WHHUMP
STAY BACK...
...YOUR RECKLESS ASSAULT HAS TRIGGERED ONE OF THE TALISMANS' DEFENSES...
ooohh...

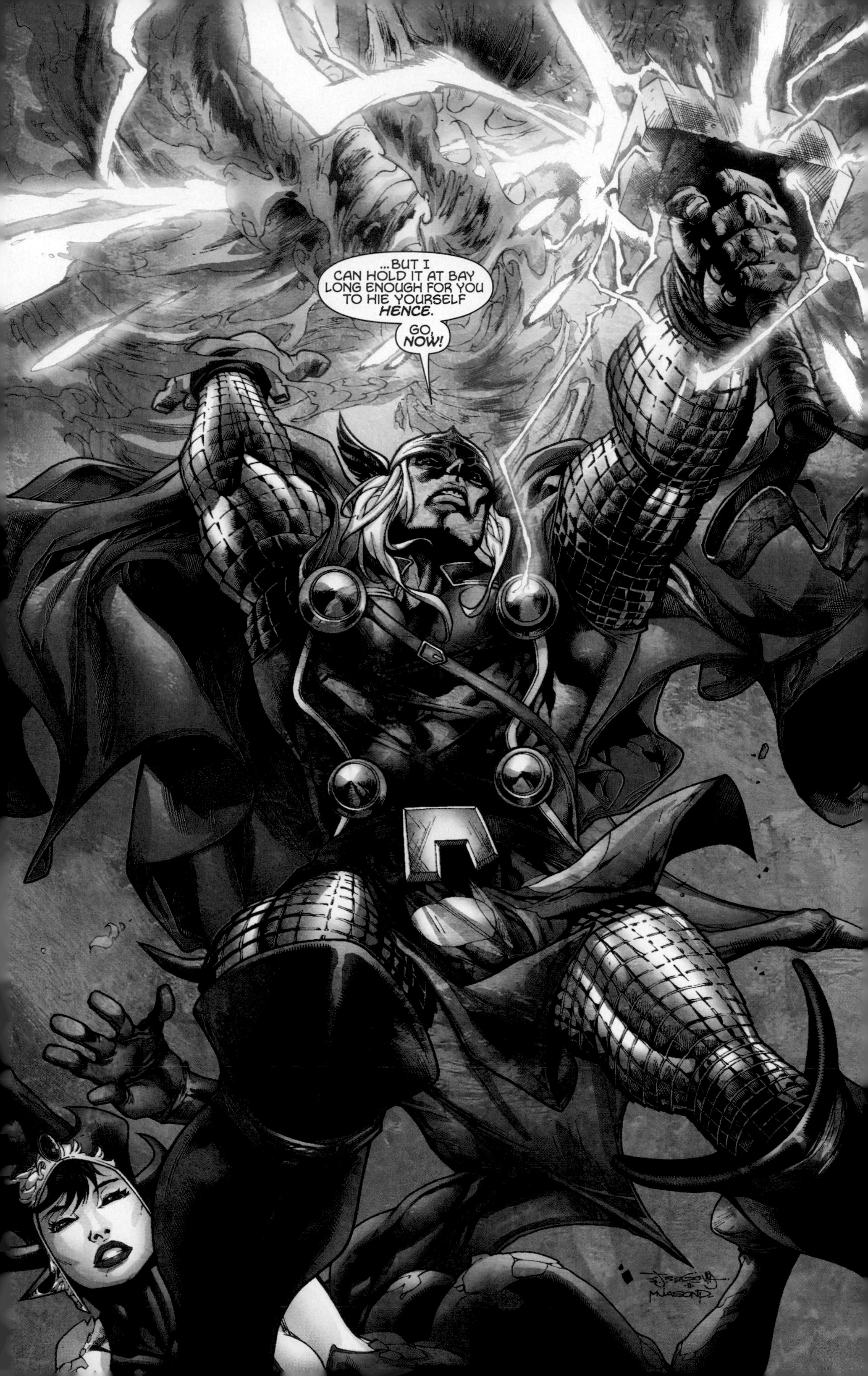
...BUT I CAN HOLD IT AT BAY LONG ENOUGH FOR YOU TO HIE YOURSELF HENCE.
GO, NOW!

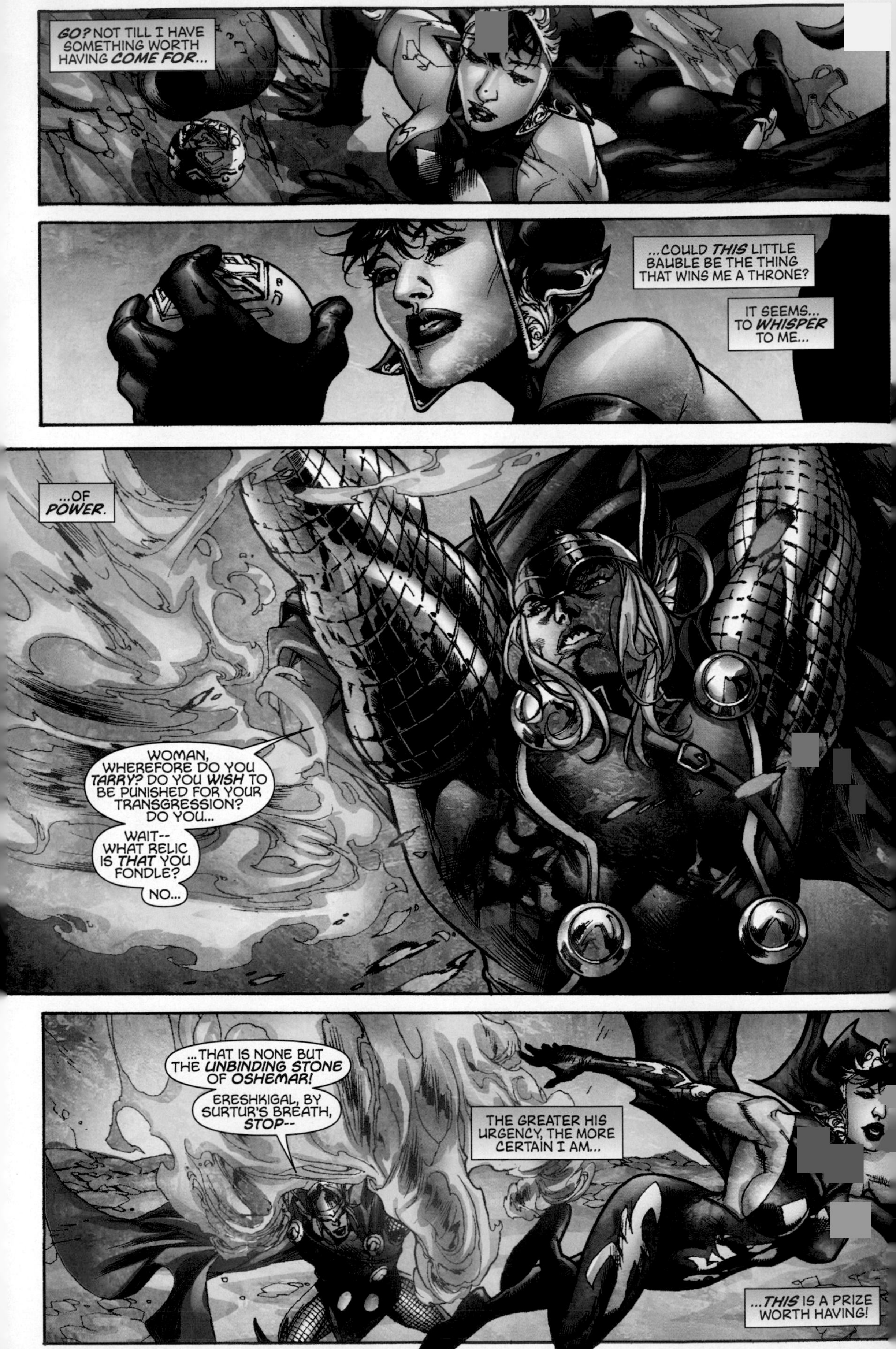
GO? NOT TILL I HAVE SOMETHING WORTH HAVING COME FOR...
...COULD THIS LITTLE BAUBLE BE THE THING THAT WINS ME A THRONE?
IT SEEMS... TO WHISPER TO ME...
...OF POWER.
WOMAN, WHEREFORE DO YOU TARRY? DO YOU WISH TO BE PUNISHED FOR YOUR TRANSGRESSION? DO YOU...
WAIT-- WHAT RELIC IS THAT YOU FONDLE?
NO...
...THAT IS NONE BUT THE UNBINDING STONE OF OSHEMAR!
ERESHKIGAL, BY SURTUR'S BREATH, STOP--
THE GREATER HIS URGENCY, THE MORE CERTAIN I AM...
...THIS IS A PRIZE WORTH HAVING!

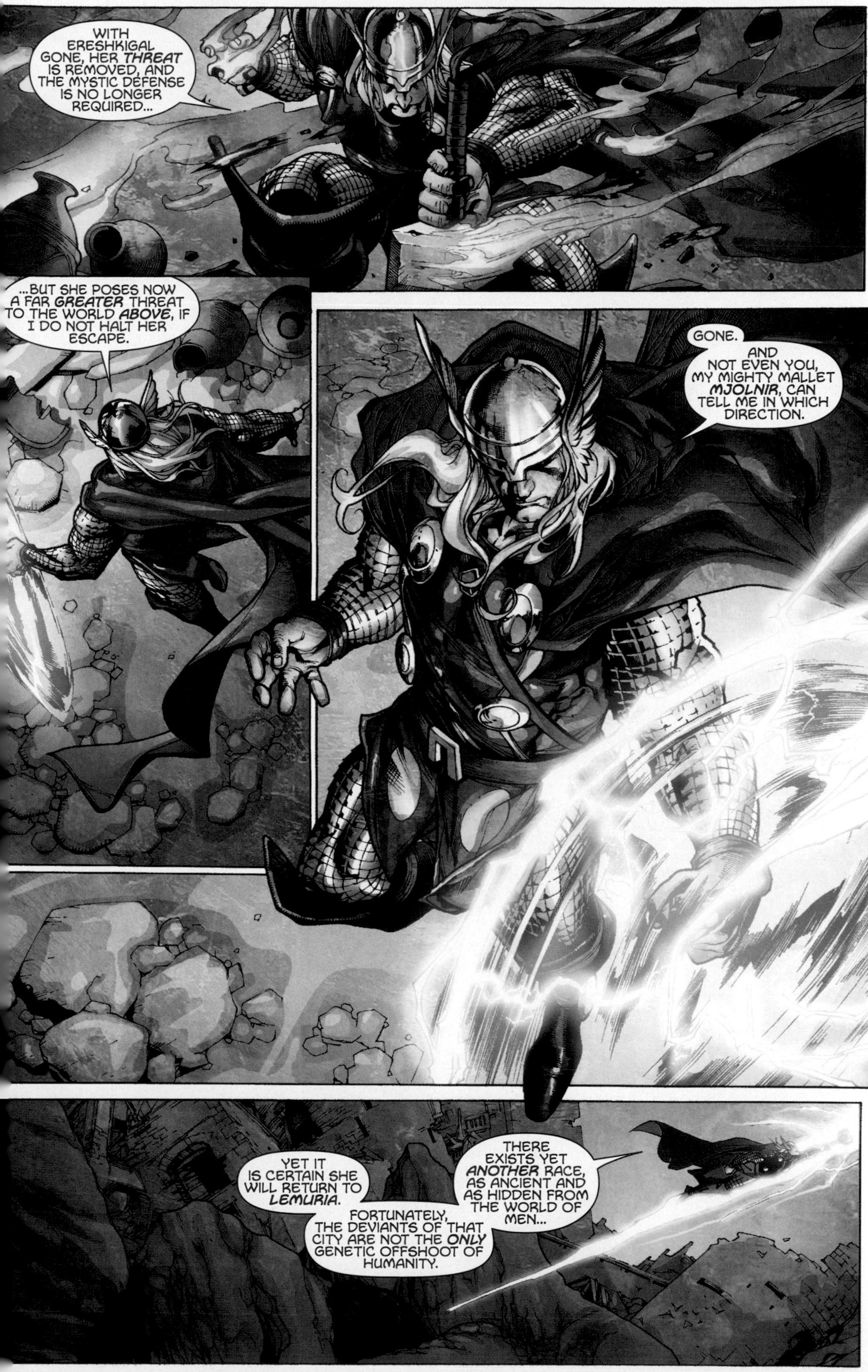
WITH ERESHKIGAL GONE, HER THREAT IS REMOVED, AND THE MYSTIC DEFENSE IS NO LONGER REQUIRED...
...BUT SHE POSES NOW A FAR GREATER THREAT TO THE WORLD ABOVE, IF I DO NOT HALT HER ESCAPE.
GONE. AND NOT EVEN YOU, MY MIGHTY MALLET MJOLNIR, CAN TELL ME IN WHICH DIRECTION.
YET IT IS CERTAIN SHE WILL RETURN TO LEMURIA.
FORTUNATELY, THE DEVIANTS OF THAT CITY ARE NOT THE ONLY GENETIC OFFSHOOT OF HUMANITY.
THERE EXISTS YET ANOTHER RACE, AS ANCIENT AND AS HIDDEN FROM THE WORLD OF MEN...

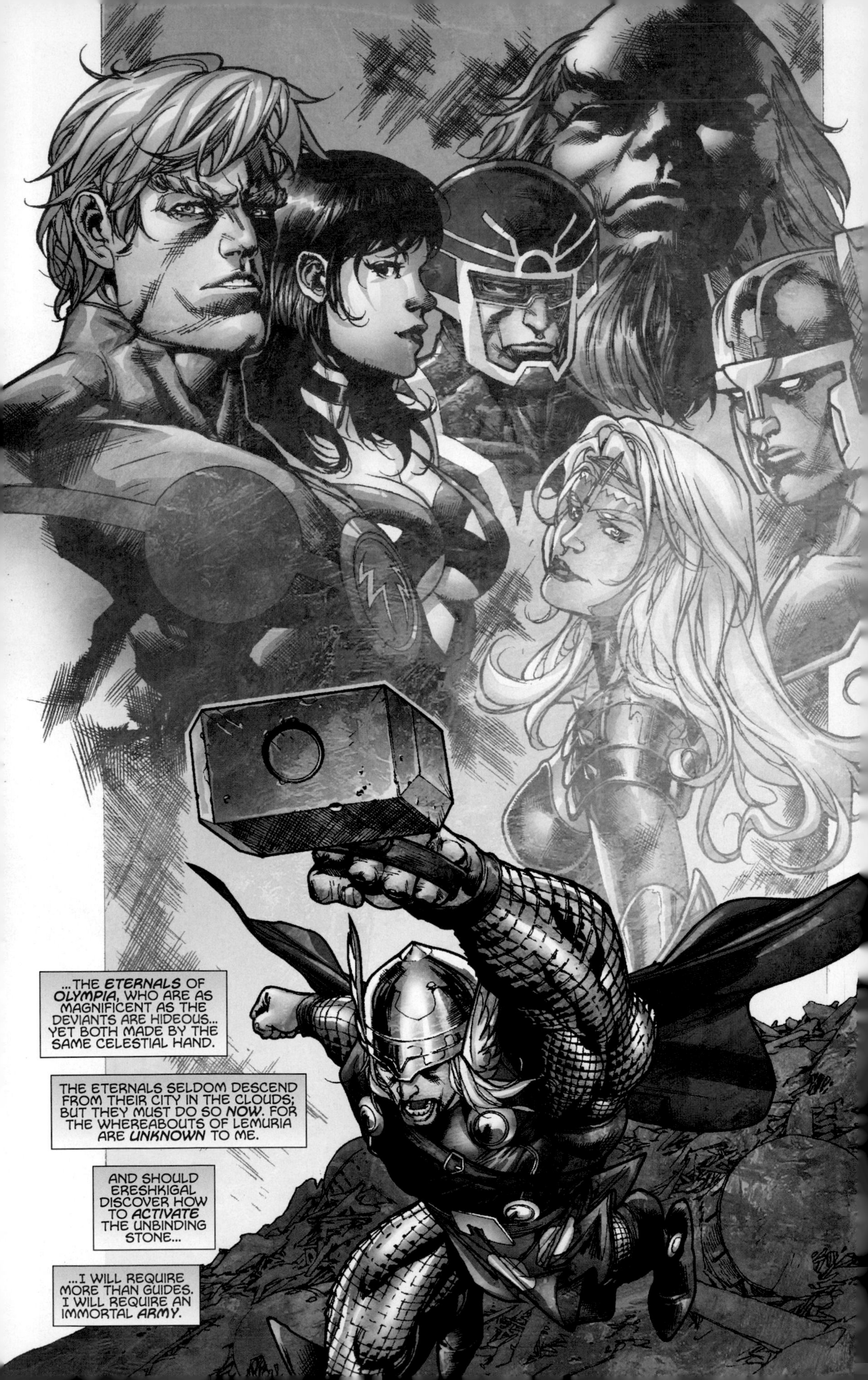
...THE ETERNALS OF OLYMPIA, WHO ARE AS MAGNIFICENT AS THE DEVIANTS ARE HIDEOUS... YET BOTH MADE BY THE SAME CELESTIAL HAND.
THE ETERNALS SELDOM DESCEND FROM THEIR CITY IN THE CLOUDS; BUT THEY MUST DO SO NOW. FOR THE WHEREABOUTS OF LEMURIA ARE UNKNOWN TO ME.
AND SHOULD ERESHKIGAL DISCOVER HOW TO ACTIVATE THE UNBINDING STONE...
...I WILL REQUIRE MORE THAN GUIDES. I WILL REQUIRE AN IMMORTAL ARMY.

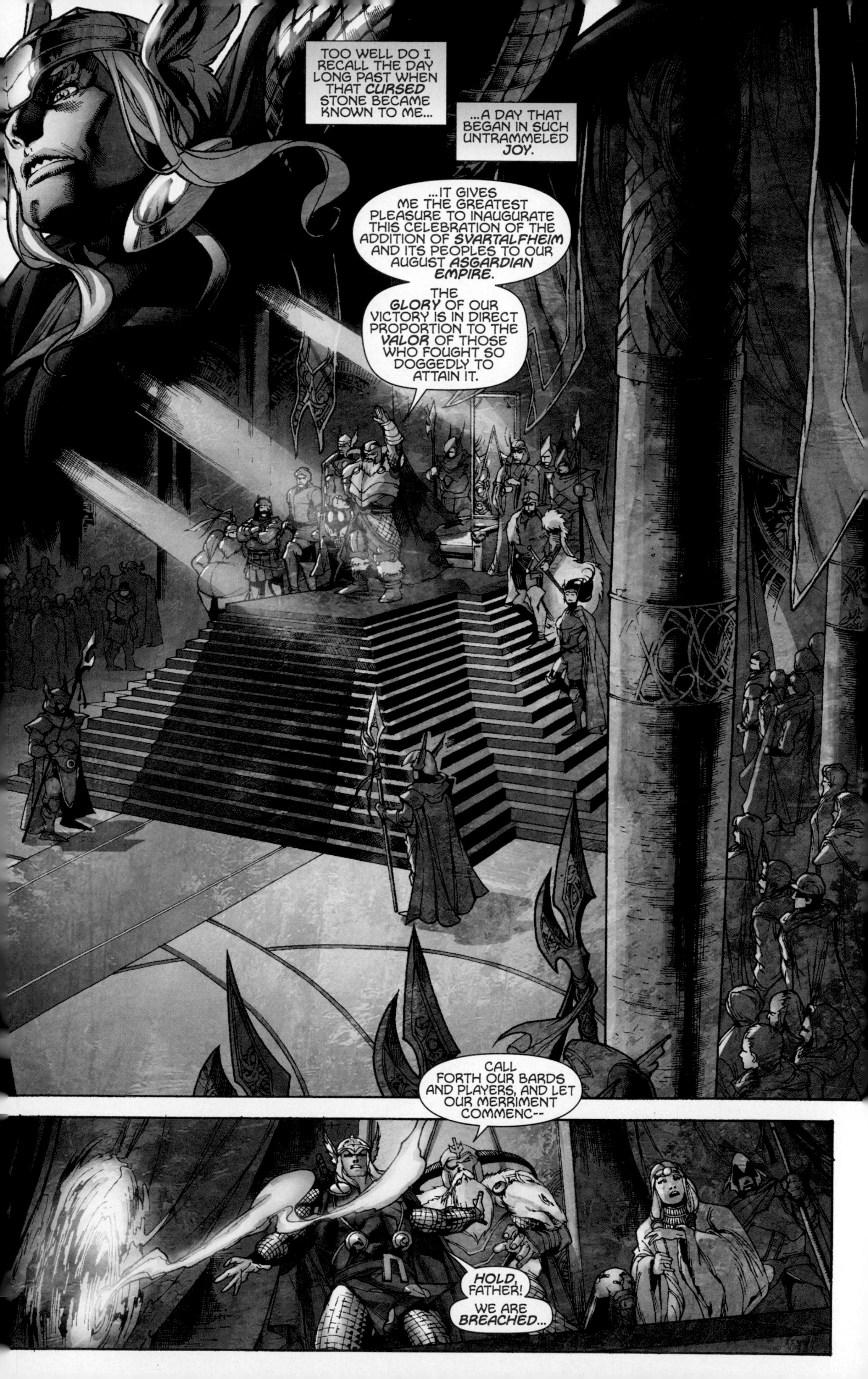
TOO WELL DO I RECALL THE DAY LONG PAST WHEN THAT CURSED STONE BECAME KNOWN TO ME...
...A DAY THAT BEGAN IN SUCH UNTRAMMELED JOY.
...IT GIVES ME THE GREATEST PLEASURE TO INAUGURATE THIS CELEBRATION OF THE ADDITION OF SVARTALFHEIM AND ITS PEOPLES TO OUR AUGUST ASGARDIAN EMPIRE.
THE GLORY OF OUR VICTORY IS IN DIRECT PROPORTION TO THE VALOR OF THOSE WHO FOUGHT SO DOGGEDLY TO ATTAIN IT.
CALL FORTH OUR BARDS AND PLAYERS, AND LET OUR MERRIMENT COMMENC--
HOLD, FATHER!
WE ARE BREACHED...

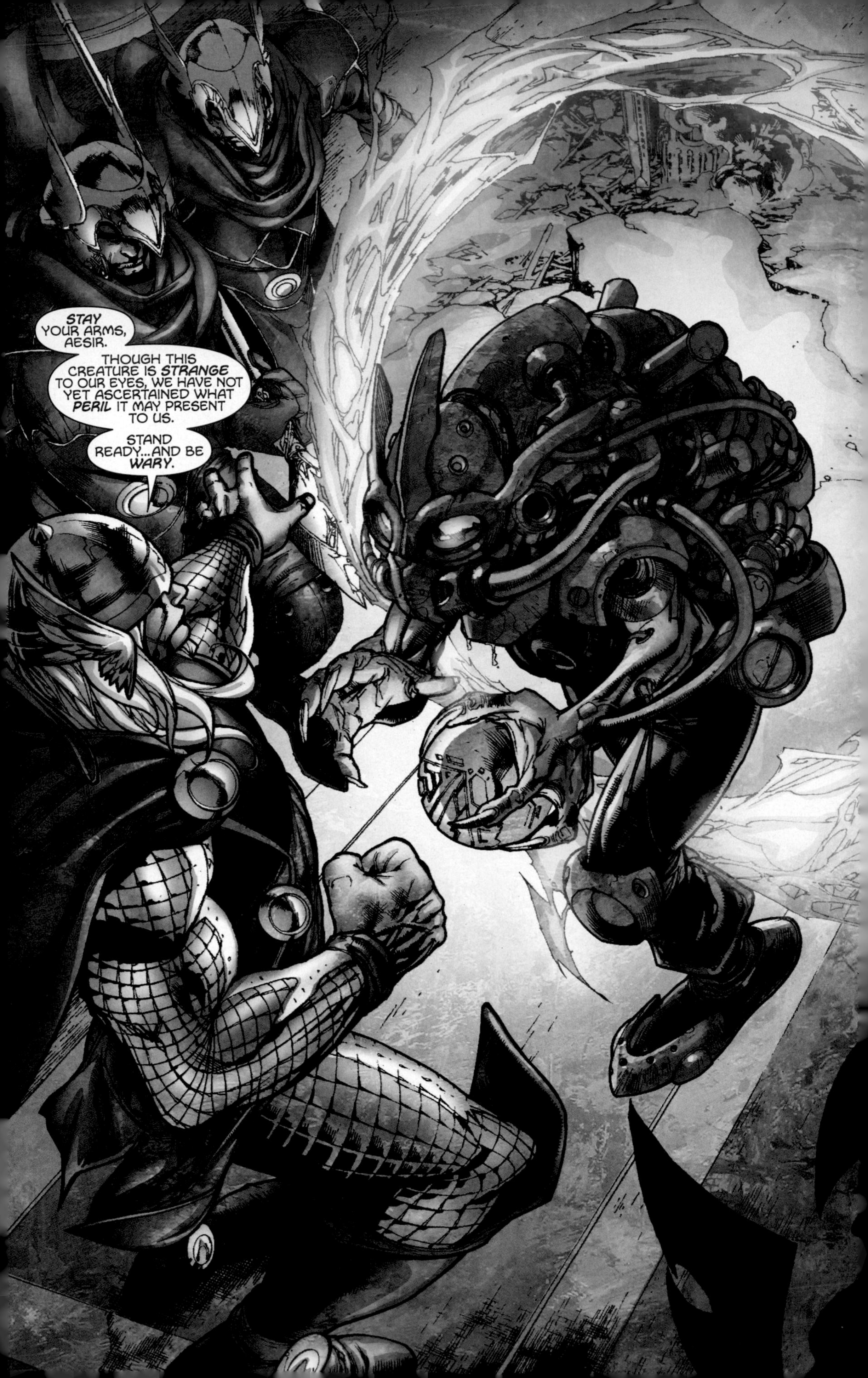
STAY YOUR ARMS, AESIR.
THOUGH THIS CREATURE IS STRANGE TO OUR EYES, WE HAVE NOT YET ASCERTAINED WHAT PERIL IT MAY PRESENT TO US.
STAND READY...AND BE WARY.

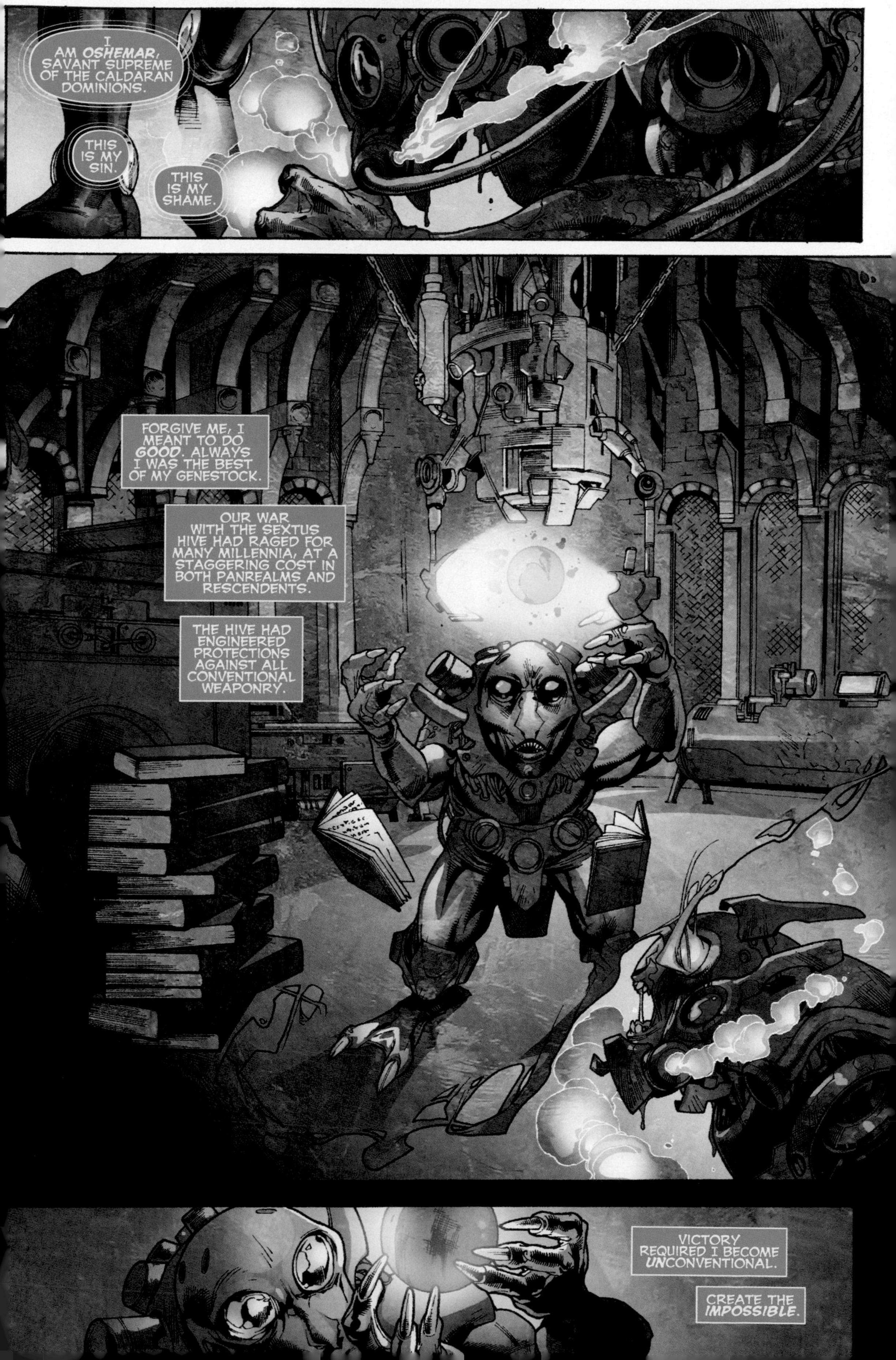
I AM OSHEMAR, SAVANT SUPREME OF THE CALDARAN DOMINIONS.
THIS IS MY SIN.
THIS IS MY SHAME.
FORGIVE ME, I MEANT TO DO GOOD. ALWAYS I WAS THE BEST OF MY GENESTOCK.
OUR WAR WITH THE SEXTUS HIVE HAD RAGED FOR MANY MILLENNIA, AT A STAGGERING COST IN BOTH PANREALMS AND RESCENDENTS.
THE HIVE HAD ENGINEERED PROTECTIONS AGAINST ALL CONVENTIONAL WEAPONRY.
VICTORY REQUIRED I BECOME UNCONVENTIONAL.
CREATE THE IMPOSSIBLE.

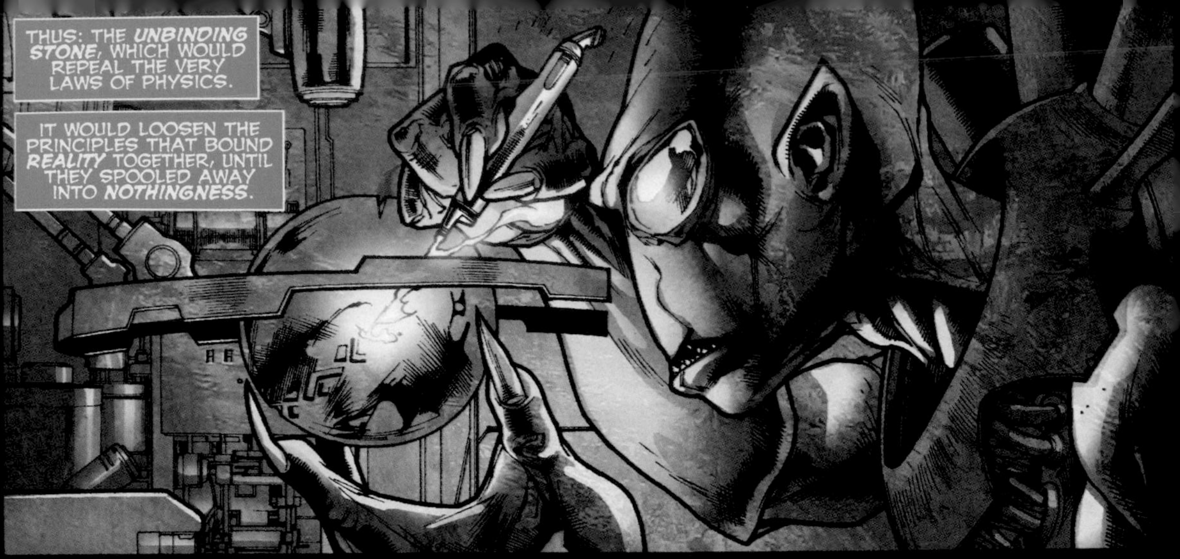
THUS: THE UNBINDING STONE, WHICH WOULD REPEAL THE VERY LAWS OF PHYSICS.
IT WOULD LOOSEN THE PRINCIPLES THAT BOUND REALITY TOGETHER, UNTIL THEY SPOOLED AWAY INTO NOTHINGNESS.

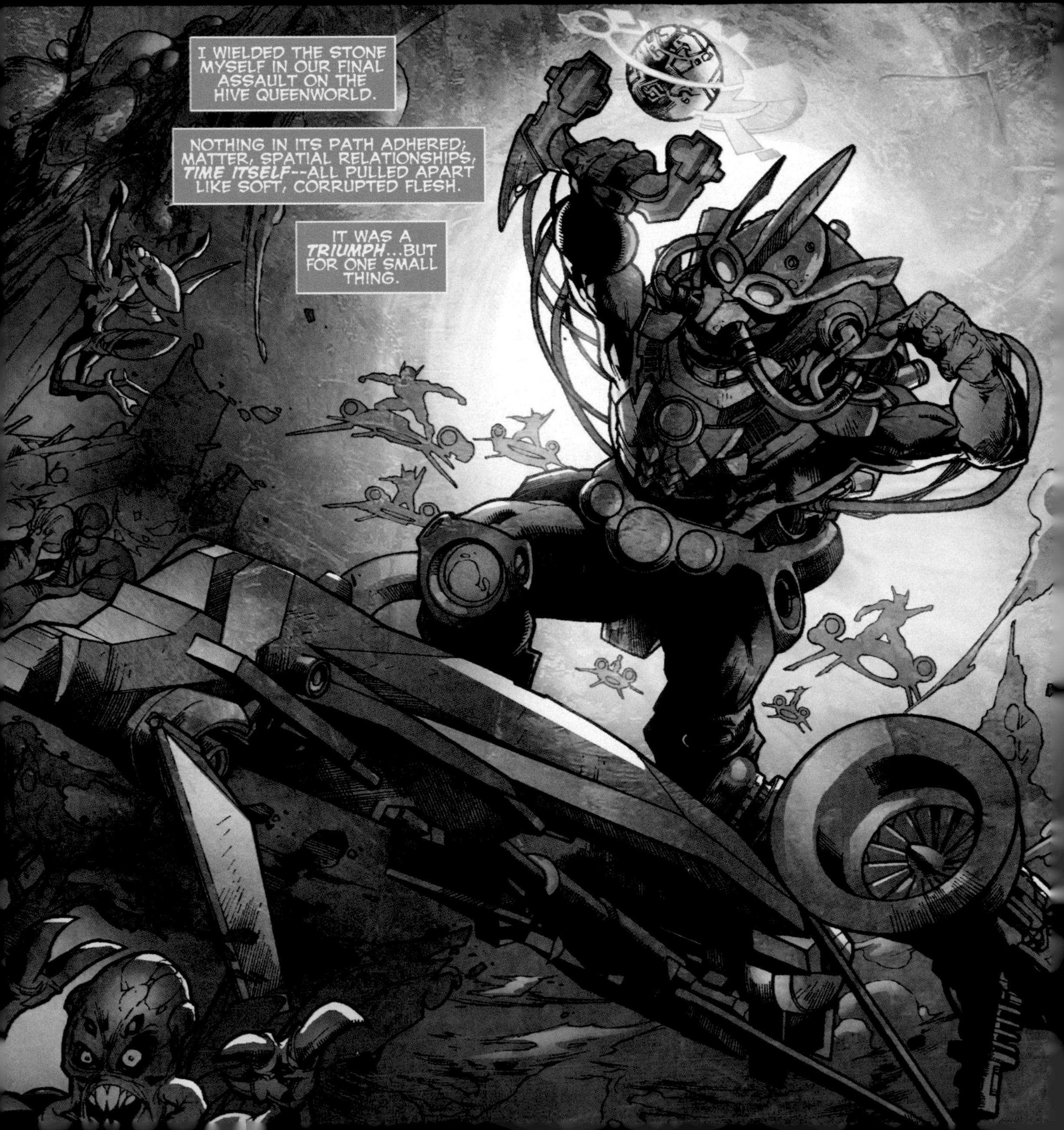
I WIELDED THE STONE MYSELF IN OUR FINAL ASSAULT ON THE HIVE QUEENWORLD.
NOTHING IN ITS PATH ADHERED; MATTER, SPATIAL RELATIONSHIPS, TIME ITSELF--ALL PULLED APART LIKE SOFT, CORRUPTED FLESH.
IT WAS A TRIUMPH...BUT FOR ONE SMALL THING.

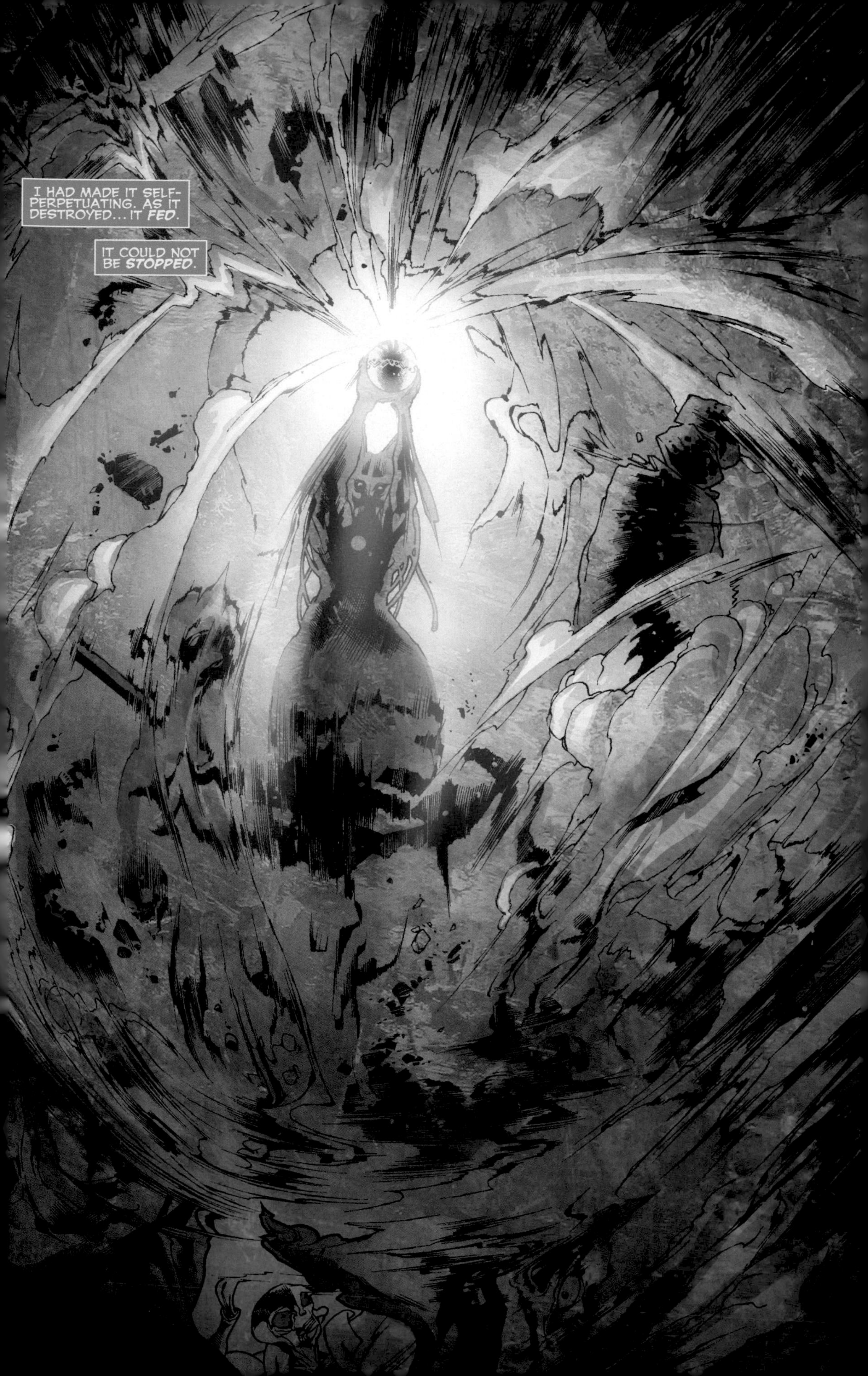
I HAD MADE IT SELF-PERPETUATING. AS IT DESTROYED... IT FED.
IT COULD NOT BE STOPPED.

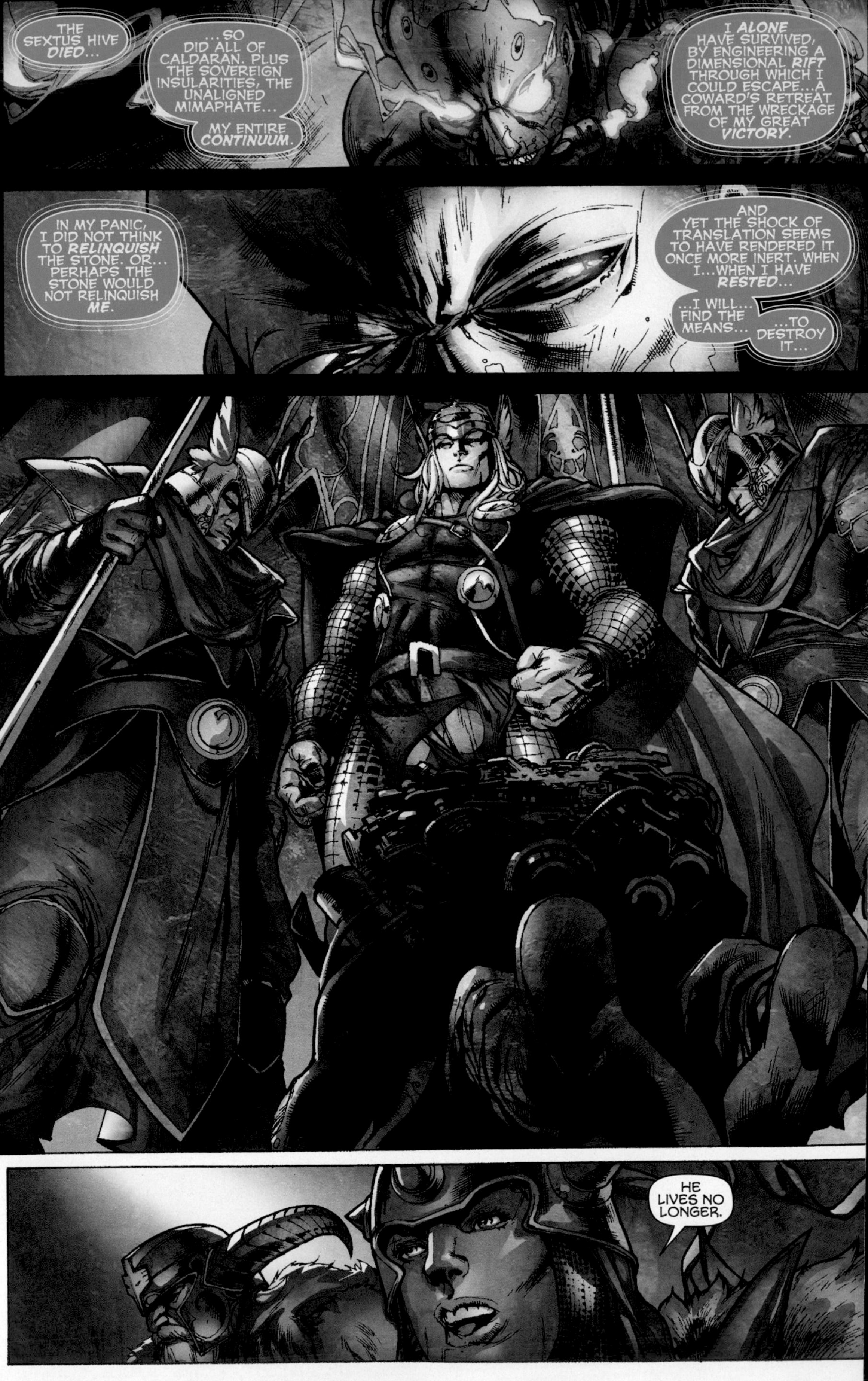
THE SEXTUS HIVE DIED...
...SO DID ALL OF CALDARAN. PLUS THE SOVEREIGN INSULARITIES, THE UNALIGNED MIMAPHATE...
MY ENTIRE CONTINUUM.
I ALONE HAVE SURVIVED, BY ENGINEERING A DIMENSIONAL RIFT THROUGH WHICH I COULD ESCAPE...A COWARD'S RETREAT FROM THE WRECKAGE OF MY GREAT VICTORY.
IN MY PANIC, I DID NOT THINK TO RELINQUISH THE STONE. OR... PERHAPS THE STONE WOULD NOT RELINQUISH ME.
AND YET THE SHOCK OF TRANSLATION SEEMS TO HAVE RENDERED IT ONCE MORE INERT. WHEN I...WHEN I HAVE RESTED...
...I WILL... FIND THE MEANS...
...TO DESTROY IT...
HE LIVES NO LONGER.

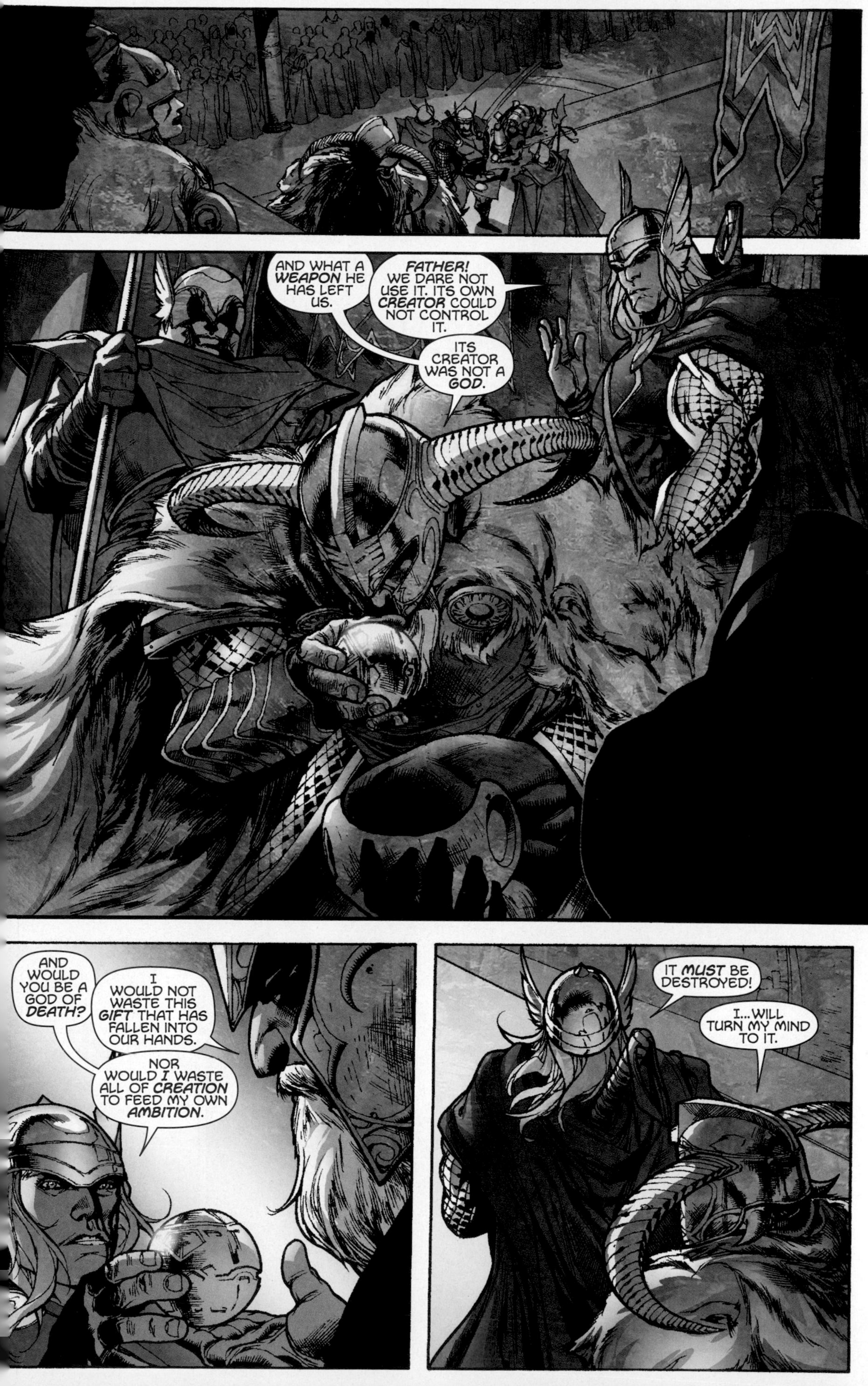

AND WHAT A WEAPON HE HAS LEFT US.
FATHER! WE DARE NOT USE IT. ITS OWN CREATOR COULD NOT CONTROL IT.
ITS CREATOR WAS NOT A GOD.
AND WOULD YOU BE A GOD OF DEATH?
I WOULD NOT WASTE THIS GIFT THAT HAS FALLEN INTO OUR HANDS.
NOR WOULD I WASTE ALL OF CREATION TO FEED MY OWN AMBITION.
IT MUST BE DESTROYED!
I...WILL TURN MY MIND TO IT.

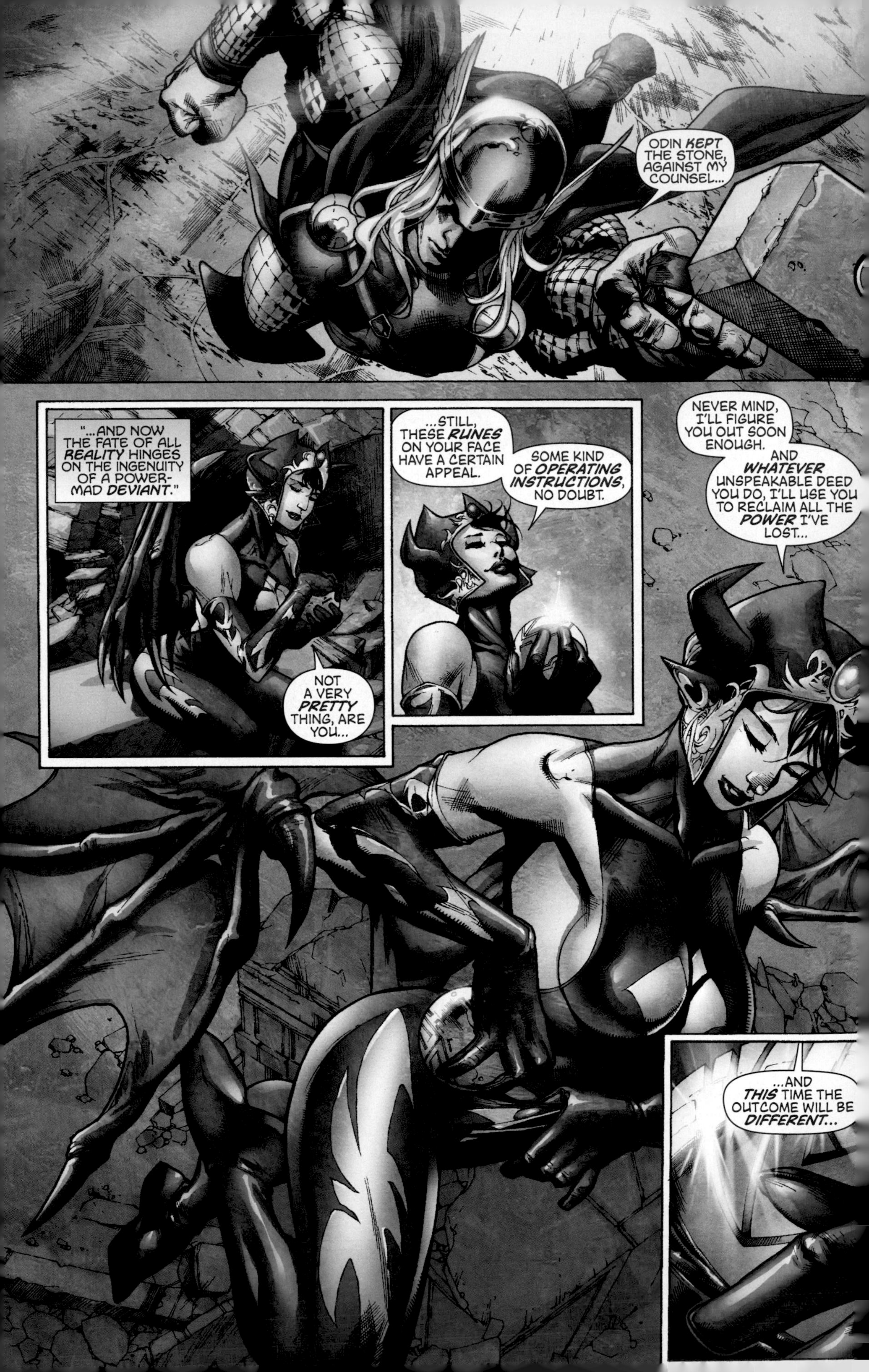

ODIN KEPT THE STONE, AGAINST MY COUNSEL...
"...AND NOW THE FATE OF ALL REALITY HINGES ON THE INGENUITY OF A POWER-MAD DEVIANT."
NOT A VERY PRETTY THING, ARE YOU...
...STILL, THESE RUNES ON YOUR FACE HAVE A CERTAIN APPEAL.
SOME KIND OF OPERATING INSTRUCTIONS, NO DOUBT.
NEVER MIND, I'LL FIGURE YOU OUT SOON ENOUGH.
AND WHATEVER UNSPEAKABLE DEED YOU DO, I'LL USE YOU TO RECLAIM ALL THE POWER I'VE LOST...
...AND THIS TIME THE OUTCOME WILL BE DIFFERENT...

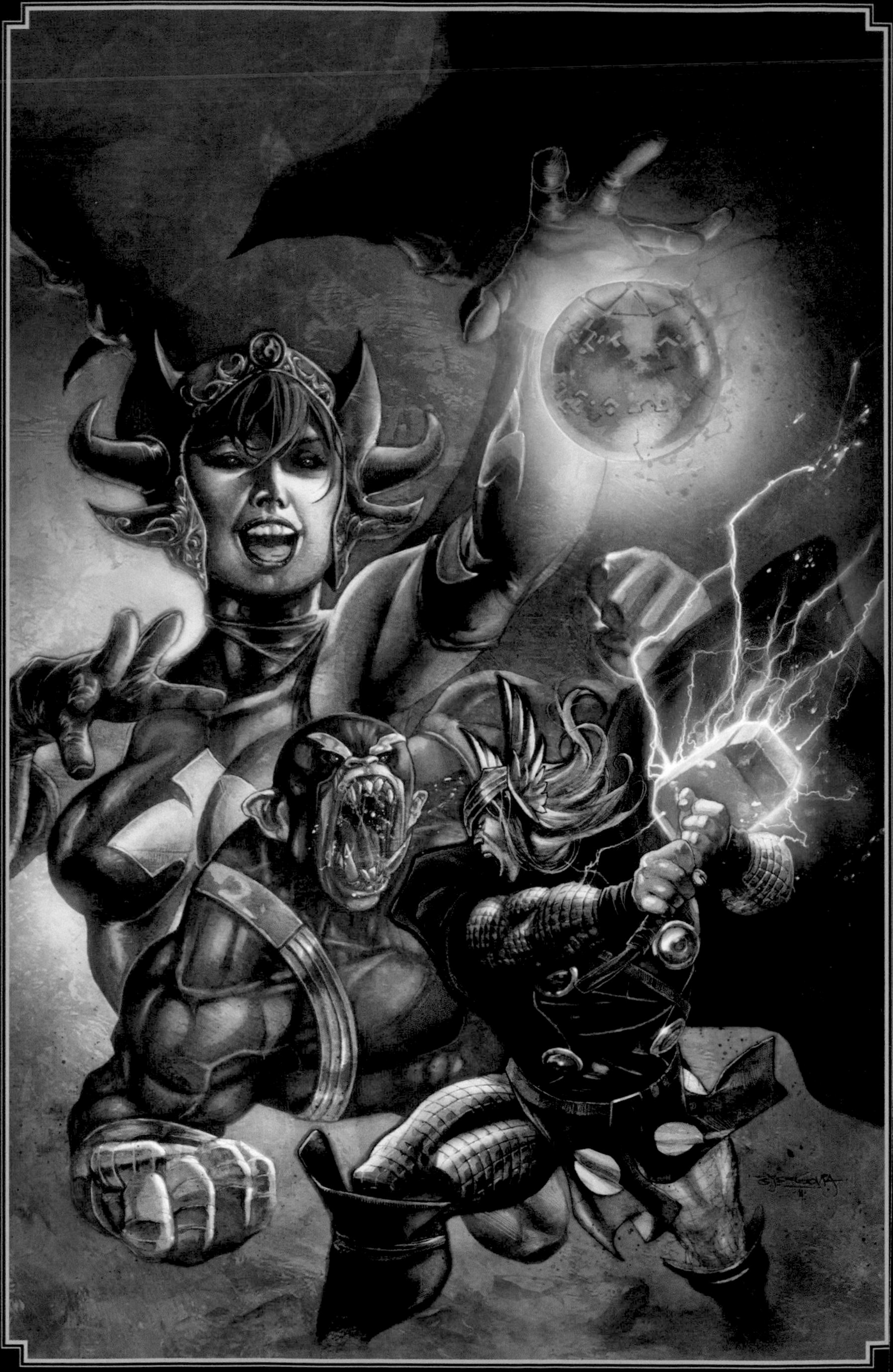

Thor: The Deviants Saga 2

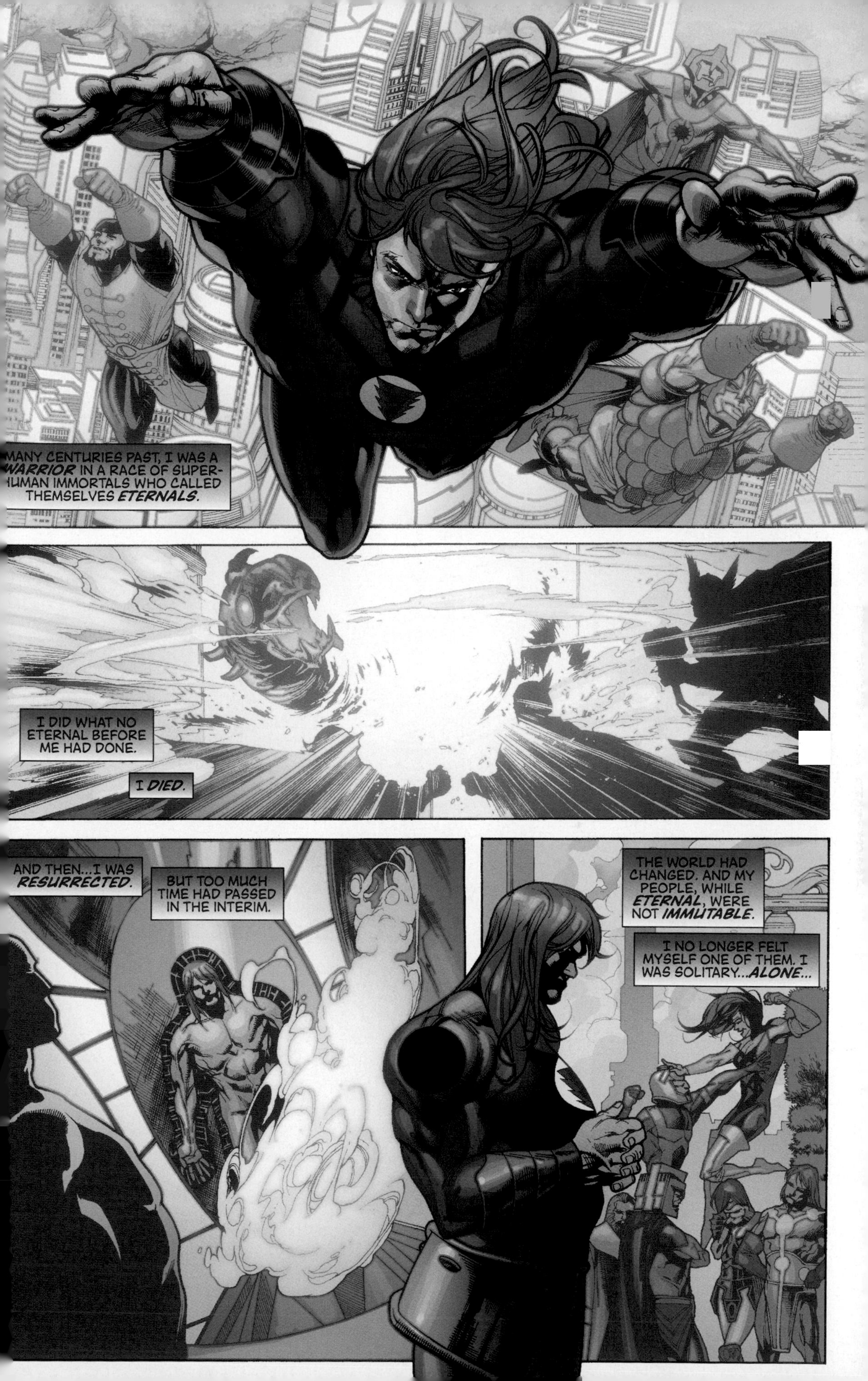
MANY CENTURIES PAST, I WAS A WARRIOR IN A RACE OF SUPER-HUMAN IMMORTALS WHO CALLED THEMSELVES ETERNALS.
I DID WHAT NO ETERNAL BEFORE ME HAD DONE.
I DIED.
AND THEN...I WAS RESURRECTED.
BUT TOO MUCH TIME HAD PASSED IN THE INTERIM.
THE WORLD HAD CHANGED. AND MY PEOPLE, WHILE ETERNAL, WERE NOT IMMUTABLE.
I NO LONGER FELT MYSELF ONE OF THEM. I WAS SOLITARY...ALONE...

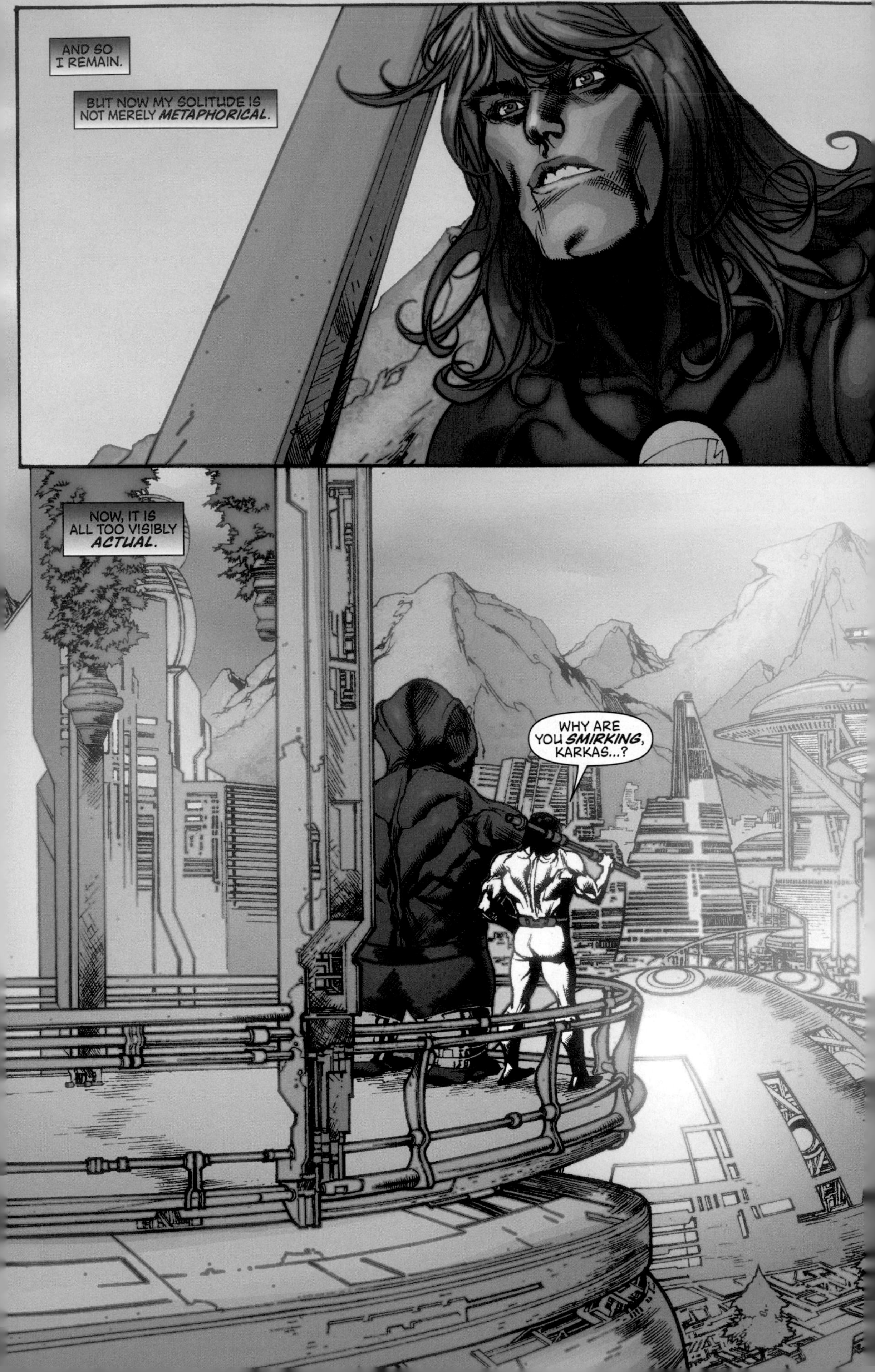
AND SO I REMAIN.
BUT NOW MY SOLITUDE IS NOT MERELY METAPHORICAL.
NOW, IT IS ALL TOO VISIBLY ACTUAL.
WHY ARE YOU SMIRKING, KARKAS...?

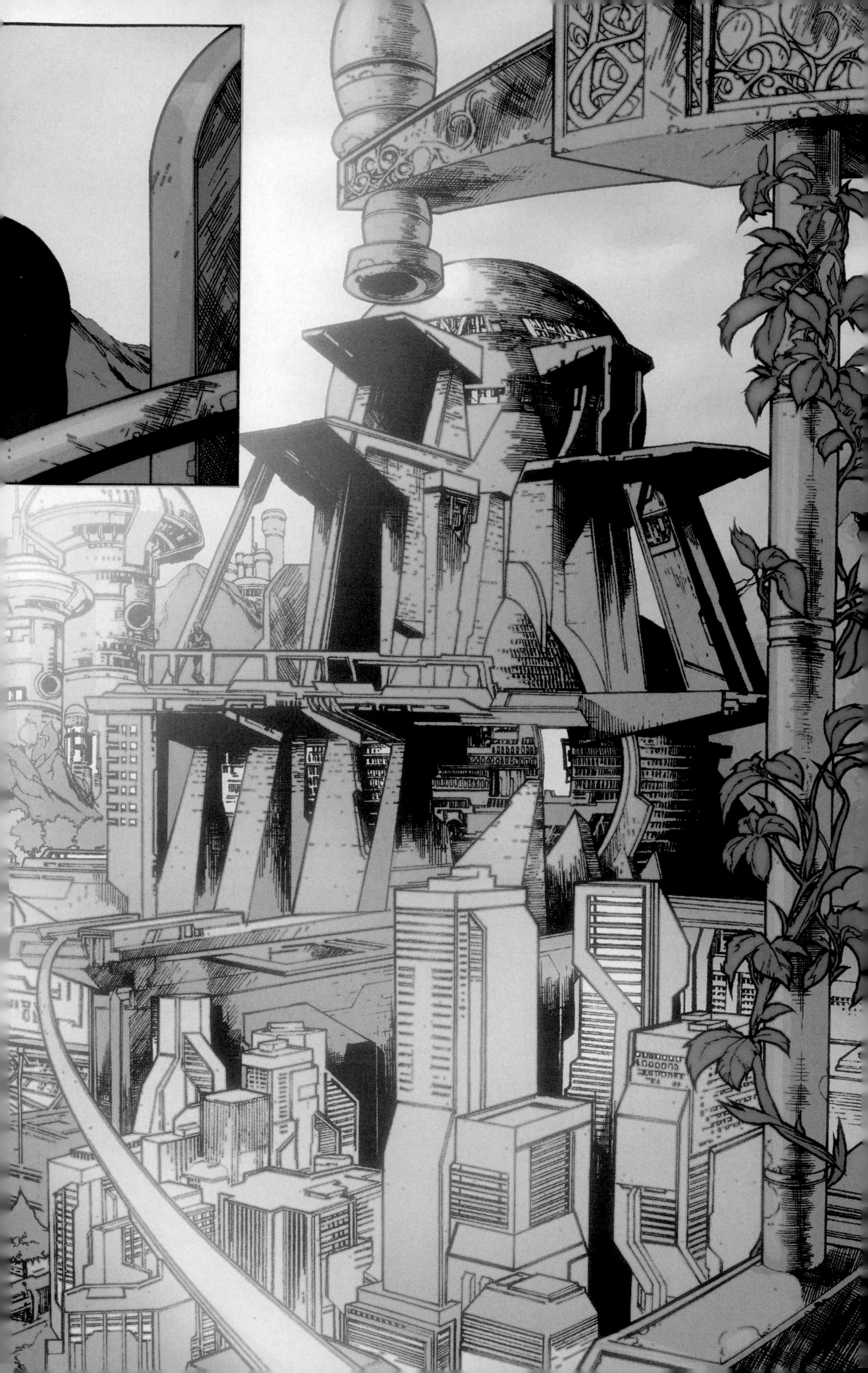

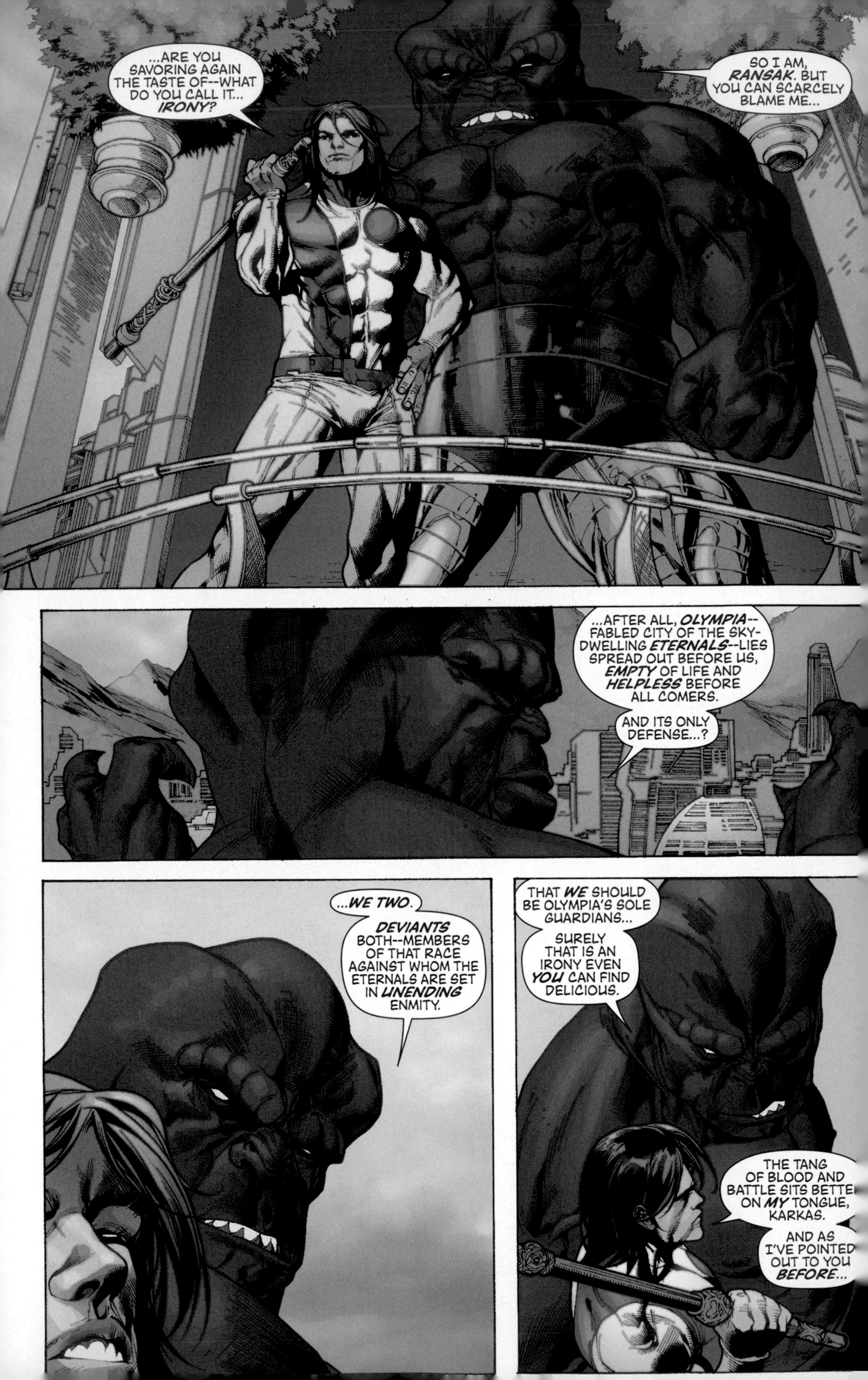
...ARE YOU SAVORING AGAIN THE TASTE OF--WHAT DO YOU CALL IT... IRONY?
SO I AM, RANSAK. BUT YOU CAN SCARCELY BLAME ME...
...AFTER ALL, OLYMPIA--FABLED CITY OF THE SKY-DWELLING ETERNALS--LIES SPREAD OUT BEFORE US, EMPTY OF LIFE AND HELPLESS BEFORE ALL COMERS.
AND ITS ONLY DEFENSE...?
...WE TWO.
DEVIANTS BOTH--MEMBERS OF THAT RACE AGAINST WHOM THE ETERNALS ARE SET IN UNENDING ENMITY.
THAT WE SHOULD BE OLYMPIA'S SOLE GUARDIANS...
SURELY THAT IS AN IRONY EVEN YOU CAN FIND DELICIOUS.
THE TANG OF BLOOD AND BATTLE SITS BETTER ON MY TONGUE, KARKAS.
AND AS I'VE POINTED OUT TO YOU BEFORE...

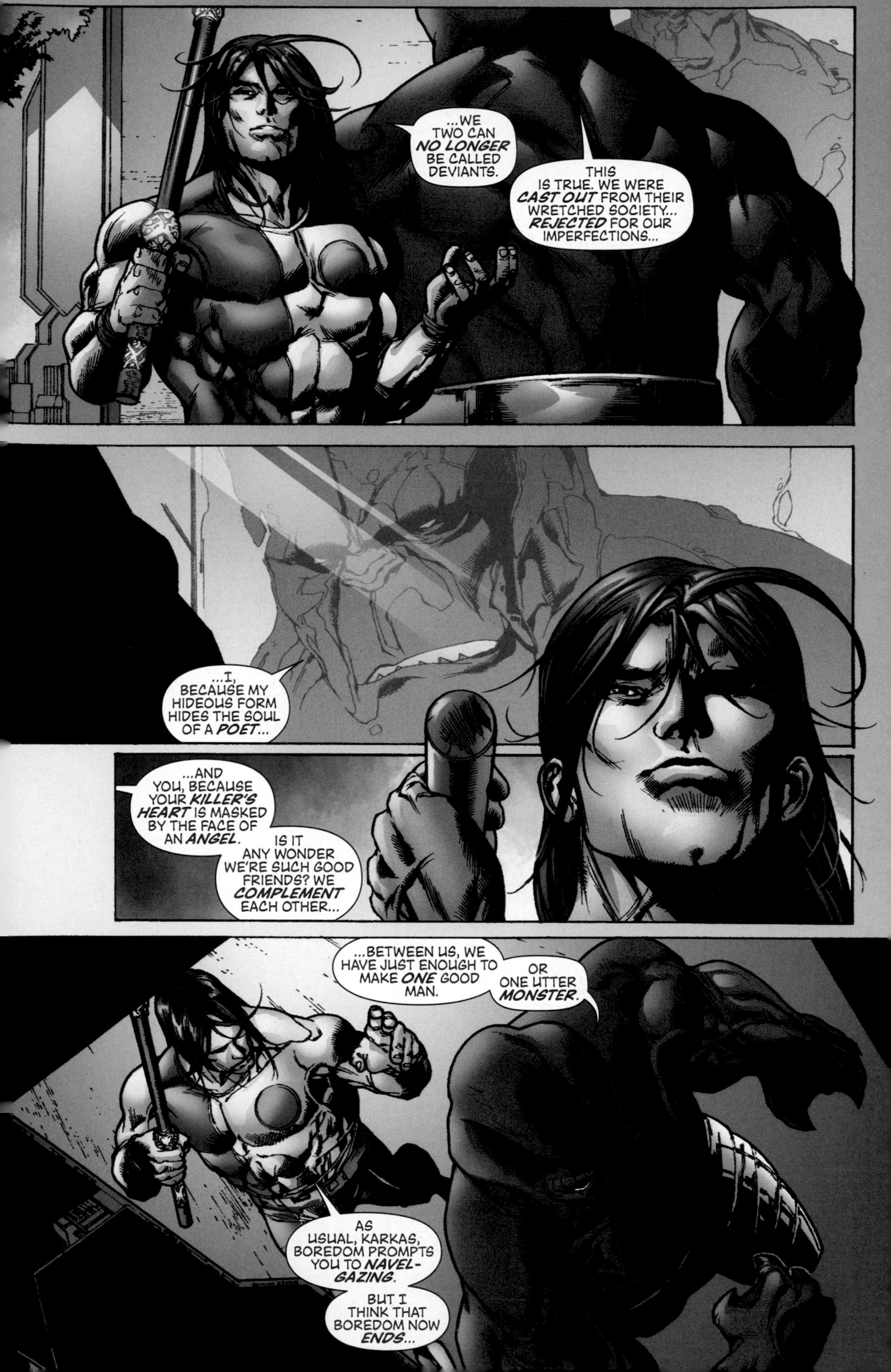

...WE TWO CAN NO LONGER BE CALLED DEVIANTS.
THIS IS TRUE. WE WERE CAST OUT FROM THEIR WRETCHED SOCIETY... REJECTED FOR OUR IMPERFECTIONS...
...I, BECAUSE MY HIDEOUS FORM HIDES THE SOUL OF A POET...
...AND YOU, BECAUSE YOUR KILLER'S HEART IS MASKED BY THE FACE OF AN ANGEL.
IS IT ANY WONDER WE'RE SUCH GOOD FRIENDS? WE COMPLEMENT EACH OTHER...
...BETWEEN US, WE HAVE JUST ENOUGH TO MAKE ONE GOOD MAN.
OR ONE UTTER MONSTER.
AS USUAL, KARKAS, BOREDOM PROMPTS YOU TO NAVEL-GAZING.
BUT I THINK THAT BOREDOM NOW ENDS...

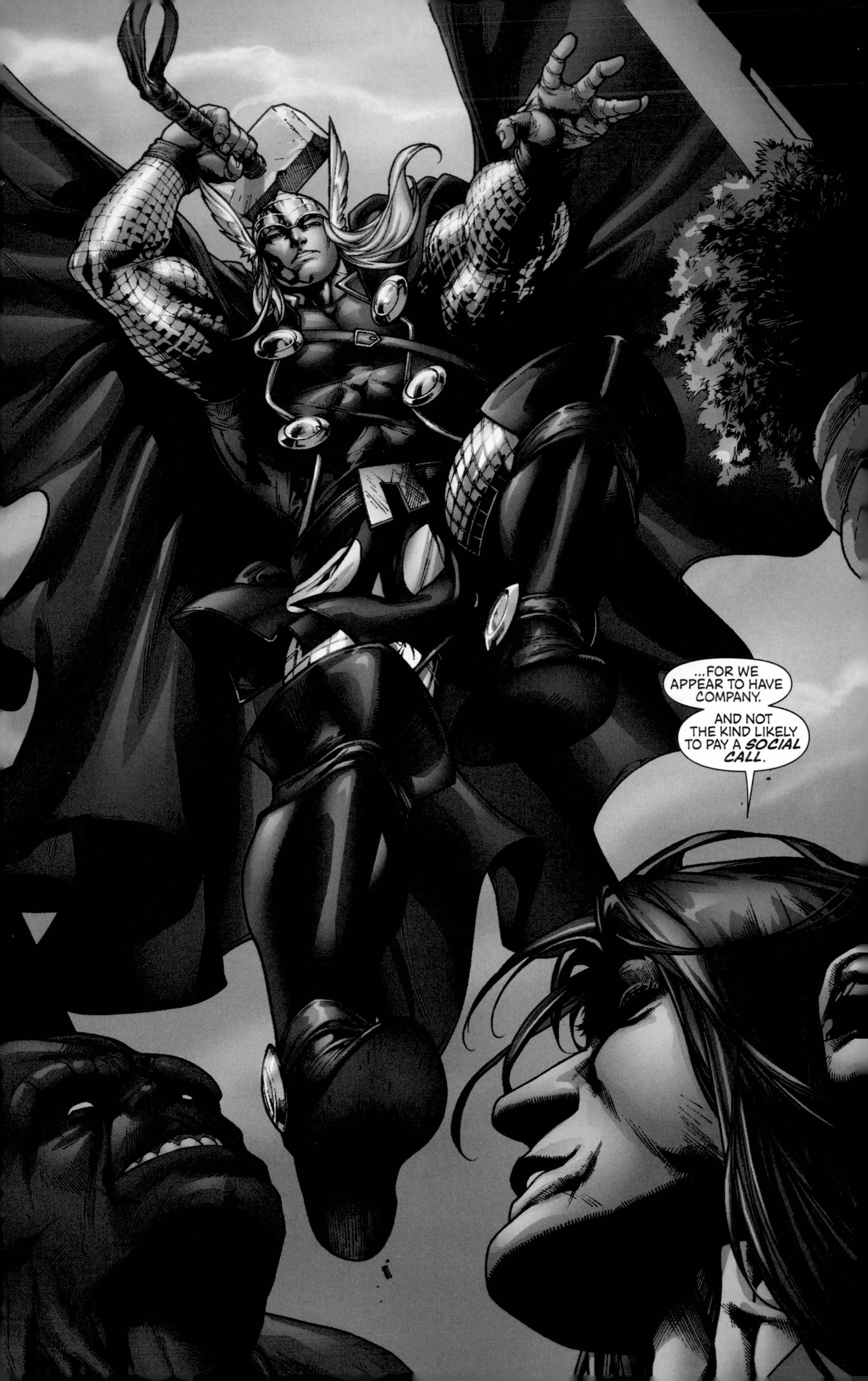
...FOR WE APPEAR TO HAVE COMPANY.
AND NOT THE KIND LIKELY TO PAY A SOCIAL CALL.

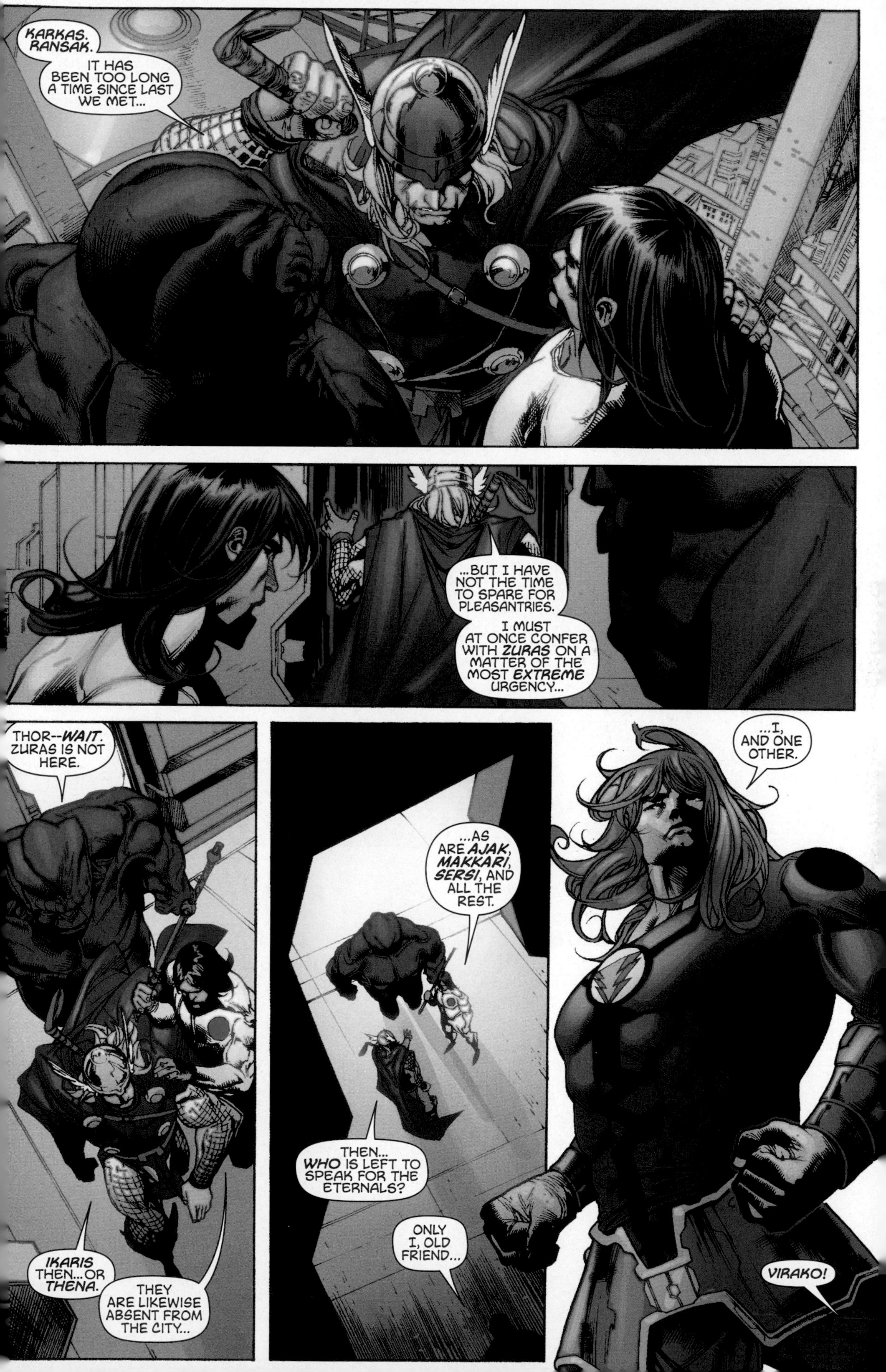
KARKAS. RANSAK.
IT HAS BEEN TOO LONG A TIME SINCE LAST WE MET...
...BUT I HAVE NOT THE TIME TO SPARE FOR PLEASANTRIES.
I MUST AT ONCE CONFER WITH ZURAS ON A MATTER OF THE MOST EXTREME URGENCY...
THOR--WAIT. ZURAS IS NOT HERE.
IKARIS THEN...OR THENA.
THEY ARE LIKEWISE ABSENT FROM THE CITY...
...AS ARE AJAK, MAKKARI, SERSI, AND ALL THE REST.
THEN... WHO IS LEFT TO SPEAK FOR THE ETERNALS?
ONLY I, OLD FRIEND...
...I, AND ONE OTHER.
VIRAKO!

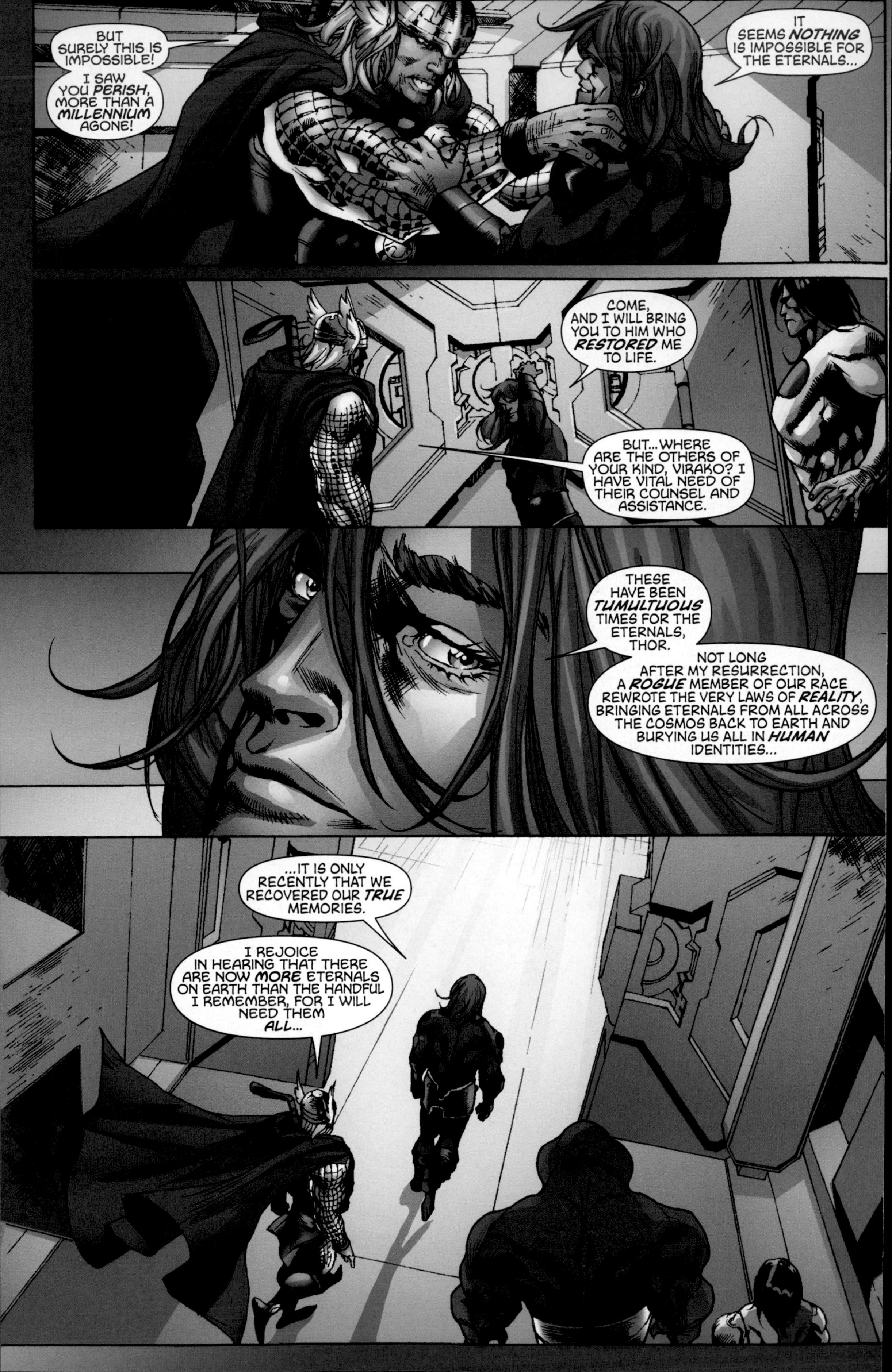
BUT SURELY THIS IS IMPOSSIBLE!
I SAW YOU PERISH, MORE THAN A MILLENNIUM AGONE!
IT SEEMS NOTHING IS IMPOSSIBLE FOR THE ETERNALS...
COME, AND I WILL BRING YOU TO HIM WHO RESTORED ME TO LIFE.
BUT...WHERE ARE THE OTHERS OF YOUR KIND, VIRAKO? I HAVE VITAL NEED OF THEIR COUNSEL AND ASSISTANCE.
THESE HAVE BEEN TUMULTUOUS TIMES FOR THE ETERNALS, THOR.
NOT LONG AFTER MY RESURRECTION, A ROGUE MEMBER OF OUR RACE REWROTE THE VERY LAWS OF REALITY, BRINGING ETERNALS FROM ALL ACROSS THE COSMOS BACK TO EARTH AND BURYING US ALL IN HUMAN IDENTITIES...
...IT IS ONLY RECENTLY THAT WE RECOVERED OUR TRUE MEMORIES.
I REJOICE IN HEARING THAT THERE ARE NOW MORE ETERNALS ON EARTH THAN THE HANDFUL I REMEMBER, FOR I WILL NEED THEM ALL...

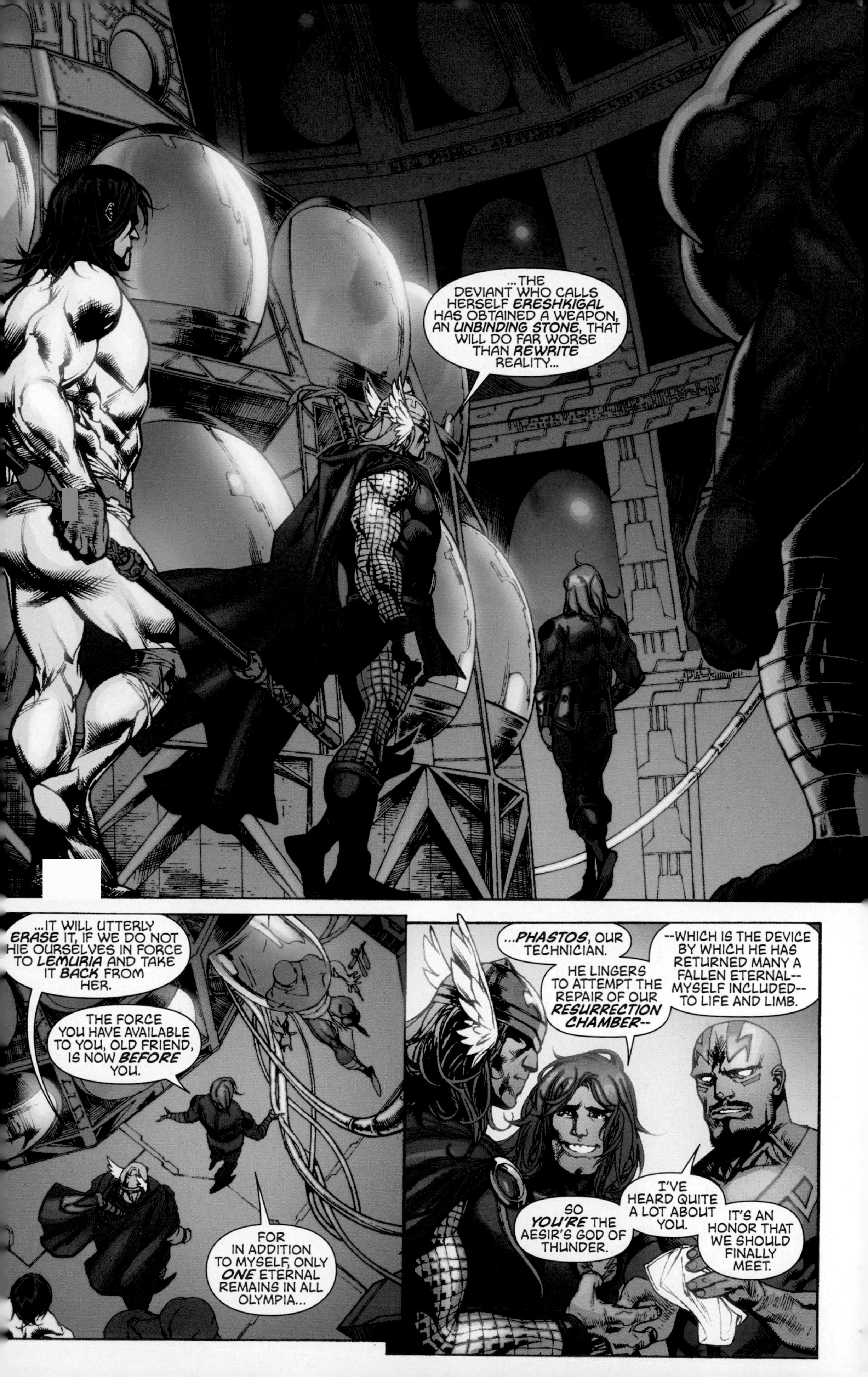
...THE DEVIANT WHO CALLS HERSELF ERESHKIGAL HAS OBTAINED A WEAPON, AN UNBINDING STONE, THAT WILL DO FAR WORSE THAN REWRITE REALITY...
...IT WILL UTTERLY ERASE IT, IF WE DO NOT HIE OURSELVES IN FORCE TO LEMURIA AND TAKE IT BACK FROM HER.
THE FORCE YOU HAVE AVAILABLE TO YOU, OLD FRIEND, IS NOW BEFORE YOU.
FOR IN ADDITION TO MYSELF, ONLY ONE ETERNAL REMAINS IN ALL OLYMPIA...
...PHASTOS, OUR TECHNICIAN.
HE LINGERS TO ATTEMPT THE REPAIR OF OUR RESURRECTION CHAMBER--
--WHICH IS THE DEVICE BY WHICH HE HAS RETURNED MANY A FALLEN ETERNAL--MYSELF INCLUDED--TO LIFE AND LIMB.
SO YOU'RE THE AESIR'S GOD OF THUNDER.
I'VE HEARD QUITE A LOT ABOUT YOU.
IT'S AN HONOR THAT WE SHOULD FINALLY MEET.

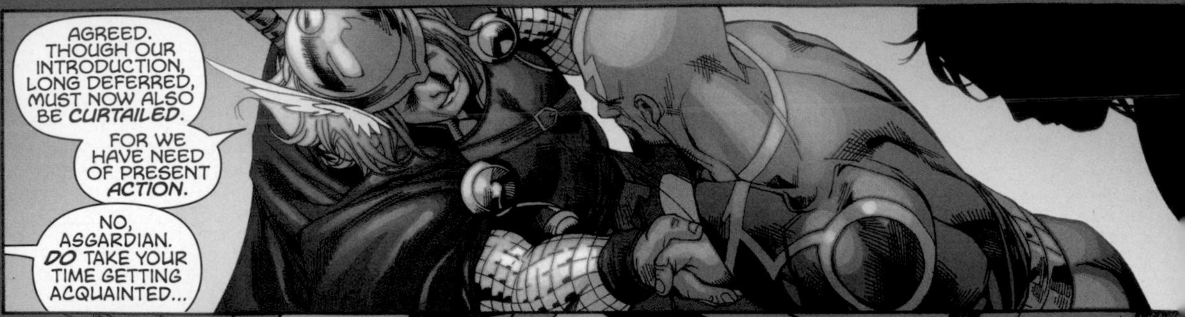
AGREED. THOUGH OUR INTRODUCTION, LONG DEFERRED, MUST NOW ALSO BE CURTAILED.
FOR WE HAVE NEED OF PRESENT ACTION.
NO, ASGARDIAN. DO TAKE YOUR TIME GETTING ACQUAINTED...

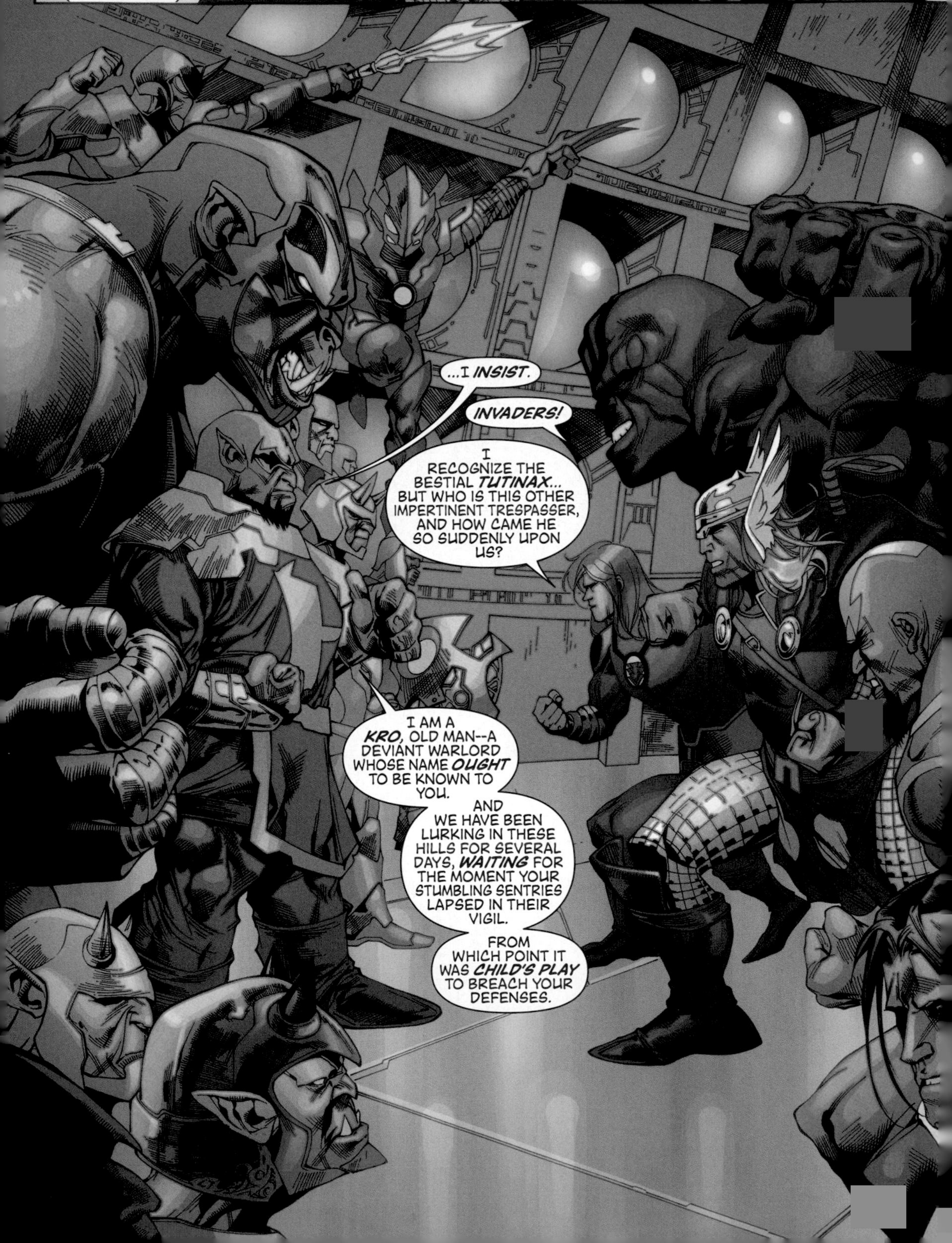
...I INSIST.
INVADERS!
I RECOGNIZE THE BESTIAL TUTINAX... BUT WHO IS THIS OTHER IMPERTINENT TRESPASSER, AND HOW CAME HE SO SUDDENLY UPON US?
I AM A KRO, OLD MAN--A DEVIANT WARLORD WHOSE NAME OUGHT TO BE KNOWN TO YOU.
AND WE HAVE BEEN LURKING IN THESE HILLS FOR SEVERAL DAYS, WAITING FOR THE MOMENT YOUR STUMBLING SENTRIES LAPSED IN THEIR VIGIL.
FROM WHICH POINT IT WAS CHILD'S PLAY TO BREACH YOUR DEFENSES.

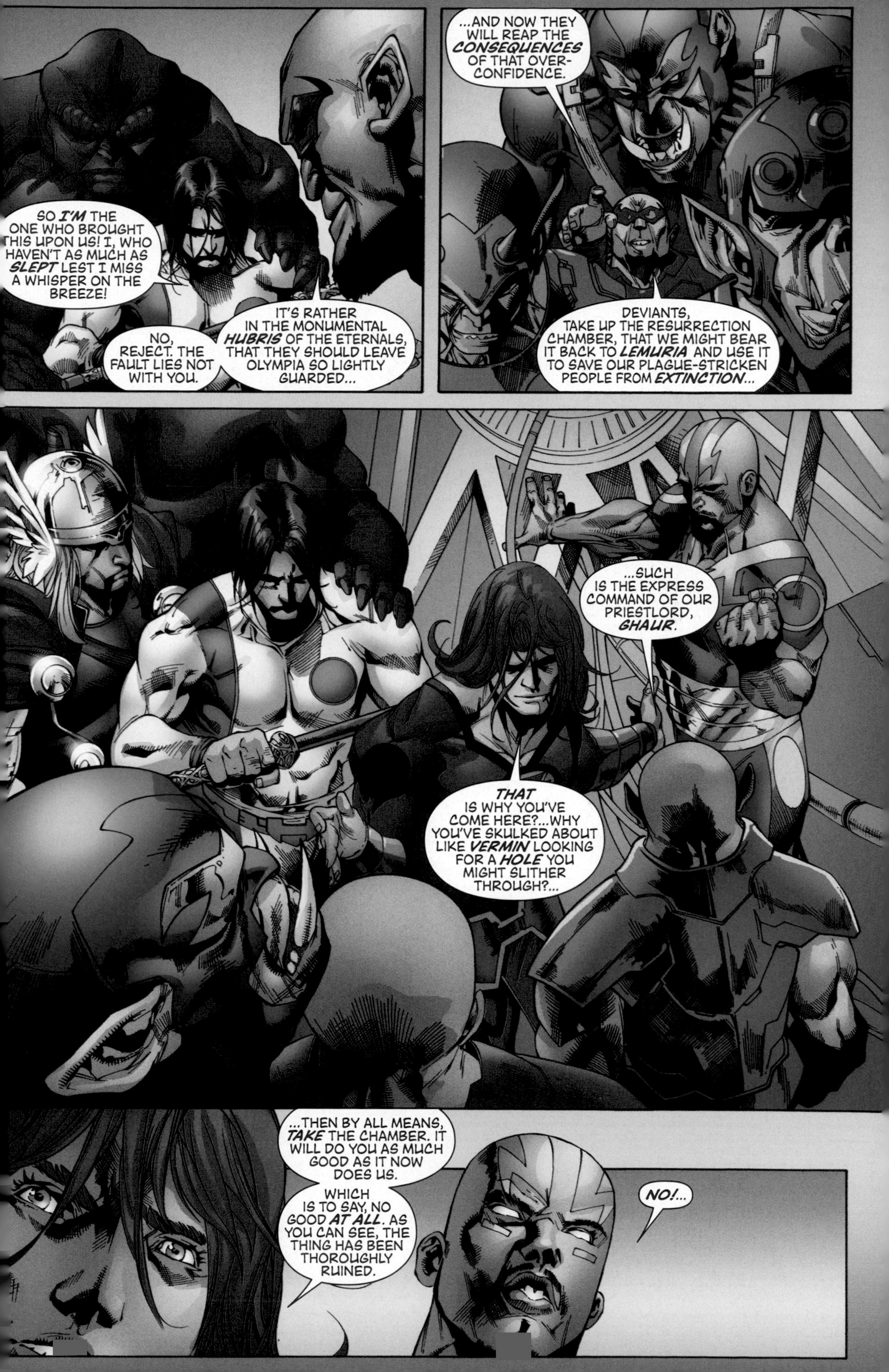
SO I'M THE ONE WHO BROUGHT THIS UPON US! I, WHO HAVEN'T AS MUCH AS SLEPT LEST I MISS A WHISPER ON THE BREEZE!
NO, REJECT. THE FAULT LIES NOT WITH YOU.
IT'S RATHER IN THE MONUMENTAL HUBRIS OF THE ETERNALS, THAT THEY SHOULD LEAVE OLYMPIA SO LIGHTLY GUARDED...
...AND NOW THEY WILL REAP THE CONSEQUENCES OF THAT OVER-CONFIDENCE.
DEVIANTS, TAKE UP THE RESURRECTION CHAMBER, THAT WE MIGHT BEAR IT BACK TO LEMURIA AND USE IT TO SAVE OUR PLAGUE-STRICKEN PEOPLE FROM EXTINCTION...
...SUCH IS THE EXPRESS COMMAND OF OUR PRIESTLORD, GHAUR.
THAT IS WHY YOU'VE COME HERE?...WHY YOU'VE SKULKED ABOUT LIKE VERMIN LOOKING FOR A HOLE YOU MIGHT SLITHER THROUGH?...
...THEN BY ALL MEANS, TAKE THE CHAMBER. IT WILL DO YOU AS MUCH GOOD AS IT NOW DOES US.
WHICH IS TO SAY, NO GOOD AT ALL. AS YOU CAN SEE, THE THING HAS BEEN THOROUGHLY RUINED.
NO!...

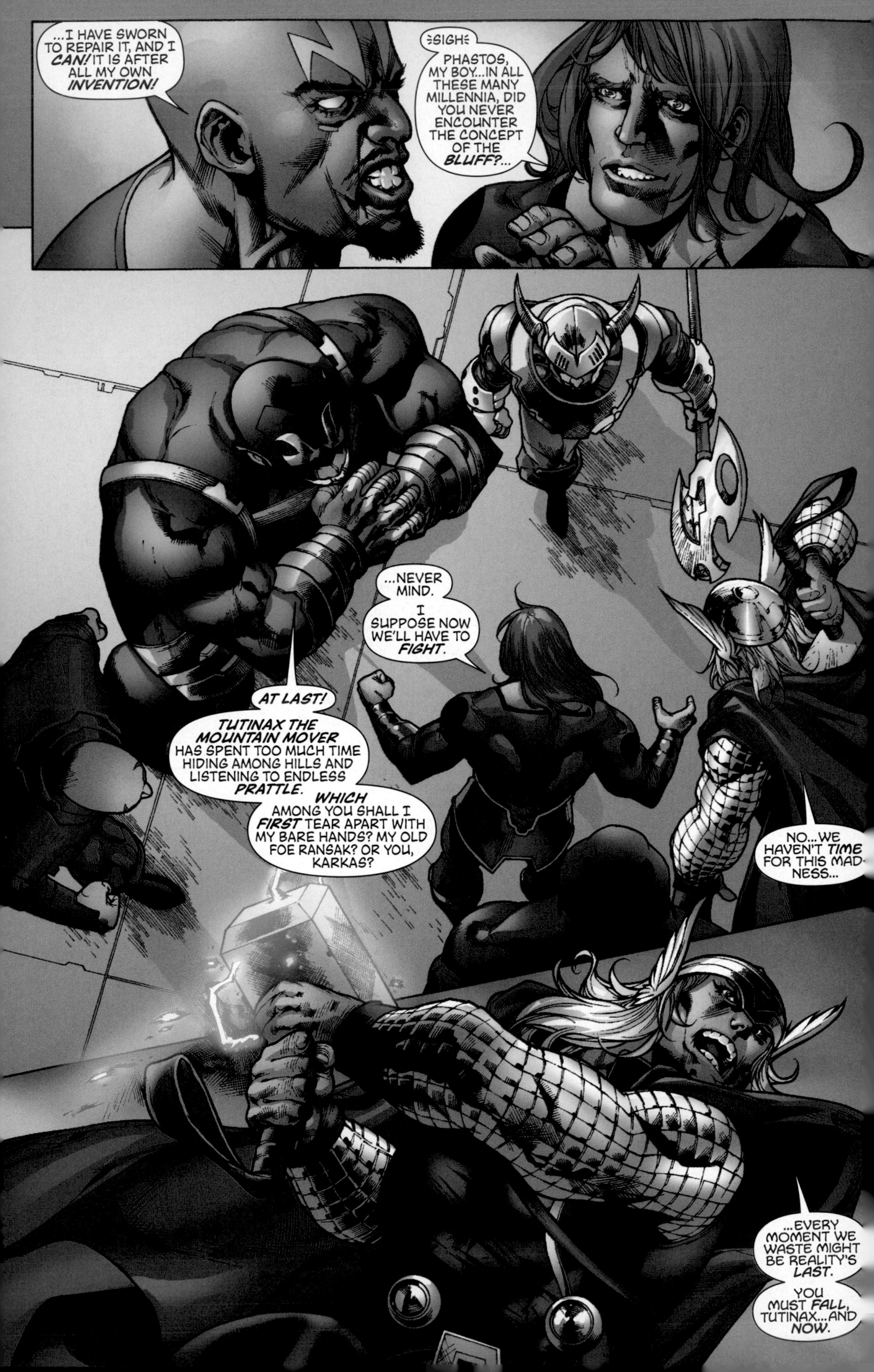
...I HAVE SWORN TO REPAIR IT, AND I CAN! IT IS AFTER ALL MY OWN INVENTION!
SIGH
PHASTOS, MY BOY...IN ALL THESE MANY MILLENNIA, DID YOU NEVER ENCOUNTER THE CONCEPT OF THE BLUFF?...
...NEVER MIND.
I SUPPOSE NOW WE'LL HAVE TO FIGHT.
AT LAST!
TUTINAX THE MOUNTAIN MOVER HAS SPENT TOO MUCH TIME HIDING AMONG HILLS AND LISTENING TO ENDLESS PRATTLE.
WHICH AMONG YOU SHALL I FIRST TEAR APART WITH MY BARE HANDS? MY OLD FOE RANSAK? OR YOU, KARKAS?
NO...WE HAVEN'T TIME FOR THIS MAD-NESS...
...EVERY MOMENT WE WASTE MIGHT BE REALITY'S LAST.
YOU MUST FALL, TUTINAX...AND NOW.

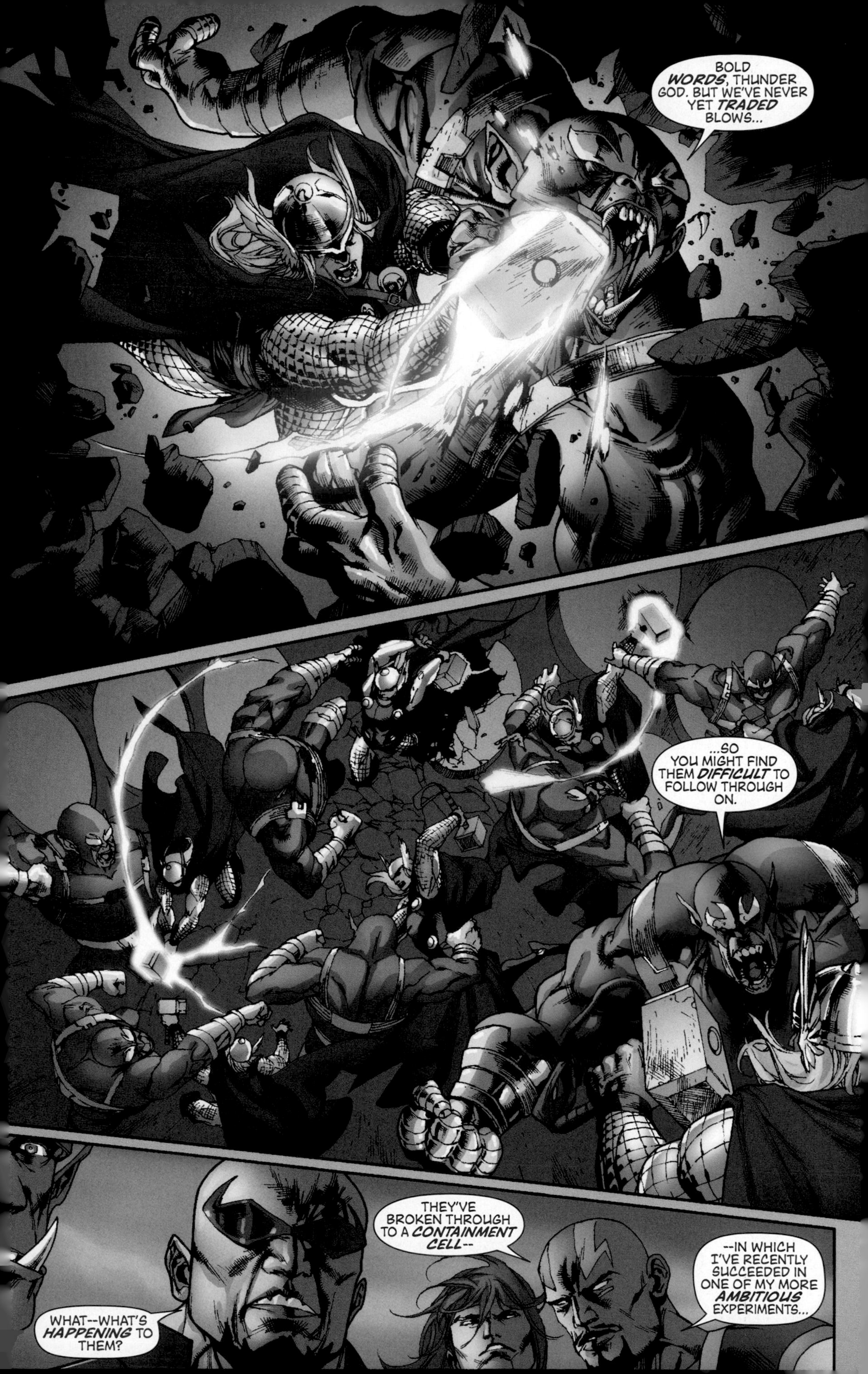
BOLD WORDS, THUNDER GOD. BUT WE'VE NEVER YET TRADED BLOWS...
...SO YOU MIGHT FIND THEM DIFFICULT TO FOLLOW THROUGH ON.
THEY'VE BROKEN THROUGH TO A CONTAINMENT CELL--
--IN WHICH I'VE RECENTLY SUCCEEDED IN ONE OF MY MORE AMBITIOUS EXPERIMENTS...
WHAT--WHAT'S HAPPENING TO THEM?

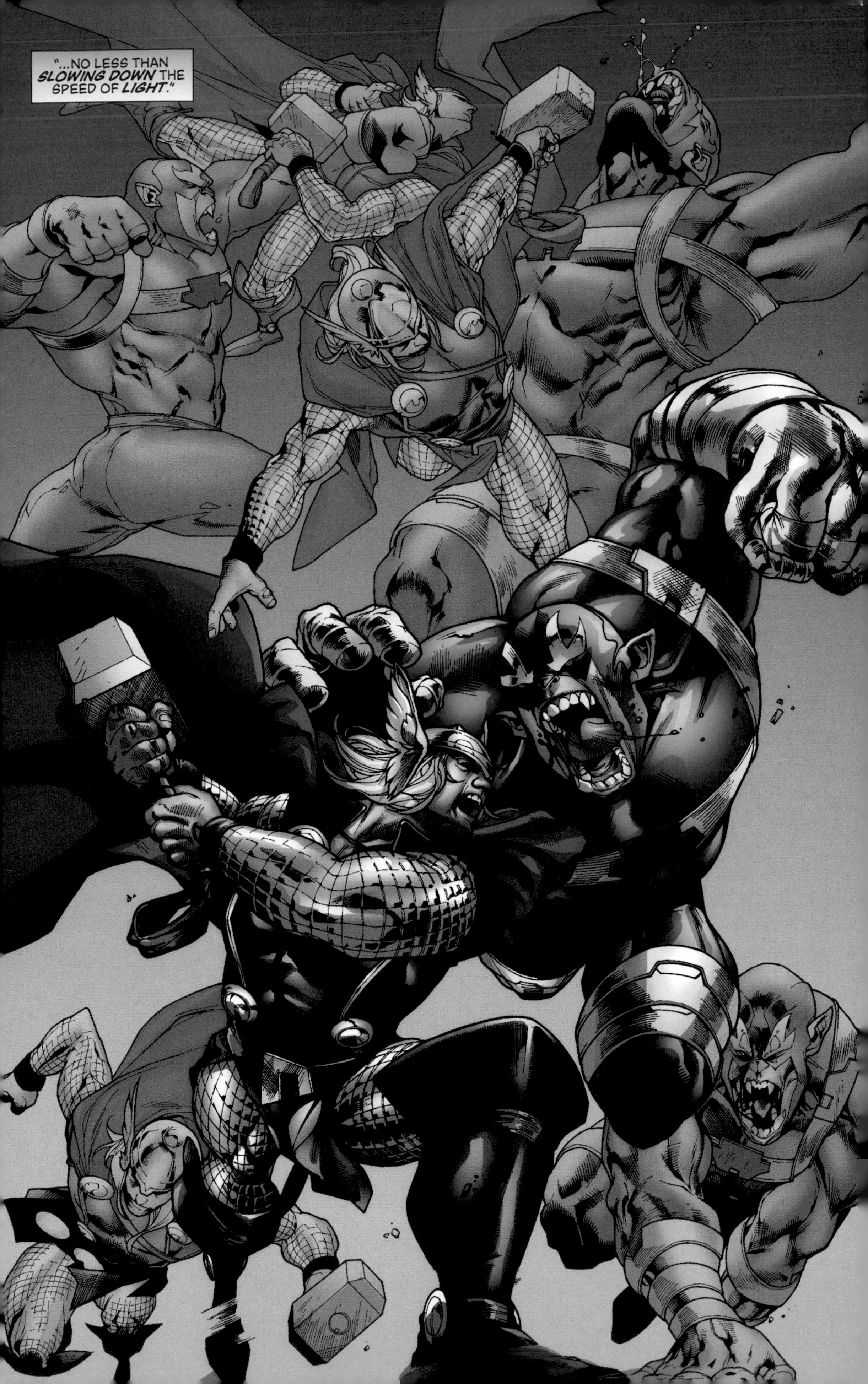
"...NO LESS THAN SLOWING DOWN THE SPEED OF LIGHT."

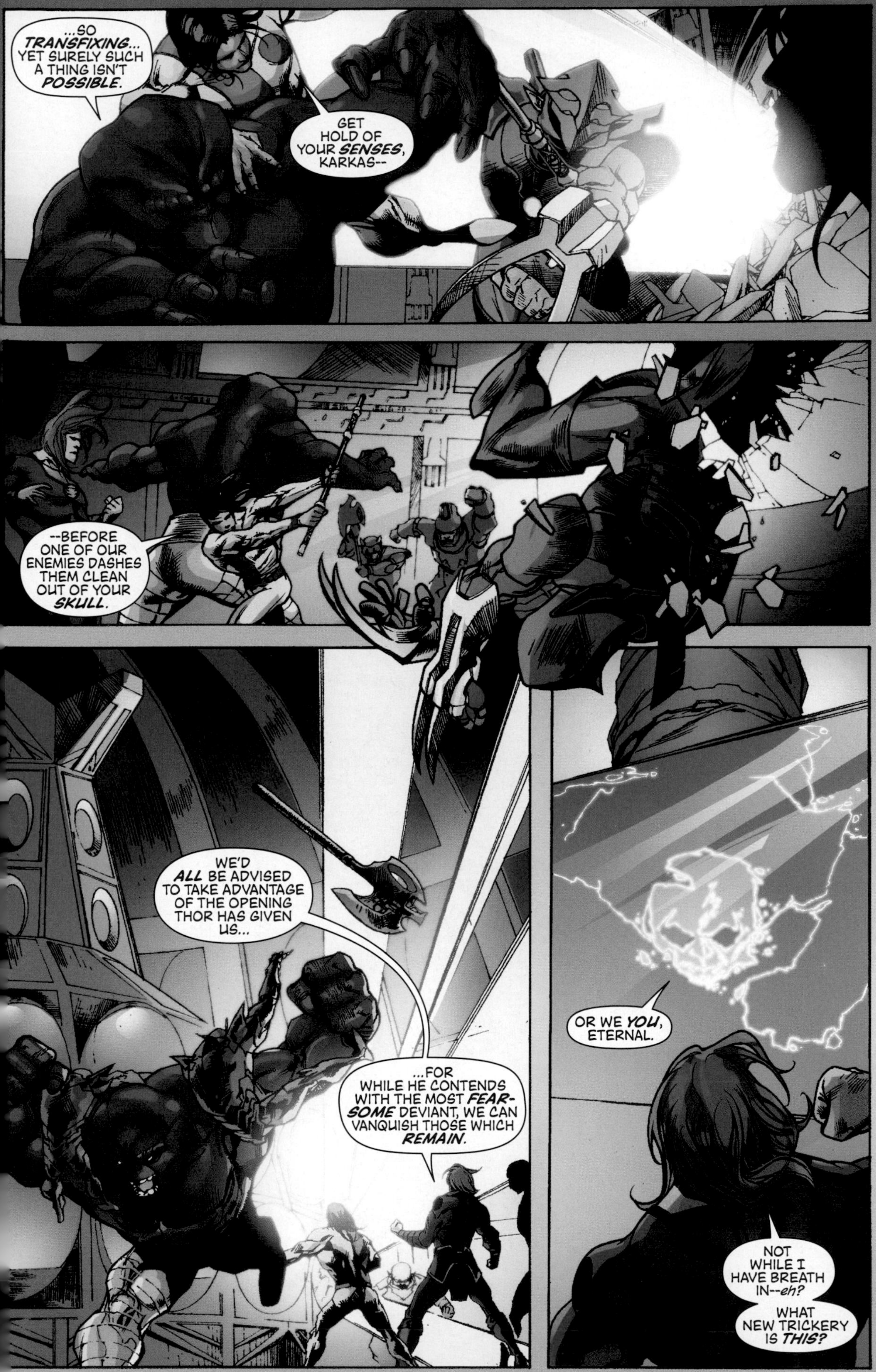
...SO TRANSFIXING... YET SURELY SUCH A THING ISN'T POSSIBLE.
GET HOLD OF YOUR SENSES, KARKAS--
--BEFORE ONE OF OUR ENEMIES DASHES THEM CLEAN OUT OF YOUR SKULL.
WE'D ALL BE ADVISED TO TAKE ADVANTAGE OF THE OPENING THOR HAS GIVEN US...
...FOR WHILE HE CONTENDS WITH THE MOST FEAR-SOME DEVIANT, WE CAN VANQUISH THOSE WHICH REMAIN.
OR WE YOU, ETERNAL.
NOT WHILE I HAVE BREATH IN--eh?
WHAT NEW TRICKERY IS THIS?

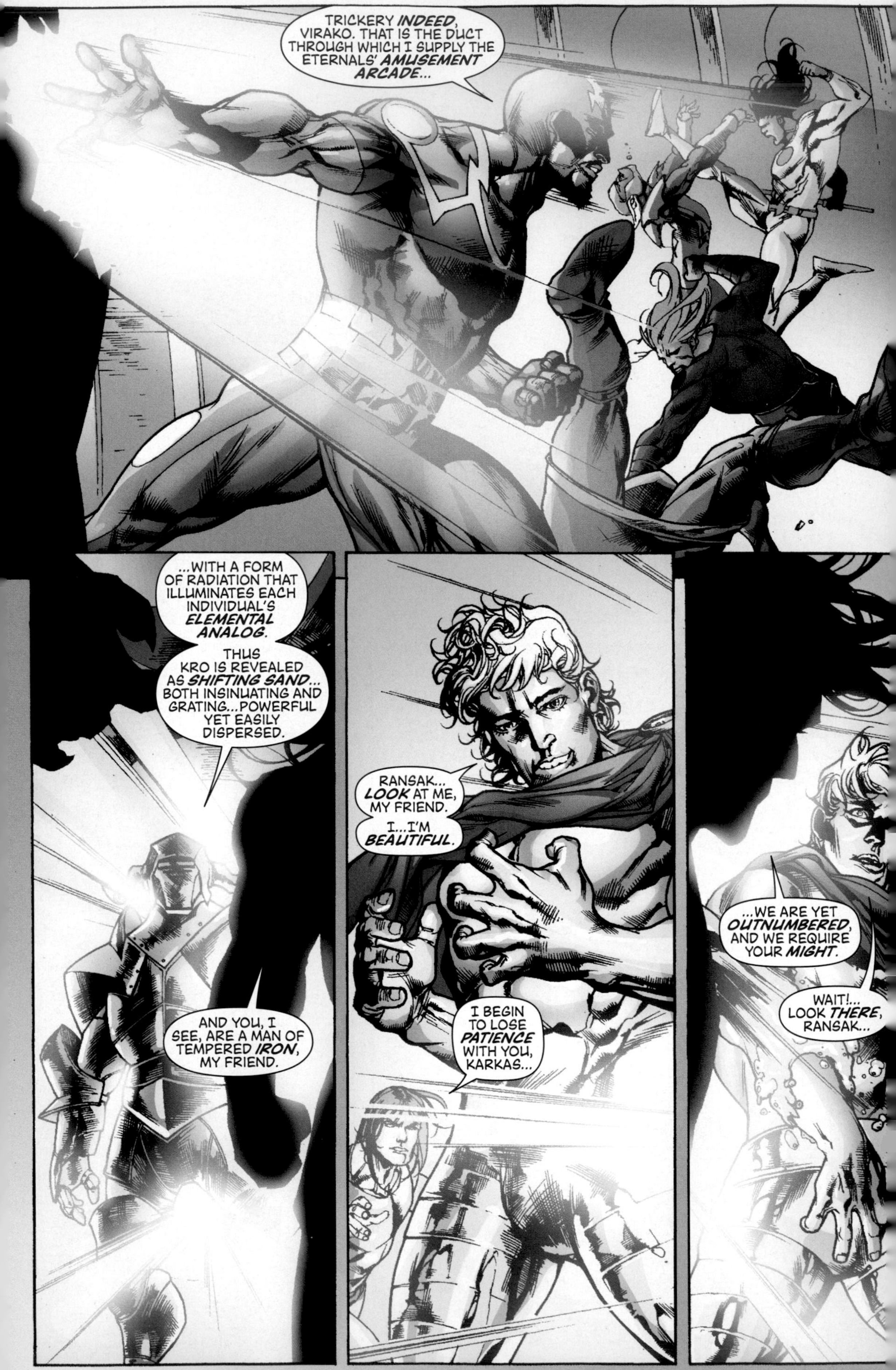
TRICKERY *INDEED*, VIRAKO. THAT IS THE DUCT THROUGH WHICH I SUPPLY THE ETERNALS' *AMUSEMENT ARCADE*...
...WITH A FORM OF RADIATION THAT ILLUMINATES EACH INDIVIDUAL'S *ELEMENTAL ANALOG*.
THUS KRO IS REVEALED AS *SHIFTING SAND*... BOTH INSINUATING AND GRATING...POWERFUL YET EASILY DISPERSED.
AND YOU, I SEE, ARE A MAN OF TEMPERED *IRON*, MY FRIEND.
RANSAK... *LOOK* AT ME, MY FRIEND.
I...I'M *BEAUTIFUL*.
I BEGIN TO LOSE *PATIENCE* WITH YOU, KARKAS...
...WE ARE YET *OUTNUMBERED*, AND WE REQUIRE YOUR *MIGHT*.
WAIT!... LOOK *THERE*, RANSAK...

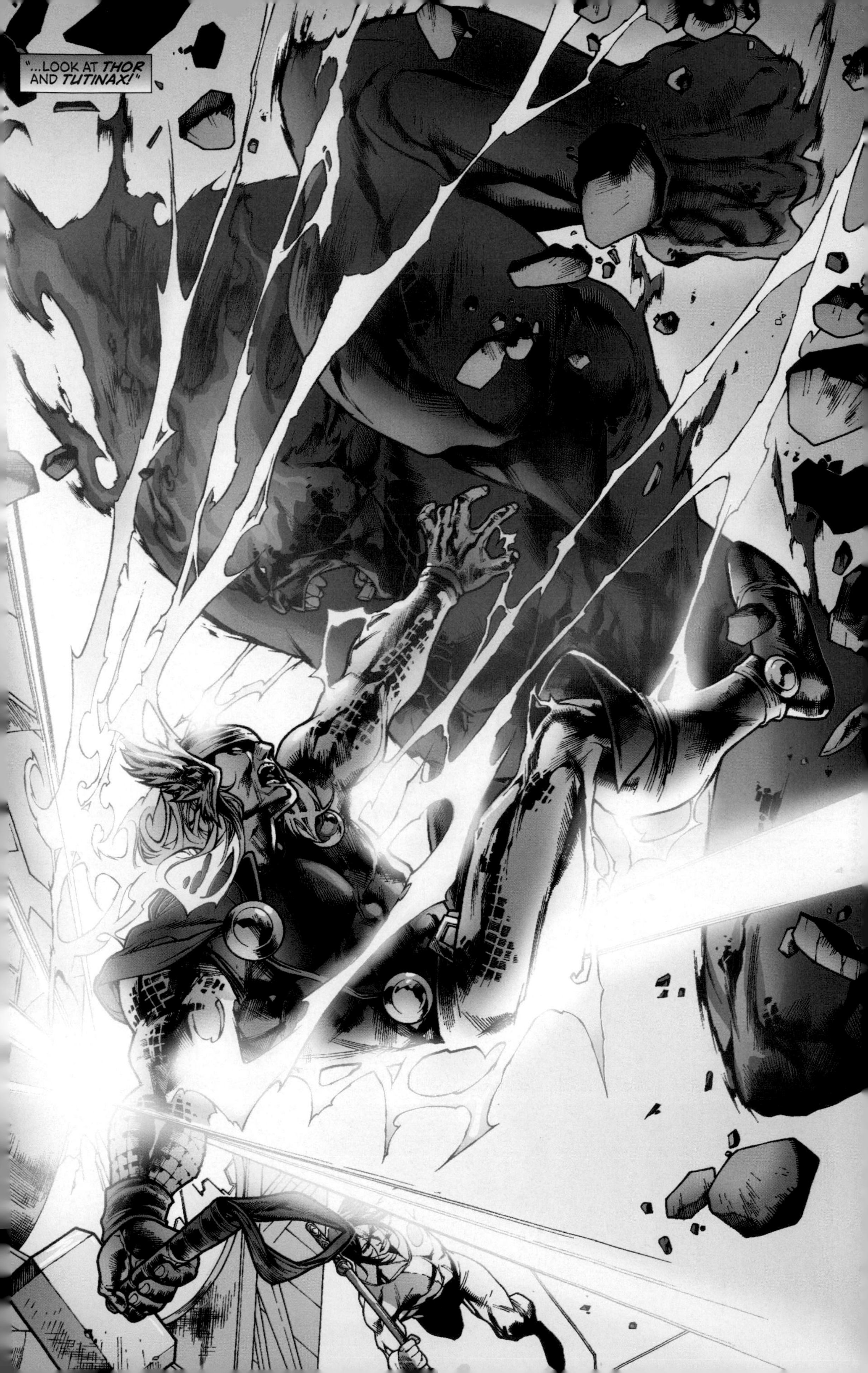
"...LOOK AT *THOR* AND *TUTINAX!*"

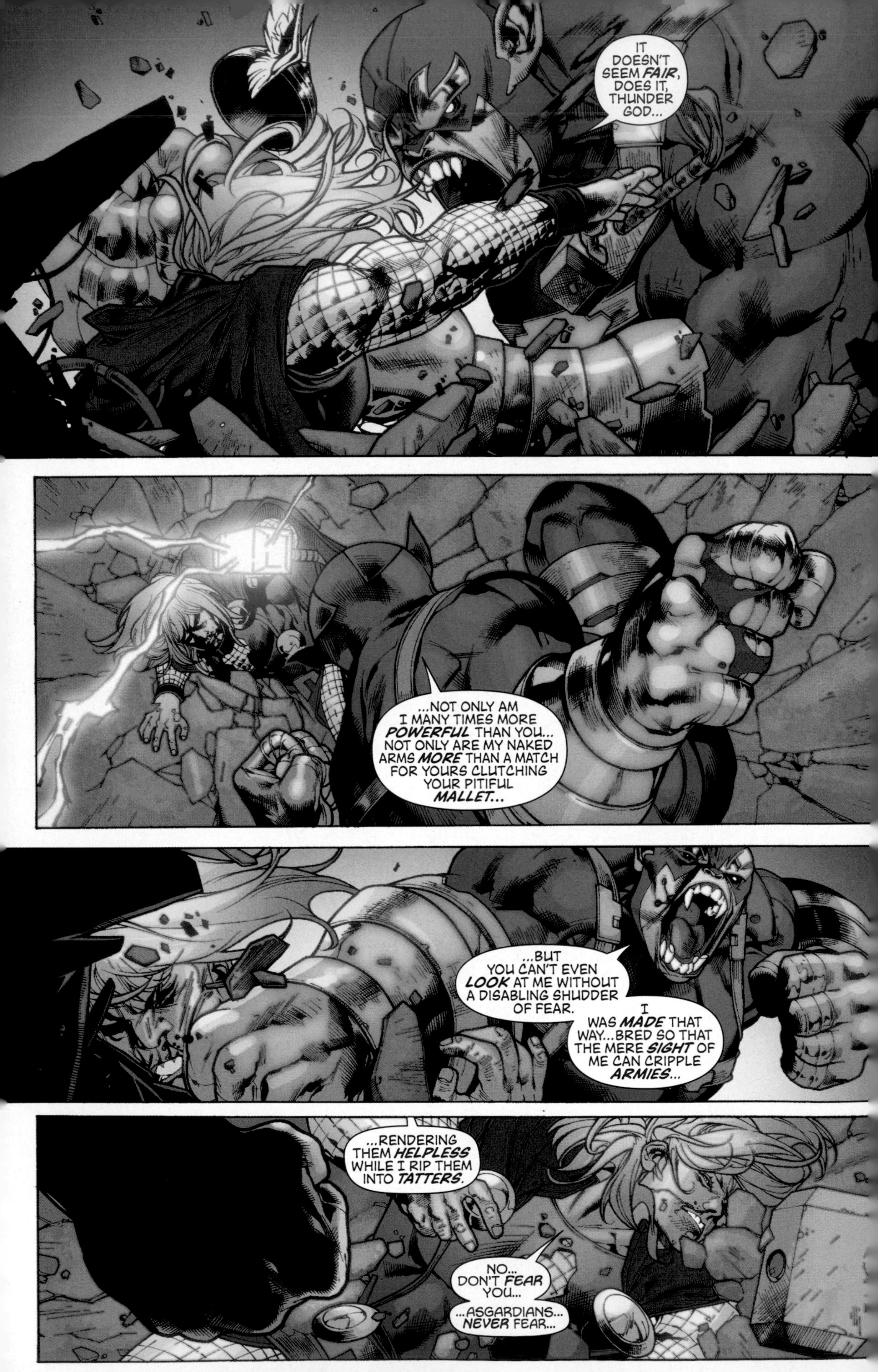
IT DOESN'T SEEM FAIR, DOES IT, THUNDER GOD...
...NOT ONLY AM I MANY TIMES MORE POWERFUL THAN YOU... NOT ONLY ARE MY NAKED ARMS MORE THAN A MATCH FOR YOURS CLUTCHING YOUR PITIFUL MALLET...
...BUT YOU CAN'T EVEN LOOK AT ME WITHOUT A DISABLING SHUDDER OF FEAR.
I WAS MADE THAT WAY...BRED SO THAT THE MERE SIGHT OF ME CAN CRIPPLE ARMIES...
...RENDERING THEM HELPLESS WHILE I RIP THEM INTO TATTERS.
NO... DON'T FEAR YOU...
...ASGARDIANS... NEVER FEAR...

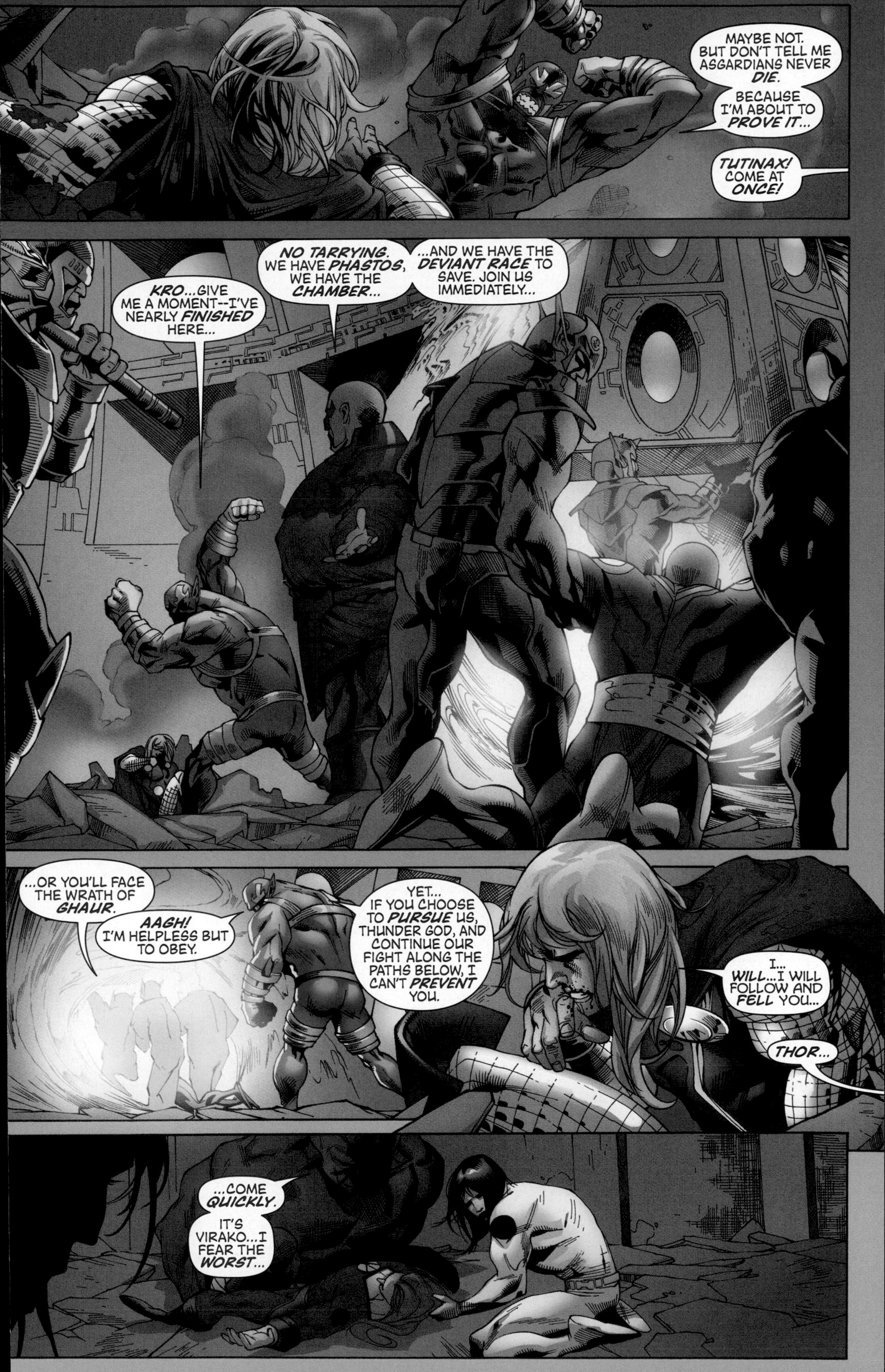
MAYBE NOT. BUT DON'T TELL ME ASGARDIANS NEVER DIE.
BECAUSE I'M ABOUT TO PROVE IT...
TUTINAX! COME AT ONCE!
KRO...GIVE ME A MOMENT--I'VE NEARLY FINISHED HERE...
NO TARRYING. WE HAVE PHASTOS, WE HAVE THE CHAMBER...
...AND WE HAVE THE DEVIANT RACE TO SAVE. JOIN US IMMEDIATELY...
...OR YOU'LL FACE THE WRATH OF GHAUR.
AAGH! I'M HELPLESS BUT TO OBEY.
YET... IF YOU CHOOSE TO PURSUE US, THUNDER GOD, AND CONTINUE OUR FIGHT ALONG THE PATHS BELOW, I CAN'T PREVENT YOU.
I... WILL...I WILL FOLLOW AND FELL YOU...
THOR...
...COME QUICKLY.
IT'S VIRAKO...I FEAR THE WORST...

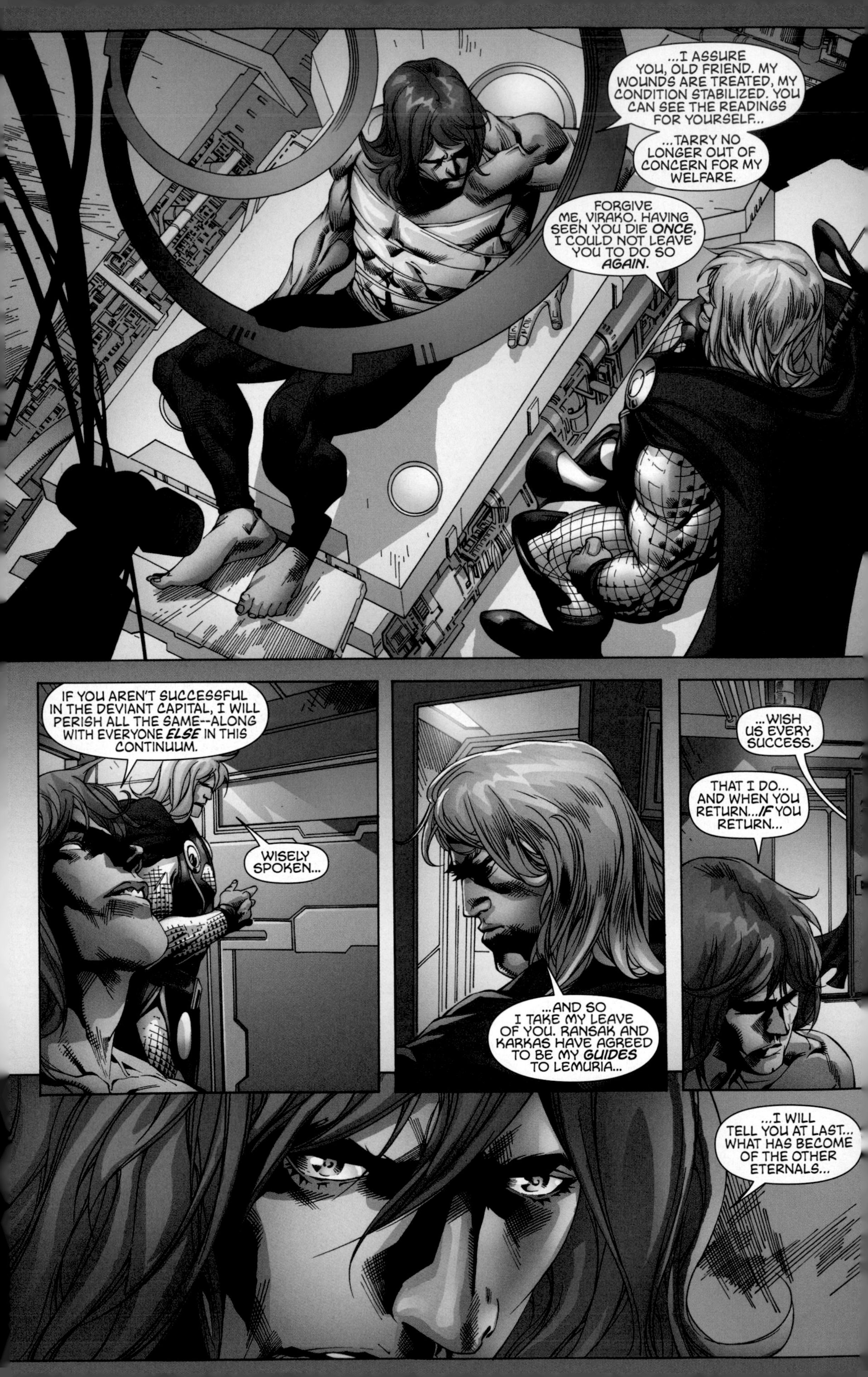
...I ASSURE YOU, OLD FRIEND. MY WOUNDS ARE TREATED, MY CONDITION STABILIZED. YOU CAN SEE THE READINGS FOR YOURSELF...
...TARRY NO LONGER OUT OF CONCERN FOR MY WELFARE.
FORGIVE ME, VIRAKO. HAVING SEEN YOU DIE ONCE, I COULD NOT LEAVE YOU TO DO SO AGAIN.
IF YOU AREN'T SUCCESSFUL IN THE DEVIANT CAPITAL, I WILL PERISH ALL THE SAME--ALONG WITH EVERYONE ELSE IN THIS CONTINUUM.
WISELY SPOKEN...
...AND SO I TAKE MY LEAVE OF YOU. RANSAK AND KARKAS HAVE AGREED TO BE MY GUIDES TO LEMURIA...
...WISH US EVERY SUCCESS.
THAT I DO... AND WHEN YOU RETURN...IF YOU RETURN...
...I WILL TELL YOU AT LAST... WHAT HAS BECOME OF THE OTHER ETERNALS...

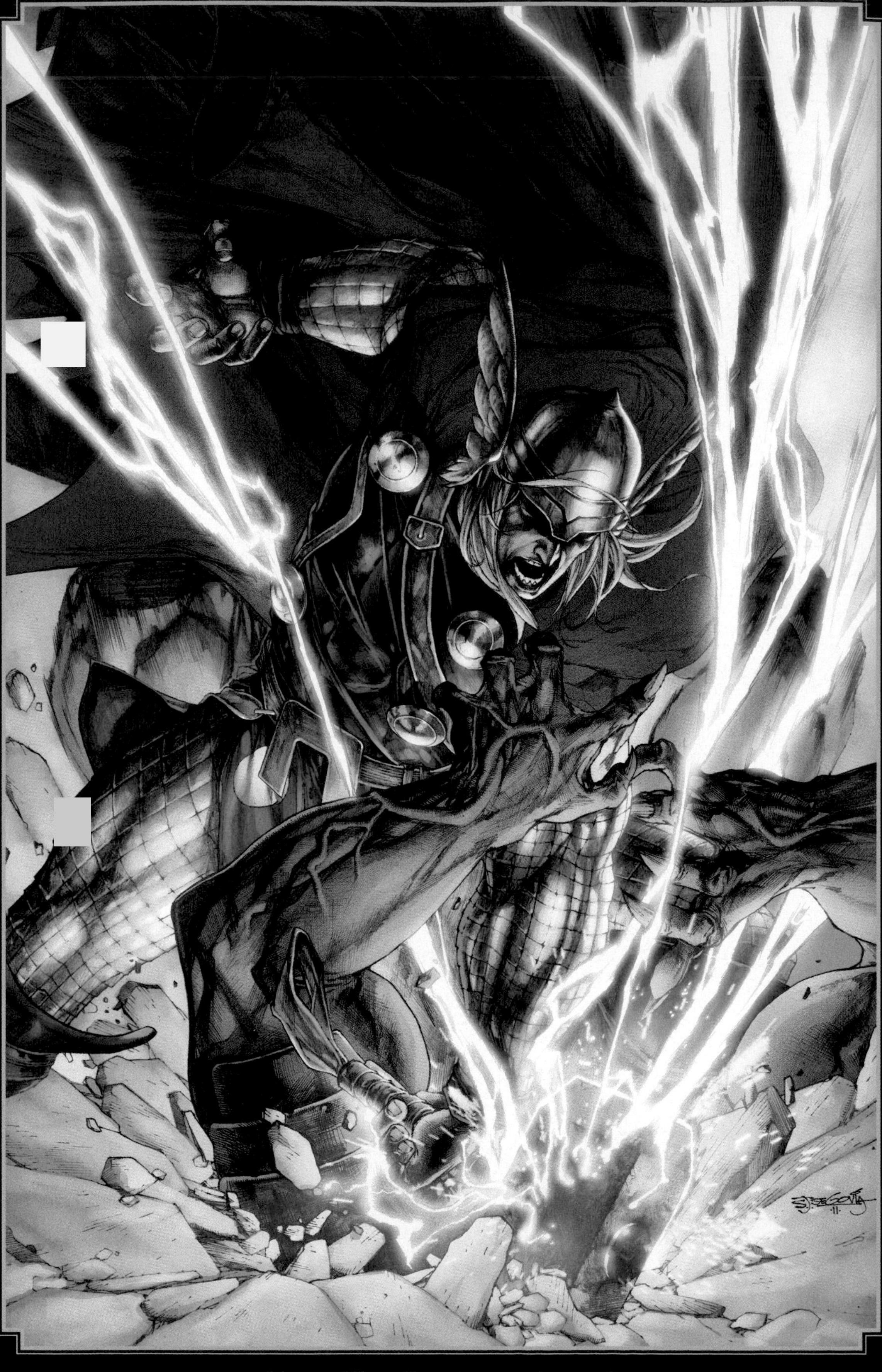

Thor: The Deviants Saga 3

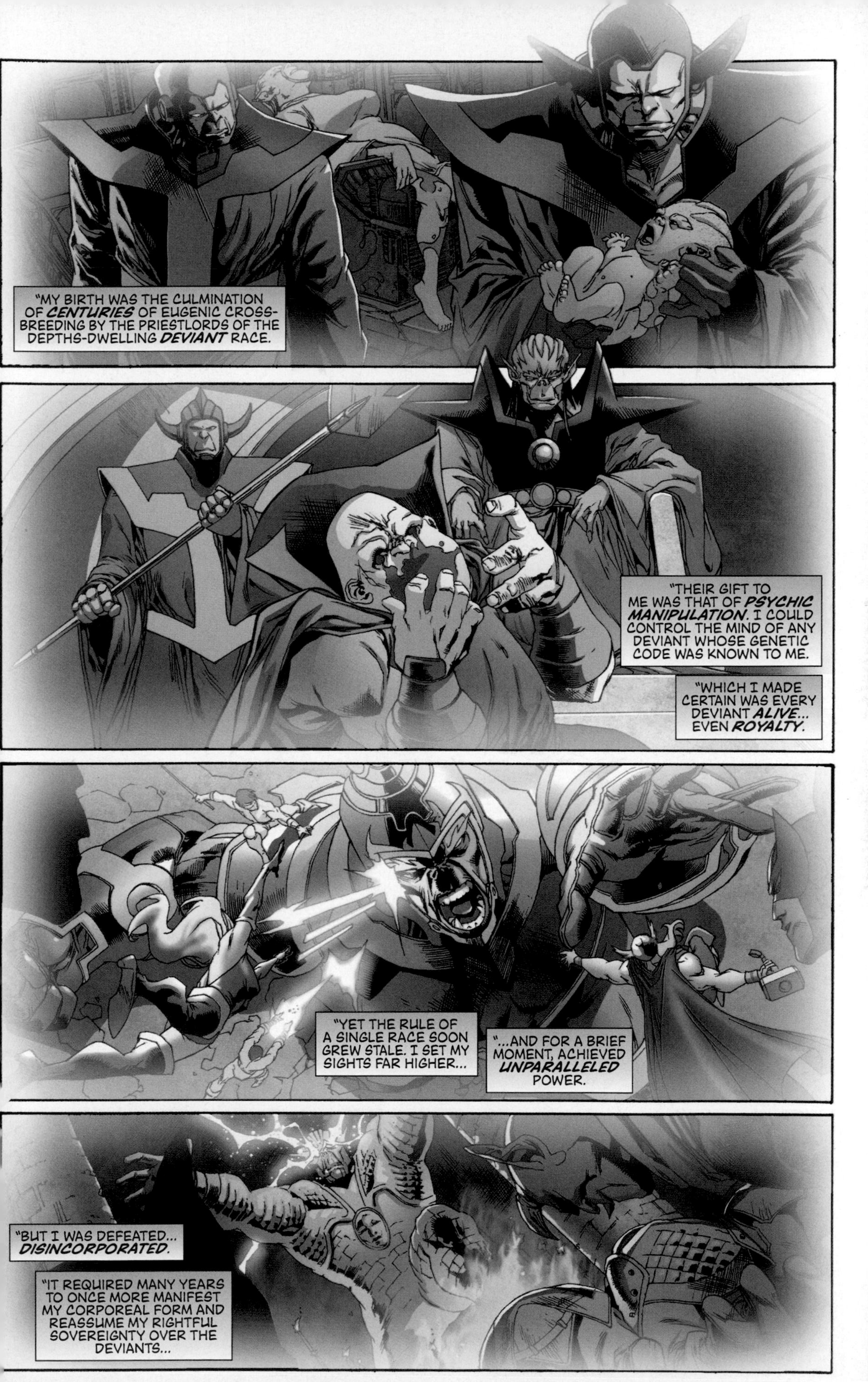
"MY BIRTH WAS THE CULMINATION OF CENTURIES OF EUGENIC CROSS-BREEDING BY THE PRIESTLORDS OF THE DEPTHS-DWELLING DEVIANT RACE.
"THEIR GIFT TO ME WAS THAT OF PSYCHIC MANIPULATION. I COULD CONTROL THE MIND OF ANY DEVIANT WHOSE GENETIC CODE WAS KNOWN TO ME.
"WHICH I MADE CERTAIN WAS EVERY DEVIANT ALIVE... EVEN ROYALTY.
"YET THE RULE OF A SINGLE RACE SOON GREW STALE. I SET MY SIGHTS FAR HIGHER...
"...AND FOR A BRIEF MOMENT, ACHIEVED UNPARALLELED POWER.
"BUT I WAS DEFEATED... DISINCORPORATED.
"IT REQUIRED MANY YEARS TO ONCE MORE MANIFEST MY CORPOREAL FORM AND REASSUME MY RIGHTFUL SOVEREIGNTY OVER THE DEVIANTS...

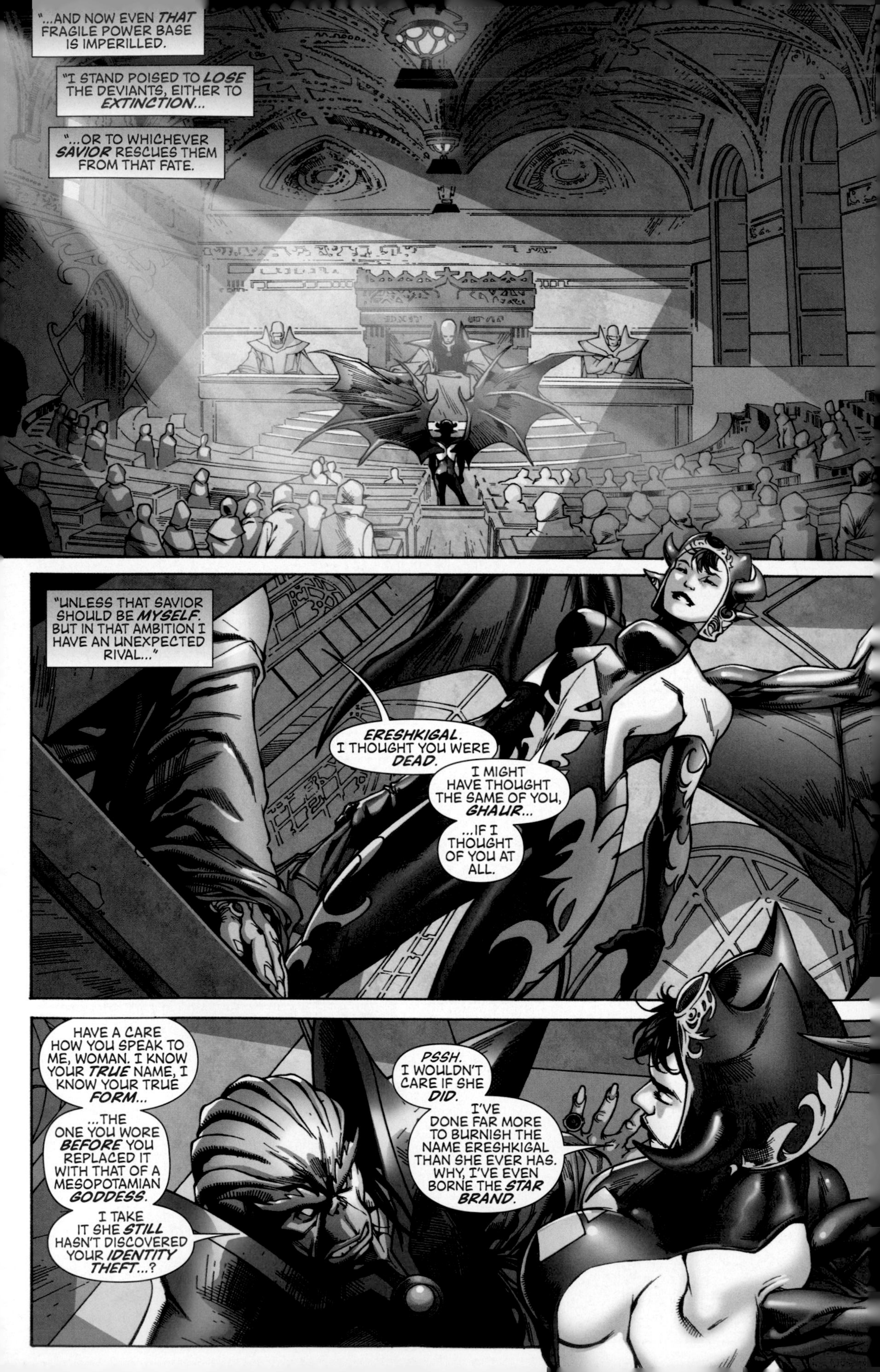
"...AND NOW EVEN *THAT* FRAGILE POWER BASE IS IMPERILLED.
"I STAND POISED TO *LOSE* THE DEVIANTS, EITHER TO *EXTINCTION*...
"...OR TO WHICHEVER *SAVIOR* RESCUES THEM FROM THAT FATE.
"UNLESS THAT SAVIOR SHOULD BE *MYSELF*. BUT IN THAT AMBITION I HAVE AN UNEXPECTED RIVAL..."
ERESHKIGAL. I THOUGHT YOU WERE *DEAD*.
I MIGHT HAVE THOUGHT THE SAME OF YOU, *GHAUR*...
...IF I THOUGHT OF YOU AT ALL.
HAVE A CARE HOW YOU SPEAK TO ME, WOMAN. I KNOW YOUR *TRUE* NAME, I KNOW YOUR TRUE *FORM*...
...THE ONE YOU WORE *BEFORE* YOU REPLACED IT WITH THAT OF A MESOPOTAMIAN *GODDESS*.
I TAKE IT SHE *STILL* HASN'T DISCOVERED YOUR *IDENTITY THEFT*...?
PSSH. I WOULDN'T CARE IF SHE *DID*.
I'VE DONE FAR MORE TO BURNISH THE NAME ERESHKIGAL THAN SHE EVER HAS. WHY, I'VE EVEN BORNE THE *STAR BRAND*.

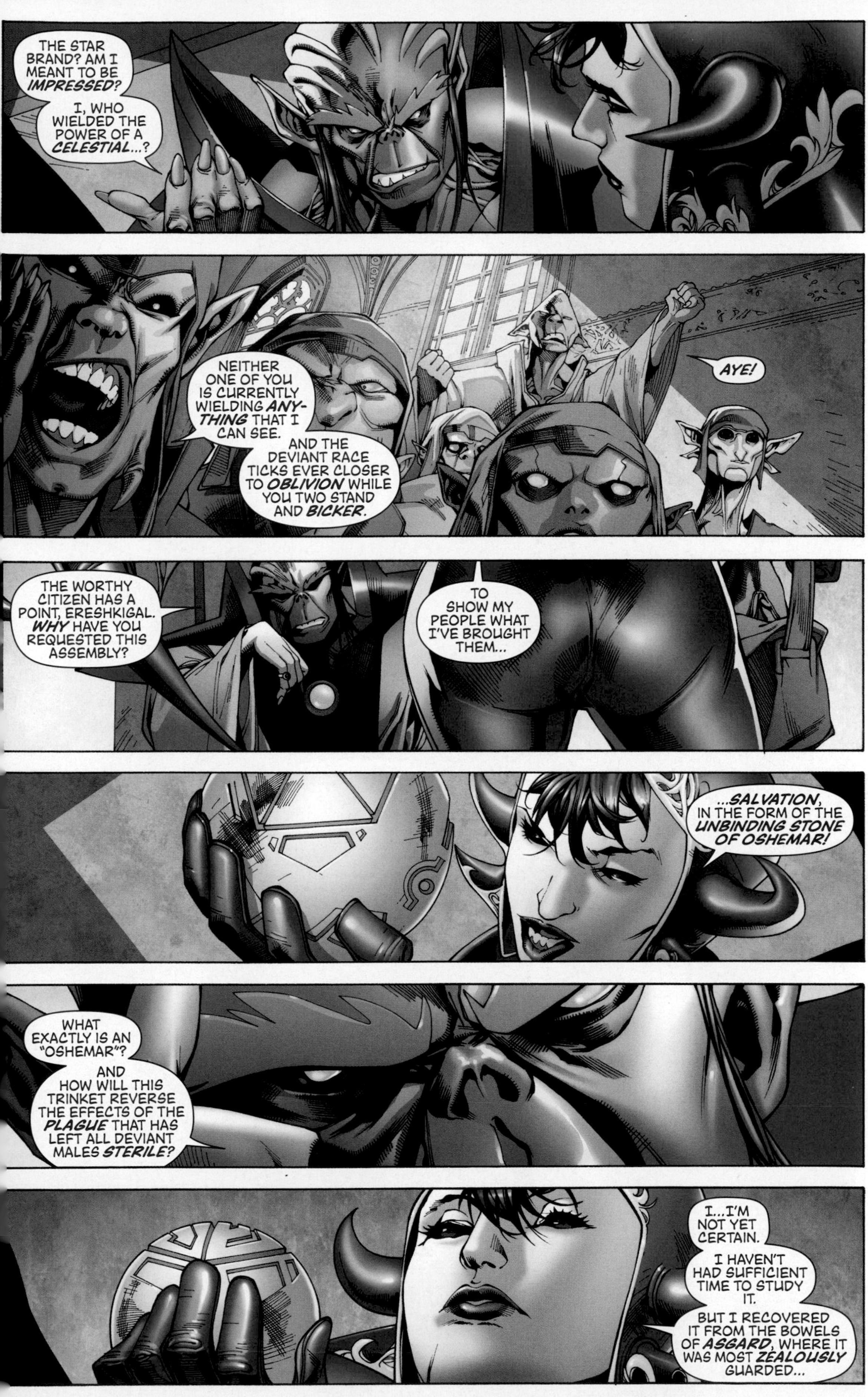
THE STAR BRAND? AM I MEANT TO BE IMPRESSED?
I, WHO WIELDED THE POWER OF A CELESTIAL...?
NEITHER ONE OF YOU IS CURRENTLY WIELDING ANY-THING THAT I CAN SEE.
AND THE DEVIANT RACE TICKS EVER CLOSER TO OBLIVION WHILE YOU TWO STAND AND BICKER.
AYE!
THE WORTHY CITIZEN HAS A POINT, ERESHKIGAL. WHY HAVE YOU REQUESTED THIS ASSEMBLY?
TO SHOW MY PEOPLE WHAT I'VE BROUGHT THEM...
...SALVATION, IN THE FORM OF THE UNBINDING STONE OF OSHEMAR!
WHAT EXACTLY IS AN "OSHEMAR"?
AND HOW WILL THIS TRINKET REVERSE THE EFFECTS OF THE PLAGUE THAT HAS LEFT ALL DEVIANT MALES STERILE?
I...I'M NOT YET CERTAIN.
I HAVEN'T HAD SUFFICIENT TIME TO STUDY IT.
BUT I RECOVERED IT FROM THE BOWELS OF ASGARD, WHERE IT WAS MOST ZEALOUSLY GUARDED...

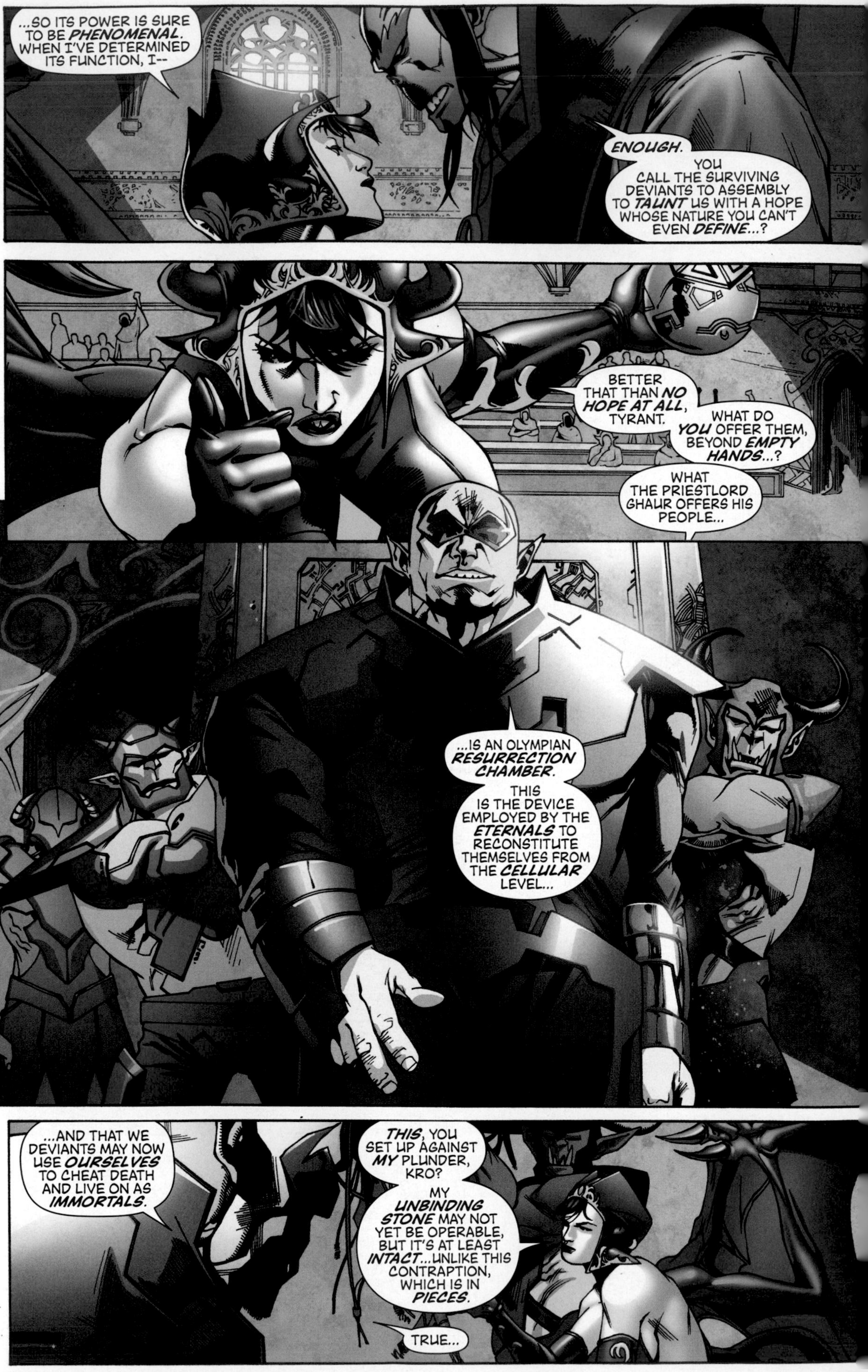

...SO ITS POWER IS SURE TO BE PHENOMENAL. WHEN I'VE DETERMINED ITS FUNCTION, I--
ENOUGH.
YOU CALL THE SURVIVING DEVIANTS TO ASSEMBLY TO TAUNT US WITH A HOPE WHOSE NATURE YOU CAN'T EVEN DEFINE...?
BETTER THAT THAN NO HOPE AT ALL, TYRANT.
WHAT DO YOU OFFER THEM, BEYOND EMPTY HANDS...?
WHAT THE PRIESTLORD GHAUR OFFERS HIS PEOPLE...
...IS AN OLYMPIAN RESURRECTION CHAMBER.
THIS IS THE DEVICE EMPLOYED BY THE ETERNALS TO RECONSTITUTE THEMSELVES FROM THE CELLULAR LEVEL...
...AND THAT WE DEVIANTS MAY NOW USE OURSELVES TO CHEAT DEATH AND LIVE ON AS IMMORTALS.
THIS, YOU SET UP AGAINST MY PLUNDER, KRO?
MY UNBINDING STONE MAY NOT YET BE OPERABLE, BUT IT'S AT LEAST INTACT...UNLIKE THIS CONTRAPTION, WHICH IS IN PIECES.
TRUE...

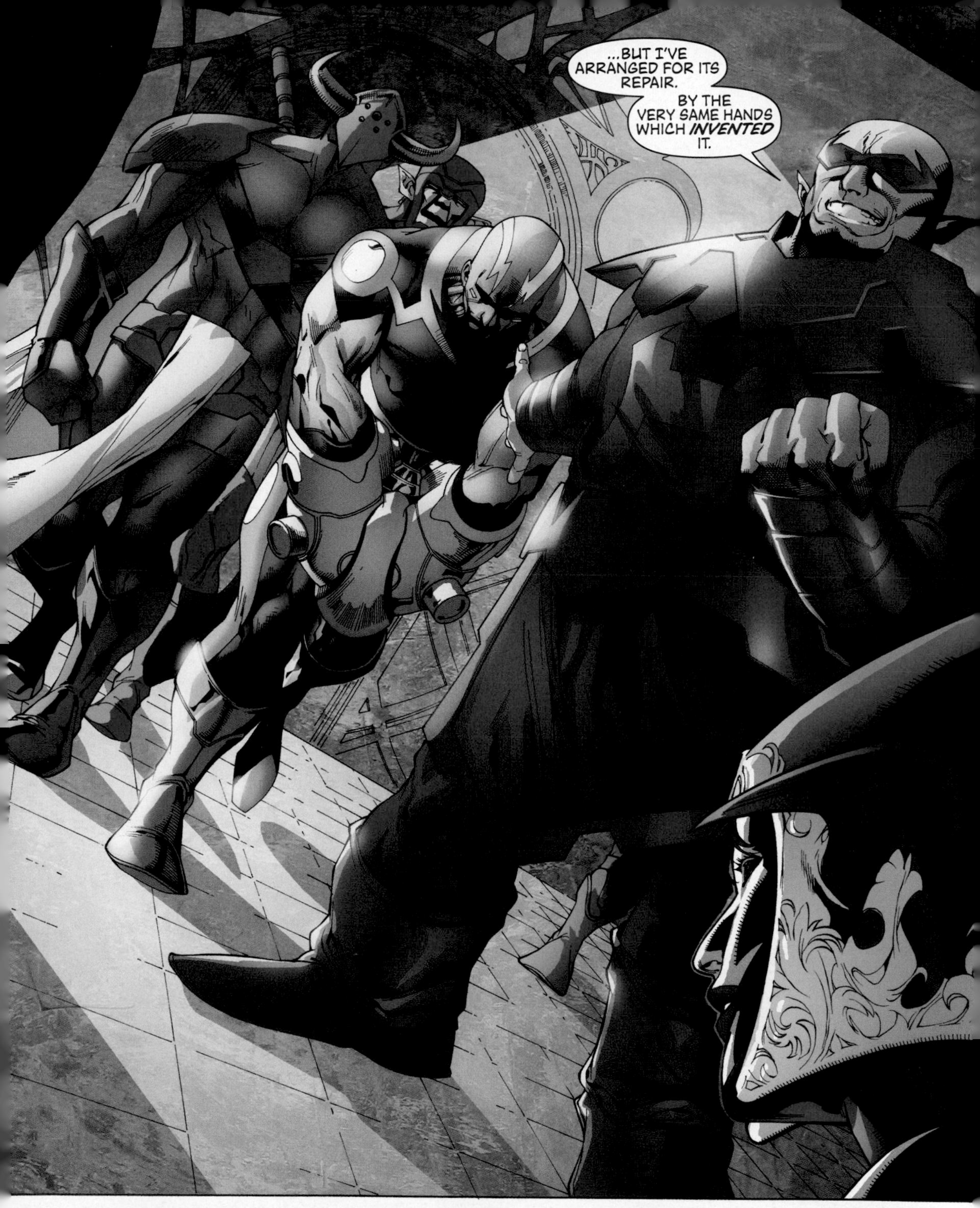
...BUT I'VE ARRANGED FOR ITS REPAIR.
BY THE VERY SAME HANDS WHICH *INVENTED* IT.

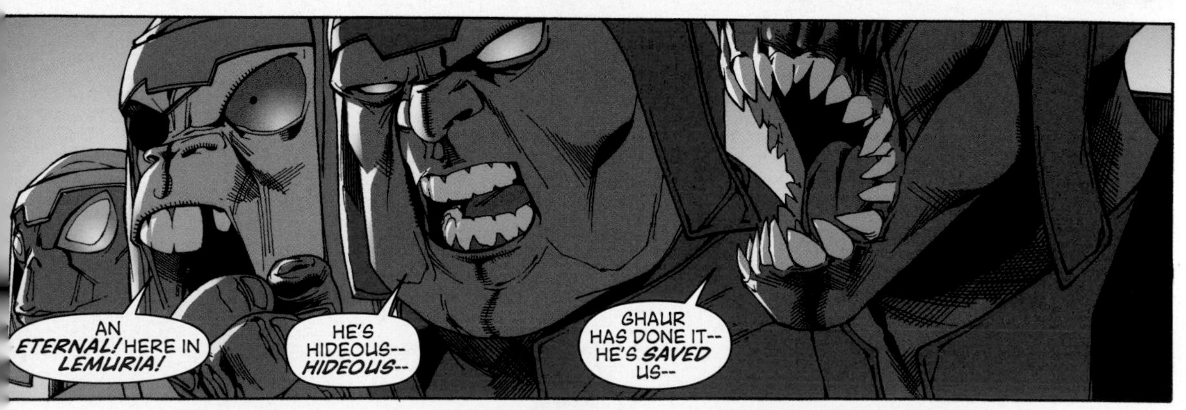
AN *ETERNAL!* HERE IN *LEMURIA!*
HE'S HIDEOUS-- *HIDEOUS*--
GHAUR HAS DONE IT-- HE'S *SAVED* US--

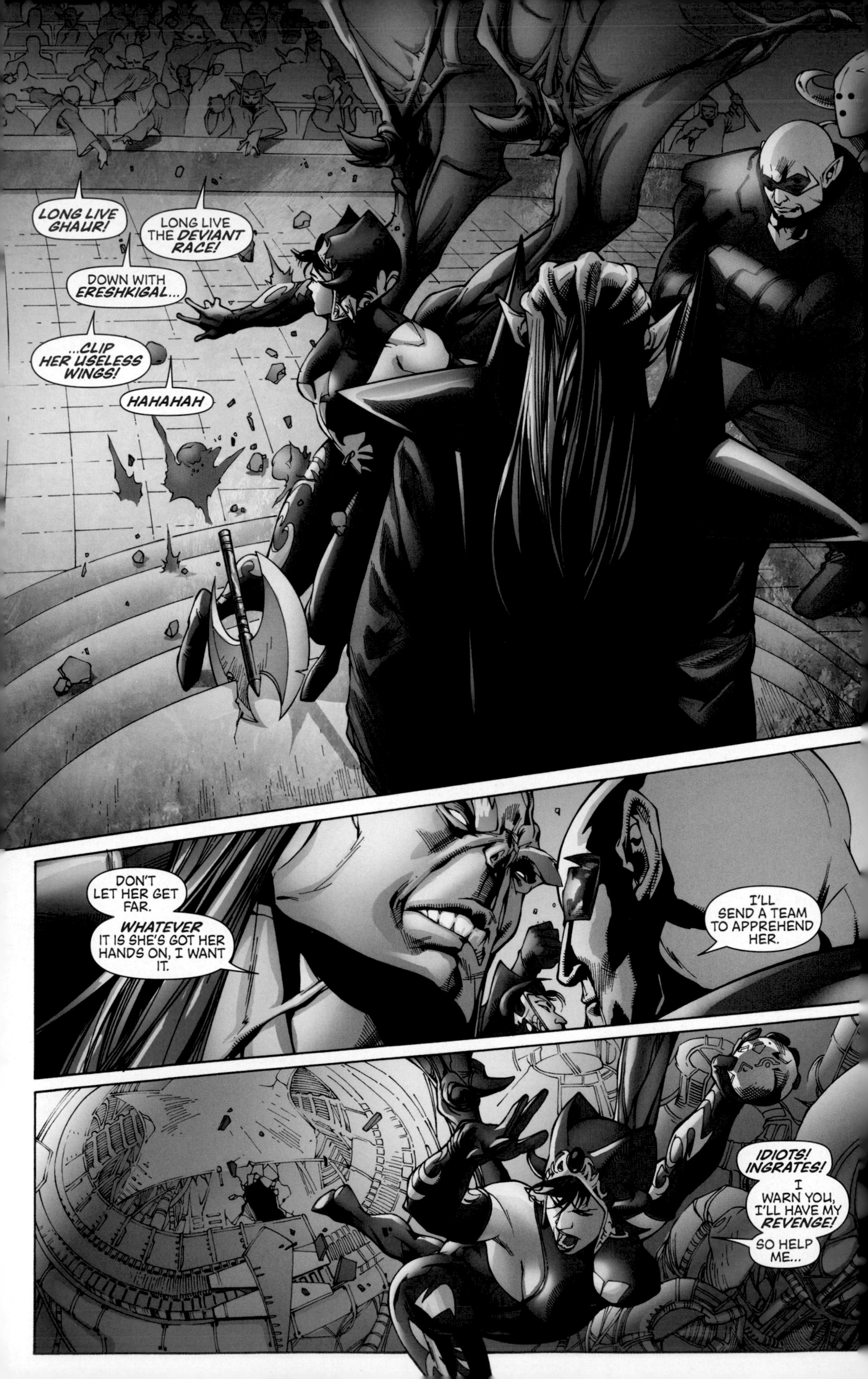
LONG LIVE GHAUR!
LONG LIVE THE DEVIANT RACE!
DOWN WITH ERESHKIGAL...
...CLIP HER USELESS WINGS!
HAHAHAH
DON'T LET HER GET FAR.
WHATEVER IT IS SHE'S GOT HER HANDS ON, I WANT IT.
I'LL SEND A TEAM TO APPREHEND HER.
IDIOTS! INGRATES!
I WARN YOU, I'LL HAVE MY REVENGE!
SO HELP ME...

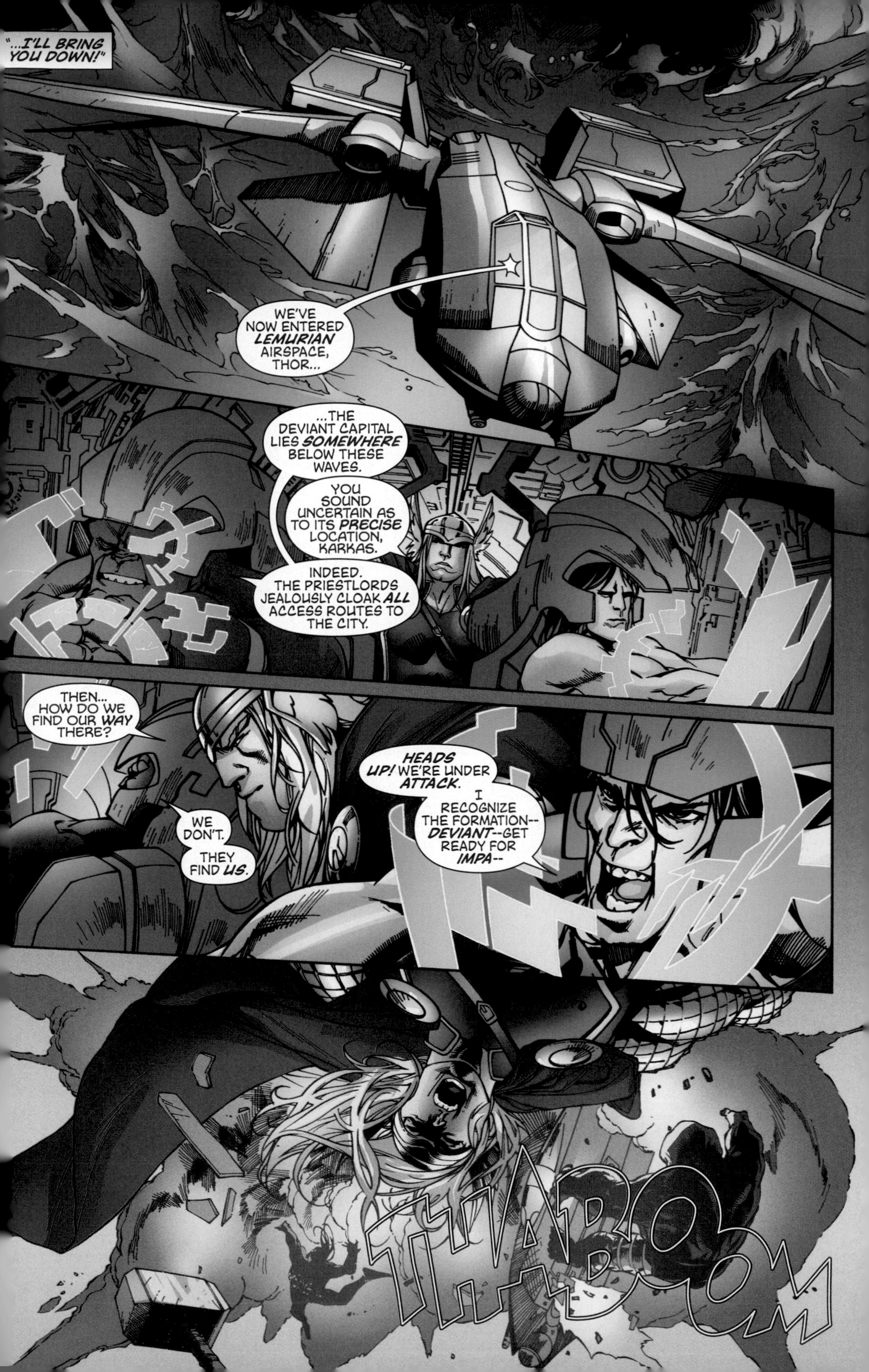

"...I'LL BRING YOU DOWN!"
WE'VE NOW ENTERED LEMURIAN AIRSPACE, THOR...
...THE DEVIANT CAPITAL LIES SOMEWHERE BELOW THESE WAVES.
YOU SOUND UNCERTAIN AS TO ITS PRECISE LOCATION, KARKAS.
INDEED. THE PRIESTLORDS JEALOUSLY CLOAK ALL ACCESS ROUTES TO THE CITY.
THEN... HOW DO WE FIND OUR WAY THERE?
WE DON'T.
THEY FIND US.
HEADS UP! WE'RE UNDER ATTACK.
I RECOGNIZE THE FORMATION--DEVIANT--GET READY FOR IMPA--
THABOOM

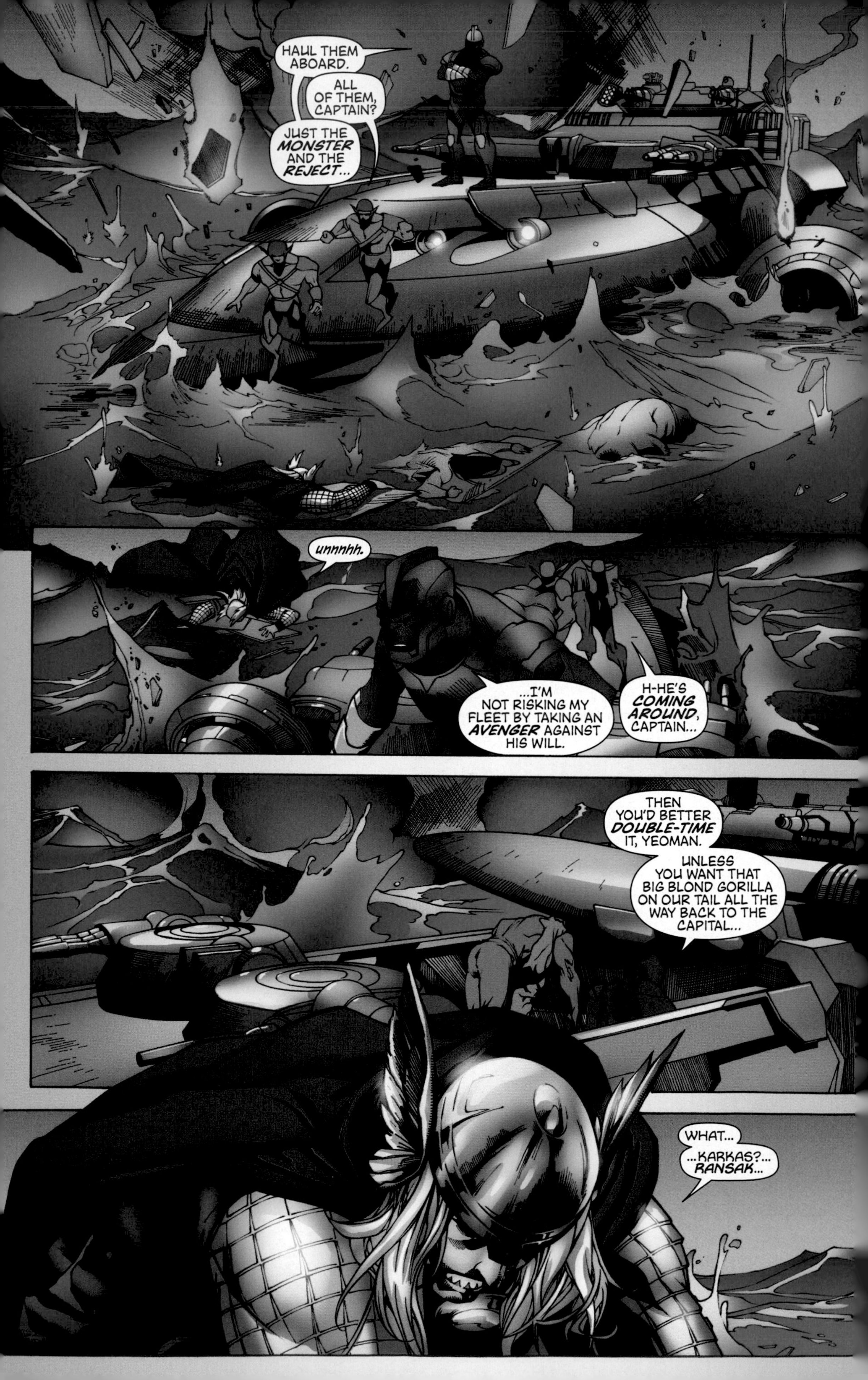
HAUL THEM ABOARD.
ALL OF THEM, CAPTAIN?
JUST THE MONSTER AND THE REJECT...
unnnhh.
...I'M NOT RISKING MY FLEET BY TAKING AN AVENGER AGAINST HIS WILL.
H-HE'S COMING AROUND, CAPTAIN...
THEN YOU'D BETTER DOUBLE-TIME IT, YEOMAN.
UNLESS YOU WANT THAT BIG BLOND GORILLA ON OUR TAIL ALL THE WAY BACK TO THE CAPITAL...
WHAT... ...KARKAS?... RANSAK...

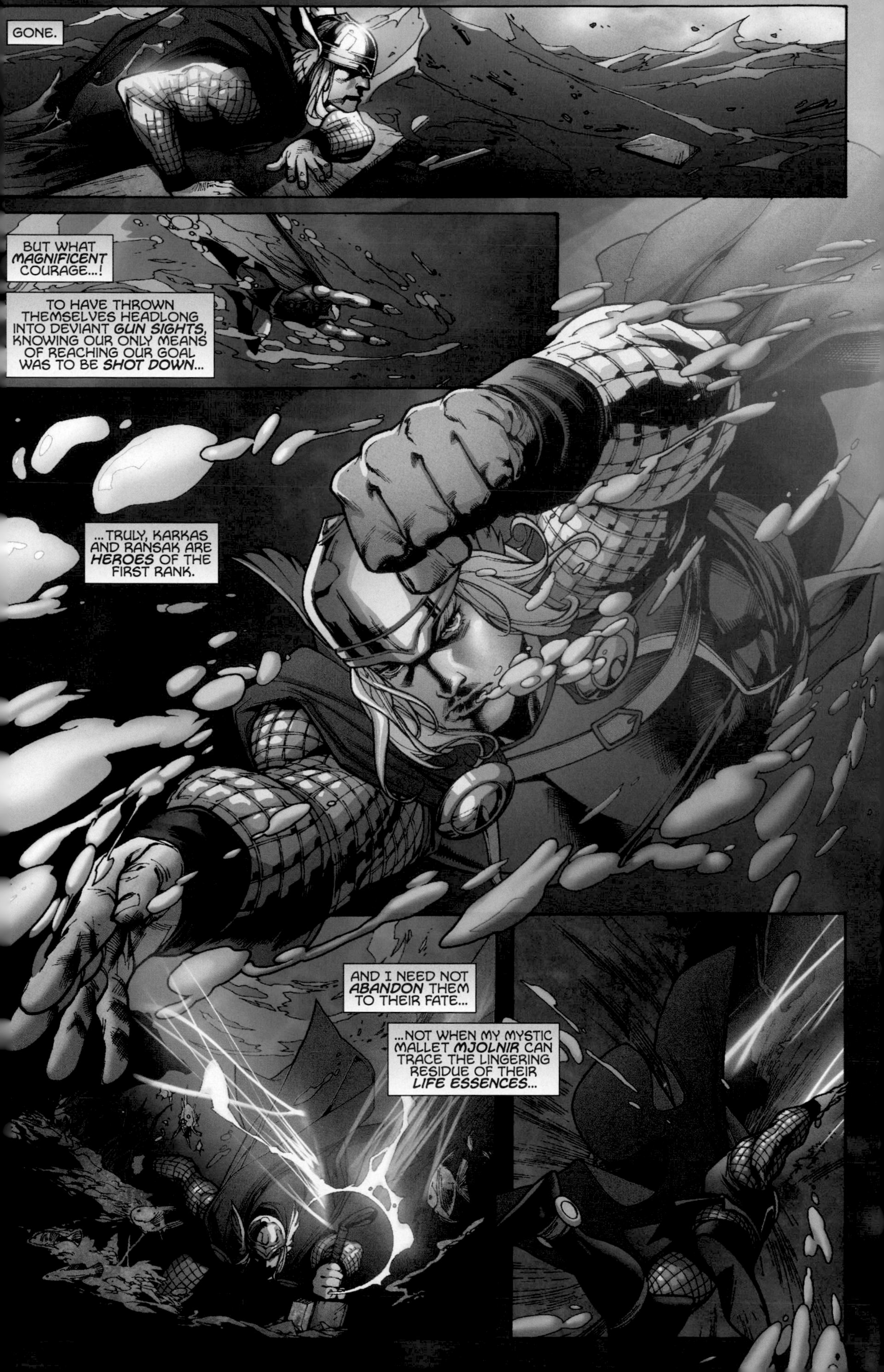
GONE.
BUT WHAT MAGNIFICENT COURAGE...!
TO HAVE THROWN THEMSELVES HEADLONG INTO DEVIANT GUN SIGHTS, KNOWING OUR ONLY MEANS OF REACHING OUR GOAL WAS TO BE SHOT DOWN...
...TRULY, KARKAS AND RANSAK ARE HEROES OF THE FIRST RANK.
AND I NEED NOT ABANDON THEM TO THEIR FATE...
...NOT WHEN MY MYSTIC MALLET MJOLNIR CAN TRACE THE LINGERING RESIDUE OF THEIR LIFE ESSENCES...

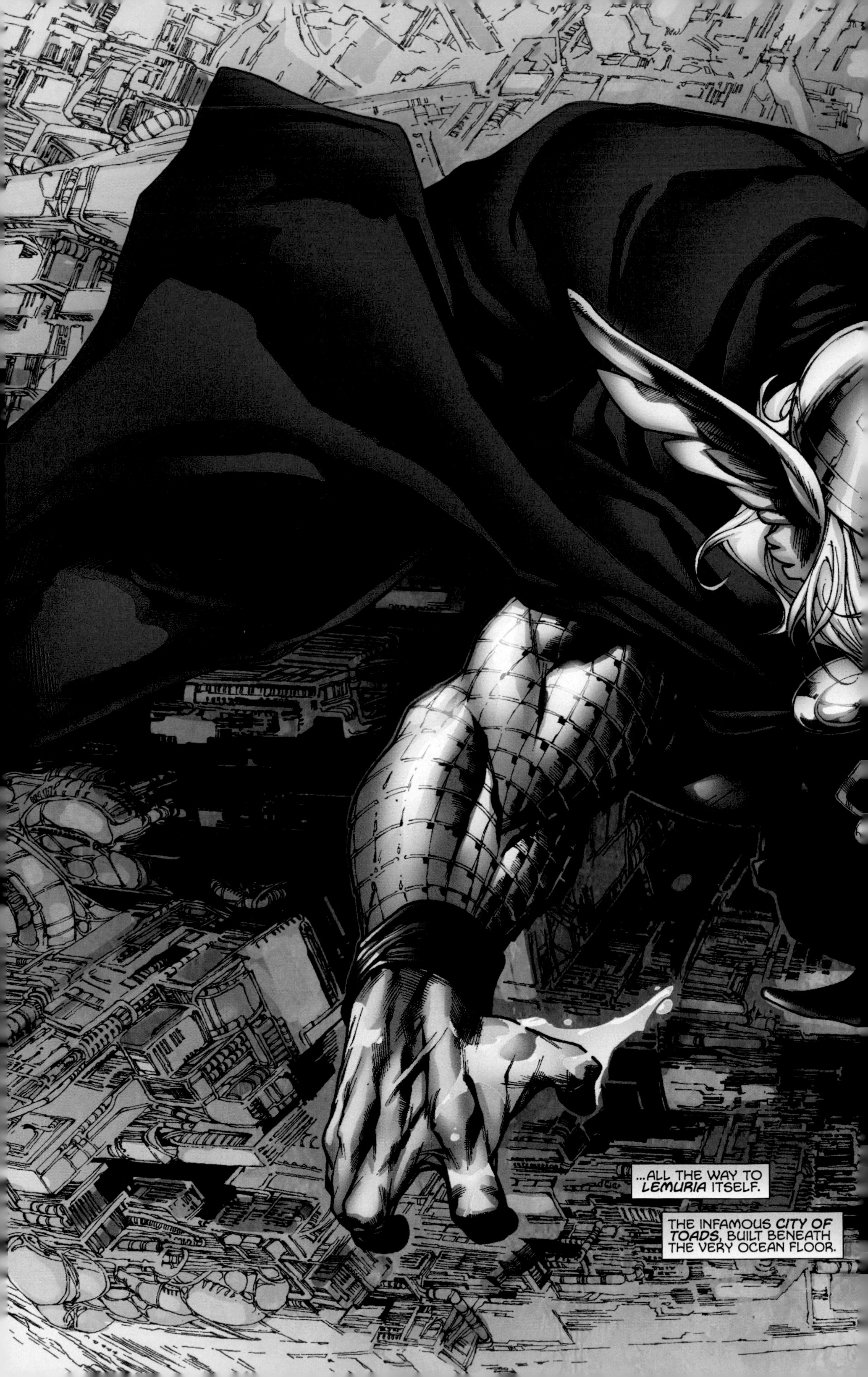
...ALL THE WAY TO LEMURIA ITSELF.
THE INFAMOUS CITY OF TOADS, BUILT BENEATH THE VERY OCEAN FLOOR.

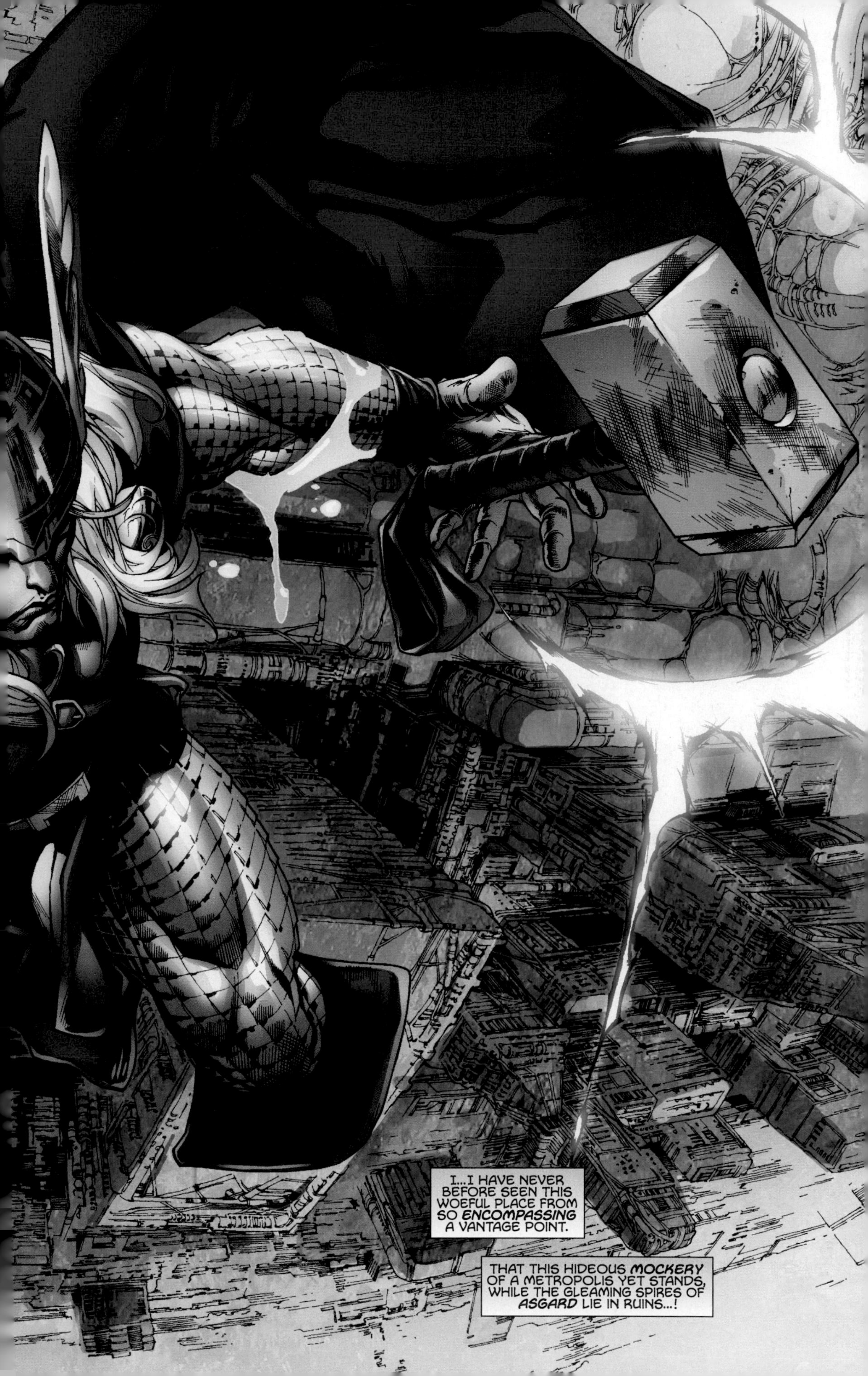
I...I HAVE NEVER BEFORE SEEN THIS WOEFUL PLACE FROM SO ENCOMPASSING A VANTAGE POINT.
THAT THIS HIDEOUS MOCKERY OF A METROPOLIS YET STANDS, WHILE THE GLEAMING SPIRES OF ASGARD LIE IN RUINS...!

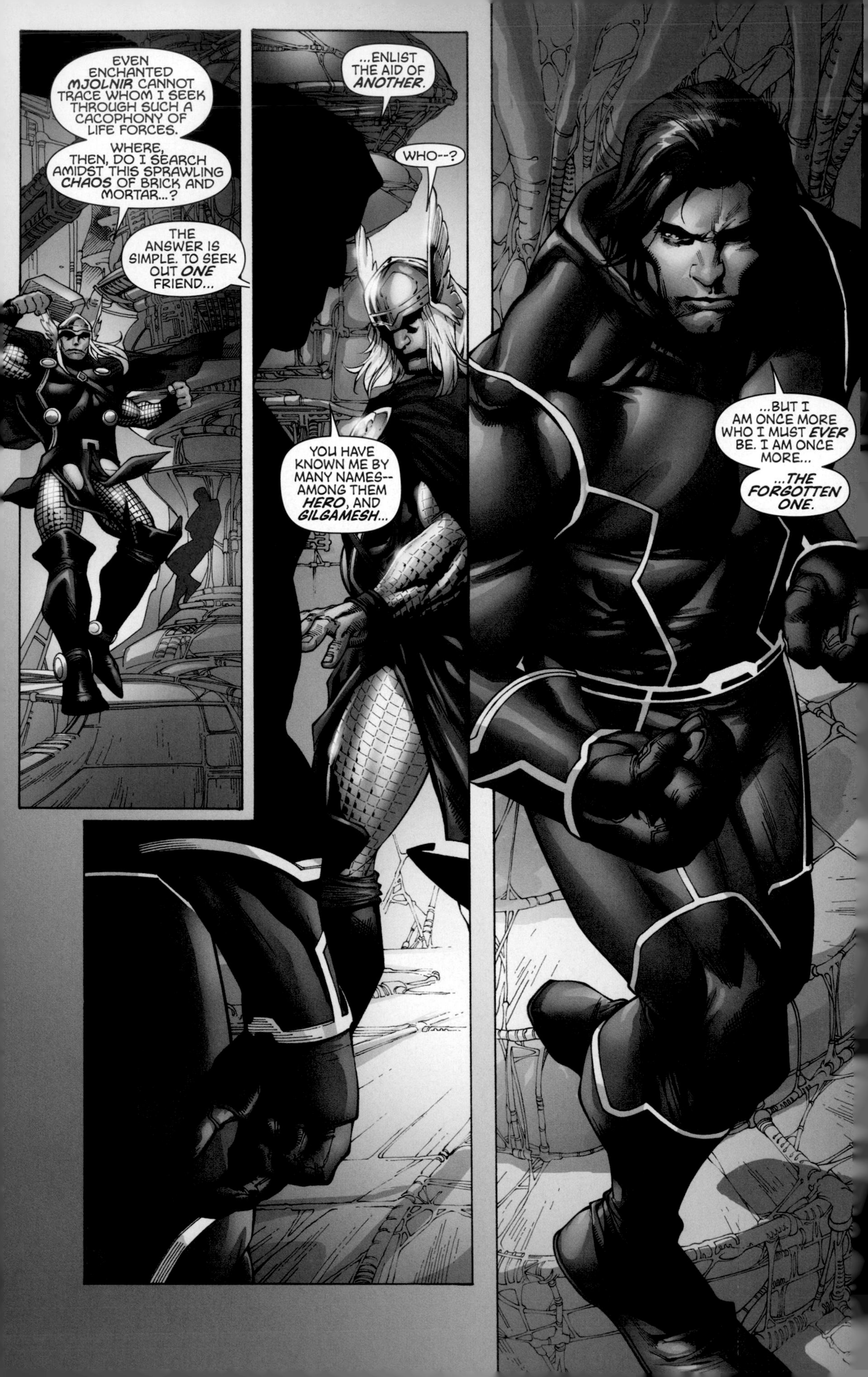
EVEN ENCHANTED MJOLNIR CANNOT TRACE WHOM I SEEK THROUGH SUCH A CACOPHONY OF LIFE FORCES.
WHERE, THEN, DO I SEARCH AMIDST THIS SPRAWLING CHAOS OF BRICK AND MORTAR...?
THE ANSWER IS SIMPLE. TO SEEK OUT ONE FRIEND...
...ENLIST THE AID OF ANOTHER.
WHO--?
YOU HAVE KNOWN ME BY MANY NAMES-- AMONG THEM HERO, AND GILGAMESH...
...BUT I AM ONCE MORE WHO I MUST EVER BE. I AM ONCE MORE...
...THE FORGOTTEN ONE.

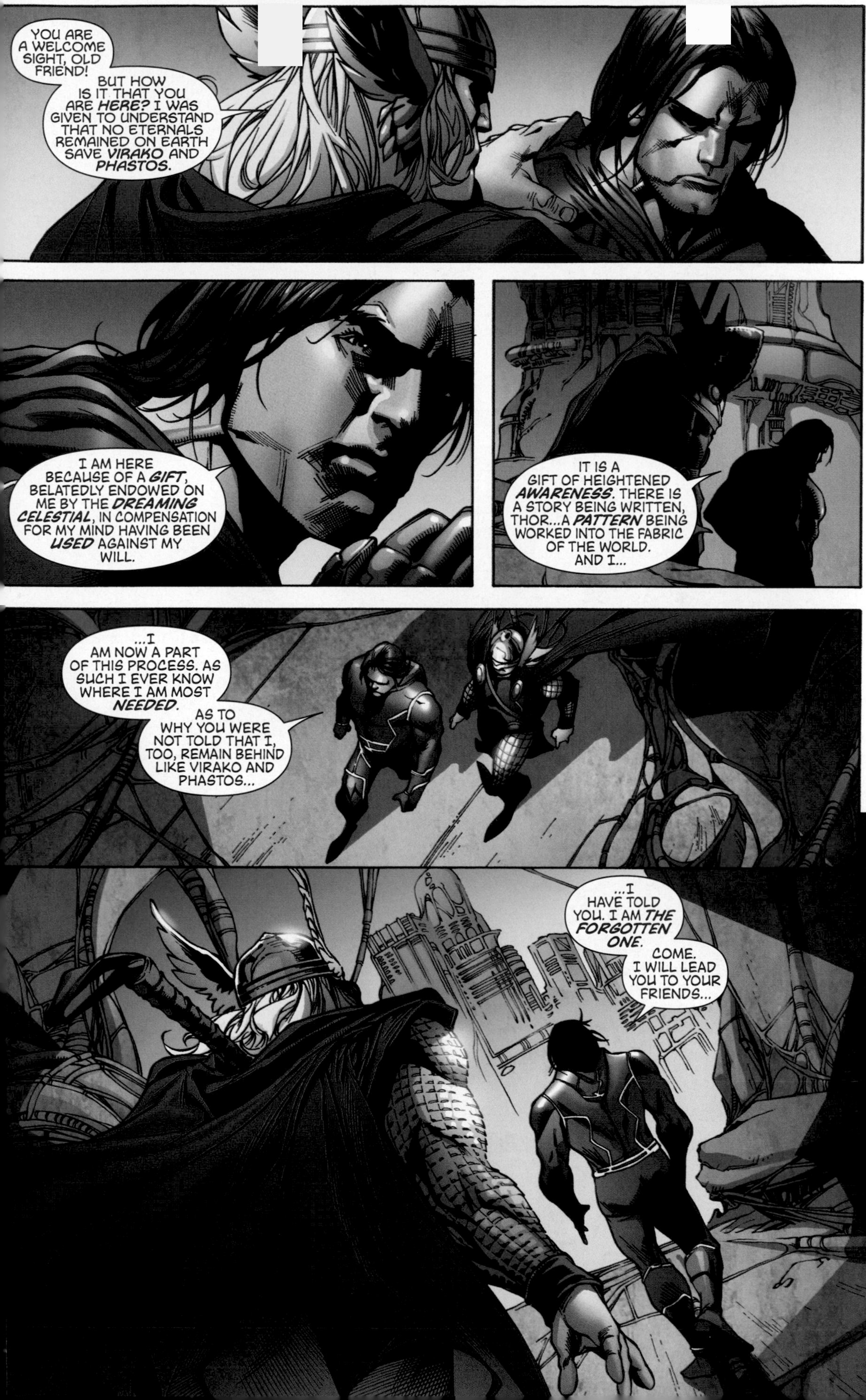
YOU ARE A WELCOME SIGHT, OLD FRIEND!
BUT HOW IS IT THAT YOU ARE HERE? I WAS GIVEN TO UNDERSTAND THAT NO ETERNALS REMAINED ON EARTH SAVE VIRAKO AND PHASTOS.
I AM HERE BECAUSE OF A GIFT, BELATEDLY ENDOWED ON ME BY THE DREAMING CELESTIAL, IN COMPENSATION FOR MY MIND HAVING BEEN USED AGAINST MY WILL.
IT IS A GIFT OF HEIGHTENED AWARENESS. THERE IS A STORY BEING WRITTEN, THOR...A PATTERN BEING WORKED INTO THE FABRIC OF THE WORLD. AND I...
...I AM NOW A PART OF THIS PROCESS. AS SUCH I EVER KNOW WHERE I AM MOST NEEDED.
AS TO WHY YOU WERE NOT TOLD THAT I, TOO, REMAIN BEHIND LIKE VIRAKO AND PHASTOS...
...I HAVE TOLD YOU. I AM THE FORGOTTEN ONE.
COME. I WILL LEAD YOU TO YOUR FRIENDS...

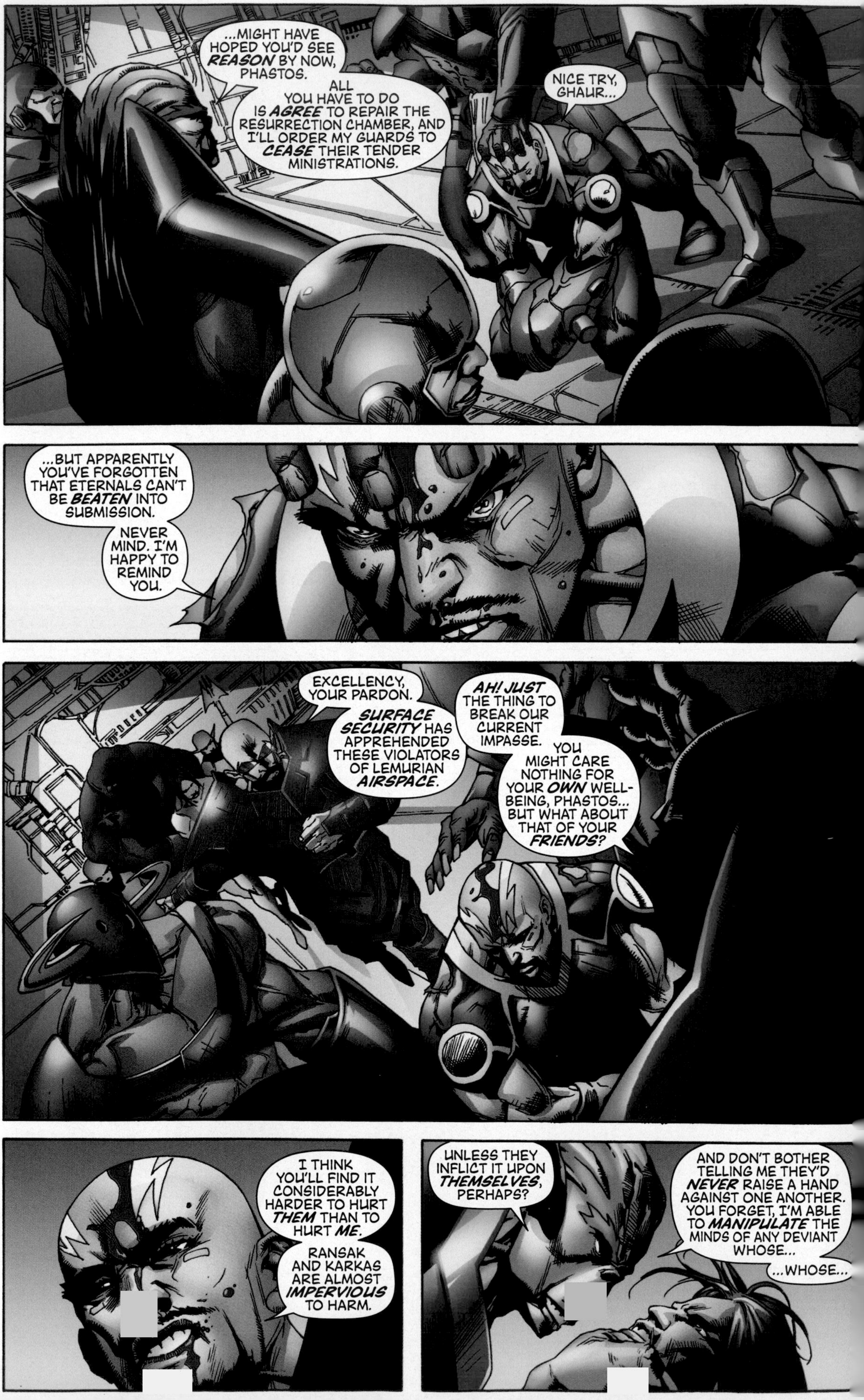
...MIGHT HAVE HOPED YOU'D SEE REASON BY NOW, PHASTOS.
ALL YOU HAVE TO DO IS AGREE TO REPAIR THE RESURRECTION CHAMBER, AND I'LL ORDER MY GUARDS TO CEASE THEIR TENDER MINISTRATIONS.
NICE TRY, GHAUR...
...BUT APPARENTLY YOU'VE FORGOTTEN THAT ETERNALS CAN'T BE BEATEN INTO SUBMISSION.
NEVER MIND. I'M HAPPY TO REMIND YOU.
EXCELLENCY, YOUR PARDON.
SURFACE SECURITY HAS APPREHENDED THESE VIOLATORS OF LEMURIAN AIRSPACE.
AH! JUST THE THING TO BREAK OUR CURRENT IMPASSE.
YOU MIGHT CARE NOTHING FOR YOUR OWN WELL-BEING, PHASTOS... BUT WHAT ABOUT THAT OF YOUR FRIENDS?
I THINK YOU'LL FIND IT CONSIDERABLY HARDER TO HURT THEM THAN TO HURT ME.
RANSAK AND KARKAS ARE ALMOST IMPERVIOUS TO HARM.
UNLESS THEY INFLICT IT UPON THEMSELVES, PERHAPS?
AND DON'T BOTHER TELLING ME THEY'D NEVER RAISE A HAND AGAINST ONE ANOTHER. YOU FORGET, I'M ABLE TO MANIPULATE THE MINDS OF ANY DEVIANT WHOSE...
...WHOSE...

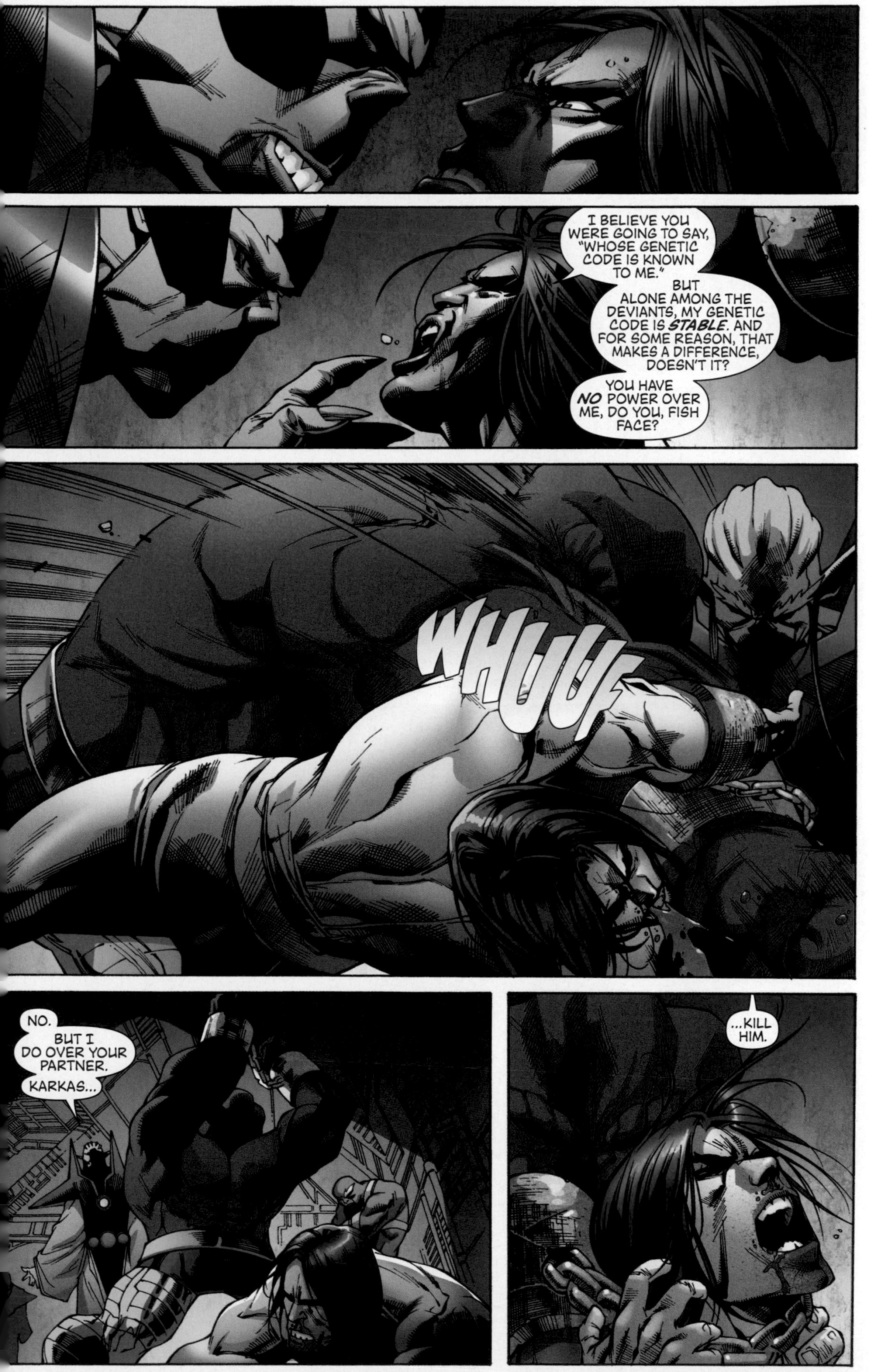
I BELIEVE YOU WERE GOING TO SAY, "WHOSE GENETIC CODE IS KNOWN TO ME."
BUT ALONE AMONG THE DEVIANTS, MY GENETIC CODE IS STABLE. AND FOR SOME REASON, THAT MAKES A DIFFERENCE, DOESN'T IT?
YOU HAVE NO POWER OVER ME, DO YOU, FISH FACE?
WHUUF
NO.
BUT I DO OVER YOUR PARTNER.
KARKAS...
...KILL HIM.

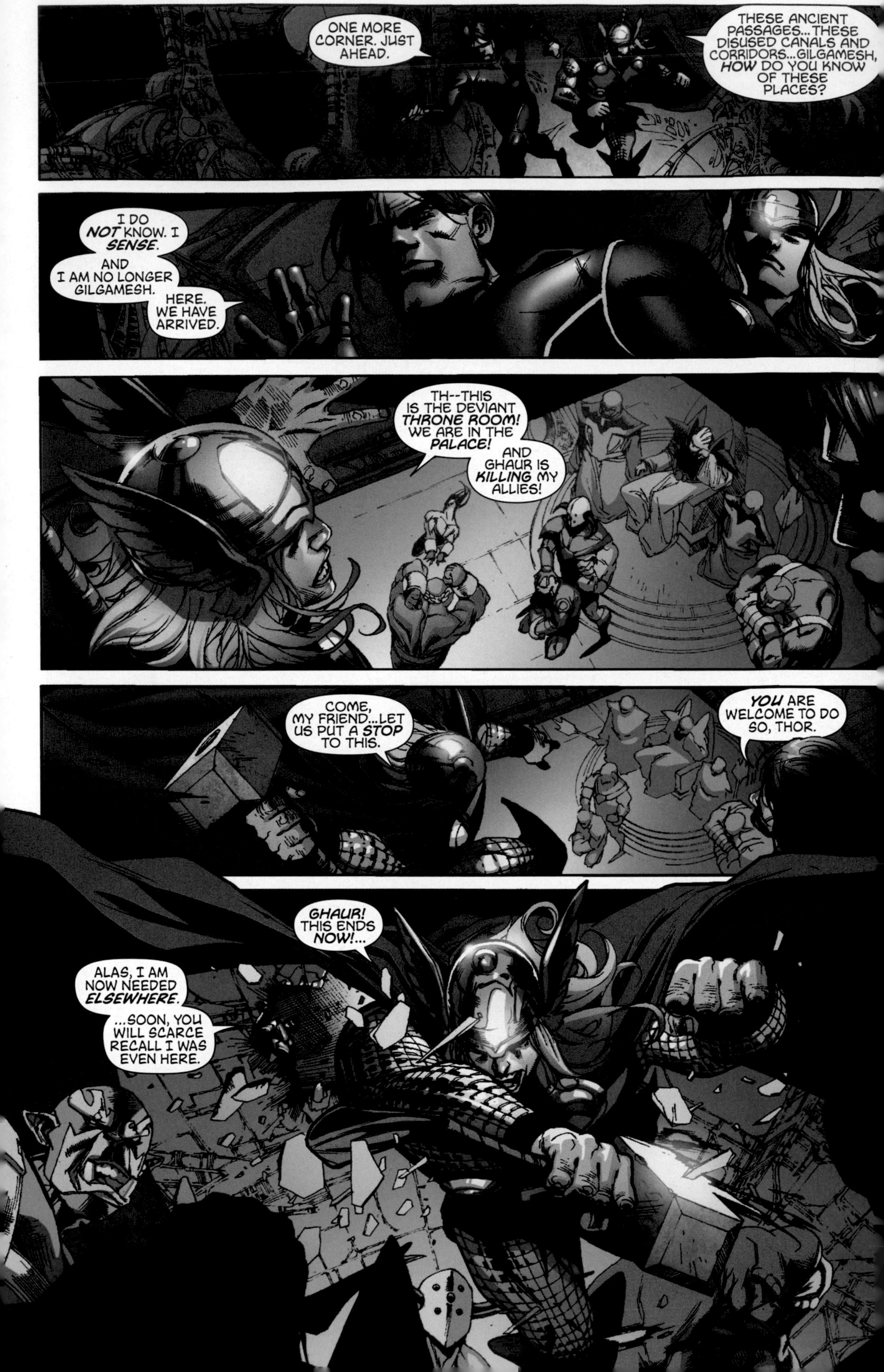
ONE MORE CORNER. JUST AHEAD.
THESE ANCIENT PASSAGES... THESE DISUSED CANALS AND CORRIDORS...GILGAMESH, HOW DO YOU KNOW OF THESE PLACES?
I DO NOT KNOW. I SENSE.
AND I AM NO LONGER GILGAMESH.
HERE. WE HAVE ARRIVED.
TH--THIS IS THE DEVIANT THRONE ROOM! WE ARE IN THE PALACE!
AND GHAUR IS KILLING MY ALLIES!
COME, MY FRIEND...LET US PUT A STOP TO THIS.
YOU ARE WELCOME TO DO SO, THOR.
GHAUR! THIS ENDS NOW!...
ALAS, I AM NOW NEEDED ELSEWHERE.
...SOON, YOU WILL SCARCE RECALL I WAS EVEN HERE.

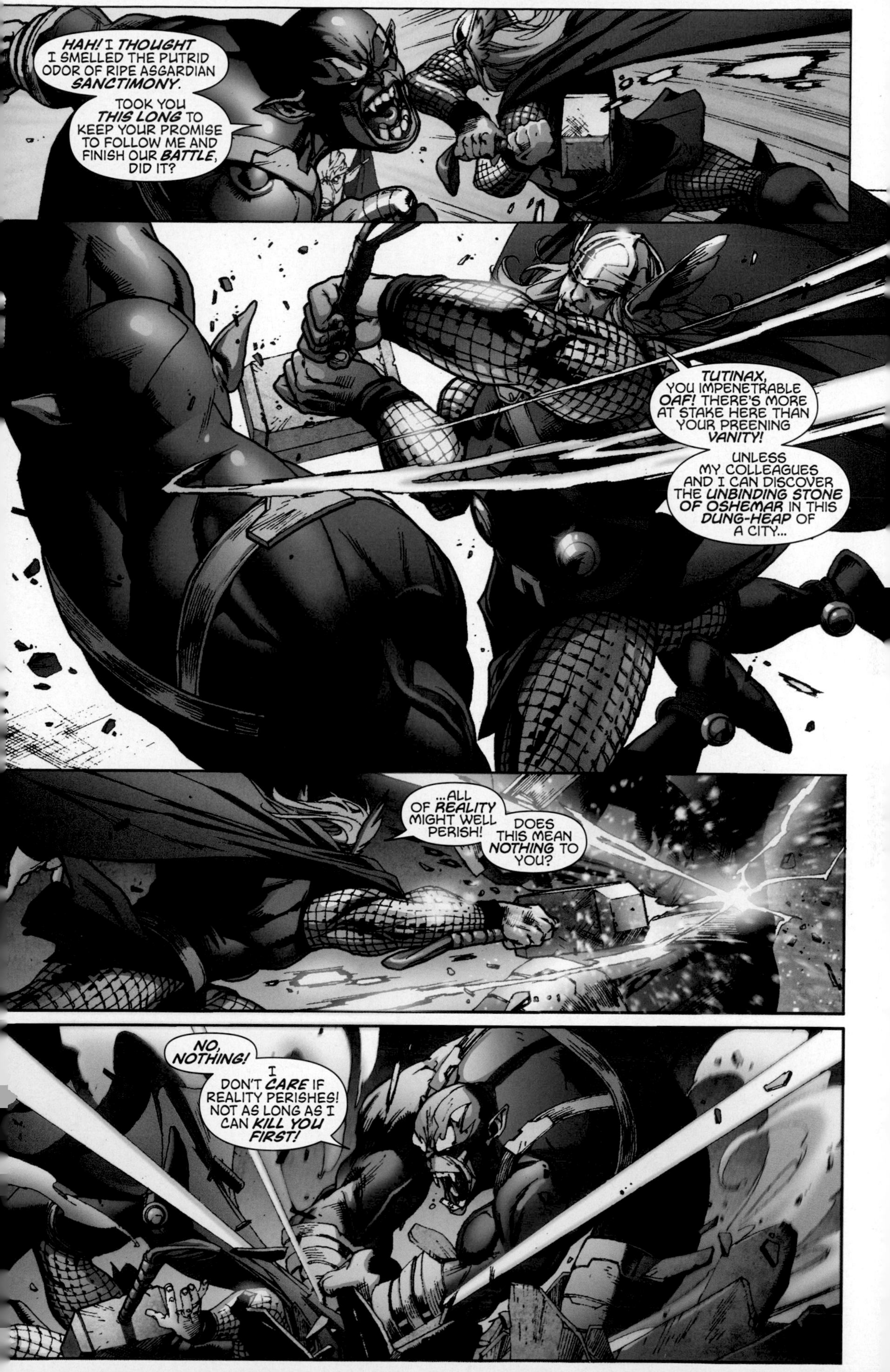
HAH! I THOUGHT I SMELLED THE PUTRID ODOR OF RIPE ASGARDIAN SANCTIMONY.
TOOK YOU THIS LONG TO KEEP YOUR PROMISE TO FOLLOW ME AND FINISH OUR BATTLE, DID IT?
TUTINAX, YOU IMPENETRABLE OAF! THERE'S MORE AT STAKE HERE THAN YOUR PREENING VANITY!
UNLESS MY COLLEAGUES AND I CAN DISCOVER THE UNBINDING STONE OF OSHEMAR IN THIS DUNG-HEAP OF A CITY...
...ALL OF REALITY MIGHT WELL PERISH!
DOES THIS MEAN NOTHING TO YOU?
NO, NOTHING!
I DON'T CARE IF REALITY PERISHES! NOT AS LONG AS I CAN KILL YOU FIRST!

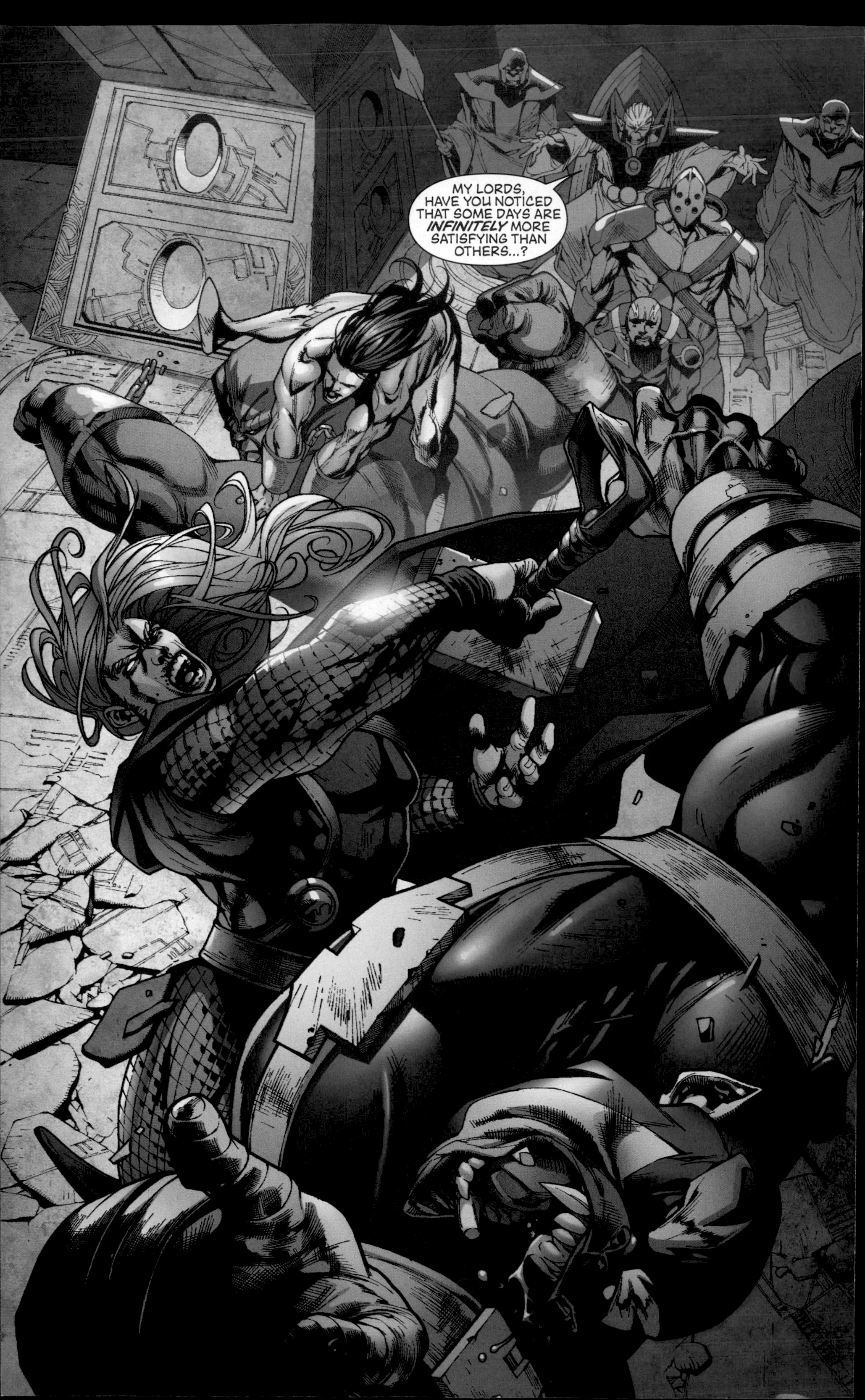
MY LORDS, HAVE YOU NOTICED THAT SOME DAYS ARE *INFINITELY* MORE SATISFYING THAN OTHERS...?

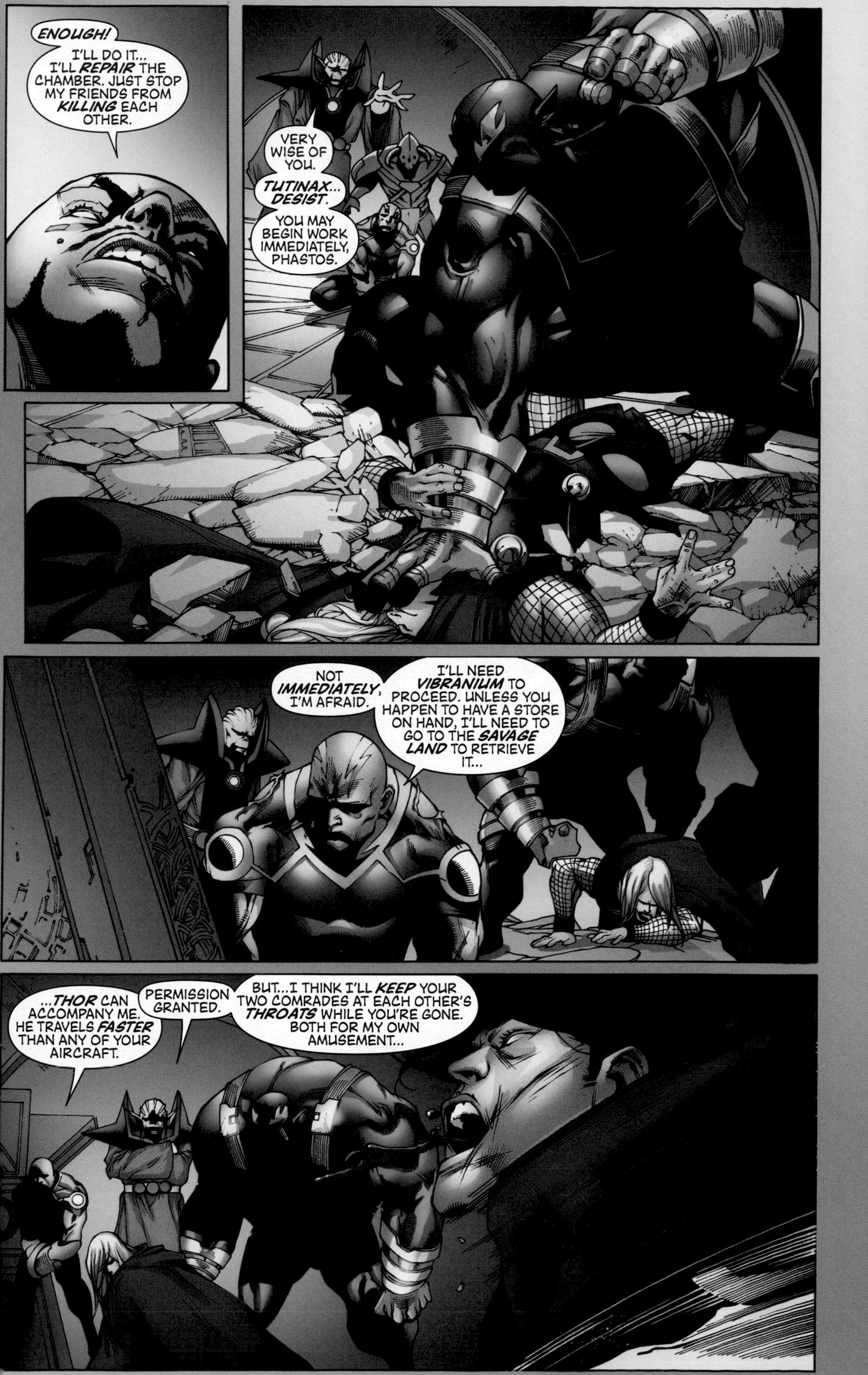
ENOUGH!
I'LL DO IT... I'LL REPAIR THE CHAMBER. JUST STOP MY FRIENDS FROM KILLING EACH OTHER.
VERY WISE OF YOU.
TUTINAX... DESIST.
YOU MAY BEGIN WORK IMMEDIATELY, PHASTOS.
NOT IMMEDIATELY, I'M AFRAID.
I'LL NEED VIBRANIUM TO PROCEED. UNLESS YOU HAPPEN TO HAVE A STORE ON HAND, I'LL NEED TO GO TO THE SAVAGE LAND TO RETRIEVE IT...
...THOR CAN ACCOMPANY ME. HE TRAVELS FASTER THAN ANY OF YOUR AIRCRAFT.
PERMISSION GRANTED.
BUT...I THINK I'LL KEEP YOUR TWO COMRADES AT EACH OTHER'S THROATS WHILE YOU'RE GONE. BOTH FOR MY OWN AMUSEMENT...

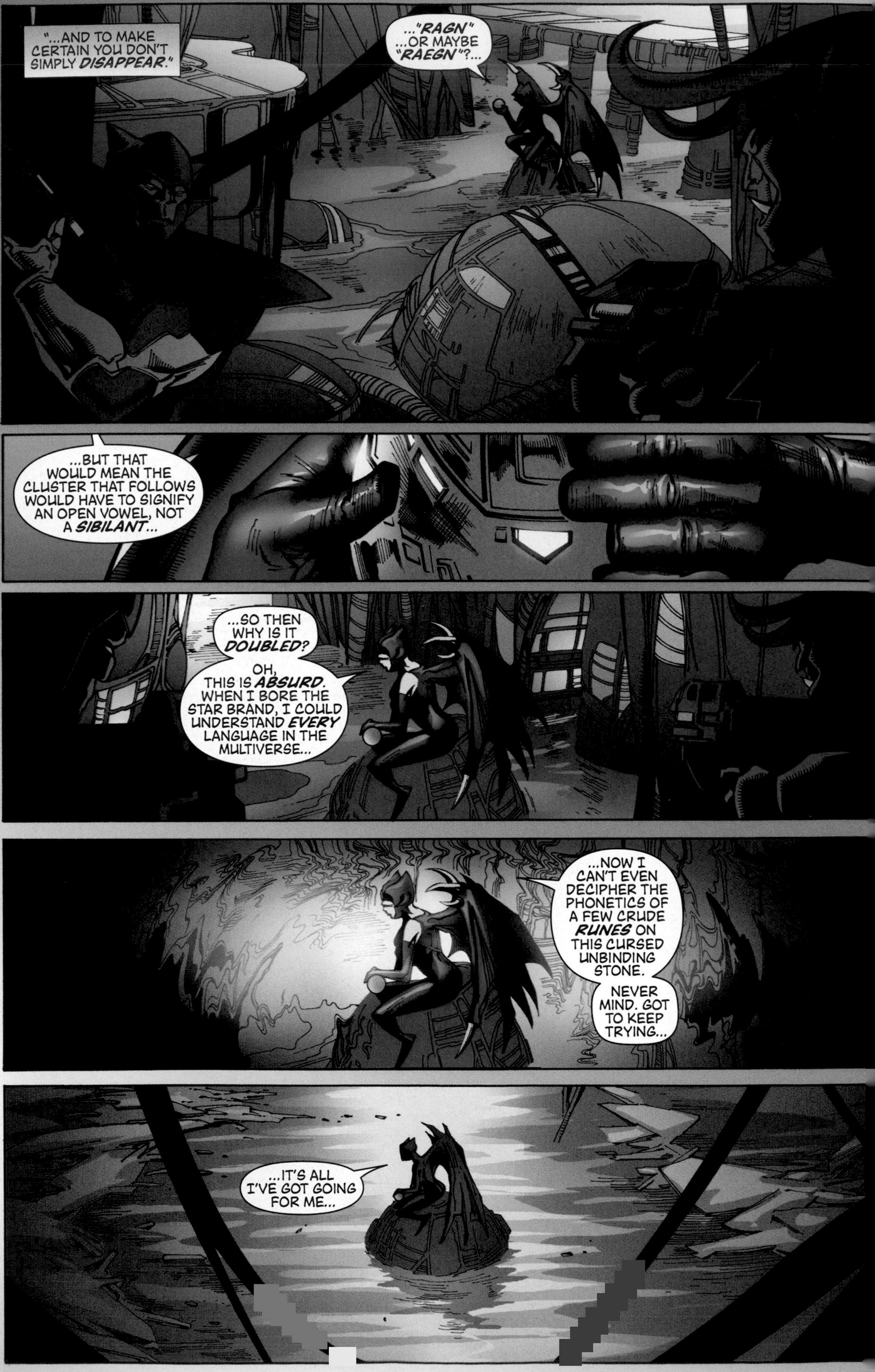
"...AND TO MAKE CERTAIN YOU DON'T SIMPLY *DISAPPEAR*."
..."*RAGN*" ...OR MAYBE "*RAEGN*"?...
...BUT THAT WOULD MEAN THE CLUSTER THAT FOLLOWS WOULD HAVE TO SIGNIFY AN OPEN VOWEL, NOT A *SIBILANT*...
...SO THEN WHY IS IT *DOUBLED*?
OH, THIS IS *ABSURD*. WHEN I BORE THE STAR BRAND, I COULD UNDERSTAND *EVERY* LANGUAGE IN THE MULTIVERSE...
...NOW I CAN'T EVEN DECIPHER THE PHONETICS OF A FEW CRUDE *RUNES* ON THIS CURSED UNBINDING STONE.
NEVER MIND. GOT TO KEEP TRYING...
...IT'S ALL I'VE GOT GOING FOR ME...

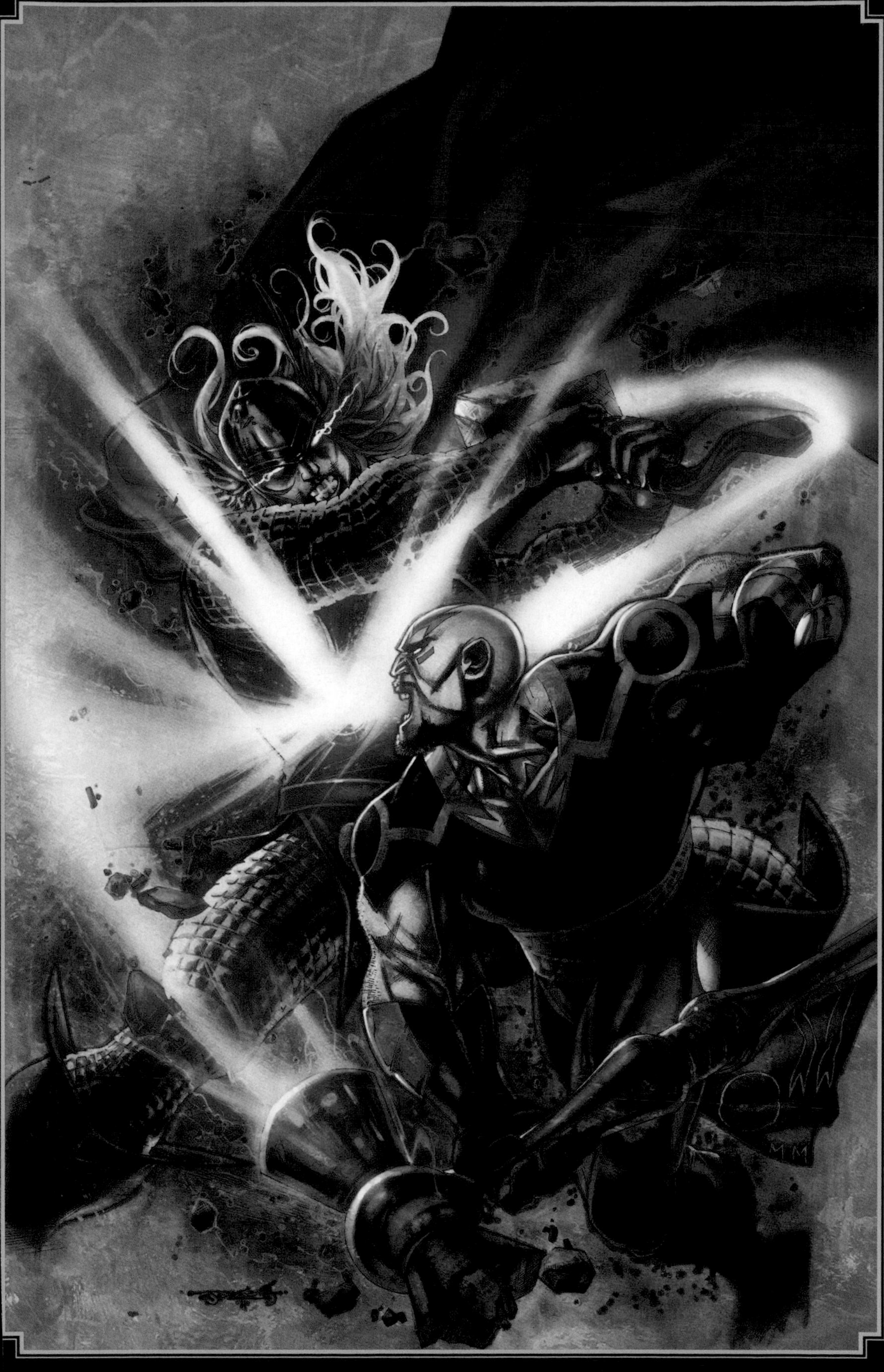

Thor: The Deviants Saga 4

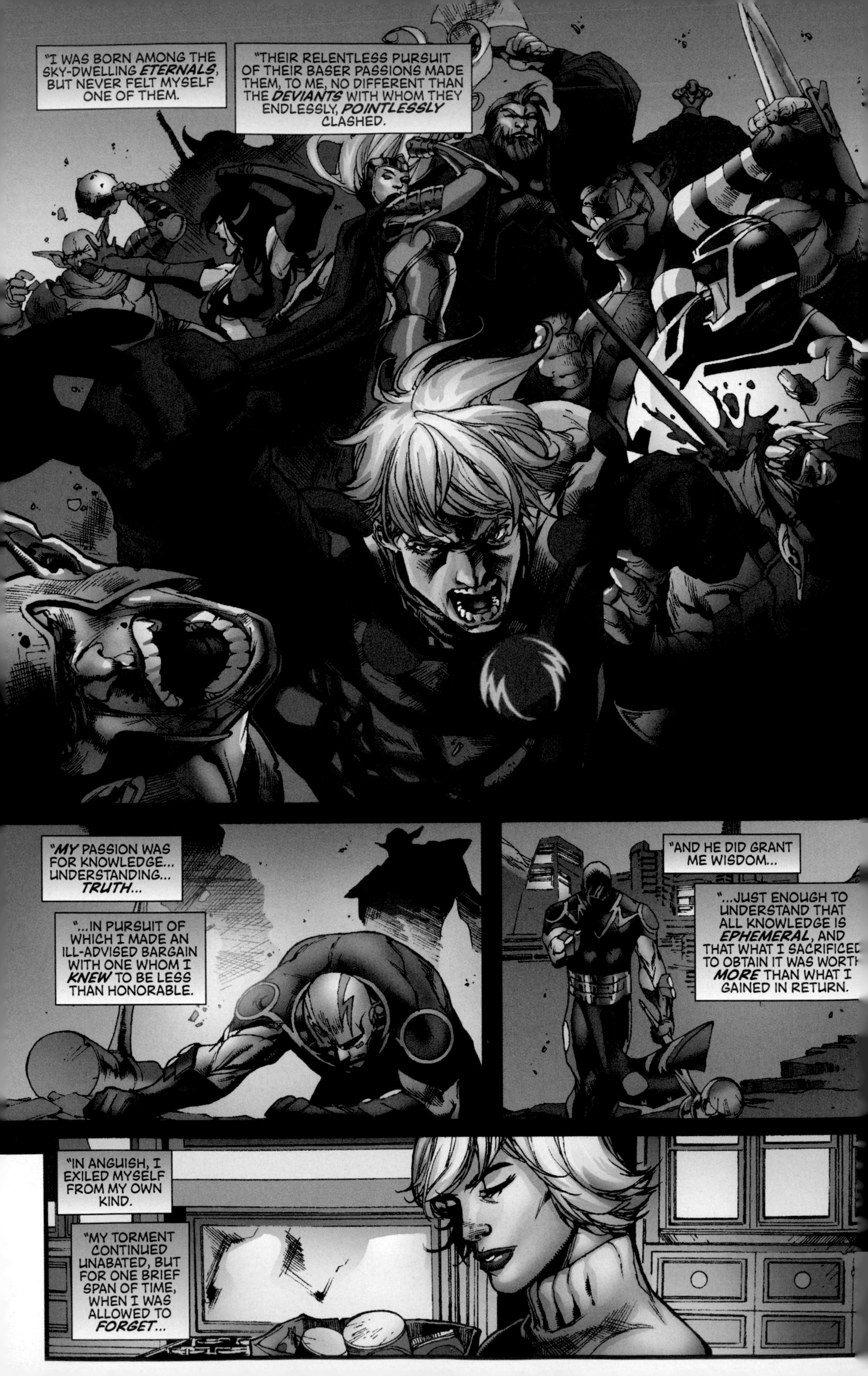
"I WAS BORN AMONG THE SKY-DWELLING ETERNALS, BUT NEVER FELT MYSELF ONE OF THEM.
"THEIR RELENTLESS PURSUIT OF THEIR BASER PASSIONS MADE THEM, TO ME, NO DIFFERENT THAN THE DEVIANTS WITH WHOM THEY ENDLESSLY, POINTLESSLY CLASHED.
"MY PASSION WAS FOR KNOWLEDGE... UNDERSTANDING... TRUTH...
"...IN PURSUIT OF WHICH I MADE AN ILL-ADVISED BARGAIN WITH ONE WHOM I KNEW TO BE LESS THAN HONORABLE.
"AND HE DID GRANT ME WISDOM...
"...JUST ENOUGH TO UNDERSTAND THAT ALL KNOWLEDGE IS EPHEMERAL, AND THAT WHAT I SACRIFICED TO OBTAIN IT WAS WORTH MORE THAN WHAT I GAINED IN RETURN.
"IN ANGUISH, I EXILED MYSELF FROM MY OWN KIND.
"MY TORMENT CONTINUED UNABATED, BUT FOR ONE BRIEF SPAN OF TIME, WHEN I WAS ALLOWED TO FORGET...

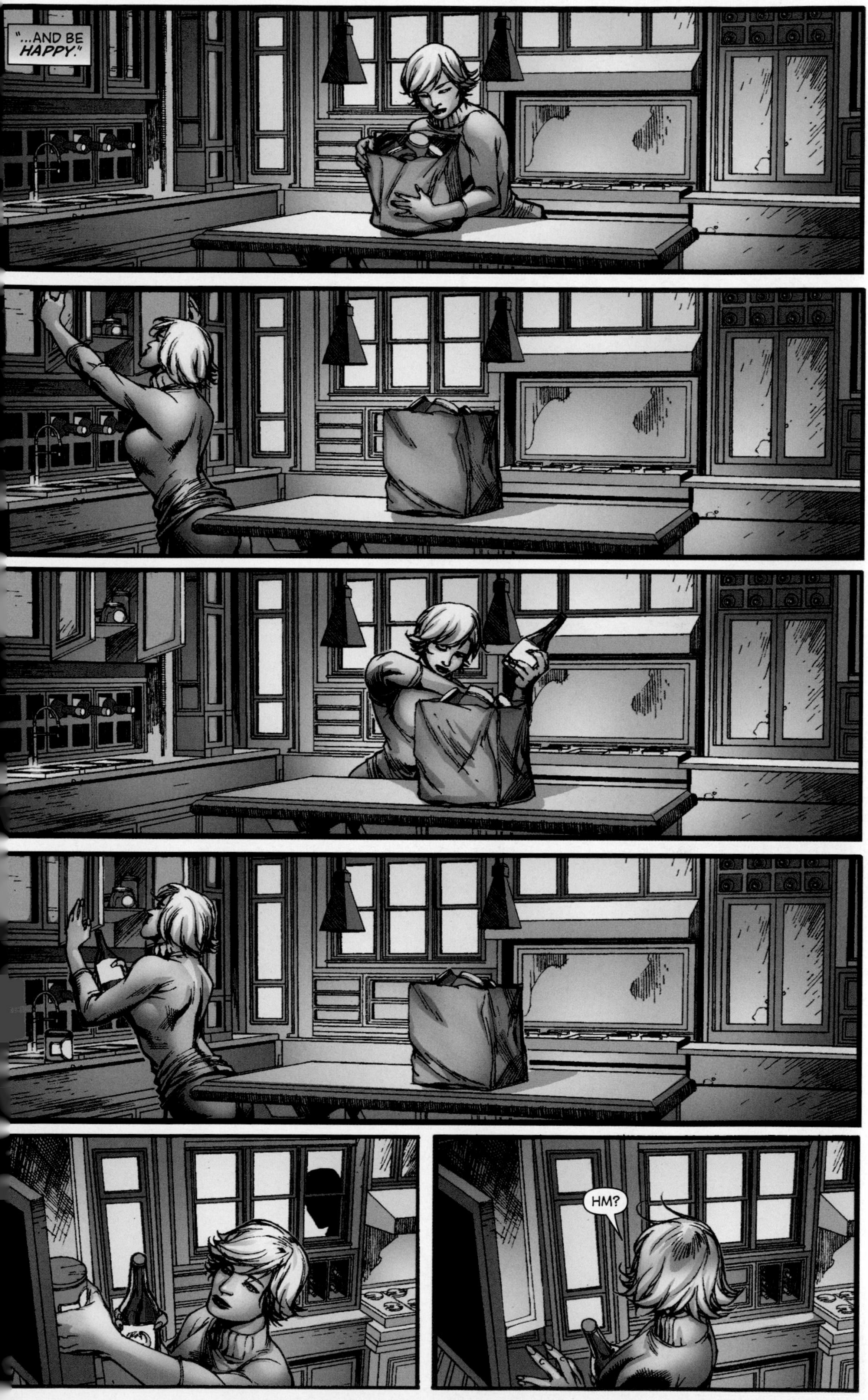
"...AND BE HAPPY."
HM?

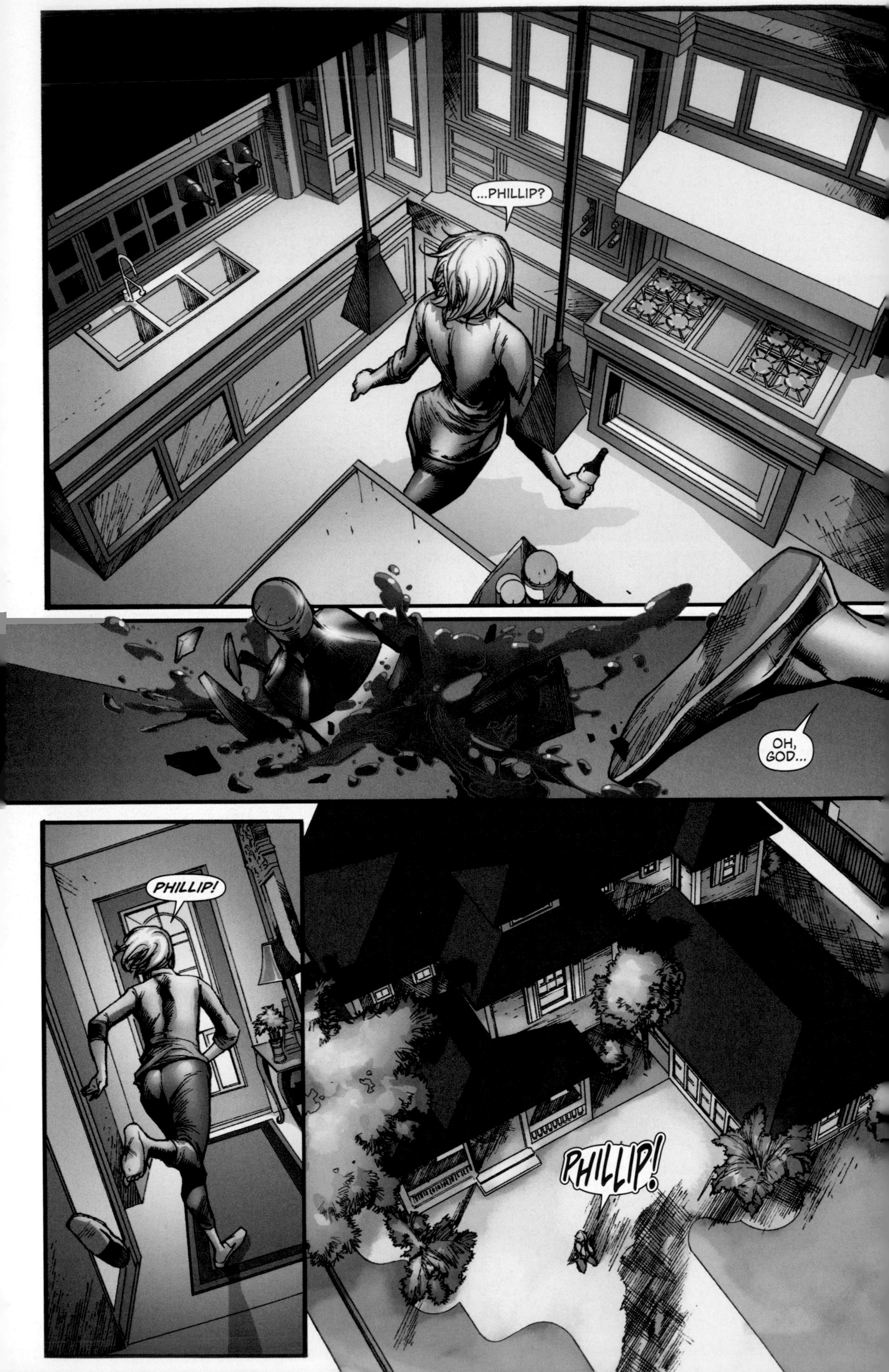
...PHILLIP?
OH, GOD...
PHILLIP!
PHILLIP!

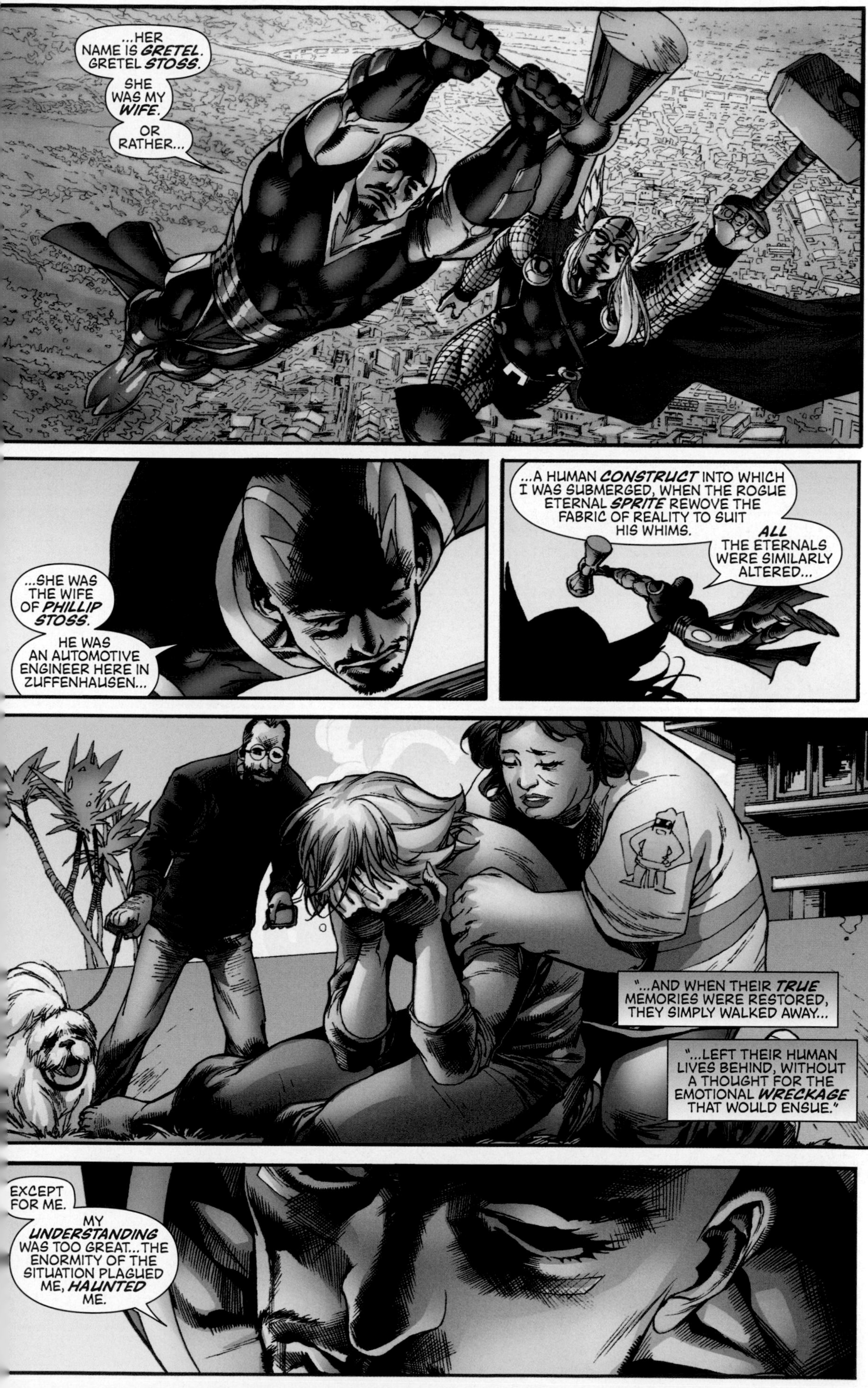
...HER NAME IS GRETEL. GRETEL STOSS.
SHE WAS MY WIFE.
OR RATHER...
...SHE WAS THE WIFE OF PHILLIP STOSS.
HE WAS AN AUTOMOTIVE ENGINEER HERE IN ZUFFENHAUSEN...
...A HUMAN CONSTRUCT INTO WHICH I WAS SUBMERGED, WHEN THE ROGUE ETERNAL SPRITE REWOVE THE FABRIC OF REALITY TO SUIT HIS WHIMS.
ALL THE ETERNALS WERE SIMILARLY ALTERED...
"...AND WHEN THEIR TRUE MEMORIES WERE RESTORED, THEY SIMPLY WALKED AWAY...
"...LEFT THEIR HUMAN LIVES BEHIND, WITHOUT A THOUGHT FOR THE EMOTIONAL WRECKAGE THAT WOULD ENSUE."
EXCEPT FOR ME.
MY UNDERSTANDING WAS TOO GREAT...THE ENORMITY OF THE SITUATION PLAGUED ME, HAUNTED ME.

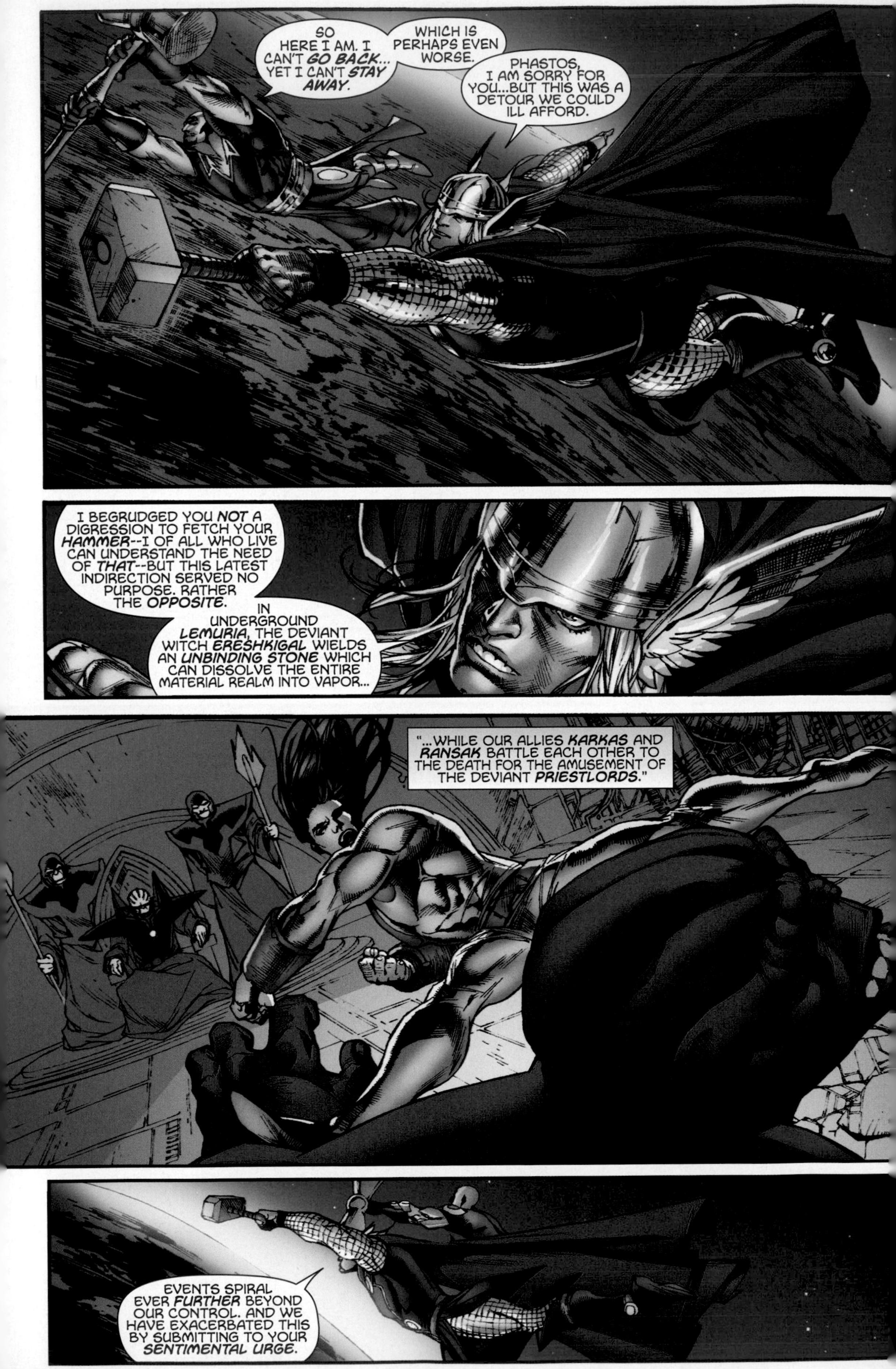
SO HERE I AM. I CAN'T GO BACK... YET I CAN'T STAY AWAY.
WHICH IS PERHAPS EVEN WORSE.
PHASTOS, I AM SORRY FOR YOU...BUT THIS WAS A DETOUR WE COULD ILL AFFORD.
I BEGRUDGED YOU NOT A DIGRESSION TO FETCH YOUR HAMMER--I OF ALL WHO LIVE CAN UNDERSTAND THE NEED OF THAT--BUT THIS LATEST INDIRECTION SERVED NO PURPOSE. RATHER THE OPPOSITE.
IN UNDERGROUND LEMURIA, THE DEVIANT WITCH ERESHKIGAL WIELDS AN UNBINDING STONE WHICH CAN DISSOLVE THE ENTIRE MATERIAL REALM INTO VAPOR...
"...WHILE OUR ALLIES KARKAS AND RANSAK BATTLE EACH OTHER TO THE DEATH FOR THE AMUSEMENT OF THE DEVIANT PRIESTLORDS."
EVENTS SPIRAL EVER FURTHER BEYOND OUR CONTROL. AND WE HAVE EXACERBATED THIS BY SUBMITTING TO YOUR SENTIMENTAL URGE.

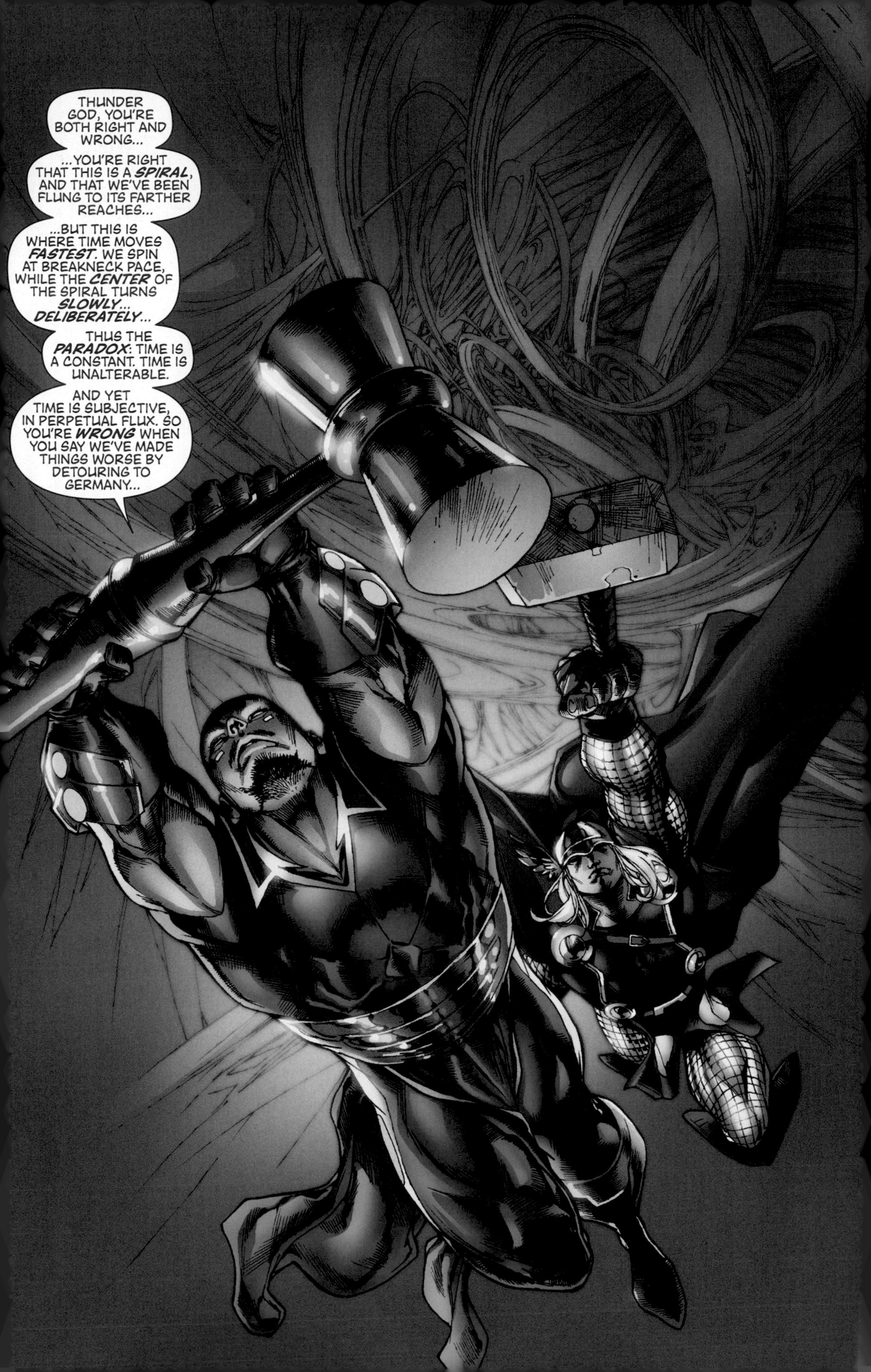
THUNDER GOD, YOU'RE BOTH RIGHT AND WRONG...
...YOU'RE RIGHT THAT THIS IS A *SPIRAL*, AND THAT WE'VE BEEN FLUNG TO ITS FARTHER REACHES...
...BUT THIS IS WHERE TIME MOVES *FASTEST*. WE SPIN AT BREAKNECK PACE, WHILE THE *CENTER* OF THE SPIRAL TURNS *SLOWLY*... *DELIBERATELY*...
THUS THE *PARADOX*: TIME IS A CONSTANT. TIME IS UNALTERABLE.
AND YET TIME IS SUBJECTIVE, IN PERPETUAL FLUX. SO YOU'RE *WRONG* WHEN YOU SAY WE'VE MADE THINGS WORSE BY DETOURING TO GERMANY...

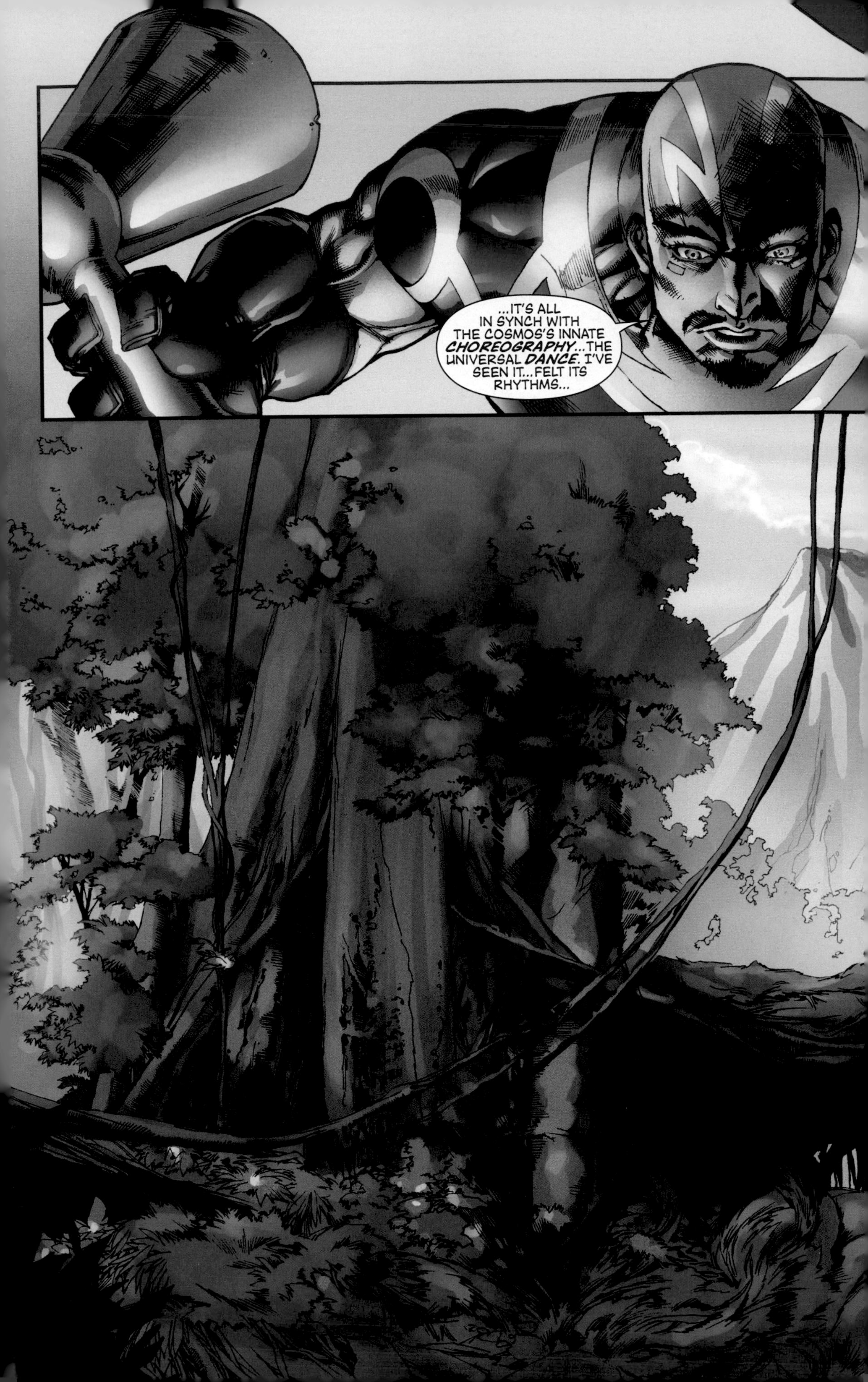
...IT'S ALL IN SYNCH WITH THE COSMOS'S INNATE CHOREOGRAPHY...THE UNIVERSAL DANCE. I'VE SEEN IT...FELT ITS RHYTHMS...

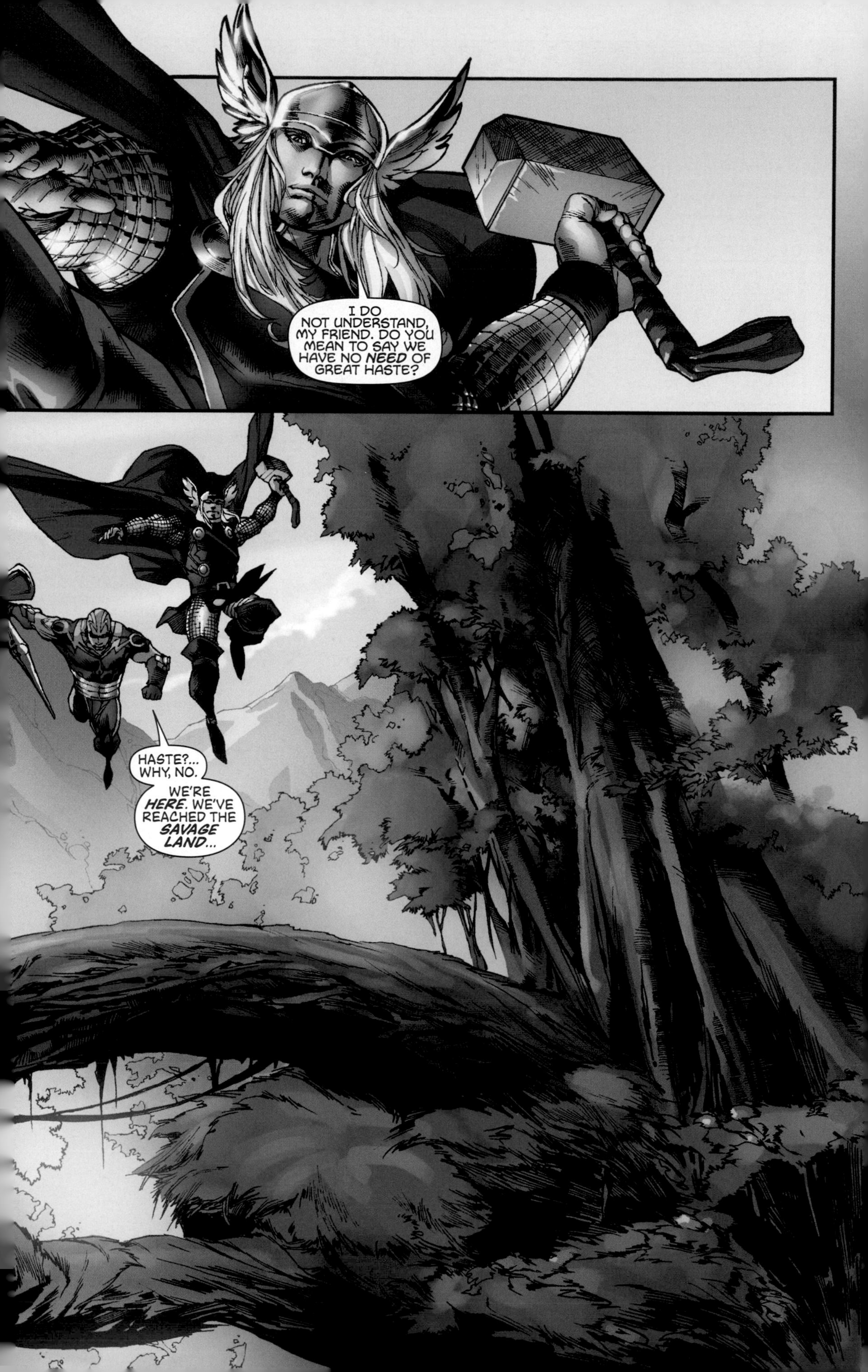
I DO NOT UNDERSTAND, MY FRIEND. DO YOU MEAN TO SAY WE HAVE NO *NEED* OF GREAT HASTE?
HASTE?... WHY, NO.
WE'RE *HERE*. WE'VE REACHED THE *SAVAGE LAND*...

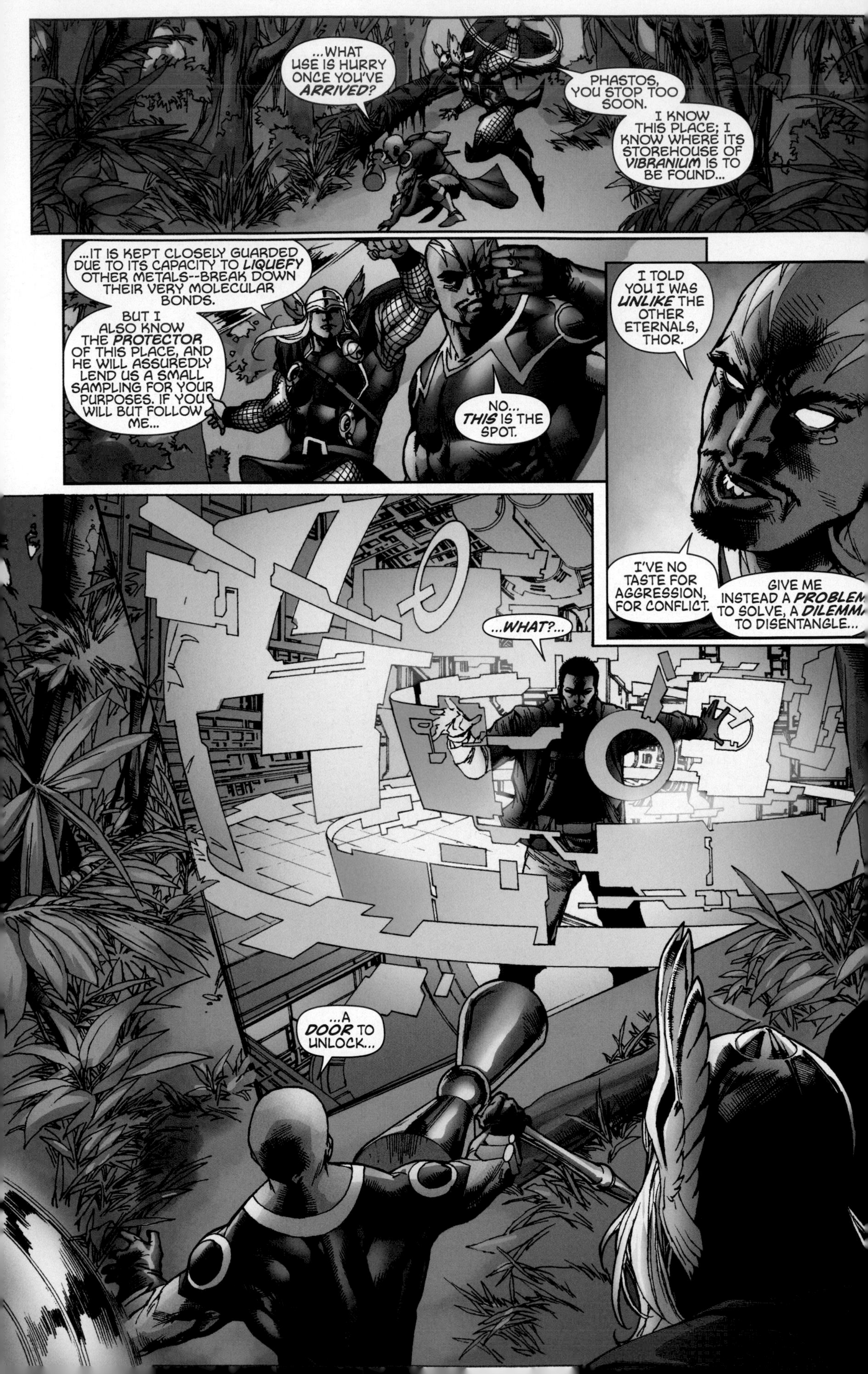
...WHAT USE IS HURRY ONCE YOU'VE ARRIVED?
PHASTOS, YOU STOP TOO SOON.
I KNOW THIS PLACE; I KNOW WHERE ITS STOREHOUSE OF VIBRANIUM IS TO BE FOUND...
...IT IS KEPT CLOSELY GUARDED DUE TO ITS CAPACITY TO LIQUEFY OTHER METALS--BREAK DOWN THEIR VERY MOLECULAR BONDS.
BUT I ALSO KNOW THE PROTECTOR OF THIS PLACE, AND HE WILL ASSUREDLY LEND US A SMALL SAMPLING FOR YOUR PURPOSES. IF YOU WILL BUT FOLLOW ME...
NO... THIS IS THE SPOT.
I TOLD YOU I WAS UNLIKE THE OTHER ETERNALS, THOR.
I'VE NO TASTE FOR AGGRESSION, FOR CONFLICT.
GIVE ME INSTEAD A PROBLEM TO SOLVE, A DILEMMA TO DISENTANGLE...
...WHAT?...
...A DOOR TO UNLOCK...

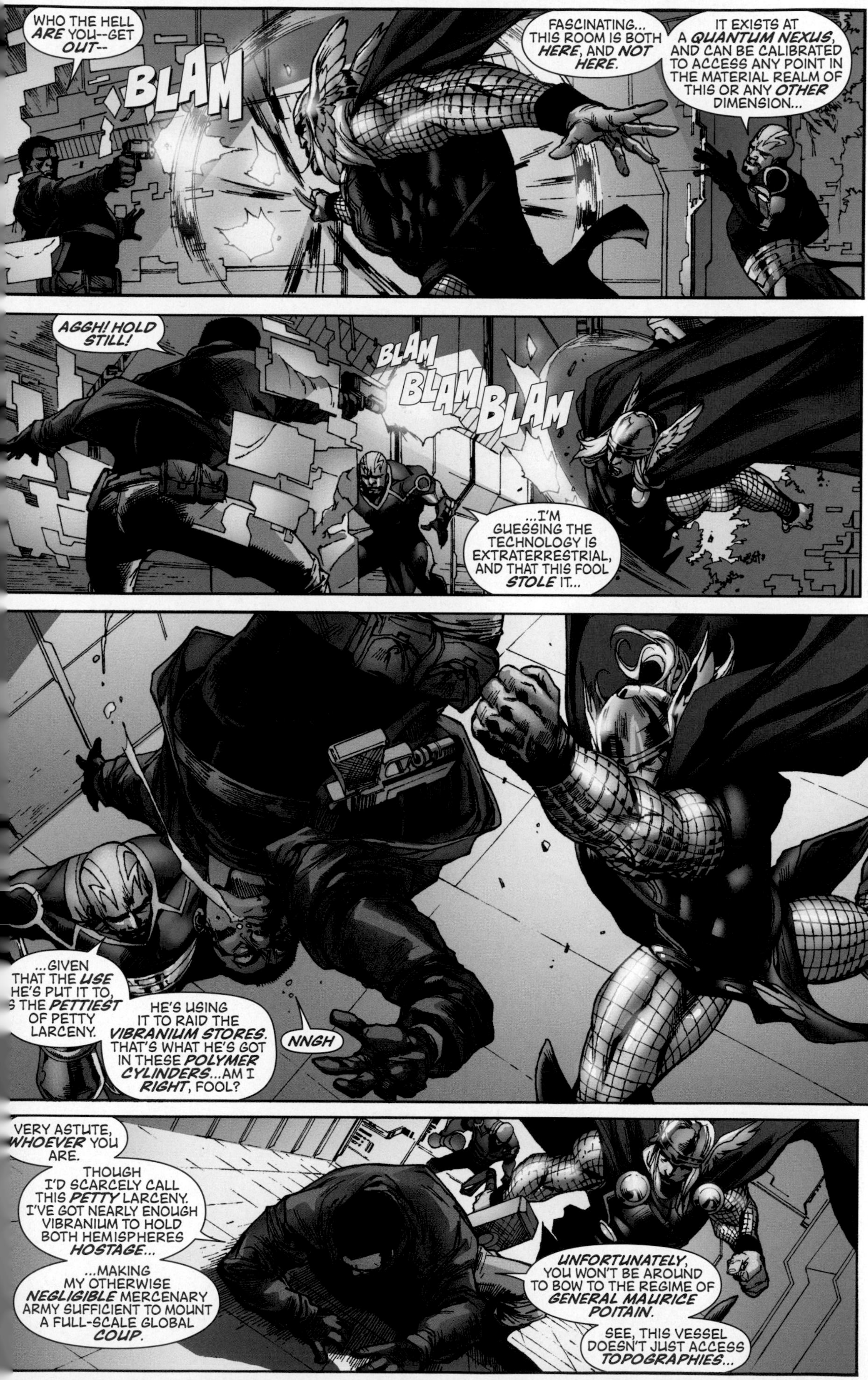
WHO THE HELL ARE YOU--GET OUT--
BLAM
FASCINATING... THIS ROOM IS BOTH HERE, AND NOT HERE.
IT EXISTS AT A QUANTUM NEXUS, AND CAN BE CALIBRATED TO ACCESS ANY POINT IN THE MATERIAL REALM OF THIS OR ANY OTHER DIMENSION...
AGGH! HOLD STILL!
BLAM
BLAM
BLAM
...I'M GUESSING THE TECHNOLOGY IS EXTRATERRESTRIAL, AND THAT THIS FOOL STOLE IT...
...GIVEN THAT THE USE HE'S PUT IT TO, IS THE PETTIEST OF PETTY LARCENY.
HE'S USING IT TO RAID THE VIBRANIUM STORES. THAT'S WHAT HE'S GOT IN THESE POLYMER CYLINDERS...AM I RIGHT, FOOL?
NNGH
VERY ASTUTE, WHOEVER YOU ARE.
THOUGH I'D SCARCELY CALL THIS PETTY LARCENY. I'VE GOT NEARLY ENOUGH VIBRANIUM TO HOLD BOTH HEMISPHERES HOSTAGE...
...MAKING MY OTHERWISE NEGLIGIBLE MERCENARY ARMY SUFFICIENT TO MOUNT A FULL-SCALE GLOBAL COUP.
UNFORTUNATELY, YOU WON'T BE AROUND TO BOW TO THE REGIME OF GENERAL MAURICE POITAIN.
SEE, THIS VESSEL DOESN'T JUST ACCESS TOPOGRAPHIES...

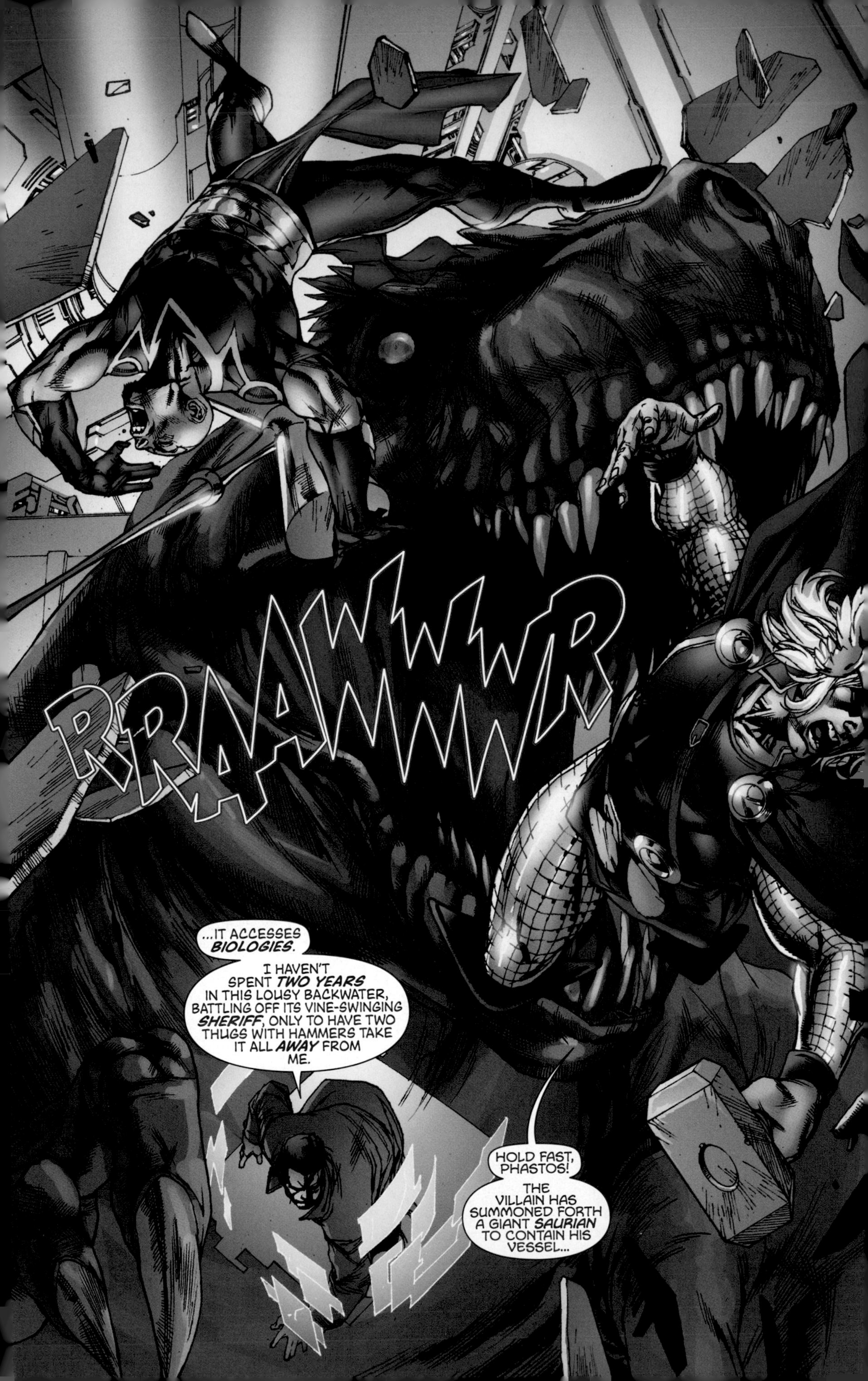
RRAAWWWR
...IT ACCESSES BIOLOGIES.
I HAVEN'T SPENT TWO YEARS IN THIS LOUSY BACKWATER, BATTLING OFF ITS VINE-SWINGING SHERIFF, ONLY TO HAVE TWO THUGS WITH HAMMERS TAKE IT ALL AWAY FROM ME.
HOLD FAST, PHASTOS!
THE VILLAIN HAS SUMMONED FORTH A GIANT SAURIAN TO CONTAIN HIS VESSEL...

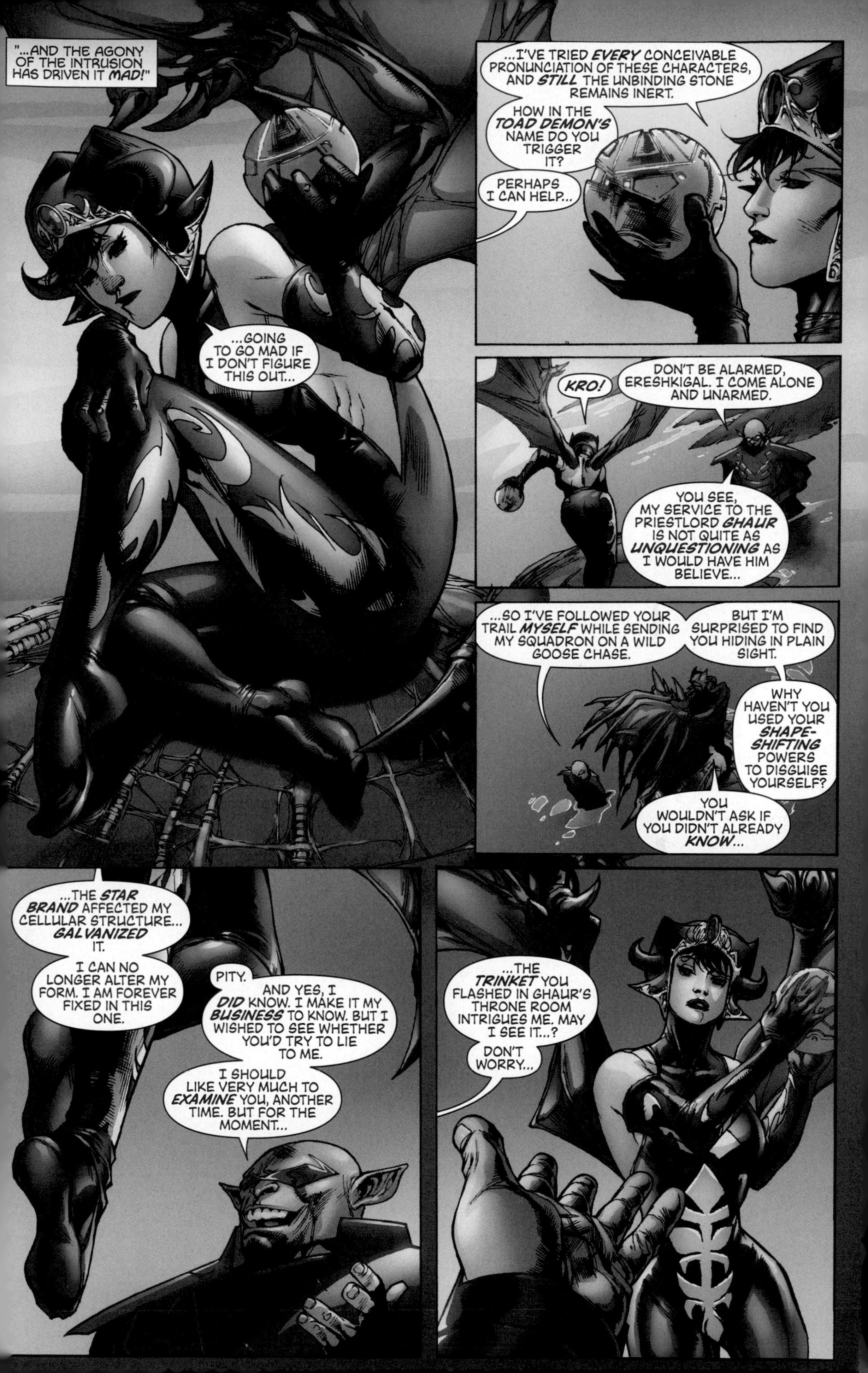
"...AND THE AGONY OF THE INTRUSION HAS DRIVEN IT MAD!"
...I'VE TRIED EVERY CONCEIVABLE PRONUNCIATION OF THESE CHARACTERS, AND STILL THE UNBINDING STONE REMAINS INERT.
HOW IN THE TOAD DEMON'S NAME DO YOU TRIGGER IT?
PERHAPS I CAN HELP...
...GOING TO GO MAD IF I DON'T FIGURE THIS OUT...
KRO!
DON'T BE ALARMED, ERESHKIGAL. I COME ALONE AND UNARMED.
YOU SEE, MY SERVICE TO THE PRIESTLORD GHAUR IS NOT QUITE AS UNQUESTIONING AS I WOULD HAVE HIM BELIEVE...
...SO I'VE FOLLOWED YOUR TRAIL MYSELF WHILE SENDING MY SQUADRON ON A WILD GOOSE CHASE.
BUT I'M SURPRISED TO FIND YOU HIDING IN PLAIN SIGHT.
WHY HAVEN'T YOU USED YOUR SHAPE-SHIFTING POWERS TO DISGUISE YOURSELF?
YOU WOULDN'T ASK IF YOU DIDN'T ALREADY KNOW...
...THE STAR BRAND AFFECTED MY CELLULAR STRUCTURE... GALVANIZED IT.
I CAN NO LONGER ALTER MY FORM. I AM FOREVER FIXED IN THIS ONE.
PITY.
AND YES, I DID KNOW. I MAKE IT MY BUSINESS TO KNOW. BUT I WISHED TO SEE WHETHER YOU'D TRY TO LIE TO ME.
I SHOULD LIKE VERY MUCH TO EXAMINE YOU, ANOTHER TIME. BUT FOR THE MOMENT...
...THE TRINKET YOU FLASHED IN GHAUR'S THRONE ROOM INTRIGUES ME. MAY I SEE IT...?
DON'T WORRY...

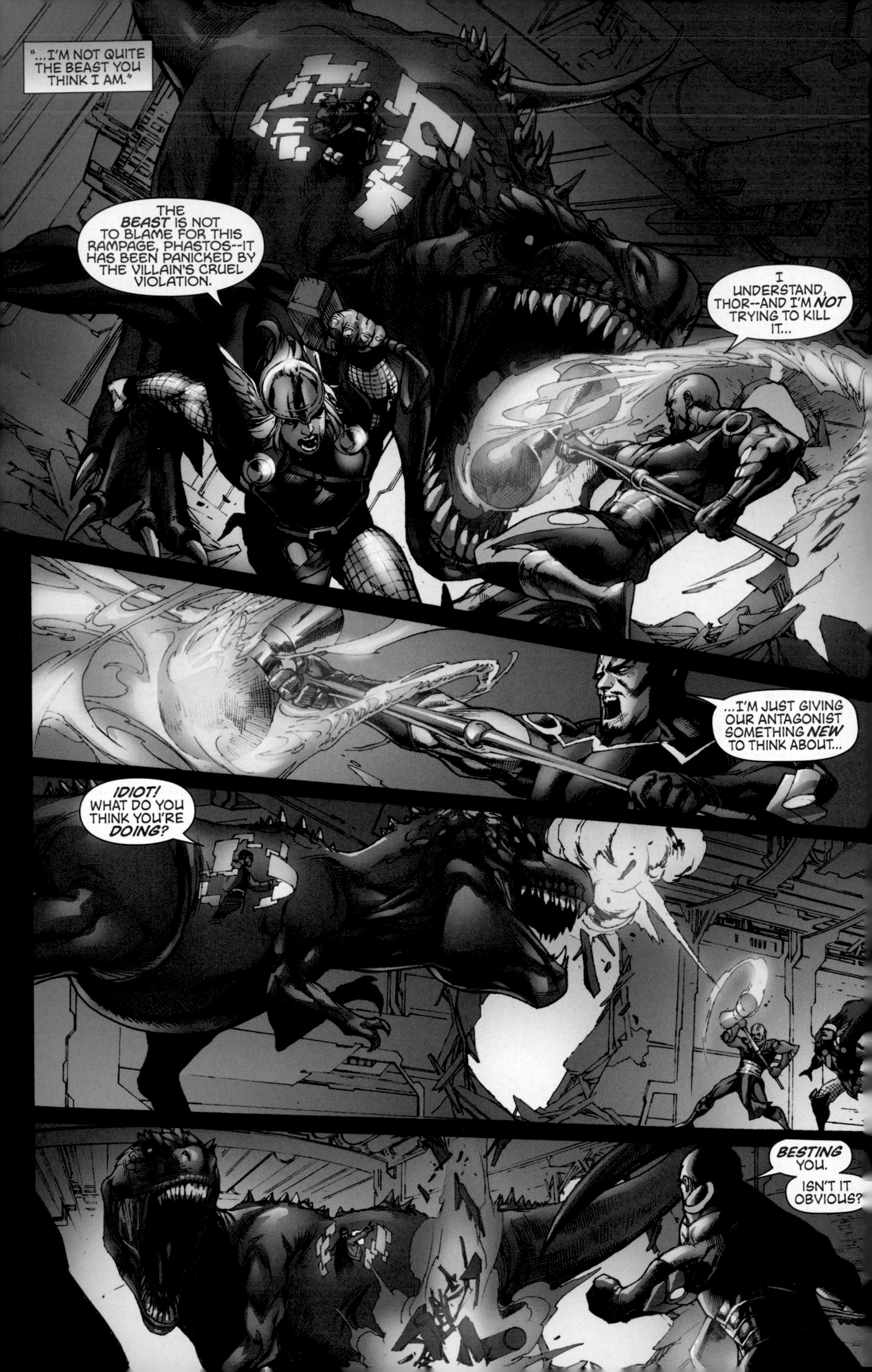
"...I'M NOT QUITE THE BEAST YOU THINK I AM."
THE BEAST IS NOT TO BLAME FOR THIS RAMPAGE, PHASTOS--IT HAS BEEN PANICKED BY THE VILLAIN'S CRUEL VIOLATION.
I UNDERSTAND, THOR--AND I'M NOT TRYING TO KILL IT...
...I'M JUST GIVING OUR ANTAGONIST SOMETHING NEW TO THINK ABOUT...
IDIOT! WHAT DO YOU THINK YOU'RE DOING?
BESTING YOU.
ISN'T IT OBVIOUS?

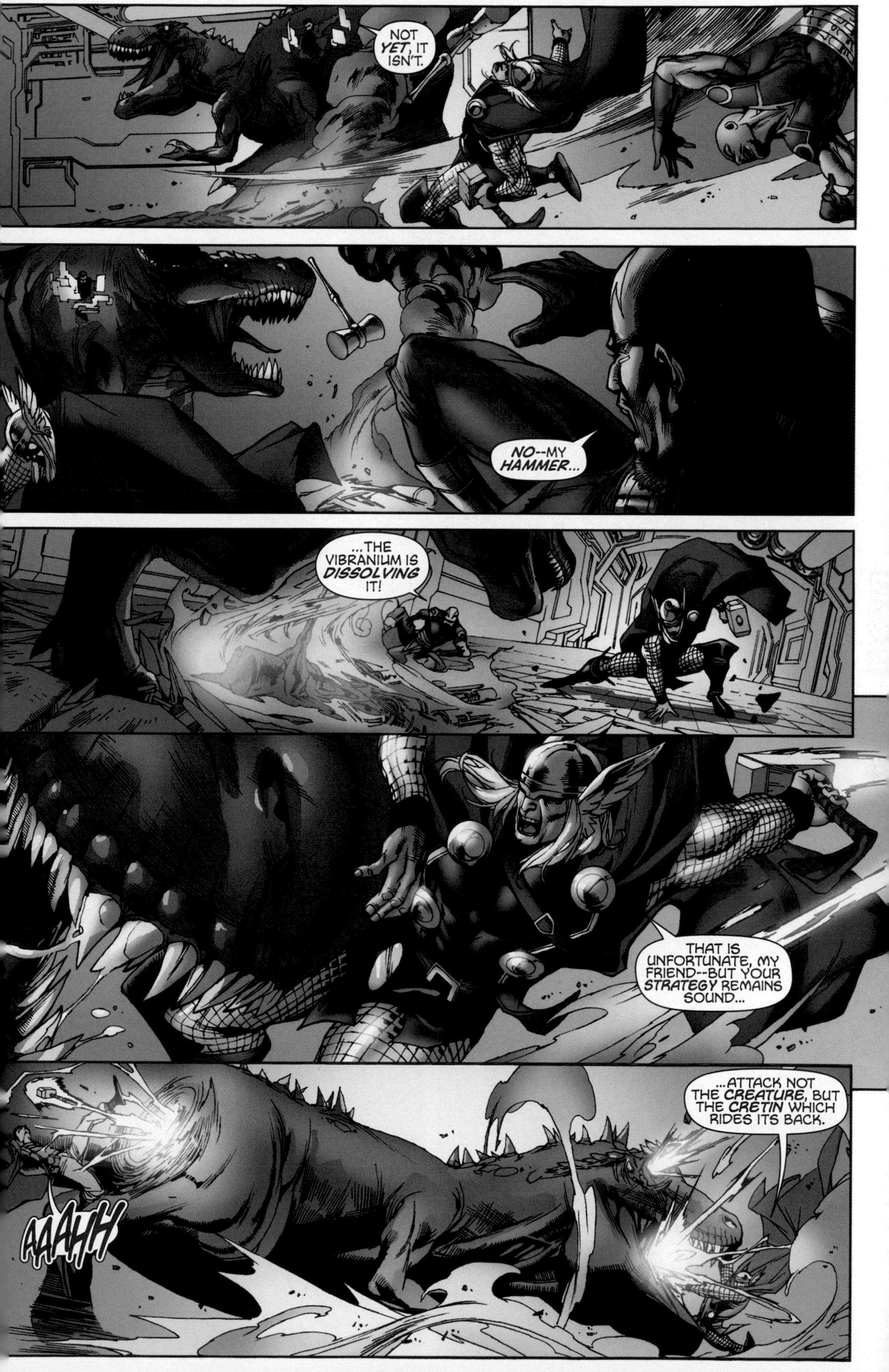
NOT YET, IT ISN'T.
NO--MY HAMMER...
...THE VIBRANIUM IS DISSOLVING IT!
THAT IS UNFORTUNATE, MY FRIEND--BUT YOUR STRATEGY REMAINS SOUND...
...ATTACK NOT THE CREATURE, BUT THE CRETIN WHICH RIDES ITS BACK.
AAAHH

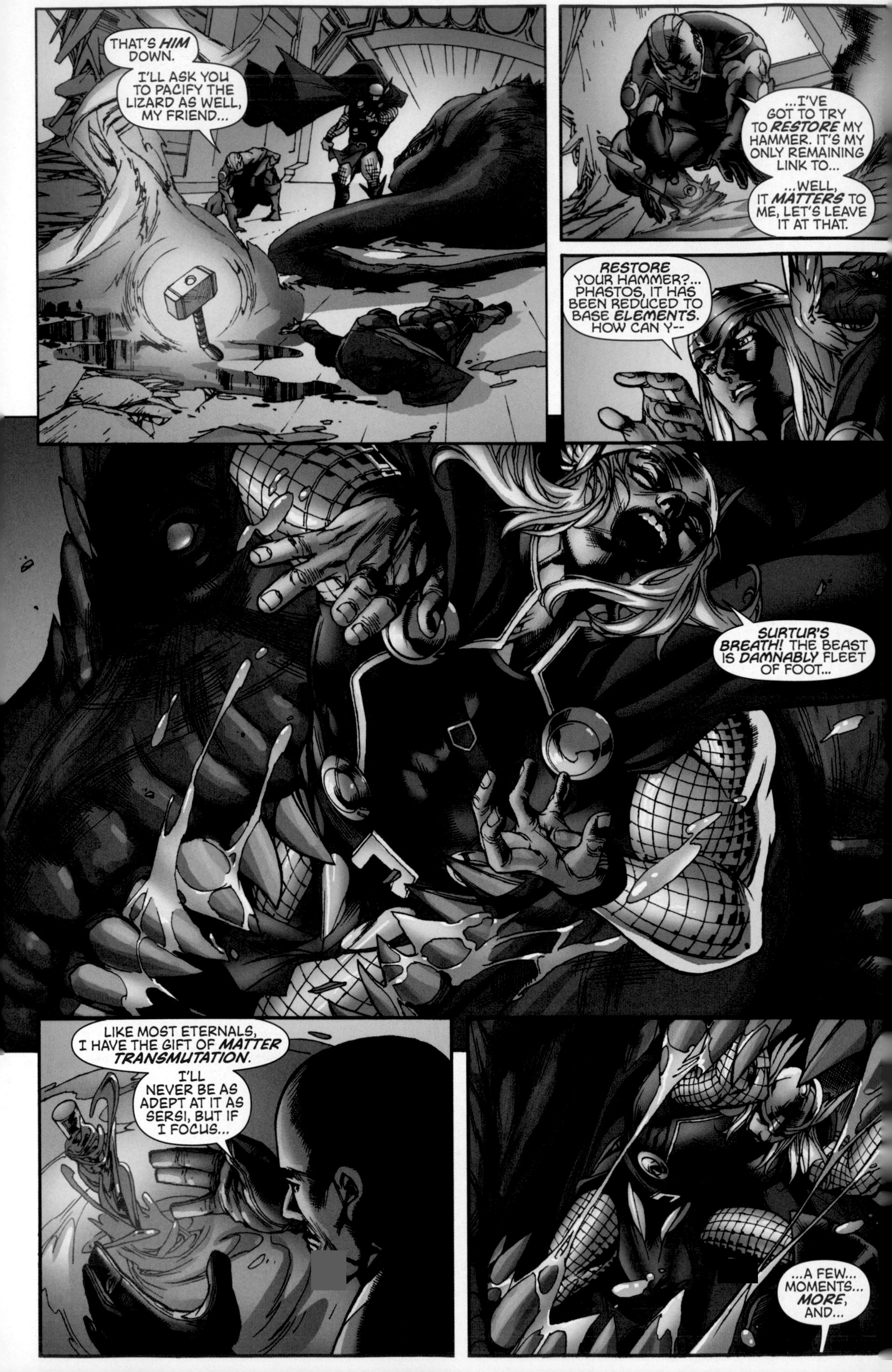
THAT'S HIM DOWN.
I'LL ASK YOU TO PACIFY THE LIZARD AS WELL, MY FRIEND...
...I'VE GOT TO TRY TO RESTORE MY HAMMER. IT'S MY ONLY REMAINING LINK TO...
...WELL, IT MATTERS TO ME, LET'S LEAVE IT AT THAT.
RESTORE YOUR HAMMER?... PHASTOS, IT HAS BEEN REDUCED TO BASE ELEMENTS. HOW CAN Y--
SURTUR'S BREATH! THE BEAST IS DAMNABLY FLEET OF FOOT...
LIKE MOST ETERNALS, I HAVE THE GIFT OF MATTER TRANSMUTATION.
I'LL NEVER BE AS ADEPT AT IT AS SERSI, BUT IF I FOCUS...
...A FEW... MOMENTS... MORE, AND...

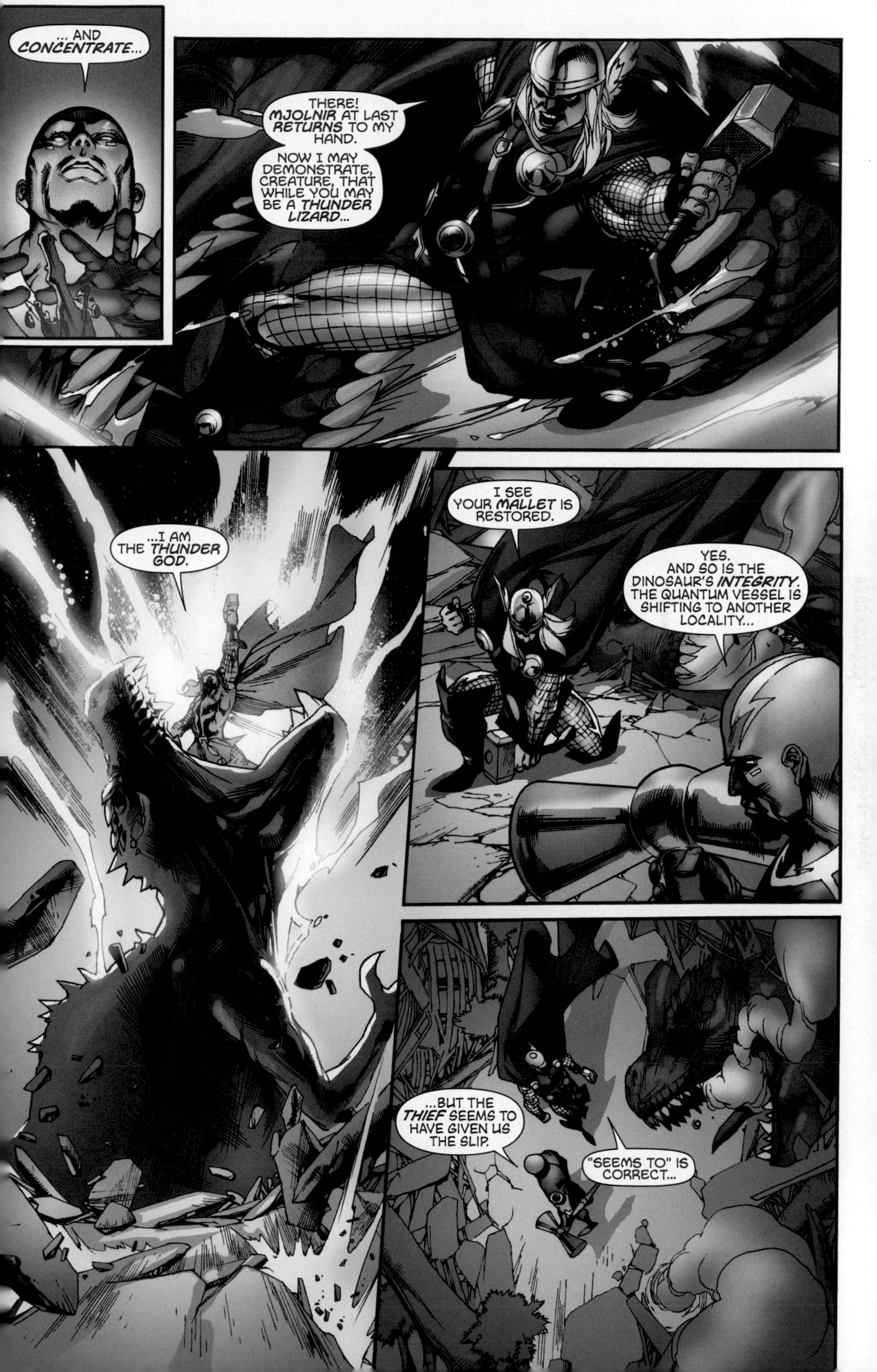
... AND CONCENTRATE...
THERE! MJOLNIR AT LAST RETURNS TO MY HAND.
NOW I MAY DEMONSTRATE, CREATURE, THAT WHILE YOU MAY BE A THUNDER LIZARD...
...I AM THE THUNDER GOD.
I SEE YOUR MALLET IS RESTORED.
YES. AND SO IS THE DINOSAUR'S INTEGRITY. THE QUANTUM VESSEL IS SHIFTING TO ANOTHER LOCALITY...
...BUT THE THIEF SEEMS TO HAVE GIVEN US THE SLIP.
"SEEMS TO" IS CORRECT...

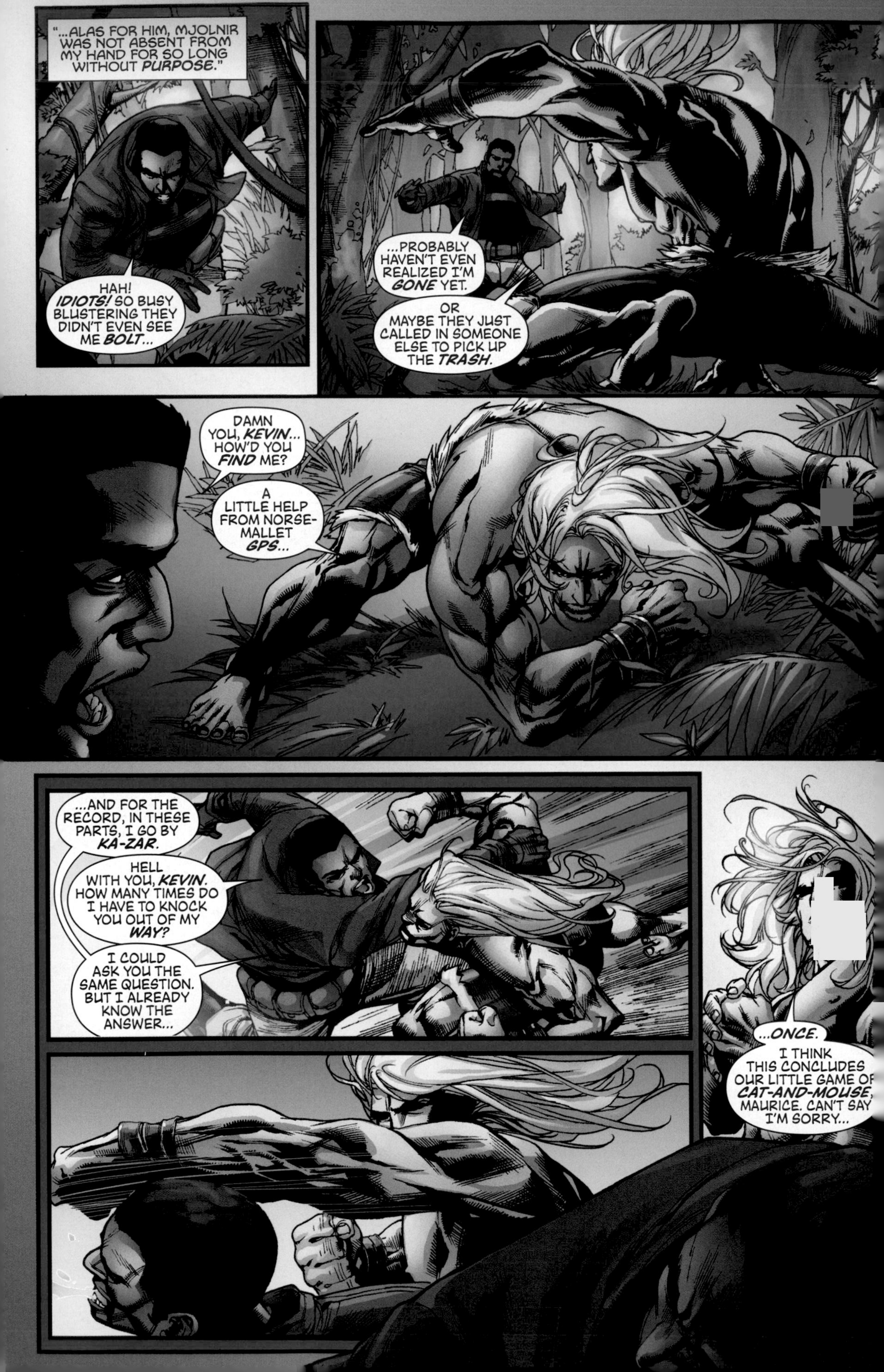
"...ALAS FOR HIM, MJOLNIR WAS NOT ABSENT FROM MY HAND FOR SO LONG WITHOUT PURPOSE."
HAH! IDIOTS! SO BUSY BLUSTERING THEY DIDN'T EVEN SEE ME BOLT...
...PROBABLY HAVEN'T EVEN REALIZED I'M GONE YET.
OR MAYBE THEY JUST CALLED IN SOMEONE ELSE TO PICK UP THE TRASH.
DAMN YOU, KEVIN... HOW'D YOU FIND ME?
A LITTLE HELP FROM NORSE-MALLET GPS...
...AND FOR THE RECORD, IN THESE PARTS, I GO BY KA-ZAR.
HELL WITH YOU, KEVIN. HOW MANY TIMES DO I HAVE TO KNOCK YOU OUT OF MY WAY?
I COULD ASK YOU THE SAME QUESTION. BUT I ALREADY KNOW THE ANSWER...
...ONCE.
I THINK THIS CONCLUDES OUR LITTLE GAME OF CAT-AND-MOUSE, MAURICE. CAN'T SAY I'M SORRY...

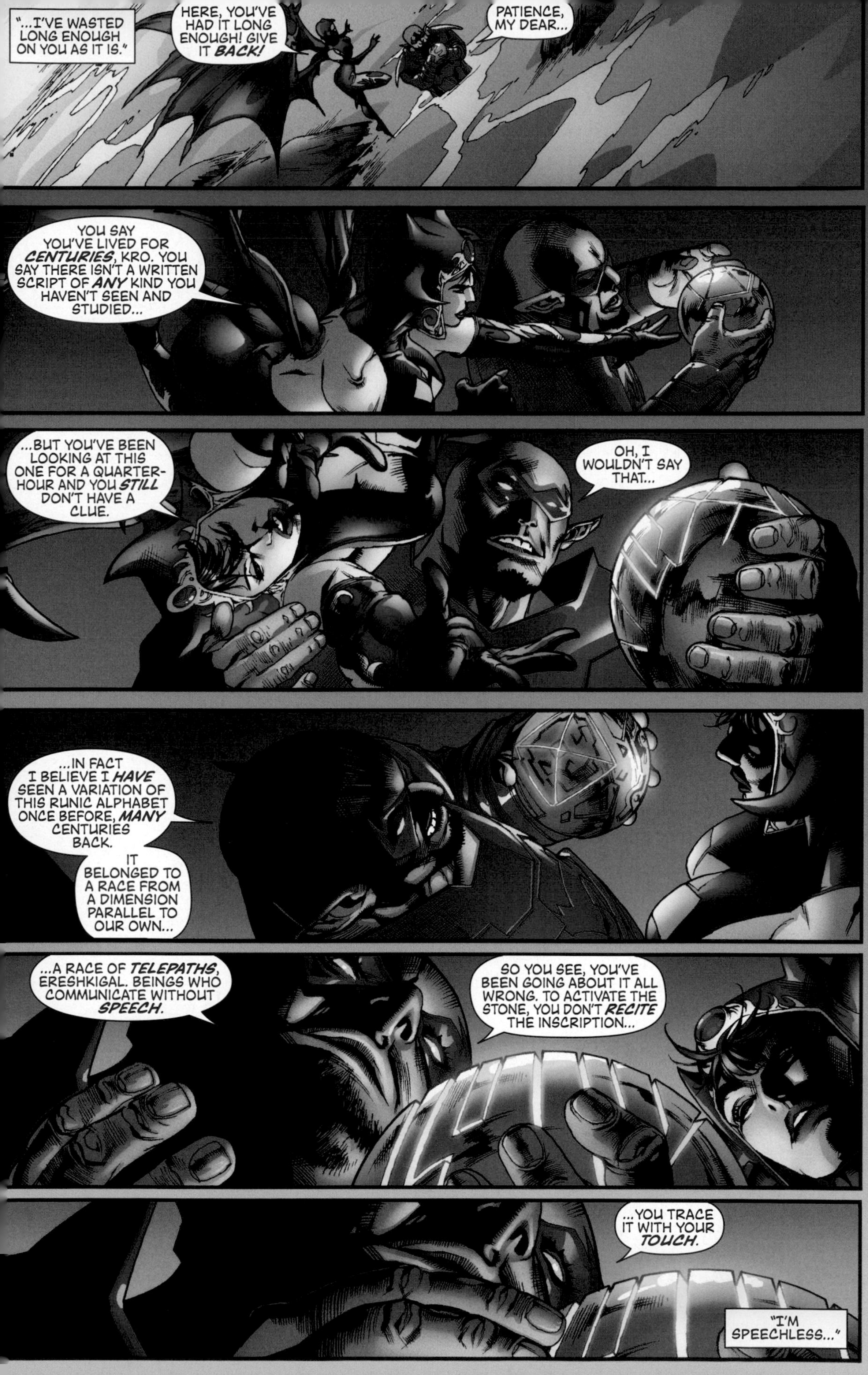

"...I'VE WASTED LONG ENOUGH ON YOU AS IT IS."
HERE, YOU'VE HAD IT LONG ENOUGH! GIVE IT BACK!
PATIENCE, MY DEAR...
YOU SAY YOU'VE LIVED FOR CENTURIES, KRO. YOU SAY THERE ISN'T A WRITTEN SCRIPT OF ANY KIND YOU HAVEN'T SEEN AND STUDIED...
...BUT YOU'VE BEEN LOOKING AT THIS ONE FOR A QUARTER-HOUR AND YOU STILL DON'T HAVE A CLUE.
OH, I WOULDN'T SAY THAT...
...IN FACT I BELIEVE I HAVE SEEN A VARIATION OF THIS RUNIC ALPHABET ONCE BEFORE, MANY CENTURIES BACK.
IT BELONGED TO A RACE FROM A DIMENSION PARALLEL TO OUR OWN...
...A RACE OF TELEPATHS, ERESHKIGAL. BEINGS WHO COMMUNICATE WITHOUT SPEECH.
SO YOU SEE, YOU'VE BEEN GOING ABOUT IT ALL WRONG. TO ACTIVATE THE STONE, YOU DON'T RECITE THE INSCRIPTION...
...YOU TRACE IT WITH YOUR TOUCH.
"I'M SPEECHLESS..."

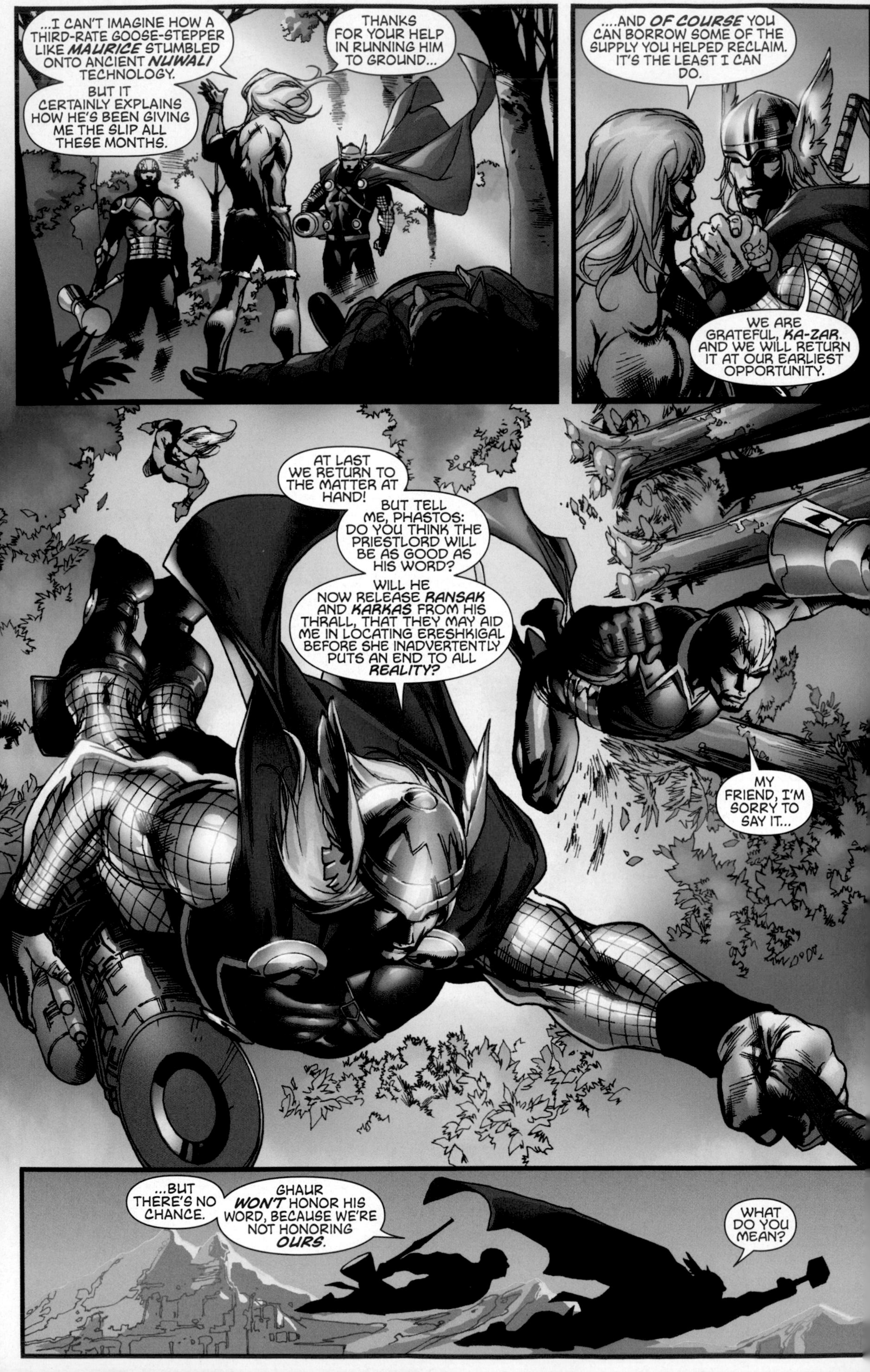
...I CAN'T IMAGINE HOW A THIRD-RATE GOOSE-STEPPER LIKE MAURICE STUMBLED ONTO ANCIENT NUWALI TECHNOLOGY.
BUT IT CERTAINLY EXPLAINS HOW HE'S BEEN GIVING ME THE SLIP ALL THESE MONTHS.
THANKS FOR YOUR HELP IN RUNNING HIM TO GROUND...
....AND OF COURSE YOU CAN BORROW SOME OF THE SUPPLY YOU HELPED RECLAIM. IT'S THE LEAST I CAN DO.
WE ARE GRATEFUL, KA-ZAR. AND WE WILL RETURN IT AT OUR EARLIEST OPPORTUNITY.
AT LAST WE RETURN TO THE MATTER AT HAND!
BUT TELL ME, PHASTOS: DO YOU THINK THE PRIESTLORD WILL BE AS GOOD AS HIS WORD?
WILL HE NOW RELEASE RANSAK AND KARKAS FROM HIS THRALL, THAT THEY MAY AID ME IN LOCATING ERESHKIGAL BEFORE SHE INADVERTENTLY PUTS AN END TO ALL REALITY?
MY FRIEND, I'M SORRY TO SAY IT...
...BUT THERE'S NO CHANCE.
GHAUR WON'T HONOR HIS WORD, BECAUSE WE'RE NOT HONORING OURS.
WHAT DO YOU MEAN?

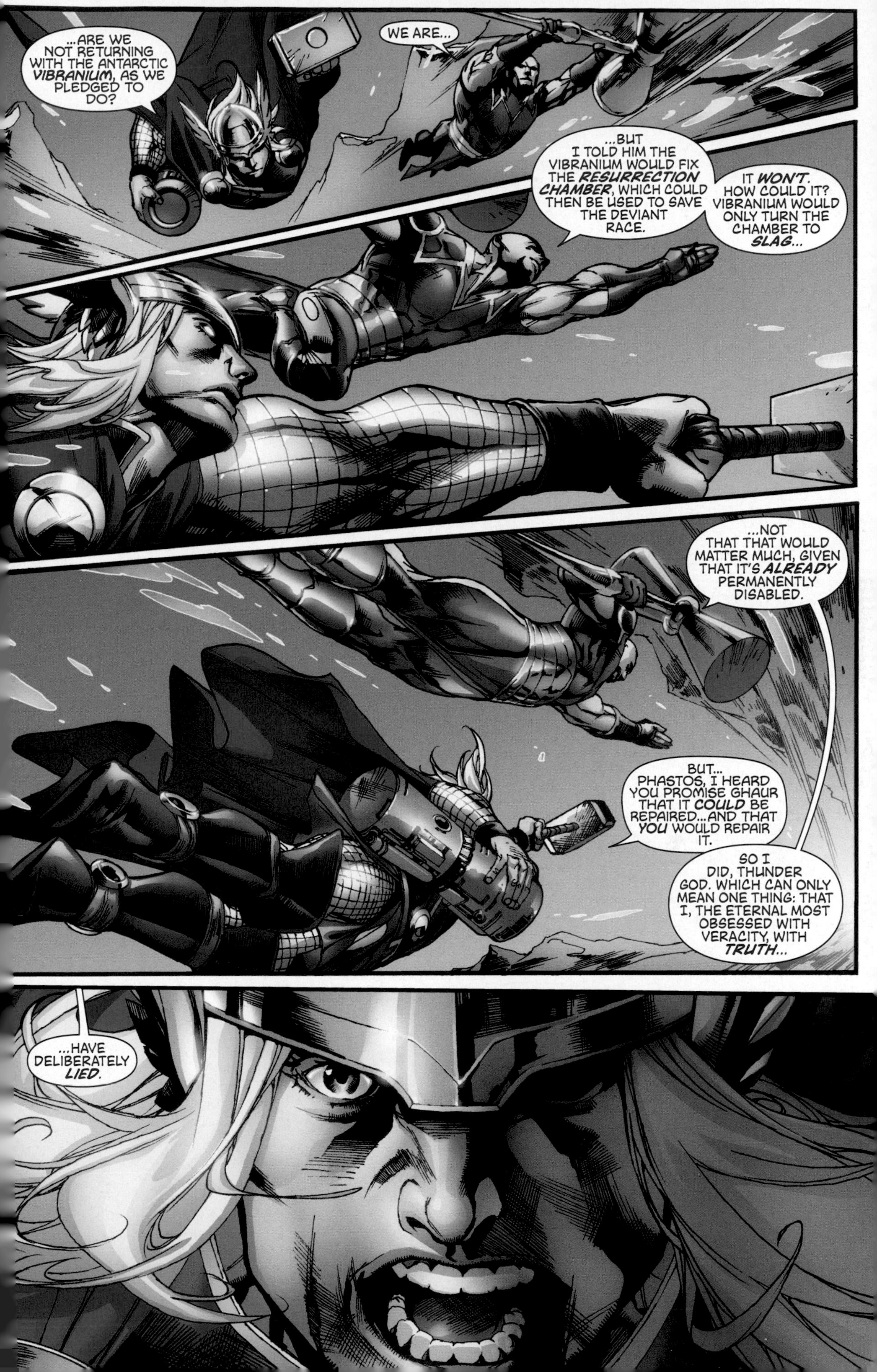

...ARE WE NOT RETURNING WITH THE ANTARCTIC VIBRANIUM, AS WE PLEDGED TO DO?
WE ARE...
...BUT I TOLD HIM THE VIBRANIUM WOULD FIX THE RESURRECTION CHAMBER, WHICH COULD THEN BE USED TO SAVE THE DEVIANT RACE.
IT WON'T. HOW COULD IT? VIBRANIUM WOULD ONLY TURN THE CHAMBER TO SLAG...
...NOT THAT THAT WOULD MATTER MUCH, GIVEN THAT IT'S ALREADY PERMANENTLY DISABLED.
BUT... PHASTOS, I HEARD YOU PROMISE GHAUR THAT IT COULD BE REPAIRED...AND THAT YOU WOULD REPAIR IT.
SO I DID, THUNDER GOD. WHICH CAN ONLY MEAN ONE THING: THAT I, THE ETERNAL MOST OBSESSED WITH VERACITY, WITH TRUTH...
...HAVE DELIBERATELY LIED.

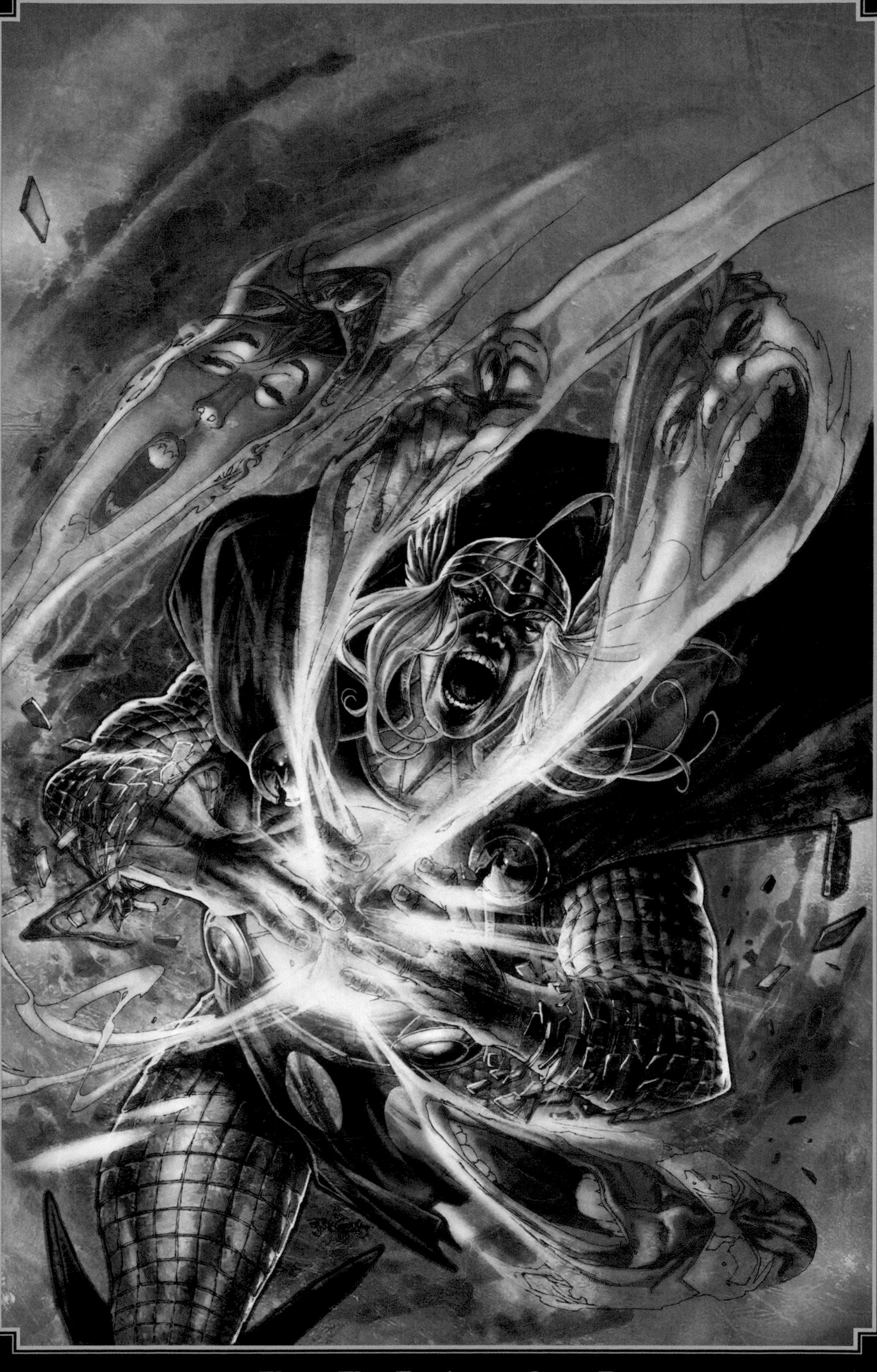

Thor: The Deviants Saga 5

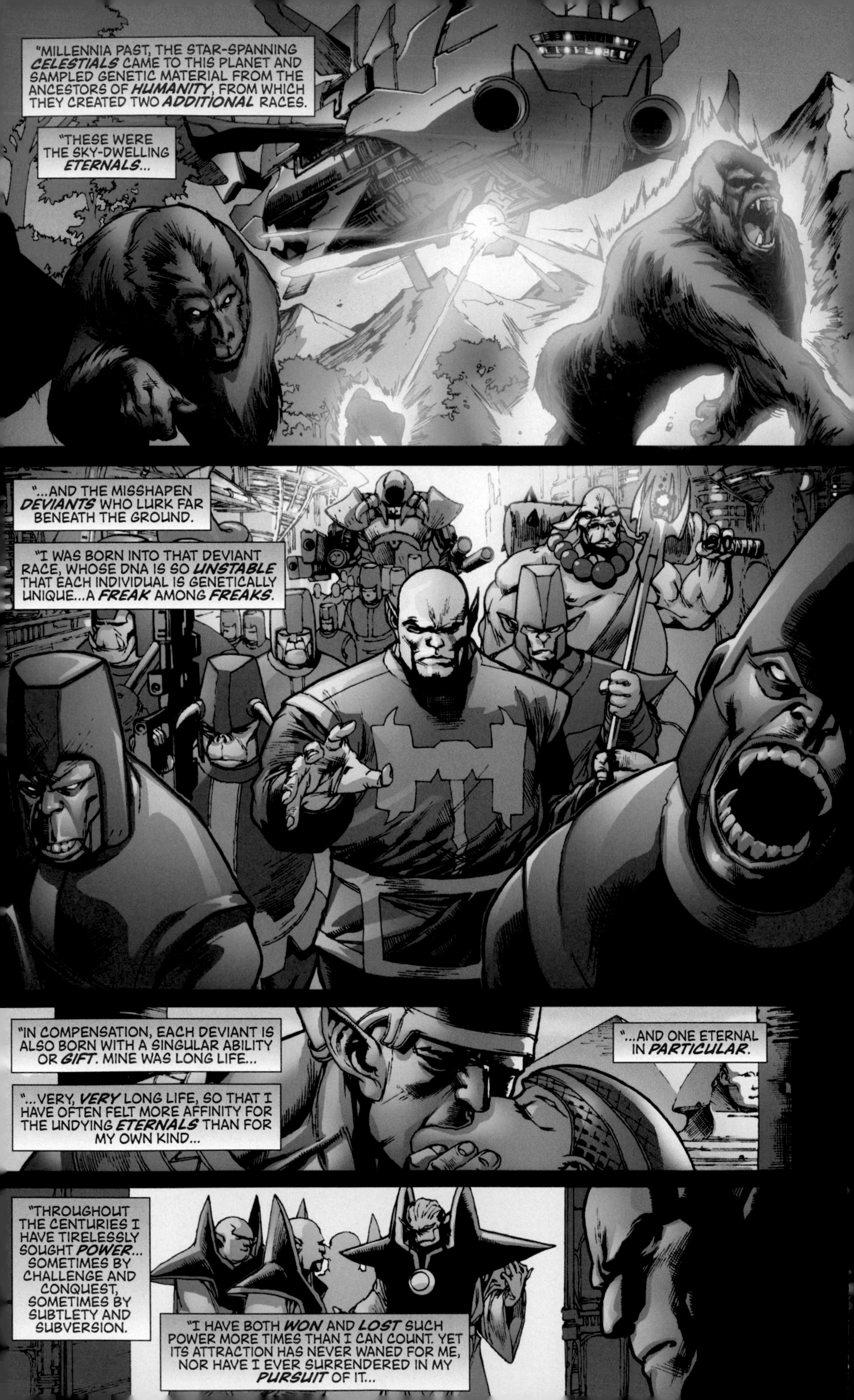
"MILLENNIA PAST, THE STAR-SPANNING CELESTIALS CAME TO THIS PLANET AND SAMPLED GENETIC MATERIAL FROM THE ANCESTORS OF HUMANITY, FROM WHICH THEY CREATED TWO ADDITIONAL RACES.
"THESE WERE THE SKY-DWELLING ETERNALS...
"...AND THE MISSHAPEN DEVIANTS WHO LURK FAR BENEATH THE GROUND.
"I WAS BORN INTO THAT DEVIANT RACE, WHOSE DNA IS SO UNSTABLE THAT EACH INDIVIDUAL IS GENETICALLY UNIQUE...A FREAK AMONG FREAKS.
"IN COMPENSATION, EACH DEVIANT IS ALSO BORN WITH A SINGULAR ABILITY OR GIFT. MINE WAS LONG LIFE...
"...VERY, VERY LONG LIFE, SO THAT I HAVE OFTEN FELT MORE AFFINITY FOR THE UNDYING ETERNALS THAN FOR MY OWN KIND...
"...AND ONE ETERNAL IN PARTICULAR.
"THROUGHOUT THE CENTURIES I HAVE TIRELESSLY SOUGHT POWER... SOMETIMES BY CHALLENGE AND CONQUEST, SOMETIMES BY SUBTLETY AND SUBVERSION.
"I HAVE BOTH WON AND LOST SUCH POWER MORE TIMES THAN I CAN COUNT. YET ITS ATTRACTION HAS NEVER WANED FOR ME, NOR HAVE I EVER SURRENDERED IN MY PURSUIT OF IT...

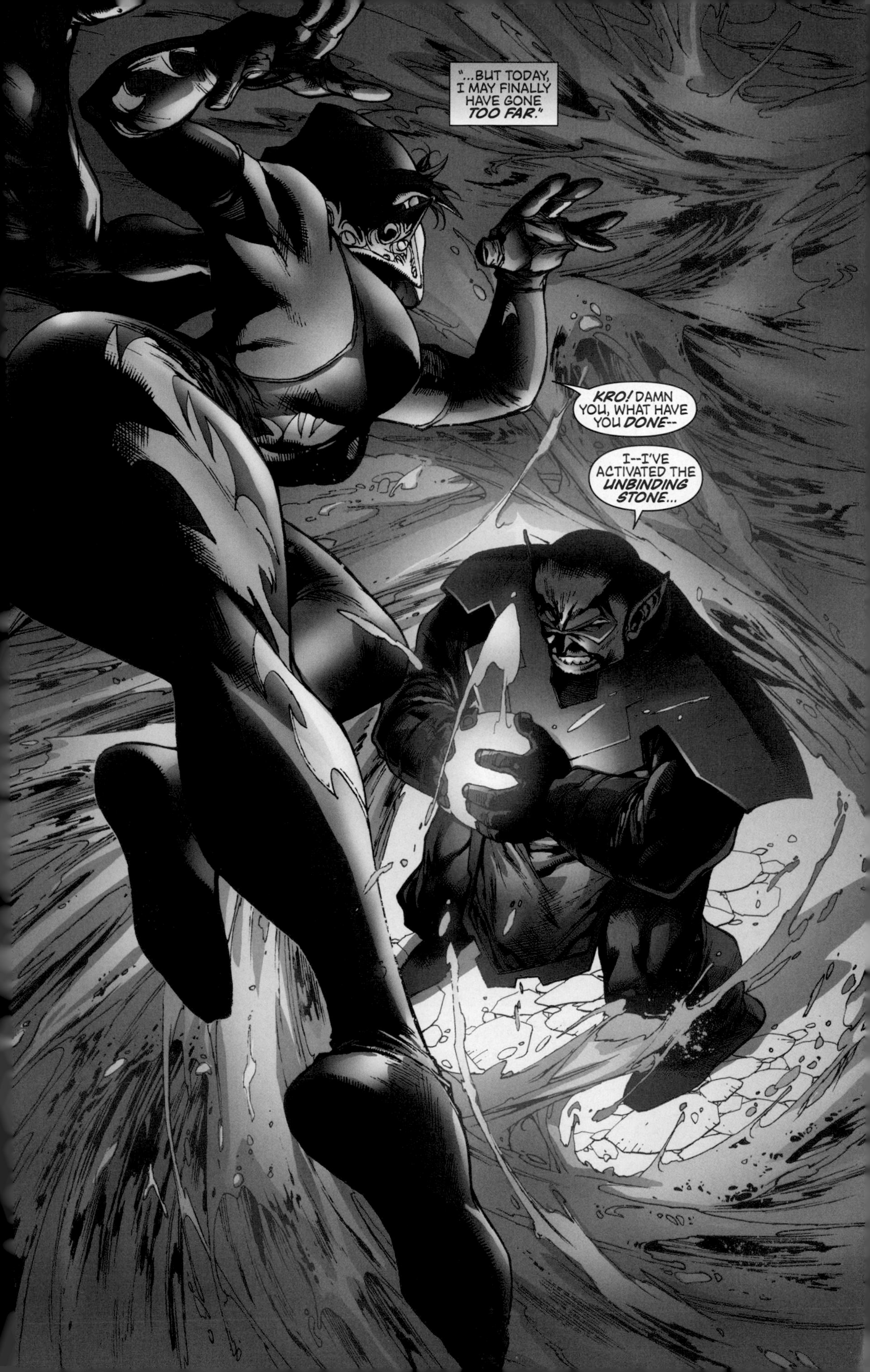
"...BUT TODAY, I MAY FINALLY HAVE GONE *TOO FAR.*"
KRO! DAMN YOU, WHAT HAVE YOU *DONE*--
I--I'VE ACTIVATED THE *UNBINDING STONE*...

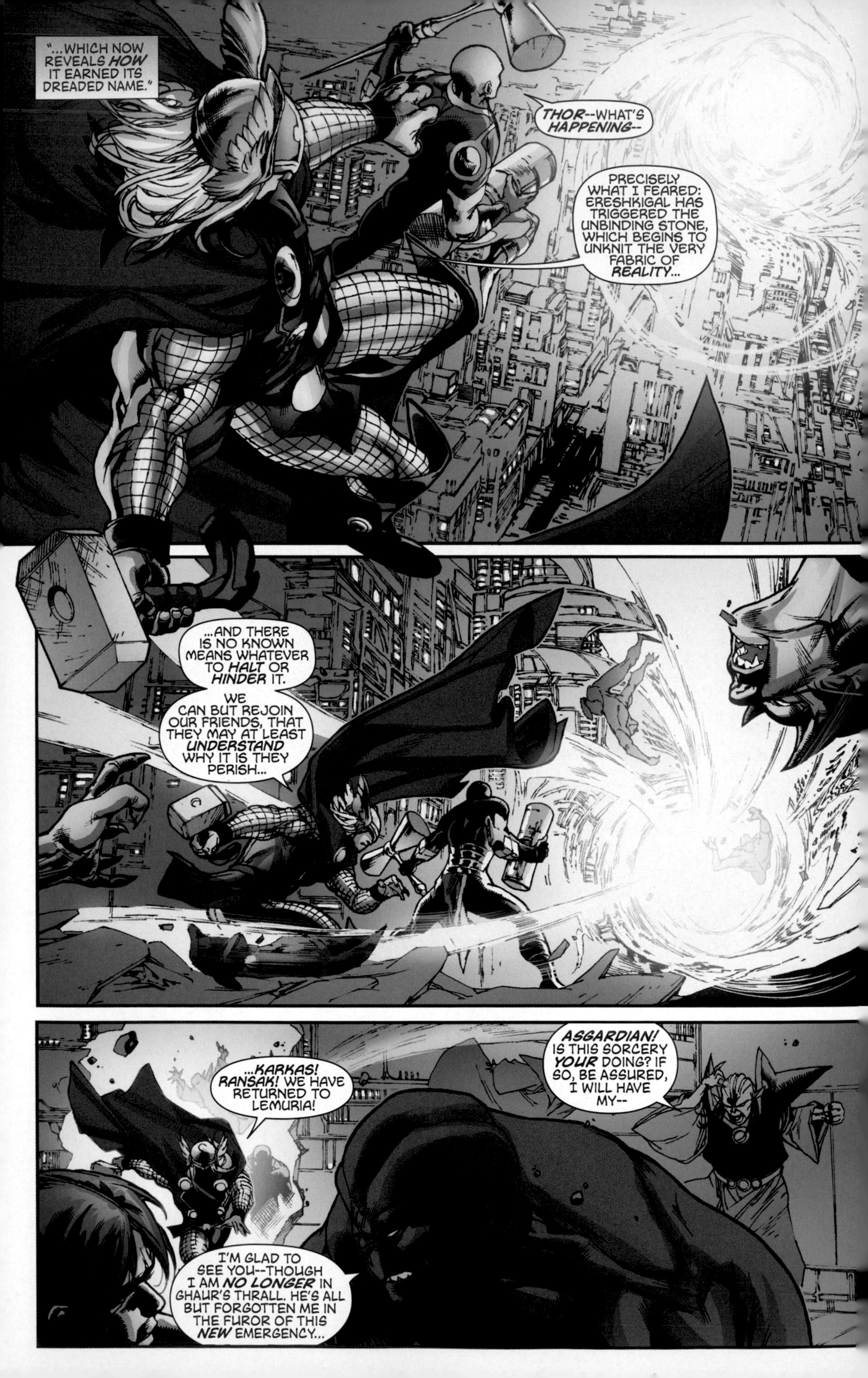
"...WHICH NOW REVEALS HOW IT EARNED ITS DREADED NAME."
THOR--WHAT'S HAPPENING--
PRECISELY WHAT I FEARED: ERESHKIGAL HAS TRIGGERED THE UNBINDING STONE, WHICH BEGINS TO UNKNIT THE VERY FABRIC OF REALITY...
...AND THERE IS NO KNOWN MEANS WHATEVER TO HALT OR HINDER IT.
WE CAN BUT REJOIN OUR FRIENDS, THAT THEY MAY AT LEAST UNDERSTAND WHY IT IS THEY PERISH...
...KARKAS! RANSAK! WE HAVE RETURNED TO LEMURIA!
ASGARDIAN! IS THIS SORCERY YOUR DOING? IF SO, BE ASSURED, I WILL HAVE MY--
I'M GLAD TO SEE YOU--THOUGH I AM NO LONGER IN GHAUR'S THRALL. HE'S ALL BUT FORGOTTEN ME IN THE FUROR OF THIS NEW EMERGENCY...

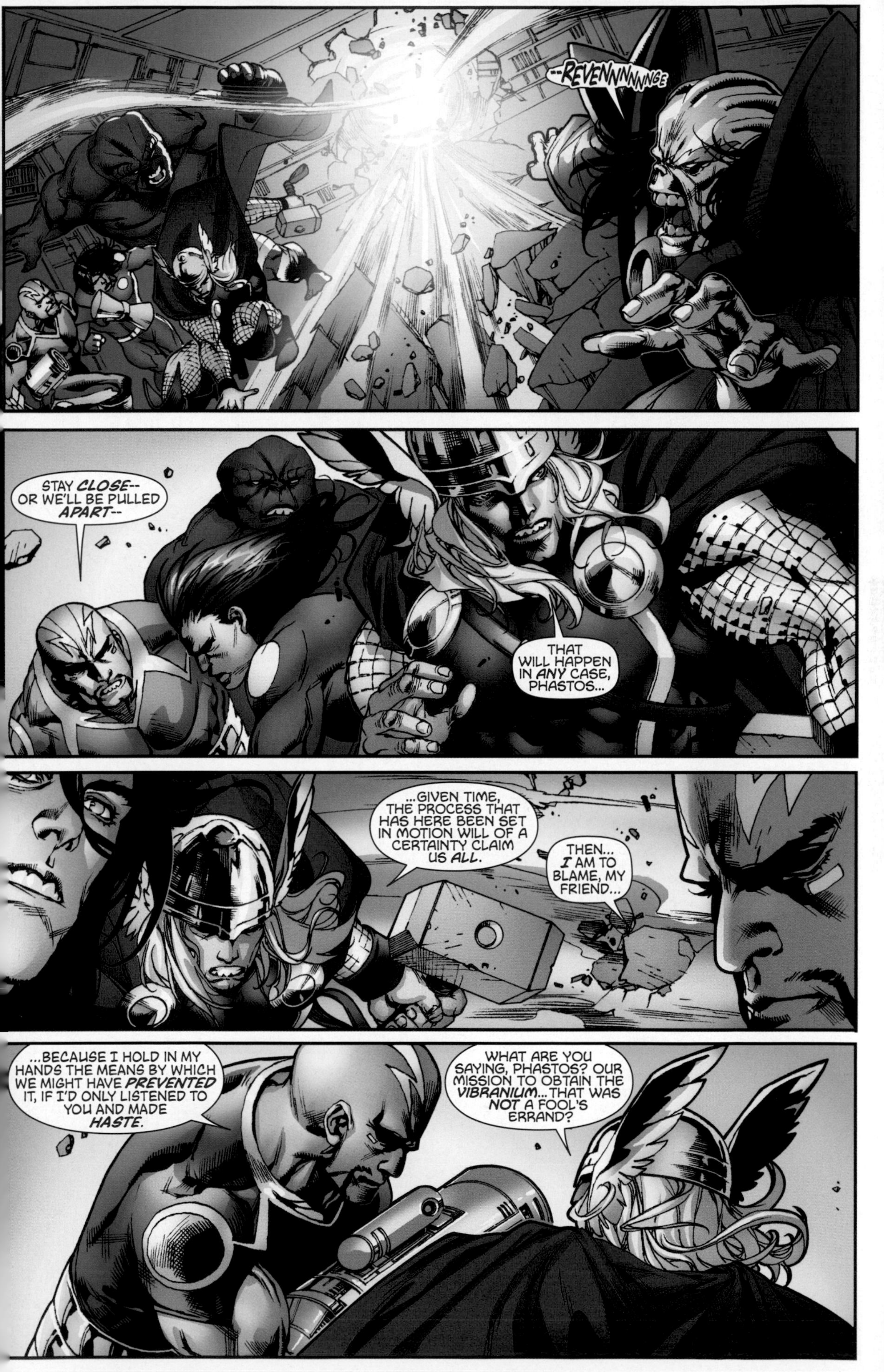
--REVENNNNNNGE
STAY CLOSE-- OR WE'LL BE PULLED APART--
THAT WILL HAPPEN IN ANY CASE, PHASTOS...
...GIVEN TIME, THE PROCESS THAT HAS HERE BEEN SET IN MOTION WILL OF A CERTAINTY CLAIM US ALL.
THEN... I AM TO BLAME, MY FRIEND...
...BECAUSE I HOLD IN MY HANDS THE MEANS BY WHICH WE MIGHT HAVE PREVENTED IT, IF I'D ONLY LISTENED TO YOU AND MADE HASTE.
WHAT ARE YOU SAYING, PHASTOS? OUR MISSION TO OBTAIN THE VIBRANIUM... THAT WAS NOT A FOOL'S ERRAND?

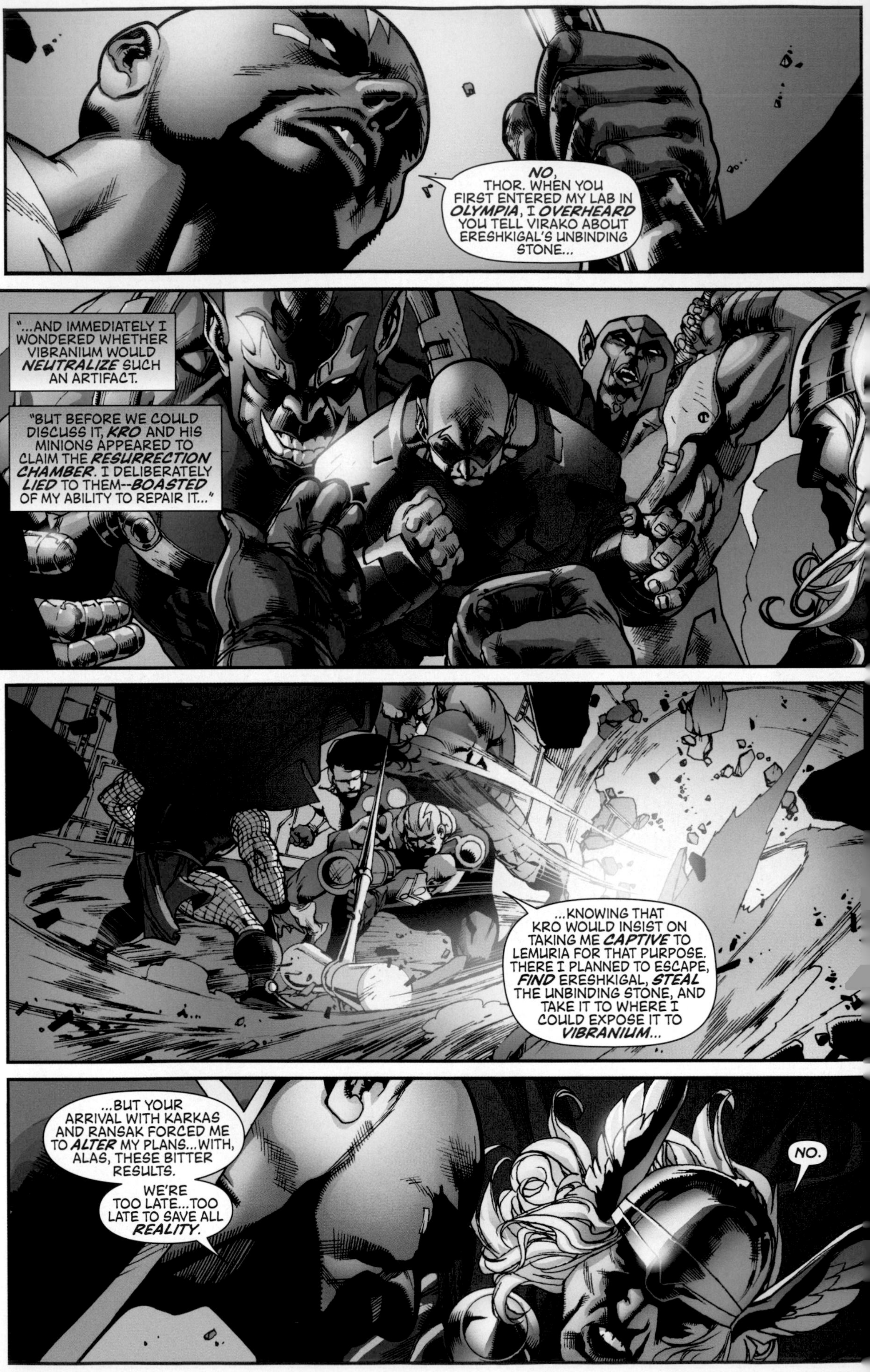
NO, THOR. WHEN YOU FIRST ENTERED MY LAB IN OLYMPIA, I OVERHEARD YOU TELL VIRAKO ABOUT ERESHKIGAL'S UNBINDING STONE...
"...AND IMMEDIATELY I WONDERED WHETHER VIBRANIUM WOULD NEUTRALIZE SUCH AN ARTIFACT.
"BUT BEFORE WE COULD DISCUSS IT, KRO AND HIS MINIONS APPEARED TO CLAIM THE RESURRECTION CHAMBER. I DELIBERATELY LIED TO THEM--BOASTED OF MY ABILITY TO REPAIR IT..."
...KNOWING THAT KRO WOULD INSIST ON TAKING ME CAPTIVE TO LEMURIA FOR THAT PURPOSE. THERE I PLANNED TO ESCAPE, FIND ERESHKIGAL, STEAL THE UNBINDING STONE, AND TAKE IT TO WHERE I COULD EXPOSE IT TO VIBRANIUM...
...BUT YOUR ARRIVAL WITH KARKAS AND RANSAK FORCED ME TO ALTER MY PLANS...WITH, ALAS, THESE BITTER RESULTS.
WE'RE TOO LATE...TOO LATE TO SAVE ALL REALITY.
NO.

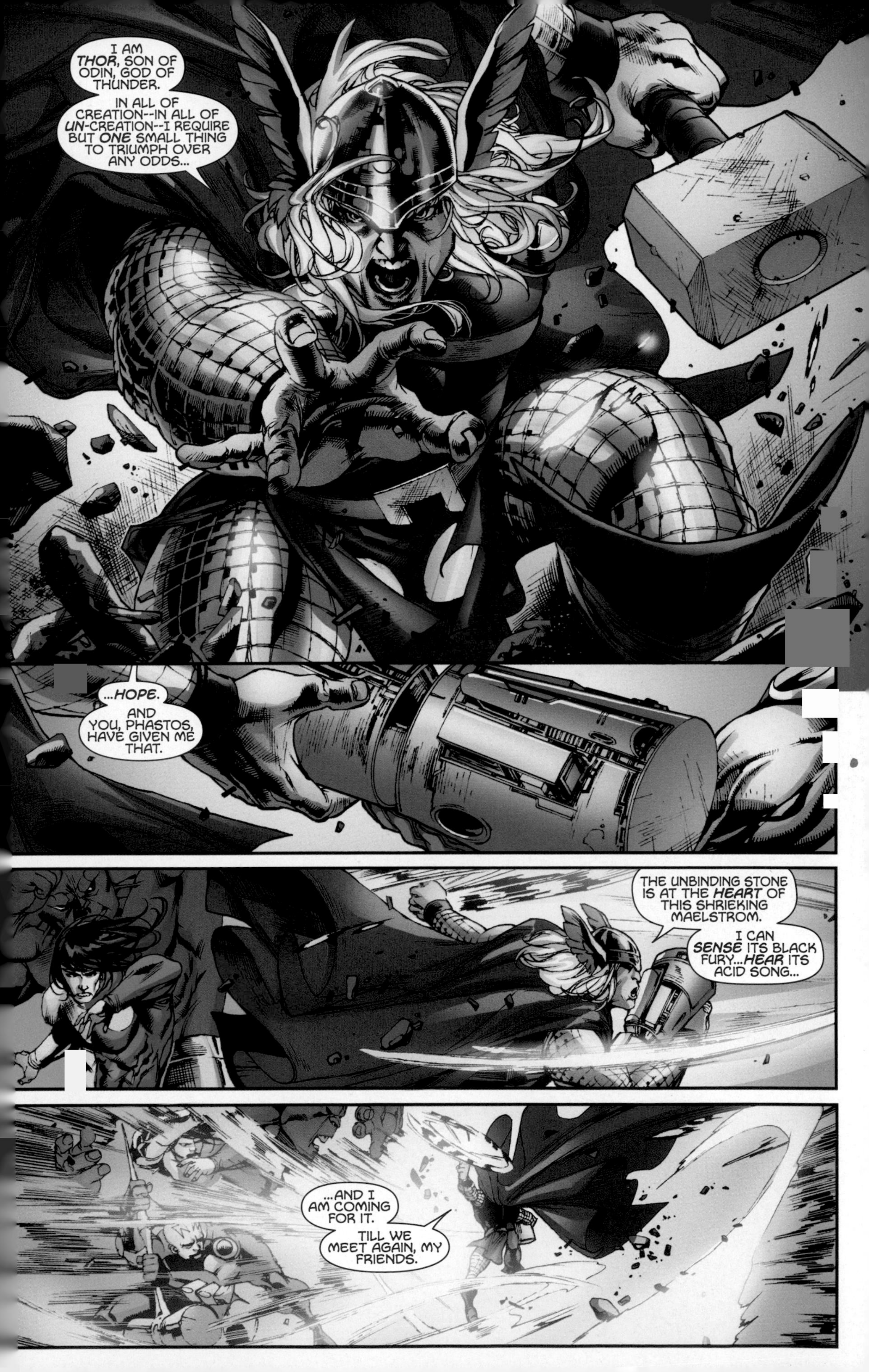
I AM THOR, SON OF ODIN, GOD OF THUNDER.
IN ALL OF CREATION--IN ALL OF UN-CREATION--I REQUIRE BUT ONE SMALL THING TO TRIUMPH OVER ANY ODDS...
...HOPE.
AND YOU, PHASTOS, HAVE GIVEN ME THAT.
THE UNBINDING STONE IS AT THE HEART OF THIS SHRIEKING MAELSTROM.
I CAN SENSE ITS BLACK FURY...HEAR ITS ACID SONG...
...AND I AM COMING FOR IT.
TILL WE MEET AGAIN, MY FRIENDS.

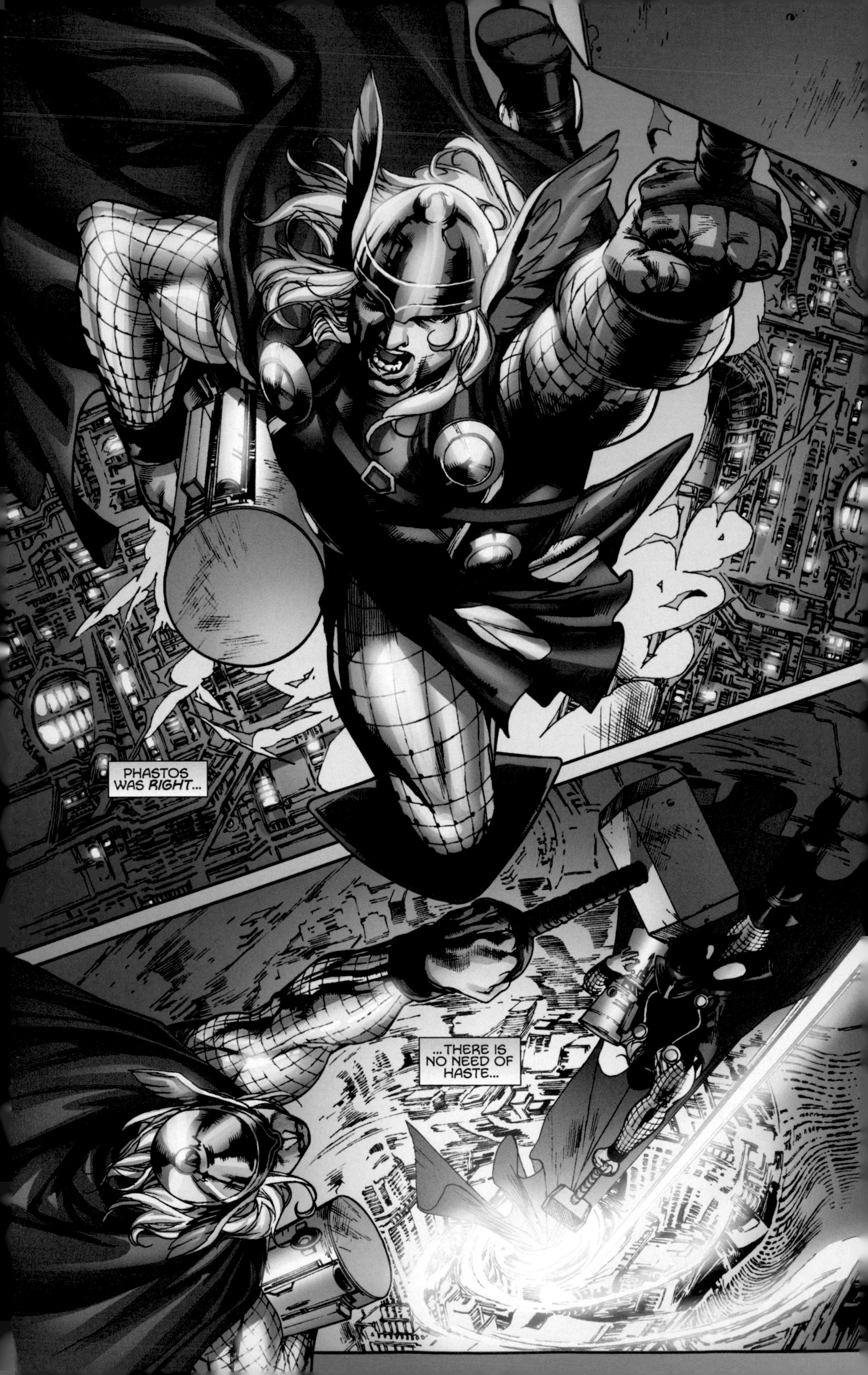
PHASTOS WAS *RIGHT*...
...THERE IS NO NEED OF HASTE...

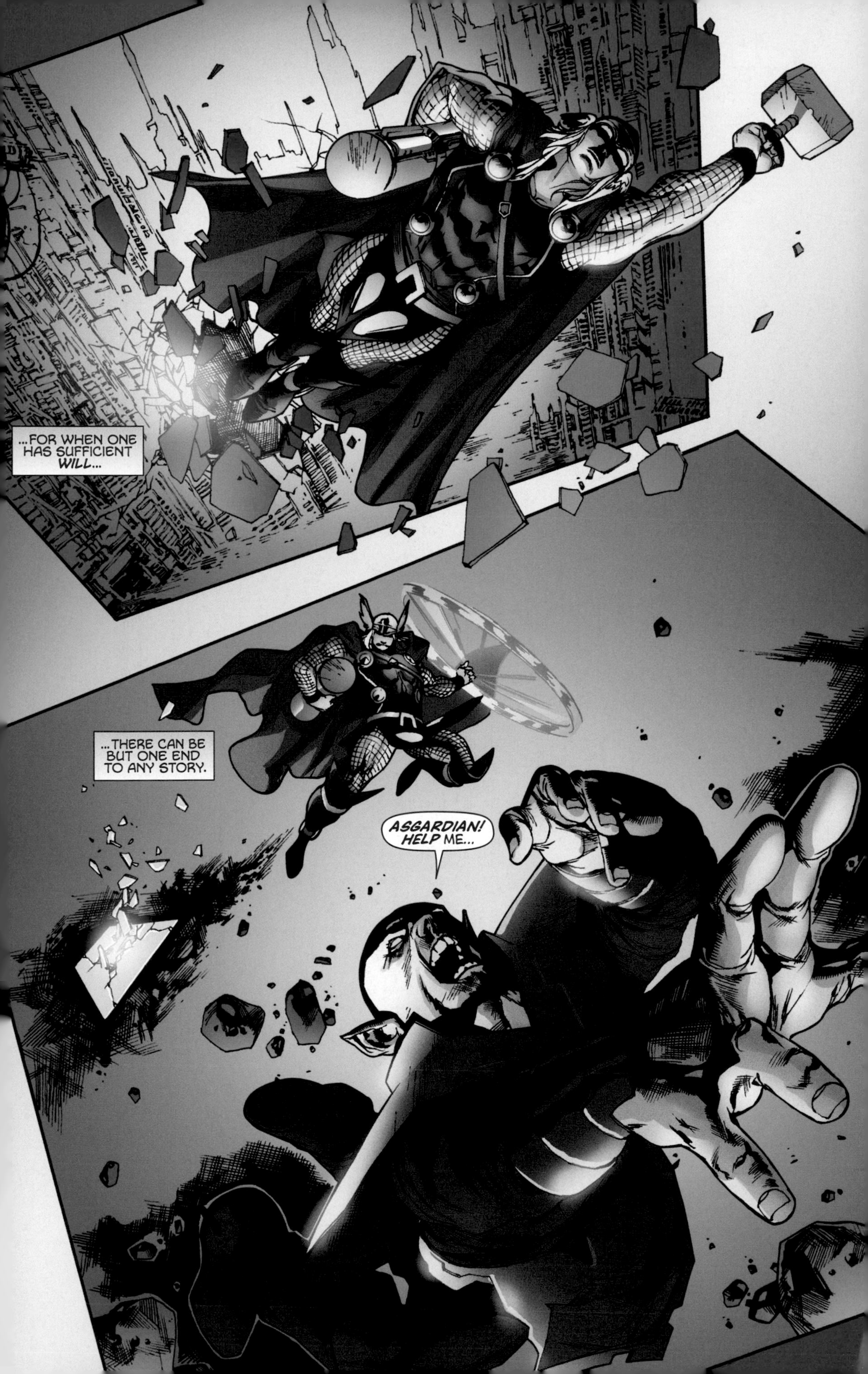
...FOR WHEN ONE HAS SUFFICIENT WILL...
...THERE CAN BE BUT ONE END TO ANY STORY.
ASGARDIAN! HELP ME...

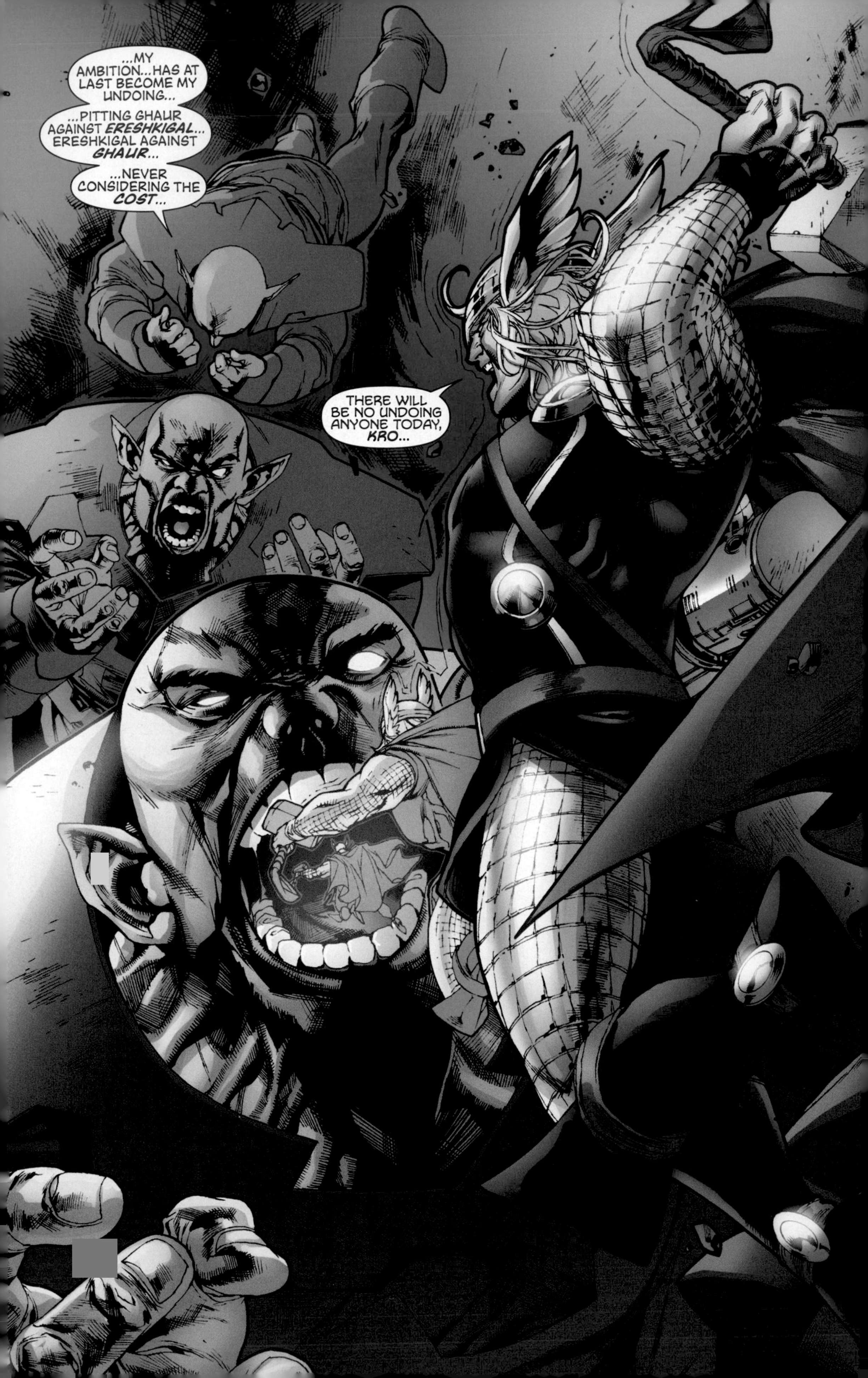
...MY AMBITION...HAS AT LAST BECOME MY UNDOING...
...PITTING GHAUR AGAINST ERESHKIGAL... ERESHKIGAL AGAINST GHAUR...
...NEVER CONSIDERING THE COST...
THERE WILL BE NO UNDOING ANYONE TODAY, KRO...

...I GIVE YOU THE WORD OF A PRINCE OF ASGARD.

YONDER HOVERS OSHEMAR'S *FOLLY*... AND *ODIN'S* TOO.

TIME NO LONGER HAS MEANING HERE. SO WHEN I SAY I HAVE BUT *SECONDS* TO ACT BEFORE THIS VOID CLOSES ABOUT AND CLAIMS ME...

...IT IS MERE *METAPHOR*.

UNLIKE THE HARD REALITY OF WHAT MUST OCCUR WHEN THE UNBINDING STONE...

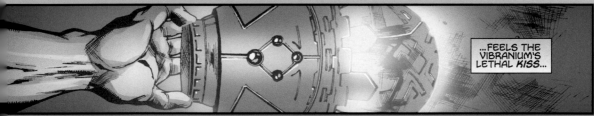

...FEELS THE VIBRANIUM'S LETHAL *KISS*...

SHHOOOM

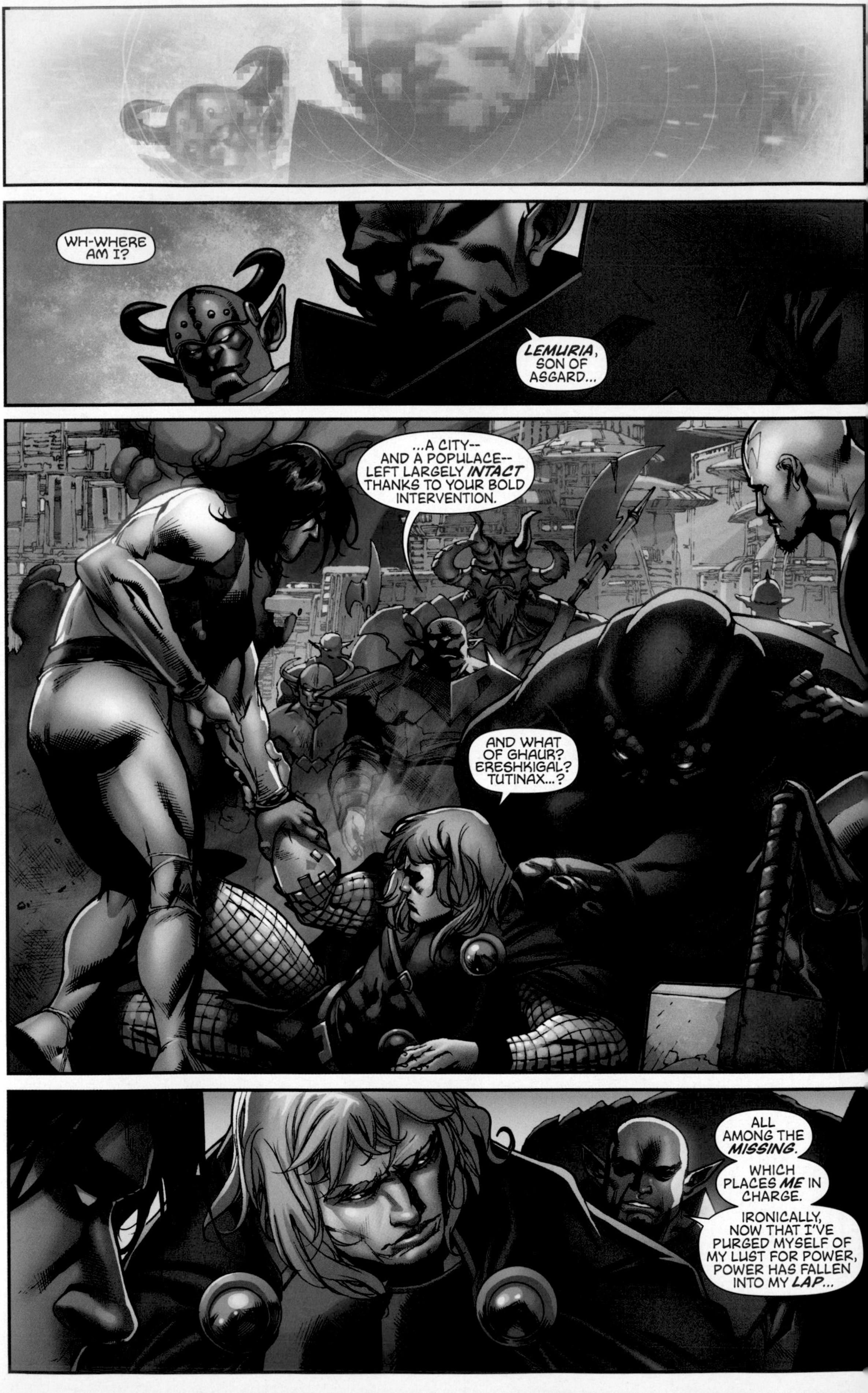
WH-WHERE AM I?
LEMURIA, SON OF ASGARD...
...A CITY-- AND A POPULACE-- LEFT LARGELY INTACT THANKS TO YOUR BOLD INTERVENTION.
AND WHAT OF GHAUR? ERESHKIGAL? TUTINAX...?
ALL AMONG THE MISSING.
WHICH PLACES ME IN CHARGE.
IRONICALLY, NOW THAT I'VE PURGED MYSELF OF MY LUST FOR POWER, POWER HAS FALLEN INTO MY LAP...

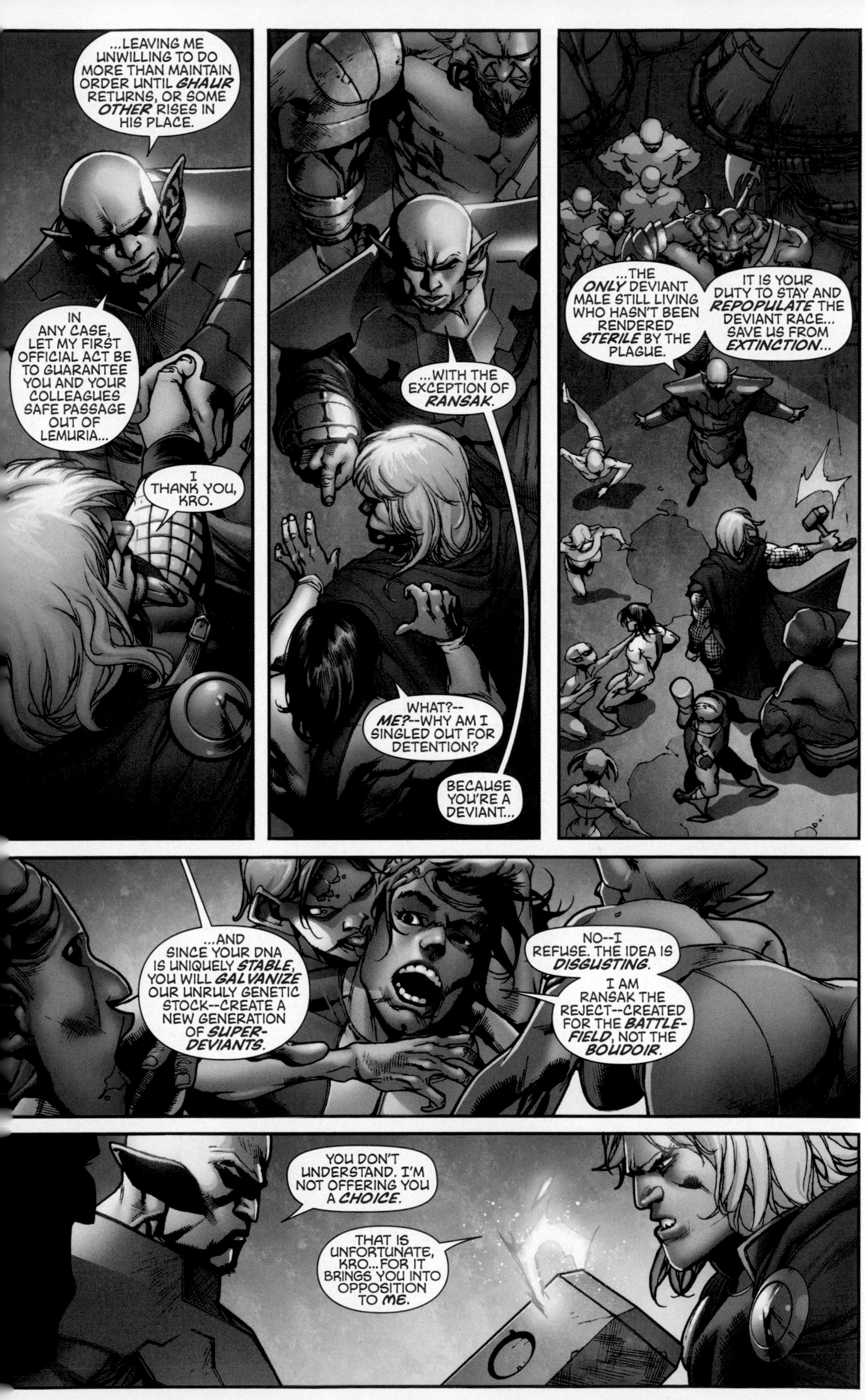
...LEAVING ME UNWILLING TO DO MORE THAN MAINTAIN ORDER UNTIL GHAUR RETURNS, OR SOME OTHER RISES IN HIS PLACE.
IN ANY CASE, LET MY FIRST OFFICIAL ACT BE TO GUARANTEE YOU AND YOUR COLLEAGUES SAFE PASSAGE OUT OF LEMURIA...
I THANK YOU, KRO.
...WITH THE EXCEPTION OF RANSAK.
WHAT?--ME?--WHY AM I SINGLED OUT FOR DETENTION?
BECAUSE YOU'RE A DEVIANT...
...THE ONLY DEVIANT MALE STILL LIVING WHO HASN'T BEEN RENDERED STERILE BY THE PLAGUE.
IT IS YOUR DUTY TO STAY AND REPOPULATE THE DEVIANT RACE... SAVE US FROM EXTINCTION...
...AND SINCE YOUR DNA IS UNIQUELY STABLE, YOU WILL GALVANIZE OUR UNRULY GENETIC STOCK--CREATE A NEW GENERATION OF SUPER-DEVIANTS.
NO--I REFUSE. THE IDEA IS DISGUSTING.
I AM RANSAK THE REJECT--CREATED FOR THE BATTLE-FIELD, NOT THE BOUDOIR.
YOU DON'T UNDERSTAND. I'M NOT OFFERING YOU A CHOICE.
THAT IS UNFORTUNATE, KRO...FOR IT BRINGS YOU INTO OPPOSITION TO ME.

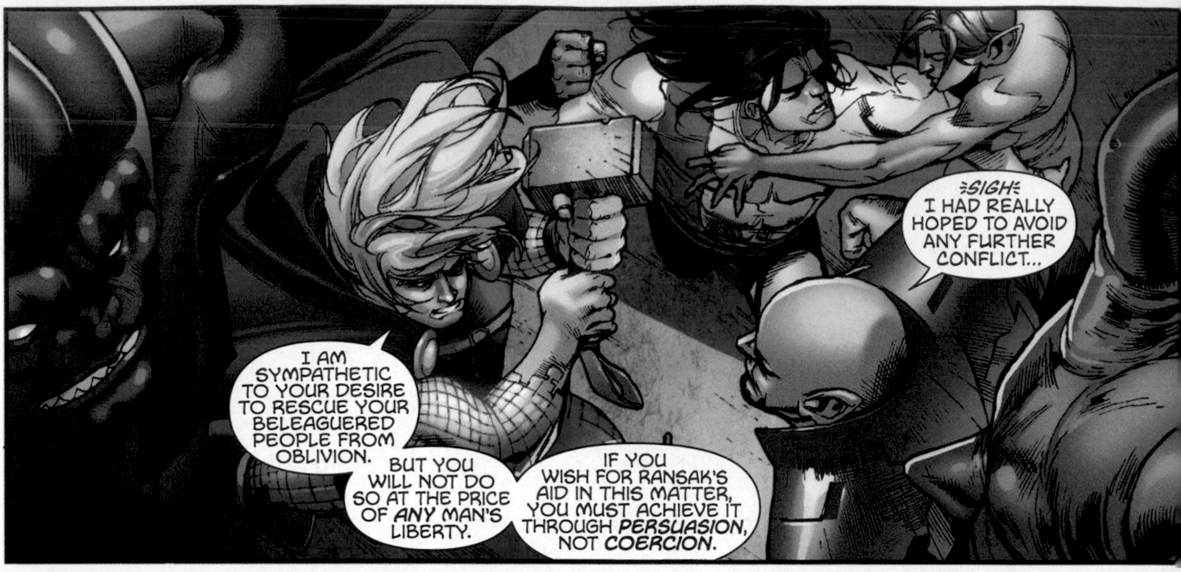

I AM SYMPATHETIC TO YOUR DESIRE TO RESCUE YOUR BELEAGUERED PEOPLE FROM OBLIVION.
BUT YOU WILL NOT DO SO AT THE PRICE OF ANY MAN'S LIBERTY.
IF YOU WISH FOR RANSAK'S AID IN THIS MATTER, YOU MUST ACHIEVE IT THROUGH PERSUASION, NOT COERCION.
SIGH I HAD REALLY HOPED TO AVOID ANY FURTHER CONFLICT...

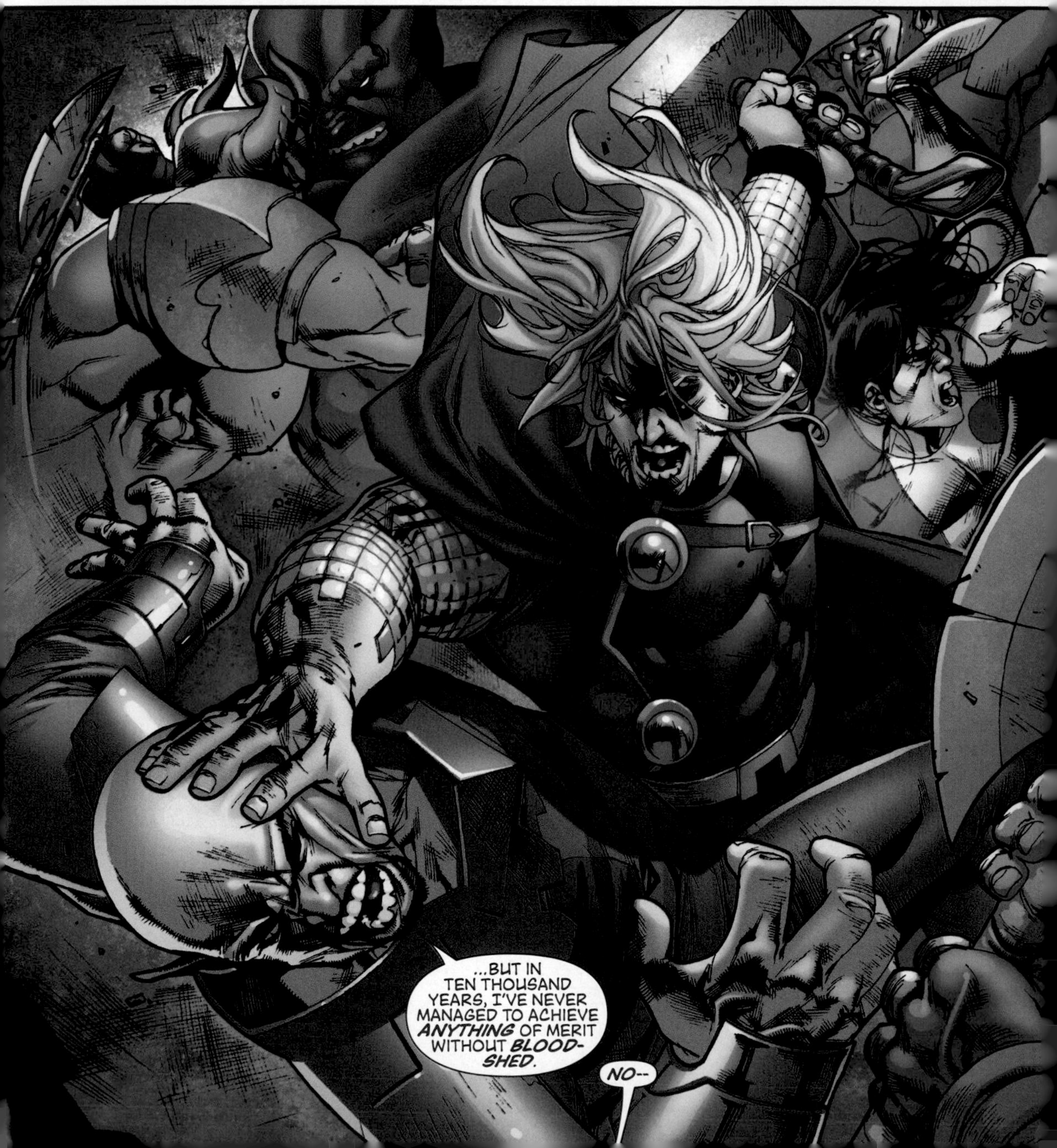

...BUT IN TEN THOUSAND YEARS, I'VE NEVER MANAGED TO ACHIEVE ANYTHING OF MERIT WITHOUT BLOOD-SHED.
NO--

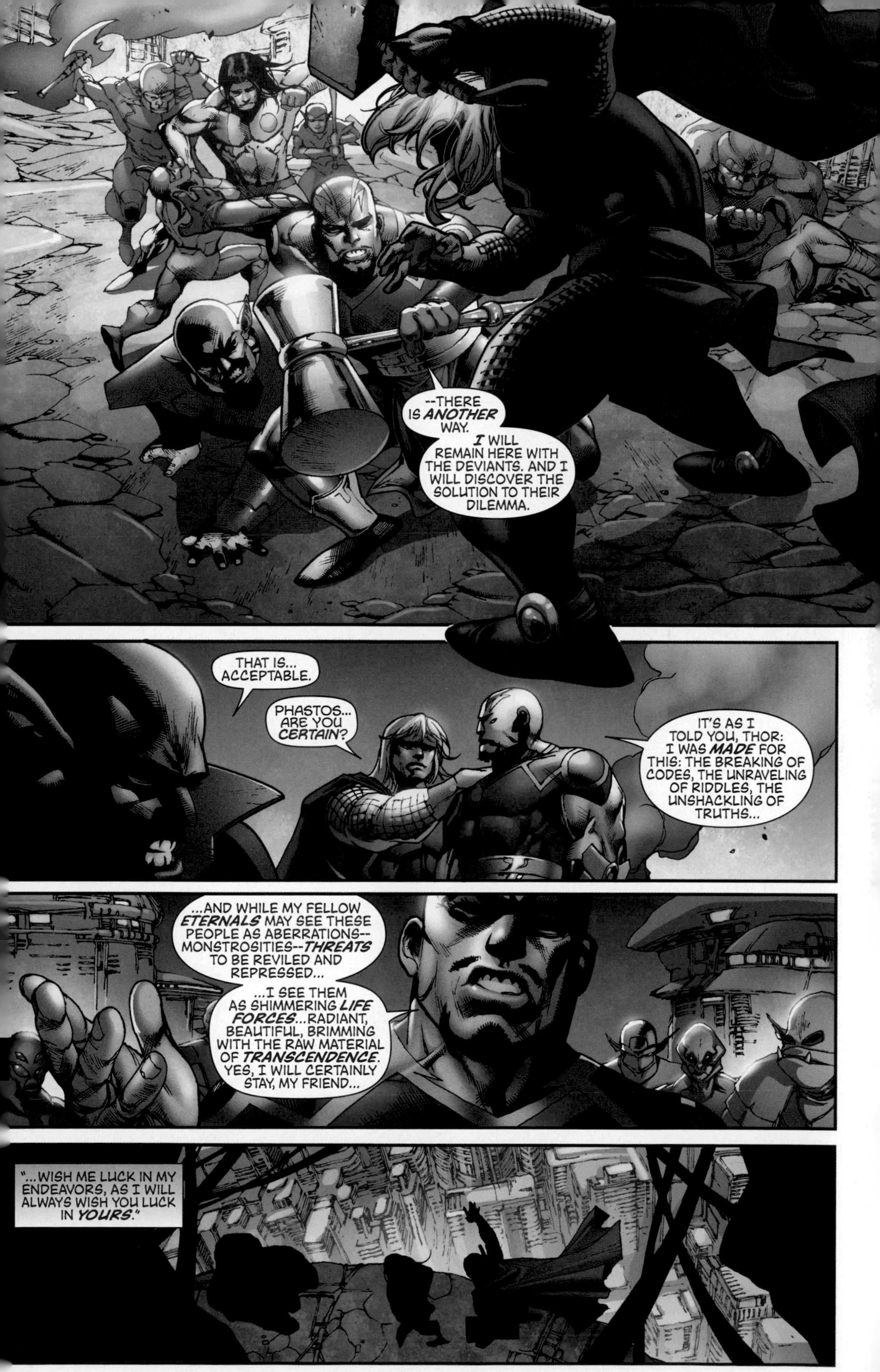

--THERE IS *ANOTHER* WAY. *I* WILL REMAIN HERE WITH THE DEVIANTS. AND I WILL DISCOVER THE SOLUTION TO THEIR DILEMMA.
THAT IS... ACCEPTABLE.
PHASTOS... ARE YOU *CERTAIN*?
IT'S AS I TOLD YOU, THOR: I WAS *MADE* FOR THIS: THE BREAKING OF CODES, THE UNRAVELING OF RIDDLES, THE UNSHACKLING OF TRUTHS...
...AND WHILE MY FELLOW *ETERNALS* MAY SEE THESE PEOPLE AS ABERRATIONS--MONSTROSITIES--*THREATS* TO BE REVILED AND REPRESSED...
...I SEE THEM AS SHIMMERING *LIFE FORCES*...RADIANT, BEAUTIFUL, BRIMMING WITH THE RAW MATERIAL OF *TRANSCENDENCE*. YES, I WILL CERTAINLY STAY, MY FRIEND...
"...WISH ME LUCK IN MY ENDEAVORS, AS I WILL ALWAYS WISH YOU LUCK IN *YOURS*."

...AND SUCH WAS HIS CHOICE, VIRAKO.

AND SUCH, TOO, THE REASON WE HAVE RETURNED TO OLYMPIA *WITHOUT* NOBLE PHASTOS.

I SEE...

...AND I AM NOT ASTONISHED. IT CERTAINLY *SOUNDS* LIKE SOMETHING HE WOULD DECIDE TO DO.

BUT I'LL MISS HIM. I AM NOW THE *SOLE* ETERNAL LEFT IN THIS CITY THAT ONCE *TEEMED* WITH THEM.

VIRAKO, YOU HAVE NOT YET DIVULGED TO ME...

...*WHERE* HAVE THE OTHER ETERNALS GONE?

THOR, YOU KNOW THAT SOME YEARS AGO, THE MAJORITY OF MY PEOPLE DEPARTED FOR THE *STARS*, LEAVING BEHIND ONLY A *HANDFUL* OF ETERNALS HERE ON EARTH...

...BUT WHEN THE ROGUE ETERNAL SPRITE *RE-WOVE* THE FABRIC OF REALITY, HE CREATED *HUMAN LIVES* FOR ALL ONE HUNDRED OF OUR RACE...

...WHICH *NEGATED* THEIR SOJOURN TO THE STARS, AND REINSTATED *ALL* ETERNALS BACK ON *THIS* WORLD.

WHEN OUR *TRUE* SELVES WERE RESTORED, THE SPACEFARING ETERNALS HAD TO DECIDE WHETHER TO *RETURN* TO THEIR FAR-FLUNG LIVES ACROSS THE UNIVERSE, OR ONCE MORE REMAIN HERE IN THE PLACE OF THEIR BIRTH.

THE DECISION WAS SO MOMENTOUS, THE ENTIRE POPULATION JOINED TOGETHER TO FORM A *UNI-MIND*--A VAST COLLECTIVE CONSCIOUSNESS WITH ITS OWN PHYSICAL FORM--TO ARRIVE AT THE ANSWER.

ONLY PHASTOS AND I ABSTAINED, AS WE HAVE NEVER FELT MUCH *AFFINITY* FOR OUR FELLOW ETERNALS...

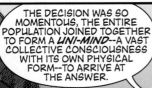

...THOUGH THEY'VE NOW BEEN GONE SO LONG ON THEIR MISSION OF DISCOVERY, I FIND MYSELF *REPENTING* THE WAY I'VE KEPT ALOOF FROM THEM...

...AND FROM MY SON *IKARIS* MOST OF ALL.

VIRAKO... THOR...LOOK *SKYWARD!*

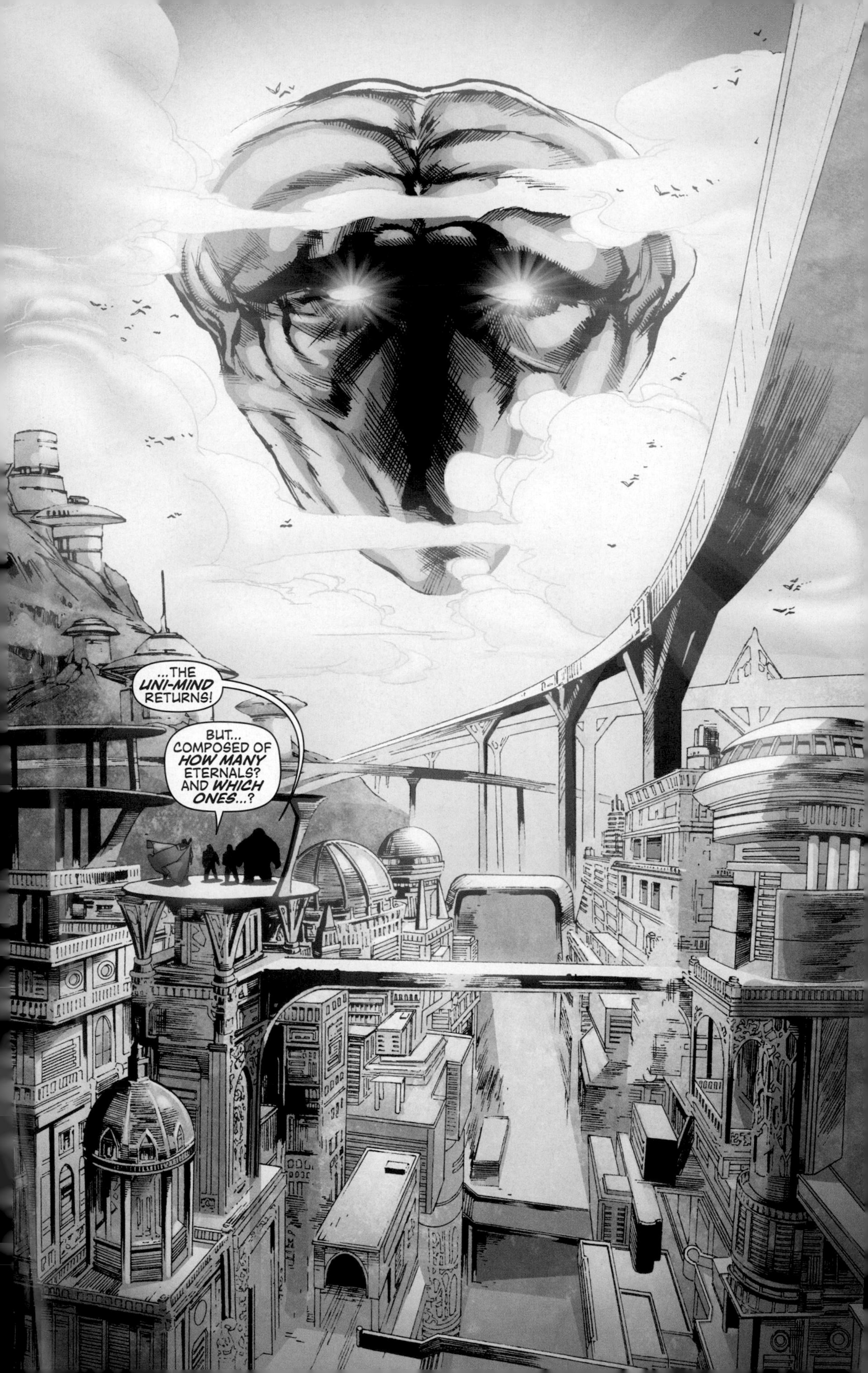
...THE *UNI-MIND* RETURNS!
BUT... COMPOSED OF *HOW MANY* ETERNALS? AND *WHICH ONES*...?

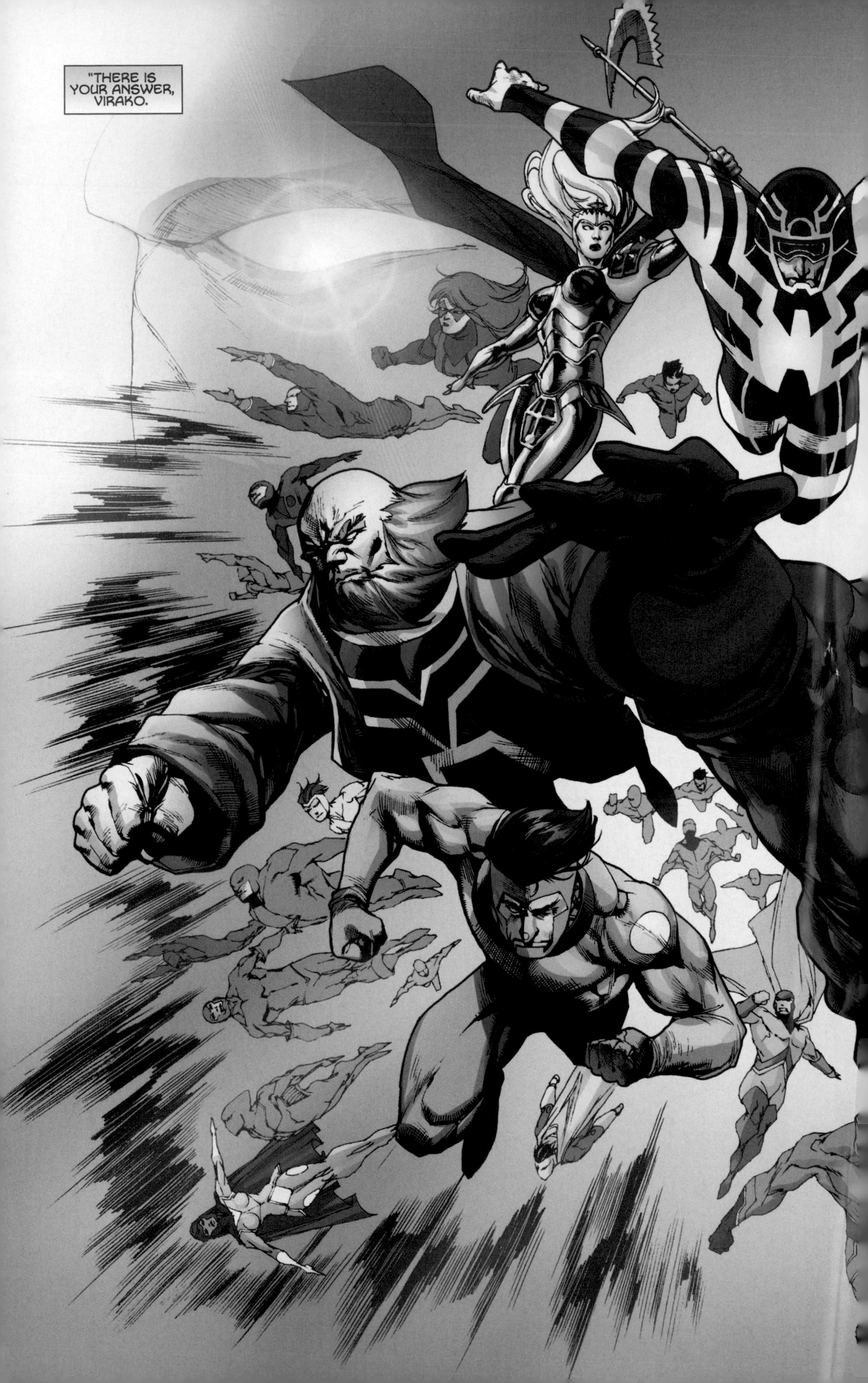
"THERE IS YOUR ANSWER, VIRAKO.

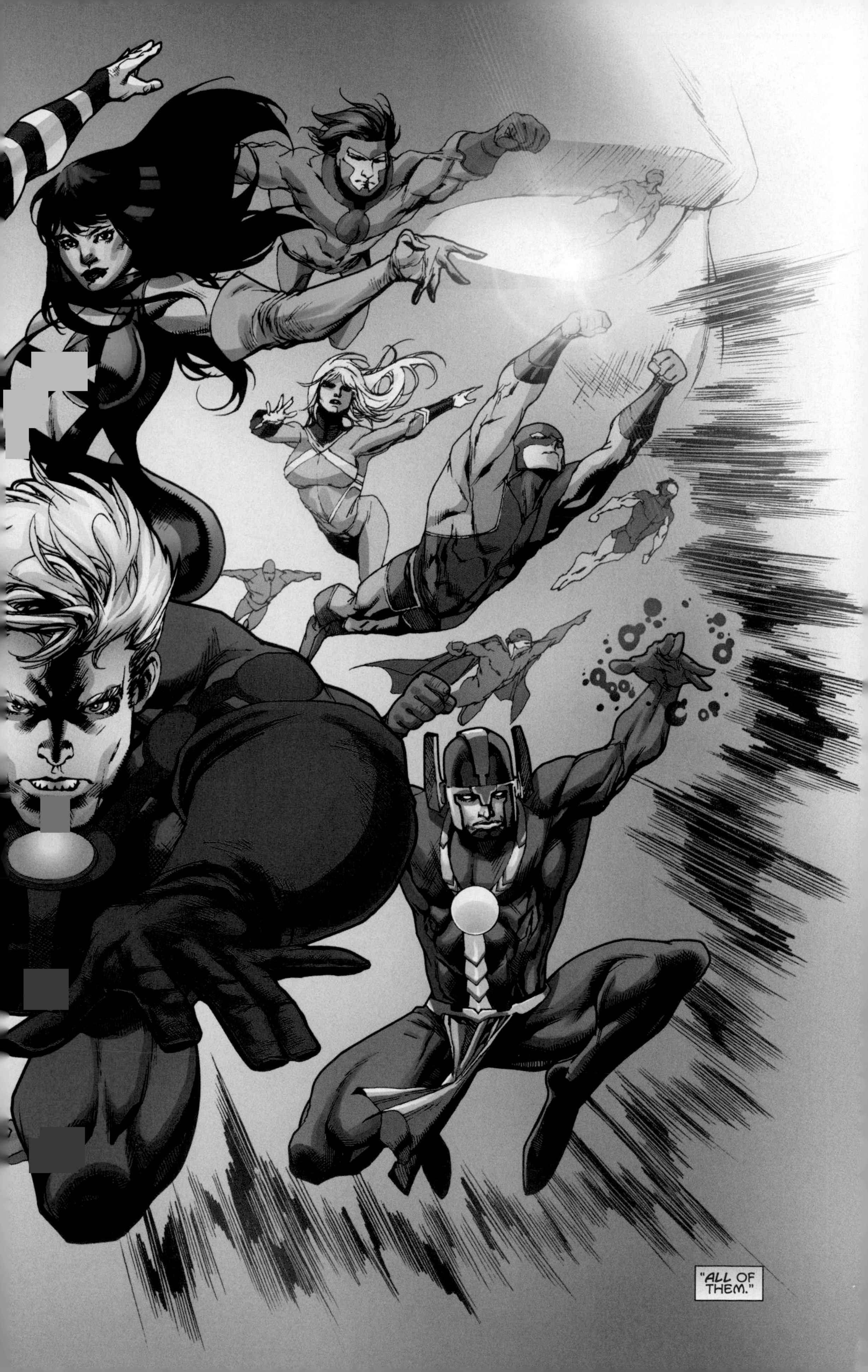
"ALL OF THEM."

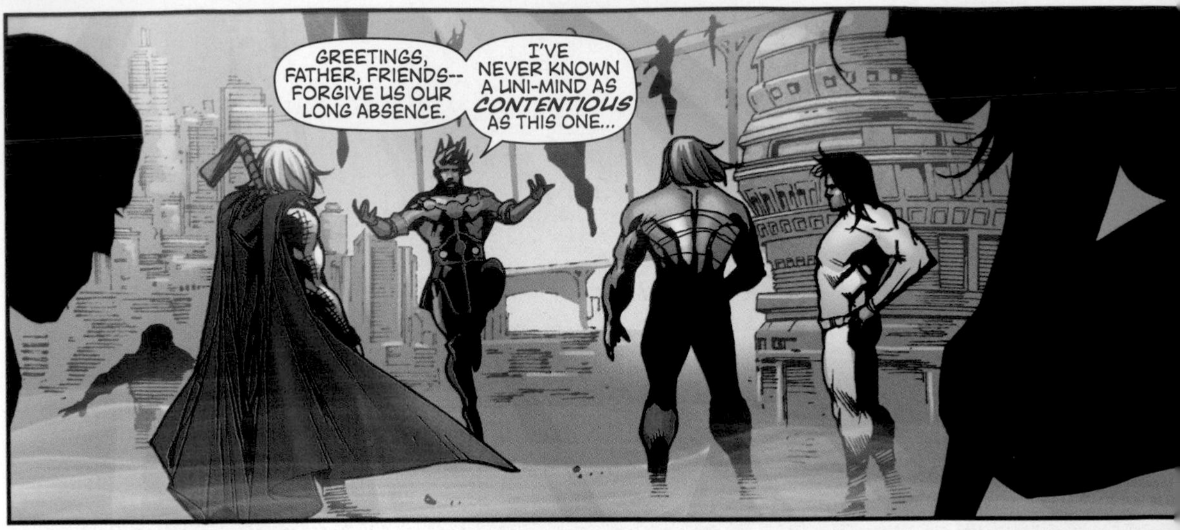
GREETINGS, FATHER, FRIENDS-- FORGIVE US OUR LONG ABSENCE.
I'VE NEVER KNOWN A UNI-MIND AS CONTENTIOUS AS THIS ONE...

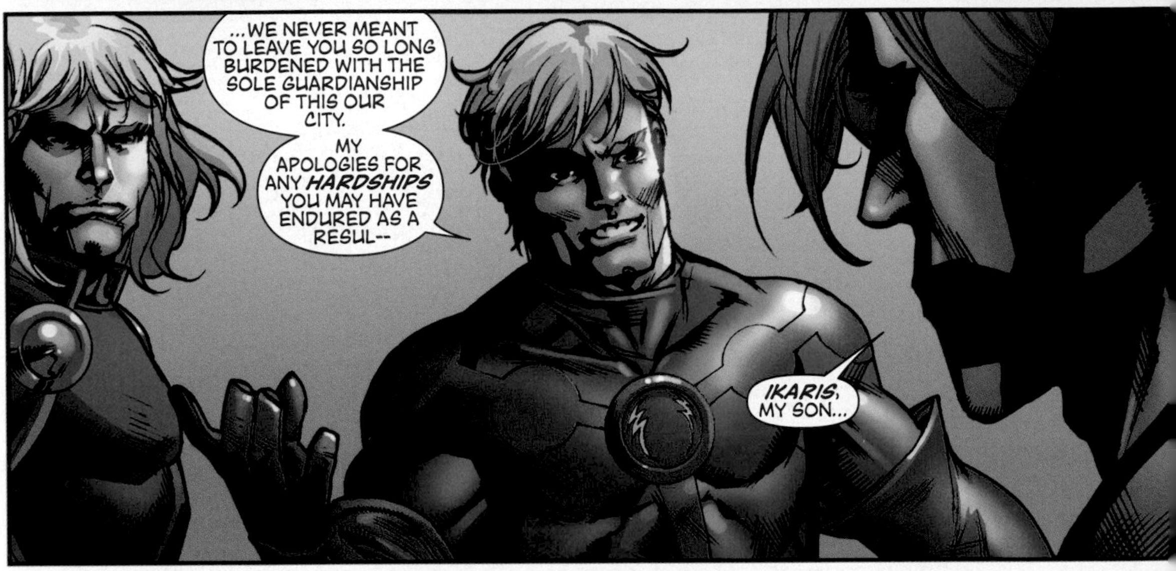
...WE NEVER MEANT TO LEAVE YOU SO LONG BURDENED WITH THE SOLE GUARDIANSHIP OF THIS OUR CITY.
MY APOLOGIES FOR ANY HARDSHIPS YOU MAY HAVE ENDURED AS A RESUL--
IKARIS, MY SON...

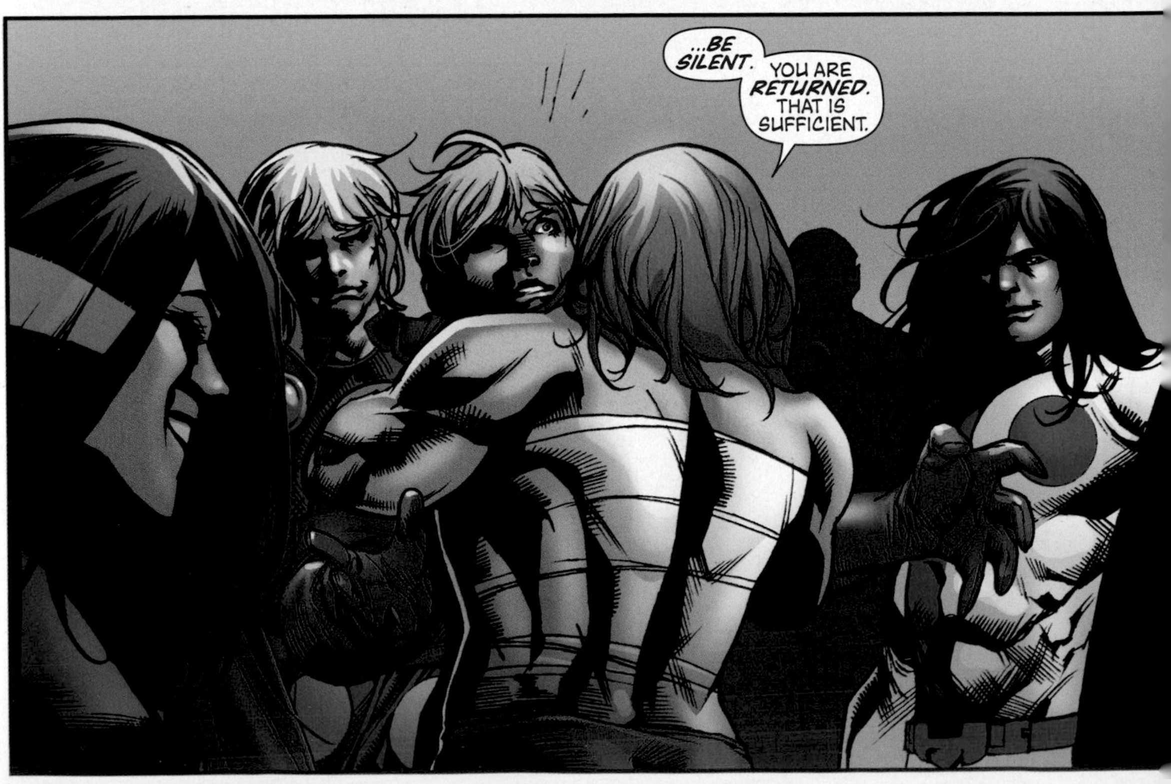
...BE SILENT.
YOU ARE RETURNED. THAT IS SUFFICIENT.

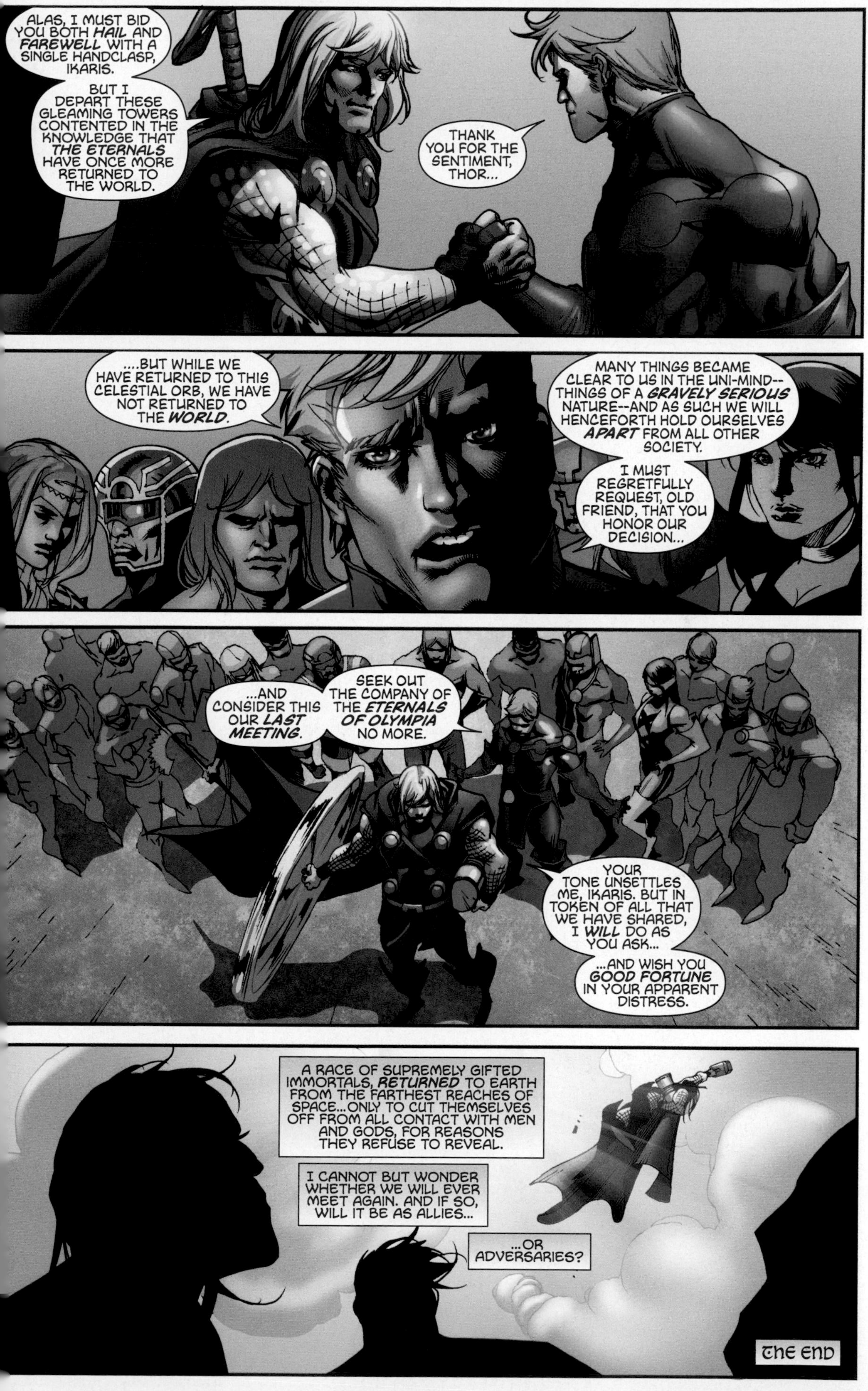
ALAS, I MUST BID YOU BOTH HAIL AND FAREWELL WITH A SINGLE HANDCLASP, IKARIS.
BUT I DEPART THESE GLEAMING TOWERS CONTENTED IN THE KNOWLEDGE THAT THE ETERNALS HAVE ONCE MORE RETURNED TO THE WORLD.
THANK YOU FOR THE SENTIMENT, THOR...
....BUT WHILE WE HAVE RETURNED TO THIS CELESTIAL ORB, WE HAVE NOT RETURNED TO THE WORLD.
MANY THINGS BECAME CLEAR TO US IN THE UNI-MIND--THINGS OF A GRAVELY SERIOUS NATURE--AND AS SUCH WE WILL HENCEFORTH HOLD OURSELVES APART FROM ALL OTHER SOCIETY.
I MUST REGRETFULLY REQUEST, OLD FRIEND, THAT YOU HONOR OUR DECISION...
SEEK OUT THE COMPANY OF THE ETERNALS OF OLYMPIA NO MORE.
...AND CONSIDER THIS OUR LAST MEETING.
YOUR TONE UNSETTLES ME, IKARIS. BUT IN TOKEN OF ALL THAT WE HAVE SHARED, I WILL DO AS YOU ASK...
...AND WISH YOU GOOD FORTUNE IN YOUR APPARENT DISTRESS.
A RACE OF SUPREMELY GIFTED IMMORTALS, RETURNED TO EARTH FROM THE FARTHEST REACHES OF SPACE...ONLY TO CUT THEMSELVES OFF FROM ALL CONTACT WITH MEN AND GODS, FOR REASONS THEY REFUSE TO REVEAL.
I CANNOT BUT WONDER WHETHER WE WILL EVER MEET AGAIN. AND IF SO, WILL IT BE AS ALLIES...
...OR ADVERSARIES?
THE END

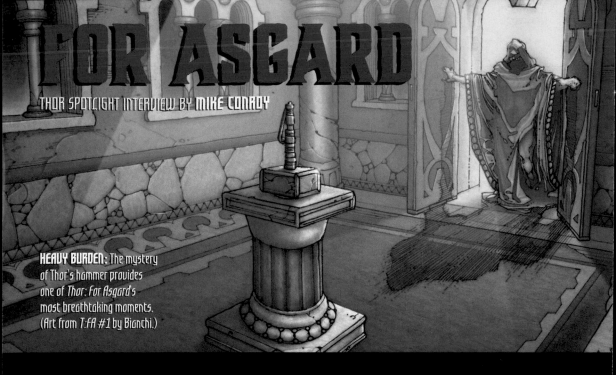

FOR ASGARD

THOR SPOTLIGHT INTERVIEW BY MIKE CONROY

HEAVY BURDEN: The mystery of Thor's hammer provides one of *Thor: For Asgard's* most breathtaking moments. (Art from *T:FA #1* by Bianchi.)

With his roots buried deep in Norse myth, Marvel's Thunder God is not your common super hero. There are many facets to his character, and Robert Rodi is only too happy to explore the road less travelled when it comes to chronicling his adventures.

As the *Astonishing Thor* writer put it, "I have to confess, I'm slightly more interested in Thor as a Norse god than as a super hero. If I had to choose between Thor the Asgardian and Thor the Avenger, it's door number one, thanks. And there aren't a lot of projects that spotlight that side of him, so I'm happy to help make up the balance. Fortunately, in this current market, there seems to be room for all kinds of different portrayals of the big guy, so we can all be happy."

Rodi started making up the balance back in 2004 when he wrote a Loki four-parter. He has, however, had an abiding fondness for ancient myths and legends. "As a kid, I had a keen interest of all world mythologies, though I learned about them mainly through movies and comics and TV. I delved into the literary sources, and other interpretations like Wagner's Ring cycle, much later."

Stan Lee and Jack Kirby introduced the Thunder God into the nascent Marvel Universe in 1962's *Journey into Mystery #83*. Comparing their interpretation with the Norse original, Rodi — who also wrote *Thor: For Asgard*, a 2009 six-parter — said, "Marvel's version is the Viking Thor as refracted through Stan and Jack's modern, urban point of view. You

look at Kirby's Asgard; it's got a kind of burnished, sci-fi look that pulls it into the post-industrial age. And Stan added the Donald Blake identity, taming the young thunder god's arrogance by saddling him with a humble human alter-ego; again, a very modern concept — that a god could actually benefit from experiencing common humanity."

It's often said that super heroes are the 20th century's version of the ancient myths and legends. It's not a view to which the writer entirely subscribes. "I'm not sure the comparison is an apt one. For the ancients, the gods were remote and virtually unknowable, and the myths about them served social and political functions. They weren't entertainment. Super heroes, by comparison, are points of identification for readers. We're supposed to get into their skin, feel what it's like to be them. It's an escape, a joyride. Two thousand years ago, you might sacrifice a goat to Apollo and hope he was in a good mood that day — but with Spider-Man, you're up there with him, swinging around town, the wind whistling in your ears."

Rodi, who admits to having been a Thor fan "forever," finds much that attracts him to the Thunder God's mythos. "I love the bigness, the sprawl, the epic scale of Asgard and its denizens. I love the idea that these charact are immortal, but not immutab The change. They're always changing Stan and Jack's Asg are very different than ever though I'm building on what the did — just as they built on what

> "...FOR THE ANCIENTS, THE GODS WERE REMOTE AND VIRTUALLY UNKNOWABLE, AND THE MYTHS ABOUT THEM SERVED SOCIAL AND POLITICAL FUNCTIONS. THEY WEREN'T ENTERTAINMENT."
> — *ASTONISHING THOR* WRITER **ROBERT RODI**

time before them. It's a wonderful wheel of story that just keeps turning and turning, on into infinity."

Moving on to discuss Asgard's major citizens, Rodi said, "Thor's the big brother, the one everybody looks up to. He's been around for millennia, he's seen and done everything, and he knows exactly who he is and what needs to be done. The only times he suffers uncertainty or self-doubt are when he's forced into a different role — as in *Thor: For Asgard*, where he's made to serve as regent for Odin, and he makes the mistake of trying to be Odin, which so undermines him he can't even lift Mjolnir anymore. But of course he gets his mojo back at the end, because he always does. He's Thor."

As for Thor's stepbrother, the Trickster God, the writer revealed his thoughts when he first discussed the Loki miniseries with his editor. "When Axel Alonso offered me the series, it was with the caveat that it had to be something special — something no one's done before. My immediate thought was, 'All right, then, after all these years, let's give Loki what he wants.' Instead of once again showing him trying to crush Asgard, let's start with that job already done: He's won, he's the victor, he's the new lord of the place. Odin, Thor, Balder, everyone else is in chains. It's Loki's town — which is where it all starts to unravel for him, because he doesn't really want to be king. He doesn't want to sit on a throne all day and hear petitions for lumber rights and sign trade agreements with Karnilla or whatever — which forces him to face what he really did want all those years, which is something else entirely. The idea was to turn Loki into a villain of almost Shakespearean complexity, like Macbeth or Richard III — someone you loathe. But at the same time, you're saying 'Man, that poor, sad bugger.'"

Explaining his Loki was all about defining the Trickster God's character, he continued, "He starts out as the God of Mischief, then graduates to being the God of Evil — but who is

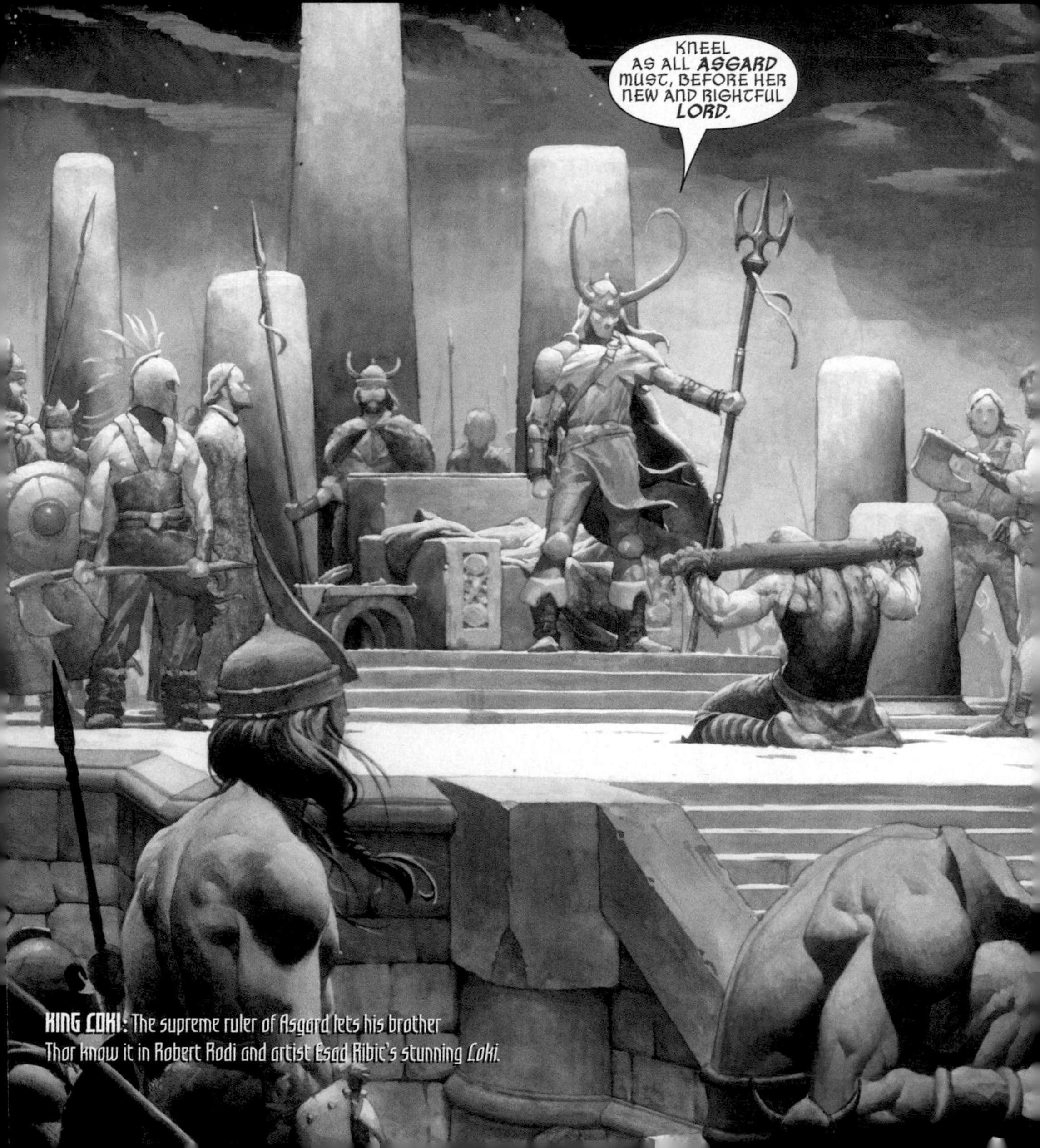
KNEEL AS ALL ASGARD MUST, BEFORE HER NEW AND RIGHTFUL LORD.

KING LOKI: The supreme ruler of Asgard lets his brother Thor know it in Robert Rodi and artist Esad Ribic's stunning *Loki*.

BIG EGO: Thor faces Ego, the Living Planet, in this "astonishing" art spread by artist Mike Choi in Rodi's *Astonishing Thor #1*.

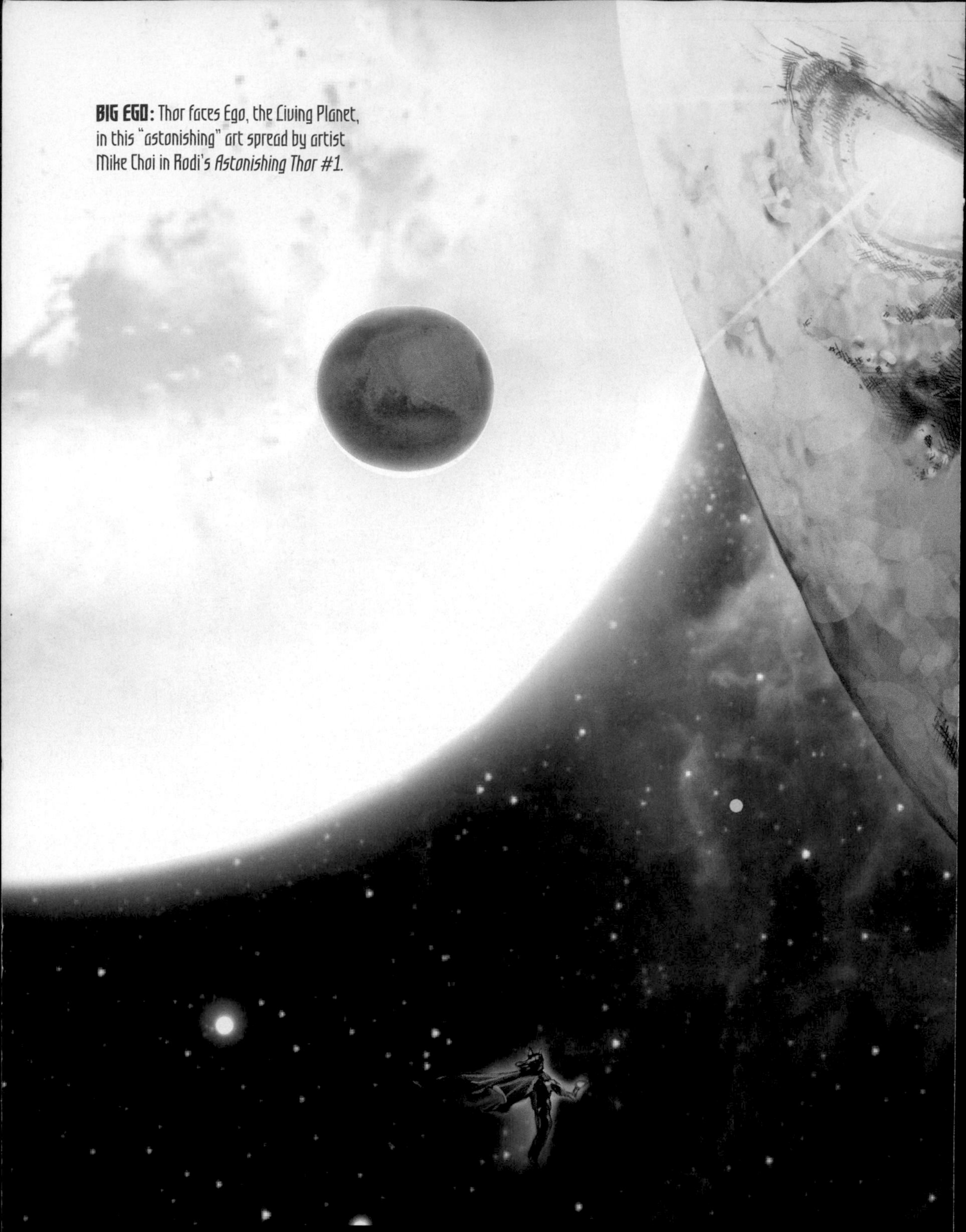

he really? What's made him the way he is, and what keeps him going? Obviously, being taken from his real family by the man who killed his father and brought up as a lesser son in that man's court — that's got a lot to do with it.

"That's the other half of the equation," Rodi said, referring to the stepbrothers' interaction. "I wanted to make the Thor/Loki relationship as credible as possible, so Loki's realization of how he really feels about Thor is at the climax of my Loki. Obviously, I don't want to be too specific about it, 'cause I'd prefer people go out and buy the darned book. But I'd like to think, when they read it, they'll think, 'Huh. That makes sense.'"

Then, there's Odin.

"He's the All-Father," Rodi said. "That about says it. He's the supreme symbol of divine authority, the court of final appeal. I gotta say, there have been occasional attempts to take Odin out of the series by one means or another, and it really never works without him. I do it in For Asgard, but with intent. Odin is off on a quest, but paradoxically that makes him more

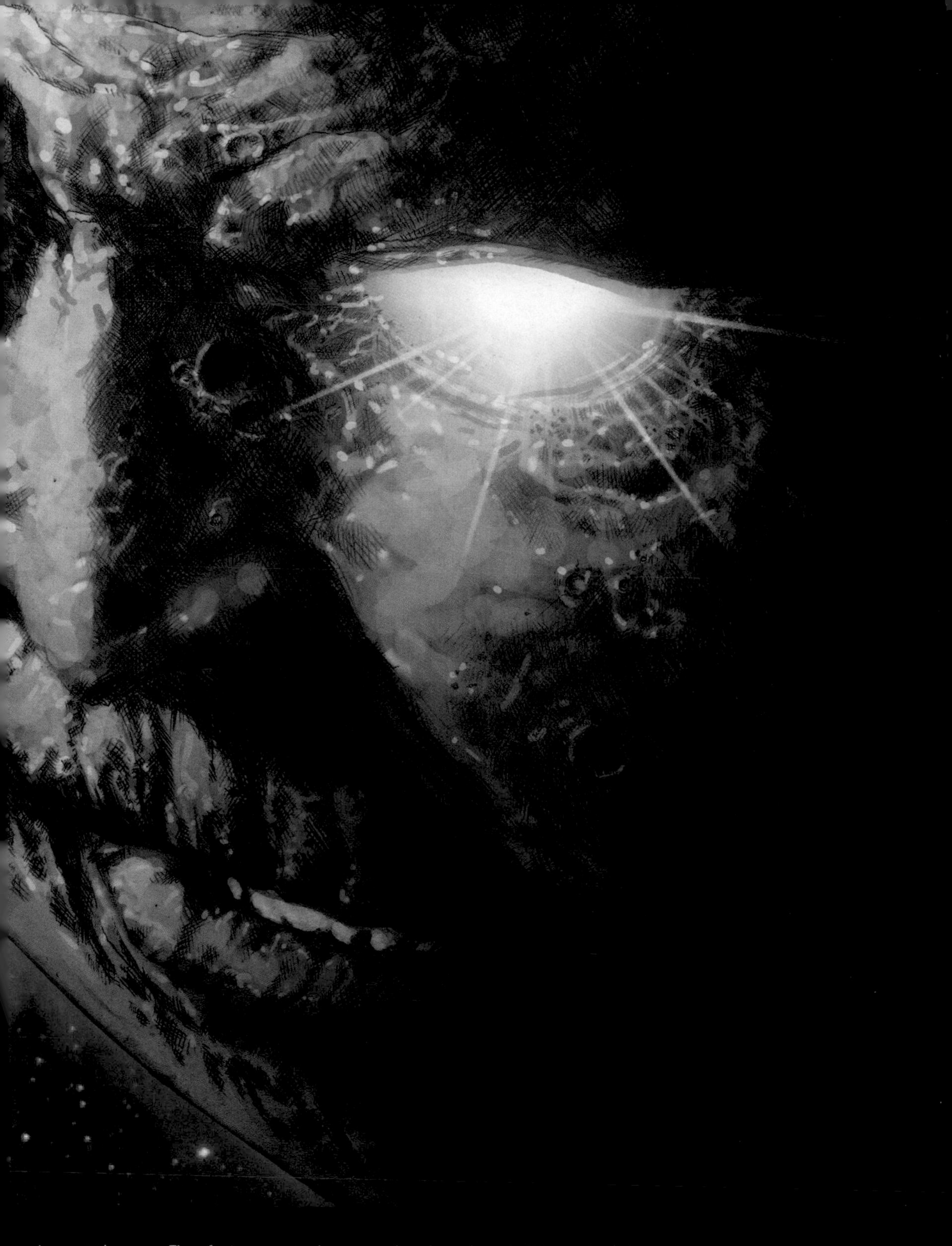

omnipresent than ever: Thor, for instance, is almost smothered by the weight of his absence."

Addressing Odin's relationship with his sons, Rodi said, "That's up to each individual writer. My own idea, floated in Loki, is that he took the infant Loki under his wing with the specific aim of turning him evil, because that would galvanize Thor's good. Uncle Ben, he's not. But we can't judge him by the standards of humanity. He's . . . well, he's Odin."

Across just three series, Rodi has added much insight to the legend of Thor — but he's not finished yet. He has several ideas in the pipeline; it won't be long until he's further expanding the characters of the Thunder God and his associates, and upon the world of Asgard.

Rodi's first two forays into Asgard, *Thor & Loki: Blood Brothers HC* and *Thor: For Asgard HC*, are already available from book retailers. And *Astonishing Thor*, his series with artist Mike Choi, is just getting started! Check with your comics retailer for the first fantastic issues! •

LOKI

PROPOSAL FOR A 4-ISSUE MINI-SERIES

Written by **Robert Rodi** • Painted by **Esad Ribić**

LOKI will take a long, hard look at one of Marvel's most complex villains. For two decades readers have heard Thor's side of the story. Now it's time to hear Loki's.

This four-issue miniseries will prove that there are always two sides to every story. Just as John Gardner's landmark novella *Grendel* deconstructed the Beowulf myth, allowing readers to see the legend from the monster's point of view, LOKI will reveal the dark nooks and crannies of Asgardian legend from the perspective of Odin's least favorite son. In this story Loki's insatiable lust for power, his conflicted sentiments toward Sif, his antipathy toward Balder, and the deep-seated feelings of longing and resentment toward his older brother, Thor, and uncaring father, Odin, will take on new meaning.

STORY

We open with LOKI in charge of Asgard. He's somehow managed to topple the All-Father ODIN from power, has had the whole court — BALDER, SIF, WARRIORS THREE — imprisoned, and he's parading his older brother THOR through the streets in triumph. Most of Asgard is, of course, horrified by the sight of Thor's humiliation, but that only delights Loki all the more. He really rubs their noses in it.

The parade over, Thor is returned to prison — or better yet, put on public display. Loki returns to his quarters, where he finds HELA, GODDESS OF DEATH, waiting for him.

He asks what she wants.

Thor, she tells him. It's no secret that she's long desired the Thunder God's soul, but never been able to win it on her own. Now that Loki has defeated him, she's come to claim it.

Loki protests; he has no intention of killing Thor. Hela scoffs; he must kill Thor. After all, if he doesn't, Thor will soon escape and take Asgard back, just as he's defeated Loki time and time again.

Loki is shocked by this. He's never considered killing Thor. All he's ever wanted was Thor's humiliation. But Hela has a point. Loki was the Trickster God; now that he's played his ultimate trick, he must become something else — as Lord of Asgard, he must change. Alter. And this transformation must begin with Thor's execution.

If he can bring himself to do it.

Loki goes off by himself, and tries to convince himself that Thor deserves to die. He recalls his boyhood, when he was brought into the Asgardian royal family — as Loki sees it, to function as a counterpoint to Thor's perfection. He's convinced that all Odin ever wanted from him was that he make Thor look good in comparison. And Thor, too, gloried in his superiority, taking every opportunity to show Loki up, make him look bad.

Even so, Loki felt no rancor at this point in his life — his stepbrother WAS perfect: beautiful, powerful, golden. He adored him. And if Thor repaid that adoration with little slights and humiliations, it was a price Loki was only too willing to pay for his company.

But then, while they were still youths, along came SIF, BALDER and the rest — and Loki was able to witness his adored brother in the company of others whom he openly loved.

And Loki realized how much he was disdained. His love turned to anger, and his anger to hatred. He took his revenge on Sif, cutting her hair — he tried to kill Balder. But his real fury was reserved for Thor, who had shown him he was not loved. So he began a long life devoted to revenge on Thor and all whom the Thunder God cared for.

While Loki is recalling all of this, we take an occasional look in on Thor, who's struggling to escape from his confinement. (Don't know exactly how Loki's holding him; we'll work that out later.)

Loki still hasn't talked himself into killing Thor. To embolden himself, he goes to see Odin, Sif and Balder, one after the other, and tells them he's going to execute the Thunder God. Each argues with Loki, and we see how Loki's version of events differs from theirs. We also begin to realize that Loki is right — these noble Asgardians have from the start looked down their noses at him, disdained him, scorned him. It was they — and Thor especially — who created the evil in him. Realizing this, Loki's pride and anger grow strong again; unwittingly, they convince him he would be right to kill his brother.

But as Loki leaves his prisoners, his will weakens again. The idea of a world without Thor is bleak to him. What would he live for? He has no real desire to rule Asgard. The hard work of sovereignty doesn't appeal to him. He's the Trickster God ... and gods can't simply change. They're elemental principles; cosmic constants.

When he's again confronted by Hela, she urges him to carry out the execution, and he refuses.

Hela taunts him: "You've defeated your enemy, you've shackled him, you've humiliated him — now you MUST kill him! If not, what would you do?"

Loki thinks for a moment, then sadly says, "I would do it all over again."

He's made up his mind: he's going to free Thor. As he says this, Hela nods her head and says, "So it shall be. There is, I fear, only one whom the great Trickster cannot trick ... himself." As she says this, she changes into Loki.

For a moment, there are two Lokis staring at each other across the panel. Then, the original one disappears, leaving only the Loki-Who-Was-Hela.

We realize that Hela was never there: the whole You-Must-Kill-Thor scenario was shape-shifter Loki's way of trying to trick himself into murdering his brother. (How he appears in two places at once remains a mystery; I'd like to inject a little of that old sense of wonder into the book. These are gods, after all.)

Having failed to trick himself, he goes off to free Thor.

As he goes, he wonders whether this act of mercy will win for him one moment of gratitude from Thor. He realizes that Thor's good opinion — his friendship, his love — is that which he has always desired, and, starved of them, have made him what he is today. He loathes Thor for his treatment of him, but he loathes himself even more for still loving his tormentor.

But he's delayed too long.

Arriving at Thor's cell, he finds that Thor has escaped, and is barreling right for Loki.

Seeing this, Loki is horrified — he protests; he was going to free Thor! Really he was! Honest!

But Thor has a major mad on; he beats the crap out of Loki.

We end with Thor standing over the defeated Loki. He says something along the lines of, Well, what have you got to say for yourself, my brother?

Loki looks up at him, at Thor, at all that beauty and perfection, those golden shoulders, and says, I would do it again ... I would do it all again ... I WILL do it all again.

THE END?

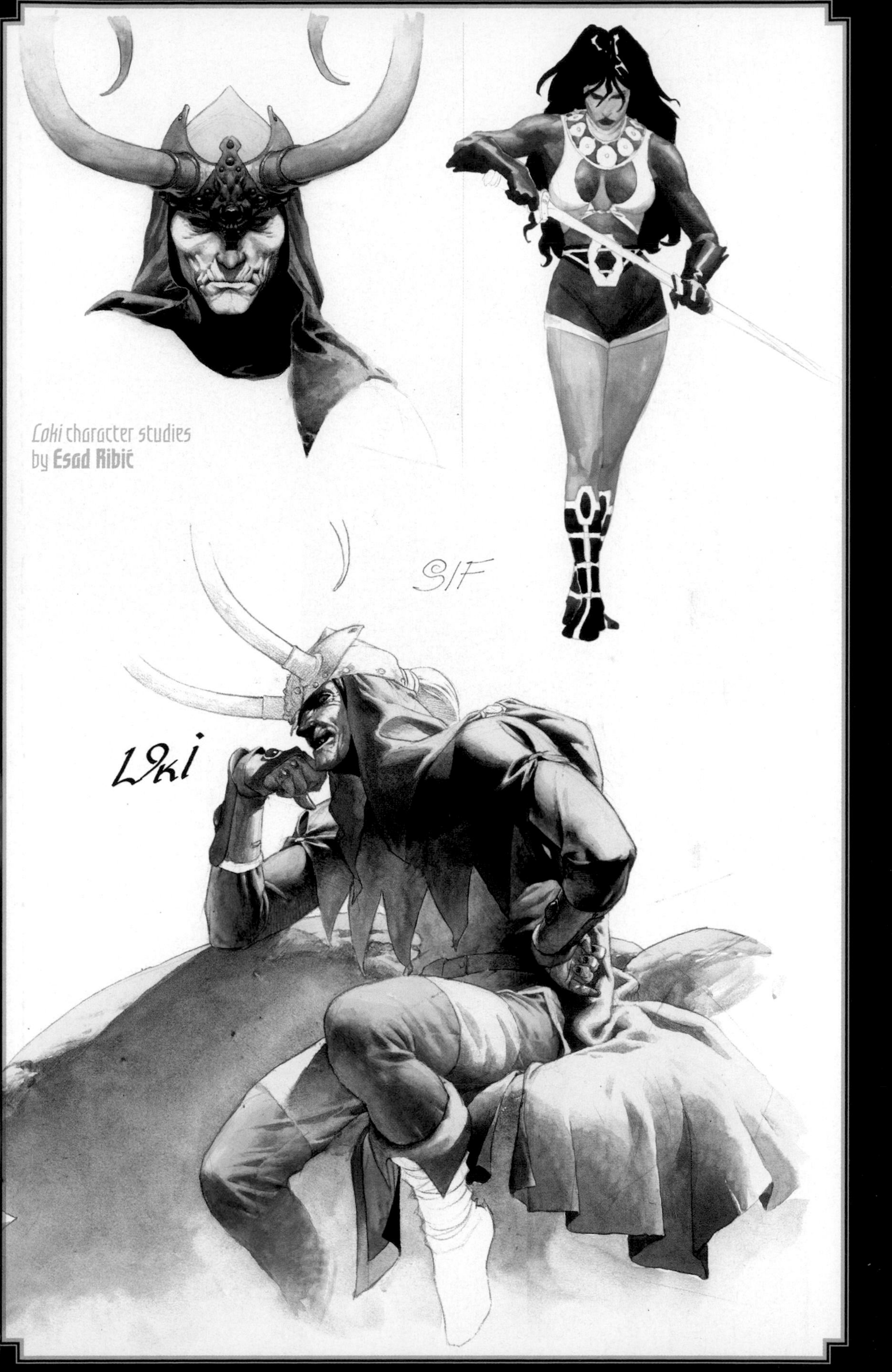
SIF
Loki

Loki character studies
by **Esad Ribić**

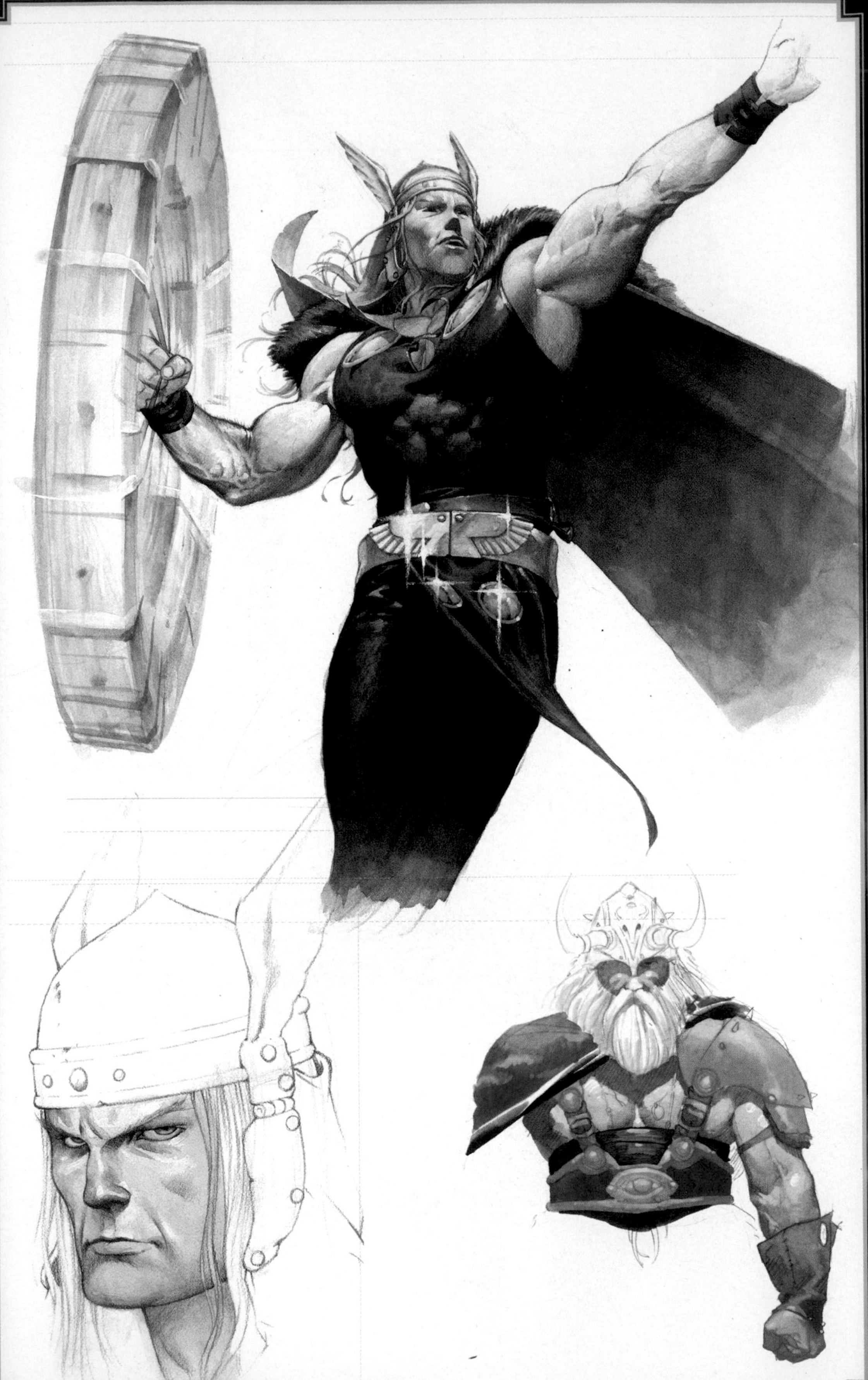

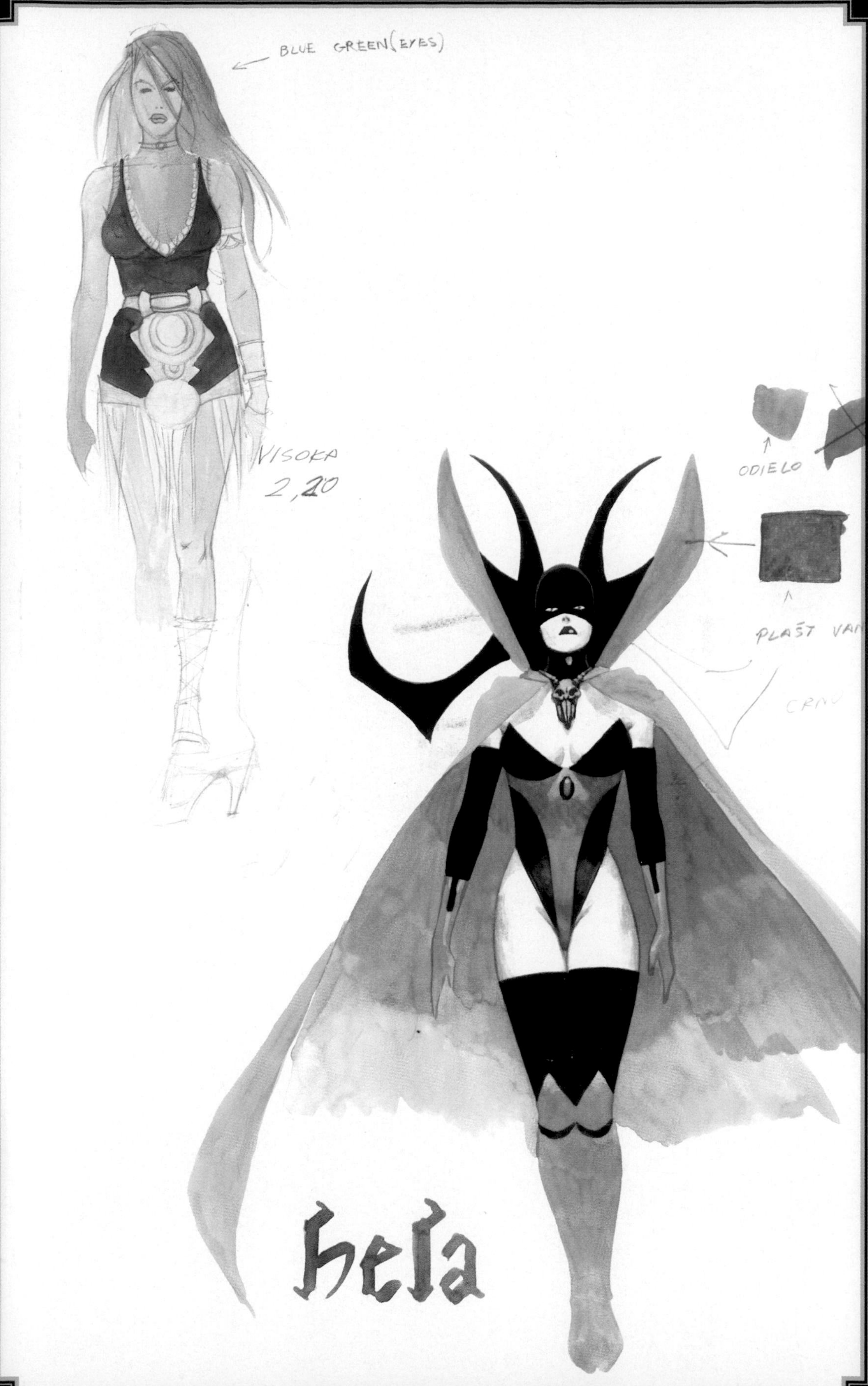
BLUE GREEN (EYES)
VISOKA
2,20
ODIELO
Hela

Loki unused cover sketches by **Esad Ribić**

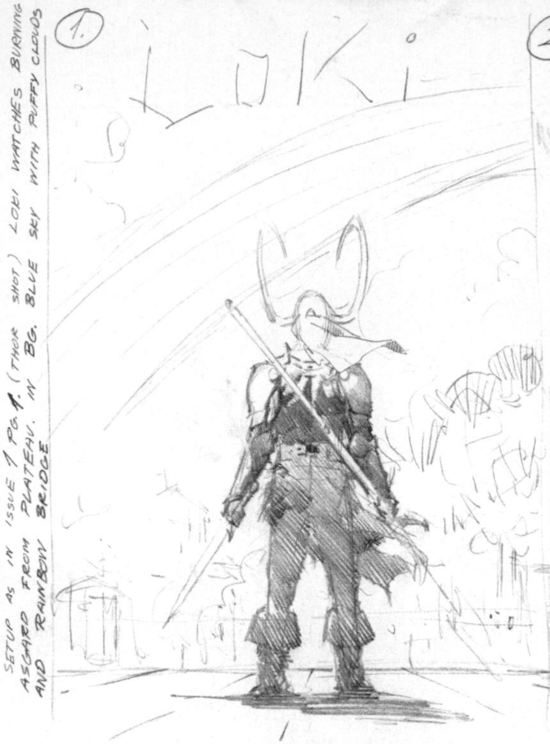
1.
SETUP AS IN ISSUE 1 PG. 1. (THOR SHOT) LOKI WATCHES BURNING
ASGARD FROM PLATEAU. IN BG. BLUE SKY WITH PUFFY CLOUDS
AND RAINBOW BRIDGE
LOKI

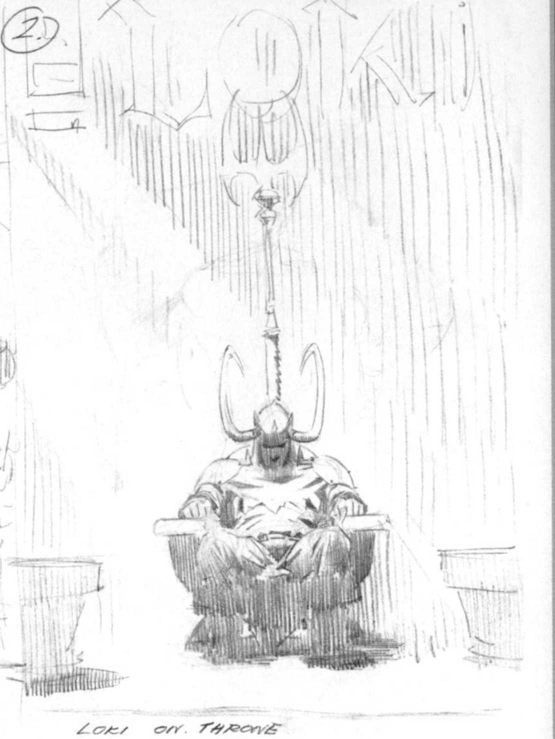
2.
LOKI
LOKI ON. THRONE

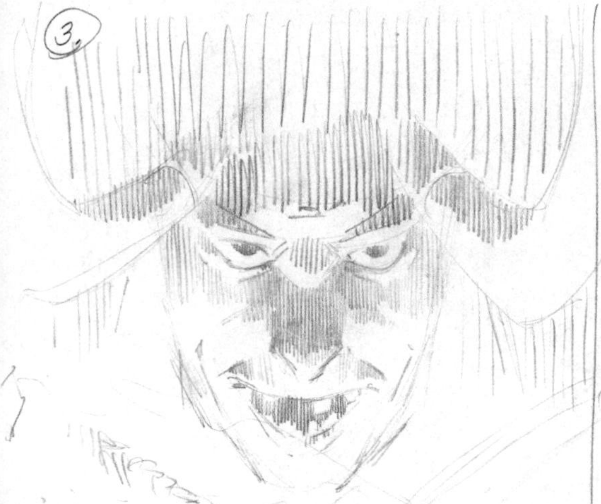
3.

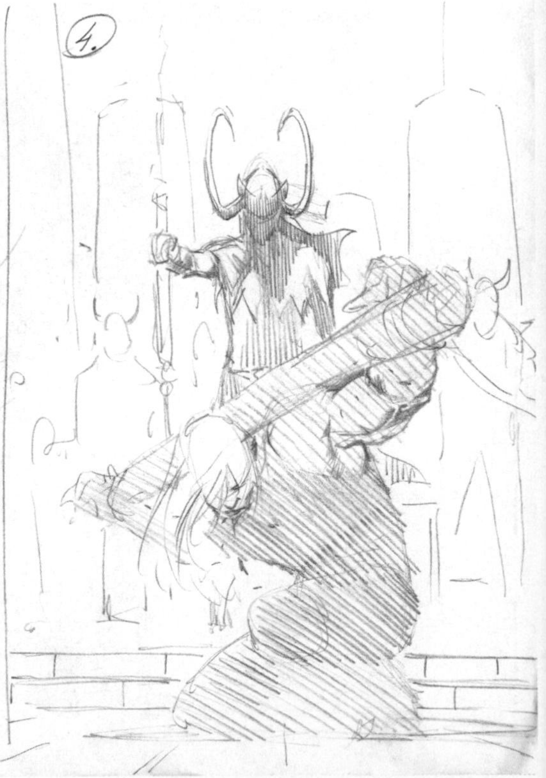
4.

Loki unused cover sketches by **Esad Ribic**

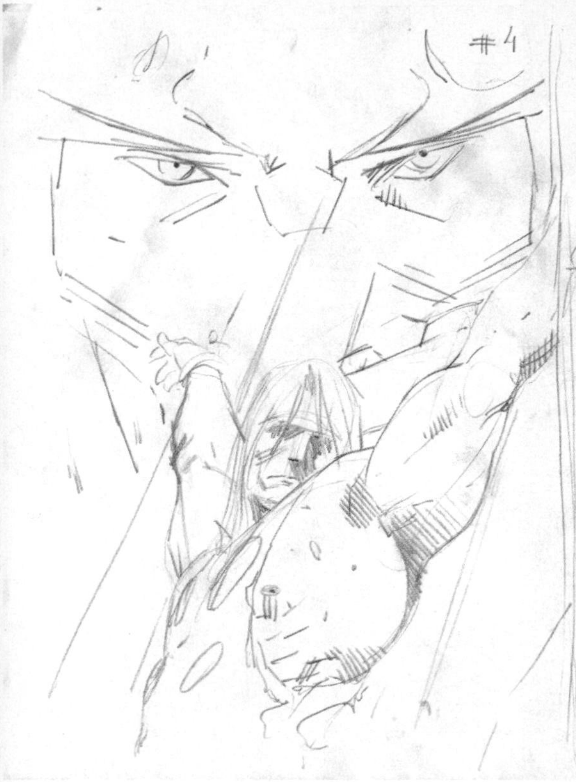
#4

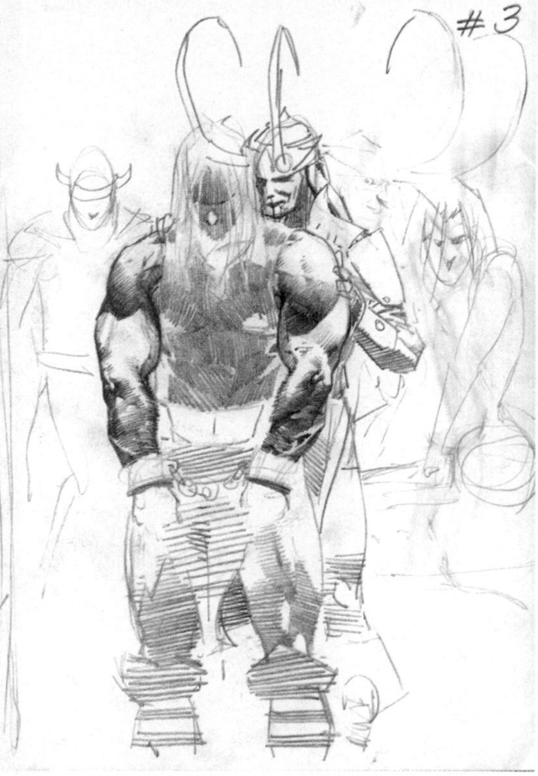
#3

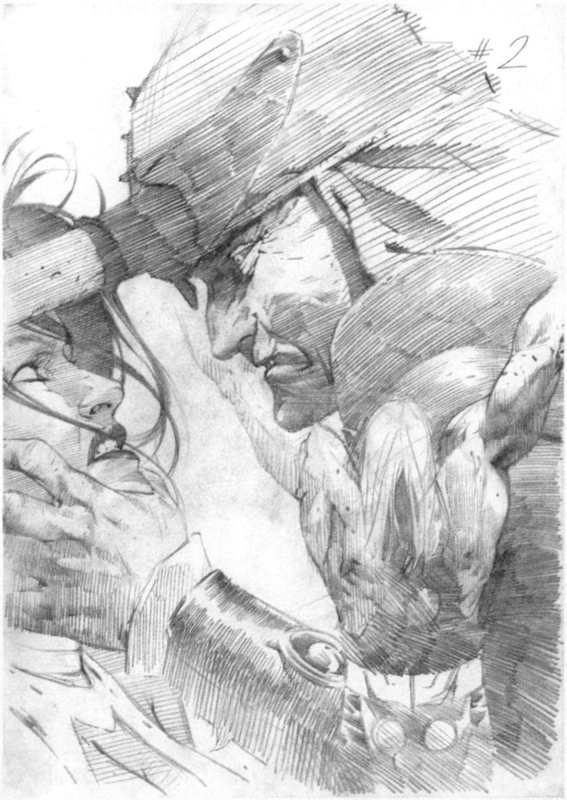
#2

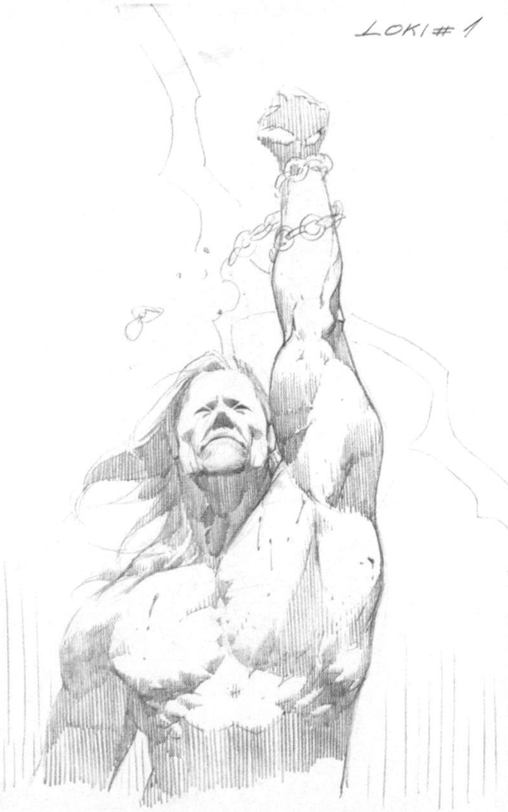
LOKI #1

Loki unused cover sketch by **Esad Ribić**

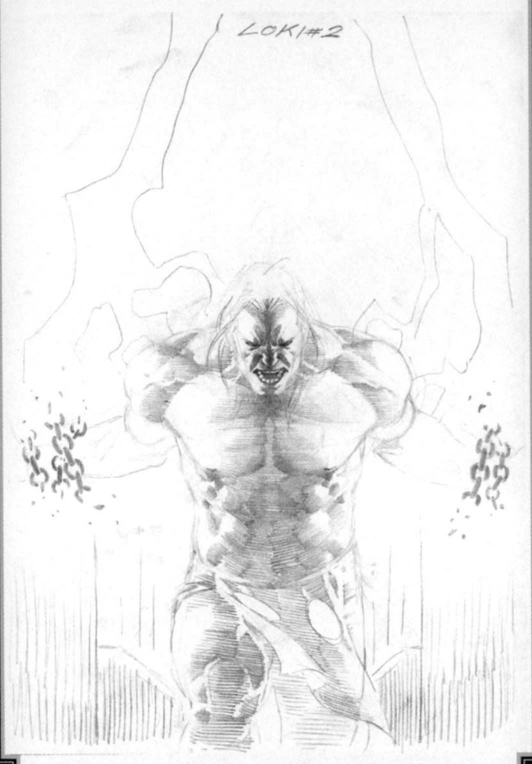
LOKI#2

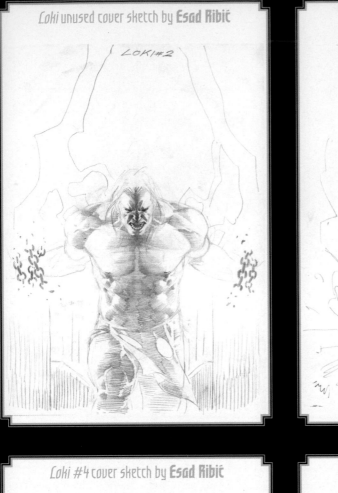

Loki #3 cover sketch by **Esad Ribić**

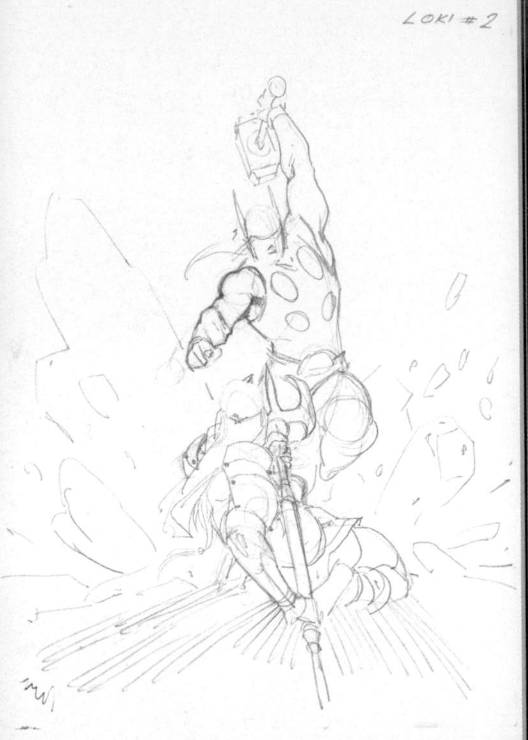
LOKI #2

Loki #4 cover sketch by **Esad Ribić**

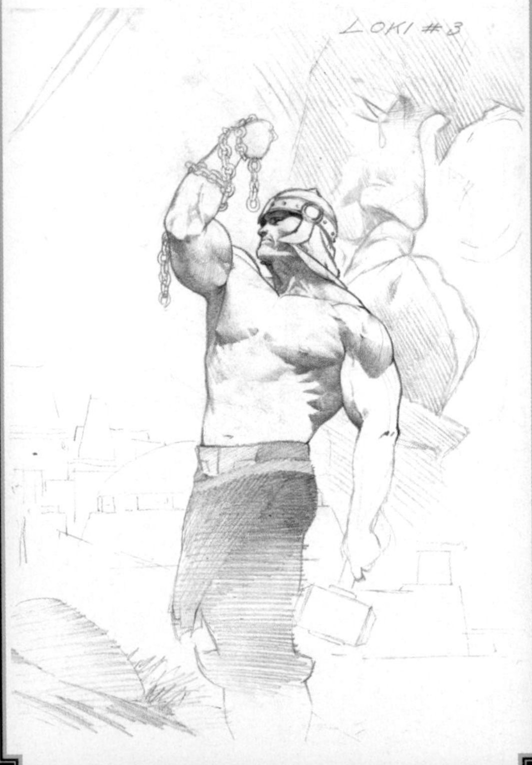
LOKI #3

Thor sketch by **Esad Ribić**

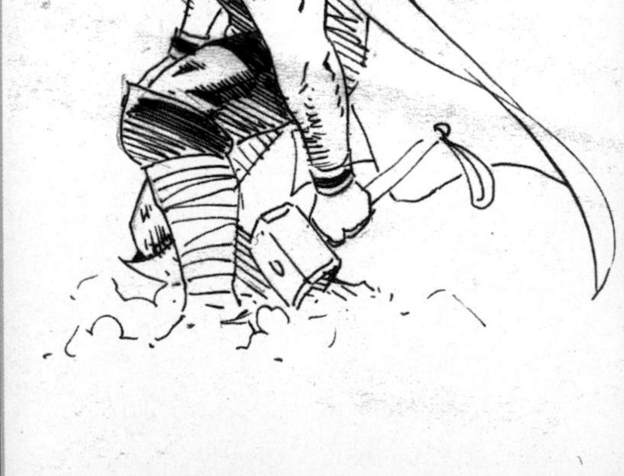

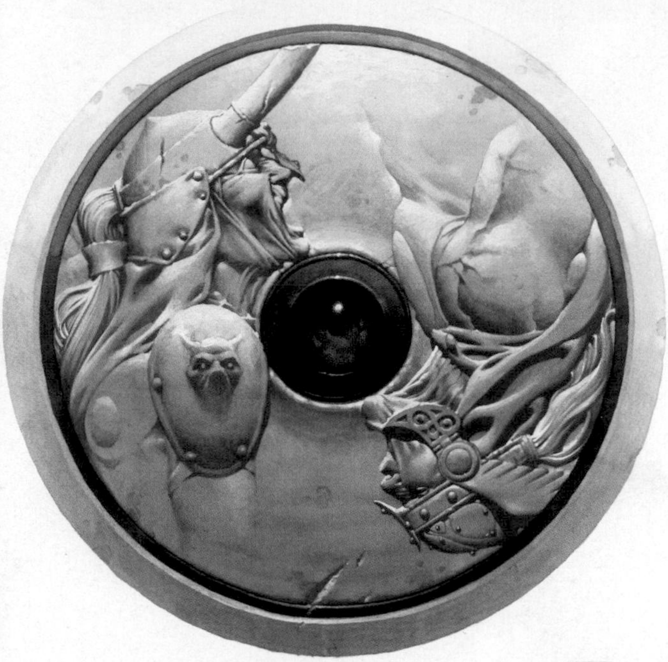

Loki shield study
by **Esad Ribić**

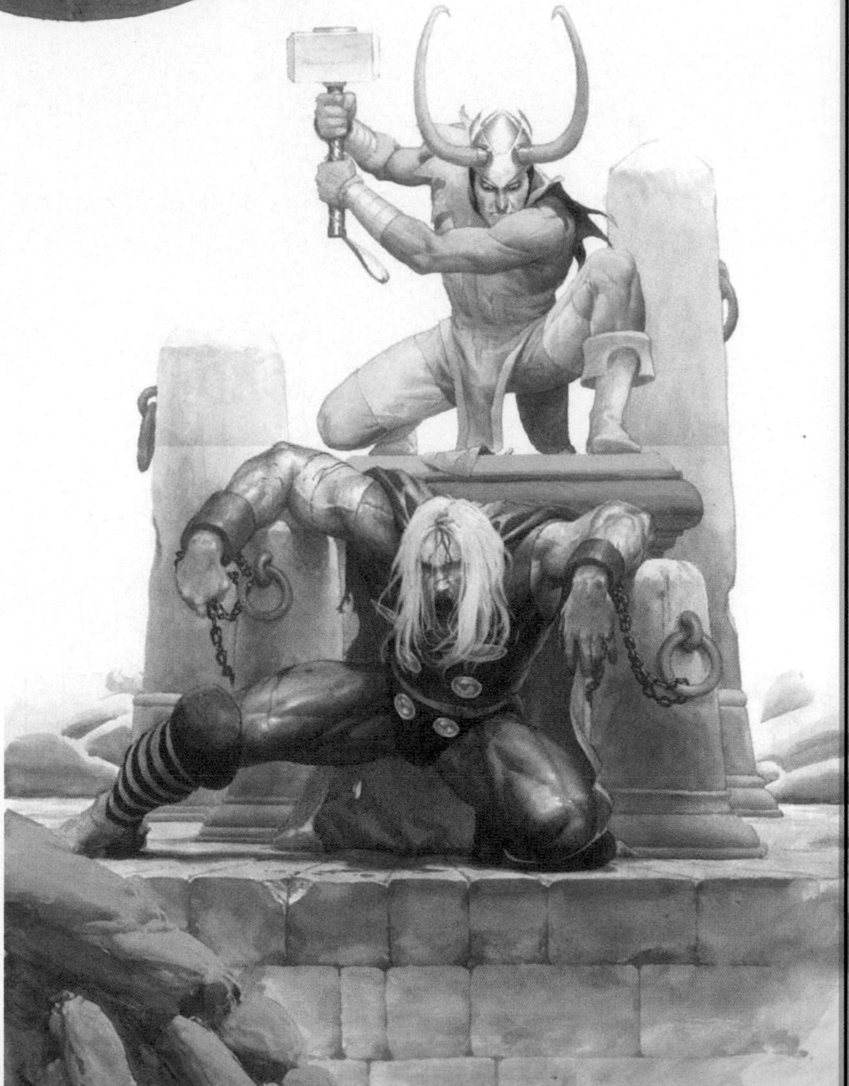

Painting for
initial *Loki* pitch
by **Esad Ribić**

Thor & Loki: Blood Brothers HC cover art by **Esad Ribić**

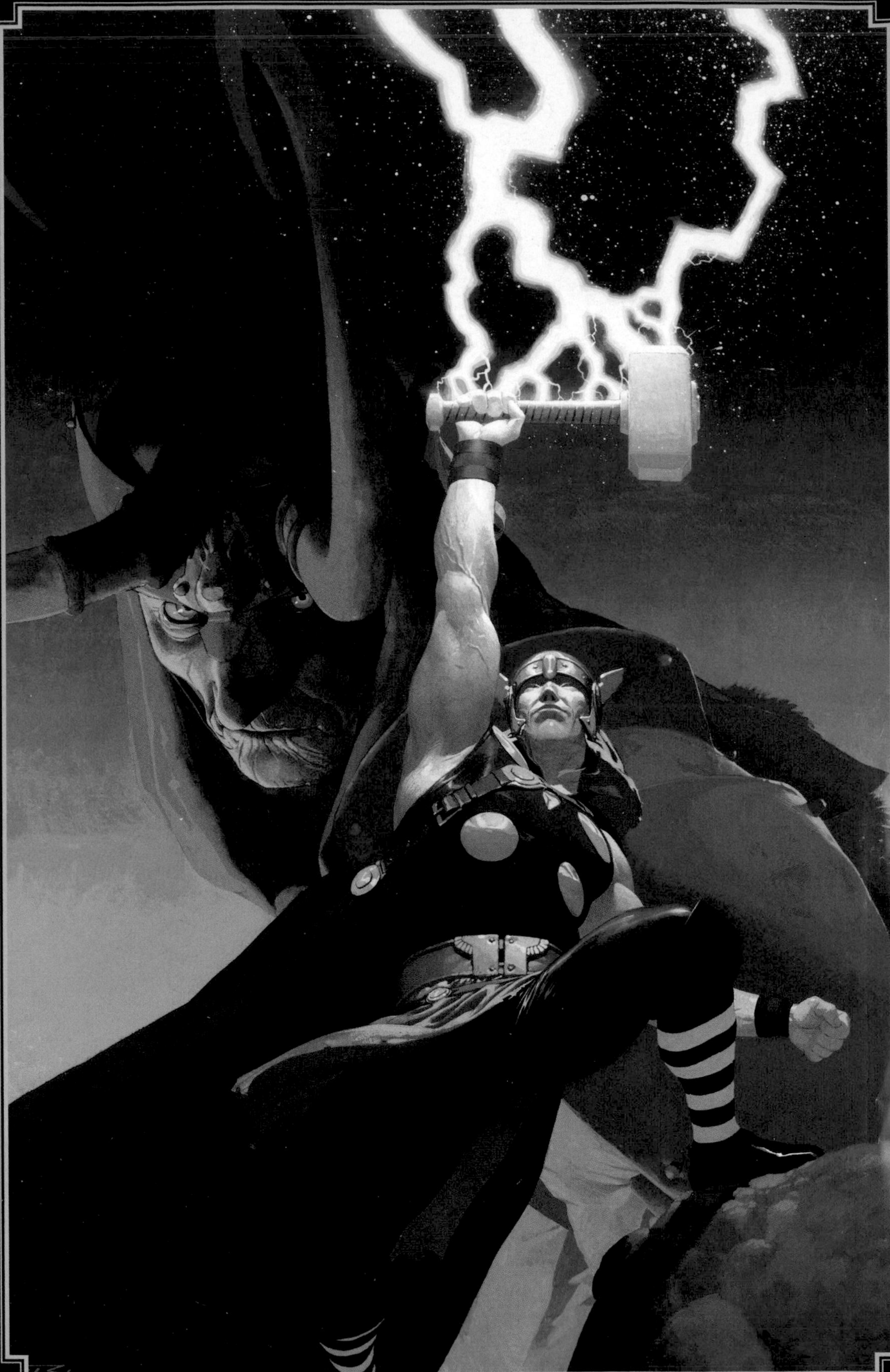